Symbols used on the maps:

The roads

Maps of large areas
- Freeway with Route Number
- Freeway under construction
- Highway, sealed, with National Route Number
- Highway, unsealed
- Highway under construction
- Major road, sealed
- Major road, unsealed
- Major road under construction
- Other road
- Vehicular track
- Underpass

Maps of small areas
- Freeway with Route Number
- Freeway under construction
- Highway, sealed, with National Route Number
- Highway, unsealed
- Highway under construction
- Major road, sealed, with Metropolitan Route Number
- Major road, unsealed
- Vehicular track
- Overpass

Other features

- Total kilometres between two main points 30
- Intermediate kilometres 5
- Number of kilometres from GPO 16
- Railway with station .... Newcastle
- Railway with town .... Eudlo
- State boundary
- Walking track
- River
- Rocks
- Reef
- Major tourist development
- Historic town
- Historic building
- Historic bridge
- Place of interest .... Caravan Park
- Other landmark .... Tower
- Homestead .... Mooloogool
- Lighthouse
- Wreck
- Vineyard

- Airport, landing ground
- Heliport
- Beacon
- Navigation light
- Park, recreational area
- Area of interest
- Building of interest
- Built-up area
- Pine forest
- Orchard
- Other timbered area
- Swamp
- Mangrove
- Beach
- Mud
- Area subject to flooding
- Lake
- Intermittent lake
- Aboriginal reserve
- Prohibited area

How to use this book:

Explore Australia begins with an Australia-wide introduction giving detailed information on planning a trip, accommodation, driving in outback conditions, breakdowns and travelling with children. From page 33 both text and maps are colour coded on a state-by-state basis.

To find out about a particular place in the text or on a map it is very important to use the index.

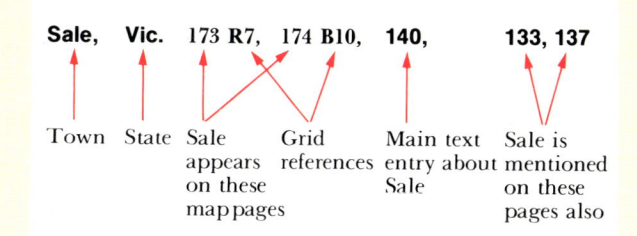

Sale,   **Vic.**   173 R7,   174 B10,   140,   133, 137

- Town
- State
- Sale appears on these map pages
- Grid references
- Main text entry about Sale
- Sale is mentioned on these pages also

The Maps

Every part of Australia is mapped in *Explore Australia*, from cities to the outback. Heavily-populated areas and places of special tourist interest are mapped in greater detail. Distance is shown by black and red markers on the maps and a scale bar at the top of each map.

Continuation of Maps

For easy continuation from one map to another there is always some overlap when maps are at the same scale. The symbol on the edges of the map pages indicates the next map page that should be turned to.

Symbols

This page has been designed to fold out for easy reference when using the maps.

Y0-CFR-278

Road distances between main cities

This distance chart shows distances by road between cities. The distances shown are in kilometres and are based on the most direct route, not necessarily the most practical.

	Adelaide	Brisbane	Canberra	Darwin	Melbourne	Perth	Sydney
Adelaide		2131	1210	3212	745	2749	1431
Albury	867	1431	350	4015	305	3525	588
Alice Springs	1690	3057	2753	1522	2435	3767	2929
Ballarat	632	1815	734	3829	113	3356	972
Bendigo	672	1710	629	3884	150	4421	867
Birdsville	1174	1570	2080	2359	2475	4636	2076
Brisbane	2131		1295	3493	1736	4390	1027
Broken Hill	509	1577	1108	3276	839	2813	1175
Broome	4036	4317	5099	1963	4781	2416	4883
Cairns	2862	1841	3139	2796	3233	6016	2868
Canberra	1210	1295		4229	655	3812	304
Darwin	3212	3493	4229		3957	4342	4060
Geelong	719	1810	729	3931	74	3468	867
Geraldton	3094	4806	4157	3895	3839	416	4333
Kalgoorlie	1965	3606	3028	4505	2710	598	3204
Katherine	2871	3152	3723	341	2592	4001	3719
Mackay	2803	1062	2357	2961	2452	5452	2090
Melbourne	745	1736	655	3957		3494	893
Mildura	400	1755	810	3465	544	3002	1033
Mount Gambier	463	2008	1007	3675	425	3212	1245
Newcastle	1608	852	479	3982	1068	4150	175
Perth	2749	4390	3812	4342	3494		3988
Port Augusta	336	1977	1399	2876	1081	2413	1575
Port Hedland	4519	4911	5582	2557	5264	1770	5551
Rockhampton	2258	671	1966	2985	2057	5061	1699
Sydney	1431	1027	304	4060	893	3988	
Tennant Creek	2197	2526	3260	1015	2942	4274	3093
Townsville	2525	1467	2765	2556	2857	5728	2494
Wagga Wagga	959	1480	257	4171	435	3565	489

Hobart to Launceston **200 kilometres**

Warning

Driving in northern and outback Australia can be extremely hazardous. During the wet season from October to March torrential rains frequently flood large areas, making roads impassable for weeks on end. When planning journeys into these areas read carefully the section on Outback Motoring in this book. Always:

- Check the road conditions before departure.
- Notify a responsible person of your planned route.
- Check that your car is in good mechanical order.
- Carry plenty of water and supplies of food.
- Stay with the car in case of breakdown.

Map of Australia

Seas and Waters:
- Arafura Sea
- Timor Sea
- Torres Strait
- Gulf of Carpentaria
- Joseph Bonaparte Gulf
- Van Diemen Gulf
- Great Australian Bight
- Spencer Gulf
- Gulf St. Vincent
- Bass Strait
- Southern Ocean
- Esperance Bay

Regions:
- Arnhem Land
- Cape York Peninsula
- Great Sandy Desert
- Gibson Desert
- Great Victoria Desert
- Nullarbor Plain
- Simpson Desert
- Sturt's Stony Desert
- Petermann Ranges
- Musgrave Range
- Flinders Ranges

States/Territories (with page references):
- Northern Territory (260 – 272)
- Queensland (305 – 336)
- South Australia (193 – 208)
- New South Wales & A.C.T. (65 – 112)
- Australia (– 259)
- Tasmania (353)

Islands:
- Melville Is
- Bathurst Island
- Groote Eylandt
- Mornington Is.
- Kangaroo Is.
- King Is.
- Flinders [Is.]

Towns and Cities:

Darwin, Jabiru, Katherine, Willeroo, Top Springs, Borroloola, Newcastle Waters, Wyndham, Kununurra, Derby, Halls Creek, Nicholson, Tennant Creek, Lake Nash, Camooweal, Mt. Isa, Cloncurry, Julia Creek, Hughenden, Charters Towers, Townsville, Cooktown, Mossman, Cairns, Mareeba, Innisfail, Normanton, Croydon, Georgetown, The Lynd, Dajarra, Winton, Middleton, Boulia, Longreach, Barcaldine, Clermont, Blackall, Alice Springs, Ayers Rock, Kulgera, Birdsville, Augathella, Charleville, Quilpie, Morven, Cunnamulla, St. George, Coober Pedy, Marree, Kingoonya, Bourke, Cobar, Coonabarabran, Nyngan, Wilcannia, Broken Hill, West Wyalong, Eucla, Madura, Cocklebiddy, Balladoni, Esperance, Kalgoorlie, Coolgardie, Penong, Ceduna, Port Augusta, Port Lincoln, Mildura, Hay, Narrandera, Wagga Wagga, Albury, Ouyen, Tailem Bend, Bordertown, Echuca, Bendigo, Ballarat, Mt. Gambier, Melbourne, Adelaide, C. Otway, Wilsons Promontory, George Town, Devonport, Smithton, Burnie, Launceston, Queenstown, Strathgordon, Hobart, Southport

Highways:
- Buchanan Hwy
- Carpentaria Hwy
- Stuart Hwy
- Tablelands Hwy
- Barkly Hwy
- Sandover Hwy
- Landsborough Hwy
- Flinders Hwy
- Mitchell Hwy
- Eyre Hwy
- Lincoln Hwy
- Flinders Hwy
- City Hwy
- Silver City Hwy
- Cobb Hwy
- Calder Hwy
- Hume Hwy
- Princes Hwy
- Glenelg Hwy
- Capricorn

National route numbers shown: 1, 8, 12, 18, 20, 24, 31, 32, 39, 41, 66, 71, 75, 78, 79, 87

Legend:
	Sealed	Unsealed
Highways	———	- - -
Other roads	——— (red)	- - - (red)
National route numbers	32	
Towns	○	

Scale: 0 100 200 300 400 500 km

EXPLORE AUSTRALIA

Lloyd O'Neil

This edition published 1986 by
George Philip & O'Neil Pty Ltd
56 Claremont Street, South Yarra 3141
for Lloyd O'Neil
First published 1980
Second edition 1981
Third edition, revised and updated, 1983
Reprinted 1984
Fourth edition 1985
Fifth edition 1986
Printed in Hong Kong
through Bookbuilders Ltd
© Concept, text and index
George Philip & O'Neil Pty Ltd
Maps © as designated:
BP Australia, 1986
George Philip & O'Neil Pty Ltd, 1986
ISBN 0 85550 494 3

The whole of the contents of this book is copyright and may not be reproduced, in whole, or in part, for any purpose without the written permission of the publisher. Action will be taken against those who unlawfully copy any part of this book.

Every effort has been made to ensure that the information in this book is accurate at the time of going to press. The publisher cannot, however, accept responsibility for any errors or omissions. The population figures given in 'Explore Australia' have been taken from the most recent census results available (June 1981).
Accommodation listed is a guide to the minimum available family accommodation in each town.

EXPLORE AUSTRALIA
TOURING FOR LEISURE AND PLEASURE

Acknowledgements

Editors
Celia Schmaler
Sue Donovan

Cartography
BP Australia Ltd
George Philip & O'Neil Pty Ltd

Researcher
Sue Crankshaw

Cartographic Consultants
Ken Ashbolt FAIC
Phil Broughton FAIC
Len Carter DIP.CART.
Ted Laker MBE, MAIC
George Ricketts MAIC
Bruno Scaggiante MAIC

Designers
Ernie Althoff
Colin Critchell
Zoe Gent-Murphy
Ian Scott

Motoring Consultant
Bryan Hanrahan

Writers
Margaret Barca
Brian Davies
Bryan Hanrahan
Colin Green
Jenny McColl
Ross Roberts
Maggie Taylor
Judy Wells

Research Assistants
Barbara Burton
Yvonne Fregon
Marjorie Harrison
Calvin Irons
Kurt Jilovsky
Tricia Randle
Rosemary Reuille Irons
Patrick Spillane
Penny Thomson
Jackie Tidey

Illustrators
Jean Cooper-Brown
John H. Kirkland
Marilyn Newland
Ian Scott

Photographers
George Althoff
John Carnemolla
Ron Clifford
David Jack
Gary Lewis
Neil McLeod
Lance Nelson
Andrew Osborne
Steve Porter
Irvin Rockman
Robin Smith
Ken Stepnell
Bruce Stewart
Doug Stone
Australian Picture Library
Ballarat Historical Park Association
Federal Pacific Hotels
Film Corporation of Tasmania
Hamersley Iron Pty Ltd
Melbourne City Council Parks, Gardens
 & Recreation Department
Overseas Telecommunications
 Commission (Australia)
Visair

This book could not have been produced without the constant help and encouragement of the following organisations, many of whom also provided photographs:

Canberra Tourist Bureau
Department of Aboriginal Affairs
Northern Territory Chief Minister's Department
Northern Territory Tourist Commission
Queensland Government Travel Centre
South Australian Government Travel Centre
South Australian Premier's Department, Publicity and Design
Tasmanian Government Tourist Bureau
The Tourism Commission of New South Wales
The Travel Centre of New South Wales
Victorian Tourism Commission
Western Australian Tourism Commission
Holiday WA Centre

The editors regret that there is not space to list individually the regional tourist authorities, national park authorities, state roads departments, state mapping authorities and the hundreds of shire councils, municipalities and corporations who contributed so much to this book.

The publishers wish to thank the companies which helped make possible the research for this project:

BP Australia Ltd
Budget Rent A Car System Pty Ltd
Ford Motor Company of Australia Limited

Contents

Inside front cover:
  Australia's Main Highways
Fold-out page:
  Symbols used on the maps
  How to use this book
Inside back cover:
  Accident Action

Explore Australia... viii
...from A to Z x
Calendar of Events xii
Planning Ahead xv
  Advance information; Useful addresses; How far ahead to start; Which way to go; Accommodation; Dividing up the dollars; Budget biters; Itineraries; Clothing; First aid kit; Useful extras; Leaving home.
Have a Good Trip xviii
  Comfortable driving; Packing; Where to set off; Checking the car.
Defensive Driving xx
  Test your rating as a safe driver; Concentration; Smooth driving; Road conditions; Positioning.
Outback Motoring xxii
  Equipping the car; Spare parts; Road conditions; Finding north; Overtaking; Animals; Survival; Water.
Breakdowns xxiv
  When the engine stops; Spark plug check; Petrol check; Checking the starter; No sound from starter; Suspected faulty electrical supply; Suspect starter motor; Ignition system check; Fuel system check; Overheating; Accidents; Motoring organisations.
Towing xxx
Child's Play xxxi
The Explore Australia Game 1
Australia's Geological Ages 2
Prehistoric Australia 4
The Australian Aborigines 6
The European Discoverers 8
Exploring an Unknown Land 10
Australian Landform Structures 12
Australian Soil Types 14
Australian Vegetation Regions 16
Trees, Grasses and Wildflowers 18

RIGHT: *Sydney Harbour Bridge, New South Wales.*

Australia's Unique Animals 20
Common Australian Birds 22
Aquatic Birds 24
Reptiles, Amphibians and Insects 26
Australia's Water Resources 28
Irrigating a Dry Continent 30
Climate and Weather Patterns 32

New South Wales
FOUNDING STATE

Introduction 33
Sydney: Australia's First City 34
  Accommodation Guide 35
Tours from Sydney 38
National Parks near Sydney 39
New South Wales from A to Z 40
Sydney's Colonial Past *opp.* 40
Bourke 42
Wines of New South Wales 43
National Parks of New South Wales 44
The Snowy Mountains 46
City on the Water *opp.* 48
Old Sydney Town 50
New England 51
The Blue Mountains 53
The Illawarra Coast 54
Caves and Caverns 55
Port Stephens 58
The Newell 59
Port Macquarie 60
The Alpine Coast 61
The Hawkesbury 63

Maps of New South Wales

Location Map 65
Central Sydney 66
North Sydney & Pacific Highway 68
Sydney & Northern Suburbs 70
Sydney & Southern Suburbs 72
Sydney & Western Suburbs 74
Tours from Sydney 76
Brisbane Water & Ku-ring-gai Chase National Parks 78
Katoomba & the Blue Mountains 80
Vineyards of the Hunter Valley 81
Newcastle 82
The Southern Central Coast 83
Coffs Harbour 84
Port Macquarie 85
Port Stephens 86
Lord Howe Island 87
Tamworth & Lismore 88
Wollongong 89
Tours from Wollongong 90
North Western New South Wales 92
North Eastern New South Wales 94
South Western New South Wales 96
Central Eastern New South Wales 98
South Eastern New South Wales 100
Bathurst & Orange 101
Sydney to Melbourne by the Main Routes 102
Kosciusko National Park Alpine Resorts 104

Australian Capital Territory

Canberra: The Nation's Capital *opp.* 56
Australian Capital Territory *opp.* 112

Maps of Australian Capital Territory

Canberra City 105
Canberra & Northern Suburbs 106
Canberra & Central Suburbs 108
Canberra & Southern Suburbs 110
Australian Capital Territory 112

Victoria
GARDEN STATE

Introduction 113
Melbourne: A Sporting City 114
  Accommodation Guide 115
Tours from Melbourne 118
Lunch in the Country 119
Victoria from A to Z 120
The Golden Age *opp.* 120
Sovereign Hill 122
Victoria's National Parks 124
The Western District 126
Alpine Country *opp.* 128
Phillip Island *opp.* 129
The Mallee 129
The Blue Dandenongs 130
The Wimmera 131
The Prom. 132
Gippsland's Lakes 133
The Great Ocean Road 134
Skiing in Victoria 135
Parks and Gardens *opp.* 136
The Mornington Peninsula 139
The Mighty Murray 140
The Grampians 142
Walhalla 143
Victoria's Wine Regions *opp.* 176

Maps of Victoria

Location Map 145
Central Melbourne 146
The Dandenongs 147
Melbourne & Suburbs 148
Melbourne & Southern Suburbs 150
The Mornington Peninsula & Westernport 152
Vineyards Close to Melbourne 154
Bellarine Peninsula & Great Ocean Road 155
Geelong 156
Ballarat 157
Tours from Melbourne 158
Lake Eildon & Southern Ranges 160
Wilsons Promontory National Park 161
North Western Victoria 162
The Wimmera 164
North Central Victoria 166
North & Eastern Victoria 168
Victorian Alpine Resorts 169
South Western Victoria 170
South Central Victoria 172
Gippsland 174
Vineyards of North Eastern Victoria 176

RIGHT: *The Flinders Ranges, South Australia.*

South Australia
FESTIVAL STATE

Introduction 177
Adelaide: An Elegant City 178
  Accommodation Guide 179
Tours from Adelaide 180
South Australia from A to Z 181
The Yorke Peninsula 181
South Australia's National Parks 182
Festival Fun *opp.* 184
The Coorong 185
Kangaroo Island 186
The Outback of South Australia 188
The Eyre Peninsula 189
The Barossa Valley 190
The Fleurieu Peninsula 191
Flinders Ranges *opp.* 192
Vineyards and Wineries *opp.* 208

Maps of South Australia

Location Map 193
Central Adelaide 194
Adelaide & Suburbs 195
Tours North from Adelaide 196
Tours South from Adelaide 198
North Central South Australia 200
Central South Australia 202
South East Corner of South Australia 204
The Eyre Peninsula 205
Northern South Australia 206
Vineyards of the Barossa Valley & Southern Vales 208

Western Australia
WILDFLOWER STATE

Introduction 209
Perth: A Friendly City 210
  Accommodation Guide 211
Rottnest Island 211
Tours from Perth 212
Western Australia from A to Z 214
Broome 215
Crossing the Nullarbor *opp.* 216
The Kimberley *opp.* 217
The Hamersley Range 217
The South West 218
The Great Southern 219
Western Australia's National Parks 220
The Goldfields 222
Western Wildflowers *opp.* 224
The Pilbara 226
The Ord River Scheme 227

Maps of Western Australia

Location Map 241
Central Perth 242
Rottnest Island 243
Perth & Northern Suburbs 244
Perth & Southern Suburbs 246
The South West Corner 248
Tours from Perth 250
Tours from Geraldton 252
Northern Western Australia 254
Southern Western Australia 256
Kalgoorlie & Coolgardie 258
The Swan Valley Vineyards 259

Contents vii

Northern Territory
OUTBACK AUSTRALIA

Introduction 230
Darwin: A Relaxed City 231
   Accommodation Guide 232
Future State 232
The Top End *opp.* 232
Tours from Darwin 233
Northern Territory from A to Z 234
Touring the Territory 234
Carrying a Camera 235
Gove 235
Tours from Alice Springs 236
Northern Territory National Parks 238
Sportsman's Territory 240
The Red Centre *opp.* 272

Maps of Northern Territory

Location Map 260
Alice Springs 261
Tours from Alice Springs 262
Darwin & Suburbs 264
The Top End 266
Central Northern Territory 268
Southern Northern Territory 270
Ayers Rock & The Olgas 272

BELOW: *Palm Valley in the Northern Territory.*

Queensland
SUNSHINE STATE

Introduction 273
Brisbane: A Sub-Tropical City 274
   Accommodation Guide 275
Mt Coot-tha 276
Tours from Brisbane 278
City of the Gold Coast 278
The Great Barrier Reef *opp.* 280
Queensland from A to Z 281
Atherton Tableland 282
Queensland's National Parks 284
Southern Reef Islands 286
Barrier Reef Cruises 287
The Gold Coast *opp.* 288
The Sunshine Coast *opp.* 289
Darling Downs 290
Capricornia 291
Gulf Country 292
The Channel Country 294
Thursday Island 296
The Far North *opp.* 296
The Whitsunday Islands 298
Cape York 300
Moreton Bay Islands 301
Tropical Islands 302
Fraser Island *opp.* 336

Maps of Queensland

Location Map 305
Central Brisbane 306
The Sunshine Coast 307
Brisbane & Northern Suburbs 308
Brisbane & Southern Suburbs 310
Tours North from Brisbane 312
Brisbane & Hinterland 314
Tours South from Brisbane 316
The Gold Coast 318
Toowoomba 320
South Western Queensland 321
South Eastern Queensland 322
North Eastern Queensland 324
Cape York Peninsula 326
North Western Queensland 327
Rockhampton & Gladstone 328
Heron Island & Great Keppel Island 329
Mackay and Brampton Island 330
The Whitsunday Group 331
Townsville 332
Magnetic Island 333
Cairns, Hinchinbrook Island & Dunk Island 334
Tours from Cairns 335
Fraser Island 336

RIGHT: *The church at Port Arthur, Tasmania.*

Tasmania
HOLIDAY ISLAND

Introduction 337
Hobart: An Historic City 338
   Accommodation Guide 339
Battery Point 339
Tours from Hobart 340
Tasmania from A to Z 341
Rural Landscapes 341
Tasmania's National Parks 342
Scenic Island State *opp.* 344
Stately Homes 346
The Bass Strait Islands 347
Tasmania's West Coast 348
Fisherman's Paradise 350
Dams for Power 351
Tasmania's Convict Past *opp.* 352

Maps of Tasmania

Location Map 353
Central Hobart & Devonport 354
Hobart & Suburbs 355
Tours from Hobart 356
Southern Tasmania 358
Northern Tasmania 360
Launceston & Burnie 362
Tours from Launceston 363
Cradle Mountain & Lake St Clair National Park 364
South West National Park 366
Port Arthur 368

Gazetteer of place names 369

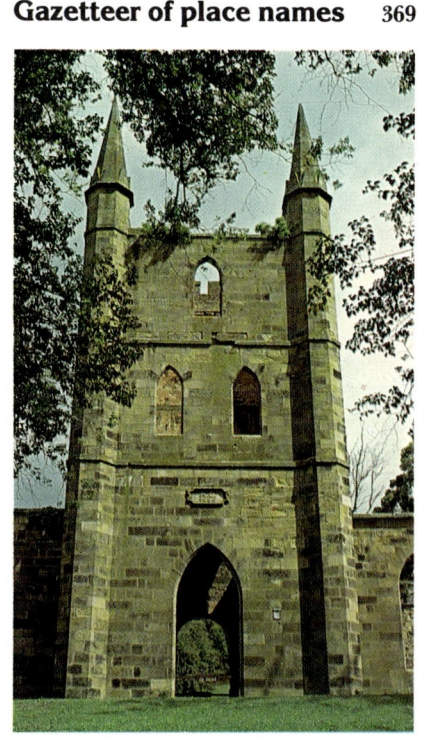

Explore Australia . . .

Darwin

INDIAN OCEAN

Perth

GREAT AUSTRALIAN

It is rather ironic that many Australians are more familiar with the beaches of Bali or the leafy byways of Britain than they are with the greater part of their own country. Possibly its sheer size is intimidating; perhaps the clichés — that Australia is just 'flat', 'arid' and 'empty' are too easily believed. As this map shows however, nothing could be further from the truth.

Three-quarters the size of all Europe, four-fifths the size of the USA, this Australian continent offers everything, from a weekend in snowfields the size of Switzerland to adventures in tropical jungles. On exploration, those flat empty areas turn out to be full of grand canyons and amazing desert ranges, and the arid stretches contradict their reputation with their sudden greenings and colourful wild flowers. With its contrasts of climate, terrain and landscape, Australia can offer you a world tour in one country — certainly enough to occupy all the holidays of a lifetime.

It's all yours to explore — wherever there's a road to take you.

GULF OF CARPENTARIA

GREAT BARRIER REEF

SUNSHINE COAST

PACIFIC OCEAN

e Springs

Brisbane

GOLD COAST

Adelaide

Sydney

Canberra

Melbourne

BASS STRAIT

Hobart

...from A to Z

A is for Ayers Rock. Where else to begin? Our national landmark, the world's largest monolith and, despite its tourist fame, still compelling and mysterious. Add to this the Alice, the Olgas, Standley Chasm and the 200 metres-high cliffs of Kings Canyon and any Red Centre trip is unforgettable.

B is for bush. The word that describes a multitude of different terrains. If you 'go bush', you will discover that it can be anything from tropical jungle to open Mallee scrub, from semi-desert, through rolling pastureland to lush valleys crowded with giant tree ferns.

C is for cities. Whether capital or provincial, each has its own character and takes a good deal of exploring. And, of course, the best way to get to know a city is to use its public transport, or your own feet.

D is for the Dreamtime. To the Aboriginal, this means the past and the future. The spirit of this world of myth and legend has been captured in paintings and drawings on rock and cave walls across the land. It is not hard to discover their whereabouts and it is an experience that should not be missed.

E is for excitement. One state has taken this feeling for itself: Western Australia. Whatever your interests, the mineral treasure troves, the glorious riot of spring wild flowers, or the giant karri, jarrah and red gum forests south-east of Perth, WA is like a country in itself.

F is for farming life. The majority of Australians live urban lives, so to spend a few days discovering rural Australia by staying on a farm or property can be an eye-opener, especially for children. Accommodation varies from the spartan to the almost luxurious. Talk to a State Government Tourist Bureau to find out more.

G is for gold. Its value has spiralled upwards and caused a modern-day gold rush across the country. If you want to fossick for your fortune, or simply try to cover your expenses, metal detectors can be hired — or you can try the good, old-fashioned panning. (Remember, you need a licence.)

H is for history. Enjoy it by seeing where it was made: if you plan a trip around the gold fields, you'll come across many beautifully preserved old towns and the fascinating remains of digging sites and mines. For a view of pioneer life, spend a day at one of the town re-creations, such as Sovereign Hill, near Ballarat, in Victoria.

I is for Innamincka, SA, across Sturts Stony Desert from the Birdsville Track.
J is for Jerilderie, NSW, the town the Kelly gang took prisoner.
K is for Kalgoorlie, WA, possibly the most famous gold town in the world.

Each of these is small, each unique, but there are thousands of similar towns lying just off the beaten track. Even if only a few people live there, there's usually an old country pub where you can discover from the locals how the town came to be, and what it is like to live in today.

L is for looking, listening and learning. Even if you normally avoid museums or exhibitions, you'll find even the smallest town is aware of its history. Many have historical societies which exhibit memorabilia from their area. The National Trust has some wonderful photographic and audio-visual displays in many of its properties. Time spent finding out about the past of an area or town will bring the place more vividly to life, and make your visit there more meaningful and enjoyable.

M is for mountains. Considering that Australia is the flattest continent, there is an impressive variety of mountains to explore. In the west, the Porongurups and the Stirling Ranges nurture plant species seen nowhere else in the world; in the north, the Warrumbungles and the Glasshouse Mountains are the 'plugs' of ancient volcanoes; and for alpine scenery, don't miss a visit to the stunning mountains of Tasmania, interlaced with deep, still lakes, or the Snowy Mountains of New South Wales with their highly developed ski resorts.

N is for National Parks. These parks preserve the beauty of the country in its unspoiled state. They have been created to include almost every variety of Australian landscape, from coastal to desert. Many provide facilities for campers and caravans. If you enjoy peace and quiet and want an opportunity to observe flora and fauna undisturbed, ask your National Parks and Wildlife Service for information.

O is for outback. Like the word 'bush', it is hard to define. To many city dwellers, 'outback' is anything more than 50 km up the road. The areas it is usually applied to cover surprising contrasts of terrain and unexpected natural beauty. Regardless of where it is, it is certainly isolated. Touring outback areas can be exciting and rewarding, but if you're not properly prepared, it can be hazardous. If you're planning a trip, research your route and read the section on outback motoring in this book.

P is for 'paradise'. Just off the Queensland coast is the Great Barrier Reef and the chain of islands sheltered by it. Many can be reached from the mainland by launch, ferry or helicopter. It's worth interrupting a motoring tour to visit some of these islands and the Reef. If you're planning to stay overnight, make your arrangements well in advance; 'paradise' is justifiably a popular place.

Q is for Queensland. The 'Sunshine State' has a more than adequate share of holiday attractions including the Great Barrier Reef, the islands and the many delights of the Gold and Sunshine Coasts. What's more, the tropical and sub-tropical hinterlands offer spectacular mountains and lush vegetation, providing a completely contrasting alternative to the sun, sand and sea of the coastal stretches of Highway One.

R is for rivers. Following them can be a delightful experience: for instance, starting at the source of the Murray, where it is only a gurgling stream, you can follow it from the Snowy Mountains to the water playgrounds of Lakes Hume and Mulwala, through rich citrus and wine growing country, past the old river ports of Echuca and Swan Hill, into the Riverina and down to its mouth at Lake Alexandrina in South Australia, 20 000 km in all.

S is for seaside. When it comes to magnificent coastal scenery, beautiful beaches and excellent surf, Victoria has much to offer. On the eastern coast is the Ninety Mile Beach, with Lakes Entrance and the Gippsland Lakes System. In complete contrast, along the western coast, the Great Ocean Road leads past wonderful sandy coves, spectacular cliffs and amazing rock formations.

T is for Tasmania. Often described as 'English', 'British' is probably more accurate. As well as leafy lanes and English-style towns like Richmond, Tasmania offers velvety fields reminiscent of Irish landscape in the north, spectacular coastline such as that found in Scotland in the south, and mountain ranges in the south-west that match up to the most wild and beautiful that Wales can offer.

U is for unique. Australian specialities like the world-famous koala (native bear) and kangaroo. Many plants are unique too, including the insect-trapping flying duck orchid! Lesser known, but equally deserving of recognition, is the *Moloch horridus,* one of the species of dragon lizards, which changes colour to suit its background. Its armour is so sharp that no animal can eat it without suffering severe injury.

V is for vineyards and —
W is for the wine with which they bless us. You don't have to be a wine expert to enjoy a sunny day discovering vineyards, watching the wine-making rituals and exploring some of the beautiful buildings of the old established wineries. Sampling is optional! Many have excellent restaurants and offer guided tours and sales facilities.

X is for 'x-traordinary'! The list is long but for some of the more bizarre — how about a cattle station the size of Belgium, Henley-on-Todd, the world's only annual regatta held on a dry river bed, or Mt Isa, the town with the longest milk run on earth — daily deliveries come from Townsville, nearly 1000 km away.

Y is for the young. Their ideas on what constitutes a good day out often differ radically from ours. Don't forget this when choosing a holiday and, for some ideas, remember that
Z is for zoos. Taronga Park in Sydney is probably the most famous in Australia, but most city zoos have been energetically improved over recent years. Fauna reserves give children the chance to see native animals in a natural environment. More exotic animals can be viewed from the safety of a vehicle at one of the many safari parks. Other stops popular with children include anything watery — swimming pools, paddlesteamers, riverside picnics; playgrounds and amusement parks; and anything odd like Queensland's 'Biggest Pineapple in the World'!

Calendar of Events

January

NSW New Year's Eve. Spectacular fireworks over **Sydney** Harbour; Surf carnival at Scotts Head Beach, **Macksville;** Festival of **Sydney** (art and cultural events), whole month; Shoalhaven aquatic carnival at **Nowra,** Australia Day weekend; Sydney to **Port Stephens** Ocean Race (yachts sail from Middle Harbour), Australia Day weekend; 'Festival of Fish and Chips' at **Brunswick Heads** (ten-day carnival featuring a pie-eating contest, woodchop competitions and sporting events); country and western festival at **Tamworth.**
VIC. The Petersville Regatta (a series of five races for keel yachts held in the second week of January on Port Phillip Bay); **Hanging Rock** race meeting (pack some food and wine and enjoy this traditional picnic race meeting on New Year's Day); Nariel Creek Folk Festival, near **Corryong.**
SA Schuetzenfest at **Hahndorf** in the Adelaide Hills (drink steins of beer at the largest German festival held outside Germany). 'Tunarama' at **Port Lincoln** (a three-day tuna fishing festival). Benson and Hedges World Series Cup (cricket).
WA **Perth** Cup (a major event in the WA Turf Club calendar), New Year's Day.
QLD Surf Carnivals, **Burleigh Heads, Coolangatta, Broadbeach, Maroochydore.**
TAS. Sydney to **Hobart** Yacht Race.
ALL STATES New Year's Day, Australia Day, public holidays.

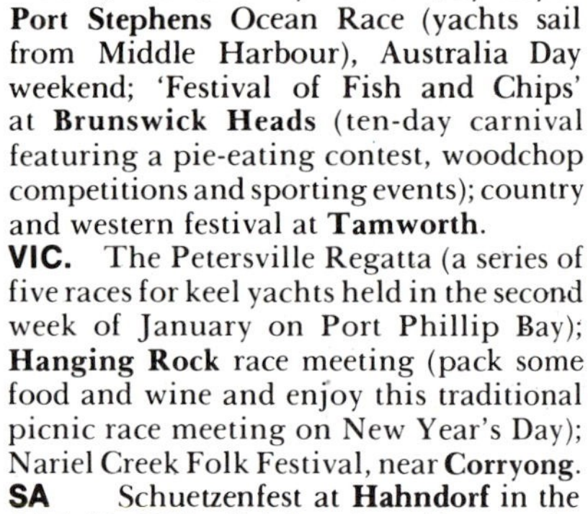

February

NSW **Cooma** Rodeo; Dahlia Festival at **Mittagong** and **Dorrigo** (dahlias bloom in gardens and window boxes. Events include wine-tasting, flower shows, sporting competitions, processions, fireworks); Game fishing championships at Shoal Bay, **Port Stephens** (the largest deep water fishing contest in the world).
ACT **Canberra** Royal Show, last weekend of month.
VIC. Formula 5000 Series (motor racing at **Sandown Park** near Melbourne); Victorian Open Golf Championship (international golfers compete for this title).
WA Festival of **Perth** begins.
TAS. Regatta Day, Hobart Cup Day, public holidays (S. Tas. only); Launceston Cup Day, public holiday (N. Tas. only); Royal **Hobart** Regatta (two-day aquatic carnival).

ACT **Canberra** Festival (parade, fairs, exhibitions, concerts, drama).
VIC. Labour Day, public holiday; **Melbourne's** Moomba Festival (ten days of concerts, sports, exhibitions, fairs, water-skiing, bird-man contest, a street parade of floats, and fireworks displays); three-day autumn horse-racing carnival, featuring the Australian Cup; Duck-shooting season opens; **Melbourne** Military Tattoo (spectacular military parade with marching and drill, Scottish country and Highland dancing, massed bands); **Ballarat** Begonia Festival (large-scale celebrations with exhibitions, fair, a parade and floral displays of begonias in bloom.
SA **Adelaide** Festival (Australia's major festival which continues for three weeks and includes performances by international artists), biennial.
WA Labour Day, public holiday.
TAS. Eight Hour Day, public holiday; Blue Gum Festival (state-wide cultural and sporting celebrations), biennial.
ALL STATES End of cricket season.

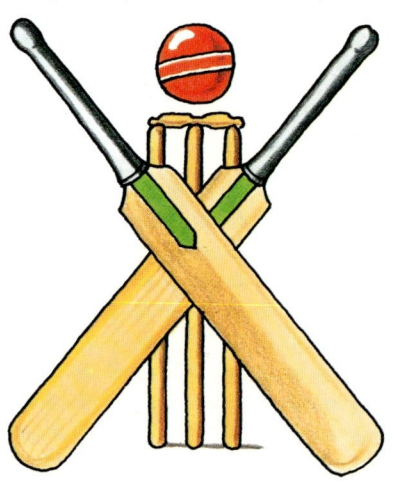

March

NSW Vintage celebrations at **Cessnock** (wine-tasting, vineyard visits, fair, dances, grape-picking and grape-treading contests).

April

NSW Highland Gathering at **Maclean** (traditional Scottish games), Easter weekend; **Sydney** Cup (one of the most popular race meetings in Australia); Bath Tub

Derby at **Tweed Heads** (a crazy race of bath tubs of all shapes and sizes); **Sydney** Easter Show (agricultural exhibits, livestock judging, equestrian events, parades, carnival); 'Blessing of the Fleet', **Ulladulla** and **Brunswick Heads** (a traditional event at Easter with a rodeo, dance, parade, street fair, fishing and sporting competitions).
VIC. Stawell Gift (one of the world's most prestigious footraces of professional runners), Easter weekend.
SA Barossa Vintage Festival (celebrates the grape harvest), biennial.
ALL STATES Anzac Day, Good Friday and Easter Monday, public holidays.

May

NSW Shoalhaven speedboat spectacular at **Nowra**; Fishing carnival at **Sussex Inlet** (fishing tournaments, also golf, tennis and bowls competitions); Big River Festival of the Arts at **Grafton** (music, drama, playwriting competitions); Thoroughbred Week at **Scone** (four days of horse sales and racing).
SA Adelaide Cup Day, public holiday.
NT 'Bangtail Muster' Parade and Sports Day at **Alice Springs**. The Camel Cup at Alice Springs (probably Australia's most unusual race meeting).
QLD Labour Day, public holiday.

June

NSW **Ballina** 10 000 footrace, Queen's Birthday weekend; **Newcastle** Folk Fair (traditional festival of folk song and dance); Skiing season begins, Queen's Birthday weekend.
ACT National Eisteddfod at **Canberra**.
VIC. **Rutherglen** Winery Walkabout, Queen's Birthday weekend; **Melbourne** Film Festival (a two-week programme of films from all over the world).
WA Foundation Day public holiday.
NT Beer Can Regatta in **Darwin** (a lighthearted race between home-made beer can boats).
QLD Pacific Festival at **Townsville** (cultural and craft fair); Australian 'Top Fuel' Championships (drag racing) at **Surfers Paradise**.
ALL STATES (Except WA) Queens Birthday, public holiday.

July

NSW Camellia Show at **Wollongong**, Racing Carnival at **Grafton**; Polo Carnival at **Scone** and **Wirragulla**; Stroud 'International Brick-throwing Contest' (an annual competition between the Australian, English, American and Canadian towns named Stroud. Events include brick- and rolling pin-throwing, gymnastics, pipe band).
VIC. Grand National Steeplechase and hurdle races at **Flemington**; Sun Tour (a major cycling road event in Australia).
NT Alice Springs Show (annual agricultural show).
QLD Saloon car racing at Copper City, **Mount Isa**; The **Doomben** Hundred Thousand (winter carnival horse race).

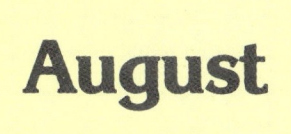

August

NSW City to Surf (annual 'fun run' from **Sydney** Town Hall to **Bondi** Beach.
NT Henley-on-Todd at **Alice Springs** (hilarious races between 'bottomless yachts' in the dry bed of the 'Todd River').
QLD Royal Brisbane Show Day public holiday. Royal National Show in **Brisbane** enjoy a carnival atmosphere. Ocean and Inland Fishing Competition at Tin Can Bay; **Birdsville** Races (a traditional outback horse racing meeting sometimes held in September); Outback Festival at **Winton**, biennial.

September

NSW Carnivale. **Sydney** and suburban week of multi-cultural activities; Rugby League finals.
VIC. Royal Melbourne Show Day, public holiday (metropolitan area only); Royal Melbourne Show at **Flemington**, (agricultural show with stock displays and judging, arena events, Grand Parade); Victorian Football League and Association finals; Tulip Festival at **Silvan** (see tulips in all their glory in the Dandenongs); Spring horse racing carnival begins, **Caulfield, Flemington, Moonee Valley.**
SA Royal Show in **Adelaide** (agricultural show); Football League finals.
WA Football League finals; **Perth** Royal Show (agricultural show and fair, parades); Wildflower Festival at **Albany**.
QLD Carnival of Flowers at **Toowoomba**; Warana Festival at **Brisbane**; Strawberry Festival at **Cleveland**; Football League finals; Canoe Sprint Regatta at **Tewantin**.

at **Blackheath** (clusters of rhododendrons bloom in their natural beauty at the Rhododendron Reserve, in the heart of the Blue Mountains); Tulip Festival at **Bowral**, the 'tulip town'; **Leura** Gardens Festival (magnificent colours of hyacinths, rhododendrons, primroses, daffodils, tulips, camellias and fuchsias fill gardens in this beautiful spot in the Blue Mountains); **Bathurst** 1000 (Australia's top motor race where international drivers reach speeds of 265 km/h around the Mount Panorama circuit.
VIC. **Warrnambool** to **Melbourne** bicycle race; Free entertainment in parks (FEIP) begins in **Melbourne;** Azalea Show at **Olinda** (colourful display in the Dandenong Ranges); **Caulfield** Cup and Guineas.
SA Labour Day public holiday; **Burra** State Folk Festival, (folk song and dance, workshops and songwriting competitions, in one of South Australia's earliest mining towns), biennial; **McLaren Vale** Bushing Festival (celebrates bottling of new vintage. Wine-tasting, 'village green' fair in Elizabethan style).
WA Queen's birthday, public holiday.
QLD Mardi Gras at **Bundaberg;** Oktoberfest at **Mount Isa**; Fun in the Sun Festival at **Cairns**.
TAS. Hobart Royal Show Day, Launceston Show Day, public holidays; Royal **Hobart** Show (agricultural show, carnival and parade); **Launceston** National Show.
ALL STATES Cricket season opens.

October

NSW Eight Hour Day, public holiday; Agricultural show and trade fair at **Wollongong**; International car rally at **Port Macquarie;** Rhododendron Festival

November

NSW Mardi Gras at **The Entrance** Tuggerah Lakes; Jacaranda Festival at **Grafton** (the whole town celebrates with dancing and a carnival in Market Square).

VIC. Melbourne Cup Day, public holiday; Melbourne Cup, **Flemington** (Australia's most famous horse race); Oaks Day ('Ladies Day'); Rhododendron Show at **Olinda** (as well as the show at the National Rhododendron Garden); Australian Open Tennis Championships; PGA and Australian Open Golf Championships; Caulfield Festival at **Caulfield**; **Geelong** Springding Festival; **Benalla** Rose Festival. **Ballarat** Rowing Regatta.
SA Christmas celebrations start early in **Adelaide** with a pageant and parade of floats down the city streets.
TAS. Recreation Day, public holiday (N. Tas. only).

December

NSW Summer Cup racing carnival at **Ballina** (12 days of Christmas Mardi Gras).
VIC. Australian Open Tennis Championships. **Kooyong** (one of the world's great tennis tournaments).
SA Proclamation Day, public holiday. Tripolis Yacht Race.
WA Christmas pageant in **Perth**; Australian Derby; H.G. Bolton International in **Perth** (this Boxing Day horse race features international jockeys).
ALL STATES Christmas Day, Boxing Day, public holidays.

Planning Ahead

Exploring by road can be a delightful way to get to know Australia. Motor travellers are their own masters, can take their time and make their own decisions. Whether a simple weekend jaunt, a fortnight interstate or a six months epic trip around the continent, however, any journey will benefit from some careful advance planning. The idea of 'throwing a bag in the back and taking off' is attractive in theory but tends to lead to strained tempers and 'No Vacancy' signs.

To experienced explorers, the information in this section already may be second nature. For the inexperienced, or naturally disorganised, these suggestions on the planning of the perfect trip could be worth reading as soon as the idea comes to mind.

Advance information

Do try to gather as much as possible, as early as possible. Good research will confirm that where you *think* you want to go is where you really *do* want to go; it will also reveal the ways, means and problems involved in arriving there and enjoying the holiday.

It is surprising how many sources of information there can be, even for the most remote areas. The first place to try is the relevant state tourist bureaus and motoring organisations. They are an excellent source for all kinds of brochures, regional maps, accommodation guides, information on national parks, rail travel and motoring hints. For information on specific areas they will put you in touch with the relevant regional tourist authority. Even if they cannot provide the information you seek, they can usually advise where best to look. Travel agents, main rail offices and airline travel centres should all be asked for as much information as possible, particularly if you are planning a fly/drive holiday or combined rail and motor travel.

Last but not least, read this book! The introductions to each state provide basic information on main areas. Once you have made a broad decision, check it out by consulting the gazetteer entries for specific towns and other points of interest. Do note that all the capital cities have been covered comprehensively but not in fine detail. For more in-depth information, visit a newsagent or bookshop on your arrival in the city and see what is available. You usually will find a pocket-sized guidebook that contains street maps, restaurant, shopping, theatre and cinema information and list major points of interest.

Useful Addresses

MOTORING ORGANISATIONS

Sydney
National Roads and Motorists' Association (NRMA)
151 Clarence Street
Sydney, NSW, 2000
Tel. (02) 260 9222

Canberra
National Roads and Motorists' Association (NRMA)
92 Northbourne Avenue
Canberra City, ACT, 2601
Tel. (062) 43 3777

Melbourne
Royal Automobile Club of Victoria (RACV)
123 Queen Street
Melbourne, Vic. 3000
Tel. (03) 607 2211

Adelaide
Royal Automobile Association of South Australia Inc. (RAA)
41 Hindmarsh Square
Adelaide, SA, 5000
Tel. (08) 223 4555

Perth
Royal Automobile Club of Western Australia Inc. (RAC)
228 Adelaide Terrace
Perth, WA, 6000
Tel. (09) 325 0551

Darwin
Automobile Association of the Northern Territory Inc. (AANT)
79-81 Smith Street
Darwin, NT, 5790
Tel. (089) 81 3837

Brisbane
Royal Automobile Club of Queensland (RACQ)
300 St Pauls Terrace
Brisbane, Qld, 4000
Tel. (07) 253 2444

Hobart
Royal Automobile Club of Tasmania (RACT)
Cnr Patrick and Murray Streets
Hobart, Tas., 7000
Tel. (002) 34 6611

TOURIST BUREAUS

New South Wales
The Travel Centre of NSW
16 Spring Street
Sydney, NSW, 2000
Tel. (02) 231 4444

Australian Capital Territory
Canberra Tourist Bureau
Jolimont Centre
Northbourne Avenue
Canberra City, ACT, 2601
Tel. (062) 49 7555

Victoria
Victour
230 Collins Street
Melbourne, Vic., 3000
Tel. (03) 619 9444

South Australia
South Australian Travel Centre
18 King William Street
Adelaide, SA, 5001
Tel. (08) 212 1644

Western Australia
Holiday WA Centre
772 Hay Street
Perth, WA, 6000
Tel. (09) 322 2999

Northern Territory
Northern Territory Government Tourist Bureau
51 Todd Street
Alice Springs, NT, 5750
Tel. (089) 521 299

Queensland
Queensland Government Travel Centre
196 Adelaide Street
Brisbane, Qld, 4000
Tel. (07) 31 2211

Tasmania
Tasmanian Government Tourist Bureau
80 Elizabeth Street
Hobart, Tas., 7000
Tel. (002) 34 6911

How far ahead to start

There is nothing worse than deciding on an area or destination and then discovering it is all booked up. Try to organise booking details anything up to one year ahead if:

a) your holiday coincides with any of the following — **School Holidays** — December to early February; May; August/September.
Christmas, New Year, Easter.
Special events or festivals such as **Melbourne Cup Week, Royal Shows.** Peak touring times for an area, such as the wildflower season in WA. (Check with the *Calendar of Events* for details of key events in all states.)

b) you plan to use *MotoRail* facilities, trans-continental trains or the Tasmanian ferry as some often are fully booked up one year in advance.

c) you require any kind of specialist accommodation such as a particular hotel, a farm, a house- or charter-boat.
Even if you take your accommodation with you, don't forget to check well in advance on bookings in camping and caravan parks in popular resort areas during peak periods. Prior permission is often required to camp in national parks or state forests.

Don't forget to book your pet into its holiday accommodation! Many kennels are booked out six months in advance — particularly for holiday times.

Which way to go

If you quail at the thought of seemingly endless kilometres of driving you should consider the alternatives: fly/drive packages and *MotoRail* facilities eliminate time-consuming motor travel and allow for concentration on the areas of particular interest. Given fuel costs, both these alternatives are not necessarily extravagances. Cost them out against the expenses involved in using your own car for the entire trip.

MotoRail: For information on this easy and non-tiring way of covering long distances, contact the state tourist bureaus or the following main state railway offices:

> **New South Wales**
> Manager, Rail Travel Centre
> 11-31 York Street, Sydney, NSW, 2000
> Tel. (02) 29 7614
>
> **Victoria**
> Manager, Passenger Operations, V/Line
> 589 Collins Street, Melbourne, Vic., 3000
> Tel. (03) 62 0771
>
> **South Australia**
> Manager, Australian National Railways
> GPO Box 1743
> Adelaide, SA, 5001
> Tel. (08) 217 4111
>
> **Western Australia**
> Interstate Booking Office, Westrail
> GPO Box S1422
> Perth, WA, 6001
> Tel. (09) 326 2733
>
> **Queensland**
> Officer in Charge, City Booking Office
> Queensland Rail
> 208 Adelaide Street, Brisbane, Qld, 4000
> Tel. (07) 225 0211

The major *MotoRail* services are:

> **Sydney—Melbourne—Sydney**
> *Southern Aurora*
> Daily, each way. (Overnight) 13 hours.
>
> **Sydney—Murwillumbah—Sydney**
> *Gold Coast MotoRail Express*
> Daily, each way. (Overnight) 17 hours.
>
> **Perth—Sydney—Perth**
> *Indian-Pacific*
> Three services a week each way. 66 hours.
>
> **Perth—Adelaide—Perth**
> *Trans-Australian*
> Two services a week each way. 44 hours. This service connects with *The Overland* to Melbourne.
>
> **Melbourne—Adelaide—Melbourne**
> *The Overland*
> Daily, each way. (Overnight) 12 hours.
>
> **Melbourne—Mildura—Melbourne**
> *The Vinelander*
> Six services a week each way. (Overnight) 10 hours.
>
> **Adelaide—Alice Springs—Adelaide**
> *Ghan*
> May-October, 2 services a week each way. November-April, 1 service a week each way. 23 hours.
>
> **Brisbane—Townsville—Cairns—Townsville—Brisbane**
> *The Queenslander*
> One service a week each way. 33 hours.
>
> **Sydney—Brisbane—Sydney**
> *Brisbane Limited*
> Daily, each way. 15 hours.

The **Abel Tasman:** Three return voyages weekly between Melbourne and Devonport in northern Tasmania. This newly commissioned luxury ship has replaced the long-serving *Empress of Australia*. Bookings should be made through your local Tasbureau office. If you are unlucky with bookings on the *Abel Tasman*, an alternative would be to plan a fly-drive holiday in Tasmania.

Campervan Rental: Fully equipped campervans are available for hire in all states. They can be hired for one or two way trips; sometimes an extra charge is made for one-way rental. Campervans vary in size and degree of luxury and hire costs vary according to the time of year. If you plan a long trip, they provide an excellent solution to the problem of accommodation costs and also allow for relaxed go-as-you-please touring.

Adventure Treks: If you are of an adventurous disposition but don't fancy going it alone to the remote outback or tropical jungle, some state motoring organisations arrange escorted group trips. You take your own car but leave the worries of organisation and navigation in really experienced hands.

Alternatively, leave the car behind. Adventure tour operators provide an amazing variety of treks to remote areas, using all kinds of transport from four-wheel drive to camels or canoes. Wilderness tours, horseback treks, trout fishing tours and packhorse and wagon tours are all available, for anything from a week's to a month's duration. Ask your travel agent or state government tourist bureau for more information.

Accommodation

State tourist bureaus, motoring organisations and booksellers all have accommodation guides, including information on camping and caravan parks. Travel agents and airline brochures can also provide information.

Hotels and motels: Major motel/hotel chains, such as Flag, Homestead, Koala, Travelodge, Zebra, cover most of the country and have head offices in each capital with facilities to book accommodation throughout Australia. Brochures detailing their accommodation are available from these offices.

For the young at heart: There are approximately 100 youth hostels throughout Australia. For information, contact the main headquartes of the Australian Youth Hostels Association, 60 Mary St, Surry Hills, NSW. (02) 212 1151

Serviced and self-service: If you are planning a stay in a city or resort area for any length of time, a sensible family alternative to motel or hotel accommodation is a serviced or self-service flat. The relevant tourist bureau has information.

Another interesting alternative is to exchange houses with another family. **Make sure you are totally satisfied with the individuals concerned and with all the details of the arrangements before committing yourself;** and check that your household insurance covers your property in this situation.

Down on the farm: Farm homestead accommodation makes a refreshing alternative. It can vary from spartan 'staff quarters' to luxurious 'country club' style. Check with state tourist bureaus or regional tourist authorities for farms and properties providing this kind of accommodation.

Stay afloat: A paddle-wheeler cruise down the Murray, a houseboat on the Hawkesbury or inland lakes or a life on the ocean wave aboard a charter yacht will add magic to any holiday. Again, tourist bureaus can supply details.

Dividing up the dollars

Although your individual mode of travel and nature of holiday will determine how you organise your budget, a few general points apply to this vital area of holiday planning. If you are doing any advance thinking on budgets, remember that any trip or holiday taken during peak holiday periods will cost more than the same holiday at other times of the year. Most accommodation, air, rail and rental prices are higher during these periods. If possible, try to arrange your trips during off-peak periods.

It is advisable to consider taking out holiday insurance. It is even more advisable to check it very carefully to see what eventualities are covered and what are not. Don't travel with large sums of cash; take travellers' cheques, Bankcard or credit cards wherever possible. Another good idea is to keep a contingency sum aside — cash if necessary, or an arrangement with your bank for an emergency drawing from another branch. This contingency should be kept intact from all the nibbling general expenses.

Budget Biters
- Admission charges
- Theatre, cinema or disco costs
- Souvenirs and presents
- Sending postcards — cards and stamps
- Snacks and drinks
- Films
- Chemists and medical expenses
- Tipping
- Car problems — garage charges and replacement of parts

If using motel accommodation you can save significantly by taking basic ingredients for breakfasts and snacks.

When you are costing your fuel budget, remember that petrol is always more expensive in the remote areas.

Itineraries

Some people like to make them and stick to them, some don't. At the very least, a rough schedule to ensure sufficient time in places of interest is a good idea.

Important factors in any itinerary include the weather — allow plenty of time for rest breaks in extreme heat — and children — they tend to have a low tolerance of long stretches of driving and too much view-admiring. In both cases, short spells of driving are best.

Clothing

Be very strict with yourself and the family when packing. All items which come into the 'I just *might* need that' category should be ruthlessly eliminated. Essentials are a warm jumper, even if it's summer, sensible comfortable shoes and as many non-crushable and drip-dry items as can be managed. Keep items like swimwear, towels, spare socks and warm sweaters in a loose bag which can be easily got at.

First aid kit

A basic first aid kit is essential. Include band-aids, some antiseptic, bandages, headache tablets, sunburn cream, insect repellent and a soothing lotion for bites. Eyedrops are a good idea, as is a thermometer, and a tourniquet, though it may sound dramatic, will certainly be missed if it is needed.

Useful extras

As well as picnic equipment, tissues, toilet paper, bags for rubbish and a polythene sheet for placing under the picnic rug if the grass is damp are all well worth taking. Gum boots usually come in handy too. Things for the children's and your car's comfort are dealt with elsewhere.

Leaving home

Everyone knows the feeling, which usually comes to mind a good distance from home: did all the windows really get locked in the flurry of leaving? Usually, all is well, but it never hurts to double check.

- Make arrangements to cancel milk, papers and mail.
- Make arrangements for watering/mowing in garden and for indoor plants. If no one is available to care for indoor plants, try putting them all together and surrounding the pots with damp peat; water thoroughly. Encasing the whole pot plant in a sealed polythene bag also helps during summer months.
- If your pet is not a good traveller, make arrangements for its safe keeping well in advance.
- If touring, try to leave at least a couple of contact addresses en route with a friend or neighbour.
- If possible, arrange for someone to keep an eye on the house. Your local police will co-operate in this.
- If turning electricity off at the mains, leave the fridge door open. Make sure that everything else that should be turned off is off.
- Check all locks on windows and doors, then check again.
- Any really valuable items, such as jewellery, are best left for safe keeping at the bank.

Have a Good Trip

Comfortable driving

Discomfort destroys concentration. Such drivers as Sir Jack Brabham, three times world motor racing champion, believe that lack of concentration is the biggest single cause of road accidents.

Almost every decently designed motor car can be set up to accommodate a driver of almost any size. Some, of course, are more sophisticated in the seat adjustments they provide than others, but it should be possible to establish a good driving position, which is the key to cutting down stress, allowing full control together with the best possible visibility, and therefore the best possible sensory intake.

You should sit almost upright, with the arms well bent so that you can take hold of the top of the steering wheel without completely straightening an arm.

If the seat has height adjustment, set it as high as is comfortable for the sake of forward vision. Set the reach of the seat so that the legs can fully depress brake and clutch pedals and still have a little movement left.

Keep both hands on the wheel all the time, but do not grip it hard or your wrists and hands will be tense. Tension leads to tiredness.

Adjust mirrors and do up seatbelts *before* driving off. If the seatbelt is of the type that tightens up on the move, pull it out an extra inch and clip a spring clothes peg across it where the webbing emerges from the runner, or from the door-post housing.

Always wear loose clothing; this rule applies to passengers too. Anything tight interferes with blood circulation and restricts movements. Wear supple, light-soled shoes. Never sandals, thongs or high heels which can get tangled up with pedals and lead to spectacular, but unscheduled, manoeuvres.

Hats with brims of useful proportions restrict vision. It is better to rely on sunvisors to combat glare or to use tinted spectacles. The best place to stow sunglasses is on top of the driver's sunvisor, secured by a thick rubber band. They can be got at quickly without taking your eyes off the road.

Gloves made of thin leather, with plenty of ventilation in the backing, are a good idea. Apart from absorbing sweat and making the wheel rim feel comfortable, stinging intruders such as bees can be grabbed and ejected without your coming to any harm. If the windscreen suddenly fogs up because of temperature change, leather or string-backed gloves will wipe it without smearing. If the hot end of a cigarette falls off it can be painlessly pinched into extinction.

Packing the car

Now that you've got yourself into the car, what about stowing away the things you want to take on the trip?

The rule that overrides every other consideration is: **put it in the boot if you can do without it inside — particularly if it's heavy.**

Remember that if a car comes to a full-stop from 60 kmh, a camera parked on the back parcel shelf will acquire an instant velocity of 60 kmh and may easily be directed towards your head. Under these circumstances the smallest camera can be classed as a very heavy object indeed. Instant flying objects of this and any other kind should be stowed in the boot.

This rule also applies to food and drink. Flying drink bottles in sudden stops are not to be risked. Sandwiches eaten on the move can mean sticky hands and crumbs dropped where they irritate. You should stop every hour on a long trip, get out and walk around for a bit to get the circulation going and to break the monotony of driving, which is the deadly killer of concentration. Use this opportunity to eat and drink if required.

If the boot is full and you have not got all your luggage in, put it on the floor in the back. It should not be able to roll under the front seat and into the front floor area. Loose things in front can and do get stuck under pedals. A shoe or a tennis ball under the brake pedal will almost guarantee full steam ahead when the anchors are needed. Any efforts to dislodge such things will be far too late in an emergency situation.

Tissues, boiled lollies and maps are about the only useful objects that are safe loose inside a car. If you *do* like to pack the kitchen sink get a roof rack or a bigger car. Towing only introduces a whole new set of problems.

When to set off

Some people like night driving. Some don't.

If the weather is clear, however, it *is* a good way of getting distance under your wheels. The best hours are usually between 1 am and 6 am when traffic is at its lightest. Obviously peak hours should be avoided in cities, but direction can be just as important as time of day.

If you are travelling west, plan to arrive before late afternoon, when the sun will be shining directly into your eyes. Going east, it is better to leave the start until mid-morning. An east-west trek across Australia can be sheer misery if you don't plan a suitable timetable.

Checking the car

All the care that you devote to your own comfort can go for nothing if you don't make sure that the car checks out, too.

On a regular basis — certainly at least once a week — you should go through this checklist.
1. When the engine is cold, check oil, water and hydraulic fluid levels. With automatic gearboxes the transmission fluid level needs to be checked too. Top up battery and screen-washer reservoirs. Check the tension and condition of the fanbelt. If it slips or breaks, you will be stuck with no fan, and no power from the alternator. Learn how to change the fan-belt, carry the necessary tools, and a spare belt.
2. Check tyre pressures with a low-priced mechanical gauge. Service station gauges often vary by up to 5 lb pressure above or below the true reading. All new cars carry a sticker that lists the correct tyre pressure. Look for it in the driver's door opening, in the glovebox, or in the boot. It may be in 'bars', or it may be in the imperial measure of pounds per square inch.

Modern steel radials are very deceptive. They look baggy even when properly inflated, and they may not look any more baggy until pressure has fallen dangerously low. Under-inflated tyres have less effective tread contact area with the road and build up more heat on the move, both of which conditions are the recipe for disaster in Australian summer heat.
3. Headlights, brake lights and signal lights should be checked for correct operation. When checking the headlights the car should be fully loaded and ready for the trip. A loaded boot can weigh down the tail so that the headlights point upwards, thus dazzling oncoming traffic.
4. All glass should be cleaned inside and out before driving. Carry a squeegee and some methylated spirit-based fluid which helps get rid of baked-on dirt, flies and condensation. Vinyl upholstery and trim sweats in hot weather and produces fumes that fog glass on the inside. This needs some kind of detergent to shift it easily. It is worth buying one of the several proprietary preparations that can be applied to inhibit formation of this film.
5. When towing anything, the hitch should be checked for security. The law in most states demands that tow bars are fitted with safety chains. Try out the tail and stop lights, marker lights and signal lights. If the van or trailer is fitted with separate brakes, try them out immediately after going on the road; don't wait for a threatening situation to arise, in case they aren't working.
6. Check that doors, windows and roof vents of a caravan are closed. Don't forget that caravan tyres need air, just like car tyres.
7. The same applies to trailing a boat, except that the lashings, as well as the trailer tyres, need to be checked.
8. Roof rack fittings can soon work loose on rough roads. If constant checking is not going to be possible, split-pin the bolts so that the nuts cannot work loose.

The fundamental rule of the road in Australia is keep to the left. A system of priority roads applies in all states but the system is not yet complete. Some intersections in almost every city and town do not have traffic lights, stop signs or give way signs.

The old rule of giving way to traffic on the right applies here, pending the installation of traffic lights or signs. Sometimes these intersections are marked by signs which read GIVE WAY TO THE RIGHT; often they are not, and you need to be highly alert all the time.

'Give way to the right' simply means that every vehicle on your right has priority over yours. Cars turning right, however, must give way to oncoming traffic turning left. This rule differs in Victoria, where cars turning right have priority over oncoming traffic turning left. To make a U-turn, you must give way to all other traffic.

The so-called diamond turn for turning right applies almost everywhere in Australia. Instead of vehicles driving around each other, they pass inside each other, with their off-sides presented to each other.

The exceptions to the diamond turn are found at several intersections in the heart of Melbourne and on some dual carriageway roads in other states. Here, those turning right pull to the extreme left of the road at traffic lights and complete the turn when the lights are green in the new direction taken. Some of these intersections are marked, some are not.

Melbourne is the last stronghold of the tram. Wherever you meet them, overtaking on the right is forbidden.

At roundabouts and traffic islands, give way to the right, or to all traffic that is on the island or roundabout before you enter it. Some have give way signs, some do not.

It is not lawful to park at the side of the road facing the opposite way to the traffic.

Never drive with only sidelights lit after lighting-up time. Although sidelights of a certain intensity are strictly legal, police are likely to stop you if your headlights are not on.

Speed and other regulations in each state vary. It is advisable to obtain a copy of current regulations from the motor transport authority in states where you plan to travel.

Defensive Driving

Defensive driving is based on the assumption that all road users other than yourself are fools, and that full allowance should, therefore, be made for them.

By doing this you are less likely to get yourself involved in accidents and you may actually help others to stay out of trouble, despite their own actions, and despite other factors such as bad weather conditions.

The keys to better driving are: **thinking ahead, position on the road, the mirror—signal manoeuvre procedure,** and **tailoring speed to fit visibility and road conditions.**

Implicit in all these things is **consideration for other road users.**

Test your rating as a safe driver

If you have never had that nasty creepy feeling that something you've done could have turned into a bad accident, you are either unique or, much more likely, you think you have nothing more to learn. The fact is that if you are really trying to improve your driving you must have the faculty to criticise and to discipline yourself. Even the most skilled and experienced driver never stops learning.

Concentration

Get to know your car: how all the controls work; how it behaves in a corner and under brakes; make yourself comfortable and relaxed. Only when you have done this can you start to develop concentration.

Concentration is all about getting into the right position, with time to spare, by anticipating the movements of traffic and of pedestrians. Don't just blindly follow the car in front. Treat it as if it has a load of fly-blown sheep carcasses. If you can't see around it or on through its windows, drop back so that you can get a view of what's ahead. If any trouble comes up in front, you will have time to use your brakes unhurriedly, and not surprise the person behind into rearranging the shape of your boot.

Being uncomfortable, tired and hungry produces the impatience that leads to bad judgement. Such lapses in concentration breed accidents.

When you're tired, admit it. You can do several things about it, such as directing the inside air vents on to your face, opening a window, turning up the radio. But no remedy is as safe and effective as stopping, getting out for a walk and perhaps having a cup of tea and a sandwich.

Are you fit to drive, anyway? Are you taking any medicine with side-effects that pep you up or slow you down? When did you last have your eyes tested or your glasses changed?

Smooth driving

With oil prices rocketing upwards, driving smoothly is paying off more and more. Smoothness is the key to economy and thinking ahead is the key to smoothness (which is not to be confused with slowness).

You, your passengers and your car will suffer much less wear and tear if acceleration is progressive. Match clutch, gear and throttle movements, and brake early. Practise braking so that the pedal effort can be tapered off as the car

If you think you're a smooth driver, try this test:

Fill an old-fashioned (metrically speaking) one-pint beer glass with water to precisely 25 mm below the rim.

Put it on top of the dash. If this is not flat enough, use some packing.

Drive off.

If you drive really smoothly, there'll be no spillage. Clumsy acceleration and braking will slop it over, as will any sudden steering movements.

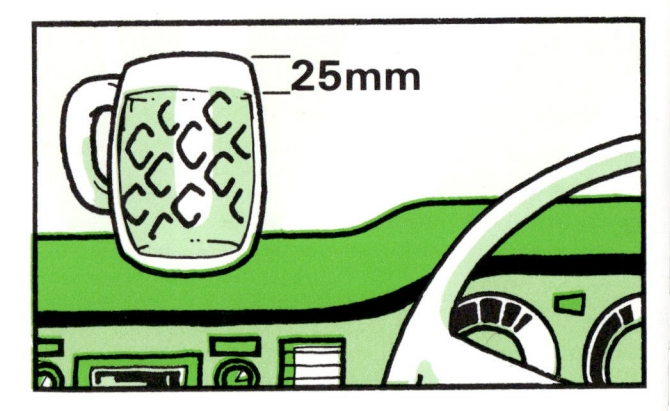

comes to a stop, and the nose does not jerk upward immediately after the actual moment of stopping.

Be economical with steering wheel movements. Turning the road wheels makes them act like brakes and wastes petrol. Power through corners on a light throttle and only open up gently as you leave the turn and straighten up.

Leave heavy acceleration and braking to racing drivers. The less of both you do, the less energy is wasted, and the more fuel saved.

Keep on thinking further and further ahead. Organise overtaking so that you don't accelerate harder or longer than is needful; for instance, you should not have to brake to match the speed of the vehicle in front of the one you've just overtaken.

Road conditions

When it rains, do not just switch on the wipers and continue driving at undiminished speed. Slippery roads mean that you have to remember all your basics and put them into practice with great delicacy.

Stopping distances increase dramatically on wet roads; and any clumsiness by a driver can lead to a skid. Driving in the wet means that *even more* anticipation is needed than in the dry.

Drive according to the visibility and keep much greater than normal distances between you and other traffic. Do not try to brake and steer at the same time, because it is an invitation to a skid. It is better to attempt only the bare minimum of braking and steering changes, and, if at all possible, to separate the two actions. If you hit the brake pedal too hard, release it as soon as the wheels skid, then depress the pedal again and repeat this action for as long as necessary. Make the smallest possible steering movements that will see you through a situation.

Never forget that the first instinct in an emergency is to try and stop. Often it's an automatic panic move when, in fact, acceleration — gentle in the wet — may be the better way out.

Trying to correct a skid when the back wheels have let go sideways is the most common way to lose road grip. It is not hard to manage but it needs practice. The way to deal with a skid is to remove the cause by lifting off the accelerator. At the same time you must steer in the direction in which the back wheels are sliding.

The tricky bit is being able to feel when the back wheels have gripped again, because this is when you must take off the sympathetic steering movement. If you don't do it quickly enough the tail will start to slide back in the opposite direction, so that the car goes 'fishtailing' down the road and probably ends up by spinning.

A front wheel skid tends to let the nose of the car drift out towards the right hand side of the road and into oncoming traffic. Try applying the handbrake, if it works on the back wheels. If it locks the back wheels they will move sideways and this will tend to point the car to the left. Apart from that you just have to sit and wait for the car to sort itself out.

The most dreaded condition in the wet is known as aquaplaning. When a road is streaming wet, or lightly flooded, tyres can ride on a wedge of water and have no contact with the hard surface at all. As long as the tyres are waterborne, steering and brakes are useless and you must not touch either, in case the car comes back into road contact with a brake locked or the front wheels turned, either of which will mean a monumental spin. The solution, again, is to back off the accelerator and wait for the aquaplaning to stop, before deciding whether brakes or steering are needed to avoid any trouble.

The main decision to make when driving on snow or ice, if your car does not have chains or studded tyres, is whether to keep moving or to stop. Fresh snow is the exception; it gives fairly good grip, but on packed and rutted snow or ice it is not much good trying to keep going if the back wheels are spinning wildly. Look for obstructions under the car; use bits of bush or gravel for packing under the driving wheels; and never forget that sometimes even the tiniest push will get a car going on a level surface.

Snow you can see; ice you often can't. If the sun seems to have thawed out an icy road, look for shiny patches in hollows under trees, and in any shadowed spots. Open the window and listen. Tyres hiss on wet surfaces, but are quiet on ice. Use a minimum of steering adjustment, brake lightly and, if there's any other traffic around, stay as far away as possible from it.

Fog is a rare phenomenon in Australia, at least to the degree of opacity that at times can blanket parts of western Europe. Nevertheless, it can mean bad trouble if you encounter it. When you come across fog, forget your itinerary and resist all pressure to hurry. The driving rules are simple:

Switch on dipped headlights; sidelights are simply not enough. Use front and back demisters. Use wipers and washers as needed; this is when you really appreciate the meaning of clean glass all around.

If someone zips past you, don't assume he has second sight and follow him. Go no faster than you can see to stop, and keep at a very respectful distance from all other traffic.

In a real murk, a correctly adjusted set of foglights is marvellous for picking up reference points, such as white lines and kerbs.

Above all, if the ordeal becomes too great, pull as far off the road as you reasonably can and wait until you feel strong enough to continue.

Positioning

On any road — from freeway to farm track — positioning is vital. Try to stagger your car in the line of traffic so that you can see well ahead — very helpful on the long and sweeping freeway type of bend.

Good positioning includes not cluttering up intersections. When turning right on a two-lane road, don't angle the car. Keep it square so that following traffic can pass by on your left.

Every manoeuvre should be based on the creed: **mirror, signal, manoeuvre.** Always be decisive and deliberate; never hurry any manoeuvre, or be hurried into it.

Long, fast Australian roads can lull you into a state of suspended judgement. The low overall speed limits can cause traffic to bunch and drivers to become bored, so that if you're in a collection of cars, all travelling at similar speeds, you get very little sense of actual speed.

To build up speed economically and easily, use level or downhill stretches as much as possible. When a speed limit sign looms up and requires you to slow down, try and arrive at the posted speed smoothly and without using the brakes.

Speed limits often lie: road conditions may be so bad that it is prudent to stop. And remember that everything can change in an instant if a semi-trailer in front jack-knifes, or a car has a blow-out. Always be able to stop in the distance you can see ahead. Keep out of queues of cars; either fall back, or overtake and keep an empty buffer space in front of and behind you. If you leave insufficient space, it will be your car that gets sideswiped.

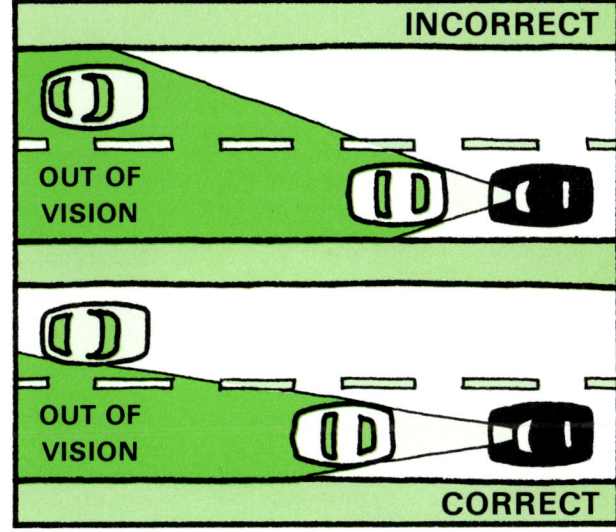

Don't sit too close to the vehicle in front — it reduces your vision.

The vehicle turning right should have pulled up square, so that the following traffic could get by.

Outback Motoring

The outback of Australia is an area so vast that you can perish for all sorts of reasons. The desolation stretches for hundreds of kilometres. In summer, daytime temperatures are around 60°C, yet at night the thermometer can record zero, or less.

Driver comfort is highly important, particularly if you are on your own. The best time to travel is in the cooler months and the dry season, roughly from May to August. Air-conditioning is the greatest comfort to fit in your car if you're going to be touring for days, weeks or months. Not only does it keep you cool; it enables you to travel with windows closed so that dust does not infest every corner of your car and its contents.

Equipping the car

An ordinary car that's in good condition, preferably with a laminated windscreen, should let you see most of the outback, mostly from bitumen roads. Four-wheel-drive is not necessary unless you want to go off the roads.

The next best thing to four-wheel-drive is a limited-slip differential. This device passes power to both driving wheels even if one has no contact with the road surface. It is better to avoid taking a fancy car. The more popular the make of car, the easier it is to get parts and service in remote places.

Anyone contemplating months away in the outback is well advised to get a workshop manual for his car and to learn how to do elementary maintenance and repair jobs.

But if you can't afford to put your car in top condition for outback motoring, you can't afford to go. Stay home and save up.

Spare parts

Don't fall into the trap of trying to take everything to cover every emergency; it's just not possible. Overloading will make a car handle badly and use a lot more petrol than it should.

The most useful spare parts to take are: fanbelt, fuel pump repair kit, a couple of spark plugs, radiator hoses, tyre repair outfit, one spare tyre, points, condenser, coil, tyre levers, assorted nuts, bolts, washers and split-pins.

Tools must include pliers and a good jack with baseplate for use on soft ground, electrical screwdriver and shifting spanner. You should have the means of removing the sump if it is holed, and enough oil to refill it. Jumper leads and a long-handled shovel are useful too.

Never be without a tube of plastic bonding goo. It will fix a sump, petrol tank or distributor cap.

Road conditions

Watch the colour of the road. Usually it's some shade of sand, broken mostly by bars of white limestone and the grey and black of toes of rock. Where the colours change, the erosion rate of the two materials differs and there is always a bump of some kind.

Once the colour change is spotted, and depending upon how fast you are going, either back off the throttle or start to brake, smoothly and early, until you are close enough to see what sort of a bump is coming up.

In **sand**, never run off the road. Stop on the road and prospect the edges on foot, or you are likely to end up bogged to the axle(s). Soft sand and mud are best negotiated at the highest reasonable speed possible in the highest gear the engine will pull. Lose momentum, and you will get stuck.

If a road disappears in a deep patch of sand or muddy water that you judge to be impassable, look for wheel or animal tracks around the area and follow them.

Do not try to find your own way around unless you are forced to do so. Prospect on foot first.

As a last resort, in really bad going, lower the tyre pressures. Do not go much below 10 lb or the tyres may roll off the rims.

This stratagem should be used only for short distances through sand and mud patches because it is very destructive to the tyres' sidewalls and causes overheating of the casings. Normal road tyres are best.

When you come to a **water** obstacle and can't tell the depth, get out and walk through it. If it is not too deep for your car, take off the fanbelt to stop water spraying around and killing the engine electrics. Then go through it slowly, but at high

---

If you cannot read a map or use a compass — or you don't have them with you — it is vital to have some means of orientating yourself if you are lost.

The most simple, rough method of finding north is to use a conventional wrist watch and the sun when it is at its lower angles.

Place the 12 on the watch in line with the sun and bisect the angle between it and the hour hand. This will give a fairly accurate indication of north.

At night the Southern Cross can be used to determine south.

When exploring sidetracks, note the time of day and position of the sun when setting out. If it is behind you, return with it in your face, unless it has passed its zenith in the meantime.

As well as this, it is a good idea to make a rough sketch of the track you are following, noting all turn-offs, and distances between them, on the speedometer, together with any landmarks, such as hills or windmills. Reconcile your return route with the sketch, point by point.

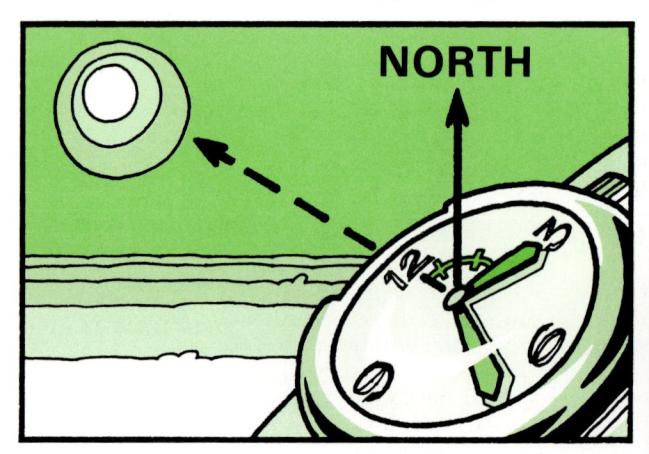

revs, in first gear, to blow water out of the exhaust pipe. If it starts to **rain**, the best action is to wait on high ground until it stops.

Bulldust holes are often almost impossible to see until you are right on top of them. These are road depressions filled with superfine dust into which a wheel will sink as if the dust were water. Watch out for them and for **cattle grids**.

A car, particularly one with a heavy load, will bore into **jump-ups** such as creek crossings as if it wants to go underground at impossibly low speeds unless a special driving technique is developed. As the nose clears the edge of the dip on entry, brake. This pulls the nose down and cocks the back up so that it also clears the entry.

Keep the brakes on until just before the deepest part of the depression has been reached. As the front wheels are about to start climbing out, release the brakes and open the throttle. This will lift the nose, preventing the springs from bottoming, giving maximum road clearance for the exit. As you get the rhythm of the road with this technique, you can speed up a bit.

Overtaking

Overtaking in dusty conditions needs great care.

If you get stuck behind a road train, which is a truck towing three or four trailers of about its own size, and perhaps equivalent in length to two semi-trailers, dust will either be coming straight back in a cloud that obscures the road, or blowing from side to side with similar effect. Stay behind the dust cloud so that you can see past the train.

When a long, straight, empty stretch of road comes up, make your move. Work up to overtaking speed before you commit yourself to the manoeuvre, so that the least time is spent on the wrong side of the road. Do not hesitate, once committed.

Unless the train driver has signalled to you somehow, you must assume that he does not know someone is trying to get by. You must also take the risk that he may swerve to avoid something while you are obscured and blinded by his dust.

In such situations it is a good idea to find an excuse to stop. There is no safe way to overtake in these circumstances.

Animals

Whether on a sealed or unsealed road, almost everywhere in the outback you will be at risk from animals: kangaroo, stock and, in the desert, even camels.

The kangaroo is by far the greatest hazard. In warm parts of the country they feed at night and sleep by day; in colder areas it may be the other way around. Whichever the case, they move in the early morning and late evening.

Bright halogen lights will often fix a 'roo for a few seconds at night, but, apart from blinding the animal, they also cause it to panic and to jump any way at any time.

Kangaroo bars are practically useless except in very low speed impacts. If the bars are strong enough to do any good, they will be so heavy that the front suspension needs to be beefed up; the stronger the bars, the more damage they will transmit to the mounting points, and you can end up after an impact at speed with an out-of-shape front-end and doors that won't open.

Survival

Getting stuck in a broken motor car can be a very dangerous matter so you must carry equipment for survival as well as spare parts and repair equipment.

Carry 20 litres of water per head. This is plenty to last a week and to refill the cooling system if it bursts. Likewise iron rations, such as dry biscuits and canned food, should be carried to cover the same period.

Water is best kept in plastic containers. Put the food in a box so that you don't have to search the whole vehicle for tins and broken biscuits.

Do not break into this supply for any other reason than an emergency. The water should be treated as almost sacred — you can go a lot longer without food than a drink.

Carry at least 40 litres of petrol in steel jerry cans. Most plastics deteriorate rapidly in contact with petrol.

THE TWO PARAMOUNT RULES OF OUTBACK MOTORING ARE:
1. If you go off the beaten track tell somebody, such as the police or a station manager, where you are going and when you expect to be back, so that they will know when and where to come looking if you're late.
2. If you do break down **do not leave your car for any reason.** A vehicle is much more easily spotted than a human, particularly from the air.

Less than 24 hours without water can be fatal in outback heat.

The first thing to conserve in a water emergency is body moisture. Keep your body covered and in any kind of shade that can be found to keep down body evaporation.

This is the main reason why you should **never leave a broken-down vehicle.** In many cases it will be the only effective shade available.

Don't forget the engine cooling water when all other supplies run out.

There is often a source of water underground, even though river or creek beds may be dry. A hole dug about one metre deep may produce a useful soak.

Where there is vegetation, use the 'Arizona still' to extract water from it, as follows:

Dig a hole about one metre across and a little more than half as deep. Put some kind of vessel in the centre to collect water.

Surround this vessel with cut vegetation. Obviously, fleshy-looking plants, such as succulents, will hold more moisture than saltbush.

Cover the hole with a piece of plastic sheet held down by closely-spaced stones, so that the hole is sealed off. Put another stone in the centre of the sheet, over the catching vessel.

The sun's heat will evaporate moisture from the plants. This moisture will condense on the plastic, run down the cone formed by the centre stone and drip off into the vessel.

Output, in uninterrupted sunlight, with the right sort of plants, should be about one litre every six hours or so.

The still takes about three hours to start producing and it will become less efficient as ground moisture is dried out. New holes will need to be dug at intervals.

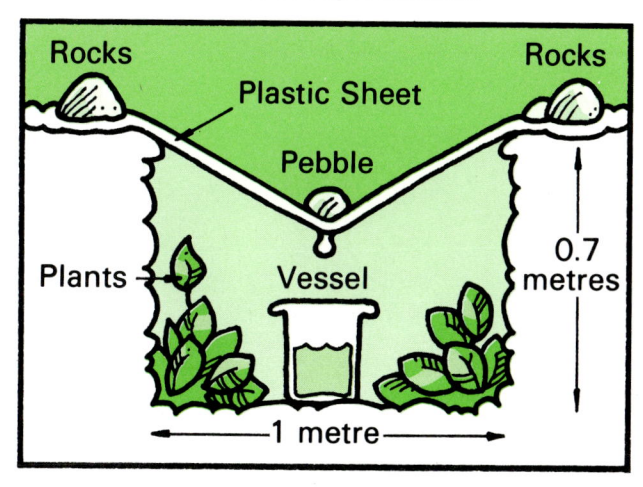

Breakdowns

The best way to avoid breakdowns is to have your car regularly and expertly serviced and to keep an eye out for any little pointers that may indicate it is getting ready to go on strike.

So many breakdowns happen because warning signs have been ignored. The average driver cannot be expected to look after a car completely but some common-sense checks are within anyone's competence.

As a matter of weekly routine — as well as before a long trip — remember **POWT**, and check the levels of petrol, oil, water and the tension of the fanbelt.

On the move, the ignition warning light may glow regularly and go out again without causing any apparent trouble. One day it may not go out and the car will catch fire.

Every now and again the water temperature needle may slide further across the gauge than it should but it usually steadies itself after a bit. The day it doesn't the cooling system may be out of water and the car will need a new engine. If you suspect something is about to go wrong, get an expert check.

When the engine stops

Try to roll the car off the road; if you can't, get help to push it off. If the car can't be moved out of traffic, switch on the four-way flasher hazard warning. If the car is in a dangerous position, such as on a blind corner, or over the brow of a hill, it is the driver's responsibility to warn other traffic. Stay with your car and get someone else to go for help.

Never attempt to work on a car while it is a hazard to other traffic.

There are only two reasons for engine failure: either it cannot get petrol and air into the cylinders, or the spark will not ignite the mixture. If the crankshaft breaks or the cylinders seize-up, neither petrol nor spark will be forthcoming.

Some people with sensitive ears claim they can tell what's basically wrong by the way an engine stops. If it splutters and dies, it's out of petrol; if it stops dead, an electrical fault is indicated.

Do not trust your ears to the extent of checking out one system completely, without first checking that there's petrol in the tank and a spark at the plugs. The system that isn't working is the one to check out thoroughly.

How to check spark at plug by earthing on engine block.

Spark plug check

Unscrew one plug, re-connect electrical lead, earth the plug body by pressing it firmly against a bare metal surface on the engine block.

With the ignition switched on, press the head of the starter solenoid under the bonnet, or have someone turn the starter from the driving seat.

The plug should produce a series of bright blue flashes. If it does not then there is a fault in the electrical system.

Petrol check

Petrol gauges are one of the most treacherous devices used to perform a vital job in a car. The tank can be bone dry yet the needle may indicate anything from empty to full.

Take no notice of it in an emergency.

Disconnect the pipe from the petrol pump to the carburettor. Turn the engine on the starter and petrol should spurt out of the pipe. If it does not, dip the tank, if you can, with a bit of wire, or undo the drain plug and have at least a 10-litre vessel to find out what may be inside.

If your car is fitted with electronic ignition *and* petrol injection, you should hope that you *are* out of petrol or the battery is flat, because these two systems are practically impervious to any kind of first aid treatment. If one or the other is fitted, don't waste time trying to fix it.

Fortunately, in this sort of situation, most cars still have neither of these complicated refinements. So you can do one more basic check before you go tracing faults in either the electric or the fuel systems.

Running with the choke in action, when it should not be, can literally drown the engine; it gets so much petrol and so little air that the mixture will not burn. If there is a strong

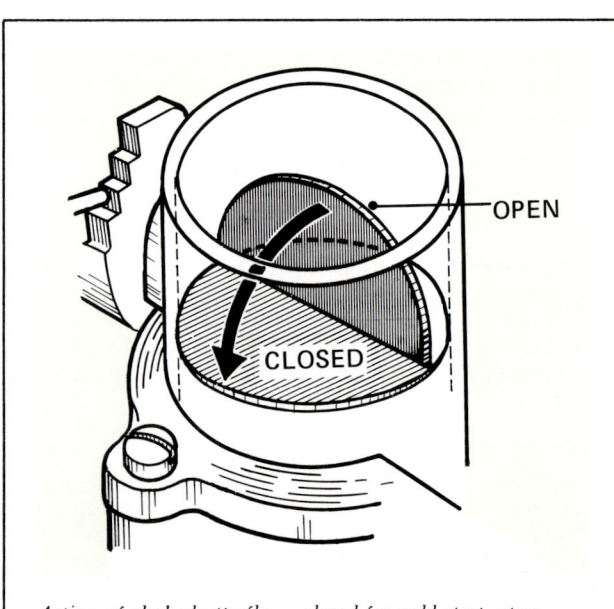

Action of choke butterfly — closed for cold start, open for running.

smell of petrol when the bonnet is raised, or a plug electrode is wet when removed, suspect the choke.

Take off the air cleaner from the carburettor. If the carburettor throat is blocked by a circle of metal hinged in the middle, push down the lower side so that it turns through 90 degrees and leaves the throat clear.

Put the air cleaner back, press the accelerator flat to the boards, and run the starter. The engine should fire after a few seconds, when you should quickly back right off the accelerator.

Never, of course, use the choke for starting when an engine is hot.

So far we have assumed that the starter motor is working. If it is not then there is obviously an electrical problem.

Checking the starter

Do not use a screwdriver or spanner on the starter motor terminals without first disconnecting the battery. Short-circuiting will produce heavy sparking that can cause flesh burns.

Zero or poor starter operation is most likely to be caused by loose, dirty or damaged battery terminal post connectors. If the battery is fitted with clamp-type connectors, slacken the nuts on the clamp bolts. If they will not pull off, put a screwdriver into the slot and expand the clamp. Connectors of the cap type are removed by taking out the central screw and twisting the cap to remove.

Any dirt or corrosion can be removed from the posts with a knife. If the corrosion is heavy, sprinkle with bicarbonate of soda and hose off; or wash with a weak solution of household ammonia and water. Treat the connectors in the same way.

Dry the metal contact surface, and smear with petroleum jelly, which will inhibit further corrosion.

Re-connect the battery and be careful not to overtighten clamps or caps. If a cap screw is loose, overtightening will easily strip the thread; better to fit a fatter screw.

One more vital operation completes this check: one battery terminal is earthed to the body of the car by a strap that is bolted usually to a sheet metal panel. Undo this connection and clean the bolt and washers with emery paper. Smear with petroleum jelly when clean and bolt firmly back in place.

Car engineers find fiendish places to put starter motors. They are seldom easy to get at. Try to check the connections for tightness. If you can, dismantle and clean the connections.

If, after all this, the starter won't go at all, or if it is noisy and slow, or runs without turning the engine, it's a workshop job.

No sound from starter

Put the dash or inside light on and operate the starter. If the motor is getting current the lights will dim and there will be a loud click as the solenoid switch engages. This is proof that the circuit is complete, so you must now look for a mechanical problem.

A likely fault is that the starter pinion is jammed. A car with manual gearbox that is on level ground can be rocked to try and free the pinion. Release the hand-brake and engage top gear. Push and pull the car so that it rocks backwards and forwards, having first made absolutely sure that the ignition is switched off. You should hear the pinion free itself. But in any case try the ignition key after a few seconds rocking.

On a slope or with an automatic transmission car, chock the road wheels and, with the gears in neutral, put a long-handled spanner on the nut that secures the crankshaft pulley and try to rock the shaft so that the pinion is thrown out.

Suspected faulty electrical supply

Dirty or loose battery connections are the most common cause. Follow cleaning and tightening procedures already outlined, then, if the starter still won't work, follow all heavy cables and check connections and terminals. Clean, tighten and re-solder where necessary.

If all connections are in order, suspect the battery itself. The best test is by hydrometer, but in an emergency try the headlights. If the lamps dim as soon as they are switched on full, then at best the battery charge is low. Switch off headlights at once.

Cold is the enemy of batteries: it slows current flow. A battery that has worked well all summer may suddenly pack up when temperatures fall.

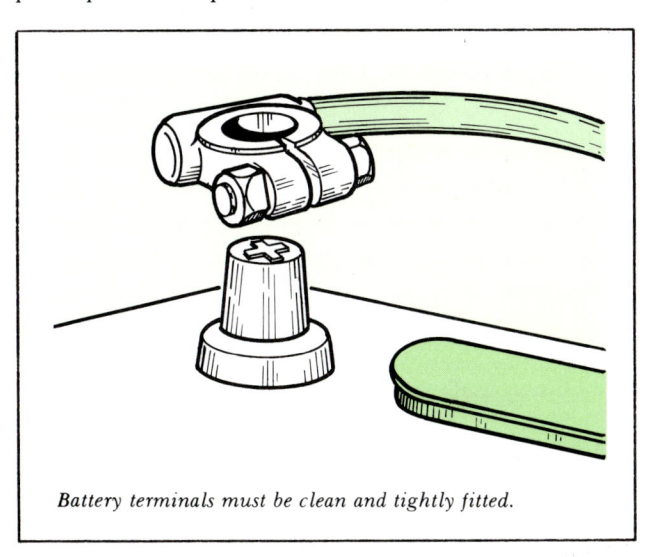

Battery terminals must be clean and tightly fitted.

Earth strap connector must be clean and tight.

Suspect starter motor

If the starter motor will not take current, the problem lies in the solenoid or in the wiring leading to it.

If the fault cannot be isolated and corrected, the car must be push-started (most automatics cannot be push-started; check the handbook) or towed to a workshop. Alternatively remove the starter and get it repaired.

This kind of fault can make the starter hum, instead of turning. The engine may have become so stiff, perhaps through overheating, that the starter is not powerful enough to turn it over.

Remove the spark plugs and see if the engine can be turned over by a spanner on the crankshaft pulley nut. If it can't then some breakage has occurred and jammed the engine. Likewise, put a spanner on the squared end of the starter motor shaft. If it will not turn there is internal trouble.

If the starter jams at times, or makes a whirring noise without turning the engine, suspect the starter drive.

Check that all nuts and bolts holding the starter casing to the engine are tight. Then clean the pinion that engages with the ring gear on the flywheel but **on no account oil or grease it**. It must be dry, or it will pick up dirt which will cause jamming.

If the pinion is badly worn, the ring gear will almost always need replacing too. This is expensive because either the engine or the gearbox has to be removed to get at the flywheel.

The quickest way to damage a starter motor is to operate it while the engine is running. Avoid this at all costs. If the starter motor turns very slowly, check the battery, and go through all other checks already outlined.

Ignition system check

The sequence in this procedure is important. Always follow it carefully.

When the engine is dead, check that the thin wire is connected tightly to the side of the distributor. Then, check the other leads going into the coil, the distributor and the spark plug leads. Switch on the ignition and try the starter. If you can see sparks and hear them snapping between the high tension leads, use insulating tape wound around the leads for a temporary repair. Replace the leads at the first opportunity.

Check the plugs, remembering that when an engine is cold and stiff to turn, the starter motor can use up so much current that there is not enough left to make healthy sparks at the plugs. The smallest loss of efficiency in part of the ignition system can, therefore, make starting impossible.

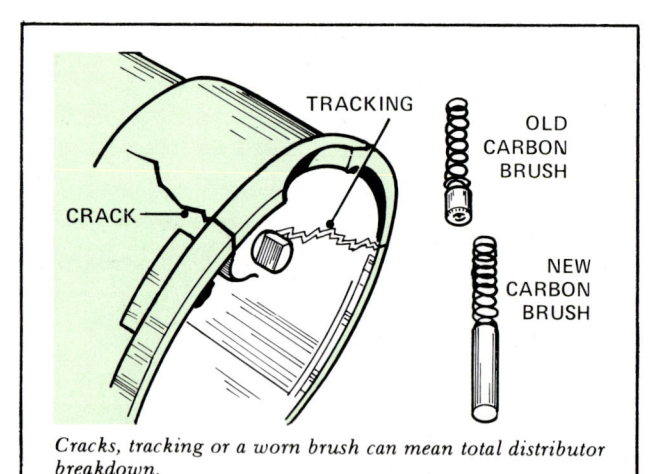

A wire brush will clean plugs but sand blasting is better. Arrow shows adjustable electrode.

This plug is almost useless.

Cracks, tracking or a worn brush can mean total distributor breakdown.

Perhaps the most common ignition problem is condensation. A highly conductive film of moisture and dirt collects on and around high tension parts, allowing current to leak to earth. You can see this filthy film, so dry off the leads and plug caps with a warm, dry cloth and try the starter again.

If it still won't go, take off the distributor cap, dry off the inside, and check that the carbon brush is not broken or damaged. (A quicker and more effective way to do these jobs is to carry a spray can of wetting agent in the car. One squirt gets rid of the film, and the effect is lasting.)

Replace the cap and try the starter again. But *do* be careful, as the search persists, not to flatten the battery or to use too much choke.

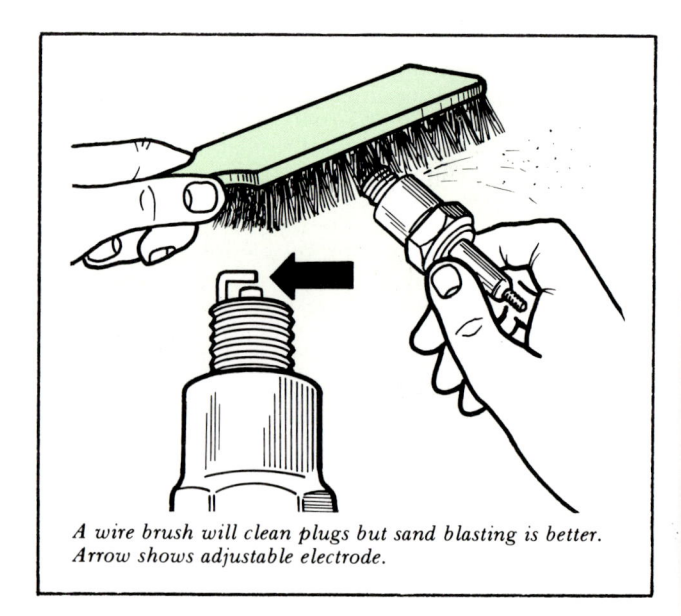

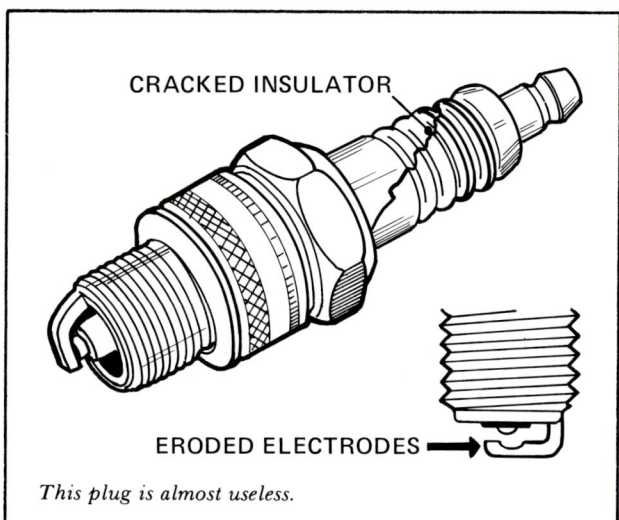

The next checkpoint is the plugs. This procedure has already been detailed. Don't forget, however, that even if there is a decent looking spark, it may not be strong enough to work under pressure in the cylinder. All you have really found out is that the coil and the distributor are functioning at a fair level of efficiency. The plugs themselves may still be at fault.

Check for cracked insulators (a good spray of wetting agent may help these get into action), clean with an emery cloth and adjust gaps.

If there's still no spark, the distributor and the coil are next on the checklist. Look at the points to see if they are blackened, pitted or just dirty.

Any of these things may be due to dirt or a faulty condenser. First try cleaning the points with petrol: use a dampened cloth, and don't flood the distributor.

Next, turn the engine, by pulling on the fanbelt until the points are closed. Turn on the ignition and open the points with a screwdriver. A bright blue spark should arch across the points as they open. If there is no spark the trouble lies in ignition circuit wiring, coil or ignition switch.

If the points do not open easily or stick in the open position, put a minute drop of oil on the pivot of the moving point and push it open and closed with the screwdriver until the movement frees up. Now go to the coil and check the high tension connections by pulling them out and pushing firmly home again.

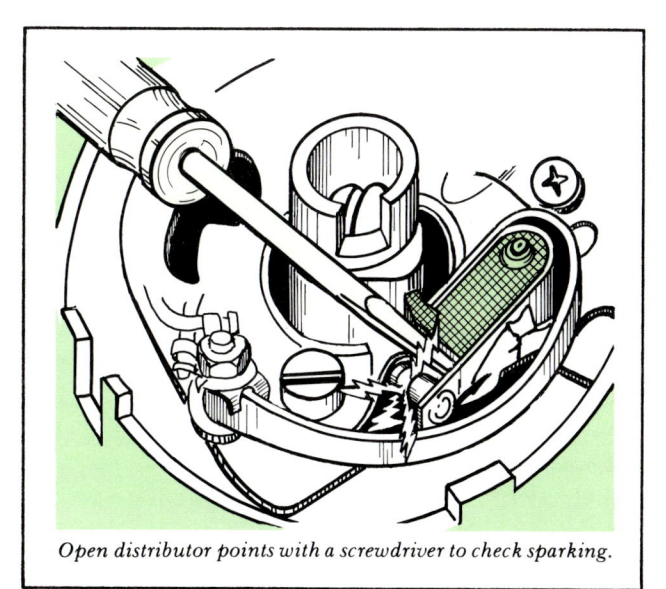

Breakdowns xxvii

Open distributor points with a screwdriver to check sparking.

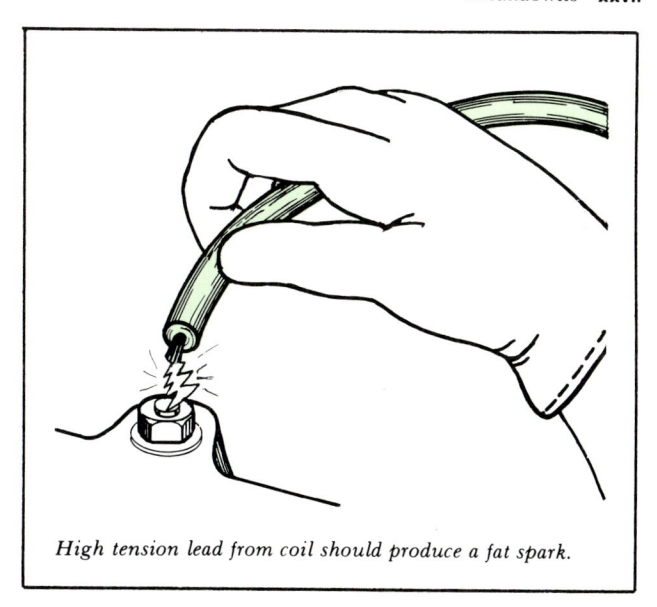

Set distributor points gap when cam opens them to maximum width.

Return to the distributor and put a test lamp (six or 12 volt) across the low tension connectors. Switch on the ignition and turn the engine slowly, by hand. The light should glow when the points close and go out when they open. If the lamp does not light, go back and test the coil. Remove the wire linking coil and the distributor and connect the test lamp between the terminal and a good earth, on the engine or a body panel. The lamp should light when the ignition is switched on. If it does not, the fault is somewhere between the coil and the ignition switch.

Check back through all leads and connectors. Then check the coil circuit by closing the distributor points and pulling the thick lead from the centre of the distributor cap. Switch on the ignition, hold the lead well back from the bare wire and position it about 5 mm from the engine block. Open the points and a healthy spark should jump from wire to engine. No spark, or just a dim flicker, means that the ignition system is really sick.

While you have the ends of the high tension wires out of their sockets, smear them with silicone grease before refitting. This will make a watertight seal and help prevent condensation from affecting the flow of current.

High tension lead from coil should produce a fat spark.

Fuel system check

If petrol is reaching the carburettor float chamber, as described earlier, the float and needle valve should be checked for flooding. Often dirt or wear are the problems with the valve, or the float is set at the wrong height.

You should be able to detect flooding because there will be a strong smell of petrol when the engine is idling and the car is stopped, and petrol consumption will be higher than normal. The smell will disappear when the engine is stopped, because the flooding also stops.

Carburettors are complicated. Do not tamper with them unless you absolutely have to. Confine yourself to cleaning and checking the needle valve and float, and blowing through the jets to make sure they are clear.

Floats usually lift out easily, or only need a split-pin removing. Shake them to find if there is fluid inside. It can be driven out by alternate heating and cooling.

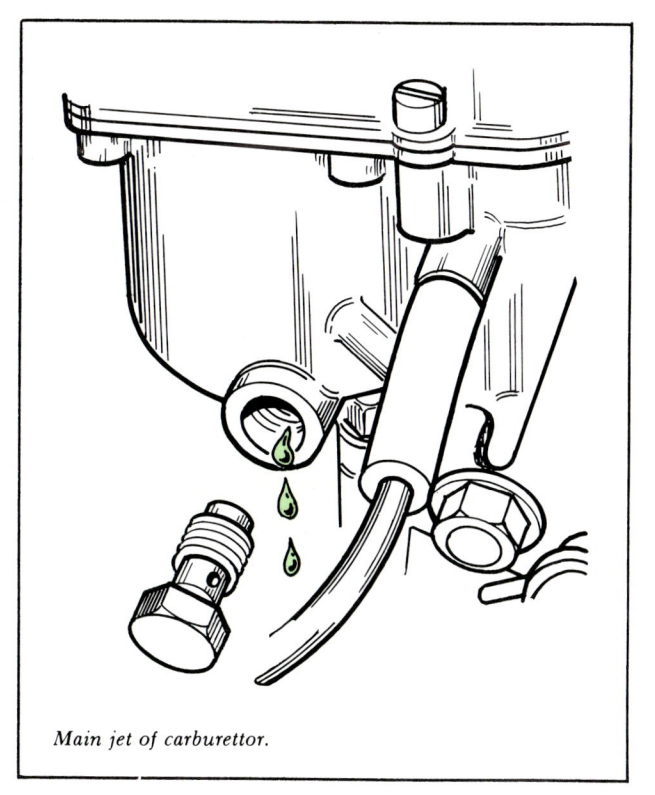

Main jet of carburettor.

Float in hot water — bubbles show leak.

A quick way to find the actual leak is to put it into hot water, when a trail of bubbles will come out of the hole. The easiest way to repair it is to use a two-part epoxy-resin glue. Any kind of repair, however, alters the float's weight and it should be replaced as soon as possible.

Water in petrol is easily detected in the float chamber. (Petrol does not mix with water and forms blobs in it.) The only solution is to throw away the entire contents. Water in the float chamber is by no means always due to condensation. Petrol from a bowser can be contaminated — by water, dirt and other substances — so clean and inspect all filters between the tank and the carburettor. If you get persistent trouble from water, dirt, or both, drain the tank completely.

If the petrol pump does not deliver fuel at the carburettor, you will need to investigate the pump itself.

If the weather is very hot, or you are towing something heavy, the problem may be fuel vaporisation. This is very hard to detect. If you suspect this is the trouble, cool the pump by parking in some shade and pouring water over the pump. Then try starting again. If the engine stays dead, most mechanical pumps have a lever below them for priming. Work this up and down.

If no petrol comes out on the carburettor side, check the bowl top screw for tightness and see if any of the screws securing the diaphragm have come loose. At the same time, take out the filter on the tank side of the pump and clean it, if necessary.

Finally, undo the petrol tank cap and the pipe, leading from tank to pump, at the pump and blow through it. You should be able to blow quite easily and hear a bubbling noise from the tank. If you can't blow into the tank, it is very likely that both line and tank inlet are blocked. About the only practical thing that is of any help these days is a long piece of fine wire.

In years gone by, a lot of people carried a hand or foot pump with an over-centre connector on the hose. You could clip this over the petrol line and pump air back into the tank, which could keep you going for quite a long while.

Electric petrol pumps are fairly rare. They are simple to check for proper operation: if the pump whirrs when the engine is switched on, the tank is probably empty; if it is silent it is either broken, or something is blocking a line; if it makes a steady ticking it is passing fuel normally.

Unless a pivot pin has fallen out, or the contact points are dirty, there is nothing much that can be done by way of first aid. Take the cap off, check the mechanism, and clean the points.

If the pump is fitted at the tank, it will never fail through vaporisation. If, however, it is fitted close to the engine, it is worth trying to treat it by wrapping it up with cool wet rags if conditions are very hot. Electric pumps seldom give up altogether. A good slap with the open palm will often jerk dirty points into action.

In the days of Rovers with running boards, bonnets split in half and opening upwards, many a driver got home with a mate standing on the running board, tickling the points into action by hand! It just might be possible with some modern cars, depending where that pump is mounted.

Overheating

If water leaks out of the cooling system or cannot circulate an engine will overheat.

Watch for the water temperature needle rocketing across the clock, or a dash warning light shining.

Drive the car off the road and switch off the engine.

Do not remove the radiator cap. Any water left may gush out in a cloud of scalding steam.

Look for steam or water escaping from all synthetic rubber water pipes, not forgetting those serving the heater. If there is no steam or water escaping, either the system is intact, or all the water has been lost.

Wait for at least 10 minutes, get a big cloth and grip the radiator cap through it. Turn your head away and **slowly** remove the cap. If steam comes out, pause until it has stopped, before turning further.

If water has been lost, you will have to top-up — but only after the car has been left to cool for 30 minutes or so. Cold water added to a hot engine can easily crack the cylinder head, the block, or both. In the meantime, leave the bonnet up and the radiator cap off.

When you are ready to top-up, start the engine and run it at a fast idle and with the heater controls set in the full hot position. Pour water into the radiator until it is close to the top of the filler.

Wait for a minute to see if the water level drops because the heater has not yet filled. Top-up again if necessary and carry out another check for leaks. If the radiator is leaking slowly, try and get to your destination. If the leak is rapid, an epoxy-resin glue fix may contain it for hundreds of kilometres.

A leaking hose can be taped up, or, if the end is split, perhaps it can be cut down in length and forced further on to its connector after releasing the clip.

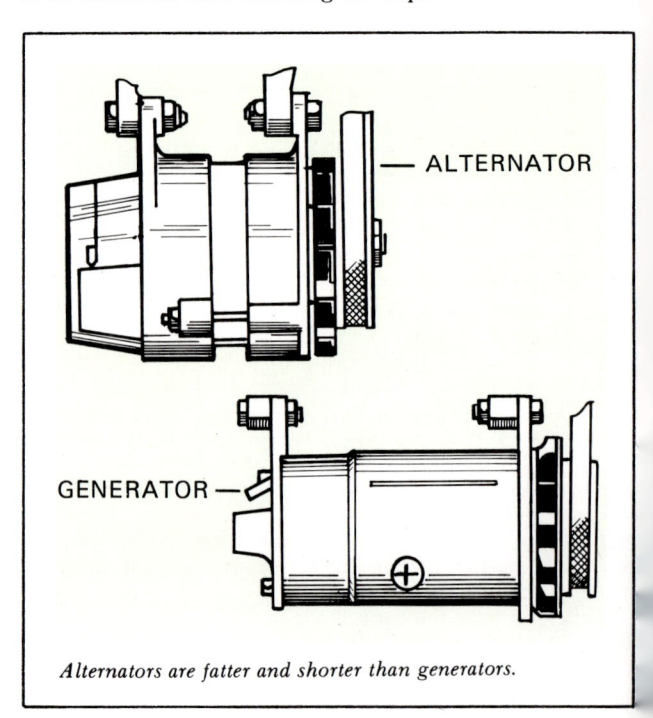

Alternators are fatter and shorter than generators.

Water leaks from the engine are often slow, such as from corroded core plugs in the block. If the head gasket has blown, however, the water may be quickly taken into the cylinders and exhausted as steam.

If you are trying to get home with a leaking cooling system, leave the radiator cap off so that pressure build-up does not occur and force the water out. Drive slowly. Watch instruments and warning lights for a repeat performance.

If there is no leak and the cooling system is full, immediately check the fanbelt. Normally it runs around three pulleys, one of which gives it the power to drive the water pump (for cooling) and the generator/alternator (for charging the battery).

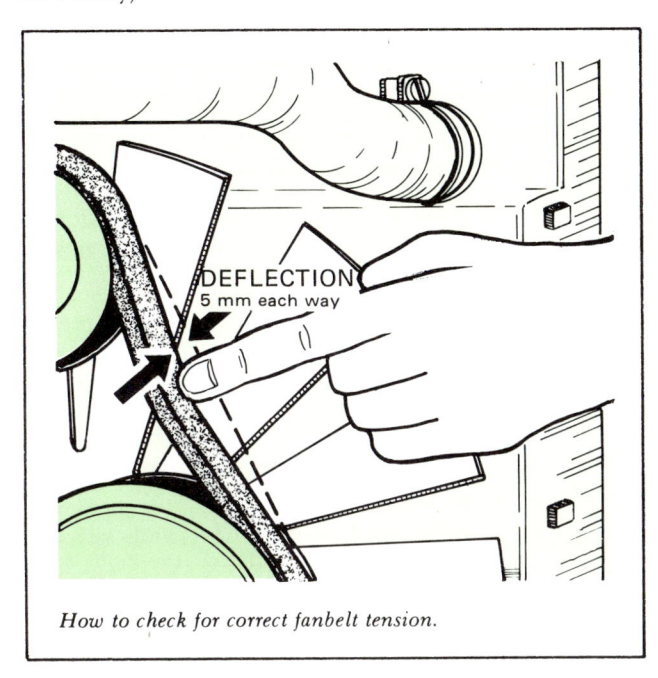

How to check for correct fanbelt tension.

Fanbelt failure is usually indicated by the ignition warning light coming on. Either the belt will have failed because it has broken (and probably fallen off), or it is slipping. Octopus straps and pantyhose have often served well as temporary fanbelts. The trick is to keep the join slim (make as small a knot as possible) so that it does not ride over a pulley rim.

A slipping belt is nearly always cured by tightening it. Just back off the three bolts that hold the generator to the engine. Get a big screwdriver or tyre lever and put it between the generator casing and the engine block. Bear down on it so that the belt tightens. Aim to leave 5 mm of free play on each side of the belt over its longest run between the pulleys. Tighten the lock nut on the adjuster bracket which is usually on top of the generator.

Follow the same procedure when fitting a new fanbelt, but, instead of pulling the generator away from the block, lever it towards the engine, so that the pulleys are as close together as possible. Slip on the new belt, lever the generator away from the block, tighten the lock nut and then the other two adjusting nuts. Start the engine. The belt is working if the ignition warning light does not show.

A new belt may stretch and start to slip. Check the tension after 200 kilometres or so.

If the overheating occurs again, the water pump or thermostat may be the problem area. These are workshop jobs.

If the ignition warning light stays on, the charging system is probably at fault.

Switch on headlights and accelerate the engine from idle speed. If the lights get brighter as you do this, the system is charging. If the lights stay at an even intensity, the system is faulty and needs expert attention.

A fully-charged battery may get you home. Bank on four or five hours of motoring in daylight, but not much more than one hour running with headlights on at night. Do not use any other electrical equipment, such as heater fan or radio and do not stop the engine if you can help it.

In all states of Australia, any accident in which someone is injured or killed *must* be reported to police at once, or within 24 hours. In Western Australia, even the smallest accident involving a car must be reported.

In any case, it is highly advisable to report to police any accident that involves substantial property damage. Police may or may not decide to attend the scene but they will at least have your report on record, which may well be useful in any legal proceedings or insurance claims.

If required by police, you *must* give your name and address and produce your driver's licence. If you do not have your licence with you, you must produce it within one week at a nominated police station, convenient to you.

Other parties involved in an accident are entitled to take note of your name and address and of the registration numbers of any cars involved.

Do not volunteer any other information. In particular, do not discuss the accident. You may find something said in the stress of the aftermath of an accident used against you if court action results. Above all, **do not admit you are at fault in any way**, even if you think you may be.

You are not obliged to make a statement to police. If you are disturbed and upset, it is better to wait until you can think clearly.

An accident that involves damage to people or property should be reported to your insurance company as soon as possible.

Each state or territory of Australia has its own motoring club or association for the general public.

All are associated with each other, under the Australian Automobile Association, and reciprocal rights are available to all members. Membership is generally available in two ways: full social and service membership, or service membership only.

If you are planning a trip you would be strongly advised to take out service membership as not only are breakdown facilities available anywhere in Australia, but a wide range of publications is offered, such as 'strip maps', books on accommodation and advice on driving conditions either free or at nominal cost.

Social membership may involve being nominated for membership, or joining a waiting list. Social members can take advantage of good accommodation, at reasonable rates, in many large centres, but there are few club premises outside the main capital cities.

The principal clubs are the National Roads and Motorists' Association (NRMA) in New South Wales and Royal Automobile Clubs in other states.

When travelling interstate it is only necessary to produce your home membership card to use the facilities of the local organisation.

In capital cities and other main population centres, the clubs provide free technical advice and tourist guidance. They also issue international driving permits.

Towing

One of the biggest problems to overcome when confronted with the prospect of towing a caravan, trailer or boat is the psychological one. With proper care, and a few simple principles in mind, however, learning to tow efficiently is far less difficult than to learn to drive a car in the first place.

The first thing to remember is that, when you are towing, you are controlling double the length, if not more, than when driving only your car. This added length will make a difference to all your road manoeuvres, such as passing, braking, cornering, reversing and parking. The last two are affected even more, but they are dealt with in detail later.

When driving **straight ahead**, you will find a maximum speed limit laid down in most states, depending on the length of your total 'rig'. Find out what this is and stick well within it. The added weight of the towed vehicle means that you should make full use of the gearbox, accelerating slowly, so as not to impose strain on the engine. Braking should also be slow and steady.

Crosswinds can affect progress on straight stretches of road. Again, the answer is to drive slowly and steadily, giving way at suitable times to drivers who wish to pass you. If you travel too fast for the conditions, the caravan will probably start to sway from side to side. When this happens, slow down *carefully* by releasing the accelerator. A sudden application of the brake will only complicate matters.

The main thing to remember when **turning** is to make the turn widely enough to give the caravan wheels room to negotiate the kerb or any other obstacles at the side of the road.

Backing and **parking** with a towed vehicle are things that should be practised, if possible, on a section of ground where you will not obstruct other traffic, such as a car park.

The most important thing to bear in mind when reversing is that you must turn the steering wheel of the car in the opposite direction to the way you would turn it if you were not towing. In other words, to swing the tail of the trailed vehicle to the left, turn the steering wheel clockwise. You should avoid getting too sharp an angle between your car and the towed vehicle. If this is happening, straighten up and start again.

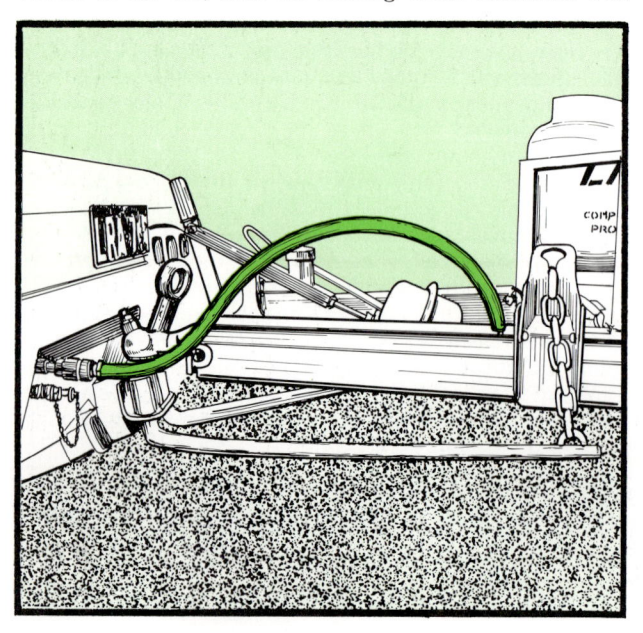

When manoeuvring in this way it is certainly a time to take note of the proverb 'more haste, less speed'. If you think it's necessary, get out of the car to inspect your position. Obviously, if you're trying to park in a busy main street this may not be possible, but if you are reversing your boat down a ramp or backing your caravan into a site, don't let spectators worry you. Campers and boating people are more likely to be able to help if you need it, so don't get embarrassed by a difficult situation. And above all, don't let the presence of an audience make you feel you have to hurry.

To **parallel park** your car and trailed vehicle, you will need a space at least a quarter as long again as the total rig. The principles involved are the same as for any parallel parking exercise, except that you must remember to turn the steering wheel in the opposite direction to normal.

Start parallel to the kerb, with the back of the trailed vehicle level with the end of the vehicle in front of the space. Turn the steering wheel clockwise, so that the van or boat swings towards the kerb. When you are about halfway into the parking space, turn the wheel anti-clockwise, so that the car also becomes parallel to the kerb. Drive forward to straighten up.

Good rear-vision mirrors, such as those on extension bars, are a vital accessory to these manoeuvres.

Two vital factors affecting any towing situation are the suitability of the 'hitch', or tow bar, and the way the car and trailed vehicle are loaded.

Seek the advice of professionals when selecting the **most suitable tow bar** for your car and the vehicle you are going to tow. A properly designed tow bar will distribute the towed weight between the front and rear wheels of the car and the wheels of the caravan. A **load equaliser** may also be required to maintain a good level position for the car and van. Having the ball of the tow bar at the correct height is also important to maintain a good level combination. If any of these points is overlooked, it will cause problems in steering and control of the whole rig. Trailers and vans that are fitted with shock absorbers (fairly rare) are much more stable on tow than those without them. Often a load equaliser is not necessary if weight distribution between car and tow is correct. If you want to know exactly what shock absorbers do for road holding, try driving a car that is not fitted with them.

When **loading the van**, luggage should be well secured, and the weight should be roughly even at the sides, front and back of the vehicle. Slightly more weight should be loaded to the front of the van's wheels so that good pressure on the tow bar is maintained. When towing an open trailer with a heavy load, such as timber, it is vital to secure the load firmly and evenly as a shifting load can be disastrous.

Before setting off, and whatever the trailed vehicle, always check and double check that the **hitch is secure**, that the **safety chains are correctly fitted** and that the **electrical connections are correct**, so that indicator lights function at the rear of the towed vehicle.

LEFT: *It is most important to make sure that all parts of the hitch are properly connected, including safety chains, brakes and electrical connections.*

Child's Play

Everyone looks forward to a family holiday but most parents dread the long car trip, when children in the back seat can get bored and end up fighting or in tears.

Children can be good travellers. They treat every trip as an adventure and are usually full of enthusiasm weeks before the journey begins. They enjoy the scenery from the car windows, love a stay in a motel and eating out, and they look forward to visiting new places. A little thought and planning by parents will help to ease the boredom of a long drive, eliminating the children's frustration and making the trip an enjoyable one for all.

- Several days before setting out for your destination, make a list of 'do's and don'ts' for the children and tell them seriously that these are rules for travelling in the car. Make it clear that they are expected to observe these rules because they are safety measures.

    1. Don't fight, scream or cry loudly when the car is in motion. This distracts the driver and can cause an accident.
    2. Don't play with door handles and locks.
    3. Do keep heads and arms inside the car — don't put them out of the window.
    4. Don't throw anything out of the window.
    5. Don't unbuckle seat belts while the car is moving.

- Any long car trip, even with frequent stops, can be tiring. Keep the children as cool and comfortable as possible. Babies and pre-school children may need their security blankets or favourite soft toy. These items can save the day if the children get upset or sleepy.

- Pack a small bag — a cosmetic bag is ideal — with packets of moist towelettes. You can purchase pop-up wet cloths in travel packs; alternatively, a damp face cloth kept in a plastic bag will help to keep the children cool.

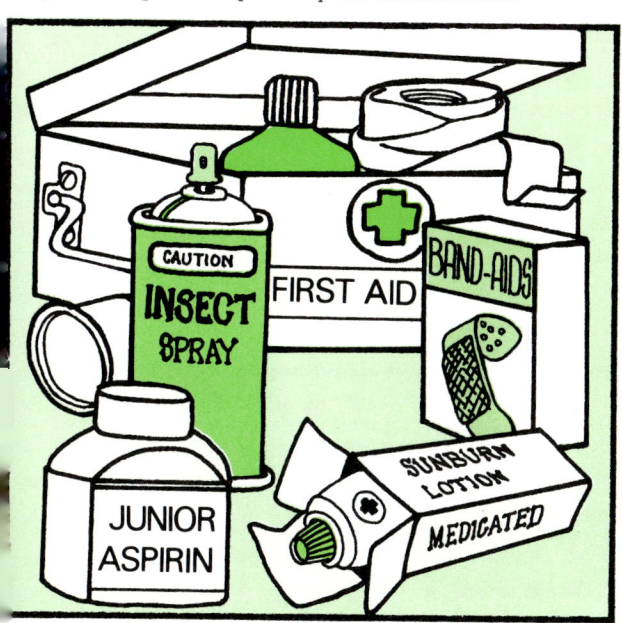

- Make sure your first aid kit contains some junior aspirin, and any other medicine with a child's dosage. It is wise to bring some insect repellent and sun block or suntan lotion as children tend to get bitten and sunburnt easily. Also bring a mosquito net to cover your baby's bassinette when you are outdoors.

- Make up a 'busy box' for the children. Take a small box — a shoe box is perfect — and keep it on the back seat where the children can reach it easily. Fill the box with small note pads, crayons or felt-tipped markers (these are better than colour pencils which break and need to be sharpened) and activity books. Choose activity books for your children's age group. Don't forget to bring your children's favourite story books.

- If your car does not have a radio, take along a transistor radio. If it has a cassette deck, include some tapes of stories and children's songs for 'quiet times'. Music soothes and lulls children to sleep.

- Although your main concern is to keep the children happy and busy during the car trip, it is important to take along some games such as snakes and ladders, Monopoly or a pack of cards to keep them amused in the motel in the evenings and on rainy days. A rubber ball and skipping rope will be welcomed by young children who like to play outdoors.

- If you have room in your car, breakfast trays are very useful as tables for colouring and drawing in the car. If not, a clipboard will serve as well.

BELOW LEFT: *Make sure your first aid box caters for children too.*

BELOW: *Choose the most comfortable approved style of safety harness or car seat recommended for your child's age group. (Photo courtesy of Safe-n-Sound.)*

- When travelling in a car with young children, make sure that you stop every hour or so as they need to stretch their legs and let off steam. Try to choose small parks and gardens to stop at which have some play equipment. If it is raining, stop at a newsagent or bookshop where the children can browse and perhaps buy a book to read.

- If a child complains of feeling sick, stop the car as soon as possible and let him out for some fresh air. Sit with him for a while and let him take a sip of water before continuing the trip.

- When approaching rest areas or a small town, ask the children if they want to go to the toilet *before* they get desperate and cannot wait.

- Even though you plan to stop for meals and snacks on your journey, you should still pack some food and drink. Children get very hungry and thirsty when travelling in a car and it is important that they eat little and often. Pack small snacks in their own lunch boxes. Avoid foods like oranges and chocolate. They are messy and tend to make children feel sick. Good snacks are sultanas, nuts (for older children only), bananas, seedless grapes, cheese cubes, celery and carrot sticks, boiled sweets. Potato chips leave a mess and make children feel very thirsty. If you are packing a lunch, avoid greasy foods. Pack easy-to-eat meals like chicken drumsticks, bite-size rolled-up pieces of cold meat with buttered bread on the side. Children can find large sandwiches difficult to handle, so remember to cut their sandwiches into small squares. Sandwich fillings require some thought: avoid anything that is mashed up or too moist.

- Avoid flasks and cups for children's drinks. Purchase milk or fruit juice in small cartons and make sure you have a good supply of drinking straws. If you take a flask of drink, take training cups for younger children and use paper or styrofoam cups with tight-fitting lids and straws for the older ones. These cups can be purchased at milk bars and take-away food places.

- Don't forget to pack a supply of small plastic garbage bags for waste paper and empty drink cans.

- When eating out at restaurants, choose those which have fast service, or have meals sent up to your hotel room.

To while away the long hours you will spend in the car with your children, here are some games for them to play.

For younger children

1. **Colour contest:** each child selects one colour, then he tries to spot cars of his chosen colour. Whoever has the first ten cars wins.

2. **Spot the mistake in the story:** either you or an older child tells a story with obvious mistakes. For example, 'Once upon a time, there was a boy called Goldilocks, and he visited the house of the seven dwarfs.'

3. **Scavenger:** make a list of 10 things you are likely to come across during your trip, e.g. farmhouse, bus stop, cow, lamb, chemist shop, man with a hat. Get the children to spot them, one at a time. Older children or parents can cross the objects out from a written list.

4. **Alphabet game:** select a letter and tell the children to spot as many things as possible beginning with that particular initial.

For older children

1. **Rhyme stories:** one person starts a story, and the next person has to make up the story with a line that rhymes. The second person also continues the story with a line of new rhyme.
   e.g. 1st person: 'I know a man called Sam'
   2nd person: 'He loves to eat sandwiches of ham.
   The more he eats the more he wants,'

2. **Cliffhangers:** one person begins a story and stops at the most exciting part, leaving the next person to continue.

3. **I packed my bag . . .** (a good memory game): each player has to name one object he puts into his bag. As each person takes his turn, he lists all the objects in order and adds a new item to the list.
   e.g. 1st person: 'I packed my bag and put an apple in it.'
   2nd person: 'I packed my bag and put an apple and a comb in it.'
   3rd person: 'I packed my bag and put an apple, a comb and a key in it.'

4. **What am I?:** this is an old favourite. One player thinks of an object or an animal and keeps it secret. The others take turns to ask him questions, which must only be answered by 'Yes' or 'No', for clues to his identity.

5. **Number plate messages:** take the letters of a number plate on a nearby car and ask the children to make a message out of it.
   e.g. WFL: what's for lunch.   EYH: eat your hat.

6. Here are a few games which take only a few minutes to prepare:
   Navigation: older children enjoy this game very much. All you have to do is to get a spare road map covering the road you are taking. The children can follow your progress with a coloured marker.

   Word scramble: prepare a list of words with jumbled up letters and get the children to unscramble them.

   Crossword: instead of giving them a crossword puzzle to do, draw squares on their note pad pages. During the trip, play a game by calling out letters at random. They can write the letters down on any square they wish, to try and make up words.

HOW TO PLAY THE EXPLORE AUSTRALIA GAME

For two or more players
1. **You will need:**
   A dice or spinner.
   Coloured counters, buttons or small coins.
2. **Decide who starts:**
   Each player throws the dice. Highest score will start; next highest goes second and so on.
3. **Move to 'START'.**
4. **Player one throws dice.** Moves forward number of squares scored. Follows instructions given in the square on which he or she lands. Other players throw dice in turn.
5. Note that short cuts, i.e. freeway to avoid city and farmer's short cut, *only* apply if you *land on the squares* where they start.
6. No second throw of dice, even if you throw a six.

the EXPLORE AUSTRALIA game

Left dog at camping ground. Go back to get him.

Littering. Miss 2 turns.

Get a good night's sleep. Go ahead 2.

CAMPING GROUND

Bogged down in river crossing. Go back 3.

FINISH

Forgot to book into a motel. Miss a turn.

Radiator boils dry. Go back to river for water.

Caught in bushfire. Miss a turn.

Luggage falls off roof. Go back 1 to collect it.

Find gold nugget in river. Go ahead 1.

Catch fish. Go to camping ground for tea.

Bridge under repair. Wait 1 turn.

Flat tyre. Go back 1.

Scenic lookout. Wait one turn, double next throw.

Slippery road. Slide back 1.

Windscreen broken. Go back to service station.

Sheep crossing road. Wait 1 turn.

New road. Go ahead 1.

Out of petrol. Go back to service station.

SERVICE STATION

Farmer tells you a short cut. Turn right next go.

Go to service station to check tyres.

Lost getting out of city. Miss a turn.

Forgot to cancel milk. Go back to start.

Drive carefully through mountains. Go ahead 4.

Take FREEWAY to avoid city.

START

Stuck in peak hour traffic. Miss a turn.

Copyright © George Philip & O'Neil Pty Ltd, 1980

Australia's Geological Ages

Era	Period	Absolute Years	Major Geological and Geographical Events	Life Forms	
C A I N O Z O I C	RECENT	10 Thousand	The sea rises and falls several times, causing erosion along the coastal areas. Volcanoes are active in eastern Aust. Minor changes on the land through stream and wind erosion.	Development of present-day animals and man.	Squatting Man
	PLEIS-TOCENE	2 Million	Spread of glaciation, especially extensive in Tasmania and south-eastern Aust. Lakes and large rivers cover the centre of the continent. Some volcanic activity on the east.	Development of man. Giant kangaroos and wombats wander extensively prior to their extinction.	**AGE OF MAN**
T E R T I A R Y	PLIOCENE	8 Million	Uplifting of the Eastern Highlands and Western Plateau.	Early evolution of man. Dominance of large carnivores. Open forests spread. Marsupials and birds continue to develop.	Man Ape
	MIOCENE	25 Million	Volcanic activity widespread along the eastern coast. In the south and west the seas encroach several times. The land bridge with New Guinea disappears beneath the sea.	Rainforests, both tropical and temperate, flourish along the east coast. Mammals become dominant living creatures.	
	OLIGOCENE	40 Million	Some volcanic activity is spread throughout the south and east.	Marsupials continue to evolve. Long-legged wading birds develop. Flowering plants abound.	Diprotodon
	EOCENE	60 Million	A great deal of the land surface has now been levelled. Shallow seas in the Carnarvon area of WA.	Dinosaurs become extinct. Mammals evolve, especially marsupials. Grasses spread.	**AGE OF MAMMALS**
M E S O Z O I C	CRETACEOUS	135 Million	Much of the continent sinks gently. Inland seas cover the area between the Great Dividing Range and the Western Plateau. When the sea eventually retreats, swamps remain.	Flowering plants grow for the first time in Aust.	Banksia
	JURASSIC	185 Million	The sea returns over part of WA and deposits sediments of sandstone, shale and limestone.	Dinosaurs at their peak. First primitive birds evolve.	Tyrannosaurus
	TRIASSIC	225 Million	Aust. possibly starts to break away from other land masses such as Asia. This process is completed in the Miocene epoch.	First dinosaurs. First primitive mammals. Reptiles now abound. Australian insects become varied.	**AGE OF REPTILES**
P A L A E O Z O I C	PERMIAN	270 Million	The Ice Age continues. Glaciers spread over a large area. Shallow seas are formed by melting ice. Coal deposits are formed in Qld, NSW and WA. Aust. probably still connected to Asia.	Trilobites become extinct. Palm-like cycads form. Spread of insects and amphibians.	Amphicentrum
	CARBONIFEROUS	345 Million	Extensive earth movements insert granitic rock. Seas cover north-east NSW and east Qld. An Ice Age begins.	Abundant insects. New forms of amphibians evolve. Widespread forests of tall land plants.	Eogyrinus **AGE OF AMPHIBIANS**
	DEVONIAN	400 Million	Volcanic activity. Shallow seas in the east lay down limestone deposits in Qld, NSW and Victoria. Most of the west and centre is now dry.	First amphibians. Many corals. Plant life becomes more complex.	Osteolepis
	SILURIAN	440 Million	Seas cover Qld, NSW and Victoria. Coral reefs build up extensive limestone deposits. Earth movements produce intensive folding.	First land plants appear and air-breathing animals commence. Primitive fishes and brachiopods abundant.	Brachiopod **AGE OF FISHES**
	ORDOVICIAN	500 Million	Extensive seas, deep in the east and shallow in the centre. First major palaeozoic mountain building and volcanic activity begins.	Life only in the seas. Graptolites, the possible forerunners of vertebrates, abound. Spread of molluscs. Culmination of trilobites.	
	CAMBRIAN	600 Million	Shallow seas cover north-west Qld and NT. Deeper seas cover NSW, Victoria and Tasmania.	Life still restricted to the sea. Trilobites predominant with many marine invertebrates.	Trilobite **AGE OF MARINE INVERTEBRATES**
	PRE-CAMBRIAN		The surface forms a vast barren landscape of mountains, deserts and lava flows. Rocks of this period are found throughout Aust. except for Victoria.	Seaweeds and soft-bodied invertebrates originate in the warm seas. Few fossils known.	Dickinsonia Worm

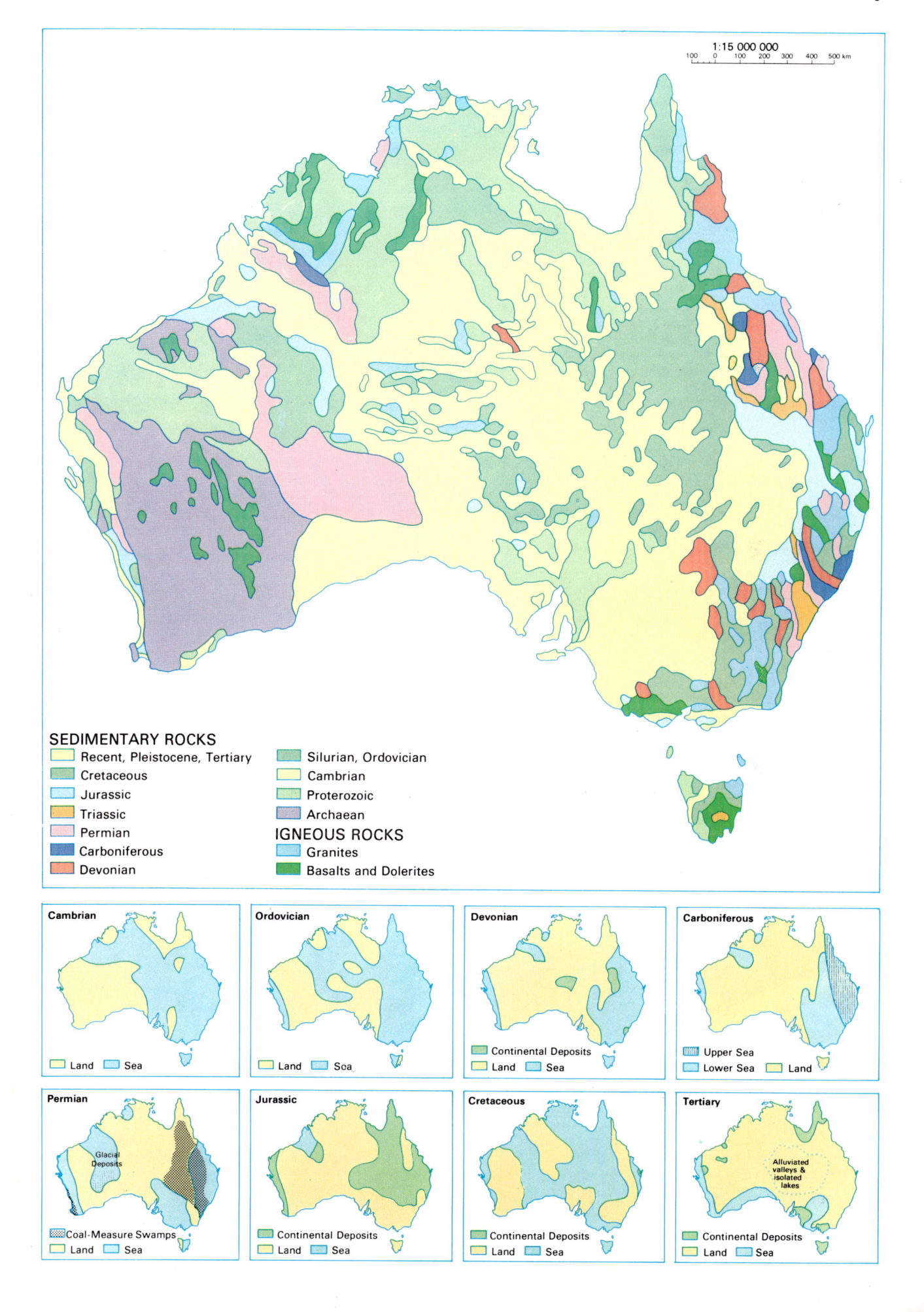

SEDIMENTARY ROCKS
- Recent, Pleistocene, Tertiary
- Cretaceous
- Jurassic
- Triassic
- Permian
- Carboniferous
- Devonian
- Silurian, Ordovician
- Cambrian
- Proterozoic
- Archaean

IGNEOUS ROCKS
- Granites
- Basalts and Dolerites

Cambrian	Ordovician	Devonian	Carboniferous
Land / Sea	Land / Sea	Continental Deposits / Land / Sea	Upper Sea / Lower Sea / Land

Permian	Jurassic	Cretaceous	Tertiary
Glacial Deposits / Coal-Measure Swamps / Land / Sea	Continental Deposits / Land / Sea	Continental Deposits / Land / Sea	Alluviated valleys & isolated lakes / Continental Deposits / Land / Sea

1:15 000 000

Prehistoric Australia

Australian prehistory has a fresh excitement. Recent finds have placed human habitation of the oldest continent as far back as 38 000 BP (Before Present), double some previous estimates. This evidence of 'modern man' — *Homo sapiens* — now compares with the earliest finds known around the world.

Many of the theories about Australia's prehistory have been reshaped by discoveries around the arid Lake Mungo region in south-west New South Wales. This ancient lake bed with its bizarre eroded landforms was best known as a local tourist attraction until 1968, when a scientist seeking information on the Australian ice ages found bones uncovered by erosion in wind-sculpted sand dunes — 'The Walls of China' — north-east of the lake.

They proved to be the broken skull of an Aboriginal woman — and 26 000 years old. The find proved to be of world significance because it was the oldest evidence in the world of a ritual cremation.

As more scientists excavated near Lake Mungo, equally rewarding discoveries were made. Another burial also dated to around 26 000 BP — and the bones were covered with ochre, earth pigments still used by Aborigines for decoration and painting. Combined with other data, this burial suggests the early Australians practised 'art' as early as any known European Stone Age cave painter.

Evidence has been slowly accumulated to outline how the Aborigines exploited the food sources around (and in) Lake Mungo before climate changes dried it up some 16 000 years ago. The lake yielded them fish and shellfish. Game abounded, especially the marsupials that still highlight Australian wildlife. Here is the oldest known proof of humans eating shellfish: heaps of mussels found next to hearths 36 000 years old.

Discoveries of grinding stones dated to the period when the lake was drying up support suggestions that Aborigines obtained grain from wild grasses as early as any other known 'modern man'.

If Lake Mungo has revealed facts about 'modern man', another recent investigation around Kow Swamp near the Murray River in northern Victoria has posed questions yet to be answered.

The skulls of 30 individuals found there have archaic features typical of a form of primitive man — *Homo erectus*. Yet these late Pleistocene remains date to as recently as 10 000 years ago.

As yet there is insufficient evidence to determine whether 'modern' and 'primitive' man co-existed in Australia for tens of thousands of years, or whether the groups derived from the same founding population.

A Killing of Giants

Experts have long assumed that the extinct giant fauna of Australia was hunted by man. Man — and the introduced dingo — are often blamed for contributing to this extinction. Not until recently did the first evidence of giant fauna being killed by humans in large numbers emerge, at a bone site at Lancefield in Victoria which was first noted in the 1840s by an early European settler digging a well.

Two metres beneath swampy ground lies a mass of bones, about 90 per cent of them from *Macropus titans*, an extinct giant kangaroo one-third as large again as modern kangaroos. With the bones is a large stone knife. Perhaps 1000 animals were killed in this swamp edge around 25 000 years ago.

Another notable recent 'special purpose' site was the flint mine discovered at Koonalda cave near the coast east of Eucla on the Great Australian Bight.

Tracks From the Past

Although the most exciting recent work in Australian prehistory has involved man, scientists have continued to expand the body of knowledge on other early life forms.

In 1971, for example, a university botanical expedition into the remote Genoa River gorge in eastern Victoria yielded what are believed to be 'footprints' as old as any in the world.

Preserved in sandstone were three sets of trackways made some 350 million years ago by amphibians believed to be among the earliest recorded land vertebrates (backboned animals). They are thought to have been made by animals similar to the genus *Ichthyostega* (found only in Greenland) and ranging in length from about 550 to 900 mm.

Below: The ancient beaches of the now waterless Lake Mungo, where erosion has revealed many exciting archaeological finds in recent years.

Opposite: An anthropologist studies the skull of an early Australian modern man, which dates back to 26 000 BP.

Australia's Fossil History

Fossils from before Cambrian times are rare anywhere. Australia is fortunate in having some remarkable 'jellyfish' fossils from the Pre-Cambrian, about 600 million years old. Since geologist Mr Reg Sprigg discovered the first of them in the Ediacara Range in South Australia in 1946, more than 1500 specimens have been collected and 25 species described, some with no resemblance to anything noted before.

Cambrian rocks are rich in fossils. Australia has possibly the best known examples of the interesting Archaeocyatha group, cone-shaped creatures which grew from the sea floor.

From the Palaeozoic Era, Australian fossils of significance include the graptolites found in great numbers and variety in Victoria, and the crocodile-like Triassic amphibian *Paracyclotosaurus davidi* discovered at St Peters in New South Wales in 1910.

Australia had its dinosaurs during the Mesozoic Era, the Age of Reptiles. The largest plant-eating Australian dinosaurs *Rhaetosaurus* and *Austrosaurus*, were about 15 metres long, less impressive sizes than the North American giants.

Giant Australian swimming reptiles included the plesiosaur *Kronosaurus queenslandicus* (which grew more than 13 metres long) and *Ichthyosaurus australis* (6 metres).

Mammals and Birds

Australia is famous for its variety of marsupials: the pouched mammals of past ages were even more remarkable, being in many cases far larger than their descendants.

Largest of all known marsupials was the extinct *Diprotodon optatum*, named in 1830 but known only by tantalising bone fragments until dozens of skeletons were found almost intact in 1892 in the dry bed of Lake Callabonna in South Australia. This animal was the size of a rhinoceros and weighed possibly two tonnes: other diprotodons were as small as a calf.

Other spectacular extinct creatures included the giant goanna *Megalania*, perhaps seven or more metres long; the flightless bird *Genyornis*, little taller than an emu but probably around four times its weight; a large ancestor of the echidna, and the intriguing 'pouched lion', *Thylacoleo*, whose distinctive teeth still puzzle scientists. Two pairs of wide side teeth (each up to 60 mm long) apparently acted as shears, although it is disputed whether *Thylacoleo* was a carnivore or herbivore.

The giant wombat *Phascolonus gigas* stood almost a metre high. Several huge kangaroos were significantly larger than today's kangaroos, the largest being *Procoptodon* standing about three metres tall and weighing possibly four times as much as the largest present kangaroo.

The fossil record has many gaps and innumerable questions remain. One of the most persistent queries is how much man contributed to the extinction of the giant fauna in relatively recent times.

Opposite: Stone tools found at Lake Mungo include grinding stones dating back to the period when Lake Mungo was filled with water.

The Australian Aborigines

The Australian Aborigines, once outcasts in their own land, have finally begun to receive the rights of other Australians. Aboriginal issues are debated as never before, and unprecedented government funding is contributing to what former Prime Minister Gough Whitlam termed the 'restoration of their lost power of self-determination in economic, social and political affairs'.

The fate of the Aborigines was almost genocide. For a long time it seemed likely that the European settlers who had seized their land and largely destroyed their unique culture, would 'smoothe their dying pillow'. But the Aborigines survived almost two centuries of oppression, neglect and racism, and their numbers are increasing so rapidly that it is probable that by the end of the century they will total around 300 000, somewhere near their population when the explorer Captain Cook 'took possession' of their land in the name of an English king in 1770. Today they number over one per cent of the Australian population, with an estimated population of 159 900 (including Torres Strait Islanders).

Scientists believe that the Aborigines migrated to Australia from Asia about 30 000 years before European settlement. They developed in isolation, hunters and foragers with no domesticated animals but the dingo, and without crops which could be cultivated. Settled across the whole continent of Australia in some 500–600 tribal groups — each with its own territory — the Aborigines spoke about 300 distinct languages, most of which had additional dialects. Although the most common group size was a band of 20–40 people, they occasionally formed large parties for ceremonial or hunting purposes.

The men were essentially hunters or fishermen. Weapons and aids included spears and clubs, stone axes and knives, boomerangs and the woomera (throwing stick) which could propel a spear 120 metres or more. They had fish nets, traps, fish hooks, various water-craft, and often used fire to flush game. They depended on their women to provide the staple diet of small animals, seeds, roots, honey, fruit and berries.

Aboriginal culture was of an awesome complexity. It linked the Aborigines to tribal land and nature through ancestral beings — past, present and future were brought together in a framework of beliefs frequently expressed through dances, songs, oral tradition, art and rigidly-defined social relationships. With no written language, one measure of a man's maturity and importance was the degree of his understanding and absorption of his tribe's rituals and mythology, handed down by the older men. Life was ordered, offering individuals social, economic and phychological security.

This was the balanced, harmonious world disrupted by the European who 'pioneered' beyond the first coastal villages. Given prevailing European attitudes to land, the dispossession and depopulation of the Aborigines was inevitable in the long term. In fact it came with brutal suddenness, more from epidemics of introduced disease than from gunfire, destroying random and futile resistance to the invaders. Aborigines died by the thousands of smallpox, venereal disease, tuberculosis, measles, influenza — killers which sometimes spread inland ahead of the first exploring parties.

In Tasmania, for example, the Aboriginal population declined from an estimated 4000 to fewer than 500 between 1800 and 1830, and was finally virtually wiped out. Three decades of European settlement in Victoria saw the Aboriginal population reduced from more than 10 000 to 2000. Disadvantaged in every way, the survivors became the 'fringe-dwellers' of Australian society, and the discriminatory pattern of poverty, health problems, high unemployment and poor education still exists in many areas.

Some Europeans had protested on behalf of the Aborigines from the earliest days of dispossession. There were well-meaning, sometimes enlightened, efforts to help. Reservations were set aside, rations issued, missions established which are still the focus of many Aboriginal settlements. But until the 1920s and 1930s the aim of much State legislation was 'protection', controlling measures which put Aborigines under the guardianship of official protectors. The result was frequently a 'reservation' philosophy, segregation which limited their movement, banned alcohol, managed property, regulated employment and often controlled interracial marriage. Public protests played a significant part in removing many of these restrictions in the 1940s, when it became obvious that improved welfare services and advanced medicines had started to reverse the population decline. In the 1950s State and Federal authorities called for assimilation, which assumed that people of Aboriginal descent would be fully integrated into the dominant European culture.

Today the policy is self-management and self-sufficiency with the encouragement of Aboriginal initiative, independence and identity. The increasing awareness of Aboriginal issues in the Australian community became evident after a 1967 referendum in which Australians voted in record numbers for changes in the Constitution, which resulted in the Federal government sharing responsibility for Aborigines with the States. Now all States but Queensland have transferred policy and coordination functions to the Federal government. In 1981, the National Aboriginal Conference, which consists of 36 members elected by Aborigines throughout Australia, assumed an advisory role to the Federal Government, to enable it to respond to the great diversity of Aboriginal aspirations and expectations.

Few Aborigines live without frequent contact with elements of the European Australian community. Many live in settlements and missions in the outback, where traditional Aboriginal culture remains strong. They have learned to put their case powerfully, especially in the controversial area of land rights. Australia has about 300 Aboriginal reserves totalling around 286 000 km^2: in the Northern Territory, where one in four citizens is of Aboriginal decent, all former reserves are now Aboriginal freehold. Much land has already been restored to Aboriginal communities, but there are still compromises to be reached before the 'unlucky Australians' achieve equality.

Below left: A mother and her children fishing for mussels, Arnhem Land, Northern Territory.

Below right: A nomadic Aboriginal tribesman, Northern Territory.

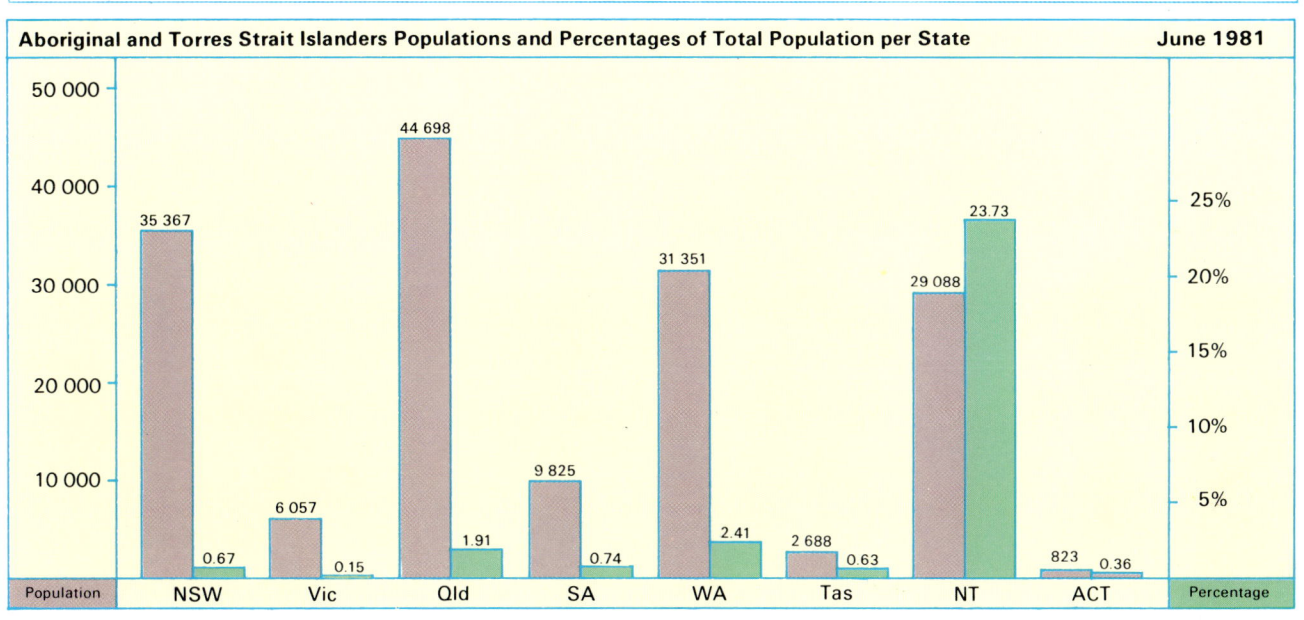

Distribution of Aborigines and Torres Strait Islanders

Based on Local Government Areas as used in the Census of 30 June 1976.

Total number of Aborigines at the 1976 Census was 160 915.

Legend:
- Fewer than 50
- 50 to 100
- 101 to 300
- 301 to 600
- 601 to 1500
- More than 1500

Aboriginal and Torres Strait Islanders Populations and Percentages of Total Population per State — June 1981

State	Population	Percentage
NSW	35 367	0.67
Vic	6 057	0.15
Qld	44 698	1.91
SA	9 825	0.74
WA	31 351	2.41
Tas	2 688	0.63
NT	29 088	23.73
ACT	823	0.36

The European Discoverers

Terra Australis — the fabulous South Land that lay, perhaps, below the Equator between the Indian and Pacific Oceans — made a fine and enduring legend. Ptolemy, the Greek mathematician, sketched it south of Asia in the second century AD. Mapmakers of the Middle Ages include it on vague charts.

Arabs, Indians and Chinese sailed the waters north of Australia for centuries before the Europeans appeared. There is no convincing evidence that they landed on Australia, although it is very likely that Malay fishermen were regular visitors.

Surprisingly, although the Portuguese, Spanish and Dutch were exploring the region from the early sixteenth century (northern Papua New Guinea was discovered in 1526), the first recorded European contact with Australia was not until early 1606. Sailing from Java in the pinnace *Duyfken*, the Dutch skipper Wilhelm Janszoon passed south of Papua New Guinea and sighted the west coast of Cape York peninsula. He mapped part of the coast, had a crew member killed in a skirmish with Aborigines and returned to Java unimpressed by the new land.

Later that year Luis Torres led two Spanish ships through the perilous strait, which today bears his name, between Papua New Guinea and Australia.

Seventeen years later the Dutchman Jan Carstensz retraced the *Duyfken's* route, reporting sourly on the land and its inhabitants. Meanwhile, the Dutch captains engaged in the East Indies spice trade discovered that the quickest route to Java was by sailing east from the Cape of Good Hope with the prevailing trade winds, then turning north after some 6400 km. The first man to miscalculate and sail far enough to sight Australia was Dirk Hartog of the *Eendracht*. In 1616 he landed at Shark Bay and left the earliest memorial of European contact, a seaman's pewter plate inscribed with his name.

Other Dutchmen followed. Some lost their ships and lives on the largely uncharted coast. In three decades they discovered much of the coast from Cape York west to the Great Australian Bight — Franz Thyssen in the *Gulden Zeepart* had mapped almost as far as Spencer's Gulf in 1627 — yet New Holland had yielded nothing of value to them. Still hoping that the South Land might lie beyond New Holland, the Governor-General of Batavia, Anthony Van Diemen, instructed Abel Tasman to search along latitude 53° South. Driven north by rough weather, Tasman came on the south-west coast of Tasmania, which he named Van Diemen's Land. Tasman explored briefly, then sailed east, discovering New Zealand before returning to Java. A second great voyage in 1644 proved that New Holland had an unbroken coast between Cape York and North-West Cape. Dutch interest in New Holland then waned.

Top left: A mid-seventeenth century Dutch map of the world.

Top right: Statue of Matthew Flinders outside St Paul's Cathedral, Melbourne.

Below left: The collier the Earl of Pembroke, *which later became the* Endeavour.

Below right: A replica of Vlamingh's plate. In 1697 Vlamingh found the original plate which had been left by Hartog on a small island he discovered off the coast of Western Australia in 1616. Vlamingh added the details of his own visit to a new plate and took the original back to Batavia.

The first English ship to reach Australia was the East Indiaman *Tryal*, wrecked in 1622 on a reef north of the Monte Bello Islands off Western Australia. Captain John Daniel in the English ship *London* also sighted the west coast in 1681, but not until the voyage of the *Cygnet* along the northwest coast in 1688 — and the subsequent publication of a journal by adventurer William Dampier — did New Holland capture the English imagination. Dampier damned the inhospitable coast and its inhabitants, but as interest in the South Seas grew the incompetent former buccaneer was appointed captain of HMS *Roebuck* and sent back to continue his discoveries. It was a shambles of a voyage that added little to the charts, yet the second book which resulted helped focus English attention on the Pacific.

Cook's Triumph

Man's interest in astronomy resulted in the English claiming the fertile east coast of New Holland. Captain Cook had taken a party of scientists to Tahiti to observe the transit of Venus across the face of the sun. Following instructions to search for Terra Australis, he then sailed south in the *Endeavour* and mapped New Zealand. Enroute to Van Diemen's Land a southerly gale forced him north, and on 19 April 1770 he sighted the east coast of Australia at what is now Cape Everard. He sailed north, exploring Botany Bay, mapping as he went until the *Endeavour* was holed by coral on the Barrier Reef and had to be beached for repairs. After charting almost the entire northern coast, he landed on an island north of Cape York and on 22 August claimed eastern New Holland in the name of King George III. Later he gave it the name New South Wales.

Enthusiastic reports of this voyage were remembered when the rebellion of the American colonies in 1776 ended the transportation of convicts to North America. The dream of the great South Land, which had excited men for centuries, soon ended in the reality of an English prison colony. Modern Australian history started in January 1788 when Captain Phillip's First Fleet arrived in Botany Bay.

Charting the Coast

Two adventurous men who had arrived in New South Wales in 1795 were to resolve the last major uncertainty about the map of New Holland. Ship's surgeon George Bass and midshipman Matthew Flinders made their first foray south from Sydney Cove in the *Tom Thumb* — only 2.5 metres long — and followed it with other hazardous journeys. Bass then sailed as far as Westernport Bay in a whaleboat, but returned to Sydney convinced by sea conditions that there was a strait between New Holland and Van Diemen's Land. Bass and Flinders proved the theory correct by sailing the sloop *Norfolk* around Van Diemen's Land.

In 1801 Flinders commenced his great work, circumnavigating the continent in the *Investigator* and meticulously mapping both the southern and much of the north-eastern coast. He ended speculation on an inland sea dividing the continent, and suggested yet another name for the Terra Incognita of the ancients — Australia.

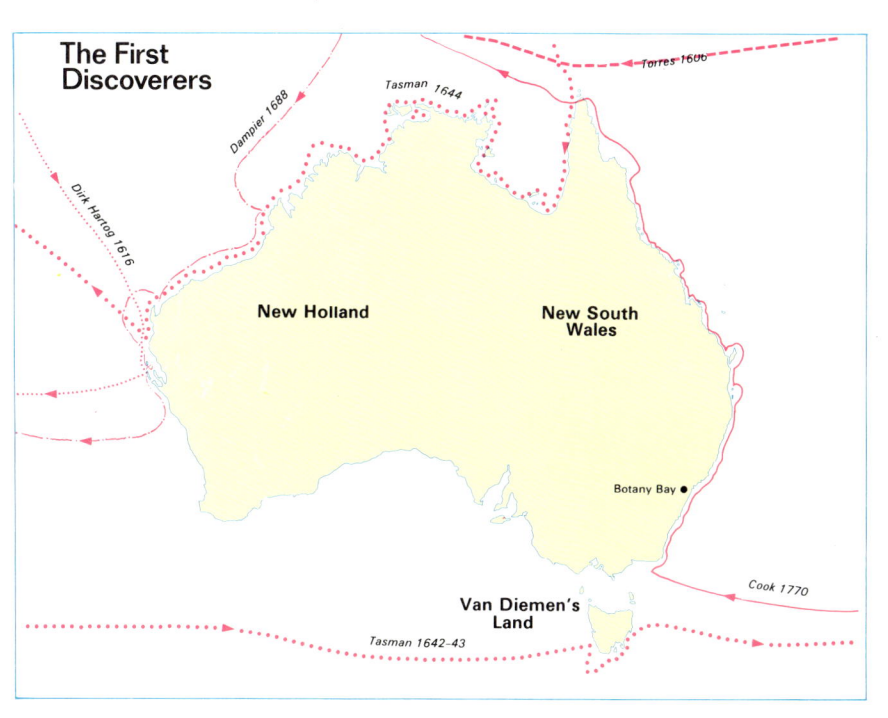

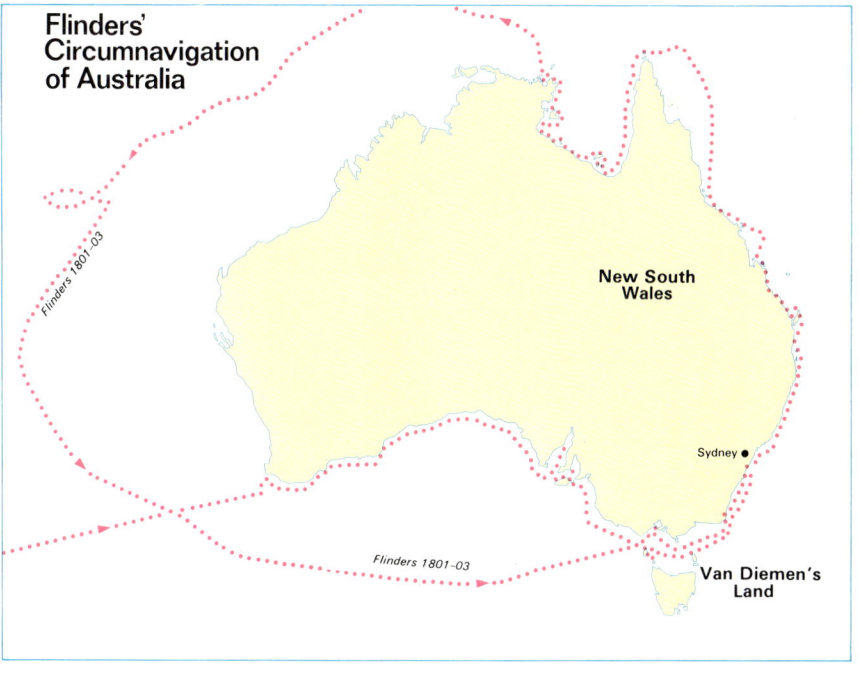

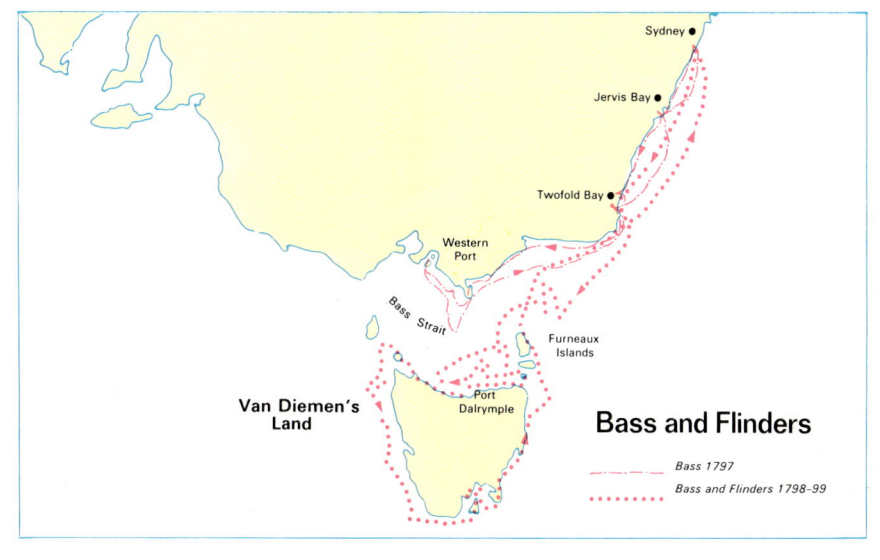

Exploring an Unknown Land

The history of Australian exploration sometimes seems as unlikely, as exaggerated, as the alien land itself: 'It does not read like history, but like the most beautiful of lies, and all of a fresh sort', Mark Twain commented. The early European settlers found the seasons reversed, the climate tending to extremes (usually heat), the animals and plants bizarre, and the geography baffling.

The sagas of exploration included men with endurance beyond belief, and also fools with no qualities other than curiosity and courage. Men carried boats towards non-existent central seas; rivers could be 40 km broad one season and then vanish for the next decade; some explorers owed their fame and lives to Aborigines, and some their lonely deaths. Some returned in triumph, or at least received a hero's burial.

The first geographic barrier facing Europeans was the Blue Mountains range — nowhere 1500 metres high — west of Sydney. For a quarter of a century its escarpments and gorges baffled expeditions, until in 1813 Gregory Blaxland, William Lawson and William Wentworth penetrated the range by following the ridges instead of the valleys. Like so many later explorers, they were driven by the need to find pastures for the colony's expanding sheep flocks. They were followed by George Evans, who completed the crossing, and John Oxley, who found rich grazing regions in 1817 and 1818 but was frustrated in attempts to follow the westward flowing Lachland and Macquarie Rivers.

Victoria was opened up by Hamilton Hume and William Hovell during their 1824 journey south across the Australian Alps to Corio Bay, now Geelong. The enigma of the westward-flowing rivers remained. Was there an inland sea, or perhaps a river outlet to the south coast? Part of the answer was provided by Captain Charles Sturt, who discovered the Darling in 1828 after being forced northwards by the reed beds of the Macquarie. In 1829 he was directed to explore the Murrumbidgee by boat, discovering Australia's major river, the Murray, in January 1830. His party made a remarkable voyage to its mouth near Lake Alexandrina: unable to rendezvous with a ship, they were compelled to battle back upstream for some 1450 km, a nightmare of exhaustion and near-starvation. Not daunted by the privations of that epic journey (including temporary blindness), Sturt searched for the supposed inland sea and the centre of Australia from 1844–46, enduring further hardships without finding fertile land.

By then men were probing inland from isolated coastal settlements, including Hobart in Tasmania (1803), the Brisbane River settlement in Queensland (1824), Swan River in Western Australia (1829), Melbourne in Victoria (1835) and Adelaide in South Australia (1836).

In 1836 Major Thomas Mitchell discovered much of Victoria's best land, including the famed sheep country of the Western District. In north-west Australia, George Grey made significant explorations in 1837 and 1839, incidentally becoming the first European to see the remarkable Aboriginal cave paintings of the Kimberley. Edward John Eyre found himself a national hero in 1841 after an incredible trek of almost 1600 km across the barren southern coastline of Australia between Streaky Bay in South Australia and King George's Sound in Western Australia. Two Aborigines in the small party murdered his European companion and deserted with supplies, leaving Eyre and the remaining Aboriginal youth Wylie to continue across the near-desert. After five weeks of extreme hardship they fortunately came upon a French whaler.

Eastern Victoria — now Gippsland — was opened up by the separate discoveries of Angus McMillan and the Pole, Paul Strzelecki, who found and named Australia's highest peak, Mount Kosciusko (2228 metres). In the north, the eccentric German migrant Ludwig Leichhardt, no bushman, discovered some of the best land in central Queensland on an arduous 3200 km trek in 1844–45 from Brisbane to Port Essington, north of modern Darwin. In 1848 he set out to cross Australia from east to west — and the entire expedition vanished without trace. Another tragedy occurred that year when Edmund Kennedy penetrated Cape York peninsula. He was fatally speared by Aborigines; three men left at a depot were never found, and six of eight men at a base camp starved to death before the relief ship arrived.

Several parties searched for the missing Leichhardt. Although unsuccessful, Augustus Gregory made two notable journeys, a west-east crossing of northern Australia in 1855–56 starting from the Victoria River, and an 1858 expedition from the Dawson Ranges in Queensland (in which he traced the Barcoo River and proved it merged into Cooper's Creek) to Adelaide.

Crossing the Continent

The first men to cross Australia from south to north were a policeman, Robert O'Hara Burke, and a surveyor, William Wills, leaders of the most costly Australian exploring party ever. They started from Melbourne with 27 camels, 23 horses and 21 tonnes of baggage. This impetuous Burke and three companions pushed northward from an advance base on Cooper's Creek without waiting for the main supplies to come up. In February 1861 they reached tidal waters on the north coast after a stern struggle: the return was frightful, one man dying of scurvy and the three gaunt survivors battling through to find the Cooper's Creek party had left the depot just seven hours before they arrived. A series of blunders by the three separated elements of the expedition resulted in Burke and Wills slowly starving to death in the wilderness.

John McDouall Stuart, an experienced bushman who had ridden with Sturt, came close to beating Burke and Wills to the north coast. Seeking the £2000 reward offered to the man who found a route for an overland telegraph from Adelaide to the north coast, Stuart made three gruelling journeys, discovering the arid centre of Australia and finally crossing the continent in 1862 after great suffering. In the west, John Forrest, Peter Warburton and Ernest Giles achieved fame with lengthy crossings of forbidding deserts and barren country.

Below left: One of the Aboriginal cave paintings discovered by Sir George Grey in the Kimberleys, north-west Australia.

Below right: An imaginary painting of exploration into the interior by T. J. Maslen, 1830.

Exploration Routes

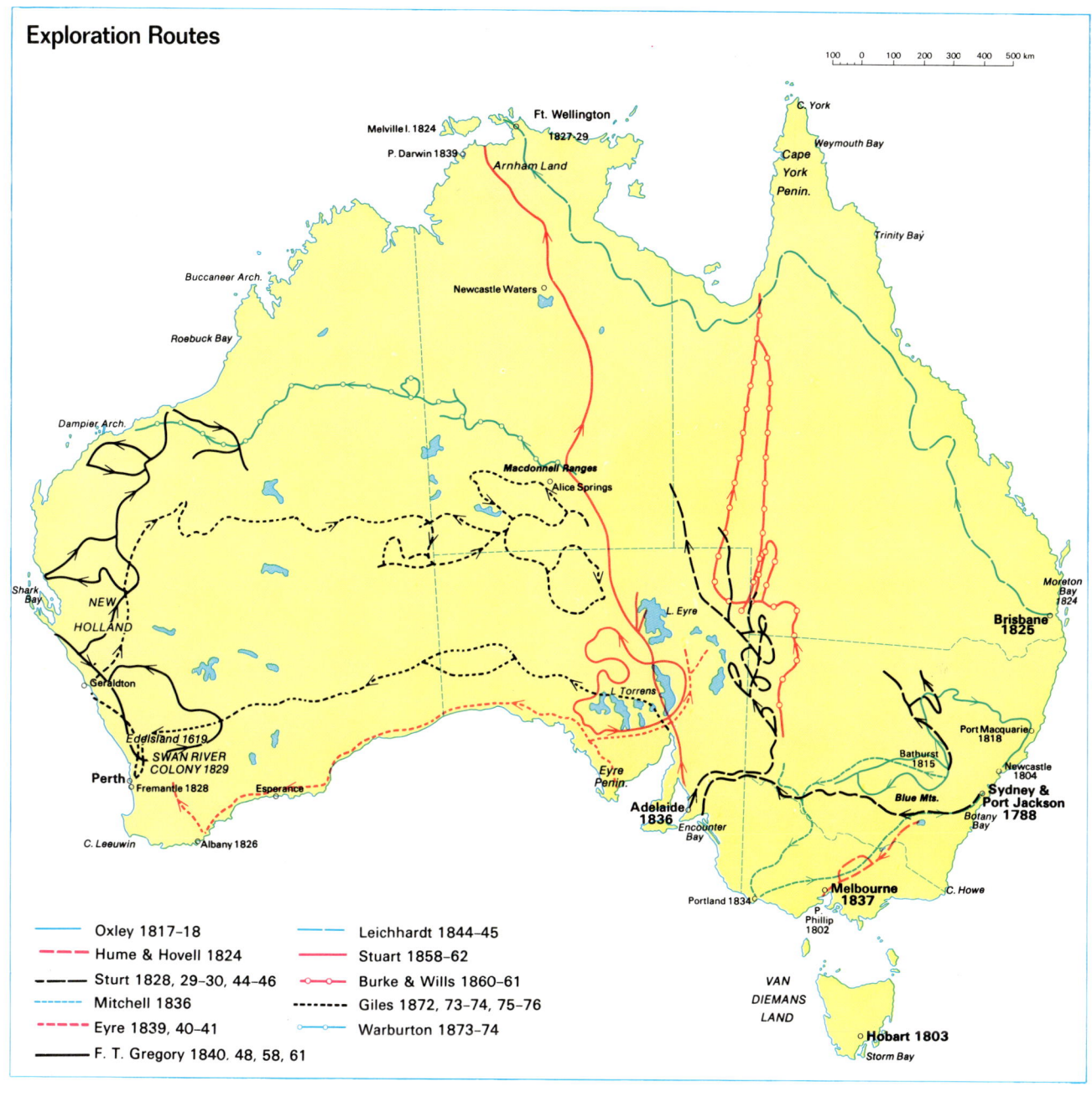

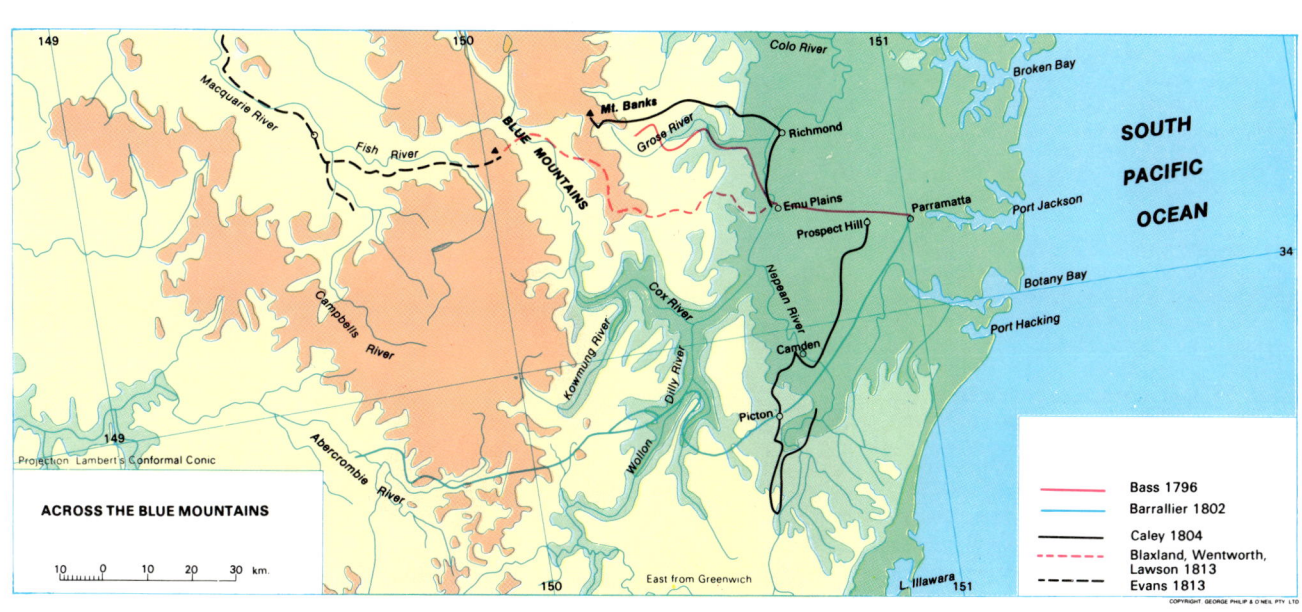

- ——— Oxley 1817–18
- – – – Hume & Hovell 1824
- — — Sturt 1828, 29–30, 44–46
- ····· Mitchell 1836
- – – – Eyre 1839, 40–41
- ——— F. T. Gregory 1840, 48, 58, 61
- – – – Leichhardt 1844–45
- ——— Stuart 1858–62
- —o—o— Burke & Wills 1860–61
- ······· Giles 1872, 73–74, 75–76
- —o—o— Warburton 1873–74

Across the Blue Mountains

- ——— Bass 1796
- ——— Barrallier 1802
- ——— Caley 1804
- – – – Blaxland, Wentworth, Lawson 1813
- – – – Evans 1813

Projection: Lambert's Conformal Conic

Australian Landform Structures

The Australian continent is made up of three major structures: the stable Western Shield; the gently-warped interior lowlands or Central Basin; and the Eastern Uplands.

The Western Shield

Nearly two-thirds of Australia is a plateau averaging between 300 and 600 metres high, but with smaller plateaux and ranges rising above the general level, and basins and troughs falling below it. This great plateau is in fact a complex of smaller units, but when regarded as a whole it constitutes the Pre-Cambrian Shield of the Australian continent. It is fundamentally composed of a basement complex of Archaean rocks, with some areas covered with younger rocks or extensive sand deposits.

The Central Basin

This region consists mainly of great sedimentary basins lying to the east of the Western Shield.

Great Artesian Basin: In this area, the Jurassic sandstones that crop out as intake beds in the north-east, pass beneath a thick cover of impervious Cretaceous claystones and Tertiary sands. The shallow folds have now been dissected into a landscape of rolling lowlands broken by tablelands and mesas. Nearly the whole area is less than 300 metres above sea level. In the area surrounding the Simpson Desert, gibber-strewn surfaces cover more than 160 000 km². Drainage in this area is directed to Lake Eyre. A combination of fine-textured alluvia, low slopes and irregular discharge of rivers, has produced many discontinuous trunk channels characteristic of the 'Channel Country' of south-western Queensland.

Riverine Plains: The riverine plains of the Murray-Darling system in the south are a composite alluvial fan sloping very gently from the points of entry of larger rivers of the Eastern Uplands. The many meandering channels of today are superimposed across the patterns of an earlier system of streams.

The Eastern Uplands

The Eastern Uplands consist of a broad belt of varied width extending from Cape York to Tasmania, and made up largely of tablelands, ranges and ridges with only limited mountain areas above 1000 metres. The highest summits are in the Snowy Mountains and Victorian Alps with slightly lower plateaux in New England and Tasmania.

Throughout this area a great variety of rocks of all ages is present and the geological structure is very complex. The older rocks are extensively mineralised. Most of the coal in Australia is found in or on the flanks of the highlands while the main hydro-electric schemes are of necessity also located in this region. The Main Divide separates the shorter, swifter-flowing rivers to the east coast from the internal drainage areas to the west, and those of the Murray-Darling system.

One of the uniting features of this region is the volcanic activity associated with Tertiary uplift. Basalt lava sheets form plateaux and upland plains from Queensland to western Victoria.

Folded mountains, western Macdonnell Ranges near Jay Creek Station, NT

Above: Channel country, western Queensland

1:15 000 000

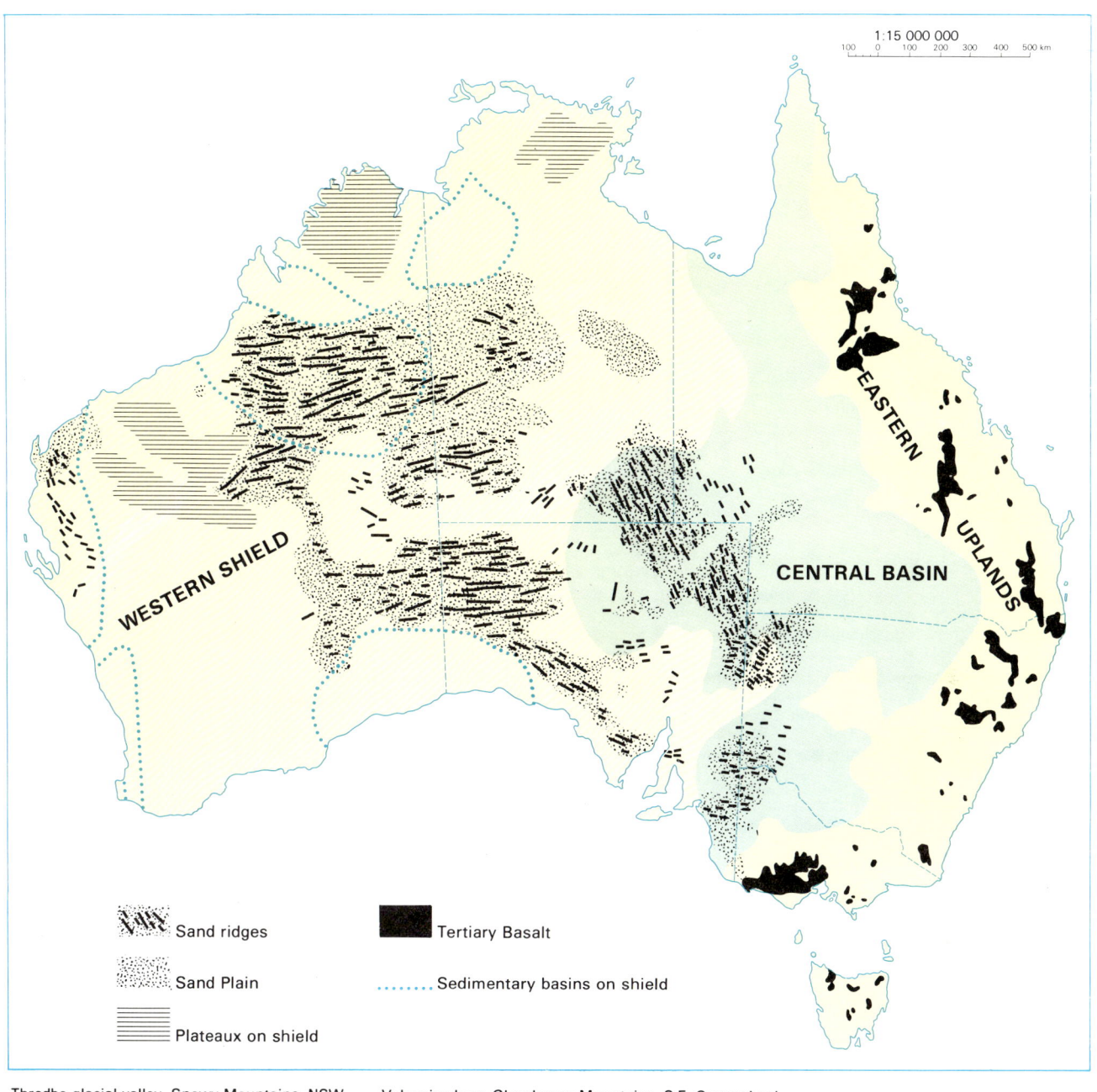

WESTERN SHIELD

CENTRAL BASIN

EASTERN UPLANDS

- Sand ridges
- Sand Plain
- Plateaux on shield
- Tertiary Basalt
- Sedimentary basins on shield

Thredbo glacial valley, Snowy Mountains, NSW

Volcanic plugs, Glasshouse Mountains, S.E. Queensland

Australian Soil Types

Soils, like other geomorphic features, are a product of their environment, and can be viewed as a function of the independent variables of climate, organisms, topography, parent rock material and time. Variations in these factors cause a distinct change in the morphology of soils.

The classification adopted in the map opposite is based on Northcote's *A Description of Australia's Soils*, published by CSIRO.

The Soil Profile

The term *soil profile* denotes the arrangement of the soil, from surface to bedrock, into layers or *horizons*, each possessing a different colour, texture and structure. A profile is a valid means of differentiating between soil types, if the soil is *mature*; that is, if it has established an equilibrium with the prevailing conditions over a long period of time.

Soil scientists have distinguished three main horizons in the soil profile:

A Topsoil
B Subsoil } True soil
C Substratum of weathered parent rock

Within each of these horizons further zones may be distinguished. Below the C horizon is the unaltered bedrock which is commonly referred to as horizon D, although it is not soil.

The A horizon contains most of the organic matter, and is therefore dark in colour. In humid areas where rainfall is reliable and moderate the A horizon may well be a *zone of eluviation* and *leaching*, through which the percolating water carries finely-divided and soluble material.

The B horizon is commonly referred to in humid areas as the *zone of illuviation*. It is a zone of enrichment from the deposition of soluble material and particles from above, and by capillary action from below.

The C horizon is the little-changed parent material from which the soil was derived, and grades down into the unaltered bedrock. The C horizon may show evidence of weathering but the original constituents of the parent material are still recognizable.

Soil Texture

Soil texture refers to the size of soil particles. Texture determines water-holding capacity, so is important in estimating rates of plant growth. *Sandy* soils are coarsely textured, porous and can hold a large amount of water. *Loams* have approximately equal percentages of sand, silt and clay with good drainage and water retention capacity. *Clays* contain 40 per cent of pore clay and relatively little sand. Due to the tightly-packed nature of clay colloids, water is prevented from moving freely through them.

Description of the Main Australian Soils

Sands: These are soils exhibiting uniform coarse-textured profiles and as a group cover 32 per cent of the Australian continent. The predominant sub-types of the sandy soils are calcareous (carbonates occur throughout the profile), bleached sands which are not calcareous (Profile 1), and brownish-earthy sands (Profile 2).

Loams: These are soils exhibiting uniform medium-textured profiles. As a group they occupy 13 per cent of Australia. Most show little or no profile development apart from some accumulation of organic matter in the surface and may be either calcareous or not calcareous (Profile 3).

Non-cracking Clays: These show uniform fine-textured profiles that do not crack open periodically. They occur in less than one per cent of the Australian continent (Profile 4).

Cracking Clays: These exhibit uniform fine-textured profiles that crack open periodically upon drying. The first main sub-type is often referred to as 'black earths', and occurs on the Darling Downs and Liverpool Plains (Profile 5). They have natural fertility but can erode easily if overworked on slopes. Other sub-types are the grey and brown, and red-brown earths (Profile 6) of the sub-humid to semi-arid zone of eastern and northern Australia. They occupy 11 per cent of Australia.

Calcareous Earths: These solonized brown soils have gradational texture profiles that are calcareous throughout (Profile 7). They have developed on calcareous materials in the semi-arid regions, notably in southern Australia, and are widely used for grazing, with some irrigated crops. They occupy 6 per cent of the Australian continent.

Massive Earths: These are soils with gradational texture profiles that are not calcareous throughout and cover 17 per cent of the Australian continent. The two principal groups are the red earths (Profile 8) and yellow earths (Profile 9) and although both are used extensively for sparse natural pastures for grazing, with irrigation availability they can support intensive farming.

Structured Earths: These are similar to massive earths in that they exhibit a gradational texture profile but their B horizon development is different. The two main groups are those with smooth or non-porous B horizons (Profile 10) and those exhibiting porous B horizons (Profile 11). They are often termed *krasnozems* (red loams), *red podzols*, *prairie soils* or *chocolate soils*. Collectively they account for under 3 per cent of the Australian land mass.

Duplex Soils: Accounting collectively for about 22 per cent of the Australian continent, duplex soils are those in which the texture suddenly becomes finer (more clayey) on passing from the A to the B horizons. The *red* duplex soils (10 per cent of total land area) have predominantly red B horizons and are commonly referred to as *desert loams*, *red podzols* or *red-brown earths* (Profile 12). The *yellow* duplex soils have dominantly yellow B horizons with sandy or loamy A horizons. They are commonly called *yellow podzols* (Profile 13). All the podzol soils are strongly leached in the surface and occur in fairly well-watered areas.

Organic Soils: These are dominated by organic matter for at least the top 30 centimetres of the profile. Generally the black or dark brown organic matter is well decomposed and humified and, under natural conditions, the soils are usually saturated for long periods. *Peats* are the most common example of this group and occur in less than one per cent of the Australian land mass (Profile 14).

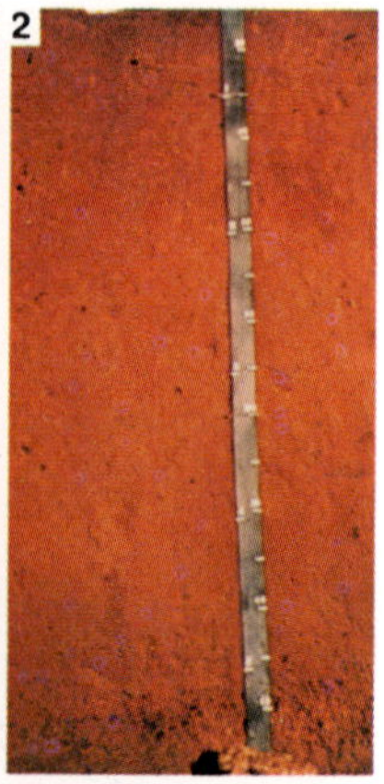

Profile 1 Bleached sand, North Stradbroke Island, Qld
Profile 2 Earthy sand, Merredin, WA
Profile 3 Shallow bleached loam, Cooroy, Qld  
Profile 4 Non-cracking clay, Bundaberg, Qld
Profile 5 Black earth, Toowoomba, Qld  
Profile 6 Red cracking clay, Woocalla, SA
Profile 7 Solonized brown soil, Coomealla, NSW 
Profile 8 Red earth, Aramac, Qld

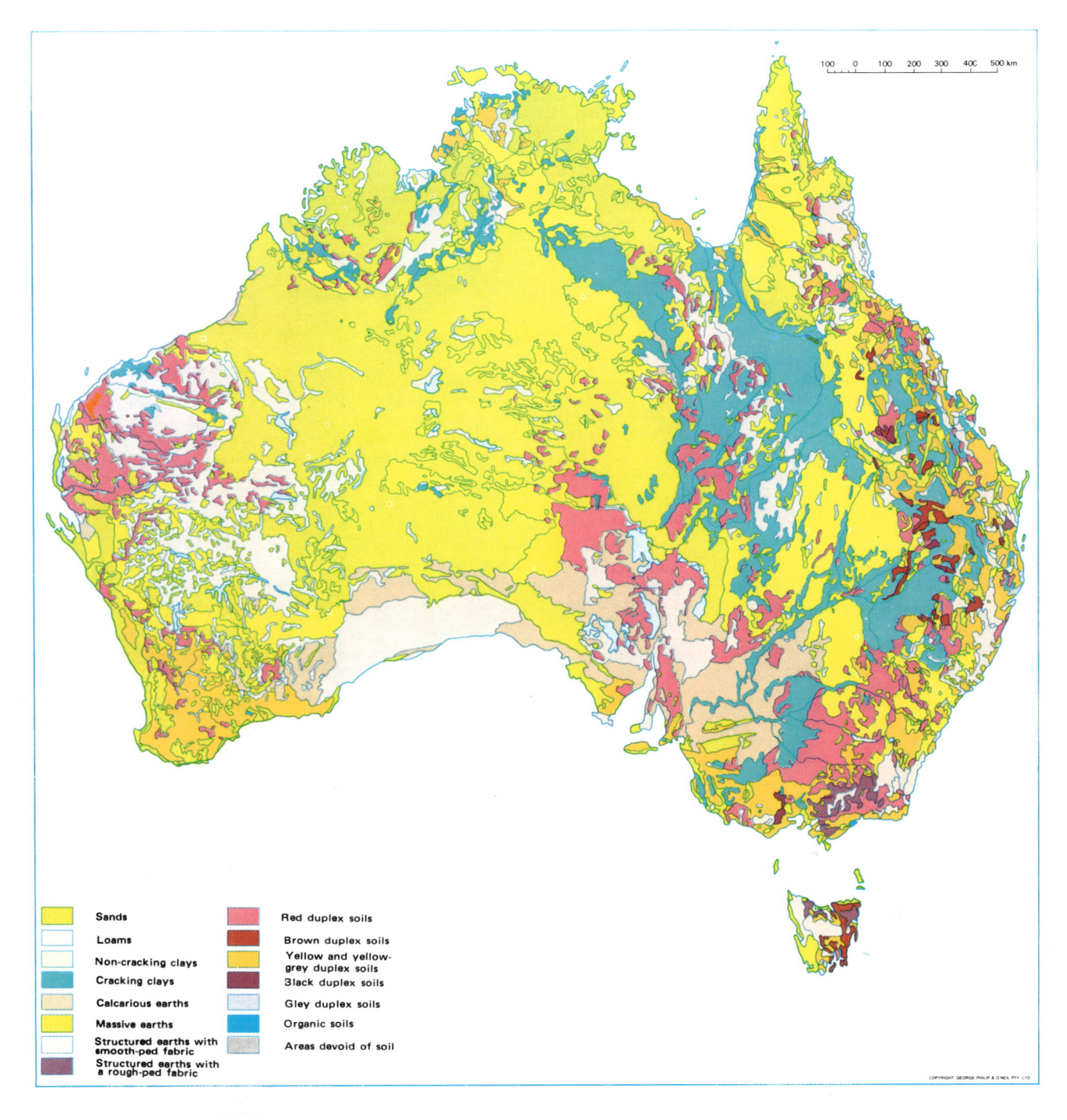

Legend

- Sands
- Loams
- Non-cracking clays
- Cracking clays
- Calcarious earths
- Massive earths
- Structured earths with smooth-ped fabric
- Structured earths with a rough-ped fabric
- Red duplex soils
- Brown duplex soils
- Yellow and yellow-grey duplex soils
- Black duplex soils
- Gley duplex soils
- Organic soils
- Areas devoid of soil

Profile 9 Yellow earth, Mareeba, Qld
Profile 10 Red podzolic soil, Mackay, Qld
Profile 11 Krasnozem, Bogong, Vic. 
Profile 12 Red-brown earth, Deniliquin, NSW
Profile 13 Yellow podzolic soil, Beerwah, Qld 
Profile 14 Peat soil, Breona, Tas.

Australian Vegetation Regions

The distinctive quality of Australian flora has been recognized since the first plant collections were made by Joseph Banks at Botany Bay in 1770. The continent has been separated from other land masses since it drifted north from Antarctica 49 million years ago. This long period of isolation has given Australia a unique flora: for example, 75 per cent of the 6000 land plants in the south-western corner of Western Australia are found nowhere else. The fact that the Australian continent was temporarily connected with New Guinea resulted in the rich tropical flora of Malaysia spreading to Australia in the Oligocene Period (about 30 million years ago) and more recently in the pleistocene Period. Thus, many of the tropical plants in our northern forests originated in Asia and arrived here via land bridges. The Australian land flora comprises over 12 000 species of flowering plants and is dominated by such conspicuous genera as *Eucalyptus, Melaleuca, Leptospermum* (family Myrtaceae), *Banksia* (family Proteaceae), *Acacia* (family Mimosaceae), *Pulteneae* (family Papillionaceae), *Casuarina* (family Casuarinaceae) and *Xanthorrhoea* (family Xanthorrhoeaceae).

affects plants distribution. Rainfall and temperature are determined largely by latitude and elevation. Not only is the amount of rainfall important to an area, but the reliability and duration of precipitation are also significant influences on plant life. For example, although coastal regions of New South Wales might receive 1000 mm of rain distributed evenly throughout the year, Alice Springs might receive its annual average of 120–150 mm in one brief but heavy downpour.

There are four very broad types of vegetation in Australia: *forests* (open and closed); *woodlands* and *grasslands; scrub* (a combination of mallee and heath) and *desert*. The distribution of these types is primarily determined by climate. Very extreme localised conditions result in specialised vegetation types such as salt marshes, mangrove swamps and tundra, which will not be discussed here.

Forests

Forests are found predominantly on the eastern coast of the continent where the rainfall ranges from 1000–2500 mm per year. A forest is a plant community dominated by trees that grow very closely together. Closed forests, particularly the northern rainforests, include trees other than eucalypts, and feature buttressing tree trunks, lianas, and low light levels at the forest floor. Cabbage Fan Palms (*Livistona australis*) and Lawyer Vines (*Smilax australis*) are examples of trees found in closed forests. Open forests are less dense and are dominated by eucalypts, including Mountain Ash (*E. regnans*) and Messmate (*E. obliqua*) which are both found in south-eastern Australia, and the Spotted Gum (*E. maculata*) which grows throughout the eastern regions of the continent.

Woodlands and Grasslands

Woodlands are found in drier areas than forests. Here, unlike the forests, the distance between trees is greater than the average height of the trees. In addition, the tree crowns are quite large. Woodland trees include the Darwin Stringybark (*E. tetrodonta*), the Western Australian Christmas Tree (*Nuytsia floribunda*) and two eastern species, the White Cypress Pine (*callitris glauca*) and the Yellow Box (*E. melliodora*). The River Red Gum (*E. camaldulensis*) is Australia's most widely-distributed eucalypt and is found near seasonal and permanent watercourses.

Woodlands frequently blend gradually into grasslands where trees and shrubs are more sporadic. In grassland Kangaroo Grass (*Themeda australis*) is found throughout much of the continent, Mitchell Grass (*Astrebla pectinata*) is dominant over large areas in the north, while the Common Wallaby Grass (*Danthonia caespitosa*) fills a similar role in southern Australia. The Blue Devil (*Eryngium rostratum*) and the Common Everlasting (*Helichrysum apiculatum*) are common grassland plants throughout our temperate regions.

Scrub

The area designated as scrub includes vegetations referred to as heath and mallee scrub. It is a community of shrubby plants in which the dominant individuals are less than 8m in height. Shrubs shorter than 6m with small evergreen leaves are common in heathlands; this vegetation is generally located on infertile soils or in areas of restricted drainage. South-west Western Australia heathlands or the Hawkesbury sand stones near Sydney may include almost as many plant species as a tropical rainforest. The Red Flowering Gum (*E. ficifolia*) and Mangle's Kangaroo Paw (*Anigozanthus manglesii*), both of Western Australia, and the eastern Saw Banksia (*Banksia serrata*) and Common Heath (*Epacris impressa*) are just a few examples of this diversity. The plant community known as mallee is dominated by eucalypts under 8 m and is restricted to the semi-arid south-western and south-eastern regions of the country. The term 'mallee' is derived from an Aboriginal word meaning 'thicket'. Mallee eucalypts consist of several slender stems rising from a single large root swelling known as a ligno tuber. Yellow Mallee (*E. incrassata*) and Erect Guinea-flower (*Hibbertia stricta*) are commonly found in mallee vegetation.

Deserts

Deserts are those regions which receive less than approximately 250 mm annual rainfall, and where evaporation exceeds precipitation throughout the year. Due to the unpredictable rainfall, flowering times are often uncertain and many plants blossom irregularly. The extreme conditions of deserts create a variety of microhabitats including saline dry lake beds and ephemeral watercourses. In addition, because so little water is available, any additional moisture can be crucial and results in a complex mosaic of plant communities. Examples of desert trees include the Coolibah (*E. microtheca*), the Ghost Gum (*E. papuana*) and the Mulga (*Acacia aneura*), while some of the perennials are Sturt's Desert Pea (*Clianthus speciosus*), Saltbush (*Atriplex vesicaria*) and Porcupine Grass (*Triodia irritans*).

Rainforest, Eastern Queensland

Wet Sclerophyll forest, Gibraltar Ranges, NSW

Dry Sclerophyll forest, Otway Ranges, Victoria
Savanna woodland (medium), Katherine, NT

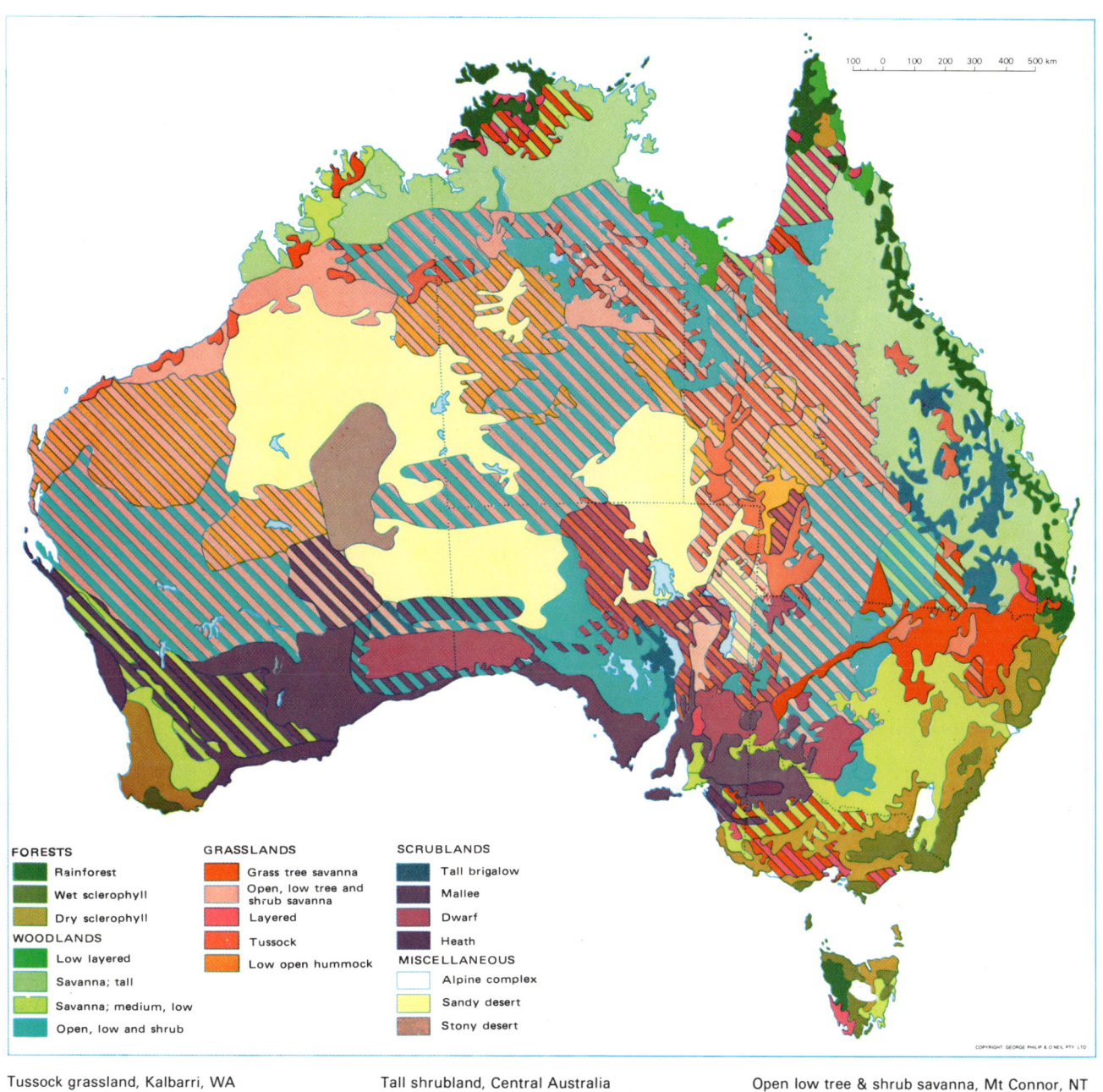

17

FORESTS
- Rainforest
- Wet sclerophyll
- Dry sclerophyll

WOODLANDS
- Low layered
- Savanna; tall
- Savanna; medium, low
- Open, low and shrub

GRASSLANDS
- Grass tree savanna
- Open, low tree and shrub savanna
- Layered
- Tussock
- Low open hummock

SCRUBLANDS
- Tall brigalow
- Mallee
- Dwarf
- Heath

MISCELLANEOUS
- Alpine complex
- Sandy desert
- Stony desert

Tussock grassland, Kalbarri, WA

Tall shrubland, Central Australia

Open low tree & shrub savanna, Mt Connor, NT

Trees, Grasses and Wildflowers

Forests

Cabbage Fan Palm
Livistona australis
28 m   Sept–Nov

Mountain Ash
Eucalyptus regnans
90 m   Jan–Mar

Messmate Stringybark
Eucalyptus obliqua
55 m   Jan–Feb

Jarrah
Eucalyptus marginata
45 m   Sept–Feb

Spotted Gum
Eucalyptus maculata
50 m   July–Aug

Hoop Pine
Araucaria cunninghamii
50 m

Purple Coral-Pea
Hardenbergia violacea
1–2 m   Aug–Nov

Grassy Woodlands and Grasslands

Western Australian Christmas Tree
Nuytsia floribunda
10–20 m   Nov–Jan

Yellow Box
Eucalyptus melliodora
16–30 m   Oct–Feb

White Cypress Pine
Callitris columellaris
18–30 m

Darwin Stringybark
Eucalyptus tetrodonta
15–30 m   July–Aug

River Red Gum
Eucalyptus camaldulensis
15–40 m   Sept–April

Mitchell Grass
Astrebla pectinata
30–100 cm   Dec–April

Scrub: Heath and Mallee

Red Flowering Gum
Eucalyptus ficifolia
6–10 m   Dec–Feb

Yellow Mallee
Eucalyptus incrassata
2–8 m   Oct–April

Pin Cushion Hakea
Hakea laurina
3–7 m   June–Sept

Coast Tea-tree
Leptospermum laevigatum
2–8 m   Sept–Nov

Saw Banksia
Banksia serrata
5–10 m   Dec–April

Desert

Ghost Gum
Eucalyptus papuana
8–20 m   Dec–Feb

Mulga
Acacia aneura
2–8 m   Irregular

Belah
Casuarina cristata
4–15 m   Nov–Feb

Coolibah
Eucalyptus microtheca
3–20 m   Aug–Feb

Berrigan
Eremophila longifolia
2–6 m   Most of year

Porcupine Grass
Triodia irritans
0.5–2 m   Nov–April

Lawyer Vine
Smilax australis
Sept-Feb

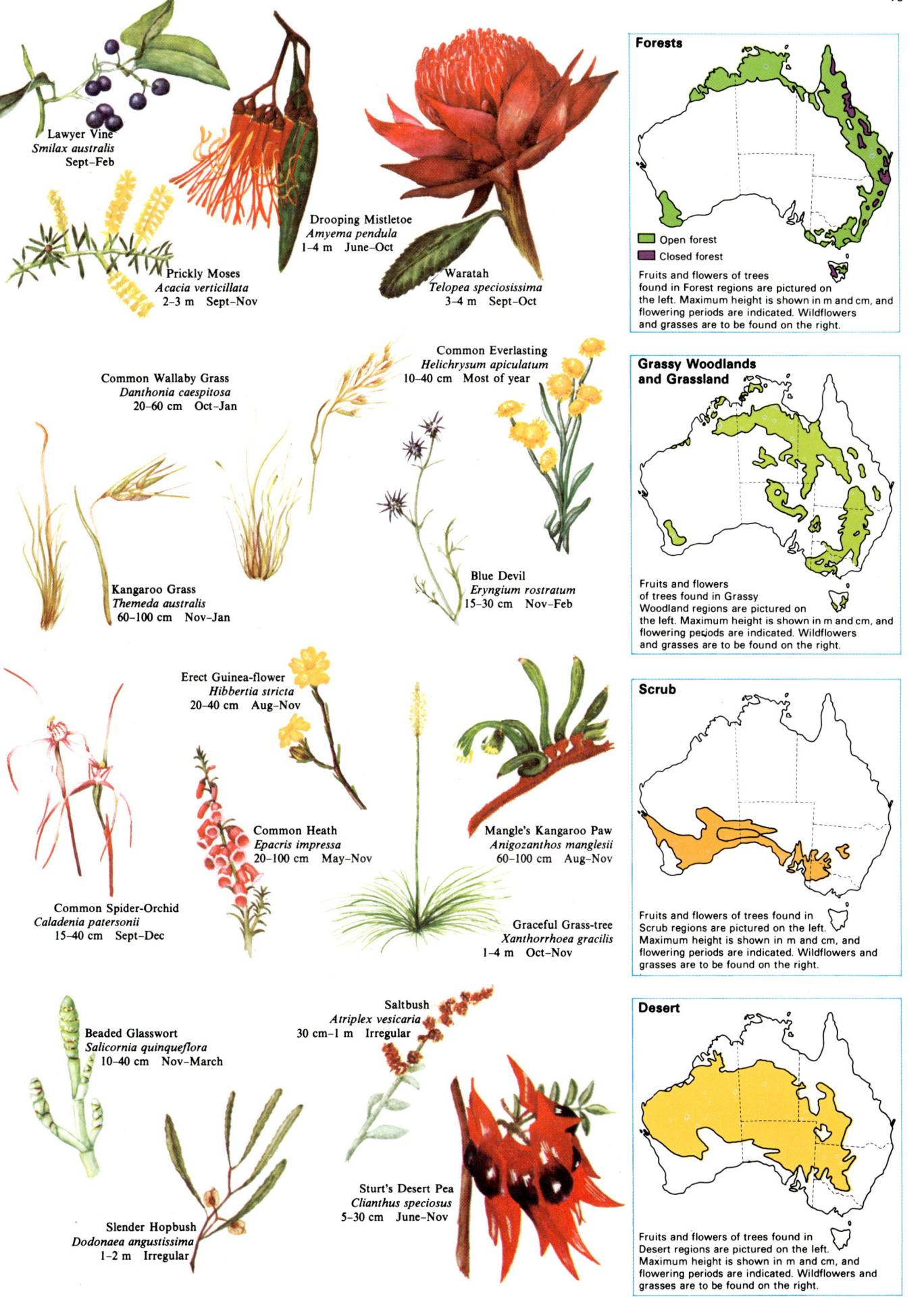

Prickly Moses
Acacia verticillata
2–3 m   Sept-Nov

Drooping Mistletoe
Amyema pendula
1–4 m   June-Oct

Waratah
Telopea speciosissima
3–4 m   Sept-Oct

Forests

Open forest
Closed forest

Fruits and flowers of trees found in Forest regions are pictured on the left. Maximum height is shown in m and cm, and flowering periods are indicated. Wildflowers and grasses are to be found on the right.

Common Wallaby Grass
Danthonia caespitosa
20–60 cm   Oct-Jan

Kangaroo Grass
Themeda australis
60–100 cm   Nov-Jan

Common Everlasting
Helichrysum apiculatum
10–40 cm   Most of year

Blue Devil
Eryngium rostratum
15–30 cm   Nov-Feb

Grassy Woodlands and Grassland

Fruits and flowers of trees found in Grassy Woodland regions are pictured on the left. Maximum height is shown in m and cm, and flowering periods are indicated. Wildflowers and grasses are to be found on the right.

Common Spider-Orchid
Caladenia patersonii
15–40 cm   Sept-Dec

Erect Guinea-flower
Hibbertia stricta
20–40 cm   Aug-Nov

Common Heath
Epacris impressa
20–100 cm   May-Nov

Mangle's Kangaroo Paw
Anigozanthos manglesii
60–100 cm   Aug-Nov

Graceful Grass-tree
Xanthorrhoea gracilis
1–4 m   Oct-Nov

Scrub

Fruits and flowers of trees found in Scrub regions are pictured on the left. Maximum height is shown in m and cm, and flowering periods are indicated. Wildflowers and grasses are to be found on the right.

Beaded Glasswort
Salicornia quinqueflora
10–40 cm   Nov-March

Slender Hopbush
Dodonaea angustissima
1–2 m   Irregular

Saltbush
Atriplex vesicaria
30 cm–1 m   Irregular

Sturt's Desert Pea
Clianthus speciosus
5–30 cm   June-Nov

Desert

Fruits and flowers of trees found in Desert regions are pictured on the left. Maximum height is shown in m and cm, and flowering periods are indicated. Wildflowers and grasses are to be found on the right.

Australia's Unique Animals

Australia's animals seem to inspire superlatives. 'Unique . . . remarkable . . . missing links . . . nature's strangest creatures . . . the platypus seems designed by a committee . . .' are typical of the comments which recur.

They enthuse the zoologist, lure the tourist, and the two best-known of them, the quaint kangaroo and the 'cuddly' koala, have become unmistakable international symbols of Australia. Australian fauna is noted for the presence of many unique animals — and the absence of many orders known elsewhere. No great apes roam in Australian forests, hoofed animals are a recent introduction, and there are no members of the order Insectivora, among others . . .

For scores of millions of years, the fauna evolved in isolation, and many different forms came from relatively few ancestral types. The marsupials, the pouched mammals, developed to a degree unknown elsewhere, many of them reflecting characteristics typical of mammalian orders in other continents.

In Australia the unique monotremes, platypus and echidna, the world's only egg-laying mammals, are to be found.

Links with the Reptiles

The monotremes are considered by some to be 'living fossils' which represent a stage in the evolution of mammals from reptiles. Best known is the furred platypus (*Ornithorhynchus anatinus*) which inhabits Australia's eastern watercourses, where it finds food in the water and mud. This 'composite' creature with webbed feet, a duckbill, and a tail resembling a beaver's, lays eggs and suckles its young. Adult males (often 600 mm long) have poison spurs on their hind legs. Burrows with exits above and below water are dug many metres deep into the banks of streams.

The other monotreme is the echidna or spiny anteater (*Tachyglossus aculeatus*) of Australia and Papua New Guinea. Echidnas are land dwellers relying on their spines and their ability to burrow partly into the ground to deter predators. They do not tunnel like the platypus, but usually live under rocks or tree roots.

Marsupials

Australia has about 230 species of mammals: almost half are marsupials, with the balance being the placental mammals and the monotremes. Marsupials lack a placenta, the womb structure which nourishes the young during pregnancy and permits the higher mammals (placental mammals) to produce almost fully developed young. The common feature of most marsupials is the possession of a pouch in which to hold the young, which are born very early, and must find their way unaided to the pouch. Considering that the young of a large kangaroo, for example, are under 20 mm long, these are some of nature's most extraordinary journeys. Not all marsupials have pouches as prominent as that of the frequently-pictured kangaroo: some have only rudimentary pouches, while the burrowing wombat's pouch opens upside down.

Most kangaroos are herbivorous — one reason for the slaughter of millions since Europeans introduced sheep and tried to eliminate competitors for the limited pasture. Some of the smaller kangaroos are insectivorous. With the exception of Queensland's tree-climbing kangaroos (similar to some found in Papua New Guinea) they are ground dwellers.

The largest are the red (*Megaleia rufa*) and great grey (*Macropus giganteus*) kangaroos, sometimes taller than a man. The smallest is the musky rat kangaroo (*Hypsiprymnodon moschatus*) less than 300 mm long. 'Wallaby' commonly denotes smaller kangaroos, 'wallaroo' those preferring rocky habitats.

Large kangaroos can bound briefly at speeds exceeding 45 kilometres per hour, and leap 11 metres or more. The heavy tail maintains balance in movement.

The koala, (*Phascolarctos cinereus*) the 'teddy bear' of scores of travel posters, is a tree dwelling marsupial. Sometimes popularly called the native bear, it is in fact related to the tunnelling wombat. It reaches around 600 mm fully grown and spends most of its life in trees, although it may walk long distances in search of the species of eucalypts whose leaves form its exclusive diet. Other tree-dwelling marsupials include tree kangaroos, the monkey-like cuscus (*Phalanger maculatus*) and various gliding possums.

The powerful, thickset wombats (*Lasiorhinus* and *Vombatus spp.*) are widespread burrowing marsupials in south-eastern Australia. Far more unusual is the small blind marsupial mole (*Notoryctes typhlops*) of inland areas. Another highly specialised Western Australian marsupial is the dramatically-striped numbat or banded anteater (*Myrmecobius fasciatus*).

The few carnivorous marsupials, members of the family Dasyuridae, include insectivorous 'mice', the native 'cats', and the Tasmanian 'tiger' and 'devil'. Some of these marsupials have evolved to resemble animals of other origins, found in other countries — this trend towards similar characteristics is called 'convergent evolution'. The Tasmanian 'tiger' or thylacine (*Thylacinus cynocephalus*) is similar to unrelated wolves on other continents.

Placental Mammals

Australia's placental mammals comprise the dingo (*Canis familiaris dingo*), marine mammals, rodents and bats.

The dingo or warrigal appears to have evolved from dogs brought from Asia by the people who became the Australian Aborigines. It is now regarded as indigenous.

There are some 50 species of native rats (only the introduced species have become widespread pests) and about 50 bat species, including nine 'flying foxes' or fruit bats.

Introduced Species

Scores of species have been introduced to Australia for pastoral use, as beasts of burden, for game purposes and sometimes for curiosity's sake. Some have created new industries — others, like the rabbit which existed in plague proportions until checked by the virus disease myxomatosis in the 1950s, came close to crippling areas of the rural economy.

Echidna

Koala

Common Wombat

Hairy-nosed Wombat

Numbat

Dingo (Desert)

21

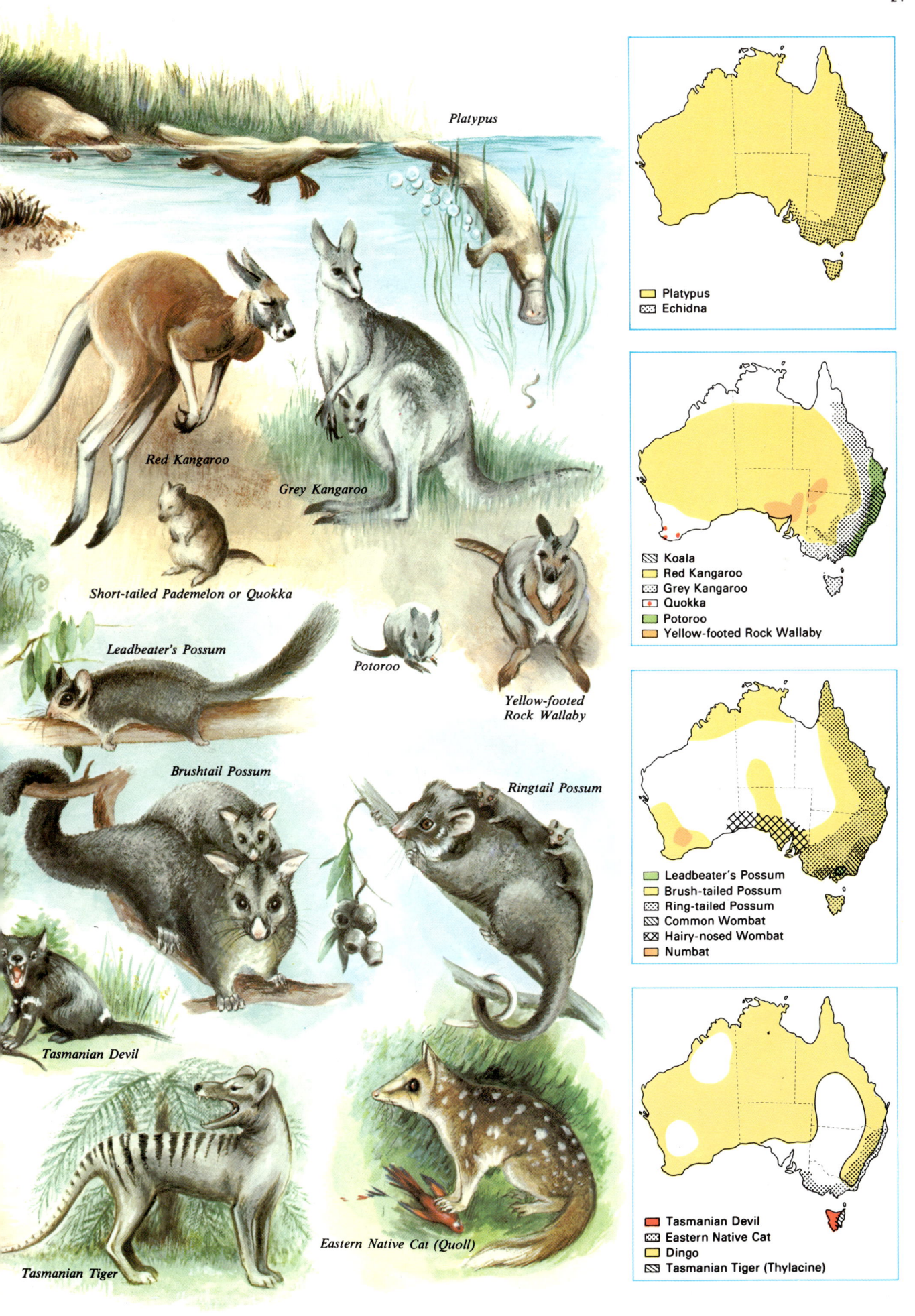

Platypus

Red Kangaroo

Grey Kangaroo

Short-tailed Pademelon or Quokka

Leadbeater's Possum

Potoroo

Yellow-footed Rock Wallaby

Brushtail Possum

Ringtail Possum

Tasmanian Devil

Tasmanian Tiger

Eastern Native Cat (Quoll)

- Platypus
- Echidna

- Koala
- Red Kangaroo
- Grey Kangaroo
- Quokka
- Potoroo
- Yellow-footed Rock Wallaby

- Leadbeater's Possum
- Brush-tailed Possum
- Ring-tailed Possum
- Common Wombat
- Hairy-nosed Wombat
- Numbat

- Tasmanian Devil
- Eastern Native Cat
- Dingo
- Tasmanian Tiger (Thylacine)

Common Australian Birds

Australia's birds, frequently colourful, occasionally bizarre, appear often in the early European journals of discovery. In 1697 the startled Dutch explorer Willem de Vlamingh found swans that were black, not white — and took three back to Batavia to prove his claim. Other newcomers marvelled at birds that 'laughed', at tall flightless birds almost as high as a man, and at scores of unfamiliar parrots exploding in gaudy swarms over inland regions.

Equally remarkable were the birds that created and paraded in elaborate bowers, and others in jungle and arid country that built incubation mounds and tended them to keep the interior temperature around 33°C. Most amazing of all were the lyrebirds, delivering concerts of great vocal range and mimicry, veiled by a gauze-like tail.

Wide Representation

Of approximately 700 birds known in Australia, some 530 are regarded as endemic. Many of the latter evolved during Australia's long geographic isolation and consequently are found only in certain defined habitats.

In contrast to the limited mammal representation in Australia, the continent has most bird orders represented. Among the significant absentees are the vultures, woodpeckers and flamingoes.

Australian bird life is dominated by the insect-eaters which comprise about 70 per cent of the bird population. Many of the world's parrots are here, 50 species of great variety, some of them favoured aviary birds around the world for a century and a half. Overseas demand remains so strong that parrots form a large part of continuing bird-smuggling operations.

Unusual Calls

Many Australian birds are noted for their calls. Outstanding is the raucous 'laugh' of the kookaburra (*Dacelo gigas*), the giant kingfisher which is also known as the laughing jackass. This popular bird with the 'crazed cackle', as an Australian author once wrote, is not a kingfisher in the literal sense, but a predator on small animals and young birds. Other common bush noises are the carolling of magpies (*Gymnorhina spp.*) and the harsh, melancholy cawing of crows (*Corvus spp.*). Also distinctive is the cracking of the whipbird (*Psophodes spp.*) and the sharp ring of the bellbird (*Manorina melanophrys*).

In terms of range and mimicry nothing matches the performance of the unique Lyrebird. There are only two species: the Superb Lyrebird (*Menura novaehollandiae*) found in many areas of eastern Australia, and the smaller Prince Albert Lyrebird (*Menura albertii*) known only in forests near the coastal junction of Queensland and New South Wales.

Males of both species are more vocal than females and give their song and dance performances around the year, except when moulting. The most spectacular concerts occur during the courting and breeding season, often on specially constructed domed mounds a metre wide. With tail extended and feathers spread forward over body and head, the lyrebird gives a performance of remarkable range that often includes mimicking the notes of other birds and even man-made noises. A single concert has been known to include up to 40 different calls.

The ancestry of lyrebirds is unknown. Their only recorded relatives are the equally remarkable Australian scrub birds (*Atrichornithidae*).

Other Distinctive Birds

Familiar from its position on the Australian Coat of Arms, the ostrich-like, flightless emu (*Dromaius novaehollandiae*) is widely distributed through inland areas, sometimes in plague proportions as far as local farmers are concerned. With the similar cassowary (*Casuarius casuarius*) of Australia and Papua New Guinea it constitutes the order Casuariiformes.

Appropriately enough, given Australia's many flowering plants, honeyeaters are well represented. Seventy species are known, ranging from pigeon-size to smaller than a canary.

Another famous group found only in Australia and Papua New Guinea comprises the bower birds (*Ptilonorhyncidae*) renown for constructing decorated bowers for display and courtship — and for highly-developed powers of mimicry. The 16 species build bowers (separate from nests) in many forms, from the common parallel row of twigs to a leaf-paved forest clearing. Decorations also vary widely, and include flowers and berries, shining objects, shell and sometimes objects of a particular colour. Some birds mix various substances to paint parts of a bower.

Notable also are the three mound-builders, birds which incubate eggs by burial rather than by normal hatching methods. The brush turkey (*Alectura lathami*) and the scrub fowl (*Megapodius freycinet*) are from tropical and sub-tropical regions, while the mallee fowl or lowan (*Leipoa ocellata*) has adapted to arid inland conditions. The procedure is generally to cover moist decaying vegetation with soil or sand, lay eggs within the mound when the temperature is determined by the male to be suitable (around 33°C) and maintain temperature by adding or removing soil daily until the chicks hatch and dig themselves out.

One particular colony of birds forms a noted tourist attraction near Melbourne. This is the rookery of fairy or little penguins (*Eudyptula minor*) on Phillip Island. The summer 'penguin parade' at dusk when the birds, members of the only penguin species resident in Australian waters, waddle in from the surf after a day's fishing, draws tens of thousands of visitors.

Another bird noted for distinctive behaviour is the brolga or native companion (*Grus rubicunda*), sole Australian representative of the crane family. Flocks of the tall brolgas routinely perform group 'dancing', with stately formal movements, on the inland plains that are their usual habitat. They are no longer found in the south-east and south-west of Australia.

Australia has only one of the world's 21 bustard species, the Australian bustard or plains turkey (*Eurodotis australis*). Widespread until decimated by early settlers, subsequent sport hunting and the marauding of introduced foxes, it is now restricted to remote areas. Bustards reach almost a metre in height.

Yellow-breasted Sunbird

Purple-crowned Pigeon

Rainbow Lorikeet

Purple-capped Lorikeet

Eastern Rosella

Scarlet Robin

Orange-winged Sittella

Azure Kingfisher

Cattle Egret

23

Mistletoe Bird

Swallow

Brown Hawk

Silvereye

Little Thornbill

Brolga

Galah

Scarlet Honeyeater

Little Kingfisher

Blue-faced Honeyeater

Lyrebird

Budgerigar

Zebra Finch

Emu

Yellow Weebill

Rainbow Bird

Crimson Chat

Purple-crowned Wren

Blue Wren

Orange Chat

Spur-winged Plover

Squatter Pigeon

Noisy Pitta

Diamond Firetail Finch

Aquatic Birds

The extent of bird migration within Australia is not known, but it is believed that at least 50 species are involved.

Many birds — mainly waders — migrate from Australia each year, crossing the Equator to breed in the Northern Hemisphere. Other species breed in Australia and travel north in autumn. Relatively few of the birds which migrate to the Southern Hemisphere come as far as the continent of Australia, most stopping in the islands to the north.

A number of tube-nosed seabirds, such as albatrosses, storm petrels and shearwaters, are found regularly in Australian waters, but seldom come ashore except to breed. Some visit Australia on their global wanderings, for example the muttonbird or short-tailed shearwater (*Puffinus tenuirostris*) which nests on southern coastlines.

Many of the duck-like birds — including geese, swans and shovellers — are also found in Australia. Two rare members of the goose family stand out. The magpie goose (*Anseranas semipalmata*) is found in the Northern Territory, north Queensland and southern Papua New Guinea. The Cape Barren goose (*Cereopsis novaehollandiae*) is restricted to southern coastal areas, notably Bass Strait. This grey bird, with its distinctive yellow bill, is about 600 mm long. It is not in fact a true goose and is currently in a subfamily of its own. For many years hunted and eaten, or shot as an agricultural pest, the species is now protected, although farmers are able to shoot the birds if a permit is obtained.

Some of the other aquatic birds are less well represented — there is only one species of pelican and five species of cormorants or shags in Australia.

25

- Blue-winged Shoveller
- Grey Teal
- Pelican
- Albatross
- Pacific Gull
- Osprey
- Cape Barren Goose
- Fairy Tern
- Avocet
- Silver Gull
- Godwit
- White-headed Stilt
- White-faced Storm Petrel
- Turnstone Non Breed
- Golden Plover
- Green Shank
- Turnstone Breed
- Hooded Dotterel
- Common Sandpiper
- Sanderling
- Terek Sandpiper
- Red-capped Dotterel
- Double-banded Dotterel
- Yellow Mouthed Drupe
- Draught Board Helmet
- Toa(d)
- Nautilus
- Cowry
- Yellow Sundial
- Jewelled Dog Whelk
- Abalone
- Spo(r)

Reptiles, Amphibians and Insects

The cautionary tales of an Australian childhood are often remembered as warnings against snakes, sharks and spiders.

Tiger snakes, 'White Death', a shark beloved of headline writers, and lurking redback spiders are just some well-publicised dangers of the outdoors which regrettably lead many Australians to kill suspect creatures first and identify them later.

While nearly 4000 Australians die annually from road accidents, about four die of snake-bite, perhaps one (on average) by shark attack. Spiders have claimed only six lives in the past 15 years. But the folklore is persistent and many Australians know more about such long-odds killers than they do about natural wonders such as Australia's giant lizards, the 'living fossil' lungfish of Queensland and Gippsland earthworms growing up to 3.6 metres long.

Australia's Reptiles

These include about 140 species of snakes, 360 lizard species, two crocodiles, 15 species of freshwater tortoises and six marine turtles.

Fewer than 20 of the terrestrial snakes have venom potentially fatal to humans. Largest, and deadliest, is the taipan (*Oxyuranus scutellatus*), growing to three metres and more. Until the development of an antivenene the bite of a large taipan was invariably fatal. Other particularly dangerous snakes are the tiger (*Notechis scutatus*), copperhead (*Austrelaps superbus*), death adder (*Acanthophis antarcticus*) and common brown (*Pseudonaja textilis*).

More than 30 species of sea-snakes found in northern waters are poisonous, but are fortunately rarely encountered by man. The yellow-bellied sea-snake (*Pelamis platurus*) — considered the world's most widely distributed snake — is common.

Two species of crocodiles were once common in northern Australia. One is harmless to man — the freshwater crocodile (*Crocodylus johnstoni*) which grows to three metres. The other, the saltwater crocodile (*C. porosus*) grows to seven metres and has frequently attacked cattle and men. Both species are now protected.

Australia's lizards range in size from the giant perentie (*Varanus giganteus*) which grows to 2.4 metres — claimed as second in size only to Indonesia's Komodo dragon lizard — down to some not 50 mm long. None are venomous. Iguanas or chameleons are unknown.

Some of the dragon lizards successfully conceal a harmless nature behind a frightening facade. The best-known of the dragon lizards, the boldly-coloured thorny or mountain devil (*Moloch horridus*) has a limited ability to change colours to match background, but is well protected by many spines. The mountain devil is one of the world's most specialised dragons. Although slow of movement, its armour is so sharp that no animal could eat it without being injured itself. It has a long adhesive tongue, particularly suited to its diet of ants. The frilled lizard (*Chlamydosaurus kingii*) unfolds a vividly-coloured neck frill of membrane. The frill is normally folded back, but under attack it opens up, umbrella-style, and sways from side to side, while it opens its brightly-coloured mouth and hisses.

Unique to Australia and Papua New Guinea, the flap-footed legless lizards (*Pygopodidae*) are often mistaken for snakes by casual observers. They lack forelegs and their hind legs are mere flaps of skin.

Goannas, known beyond Australia as monitors, are common. These are among the most spectacular lizards. The sight of a couple of two-metre perenties fighting tooth and claw seems more in keeping with prehistoric times, than the present day.

Noteworthy among Australia's abundant skinks (*Scincidae*) is the large blue tongue skink (*Tiliqua spp.*) which discourages predators with a spectacular open-mouthed display.

Of the six turtles, the green turtle (*Chelonia mydas*) is fated to be popular as turtle soup, while the luth or leathery turtle (*Dermochelys coriacea*) is renowned for weighing half a tonne and reaching three metres in length. Both are found only in northern waters.

The Amphibians

Australia has approximately 130 species of frogs, but no salamanders or newts. There is only one toad, the giant South American Cane toad (*Bufo marinus*) which was introduced in 1935 to control cane-borer beetles. Since then it has spread in plague proportions along the north-east coast. Australia's native frogs include a diverse array of tree frogs, marsh frogs and burrowing frogs.

As in the case of many fish adapted to the frequent droughts of the inland, certain burrowing frogs are well-equipped to survive in dry conditions. The waterholding frog (*Cyclorana platycephalus*) fills its bladder with water, burrows into the soil, secretes a cocoon which prevents water loss, and hibernates there for months, if necessary.

Some Invertebrates

Australia has at least 50 000 insect species, many of which are endemic. There are some 350 species of butterflies and 7600 species of moths — including the world's largest moth, the giant Atlas moth (*Coscinocera hercules*) of northern Queensland. There are some 18 000 beetle species and 900 species of ants. The magnetic termite (*Amitermes meridionalis*) creates one of northern Australia's natural wonders — nests about four metres high, three metres long and a metre wide, with the narrow ends pointing approximately north-south.

The venomous redback spider (*Latrodectus mactans*) is frequently found in rubbish heaps, old machinery and, traditionally, in outside toilets. The male redback is almost one-third the size of the female and is reputed to be non-poisonous. The Sydney Funnelweb spider (*Atrax robustus*), possibly the world's most toxic spider, is unusually aggressive and will strike at objects of almost any size. Although the males generally die upon reaching maturity at seven or eight years, a seventeen-year-old female has been recorded.

Another curious invertebrate of startling appearance is the giant earthworm (*Megascolides australis*) of Victoria's Gippsland district, growing to 3.6 metres in length and 25 mm in diameter.

Taipan
Oxyuranus scutellatus
1.5–4 m

Tiger snake
Notechis scutatus
1–2 m

Bearded Dragon
Amphibolurus barbatus
70 cm

Frilled Lizard
Chlamydosaurus kingii
90 cm

Waterholding Frog
Cyclorana platycephalus

Saltwater Crocodile
Crocodylus porosus
5–7 m

east–west aspect

Magnetic termite mound
(1–2 m in height)

north–south aspect

Magnetic Termite
Amitermes meridionalis
5 mm

Copperhead
Austrelaps superbus
1–1.5 m

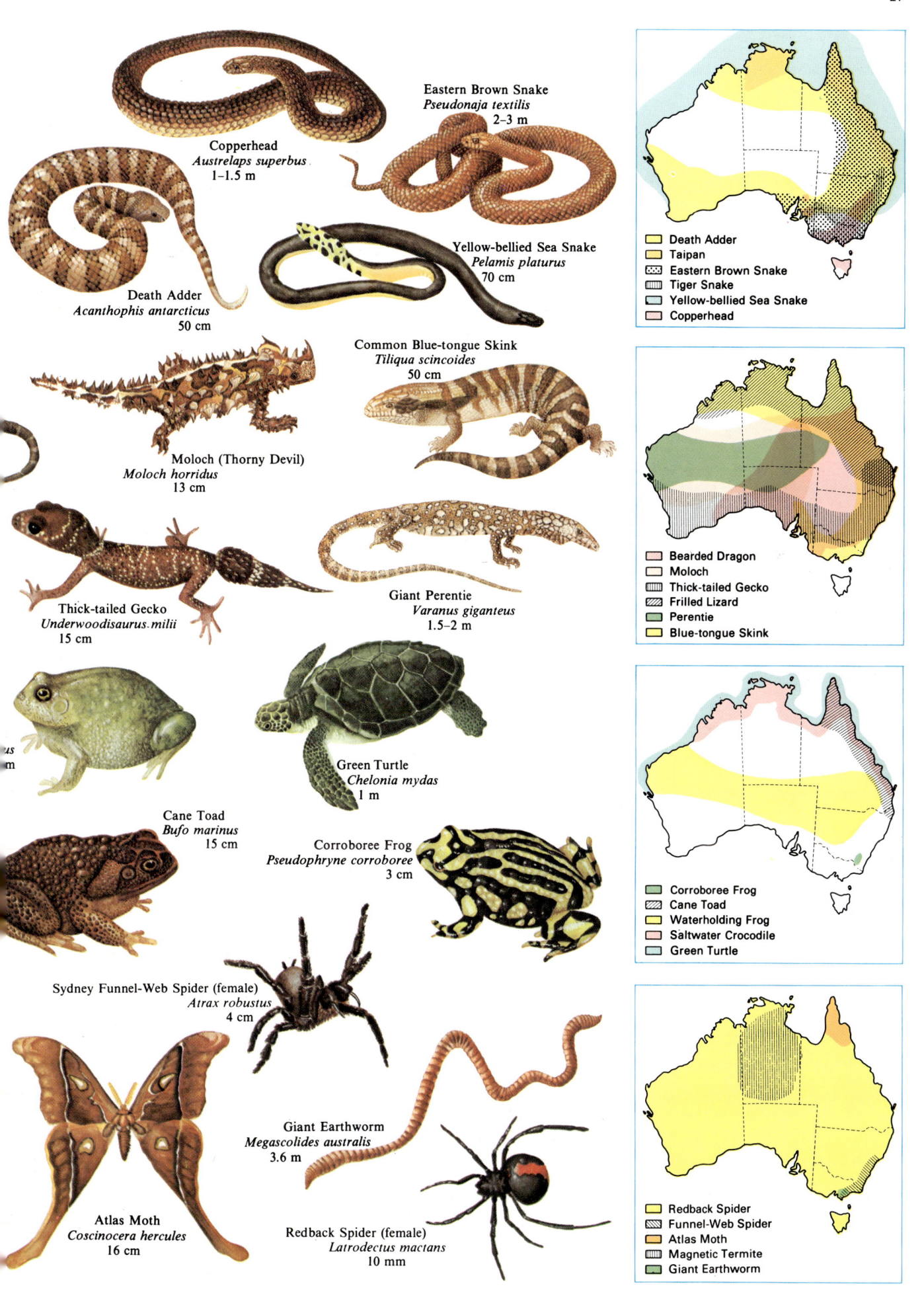

Eastern Brown Snake
Pseudonaja textilis
2–3 m

Death Adder
Acanthophis antarcticus
50 cm

Yellow-bellied Sea Snake
Pelamis platurus
70 cm

Common Blue-tongue Skink
Tiliqua scincoides
50 cm

Moloch (Thorny Devil)
Moloch horridus
13 cm

Thick-tailed Gecko
Underwoodisaurus milii
15 cm

Giant Perentie
Varanus giganteus
1.5–2 m

Green Turtle
Chelonia mydas
1 m

Cane Toad
Bufo marinus
15 cm

Corroboree Frog
Pseudophryne corroboree
3 cm

Sydney Funnel-Web Spider (female)
Atrax robustus
4 cm

Atlas Moth
Coscinocera hercules
16 cm

Giant Earthworm
Megascolides australis
3.6 m

Redback Spider (female)
Latrodectus mactans
10 mm

☐ Death Adder
☐ Taipan
☐ Eastern Brown Snake
☐ Tiger Snake
☐ Yellow-bellied Sea Snake
☐ Copperhead

☐ Bearded Dragon
☐ Moloch
☐ Thick-tailed Gecko
☐ Frilled Lizard
☐ Perentie
☐ Blue-tongue Skink

☐ Corroboree Frog
☐ Cane Toad
☐ Waterholding Frog
☐ Saltwater Crocodile
☐ Green Turtle

☐ Redback Spider
☐ Funnel-Web Spider
☐ Atlas Moth
☐ Magnetic Termite
☐ Giant Earthworm

Australia's Water Resources

Australia's water resources are puny by most world standards. 'Making the most of our water' has long been a national catchcry — especially from rural politicians.

One result has been that Australia currently has 49 dams and reservoirs with capacities of at least 100 million cubic metres. Completed in 1974, Tasmania's Lake Gordon is currently the largest storage with a gross capacity of 11 671 million cubic metres. Next are Lake Argyle (5720 million cubic metres), storage for the $100 million-plus Ord River project in Western Australia, and Lake Eucumbene (4807 million cubic metres), heart of the $800 million Snowy Mountains Hydro-Electric Scheme in New South Wales. Victoria's recently completed Dartmouth Dam (4000 million cubic metres) will be used for both hydro-electric and irrigation purposes.

But there are practical and economic limits to the building of such huge storages. In highly-populated south-eastern Australia for example, development of surface water in some areas has already reached around 60 per cent of the total resources, close to the feasible limit.

In addition, the days of unquestioned grandiose water storage proposals are probably over. The familiar response to the problem — 'bigger and better dams' — and other long-standing assumptions about water conservation are under increasing public scrutiny. 'Damning dams' has become respectable, whether on economic or environmental grounds. Although a national outcry failed to 'Save Lake Pedder' from submersion in the name of Tasmanian hydro-electric power, other storage proposals are being defeated or modified by community pressure.

Water Sources

Australia's location in the 'dry latitudes', together with the absence of significant mountains, is largely responsible for the continent having easily the lowest average annual rainfall of the inhabited continents.

Australia's average rainfall is only 470 mm compared with the average 720 mm falling on the world's land surfaces, while the annual flow of all Australian rivers (345 374 million cubic metres, around 10 per cent of rainfall) represents a depth of water over the continent of only 60 mm, about one-fifth the average for the other continents. The annual discharge of Australia's largest river, the Murray, is reached in nine days by the Mississippi and only one and a half days by the Amazon.

A third of Australia has no rivers. River flows vary greatly, especially in the north where rivers carrying 30 000 cubic metres a second in flood may disappear entirely in the dry season.

Water drawn from underground provides about 20 per cent of the national water supply and is more important than surface water over 60 per cent of the country. These artesian waters, often too mineralised for irrigation or human consumption, are usually suitable for stock.

Eildon Reservoir, east-central Victoria. The Goulburn River has been regulated by Lake Eildon to provide irrigation for large areas to the north-east.

Largest of the twelve major water-bearing basins is the Great Artesian Basin lying under almost a quarter of Australia. Some 6000 bores tap it: for almost a century it has yielded about 600 million cubic metres of low-salinity groundwater annually.

Some good quality groundwater is available, primarily near the higher rainfall areas of the east, but intense use in some regions has already made it necessary to recharge depleted aquifers artificially, notably in the Burdekin Delta where waters are drawn on for sugar cane irrigation.

Water Uses

The long battle to 'droughtproof' Australian towns and cities is not yet finally won, although the days of restrictions on domestic water supply to the major cities are disappearing.

Irrigation is an important element of the rural scene, with some 1 500 000 hectares under irrigation, about two-thirds of them along the Murray and its tributaries.

Hydro-electricity provides about one-fifth of national annual electricity consumption, which exceeds 90 million kWh. Tasmania contributes about half the hydro-electricity, thanks to the abundant and reliable rainfall which makes it the only State able to operate hydro-electric plants continuously. The Snowy Mountains Hydro-Electricity Scheme, a quarter century in the making, is the nation's greatest engineering feat. Completed in 1974 at a cost of $800 million, it has seven power stations, a pumping station, 16 large and many smaller dams, over 145 km of tunnels and 80 km of aqueducts. Total generating capacity is about 4000 MW and it also provides about 2344 million cubic metres of additional water annually for irrigation by diverting water inland from coastal watersheds to the Murray and Murrumbidgee rivers.

Artesian supplies are being increasingly exploited for town water needs and sometimes irrigation, but the most widespread use is for stock watering. Much of the nation's pastoral industry is dependent on artesian bores.

Problems

Water quality and quantity are affected by many things beyond rainfall. Within only seven years of European settlement in Australia the authorities had to issue proclamations forbidding pollution of the Tank Stream — Sydney's major water supply. Pollution continues to affect some surface waters and this often extends to groundwater supplies. Sewage, industrial and agricultural effluents and mining wastes are frequent pollutants.

Artesian waters are not inexhaustible. Reductions of flow in some basins have caused concern since the turn of the century and there are now strict controls and licensing restrictions to lessen wastage of bore water.

Equally disturbing is the incidence of salinity in ground water and surface supplies that has resulted from expanding agricultural and irrigation schemes. In south-western Australia around 4 million hectares of land have been made sterile and difficult to till because removal of the natural vegetation caused the water table to rise, and high-salinity groundwater has affected both soil and surface water. Some urban water storages have been threatened.

A similar danger faces the Murray Valley basin in south-east Australia. Heavy flood irrigation and vegetation removal have combined to harm soil and surface water. In Victoria alone an estimated 30 000 hectares of valuable land have been laid waste. The increasing salinity of the Murray causes great concern: salt content in its upper reaches is less than 30 milligrams per litre total dissolved solids, yet during the 1967-68 drought the salt content downstream in South Australia exceeded 600 milligrams per litre. Current Victorian proposals to start correcting the salinity may cost an initial $40 million. These include pumping saline water to drying pans, and increasing the number of trees (especially the river red gum, *Eucalyptus camaldulensis*) fivefold.

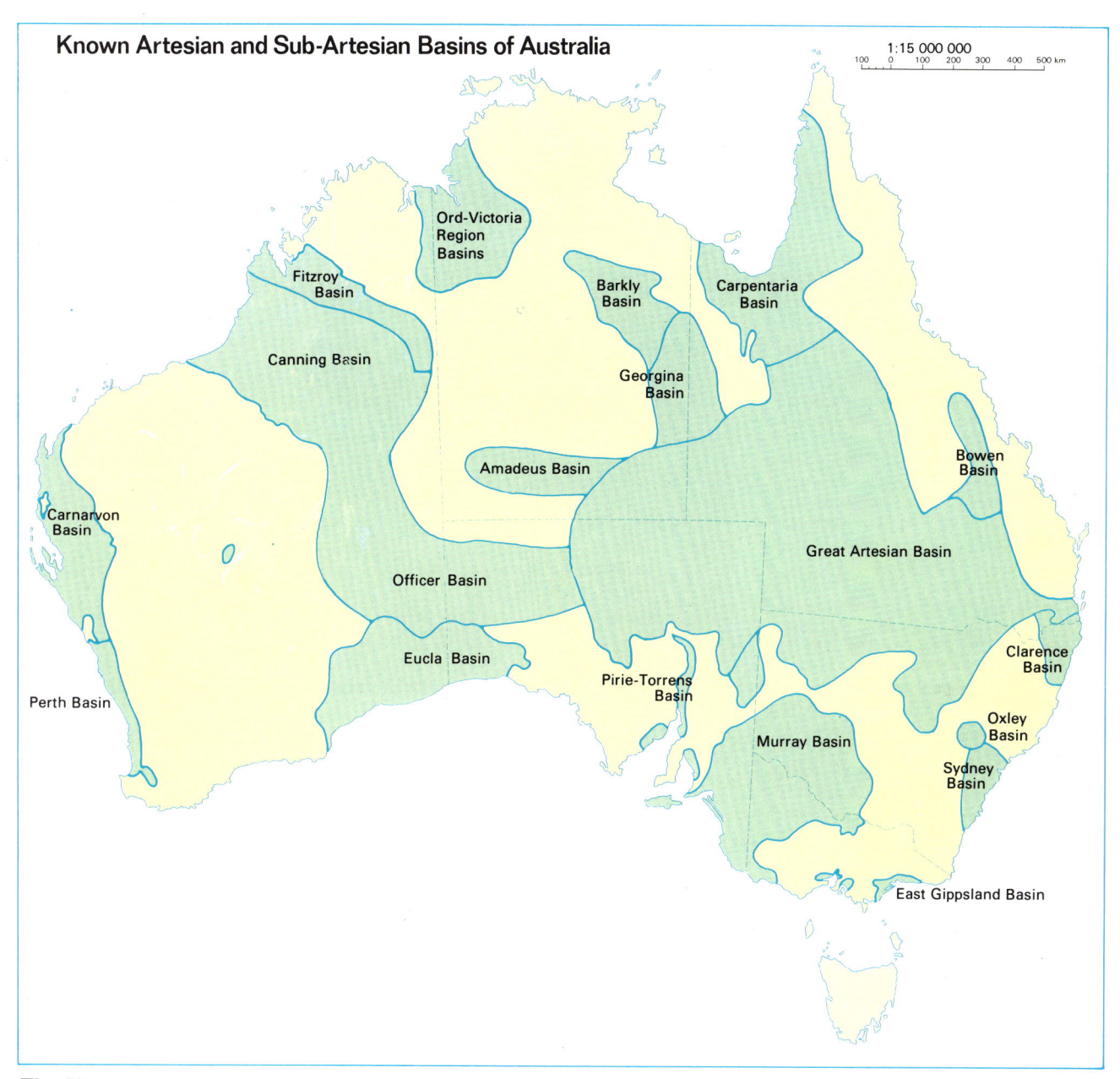

Known Artesian and Sub-Artesian Basins of Australia

1:15 000 000

Basins shown on map:
- Fitzroy Basin
- Ord-Victoria Region Basins
- Barkly Basin
- Carpentaria Basin
- Canning Basin
- Georgina Basin
- Bowen Basin
- Carnarvon Basin
- Amadeus Basin
- Great Artesian Basin
- Officer Basin
- Clarence Basin
- Eucla Basin
- Oxley Basin
- Perth Basin
- Pirie-Torrens Basin
- Murray Basin
- Sydney Basin
- East Gippsland Basin

The Future

The national agency charged with investigating the quantity and quality of water resources through the co-operation of State and Federal authorities is the Australian Water Resources Council. The problems are complex and the solutions certain to be costly: some of the most useful answers appear to lie in the fields of more efficient management and public awareness of water conservation, rather than in expensive additional storages, the contentious possible benefits of cloud-seeding or such Space Age techniques as nuclear desalination of seawater.

A vertical infra-red photograph of irrigated vineyards near Berri, South Australia. The vegetation (leaves) can be identified by the shades of red. The areas that are patchy indicate the effects of inadequate irrigation techniques resulting in salt accumulations on the surface. Salination is a problem where evaporation is high and the water is spread by shallow gravity flows through the fields.

Irrigating a Dry Continent

Irrigation has remained something of a national article of faith since the Canadian-born Chaffey brothers drew on their Californian experiences to pioneer irrigation in Australia in 1866.

Irrigation has brought immense benefits to Australia. Yet the Chaffeys' bold venture on a run-down cattle station on the Victorian side of the Murray River at Mildura ended in their bankruptcy in 1895. Mildura endured — and now thrives as the centre of national dried-fruit production — but after almost a century, irrigation is not without its troubles.

Problems of orderly marketing of the produce grown on irrigated land recur, and a traditional market shrank with Britain's entry into the Common Market. Salinity in various forms endangers some areas, and the costs of combating it will be formidable.

On the ambitious Ord River project in remote north-west Western Australia, the first large-scale attempt at tropical irrigation, the problems have so far outweighed the profits. Cotton growing has been abandoned, while the search continues for crops with sufficient return to overcome high transport costs and the hazards of insect and bird pests.

Australia now has around 1 475 000 hectares under irrigation, comprising (rounded figures) New South Wales 602 000 hectares; Victoria 557 000; Queensland 186 000; South Australia 78 000; Western Australia 28 000; Tasmania 22 000; Northern Territory 900 and Australian Capital Territory 200. Water is supplied for orchards, vineyards, pastures, vegetables, fodder and grain crops, and for domestic and stock purposes. In Victoria alone, the value of irrigation production exceeds $250 million annually.

Irrigation Methods

Flood irrigation is by far the most dominant form of irrigation in Australia. Other techniques are spray, furrow and trickle (drip) irrigation.

Flood irrigation is used to inundate bays of farmland, especially for pastures and rice (which has been grown since 1924 in the Murrumbidgee Irrigation Area of New South Wales). Wheat and millet are among other crops flood-irrigated.

Furrow irrigation — a form of flood irrigation — is employed for vegetables and row crops, particularly tomatoes and cotton. Spray irrigation is usually used when water is pumped direct from rivers: it *must* be used over uneven ground or on sandy soils. Most citrus growers use spray irrigation and it is also commonly employed for vegetables and pastures. One sidelight of the widespread salinity problem is that some citrus growers have been forced to instal under-tree sprinklers to prevent defoliation caused by overhead sprinkling of saline water.

Murray River Valley Irrigation

About two-thirds of Australia's irrigated land is in south-east Australia, along the Murray River and its tributaries. The Murray forms the largest part of the New South Wales-Victorian border before it passes into South Australia.

Large storages on the upper reaches of the Murray, Murrumbidgee, Lachlan and Goulburn Rivers store more than nine km^3 of water for irrigation areas: an additional annual average 2.3 km^3 is diverted inland to the Murray and Murrumbidgee by the Snowy Mountains Scheme, enough to irrigate an extra 2600 km^2 and increase productivity by around $60 million.

Generally in the upper reaches of the rivers water is tapped by weirs and gravity canals: lower down it is usually pumped out.

The irrigation season usually runs from September to April. Canneries at Shepparton in Victoria and Leeton in New South Wales process much of the fruit and vegetables. Canned fruit remains a significant export item. In South Australia, Berri and Waikerie are noted for citrus production. The Murray Valley area yields large amounts of rice, fruit, vegetables, fodder crops and wheat, wine, fat lambs, wool and dairy products from irrigated pastures.

The Ord: Expensive Experiment?

The Ord River project, conceived when 'develop the North' was a virtually unquestioned slogan, has yet to prove its economic worth. The first major irrigation scheme opened for significant development with the completion in 1971 of the Lake Argyle storage, then the nation's largest storage with a gross capacity of 5.7 km^3. Federal and State spending on capital works exceeded $50 million and the project has the potential to irrigate 70 000 hectares of alluvial land east of the Kimberley.

Until 1975 commercial agriculture production on the Ord had been almost exclusively cotton, which required large amounts of costly nitrogenous fertilisers, and pesticides to combat serious insect plagues. These factors, combined with steep transport costs, forced abandonment of cotton growing following the 1974 crop.

Currently there are 23 Ord farms with commercial production on only an estimated 2900 hectares, comprising grain sorghum (2420 hectares), rice (280), wheat (80) and peanuts (120). Further expansion will depend on scientists identifying crops with sufficient return to cover high freight charges, and not requiring excessive amounts of fertiliser or pesticide.

Research is now oriented towards assessing new varieties of sorghum and rice, sugar cane, grain legumes such as chick peas and mung beans, and fibrous plants like kenaf used for making paper pulp, with by-products suitable for stock feed. A pilot sugar farm has produced, to date, high yields and there is currently a proposal before the state government for the establishment of a sugar industry.

Other Irrigation Areas

In northern New South Wales the Keepit dam in the Namoi Valley provides irrigation for the Wee Waa-Narrabri district, Australia's most important cotton region, producing more than 100 000 bales annually.

About a third of Queensland's irrigated land grows sugar cane. Unlike other States, most water is pumped privately from rivers or underground sources.

Western Australia has more than 12 000 hectares of irrigated land in the coastal plain south of Perth, fed from dams in the Darling Range. At Carnarvon almost 150 plantations draw water from the Gascoyne River.

Tasmania's abundant and reliable rainfall meant that the island had few irrigated areas until recent years. Spray irrigation has come into increasing use, and private pumping from streams accounts for most needs.

Above: Lake Argyle, part of the controversial Ord River Scheme, is the largest man-made lake in Australia.

Opposite: Irrigated strip pasture and the River Murray, near Mannum, South Australia.

The River Murray System

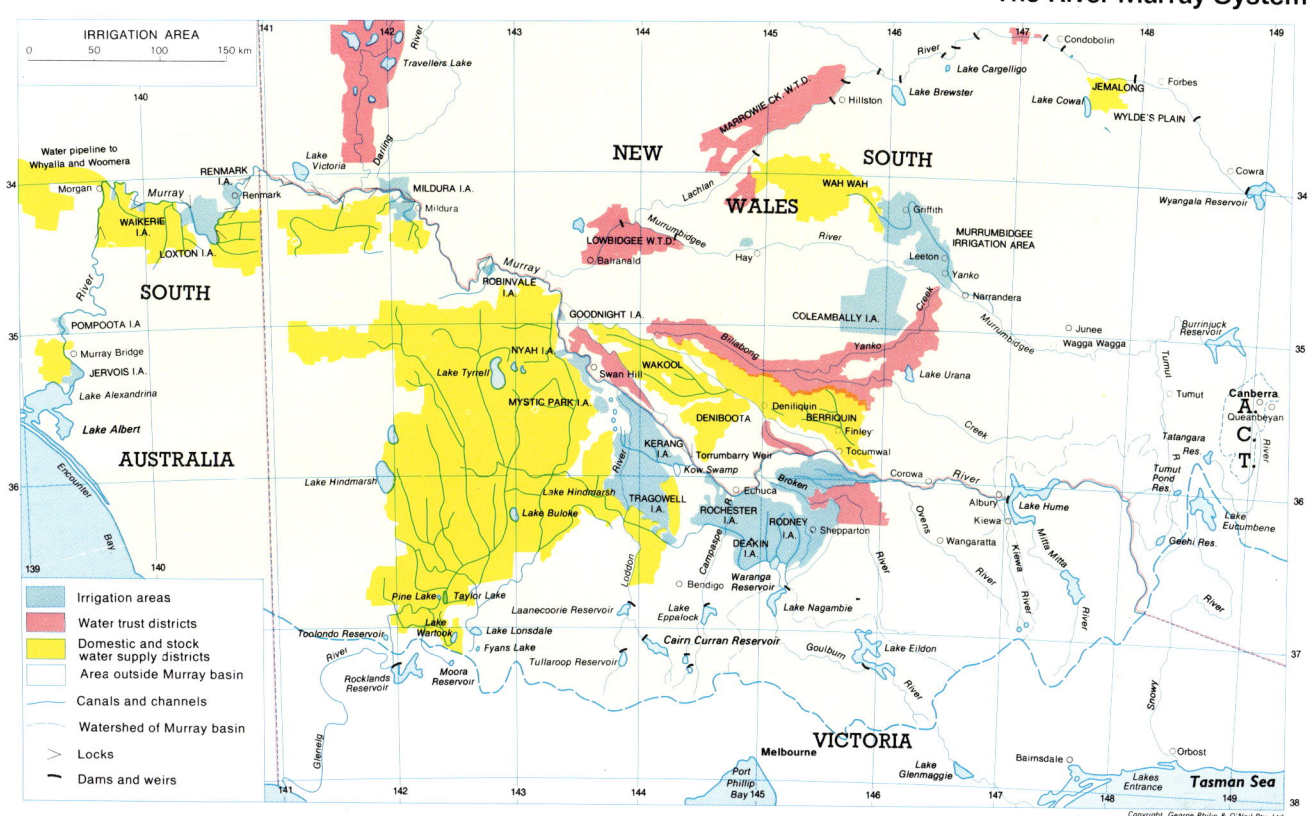

Climate and Weather Patterns

Australia's climate encourages suntans and grim jokes, not widespread human settlement. One-third of this driest of inhabited continents is desert, while another third is suitable only for grazing relatively small numbers of animals over huge areas.

To visitors from kinder climates, the seasons turn slowly, while contrast and caprice characterise the weather. The images of climate are often those of disaster: drought, floods, cyclones and, always, heat. Cities of millions sometimes have found their water supplies threatened. For three-quarters of Australia, evaporation loss exceeds rainfall in all months.

Rainfall Patterns

Fifty per cent of Australia has an annual median rainfall below 300 mm. Eighty per cent receives less than 600 mm.

Almost all Australians live along the relatively well-watered coastal fringes, especially the eastern 'fertile crescent' where the continent's only significant mountain range encourages regular rainfall. The general aridity means that Australia supports 14 500 000 people over a land mass approximating that of the USA with its population exceeding 220 000 000.

The dominant cause of this aridity is the continent's position on planet Earth, astride latitude 30°S. All the world's hot deserts lie on the 30s, the 'dry latitudes' where subtropical high pressure systems (anticyclones) prevail. Australia is also unfortunate in being the flattest continent — average elevation under 300 metres — with only the modest Eastern Highlands able to trap rain from the weather systems crossing their path. Although heat discomfort is significant over most of Australia, the continent's low relief and the moderating effects of surrounding oceans mean that low temperatures are not as extreme as in other continents.

During the winter (May-October) period, high pressure systems dominate the central and northern parts of Australia. Northern Australia is affected by mild, dry south-east trade winds and southern Australia by cool, moist westerlies associated with the Sub-Polar low pressure belt. Outbreaks of cold weather typically occur in southern Australia when intense depressions over the Southern Ocean force cold air northwards.

The summer period (November-April) sees the anticyclones taking a more southerly path from west to east, resulting in general easterly winds over the continent. Heat waves occur when an anticyclone's eastward movement is blocked and winds subsequently back northerly. Northern Australia has a monsoon season (the 'Wet') between November and April, resulting from an indraught of moist air.

Tropical cyclones (hurricanes) are random summer hazards between November and April. On average about three Coral Sea cyclones affect the Queensland coast each year while around two affect north-western Australia.

Erratic Rainfall

Australia's significant rainfall is concentrated on its east, south and north fringes with the Eastern Highlands being responsible for the heaviest regular falls. North Queensland's east coast averages around 4400 mm annually. Another very wet region is western Tasmania, with more than 2500 mm a year.

The nation's driest area comprises some 180 000 km² around Lake Eyre in South Australia, with annual rainfall averaging 130 mm. This is the forbidding zone of salt 'lakes' that may fill once in a lifetime with cyclonic rains that have drained across half a continent.

If scarcity of rainfall is the greatest check on agricultural and pastoral expansion, the general unreliability of rainfall is almost as inhibiting. Reasonably reliable rainfall is encountered only in restricted areas of southern Australia — southern Victoria, Tasmania and south-west Western Australia. Generations of Australians have complained of too many droughts broken by too many floods. Between 1864 and 1973 eight major droughts affected the greater part of Australia and at least seven other lesser droughts afflicted wide areas.

The rainfall variability over four-fifths of Australia is above the world average for comparable rainfall totals. An extreme example of erratic rainfall caused by Australia's variable weather is Onslow in Western Australia, where rain from tropical cyclones contributes randomly to wild fluctuations. Onslow's recorded annual rainfall totals range between 15 mm in 1912 and 1085 mm in 1961, while between 1921-24 its totals were successively 566, 69, 682 and 55 mm.

Even in heavy rainfall areas there may be great variability. Queensland's Tully, which has Australia's highest median rainfall (4400 mm), has had annual rainfalls as high as 7899 in 1950 and as low as 2489 mm in 1961.

Over most of Australia there are less than 50 rain-days a year when rainfall reaches 0.25 mm or more. Central Australia has less than 25 rain-days annually, while rain-day frequencies of 150 and above are known only in Tasmania, southern Victoria, areas along Queensland's north coast and in the extreme south-west of Western Australia.

Temperature

Australia lies between latitudes 10–40°S with more than 50 per cent of Queensland, 40 per cent of Western Australia and 80 per cent of the Northern Territory in the tropics. The remaining 60 per cent of Australia is in the temperate zone.

Hot weather prevails generally. Average annual temperatures vary from around 27°C in the far north to 13°C in the far south. January (summer) and July (winter) average temperatures range from 29°C and 24°C in the north to 18°C and 10°C in the south. Average daily hours of sunshine in the major cities are Sydney 6.7, Melbourne 5.7, Brisbane 7.5, Adelaide 6.9, Perth 7.9, Hobart 5.9, Darwin 8.5 and Canberra 7.2.

Marble Bar in the north-west of Western Australia earned an unenviable place in folklore as the nation's hottest town, especially after its record unbroken spell of 160 days of at least 38.4°C (100°F) between 31 October 1923 and 7 April 1924. The highest record temperature was 53.1°C at Cloncurry in Queensland on 16 January 1889.

Australia's lowest temperatures have been recorded in the Snowy Mountains area of the Australian Alps, one of few regions to have snow on the ground in winter. Charlotte Pass in New South Wales (elevation 1750 metres) has twice recorded –22.2°C. Snow covers much of the Australian Alps above 1500 metres between late autumn and early spring, sometimes falling widely down to 1000 metres, but rarely below that.

Evaporation is very significant in water conservation and, over approximately 75 per cent of Australia, evaporation from water surfaces exceeds rainfall in all months. In central and north-west Australia the evaporation rate is ten times the rainfall.

The graphs below show the monthly average rainfall and max. and min. temperatures for 10 cities.

Cyclone Tracy which devastated Darwin on Xmas Day 1974, was the most destructive cyclone ever recorded on the Australian mainland.

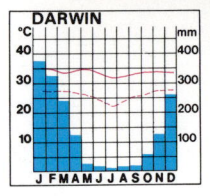

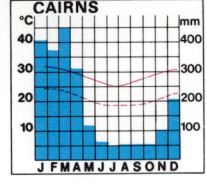

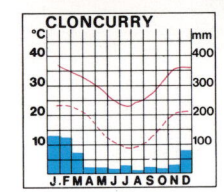

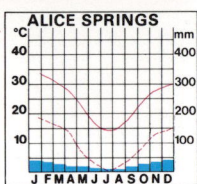

1:60 000 000

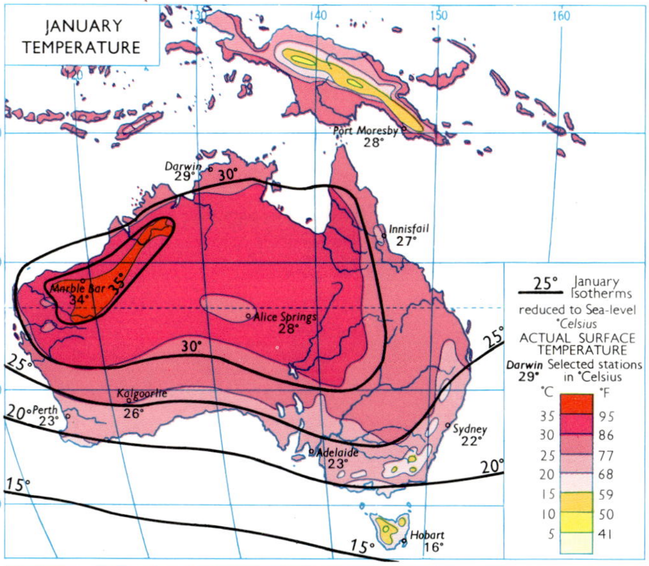

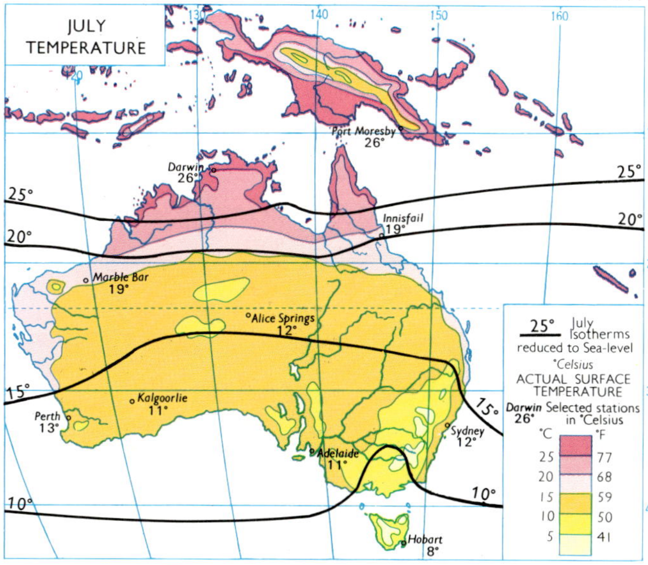

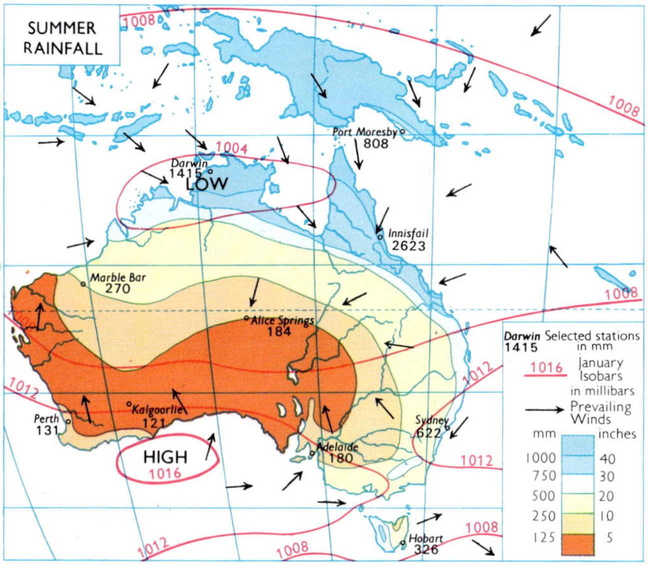

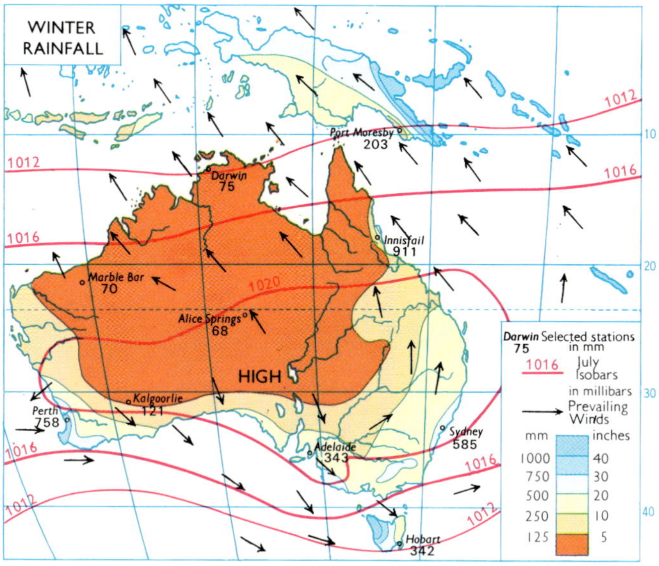

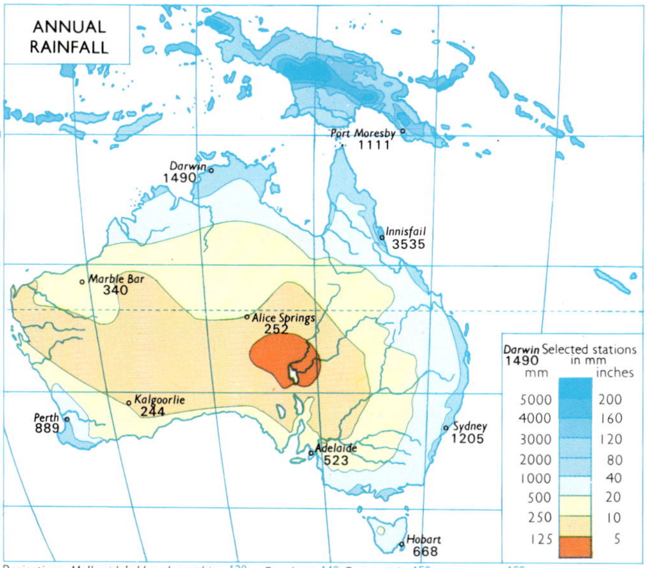

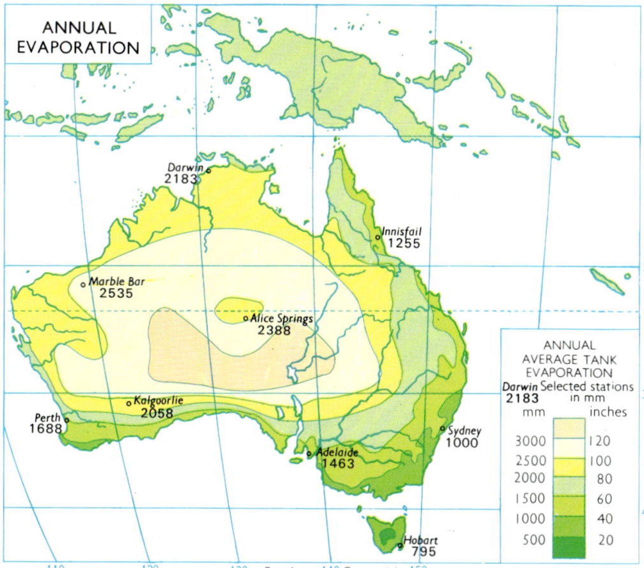

Projection: *Mollweide's Homolographic* 130 East from 140 Greenwich 150 160 110 120 130 East from 140 Greenwich 150

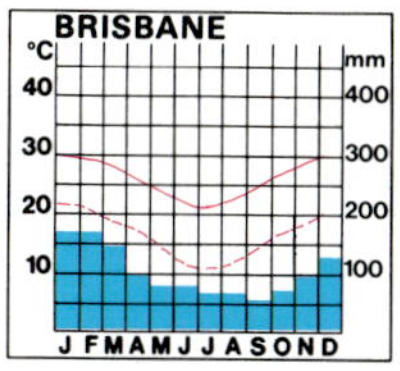

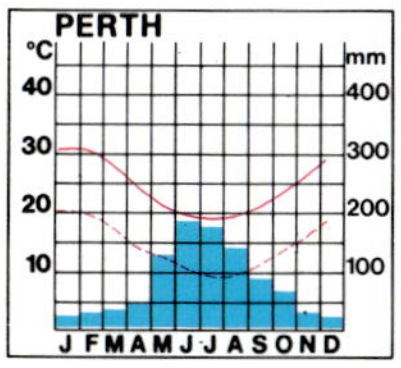

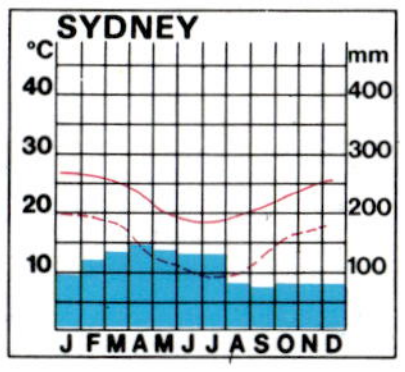

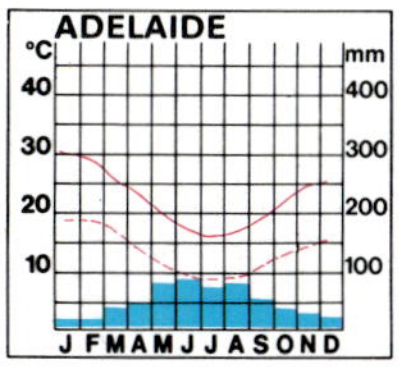

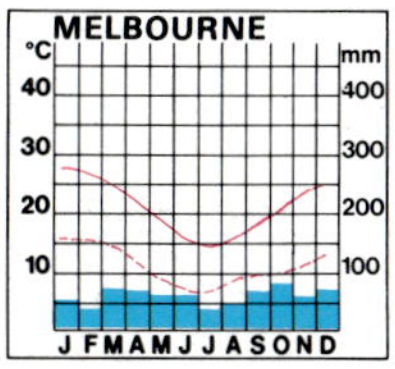

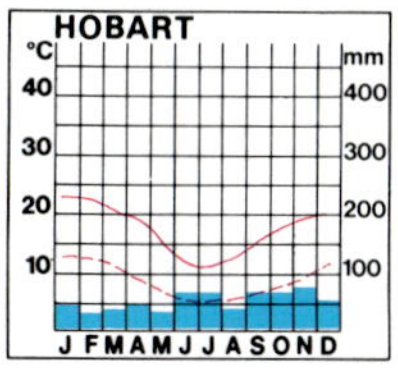

Far left: Multi-storey office blocks tower over Sydney's bustling city centre

Left: The Three Sisters, one of the many spectacular sights in the Blue Mountains

Above: Gentle pastoral scenery in northern New South Wales. Mount Warning is in the background.

Right: The Carillon and Captain Cook Memorial water-jet on Lake Burley Griffin, Canberra, ACT.

New South Wales
FOUNDING STATE

In 1770, Captain Cook took possession for the British of all Australian territories east of the 135th meridian of east longitude and named them New South Wales. Today, the founding state has shrunk somewhat and occupies just 10 per cent of the continent. It is a state of contrasts, containing Australia's largest city, extremes of country ranging from sub-tropical to alpine and covering an area of 801 428 square kilometres.

Governor Phillip established Sydney as a penal colony in 1788 and worked hard to develop the new town. After his departure in 1792, however, much of this work went to rack and ruin under the dominance of the infamous 'Rum Corps' and the city was left in chaos. Harassed motorists can blame the Rum Corps for the frustrations of driving in Sydney's inner centre. In 1810, however, the city was saved by the redoubtable Governor Macquarie.

In 1813, Blaxland, Lawson and Wentworth discovered the lands to the west of the Blue Mountains. Further exploration quickly followed and settlement fanned out from Sydney. Sydney itself thrived and its citizens agitated against the stigma of the penal presence with the result that transportation ended in 1840. The gold rushes of the 1850s swelled the population and led to much development throughout the state. With the granting of responsible government in 1856, the founding state was well on its way.

Today New South Wales is the most populated state and its central region, around Sydney, Newcastle and Wollongong-Port Kembla, has been described as 'the heart of industrial Australia'. New South Wales produces two-thirds of the nation's black coal from huge deposits under the Hunter Valley, the Blue Mountains and the Illawarra Region. Its other main source of mineral wealth is the zinc-lead-silver mines of Broken Hill. Primary production is diversified and thriving — New South Wales is the nation's main wheat producer and has more than one-third of the nation's sheep population.

The state divides itself into four natural regions — the sparsely populated western plains, which take up two-thirds of the state; the high tablelands and peaks of the Great Dividing Range; the pastoral and farming country of the Range's western slopes; and the fertile coastal region.

The climate varies with the landscape: sub-tropical along the north coast; temperate all year round on the south coast; the north-west has fearsome dry summers; and the high country has brisk winters with extremes of cold in the highest alpine areas. Sydney has a midsummer average of 25.7°C, a midwinter average of 15.8°C and boasts sunshine 342 days a year.

Lively and sophisticated, Sydney offers the shopping, restaurants and nightlife you would expect from a great cosmopolitan city, yet within a 200 kilometre radius, you can enjoy much of New South Wales' best country. Superb beaches, the intricate bays and inlets of Pittwater, the Hawkesbury and Tuggerah Lakes and the breathtaking Illawarra coastline. Even the Blue Mountains and the Jenolan Caves can be reached in a day trip. Most of the state's highways lead out from the capital. The Pacific runs north to Port Macquarie and the industrial city of Newcastle. Inland, you can sample the products of the rich Hunter Valley vineyards. Further north, the country becomes hilly and sub-tropical, with irresistible golden beaches, and with the New England tablelands inland — high mountain and grazing country, at its best in autumn.

The state's extreme north and west is still frontier territory; with limited tourist facilities. If you enjoy getting off the beaten track, and if you and your car are well prepared, the region can be very rewarding. Highlights include the spectacular Nandewar and Warrumbungle Ranges, Lightning Ridge and the green oasis of Broken Hill, the state's storehouse of mineral wealth.

You'll be able to see many relics of the early gold and agricultural history of the rich central tableland and plains region in and around towns such as Bathurst, Dubbo, Wellington, Griffith and Wagga. Towards the Victorian border, where the Murray River forms a natural boundary, irrigation greens the countryside and supports many vineyards and citrus groves. The Murray River towns retain much of the history of the river boat era when the Murray was a major transport route.

The Princes Highway leads south from Sydney down the Illawarra Coast, famous for its panoramic views, excellent beaches and numerous national parks. Good fishing of all kinds can be enjoyed and there's splendid bushwalking and climbing in the nearby foothills of the southern highlands.

The Snowy Mountains area includes the natural grandeur of the Kosciusko National Park and the man-assisted grandeur of the Snowy Mountains hydro-electric scheme.

In 1908, an area of 900 square miles (2331 square kilometres) was set aside from New South Wales to become the Australian Capital Territory and Canberra became the official seat of the Australian Government on 9 May, 1927.

Inhabitants of the ACT are fortunate in being within easy reach of both the mountains and the coast. Canberra is a unique place to visit, with unspoiled countryside minutes away, excellent roads, and a beautifully laid out city centre.

Sydney
AUSTRALIA'S FIRST CITY

Sydney, with its population of over 3½ million, is Australia's largest city, and was the first site of settlement on the Australian continent.

Captain Cook noted the entrance to Sydney Harbour as he navigated the east coast of Australia in 1770. He called it Port Jackson in honour of the then Secretary of the British Admiralty, Sir George Jackson. The British Government subsequently decided to set up a penal colony in 'New Holland', as the continent was known, both as an outlet for Britain's convict population and as a permanent British presence in the South Pacific. Command of the expedition to start the colony was entrusted to Captain Arthur Phillip.

Having looked at Botany Bay and decided it was unsuitable, Phillip moved north to Port Jackson. The narrow bay in which he anchored he dubbed Sydney Cove, and on its shores on 26 January 1788, he raised the flag and proclaimed the settlement that was to become Sydney.

Thus, for many years the gateway to Australia was Phillip's Sydney Cove, some 11 km from the towering bluffs that flank the harbour mouth — North Head and South Head. Both headlands, particularly South Head, command a breathtaking view back along the harbour to the city — like zoom lens automatically drawing the focus to the metropolitan skyline, the **Opera House** and **Harbour Bridge**.

The Bridge and the Opera House may be Sydney's landmarks, but the Harbour is its pride and joy. Its innumerable arms extend in all directions, the product of a drowned valley system that finds bottom in the depths of the Pacific.

Sydney's city 'proper' is bounded by the harbour north and west and cut off to the east by the green parklands of the **Botanic Gardens** and **The Domain**.

Within those boundaries Sydney is an exciting and rewarding city to walk around — elegant, raucous, handsome, solemn, Georgian, Edwardian, Victorian and dazzlingly contemporary.

Where the First Fleet dropped anchor, the shoreline has become a neat U-shaped waterway with major wharves on either arm and the harbour ferry terminals at its base.

Circular Quay was built in the 19th century to handle overseas shipping and, in the final great era of sail, the days of the superb clipper ships, Sydney Cove was a forest of majestic masts, with clippers tied up — several abreast.

Across the water from the Quay, the Harbour Bridge disgorges its congested traffic into Sydney's 'mini-twin', **North Sydney**, a high-density, high-rise satellite that took shape in the 1960s when space and traffic were becoming intolerably congested in the city.

Under the shadow of the bridge to the west is **Pier One**. Originally the disembarkation point for new immigrants, the Pier has been re-modelled to preserve its original atmosphere. It has many shops, cafes (especially good for seafood) and a tavern decorated in old Sydney style.

Standing sentinel at the eastern end of **Sydney Cove**, almost flowing out of the water, as its designer Joern Utzon intended it to be, like sails scudding up from the waves, is the Sydney Opera House. Excellent tours of the Opera House are available seven days a week; the length of the tour depends on how many rehearsals are taking place.

By day, conventional, commercial Sydney reasserts itself. The western shore of the Quay is dominated by the **Sydney Cove Passenger Terminal**, Sydney's largest passenger berth with deep anchorage enough for ships of 40 000 tonnes.

Its sandstone neighbour is the **NSW Maritime Services Board**. Commercial blocks face them on the opposite side and linking the two is the span of the **Cahill Expressway** enabling traffic to and from the Harbour Bridge to bypass the city. Below the overhead roadway is the elevated section of Sydney's **underground railway**, which breaks into daylight at Circular Quay railway station and, below that again, **Circular Quay Plaza**, one of the city's major bus terminals.

In line with Sydney's boundaries the city's bus services terminate at three main points: Circular Quay in the north, **Wynyard Square** in the west, and, in the south, **Central Railway Station**, the outlet for all country and interstate train services. The red Sydney Explorer tourist bus runs every 20 minutes around the city.

'Down-town' has that slightly seedy, railway-air about it, while the Quay remains typically 'waterfront'. One old-style Sydney pub on one side of the Circular Quay Plaza is worth a visit, particularly since it is an early-opener — 'The Ship Inn'. It opens at 6.30 am, officially to cater for nightshift-workers, although anyone may patronise it.

Aloof from these, and from their high-rise neighbours, in the centre of the Plaza, the old **Customs House** continues to preside over the scene, a monument in sandstone to 19th century Sydney. Its time-honoured clock is surrounded by tridents and dolphins. The coat of arms above the entrance is one of the best stone carvings in Australia.

Immediately behind Circular Quay Plaza, a series of maritime-flavoured laneways and narrow streets culminates in **Macquarie Place** and its sheltering canopies of giant Moreton Bay fig trees. An anchor and a cannon from Phillip's flagship *HMS Sirius* are preserved in the park, which they share with gas lamps, an 1857 drinking fountain, an ornate Victorian 'gents' (classified by the National Trust) and a weathered obelisk, from which distances to all points in the colony used to be measured.

In the surrounding laneways look for Len Evans restaurant (gourmet cuisine) in Bulletin Place; The Basement, a

RIGHT: *A view of the Sydney skyline looking across Farm Cove.*

fashionable jazz restaurant, in Reiby Place; and in nearby Young Street one of the world's smallest churches, the tiny **St Vincent de Paul** chapel at 5 Young Street, run by the Marist Fathers.

Government House is an imposing neo-Gothic sandstone mansion of the 1840s, not open to the public, but easily admired from the adjacent Botanic Gardens. Between the entrances to both, the fortress-like lines of the NSW Conservatorium of Music successfully conceal the building's origin as stables, designed in 1816 by the renowned convict architect, Francis Greenway, and completed in 1821 to go with an earlier Government House on the site.

The Botanic Gardens, more than 24 hectares of formal landscaping, were originally dedicated in 1816. Today they are a perennial landscape of colour as more than 4000 native and exotic plants bloom throughout the year. In one small corner there's a stone wall, nearly 200 years old, marking the original plot of the colony's first vegetable garden, planted at the direction of Governor Phillip.

The other side of the roadway, the western side of Macquarie Street, is typical of Sydney high-rise, with one of the most striking buildings, the **State Government Office** block, standing diagonally opposite the **Library of New South Wales**.

In the Library's **Mitchell** and **Dixson** wings is one of the world's great repositories of national archives and memorabilia, a priceless collection of Australiana and historical records — much of it frequently on view.

Adjacent to the Library are two of Sydney's oldest buildings — the **New South Wales Parliament** and the old **Colonial Mint Building** (now a museum) — both of them the wings of the first colonial hospital. Between them now — in all its dour Victorian splendour — is the present **Sydney Hospital**, a city institution which opened in 1879.

The original colonial hospital, of which Parliament House and the former Mint were part, was known as the Rum Hospital. When coins were short in the colony, rum was the currency and the builders were paid in casks of the spirit. Behind the buildings, the Domain — a Sunday afternoon forum for 'soap-box' orators — separates the rear of Macquarie Street from the **Art Gallery of New South Wales**.

Macquarie Street finally leads into **Queens Square**, arguably one of Sydney's most elegant precincts. The square is encircled by **Hyde Park**, the towering **Law Courts** building and Francis Greenway's pre-1820 masterpieces — **St James's Church** and **Hyde Park Barracks** (now a museum). Flowing harmoniously on from the old barracks are two great neo-Gothic triumphs of the 19th century — the **Registrar-General's** building and **St Mary's Roman Catholic Cathedral.**

Hyde Park is now divided into two sections by the broad avenue of **Park Street**

RIGHT: *A view of famous Hyde Park showing St Mary's Cathedral.*

HOTELS
Hotel International,
117 Macquarie St, Sydney.
(02) 230 0200
Sydney Hilton,
259 Pitt St, Sydney.
(02) 266 0610
Sydney Regent,
199 George St, Sydney.
(02) 238 0000

FAMILY AND BUDGET
Cameo Inn,
626 New South Head Rd, Rose Bay.
(02) 371 7000
Great Southern,
717 George St, Sydney.
(02) 211 4311
Wybalena House YWCA,
5 Wentworth Ave, Sydney.
(02) 264 2451
York Apartments,
5 York St, Sydney.
(02) 264 7747

MOTEL GROUPS: BOOKINGS
Flag (02) 267 5555
Homestead (02) 264 3166
Travelodge (02) 267 2144

This list is for information only; inclusion is not necessarily a recommendation.

---

which connects the city with **Kings Cross**. One half is dominated by the **Archibald Fountain** — a legacy to the city from the first publisher of the *Bulletin* — and the other by a **Pool of Remembrance** and the **Anzac War Memorial**. On the eastern boundary of the park, on College Street, stand the **Australian Museum**; one of Sydney's oldest colleges, **Sydney Grammar School**; and two high-rise neighbours — the **Returned Servicemen's League** headquarters and a major **NSW Police Department** block.

On the city side of Hyde Park runs **Elizabeth Street**. No longer the major city artery it once was, these days it serves as a vital, almost continuous, bus feeder route, particularly where the two underground railway stations, St James and Museum, disgorge. It is still, however, noteworthy for the headquarters of one of Australia's great retailing empires, **David Jones**; another of Sydney's historic buildings, the **Great Synagogue**; and the administrative headquarters of the ABC, **Broadcast House**.

David Jones, on the corner of Elizabeth and Market Streets, is a Sydney landmark. 'I'll see you on DJ's corner' was, and still is, a regular Sydney rendezvous. From here, Elizabeth Street continues north to the spacious semi-circle of **Chifley Square**, named in honour of a former Prime Minister, J. B. Chifley. Looking on to the square are the **Goodsell Building**, one of the headquarters of the NSW Public Service; one of Sydney's top hotels, the **Sheraton Wentworth**; one of the major federal public service buldings in Sydney, the **Commonwealth Centre**, a 'regular tourist call' because it houses Commonwealth Health and Immigration departments, and the TAA building (the old Qantas House).

In a wedge-shaped sector of blocks made by Bent, Bridge, Young, Phillip and Loftus Streets stand the office buildings of colonial New South Wales — elaborate and ornate in Sydney's superb Hawkesbury sandstone on which the city is built. Mostly late-Victorian, the buildings still serve their original purposes for the state departments of Lands, Education, Agriculture and Public Works and so on — although the Colonial Secretary's building is now an annexe of the Premier's Department.

All are massively solid and set with either statues, gargoyles, handsomely-worked stone, or all three. Within them, cedar-lined offices open on to marbled corridors, wrought-iron balustrades and ceilings so high and arched as to be almost vault-like. Those ministerial offices still within them are treasure-troves of priceless colonial artefacts and design — from grandfather clocks to richly-panelled fireplaces.

The disordered pattern of the surrounding streets is a product of the complete lack of planning that occurred once Governor Phillip was recalled from Sydney. Bullock-tracks and wandering cow-paths determined the town-plan until Governor Macquarie attempted to impose order some 20 years later! Today, the raffish result contributes to Sydney's charm — as it also ensures the narrowness and congestion of the city streets.

Castlereagh Street, parallel with Elizabeth Street, also loses itself in the tangle of colonial office blocks above the Quay. North of Martin Place, it is part of Sydney's merchant belt. It hosts banks, insurance company offices, the Taxation Department, shipping companies and airline offices. South of Martin Place the character of the area changes. One of the newest high-rise complexes in Sydney is the **MLC Centre**. This building dominates almost a whole block, and contains suites of luxurious offices above, and, at ground level, some exclusive and very expensive shops. These comprise mostly jewellers and fashionable boutiques. The complex also houses a convenient fast food area, Australia Tavern, a cinema, 'The Dendy', and for the theatre-goer, Sydney's prestigious Theatre Royal.

There are more cinemas nearby and a less expensive shopping complex — **Centrepoint** where you can visit **Sydney Tower**. It has two observation decks, plus high-powered binoculars and a video television camera so you can see Sydney's landmarks. There is an a la carte revolving restaurant for 220 people (level 1) and a self-serve revolving restaurant for the family (level 2).

Only two of Sydney's north-south arteries actually make a complete journey from Circular Quay to Central Railway Station: **Pitt Street** and **George Street**. Perhaps it's this that sets them apart from the rest of the city's streets; the continuity seems to have allowed them to develop and flow through parallel rhythms of liveliness — commerce, restaurants, bustle and entertainment. Of the two, Pitt Street is probably the more exciting, except for George Street's carnival-thronged evenings along its entertainment section where cinema complexes, fast-food houses and pin-ball alleys, all-night book shops and erotic movie houses compete for the jostling crowd's attention. Footpaths are jammed and the traffic blares.

In both there's little trace of colonial Sydney, although handsome turn-of-the-century commercial buildings remain carefully watched over by devoted citizens and the National Trust for fear developers' ambitions exceed their senses of history and good taste.

Between King and Park Streets, Pitt Street comes into its own: department stores, including Grace Bros. and Centrepoint; another popular sporting club, **City Tattersalls**; the Pitt Street side of the **Methodist Church's Wesley HQ**; cinemas, one a complex of several — the Lyceum, the Ascot and the Pitt Centre; and, dominating the two blocks, the sumptuous **Sydney Hilton Hotel**, now out-rivalled by its soaring neighbour, Sydney Tower — Sydney's tallest.

Pitt Street too peters out into the nondescript as it goes south towards Central Railway, with some second-hand stores, the **People's Palace**, and a laneway that leads to a 19th century Police HQ build-

RIGHT: *The Harbour Bridge is a vital link between Sydney and its northern suburbs*

ABOVE: *Archibald Memorial Fountain, a popular place in Hyde Park.*

ing, now more a city watch-house and serving as cells for the grim **Central Criminal Court** building on one of the cross streets, Liverpool.

Further south, occupying the site once filled by Sydney's municipal markets is the brand new **Sydney Entertainment Centre**. It is an important venue for pop concerts given by overseas and Australian artists but is also used for conventions and for filming TV commercials.

Another part of the old markets has been redeveloped as a campus for the NSW Institute of Technology and across the railway tracks the huge old **Power House**, a well-known Sydney landmark, will house the Museum of Applied Arts and Sciences.

Apart from its entertainment area that makes its nights so boisterous, by day George Street boasts a number of Sydney's most important and very interesting buildings, from the old to the new. The newest was, until only a few years ago, Sydney's and Australia's tallest building — the **Australia Square Tower**. Tall and circular in shape, the 48th floor has an observation platform and there is a revolving restaurant, the 'Summit'. It has since been surpassed in height by the AMP and MLC buildings, and now more recently, by the Sheraton Wentworth Hotel situated opposite on Phillip Street.

South from here are Wynyard Underground Railway Station, the GPO, Sydney's Victorian massif, and the remarkable **Queen Victoria Building** which monopolises an entire block. This latter is being restored by the Sydney City Council, including the reburnishing of its enormous copper domes which once loomed over an older, smaller, city skyline. A landmark of that old city is to be found opposite the Queen Victoria building through the George Street entrance to the Hilton Hotel — in the hotel's basement, also restored precisely to its original ornate detail, is the Marble Bar of the old Adams Hotel which stood on the site of the Hilton. It is one of the great pieces of Victoriana of its type.

Sydney has several shopping arcades that run off Pitt and George Streets. One of these, The Strand, is particularly noteworthy, having been restored to its 1891 standard of splendour.

The **Town Hall**, Sydney, now dwarfed but not overshadowed by a modern council administration block, is Italian Renaissance in style, built of mellow brown sandstone, completed in 1874. A graceful shaded pedestrian plaza to set both buildings off separates it from Sydney's Anglican Cathedral, **St Andrew's**. Built in stages from 1839 onwards, each stage was apparently complete, but it was not until the final additions and alteration that the present main entrance on to George Street finally opened in 1949.

Opposite St Andrew's is one of Sydney's three great art-deco cinema houses, the **Regent**, now classified by the National Trust. The Regent has a neglected air

ABOVE: Vaucluse House, once owned by William Wentworth.

about it: the formal cinema-going days it once catered for long gone, and taken over by the razzle-dazzle of the Hoyts Cinema complex of eight cinemas, bars, pin-ball alleys, trinket-shops and complete one-stop-shopping. Another cinema complex, the Village trio, is nearby.

West of George Street lies **Dixon Street**, Sydney's 'China Town' — a traditional area of restaurants, warehouses, speciality stores and Chinese grocers, where even the banks and service stations are labelled in Chinese script, not English.

Of the city's cross-streets, two are noteworthy — **Park Street** because it leads to Kings Cross, and **Martin Place**, the authentic heart of the city. Both are wide, handsome boulevards.

Martin Place, with its memorial **Cenotaph** to Australia's war dead, is the annual stage for the city's Anzac Day march; every other day of the year — now that it is closed to traffic — it is thronged with lunch-hour Sydneysiders enjoying its fountains, benches, buskers, flower-stalls and street theatre forums to the full. When the car was banished from Martin Place, the people of Sydney took it over as a people's enclave in the heart of the concrete jungle.

Returning to Park Street, the way inevitably leads to Kings Cross, Sydney's version of Soho and Greenwich Village, with its own unique flavour because neither of the others catches a Sydney Harbour breeze or a glimpse of blue water from its canyons. Whatever 'the Cross' has borrowed from other cities for its strip-joints, gaudy night spots and colourful characters, it has its own Bohemian traditions to draw on. In its background are **Garden Island** naval dockyard — with the fleet nearly always in — and the encircling apartment houses of select **Elizabeth Bay**. On its boundaries are once-notorious **Darlinghurst**, including historic Darlinghurst Gaol where bushrangers were hanged, and inner-city

RIGHT: Enjoying the sun on the Corso, Manly.

Woolloomooloo — the famous 'Loo — cramped houses and narrow streets that predictably will become very costly in the race for fashionable living at Kings Cross.

Individual restaurants and bars are too numerous to list, but among the Cross's major hotels are the Chevron, the Rex, the Sebel Town House, the Crest, the Hyatt, the Boulevarde and the Gazebo. There are an even greater number of erotic movie-houses and speciality book shops — with the red-light-district flavour that seems to go with them. A less controversial 'Cross' landmark is the dandelion-shaped **El Alamein Fountain** commemorating the World War 2 battle.

In the other direction, Darlinghurst Road and Bayswater Road lead to Sydney's 'trendiest' area, **Paddington**, a suburb of steep hills and unplanned streets, picturesque terrace houses — hardly one without ornate Victorian wrought-iron railings and fences and lots of trees.

Prosperous 'counter-culturalists' compete with fashionable professional men in the real-estate market for very high-priced houses. The old-fashioned pubs are now terribly chic; well-spoken children and very large dogs exercise on expensive streets, once the domain of street-urchins, before Paddington underwent its fashionable revival back in the late fifties.

Paddington's counterpart on the other side of Sydney, **Glebe**, bordering historic **Sydney University**, isn't quite so restorable, not quite so leafy or picturesque, and certainly not as expensive, but twice as determined to outshine its eastern rival.

Both suburbs, at every turn of a corner, shield something old and handsome in weathered sandstone: a church, an old cottage, a priory or a hall from Sydney's past. For that alone both are worth a visit.

But so is the rest of Australia's first city: from Paddington's neighbours, **Woollahra** and **Rushcutters Bay** through the harbour-side suburbs of exclusive **Double Bay**, **Rose Bay** and **Vaucluse** to The Gap and South Head — or across the Harbour by the ferry, hydrofoil or Harbour Bridge to **Manly** and the long line of beaches stretching north to **Palm Beach**, competing in terms of wealth and privilege with the precipitous bush gorges and superior heights of the elegant **North Shore** suburbs. Beyond all that again lies the metropolitan heartland of Sydney's great urban sprawl — 75 km now from the Harbour across the vast, flat western suburbs to the foothills of the **Blue Mountains** that once hemmed in the first settlers, but which are no longer a barrier to modern Sydney's unbounded ambition.

It is not possible to list all of Sydney's restaurants. In Sydney, one can dine out on the cuisines of virtually every nation in the world. It should be mentioned that Sydney is famous for its rock oyster and the Balmain Bug — an odd-looking but tasty crustacean. On the Hawkesbury River at Berowra is the famous Berowra Waters Inn, ranked as the best restaurant in Australia. The choice of cinema, live theatre, theatre restaurants is just as comprehensive.

Tours from Sydney

Sydney's range of available days out and about is almost unrivalled for its variety of scenery, sites and recreation areas.

In the frantic rush to get out of the city, however, it is easy to overlook two of Sydney's greatest assets, Royal National Park, little more than an hour's drive from the GPO, and Ku-ring-gai Chase National Park, 40 km north of the city.

Harbour Cruises from Circular Quay, Wharf 6.

An ideal way to view Sydney and its harbour is by boat. Several cruises are available. The Urban Transit Authority runs a two and half hour harbour cruise at 1.30 pm on Wednesdays and all school holidays, and at 2.30 pm on Saturdays, Sundays and public holidays.

A two and a half hour cruise up the Parramatta and Lane Cove Rivers leaves at 2 pm on Sundays and public holidays. 'Coffee cruises' operated by Captain Cook Cruises run twice daily at 10 am and 2 pm through Main and Middle Harbours and the same company's luncheon cruises travel up the Parramatta and Lane Cove Rivers, leaving at 12.30 pm daily. The *John Cadman* makes a 'dinner cruise' at 7.30 pm daily and on Sundays at lunch time.

The Maritime Services Board conduct tours to Fort Denison, one of the most historical relics in Australia, from Tuesday to Saturday at 10 am, 12.30 pm and 2 pm, and on Sunday at 9.45 am and 12.30 pm.

El Caballo Blanco, Catherine Field, 60 km from Sydney via the Hume Highway and Camden Valley way.

At this Spanish-style complex, you can see performances by Andalusian dancing horses. Open 10 am to 5 pm Wednesday to Sunday and public holidays.

Australia's Wonderland, Eastern Creek, 40 km from Sydney via the Great Western Highway.

This large amusement park boasts a giant wooden roller coaster, a shoot-the-rapids rafting ride and performing pirates. Open from 10 am to 8 pm every day during school holidays and on weekends and public holidays between August and May.

Historic Camden and Campbelltown, 60 km from Sydney via the Hume Highway.

Lovers of history will enjoy a relaxed stroll around these two early towns of New South Wales. Although most of the historic buildings are not open for inspection, you can still spend a pleasant day viewing them from the outside and taking in the atmosphere. A 'guided walk' booklet is available from the Camden Tourist Association.

Taronga Zoo Park, twelve minutes by ferry from Circular Quay, Wharf 5.

Australia's largest zoo, Taronga is set in 30 hectares of harbourside bushland which give it a magnificent and unique setting. Of particular interest are the displays of Australian native animals and the nocturnal house. Children will enjoy patting the young, tame animals at the Friendship Farm.

BELOW: *A harbour cruise is a relaxing and pleasant way to see many of Sydney's attractions.*

Palm Beach, 48 km from Sydney via Pittwater Road.

This beautiful beach in bush surroundings offers swimming and boating facilities and a choice of ocean or Pittwater beaches. The drive from Sydney through Manly reveals many of Sydney's lovely northern beaches and it is tempting to stop at every one.

Captain Cook's Landing Place, Kurnell, about 40 km from Sydney via the Princes Highway and Captain Cook Bridge.

The site of the first recorded landing by Europeans on the east coast of Australia in 1770 is set aside as an historic site on a pleasantly laid out reserve. An excellent museum displays items related to Captain James Cook's life and discoveries. A short 'historical walk' takes visitors past several interesting points. There are picnic and barbecue facilities in the grounds.

Warragamba Dam, 68 km from Sydney via the Great Western Highway and St Marys.

On Lake Burragorang, the dam may be inspected at certain times. There are attractive gardens and picnic areas around the lake. The nearby African Lion Safari and Dolphinarium features more than fifty lions and tigers roaming free. The children will enjoy the pets' corner, parrot circus and kangaroo reserve, as well as trampolines, miniature railway and pony rides. There are regular shows at the Dolphinarium and Sea Lion Circus.

Windsor and Richmond, 60 km from Sydney via the Great Western Highway and Windsor Road.

These two towns on the Hawkesbury River are full of reminders of New South Wales's earliest settlement. Of the many buildings, George Street, Thompson Square and the Doctor's House in Windsor are probably the most impressive, but the court-house and the many churches and hotels in both towns are all of interest. The Hawkesbury Museum and Tourist Information Centre at 7 Thompson Square, Windsor, is housed in an old colonial building. It contains various items of historical interest relating to pioneer days.

Parramatta, 22 km from Sydney via the Great Western Highway.

Although it has now become a suburb of Sydney, Parramatta retains its individuality and has some charming and interesting buildings. Old Government House, beautifully restored and maintained by the National Trust, is one of the most impressive and the system of having a guide in charge of each room lends itself to a leisurely and informative tour of the building. In complete contrast of style, Experiment Farm Cottage in Ruse Street, also run by the National Trust, shows how the early rural settlers lived. Elizabeth Farm, in Alice Street, is the oldest surviving building in Australia, having been built in 1793.

BELOW: *The lovely garden at Experiment Farm is reminiscent of an English cottage garden.*

Katoomba and the Blue Mountains, 104 km from Sydney via the Great Western Highway (or mini fare excursion, Public Transport Commission).

There are enough attractions in this area west of Sydney to warrant a pleasant weekend away from the city. Katoomba has several old-style hotels from which you can explore the Three Sisters, travel on the world's steepest railway or a scenic skyway, see the Jenolan Caves, and visit the Norman Lindsay Gallery at Springwood.

Old Sydney Town, near Gosford, 88 km from Sydney via the Pacific Highway (or by rail tour).

This excellent, full-scale re-creation of Sydney Cove in the early 1800s will be particularly enjoyed by children. Soldiers and convicts mingle with visitors and demonstrate the hard life that was endured by Australia's first European settlers. Old Sydney Town is open from Wednesdays to Sundays, on public holidays, and daily during NSW school holidays. Barbecue and picnic facilities, a kiosk and a restaurant are all available.

The Hunter Valley Vineyards, 180 km from Sydney via the Pacific Highway (see map 81).

Although it is possible to do this trip in a day it certainly wouldn't do the area justice — and it is definitely not a good idea if you plan to do any winetasting!

The best time to visit the Hunter Valley is at vintage time when you can see the grapes being fermented in great open vats. Picking starts any time from the end of January, but this can vary considerably, and sometimes doesn't start until well into February.

Most wineries welcome visitors. It is, however, well worth while visiting a few of the smaller wineries as well. Tyrrell's and Drayton's wineries were established within a few years of each other in the 1860s, and at Tyrrell's you can still see the classic hand presses being used during vintage and fermentation.

Most of the wineries are open from Mondays to Saturdays from 9 am to 5 pm; some are open on Sunday afternoons as well from 12 noon to 5 pm. Inspections can be arranged with the wineries direct or by calling at the Tourist Information Centre, cnr Mt View and Wollombi Roads, Cessnock, phone (049) 90 4477.

Canberra 300 km from Sydney via the Hume and Federal Highways. (See maps 108/9 and 110/11.)

A minimum of two days is really necessary to do justice to the model city of Canberra, with its beautiful tree-lined streets and interesting architecture. The best time to visit is in the spring or autumn, when it is startlingly beautiful, and a drive around the city during any season is a must.

The city is built on the shores of the man-made Lake Burley Griffin, and a good place to start your tour is at Parliament House, overlooking the lake. Visitors can watch proceedings of both the House of Representatives and the Senate when they are in session and, when not in session, conducted tours of both chambers are available.

Behind Parliament House is Capital Hill where the construction of the new Parliament House due to be opened for Australia's bicentenary in 1988, is taking place. From Capital Hill, Adelaide Avenue leads past the Prime Minister's Lodge to the Royal Australian Mint where you can see coins being made. The Mint is open from 9 am to 4 pm Mondays to Fridays.

Near Parliament House the National Library houses over a million books including Captain Cook's journal, and diaries of famous explorers. It is open from 9 am to 10 pm although the exhibition area closes at 4.45 pm.

Two splendid buildings, the High Court, opened in May 1980, and the National Gallery opened in 1982 are within a short stroll of the National Library along the picturesque shores of Lake Burley Griffin.

Looking down on Anzac Avenue is the Australian War Memorial Museum which houses an extremely good collection of war relics. The displays and dioramas make it interesting even for children and they'll also enjoy looking at the old aircraft on display.

Although the Botanic Gardens on the lower slopes of Black Mountain are used primarily for scientific and educational purposes, visitors are welcome and the gardens are fast becoming one of Canberra's greatest attractions. Several very good brochures are available from the Display Room. These give details of walks around the gardens and point out the many different Australian plants.

You can take a sight-seeing cruise on the Lake where you can see the Captain Cook Memorial, the second highest fountain in the world, 137 metres high, constructed to celebrate the bicentenary of the European discovery of eastern Australia.

A number of coach operators offer tours to Canberra from Sydney if you prefer not to tackle the drive yourself.

National Parks near Sydney

Dedicated in 1879, the second national park to be proclaimed anywhere in the world, the Royal National Park, 36 km south of Sydney, covers 15 000 hectares of Sydney bushland, which survives in much the same condition it was in before the coming of Europeans. It is now, however, a place of sealed roads, picnic and barbecue areas, swimming enclosures and boats for hire.

The Park is situated on land which was inhabited by the Dharawal tribe of Aborigines and a wealth of items from that period has been found there: bone spear points, stone scrapers, cave paintings, rock engravings and so on. Park officers run informative sessions on the Aboriginal culture of the region during school holiday periods.

There are caravan, camping, bush walking and barbecue facilities at Royal National Park. Located so close to Sydney, it is an ideal place simply for a day on the beach or bushwalking, or for a longer camping holiday. A charge is made for admission but this money is used for park maintenance.

North of Sydney, the Ku-ring-gai Chase National Park offers similar facilities to the Royal, though it cannot claim to be 100 years old, like its southern 'sister'. Set around a flooded river valley, it offers some superb coast and river scenery. Boats can be hired for a day on the water. Birdwatchers will try to spot the shy lyrebird and will also see many species of water birds.

The Park covers 14 709 hectares and on the opposite (northern) banks of Broken Bay and the Hawkesbury River, a further 8103 hectares is set aside as the Brisbane Water National Park. There is no camping here, but picnic and barbecue facilities are available. The Aboriginal rock engravings discovered in this area are of particular interest.

Many Sydneysiders will enjoy re-visiting these national parks time and time again, and an annual permit covering entry to all the state's parks is available from Park Offices or Visitors' Centres.

New South Wales from A to Z

Aberdeen Population 1410.
Pioneer Henry Dangar first looked north to the Liverpool Plains from Aberdeen. These days the town is highly industrialised but, with the Hunter River as its northern boundary, there are scenic views north and south from the hills around the town. **Accommodation:** 3 hotels, 1 caravan park.
Map ref. 95 J13, 99 J1

Adaminaby Population 378.
This small town on the Snowy Mountains Highway is renowned as a base for cross-country skiers and the ski area of Mt Selwyn is nearby. It is the stepping off point for Lake Eucumbene, which has five holiday resorts around its shores. These offer varied accommodation, including caravan and camping parks, cottages, units and four-berth cruisers. These may be hired at Buckenderra. Fishing is excellent and boats may be hired. Providence Portal is the only place in the Snowy Mountains where water can be seen gushing from one of the giant tunnels into the lake. The Yarrangobilly Caves and thermal pool are just off the Snowy Mountains Highway, north of town. **Accommodation:** 1 hotel, 2 motels, 1 caravan/camping park.
Map ref. 100 D8, 104 H3

Adelong Population 806.
Fossickers and historians will find plenty to interest them in this picturesque tablelands town on the Snowy Mountains Highway. A Gold Rush Carnival is held each summer for one week. In the mid 1850s, it produced 200 tonnes of gold and attracted 20 000 hopeful miners. **Of interest:** The main street, from Campbell to Neil Sts, has been classified by the National Trust and some buildings such as the Bank of NSW are rated as being of great historic interest. **In the area:** Oasis coloured sheep farm. The cascade falls at Adelong, 2 km north on the Tumblong-Gundagai Road, offer a scenic picnic area and barbecue facilities. Gold fossicking area here and along Adelong Creek. Local old gold reef mines. **Accommodation:** 2 hotels, 1 motel, 1 caravan park.
Map ref. 97 R11, 98 C11, 100 B6

Albury Population 35 072.
This principal city of the Murray district has been developed as part of the Albury-Wodonga decentralised city by the NSW and Victorian governments. It is situated on the north bank of the Murray River, 596 km from Sydney, and makes a convenient stop-over point for motorists driving via the Hume Highway between Sydney and Melbourne. It is an important distribution centre for the district's produce and many secondary industries are locating their facilities there. **Of interest:** Botanic Gardens, Wodonga Place. Ettamogah Wildlife Sanctuary, 11 km to the north, displays Aboriginal artefacts, rock and mineral samples, Australian flora and fauna. The Folk Museum, housed in a former hotel named the Turk's Head. 'William Hovell Tree', opposite the junction of Hume St and Wodonga Place, is an old river gum, marked by Hovell in 1824 when he and fellow explorer Hamilton Hume discovered the Murray on their overland expedition from Sydney Town to Port Phillip. **In the area:** Hume Weir, about 12 km to the east, is a man-made inland lake ideal for water sports. The roadway over the wall of the dam links New South Wales with Victoria. There is a trout farm at the northern end of the weir where rainbow trout may be fed. Jindera Pioneer Museum is 16 km north-west. **Accommodation:** Albury/Wodonga 27 motels, 9 caravan/camping parks.
Map ref. 97 P13, 167 R4, 168 B4

Ardlethan Population 602.
Ardlethan is just off the Newell Highway, south of West Wyalong. The enormous open-cut mine, which is over 150 m deep, can be viewed Wednesdays 2 pm and Fridays 10 am. **Accommodation:** 1 hotel, 1 motel.
Map ref. 97 P8

Armidale Population 18 922.
Situated midway between Sydney and Brisbane in the New England Ranges (altitude 1035 m), this important city is an attractive tourist centre and a convenient stop-over for Sydney-Brisbane travellers. **Of interest:** University of New England, 5 km north-west of city. The Howard Hinton Art Collection, in college of advanced education, claimed to be the most valuable provincial art collection in Australia. Folk Museum with its display of pioneer relics, set in classified National Trust building. St Mary's Roman Catholic Cathedral, magnificent Gothic revival cathedral, built 1912. St Peter's Anglican Cathedral. Art Gallery, Rusden St. Central Park, a pleasant city park, has a useful relief map of area. **In the area:** River State Forest, 65 km to the east, is an area of 31 000 ha, with forest roads leading through magnificent stands of rainforest. Wollomombi Falls, 39 km to the east, are the highest falls in Australia, plunging 457 m. The Chandler Falls and Dangars Falls are among the finest falls in NSW. The gold-mining ghost town of Hillgrove once had a population of 3000. There are now many buildings still intact, including a rural life and industry museum with old mining equipment. Wild pig hunting, duck and quail shooting. **Accommodation:** 3 hotels, 10 motels, 2 caravan/camping parks.
Map ref. 95 L8

Ashford Population 594.
This small New England town is the centre of a tobacco-growing district. **Of interest:** Network of limestone caves and the spectacular Macintyre Falls north-west of the town. Bushwalking, swimming, fishing, camping, barbecue facilities. **Accommodation:** 1 caravan/camping park.
Map ref. 95 K4

Ballina Population 9738.
A fishing town and family holiday resort at the mouth of the Richmond River. **Of interest:** Ballina Maritime Museum includes a steam riverboat exhibit and the *La Balsa* raft, which sailed from South America. Shaws Bay Hotel at East Ballina is a gracious two-storey building, formerly named Fenwick House. It has a red cedar dining room and staircase made from local cedar and carved in Spain. The ship-building yards of the engineering company. The Tropical Fruit Research Station has tours on Monday and Thursday at 10 am, excluding public holidays. **In the area:** Lake Ainsworth to the north of Ballina along the coast road. Freshwater lake with safe paddling and swimming for children. Broadwater Sugar Mill, on Pacific Highway at Broadwater, 19 km south of Ballina, may be inspected on weekdays. (Covered shoes must be worn.) **Accommodation:** 16 motels, 9 caravan/camping parks.
Map ref. 95 R3

Balranald Population 1442.
On the Murrumbidgee River, 438 km from Melbourne in wool, cattle, wheat, fruit and timber area. **Of interest:** Yanga Lake, 7 km south-east of the town, offers good fishing and water sports. **Accommodation:** 1 hotel, 3 motels, 2 caravan/camping parks.
Map ref. 96 H9, 163 O6

Barraba Population 1679.
Surrounded by magnificent mountain scenery on the Manilla River in the Nandewar Ranges, Barraba is the centre for an agricultural and pastoral area and an ideal base for exploring the eastern part of Nandewar Mountains. **Of interest:** Breathtaking views from Mt Kaputar's summit which can be reached by a good road from Narrabri. The Horton River Falls and Horton Valley lie west of Barraba towards Mt Kaputar National Park and offer picnic and barbecue facilities. **Accommodation:** 3 hotels, 1 motel, 2 caravan/camping parks.
Map ref. 95 J7

SYDNEY'S COLONIAL PAST

At the first settlement at Sydney Cove Captain Watkin Tench of the Marines wrote 'to proceed on a narrow, confined scale in a country of the extensive limits we possess, would be unpardonable ... extent of Empire demands grandeur of design'.

Such 'grand design' began in 1810, when the vision of the new Governor, Lachlan Macquarie, was put into practice by the convict architect Francis Greenway, giving us a heritage of splendid buildings, many of which are landmarks today. It continued through nearly a century of growth and lofty ideals to create a prosperous and busy metropolis — a great symbol of colonial aspirations.

BELOW: *Sydney's first settlers built the Observatory on this high ground to watch out over the Harbour.*

As it developed, Sydney was both 'mean and princely' — a mixture of broad, tree-lined avenues and narrow streets and alleys, grand buildings, and crowded cottages and terraces. Its switchback, craggy hills around the sprawling indented harbour made orderly Georgian-style planning impossible, and the grand outlines of earlier days soon became blurred by the city's growth from first settlement to colonial seat, to state capital, to modern city.

In modern Sydney, however, with its gleaming towers, its crowds and its traffic, substantial and fascinating remnants of old Sydney remain. Some parts of the city, such as The Rocks area, adjacent to Circular Quay, are almost pure history. The old pubs and band-stands, sandstone cottages and terrace houses, the Argyle Cut and Agar Steps,

ABOVE: *Macquarie Lighthouse.*

BELOW: *The Argyle Tavern, The Rocks.*

the Garrison Church and the village green are an oasis separated from the bustling city by Flagstaff Hill, where the old Observatory stands, and the **Harbour Bridge**.

There are many other inner suburban areas that are reminiscent of the feeling of old Sydney. Paddington is the showplace historic suburb, with its picturesque terraces and cottages, many of them superbly restored by proud owners. The narrow streets of this once working-class suburb provide an intimate, neighbourly feeling. Balmain, Leichhardt and Redfern are becoming popular as the advantages of inner suburban living and sandstone cottages attract owners who are conscious of the aesthetic quality of the old houses.

In the city itself, the street which best reflects the past is probably Macquarie Street, which overlooks the Domain where Government House, the National Gallery and the Conservatorium of Music are situated. Governor Macquarie planned for the east side of the street to be occupied by official buildings and for the west to contain town houses of wealthy citizens, which are now mainly occupied by members of the medical profession.

Among other interesting buildings in Macquarie Street are Parliament House, a verandahed sandstone building which was known as the Rum Hospital; the adjoining Mint Building of the same age; the Richmond Villa in Gothic style — now in Kent Street; Sydney Hospital; the Royal College of Physicians; and the Hyde Park Barracks (1819), now the Law Courts. In nearby Queens Square is the classically designed St James's Church.

At the harbour end of Mrs Macquarie's Road is a natural reminder of the Macquarie era — a sandstone shell known as Mrs Macquarie's Chair. The Governor's wife is said to have sat here and gazed out upon the great harbour, now one of the world's busiest and most picturesque waterways.

There are a number of other major buildings in or near to the city. Buildings like Elizabeth Bay House, in Regency style, now beautifully restored and showplace for the rich furnishings of the time when it looked out over a harbour verged by cliff and woodland; the General Post Office in Martin Place, completed in 1887 in classic Renaissance style; the Great Hall of Sydney University, and St Andrew's Cathedral, both designed by Edmund Blacket; St Mary's Cathedral, designed by William Wardell; the Greek Revival Courthouse in Taylor Square, designed by Mortimer Lewis; Vaucluse House, former home of William Charles Wentworth, the father of the NSW Constitution. But perhaps the most striking example of colonial

ABOVE: *Much of the intricate iron lace work of Paddington's terrace houses has been restored to its former glory.*

BELOW: *An enjoyable day can be spent wandering around The Rocks. An incredible variety of early buildings is crammed into this small area.*

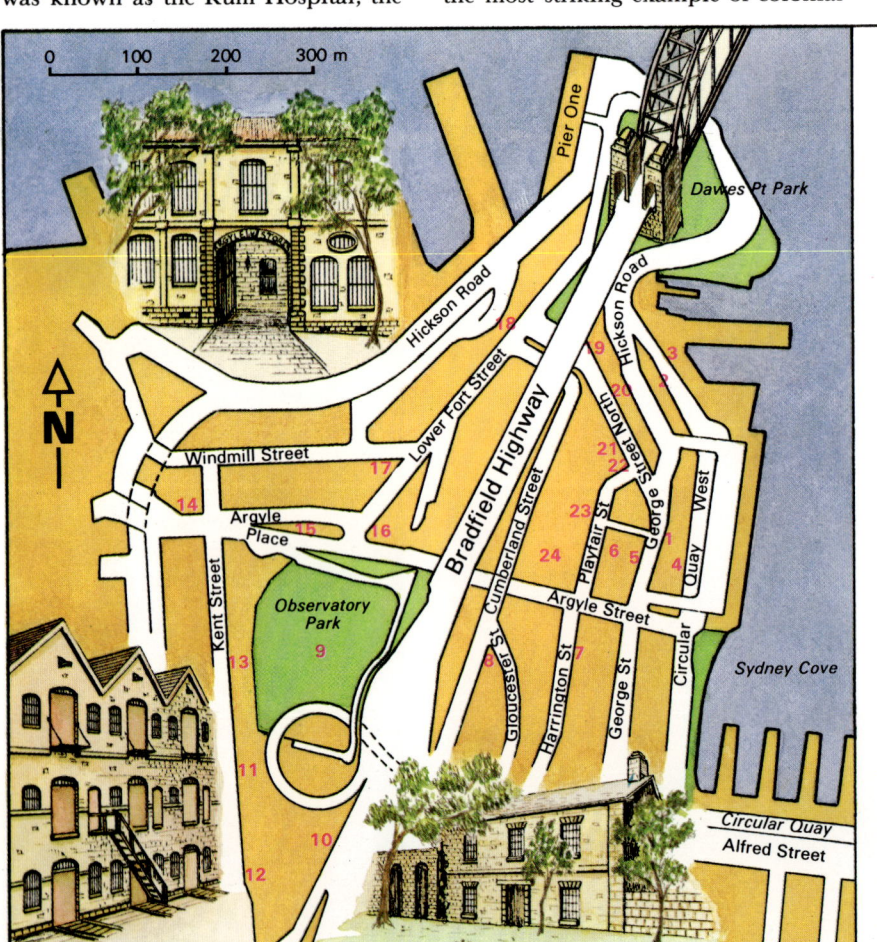

1. The Rocks Visitors' Centre
2. Campbells Storehouse
3. Campbells Wharf
4. Cadmans Cottage
5. Unwins Stores
6. The Coachhouse
7. Reynolds Cottage
8. Australian Hotel
9. Fort Phillip
10. National Trust Centre
11. Agar Steps and Carlson Terrace
12. Noahs Ark and Richmond Villa
13. Seaforth and Winsbury Terraces
14. Lord Nelson Hotel
15. Argyle Place
16. Holy Trinity (Garrison) Church
17. Hero of Waterloo Hotel
18. Georgian residences, Lower Fort Street
19. Geological & Mining Museum
20. Metcalfe Bond and Arcade
21. Sergeant Majors Row Terrace
22. The Counting House and Union Bond
23. Argyle Terrace
24. Argyle Centre

Sydney's Colonial Past

ABOVE: *The castle-like exterior of Sydney's Conservatorium of Music, formerly Government House Stables. The original building was designed by colonial architect Francis Greenway in 1821.*

BELOW: *It is hard to believe that these old workmen's cottages facing the village green in Argyle Place are only minutes away from the heart of Australia's largest city. The area is enhanced by attractive street furniture such as pillar boxes and lamp posts of the early 1900s.*

ABOVE: *The General Post Office in Martin Place is classified by the National Trust.*

BELOW: *Elizabeth Bay House, a superbly restored Palladian villa, was built in 1838 by architect John Verge and has been beautifully restored.*

New South Wales

ABOVE LEFT: *Berrima's gaol is a beautifully preserved sandstone building.*

ABOVE: *Victoria Barracks, built in 1836 by colonial engineer, George Barney.*

ABOVE: *Experiment Farm Cottage, Parramatta.*

BELOW: *The Doctor's House, Windsor, lived in by doctors since 1876.*

architecture in Sydney is Victoria Barracks in Darlinghurst. This two-storeyed sandstone building of severe Georgian style, 74 metres long, with white painted upper and lower verandahs, is a model of elegance.

As settlement extended from the harbourside colony, villages were established, first in the upper Hawkesbury region to the north-west, then to the south and, finally, as the Blue Mountains were breached, out to the western plains and throughout New South Wales.

In the upper Hawkesbury valley are the sister towns of Windsor and Richmond, beautifully sited on the river and retaining the peaceful charm and many of the buildings of their earlier days. Windsor has a number of fine buildings — Claremont Cottage, St Matthew's Anglican Church, the Macquarie Arms, Tebbutt's Observatory, Doctor's House, the Toll House, the court-house, to name but a few. At Richmond are the mansion Hobartville, Toxana House, St Peter's Anglican Church, the School of Arts and Belmont.

In the southern highlands the settlements of Campbelltown, Camden, Moss Vale, Berrima and Bowral are full of historic interest. Berrima is perhaps the best example of a colonial town, as the Berrima Village Trust has preserved it as it was in the nineteenth century. Sited in a valley, it contains a number of fine sandstone buildings grouped around a central common, among them the gaol and court-house, the Surveyor General Inn, the Church of the Holy Trinity, 'Harper's Mansions' and 'Allington'. There are many other historic towns and properties throughout New South Wales bearing the hallmarks of a nation's foundation, though Berrima is the best preserved.

Batemans Bay Population 4924.
Crayfish and oysters are the speciality of this attractive resort town on the Princes Highway. The charming site, at the estuary of the Clyde River 294 km south of Sydney, makes it an ideal picnic and bushwalking spot. **Of interest:** Batehaven Birdland, with its native and exotic birds, wildlife, rainforest trail, picnic and gas barbecues. Excellent swimming, surfing and fishing, and outstanding bowling club. **In the area:** Shell Museum, 1 km east of the town, has shells from all over the world on display. Tollgate Island Wildlife Reserve includes penguins among its inhabitants. Araluen, an old gold-mining town to the north-west. **Accommodation:** 2 hotels, 11 motels, 7 caravan/camping parks.
Map ref. 100 G7

Bathurst Population 19 640.
This sedate old city, 209 km west of Sydney on the Macquarie River, has many historic connections. It is the centre of a pastoral, fruit and grain growing district, and the birthplace of former Prime Minister Chifley. **Of interest:** Abercrombie House, 8 km from centre of town, is a huge baronial-style mansion of the late 1870s. Ben Chifley's Cottage, in Busby St. The Folk Museum in the historic court-house, 1 George St displays relics of the area, including Aboriginal artefacts, and the remains of Old Government House of 1817, furnished in the style of the day. Mitchell College of Advanced Education. Mitchell Regional Art Gallery. Bathurst Museum of Applied Arts and Sciences. **In the area:** Bathurst Gold Diggings, Karingal Village, Mt Panorama, is an authentic reconstruction of a gold-mining area and shows restored machines in action. A film on gold discoveries can be seen at the Information Centre in the village. Sir Joseph Banks Nature Reserve, on Mt Panorama, is home for koalas, kangaroos and wallabies in 41 ha of bushland with magnificent views. Organised tours daily can be arranged with the Bathurst Tourist Bureau. Abercrombie Caves, 72 km south of Bathurst on the Bathurst-Goulburn Road, are open for inspection at certain times. (Check with the Tourist Information Centre.) This limestone cave system contains the spectacular Arch Cave, considered to be one of the finest natural arches in the world, and is larger than the Grand Arch at Jenolan Caves. Mt Panorama offers magnificent views from its summit and picnic shelters in McPhillamy Park. The motor car and motor cycle races held at Mt Panorama Circuit every October and Easter are a great tourist attraction. Hill End historic township is 80 km north-west of Bathurst. This former gold-field is now an historic site. **Of interest:** Many original buildings still stand, some of them restored to their former glory. Park Headquarters and Information Centre in old Hill End Hospital. Equipment for panning and fossicking may be bought or hired in the village. Nearby are other old gold towns including Rockley, O'Connell and Sofala. **Accommodation:** 4 hotels, 9 motels, 1 caravan/camping park.
Map ref. 98 G5, 101

Batlow Population 1354.
This timber milling and former gold-mining town in the Great Dividing Range south of Tumut is in a district renowned for its apples, pears and berry fruits. An apple blossom festival is held each October. **Of interest:** The 'Big Red Apple' tourist complex just north of the town has magnificent views of the Bogan Ranges, a restaurant, barbecues, displays. **In the area:** Hume and Hovell's Lookout: spectacular view over Blowering Reservoir at site where the explorers paused in 1824. Picnic area. Excellent walks and drives through scenic forest on south-west slopes of Bago State Forest. Blowering Reservoir. Picnic and barbecue areas. Paddy's River Dam, built by Chinese after a gold strike in the 1850s. **Accommodation:** 1 hotel, 1 motel, 1 caravan park.
Map ref. 97 R11, 98 D11, 100 B6

Bega Population 4388.
It is possible to swim and ski on the same day when staying at Bega, set as it is, between the beach and the best Kosciusko snow resorts. This town at the junction of the Princes and Snowy Mountains Highways, which join Sydney, Melbourne and Canberra, is important for its position. **Of interest:** Bega cheese factory and Kameruka dairy estate can be inspected. Bega Historical Museum. Yarranung and Rotolactor farms, children can see cows being milked. **In the area:** Dr George Lookout and Bega Valley Lookout for fine views. Wallgoot Lake for water sports. Mimosa Rocks National Park, just north of Tathra is a natural park with nearby hotel, motel and lodges. Swimming, fishing and bushwalking. Historic village of Candelo, 39 km south-west of Bega, via Kameruka, is a small nineteenth century village untouched by time. **Accommodation:** 3 hotels, 5 motels, 2 caravan/camping parks.
Map ref. 100 F10

Bellingen Population 1593.
Attractive tree-lined town on the banks of the Bellinger River in the rich dairylands of the Bellinger Valley. In pioneer days it was a timber-getting and shipbuilding centre. **Of interest:** River walks in picturesque setting. A scenic island in the river. Picnic spot at Thora, at the foot of Dorrigo Mountain. Several beautiful state forests for bushwalking and horseriding. Trout fishing in the streams on the Dorrigo Plateau beyond Bellingen. **Accommodation:** 1 motel, 1 caravan/camping park.
Map ref. 86 D6, 95 P8

Bermagui Population 827.
Fishing in all forms — lake, estuary, deep sea and big game — is excellent in this delightful small port 13 km from the Princes Highway. It was much publicised for its fishing by American novelist-sportsman Zane Grey in the 1930s. **Of interest:** Beautiful rock pools, rugged coast and unspoiled country. Wallaga Lake National Park, 8 km to the north, is good for boating, fishing, swimming, bushwalking and picnicking. Montague Island, 23 km north, is a mecca for big-game fishermen from all over the world and was another of Zane Grey's favourite spots. Cobargo, on the Princes Highway to the west, is an unspoiled old town with an interesting gallery, a pottery and a motel. **Accommodation:** 1 hotel, 2 motels, 5 caravan/camping parks.
Map ref. 100 G9

Berrima Population 685.
A unique historic village on the Hume Highway, 137 km south-west of Sydney, Berrima is an important part of Australia's national heritage. It has hardly changed since early last century. Founded in 1829 by NSW Surveyor General, Sir Thomas Mitchell, it was planned to be the chief centre for the southern part of the state. Buildings were constructed of local sandstone and designed to suit local conditions, giving it a purely Australian character. The Berrima Village Trust was set up in 1963 to preserve it. **Of interest:** Berrima court-house (1838), scene of Australia's first trial by jury; Berrima gaol (1839), closed as a gaol in 1919, used as internment camp in World War I, now a training centre for rehabilitation of young prisoners; The Surveyor-General Inn, the oldest continuously licensed inn in Australia still trading within its original walls; and the public school building, still in use. Also, the old bakery, the Victoria Inn, the Colonial Inn, the Barn, Geranium House, Harper's Mansion, churches and rectories, an oak tree planted by Sir Henry Parkes, the district historical museum. **Accommodation:** 1 hotel, 2 motels.
Map ref. 90 I7, 98 I8, 100 G3

Berry Population 1220.
Old English trees add to the charm of this picturesque township on the Princes Highway, 18 km north of Nowra. In the midst of rich dairying country, it was founded by David Berry, the brother of Alexander who was the first settler in the Shoalhaven area. **Of interest:** Several buildings have National Trust classifications, including the historical museum. Historic Coolangatta, on the site of the first settlement in the area by Alexander Berry in 1822, is a group of convict-built cottages which have been restored and converted into motel units. **Accommodation:** 1 hotel, 2 motels.
Map ref. 91 N10, 99 J9, 100 H4

Bingara Population 1257.
Diamonds, sapphires, tourmalines and gold may be found in the local creeks and rivers of this fascinating little town. **Of interest:** Glacial area at Rocky Creek. All Nations Gold Mine, which closed in 1946. Historical Society Museum is a slab building, thought to be the town's first hotel, and is classified by the National Trust. It houses a collection of old furniture and photographs depicting early days of the district. Good river fishing and sports facilities in the town. **In the area:** Upper Bingara Goldfields, where there are the remains of old gold and copper mines, and a Chinese cemetery. The creek is a good spot for gold-panning. **Accommodation:** 1 hotel, 1 motel, 1 caravan/camping park.
Map ref. 95 J5

Blayney   Population 2694.
On the Mid Western Highway between Cowra and Bathurst, Blayney is close to the famous historic village of Carcoar. Reminiscent of an English village, and the scene of NSW's first bank hold-up in 1863, Carcoar has an hotel, picnic areas, an antique shop specialising in porcelain, and the Stokes Stable Museum. The court house (1882) is being restored by the local historical society. **In the area:** Carcoar Dam, 9 km north-west of town via the Mid Western Highway, has attractive picnic areas. Also fishing, water sports and overnight camping. **Accommodation:** 1 hotel, 1 motel.
Map ref. 98 F5

Bombala   Population 1504.
This small town on the Monaro Highway in the Great Dividing Range serves the surrounding timber, sheep, cattle and agricultural district. **Accommodation:** 3 hotels, 2 motels, 1 caravan/camping park.
Map ref. 175 N2, 100 E11

Bourke   Population 3326.
Anything 'back o' Bourke' is the real outback. Bourke itself is the service centre of a vast area of sheep country, which produces up to 55 thousand bales of wool a year. It is claimed to be the largest railhead for wool shipment in the world. **Of interest:** Courthouse. Cobb and Co. sign on the outside wall of the Carrier Arms Hotel, which was once the coach booking office. Fort Bourke stockade site, south of Bourke, where a memorial and rebuilt stockade marks the site on which explorer Major Mitchell built a stockade against hostile Aborigines in 1835. Every Easter there is a festival of sport held. Good river fishing and swimming, golf, tennis, bowls. Rodeo championships are held annually in late winter. Various activities organised each week preceding and including the Queen's Birthday weekend in June. **Accommodation:** 6 hotels, 4 motels, 3 caravan/camping parks.
Map ref. 93 M6

Bowral   Population 6862.
This popular family resort in picturesque setting is the centre of a dairying, fruit-growing and mixed farming district. **Of interest:** Mount Gibraltar Reserve, a 24 ha bird and animal sanctuary. A tulip festival is held each September-October. **In the area:** Wombeyan Caves, five interesting limestone caves open for inspection, all easily accessible by graded paths. There are picnic areas and tennis courts at the caves. Riding schools and excellent sporting facilities. **Accommodation:** 5 hotels, 6 motels.
Map ref. 91 J6, 98 I8, 100 H3

Braidwood   Population 944.
This old town, 84 km south of Goulburn, has been declared an historic village by the National Trust. It has many interesting old sandstone buildings, including churches, homesteads, flour mills. Bedervale homestead is open first Sunday of each month. Museum is open between Thursday and Monday 10 am to 4 pm. **Of interest:** Potteries, silversmith and a few antique shops. **Accommodation:** 2 hotels, 1 motel.
Map ref. 98 G11, 100 F6

Brewarrina   Population 1236.
An Aboriginal word for 'good fishing' which is still very appropriate. Pastoral activities include grazing and wheat production. **Of interest:** Aboriginal fisheries in the bed of the Darling River. Festival of fisheries during May school holidays. Two-day rodeo late August. **Accommodation:** 2 hotels, 1 motel, 1 caravan/camping park.
Map ref. 93 O6, 94 A6

Broken Hill   Population 26 913.
This artificial oasis in the arid wastelands of far western NSW was created to serve the miners in the incredibly rich silver-lead-zinc mines of the Barrier Range. The green parks and colourful gardens of this modern city, 1170 km west of Sydney, seem unreal in the setting of the surrounding desolation. The city's water supply comes from local water storage schemes and from the Menindee Lakes dam on the Darling River. As well as being a lesson in human ingenuity in overcoming a harsh environment, Broken Hill has its own unique system of handling industrial relations. Since 1925, when all unions affiliated in the Barrier Industrial Council, this body has controlled many aspects of the city's life. The mines produce two million tonnes of ore annually. **Of interest:** Gladstone Mining Museum. Several art galleries, including the Civic Centre Galleries and Pro Hart Gallery in Wyman St. Mine tours include Delprat's Mine and Morgan Mine. For details see Tourist Information Centre, Argent St. Moslem Mosque, built in 1891 by the Afghan community which then lived in the town. The Silver Tree, Civic Centre, which was commissioned by Charles Rasp, the discoverer of the Broken Hill ore-body in 1883 Historic streetscape in Argent St classified by the National Trust, comprising Post Office, Town Hall facade, police station, technical college and courthouse. Imperial Lake, well-stocked with trout and perch. Swimming and sailing are allowed in good rainfalls. Royal Flying Doctor Service is open for inspection. **In the area:** The ghost town of Silverton, on the road to Umberumberka Reservoir, is where silver chlorides were discovered in 1883. In two years the population rose to 3000, but in 1889 the field closed and almost everyone made for what is now Broken Hill. It retains many interesting buildings, including the gaol. Mootwingie historical site covers about 486 ha in the Bynguano Ranges. Here, a wealth of Aboriginal relics, such as campsites, tools, rock carvings and paintings, can be found. Visitors' Centre run by the ranger. Visitors are warned that water may be scarce. No petrol available. **Accommodation:** 8 hotels, 10 motels, 2 caravan/camping parks.
Map ref. 92 B12, 96 B1

Brunswick Heads   Population 1877.
This small town at the mouth of the Brunswick River is renowned for its outstanding fishing. Boats and canoes can be hired, and a large commercial fishing fleet is based in the boat harbour. Also good for surfing, swimming and water-skiing. **Of interest:** Minyon Falls, Cape Byron lighthouse and lookout, and Peach Mountain lookout. **Accommodation:** 1 motel, 6 caravan/camping parks.
Map ref. 95 R2

Bulahdelah   Population 972.
Situated on the Pacific Highway at the foot of Alum Mountain, Bulahdelah is a good base for a bushwalking holiday. **Of interest:** The mountain, which has huge alum deposits, is well-known for its rare varieties of rock orchids. **In the area:** Myall Lakes National Park, 12 km east of town, has spectacular headlands with long expanses of beach and superb rainforest. Ten thousand hectares of lakes. Great variety of flora, fauna and rock formations. Bush camping is permitted in most areas. **Accommodation:** 1 hotel, 3 motels.
Map ref. 99 N2

Bundanoon   Population 1018.
Oaks and golden poplars line the lanes of this charming little township. On the edge of a plateau, lush farms with grassy slopes contrast with rugged mountain gorges beyond. **Of interest:** Bushland trails lead to wildlife sanctuaries in the nearby mountain country, bellbird forests and Glow Worm Glen. Entrance to Morton National Park. Ranger station and camping facilities at Gambells Rest. **Accommodation:** 1 hotel, 3 motels, 1 caravan/camping park.
Map ref. 90 I9, 98 I9, 100 G4

Bourke

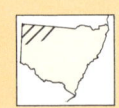

Once you go beyond Bourke you are well and truly off the beaten tourist track — and for a very good reason: the far west of NSW is harsh and forbidding with seemingly endless red plains broken by occasional low rocky ranges and sluggish creeks. From November to March it is unpleasantly hot and dusty and flies abound. Secondary roads are rough, and running out of petrol, food or water can soon become, literally, a matter of life and death. In its own way, however, the far west is one of the state's most fascinating and uniquely Australian areas. It is the 'real outback' of Australian folklore.

Before setting out read the section on outback motoring. If you prepare for your trip carefully and stay on the Barrier Highway, you could have a fascinating holiday. But before you venture on to secondary roads to see some of the quaint little mining towns in the area, consult the locals about road conditions. For the less intrepid, the best way to get to Bourke is by air.

Wines of New South Wales

A vineyard holiday takes you through peaceful, ordered countryside and gives you the chance to learn more about wine and its making at first-hand. It also gives you a perfect excuse for tasting wines and, later, sampling them with a meal in a first-class restaurant in the area. The obvious place to head for in NSW is the famous Hunter Valley. It is not far from Sydney (two hours' drive each way) and must rate as one of the most important wine-growing districts in Australia. Although it is just possible to do a day trip from Sydney to the Hunter, it is well worth booking into a motel in the area for at least one night, to do justice to it.

It is Australia's oldest commercial wine-producing area, wine having first been made there in the 1830s. The Hunter's table wines — both red and white — still rank as among the best in Australia.

Most of the early colonial vineyards have vanished and all but two or three family concerns have been taken over by the larger companies with such well-known names as Lindemans and Hermitage, and their wineries can be visited.

The high reputation of the district is maintained by such well-known properties as Mount Pleasant, Dalwood, Oakvale, Ben Ean, Draytons Bellevue and Glen Elgin.

Pokolbin, a few kilometres inland from Cessnock, is the heart of the Hunter. The whole district has had a remarkable revival in the last few years and a score of new vineyards has been established.

Most wineries welcome visitors and are open for inspection and wine tastings on weekdays. Several of them have picnic grounds, barbecue facilities and high-class restaurants.

There are many good restaurants in the area, including the Cellars at Hungerford Hill, Blaxland's at Pokolbin and the Casuarina at North Pokolbin.

The Hungerford Hill Wine Village at Pokolbin goes all out to cater for the tourist — wine tastings, wine sales of the complete range of Hungerford Hill wines, accommodation at the Motor Inn, specialty shops, superb restaurant, barbecue facilities, adventure playground and so on, phone (049) 98 7666.

It is best to go at vintage time — usually around February in the Hunter — if you want to see a vineyard in full swing. However, this is the most hectic time of year for vignerons, so don't expect their undivided attention. If you want to get an idea of the range of wineries in the district, it is worth seeing Tyrrell's and Drayton's wineries for a glimpse of the more traditional family approach, and Lindeman or Hermitage for the modern 'big company' style.

Not far from **Camden**, Gledswood is the birthplace of Australia's wine industry. The first vines were planted in 1827 and the winery was re-established as Gledswood Cellars in 1970. The winery offers wine tastings and purchases, an art gallery and shearing demonstrations. Barbecue facilities are available. Hay rides and candlelit dinners can be arranged for parties.

You could have an equally enjoyable wine-tasting holiday in the Riverina town of **Griffith**, the other main wine-growing area of the state. **Mudgee**, 261 kilometres north-west of Sydney, is also gaining a reputation as a wine area. Other smaller vineyards are scattered throughout the state — some of them quite close to Sydney.

National Parks of New South

The national parks of New South Wales are extremely popular with residents and tourists, who return time and time again to these unspoiled scenic retreats which offer a wide range of activities for holiday makers.

Most of the state's parks are found along the coast, with their rugged headlands, quiet inlets and sweeping beaches pounded by the crashing surf. The easy accessibility of these coastal parks accounts for their popularity.

Among the 65 parks is Australia's first, The Royal National Park, just 36 kilometres south of **Sydney**. Established in 1879, this was the second national park declared in the world; America's Yellowstone was the first. Royal National Park has 15 015 hectares of heath-covered sandstone plateau country, broken here and there by fine surf beaches, and the Hacking River runs through almost the entire length of the park. From August to November, the area is ablaze with the colourful wild flowers of more than 700 species of plants, trees and shrubs which, in turn, attract over 250 species of birds. Visitors to this park can enjoy picnicking at one of the many picturesque spots along the coast. Activities are mainly for sun lovers: surfing, swimming, canoeing, beach fishing, and bushwalking. You can hire a boat (Tel. (02) 521 6467) at **Audley** (77 012) and row leisurely up the Hacking River, following its twisting course under a canopy of figs and coachwoods decked with tree ferns.

Just north of Sydney are two prominent national parks, situated in the Hawkesbury River district. Brisbane Water and Ku-ring-gai Chase National Parks are renowned for their sheltered creeks and inlets and bushland walking tracks adorned with wild flowers.

Ku-ring-gai Chase, established in 1894, comprises 14 717 hectares of open rainforest, eucalypt forests, scrub and heath and is home for a wide range of birdlife including the lovely lyrebird, honeyeaters, waterbirds, colourful parrots and lorikeets. A small colony of koalas dwells in the eucalypt forest while hundreds of Aboriginal rock carvings are found on sandstone slabs close to the road and tracks.

Nearby is Dharug National Park, its sandstone cliffs rising high above the meandering Hawkesbury River. This park houses magnificent waterfalls set in forests of coachwood, sassafras and eucalypts and framed by colourful wild flowers including Christmas bells, spider flowers and boronias.

Further inland, to the west of Sydney are many splendid parks nestling in mountains which give panoramic views of the surrounding areas. Year after year, innumerable visitors return to the Blue Mountains National Park, where mysterious blue mists shroud the immense valleys of the Grose River, creating ever-changing patterns of colours: green, mauve, blue and purple.

At **Katoomba**, pillars of weathered sandstone rise abruptly like isolated church spires: these are The Three Sisters, the most popular tourist attraction in the Blue Mountains. The 215 946-hectares park is also a sanctuary for grey kangaroo, wallabies, platypuses and many species of birds, including the unique rock warbler.

The New England National Park, which preserves one of the largest remaining areas of rainforest in New South Wales, is 576 kilometres northwest of Sydney. Its 29 823 hectares cover three distinct zones: sub-alpine with tall snow gums, temperate forests of ancient Antarctic beeches and true sub-tropical rainforests, rich in ferns and orchids. There is a diverse range of flora and fauna, with trackless wilderness for experienced bushwalkers.

One park popular throughout the year is Warrumbungle National Park, located on the western slopes of the Great Divide, 491 kilometres northwest of Sydney. Here is some of the most spectacular scenery of the nation.

At Warrumbungle, east meets west: the dry western plains and moist eastern coast meet to give high peaks covered with snow gums, and lower forests filled with fragrant native trees and shrubs. There are sheltered gorges, permanent springs and walks and climbs to suit everyone, with trails leading to lookout points where hikers are rewarded with the fascinating colours of sunrise and sunset. Spring and summer months lure many visitors with the colourful display of wild flowers and brightly plumaged birds.

Wales

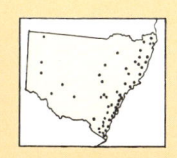

The largest national park in New South Wales is Kosciusko, with its 645 527 hectares of glacial lakes, limestone caves, grasslands, heaths and woodlands. Situated 487 kilometres south-west of Sydney, this park is of particular significance because it embraces a large area of the continent's only extensive alpine region and contains Australia's highest mountains as well as the sources of the important Murray, Snowy and Murrumbidgee Rivers. Here are the most extensive snowfields of the nation, housing developed ski resorts, including the famous **Thredbo, Perisher Valley, Smiggin Holes** and **Charlotte Pass**. There are easy grades for beginners and slopes for expert skiers. Although Kosciusko is associated with winter sports, it is also a superb summer retreat with its crisp, clean air, crystal clear lakes and a wonderful display of alpine wild flowers. This is a popular venue for those who enjoy camping, fishing, boating and bushwalking.

In the far west of New South Wales are two outstanding national parks. Kinchega, 1018 kilometres west of Sydney, houses beautiful saucer-shaped overflow lakes of the Darling River. These lakes provide a most important breeding ground for a wide variety of waterbirds, including herons, ibises, spoonbills and black swans. There are good walking tracks through forests of red river gums and fishing is good.

The most remote national park in the state is Sturt, 1200 kilometres from Sydney. This is an ideal place for those who want to get away from it all and experience the real Australian outback. The 304 280 hectares comprise scenic open deserts, endless red sand dunes, rocky ridges, lakes and billabongs. If you prepare yourself and your equipment well, you can camp anywhere and enjoy bushwalking over the sand plains and seeing the wild flowers which include the scarlet and black blooms of Sturt's desert rose. Here also are relics of an early settlement, when the area was used solely for grazing.

For more information about national parks of New South Wales, contact the National Parks and Wildlife Service, ADC Building, 189-193, Kent Street, Sydney, NSW 2000.

Byron Bay Population 3187.
Surfers from near and far gravitate to Watego's Beach, on Cape Byron. It is one of the best beaches for surfboard riding on the east coast, due to its northerly aspect. Australia's most powerful lighthouse is situated nearby at Cape Byron, the most easterly point of the Australian mainland. Dairy products, bacon, beef and tropical fruits are produced locally. **Of interest:** Lighthouse and lookout, 5 km south-east of Byron Bay (open during school holidays). The Everglades, Suffolk Park, to the south of the town. **Accommodation:** 2 hotels, 5 motels, 4 caravan/camping parks.
Map ref. 95 R2

Camden Population 9000.
It was in the Camden district that pioneer John Macarthur was granted two properties in 1805, where he began his famous merino sheep-breeding experiments. It is also the birthplace of the Australian wine industry. Located 60 km south-west of Sydney on the Camden Valley Way, many historic buildings still remain. **Of interest:** The Church of St John the Evangelist, Menangle Rd (built 1840-49). Camden Park (1834) and Denbigh (1817-27) all have National Trust classifications. Also Brownlow Hill (1835), Hassall Cottage, Macquarie Grove (1817), Kirkham Stables (1816) and Wivenhoe (1837). Gledswood Cellars, on the Camden Valley Way, is the original old winery built as a coach house in 1810, with the first vines having been planted in 1827. There is an aviation museum at Camden Airport, Narellan. El Caballo Blanco, Spanish dancing stallions. **In the area:** A sophisticated milking machine, a rotolactor, may be seen at Menangle. **Accommodation:** 2 hotels, 3 motels, 1 caravan/camping park.
Map ref. 77 K12, 100 H2

Camden Haven Population 3161.
A fisherman's dream, consisting of the three fishing villages, Laurieton, North Haven and Dunbogan, all less than 3 km apart, 44 km south of Port Macquarie. **Of interest:** Wealth of oysters, lobsters, crabs, bream and flathead, in local rivers and lakes. Seafront well-known for wonderful fishing. Delightful bushwalks along the seafront and around lakes. Panoramic views from pinnacle of North Brother Mountain. **Accommodation:** Laurieton, 1 hotel, 3 motels, 2 caravan/camping parks. North Haven, 2 motels, 3 caravan/camping parks.
Map ref. 95 O11

Campbelltown Population 37 140.
Named by Governor Macquarie on his second visit to the infant settlement in 1820 in honour of his wife's family, Campbelltown is now a satellite city of Sydney. **Of interest:** Many historic buildings, including Glenalvon (1840), early houses at 284-298 Queen St and St Peter's Church (1824). Fisher's Ghost Creek, which flows through the city, is a reminder of a convict murder, in which the victim's ghost allegedly pointed out his missing body in the creek, and brought the murderer to justice. **Accommodation:** 1 motel.
Map ref. 77 L12, 99 J7, 100 I 2

Canowindra Population 1720.
Bushranger Ben Hall and his gang commandeered this township in 1863. With the police locked up in their own cells, the bushrangers and townspeople joined forces for several days of compulsory revelry! An obelisk downstream from the town commemorates the event. Situated north of Cowra, on the Belubula River, Canowindra is noted for its curving, graceful main street, and its many notable public buildings that have been classified by the National Trust. **Accommodation:** 1 hotel, 1 motel, 1 caravan/camping park.
Map ref. 98 E6

Casino Population 9743.
This important commercial centre on the middle reaches of the Richmond River could be dubbed the city of parks. There are about 20 in all, most with good picnic facilities. **Of interest:** Aboriginal rock carvings 20 km outside the town on the Tenterfield Road. Casino Folk Museum. Fresh water fishing on Cooke's Weir and the Richmond River. **Accommodation:** 3 hotels, 5 motels, 2 caravan/camping parks.
Map ref. 95 P3

Cessnock Population 16 916.
Many of the excellent Hunter River table wines are produced in the Cessnock district. The city itself is highly industrialised, its economy based on both wine and coal. **Of interest:** Many wineries may be inspected in the Pokolbin area. Tourist Information Centre, cnr Mt View and Wollombi Rds. **In the area:** The picturesque village of Wollombi has a wealth of historic buildings, including the beautiful St John's Anglican church, the old court-house (now Endeavour Museum), and the two-storey sandstone post office. Watagan Mountains and State Forest to the south-east. Heaton, Hunter's and Flat Rock Lookouts all have picnic and barbecue facilities and natural rugged beauty. **Accommodation:** 4 hotels, 2 motels, 2 caravan/camping parks.
Map ref. 81 H12, 83 C5, 99 K3

Cobar Population 3583.
A progressive copper-mining town with wide tree-lined streets, Cobar is on the Barrier Highway, 723 km north-west of Sydney. Since the opening of the CSA Copper Mine in the mid 1960s, and the introduction of a channel water supply, the town has been transformed from an arid landscape to a green oasis. The CSA Mine, which is the most highly mechanised mine in Australia, has an annual output of 600 000 tonnes of copper and copper/zinc ores. Wool is the main local primary industry. **Of interest:** Fine early architecture including court-house and police station, the Catholic church and the Great Western Hotel, which has the longest iron lace verandah in the state. Above-ground tours of the CSA Mine take place on Friday afternoons, or by special arrangement. Further details from Tourist Information Centre in the main street. Pastoral, Mining and Technological Museum. **In the area:** Commonwealth Meteorological Station, 4 km north-west of Cobar, can be inspected by telephoning the officer in charge, on Cobar 36 2149. Mt

Grenfell Aboriginal cave paintings, 40 km west of Cobar along Barrier Highway, near the Mt Grenfell homestead. Permission to inspect must be obtained at the homestead (Telephone: Cobar 36 4223). The paintings are of human and animal figures which densely cover rock shelters. There is a picnic and barbecue area nearby with Olympic swimming pool in picnic area. **Accommodation:** 3 hotels, 4 motels, 1 caravan/camping park.
Map ref. 93 M11

Coffs Harbour Population 16 020.
Known as the capital of the Banana Coast, this large, popular resort town, 580 km north of Sydney on the Pacific Highway, is also a progressive timber port. The surrounding districts produce timber, bananas, vegetables, dairy products and fish. Coffs Harbour is really two towns — one on the highway, and the other near the artificial harbour and railway station. **Of interest:** The Big Banana, 3 km north of Coffs Harbour along the Pacific Highway. Open 8.30 to 5.30 daily. This unusual concrete landmark in the form of a huge banana has displays inside illustrating the banana industry. Shops and licensed restaurant nearby, coastline views from the surrounding area. Pet Porpoise Pool, near the entrance to Coffs Harbour, is a sea circus with performing porpoises and seals, native fauna sanctuary. Catamarans for hire (weather permitting) Fun Bikes at Northside shopping centre. **In the area:** Kumbaingeri Wildlife Sanctuary, 14 km north of Coffs Harbour, has Australian animals and birds, and deer, foxes, peacocks and pheasants. Shetland ponies for hire. Bruxner Park Flora Reserve, Korora, is a dense tropical jungle area of vines, ferns and orchids. It has bushwalking tracks and a picnic area at Park Creek. **Accommodation:** 4 hotels, 25 motels, 10 caravan/camping parks.
Map ref. 84 F11, 86 B4, 95 P7

Coleambally Population 565.
The state's newest town, officially opened in June 1968, is the centre of the Coleambally Irrigation Area. It is south of the Murrumbidgee River and separate from the Murrumbidgee Irrigation Area. Rice is the main crop of the 70 000 ha under irrigation, with an annual value of more than 6 million dollars. The town has a modern shopping centre and a rice mill. **Accommodation:** 1 hotel, 1 motel.
Map ref. 97 M9

Condobolin Population 3355.
On the Lachlan River, 475 km west of Sydney, Condobolin is the centre of a red-soil plains district producing wool, fat lambs, fruit and mixed farm products. **Of interest:** Community Crafts Centre, corner of Bathurst and Dennison Sts. Racing and trotting clubs, golf course, tennis courts, bowling greens and Olympic swimming pool. **In the area:** Aboriginal relics 40 km west of town including a monument marking the burial place of one of the last Lachlan Aboriginal chiefs. Agricultural Research Station 10 km east of town. **Accommodation:** 4 hotels, 3 motels, 1 caravan/camping park.
Map ref. 97 P4, 98 A4

Cooma Population 7978.
This lively, modern tourist centre at the junction of the Monaro and Snowy Mountains Highways, on the Southern Tablelands of NSW, was once dubbed Australia's most cosmopolitan town. Thousands of migrants from many different countries worked here on the Snowy Mountains Scheme. Today it is a busy tourist centre all year round, and the jumping off point for the Snowies. Motorists should check their tyres, and stock up on petrol and provisions. Before setting off for the snow country, a hot meal would be a good idea. **Of interest:** Cooma Visitors' Centre, adjacent to Centennial Park in Sharp St, is a good starting point for the tourist. Travellers' Rest Pioneer Museum, 6 km west of Cooma, was built as an hotel and Cobb & Co. staging post in 1861. It is the largest museum in the area, with a small village attached, including stables, police station and kangaroos. Fairy Tale Park, 3 km west of Cooma, is in a bushland setting on the slopes of Mt Gladstone. It has miniature buildings and ceramic figures depicting fairy tales; Hunters Lodge Restaurant offers lunch daily, dinner Friday, Saturday and Sunday. At Clogs Cabin you can see a Dutch craftsman demonstrating clog-making. Raglan Gallery, built in 1854, was originally used as an hotel and bank. It has paintings, pottery and Oriental rugs on display. Southern Cloud Park, on the Snowy Mountains Highway 500 m west of Cooma, displays the remains of the *Southern Cloud*, which crashed here in 1931 but was not found until 1958. A recorded tape tells the story. In the Avenue of Flags, Centennial Park, the flags of 27 countries were unfurled in 1959 to commemorate the tenth anniversary of the Snowy Mountains Hydro-Electric Authority, in recognition of the varied nationalities of the people who worked there. Take the historic Lambie St walk where you will see 21 buildings classified by the National Trust, each marked with a plaque. **Accommodation:** 7 hotels, 19 motels, 1 caravan park, 2 caravan/camping parks.
Map ref. 100 D8

Coonabarabran Population 3001.
A tourist-conscious town in timber, wheat and sheep country on the Castlereagh River, 491 km north-west of Sydney. **Of interest:** Miniland, 8 km west of the town, has life-size models of prehistoric animals displayed in a bushland setting. Kiosk, picnic and barbecue facilities, and an historical museum. Miniland won an Australian National Travel Association award in 1974. One and two-day pack horse safaris through exciting mountain country. Further information from local travel centre in John St. Warrumbungle Mineral Museum, in the main street, has a collection of fine minerals found in the Warrumbungle Range, including the beautiful crystalline stilbite and heulandite. **In the area:** Warrumbungle National Park. The final 10 km approaching this is a rough road and drivers should proceed with caution, but bushwalking, rock climbing and nature study are ideal pursuits in this ancient volcanic range. Map of walking tracks is available from park headquarters at Canyon Camp. Caravan park and camping. Siding Spring Observatory, 24 km west of Coonabarabran, has the largest optical telescope in the southern hemisphere. The approach is too steep for caravans. Pilliga Scrub, Baradine, 44 km north-west of Coonabarabran. This 390 000 ha forest consists mainly of white cypress pine and broom plains of dense heath and scrub. Location of picnic areas can be obtained at Baradine Forestry Office. **Accommodation:** 3 hotels, 6 motels, 2 caravan/camping parks.
Map ref. 94 G10

Coonamble Population 3090.
This town on the Newell Highway is situated in the Western Plains, where the slopes end and the vast Western Plains begin, 518 km north-west of Sydney. It serves a district which produces wheat, wool, lamb, beef, cypress pine and hardwood timber. **Of interest:** Police station and stables museum. **In the area:** Yowie Bore, 20 km north of town on Castlereagh

The Snow

The Snowy Mountains are a magnet to tourists all year round. The combination of easily accessible mountains, alpine heathlands, forests, lakes, streams and dams is hard to beat. In winter warmly rugged-up skiers flock to the snug well-equipped snow resorts of the area. As the snow melts, anglers, bushwalkers, water-skiers, and boating enthusiasts move in. Almost as many holidaymakers stay at the ski resorts in summer as in winter.

The creation of the Snowy Mountains Hydro-Electric Scheme was indirectly responsible for boosting tourism in the area. The roads built through the previously inaccessible

Mountains

mountain country helped to open up the area which is now used for winter sports.

All the snow resorts of the Snowy Mountains are within the Kosciusko National Park which is the largest National Park in the state and which includes the highest plateau in the Australian continent. Mount Kosciusko (2173 m) is its highest peak.

The major ski areas are: Thredbo, Perisher Valley, Smiggin Holes, Guthega and Charlotte Pass in the southern part of the Kosciusko National Park, and Mt Selwyn in the north.

The resorts are easily accessible and the major centres have first-class amenities such as chairlifts, ski-tows, motels, hotels, restaurants, lodges, apres-ski entertainment, and expert instruction. The snow sports season usually starts in late May or early June and continues until mid or late October.

Charlotte Pass, 98 km from Cooma and 8 km from the summit of Mt Kosciusko (104 C9). A convenient base for ski tours to some of Australia's highest peaks and most spectacular ski runs.

Perisher Valley (104 D9), 90 km from Cooma. One of the highest and most popular ski resorts in the area; caters for downhill and cross-country skiers. Ski hire and instruction.

Smiggin Holes (104 E8), 89 km from Cooma. Linked to Perisher by ski lifts and a free shuttle bus service. Ski hire and instruction.

Thredbo Village (104 C10), 96 km from Cooma at the foot of the Crackenback Range. This world class resort has the only giant slalom course in Australia approved by the world skiing control board. It is the site for international skiing events. Wide range of facilities for skiers at all levels; Merritt's Spur has been specially developed for beginners. Ski hire and instruction. The chairlift to the summit of Mt Crackenback operates through the summer. Thredbo has a wide range of amenities, restaurants and entertainment.

Skiing is fun but, like any other sport, it has its risks of injury. It is also a strenuous sport, so do not overdo it when you go on the slopes. All ski resorts have teaching facilities if you need to take lessons. Choose slopes that suit your ability, check your equipment and watch the weather. Be alert for signs of exposure (hypothermia) — weariness, reluctance to carry on, clumsiness, loss of judgement and collapse. Avoid skiing alone. If you must, then tell someone you are going skiing. If you get lost, stay where you are or retrace your tracks. Cross-country skiing requires careful planning. Tell someone in authority exactly where you are going, travel in groups, watch the weather, bring plenty of food, especially glucose sweets, and take enough equipment for your survival. Protect yourself against sunburn. Don't allow children to become too fatigued and make sure they wear waterproof clothing.

Highway, can be inspected any time. Water from the bore is hot and supplies five properties with stock water. Nearby Macquarie Marshes are an enormous breeding ground for birds. **Accommodation:** 1 hotel, 2 motels, 1 caravan/camping park.
Map ref. 94 D9

Cootamundra Population 6540.
This town on the Olympic Way, 427 km from Sydney, is an important stock-selling centre for the surrounding pastoral and agricultural country. On the main Sydney-Melbourne railway, it is also an important junction for branch lines serving NSW. Gold is mined in the nearby settlements of Cullinga and Muttama. **Of interest:** Pioneer Park, on southern outskirts of town. Panoramic views in natural reserve. Good picnic spot. **In the area:** Beaufort Herb Farm, 8 km north of town. Hundreds of varieties of herbs, potted and dried, for sale. **Accommodation:** 7 hotels, 3 motels, 1 caravan/camping park.
Map ref. 97 R9, 98 C9, 100 B4

Corowa-Wahgunya Pop. 3390.
Corowa, on the NSW side of the Murray River, 56 km downstream from Albury, serves a district which is famous for its wine grapes and wineries. **Of interest:** Bangerang Railway in Ball Park offers train rides on the second Sunday of each month and public holidays. Lindeman's Winery, 5 km north. **In the area:** Mulwala, on Lake Mulwala, is an ideal spot for water sports. It has a motel/boatel, where boats can be moored just outside the suites. **Accommodation:** Corowa, 6 hotels, 11 motels, 2 caravan/camping parks.
Map ref. 97 N13, 167 O4, 176 A2

Cowra Population 7900.
The peaceful air of this well-established old town belies its dramatic recent history. On 4 August 1944, Japanese prisoners made a mass attempt to escape from a nearby prisoner-of-war camp, and 247 of them, as well as four Australian guards, died in the struggle. Many of the Japanese committed suicide. Cowra, on the Lachlan River, is the centre of a rich pastoral and agricultural district. **Of interest:** Japanese War Cemetery, 5 km north of town beside the Cowra-Canowindra Road. Built at the expense of the Japanese government to honour the memory of the Japanese servicemen who died in Australia during the war. An Australian War Cemetery is beside it. Memorial Cairn, 2 km south-east of the cemetery, off Binni Creek Road, was erected at the site of the Japanese escape attempt. A plaque gives a brief account. Agricultural Research Station, 5 km north of town and east off the main Cowra-Canowindra road. William Farrer worked on the development of rust-resistant wheat at this experimental farm, established in 1903, and it is still the base for a mobile research unit. **In the area:** Wyangala Dam, state recreation area 40 km south-east of town, is a popular resort for water sports, camping and hiking. There is a well-equipped caravan park on the waterfront. Modern amenities in Country Club including games and TV room for children. **Accommodation:** 4 hotels, 5 motels, 3 caravan/camping parks.
Map ref. 98 E6, 100 C1

Crookwell Population 2063.
On the Crookwell Road, 37 km north-west of Goulburn. Once gold-mining and bushranger country, Crookwell is now the centre of a rich agricultural and pastoral district, producing top quality apples, pears, cherries and potatoes. **Of interest:** Crookwell Potato Co-operative: modern potato-grading machinery can be seen in use. Crookwell Memorial Park. Redground Lookout, 8 km north-east of Crookwell. **In the area:** Many quaint villages associated with gold, copper and bushrangers: Tuena, Peelwood, Laggan, Bigga, Binda and Roslyn (birthplace of the poet Dame Mary Gilmore). **Accommodation:** 2 hotels, 1 motel, 1 caravan/camping park.
Map ref. 98 F8, 100 E3

Culburra-Orient Point Pop. 2068.
Famous for its prawning, this unspoiled resort is situated east of Nowra on a magnificent ocean beach near Wollumboola Lake. **Of interest:** Surfing, swimming, lake, shore and rock fishing. The beach is patrolled in the summer holidays. **Accommodation:** 1 caravan/camping park.
Map ref. 91 O13, 99 J10

Deniliquin Population 7354.
At the centre of the largest complex of irrigation areas in Australia, on the Edward River, 771 km south-west of Sydney, Deniliquin has the largest rice mill in the Southern Hemisphere. The northern part of the district is famed for merino sheep studs such as Wanganella and Boonoke. **Of interest:** Tours of rice mill and irrigated properties can be arranged through Tourist Information Centre, End St. Pioneer Garden Centre, which houses antique steam pump display. Waring gardens, weir and syphon. Island Sanctuary, off Cressy St footbridge, has free-range animals and birds. **Accommodation:** 4 hotels, 3 motels, 4 caravan/camping parks.
Map ref. 97 K12

Dorrigo Population 1192.

Magnificent river, mountain and forest scenery make this important timber town worth seeing. **Of interest:** Dorrigo Pottery, on Tyringham Road. Potter working on premises. Dorrigo National Park, 5 km east of Dorrigo, is an area of sub-tropical rain forest with wide variety of birds and animals. **In the area:** The New England National Park, part of the eastern escarpment of New England Plateau, has wide range of vegetation with lodge and cabin accommodation available within the reserve. Excellent trout fishing in the district. **Accommodation:** 1 hotel, 1 motel, 1 caravan/camping park.
Map ref. 86 C8, 95 O7

Dubbo Population 23 986.

This pleasant city on the Macquarie River, 420 km north-west of Sydney, is an important rail junction for the surrounding district which produces wheat, wool, fat lambs and some fruit and vegetables. **Of interest:** Old Dubbo Gaol is an historic gaol with the old gallows on display. Court-house. Dubbo Museum, Macquarie St. Victoria Park, a sporting centre, gardens and animal and bird enclosure. Western Plains Zoo, 5 km south-west of Dubbo. Administered by Zoological Parks Board of NSW, and sister to Sydney's Taronga Park, it is claimed to be Australia's greatest open range wildlife park, with free-roaming animals from six continents. Includes Friendship Farm, where children may pet and feed young animals. Picnic and barbecue areas. **Accommodation:** 10 hotels, 23 motels, 5 caravan/camping parks.
Map ref. 94 E13, 98 E1

Dungog Population 2126.

These days an ideal base for bushwalking enthusiasts, Dungog was established in 1838 as a military post to help put down bush ranging in the area. Situated on the upper reach of the William River, it is on one of the main access routes to Barrington Tops National Park. **In the area:** Telegherry Forest Park, with walking trails along the Telegherry River, barbecue, picnic, swimming and camping spots. Scenic waterfalls with pleasant walking trails nearby. Duncan Park. Barrington Tops National Park, a fascinating plateau and source of several rivers. The Barrington Brush is noted for unusual native flora and rich variety of wildlife. Chichester Dam, along the Bandon Grove Road, is a beautiful lake in a picturesque mountain setting, an ideal spot for a barbecue. **Accommodation:** 3 hotels, 1 motel, 1 caravan/camping park.
Map ref. 99 L2

Eden Population 3107.

Quiet, former whaling town on Twofold Bay, 512 km south of Sydney, with an outstanding natural harbour. Today fishing and timber-getting are main industries. **Of interest:** The Whaling Museum includes the skeleton of notorious 'Tom the killer whale' and 70 million-years old snail fossils. **In the area:** Ben Boyd National Park, extending north and south of Eden, has outstanding scenery of rugged cliffs, backed by forested hills, and is ideal for fishing, swimming, camping and bushwalking. Ruins of nearby former rival settlement Boydtown, including convict-built Sea Horse Inn which still functions as a licensed inn, with snacks; ruined church and unfinished lighthouse. Good, safe beach. Excellent fishing. **Accommodation:** 1 hotel, 6 motels, 6 caravan/camping parks.
Map ref. 100 F11, 175 P3

Eugowra Population 577.

'The great gold-escort robbery' occurred near this small town on the Forbes-Orange road in 1862. It was the only big gold-escort robbery in NSW. **Of interest:** Escort Rock, 3 km east of town, where bushranger Frank Gardiner and his gang hid before ambushing the Forbes gold-escort. The rock is on private property, but a plaque on the road gives details and visitors may go through an unlocked gate to see it. Good picnic facilities. Eugowra Museum contains an Aboriginal skeleton and artefacts, a collection of gemstones and early farm equipment and wagons. **Accommodation:** Limited.
Map ref. 98 D5

Evans Head Population 1802.

This holiday and fishing resort, and centre of the NSW prawning industry is just off the Pacific Highway at Woodburn. It has safe surf beaches and sandy river flats. Rock, beach and ocean fishing, boating, windsurfing. **Of interest:** Broadwater National Park is adjacent to the coastline between Evans Head and Broadwater, activities enjoyed here include bushwalking, fishing and swimming. Bundjulung National Park at south Evans Head has emus, wallabies, koalas and Aboriginal relics. Good sports facilities in town. Highly recommended seafood restaurant, run by trawler fishermen. **Accommodation:** 1 hotel, 1 motel, 1 caravan park, 1 caravan/camping park.
Map ref. 95 Q4

Finley Population 2193.

This town on the Newell Highway, near the intersection with the Riverina Highway, has become the mecca for stock car racing enthusiasts. A *mardi gras* parade and many special sporting events are held here annually on New Year's Eve. **Accommodation:** 3 hotels, 4 motels, 1 caravan/camping park.
Map ref. 97 M12, 167 J1

Forbes Population 8029.

Bushranger Ben Hall is buried in the cemetery of this former gold-mining town 386 km west of Sydney, on the Lachlan River. He was shot by police just outside the town in 1865. Today the town's industries include a meatworks, butter factories, a cannery and a flour mill. **Of interest:** Historical museum, containing relics associated with Ben Hall, including a silver coin that was in his pocket when he was shot, and a locket with a portrait of his sister, also found on his body. Also local historical photographs and displays. Forbes cemetery, along the Bogan Gate Road, contains the graves of Ben Hall and Ned Kelly's sister, Kate Foster. Historical sites include a memorial in King George V Park, where 'German Harry' discovered gold in 1861, and another memorial, marking the spot where explorer John Oxley first passed through Forbes, is in a small park in Dowling St. **In the area:** Lachlan Vintage Village, 1 km south of Forbes, is open daily but has no activated displays on Mondays or Tuesdays. A re-creation of the gold-rush era on a 73 ha site. Activities include gold-panning, wheat stripping, hay baling and farriery. A licensed restaurant is open from Wednesday to Sunday. Barbecue and picnic facilities. Sandhills Vineyard, 6 km from Forbes in Eugowra Road, is open for tasting and sale of red and white table wines. Picnic and barbecue facilities. **Accommodation:** 4 hotels, 4 motels, 4 caravan/camping parks.
Map ref. 97 R5, 98 C5

Forster-Tuncurry Population 9261.

Twin towns on opposite sides of Wallis Lake, a holiday area of the Great Lakes district, Forster and Tuncurry are connected by a bridge. Launches and boats may be hired for lake and deep sea fishing. Renowned for its good fishing, including flathead, bream and whiting, as well as oysters and prawns. **Of interest:** Forster Arts and Crafts Centre. Vintage Car Museum, 3 km south of Forster. Follyfoot Farm Horseriding School, on Lakes Way, Forster, offers supervised rides through beautiful and lake areas. The 'Ton of Fun' Amusement Park is situated at Fallford. There is a skating rink, bicycle hire, mini-golf and many more amusements in the area. The Green Cathedral, at Tiona on the shores of Wallis Lake, 13 km south of Forster, is an unusual open-air 'cathedral'. **In the area:** Myall Lakes National Park. **Accommodation:** 2 hotels, 16 motels, 18 caravan/camping parks.
Map ref. 95 N13, 99 N2

Gerringong Population 1775.

Spectacular views of white sand and rolling breakers can be seen from this resort, 11 km south of Kiama on the lovely Illawarra coast. **Of interest:** Surfing and swimming at local beaches (Werri, Gerroa, Seven Mile Beach). Bushwalks through Seven Mile National Park. Picnic and barbecue facilities. There is a memorial to pioneer aviator, Sir Charles Kingsford Smith, at the northern end of Seven Mile Beach, the site of his take-off to New Zealand in the *Southern Cross* in 1933. **Accommodation:** 1 hotel, 1 motel, 3 caravan/camping parks.
Map ref. 91 O10, 99 J9, 100 I 4

Gilgandra Population 2700.

Gilgandra is a small town at the junction of the Newell, Oxley and Castlereagh Highways, in timber, wool and cereal-growing country. **Of interest:** The Gilgandra Observatory and Display Centre has a 300 mm (12 inch) telescope and an audio-visual display of American Gemini flights and the Apollo moon landing. There is also an historical display of pioneer days of district. **Accommodation:** 2 hotels, 3 motels, 1 caravan/camping park.
Map ref 94 E11

CITY ON THE WATER

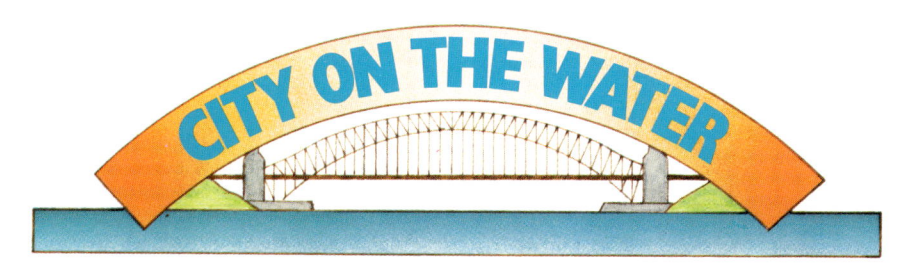

In the arid continent of Australia, Sydney stands out, set as it is around the bays and inlets of Port Jackson, with more than 250 kilometres of unspoiled foreshore, scalloped with white sandy beaches. The South Pacific licks the sheltered coves and thunders in on some of the best surf beaches in the country. The climate is mild, the water warm and comfortable enough for swimming nine months of the year.

Sydneysiders are rightly proud of their city — it is the cradle of Australian history and, industrially and commercially, the focal point of the South Pacific. The people are relaxed yet sophisticated, usually content to spend their leisure time lying in the sun, sailing, swimming, surfing or cruising. The water that surrounds them has a great impact on their lifestyle: office workers can commute by ferry and spend their lunch hours by the foreshore, enjoying the cool sea breeze in hot summer months.

Sydney owes a lot to its harbour: first discovered in 1770 by Captain James Cook who named it Port Jackson, in 1788 Captain Arthur Phillip declared it 'the finest harbour in the world'. Today, it is the world's best *natural* harbour, due to its vast size, its protection from storms, uniform depth, small tides, freedom from silting, its lack of navigational hazards and its wharves, conveniently situated close to the city's business centre. As it embraces more than 55 square kilometres of water, it caters for more than 4000 vessels each year.

Each weekend, the harbour bustles with activity. Sydneysiders take their pleasure crafts on the water — sailboats, speedboats, yachts and launches — to join the busy harbour traffic of ferries and hydrofoils, with sailboats bringing bursts of colour amidst massive container ships and luxury liners. Sydney Harbour is also the venue of many boating classics, including the Sydney to Hobart Yacht Race which sets out from Sydney on Boxing Day each year, escorted to the Heads by a colourful fleet of pleasure boats.

This beautiful piece of water is dominated by two impressive structures — the Sydney Harbour Bridge and the Opera House. The Harbour Bridge, affectionately known as 'the old coathanger', is the world's largest single span arch bridge, offering the only direct link to the developing twin city of North Sydney. In addition to railway tracks and traffic lanes, this bridge has a special track for bicycles and a footway for pedestrians.

RIGHT: *Pier one is just a short walk from the historic Rocks area.*
BELOW RIGHT: *Sydney's two famous landmarks, the Opera House and the Harbour Bridge, form a spectacular backdrop to the annual blessing of the fishing fleet.*
BELOW: *Yachts are a part of the scene of Sydney Harbour.*

New South Wales

At Bennelong Point, the Sydney Opera House rises 70 metres above the water like a cluster of gleaming white sails billowing in the wind. It is one of the world's best-known pieces of modern architecture and was the brainchild of Copenhagen architect Joern Utzon. Having been the subject of controversy for more than two decades, the Opera House is now the unofficial emblem of Sydney.

Between these two magnificent pieces of architecture is Sydney Cove — the birthplace of city, state and nation. In 1788, Captain Arthur Phillip chose this inlet to establish the first colony because of its deep bay and running stream of fresh water.

In the heart of Sydney lies Circular Quay, dwarfed by skyscrapers, with the City Circle Railway passing immediately overhead, and the Cahill Expressway forming a canopy over the railway. The nucleus of the network of ferry services, it links the city to its suburbs and popular beaches: Manly, Mosman, Neutral Bay, Woolwich, Taronga Zoo. You can even catch a ferry to Luna Park (open Fri-Sun and public holidays) at Milson's Point for some lively fun. There are also special cruises which go to Middle Harbour and the Lane Cove and Parramatta Rivers. Most ferry routes pass close to Fort Denison, a fortress island (which has never fired a shot in anger) also known as 'Pinchgut', where convicts were once marooned with a diet of bread and water.

The ferry to Manly dates back to 1847. This resort-suburb is often advertised as being 'seven miles from Sydney and a thousand miles from care'. Named by Captain Phillip after the 'manly' behaviour of Aborigines, this suburb can be reached by a 35-minute ferry ride or a 13-minute journey in a hydrofoil. Manly stands at the gateway to Sydney Harbour and, each summer, its popularity doubles its population due to the mild climate and the 18 harbour and ocean beaches nearby. It is also possible to hire an aqua cab (water taxis) to take you to any point around the harbour.

Between Grotto Point and Middle Head is the lovely fishing and boating haven of Middle Harbour. The Spit Bridge opens for vessels visiting the many channels and bays, rich in coves and little beaches.

Along the north shore of Port Jackson are several well-known beaches: Chowder Bay, where American whalers concocted their famous dish using Sydney rock oysters; Neutral Bay where ships from foreign countries once

RIGHT: *The sail-like roofs of the Opera House reflect the spirit of Sydney and make a spectacular sight, framed against the blue waters and sky of a bright Sydney day.*

anchored; and the picturesque Mosman Bay and Chinamans Beach, a favourite haunt of artists.

The south shore is dominated by a chain of unbroken greenery, with almost 100 hectares of grasslands in the Domain and the Royal Botanic Gardens. Each day, office workers flock to the gardens for a quiet lunch break, a stroll along the foreshore, or a quick game of cricket.

Sydney is also renowned for its fine surf beaches. Brightly coloured beach umbrellas and suntanned bodies spread out on the white sands while surfers ride the crests of waves that crash in from the Pacific. The northern beaches, from Manly to Palm Beach, are more scenic than those in the south, but Bondi, just seven kilometres from the general post office, is the most popular

BELOW: *Beautiful sand and surf are the attractions of Bondi Beach.*

metropolitan beach. Coogee, Cronulla and Mona Vale are also popular beaches, while the smaller ones at Clovelly and Tamarama offer quiet seclusion in the crowded summer months. The 34 surfing beaches of Sydney are patrolled by volunteer life savers who stage large-scale carnivals to demonstrate their skills.

Some beaches are protected with sharkproof enclosures, as shark scares are not uncommon in Sydney. In all the history of this city, however, there have probably been less than 20 people killed by sharks. Rock pools are abundant and are ideal for children. It is not advisable to swim in the harbour and surfers should take heed of flags placed on the sand, as they mark the areas safe for surfing on that day.

BELOW: *Surfboards make a splash of colour at Manly.*

Glen Innes Population 6052.
This mountain town was the scene of many bushranging exploits last century. In a beautiful setting, at an altitude of 1073 m, it is now the progressive centre of a lush dairying and farming district, where sapphire mining is an important industry. Tin is also mined. **Of interest:** Land of the Beardies, an enormous folk museum housed in the town's first hospital, is set in extensive grounds and includes a reconstructed slab hut, period room settings and pioneer relics. **In the area:** Gibraltar Range National Park, 68 km to the east of Glen Innes, is an area of lush sub-tropical rainforest noted for wild flowers and wildlife (including platypuses). Bushwalking, swimming and fishing; camping and barbecue facilities at park headquarters at Dandahra Creek. Balancing Rock (on private property) can be seen from Stonehenge Reserve where there are other unusual rock formations and picnic facilities. At Dunvegan Sapphire Reserve on the Reddeston Creek you can hire tools and go fossicking for sapphires. Camping, barbecueing, swimming and bushwalking. Guy Fawkes River National Park is a wild, river area for canoeing, bushwalking and fishing. No roads. Check with National Parks and Wildlife service at Armidale or Grafton before setting out. Mushroom Rock, near Backwater, is a unique rock formation with fossicking areas for garnets, zircons, topaz and sapphires nearby. Convict-carved road tunnel, half-way between Glen Innes and Grafton on a road which passes through beautiful mountain and riverside country. Rangers Valley Dam north of Glen Innes is a privately owned 162 ha dam, used for water sports in warm months. An aquatic carnival is held each November. **Accommodation:** 4 hotels, 8 motels, 4 caravan/camping parks.
Map ref. 95 M5

Gloucester Population 2488.
This quiet town lies at the foot of a range of monolithic hills called the Bucketts. At the junction of three tributaries of the Manning River, it is excellent for trout and perch fishing. **Of interest:** The Bucketts, immediately west of the town. Lookouts at Copeland Tops and Kia-Ora Lookout. Gloucester Park, an outstanding sporting complex. Tourist Information, Shire Council Chambers, Queen St. **Accommodation:** 2 motels, 1 caravan/camping park.
Map ref. 95 M12, 99 M1

Gosford Population 38 205.
The main tourist centre of the beautiful Brisbane Water area, Gosford is 85 km north of Sydney. **Of interest:** Henry Kendall's Cottage, built as an inn in 1838, where the poet lived from 1874-5. There are picnic facilities in pleasant grounds. Eric Worrell's Reptile Park has taipans, pythons, goannas and platypuses on display. Nearby Old Sydney Town, a recreation of a pioneer settlement. Somersby Falls, near Old Sydney Town, is an ideal picnic spot. **In the area:** Park Family Fun Centre, Forresters Beach, 31 km from Gosford. The Ferneries, Oak Road, Matcham, 11 km from Gosford, is an area of ferny rainforest with paddle boats, a playground, picnic and barbecue areas and Devonshire teas. Bouddi National Park, 17 km south-east of Gosford, offers bushwalking, camping, fishing and swimming. Brisbane Water National Park — beautiful waratahs and Christmas bells in spring. Bushwalking, camping and barbecue facilities. State Forests of the Watagan Mountains, Wyong — magnificent coastal lookouts. Abundant flora and wildlife. Barbecue and picnic facilities, tank water. **Accommodation:** 3 hotels, 9 motels, 2 caravan/camping parks.
Map ref. 77 Q1, 78 A2, 83 E13, 99 K5

Goulburn Population 21 755.
This interesting provincial city, steeped in early colonial history (it was proclaimed a town in 1833), is on the Hume Highway 209 km south-west of Sydney. It is the centre of a wealthy farming district (including wool, wheat, stud cattle and horses) at the junction of the Wollondilly and Mulwarry Rivers beyond the Southern Highlands. **Of Interest:** Riversdale, National Trust coaching house (built 1840) in lovely gardens, is open daily except Tuesdays. St Clair History House (built about 1843), a twenty-room mansion, restored by the local historical society. Garroorigang and Hume Dairy, South Goulburn, (built 1857) is mostly in its original condition. Although lived in, it is open daily for inspection. Other historic buildings are Goulburn courthouse, the Cathedral of St Saviour and the Cathedral of St Peter and St Paul. **In the area:** Pelican Sheep Station, 10 km south from Goulburn along the Braidwood Road (groups may inspect by arrangement with Eric Sykes, c/o the station). Shearing, wool preparation and sheepdog demonstrations. The Big Merino, a 15-metre high sculptured relief of a ram, provides an appropriate setting for a display of wool products and Australiana. Goulburn Steam Museum, Crockwell Road (closed Mondays and Tuesdays), offers rides on 'Leisureland Express'. Barbecue facilities by Wollondilly River at Marsden Weir. Applied Arts and Sciences Museum includes a collection of local rocks and minerals, model steam engines and local wool samples. Rock Hill War Memorial, the city's best-known landmark, built in memory of local men who served in World War I. **Accommodation:** 7 hotels, 12 motels, 3 caravan/camping parks.
Map ref. 90 C12, 98 G9, 100 F4

Grafton Population 17 005.
A garden city, famous for the magnificent jacaranda, wheel and flame trees lining its wide streets. Situated on the Pacific Highway at its junction with the Gwydir Highway, 665 km north of Sydney. A colourful Jacaranda Festival is held annually in the first week of November. **Of interest:** Schaeffer House, built at the turn of the century by the city's first architect. Now a district historical museum. Glenugie Peak, south of the town, has picnic grounds and good walking trails to its summit, which offers panoramic views. The ice-cream factory in Fry St is open for inspection at 2 pm weekdays. Susan Island in the Clarence River opposite the city is a recreation reserve covered with rainforest and rich in birdlife. **In the area:** Maclean Lookout offers magnificent views of the Clarence Valley, the canefields and the coastline. Lake Hiawatha, 10 km from the coast, is a freshwater lake with an excellent bird and wildlife area. (No boating.) Guy Fawkes River National Park, west of Grafton, is a wild river area suitable for canoeing, fishing and bushwalking. No roads or facilities, and access is difficult. **Accommodation:** 3 hotels, 7 motels, 3 caravan/camping parks.
Map ref. 95 P5

Grenfell Population 2070.
The birthplace of famous poet and short-story writer Henry Lawson, and the background for many of his verses and stories, this small town on the Mid Western Highway 377 km west of Sydney was named for a gold commissioner, who was killed by bushrangers soon after the discovery of gold in 1866. **Of course:** Henry Lawson Obelisk, next to Lawson Park on the site where the poet is believed to have been born. A Henry Lawson Festival is held in the town every June. **In the area:** Weddin Mountains National Park, 18 km to the south-east for bushwalking and picnicking and crescent-shaped mountain range. Abundant flora and fauna. Barbecue and picnic facilities are available. **Accommodation:** 5 hotels, 1 motel, 1 caravan/camping park.
Map ref. 98 D6, 100 B1

Griffith Population 13 187.
Developed as a model settlement, Griffith was planned by Walter Burley Griffin, the architect of Canberra. Industries include fruit-processing and canning, wine-making, flour- and rice-processing. Griffith produces 80% of the state's wines and is the second largest wine producing area in Australia. **Of interest:** Pioneer Park Museum, just north of town, with drop-log homestead, gaol house, log smokehouse, country school, chemist shop and pioneer church. Lake Wyangan Picnic Grounds. Water-sports, picnic and barbecue facilities and fully serviced paddle boats. **In the area:** Cocoparra National Park, 19 km north-east of Griffith. Fruit and vegetable canneries and wineries can be inspected. Tourist Information Centre is at the corner of Banna Ave and Jondaryan Ave and is open every day. A highlight of the Griffith social calendar is a three-day Vintage Festival, held over Easter during years of odd number. **Accommodation:** 7 motels, 1 caravan park. 1 caravan/camping park.
Map ref. 97 N8

Gulgong Population 1740.
This fascinating old gold-mining town, 29 km north-west of Mudgee, is known as 'the town on the $10 note'. In its heyday in the 1870s it was packed with fortune hunters from all over the world. Some of its former glory remains in the form of many restored buildings, but none of those depicted on the $10 note remain. **Of interest:** Buildings worth seeing include

Old Sydney Town

Wandering through the streets of Old Sydney Town is like going back in a time machine, or stumbling on to a busy film set. You may happen upon a public flogging, a duel or an escape bid by a desperate convict.

This non-stop street theatre is all part of an amazing reconstruction of the infant colony of New South Wales transposed to bushland at Somersby, 70 km north of Sydney.

All the staged events are based on things that really happened — such as court cases based on actual trials — and all the buildings have been re-created as authentically as possible from carefully researched material.

The guidebook on sale at the entrance gives details of all the activities and buildings.

To get to Old Sydney Town, take the Newcastle Tollway at the first Gosford turn-off and follow the signs for seven kilometres, or there is a longer route along the Pacific Highway. An alternative, and more relaxing, way to get there is by rail tour.

There is so much to see and do at the complex that it is worth setting aside a whole day, and children in particular should have an enjoyable time. There are barbecue and picnic facilities, a restaurant and a kiosk.

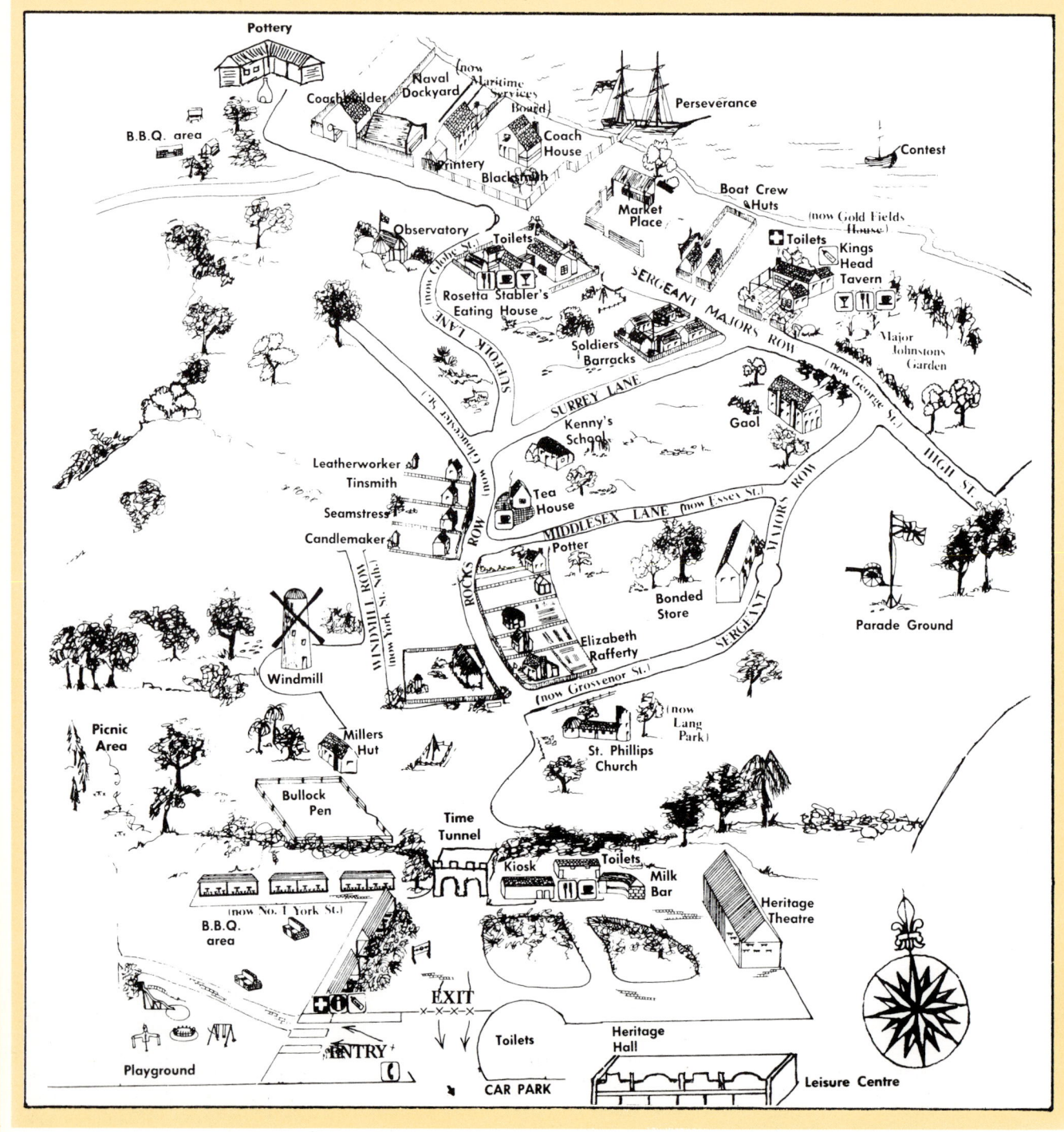

The Prince of Wales Opera House in Mayne St, the Ten Dollar Town Motel (formerly the Royal Hotel) at corner of Mayne and Medley Sts, American Tobacco Warehouse and Fancy Goods Emporium. The Coffee House in Mayne St, and the Gulgong Pioneers Museum, corner of Herbert and Bayly Sts. **In the area:** Henry Lawson's boyhood home memorial, at the remains of the demolished cottage there is a plaque that was unveiled by Lawson's widow. **Accommodation:** 4 hotels, 2 motels, 1 caravan/camping park.
Map ref. 94 G13, 98 G2

Gundagai Population 2308.
Much celebrated in song and verse, this prosperous town on the Murrumbidgee River, 403 km south-west of Sydney, has become part of Australian folklore. Its rich history includes Australia's worst flood disaster in 1852, when 89 people drowned; nearby gold rushes and many bushranging attacks. Today it is the centre of a rich pastoral and agricultural district which produces wool, wheat, fruit and vegetables, and is a convenient overnight stopping place for motorists along the Hume Highway. **Of interest:** Dog on the Tuckerbox, 'five miles from' or 8 km north of Gundagai. Monument to pioneer teamsters and their dogs, celebrated in the song by Jack O'Hagan. Nearby kiosk, fern house and ruins of the old Five Mile Pub, where teamsters and gold miners once broke their journeys. Marble carving of cathedral, comprising over 20 000 pieces, by Frank Rusconi, the sculptor of the tuckerbox dog, on display in the Tourist Information Centre, Sheridan St. Outstanding collection of early photographs with letters and possessions of the poet Henry Lawson on display at Gabriel Gallery, Sheridan St. Historical museum. The court-house (built in 1859 and still in use), classified by National Trust as a building of great architectural merit, was the scene of many historic trials, including that of the notorious bushranger, Captain Moonlight. **In the area:** Mount Parnassus lookout and scenic drive. **Accommodation:** 2 hotels, 5 motels, 1 caravan park, 1 caravan/camping park.
Map ref. 97 R10, 98 C10, 100 B5

Gunnedah Population 8909.
Prosperous town in the highly fertile Liverpool Plains district, at the junction of the Namoi and Mooki rivers. The centre of rich pastoral and agricultural country, it has one of the largest stock-marketing and killing centres in NSW. **Of interest:** Keepit Dam and State Recreation Centre, east of Gunnedah. The 425 000 megalitre dam and 6 megawatt hydro-electric power station is also a centre for water sports. Bushwalking, barbecue and camping facilities. There is a good road to the Porcupine Lookout 3 km from town where there are excellent views and picnic facilities. **Accommodation:** 6 hotels, 5 motels, 1 caravan/camping park.
Map ref. 94 I9

Gunning Population 438.
In the centre of lush pastoral country on the Hume Highway between Goulburn and Yass. **Of interest:** Pye Cottage, a slab-style pioneer cottage. The Post Office, Royal Hotel, old Court-house now a church, Police Station and many more interesting buildings. **Accommodation:** 1 hotel, 1 motel.
Map ref. 98 F9, 100 E4

Guyra Population 1840.
Aboriginal for 'fish may be caught', Guyra's local streams are excellent for trout and eel. At 1300 m, this small town in the Great Dividing Range is one of the highest in NSW. **Of interest:** Chandler's Peak for spectacular views. Ebor Falls and picnic reserve. Unusual balancing rock formation and gem fossicking at Backwater. **Accommodation:** 1 motel, 1 caravan/camping park.
Map ref. 95 M7

Harden-Murrumburrah Pop. 2070.
Twin towns on the Friendly Way, 357 km by road south-west of Sydney. Settled in 1830, and later important as the district's railway centre. **Of interest:** Harden-Murrumburrah Historical Museum. Newson Park, in Harden, with aviary, gardens and picnic/barbecue area. Barwang Vineyard, where wines may be sampled and bought. **Accommodation:** 1 motel, 1 caravan/camping park.
Map ref. 98 D8, 100 C3

Hartley Population under 200.
This historic village just off the Great Western Highway, 134 km west of Sydney, used to be an important stop-over for travellers in the early colonial days. Situated in the Hartley Valley, it is now administered by the National Parks and Wildlife Service. **Of interest:** Convict-built court-house, opened in 1837, designed by colonial architect Mortimer Lewis, and recognised as one of the few examples of colonial architecture in its original state. The historic site includes the Royal Hotel (early 1840s), Old Trahlee Cottage, Post Office (1846), St Bernard's Church and Presbytery (1842), the Farmer's Inn, Ivy Cottage and Shamrock Cottage. **Accommodation:** Limited.
Map ref. 100 G1

Hay Population 2958.
Hay serves as the commercial centre for the huge area of semi-arid grazing country on the Murrumbidgee River at the junction of the Cobb, Mid Western and Sturt Highways. Many world famous sheep studs are in the area. **Of interest:** Sandy river beaches along the Murrumbidgee for swimming, boating and fishing. Hay Gaol Museum, Church St, exhibits pioneer relics, including a Cobb and Co. coach, used in the film *Mad Dog Morgan*. Hay Park, with aviary, picnic and barbecue area, children's playground and pond. Ornate wrought-iron fountain (1883) and plaque in Lachlan St commemorate the epic journey of explorer Charles Sturt along the Murrumbidgee and Murray rivers in 1829-30. **In the area:** A weir built on the Murrumbidgee River 12 km west. Famous sheep studs of Mungadal, Uardry and Cedar Grove. **Accommodation:** 7 hotels, 4 motels, 2 caravan/camping parks.
Map ref. 97 K8

New England

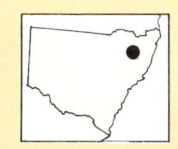

If you pull over for a rest in the New England area, it's worth keeping your eyes on the ground — despite the lovely scenery. Some of the best fossicking specimens in the district have been found by the roadside. Jaspers, serpentine, all kinds of quartz, crystal and chalcedony are found right through this area. Not to mention sapphires, diamonds and gold, though these require a little more effort to find.

The round trip from **Tamworth**, through **Manilla**, **Barraba**, **Bingara**, **Inverell** to **Glen Innes** and back, is known as 'The Fossickers' Way' (Tourist Drive 15) and brown shields have been placed at intervals to guide the motorist. This route runs across the mighty Copeton Dam which holds two and a half times as much water as Sydney Harbour.

Glen Innes and Inverell have nearby sapphire reserves where fossickers may hire tools and try their luck. Anything you find is yours; but remember, you must have a fossicker's licence. The largest find in the Nullamanna Fossicking Reserve, near Inverell, to date is a 70-carat blue, valued at three thousand dollars.

The New England district is the largest area of highlands in Australia, and has plenty to offer besides gemstones. The countryside is varied and lovely with magnificent mountains and streams cascading into spectacular gorges, contrasting with the rich black-soil plains of wheat and cotton to the west.

Fishing is excellent, with trout in the streams of the tablelands and cod and yellow-belly in the rivers of the plains and north-west slopes. (An inland fishing licence is required.) You can also fish, picnic, swim, sail or water-ski at Lake Keepit and the Copeton Dam.

Holbrook Population 1276.
This small town 521 km south-west of Sydney on the Hume Highway is a noted stock-breeding centre. **Of interest:** Commander Holbrook submarine in Holbrook Park, a replica of the submarine in which the late Commander N. D. Holbrook won the VC early in World War I. The town (formerly Germanton) was renamed in his honour. Woolpack Inn Museum on Hume Highway, located in a former hotel built in 1860, has exhibits including complete plant of an old cordial factory, a bakery, horse-drawn vehicles and farm equipment, together with records and letters of Commander Holbrook. The Tourist Information Centre is in the museum. **Accommodation:** 2 hotels, 4 motels, 1 caravan/camping park.
Map ref. 97 Q12, 168 D2

Inverell Population 9734.
Known as 'Sapphire City', this interesting town is in the midst of fertile farming land, also rich in minerals. Industrial diamonds, sapphires, zircons and tin are mined and silver, phosphates and bauxite deposits have been found. **Of interest:** Court-house, classified by National Trust. Pioneer village with buildings dating from 1830 which have been moved from their original sites and include the Grove Homestead, Paddy's Pub and Mt Drummond Woolshed. **In the area:** Gilgai Red Vineyard. Red and white wines for tasting and for sale. Northumbria cashmere goat and craft farm, 23 km south. Tours arranged through Inverell Tourist Centre. Copeton Dam and state recreation area offers boating, water-skiing, swimming and fishing on a 1450 m-long dam together with bushwalking, rock-climbing, two children's adventure playgrounds, barbecues and picnic facilities. **Accommodation:** 1 hotel, 5 motels, 1 caravan/camping park.
Map ref. 95 K5

Jerilderie Population 1075.
The Kelly gang held this small town on the Newell Highway for two days in 1879. They locked the police in the gaol, cut the telegraph wires and robbed the bank of a large sum of money. Today it is the centre of the largest merino stud area in NSW. **Of interest:** Telegraph Office Museum, Powell St, where relics of the Kelly gang can be seen. **Accommodation:** 2 motels, 2 caravan/camping parks.
Map ref. 97 M11

Jindabyne Population 1602.
Nestling on the shores of Lake Jindabyne in the Snowy Mountains, this small town attracts fishermen, water-sports enthusiasts and skiers. Snowy River Information Centre, Petamin Plaza. **Of Interest:** Lake Jinabyne is well stocked with trout and ideal for boating and water-skiing. **In the area:** The Information Centre of Kosciusko National Park is 20 km west of town on the Mt Kosciusko Road. Open daily, it provides information and a winter shuttle bus service to Smiggin Holes and Perisher Valley; and a caravan park and cabins. **Accommodation:** 2 hotels, 2 motels, 2 caravan/camping parks.
Map ref. 100 C9, 104 G9

Junee Population 3993.
Junee is an important railhead town and commercial centre of a mixed farming area, 482 km south-west of Sydney. **Of interest:** Several historic buildings including Monte Cristo, a beautifully restored Victorian homestead, off the Olympic Way. Afternoon tea and lunch by arrangement (tel: 241 1637). **In the area:** Scenic road to Mount Ulandra. **Accommodation:** 4 hotels, 1 motel, 1 caravan/camping park.
Map ref. 97 Q9, 98 B9, 100 A4

Katoomba-Wentworth Falls
Population 13 942.
Visitors are big business in Katoomba, the highly developed tourist centre of the magnificent Blue Mountains. At least half a million people visit the area each year. Katoomba and the smaller towns of Leura and Wentworth Falls have many interesting features as well as the superb mountain scenery for which they are famous. Originally developed as a coal mine last century, it was not long before Katoomba was attracting wealthy Sydney holiday-makers. Word of the area's attractions spread and guest and holiday houses sprang up almost overnight. The coal mine foundered but Katoomba continued to develop. Since the construction of the fast electric train service from Sydney, it has become almost a dormitory town. **Of interest:** Scenic Skyway, Violet St/Cliff Drive. The first horizontal passenger-carrying ropeway in Australia, it travels about 350 m across the mountain gorge above Cooks Crossing, giving magnificent views of Katoomba Falls, Orphan Rock and the Jamison Valley. The Skyway Building houses a revolving restaurant, an amusement area and a souvenir shop. Built in 1880s by the founder of the Katoomba coal mine to bring out the coal and transport the miners. Reputed to be the steepest railway in the world, it descends into the Jamison Valley at an average incline of 45°, through a sunlit, tree-clad gorge approximately 445 metres in length. Famous rock formations (The Three Sisters and Orphan Rock) and falls (Leura Cascades and Katoomba Falls) are floodlit at night. Yester Grange, a 73-square house built in the 1870s, on 4.7 hectares has been restored and furnished to their late Victorian splendour. Details of planned tourist drives from Tourist Information Centre in Katoomba St. The Explorer's Tree, marked by one of the explorers (Blaxland, Lawson or Wentworth) on their first crossing of the Blue Mountains in 1813. It is not known which of them made the marking. The Explorer's Tree Birdland, off the Great Western Highway at the Explorer's Tree, a tropical, indoor free-flight aviary. Everglades, the National Trust's Blue Mountains garden, Denison St, Leura. At the head of the Jamison Valley, with panoramic views over the Blue Mountains, it is one of the most beautiful gardens open to the public in Australia. Gently graded paths meander over 2.8 ha of landscaped terraces, each with its own character. Particularly lovely in spring with its display of bluebells, daffodils and azaleas. Devonshire teas and lunches served at the poolside restaurant at weekends and holidays. Deer Park, Little Switzerland Road, Wentworth Falls, has animals in natural surroundings, an aviary, an antique museum, children's play area, barbecue and picnic facilities. **In the area:** Surrounded by a 2430 ha wildlife reserve, Jenolan Caves contain some of the most splendid underground caves and above-ground arches found in Australia. They are about 80 km drive from Katoomba. **Accommodation:** 5 hotels, 12 motels, 3 caravan/camping parks.
Map ref. 76 E7, 80 D5

Kempsey Population 9034.
The main attraction of this industrial town in Macleay river valley, 480 km north of Sydney, is probably the Trial Bay Gaol, 35 km to its north-east on the shores of Trial Bay. A Sydney brig, *The Trial* was stolen by convicts and wrecked there in 1816, and the front section has been restored and now houses a museum and kiosk. There are also good picnic facilities in the surrounding Arakon State Recreation Area. **Of interest:** Beranghi Folk Museum, South Kempsey. **In the area:** Smoky Cape Lighthouse, near South West Rocks 31 km north of Kempsey, is open for inspection on Tuesdays and Thursdays. Hat Head National Park, 21 km to the north-east of the town, is a coastal strip which abounds in native flowers and birdlife and offers good swimming, fishing, bushwalking. There are superb panoramic views from Yarrahapinni Lookout at the summit of Yarrahapinni Mountain, 55 km north of Kempsey. Several farms (including a strawberry farm and a bee farm) are open for inspection. **Accommodation:** 6 hotels, 9 motels, 5 caravan/camping parks.
Map ref. 87 L4, 95 O10

Kiama Population 7716.
The spectacular Blowhole is the best-known attraction of this resort town. Discovered by explorer George Bass in 1797, it sprays water up to heights of 60 m. It is floodlit until 9.30 pm each evening. Kiama is the centre of a prosperous dairying and mixed farming district. **Of interest:** Little Blowhole. Although smaller, it sometimes outblows its famous brother. Cathedral Rocks, at Jones Beach, a scenic rocky outcrop, is best viewed at dawn. Kiama Beach is good for surfing, swimming and fishing. Historical Museum. Eight terrace houses on the Princes Highway have been renovated into specialty shops including crafts and pottery. **Accommodation:** 5 motels, 3 caravan/camping parks.
Map ref. 91 O8, 99 J9, 100 I4

Kyogle Population 3070.
Kyogle makes a good base for exploring the beautiful mountains nearby. It is also the centre of a lush dairy and mixed farming area on the upper reaches of the Richmond River near the Queensland border. **In the area:** Mt Warning and Mt Warning National Park, 16 km north of Kyogle, have excellent walking tracks to the summit of this former volcano. The National Park at the base of the mountain has dense rainforest vegetation. Mt Linde-

say is 45 km north of Kyogle, astride the NSW/Queensland border and has magnificent views. Wiangaree State Forest, north-east of Wiangaree, 30 km north of Kyogle, is a beautiful rainforest with elevated coastal views. Toonumbar Dam, 31 km west of Kyogle, offers bushwalking and barbecue areas, and there is freshwater fishing and camping at Bell's Bay. The many attractive picnic spots in the area include Grady's Creek, Moore Park, Tooloom Falls and the scenic area at Nimbin Rocks. **Accommodation:** 1 hotel, 1 motel, 1 caravan/camping park.
Map ref. 95 P2

Lake Cargelligo Population 1240.
Many species of birds, including pelicans, wild ducks, geese and black swans, make their home in this lake sanctuary, 586 km west of Sydney. A small township, of the same name as the lake, serves the surrounding agricultural and pastoral district. **Of interest:** Fishing, boating, water-skiing and swimming on parts of the lake, which is controlled by the Water Resources Commission. Other bird species include galahs, white cockatoos and, at times, the rare black cockatoo, and other colourful members of the parrot family. **Accommodation:** 3 hotels, 2 motels, 1 caravan/camping park.
Map ref. 97 N5

Leeton Population 6498.
One of the largest fruit canneries in Australia can be inspected in this pretty town, 550 km from Sydney. Rice mills and fruit-packing sheds may also be inspected. In the southern section of the Murrumbidgee Irrigation Area, Leeton is the centre of a fruit, rice and livestock district. **Of interest:** Gogeldrie Weir, 22 km south-west of Leeton. Gas barbecues. Fishing, boating and water-skiing nearby. Yanco Agricultural High School 10 km and Murrumbidgee College of Agriculture 8 km are south towards Narrandera. Tourist Information Centre, Shire Council Chambers, Chelmsford Place, for details of cannery tours. **Accommodation:** 2 hotels, 3 motels, 3 caravan/camping parks.
Map ref. 97 O8

Lightning Ridge Population 1112.
Small opal-mining township in the famous Lightning Ridge opal fields, 74 km north of Walgett, via the Castlereagh Highway. The extremely valuable black opal can be found in this opal field, which attracts gem fossickers from all over Australia. **Of interest:** The Diggers Rest Hotel, in the main street, is the centre of the township's social life. Licensed restaurant. Other attractions include artesian bore baths, Bird of Paradise Underground Showrooms, Bottle House Museum, Lorne Puddling Tank and Spectrum Opal Mine Workshop and Showrooms. Mine tours. **Accommodation:** 3 motels, 3 caravan/camping parks.
Map ref. 93 R4, 94 C4

Lismore Population 24 033.
The centre of a closely settled and intensively cultivated rural area producing dairy products, tropical fruits, beef, timber and fodder crops, Lismore is situated on

The Blue Mountains

The Blue Mountains have been a favourite holiday resort for Sydney-siders for more than a century. Rising from the coastal plain 65 km west of Sydney, they combine a unique blend of superb mountain scenery and outstanding geographical features with a plethora of highly developed tourist attractions and accommodation. Hundreds of thousands of tourists visit them each year.

The towering cliffs of the Blue Mountains presented a seemingly impassable barrier to the early settlers until Blaxland, Lawson and Wentworth made their historic crossing in 1813 — thus opening up much needed pasture-land beyond.

In the late 1870s, the well-to-do of Sydney discovered the area's charms as a resort, and started to build elaborate holiday houses to escape the summer heat of the coast. At first they travelled by Cobb and Co., later by train. Now the mountains are only a few hours away from Sydney by road or rail. One-day round-trip coach tours run daily between Sydney and Katoomba.

The Blue Mountains are justly famous for their spectacular scenery of high precipices rising from densely wooded valleys. Their highest point is about 1100 metres above sea level. Although the area has been intensively developed for tourism, deep gorges and high rocks make much of the terrain inaccessible, except to skilled bushwalkers and mountaineers.

The panoramic Blue Mountains National Park, which covers an area of 100 865 ha, is the second largest National Park in the state. Visitors centres are at Glenbrook and Blackheath.

The City of Blue Mountains incorporates 24 towns and villages including the main towns of **Katoomba, Blackheath, Wentworth Falls** and **Springwood.** All these towns depend on tourism and are geared for the holiday trade. They offer a wide range of accommodation from cottages and guest houses to luxurious hotels and motels, and excellent sporting facilities of all kinds. The area is famous for its bushwalking and horseriding trails.

WHY ARE THE BLUE MOUNTAINS SO BLUE?

The whole area is heavily timbered with eucalypts which constantly disperse fine droplets of oil into the atmosphere. These droplets cause the blue light rays of the sun to be scattered more effectively, thus intensifying the usual light refraction phenomenon (known as Rayleigh Scattering) which causes distant objects to appear blue.

The Illawarra Coast

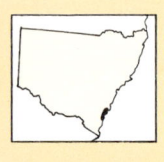

The magnificent panoramic views along the rugged Illawarra coast more than compensate for the sometimes winding route of the Princes Highway, which runs the length of it. 'Illawarra' is a corruption of an Aboriginal word appropriately meaning 'high and pleasant place by the sea'. Stretching from Sydney, south to Batemans Bay, the Illawarra coast is bounded on the west by the Southern Highlands.

Fine surf beaches stretch along this beautiful craggy coastline, which is liberally dotted with mountain streams, waterfalls, inlets and lakes — ideal for prawning and water sports.

Australian wild flowers and fauna abound in the many reserves along the coast, and distinctive trees include cabbage-palms, tree-ferns and giant fig trees.

This is the unlikely setting for the state's third largest city — the giant **Wollongong-Port Kembla** complex — and the site of Australia's largest steelworks. Despite heavy industrialisation, it has many tourist attractions, scenic lookouts and beautiful beaches.

The other main towns on the coast are **Shellharbour**, a popular holiday resort and residential town south of Lake Illawarra; **Kiama**, the centre of a prosperous dairying and mixed farming district; **Nowra**, the main town of the fascinating Shoalhaven River district, and **Ulladulla**, a picturesque little fishing town and popular summer holiday resort.

the Richmond River (now renamed the Wilson River) 821 km from Sydney. It is best known for its beautiful parks and gardens. **Of interest:** Historical museum. Tucki Koala Reserve, adjacent to the Lismore-Woodburn road, with an old Aboriginal ceremonial ground nearby. Lumley Park has an open-air pioneer transport museum, on the Bruxner Highway at Alstonville. Three km south of Nimbin are the spectacular volcanic Nimbin rocks. At Lismore Lake, less than 3 km south of the town, there are picnic facilities, gas barbecues and a pleasant lagoon for swimming, also a children's adventure park. **In the area:** Nightcap National Park, 25 km north of town on Dunoon Road, has outstanding views and abundant wildlife. **Accommodation:** 8 hotels, 12 motels, 4 caravan/camping parks.
Map ref. 88, 95 Q3

Lithgow Population 12 793.
This important coal-mining city on the north-west fringes of the Blue Mountains is a must for railway enthusiasts. The city itself is highly industrialised with a power station, textile mill, clothing factory, brickworks and brewery, but the surrounding countryside is beautiful. **Of interest:** Zig Zag Steam Railway, 10 km east of town via Bell Road. (11-4.00 Saturdays, 10-4.00 Sundays and public holidays.) Breathtaking stretch of railway which was regarded as an engineering masterpiece when it was built in 1868. After falling into disrepair, it was recently restored by enthusiasts. Car parking and picnic facilities. Eskbank House, Bennett St, built in 1841 by Thomas Brown, who discovered the Lithgow coal seam, is now a museum with a fine collection of nineteenth-century furniture and vehicles, and displays depicting the industrial history of the area. Hassan Wall's Lookout, 5 km south of town, off Great Western Highway. Sweeping views of Mt Blaxland, Mt Victoria, Mitchell's Pass and the Jenolan State Forest. **In the area:** Historic village of Hartley, 9 km south-east of town, just off Great Western Highway, has a convict-built court-house (1837) of outstanding architectural and historic interest. **Accommodation:** 1 hotel, 3 motels.
Map ref. 76 C4, 98 H5

Liverpool Population 92 709.
Situated 32 km from Sydney, Liverpool has developed into a major retail and commercial centre. Several outstanding examples of colonial architecture remain, including Francis Greenway's Church of St Luke and the State Hospital and Asylum, built in 1822. **Accommodation:** 4 hotels, 8 motels.
Map ref. 75 O12, 77 M9, 99 J7, 100 I 2

Macksville Population 2352.
This is an attractive town on the Nambucca River, south of Nambucca Heads. **Of interest:** Mary Boulton Pioneer Cottage, River St, is a charming replica of a pioneer cottage and includes furniture and costumes and a museum of horse-drawn vehicles in its collection. The 'Pub with No Beer', made famous by the song, is at Taylors Arm, up-river from Macksville. Called the Cosmopolitan, it is an interesting old pub (built 1903), surrounded by lawns and trees, and has a shady barbecue and picnic area. **In the area:** The Joseph and Eliza Newman Folk Museum at Bowraville, an unspoiled old country town. **Accommodation:** 1 hotel, 3 motels, 1 caravan park.
Map ref. 86 G5, 95 P8

Maclean Population 2016.
Fishing and prawning fleets are based at this resort town on the delta of the Clarence River, about 740 km north of Sydney. Fishermen from here and from the nearby towns of Yamba and Iluka catch about 20 per cent of the state's seafood. Sugar cane, maize, bananas and mixed farm crops are grown under intensive cultivation in the area. **Of interest:** Sugar mill on Harwood Island. **In the area:** The Iluka rainforest, the blue pool and surfing beach at Angourie. **Accommodation:** 3 hotels, 2 motels, 1 caravan park, 2 caravan/camping parks.
Map ref. 95 Q5

Maitland Population 38 863.
This coal-mining city on the Hunter River, 28 km from Newcastle, dates back to the early days of the colony. Many beautiful old buildings remain. The city's winding High St has been recorded by the National Trust as a Conservation Area. First settled in 1818 when convicts were put to work as cedar getters, it was a flourishing township by the 1840s. Today it is a market town and industrial centre. **Of interest:** National Trust properties Grossman House, furnished as a Victorian gentleman's town house, and Brough House, which houses the city's art collection. **In the area:** Homesteads Aberglasslyn, Anambah and Dunmore. Windermere Colonial Museum, Lochinvar, built of sandstock brick by convict labour in the 1820s, was later occupied by William Charles Wentworth. Morpeth Town has quaint shops, historic buildings, superb iron lace and old hitching posts. Nature Wonderland, 3 km south-west of Maitland. **Accommodation:** 1 hotel, 4 motels.
Map ref. 83 F3, 99 L3

Manilla Population 1884.
This small town set in beautiful countryside boasts Dutton's Meadery, the only meadery in the state. Visitors can sample and buy fresh honey and mead. **In the area:** Manilla Ski Gardens on Keepit Dam. **Accommodation:** 4 hotels, 1 motel, 2 caravan/camping parks.
Map ref. 95 J8

Menindee Population 453.
It was at this small township, that now serves the surrounding country population, that the ill-fated Burke and Wills stayed in 1860 on their journey north. **Of interest:** Maiden's Hotel (where they lodged), still run by the Maiden family, who took over the licence in 1890. Menindee Lakes, upstream from the township, is a water-storage scheme which guarantees an unfailing water supply to Broken Hill. The 16 200 ha lake is good for yachting and swimming, while nearby Copi

Hollow attracts water-skiers and power boat enthusiasts. Kinchega National Park, immediately west of town, has about 43 975 ha of grey soil plains and red sand ridges. Emus and red kangaroos abound. **Accommodation:** 1 caravan/camping park.
Map ref. 92 E13, 96 E2

Merimbula Population 2899.
Excellent surfing, fishing and prawning make this small sea and lake town a popular holiday resort. Its sister village of Pambula also offers fine fishing and surfing. Boats can be hired. **Of interest:** Old School Museum, main street, a fine stone building originally used as a school, now houses an interesting historical display. **In the area:** Brogo Valley Rotolactor where cows are milked at 3 pm on a rotary turnstile. **Accommodation:** 8 motels, 2 caravan/camping parks.
Map ref. 100 F10, 175 P2

Merriwa Population 944.
This small township in the western section of the Hunter region is noted for its many historic buildings. **Of interest:** Church of England, Catholic Church, police station and court-house. Convict-built Flags Road. Historical museum housed in an 1857-built stone cottage. **In the area:** Official gem-fossicking area 27 km to the south-west. Great variety of rocks and petrified wood. Cassilis, a small town noted for its historic sandstone buildings. Ulan coal mine has pit ponies and antique coal-extraction equipment on view. Aboriginal hands painted on rocks in the caves just off the Mudgee Road, 32 km from Cassilis. **Accommodation:** 1 motel, 1 caravan/camping park.
Map ref. 94 I 13

Mittagong Population 4266.
An interesting tourist and commercial town, Mittagong is the main centre of a mixed farming, dairying and vegetable growing area. Coal, trachyte and building marble are mined locally. **Of interest:** Ghost town of Joadja, west of the town, a former kerosene shale-mining village, is on private property. It comprises an old cemetery, stone church, school house, row of miners' cottages and brick kilns set in dense bush. There are barbecue facilities but no water. For visiting time, check with Tourist Information Centre, Mittagong. Victoria House has the largest display of embroidery and needlework in Australia, open daily. The Wombeyan Caves are 60 km from town. **Accommodation:** 2 hotels, 4 motels, 1 caravan/camping park.
Map ref. 91 J6, 98 I8

Molong Population 1374.
The grave of Yaranigh, the faithful Aboriginal guide of explorer Sir Thomas Mitchell, is 4 km east of this Mitchell Highway town. Yaranigh was buried there in 1850, according to the rites of his tribe. The grave is marked by a headstone which pays tribute to his courage and fidelity. Four trees, one dead but preserved for its Aboriginal carvings, mark the four corners of the burial ground. **Of interest:** Mitchell's Monument, 21 km south of

Caves & Caverns

Magical underground limestone caves are one of the geographical wonders of NSW. Glittering limestone stalactites and stalagmites, caused by the ceaseless dripping of limestone-impregnated water over tens of thousands of years, glow eerily in vast cathedral-like caves. These incredibly delicate formations of ribbed columns, frozen cascades and waterfalls and delicate tinted 'tapestries' and 'shawls' look like part of a subterranean fairyland.

The **Jenolan Caves** (76 B10) are the most famous and centrally sited of these caves. Since they were first opened in 1866, several million people have visited them. Situated on a spur of the Great Dividing Range, a few kilometres to the south-west of the Blue Mountains, they are open daily from 9 am to 5.30 pm. The caves are surrounded by a 2430 ha flora and fauna reserve with delightful walking trails and picnic facilites. An old-world style guest house, Caves House, provides first-class accommodation.

The **Wombeyan Caves** (98 H8) are set in a pleasant valley in the Southern Highlands, 193 kilometres south-west of Sydney. They can be reached from the Wombeyan turn-off, 4 kilometres south of Mittagong. From here a well-surfaced but narrow road winds for 65 kilometres through spectacular mountain scenery. The alternative route, and the one recommended for caravanners, is via Goulburn, Taralga and Richlands. Five of these caves are open for inspection and are easily accessible by graded paths. These are the Wollondilly, Kooringa, Fig Tree, Mulwaree and Junction Caves. They are fully developed for visitors, with steps and hand-rails. Open daily between 9 am and 4 pm for self-guided tours; guided tours are available. There is a modern caravan park nearby with on-site caravans. The nearest hotel accommodation is at Taralga, 35 km away.

The **Yarrangobilly Caves** (100 C7) just off the Snowy Mountains Highway, 113 kilometres north of Cooma, are open daily for self-guided tours between 10 am and 4 pm. At weekends, school holidays and public holidays, guided tours are available at 11 am, 1 pm and 3 pm, subject to demand. About 60 caves are known in the area but only four have been developed and are open for inspection — The Glory Hole, North Glory, Jersey and Jillabenan. An added attraction here is a thermal pool, built out of what was originally a mineral spring. The pool is at a constant temperature of 27° Celsius all the year round, and the water is slightly mineralised. The reserve surrounding the caves contains some of the most beautiful unspoiled country in the state. But bring your own food and drink as none is available in the area.

town, marks the spot the explorer used as a base for many of his expeditions. Yarn Market, Bank St, open daily. Spinning and weaving demonstrations. Annual sheep-dog trials held in March. **Accommodation:** 2 hotels, 1 motel, 1 caravan/camping park.
Map ref. 98 E4

Moree   Population 10 455.
Situated on the Mehi River, this town has suffered serious damage from flooding several times. It is best-known for its artesian bore baths, said to relieve arthritis and rheumatism. There is also a heated Olympic swimming pool. **Of interest:** Mary Brand historic cemetery. Meteorlogical Station. **In the area:** Pecan nut farm. The Overseas Telecommunications Station, with its huge parabolic dish antenna which relays international telecommunications to and from Australia. Large display of global maps showing positions of satellite stations. **Accommodation:** 6 hotels, 8 motels, 5 caravan/camping parks.
Map ref. 94 H4

Moruya   Population 2003.
Many famous old dairying estates were founded near this town which was once a gateway to the Araluen and Braidwood goldfields. Situated on the Moruya River 322 km from Sydney, it is now a dairying, timber and oyster-farming centre. Granite used in the pylons of the Sydney Harbour Bridge was quarried in the district. **Of interest:** Coomerang House and Bodalla, south of town, home of famous nineteenth-century industrialist and dairy farmer Thomas Sutcliffe Mort. Mort Memorial Church, historic cemetery at Moruya Heads. Nerrigundah, to southwest, former gold-mining town in beautiful setting. Eurobodalla Historic Museum depicts discovery of gold at Mogo and general history of district. Fishing, surfing or any water sports. **Accommodation:** 2 hotels, 4 motels, 4 caravan/camping parks.
Map ref. 100 G8

Moss Vale   Population 4414.
This market town not far from Berrima serves a dairying, meat, stud horse and fruit-growing district. **Of interest:** Throsby Park House, proclaimed for preservation by the National Trust. Built between 1834 and 1837 by the first settler in the district. Morton National Park, an area of bushland with deep gorges, waterfalls and tracks is a haven for experienced bushwalkers. **Accommodation:** 3 hotels, 2 motels, 2 caravan/camping parks.
Map ref. 98 I9, 100 H4

Mudgee   Population 6013.
This attractively laid-out town is the centre of a productive agricultural area, on the Cudgegong River 264 km northwest of Sydney. Wine grapes, fine wool, stud sheep and cattle, and honey are among the local produce. **Of interest:** Many fine buildings in the town centre, including St John's Church of England, built in 1860, St Mary's Roman Catholic Church, the railway station and the town hall. Some of these are floodlit at night. Colonial Museum, in Market St. Cudgegong River Park, 14 km from Mudgee, is on the eastern foreshores of the Burrendong Dam and has excellent fishing and water sports. For information about camping sites telephone park ranger on (063) 73 0378. Glenroch and Mudgee Honey Companies. **In the area:** Many local wineries open for inspection. **Accommodation:** 7 hotels, 6 motels, 3 caravan/camping parks.
Map ref. 98 G3

Mullumbimby   Population 2234.
Situated west of Brunswick Heads in lush sub-tropical country, Mullumbimby is approximately 850 km from Sydney. **Of interest:** Cedar House, Dalley St, is a beautifully restored and furnished old house containing a phonograph collection and vintage vehicles. **In the area:** Nightcap National Park is north of town and the Tuntable Falls are to the south. **Accommodation:** Limited.
Map ref. 95 Q2

Murrurundi   Population 861.
This picturesque town on the New England Highway, set in a lush valley on the Pages River, is overshadowed by the Liverpool Ranges. **Of interest:** Old church containing 1000 pieces of Italian marble. **In the area:** Timor Limestone Caves, 43 km east. The Burning Mountain at Wingen. Chillot's Creek, where the huge diprotodon remains, now in Sydney Museum, were found. **Accommodation:** 2 motels, 1 caravan/camping park.
Map ref. 95 J11

Murwillumbah   Population 7806.
In the centre of a banana and sugar cane growing district near the Queensland border, Murwillumbah is 32 km from the mouth of the Tweed River. **Of interest:** CSR Sugar Mill, Condong, 1.5 km north of Murwillumbah on the Pacific Highway, is open between June and December, in fine weather only. **In the area:** Kookendoon Wildlife Sanctuary at Dungay, 8 km north of the town on the Tomewin Road. Mount Warning National Park, has a safe walking track to the summit (1156 m). **Accommodation:** 4 hotels, 4 motels, 4 caravan/camping parks.
Map ref. 95 Q1

Muswellbrook   Population 8549.
A coal-mining town in the Upper Hunter Valley, also produces fodder crops, stud cattle and horses, sheep and dairy products. **Of interest:** Fellowes Zoo, 4 km west of Muswellbrook on the Wybong Road. Matt Peel's Quarter Horse Stud and Rural Museum, 12 km west of the town. Many of the vineyards in the area have tastings and sales. **Accommodation:** 7 motels, 2 caravan/camping parks.
Map ref. 95 J13, 99 J2

Nambucca Heads   Population 4053.
At the mouth of the Nambucca River, 552 km north of Sydney, this beautifully sited resort is ideal for boating, fishing and swimming. **Of interest:** Breath-taking views from local lookouts, especially Yarrahapinni Lookout, which commands one of the most impressive coastal panoramas in the state. River Cruises on the Nambucca Princess. Orana Minerals Museum and Nambucca Historical Museum. **Accommodation:** 1 hotel, 9 motels, 6 caravan/camping parks.
Map ref. 86 F4, 95 P8

Narooma   Population 2758.
This popular fishing resort at the mouth of the Wagonga River on the Princes Highway, 360 km south of Sydney, is well-known for its mud oysters. **Of interest:** Tuross and other nearby lakes and inlets. Mystery Bay near Lake Corunna, famous for coloured sands and strange rock formations, and other interesting inlets and lakes north and south of the town. **In the area:** Historic village of Tilba 15 km south of Narooma on Princes Highway. Founded in 1894, it is virtually unchanged since 1904 (apart from its cheese factory), with buildings in original nineteenth-century condition. Classified as an 'unusual mountain village' by the National Trust. **Accommodation:** 1 hotel, 15 motels, 4 caravan/camping parks.
Map ref. 100 G9

Narrabri   Population 7290.
This town has two agricultural research stations, a solar observatory and a cosmic ray station nearby. Situated between the spectacular Nandewar Range and the extensive Pilliga scrub country, it has recently become a phenomenally successful cotton-producing centre with more than 50 000 ha under cultivation. A cotton festival is held in late October. **Of interest:** Myall Vale Research station on the Wee Wah Road; the radioheliograph, 24 kilometres west on the Culgoora Road; and the Plant Breeding Institute 9 kilometres north on the Newell Highway. **In the area:** Mt Kaputar National Park, in Nandewar Range east of town, contains more than 27 000 ha of spectacular volcanic blue mountain country. Visitors' centre at Dawsons Spring. **Accommodation:** 3 hotels, 5 motels, 2 caravan/camping parks.
Map ref. 94 H7

Narrandera   Population 5013.
This pastoral and wheat town near the intersection of the Sturt and Newell Highways is 580 km south-west of Sydney, at the gateway of the Murrumbidgee Irrigation Area. **Of interest:** Lake Talbot swimming pool complex in bushland sanctuary. Water-skiing, fishing, sailing in the lake. Narrandera Park and Miniature Zoo. MIA Tourist Information Centre, East St. **In the area:** Koala Regeneration Centre, 3 km from town. Inland Fisheries Research Station, 6 km south-east of town. NSW Forestry Commission Nursery, near Lake Talbot swimming pool. Berembed Weir, 40 km from town. **Accommodation:** 2 hotels, 5 motels, 1 caravan/camping park.
Map ref. 97 O9

Narromine   Population 2994.
On the Macquarie River, 457 km from Sydney, is the centre of a first-class citrus fruit growing district. **Of interest:** Citrus Packers Co-Op. **Accommodation:** 1 motel, 1 caravan/camping park.
Map ref. 94 D13, 98 D1

Canberra, The Nation's Capital

Canberra, Australia's modern capital city, was built on an undulating plain in an amphitheatre of the Australian Alps, 300 kilometres south-west of Sydney. The Molonglo River, a tributary of the Murrumbidgee, runs through the city and was dammed to create Lake Burley Griffin around which Canberra has been developed. The city is within the Australian Capital Territory, an area of plains, hills and mountains.

It is one of the world's best-known fully-planned cities and over the last 60 years has become an increasing source of pride and interest for Australians and for overseas visitors. Its impressive public buildings, its areas of parkland and bush reserves, its leafy suburbs and broad tree-lined streets have resulted from brilliant planning by its architect, Walter Burley Griffin, and from care and pride taken in its development over the years. Its architecture and its atmosphere are unique and stimulating in that there is so little that is more than fifty years old. Because of this the city has something of the air of being too contrived and self-conscious, but it contains so much that will educate, absorb and stimulate the visitor that this somewhat sterile quality can be soon forgotten.

The land on which the city is sited was first discovered in 1820 by a party of explorers led by Charles Throsby Smith. The area became known as Limestone Plains and was destined for settlement as grazing property. The first white settler, Joshua Moore, took up a thousand acres of land on the Murrumbidgee River in 1824 and named his

BELOW: *Canberra, model city, national capital and an academic and diplomatic centre. Only 70 years ago this was open farming and grazing land.*

ABOVE: *The carillon on Aspen Island, a gift to Canberra from the British Government, marking the city's half century.*

Australian Capital Territory

ABOVE: *A view of Canberra illustrating Walter Burley Griffin's meticulous planning for the national capital.*

ABOVE: *The High Court of Australia. The first sitting of the High Court was in June 1980. The High Court is open for public inspection 10.00 am to 4.00 pm most days of the year.*

property Canberry, an Aboriginal word meaning 'meeting place'. A year later, Robert Campbell, a wealthy Sydney merchant, took up 4000 acres of land which formed the first part of the Duntroon estate.

When the land on which the city is now built was acquired by the Commonwealth Government in 1911, it contained only two small villages. The site for a national capital had been decided only after prolonged wrangling between state and federal authorities.

Construction of the first public buildings started in 1913, and in 1914 a rail service was opened between Sydney and the new capital. The Depression and World War 2 slowed down building construction, but the rate of development has been quite spectacular since the mid-1950s and the population is now almost 250 000.

The present Parliament House, a low white building, was completed in 1927. Parliament House, a number of government department buildings and hostels for public servants were among the first buildings in the national capital. They are now dwarfed by the grand buildings of later development which have turned Canberra into a gleaming showplace.

The new Parliament House, being constructed on Capital Hill above and behind its predecessor, is due to open for Australia's bicentenary in 1988. Alongside the building site is the Exhibition Centre with displays including construction photographs, a large model of the new building and architect's drawings. The centre is open daily from 9 am to 6 pm except Christmas Day and Good Friday.

The city took on a new character in 1964 when Lake Burley Griffin was created. The shoreline totals 35 kilometres and the lake has become popular for rowing, sailing and fishing.

In recent years Canberra has spread outwards into the plains, with satellite towns at Belconnen, Woden, Tuggeranong and Weston Creek, but the focus still remains on the city centre and the modern architectural development around Lake Burley Griffin.

Black Mountain, close to the city centre and the shore of the lake, is topped by a telecommunications tower. Visitors can go up to public viewing galleries and a revolving restaurant. On the lower slopes of Black Mountain are Canberra's famous Botanic Gardens. They follow Walter Burley Griffin's original plan for a garden devoted to plants and trees native to Australia. The superbly laid out gardens, with arrowed walks which allow for varying degrees of stamina, take visitors through areas of foliage indigenous to various Australian regions. A highlight is the rainforest area, where a misting system has been installed to create simulated rainforest conditions.

The Australian War Memorial houses a huge collection of relics and paintings from all theatres of war. Its cloisters, pool of reflection, hall of memory and many galleries of war relics provide an

ABOVE: *Canberra's Botanic Gardens, on the lower slopes of Black Mountain.*

ABOVE RIGHT: *In autumn Canberra's beautifully treed areas take on breathtaking colours.*

unforgettable experience. Near Parliament House is the National Library of Australia which contains a fascinating historic collection and an interesting exhibition area. On Lake Burley Griffin are the Carillon, a three-column bell tower which was a gift from the British Government to mark Canberra's Jubilee, the Captain Cook Memorial, a towering water jet, and Canberra Planning Display at Regatta Point which has a pavilion with exhibits showing Canberra's development.

Diplomatic missions bring an interesting international flavour to the city's architecture. It is well worth driving around the suburbs of Red Hill, Forrest and Yarralumla to view the various embassy buildings there. The Royal Australian Mint has plate glass windows in its visitors' gallery giving excellent views of the money-making process. The Australian National Gallery, the High Court of Australia, the Australian National University and the Law Courts are all places of absorbing interest to the visitor.

Canberra has many attractions. Cockington Green is a quaint miniature English village. Tourist information is available at the Canberra Tourist Bureau, Northbourne Avenue, Canberra City, or at the Visitors Information Centre, Northbourne Avenue, Dickson, on the main road from Goulburn. Driving in Canberra can be confusing; it is wise to study a map before beginning to tour the city.

RIGHT: *Canberra's Botanic Gardens, exhibit many native Australian plants.*

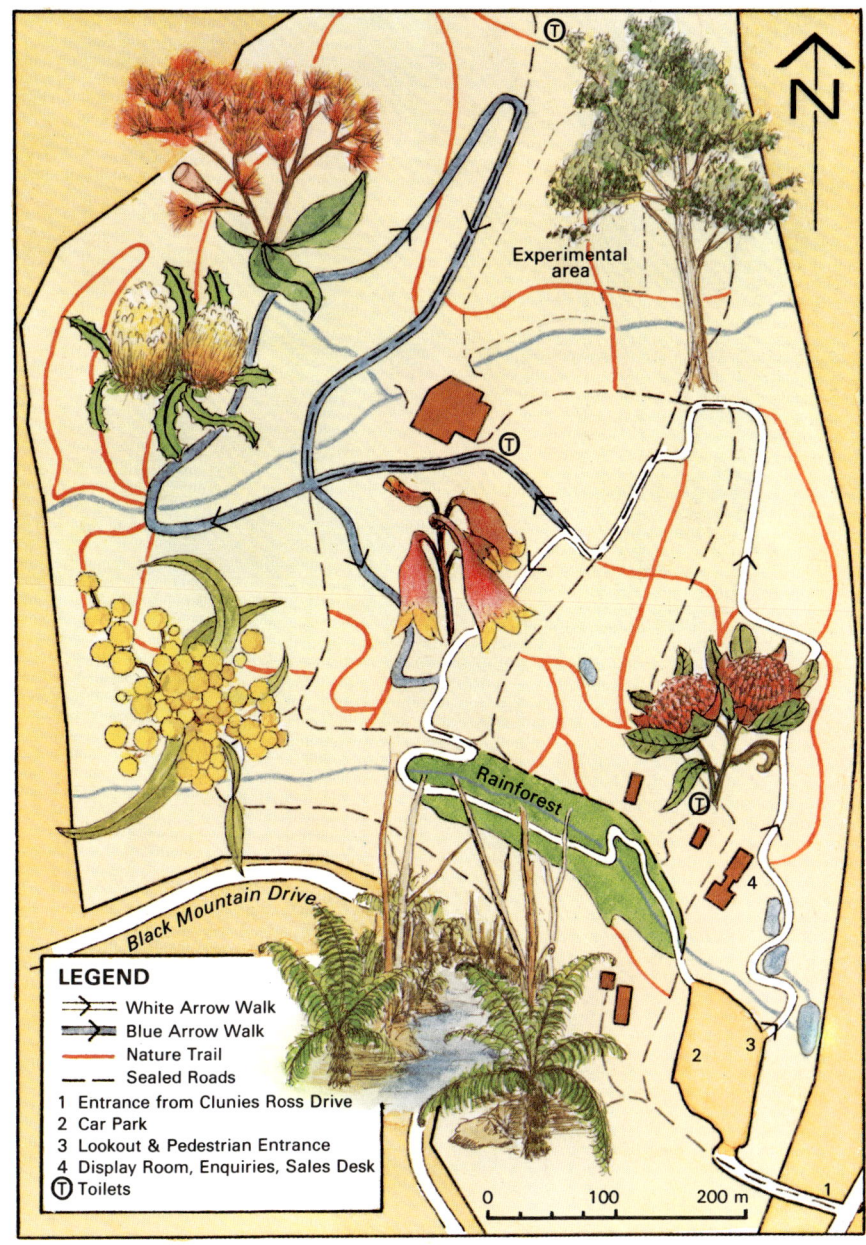

LEGEND
- White Arrow Walk
- Blue Arrow Walk
- Nature Trail
- Sealed Roads
1. Entrance from Clunies Ross Drive
2. Car Park
3. Lookout & Pedestrian Entrance
4. Display Room, Enquiries, Sales Desk
- T Toilets

Australian Capital Territory

ABOVE: *The Australian National Gallery which houses the National Collection of Art.*

ABOVE RIGHT: *Government House, Yarralumla.*

ABOVE: *Academy of Science, Canberra. Around the base of its much-photographed copper coloured dome is a water-filled moat.*

Canberra Population 219 331

As well as being Australia's capital, Canberra is a model city. Its unique concentric circular streets, planted with more than four million trees and shrubs, are set graciously on the shores of the artificial Lake Burley Griffin. Many embassies and consular buildings follow the style of their own national architecture, adding an international flavour to the city. This is reinforced by the wide range of cosmopolitan restaurants. The superb Australian War Memorial is Canberra's top tourist attraction. When Parliament is in session you can watch proceedings from the visitors' gallery. Half-hourly tours are conducted through Parliament House. Visit the new Parliament House site. You can see money being made — literally — at the Royal Australian Mint; or visit the Australian National Gallery, with its magnificent collection, the National Library or the High Court of Australia. The city's parks include the Botanical Gardens and the Tidbinbilla Nature Reserve, which has native animals. Frequent cruises operate on the lake. A wide range of accommodation — from international star-class hotels to motels — can be arranged at the Canberra Tourist Bureau, Northbourne Ave, Canberra City. **Accommodation:** 19 hotels, 33 motels, 1 caravan park, 3 caravan/camping parks.
Map ref. 100 D6, 105

Jervis Bay

This fine natural port has never been developed commercially. It was the site of the Royal Australian Navy Training College, established in 1915. In that year its jurisdiction was transferred from NSW to the ACT, to give the Federal Capital sea access. Fifteen years later, the Naval College was transferred to Flinders in Victoria. then in 1958 the Navy returned to Jervis Bay. **Of interest:** Several pleasant holiday resorts, ideal for swimming, fishing, boating and bushwalking.
Map ref. 99 J10

LEFT: *Australian War Memorial. This Byzantine structure honours Australia's service men and women.*

Nelson Bay Population 7930.
This beautiful bay is the main anchorage of Port Stephens, about 60 km north of Newcastle. **Of interest:** Excellent fishing. Cruises leave on Tuesday, Wednesday and Thursday mornings. Gemstone House, Shoal Bay Road. **In the area:** Abundant native flora and fauna. Golf course. **Accommodation:** 1 hotel, 5 motels.
Map ref. 99 M3

Newcastle Population 258 956.
Newcastle is the sixth largest city of Australia, at the mouth of the Hunter River, 167 km north of Sydney. Massive industrial, commercial and transportation complex, and one of the country's most important centres for the manufacture of steel and steel products. Its busy port is the clearing point for the coal production of the northern NSW coalfields and other exports. For nearly a century it was mainly a coal-mining town, until the BHP steelworks opened in 1915. Set in attractive country, Newcastle has all the facilities of a modern city. **Of interest:** Many surf beaches, nine of which have surf patrols over summer. Blackbutt Reserve at New Lambton Heights, is about 166 ha of natural bushland with kangaroos, koalas and native birds. Civic centre and park, with several buildings of architectural note and public interest nearby, including Newcastle Region Art Gallery and City Hall. BHP Steelworks at Port Waratah. Newcastle Maritime and Military Museums, Fort Scratchley. Newcastle local history museum. King Edward Park, overlooking the ocean at Newcastle South, has sweeping lawns and fine views and is a popular picnic spot. A wide variety of excursions into the Hunter Valley for wine tasting can be experienced. **Accommodation:** 27 hotels, 30 motels, 13 caravan/camping parks.
Map ref. 82 I6, 83 I5, 99 L4

Nowra-Bomaderry Pop. 17 885.
Rapidly becoming a popular tourist centre, Nowra is the principal town of the Shoalhaven River district. Bomaderry is directly opposite on the northern side of the river. **Of interest:** The Shoalhaven River is excellent for fishing, water-skiing, canoeing and sailing. Several beautiful beaches within a 30 km radius. Hanging Rock, near town, for fine views. Riverside Animal Park displays native fauna and peacocks in a rainforest setting. **In the area:** Kangaroo Valley has many interesting old buildings including The Friendly Inn (classified by the National Trust) and the pioneer farm museum, a reconstruction of a typical dairy farm of the 1880s. Visitors can view the HMAS *Albatross* Naval Air Station daily from 10 am to 4 pm. Built during World War 2, it is Australia's only RAN air station. Two hangers are converted to a navy museum. Fitzroy Falls. **Accommodation:** Nowra, 9 motels. Bomaderry, 1 hotel, 1 motel, 1 caravan/camping park.
Map ref. 91 M12, 98 I10, 100 H5

Nyngan Population 2485.
The centre of a wool-growing district on the Bogan River, 603 km north-west of Sydney, with an early history of hostility with Aborigines. **Of interest:** The grave of the botanist with Major Mitchell's party, who was speared by Aborigines in 1835, is on private property. (Inspection by arrangement with manager Mr Ian Shaw: 88-3165.) **In the area:** Bird sanctuary in the Macquarie Marshes, 64 km to the north. **Accommodation:** 5 hotels, 2 motels, 2 caravan/camping parks.
Map ref. 93 P11, 94 A11

Orange Population 27 625.
A prosperous old city set in rich red volcanic soil, famous for its fruit. Orange is situated 264 km from Sydney on the slopes of Mt Canobolas. The area also produces fat lambs, cattle, pigs and fodder crops. An obelisk marks the birthplace of the city's most famous citizen, poet A.B. (Banjo) Paterson. One of his best-known poems, 'Clancy of the Overflow', is engraved upon it. **Of interest:** Campbell's Corner, 8 km south of town on the Pinnacle Road, is an attractive roadside picnic and barbecue spot with many European trees. Cook Park has a begonia conservatory (begonias flower from February to May), European trees, duck ponds, a fernery and a picnic area. There is a BMX bike park near Ridley Oval and also one at Glenroi. Bikes can be hired in Orange. The Historical Museum in the Cultural Centre, Sale St, displays mining relics of Ophir and Lucknow and a 300-years-old Aboriginal carved tree. Orange Civic Centre, in Byng St. This $5-million complex comprises a theatre, art gallery, exhibition rooms, bar and restaurant. The city's original art exhibition is also housed in the Civic Centre. **In the area:** The Agriculture Research Centre, 5 km from the city centre, was completed in 1980. Field days are held for farmers to inspect new developments. 'Once Upon a Time Land' at Nashdale, on the western slopes of Mt Canobolas, is a good spot to entertain young children. It has recreations of fairy-tale and nursery rhyme characters, merry-go-round and picnic area. Ophir goldfields, 27 km north of Orange, were the site of first discovery of payable gold in Australia in 1851. Still a fossicking centre, it is now also a flora and fauna reserve, with picnic area, and walking trails to historic gold tunnels. Apple stop at Lucknow Village, 10 km east of Orange, open daily. Toll Bar Gem Gallery, 1 km east of Orange, has a mineral and fossil collection. Golden Memories Museum, Millthorpe 22 km from Orange displays over 5000 exhibits, including museum, grandma's kitchen, a blacksmith's shop and an arts and craft centre. Lake Canobolas Park, 8 km south-west of town via the Cargo Road, is a lovely lake used for recreation. A deer park, children's play equipment and barbecue area nearby, trout fishing and pedal boats in season, camping area with hot showers. Mt Canobolas Park, 14 km south-west of Orange. A detailed plan of the park showing walking trails is available from Orange Visitors' Centre, Civic Gardens, Byne St. It is 1500 ha of bird and animal sanctuary. **Accommodation:** 5 hotels, 9 motels, 2 caravan/camping parks.
Map ref. 98 F5, 101

Parkes Population 9047.
This developing country centre, 364 km west of Sydney on the Newell Highway, has a wide variety of tourist attractions. It is often referred to as Gateway to the stars. Parkes was first settled in 1862 when reef gold was discovered and it is now the commercial and industrial centre of an important agricultural area. Motor Museum and Craft Corner displays vintage and veteran vehicles, as well as local arts and crafts. Pioneer Park Museum, in Pioneer St, a pioneer school and church, and early farming machinery and transport. Kelly Reserve (the Tourist Centre location), on the northern outskirts of town, is a lovely bush setting for picnics. Gas barbecues are available. There are imposing views from the Shrine of Remembrance at the eastern end of Bushman St. **In the area:** Mugincoble Wheat Sub-Terminal, 8 km south-east of Parkes. Radio Telescope, 23 km north of the town, open daily, has a visitors' centre with many educational aids to explain the use of the giant saucer-shaped telescope. **Accommodation:** 8 hotels, 8 motels, 5 caravan/camping parks.
Map ref. 98 D4

Parramatta Population 130 935.
Parramatta has merged into the suburbs of Sydney but once it was regarded as the 'interior' of the colony. It became the second settlement in Australia when it was chosen as the farming area for the infant colony at Sydney Cove in 1788. Many unique historic buildings remain, including Old Government House and Elizabeth Farm House, the latter built in 1793 by John Macarthur, and believed to be the oldest farmhouse in Australia. **Accommodation:** 1 hotel, 2 motels.
Map ref. 70 C13, 72 C2, 99 J6, 100 I1

Penrith Population 77 727.
This historic town on the Great Western Highway, 55 km from Sydney, has almost been absorbed by the city. After the opening of the Blue Mountains road in 1815 a court-house and a small gaol were built here. Today it makes a pleasant day trip from Sydney, which can be combined with a visit to the lion park at nearby Warragamba Dam or to Australia's Wonderland at Eastern Creek. **Accommodation:** 1 hotel, 3 motels.
Map ref. 74 B3, 77 J7, 99 J6, 100 I1

Picton Population 1817.
Picton, named after Sir Thomas Picton, hero of Waterloo, is 80 km south-west of Sydney on the Hume Highway. The old buildings and quiet hills of this small town seem to echo the past. **Of interest:** The old railway viaduct over Stonequarry Creek, the Tollkeepers Cottage and St Mark's Church of England. Jarvisfield, the old family home of pioneer landowners, is now the clubhouse of the Antill Park Golf Club. **In the area:** Wirrimbirra Sanctuary, on the Hume Highway about 13 km south of Picton, is a sanctuary for native flora and fauna. It comprises a large area of bushland and has cabins to accommodate overnight visitors. **Accommodation:** 1 hotel.
Map ref. 91 L1, 98 I7, 100 H2

Port Stephens

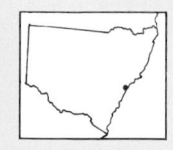

The white volcanic sand and aquamarine waters of the beaches of **Port Stephens** (99 N3) have a distinctly tropical look, and the annual average temperature is within about four degrees Celsius of that of the Gold Coast. This large deepwater port, less than an hour's drive from Newcastle, is one of the most unspoiled and attractive seaside holiday areas on the NSW coast. Two-and-a-half times the size of Sydney harbour and almost enclosed by two volcanic headlands, the circular harbour is fringed by sheltered white sandy beaches backed by stretches of natural bushland. In spring, wild flowers grow in profusion.

The deep, calm waters of the harbour are ideal for boating and offer excellent fishing. A wide range of boats — from aquascooters and catamarans to sailing and power boats — can be hired. Big-game fishing waters are within reach outside the harbour but local fishing clubs warn against leaving the heads unless you are an experienced sailor with a two-motor boat. The best way to reach these waters is aboard the charter boats *Waranah*, *Jamala* and *Wendy Gai*, which are licensed to take fishermen and sightseers outside the heads. Early in the afternoon you can watch the local fishing fleet coming into **Nelson Bay**, the main anchorage of the port.

Restaurants in the area — not surprisingly — offer fresh seafood as a speciality. At Salamander Bay, you can sample a superb lobster supreme, washed down by a fine Hunter Valley wine. What more could you ask? For dedicated oyster-lovers, a trip to Moffat's Oyster Barn, Swan Bay, is a must. As well as seeing oysters under cultivation and learning about their four-year life cycle, you can enjoy a delicious meal of oysters. (Bookings, (049) 97 5433.) If you go by boat, make sure you don't run aground on an oyster lease!

You can hire almost anything in the area: bicycles — how about a tandem? — beach umbrellas, fishing tackle, horses; there are good golf courses, putt putt golf, bowling greens and all the usual sporting facilities.

For-surfing, you can visit the spectacular ocean beaches which stretch in both directions outside the harbour. Within about six kilometres are Zenith, Wreck and Box Beaches, Fingal Bay and the strangely-named Fly Roads.

Other local attractions include a shell museum, a gemstone house, an aquarium and art gallery. A lion park at Raymond Terrace caters for children, with an Indian village, Fort Courage, flying foxes and a swing bridge, as well as a wide variety of wildlife including, of course, lions. Barbecue areas are scattered throughout the park. Good accommodation, including hotels, motels and modern holiday flats, is available throughout the area and there are eight caravan and camping parks. The main resorts, apart from Nelson Bay, are **Shoal Bay**, **Soldiers' Point** and **Lemon Tree Passage** on the south shore; **Tea Gardens** and **Karuah** on the north. The Tourist Information Centre in Stockton Road, Nelson Bay, will give more detailed information about the area, including nearby attractions such as the Myall Lakes and the Hunter Valley.

Port Macquarie Population 19 572.
Founded as a convict settlement in 1821, and one of the oldest towns in the state, Port Macquarie is now a major holiday resort, situated at the mouth of the Hastings River, 423 km north of Sydney. **Of interest:** St Thomas's, convict-built church which was designed by the famous convict architect T. Owen. Historic cemetery. The Hastings Historical Museum, Clarence St, has convict and pioneer relics. Sea Acres Sanctuary, Pacific Drive, 5 km south of town, is an area of more than 30 ha of rainforest, flora and fauna. Port Macquarie Observatory, from where the moon, planets and stars can be observed. Children will enjoy the Fantasy Glades, a re-creation of the story of Snow White, with birds, animals, bushwalks, children's playground and kiosk. Also the King Neptune Marine Park, at the mouth of the Hastings River, which has performing seals and dolphins, sharks, turtles and fairy penguins. Peppermint park has slides, skateboard areas and roller skating. River cruises available daily. **In the area:** Exceptionally good fishing and all water sports. **Accommodation:** 2 hotels, 40 motels, 18 caravan/camping parks.
Map ref. 85 G5, 87 P2, 95 P11

Queanbeyan Population 19 383.
Adjoining Canberra, Queanbeyan has a special relationship with the Australian capital. First recorded as a holding under the name of Queen Bean, it was proclaimed a town under the present spelling in 1838. **Of interest:** History museum. Jerrabomberra Hill lookout, 6 km east of town, for city views, and Bungendore Hill lookout, 6 km to the north-east, for pleasant rural views. **Accommodation:** 4 hotels, 12 motels, 2 caravan/camping parks.
Map ref. 98 F11, 100 E6, 112 G6

Quirindi Population 2851.
Appropriately named after an Aboriginal word meaning 'nest in the hills' this town in the Liverpool Ranges was proclaimed in 1856. One of the first towns in Australia to organise the game of polo, it still holds an annual polo carnival in the first week of August. **Accommodation:** 5 hotels, 2 motels, 1 caravan/camping park.
Map ref. 95 J11

Raymond Terrace Pop. 7548.
Several historic buildings remain in this town which was an important wool-shipping centre in the 1840s. **Of interest:** Buildings include the court-house, built in 1838 and still in use; 'Irrawang', built in 1830 as the homestead of pioneer James King; the Church of England and rectory, built of hand-hewn sandstone in the 1830s. Drive-through lion safari and Adventure Island, Six Mile Road, with children's playground, flying foxes, Indian village, Fort Courage and an old fire-engine. Tomago sandbeds. 26 800 ha of water-bearing sands replenished entirely by rainfall and now being developed as a major source of Newcastle's water supply. **Accommodation:** 1 hotel, 2 motels, 2 caravan/camping parks.
Map ref. 83 H3, 99 L3

Richmond Population 15 490.
Sister town to Windsor, 8 km away. Richmond was proclaimed a town in 1810. **Of interest:** Hobartville, Castlereagh Road. Richmond Estate Winery, North Richmond with premium quality wines grown on the estate. Toxana, Windsor Street, building 1841. St Peter's Church, Windsor St (1841) and graveyard with many notable pioneers including road-builder William Cox and Australia's convict chronicler Margaret Catchpole. RAAF Station, Windsor-Richmond Road, is the oldest Air Force establishment in Australia, having been used for civilian flying as early as 1915. The Hawkesbury Agricultural College, is south of Richmond. The foundation stone of this important college was laid in 1895. Tourist Information Centre, Thompson Square, Windsor. **Accommodation:** 1 hotel, 2 motels.
Map ref. 77 J5, 99 J6, 100 I 1

Rylstone Population 646.
Aboriginal hand paintings on a sandstone rock overhang can be seen just out of Rylstone, which is west of the Great Dividing Range on the Cudgegong River, north-east of Bathurst. Visitors to the rock paintings should check with the local shire council before setting out. **Of interest:** Fern Tree Gully, 16 km north of town on the Bylong Road. Magnificent tree ferns and other native flora. Glen Davis, 56 km south-east of Rylstone on Capertee River, situated deep in the Capertee Valley, surrounded by sheer cliff faces. Many camping spots and fishing areas on the upper reaches of the Capertee River. **Accommodation:** 1 hotel, 1 caravan/camping park.
Map ref. 98 H3

Sawtell Population 5963.
This peaceful family holiday resort, 8 km south of Coffs Harbour, has safe beaches and tidal creeks for fishing, swimming and surfing. There are enchanting walks and drives in the surrounding bush and mountains, including the unspoiled Sawtell Reserve. **Of interest:** Lazy Daisy Caravan Ranch, Bonville, is a 'Wild West' town, with swimming pool, miniature train, mini golf, paddle boats, roller skating, farmyard animals and, believe it or not, a dancing camel. There are also barbecue facilities. **Accommodation:** 1 hotel, 2 motels, 2 caravan/camping parks.
Map ref. 86 B4, 95 P7

Scone Population 3950.
This pleasant town set in beautiful country on the New England Highway north of Sydney is an important stock-selling centre. The area is noted for its thoroughbred horse, cattle and sheep studs. **Of interest:** Scone Historical Society Museum. Scone mare and foal sculpture. **In the area:** Burning Mountain at Wingen, a deep coal seam which has been smouldering for at least one thousand years. Lighting of fires prohibited. Glenbawn Dam, ideal for all water sports and has picnic and barbecue facilities. State Forest, 80 km to the north-east (road sometimes closed by snow), for scenic drives and walks. **Accommodation:** 1 hotel, 4 motels, 1 caravan park, 1 caravan/camping park.
Map ref. 95 J12, 99 J1

Shellharbour Population 1754.
This attractive holiday resort south of Lake Illawarra is one of the oldest towns in the area. It was a thriving port in the 1830s but its importance declined after the opening of the south coast railway. Today it is a residential and seaside holiday town for the people of Wollongong. **Of interest:** Fine beaches for fishing, surfing and boating on Windang Peninsula. **In the area:** Jamberoo Falls. **Accommodation:** 1 hotel, 1 motel, 1 caravan/camping park.
Map ref. 91 P7, 99 J9, 100 I 4

Singleton Population 9572.
This important coal-mining town on the upper Hunter River is one of the oldest in NSW, having been proclaimed a town in 1836. Today it is the market and manufacturing centre for a dairy, meat, wine grapes and vegetable growing district. **Of interest:** Historic museum at Burdekin Park, housed in the 1841-built gaol. Exhibits include a convict's conditional pardon, an original government rum jar, early tools and clothes, a convict's cell in original condition. **In the area:** Lake Liddell, 26 km to the north-west, is good for water sports and picnics. The adjacent Liddell Power Station can be inspected by arrangement. **Accommodation:** 1 hotel 3 motels, 1 caravan/camping park.
Map ref. 83 A1, 99 K3

The Newell

With its excellent bitumen surface and long, straight stretches, the Newell Highway provides fast and easy driving right across NSW. Travel between Melbourne and Brisbane is up to six hours quicker by this than by any other route. The driving time you save could be put to good use enjoying the many interesting towns and attractions along the way.

From the Murray River town of **Tocumwal** to the Queensland border town of **Goondiwindi**, the highway runs through a wide range of scenery and is well served with motels, roadside cafés and service stations.

In **Narrandera** there is an excellent caravan park with on-site cabins and vans on the edge of Lake Talbot — a popular water sports centre. Beyond **West Wyalong** to the north is Lake Cowal which is the largest natural lake in NSW and an important bird sanctuary; out of **Forbes**, further north is a major tourist attraction — the Lachlan Vintage Village which is a re-creation of a nineteenth-century gold-mining town.

There's plenty to see in **Parkes**, including a vintage car museum and the Henry Parkes Museum; **Dubbo** boasts what is probably the most popular tourist attraction on the Newell — the superb Western Plains Zoo, claimed to be the best open range wildlife park in Australia. The old Dubbo gaol, gallows and museum are also worth seeing.

From Dubbo the highway passes through the spectacular volcanic Warrumbungle National Park, which is ideal for bushwalking. If you've got children aboard, don't miss the award-winning fantasy park, 'Miniland', with its life-size prehistoric animals, just west of **Coonabarabran**. Once you get beyond the Warrumbungle Ranges the scenery changes dramatically to the sombre Pillaga scrub country, and the New England town of **Moree**, which is not far from the Queensland border, is famed for its artesian baths.

Stroud Population 522.
This small country town, 75 km north of Newcastle, is worth visiting for its many historic buildings. The finest is the convict-built Anglican Church of St John, built in 1833 of local clay bricks. It has beautiful stained glass windows and cedar furnishings. Other interesting buildings include the rectory of St John's (1836), Stroud House (1832), Parish House (1837), the court-house and the post office. An underground silo (one of eight built in 1841) at Silo Hill Reserve. For further information about historic buildings contact Great Lakes Shire Council, Forster. **Accommodation:** Limited.
Map ref. 99 M2

Swansea, Belmont and Toronto Population 16 973.
These are the main resorts on Lake Macquarie, the largest seaboard lake in Australia. The northern shores are heavily developed but the lake is still pleasant for swimming, yachting and fishing. **Of interest:** *MV Wangi Queen*, a double-decker ferry, cruises the northern lake at weekends, leaving from Toronto Wharf. Natchez floating restaurant, sails daily from Belmont south foreshore. Dobell House, 47 Dobell Drive, Wangi Wangi. Retained as it was when the artist William Dobell lived there, with exhibition of paintings. **Accommodation:** Swansea, 4 motels, 3 caravan/camping parks. Belmont, 1 hotel, 6 motels, 1 caravan park, 1 caravan/camping park. Toronto, 1 hotel, 2 motels, 1 caravan/camping park.
Map ref. 83 G8, 99 L4

Tamworth Population 29 656.
This progressive, prosperous city at the foot of the Wentworth Mounds in the rich Peel Valley serves as the country music capital of Australia. Many thousands of fans flock here for the Australasian country music awards which have been held here each Australia Day weekend since 1973. The proceedings are broadcast live to more than 30 radio stations. Tamworth, with its attractive public buildings and beautiful parks and gardens, has much to offer the tourist. It is the headquarters for East-West Airlines, which operates a fleet of aircraft to 30 centres in NSW, Queensland, Hobart and Alice Springs and is the commercial and industrial centre of a rich, mixed farming district. **Of interest:** Country music hands of fame cornerstone at CWA Park has hand imprints of most Australian country stars, including Tex Morton, Slim Dusty and Smokey Dawson. Bronze roll of renown plaques for country music stars at Radio Centre, Calala. Calala Cottage, classified by the National Trust has been restored by Tamworth Historical Society, open Tues-Sun 2-4 pm. Minamucca House, Victorian mansion. Old Mill Cottage, on site of the town's first flour mill, now houses arts and crafts. City Art Gallery has works of Hans Heysen, Will Ashton and Turner on show. Wewsal Pottery. Oxley Gallery. Dunst Pottery Studio. Endeavour Drive and Oxley Park is a wildlife sanctuary, offering bushwalks, barbecues and picnic facilities. Oxley Lookout offers panoramic city views and barbecue area. There is a visitor's centre for further tourist information. **In the area:** The historic gold-mining township of Nundle, 63 km south-east of town, has a picturesque old court-house. It is one of the best areas in the state for crystals and fossicking for precious stones is one of the main attractions of the area. **Accommodation:** 6 hotels, 19 motels, 3 caravan/camping parks.
Map ref. 88, 95 K9

Taree Population 14 696.
Attractively laid-out, Taree serves as the manufacturing and commercial centre of the Manning River district, on the Pacific Highway 340 km north of Sydney. **In the area:** There is easy access by car to the top of Ellenborough Falls, on the Bulga Plateau 50 km north of Taree. Crowdy Bay National Park, 40 km east of Taree, is a coastal stretch with beautiful wild flowers in spring and is pleasant for fishing, swimming, bushwalking. Bundary Riding School, on Pacific Highway at Kooraingat, offers farm and forest rides, barbecue and picnic area. There are fine surfing beaches on the coast about 16 km away and upland streams liberally stocked with rainbow and brown trout add to the attractions of this area. **Accommodation:** 4 hotels, 20 motels, 2 caravan/camping parks.
Map ref. 95 N12, 99 N1

Temora Population 4350.
An industrial centre for the rich wheat district of northern and western Riverina, which also produces oats, barley, fat lambs, pigs and cattle. **Of interest:** Rock and Mineral Museum. Temora Rural Museum with working displays including a printing press and farm machinery. Barbecue facilities. **Accommodation:** 2 hotels, 3 motels, 1 caravan/camping park.
Map ref. 97 Q8, 98 B8

Tenterfield Population 3402.
This market town serves a prosperous farming district which produces high quality apples, livestock, fat lambs and tobacco. The area is noted for its contrasting scenery. **Of interest:** Bald Rock National Park, over 2000 ha of natural bushland. Bald Rock itself, a large granite monolith, can be climbed on its north-east side and gives panoramic views of Qld and NSW from its summit. Spectacular Boonoo Boonoo Falls, 32 km north, have a rough access road but are worth visiting. Centenary Cottage, built in 1871, has many items of local historical interest on display. Hillview Doll Museum exhibits more than 1000 dolls including locally-made 'apple-head' dolls. Historic Stannum, an ornate Victorian house (privately owned, not open to the public) was built in 1888. Among its features are an Italian marble fireplace and cedar corkscrew staircase. Sir Henry Parkes Memorial School of Arts, displays of relics relating to Sir Henry Parkes who made his famous Federation speech in this building in 1889. Thunderbolt's Hideout, 11 km from town, is where notorious bushranger Captain Thunderbolt stabled his horse and camped in a small cave. **Accommodation:** 5 hotels, 5 motels, 4 caravan/camping parks.
Map ref. 95 N3

Terrigal-Wamberal Pop. 7453.
Excellent surfing is one of the main attractions of this popular holiday resort on the Central Coast. **Of interest:** Bouddi National Park to the south, for bushwalking, camping, fishing and swimming. **Accommodation:** 1 hotel, 3 motels, 1 caravan/camping park.
Map ref. 77 R1, 83 F13

The Entrance Population 37 831.
This highly developed resort at the ocean entrance to Tuggerah Lake attracts thousands of campers, tourists and day-trippers from Sydney. All popular sporting facilities and entertainments are available. **Of interest:** The lake is excellent for prawning, and the ocean beaches good for fishing and swimming. Famous Kim's Restaurant and holiday cabins nearby on the safe, unspoilt beach at Toowoon Bay. **Accommodation:** 3 hotels, 10 motels, 1 caravan park, 4 caravan/camping parks.
Map ref. 83 F12, 99 L5

The Rock Population 693.
This small township, 32 km south-west of Wagga Wagga, is noted for its unusual scenery and has an interesting flora and fauna reserve with walking trails through wild flowers and trees to the summit of The Rock (about 365 m). One species of flower, groundsel, is believed to be unique to this area in Australia. **Accommodation:** 1 motel.
Map ref. 97 P11, 98 A11

Port Macquarie

The emphasis is on family fun at this popular coastal resort on the Hastings River — roughly midway between Sydney and the Queensland border.

A marine park with tropical fish, sharks, dolphins and crocodiles, and Fantasy Glades, a miniature fairyland in a bushland setting, are two of its top tourist attractions. Two putt putt golf courses and a riding school (with mini-bikes as well as horses) are also popular with holidaymakers. Dozens of take-away food places and a wide range of restaurants cater for the holiday crowds.

But there is another side to Port Macquarie. It is one of the oldest towns in NSW, originally founded in 1821 and developed as a convict settlement until 1830.

The convict-built St Thomas's Church in Hay Street is a legacy of the town's colourful past, as is the old cemetery in Gordon Street.

Port Macquarie has good surf beaches and is exceptionally good for fishing, particularly when the bream run in winter. A lush prehistoric rainforest sanctuary, just south of the town, shows how the area once looked. Strangler figs, a thousand years old, and a rich variety of bird and animal life are a feature of the 30-hectares reserve.

Tibooburra Population 134.
The name of this former gold town, 337 km north of Broken Hill, comes from an Aboriginal word meaning 'heaps of boulders'. It is surrounded by granite outcrops and used to be known as The Granite. **Of interest:** Many buildings of local stone, including the court-house (1888), the Family Hotel (1888), Braybrook's House (1888) and Tibooburra Hotel (1890). Many nearby gold-fields; more details available from the National Parks and Wildlife Service in the old court-house. Sturt National Park. Semi-desert 188 000 ha area, noted for its wildlife and geological features. Visitors are requested to contact the park ranger. **In the area:** Former gold township of Milparinka to the south. Today the Albert Hotel is the only active concern. Sandstone structures, which were once the court-house, police station, bank and post office, still remain. **Accommodation:** 1 hotel, 1 caravan/camping park.
Map ref. 92 C4, 322 A13, 321 H13

Tingha Population 868.
This small tin-mining town has an outstanding museum. A tin dredge is still operating at Copes Creek. **Of interest:** Smith's mining and national history museum on the banks of Copes Creek has a mineral and gemstone collection from New England area and other parts of Australia together with Aboriginal artefacts, antiques and period clothes. **Accommodation:** 1 hotel, 1 caravan park.
Map ref. 95 K6

Tocumwal Population 1174.
This peaceful Murray River town, on the Newell Highway, is ideal for swimming, fishing and boating. **Of interest:** A huge fibreglass codfish in the town square represents an Aboriginal legend about a giant Murray cod which lived in the nearby blowhole. Picnic area with lawns and sandy river beach, 200 m from the town square. **In the area:** The aerodrome can be inspected from Monday to Saturday. It was the largest RAAF base in Australia during World War 2 and is now popular with gliding enthusiasts. The Rocks, 11 km north-east of the town, is a stone quarry which has been in use for more than 50 years. It is now a popular picnic spot. **Accommodation:** 1 hotel, 4 motels, 2 caravan/camping parks.
Map ref. 97 M12, 167 J2

Toukley Population 6520.
Resort at bottleneck between Budgewoi and Tuggerah Lake. **Of interest:** Excellent prawning and boating on lake. Good fishing, swimming and surfing on ocean beaches. Norah Head lighthouse. Edward Hargraves' cottage in Norahville, (not open to public). **Accommodation:** 1 hotel, 5 motels, 7 caravan/camping parks.
Map ref. 83 G11

Tumbarumba Population 1536.
Bushranger 'Mad Dog' Morgan raided this town and shot a policeman in 1854, in the days when it was a gold-mining town. Situated in the foothills of the Australian Alps, 50 km south-west of Sydney and 440 km north-east of Melbourne, it is the

The Alpine Coast

The southern coast of NSW — from Batemans Bay down to the Victorian border — is a fisherman's paradise. Hemmed in by the Great Dividing Range, it is one of the finest areas for fishing in southern Australia. It is also a haven for anyone who enjoys swimming, surfing or bushwalking in an unspoiled setting.

One of the attractions of this stretch of coast is the variety of country. You'll see superb white surf beaches, and crystal clear blue sea against a back-drop of craggy mountains, gentle hills, lakes, inlets and forests. The coast is dotted with quaint little fishing and holiday resorts, which have a wide range of hotel, motel and holiday flat accommodation, as well as many caravan parks. They are not highly commercialised, although many of them triple their population in the peak summer months. Boats of all kinds can be hired at the major resorts.

Peaceful **Batemans Bay**, at the estuary of the Clyde River, has become very popular with Canberra people since the road linking the Monaro and Princes Highways was updated. **Narooma**, **Montague Island** and **Bermagui** are famous for their big-game fishing. Black marlin, blue fin and hammerhead sharks are the main catch. Narooma also boasts an 18-hole cliff-side golf course where you tee off from the third hole across a narrow canyon.

Bega, to the south, is the unofficial capital of the area and is an important dairying and cheese-making centre. Its proud boast is that you can ski in the Snowies and surf in the Pacific on the same day, as it is about 10 minutes inland from the coast and 90 minutes from the snowfields. Further south is the popular holiday resort of **Merimbula** and its sister village of **Pambula**.

The southernmost town of the region is the quaint old fishing village of **Eden**, and its former rival settlement, **Boydtown**, which is now a ghost town. They are both reminders of the colourful whaling days of the last century.

Fishing is excellent all along the coast. You can catch a wide variety of fish — including rock cod, bream and jewfish — from the beach or net crayfish off the rockier parts of the coast. Prawning is good in the scattered inlets; and trout and perch can be caught in the many short rivers draining from the mountains.

Because of its position, this part of the coast attracts tourists from Victoria and Canberra, as well as from other parts of NSW. The best time to go is in summer and autumn as it can be cold and wet at other times, but you must book well ahead in the peak summer holiday period.

ideal base for day trips to the Snowy Mountains and Mount Selwyn ski slopes. **Of interest:** Magnificent mountain scenery, fishing and bushwalking. **In the area:** Paddy's River Falls, 16 km to the south, has spectacular cascades dropping 60 metres. Tooma historic hotel and store. **Accommodation:** 2 hotels, 1 motel, 2 caravan/camping parks.
Map ref. 97 R12, 100 B7, 168 H2

Tumut Population 5816.
A progressive town on the Snowy Mountains Highway, Tumut is almost equidistant from Sydney (435 km) and Melbourne (495 km). Close to ski resorts and the great dams of the Snowy Mountains Hydro-electric Scheme, which are excellent for water sports, it attracts tourists all the year round. Spectacular mountain scenery, pine forests, distinctive seasons and European trees add to its charm. A festival of the falling leaf is held annually. The huge Snowy Mountain Trout Farm at Blowering Dam is the largest commercial trout farm in Australia. **Of interest:** Tourist Information Centre, for details of inspections of local power stations, pyneboard, marble and millet broom factories. **In the area:** Talbingo Dam and Reservoir, the tallest rock-filled dam in Australia, is set in beautiful steep wooded country and renowned for large trout. Blowering Lake, 10 km south of town, is a major centre for water sports and fishing for rainbow trout, brown trout and perch. Blowering Trout Farm, near the dam, is open to the public. There is excellent fishing on the Tumut River and the Goobarragandra River which is good for white water canoeing. The historic gold rush and skiing town of Kiandra is nearby. Electrically lit Yarrangobilly limestone caves and thermal pool are 60 km from town via the winding Snowy Mountains Highway. **Accommodation:** 5 hotels, 6 motels, 2 caravan/camping parks.
Map ref. 98 D11, 100 B6

Tweed Heads Population 5120.
This tourist resort on Point Danger, astride the NSW/Queensland border, is the twin town of Coolangatta, Queensland. **Of interest:** Twin Towns Service Club. Waterworld has a waterslide, paddle boats and a pin ball parlour. Captain Cook Memorial and laser beam lighthouse. The world's first laser beam lighthouse — switched on in 1971. Nearby, the memorial to Captain Cook has been made from cast-iron ballast believed to have been dumped overboard by Cook in the Great Barrier Reef in 1770 when the *Endeavour* was nearly wrecked. The iron has been remoulded into the shape of the capstan of the *Endeavour*. **In the area:** Terranora Lake, 5 km south-west of Tweed Heads, on the Terranora Road, has pleasant fishing, boating and oyster leasing. There are panoramic coastline views from the surrounding hills. From Razorback Lookout, 3 km from Tweed Heads, there are magnificent views all around the Tweed Valley and the Gold Coast. **Accommodation:** 2 hotels, 10 motels, 7 caravan/camping parks.
Map ref. 95 R1

Ulladulla Population 6016.
Ulladulla, a picturesque fishing town, and nearby Milton are at the northern end of a stretch of beautiful coastal lakes and lagoons with white sand beaches. A colourful blessing of the fleet ceremony is held each Easter. **Of interest:** Bendalong for surfing and swimming. Lakes Conjola, Burrill and Tabourie for swimming, fishing and water-skiing. Mollymook, to the north, for surfing, excellent fishing and golf. Bushwalkers can climb Pigeon House Mountain, a rocky outcrop at the south end of Morton National Park, right to the top. Advised to take drinks. **Accommodation:** 1 hotel, 7 motels, 1 caravan park, 4 caravan/camping parks.
Map ref. 98 I 11, 100 H6

Uralla Population 2090.
'Gentleman' bushranger Captain Thunderbolt was shot dead by a local policeman in 1870, after a furious battle in the swampy country south-east of this New England town. Rich gold discoveries were made in the vicinity in the 1850s. **Of interest:** An interesting fossicking area near the Old Rocky River diggings. Thunderbolt's grave in the Uralla cemetery. 'Gostwyck', one of the oldest properties in the New England area occupies about 5000 ha. **Accommodation:** 2 hotels, 2 motels, 2 caravan/camping parks.
Map ref. 95 L8

Urunga Population 2045.
One of the best fishing spots on the north coast, 32 km south of Coffs Harbour at the mouth of the Bellinger and Kalang Rivers. It is separated from the ocean by a broad lagoon. **Of interest:** Safe river swimming pool for children, with picnic reserve. **Accommodation:** 4 motels, 1 caravan park, 4 caravan/camping parks.
Map ref. 95 P8

Wagga Wagga Population 36 332.
Often referred to simply as 'Wagga', this prosperous city on the Murrumbidgee River, 517 km from Sydney, is a centre of agricultural and soil conservation research and site of many educational and research establishments. **Of interest:** Botanic Gardens and Zoo, Willans Hill. **In the area:** Lake Albert, to the south of Wagga, is excellent for water sports. Murray Cod Hatcheries and Fauna Park. Agricultural Research Institute, 9 km north of Wagga, off the Coolamon Road. Wallacetown Historical Arms Museum, 20 km north of Wagga on Olympic Way. **Accommodation:** 2 hotels, 11 motels, 2 caravan/camping parks.
Map ref. 97 Q10, 98 B10

Walcha Population 1674.
Small town on the Oxley Highway on the eastern slopes of the Great Dividing Range. **Of interest:** Pioneer Cottage. A tiger moth plane, the first to be used for crop-dusting in Australia, is also on display. **In the area:** Apsley Gorge National Park, 20 km east of town, has spectacular two-drop falls. Tia Falls near the southern boundary of park. **Accommodation:** 2 hotels, 2 motels, 1 caravan/camping park.
Map ref. 95 L9

Walgett Population 2157.
The famous 'Light of the World' opal weighing 450 g was found in 1928 at Grawin, not far from this small pastoral town, near the junction of the Namoi and Barwon Rivers. Another rich find in 1970 resulted in a rush of about 200 miners to Glengarry. Walgett is the nearest sizeable town to these opal fields. **Of interest:** Grawin and Glengarry opal fields. Motorists are warned that water is scarce, and a supply should be carried. Drive west of Walgett for 48 km to Cumborah and continue for another 13 km, then turn left off the main road on to a track for 6 km to Grawin. Directions about the track to Glengarry are available at the store. **In the area:** Narran Lake, about 96 km west of Walgett via the Cumborah Road, is one of the largest natural inland lakes in Australia, abundant in animal and bird life. No facilities for private visits, but special tours in light aircraft can be arranged through Walgett Aero Club, c/o Shire Council Chambers, Walgett, NSW 2385. (068) 28 1399. Walgett has a swimming pool and other sporting facilities. **Accommodation:** 2 hotels, 4 motels, 1 caravan/camping park.
Map ref. 93 R6, 94 D6

Warialda Population 1340.
Small town on Gwydir Highway west of Inverell, in a stud farm district. **Of interest:** Private gemstone collection at 'Mt View', where visitors can watch cutting, polishing and setting of stones. Some fossicking is allowed. Large aviary of birds. **Accommodation:** 1 hotel, 1 motel, 1 caravan/camping park.
Map ref. 95 J4

Warren Population 2153.
In a cotton-growing district on the Macquarie River, this Oxley Highway town offers excellent fishing. Cod, yellow-belly, bream and catfish are plentiful. **Accommodation:** 1 motel, 1 caravan/camping park.
Map ref. 93 R11, 94 C11

Wauchope Population 3644.
Nearby Timbertown, a major re-creation of a typical timber town of the 1880s, has put Wauchope on the tourist map. The town itself is the centre of a timber-getting, dairying, beef cattle and mixed farming area on the Oxley Highway, 19 km from the mouth of the Hastings River. **Of interest:** Timbertown, on the fringes of Broken Bago State Forest, 3 km west of Wauchope. (Open 10 am to 5 pm daily.) Attractions include a working bullock team, horse-drawn wagons, a blacksmith, a steam-powered train, and sleeper-cutting demonstrations. A modern exhibition hall with restaurant is at entrance. Hastings Dairy Co-Operative, Randall St, can be inspected promptly at 9.30 am weekdays, to see production of cheese. **In the area:** Fernvale Nursery is well-known for its varieties of native plants, elkhorns, staghorns and orchids. Picnic facilities. Nearby Bellangry State Forest, noted for its magnificent stands of hardwood trees, as well as large areas of brushwood rainforests. **Accommodation:** 2 hotels, 1 motel.
Map ref. 87 Q4, 95 O11

Wee Waa Population 1904.

This small town near the Namoi River serves a first-class cotton and wine grape growing district. Local wines have won over 30 medals at Australia-wide shows, and the district has the highest cotton yield in Australia, with an average of about 5.5 bales per hectare. **Of interest:** Cubbaroo Winery, 45 km to the west, produces prize-winning wines. Tasting room, banquet hall and barbecues. Namoi Cotton Co-Op and Ginnery and Yarramin Gin are open for inspection. Yarrie Lake, 24 km south, is suitable for boating and fishing. **Accommodation:** 2 motels, 1 caravan park.
Map ref. 94 G7

Wellington Population 5280.

Limestone caves are one of the many interesting features of this town at the junction of the Macquarie and Bell Rivers, 362 km north-west of Sydney. **Of interest:** Wellington Caves, 9 km from the town, may be inspected. Clock museum nearby, picnic facilities, kiosk, aviary and caravan park in grounds. Next to the caves is the 18-hole Wellington Golf Club which is open to the public. Historical Museum, situated in a two-storey building (1883), originally a bank. The Phonograph Parlour — a collection of antique sound equipment and records. From Mt Arthur Reserve there are walking trails to Binjang with lookout at the summit. Maps of other walking trails are available from Wellington Visitors' Centre in Cameron Park, an attractive park on the western side of the main street. **In the area:** Wellington wineries: Glenfinlass Wines, 8 km south-west of town beside the Parkes Road, a chateau-style winery specialising in dry red wines. (Open Saturdays only.) Markeita Cellars, 16 km south of town in the village of Neurea, produces red table wines. Burendong Dam: drive across the road built on the wall and continue to the spillway for a really good view. Areas for water-skiing, sailing, power-boat and fishing enthusiasts nearby. Rangers in these areas supervise activities and there are facilities for day and overnight visitors. **Accommodation:** 7 hotels, 3 motels, 2 caravan/camping parks.
Map ref. 98 F2

Wentworth Population 1130.

One of the famous Murray River paddle steamers, *Ruby*, is a reminder of an earlier era in this small town 1056 km west-south-west of Sydney, near the junction of the Murray and Darling Rivers. Today *Ruby* rests in Fotherby Park, near the Darling River bridge. Wentworth is the centre of three long-established irrigation settlements, Pomana, Curlwaa and Coomealla, which produce citrus and vine fruits. Wool is the main local industry. **Of interest:** Folk Museum and Arts Centre, displaying pioneer relics and the largest known collection of riverboat photographs in Australia. The old gaol, built in 1879-81, has been recently restored. A stretching rack and whipping stool are among the more macabre exhibits. **Accommodation:** 2 hotels, 3 motels, 1 caravan/camping park.
Map ref. 96 D8, 162 F2

The Hawkesbury

If you want to get away from it all, hiring a houseboat or a rowing boat on the beautiful Hawkesbury River could be the answer. You can pull in to explore little coves, stop to picnic at quiet beaches, dine at riverside restaurants or simply admire the tranquillity of the scene. When English novelist Anthony Trollope was in Australia last century, he was charmed by the Hawkesbury and wrote: 'To me it was more enchanting than those waters of either the Rhine or the Mississippi.'

It is unchanged today and the majestic unspoiled scenery between **Wisemans Ferry** and **Broken Bay** gives the Hawkesbury its reputation for being the most beautiful river on the Australian continent.
You can hire craft of all types — from small rowing dinghies to large cruisers and houseboats — at Bobbin Head. Halvorsen Boats (02) 457 9011 hire out 8-metre 5-berth, 9-metre 7-berth and 11-metre 9-berth boats.

TEN RULES FOR SAFE BOATING

1. Tell someone where you are going.
2. Carry adequate equipment.
3. Carry effective life jackets.
4. Know the rules, distress signals and local regulations.
5. Watch the weather.
6. Don't overload the craft.
7. Carry enough fuel and water.
8. Guard against fire.
9. Ensure engine reliability.
10. Don't drink (alcohol) while boating.

West Wyalong Population 3778.

This former gold-mining town, at the junction of the Mid Western and Newell Highways, is now the business centre of a prosperous wheat, wool and mixed farming area. **Of interest:** District Museum includes a scale model of a goldmine, historical displays, and locally-found fossils. **In the area:** Lake Cowal, 48 km north-east of town, via either Blow Clear or Clear Ridge Roads, is the largest lake in NSW, when it's full. It is also an important bird sanctuary and breeding ground for waterfowl. Most of the lake is privately-owned. Public accesss to the reserve on the western bank. West Wyalong has a trotting track and other sporting facilities. Good fishing and shooting in the area. **Accommodation:** 7 hotels, 8 motels, 2 caravan/camping parks.
Map ref. 97 P7, 98 A7

White Cliffs Population 210.

The opalised skeleton of a plesiosaur, found in a local mine, is on display in this small opal-mining town, 98 km north-west of Wilcannia. A few opal gougers still work in the area. **Of interest:** A walk-in opal mine museum, where opal seams and fossils can be seen *in situ*. Ultra-violet opal displays and opal-cutting demonstrations. Clancy's Hut, an early miner's home, classified as being of historic significance, the old police station, now used as an art gallery, and underground dug-outs, where residents live to avoid the heat. **Accommodation:** 1 hotel, 1 caravan/camping park.
Map ref. 92 F9

Wilcannia Population 934.

Once the 'queen city of the west', this quaint township still has many impressive sandstone buildings. It was once a key inland port in the days of paddle-steamers. Gradually declining in the early 1920s with the advent of the car, today it is the service centre for a far-flung rural population. **Of interest:** Historic buildings, including the post office, the prison and court-house and the Athenaeum Chambers, which house the local Tourist Information Centre. Also the lift-up bridge across the Darling River, and the paddle-steamer wharf just upstream. **In the area:** Opal fields at White Cliffs. **Accommodation:** 2 motels, 1 caravan/camping park.
Map ref. 92 G11

Windsor Population 13 490.

An exciting town for lovers of history and early architecture, Windsor is one of the oldest towns in Australia, situated 56 km north-west of Sydney. **Of interest:** St Matthew's Church, Moses St, is the oldest Church of England church in Australia, convict-built and designed by Francis Greenway in 1817. The nearby graveyard is even older. Court house, Court St, another Greenway building. The Doctor's House, Thompson Square, built in 1844, is now privately owned. Many other fine buildings in historic George St and Thompson Square. Hawkesbury Museum and Tourist Information Centre, Thompson St, was formerly the Daniel O'Connell Inn, built in the 1840s. **In the area:** Australiana Village, 6 km from Windsor.

Rose Cottage, the oldest timber dwelling in Australia. A wagon and buggy collection. Picnic and barbecue facilities and a lake with paddle boats. Tizzana Winery, Ebenezer, has a good range of fortified wines. There are barbecue facilities and single bottles are sold. Ebenezer Presbyterian Church, claimed to be oldest church in Australia still holding regular services, was built in 1809. An old cemetery and school house (1817) are nearby. Tijuana Fruit Winery, Glossodia, produces fruit-based wines. Barbecue facilities. Paradise Gardens, Cattai, 14 km to the north-east, is a children's activity centre, including a playground, pony rides, swimming, golfing, 'Prehistoric World' and 'Enchanted Forest'. Licensed restaurant and kiosk. **Accommodation:** 1 hotel, 1 motel.
Map ref. 77 K5, 99 J6, 100 I1

Wingham Population 3937.
The oldest town on the Manning River, 13 km up river from Taree, Wingham was established in 1843. **Of interest:** The Brush, close to town centre, is an unusual park consisting of dense scrubland, with orchids, ferns, Moreton Bay fig trees and sub-tropical flowers growing in natural state. From September to May each year, thousands of flying foxes live here. **Accommodation:** 2 hotels, 1 motel.
Map ref. 95 N12

Wisemans Ferry Pop. under 200.
Situated on the southern side of the Hawkesbury River, 66 km north-west of Sydney, Wisemans Ferry is an important recreational area for those interested in water sports. Two vehicular ferries provide transport across the river. **Of interest:** Wisemans Ferry Inn named after the founder of the original ferry service and innkeeper. Said to be haunted by his wife, whom he allegedly pushed down the front steps to her death! Dharug National Park, on north side of the river, named after an Aboriginal tribe, is important for its wealth of Aboriginal rock-engravings thought to be 8000 years old. The old convict-built Great Northern Road is of particular interest. Bushwalking, camping. Barbecue facilities. **Accommodation:** 2 caravan/camping parks.
Map ref. 77 M1, 99 J5

Wollongong-Port Kembla
Population 203 601.
This heavily industrialised centre is the third largest city in New South Wales. Greater Wollongong is an aggregate of several once independent towns, which have expanded rapidly over the past 30 years. Coking coal, pig iron, steel, tinplate and steel products are among its main secondary industries. The largest steelworks in Australia is at Port Kembla. On a site of 800 ha, with 20 000 employees, it has a steel-making capacity of 5.5 million tonnes per annum. Dairying and fishing are the main surviving primary industries in the district. **Of interest:** Many beautiful surfing beaches and rock pools, north and south of Wollongong. Lake Illawarra, stretching from the South Pacific Ocean to the foothills of the Illawarra Range, for good prawning, fishing and sailing. Wollongong Harbour. Fishing fleet and fish market. Historic lighthouse. Many lookouts with superb views of the coast, including Bald Hill Lookout, which was the site of the aviator Lawrence Hargrave's first attempt at flight in the early nineteen hundreds. Now a favourite spot for hang-gliders. Port Kembla steelworks can be inspected. Book at Visitors' Centre, Port Kembla. **In the area:** Mt Kembla Village, where there was a tragic mining disaster in 1902. Monument in church. Miners' huts still stand. Several historic buildings including Historical Museum housed in the former post office, pioneer kitchen, blacksmith's shop, and a reconstruction of the Mt Kembla disaster. Symbio Animal Gardens, Helensburgh, a delightful spot for children to see free-roaming wombats, kangaroos, donkeys and other animals. Macarthur Estate Wines, Wilton. Wine-tasting, restaurant, picnic and barbecue area. Sole's Wild Australia. **Accommodation:** 3 hotels, 7 motels, 3 caravan/camping parks.
Map ref. 91 P5, 99 J8, 100 I3

Woodburn Population 647.
A pleasant town on the Pacific Highway, astride the Richmond River, Woodburn offers access to the inland and northwards through Casino and Lismore to Evans Head on the coast. **Of interest:** Riverside Park. Monument and remains of settlement at New Italy, the result of the illfated Marquis de Rays' expedition in 1880. **Accommodation:** 1 hotel, 1 motel.
Map ref. 95 Q3

Woolgoolga Population 2079.
This charming seaside town on the Pacific Highway, 26 km north of Coffs Harbour, is excellent for crabbing, prawning and whiting fishing. Good surf beach. **Of interest:** Adventure Village, including a dwarf's house, New Guinea village, swing boats, train and donkey rides, picnic and barbecue facilities. Guru Nanak Sikh Temple, River St, the place of worship for the town's Indian population, is open at weekends. **In the area:** Sam's Place, 5 km north at Mullaway, has pottery demonstrations and a restaurant (closed Mondays). Yuralgin National Park, 10 km north of Woolgoolga, offers bushwalking, fishing, swimming, picnic and camping areas in a beautiful stretch of unspoiled beaches and dunes. **Accommodation:** 6 motels, 5 caravan/camping parks.
Map ref. 95 P7

Woy Woy Population 12 206.
Situated 90 km north of Sydney and about 6 km south of Gosford, it has virtually become a dormitory suburb. **Of interest:** Boating, fishing, swimming. The centre for the Brisbane Water National Park to the south-west. Noted for spring wild flowers. Bushwalking, camping, barbecue facilities. **Accommodation:** 1 motel.
Map ref. 77 Q2, 78 E3

Wyong Population 3902.
This town on the Pacific Highway, 23 km north of Gosford, is pleasantly situated between Tuggerah Lake and the State Forests of the Watagan Mountains. **Of interest:** Water sports and prawning on the lakes. Bushwalking and camping in the 80 600 ha forests. Races, golf, swimming and fishing. **Accommodation:** 2 hotels, 1 motel, 2 caravan/camping parks.
Map ref. 83 E11, 99 L5

Yamba Population 3101.
This prawning and fishing town, at the mouth of the Clarence River, offers sea, lake and river fishing. **Of interest:** Yuraygir National Park, about 5 km south of town. Swimming, fishing and bushwalking in an area dominated by sand ridges and banksia heath. Lake Wooloweyah, 4 km from town along Angourie Road, is excellent for fishing and prawning. The Blue Pool at Angourie. Only 50 m from the ocean, the pool is of unknown depth and origin. Popular swimming and picnic spot. **Accommodation:** 1 hotel, 6 motels, 3 caravan/camping parks.
Map ref. 95 Q4

Yass Population 4283.
At the junction of two major highways (the Hume and the Barton) this interesting old town is on the Yass River, surrounded by beautiful rolling country, 296 km south-west of Sydney. **Of interest:** Grave of explorer Hamilton Hume, who discovered the Yass Plains in 1824. Cooma Cottage, built in 1830 (not open), where Hume lived for more than 40 years. Hamilton Hume Museum, Comur St, contains many pioneer relics, some associated with the explorer. The courthouse in Comur St, and the police station in Rossi St, have been classified as 'an essential part of Australia's heritage' by the National Trust. **In the area:** Burrinjuck State Recreation Area, for bushwalking and water sports on the manmade lake. Wee Jasper and Micalong Creeks for trout fishing. Carey's Cave, at Wee Jasper, consist of seven chambers of superb limestone formations. Open on Sundays from 1pm. **Accommodation:** 4 hotels, 5 motels.
Map ref. 98 E9, 100 D4

Young Population 6906.
Attractive former gold-mining town in the western foothills of the Great Dividing Range, 395 km west-south-west of Sydney. Today cherries and prunes are the area's best-known exports, as well as flour, steel, tiles and magnesium oxide factories. **Of interest:** Lambing Flat Historic Museum contains fascinating reminders of the town's colourful history, including the historic 'roll-up' flag carried by the gold-miners during the infamous anti-Chinese Lambing Flat riots of 1861. Chinaman's Dam, formerly used by Chinese gold-diggers for sluicing, is now a picnic area, with safe swimming for small children, canoeing and sailing. Backguard Gully plus historic Pug-Mill, on Boorowa Road, has been restored as an example of early gold-mining methods. **In the area:** At Murringo Village is the home of crystal designer and engraver Helmut Heibel. **Accommodation:** 3 hotels, 6 motels, 1 caravan/camping park.
Map ref. 98 D8, 100 B3

Maps of New South Wales

Location Map

SYDNEY & WESTERN SUBURBS	74 - 75
BRISBANE WATER & KU-RING-GAI CHASE N.P.	78 - 79
KATOOMBA & THE BLUE MOUNTAINS	80
VINEYARDS OF THE HUNTER VALLEY	81
NEWCASTLE	82
COFFS HARBOUR	84
PORT MACQUARIE	85
PORT STEPHENS	86
LORD HOWE ISLAND	87
TAMWORTH & LISMORE	88
WOLLONGONG	89
BATHURST & ORANGE	101
SYDNEY TO MELBOURNE BY THE MAIN ROUTES	102 - 103
CANBERRA CITY	105
CANBERRA & NORTHERN SUBURBS	106 - 107
CANBERRA & CENTRAL SUBURBS	108 - 109
CANBERRA & SOUTHERN SUBURBS	110 - 111
AUSTRALIAN CAPITAL TERRITORY	112

66 Central Sydney

0 500 1000 1500 2000 m
J K L M N O P Q R
73
1 2 3 4 5 6 7 8 9 10 11 12 13
PORT JACKSON
Clark Island
Wharf
Woollahra Point
Point Piper
Felix Bay
Lady Martins Beach
WOLSELEY CR
WYUNA RD
WENTWORTH RD
WENTWORTH PL
Point Piper
R.M.Y.C.
Marina's
WUNULLA RD
WOLSELEY RD
Rose Bay
Rose Bay Park
Marina
Darling Point
Blackburn Cove
YARRANABBE RD
THORNTON RD
HAMPDEN RD
ETHAM AV
SUTHERLAND CR
Double Bay
Redleaf Pool
Seven Shilling's Beach
Darling Point
Cranbrook School
ROSE BAY AV
ASTON PL
CRANBROOK RD
BERESFORD RD
SALISBURY RD
O'SULLIVAN RD
Woollahra Park
Yarranabbe Park
MITCHELL RD
YARRANABBE RD
EASTBOURNE RD
Macleay Point
Marina
Wharf
VICTORIA RD
POWELL ST
Rose Bay
BALFOUR RD
Scots College
PLUMER RD
Rushcutters Bay
Marina's
Cruising Yacht Club
POINT RD
MARATHON RD
AV
ST
BEACH ST
STAFFORD ST
SHERBROOKE
WILLIAM ST
PRESTON AV
GINAHGULLA RD
NEW BEACH RD
The Reg Bartley Oval
Park
MONA RD
GREENOAKES AV
CROSS ST
Double Bay
GUILFOYLE AV
SOUTH ST
OCEAN AV
BAY ST
St Marks Rd
COOPER ST
FAIRFAX RD
RUPERTS WOOD AV
KAMBALA RD
DRUMALBYN RD
DARLING
TARRANT
KULGOA RD
BULKARA RD
Bellevue Hill
VICTORIA RD
ROAD
BELLEVUE
HENRIETTA
HOLT ST
ANDERSON RD
PATTERSON RD
COURT RD
MANNING
Railway
Viaduct
76
NEW SOUTH HEAD RD
Edgecliff
Edgecliff
Weigall Sports Ground
White City Tennis Courts
Sydney Grammar Prep. School
NEILD AV
LAWSON ST
GOODHOPE ST
GLENMORE RD
CAMBRIDGE ST
Oval
Trumper Park
ROYLSTON ST
HAMPDEN ST
CECIL ST
SUTHERLAND ST
PINE HILL AV
FOREST RD
GLENDON RD
KIAORA RD
EPPING RD
CARLOTTA RD
Underground
EDGECLIFF RD
ALBERT ST
Railway
THORNE ST
Rosemont Av
ROSLYNDALE AV
WARREN RD
SUTTIE RD
RANFURLEY RD
HOLLAND RD
STREATFIELD RD
COOPER PARK RD
NORTHLAND RD
MARCH ST
FAIRWEATHER ST
VIVIAN ST
FOSTER AV
ROSSLYN ST
RIVERS ST
LENNOX ST
BRADLEY AV
RIDDELL ST
COOPER RD
CASCADE ST
GURNER ST
HEELEY ST
BROUGHTON ST
HARGRAVE ST
HARRIS ST
OCEAN ST
TRELAWNEY ST
FULLERTON RD
Lough Playing Field
COOPER PARK
STAFFORD ST
UNDERWOOD ST
WINDSOR ST
TARA ST
HOLDSWORTH ST
WELLINGTON ST
WEEROONA AV
GLENCOE RD
LINDEN AV
WALLAROY RD
EDWARD ST
SMALL ST
RAINE ST
KENDALL ST
Paddington
WILLIAM ST
DUDLEY ST
QUEEN ST
UNDERWOOD ST
VICTORIA RD
PADDINGTON ST
TAYLOR ST
CALEDONIA ST
MORRELL ST
ALTON ST
FORTH ST
NELSON ST
ATTUNGA ST
GREYCAIRN PL
STANLEY ST
CHESTER ST
MILTON AV
BATHURST ST
VIEW ST
FLETCHER ST
ADELAIDE ST
Bon Accord Av
OXFORD ST
ELIZABETH ST
GEORGE ST
RENNY ST
REGENT ST
GORDON ST
BENT ST
STEWART ST
LEINSTER ST
MONCUR ST
SPICER ST
QUEEN ST
Woollahra
JERSEY RD
SMITH ST
QUEEN ST
JAMES ST
JOHN ST
WALLIS ST
BONDI JUNCTION
EDGECLIFF RD
MAGNEY RD
SABER ST
ROWE ST
GROSVENOR ST
JUNCTION ST
BY-PASS
BENEDEN ST
PAUL ST
WAVERLEY CR
GOWRIE AV
GRAFTON ST
Railway
NEWLAND ST
Train Bus Exchange
Plaza
Bondi Junction
Oxford Mall
OXFORD ST
PINE AV
BONDI RD
Centennial Square
Moore Park
Barracks
Reservoirs
Centennial Park
Moore Park
Cricket Ground
ROAD RD
COOK RD
MITCHELL ST
LANG RD
YORK RD
ST JAMES RD
GOWRIE ST
RUTHVEN ST
MILL HILL RD
DENISON ST
SPRING ST
LAWSON ST
EBLEY ST
Res
KEIRAN ST
WALTER ST
RATTRAY ST
MACKENZIE ST
Bondi Junction
BRONTE RD
WAVERLEY ST
DALLEY ST
LLANDAFF ST
BOTANY ST
COUNCIL ST
HOLLYWOOD AV
ALLENS PDE
ALLENS
BOTANY PDE
PL
PORTER ST
JAMES ST
Waverley Park

68 North Sydney & Pacific Highway

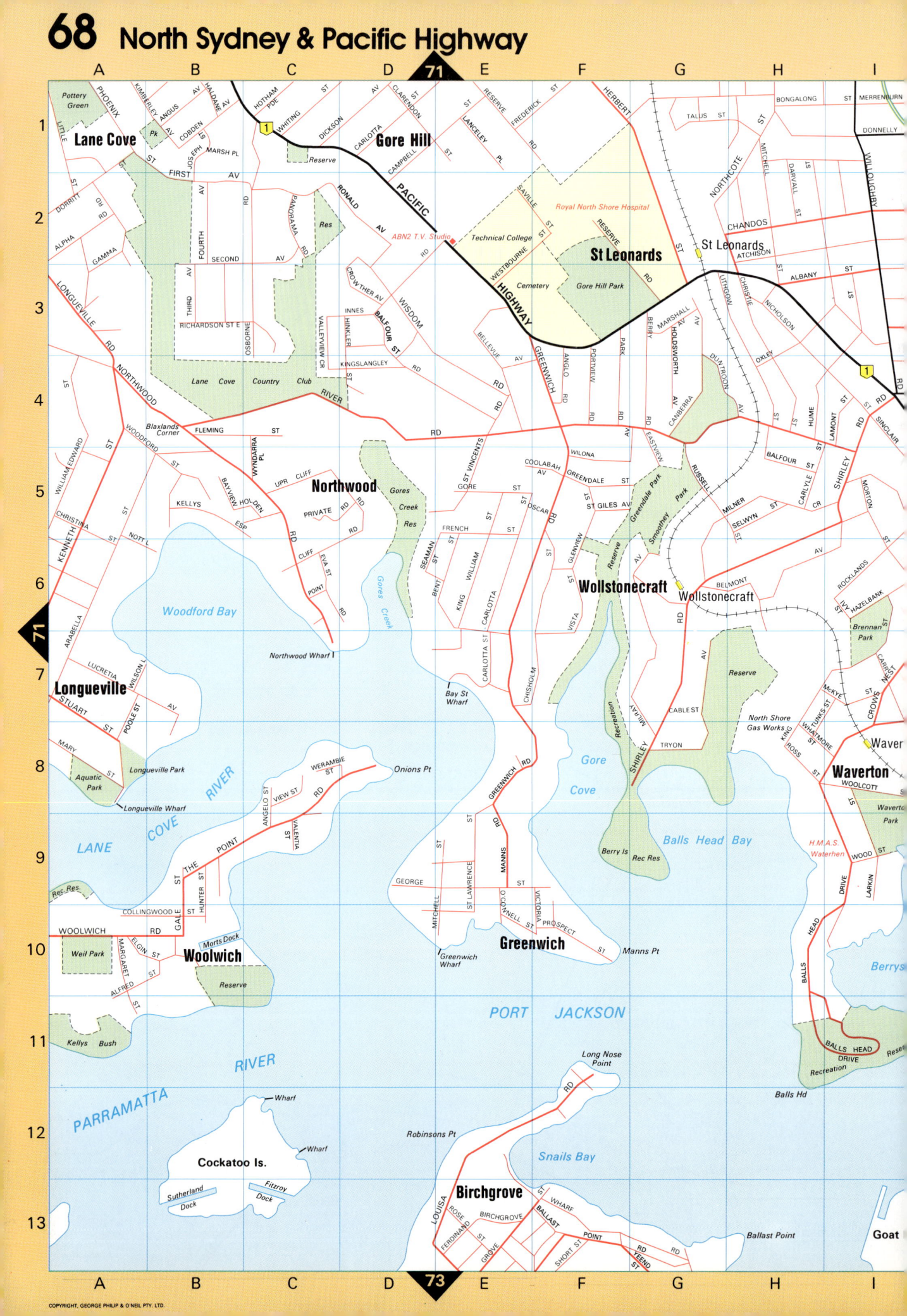

0
500
1000
1500
2000 m
71
66
J
K
L
M
N
O
P
Q
R
1
2
3
4
5
6
7
8
9
10
11
12
13
Cammeray
CAMMERAY PARK & GOLF LINKS
Green Park
Primrose Park
Cremorne
Crows Nest
MILITARY RD
FALCON ST
PACIFIC HIGHWAY
WARRINGAH EXPRESSWAY
ST. LEONARDS PARK
Music Shell
Oval
North Sydney Oval
Bowling Green
War Memorial
Footbridge
Mater Misericordiae Hosp
Nth Sydney Girls High Sch
Nth Sydney Public School
North Sydney
Forsyth Park
Bowling Green
Neutral Bay
Anderson Park
Victoria Cross
Graythwaite Hospital
Nth Sydney
Res
Steps
Lavender Bay
Watt Pk
Clark Pk
Ferry Wharf
Milsons Point
Milson Park
Kesterton Park
Hayes St Wharf
Neutral Bay
Kurraba Wharf
High St Wharf
Careening Cove
Shell Cove
Recreation Reserve
Cremorne Pt
The Hodgson Lookout
Kurraba Point
Wudyong Point
Royal Sydney Yacht Squadron
Lavender Bay
McMahons Point
McMahons Pt Wharf
McMahons Point
Luna Park
Olympic Pool
Stanton Lookout
Kirribilli
Jeffrey St Wharf
Kirribilli House
Admiralty House
Milsons Point
Beulah St Wharf
Kirribilli Point
Blues Point
PORT JACKSON
SYDNEY HARBOUR BRIDGE
BRADFIELD HIGHWAY
Fort Denison
Maritime Services Board Depot
Millers Point
Pier One
Dawes Pt Pk
Dawes Point
Walsh Bay
N

70 Sydney & Northern Suburbs

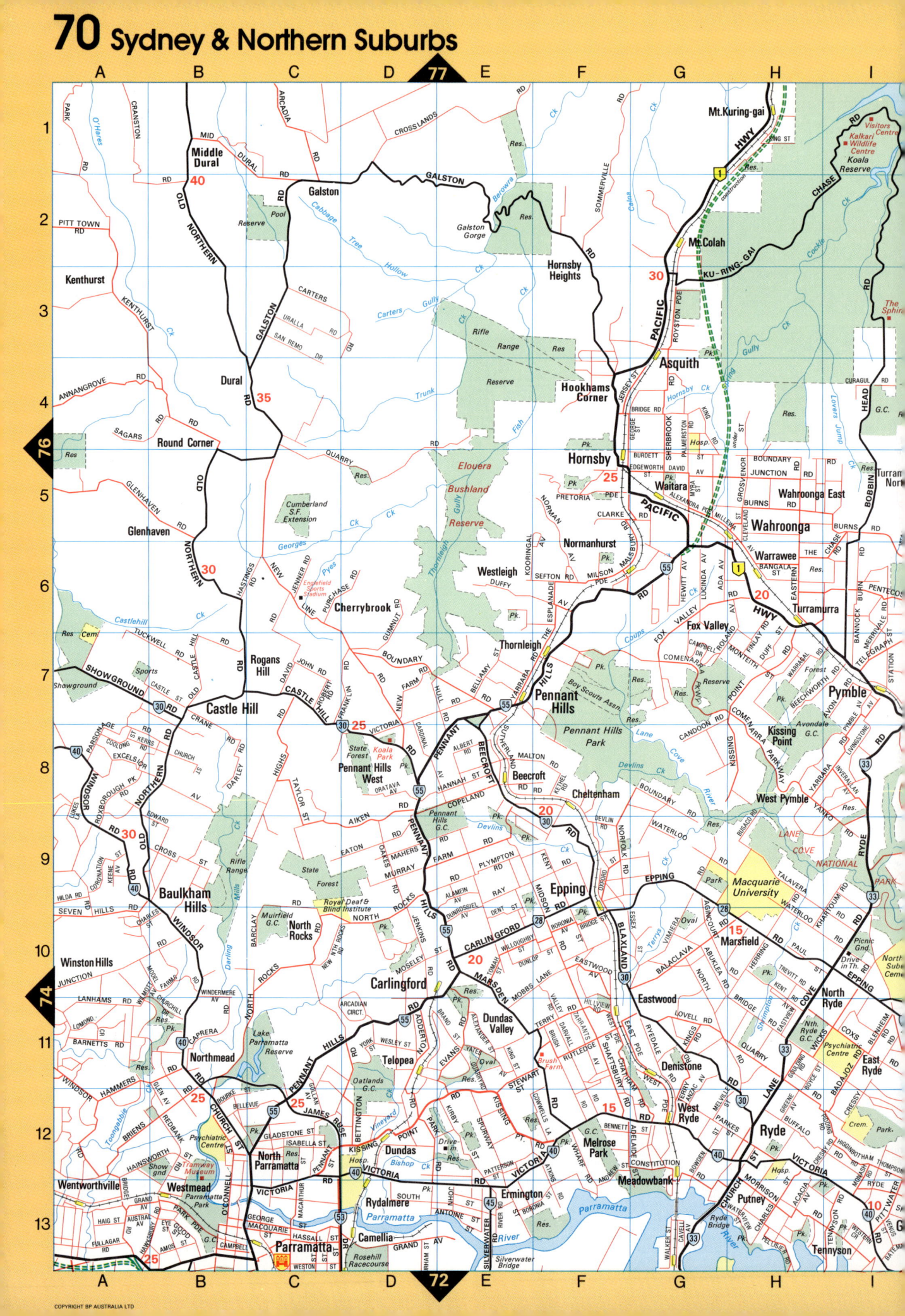

77

0 1 2 3 4 5 6 km
J K L M N O P Q R
1 2 3 4 5 6 7 8 9 10 11 12 13
KU-RING-GAI CHASE
NATIONAL
PARK
Aerodrome
Duffys Forest
Waratah Park
NSW Gun Club
Terrey Hills
McCARRS CREEK RD
MONA VALE RD
Bahai Temple
Ingleside
Monash G.C.
Elanora
Elanora GC
Mona Vale
Bayview G.C.
Mona Vale GC
Mona Vale Beach
Warriewood
Warriewood Beach
Turimetta Head
Turimetta Beach
Narrabeen Head
Narrabeen North
Narrabeen
Narrabeen Lagoon
Camping Area
PITTWATER RD
BARRENJOEY RD
The Basin
Showground
Ku-ring-gai Wildflower Garden
Police Driving School
St. Ives North
St. Ives
Davidson Park
Pony Club
National Fitness Camp
Wheeler Heights
Collaroy Plateau
Cromer G.C.
Cromer
Collaroy
Long Reef Golf Club
Long Reef Beach
Long Point
Dee Why Lagoon
Dee Why Beach
Dee Why
Belrose
Oxford Falls
WAKEHURST PARKWAY
Davidson
Frenchs Forest
Warringah
Drive-in
Film Studios
Beacon Hill
Narraweena
Brookvale
North Curl Curl
Dee Why Head
Curl Curl
Harbord Lagoon
Harbord
Harbord Beach
Curl Curl Head
Queenscliff Beach
Queenscliff
North Steyne Beach
Manly
Manly Beach
Fairlight
Marine land
Manly Cove
North Manly
Manly Vale
Manly Golf Course
North Balgowlah
Balgowlah
Balgowlah Golf Course
Balgowlah Heights
Clontarf
Military Res.
Dobroyd Head
Cannae Point
Grotto Point
Inner North Head
Outer North Head
Quarantine Station
Military Reserve
North Head
North Harbour
Gordon
Killara
East Killara
Lindfield
East Lindfield
Roseville G.C.
Roseville Bridge
Roseville
Roseville East
Forestville
Killarney Heights
Allambie Heights
Manly Warringah War Memorial Park
Old Manly Resr
Bantry Bay
Castle Cove
Middle Harbour
Garden & Res.
North Arm
Middle Cove
Sugarloaf Bay
Sugarloaf Point
Powder Hulk Bay
South Arm
Castlecrag
Sailors Bay
Bluff Head
Seaforth
The Spit Bridge
The Spit
Beauty Point
Wy-ar-gine Point
Balmoral
Hunters Bay
Rocky Point
Spit Junction
Mosman
Middle Head
Obelisk Bay
Georges Heights
Georges Head
Chowder Bay
Chowder Point
Clifton Gardens
Taronga Pk Zoo
Taylors Bay
Cremorne
Cremorne Point
Neutral Bay
Mosman Bay
North Sydney
Waverton
Crows Nest
St. Leonards
Wollstonecraft
Greenwich
Naremburn
Cammeray
Northbridge
Long Bay
Fig Tree Pt.
Willoughby
Willoughby North
Chatswood
Chatswood West
Fullers Bridge
Lane Cove West
Lane Cove
Artarmon
Channel 9
Channel 2
Gore Hill
Longueville
Riverview
Linley Pt
Fig Tree Bridge
Hunters Hill
Tarban Ck Bridge
Woodford Bay
Tambourine Bay
Burns Bay
Lane Cove River
Gore Cove
Berry Bay
Port Jackson
Inner South Head
Military Reserve
Lady Bay
Camp Cove
Green Point
Watsons Bay
The Gap
Village Point
Vaucluse Bay
Vaucluse Point
Shark Bay
Outer South Head
SOUTH PACIFIC OCEAN
PACIFIC HWY
WARRINGAH FWY
MILITARY RD
SYDNEY RD
CONDAMINE ST
PITTWATER RD
WARRINGAH RD
EASTERN VALLEY WAY
BOUNDARY ST
FULLERS RD
FOREST WAY

73

72 Sydney & Southern Suburbs

73

74 Sydney & Western Suburbs

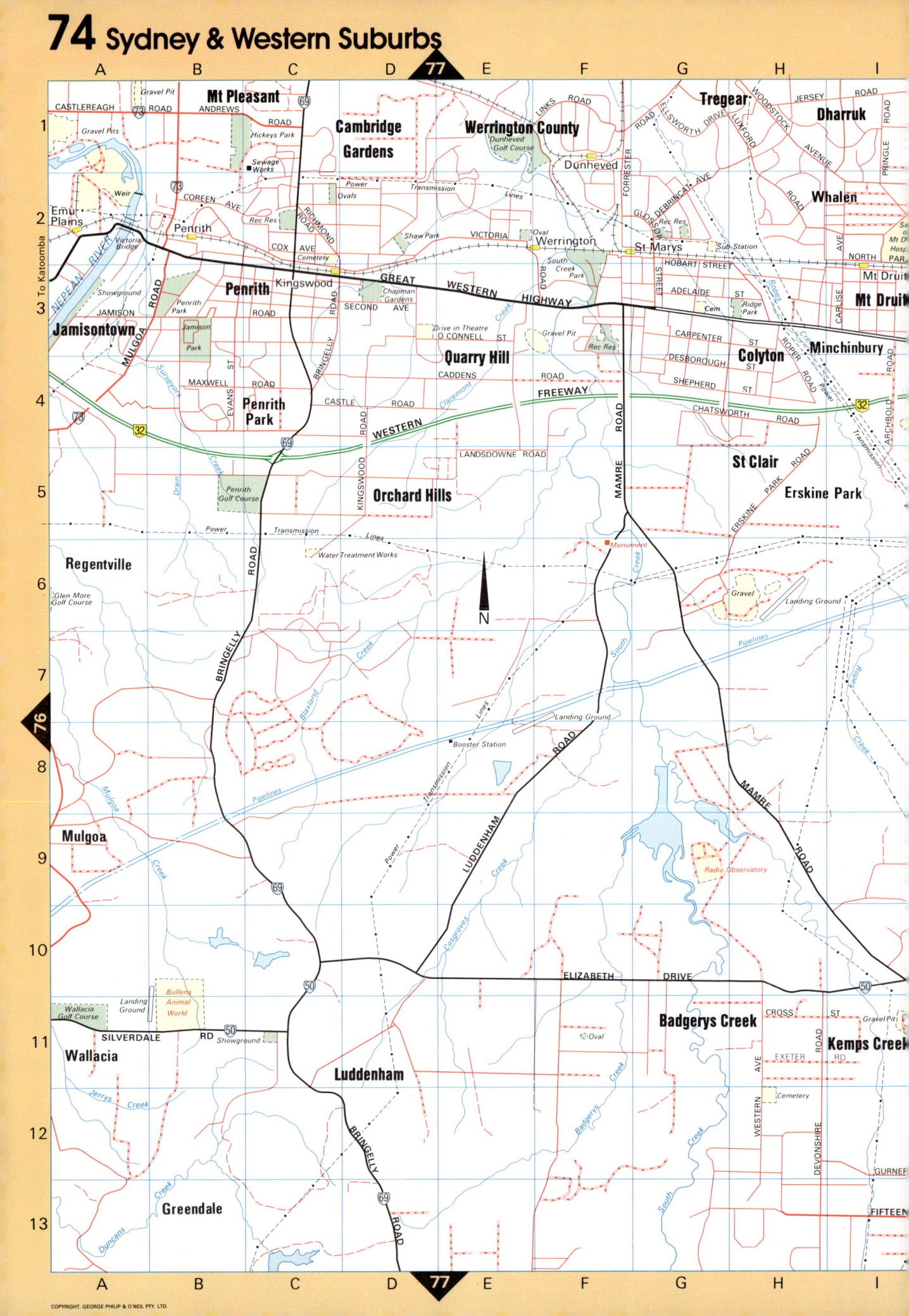

0 1 2 3 4 5 6 7 8 9km

J K L M 77 N O P Q R

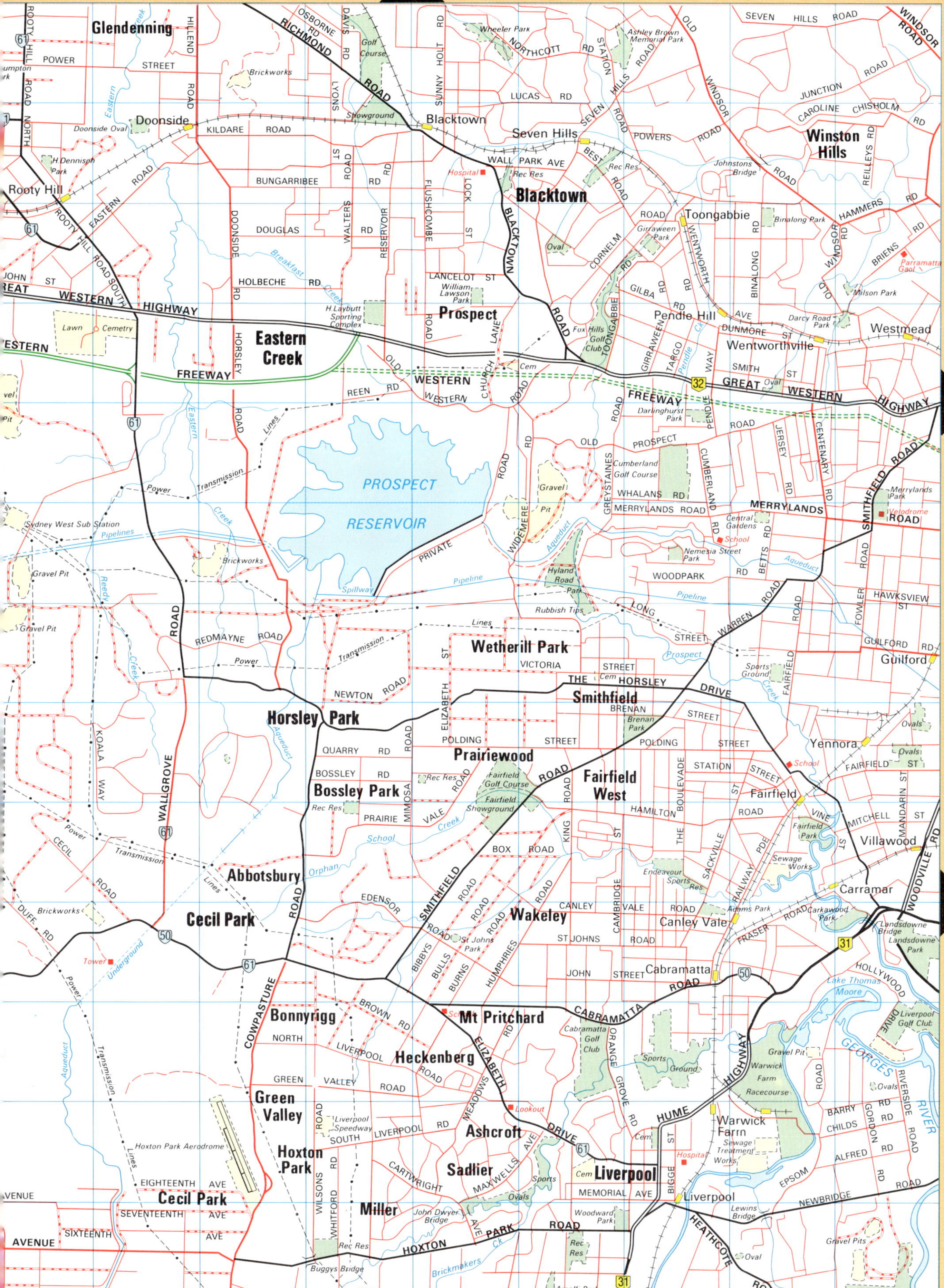

J K L M 77 N O P Q R

76 Tours from Sydney

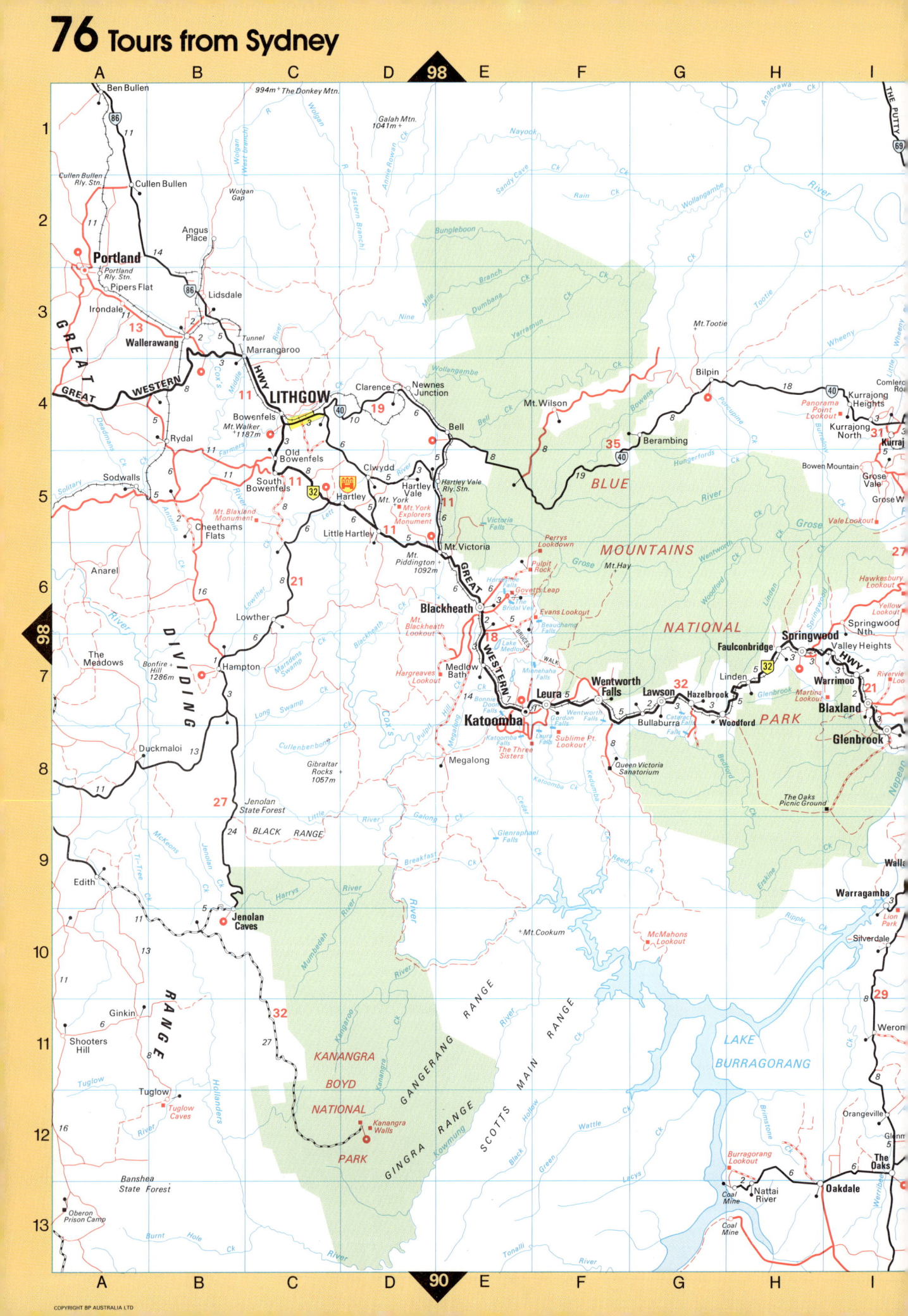

77

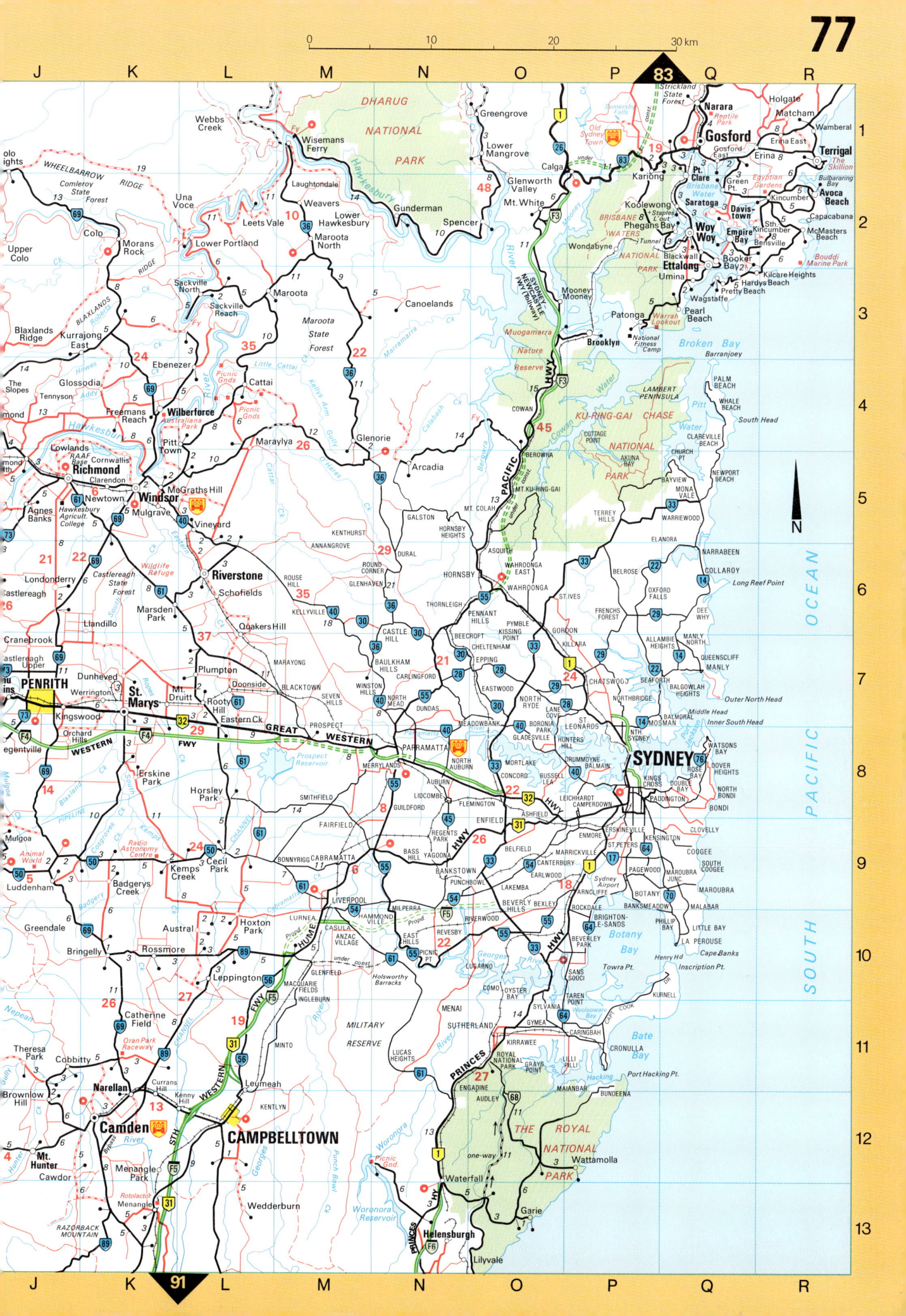

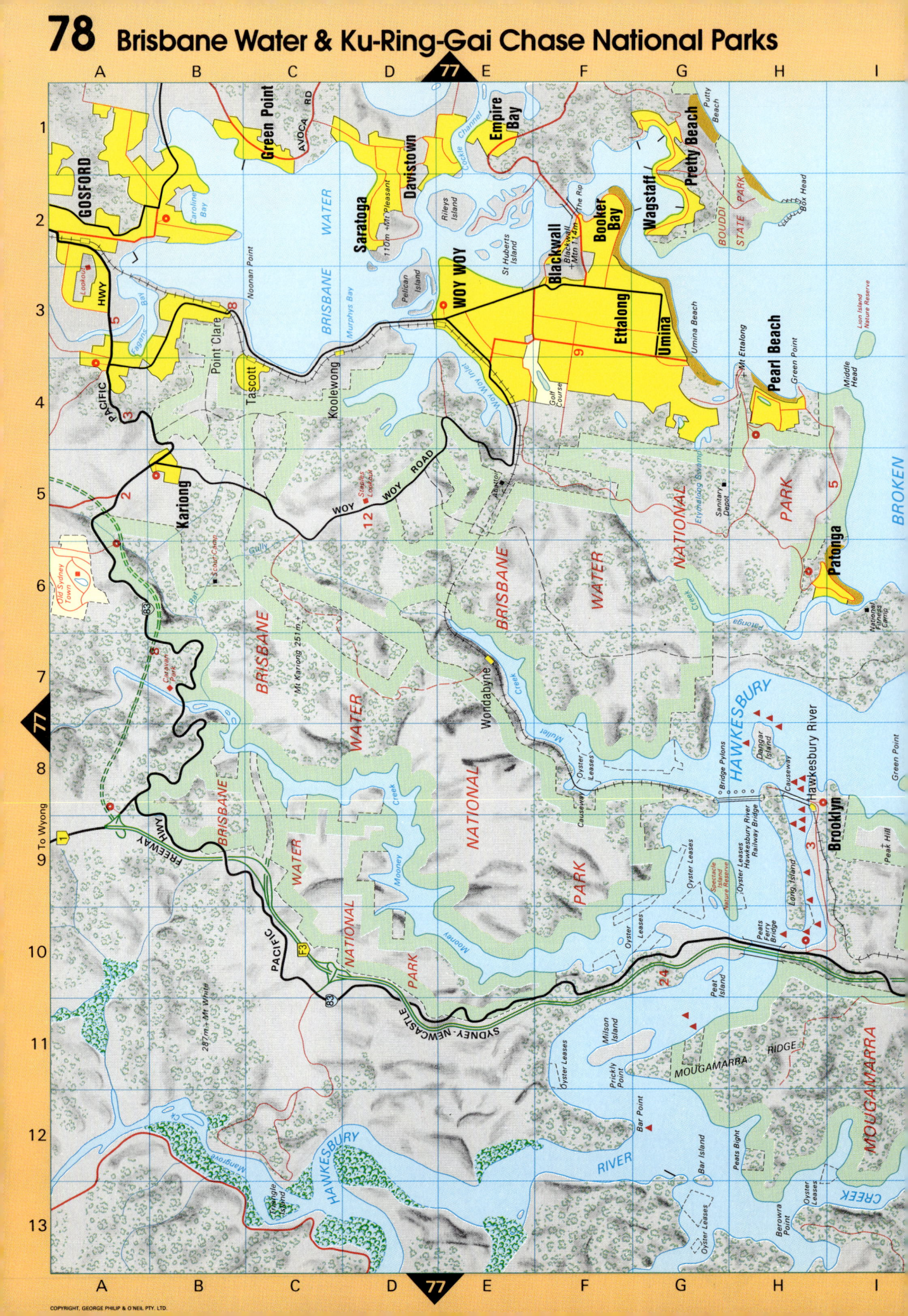

78 Brisbane Water & Ku-Ring-Gai Chase National Parks

0 1 2 3 4 5 6 7 8 9 10 km
J K L M N O P Q R
1 2 3 4 5 6 7 8 9 10 11 12 13
SOUTH PACIFIC OCEAN
Barrenjoey Head
Palm Beach
Whale Beach
Little Head
Bangalley Head
Careel Bay
Avalon
Bilgola
Bilgola Head
Golf Course
Bungan Head
Newport Beach
Mona Vale
Mona Vale Beach
Turimetta Head
Narrabeen Beach
Narrabeen
Narrabeen Lake
Newport
Church Point
Scotland Island
Taylors Point
Stokes Point
Soldiers Point
Great Mackerel Beach
West Head
Lookout
PITT WATER
Towlers Bay
BARRENJOEY ROAD
PITTWATER RD
MONA VALE RD
Ingleside
Drive-in Theatre
Elanora Heights
Golf Course
WEST HEAD ROAD
Juno Point
Eleanor Bluffs
Challenger Head
Refuge Bay
CREEK
KU-RING-GAI CHASE NATIONAL PARK
McCARRS CREEK ROAD
McCarrs
Scout Camp
The Sugarloaf 196m
Terrey Hills
Duffys Forest
Tollgate
CORAL AND CANDLE CREEK ROAD
Akuna Bay Marina
Coal and Candle Creek
Smiths Creek
COTTAGE CREEK RD
Cottage Point
COWAN
Shark Rock Point
Jerusalem Bay
SYDNEY-NEWCASTLE FREEWAY
Tollgates and Weighing Station
Cowan
RESERVE
PACIFIC HWY
Berowra Heights
Berowra
BEROWRA
Mount Kuring-Gai
Bobbin Head
Park Headquarters
KU-RING-GAI CHASE RD
BOBBIN HEAD ROAD
St Ives Chase
Police Driving School
MONA VALE ROAD
Golf Course
To Hornsby
77

Katoomba and the Blue Mountains

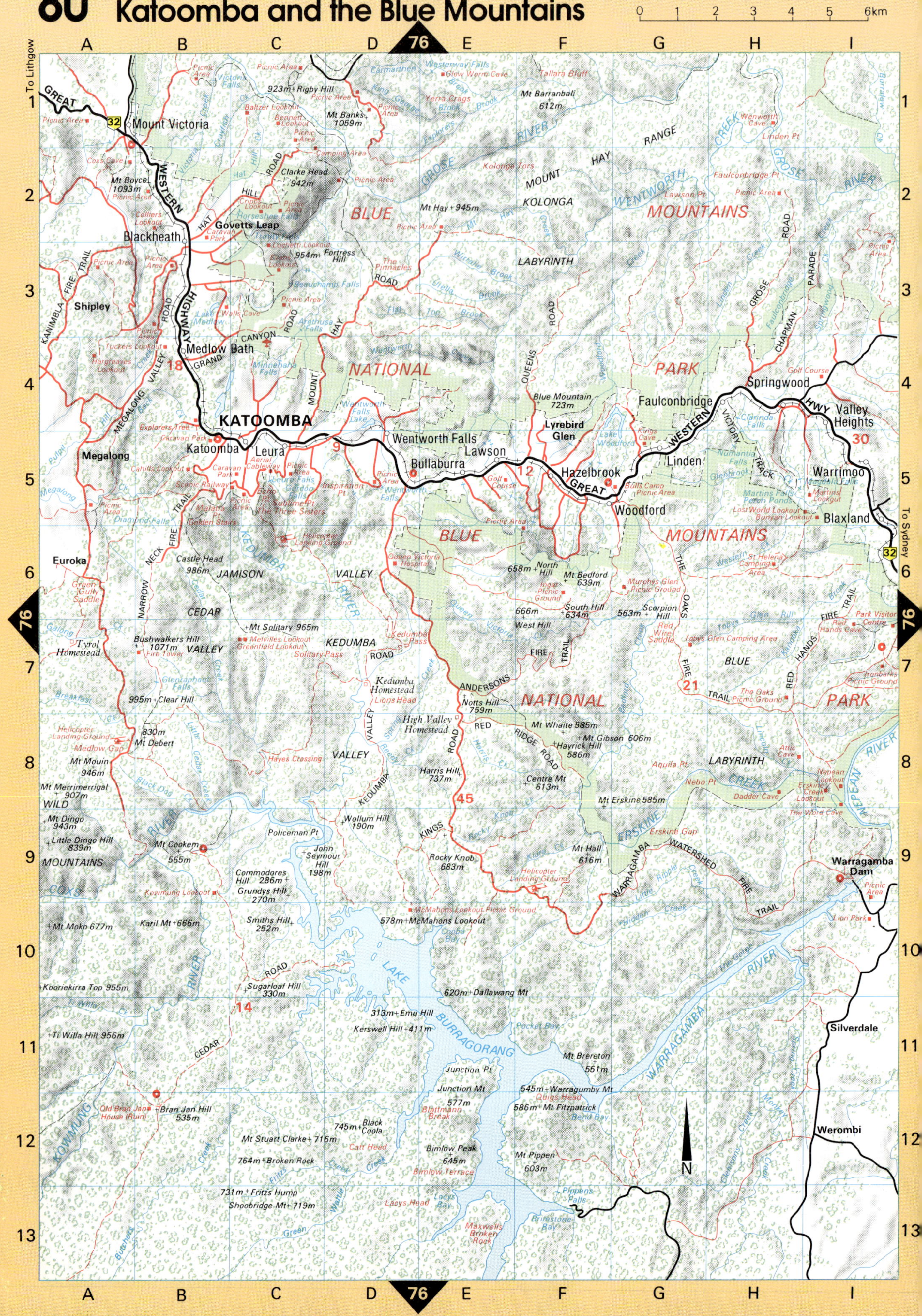

Vineyards of the Hunter Valley

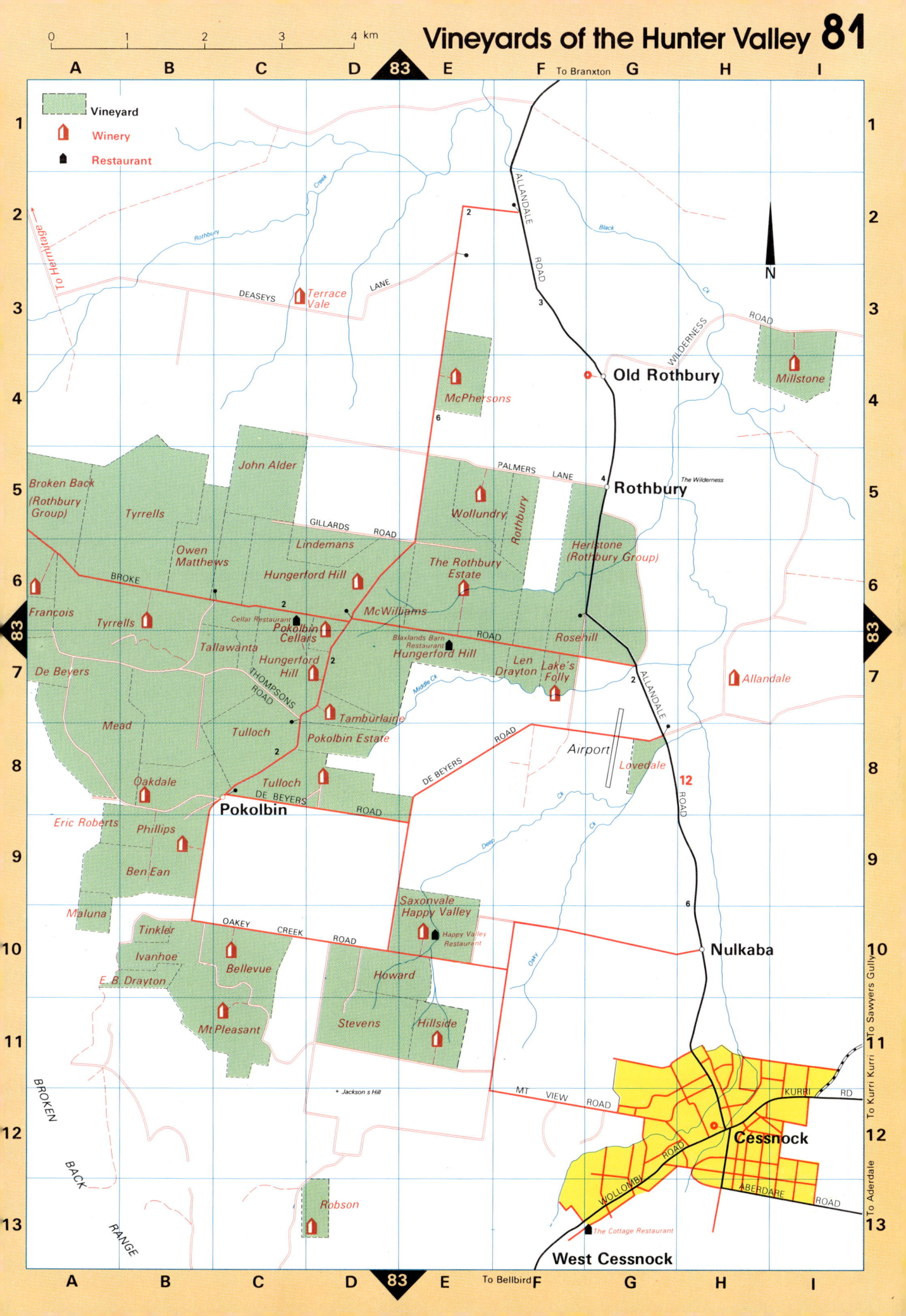

82 Newcastle

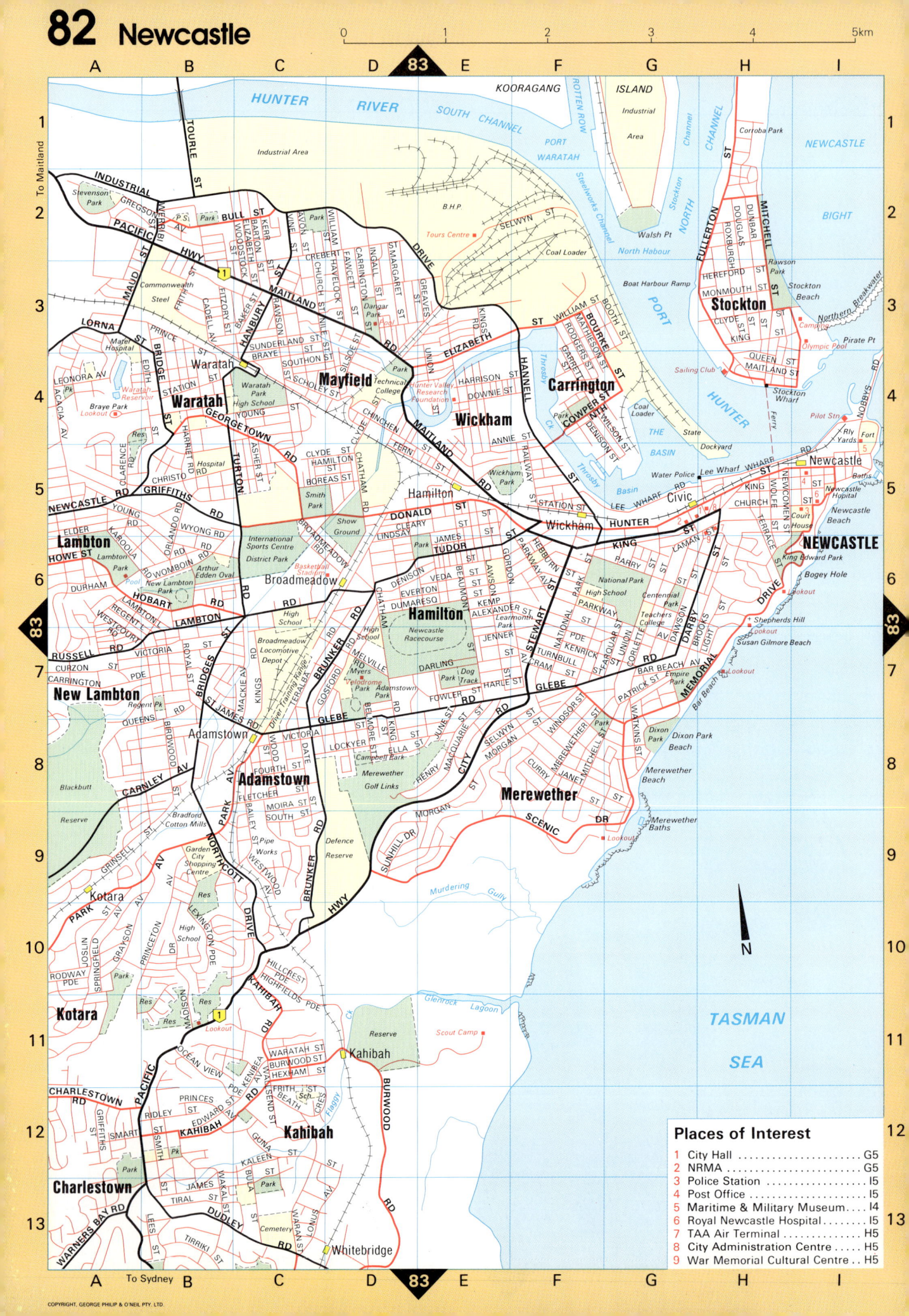

Places of Interest
1. City Hall G5
2. NRMA G5
3. Police Station I5
4. Post Office I5
5. Maritime & Military Museum .. I4
6. Royal Newcastle Hospital ... I5
7. TAA Air Terminal H5
8. City Administration Centre .. H5
9. War Memorial Cultural Centre .. H5

The Southern Central Coast 83

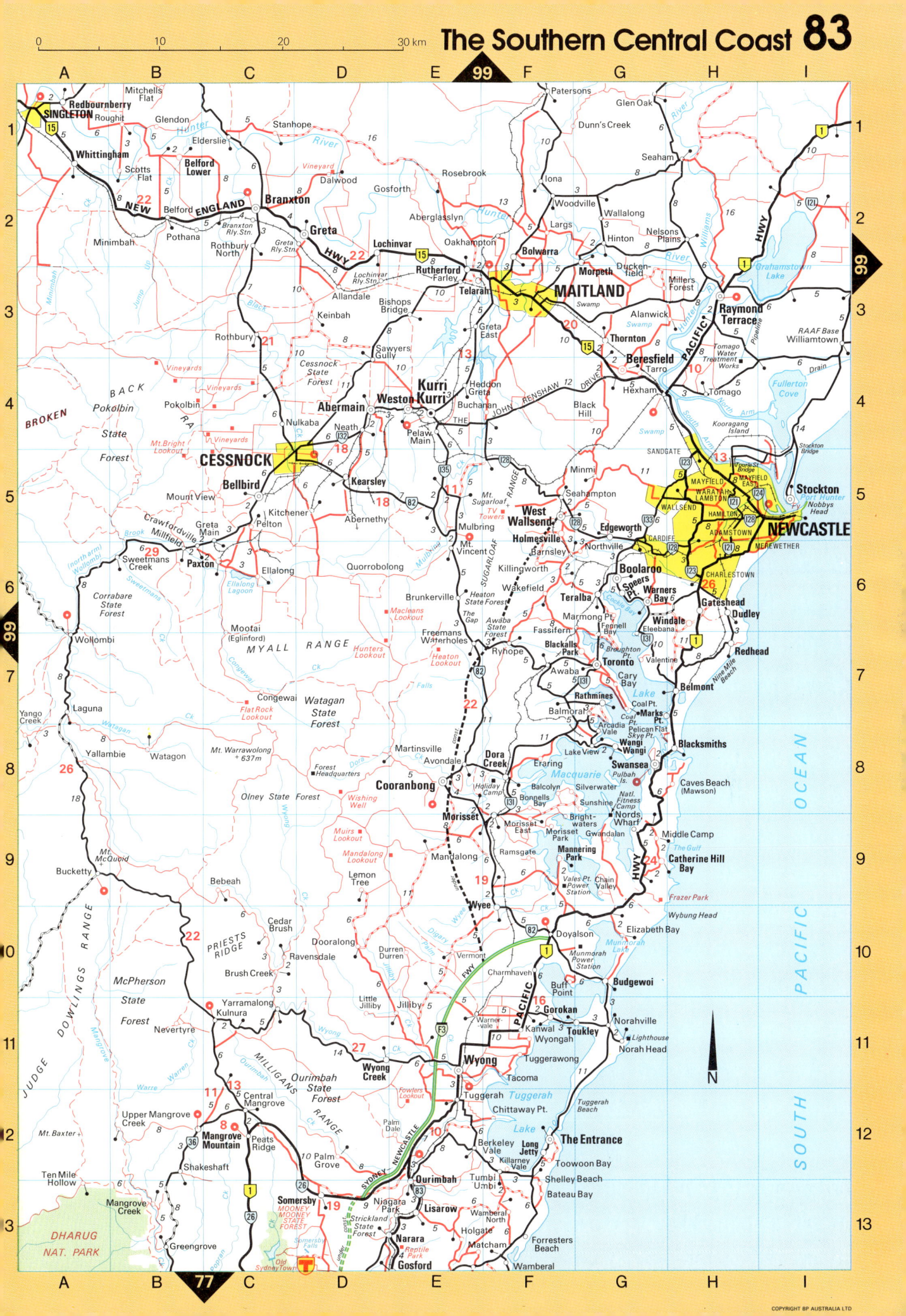

84 Coffs Harbour

PLACES OF INTEREST

1. Banana Bowl A8
2. Midway Motel C8
3. Park Beach Hotel Motel C6
4. Bowling Club D6
5. Post Office E6
6. Porpoise Pet Pool F6
7. Recreation & Sporting Club ... F12
8. NRMA Depot F11
9. Coffs Harbour Post Office F11
10. RSL Club F10
11. Civic Centre F10
12. Library F10
13. Fire Station F10
14. Tourist Information Centre .. G10
15. Police Station & Court House G11
16. Ambulance Station G11
17. NRN-11 TV Studio H12
18. Beacon Hill Lookout I5
19. Deep Sea Fishing Club I5
20. Coastal Patrol G5
21. Yacht Club G5
22. Deep Sea Fishing & Island Cruises . G4

Port Macquarie 85

Places of Interest

1. Marina Caravan Park D3
2. Jordans Caravan Park C3
3. Hastings River Caravan Park A4
4. Hibbard Post Office A4
5. Leisure World Caravan Park A4
6. Surfrider Motel D5
7. Bowling Club D5
8. Tennis Courts E5
9. Croquet Lawns E5
10. Port Macquarie Post Office E5
11. Tourist Information Centre E5
12. Court House F5
13. Caravan Park F5
14. Observatory G5
15. Bowling Club G5
16. Belair Motel D6
17. John Oxley Motel D6
18. Coolibah Motel D6
19. Olympic Motel D6
20. Hastings District Hospital D6
21. Celtic Motel E6
22. Thrumster Village Pottery A8
23. Mid Pacific Caravan Park A9
24. Caratel Caravan Park G8
25. Taskers Caravan Park G8
26. Flynns Beach Caravan Park H8
27. Obelisk H8
28. Ambulance Station E5
29. Fantasy Glades H9
30. Police Station F5
31. Transit Hill Lookout F11
32. Bermuda Breezes Country Motel G12
33. Marbuk Stables F13

86 Port Stephens

Lord Howe Island 87

88 Tamworth & Lismore

Wollongong 89

Places of Interest

1	Ambulance Station	E10
2	Coniston Post Office	D12
3	Corrimal Post Office	E2
4	Department of Motor Transport (Registry)	E11
5	Fairy Meadow Post Office	E5
6	Fairy Meadow Police Station	E5
7	Fig Tree Post Office	A12
8	Mt Keira Post Office	A9
9	NRMA	E10
10	Wollongong Court House	E10
11	Wollongong Library	E10
12	Wollongong Police Station	E10
13	Wollongong Town Hall	E10

90 Tours from Wollongong

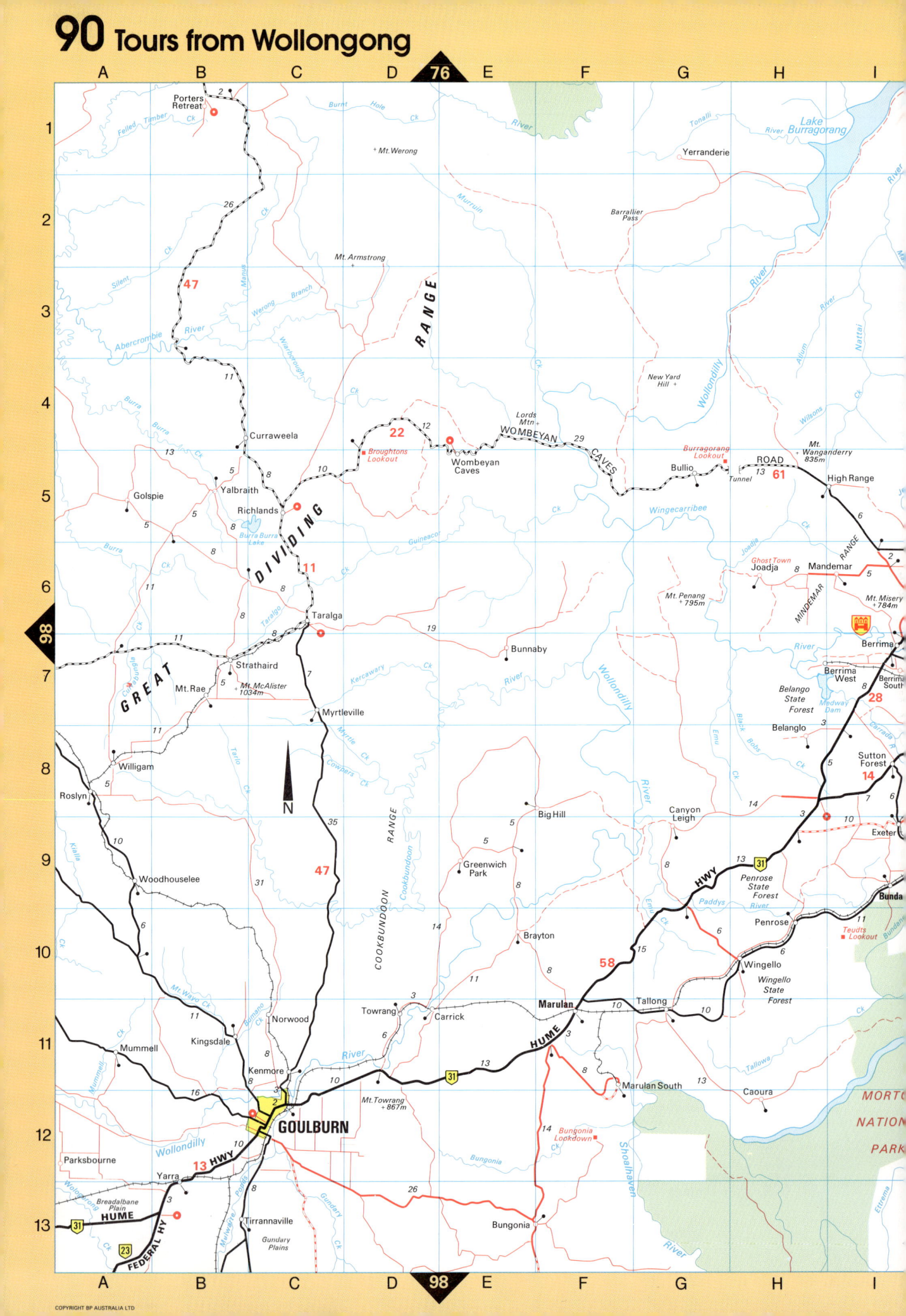

91

92 North Western New South Wales

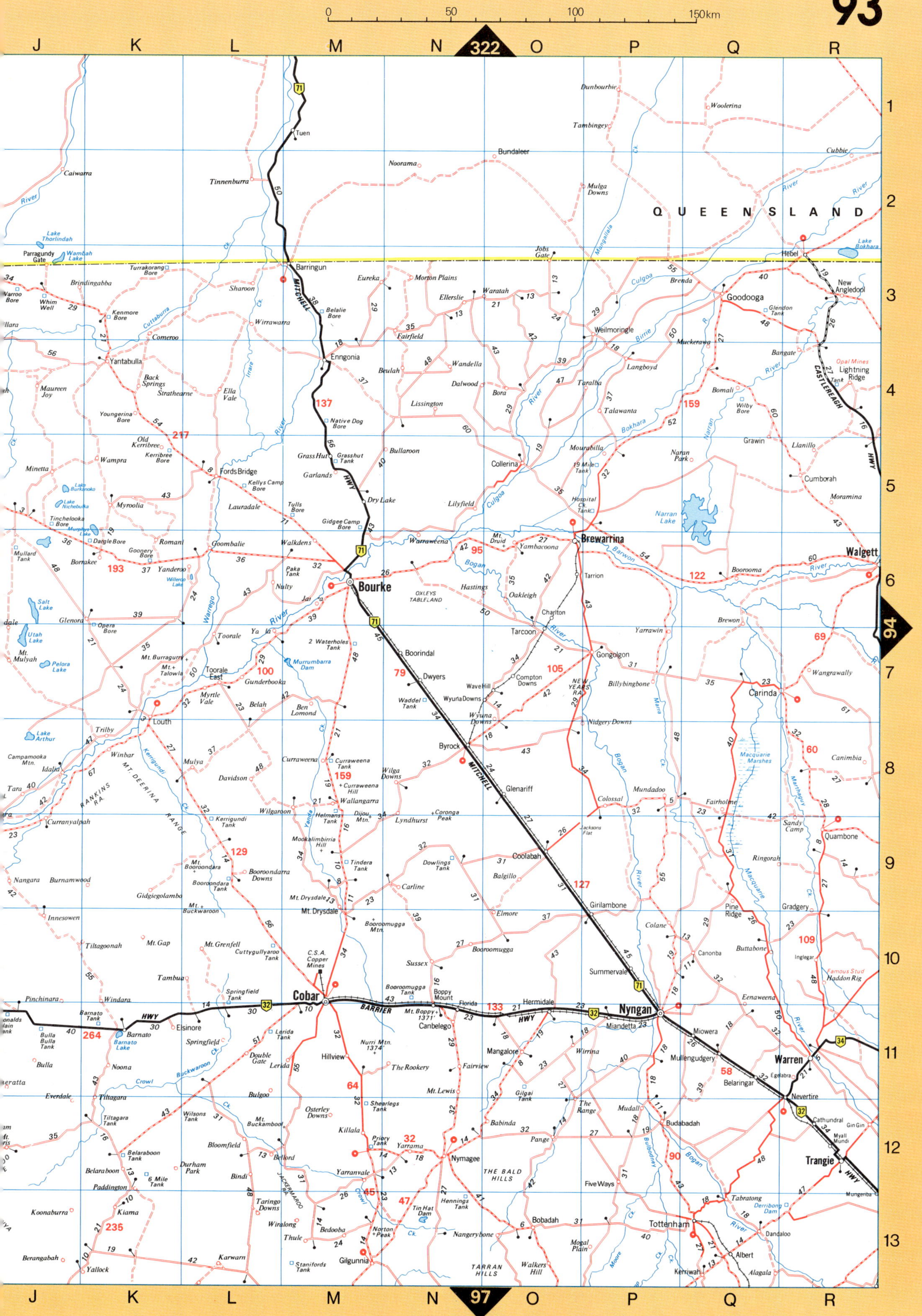

0 50 100 150km
322
94
97
QUEENSLAND
Barringun
Tuen
Tinnenburra
Caiwarra
Noorama
Bundaleer
Dunbourbie
Woolerina
Tambingey
Cubbie
Mulga Downs
Lake Thorlindah
Parragundy Gate
Wambah Lake
Jobs Gate
Hebel
Lake Bokhara
Turrakorang Bore
Brindingabba
Sharoon
Eureka
Morton Plains
Ellerslie
Waratah
Brenda
Goodooga
New Angledool
Whim Well
Kenmore Bore
Belalie Bore
Glendon Tank
Wirrawarra
Comeroo
Fairfield
Weilmoringle
Muckerawa
Yantabulla
Enngonia
Wandella
Beulah
Dalwood
Bora
Taralba
Langboyd
Bangate
Opal Mines
Lightning Ridge
Maureen Joy
Back Springs
Strathearne
Ella Vale
Lissington
Talawanta
Bomali
Wilby Bore
Youngerina Bore
Native Dog Bore
Old Kerribree
Kerribree Bore
Wampra
Bullaroon
Collerina
Mourabilla
Naran Park
Grawin
Llanillo
Grass Hut
Grasshut Tank
Garlands
19 Mile Tank
Cumborah
Minetta
Fords Bridge
Kellys Camp Bore
Lake Burkanoko
Lake Nichebulka
Myroolia
Lauradale
Tulls Bore
Dry Lake
Lilyfield
Hospital Ck. Tank
Moramina
Tinchelooka Bore
Murphys Lake
Dangle Bore
Gidgee Camp Bore
Narran Lake
Romani
Goombalie
Walkdens
Warraweena
Mt. Druid
Yambacoona
Brewarrina
Mullard Tank
Bomakee
Goonery Bore
Yanderoo
Willero Lake
Paka Tank
Nulty
Bourke
Hastings
Oakleigh
Tarrion
Booroma
Walgett
Salt Lake
OXLEYS TABLELAND
Glenora
Opera Bore
Utah Lake
Mt. Mulyah
Pelora Lake
Toorale
Toorale East
Mt. Burragurry
Mt. Talowla
Charlton
Tarcoon
Yarrawin
Brewon
2 Waterholes Tank
Boorindal
Gongolgon
Murrumbarra Dam
Gunderbooka
Myrtle Vale
Belah
Dwyers
Compton Downs
Wave Hill
Wyuna Downs
Billybingbone
Wangrawally
Carinda
Waddel Tank
NEW YEARS RA.
Ben Lomond
Louth
Lake Arthur
Trilby
Nidgery Downs
Campamooka Mtn.
Idalia
Winbar
Byrock
Mulya
MT. DEERINA RANGE
RANKINS RA.
Davidson
Curraweena
Curraweena Tank
Wilga Downs
Curraweena Hill
Macquarie Marshes
Canimbia
Glenariff
Tara
Wallangarra
Colossal
Mundadoo
Fairholme
Curranyalpah
Wilgaroon
Helmans Tank
Dijou Mtn.
Lyndhurst
Coronga Peak
Jacksons Flat
Sandy Camp
Quambone
Kerrigundi Tank
Mookalimbirria Hill
Nangara
Burnamwood
Mt. Booroondara
Booroondara Tank
Booroondarra Downs
Tindera Tank
Dowlings Tank
Coolabah
Balgillo
Ringorah
Gidgiegolamba
Carline
Mt. Drysdale
Mt. Buckwaroon
Elmore
Girilambone
Innesowen
Booroomugga Mtn.
Colane
Pine Ridge
Gradgery
Tiltagoonah
Mt. Gap
Mt. Grenfell
Cuttygullyaroo Tank
Sussex
Booroomugga
Canonba
Buttabone
Inglegar
C.S.A. Copper Mines
Summervale
Famous Stud
Haddon Rig
Tambua
Springfield Tank
Booroomugga Tank
Boppy Mount
Pinchinara
Windara
Cobar
Florida
Hermidale
Nyngan
Eenaweena
Barnato Tank
BARRIER HWY
MITCHELL HWY
CASTLEREAGH HWY
Mt. Boppy 1371'
Canbelego
Miandetta
Miowera
Barnato
Elsinore
Barnato Lake
Lerida Tank
Springfield
Nurri Mtn. 1374'
Mangalore
Wirrina
Bulla Bulla Tank
Bulla
Noona
Double Gate
Lerida
Hillview
The Rookery
Fairview
Mullengudgery
Warren
Belaringar
Egelabra
Everdale
Tiltagara
Crowl
Bulgoo
Mt. Lewis
Gilgai Tank
The Range
Mudall
Nevertire
Tiltagara Tank
Wilsons Tank
Osterley Downs
Shearlegs Tank
Babinda
Budabadah
Cathundral
Gin Gin
Mt. Buckambool
Killala
Myall Mundi
Bloomfield
Priory Tank
Yarrama
Pange
Belaraboon Tank
Belaraboon
Durham Park
Bellord
Nymagee
Trangie
6 Mile Tank
Bindi
Yarranvale
THE BALD HILLS
Five Ways
Paddington
JACKAROO RA.
Mungenba
Kiama
Taringo Downs
Hennings Tank
Tin Hat Dam
Tabratong
Derribong Dam
Koonaburra
Wiralong
Bedooba
Norton Peak
Nangerybone
Bobadah
Tottenham
Dandaloo
Thule
Mogal Plain
Berangabah
Yallock
Karwarn
Stanifords Tank
Gilgunnia
TARRAN HILLS
Walkers Hill
Kerriwah
Albert
Alagala
Warrego River
Darling River
Bogan River
Culgoa River
Birrie River
Barwon River
Macquarie River
Marthaguy Ck.
Yanda Ck.
Bulbodney Ck.
Kerrigundi Ck.
Cuttaburra
Irrara Ck.
Mungallala Ck.
Narran R.
Bokhara
Marra Ck.
Buckwaroon Ck.
J K L M N O P Q R
1 2 3 4 5 6 7 8 9 10 11 12 13

94 North Eastern New South Wales

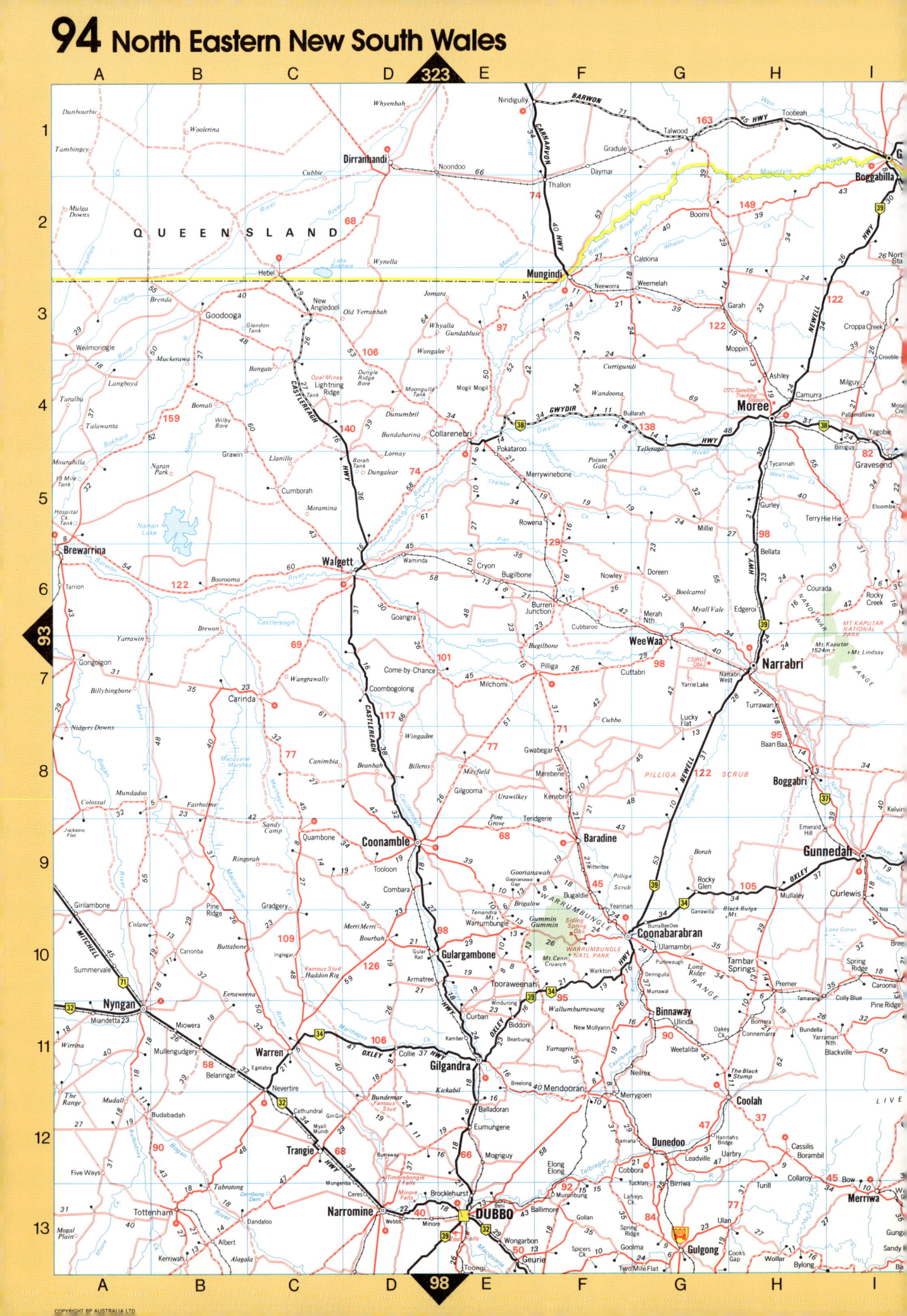

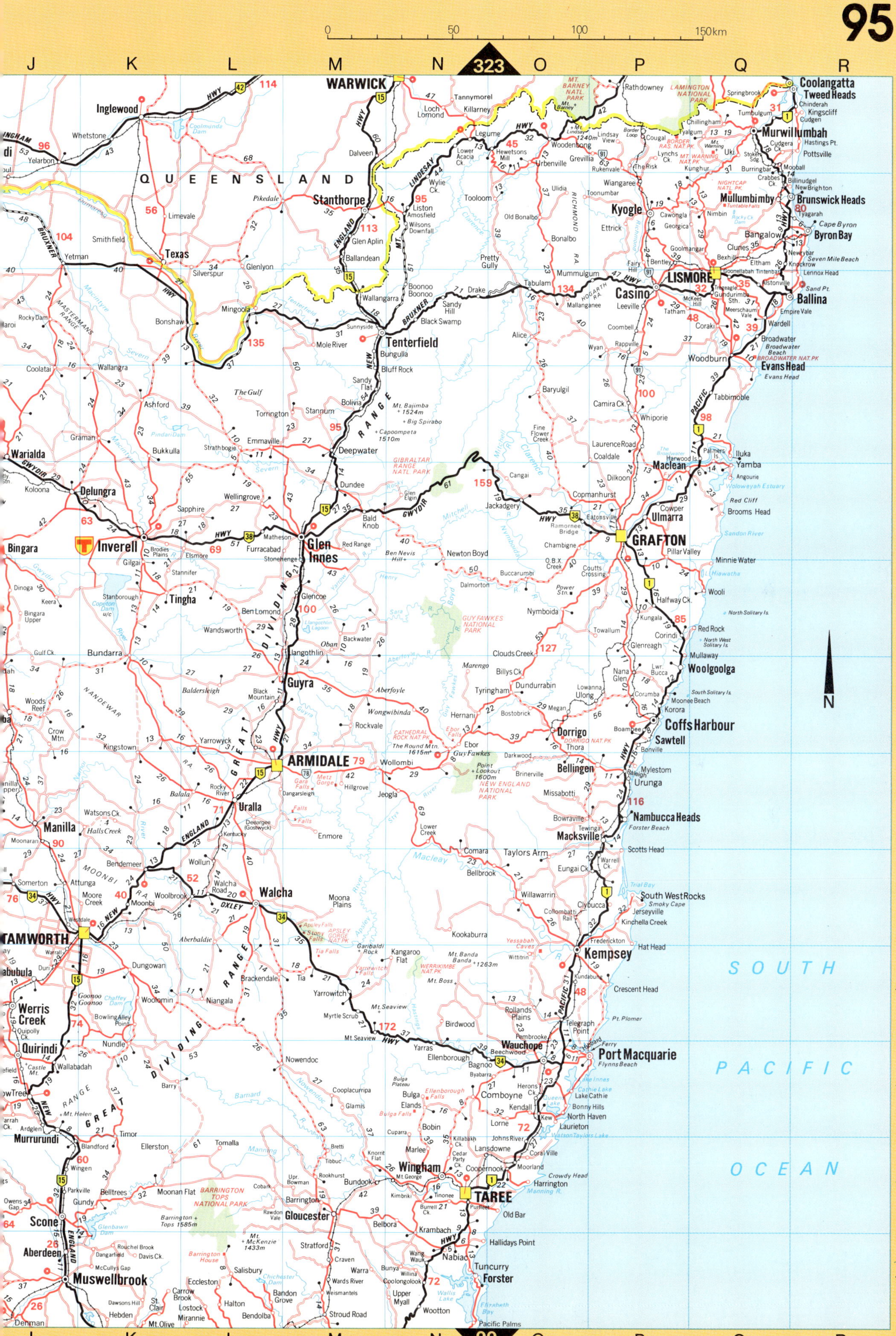
0 50 100 150km
J K L M N 323 O P Q R
1 2 3 4 5 6 7 8 9 10 11 12 13
QUEENSLAND
SOUTH PACIFIC OCEAN
N
WARWICK
Inglewood
Texas
Stanthorpe
Wallangarra
Tenterfield
Coolangatta
Tweed Heads
Murwillumbah
Mullumbimby
Brunswick Heads
Byron Bay
Kyogle
LISMORE
Casino
Ballina
Evans Head
Woodburn
Maclean
Yamba
Iluka
GRAFTON
Ulmarra
Warialda
Delungra
Bingara
Inverell
Tingha
Glen Innes
Deepwater
Emmaville
Guyra
ARMIDALE
Uralla
Walcha
Woolgoolga
Coffs Harbour
Sawtell
Dorrigo
Bellingen
Urunga
Nambucca Heads
Macksville
South West Rocks
Kempsey
Wauchope
Port Macquarie
Manilla
TAMWORTH
Werris Creek
Quirindi
Murrurundi
Scone
Aberdeen
Muswellbrook
Gloucester
Wingham
TAREE
Harrington
Forster
Tuncurry
Nabiac
Laurieton
GUY FAWKES NATIONAL PARK
NEW ENGLAND NATIONAL PARK
BARRINGTON TOPS NATIONAL PARK
GREAT DIVIDING RANGE
NEW ENGLAND HWY
GWYDIR HWY
OXLEY HWY
PACIFIC HWY
BRUXNER HWY
99

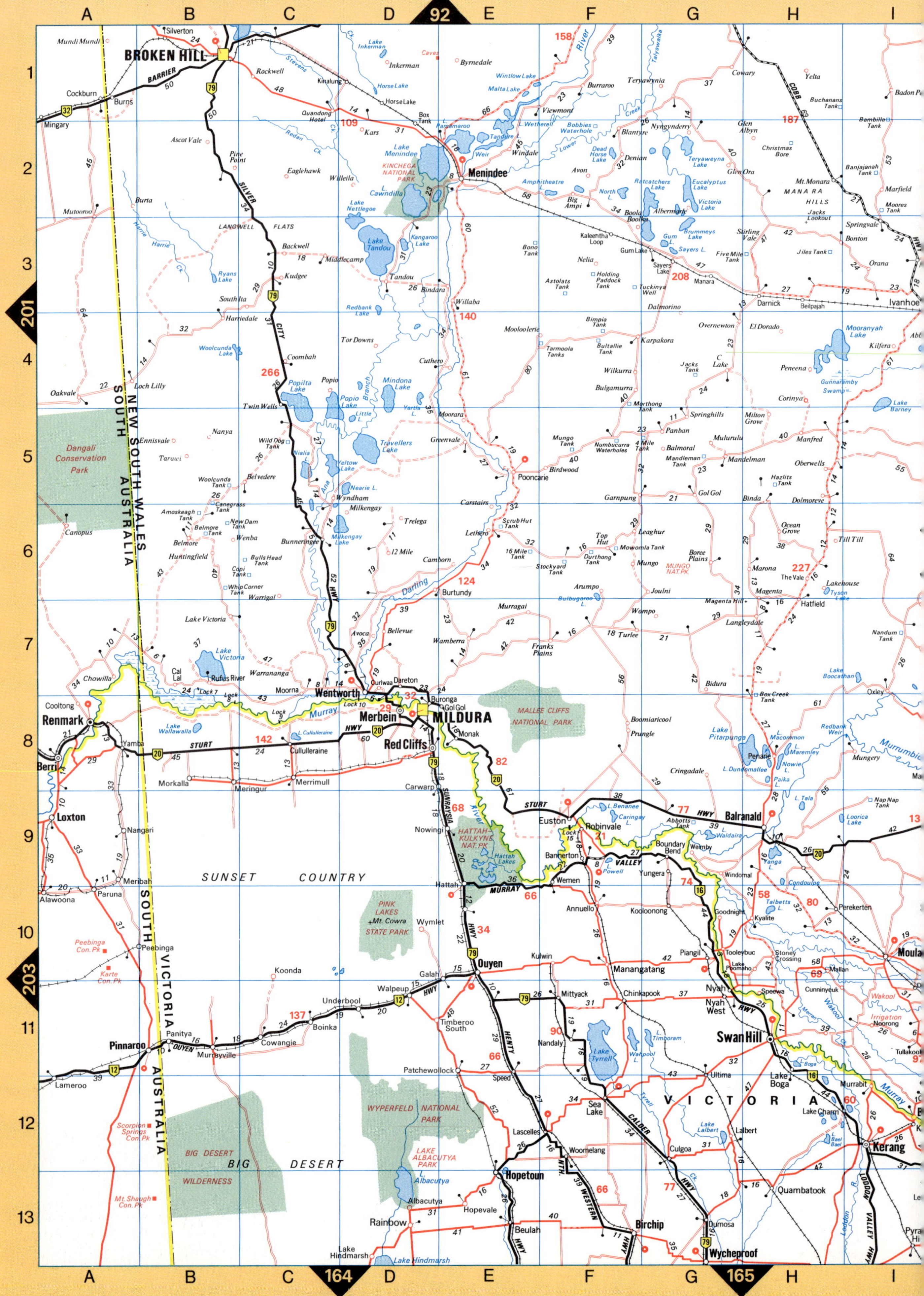
A
B
C
D
E
F
G
H
I
92
164
165
201
203
1
2
3
4
5
6
7
8
9
10
11
12
13
Silverton
Mundi Mundi
BROKEN HILL
BARRIER
Cockburn
Burns
Mingary
Rockwell
Stevens
Kinalung
Quandong Hotel
Kars
Horse Lake
Box Tank
Lake Inkerman
Inkerman
Caves
Byrnedale
Winlow Lake
Malta Lake
Burraroo
Teryawynia
Cowary
Yelta
Badon P
Ascot Vale
Pine Point
Eaglehawk
Willeila
Lake Menindee
KINCHEGA NATIONAL PARK
L. Cawndilla
Menindee
Weir
Windale
Viewmont
L. Wetherell
Bobbies Waterhole
Blantyre
Nyngynderry
Glen Albyn
Christmas Bore
Bambilla Tank
Buchanans Tank
Avon
Dead Horse Lake
Denian
Teryaweyna Lake
Glen Ora
Banjajanah Tank
Marfield
Amphitheatre L.
Big Ampi
North L.
Ratcatchers Lake
Eucalyptus Lake
Mt. Monara
MANARA HILLS
Victoria Lake
Moores Tank
Jacks Lookout
Burta
Mutooroo
Harrie Ck.
LANGWELL FLATS
SILVER
Lake Nettlegoe
Lake Tandou
Kangaroo Lake
Backwell
Middlecamp
Kudgee
Tandou
Bindara
Ryans Lake
South Ita
Harriedale
Bono Tank
Kaleentha Loop
Boola Boolka
Albermarle
Gum L.
Sayers L.
Brummeys Lake
Stirling Vale
Five Mile Tank
Jiles Tank
Springvale
Bonton
Orana
Gum Lake
Sayers Lake
Nelia
Holding Paddock Tank
Astolats Tank
Tuckinya Well
Manara
Dalmorino
Darnick
Beilpajah
Ivanhoe
Willaba
Redbank Lake
Tor Downs
CITY
Coombah
Woolcunda Lake
Loch Lilly
Oakvale
Mooloolerie
Bimpia Tank
Tarmoola Tanks
Bultallie Tank
Karpakora
Overnewton
El Dorado
Mooranyah Lake
Kilfera
Wilkurra
Jacks Tank
C Lake
Peneena
Gunnaramby Swamp
Bulgamurra
Corinya
Lake Barney
Popio
Popiltah Lake
Mindona Lake
Popio Lake
Little L.
Cuthero
Yertla L.
Twin Wells
Moorara
Morthong Tank
Springhills
Milton Grove
NEW SOUTH WALES
SOUTH AUSTRALIA
Dangali Conservation Park
Ennisvale
Nanya
Tarawi
Wild Dog Tank
Nialia Lake
Travellers Lake
Greenvale
Mungo Tank
Numbucurra Waterholes
4 Mile Tank
Panban
Mulurulu
Balmoral
Mandleman Tank
Manfred
Mandelman
Oberwells
Pooncarie
Birdwood
Yeltow Lake
Belvedere
Woolcunda Tank
Nearie L.
Wyndham
Garnpung
Gol Gol
Binda
Hazlits Tank
Dolmoreve
Canegrass Tank
Milkengay
Carstairs
Amoskeagh Tank
Canopus
New Dam Tank
Belmore Tank
Belmore
Wenba
Trelega
Scrub Hut Tank
Leaghur
Ocean Grove
Milkengay Lake
Bunneringee
Lethero
Top Hut
Mowomla Tank
Till Till
Huntingfield
Bulls Head Tank
12 Mile
16 Mile Tank
Durthong Tank
Boree Plains
Camborn
Stockyard Tank
Mungo
MUNGO NAT. PK.
Marona
The Vale
Copi Tank
Whip Corner Tank
Warrigal
Darling
Burtundy
Arumpo
Bulbugaroo L.
Joulni
Magenta
Lakehouse
Tyson Lake
Magenta Hill
Hatfield
Lake Victoria
Murragai
Wompo
Langleydale
HWY
Avoca
Bellevue
Wamberra
Franks Plains
Turlee
Nandum Tank
Lake Victoria
Chowilla
Cal Lal
Rufus River
Warrananga
Lock 7
Lock 8
Moorna
Wentworth
Curlwaa
Dareton
Buronga
Gol Gol
Lock 10
Lock 9
Lock 11
Murray
Bidura
Lake Boocathan
Oxley
Cooltong
Renmark
Lake Wallawalla
L. Cullulleraine
Merbein
MILDURA
MALLEE CLIFFS NATIONAL PARK
Box Creek Tank
Boomiaricool
Prungle
Lake Pitarpunga
L. Macommon
L. Marameley
Redbank Weir
Murrumbidgee
Mungery
Monak
Yamba
STURT
Cullulleraine
Red Cliffs
Berri
Penarie
Nowie L.
Paika L.
L. Dundomallee
Cringadale
Morkalla
Meringur
Merrimull
Carwarp
SUNRAYSIA
Loxton
Euston
L. Benanee
Caringay L.
Abbotts Tank
Balranald
L. Tala
Nap Nap Tank
Loorica Lake
Nangari
Nowingi
HATTAH-KULKYNE NAT. PK.
Hattah Lakes
Robinvale
Lock 15
Waldaira L.
Boundary Bend
Weimby
Yanga L.
SUNSET COUNTRY
Meribah
Paruna
Alawoona
Bannerton
VALLEY
Powell
Yungera
Wemen
Windomal
Condoulpe L.
Hattah
Annuello
Kooloonong
Talbetts L.
Perekerten
Goodnight
Kyalite
PINK LAKES STATE PARK
Mt. Cowra
Wymlet
Peebinga Con. Pk
Peebinga
Karte Con. Pk
Koonda
Ouyen
Kulwin
Manangatang
Piangil
Tooleybuc
Stoney Crossing
Mallan
Moulamein
Lake Poomaho
Galah
Walpeup
Underbool
Mittyack
Chinkapook
Nyah
Nyah West
Speewa
Cunninyeuk
Wakool
Irrigation
Noorong
Tullakool
Boinka
Timberoo South
HENTY
Nandaly
L. Timboram
Walpool L.
Lake Tyrrell
Swan Hill
Pinnaroo
Panitya
OUYEN
Murrayville
Cowangie
VICTORIA
Patchewollock
Speed
Ultima
Lake Boga
Murrabit
Lameroo
Sea Lake
CALDER
Tyrrell
L. Boga
Lake Charm
WYPERFELD NATIONAL PARK
Scorpion Springs Con. Pk
Lascelles
Woomelang
Lake Lalbert
Lalbert
Bael Bael L.
Kerang
BIG DESERT WILDERNESS
BIG DESERT
LAKE ALBACUTYA PARK
L. Albacutya
Hopetoun
Culgoa
NTH.
WESTERN
Quambatook
LODDON VALLEY
Mt. Shaugh Con. Pk
Albacutya
Hopevale
Rainbow
Beulah
Birchip
Dumosa
Lake Hindmarsh
Wycheproof
Loddon R.
Pyramid Hill

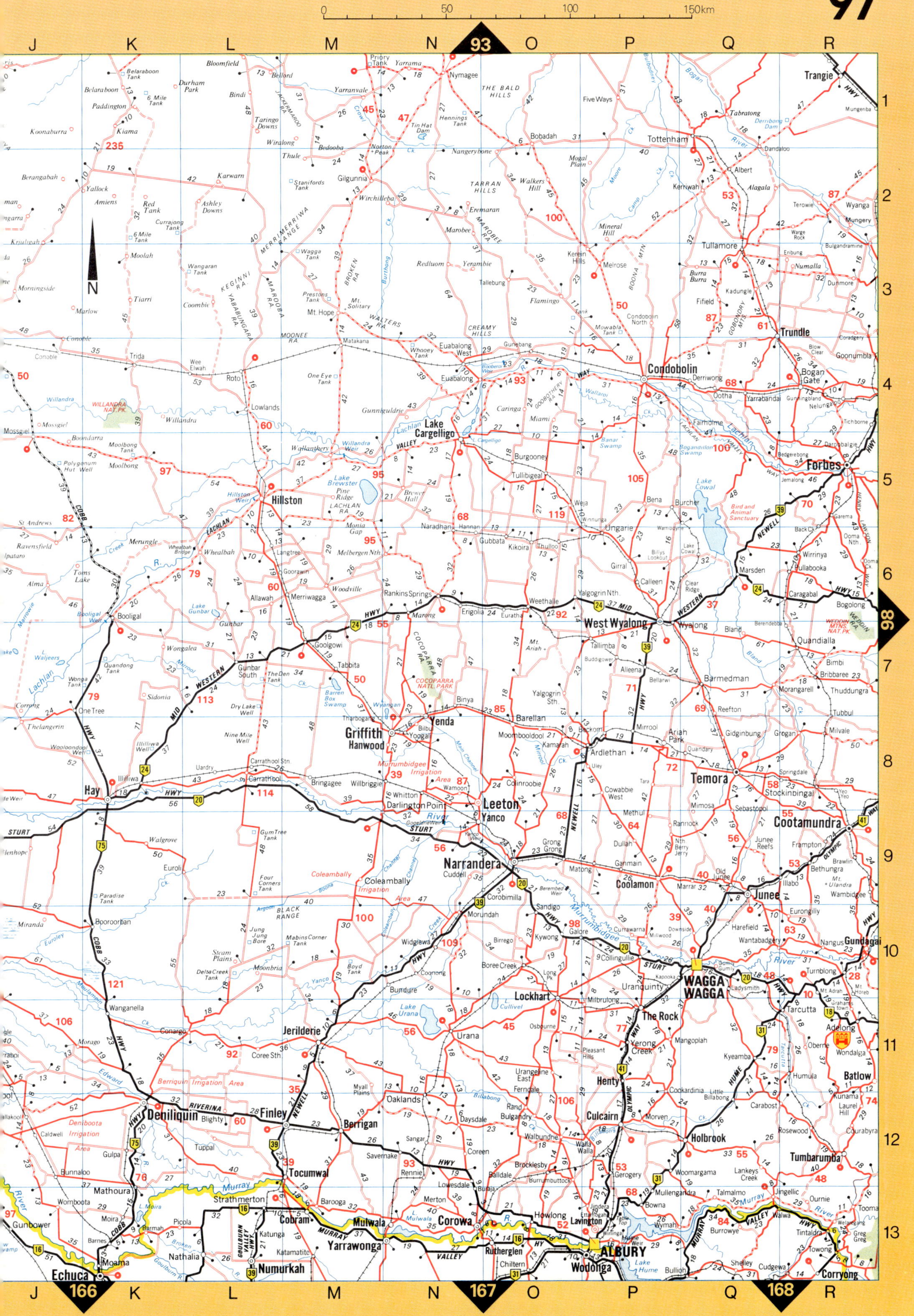

98 Central Eastern New South Wales

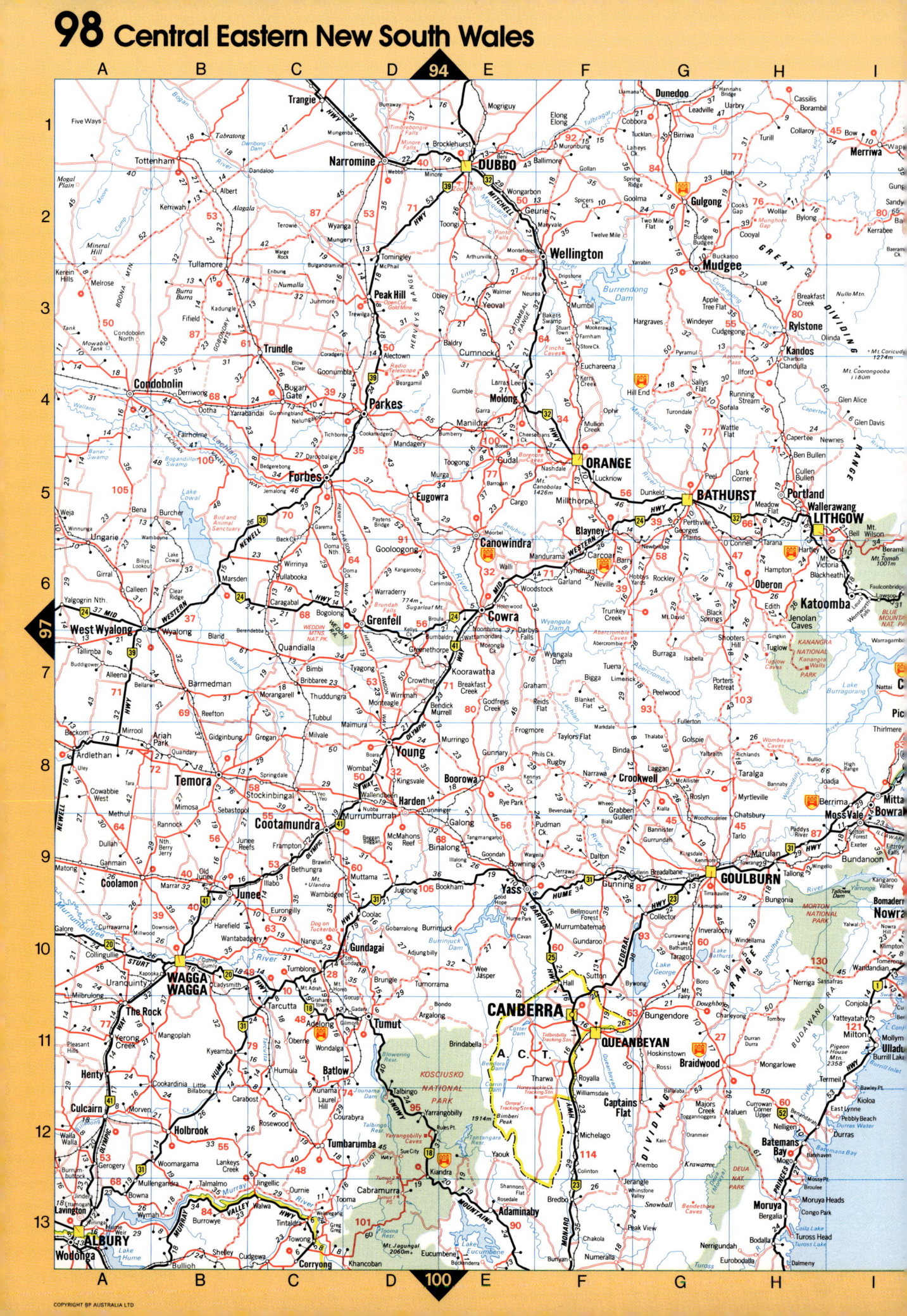

0
50
100
150km
95
J K L M N O P Q R
1 2 3 4 5 6 7 8 9 10 11 12 13
TAREE
Harrington
Manning R.
Old Bar
Hallidays Point
Tuncurry
Forster
Nabiac
Krambach
Gloucester
Barrington
Bundook
Cobark
Upr. Bowman
Stratford
Craven
Warra
Bunya
Wards River
Weismantels
Stroud Road
Stroud
Booral
Bulahdelah
Wootton
Bungwahl
Pacific Palms
Sugarloaf Bay
Seal Rocks
Myall Lake
MYALL LAKES NAT. PK.
The Broadwater
Tamboy
Broughton Is.
Tea Gardens
Hawks Nest
Port Stephens
Nelson Bay
Raymond Terrace
Williamtown
Karuah
Port Hunter
Stockton
NEWCASTLE
Belmont
L. Macquarie
Swansea
Toronto
Cooranbong
Morisset
Wyee
Doyalson
Budgewoi
Norah Head
Tuggerah Lake
The Entrance
Ourimbah
Gosford
Wyong
Kulnura
Calga
BRISBANE WATER NAT. PK.
Broken Bay
Palm Beach
KU-RING-GAI CHASE NAT. PK.
HORNSBY
Mona Vale
Narrabeen Lagoon
Long Reef
Port Jackson
SYDNEY
PARRAMATTA
LIVERPOOL
PENRITH
Windsor
Wilberforce
Pitt Town
Ebenezer
Kurrajong
Botany Bay
CAMPBELLTOWN
ROYAL NATL. PK.
Appin
Garie
Stanwell Park
Coledale
Bulli
Corrimal
WOLLONGONG
Unanderra
Red Pt.
Port Kembla
Lake Illawarra
SHELLHARBOUR
Bass Pt.
Bombo
Kiama
Gerringong
Shoalhaven Heads
Orient Pt (Crookhaven Heads)
Culburra
L. Wollumboola
Worrain Beach
Currarong
Jervis Bay
Scone
Aberdeen
Muswellbrook
Denman
Singleton
Branxton
MAITLAND
CESSNOCK
Kurri Kurri
Abermain
Bellbird
Wallsend
Millfield
Wollombi
Broke
Bulga
Howes Valley
Mt. Yengo 668m
Mt. Poppong 365m
Paynes Crossing
Bucketty
St.Albans
DHARUG NATL. PARK
Colo Heights
Wisemans Ferry
Dungog
Gresford
Paterson
Vacy
Clarence town
Seaham
Woodville
Morpeth
Lochinvar
Glendon Brook
Mt.Olive
Liddell
Ravensworth
Camberwell
Jerrys Plains
Warkworth
Mt.Thorley
Hebden
Dawsons Hill
St. Clair
Carrow Brook
Lostock
Mirannie
Eccleston
Halton
Bendolba
Trevallyn
Salisbury
Chichester Dam
Bandon Grove
BARRINGTON TOPS NATIONAL PARK
Barrington Tops 1585m
Mt. McKenzie 1433m
Barrington House
Moonan Flat
Belltrees
Gundy
Parkville
Glenbawn Dam
Rouchel Brook
Dangarfield
Davis Ck.
McCullys Gap
Owens Gap
Upper Myall
Coolongolook
Wang Wauk
Belbora
Tinonee
Kimbriki
Burrell Ck.
Purfleet
Wallis Lake
Elizabeth Bay
Limeburners Ck.
HWY
PACIFIC
ENGLAND
N
SOUTH PACIFIC OCEAN

100 South Eastern New South Wales

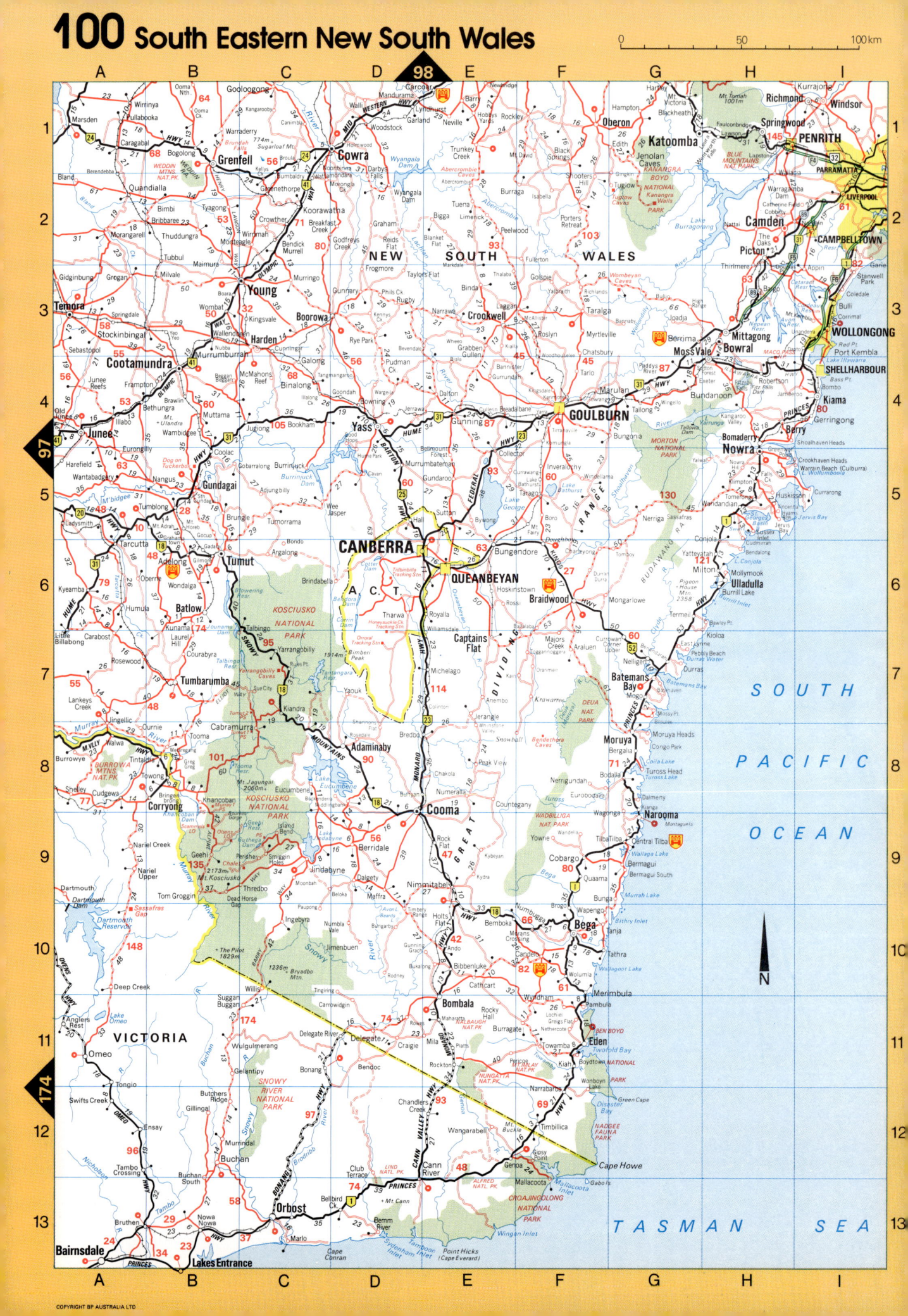

Bathurst & Orange 101

102 Sydney to Melbourne by the Main Routes

If you value views more than speed, take the meandering Princes Highway (1048 km from Melbourne to Sydney). In parts the road narrows and winds, making progress slow, but what you gain in panoramic views and delightful stopping places more than makes up for the extra driving time. The scenery — particularly along the lovely rugged Illawarra coast — is unsurpassed; and the whole area is dotted with enticing fishing and resort towns. These include Eden, Bega, Narooma and Batemans Bay. You will need to book accommodation well ahead during holiday periods.

If you are in a hurry, you will save a good two hours by taking the excellent Hume Highway (885 km from Melbourne to Sydney). A word of warning: many trucks favour this well-maintained highway, which can be frustrating to the motor car driver, and demands the utmost concentration. Suggested stop-overs are Albury-Wodonga, Gundagai, Yass or Goulburn. If your schedule allows, stop for a stroll through the charming historic village of Berrima.

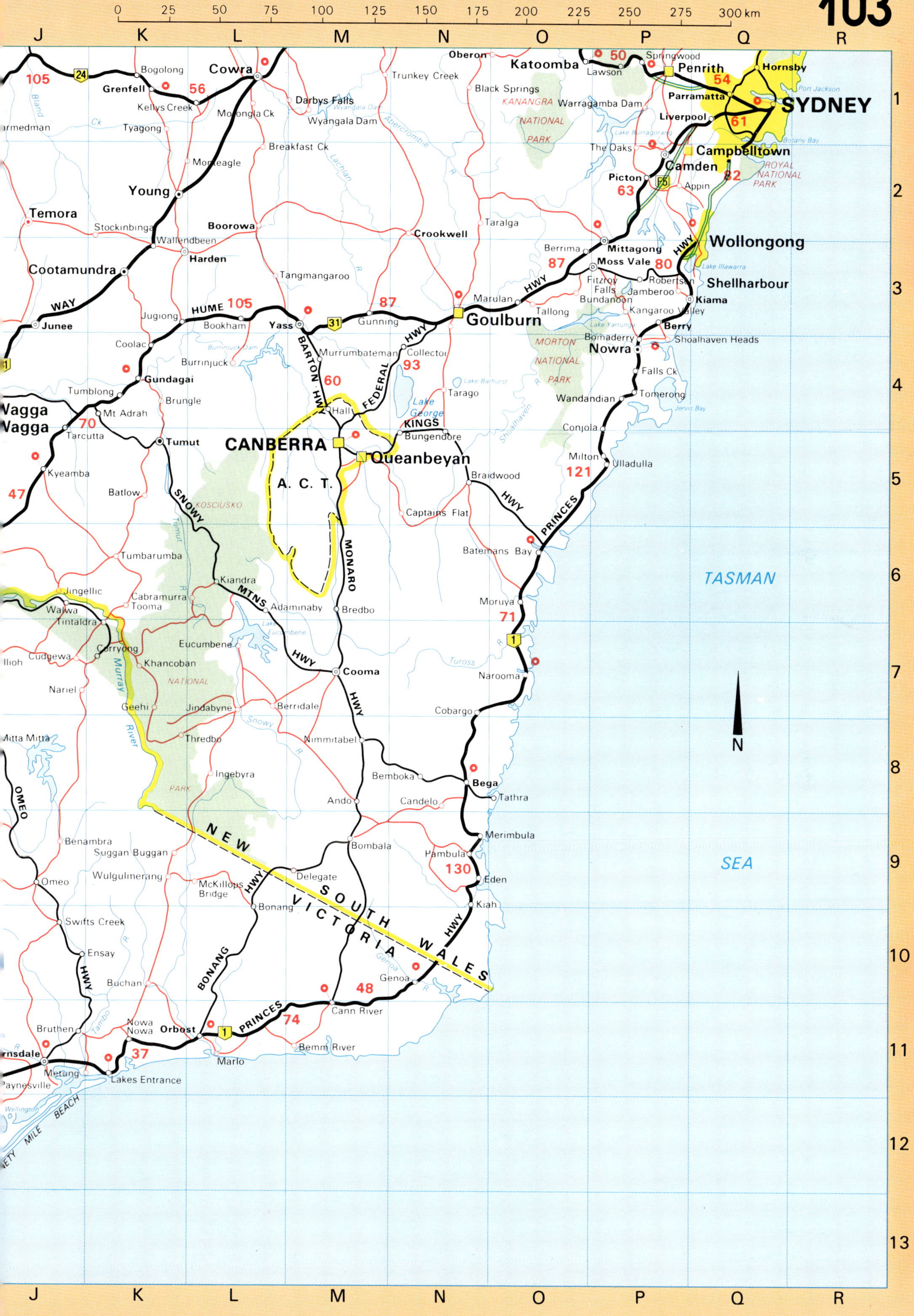

0 25 50 75 100 125 150 175 200 225 250 275 300 km
J K L M N O P Q R
1 2 3 4 5 6 7 8 9 10 11 12 13
SYDNEY
Hornsby
Penrith
Springwood
Lawson
Katoomba
Oberon
Parramatta
Liverpool
Port Jackson
Botany Bay
Campbelltown
Camden
Picton
The Oaks
Appin
ROYAL NATIONAL PARK
Wollongong
Lake Illawarra
Shellharbour
Kiama
Berry
Shoalhaven Heads
Nowra
Bomaderry
Falls Ck
Tomerong
Jervis Bay
Wandandian
Conjola
Milton
Ulladulla
Batemans Bay
Moruya
Narooma
Cobargo
Bega
Tathra
Merimbula
Pambula
Eden
Kiah
Genoa
Cann River
Bemm River
Marlo
Orbost
Nowa Nowa
Lakes Entrance
Metung
Paynesville
Bruthen
Buchan
Ensay
Swifts Creek
Omeo
Benambra
Suggan Buggan
Wulgulmerang
McKillops Bridge
Bonang
Delegate
Bombala
Candelo
Ando
Bemboka
Nimmitabel
Cooma
Berridale
Jindabyne
Thredbo
Ingebyra
Eucumbene
Lake Eucumbene
Adaminaby
Kiandra
Cabramurra
Tooma
Khancoban
Geehi
Corryong
Cudgewa
Nariel
Tintaldra
Walwa
Jingellic
Tumbarumba
Batlow
Tumut
Kyeamba
Tarcutta
Mt Adrah
Wagga Wagga
Tumblong
Gundagai
Brungle
Coolac
Jugiong
Junee
Cootamundra
Harden
Wallendbeen
Stockinbingal
Temora
Young
Monteagle
Tyagong
Kellys Creek
Grenfell
Bogolong
Cowra
Mogongla Ck
Darbys Falls
Wyangala Dam
Breakfast Ck
Boorowa
Crookwell
Taralga
Trunkey Creek
Black Springs
KANANGRA NATIONAL PARK
Warragamba Dam
Lake Burragorang
Mittagong
Berrima
Moss Vale
Robertson
Fitzroy Falls
Bundanoon
Jamberoo
Kangaroo Valley
Marulan
Tallong
Lake Yarrunga
MORTON NATIONAL PARK
Goulburn
Gunning
Tangmangaroo
Yass
Bookham
Burrinjuck
Burrinjuck Dam
Murrumbateman
Collector
Lake George
Lake Bathurst
Tarago
Bungendore
Hall
CANBERRA
Queanbeyan
A. C. T.
Captains Flat
Braidwood
Bredbo
KOSCIUSKO NATIONAL PARK
Tasman
TASMAN SEA
N
HUME HWY
BARTON HWY
FEDERAL HWY
KINGS HWY
MONARO HWY
SNOWY MTNS HWY
PRINCES HWY
BONANG HWY
OMEO HWY
NEW SOUTH WALES
VICTORIA
NINETY MILE BEACH
Lake Wellington
Murray River
Snowy R
Tumut
Shoalhaven
Lachlan
Abercrombie
Tuross
Tambo
Genoa
Bland Ck
24 31 1 F5
105 56 87 60 93 54 61 82 63 50 80 121 71 70 47 130 48 74 37

104 Kosciusko National Park Alpine Resorts

Canberra City 105

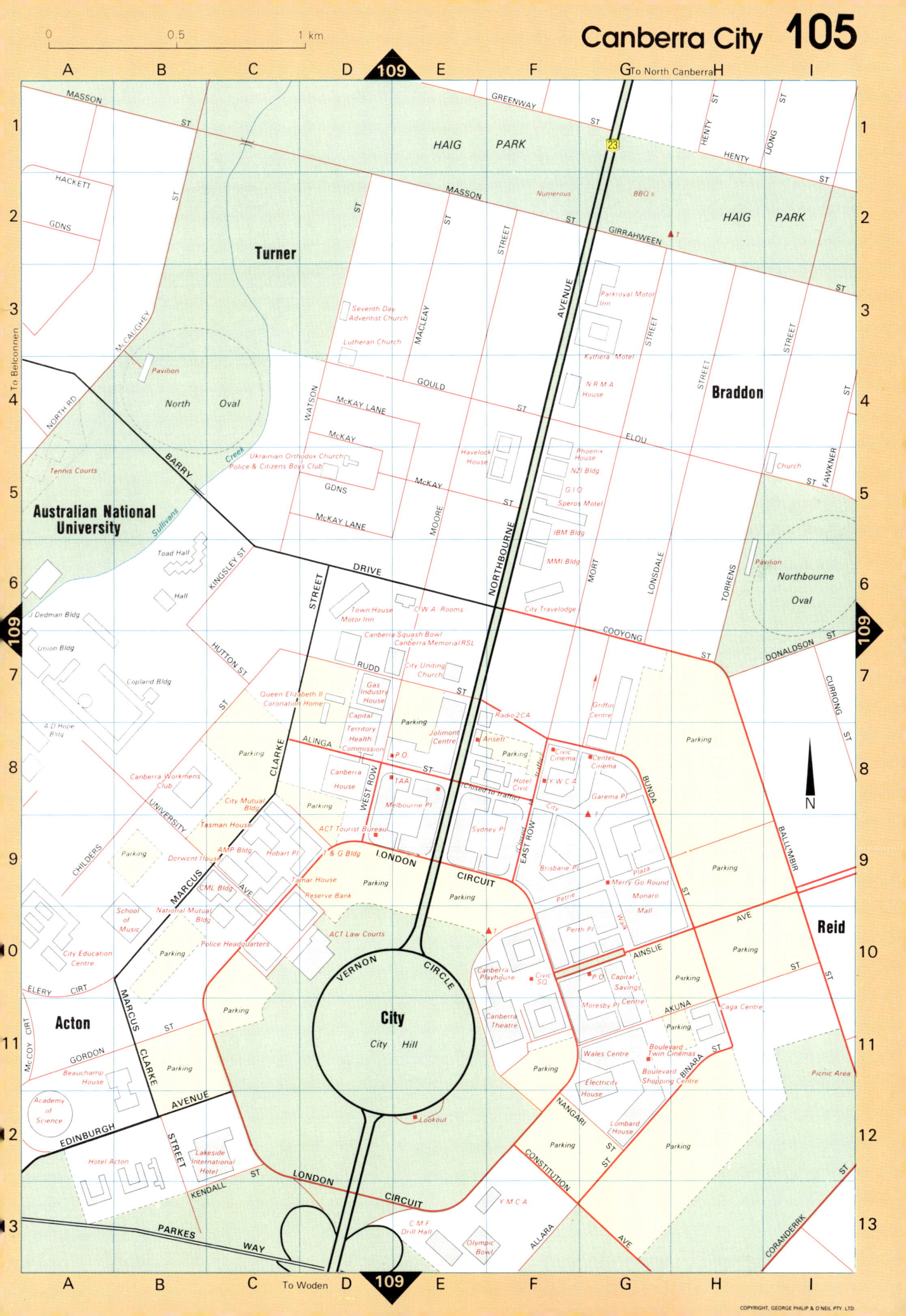

106 Canberra & Northern Suburbs

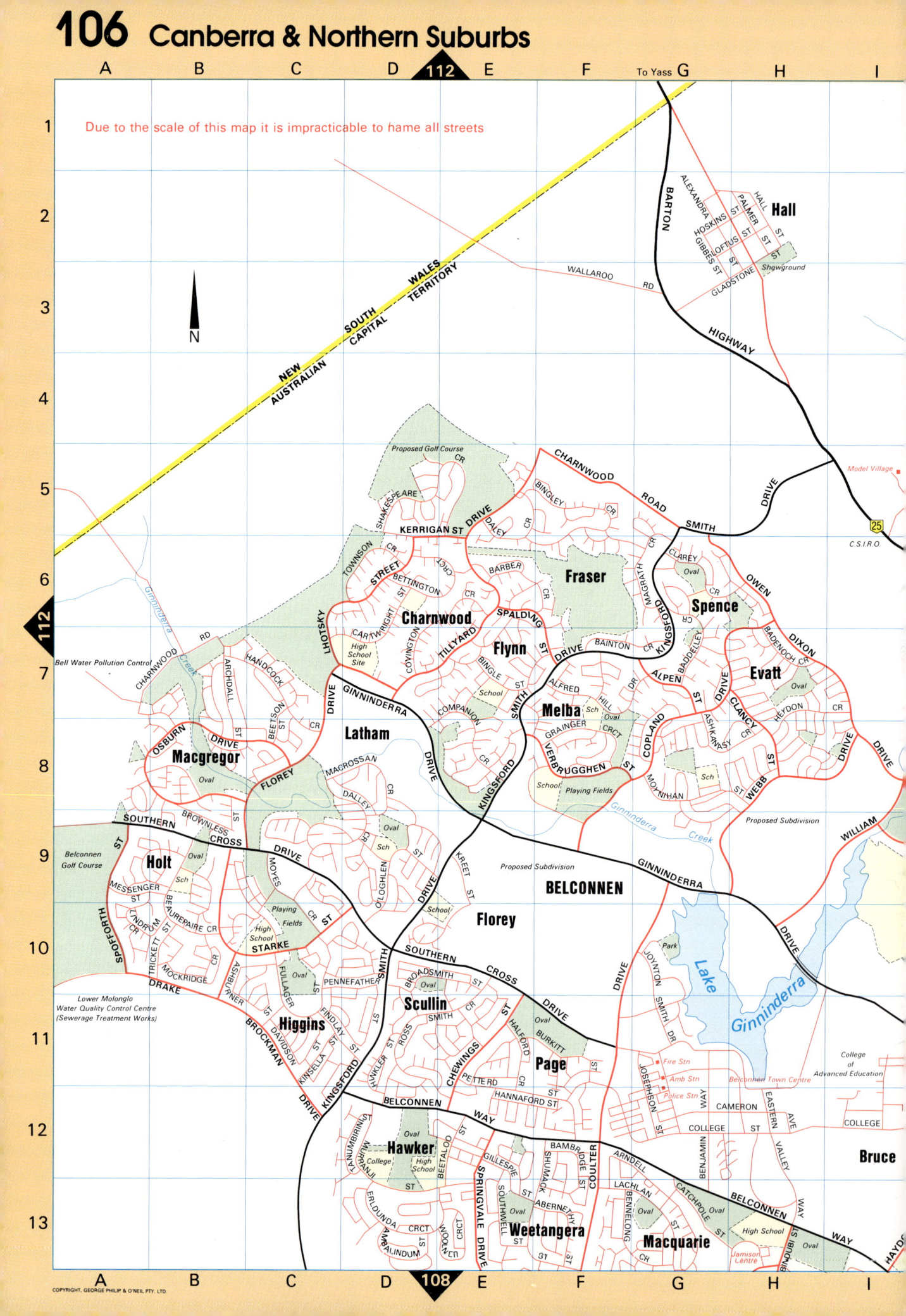

107

108 Canberra & Central Suburbs

Due to the scale of this map it is impracticable to name all streets

109

DIPLOMATIC MISSIONS

#	Country	Ref
1	Arab Republic of Egypt	L13
2	Argentina	K12
3	Austria	K13
4	Bangladesh	J9
5	Belgium	J9
6	Britain	K8
7	Burma	K13
8	Canada	K8
9	Chile	K13
10	Cyprus	L13
11	France	K8
12	German Republic	K13
13	Germany	J9
14	Greece	L11
15	Holy See	N6
16	Hungary	J9
17	India	K13
18	Indonesia	K8
19	Iran Imperial	K11
20	Ireland	L13
21	Israel	J9
22	Italy	K9
23	Japan	J9
24	Jordan	L6
25	Korea	K12
26	Laos	I13
27	Lebanon	J9
28	Malaysia	K8
29	Malta	K13
30	New Zealand	K8
31	Nigeria	K9
32	Pakistan	L10
33	Papua-New Guinea	K13
34	Peru	K11
35	Philippines	K9
36	Polish Peoples Republic	K11
37	Portugal	K12
38	Singapore	K13
39	South Africa	K8
40	Sri Lanka	L10
41	Sweden	J9
42	Switzerland	K10
43	Thailand	J9
44	The Netherlands	J9
45	Turkey	K12
46	USSR	M11
47	USA	K9
48	Uruguay	L11
49	Vietnam	K13
50	Yugoslavia	L13

110 Canberra & Southern Suburbs

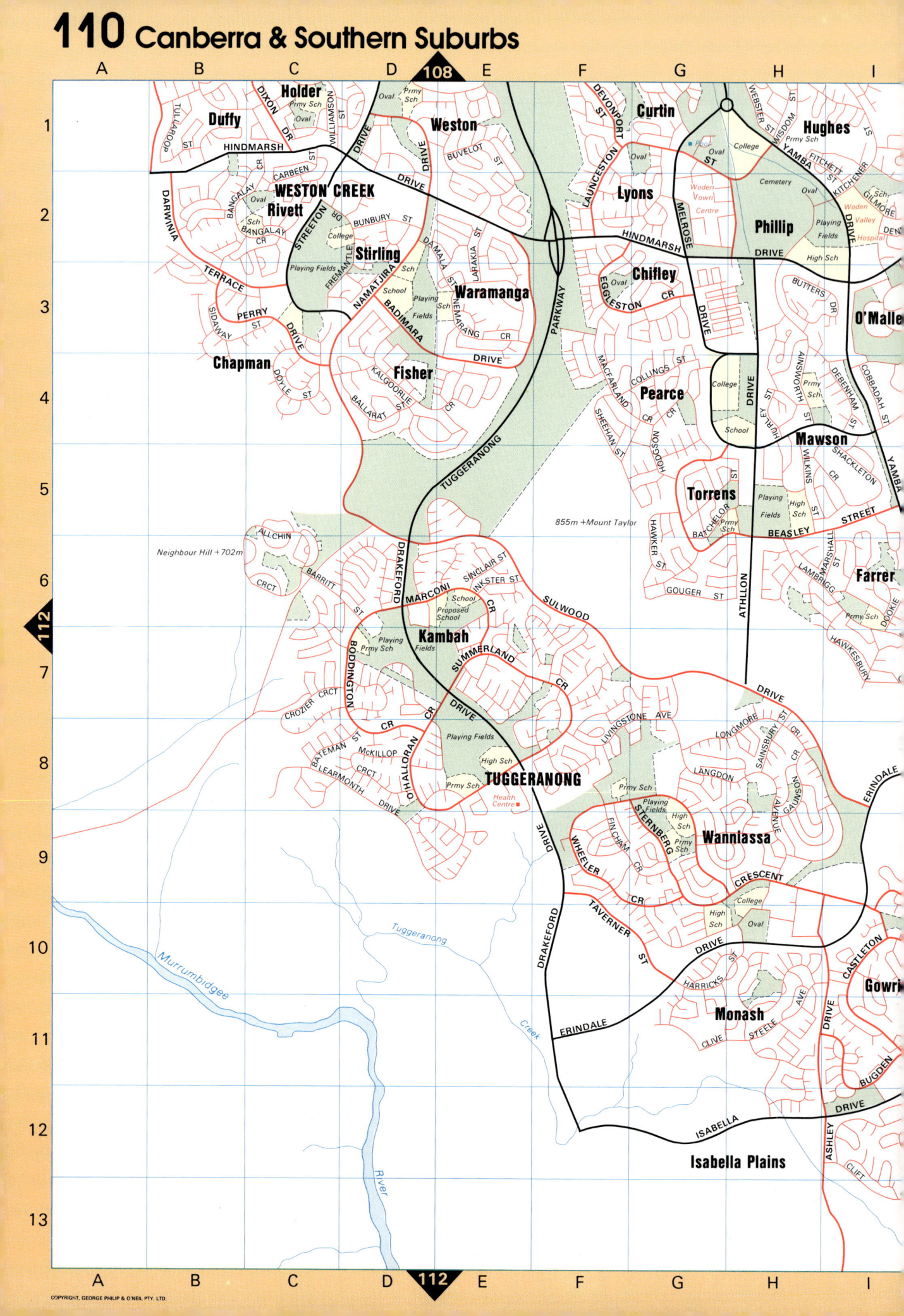

111

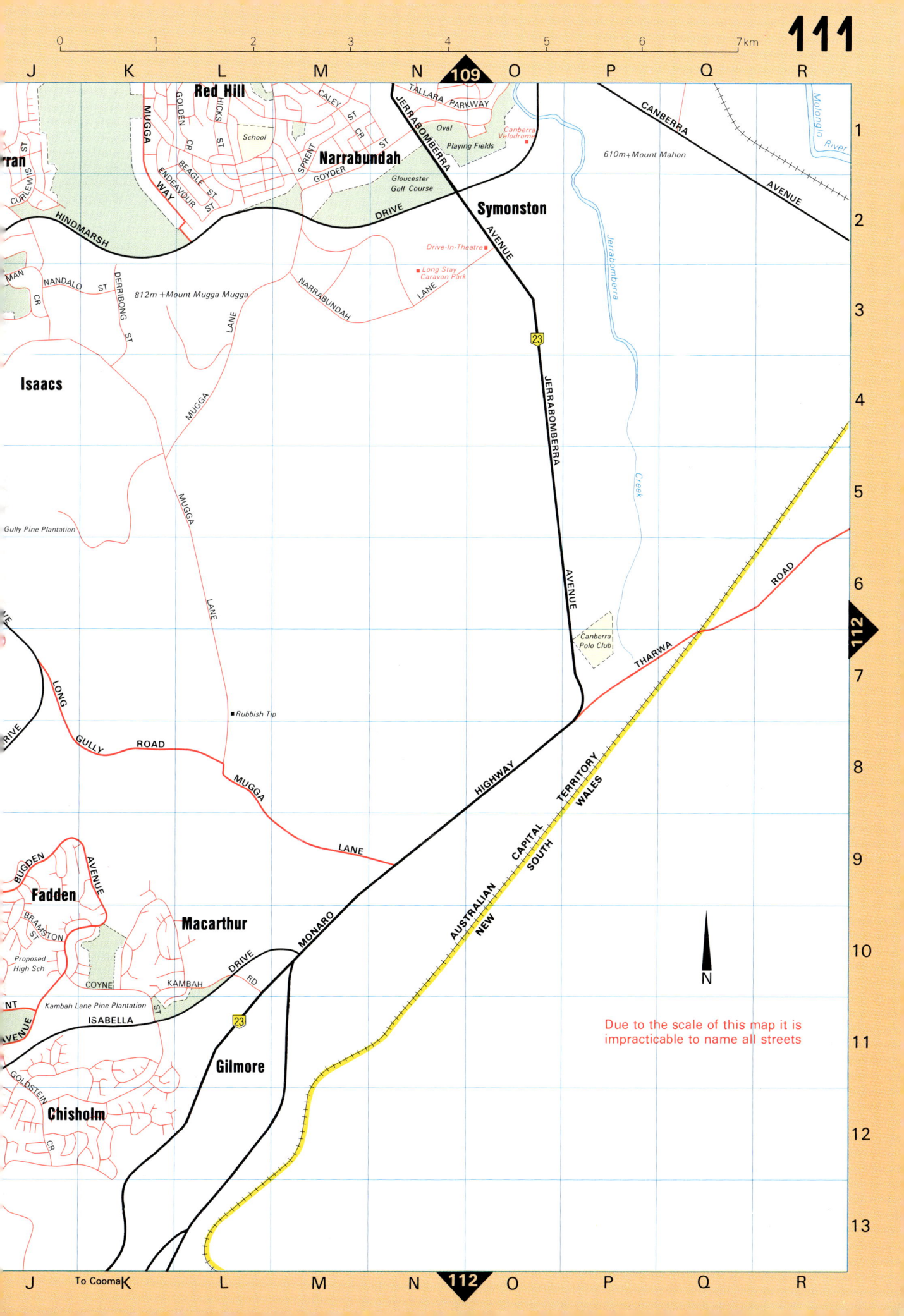

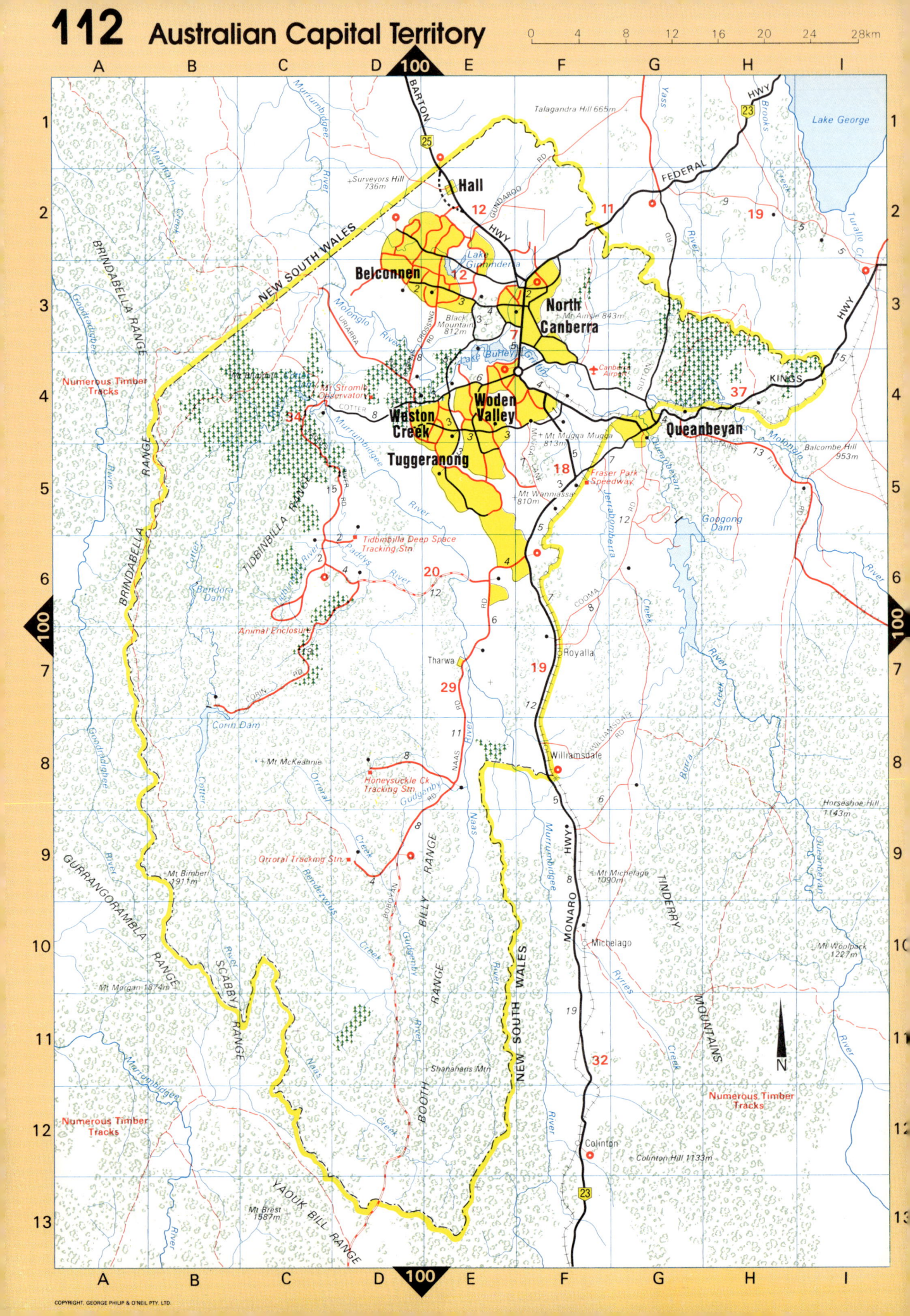

112 Australian Capital Territory

AUSTRALIAN CAPITAL TERRITORY

The ACT is a 250 000 hectares area which has an air of spaciousness and grace enhanced by the beautiful valley of the Molonglo River and the surrounding hills, mountains and pastureland, typical of eastern rural Australia.

There are four distinct seasons, a warm spring, a hot dry summer, a brilliant cool autumn, and a cold winter with occasional snow. Perhaps the best time to visit the ACT is in the autumn, when there is a magnificent display of golden foliage. Over three million Australian and overseas visitors come to the ACT each year.

Despite the gleaming modern style of the city of Canberra, there are still interesting vestiges of the old Limestone Plains settlement which existed before the city was developed. The sandstone homestead of the Duntroon estate, now the Officer's Mess at Duntroon Royal Military College, is the finest old house in the ACT. The single-storey part of the house was built in 1833 and the two-storey extension was completed in 1856.

The Church of St John the Baptist, begun in 1841, records on its tombstones and other memorials much of the area's early history. The adjacent school house containing relics of this history is regularly open to visitors. Many of the stained glass windows of St John's Church commemorate members of the pioneer families, including Robert Campbell, the founder of Duntroon estate. Blundell's farmhouse built in 1858 by Campbell for his ploughman has been furnished by the Canberra and District Historical Society with pieces contemporary to the district's early history.

There are a number of lookouts on the surrounding hills which give superb views of the city. The Telecommunication Tower on Black Mountain is the highest. Mount Ainslie offers fine views of central Canberra and Lake Burley Griffin. Red Hill overlooks the new Parliament House site, south Canberra and the Woden Valley. Mount Pleasant has memorials to the Royal Regiment of Australian Artillery and the Royal Australian Armoured Corps at its summit.

RIGHT: *Duntroon. This fine old sandstone house was once the homestead of the Duntroon Estate, now it serves as the Officers' Mess at Duntroon Military College.*

At the Tidbinbilla Nature Reserve, an area of more than 5000 hectares has been developed to enable visitors to see Australian flora and fauna in their natural surroundings. Another favourite spot is the Cotter Dam and Reserve where there are pleasant picnic and camping areas, river swimming and a children's playground. Nearby is the Mount Stromlo Observatory, its large silver domes and buildings housing the huge telescope of the Department of Astronomy of the Australian National University. Further out from the city is the deep space tracking station at Tidbinbilla which is one of the most technologically advanced in the world.

BELOW: *Tidbinbilla Tracking Station is one of the most technologically advanced deep space tracking stations in the world.*

BELOW: *Cotter Reserve is a lovely spot on a sunny day for a picnic, a swim or a barbecue lunch.*

Far left: Lorne is a resort popular for family holidays in the summer months.

Left: The Twelve Apostles, one of many spectacular landforms to be found on Victoria's ocean coast.

Above: Rich farming land at Yarra Glen is typical of much of Victoria's countryside.

Right: The Victorian Arts Centre with its imposing spire, theatre and concert hall.

Victoria
GARDEN STATE

Victoria is an ideal state for the motoring tourist. It is quite easy, during one day's drive, to explore mountain country, pastoral landscape, spectacular coastline, yet still arrive at your destination in time to watch the sunset.

The Garden State's earliest explorers, of course, were from a pre-motor age. What they saw did little to arouse their enthusiasm. After an unsuccessful attempt at settlement in the Port Phillip area in 1802, it was not until 1834 that parties from Van Diemen's Land, searching for more arable land, settled along the south-west coast of Victoria. Their glowing reports prompted John Batman and John Fawkner to investigate the Port Phillip area. They liked what they saw and purchased land on opposite sides of the Yarra from Aboriginal tribes. The Colonial Office in London expressed disapproval of these transactions, but in those times possession was nine points of the law. A squatting colony grew up rapidly in the district and the new town was named Melbourne after the British Prime Minister of the day.

Nervous of inheriting the penal system of settlement, Victoria sought separation from New South Wales; it was granted in 1851. At about that time, gold was discovered near Ballarat and the state's population more than doubled within a year. Apart from a serious, but short-lived, setback caused by land speculation in the early 1890s, Victoria has gone from strength to strength ever since.

Today, Victoria is the most closely settled and industrialised part of the nation, responsible for about one-third of the gross national product. Melbourne has been traditionally regarded as the 'financial capital' of the country.

Melbourne's inner areas are graced by spacious parks and street upon street of elegant and well preserved Victorian and Edwardian architecture, contrasting strongly with modern tower blocks.

Beyond the city, the Dandenong Ranges, 50 kilometres to the east, are noted for their forests of eucalypts, graceful tree ferns, their many established European-style gardens and an increasing number of good restaurants and galleries. Phillip Island, just a few hours' drive away, is famed for its unique fairy penguin parade as well as for its good surfing. To the east and west, the Mornington and Bellarine Peninsulas provide Melbourne with its seaside playgrounds, extremely popular during the summer months.

Summer can be unpredictable in Victoria, particularly along the coastal regions. Despite its rather volatile weather, however, the state enjoys a generally temperate climate. Spring, late summer and autumn provide the most settled and pleasant touring weather. The state's road system is good and penetrates to all but a few remote areas. Much of the state can be reached easily in a day's driving.

Each of Victoria's five main geographical regions has its own special attraction. The central and western districts, due north and west of Melbourne, offer touring highlights such as the historic gold rush areas, with well-preserved, attractive towns such as Bendigo, Castlemaine and Ballarat — which is always popular during its March Begonia Festival — and the Grampians, Victoria's most beautiful natural garden, particularly with its spring wild flowers. Travelling south from these impressive ranges brings you into the western district where rich grazing land is dotted with splendid old properties. No exploration of this region would be complete without a drive along the Great Ocean Road, which runs for 320 kilometres along the dramatic south-west coast. The rock formations in the Port Campbell National Park are probably its most spectacular sights, but along its length there are excellent beaches and pleasant small resort towns.

The north-east alpine region has equally magnificent scenery and is dotted with well patronised winter ski resorts. Although popular in spring and summer, this unspoiled region would hardly ever be described as crowded and the wild flowers, sweeping views and clear air can be enjoyed with a fair degree of solitude. Fishing, bushwalking and climbing are well provided for and, down in the foothills, the Eildon Reservoir and Fraser National Park area are popular for water sports.

Gippsland stretches to the south-east; it contains some of the state's most beautiful and varied country. Rolling pastures lead to densely wooded hill country, still relatively unpopulated and peaceful. National parks such as the Tarra and Bulga and the famous Wilsons Promontory Park, with its lush growth and secluded beaches, are all well worth visiting. The coastal region of Gippsland includes the Ninety Mile Beach bordering the Gippsland Lakes System, Australia's largest inland waterway network.

Following the Murray can be an interesting way of exploring Victoria's north. For those so inclined, the gambling freedoms of New South Wales are just across the river! The river begins as a narrow fast alpine stream, and changes to a broad expanse near the aquatic playgrounds of Lakes Hume and Mulwala; it has waterbird and wildlife reserves, sandy river beaches and offers fascinating glimpses of life in the riverboat era at towns such as Echuca and Swan Hill. Perhaps the Murray sums up the contrasting landscape which is Victoria, the Garden State.

Melbourne
A SPORTING CITY

At first glance Melbourne looks like any other modern city with its skyline chock-a-block with concrete and glass giants. If you look a little closer, however, you'll find the real Melbourne: clanging trams, swanky boutiques, friendly taxi drivers, Australian Rules football, fickle weather, and 'BYOs' (restaurants to which you bring your own liquor) by the hundred. Add to this Melbourne's traditional virtues of tree-lined boulevards, glorious parks, elegant buildings and imposing Victorian churches and banks — and the Melbourne Cricket Ground — and you'll have some idea of the city.

In recent years it has become a polyglot society with its huge influx of migrants from many countries such as Albania, Italy, Lebanon, Yugoslavia and, particularly, Greece. The city has one of the largest Greek-speaking populations in the world. This cosmopolitan influence is reflected in Melbourne's bustling markets, delicatessens and restaurants. Eating out has become one of the great Melbourne pastimes and the city and its suburbs offer a vast range of restaurants of almost every nationality imaginable.

At the head of Port Phillip Bay and centred on the north bank of the Yarra River, Melbourne's population of over three million lives in the flat surrounding suburbs which stretch in all directions — particularly round the east coast of the bay right out to the blue hills of the Dandenongs.

Founded by John Batman in 1835, Melbourne soon entered a boom period with the discovery of gold in the state in 1851. The goldfields of Bendigo, Ballarat and Castlemaine attracted fortune hunters from all over the world, and by 1861 Melbourne had become Australia's largest city. By the end of the century it was firmly established as the business and cultural centre of the colony.

Today Melbourne's traditional position as the financial and cultural centre of the nation has been challenged by Sydney, but it still has an unruffled elegance and style all its own. Melbourne was the only Australian capital to retain its network of electric trams and the clang of the old green thunderers adds a special flavour to the city. Some of these have been given a new lease of life after being decorated by leading artists, while others have been replaced by new orange trams.

Melbourne has a huge range of retail stores and shopping in the city and in suburbs such as fashionable **South Yarra** is one of the joys of the city. Several other suburbs such as **Carlton**, **Prahran** and **Camberwell** rival the city centre with their retail stores and restaurants.

The **Victorian Arts Centre**, comprising a three-theatre complex and national art gallery, is popular with the traditionally keen Melburnian theatre and concert goers.

Melburnians are also great sports lovers and this is reflected in the huge crowds that attend cricket and Australian Rules football matches. A peculiarly Melbourne phenomenon is 'football fever' which grips the city each year with enthusiasm building up to mass hysteria on Grand Final day in September.

Horse racing is another popular Melbourne spectator sport and the Melbourne Cup at **Flemington Racecourse** brings Australia to a halt for three minutes each first Tuesday in November. Melbourne's other main racecourses are at **Caulfield**, **Moonee Valley** and **Sandown Park**. The annual Moomba Festival in March is another outstanding event on the Melbourne calendar.

Melbourne's climate ranges from biting cold in winter to sweltering hot in summer with just about every variation in between — sometimes all on the same day!

The **World Trade Centre** on the corner of Flinders and Spencer Streets hosts international trade displays. Further along Flinders Street is the **Flinders Street Station** complex with its restaurants and shops. It is the main terminus for the suburban rail system. Melbourne's **Underground Rail Loop** has three stations located on the edge of the central business district. Above ground, the **City Explorer** tourist bus departs Flinders Street Station hourly stopping at some of Melbourne's major attractions. To get a different view of Melbourne, take a river cruise on the Yarra departing from the **Princes Walk Terminal** — the bluestone walls contain a restaurant.

The city centre is compact, its wide streets laid out in an orderly grid system. Take a tram to the top of Collins Street and wander down it — Collins Street somehow epitomises Melbourne.

Looking down on Collins Street, in Spring Street, is the elegant **Old Treasury Building**, which was built in 1853, and just down from Spring Street is the august **Melbourne Club**, mecca of Melbourne's Establishment. On the opposite side of the street on the Exhibition Street corner is **Collins Place** — a multi-storey complex which houses the **Regent Melbourne** in one of its high towers. Called the 'City within a City', many of the shops and boutiques in this complex are open all weekend. Another tall building, **Nauru House**, can be seen diagonally opposite.

Continuing down the hill you will see fashionable boutiques and two old churches, the **Uniting Church** and **Scots Church**; and between Russell and Swanston Streets there are pavement tables shaded by colourful sunshades. Opposite these is a unique Melbourne institution — **Georges** — Australia's most elegant department store. Just down the hill is the graceful porticoed **Baptist Church**, built in 1845. Melbourne's imposing **Town Hall** and soaring **St Paul's Cathedral** in Swanston Street provide an attractive contrast to the modern **City Square** on the corner of Collins and Swanston Streets. With its huge glass canopy, cafes, bistros, shops and shady trees and fountains, this is an ideal place for browsing or meeting a friend — in all weathers.

LEFT: *Rowing on Melbourne's Yarra River.*

Further down Collins Street is the elegant old **Block Arcade** with its mosaic floor, glass and iron lace roof and stylish shops. The small lane at the back of this arcade (Block Place) leads through to Little Collins Street and to another gracious old arcade. This is the **Royal Arcade** where, every hour, the huge statues of mythical figures, Gog and Magog, strike the hour. This arcade leads through to the **Bourke Street Mall**, between Elizabeth and Swanston Streets. Several department stores and fashion chains including **Myer**, Australia's largest department store, front on to the mall. The shopping complex, **Centre Point**, on the opposite side is a handy place to browse under shelter, or to stop for a snack in one of its many coffee bars. You can sit and watch city buskers from the seats provided in the mall but beware of the orange and green trams — the only traffic apart from delivery vehicles allowed in this block.

An appealing combination of bookshops and bistros has sprung up in the uppermost block of Bourke Street. The front bar at Pellegrini's — a bustling Italian restaurant — is a great favourite with children, and their BYO restaurant at the rear is an Italian-style cafeteria where you make your selection from mouth-watering hot and cold dishes. Just down from here is one of Australia's great restaurants, The Florentino. Style and discreet elegance have been the hallmark of The Florentino for many years. On the opposite side of the street on the Spring Street corner is one of the last of Melbourne's grand old hotels, the elegant twin-towered **Windsor**, which looks over Melbourne's peaceful **Treasury Gardens**. Proudly surveying the city from Spring Street is the impressive classical-style **State Parliament House**. The plush Corinthian style of the Legislative Council Chamber is a legacy of Melbourne's golden era. The spires of massive bluestone **St Patrick's Cathedral** can be seen beyond. One of Melbourne's most elegant old theatres, The **Princess**, is also in Spring Street.

At the top of Little Bourke Street is **Gordon Place**, a unique old building designed by the colonial architect William Pitt in 1883. The building is now an attractive apartment complex. This is a luxurious alternative to hotel accommodation. Weekly and long-term stay tariffs are available. It has 60 self-contained suites, a glass-roofed restaurant to seat 120 people, reception rooms, food shops, a 20 metre salt water pool, indoor spas and gymnasium.

If you like Chinese food don't miss Melbourne's **Chinatown** in Little Bourke Street between Exhibition and Swanston Streets. This fascinating conglomeration of dozens of oriental restaurants and quaint grocery shops and mixed stores dates back to Melbourne's post gold rush days when it became the city's Chinese quarter. Look up at the buildings and you will see that many of them are a mixture of oriental and occidental styles. The general standard of the restaurants is good and prices vary from fairly cheap to very expensive. Among the outstanding restaurants are The Oriental Gourmet,

HOTELS
Menzies at Rialto,
495 Collins Street, Melbourne.
(03) 62 0111
Regency Melbourne,
Cnr Lonsdale and Exhibition Sts, Melbourne.
(03) 662 3900
Windsor,
103-115 Spring St, Melbourne.
(03) 63 0261

FAMILY AND BUDGET
Lygon Lodge,
204-220 Lygon St, Carlton.
(03) 347 7033
Spencer,
44 Spencer St, Melbourne.
(03) 62 6991
The Victoria,
215 Little Collins St, Melbourne.
(03) 63 0441
YWCA,
489 Elizabeth St, Melbourne.
(03) 329 5188

MOTEL GROUPS: BOOKINGS
Flag (03) 698 7737
Homestead (03) 63 7666
Travelodge (03) 690 6111

This list is for information only; inclusion is not necessarily a recommendation.

The Flower Drum and The Empress of China.

Just half a block away in Lonsdale Street, Greek music cafés and flaky pastry shops make Melbourne a mini-Athens for a couple of blocks. Around the corner in Swanston Street are several bookshops including Mary Martin's, housed in a galleried building with stained glass windows and a relaxed atmosphere. It is one of the few Melbourne shops open on Sundays.

The **Science Museum** in Swanston Street has many interesting exhibits including Australia's first plane and car. This imposing old building also houses the **Planetarium** (where slides are projected on the ceiling of the dome); the magnificent domed **State Library**; the **La Trobe Library;** and the **National Museum** which includes a large collection of Australiana, natural history exhibits — including the legendary racehorse Phar Lap — and the **Children's Museum**, the first of its kind in Australia.

A block away, opposite the Russell Street Police Station, is the grim **Old Melbourne Gaol** and Penal Museum with its chillingly macabre exhibits including the gallows where folk hero Ned Kelly swung.

More cheerful sights such as cheeses, sausages and decoratively arrayed vegetables can be seen at Melbourne's bustling **Victoria Market**, at the corner of Peel and Victoria Streets, held on Fridays, Saturdays and Sundays. Opposite the market on the corner of Queen and Franklin Streets is the fascinating **Queen Victoria Arts and Craft Centre** open daily. From here it's only a short stroll to the beautiful **Flagstaff Gardens**, once used as a pioneer graveyard and later a signalling station. Today they are a pleasant place to relax with shady old trees and a children's playground. Facing the park in King Street you can see **St James' Old Cathedral** which was built in 1839.

The lower part of the city is the sedate legal and financial sector. Back towards the city centre along William Street are the former **Royal Mint** and the **Supreme Court** and **Law Courts** which were built between 1877 and 1884. At the bottom end of Collins Street is the luxury hotel **Menzies at Rialto.** The elaborate Rialto Building and its neighbours, erected between 1889 and 1893, have been retained as a facade to this towering hotel and office complex.

In complete contrast, two of Melbourne's finest city parks — the quiet old **Treasury Gardens** and the beautiful **Fitzroy Gardens,** lie to the eastern boundary of the central city 'grid'. The Fitzroy Gardens have superb avenues of huge English elms planted along gently contoured lawns, giving them a serene beauty all year round. Attractions within the gardens include **Captain Cook's Cottage**; the **'Fairy Tree'**; a model Tudor village; a restaurant and kiosk and a children's playground. In summer the Fitzroy Gardens and other city parks have a

BELOW: *Crowds gather at the Foster's Melbourne Cup, the race that is said to bring Australia to a standstill each November.*

ABOVE: *The Jam Factory shopping centre displays some of the old machinery from its jam-making days.*

programme of free entertainment including art shows, children's plays, jazz and ballet.

The **Carlton Gardens**, north-east of the city, flank the **Exhibition Buildings** — a grandiose domed hall originally built for the Great Exhibition in 1880 and still used for trade fairs. The southern side of the gardens has an ornamental pond and ornate fountain and the northern section an adventure playground and mini-traffic circuit popular with junior cyclists.

The **Victorian Arts Centre** is just over Princes Bridge on St Kilda Road and comprises the **National Gallery of Victoria**, the **Melbourne Concert Hall**, the **Theatres** and the imposing **Spire**. The National Gallery features a fine collection of Australian and overseas masterpieces, and the intricate stained-glass ceiling of the Great Hall, designed by Australian artist Leonard French. The Concert Hall is used for symphony music and a variety of other concerts. It also contains the **Performing Arts Museum**. The Theatres include the State Theatre for opera, ballet and large musicals, the Playhouse for drama and the Studio for experimental theatre.

The **King's Domain**, across St Kilda Road, is a huge stretch of shady parkland where you'll see the **Myer Music Bowl** — the site of many outdoor concerts; the tower of **Government House**; the imposing pyramid-style **Shrine of Remembrance** which dominates St Kilda Road and is open to the public; the **Old Observatory** in Birdwood Avenue and, just past this, **La Trobe's Cottage**, Victoria's first Government House. This quaint cottage with many original furnishings — a reminder of Melbourne's humble beginnings — was brought out from England by the first Governor La Trobe in pre-fabricated sections. It is now a National Trust property, furnished in the original style and open daily. The entrance to the old **Royal Botanic Gardens** is nearby. These lush, beautifully landscaped gardens with gently sloping lawns, attractively grouped trees and shrubs, shady ferneries and ornamental lakes, are a peaceful retreat for city-dwellers. Many of the majestic old oaks in the western end of the gardens are more than 100 years old. The kiosk, open daily, serves teas and lunch.

If you walk through the gardens you will come to shady **Alexandra Avenue** which runs beside the Yarra River. Barbecues are dotted along the Yarra's grassy banks. At weekends you can hire bicycles near the gates of the Botanic Gardens and ride along a scenic **riverside bicycle track**, or you can take a ferry trip from Princes Bridge to Morrell Bridge or historic **Como House**.

Nearby **Albert Park**, just south of St Kilda Road, is another good place for families — and sports enthusiasts. There are coin-in-the-slot barbecues on the edge of the huge Albert Park Lake and boats are for hire at the Jolly Roger boat shed. You can also hire bicycles here on weekdays, but look out for joggers if you circle the lake. Rob's Carousel Restaurant, which overlooks the lake, caters for children with a special junior menu, and there is another Rob's Restaurant on the opposite side of the lake.

Melbourne's safe city beaches are within a few blocks of the park. **Albert Park Beach** has a brightly-equipped playground with a tunnel slide on to the sand. In summer you can hire wind surfers on the beach near Fraser Street, West St Kilda.

Cosmopolitan **St Kilda** is one of the few places in Melbourne which throngs with life at weekends. A combination of London's 'Soho' and an old-fashioned fun resort, **Luna Park**, and the enormous **Palais Theatre** are relics of the days when St Kilda was Melbourne's leading seaside playground. A weird and wonderful collection of art and craft stalls appears on the **Esplanade** on Sundays and **Acland Street** offers book shops, art galleries and luscious tempting continental cakes.

Just outside St Kilda at 192 Hotham Street, Elsternwick, is **Rippon Lea**, a National Trust property open daily. This huge Romanesque mansion is famed for its beautiful English-style landscaped gardens, which contain ornamental ponds and bridges, sweeping lawns, herbaceous borders and peacocks in a superb old fernery.

Two of Melbourne's wealthiest suburbs are **South Yarra** and **Toorak**. Como, another magnificent National Trust mansion, is in Como Avenue, off Toorak Road. Set in pleasant gardens, which once spread right down to the river, charmingly balconied Como is a perfectly preserved example of 19th century colonial grandeur.

Although many of Toorak's and South Yarra's grand old estates have been subdivided, there is no shortage of imposing gates and high walls screening huge mansions. You could easily spend the best part of a day strolling down **Toorak Road**. This is a place to see and be seen — where there are probably more swanky boutiques, expensive restaurants and gourmet foodshops per metre than in any other part of Melbourne. Outstanding restaurants in the district include Maxim's — one of Melbourne's great restaurants and surprisingly good value at lunchtime; Two Faces, which vies with Glo Glo's as leader of the culinary Establishment; and Pickwick, for a sumptuous atmosphere. For cheaper eating there are plenty of spaghetti and pizza bars to choose from.

Another of Melbourne's great shopping streets — **Chapel Street** — crosses Toorak Road in South Yarra. Here yet more fashion boutiques and antique and jewellery shops abound, but the air is not quite so rarefied nor are the price tags quite as high. The **Jam Factory** is a huge red brick building which still looks like a factory from the outside but inside there is an arcade of shops, an attractive glass-topped courtyard and a restaurant. Further on towards Malvern Road, Chapel Street becomes more cosmopolitan and the emphasis shifts from fashion to food. The **Prahran Market** is just round the corner in Commercial Road. This market springs to life on

BELOW: *The Exhibition Buildings are used for trade and industrial displays, conferences and social functions.*

ABOVE: *Cycling by the Yarra.*

Tuesdays, Fridays and Saturday mornings. Catch a tram down nearby **High Street** to Armadale and you'll come upon Melbourne's antique area. Arts and crafts galleries and antique shops — and more antique shops — stretch along High Street for several blocks.

As Melbourne's city centre has become more impersonal her once depressed inner suburbs north of the Yarra have been recharged with life. Theatres, theatre restaurants, antique shops, fashion boutiques and dozens of BYOs have bloomed in former slums such as **Carlton**, **North Fitzroy** and **Richmond**. Most of the elegant iron-lace terrace houses in the more fashionable inner suburbs have been lovingly restored but these areas still have a lively mixture of migrants and Australian old-timers. Carlton — the site of **Melbourne University** — also has one of the largest concentrations of beautiful Victorian houses in Melbourne. Its shady wide streets and squares of restored terraces can make you forget that you are within easy walking distance of a modern city.

Lygon Street has the essence of Carlton, with its Italian restaurants, delicatessens, book shops, boutiques and 'arty' shops. Have lunch and take in the Carlton scene at Jimmy Watson's — Melbourne's oldest wine bar at 333 Lygon Street. The wine is good but cheap, the food self-service and the atmosphere frenetic — with everyone talking at once. If the weather is good the clientele spills out into the rear courtyard. Another informal eating place with courtyard is the Caffe Paradiso, nearby at 368 Lygon Street.

Through Melbourne University grounds — a mixture of original ivy-clad buildings and modern blocks — you'll come to **Parkville**. This is another little pocket of gracious Victorian terraces and shady streets. And at the **Melbourne Zoo**, just across nearby **Royal Park**, you can see

RIGHT: *The Zoo's walk-through aviary keeps visitors and birds happy!*

families of lions at play from the safety of a 'people cage' — an enclosed bridge which takes you right through the lions' large, natural-looking enclosure. This innovation is typical of the zoo's policy of providing enclosures for the animals which are as large and as natural as possible, with a minimum of bars. The zoo also has an amusement park and kiosk.

Another old inner suburb worth exploring is Fitzroy which is similar in character to Carlton. Raffish Brunswick Street, Fitzroy, has an interesting mixture of antique shops, pubs, milk-bars and first-class BYOs. Mietta's at 533 Brunswick Street has a reputation for imaginative menus based on fresh foods in season.

East Melbourne, another extremely well preserved area of beautiful terrace houses, has such 'grand old ladies' as **Clarendon Terrace** (in Clarendon Street) with its graceful colonnaded central portico and **Tasma Terrace** in Parliament Place, which now houses the National Trust Preservation Bookshop.

Swan Street, Richmond has one of the best selections of Greek restaurants in Melbourne. There's no need to book: if one is full you can always try the next one down. Most are cheap and unpretentious with excellent food enhanced by Greek music and a lively atmosphere.

It is possible in Melbourne to dine and see the sights at the same time. The Colonial Tramcar Company runs a restaurant aboard a tram thus allowing patrons to enjoy a meal in elegant style while travelling through Melbourne and some of its suburbs. Another novel way to dine is aboard the Latour Double Decker Bus. Diners are able to sample fine Victorian wines and enjoy international cuisine while touring Melbourne's sightseeing attractions.

West of the city is Melbourne's oldest suburb, **Williamstown**, founded in the 1830s. This fascinating former maritime village has many quaint old seafront pubs, historic churches, fishermen's cottages and relics of its days as an important seaport. Because it was shielded from modern development until the completion of the

ABOVE: *The* Polly Woodside.

West Gate Bridge to the city centre, much of Williamstown has changed little and retains a strong seafaring character. At weekends you can see over the **Maritime Museum** ship *HMAS Castlemaine* — a World War 2 minesweeper restored by the Maritime Trust, and picnic along the grassy foreshore. You can also see model ships, early costumes and relics at Williamstown **Historical Museum** in Electra Street and look over a superb exhibition of old steam locomotives at the Railway Museum in Champion Road, North Williamstown.

Another historic ship, the *Polly Woodside* — a square-rigged commercial sailing ship built in 1885 — is moored at the old Duke and Orr's Dry Dock near Spencer Street Bridge, South Melbourne.

For more detailed information on Melbourne there are a number of guide books available. Victour, 230 Collins Street, (03) 619 9444 can provide maps, brochures and other information for visitors.

Tours from Melbourne

Many interesting trips can be taken in a day from Melbourne. For some of the outings mentioned, it is recommended that you plan an overnight stop to enjoy fully the areas surrounding the destination in a leisurely fashion.

Ballarat and Sovereign Hill, 110 km from Melbourne via the Western Highway.

It is well worth making an overnight stop in Ballarat to do justice to this extremely interesting city. Ballarat is one of Victoria's most attractive old cities and nearby Sovereign Hill is a brilliant re-creation of a typical mining village of the 1850s, with a working model mine to inspect, period shops to explore and a good variety of meals and refreshments available. Other attractions in Ballarat are the Begonia Festival and gardens and the Eureka Stockade.

Phillip Island, 140 km from Melbourne via the Mulgrave Freeway and the South Gippsland and Bass Highways.

This large island in Westernport Bay offers the attractions of excellent surf and swimming beaches, koalas and the unique nightly parade at dusk of fairy penguins up to their burrows at Summerland Beach. Churchill Island, in Westernport Bay is now open to tourists.

The Dandenong Ranges, 49 km from Melbourne via the Burwood Highway.

One of the most popular tourist attractions in Victoria, these lushly forested ranges are interlaced with a network of attractive roads and a number of charming townships. The Dandenongs provide an ideal outing for nature lovers, garden enthusiasts or those who like simply to browse through a variety of antique shops, craft shops or galleries. Many of the restaurants tucked away in these hills offer delicious Devonshire teas and excellent meals. Barbecue and picnic areas are scattered throughout the Dandenongs. If possible, try to get there on a weekday, as the narrow roads become busy at weekends.

Port Phillip Bay Cruises from Station Pier, Port Melbourne.

The *Spirit of Victoria* makes four- and six-hour trips around the Bay and the bayside resort towns of Queenscliffe, Sorrento and Portarlington Wednesdays to Sundays. For departure times, contact (03) 62 6997.

RIGHT: *The tulip gardens at Silvan are ablaze with colour in Spring.*

Leisureland Fair 40 km from Melbourne via Hastings-Dandenong Road.

This adventure playground is very popular with children and features a paddleboat, rollercoaster and bike track. Open 11 am to 5 pm Saturdays and Sundays, public holidays and school holidays. There are picnic and barbecue facilities, and a kiosk.

Healesville Sanctuary, 60 km from Melbourne via the Maroondah Highway.

Just outside the peaceful township of Healesville, on Badger Creek Road, is the Healesville Sanctuary which houses one of the best collections of native wildlife in Australia. Many of the animals roam freely in their natural environment; there are 'walk through' aviaries, excellent nocturnal displays and, at certain times, the amazing duck-billed platypus can be viewed. Open daily, 9 am to 5 pm. Picnic and barbecue facilities. Free parking.

Werribee Park, 35 km from Melbourne via the Princes Highway, west.

Just outside the township of Werribee, Werribee Park is a large estate with a magnificent Italianate mansion of 60 rooms which was built in the 1870s for the Chirnside brothers. These brothers had established a pastoral 'empire' in the Western District. Now owned by the Victorian Government, it is open daily 10 am to 4 pm. There are extensive formal gardens, a friendship farm, restaurant, kiosk, picnic facilities, electric barbecues, a golf course and tennis courts. The grounds are open until 8 pm during daylight saving time, 6 pm in winter.

The Kinglake National Park and Yarra Glen, about 60 km from Melbourne via the Maroondah Highway or route 46.

This tour takes in a variety of mountain and river country, with some attractive townships and historic buildings along the way. **St Andrews** Community Market, held on Saturday mornings, sells local produce, arts and crafts. There is an attractive country pub which serves lunches. The House of Bottles, Parkland Road, **Kinglake**, is a house and windmill completely made of bottles. In the Kinglake National Park, the Jehosaphat Valley picnic area makes a good stopping point. At **Dixons Creek**, Chateau Yarrinya Winery is open on weekdays for inspection and tastings. The Gulf Station Homestead, 2 km north of Yarra Glen, is more than 100 years old and is classified by the National Trust. The route from Yarra Glen homewards leads through the beautiful rolling countryside of the Christmas Hills area. 'Montsalvat' in Hillcrest Avenue, **Eltham**, is an artists'

ABOVE: *The Sir Colin MacKenzie Fauna Park at Healesville displays Australia's native animals, like these kangaroos, in their natural habitat.*

colony built in the Gothic style during the Great Depression. The craft shop is open daily from 9 am to 5 pm and the interior of the magnificent mud-stone Great Hall is open daily from mid-day to 5 pm. Afternoon tea is available. The Diamond Valley railway, lower Eltham Park, has a display of working models of steam trains with track running through landscaped grounds; there are picnic facilities. Nearby **Warrandyte** is well known for its community of artists and potters and has a number of art and craft galleries, antique shops and nurseries.

Mount Macedon and Hanging Rock, 80 km from Melbourne via the Calder Highway. Hanging Rock can be reached via either Mt Macedon or Woodend.

On Ash Wednesday 1983, bushfires that were among the worst this country has known destroyed about half of the beautiful gardens and nurseries in the Macedon area. They were known for their beautiful displays of azaleas and rhododendrons and for the autumn colours of the many English trees. Despite the destruction of the fire, the gardens that remain are still worth visiting and plans are already under way to rebuild. Hanging Rock itself is a strange massive outcrop, volcanically formed, made famous by Joan Lindsay's book and the subsequent film 'Picnic at Hanging Rock'. It can be climbed quite easily, but note carefully the track to be followed. There is a picnic area at its base, with barbecues, kiosk and toilets. For a longer tour, continue along the Calder Highway to the historic gold towns of **Kyneton, Castlemaine** and, nearby, **Maldon**, all well worth exploring. A pleasant route back to Melbourne is via the hilly resort town of **Daylesford,** thence to **Ballan** and **Bacchus Marsh.**

RIGHT: *The upper reaches of the Yarra River are a popular weekend haunt, offering peaceful seclusion relatively close to Melbourne.*

The Mornington Peninsula, 94 km from Melbourne to its furthest point, via the Nepean Highway.

Fortunately, all of this attractive area is within easy driving distance of Melbourne and many different drives can be enjoyed. A round trip via **Frankston**, **Rosebud**, **Flinders**, **Hastings** and back via Frankston will reveal a good cross section of the Peninsula: the densely settled Port Phillip Bay side with its sheltered beaches, the surf beaches at the Peninsula's ocean end, which also stretch along some of the Westernport Bay side, the pleasant, less populated, resort areas on Westernport Bay and, in driving across the Peninsula, its charming, still rural, inland countryside. The Nepean Highway leads right through to **Portsea**, 94 km from Melbourne, and the Princes and South Gippsland Highways lead to **Tooradin**, 66 km from Melbourne. Traffic jams along the coastal roads are common during summer holidays and weekends.

Warburton and the Upper Yarra Dam, 120 km (to Cumberland Junction), via the Maroondah and Warburton Highways.

This tour through the high country offers excellent scenic driving through the beautiful country around Lake Mountain. It is not a journey to be undertaken in the winter months as much of the route can be snow-covered. The Upper Yarra Dam, just off the Warburton Highway, is a most pleasant spot to stop for a picnic and the road on across Lake Mountain offers superb views. A slightly shorter route is via the Acheron Way.

Lunch in the country

Most country towns have several pubs which serve counter lunches and teas, as well as a variety of cafes and takeaway food shops. If, however, you enjoy the idea of a more relaxed meal in a restaurant a few of the more popular restaurants within a morning's drive of Melbourne are listed below. (BYO means you can take your own liquor to the restaurant.)

Knockers, 182 Ocean Beach Road, Sorrento (85 km from Melbourne), BYO. Open daily in the summer, weekends in the winter. Offering a pleasant general menu, the restaurant encourages family sittings at 6 pm with children's serves at half-price.
(059) 84 1246.

Potter's Restaurant, Jumping Creek Road, Warrandyte (28 km from Melbourne), BYO. Open for lunch and afternoon tea Tuesdays to Sundays and dinner Wednesdays to Saturdays. Part of Potter's Cottage, which is an interesting craft centre, this restaurant has a pleasant, casual atmosphere and excellent home cooking served on pottery plates. There is a jazz band on Fridays and a pianist entertains diners on Thursdays and Saturdays and a trio on Fridays.
(03) 844 2270

Cotswold House Restaurant, Blackhill Road, Menzies Creek (40 km from Melbourne), fully licensed. Open for dinner Thursdays to Saturdays and lunch Tuesdays to Sundays. Set in a charming old timber house that has been classified by the National Trust, the dining room overlooks sweeping lawns where ducks and geese roam freely.
(03) 754 7884

Kenloch, Mt Dandenong Road, Olinda (48 km from Melbourne), fully licensed. Open Wednesdays to Sundays for lunch and Fridays and Saturdays for dinner. In a gracious old house set in beautiful gardens, there is good food and an excellent wine cellar.
(03) 751 1008.

Clover Cottage, Manuka Road, Berwick (45 km from Melbourne), fully licensed. Lunch is served Wednesdays to Saturdays on the Strawberry Terrace, and lunch on Sundays and dinner Wednesdays to Saturdays is served banquet-style in the main dining room of this Georgian mansion set in beautiful surroundings.
(03) 707 1048.

Fiddler's Green, Main Road, Olinda (45 km from Melbourne), BYO. Open daily for lunch, Devonshire tea and dinner, specialising in Swiss and Australian cooking.
(03) 751 1176.

Wiener Wald, cnr Olinda-Monbulk Road and Mt Dandenong Tourist Road, Olinda (45 km from Melbourne), fully licensed. An Austrian style restaurant and wine bar serving good, reasonably priced food. Open for lunch and Devonshire tea Wednesdays to Sundays and Public Holidays and dinner Fridays to Sundays.
(03) 751 1120.

Muddy Creek, Boundary Road, Narre Warren East (51 km from Melbourne, near Berwick), BYO. Open for lunch Sundays and dinner Wednesdays to Saturdays. Good freshly prepared food in rustic surroundings.
(03) 796 8391.

Victoria from A to Z

Alexandra Population 1753.
Alexandra is a farming and holiday centre, 24 km west of Lake Eildon. **Of interest:** Some older buildings, including the Post Office and Law Courts. Graceburn Park Farm, Spring Creek Road, 10 km north, has farm displays and a farm animal nursery. **In the area:** The Fraser National Park, 12 km east. Every Easter, Alexandra holds the National Billy Goat Derby on a specially made track. The Community Market sells local produce, livestock and arts and crafts. It is usually held on the last Saturday of every month. A short drive south of the town is the McKenzie Nature Reserve, an area of virgin bushland with an abundance of orchids in winter and spring. Spring Creek Craft House in Vickery St sells arts and crafts, wools, fleeces and gourmet foods. Taggerty, 18 km south in the Acheron Valley, offers good trout fishing. The Rubicon Falls are nearby. **Accommodation:** 2 hotels, 1 motel, 3 caravan/camping parks.
Map ref. 160 F4, 167 K12, 173 K1

Anglesea Population 1460.
This attractive seaside town on the Great Ocean Road was badly affected by bushfires in 1983. It has excellent swimming and surfing. It has an interesting golf course, noted for its wildlife. Behind the town there is an open-cut brown coal mine and power station which provides electricity to the Alcoa aluminium refinery at Geelong. **Of interest:** The Angahook Forest Park, a very attractive reserve with many walking tracks. Features include Iron Bark Grove, Currawong Falls, Treefern Grove and the Melaleuca swamp. Excellent opportunities for nature lovers to observe a wide variety of flora and fauna. Access from either Anglesea or Airey's Inlet, also burned in the bushfires, 10 km along the Great Ocean Road. **Accommodation:** 2 motels, 3 caravan/camping parks.
Map ref. 155 D11, 172 C9

Apollo Bay Population 921.
The Great Ocean Road leads to this attractive coastal town, the centre of a rich dairying and fishing area. The largest fish freezing base in the state is located here. The wooded mountainous hinterland offers memorable scenery and there is excellent sea and river fishing in the area. The rugged and beautiful coastline has been the scene of many shipwrecks in the past. **Of interest:** The Otway National Park is excellent for bush walking. The Otway mountains and forests in the back country, including Turton's Pass. In the valley of the Barham River are the attractive Paradise picnic grounds and along the ridge to the north-west is Melba Gully, a 49 ha park, which has beautiful ferns, mosses, native trees and native birds. Lavers Hill, tiny now in comparision with the booming timber centre of its heyday, is 3 km west. **Accommodation:** 4 motels, 3 caravan/camping parks.
Map ref. 171 Q12

Ararat Population 8335.
The Ararat area gold boom came in 1857. It was short lived, however, and sheep farming became the basis of the town's economy. Today the town is the commercial centre of a prosperous farming and wine growing region. The area also produces fine merino wool. The first vines in the district were planted by Frenchmen in 1863 and the little town of Great Western, 16 km north-west of Ararat, gave its name to some of Australia's most famous champagnes and wines. **Of interest:** Alexandra Park and Botanical Gardens, noted for their begonia hothouses. The Langi Morgala Folk Museum, Queen St, which includes a collection of Aboriginal weapons and artefacts. Ararat art gallery, regional gallery specialising in wool and fibre pieces by leading craftsmen. Highland sports meeting at New Year and Queen's Birthday weekend chess tournament which attracts players from all over Australia. The town boasts some beautiful bluestone buildings, such as the Post Office, and has a splendid Town Hall, Civic Square and War Memorial. **In the area:** The Langi Ghiran State Forest, 13.5 km east off the Western Highway, has scenic walks to the nearby reservoir, picnic and barbecue facilities and a children's playground. Buangor, 5 km on, has the century-old Buangor Hotel, which provides meals, and, opposite, an old Cobb and Co. changing station, built about 1860. In the street behind the hotel, Hovey's blacksmith forge is still in use. Mt Buangor State Forest and Fern Tree Waterfalls, with picnic facilities, are 18 km further on. Several wineries are in the area, such as Seppelt's Great Western Vineyards, 16 km west of Ararat, which specialise in dry red wines and champagnes. The vineyard was established in 1865, and its underground cellars have been classified by the National Trust. Best's Wines are 2 km on through Great Western and are open for inspection, tastings and sales. Montara Winery is 3 km south of Ararat on the Chalambar Road. Historic gold areas are Cathcart, a few km west, and, further west, Mafeking, once a bustling settlement with 10 000 people. There are picnic facilities at Mafeking. Take care when walking in the area for there are many deep mine shafts. Just north of Great Western are the Malakoff goldfields. **Accommodation:** 4 hotels, 5 motels, 2 caravan/camping parks.
Map ref. 165 L13, 171 M1

Avoca Population 1032.
In the Central Highlands region, Avoca was established with the discovery of gold in the area in 1852. It is at the junction of the Sunraysia and Pyrenees Highways and the surrounding Pyrenees Range foothills offer attractive bushwalking and are the home of numbers of kangaroos, wallabies and koalas. **Of interest:** Early bluestone buildings in Avoca classified by the National Trust include the old gaol, powder magazine, court-house and one of the state's earliest pharmacies. The Avoca and Wimmera Rivers and the Bet Bet Creek are popular for fishing. There are a number of wineries in the Central Highlands region, within easy driving distance from Avoca. They include the Remy Martin Vineyards, 8 km west on the Vinoca Road, specialising in red wines and champagnes, open weekdays for cellar door sales. Mt Avoca 7 km west, open 10 am to 5 pm Mondays to Saturdays and 12 pm to 5 pm Sundays. The Taltarni vineyards, 16 km west, have tours and tastings on Mondays to Saturdays between 9 am and 4.30 pm. **Accommodation:** 1 caravan/camping park.
Map ref. 165 O12

Bacchus Marsh Population 6222.
The trees of the Avenue of Honour provide an impressive entrance to Bacchus Marsh, 49 km from Melbourne on the Western Highway. This old established town is situated in a fertile valley, once marshland, between the Werribee and Lerderderg Rivers. **Of interest:** The home of the town's founder, Captain Bacchus, known as the Manor House, in Manor St, now privately owned. In the main street, an original blacksmith's shop and cottage. The court-house, lock-up and National Bank have all been classified by the National Trust. The Border Inn opened in 1850 and its founders are thought to have provided the first coaching service stop in Victoria. **In the area:** Werribee and Lerderderg Gorges both provide attractive surroundings for picnics, bushwalking and swimming. To the north, the Wombat State Forest, to the south-west, the Brisbane Ranges and the Anakie Gorge, and to the north-east, the Bull Mallee Reserve — these areas are rich in natural flora and fauna and are popular with fishermen and bushwalkers. On the Western Freeway, the Bacchus Marsh Lion and Tiger Park, with picnic facilities. Also on the Western Freeway, St Anne's Vineyard, with an old bluestone cellar, built from the remains of the old Ballarat gaol, daily tastings, and sales. Tourist information from the Shire Offices, Main Street. **Accommodation:** 4 hotels, 2 motels, 1 caravan/camping park.
Map ref. 154 C8, 158 G11, 172 D4

THE GOLDEN AGE

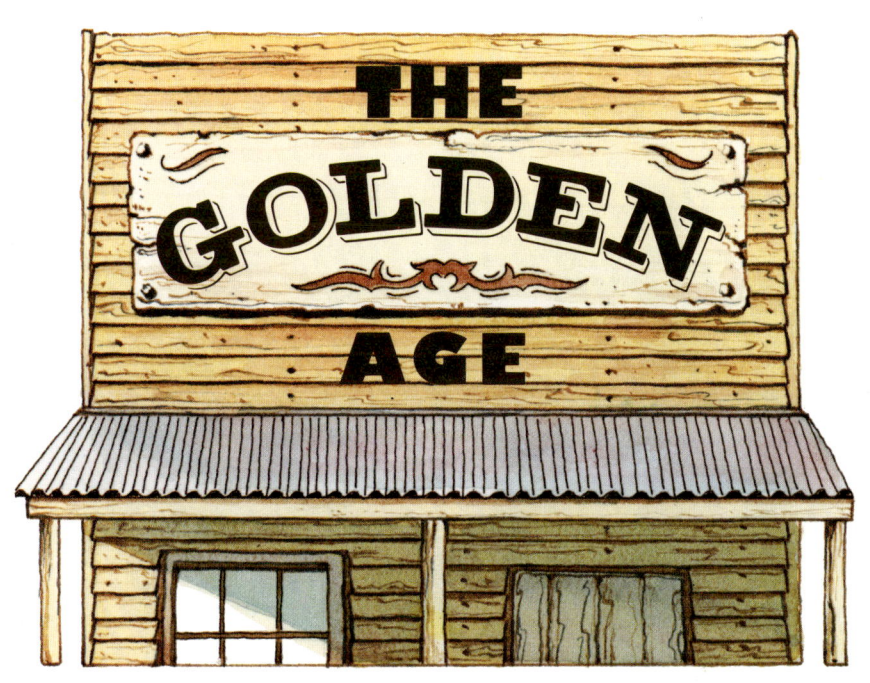

The cities and towns of the goldfields region of Victoria came to a peak of style and affluence in the 1880s, an affluence built on the first gold discoveries in the 1850s. The towns display all the frivolity and grandeur of Victorian architecture, having grown up in an age when it was believed that gold and wealth were going to be a permanent benefit in Victoria.

The two major cities of the region are Ballarat and Bendigo but there are many other towns, large and small, dotted around. They all have beautiful old houses and public buildings, and many have other trappings of the past, statues, public gardens sometimes with lakes, ornamental bandstands and grand avenues of English trees. Spring and autumn are the best seasons to visit this region as there are not the extremes of summer and winter temperatures and the flowers and foliage are at their best.

It is a quiet region now. The remaining small towns serve the rich pastoral district and any secondary industries and services are centred on the two cities.

It was once, however, an area of frantic activity. Gold was discovered at Clunes in 1851 and within three months 8000 people were on the diggings in the area between Buninyong and Ballarat. Nine months later there were 30 000 adult men on the goldfields and four years later one hundred thousand. The population of the city of Melbourne dwindled alarmingly and immigrants rushed to the diggings from Great Britain, America and many other countries. Ships' crews, sometimes even captains, abandoned their vessels and trekked to the diggings to try their luck. Tent cities sprang up on the plains as men dug and panned for gold. There were remarkable finds of huge nuggets in the early days but, as time went by, the amount of gold obtained by panning in the rivers and by digging grew less and less. They were remarkable communities, 'shanty' towns, with streets crowded day and night, with pubs and dancing rooms, hawkers, traders and continuous sounds of music and revelry.

As time went on the surface gold was worked out and it was followed by expensive company-backed operations, mining in deep shafts, stamping and crushing the ore in steam-powered plants on the surface.

The success of these methods heralded a new era, that of the company mines, outside investors and stock exchange speculation. It led to a more stable workforce and to the well-established communities which slowly evolved into the towns of the region today. As the pastoral potential began to be fully exploited, it was the perfect scene for expansion and optimism.

BELOW: *The poppet head was a familiar sight on the goldfields. It supports the winding mechanism above the shaft.*

BELOW: *Old diggings are still in evidence around Bendigo.*

BELOW: *Chinese were among the many nationalities who flocked to Victoria's goldfields in the 1800s. These gravestones are at Bendigo.*

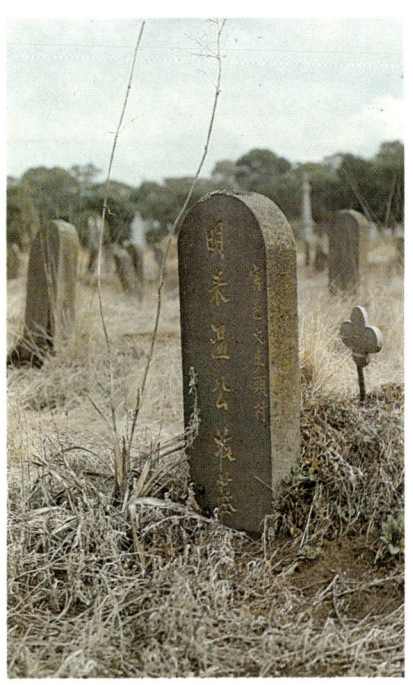

Victoria

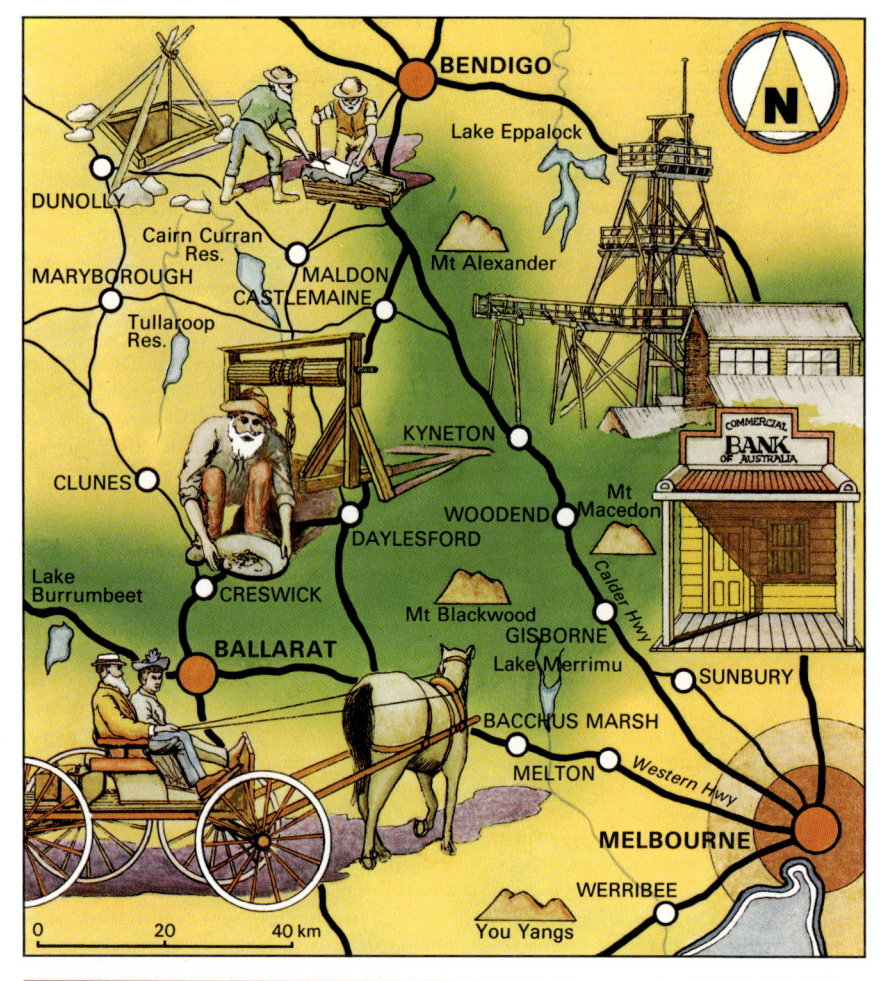

The years between 1870 and 1890 saw the towns embellished with fine civic buildings, mansion houses, solid town houses, churches, hotels and all the trappings of affluence. Thus Ballarat, Bendigo, Castlemaine and, to a lesser extent, Clunes, Creswick, Daylesford and Maldon became extraordinary *nouveau riche* visions of the current British taste.

The Western Highway between Melbourne and Ballarat is at its most scenic as it rises into the Pentland Hills. Rounded volcanic hills circle Bacchus Marsh, which is approached by a magnificent avenue of American elms commemorating those who died in the Great War. Bacchus Marsh is adjacent to the Lerderderg and Werribee Rivers, which enter dramatic gorges close to the town. Just off the highway are the small rural towns of Myrniong and Ballan, Gordon and Bungaree. South of the highway near Bungaree is Dunnstown, dominated by its bluestone distillery and the bulk of Mount Warrenheip, where an excellent view of the district can be had from the summit.

A turn-off to the south near Ballarat leads to Buninyong, the scene of one of the first gold strikes in Victoria. This impressive township with a grand tree-lined main street has a number of striking buildings — the Crown Hotel and white-walled Uniting Church are of the 1860s while the combined council chambers and court-house of 1886 are in rich Italianate design, unified by a central clocktower.

The city of Ballarat was laid out to the west of the diggings within twelve months of the first discovery of gold. The design included a magnificent chief thoroughfare, Sturt Street, wide enough for future plantations and monuments. The primitive buildings of early settlement were gradually replaced by boom-style architecture in the 1880s. Italianate, Romanesque, Gothic and French Renaissance styles mingle together; porticoes, colonnades and ornamental stone facades view with verandahs of lavish cast-iron decoration. There are many superb buildings, the most notable being the post office, the railway station, the town hall, the stock exchange, the former Ballarat gaol, the Wesley Church, the George Hotel, Reids Coffee Palace, the Bailey Mansion, the Roman Catholic bishop's

ABOVE LEFT: *If you set off on an excursion into this area armed with a gold pan or metal detector, you may well return richer than when you left!*

LEFT: *The beautifully proportioned verandahed facades of Ballarat's buildings were practical as well as pleasing to the eye, shielding the residents from winter rains and summer heat.*

residence, Loreto Abbey and the art gallery. It is a city of many beautiful gardens, particularly the Botanical Gardens adjacent to Lake Wendouree, famous for the begonia display in March.

Beyond Ballarat, on the Midland Highway is Creswick, a picturesque valley town with a wonderfully ornate town hall. The bluestone tower of St John's Church dominates the town's western hill and on the hilltop across the valley is a Tudor-style hospital building which is now a school of forestry.

To make a turn off the highway to Clunes is well worthwhile. Gold was first discovered here in July 1851 but it proved difficult to get supplies to this remote township, so the rush was limited and the later discoveries at Buninyong and Ballarat quickly diverted attention. Of particular interest in Clunes are the rich verandahed facades in the shopping area of Fraser Street and the elegant style of the banks, hotels, post office and town hall.

North-east of Ballarat up the Midland Highway is Daylesford, another former gold-mining town set in picturesque wooded hills around Wombat Hill Gardens and Lake Daylesford. The town has a number of churches in the 'Gothic revival' style and an imposing town hall, post office and school. On the hill are groves of rhododendrons, exotic trees and a lookout tower which provides a view of Mount Franklin, a perfectly preserved volcanic crater, and Mount Tarrengower. Several kilometres north of Daylesford are natural springs containing lime, iron, magnesia and other minerals. This is the famed Hepburn Spa which attracted visitors in the nineteenth century for its medicinal properties. Bottling mineral water is still the town's main industry.

Further north on the road to Bendigo is Castlemaine, a larger town and one of the most picturesque in the region. The blocks in the centre of the town have remained virtually unaltered since its early days, for the prosperity of the 1860s diminished and the town settled down to a quieter rural life. One of the most notable buildings is the Castlemaine market, an unusual Palladian inspired building which was restored in 1974 and which now contains a museum portraying the history of the town and the Mount Alexander goldfields. The town boasts some other fine buildings, including the great post office in Italianate style with a central clock-tower, the former telegraph office, the

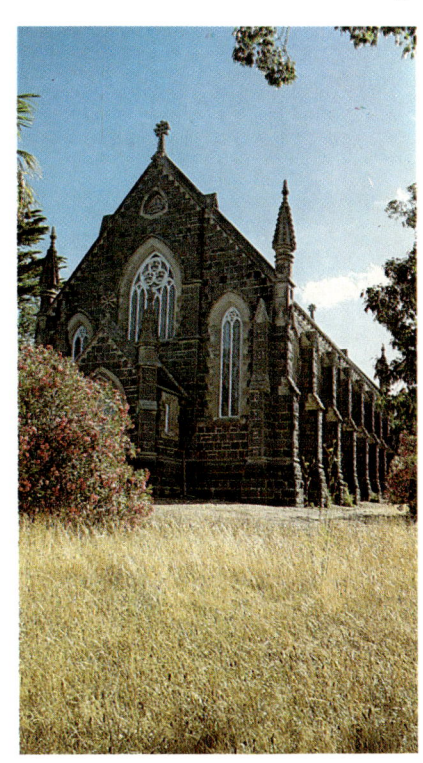

BELOW: *One of Bendigo's unique 'talking trams' which provides a taped commentary for visitors as it takes them through the streets. Wide streets, statues and green areas all add to the attraction of this historic city.*

ABOVE: *During its brief spell of prosperity, the people of Clunes built this English-style church of stone blocks.*

BELOW: *This magnificent building, typical of the grand style of architecture adopted in Victoria's gold rush, houses Maryborough's railway station.*

Victoria

ABOVE: *The Crown Hotel at Buninyong, is a reminder of Victoria's golden age.*

ABOVE: *The red brick CBC Bank building in Castlemaine is decorated with stone.*

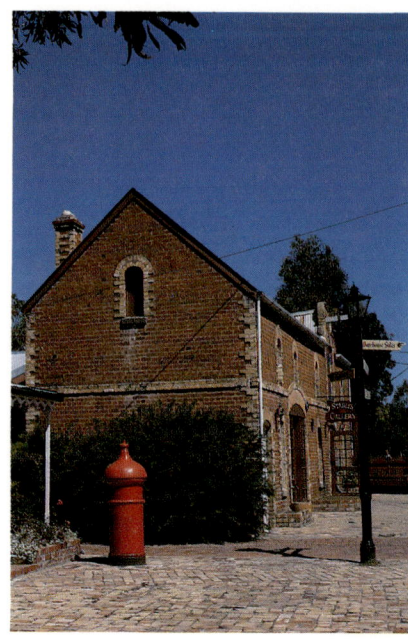

ABOVE: *Bendigo Pottery is a major tourist attraction in Bendigo.*

mechanics institute, the Imperial Hotel and the Commercial Banking Company building. High on a hill above the town are the stone and redbrick gaol and the obelisk, built in 1862 to commemorate the Burke and Wills ill-fated expedition.

Nearby Maldon was declared a notable town by the National Trust in 1962. The winding streets are flanked by low buildings, deep verandahs shading the bluestone pavements which were laid in 1866. The buildings of the greatest proportions are the hotels, mostly ornamented with cast iron.

BELOW: *The splendid Shamrock Hotel is one of 26 buildings in Bendigo constructed between 1856 and 1896 that have been classified by the National Trust.*

The city of Bendigo is the jewel of the region and is Victoria's most outstanding example of a boom town. Gothic- and classical-styled buildings have been designed in vast proportions, richly ornamented and combined with the materials of the age, cast iron and cast cement.

The post office and law courts are among the most impressive high Victorian public buildings in Australia. Opposite the post office is the Shamrock Hotel — a massive verandahed structure which boasted 100 rooms, each with an electric light and an electric bell. Many of Bendigo's important buildings were designed by the German architect, William Charles Vahland. His work included the Benevolent Asylum and Hospital, the school of mines, the Mechanics Institute, the town hall, the masonic hall, the Princess Theatre, four banks and the handsome Alexandra fountain at Charing Cross, the centre of Bendigo. The works are splendidly opulent, as if borrowed from all the styles and ages of the world.

The goldfields region can be enjoyed in three days, or three weeks, according to time and taste. Reasonably priced accommodation is available throughout the region. More detailed information can be obtained from Victour, the Gold Centre Tourism Limited or Tourist Information Centres and towns within the region.

BELOW: *Bendigo's Post Office.*

Bairnsdale Population 9457.
This Gippsland trade centre and holiday town is at the junction of the Princes Highway, the Omeo Highway and the road east to Lakes Entrance and makes an excellent touring base. It is a pleasant town with good sporting facilities and gardens. **Of interest:** St Mary's Church has some interesting and complex wall and ceiling murals by an Italian artist. The Bairnsdale Recreation Centre, opened in 1982 has many attractions including a sports hall measuring 34 m x 45 m, and the local swimming pool has a slide which is 10 m high and 39 m long. **In the area:** Lindenow, 19 km west, is close to the Glenaladale National Park. This has good bushwalking tracks and, in a gorge on the Mitchell River, the Den or Nargun, a famous Aboriginal ceremonial ground. The Mitchell River empties into Lake King at Eagle Point Bluff, where the world's second longest silt jetties can be seen. Metung is a picturesque fishing village on the shores of Lake King, with some solid pioneer holiday homes still standing. It has an hotel, holiday flats and a caravan park. McLeod's Morass is about 10 km out of Bairnsdale on the way to Paynesville and has holiday flats and caravan and camping parks. A drive north along the Omeo Highway passes through the very beautiful Tambo River valley, which is stunning in spring when the wattles are in bloom. Tourist information from South East Coast Tourism Limited, 240 Main Street, Bairnsdale. **Accommodation:** 6 hotels, 8 motels, 3 caravan/camping parks.
Map ref. 174 E8

Ballan Population 681.
A small township on the Werribee River, noted for its mineral springs. **Of interest:** Pykes Creek Reservoir, with good trout fishing. Caledonian Park, picnic areas, swimming and golf course nearby. **Accommodation:** 1 hotel, 1 caravan park.
Map ref. 154 B8, 158 E10, 172 C4

Ballarat Population 62 640.
Ballarat is Victoria's largest inland city, situated in the Central Highlands. Its inner areas retain much of the charm of its gold boom era, with many splendid original buildings still standing and parks and gardens adding to its attractive appearance. The begonia is the city's floral emblem and the annual Begonia Festival in March attracts many enthusiasts. Ballarat was just a small rural township in 1851, when its enormously rich alluvial goldfields were discovered. Within two years, it had a population of nearly 40 000. Australia's only civil battle occurred here when miners refused to pay Government licence fees and fought with police and troops at the Eureka Stockade. Today Ballarat is a bustling city with the added attraction of many galleries, museums, antique and craft shops. It has excellent recreational facilities and beautiful garden areas, making it most attractive to visitors. The Royal South Street Eisteddfod, which focuses on music and the dramatic arts, is held each September/October. Bridge Street Mall in the centre of the city has many shops to offer in a relaxed atmosphere.
Of interest: Man-made Lake Wendouree is popular for all kinds of water sports. Visitors can tour it aboard the paddle cruiser *Sarah George* listening to a commentary on the history of the city. Adjoining the lake area are the 40 ha of peaceful Botanic Gardens, containing splendid begonia conservatories. Located here is Prime Ministers' Avenue, which contains a bust of every Australian Prime Minister. Adam Lindsay Gordon's cottage and an elegant statuary pavilion are nearby. The Tourist Tramway takes visitors for rides around the gardens at weekends, public and school holidays. There are also restaurant and refreshment facilities there. Ballarat's most notable gallery is the Fine Art Gallery in Lydiard St Nth, with its comprehensive collection of Australian art, including works by the Lindsay family. Montrose Cottage, Eureka St, was the first masonry cottage built on the goldfields and is classified by the National Trust. Beside it is the Eureka Museum, displaying a large collection of gold era relics. Golda's World of Dolls, displaying antique and modern dolls.
The Old Curiosity Shop has a fascinating collection of pioneer relics. In Stawell St Sth is the Eureka Stockade Park, which has a life-size replica of the famous battle. It has barbecue and picnic facilities and a swimming pool. Adjoining Sovereign Hill, is the Gold Museum, which contains a rich display of gold history. There is a large collection of gold coins and a display of the uses of gold 'today and tomorrow'.

In the area: Sovereign Hill is a major tourist attraction just outside the centre of Ballarat. It is a reconstruction of a goldmining settlement with the working displays of great interest to adults and children alike. Excellent barbecue facilities, kiosk, restaurant and a licensed hotel offer refreshment. Kryal Castle, 8 km east of the city on the Western Highway, is a rather amazing reconstruction of a medieval castle and offers entertainment for all the family. Displays of jousting, sword-fighting and so on take place each day and there is a licensed restaurant. At the western edge of the city is the 22 km Avenue of Honour and Arch of Victory which honour those who fought in World War I. Lake Burrumbeet is 32 km north-west and offers a variety of water sports, picnic spots and excellent trout fishing. The 30 m high Lal Lal Falls on the Moorabool River are 25 km south-east of the city. Another attractive picnic spot is at the White Swan Reservoir, north of Ballarat off the Daylesford Road, with lawns, water views, picnic and barbecue facilities. Tourist information is available from the Gold Centre Tourism Limited, 202 Lydiard Street, North Ballarat. Craig's Royal Hotel, 10 Lydiard St, offers dining in gracious, old world surroundings. Several other hotels serve counter meals and a number of motels have licensed restaurants. La Scala Restaurant is located in a century old bluestone warehouse in Lydiard Street. **Accommodation:** 5 hotels, 21 motels, 5 caravan/camping parks.
Map ref. 157 E6, 158 A9, 171 Q3, 172 A3

Beaufort Population 1214.
This small town on the Western Highway, midway between Ballarat and Ararat, has a gold-rush history, like so many of the other towns in this area. The discovery of gold at Fiery Creek swelled its population in the late 1850s to nearly 100 000. Today Beaufort is primarily a centre for the surrounding pastoral and agricultural district. **Of interest:** The Mt Cole State Forest, part of the Great Dividing Range, is 16 km north-west, via Raglan. This is a peaceful natural area ideal for bush walks, picnics and the observation of some native flora and fauna. It has camping grounds. Lake Goldsmith is 14 km south of Beaufort. Each April and November a Steam Rally is held 2 km east of the lake. Tourist information from the map opposite the Rotunda. **Accommodation:** 3 hotels, 1 motel, 1 caravan/camping park.
Map ref. 171 O3

Beechworth Population 3154.
Once the centre of the great Ovens goldmining region, Beechworth lies 24 km off the Ovens Highway, between Wangaratta and Myrtleford on the Old Sydney Road. It is one of Victoria's best preserved and most beautiful old gold towns, magnificently sited on the edge of the Alps. Its public buildings are of architectural merit and more than 30 of them have been classified as historically important by the National Trust. The fabulously rich alluvial goldfield at Woolshed Creek was discovered by a local shepherd during the 1850s. More than 85 000 kg of gold were mined in 14 years. A story is told of Daniel Cameron, campaigning to represent the Ovens Valley community; he rode through the town at the head of a procession of miners from Woolshed, on a horse shod with golden shoes. Sceptics claim they were merely gilded, but the tale is an indication of what Beechworth was like during the 'boom era', when its population was 8000 and it boasted 61 hotels and a theatre at which international celebrities performed.
Of interest: Post Office and tower clock, The Powder Magazine, built of local granite in 1859, restored and furnished as a museum. Five Government buildings built of local honey-coloured granite in the 1850s. The Robert O'Hara Burke Memorial Museum, with relics of the gold rush and a new group of 16 mini-shops depicting the main street as it was more than 100 years ago. The Harness and Carriage Museum, in century-old stable buildings, run by the National Trust. In front is Tanswell's Hotel, a privately restored, gracious, lacework building, offering accommodation and a good restaurant. In the old gaol is a cell in which Ned Kelly was held. The restored Bank of Victoria building houses the Rock Cavern with a gemstone collection. At nearby Woolshed Creek is Kelly's Lookout. On the road to Chiltern, at Beechworth Cemetery, are Chinese burning towers and a Chinese cemetery.
In the area: Waterfalls at Reid's Creek, Woolshed and Clear Creek. At Chiltern, to the north, 'Lake View' the home of Henry Handel Richardson (pen name of Ethel

Florence Lindsay Richardson), has been restored and landscaped by the National Trust and is open daily. Tourist information from the Rock Cavern, Ford Street. Many good restaurants in the town. **Accommodation:** 4 hotels, 2 motels, 2 caravan/camping parks.
Map ref. 167 P6

Benalla Population 8151.
This small city on the Hume Highway is 40 km south of Wangaratta. Lake Benalla has recently been created in the Broken River, which runs through the city, and there are recreation and picnic facilities there, with a protected sanctuary area for birdlife. During the late 1870s Benalla was a focal point of the activities of the notorious Kelly Gang who were eventually captured at nearby Glenrowan in 1880. **Of interest:** Some splendid Rose Gardens; Benalla's popular Rose Festival is held in October/November. The impressive Art Gallery is on the shores of the lake and contains the important Ledger Collection of Australian paintings. Benalla's Pioneer Museum has Ned Kelly's cummerbund on display. **In the area:** Lake Mokoan, 11 km to the northeast, offers swimming, boating and picnic facilities. South of the Midland Highway is Reefs Hill forest reserve, with 2030 ha of forest and a wide variety of native flora and fauna. Pleasant day trips can be taken to the King Valley and the spectacular Paradise Falls. There are some interesting vineyards in the area, including Brown's and Bailey's. Restaurants include the Loaded Dog, the Mandalay and Georgina's. General information from the Regional Community Information Centre, Mair St. **Accommodation:** 4 motels, 2 caravan/camping parks.
Map ref. 167 M8

Bendigo Population 52 739.
This is one of Victoria's most famous gold-mining towns. It is at the junction of five highways and is centrally located for trips to many of the other gold towns in the surrounding areas. Its history is indeed golden: the rush began here in 1851 and gold production continued for 100 years. The affluence of the period can still be seen today in many splendid public and commercial buildings. Built in 1897 the historic Shamrock Hotel has been restored to its original charm.
Of interest: A drive around the city's streets reveals many attractive lacework-verandahed buildings; the Sacred Heart Cathedral, the largest outside Melbourne, with a splendid 92 m high spire, the Alexandra Fountain at Charing Cross and the elaborate Renaissance-style Post Office. The Bendigo Art Gallery, View St, has some interesting collections. The Central Deborah Mine is a vivid reminder of Bendigo's history. It has been restored to working order and can be inspected daily. The famous Bendigo Vintage 'Talking Trams' have their terminus here. They run daily and a taped commentary gives information about the many points of interest along the 8 km trip. The Chinese Joss House, Emu Point, was built by the many Chinese miners who worked the diggings here. It is classified by the National Trust and is open for inspection. The Dai Gum San Wax Museum contains life-size wax models which depict aspects of life in ancient and modern China. Dudley House, classified by the National Trust, is a gracious old home in lovely gardens now housing an historical display. At Myers Flats, Sandhurst Town is a re-creation of a colonial town, complete with gold diggings, a eucalyptus distillery, display of antique vehicles and a working 2 ft gauge railway. The Bendigo Pottery, Midland Highway, Epsom, 7 km, is Australia's oldest pottery. Inspection tours are offered and pottery can be purchased. The Stables Gallery is a popular spot for lunches and Devonshire tea. Picnic facilities available. Bendigo's Easter Fair features Sun Loong, the ceremonial Chinese dragon more than 30 m long.

In the area: Hartland's Eucalyptus Factory and Historic Farm, Whipstick Forest, off Neilborough Road, was built in 1890 to process the oil from the surrounding scrub. The method of production can be inspected and there is also a cottage with relics of local history and picnic and barbecue facilities. The mohair farm at Lockwood is open daily and has guided tours. Bendigo's restaurants include 20 BYO and 5 licensed restaurants and a good selection of cafes and take-away food shops. Tourist information from the Bendigo Trust Information Centre, Charing Cross. **Accommodation:** 10 hotels, 17 motels, 9 caravan/camping parks.
Map ref. 154 B1, 166 C9

Sovereign Hill

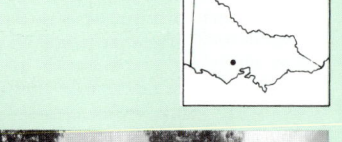

The re-created goldmining township of **Sovereign Hill** near Ballarat is a fascinating place for a day's outing to interest all the family.

Gold was discovered in Ballarat in 1851, and a visit to the Red Hill Gully Diggings at Sovereign Hill will show you something of the life of those early days. Your visit is not complete without a chance to pan for 'colour' for yourself. A friendly digger will give you a lesson, but you must be sure to purchase your licence first or you may find yourself being arrested by the watchful trooper!

Main Street is lined with faithfully re-created shops and businesses of the 1851-1861 period. These are based on actual shops and businesses that were operating in Ballarat at that time. Perhaps you'll be tempted by the aroma of freshly-baked bread from the wood-fire brick oven of the Hope Bakery. Next door you may dress in top coat or crinoline and be photographed in true Victorian pose. Across the road, mid-19th century printing presses in the Ballarat Times office are used to put your name on a WANTED poster, similar to that issued for Lalor and Black after the uprising at the Eureka Stockade in 1854.

Few can even pass the well-stocked Grocery without a surge of nostalgia for days gone by. The tiny sweetshop nearby sells all manner of sweets made to Victorian recipes at Brown's confectionery factory, further up the street.

For those with larger appetites you may wine and dine at the United States Hotel or take a digger's lunch of soup, roast meat and apple pie at the New York Bakery. For some energetic relaxation, try your hand at 9-pin bowling on the 131-ft long alley in the Empire Bowling Saloon. The accommodation complex, Government Camp, provides comfortable and inexpensive lodging.

During school terms you will be enchanted to watch a 'class of 1856' at the Red Hill National School. Here children dress in period costume,

Birchip Population 895.
On the main rail link between Melbourne and Mildura, Birchip gets its water supply from the Wimmera-Mallee stock and domestic channel system. The area was the last unsettled land left in Victoria and the township was not established until 1882. **Of interest:** The junction of the two major irrigation channels constructed in the early 1900s, north of town. Sections of original Dog Fence, the vermin-proof barrier constructed in 1883 between the Murray near Swan Hill and the S.A. border. Tchum Lake, with facilities for motor boats is 8 km to the east. Tourist information can be obtained from the motel. **Accommodation:** 2 hotels, 1 motel, 1 caravan/camping park.
Map ref. 165 L4

Boort Population 863.
A pleasant rural and holiday town on the shores of Lake Boort. The lake is popular for water sports, has a lakeside speedway, picnic facilities and beaches and offers trout and red fin fishing. There is prolific native birdlife in the area. **Accommodation:** 1 motel, 1 caravan/camping park.
Map ref. 165 P5, 166 A4

Bright Population 1545.
In the heart of the beautiful Ovens Valley and at the foothills of the Victorian Alps, Bright is an attractive tourist centre and a base for winter sports enthusiasts. The area is excellent for bushwalking, trout fishing and is very photogenic, particularly in autumn. The discovery of gold was responsible for the town's beginnings. Tensions between white and Chinese miners led to the notorious Buckland Valley riots of 1857 in which the Chinese were driven from their claims with some brutality. The remains of the alluvial goldfields can still be seen about the area. There is a good variety of restaurants, counter meals, cafes and take-away food shops. Bright caters for skiers with a number of ski hire shops which stay open late during the winter season.
Of interest: The many English and European trees in Bright have spectacular autumnal colours and Bright holds an annual Autumn Festival with many activities and displays. The Old Mill Amusement Park offers varied entertainments for children and adults, also barbecue and picnic facilities. Bright's Historic Museum is located in the old Railway Station. The Ovens River runs through the town and the areas along its banks are very pretty and popular with picnickers and campers.
In the area: Pleasant walking tracks lead to excellent views at Clearspot Lookout, from Bakers Gully Road, and Huggins Lookout from Deacon Avenue. The Alpine Road to Mt Hotham gives superb views of Mt Feathertop, the Razor Back and Mt Bogong. Harrietville is a tiny tranquil township, 18 km from Bright. The Stony Creek Trout Farm and the Pioneer Park open-air museum are of interest. Porepunkah, 6 km north-west of Bright, is at the junction of the Ovens and Buckland Rivers and convenient to the access road to Mt Buffalo. It has a hotel, caravan park and ski hire shop. Tourist information from the Caltex Sevice Station, corner of Gavan and Anderson Sts. **Accommodation:** 7 motels, 5 caravan/camping parks. It is advisable to book early during the popular holiday and school holiday seasons.
Map ref. 167 R9, 168 B9

Broadford Population 1580.
A small town off the Hume Highway, near to Mt Disappointment, the State Forest and Murchison Falls. Picnic facilities at Anderson's Gardens, a natural forest setting at the entrance to the State Forest. In the town there are barbecues and picnic facilities, and parkland with a replica of a drop-slab pioneer cottage. **Accommodation:** 2 hotels, 1 caravan/camping park.
Map ref. 154 F5, 159 M4, 166 G12, 172 H1

Buchan Population 220.
This small township, set in the heart of Gippsland mountain country north-east of Bairnsdale, is famous for its remarkable series of limestone caves. The two main caves, Royal and Fairy, have been opened up and conducted tours begin at 10.00 am, 11.00 am, 1.15 pm, 2.30 pm and 3.45 pm each day. In the hills behind the caves, there is a park and spring-fed swimming pool. **Accommodation:** 1 motel, 2 caravan/camping parks.
Map ref. 174 H6

Camperdown Population 3545.
This south-western town on the Princes Highway has an English-style charm due to its many gracious buildings and avenues of elms. It is the centre for a rich

---

learn from actual 1850s texts, and are totally involved in living the life of a mid-19th century goldfields child.

The towering poppet head, the hiss of steam and the thunder of the stamper battery will draw you to the Sovereign Quartz Mine. Take a guided tour of the underground area; you'll see examples of early mining techniques and even some original workings of the 1880s period.

As you wander through the streets you will meet costumed diggers and businessfolk, and ladies in bell-shaped crinolines and bonnets. Stop and talk to them and you will learn more about life in the days of the 'rush'.

Sovereign Hill is open from 9.30 a.m. to 5.00 p.m. daily, except Christmas Day. There are admission charges, and ample parking is available. Enquires to the Marketing Department, Sovereign Hill Post Office, Ballarat, 3350.

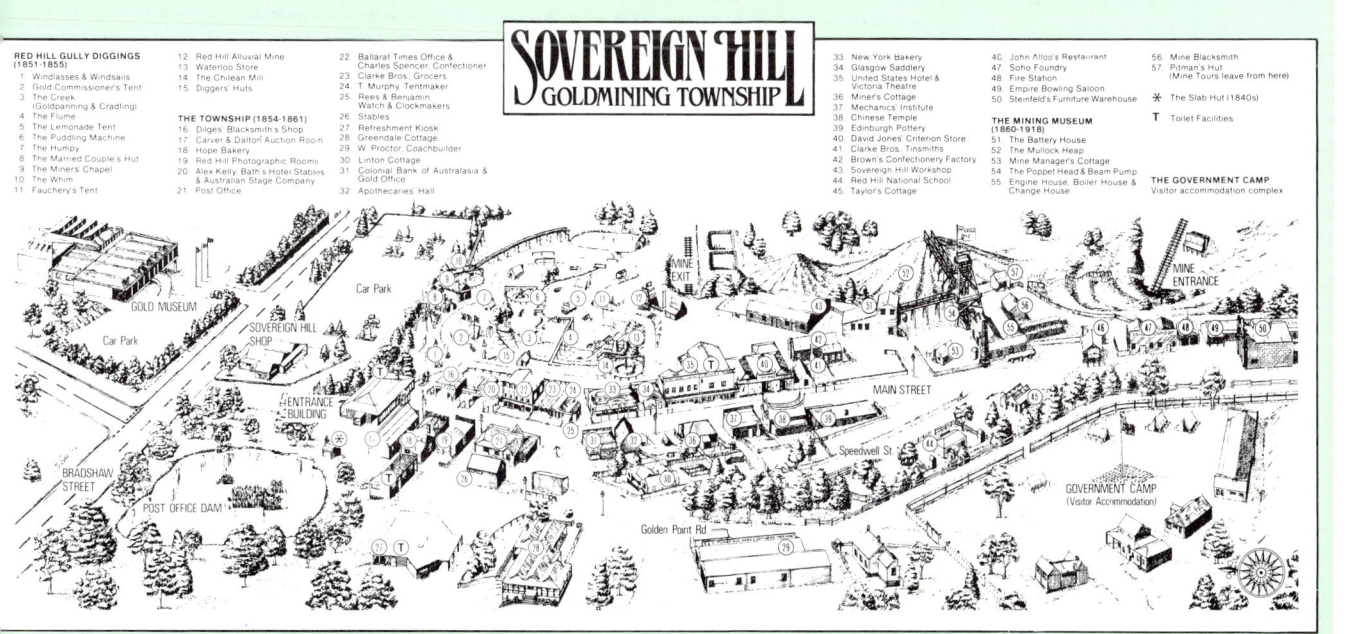

SOVEREIGN HILL GOLDMINING TOWNSHIP

RED HILL GULLY DIGGINGS (1851-1855)
1. Windlasses & Windsails
2. Gold Commissioner's Tent
3. The Creek (Goldpanning & Cradling)
4. The Flume
5. The Lemonade Tent
6. The Pudding Machine
7. The Humpy
8. The Married Couple's Hut
9. The Miners Chapel
10. The Whim
11. Fauchery's Tent
12. Red Hill Alluvial Mine
13. Waterloo Store
14. The Chilean Mill
15. Diggers' Huts

THE TOWNSHIP (1854-1861)
16. Diges Blacksmith's Shop
17. Carver & Dalton Auction Room
18. Hope Bakery
19. Red Hill Photographic Rooms
20. Alex Kelly, Bath's Hotel Stables & Australasian Stage Company
21. Post Office
22. Ballarat Times Office & Charles Spencer, Confectioner
23. Clarke Bros, Grocers
24. T. Murphy, Tentmaker
25. Rees & Benjamin, Watch & Clockmakers
26. Stables
27. Refreshment Kiosk
28. Greendale Cottage
29. W. Proctor, Coachbuilder
30. Linton Cottage
31. Colonial Bank of Australasia & Gold Office
32. Apothecaries' Hall
33. New York Bakery
34. Glasgow Saddlery
35. United States Hotel & Victoria Theatre
36. Miner's Cottage
37. Mechanics' Institute
38. Chinese Temple
39. Edinburgh Pottery
40. David Jones' Criterion Store
41. Clarke Bros. Tinsmiths
42. Brown's Confectionery Factory
43. Sovereign Hill Workshop
44. Red Hill National School
45. Taylor's Cottage
46. John Alloo's Restaurant
47. Soho Foundry
48. Fire Station
49. Empire Bowling Saloon
50. Steinfeld's Furniture Warehouse

THE MINING MUSEUM (1860-1918)
51. The Battery House
52. The Mullock Heap
53. Mine Manager's Cottage
54. The Poppet Head & Beam Pump
55. Engine House, Boiler House & Change House
56. Mine Blacksmith
57. Pitman's Hut (Mine Tours leave from here)
* The Slab Hut (1840s)
T Toilet Facilities

THE GOVERNMENT CAMP
Visitor accommodation complex

pastoral district and also famous for fishing in numerous volcanic crater lakes in the area. **Of interest:** The lookout at Mt Leura, an extinct volcano, gives a view over 38 of the crater lakes in the vicinity and across to the plains grazing country. Lake Corangamite, a salt lake just to the north, is Victoria's largest, and other excellent fishing lakes include Bullen Merri, very near the town, and Purrumbete, a few km south-east, which is well stocked with Quinnat salmon. It also has excellent water sports facilities, picnic spots and a caravan park. **In the area:** Cobden, 13 km south, is a peaceful dairying town. Timboon, a few km further south, is a timbered township on a very picturesque road leading to the tiny village of Port Campbell. This small seaside resort has good rock fishing and is close to a spectacular stretch of scenery along the Great Ocean Road. This is the area of the Port Campbell National Park, which has camping and caravan facilities. Port Campbell has a hotel and 2 motels. Tourist information from West Coast Tourism Limited, 83 Ryrie Street, Geelong. **Accommodation:** 2 hotels, 2 motels, 1 caravan/camping park.
Map ref. 171 N8

Cann River Population 345.
A popular halfway stop for Sydney-Melbourne motorists using the Princes Highway. Excellent fishing and bushwalking in the rugged hinterland. **Of interest:** Croajingolong National Park, which takes in all the coastline from Sydenham Inlet to the NSW border, incorporating the Captain James Cook, Wingan and Mallacoota National Parks. **Accommodation:** 1 hotel, 2 motels, 2 caravan/camping parks.
Map ref. 175 L6

Casterton Population 1945.
Given the Roman name meaning 'walled city' because of lush hills surrounding the valley, Casterton is on the Glenelg Highway, not far from the South Australian border. The Glenelg River runs through the town and as well as providing excellent fishing and mineral and gem fossicking along its banks, it also offers water skiing at Rocklands and Nelson. Launch trips can be taken at Nelson to the river's mouth on the coast at Discovery Bay. **Of interest:** Casterton Historical Museum in the old Railway Buildings. Goodman Park, with picnic facilities. Bryan Park, the Soldiers Memorial park, has a children's playground. **In the area:** The Warrock Homestead, classified by the National Trust, is a unique collection of buildings and is open for inspection. Twice a year there are displays of traditional working life. The area surrounding Casterton is mainly grazing land with rolling hills and areas of natural forest with wildflowers in abundance, each October-November. Baileys Rocks are an interesting collection of giant granite boulders of a unique green colour. Tourist information from the Shire Office, Henty St. **Accommodation:** 2 hotels, 1 motel, 1 caravan/camping park.
Map ref. 170 D4

Castlemaine 7534.
Along with Kyneton and Maldon, Castlemaine epitomises the gold-mining towns of north-western Victoria. A very attractive and interesting town, it is built on low hills at the foot of Mt Alexander, on the Calder Highway, 119 km from Melbourne. During the 1850s and '60s, enormous quantities of gold were found in its surface fields. This gold boom saw Castlemaine grow very rapidly and many of the fine old buildings which remain today were built during this period. The boom was eventually brought to an end by disease in the camps and a decline in the supply of surface gold. **Of interest:** The Town Market, built in 1861 for seven thousand pounds. An impressive building, it is now restored and is operated by the National Trust. It houses audio-visual displays, photographs and relics of the town and district in its heyday. Other splendid buildings are the Midland and Imperial hotels, both with verandahs decorated with iron lacework. The courthouse, town hall and library, 'Buda', Leviny Homestead, the art gallery and museum in Lyttleton St and the Claremont Gallery with its arts and crafts are all worth visiting, as is the old sandstone prison. **In the area:** The Wattle Gully Gold mine at Chewton, closed for a brief period, is now operational again. There is a pottery at Newstead and an interesting private gallery on the Burnett Road in North Castlemaine, on a 4 ha property with a recently restored homestead. Harcourt has good fishing and picnic spots and nearby on Mt Alexander there is a koala reserve. Vaughan boasts an interesting Chinese cemetery and mineral springs, with good picnic spots in the area. The Duke of Cornwall mine buildings, Fryerstown. Guildford, once the largest Chinese camp on the goldfields, has an art gallery and antique display. **Accommodation:** 2 hotels, 2 motels, 2 caravan/camping parks.
Map ref. 154 A4, 158 E2, 166 C11

Charlton Population 1377.
A supply centre for a rich wheat district, Charlton is at the intersection of the Calder and Borung Highways in north central Victoria. It has a good shopping centre and sports facilities. **Of interest:** Wooroonook Lake, for swimming and boating. The Avoca River gives good fishing. The Wychitella State Forest is 27 km to the east, with a collection of interesting native flora and fauna, including the Lowan, or Mallee Fowl. **Accommodation:** 2 hotels, 1 motel, 1 caravan/camping park.
Map ref. 165 N6

Chiltern Population 867.
Halfway between Wangaratta and Wodonga, Chiltern is 1 km off the Hume Highway. It was once a gold-mining boom town with 14 suburbs. Many of its attractive buildings have been classified by the National Trust. **Of interest:** The home of well-known author Henry Handel Richardson, 'Lake View', National Trust, open daily for inspection. The former Grape Vine Hotel boasts the largest grape vine in Australia. North Hill Clock

Victoria's

Although it is Australia's smallest mainland state, Victoria houses some 40 national, state and coastal parks, all of which offer something for everyone in every season.

Victoria's parks reflect the wide range of her landforms: alps, open grasslands, desert mallee, tropical fern gullies, ash forests and volcanic plains. Spring and summer are the best seasons to visit, when wild flowers bloom in natural surroundings and sun lovers can head for parks along the coast to swim, surf, canoe, boat or fish. Autumn, with its mild weather, beckons the bushwalker, and winter means skiing at alpine parks.

Several parks contain rock formations of great geological interest. At Organ Pipes National Park, a series of hexagonal basalt columns rises more than 20 metres above Jacksons Creek. These 'organ pipes' were formed when lava cooled in an ancient river bed. Other forms of lava can be seen at Mount Eccles, an extinct volcano. A lava canal, lava cave and the formation called the Stony Rises are exceptional features here, while the crater contains the tranquil Lake Surprise. More well-known and unusual rock structures are found at Port Campbell: 'London Bridge', 'The 12 Apostles', 'The Arch' and 'Loch Ard Gorge' are majestic formations sculpted out of soft limestone cliffs by the restless sea.

National Parks

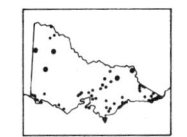

Victoria's mild and fairly wet climate combined with her rich soils produces vast areas of dense forest, particularly in the uplands. These are particularly attractive to bushwalkers, who will find a wide range of trees, mainly eucalypts, but also forests of native pine, alpine ash, banksias and paperbark scrubland. In summer, many bushwalkers prefer the parks along the coast, such as the Nepean parks, Cape Schanck, The Lakes and Wilsons Promontory. Of these, Wilsons Promontory National Park is the best-known and one of the most popular.

Another favourite haunt of bushwalkers is Kinglake National Park, where wooded valleys, fern gullies and timbered ridges provide a perfect setting for two breathtakingly beautiful waterfalls, Masons and Wombelano Falls. From a lookout point, visitors can take in a panoramic view of the Yarra Valley, Port Phillip Bay and the You Yangs Range.

Just 35 kilometres east of Melbourne is the green wonderland of Ferntree Gully National Park. Part of the Dandenong Ranges, this park comprises layers of vegetation similar to a tropical rainforest. Huge fronds of ferns form a canopy overhead, screening the sun and creating a cool, moist environment in which mosses, delicate ferns and flowers, including over 30 species of orchids, all thrive. There are more than 20 species of native animals, including echidna, platypuses, ring-tailed possums and sugar gliders, in the park; kookaburras, rosellas, cockatoos and the spectacular looking rufous fantail often visit picnic areas. You can also hear the calls of over 100 species of birds, but you may be fooled by the lovely, but shy, lyrebird, which can mimic all these calls.

One natural park best visited in winter is Wyperfeld, located in the arid north-western corner of Victoria. The 100 000 hectares preserve unique mallee flora and wildlife, and over 450 species of plants and colourful wild flowers. There are also over 200 species of birds, including the rare lowan, or mallee fowl.

Winter months bring snow to the alpine parks. Mount Buffalo draws skiers and holidaymakers for downhill and cross-country skiing. In milder weather, Mount Buffalo, with its bubbling streams and cascading waterfalls, offers visitors many activities including swimming, boating, horse riding and camping at the picturesque Lake Catani. More than 400 species of plants and flowers bloom on this plateau. Amongst them is the delicate snow gum. Another winter haven is the Baw Baw National Park, ideal for ski-touring and long-distance walking. Climbers can also attempt the big challenge of a rocky razor-back edge at Cathedral Range State Park. Canoeists will find excitement shooting the rapids or exploring the gorge of Snowy River National Park, while bushwalkers can hike through forests of native pine, alpine ash, messmate and gum. This national park is an important habitat for the rare brush-tailed rock wallaby.

Croajingolong National Park has 86 000 hectares of coastline and hinterland stretching from Sydenham Inlet to the New South Wales border. The area contains rainforest, woodland, ocean beaches, rocky promontories, inlets and coves. There are several rare animals here, such as the smoky mouse and the ground parrot. An array of wild flowers thrives on the land which still retains the natural charm seen by Captain James Cook when he arrived in Australia over 200 years ago. There is a wide range of activities for visitors at Croajingolong, with a resort centre at **Mallacoota** and other towns along the Princes Highway offering comfortable accommodation and fine food.

The Grampians National Park is the state's newest and largest. Its 167 000 hectares comprise marvellous scenery, wildlife and tourist facilities. **Halls Gap** (165 J12) offers good accommodation.

National parks have become more and more popular as leisure time has increased and the Victorian government is continually reviewing the designated areas and creating new parks for people to enjoy. For more information, contact the Department of Conservation, Forests and Lands at 240 Victoria Parade, East Melbourne 3002.

Museum. Tourist information, corner Main and Conness Sts. **Accommodation:** 1 caravan/camping park.
Map ref. 167 P5, 176 G7

Clunes Population 761.
The first reported find of gold in the state was made on a hillside in this small town some 40 km north of Ballarat. The town is quiet and pleasant with some solid sandstone buildings erected during the gold boom. Surrounding the town are a number of rounded hills which are extinct volcanoes and a good view of them all can be obtained about 3 km out of town on the road to Ballarat. **Of interest:** The William Barkell Historical Centre, several public buildings classified by the National Trust. **Accommodation:** 1 hotel, 1 motel, 1 caravan/camping park.
Map ref. 165 Q13, 166 A13, 171 Q1, 172 A1

Cobram Population 3817.
Magnificent wide sandy beaches are a feature of the stretch of the Murray River at Cobram. The river area offers good picnicking spots and a variety of water sports can be enjoyed. This is fruit-growing country and Cobram is well-known for its 'Peaches and Cream' festival held Australia Day weekend every odd year, e.g. 1983, 1985 etc. **Accommodation:** 2 motels, 3 caravan/camping parks.
Map ref. 167 K3

Cohuna Population 2178.
Between Kerang and Echuca on the Murray Valley Highway, Cohuna is beside Gunbower Island, formed by the Murray on the far side and Gunbower Creek just across the highway from the town. This island is covered in red gum and box forest which provides a home for abundant water fowl and birdlife, as well as kangaroos and emus. The central zone of the forest is a sanctuary. The forest is subject to flooding and a large part of the island has breeding rookeries during the flood periods. Picnic and barbecue facilities can be found on the island and forest tracks give access for driving and riding. Maps are available from the Forests Officer or from stores in Cohuna.
Of interest: The Cohuna swimming pool features a 45 metre water slide. The pool is open daily from November to Easter.
In the area: Box Bridge, at Kow Swamp, south of Cohuna, also a sanctuary, has picnic spots and good fishing. Mount Hope, 110 m high, is popular for easy rock climbing; it has good views from its summit and beautiful wild flowers in spring. Picnic facilities. Torrumbarry Lock, 40 km from Cohuna, has its entire weir structure removed from the river during winter. In summer you can water-ski above the weir. **Accommodation:** 2 motels, 2 caravan/camping parks.
Map ref. 166 C2

Colac Population 10 587.
Colac is situated on the eastern edge of the volcanic plain which covers much of the Western District of Victoria. It is the city centre of a prosperous, closely settled agricultural area and is sited on the shores

The Western District

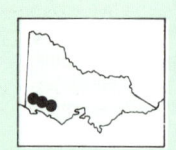

Some famous Australians have been born and bred in this south-western part of Victoria, including a Prime Minister or two. Many have been members of the wealthy landowning families whose gracious homesteads are dotted about this beautiful pastoral area. The Western District supports one-third of Victoria's best sheep and cattle — and the merino wool is acknowledged to be the finest in the land.

Many of the Western District towns boast some splendid original buildings. Of special interest are **Hamilton** — looked upon as the 'capital' of the area — and the attractive little towns of **Coleraine** and **Casterton**. **Ararat**, situated close to the Langi Ghiran State Forest, is a popular spot for picnics and bushwalks. Several of the district's historic homesteads are open for inspection, including 'Warrock', which has 33 original farm buildings still in operation, and 'Muntham', a property established by Edward Henty in 1837. Both are near Casterton.

The production of champagne and fine wines is another of the district's claims to fame. The champagne area, situated around the township of **Great Western**, is a pleasure to explore.

The heart of the district is fairly flat grazing land. To the east, the volcanic lake area around **Camperdown** offers great fishing and is well developed for water sports. To the south, a rugged coastline stretches from **Anglesea** to the tiny hamlet of **Nelson**, at the mouth of the Glenelg River. To the north, the high rocky ranges of the Grampians break through the gentle rolling countryside. An excellent scenic route to the Grampians from the Western District is along the Mt Abrupt Road from **Dunkeld**.

of Lake Colac, which has good fishing and a variety of water sports. On its foreshore, beautiful Botanic Gardens cover an area of 18 ha. **In the area:** Alvie and Red Rock Lookout from which 30 of the surrounding volcanic lakes can be seen. Lake Corangamite is Victoria's largest salt lake and the beautiful Otway Ranges lie to the south. Winding roads pass through them, revealing lush and beautiful mountain scenery, and lead down to the coast. Birregurra, about 20 km east of Colac, has some interesting old buildings. Colac holds the Kanyana Festival — ten days of sporting and agricultural events, exhibitions and concerts — each March. **Accommodation:** 1 hotel, 3 motels, 4 caravan/camping parks.
Map ref. 171 P9

Coleraine Population 1232.
Situated in the attractive Wannon River valley, 35 km west of Hamilton, this area was first settled by the Henty and Winter brothers in 1837 for pastoral grazing. The primary products of the area are still pastoral and agricultural. **Of interest:** The Wannon and Nigretta Falls, between Coleraine and Hamilton. Adjacent to the township, at Points Lookout, there is a unique planting of over 700 species of native trees and shrubs. There are a number of interesting historic homesteads in this area. Glendinning, near Balmoral, 50 km to the north, maintains a wildlife sanctuary and offers farm holiday accommodation (details from the manager). Just outside Balmoral is the Rocklands Reservoir, noted for excellent fishing and boating, with a caravan park. Tourist information from West Coast Tourism Limited, 83 Ryrie Street, Geelong. **Accommodation:** 2 hotels, 1 caravan/camping park.
Map ref. 170 F4

Corryong Population 1320.
Situated in alpine country, Corryong is at the gateway to the Snowy Mountains. The town holds the Nariel Creek folk music festival twice a year, at New Year and Labour Day weekend. The district offers superb mountain scenery and excellent trout fishing. The Murray, near Corryong, is still a brisk and gurgling stream running through forested hills. Jack Riley, 'The Man from Snowy River', came from these parts and his grave is in Corryong cemetery. 'The Man from Snowy River' museum has an antique ski collection and a replica of Riley's original shack. The Cudgewa Bluff Falls area, 27 km from Corryong, has excellent scenery and bushwalking tracks. **Accommodation:** 2 motels, 2 caravan/camping parks.
Map ref. 168 G5

Cowes Population 1563.
This is the main town on Phillip Island, a popular resort area in Westernport Bay, linked to the mainland by a narrow bridge at San Remo. Cowes is on the northern side of the island and is the centre for hotel and motel accommodation. It has a pleasant beach, safe for children. The town has a number of arts and crafts shops, an amusement centre and a variety of restaurants, licensed and BYO, as well

as cafes, pizza houses and take-away food shops. The Cowes Tourist Information Centre is at 71 Thompson Ave and bookings for island tours and cruises can be made there. **Accommodation:** 13 motels, 10 caravan/camping parks.
Map ref. 153 O11, 172 I10

Creswick Population 2036.
This charming old town, 18 km north of Ballarat, originated with the discovery of one of the richest alluvial goldfields in the world. At one time during the boom, its population swelled to 60 000. **Of interest:** Mullock heaps can still be seen in the goldfields area and gold panning is popular in the numerous streams. The surrounding volcanic bushland and forest areas are of interest to field naturalists and bushwalking enthusiasts. The Creswick Historical Museum, Albert St, has a magnificent winding staircase and a good collection of the early history of the area, including some Lindsay paintings and sketches. At the local cemetery, some interesting early miners' graves, and a Chinese section. There are barbecue and picnic facilities at the Koala Park, Creswick Road. **In the area:** Olympic pool and wildlife reserve at Calambeen Park. At Smeaton, north of Creswick, Smeaton House, an elegant house built in the 1850s. Tourist Information rotunda, corner Raglan and Cambridge Sts. **Accommodation:** 1 motel, 1 caravan/camping park.
Map ref. 158 A7, 171 R2, 172 B2

Daylesford Population 2383.
Both Daylesford and nearby Hepburn Springs are popular holiday centres, set in attractive hill country. They are both 'spa' towns, with mineral springs. The bathhouse at Hepburn Springs is open daily from 10 am to 12 noon and 1.30 pm to 6 pm with extended hours during the summer months and school holidays. Daylesford rambles up the side of Wombat Hill, at the top of which are the Botanical Gardens with a lookout tower offering commanding views. **Of interest:** Jubilee Lake is a good spot for a picnic, as is the Central Springs Spa Reserve. There is an historical museum in the former School of Mines, Parma House, Hepburn Springs, built in 1853. **In the area:** Breakneck Gorge, Loddon, Sailors and Trentham Falls and, 13 km north, Mt Franklin, an extinct volcano. **Accommodation:** 1 motel, 3 caravan/camping parks.
Map ref. 154 A6, 158 D6, 166 C13, 172 C2

Dimboola Population 1675.
The word 'dimboola' is Ceylonese and means 'land of figs'; it was chosen by a local surveyor on returning from a trip to Ceylon. It is a peaceful town on the tree-lined Wimmera River, 35 km north-west of Horsham. **In the area:** The Little Desert National Park is nearby. Power boats can be hired to travel along the river to its edge or it can be approached by road through Kiata, 26 km west, where mallee fowl can be seen in the Lowan Sanctuary throughout the year. Wail, 11 km south of Dimboola, has a well-stocked forest nursery run by the Department of Conservation, Forests and Lands. **Accommodation:** 2 hotels, 1 motel, 1 caravan/camping park.
Map ref. 164 G7

Donald Population 1509.
At the junction of the Sunraysia and Borung Highways, Donald is situated on the Richardson River and in a Wimmera district renowned for its fine wheat, sheep and fat lambs. **Of interest:** Agricultural museum, railway steam engine, and historic water pump by the lake. **In the area:** Lake Buloke has good duck and quail shooting in season. **Accommodation:** 2 hotels, 1 motel, 1 caravan/camping park.
Map ref. 165 L7

Drouin Population 3492.
Drouin is on the Princes Highway not far from Warragul and the Latrobe Valley. A large milk products factory and a plastics factory are two of the major industries. **Of interest:** In the main street, there is an old brick police station, with exhibits organised by the Buln Buln Historical Society. **In the area:** The Tarago River runs through attractive camping and picnic spots at Glen Cromie, where there is a nature reserve, and Picnic Point, on the Princes Highway west of the town. Neerim South has a picnic and barbecue area at the Tarago Reservoir. Gumbuya Park, about 25 km west of Drouin on the Princes Highway between Garfield and Tynong, is the largest game and bird park in Australia. There are picnic facilities, an adventure playground and plants for sale. Tourist information from South East Coast Tourism Limited, Silkstone Road, Korumburra. **Accommodation:** 2 hotels, 2 motels, 3 caravan/camping parks.
Map ref. 173 L8

Drysdale Population 1127.
This is primarily a service centre for the local farming community on the Bellarine Peninsula. Nearby Clifton Springs had a brief burst of fame in the 1870s when the therapeutic value of its mineral spring water was discovered. **In the area:** Coryule homestead. Just outside the township, the Lake Lorne picnic area. **Accommodation:** Limited.
Map ref. 155 H7, 172 E8

Dunkeld Population 432.
On the Glenelg Highway, 31 km from Hamilton, Dunkeld lies at the southern end of the Grampians and is conveniently located for trips to the Victoria Valley, the Chimney Pots and Billywing Plantation. **Accommodation:** 1 motel, 2 caravan/camping parks.
Map ref. 170 I4

Dunolly Population 621.
A small township in north central Victoria, in the heart of the gold country. The 'Welcome Stranger', the largest nugget ever discovered, was found 15 km away at Moliagul. The district has produced more nuggets than any other goldfield in Australia; 126 were unearthed in the town itself. There is a 'Gold Rush Weekend' each October. **Of interest:** Some handsome original buildings in the main street. The Goldfields Historical Museum is open at weekends and has replicas of some of the most spectacular nuggets. Dunolly Gold Wines has the oldest existing licence in the state. More than 40 types of wine are blended and bottled there and may be sampled on weekdays. The Kurrajong gallery and pottery is in an old bakery. **In the area:** The Melville Caves, 30 km north, were the haunt of bushranger Captain Melville. Laanecoorie Reservoir, 16 km east, is a pleasant picnic spot. The countryside around Dunolly abounds with wild flowers in spring and many native birds and animals can be seen. Enthusiasts can pan for gold in the local creeks. **Accommodation:** 1 caravan/camping park.
Map ref. 165 P10, 166 A10

Echuca Population 7946.
This town is at the junction of the Murray, Campaspe and Goulburn Rivers and was once Australia's largest inland port. An iron railway bridge leads to the NSW town of Moama across the Murray. **Of interest:** The Port of Echuca, restored to the period of its heyday, includes the paddle steamers *Adelaide* and *Pevensey*, the Star Hotel, with its huge underground bar and the Bridge Hotel, built by Henry Hopwood, one of the early residents who ran the original punt service across the river. The Bridge has a good restaurant. Cruises can be taken on the modern paddle steamer *Canberra* from this point. A scenic tour starting from the Tourist Centre in Heygarth St has green arrows to guide visitors on a tour of the city and of Moama. The Alambee Auto and Folk Museum, the Port of Echuca Museum and the Murray Museum, with its impressive collection of early glass and earthenware, are all of interest to visitors. **In the area:** The Barmah Redgum Forest covers an area of 50 000 ha and has a Murray River frontage of about 192 km. The road beside the Barmah Hotel leads to the forest and lakes. Check with the Tourist Information Centre, Heygarth St, about the road conditions. **Accommodation:** 8 motels, 5 caravan/camping parks.
Map ref. 166 F5

Edenhope Population 827.
On the Wimmera Highway, just 30 km from the border, Edenhope is surrounded by interesting lake country and is situated on the shores of Lake Wallace, a haven for water birds. When full, the lake is popular for water sports and has a boat ramp, golf course and tennis courts nearby. **Of interest:** A cairn in the township commemorates the visit of the first all-Aboriginal cricket team to England. The team was coached by T. W. Willis, who was also the founder of Australian Rules football. **In the area:** Harrow, 32 km south-east, is one of Victoria's oldest inland towns, with many interesting buildings (some still in use), including the Hermitage Hotel (1851) and the log gaol (1862). Just over the SA border, the Naracoorte Caves Conservation Park. The Rocklands Reservoir, 65 km east of Edenhope, is part of the Wimmera-Mallee irrigation system. It is popular for fishing and boating, and has launching facilities and caravan and camping areas on its western shores. **Accommodation:** 1 hotel, 1 motel, 1 caravan/camping park.
Map ref. 164 C12

Eildon Population 737.

Built to irrigate a vast stretch of northern Victoria and to provide hydro-electric power, Lake Eildon is the state's largest man-made lake and is a very popular resort area, surrounded by the beautiful foothills of the Alps. There are excellent recreational facilities around the foreshores, two major boat harbours, launching ramps, picnic grounds and lookout points. The towns of Eildon and Bonnie Doon are popular holiday centres. There are a number of restaurants and take-away food shops in Eildon. Power, rowing and houseboats can be hired at the boat harbours. **Of interest:** Snob's Creek Fish Hatchery is near Eildon township and millions of trout are bred there and used to stock lakes and rivers. Open daily, it offers tours and picnic facilities in park surroundings. There is a Fauna Sanctuary nearby. The Snob's Creek Falls are an impressive 107 m cascade. **In the area:** Mt Pinniger (543 m) gives a panorama of Mt Buller and the Alps. Jamieson, an old mining town on the south side of Lake Eildon, stands at the junction of the Goulburn and Jamieson Rivers and is surrounded by dense, bush-clad mountain countryside. It has holiday cabins and a limited number of hotels and motels. A mercury mine, 26 km east, can be reached by a bridle track skirting the river gorges. Mt Skene, 48 km from Jamieson, is usually spread with wild flowers from December to February (the road is closed in winter. There is no closed season for trout in Eildon Lake, which is also stocked with Murray cod and redfin. An Inland Fishing Licence is required for anyone over the age of sixteen. **Accommodation:** 2 motels, 5 caravan/camping parks. Book well ahead at Christmas and Easter.
Map ref. 160 H4, 167 L13, 173 L1

Emerald Population 2857.

The Puffing Billy railway serves this pretty township, which was the first settlement in the Dandenong Ranges. Situated on a high ridge, it has a number of interesting galleries and craft shops, and lavender farms nearby. Emerald Lake which has waterslides and paddleboats is one of the hills' prettiest and best-equipped picnic and swimming sites.
Map ref. 147 H12

Euroa Population 2713.

A small town on the Hume Highway, Euroa is a good base from which to explore the Strathbogie Ranges and tablelands. **Of interest:** The Seven Creek Run Woolshed. This will eventually house the Australian Wool Museum. The scenic drive to Gooram Falls is recommended. It was here that the Kelly gang pulled off a daring robbery, rounding up more than 50 people at nearby Faithfull Station and then making off with £2200. Every December, the Kelly raid is re-enacted in costume. The Faithfull Creek homestead was burnt down in the 1939 bushfires, but the ruins remain. Nearby is the Faithfull Creek Waterfall, with picnic facilities. **Accommodation:** 2 motels, 1 caravan/camping park.
Map ref. 154 I1, 167 J9

Foster Population 1038.

A picturesque small township within easy reach of Corner Inlet, Waratah Bay and Wilson's Promontory on the south east coast of Victoria. **In the area:** Walkerville and Waratah Bay are two pleasant beach resorts. Cape Liptrap gives excellent views of the rugged coastline and Bass Strait. There is a good surf beach at beautiful Sandy Point. Just behind, the protected waters of Shallow Inlet are popular for fishing and swimming. Port Franklin is another small fishing village on Corner Inlet. Turton's Creek, 18 km north of Foster, is an old gold rich village where lyrebirds can sometimes be seen in the tree-fern gullies nearby. Foster is the service town for Wilson's Promontory National Park. **Accommodation:** 2 motels, 1 caravan/camping park.
Map ref. 173 N11

Geelong Population 125 269.

The largest provincial city in Victoria, Geelong is a rapidly expanding industrial centre on Corio Bay. Its principal trade is crude and refined petroleum products and it is a traditional wool selling centre. The Corio Bay area was first settled in the 1830s and, apart from a rush to the diggings during the gold boom, Geelong has grown and prospered steadily. It is a pleasant and well laid out city with more than 14 per cent of its area reserved for parks and sports grounds.
Of interest: The Botanical Gardens in Eastern Park overlooking Corio Bay. Johnstone Park includes the art gallery, war memorial library and city hall. Queens Park has a golf course, sports oval and walks from there lead to Buckley's Falls. Geelong boasts many interesting buildings, more than 100 of them with National Trust classifications. They include Merchiston Hall, Garden St, East Geelong, an eight-roomed stone house built in 1856 for an early settler, James Cowie. In North Geelong, Osborne House, Swinburne St, is a bluestone mansion built in 1858. At Eastern Beach is the beautiful Corio Villa, a prefabricated iron house built in 1856. 'The Heights', Aphrasia St, Newtown, is a 14-roomed prefabricated timber mansion built in 1855 for Charles Ibbotson. It is open to the public. Also open is Barwon Grange, Fernleigh St, Newtown. The oldest Anglican church in Victoria still in continuous use is Christ Church, Moorabool St. Also of interest, the Customs House in Brougham Place and Dennys Lascelles Wool Store in Moorabool St.
In the area: Fyansford, on the outskirts of the city, is one of the oldest settlements in the region. The old Monash Bridge across the Moorabool River is thought to be one of the first reinforced concrete bridges in Victoria. Interesting buildings include the 'Swan Inn', the Balmoral Hotel (1854), now an art gallery, and the Fyansford Hotel. There is an old paper mill with a bluestone tower at Buckley's Falls. From the Brownhill Observation Tower at Ceres there is an excellent view of the surrounding areas. Batesford, 10 km north of Geelong, is now a picturesque market garden township, with a history of vineyards. The Idyll vineyard on the Ballan Road is open for tastings and sales. The sandstone 'Travellers Rest Inn' was built in 1849 and is across the Moorabool River from the present hotel. Lara (population 4231), east of Geelong, was swept by bushfires in 1969, but some interesting buildings remain. It is at the foot of the You Yangs, a range of granite hills, with a forest reserve and wildlife sanctuary. The Twin Lakes, a 486 ha fauna sanctuary 19 km from Geelong, is a breeding haven for kangaroos, emus, koalas and wildfowl. Some 46 km along the Midland Highway is Meredith, one of the oldest towns in Victoria, and once an important stopping place for diggers on their way to the gold fields. The shire hall, railway station, and bluestone state school are of interest. Anakie and the Anakie Gorge can be approached from Geelong, via Batesford. The township is at the foot of the Brisbane Ranges, a National Park area. There are many species of fern and flowering plants in the park; walking tracks lead to the gorge and adjoining wildlife sanctuary. On Mt Elephant, the Fairy Park is a display of quaint miniature houses and scenes from fairy tales, which children can enjoy. Hickinbotham Winemakers, 4 km north of the township on Staughton Vale Road, is open Saturdays and produces local wines. Steiglitz, a few km north of Anakie, has a popular camping ground an interesting old court-house dating back to 1875. The trip to Batesford, Anakie and Steiglitz makes a pleasant day trip from Geelong, as does an exploration of the Bellarine Peninsula, including the towns of Queenscliff, Portarlington, Ocean Grove and Barwon Heads. Venturing a bit further afield, a trip down the Great Ocean Road from Torquay to Lorne is well worth while, as the coastal scenery is spectacular. Geelong has excellent sporting facilities including a race-course, trotting and greyhound courses and three first-class golf courses. There are boat ramps on the Corio Bay beaches and the area offers good river and bay fishing. Tourist information centre at 83 Ryrie St. **Accommodation:** 8 hotels, 20 motels, 10 caravan/camping parks.
Map ref. 154 C11, 155 E7, 156, 172 D8

Gisborne Population 1747.

Once a stopping place for coaches and foot travellers on their way to the Castlemaine and Bendigo goldfields, Gisborne is now a quiet and attractive township on the road to Woodend and Kyneton. **Of interest:** Barringo Wildlife Reserve, Calder Highway, an area of natural bushland with herds of deer, many wallabies and kangaroos and a lake stocked with trout. **Accommodation:** 1 motel.
Map ref. 154 D7, 158 I8, 172 E3

Goroke Population 370.

Spring is an excellent time to visit this tiny town close to the Little Desert National Park. Lake Charlegark, 26 km west of the town, has picnic spots, water skiing and cod fishing. There is a Murray cod hatchery open daily. **Accommodation:** Limited.
Map ref. 164 D9

ALPINE COUNTRY

To the east and north-east of Melbourne, the gently rounded peaks of the Victorian Alps stretch, seemingly endlessly, under clear skies. They are much lower than Alpine ranges in other parts of the world, lacking in sheer escarpments and jagged peaks, but they still stand majestic especially when covered in snow. These blue ranges are not high enough to have a permanent cover of snow, but the expanses of the rolling mountains are ideal for cross-country skiing as well as for the more popular downhill variety.

The skiing season officially opens on the Queen's Birthday weekend each June and closes in October — but it often actually extends beyond these dates. Each year, thousands of people flock to the snow: for downhill racing, for leisurely Nordic or cross-country skiing, or just to enjoy the beauty of nature at its best. Children can have a great time throwing snowballs and building snowmen.

There is bountiful fishing in the lakes and trout streams. Sailing, swimming, canoeing and water-skiing are popular sports in the summer months. Many riding schools in the valleys provide a leisurely pastime for those who want to explore the countryside. For the more energetic, bushwalking in the beautiful rugged country is a must. Although the Alps look so beautiful in summer, they can still claim the life of an ill-prepared bushwalker. So make sure you have the necessary equipment and knowledge to tackle this recreation activity; and always tell someone where you are going and when you expect to be back. For more information about the area contact Victour, 230 Collins Street, Melbourne.

LEFT: *Snow-covered Mt Buller is popular with skiers.*

BELOW: *The Cathedral, Mt Buffalo, one of the many granite tors that dominate this area.*

ABOVE: *King Valley, a year round destination for outdoors enthusiasts.*

ABOVE: *Horse riders at Marysville.*

BELOW: *Spring wattles at Falls Creek.*

PHILLIP ISLAND

Situated at the entrance to Westernport Bay, 124 kilometres south-east of Melbourne, Phillip Island is a year-round destination for those who want to 'get away from it all'.

Once over the narrow bridge at San Remo, the visitor is greeted by wide open spaces, most of the native bush having been cleared, leaving only isolated clumps of gums and eucalypts.

With an area of 10 300 hectares, Phillip Island is unusual, in that animals and birds live freely alongside man. The greatest attraction for visitors are the fascinating fairy penguins on Summerland Beach. The penguins spend the day out at sea, catching whitebait for their young. Each evening, at sunset, these adorable little creatures return from the sea in small groups and waddle up the beach to their sand-dune burrows. Amazingly, they appear not to be worried by the glaring floodlights or by their large audience, and will come up within hand's reach if you remain still and quiet.

At the south-west tip of the island, The Nobbies, is a cluster of tall rocks where 5000 fur seals live and breed. You can watch the seals sunbathing on the rocks from telescopes up on the headland. Nearby is the blowhole, which is a spectacular sight in rough seas.

BELOW: *Children love spotting koalas.*

ABOVE: *Cowes Beach, in the shelter of Westernport Bay, is safe and popular for bathing.*

BELOW: *Fairy Penguins provide unique entertainment each evening at dusk at Summerland Beach.*

Take the road down to Cape Woolamai, a rugged granite headland where diamonds were once found. The breathtaking view includes thundering surf and curiously shaped rock formations of pinnacles and colonnades. Down on the sand dunes are rookeries where the mutton birds breed. The shy koalas also make their home on this island, where they can be viewed easily in their natural habitat.

The Len Lukey Memorial Museum and gardens is ideal for a day out. It has a large motor and antique museum, barbecues, wildlife park, roller skating and swimming pool.

Children would enjoy a visit to the Kingston Gardens Zoo, where a variety of animals live in a farmland setting. Wombats, kangaroos, wallabies, turkeys, goats, donkeys, cockatoos and lambs wander freely.

Some unusual species of birds make their homes in The Nits at Rhyll, a fishing resort on the northern side of the island. Pelicans, ibis, royal spoonbills, swans and gulls inhabit the swamplands there.

Also on the north coast is Cowes, the most popular summer resort on Phillip Island. Its unspoilt beaches are sheltered for safe swimming, yachting and other water sports. There is a ferry service which runs from Cowes to Stony Point across Westernport Bay.

For more detailed information and local guide, call at the tourist information centre near the Post Office just minutes from the bridge to Phillip Island.

BELOW: *Fur Seals. Colonies of these creatures lie sunbathing on Seal Rocks and can be viewed by telescope from the headland.*

Halls Gap Population 265.
Beautifully sited in the heart of the Grampians, this little township is the tourist and accommodation centre of the Grampians area. It is adjacent to the Wonderlands Forest Park and Lake Bellfield and is the focus of a network of scenic roads which run through the ranges. There are shops, an art gallery and pottery and also a swimming pool and golf course. The guide service to the Grampians is located in Halls Gap and tourist information can be obtained from the newsagency. The Grampians are famous for their wild flowers and Halls Gap holds an annual spring wild flower exhibition. **Accommodation:** 6 motels, 4 caravan/camping parks.
Map ref. 165 J12, 171 J1

Hamilton Population 9749.
Known as the 'wool capital of the world', Hamilton is a prosperous and pleasant city less than an hour's drive from the resort towns of Portland, Port Fairy and Warrnambool on the south coast and the Grampian Ranges to the north. **Of interest:** An outstanding art gallery, in Brown Street, has varied collections of the decorative arts and includes a number of watercolours and etchings by Paul Sandby. In the city centre, Lake Hamilton has a sandy beach, water sports and picnic facilities. It is also stocked with trout. There is a small zoo at the Botanical Gardens, with a free flight aviary, a duckpond and a playground. A drive through the town centre reveals many splendid old public buildings and gracious homes. **In the area:** The Wannon, 15 km, and Nigretta Falls, 15 km away, are worth a visit, as it the Mt Eccles National Park, near Macarthur, some 33 km from Hamilton on the Port Fairy Road. Mt Eccles, and its crater Lake Surprise, is one of three extinct volcanoes around this district — the other two are Mt Rouse at Penshurst, some 30 km south-east of Hamilton, and Mt Napier, 16 km south of the city. On the Portland Road the Warrawong open farm, 24 km south of Hamilton, gives a picture of day-to-day farm activities, and has arts and crafts for sale as well as picnic and barbecue facilities. A pleasant day trip from Hamilton is the Grampians Tour, about 250 km, to Dunkeld, Halls Gap, Ararat and back via Glenthompson. This trip includes the picturesque Victoria Valley and the wineries of the Great Western area, as well as the attractions of the Grampians. Tourist information from West Coast Tourism Limited, 83 Ryrie Street, Geelong. **Accommodation:** 6 hotels, 8 motels, 2 caravan/camping parks.
Map ref. 170 H5

Healesville Population 4526.
Surrounded by mountain forest country, Healesville is about an hour's drive from Melbourne along the Maroondah Highway. It has been a popular resort town since the turn of the century, as the climate is cool and pleasant in summer and the area offers excellent bushwalks and scenic drives. **Of interest:** Just outside the town, on Badger Creek Road, the famous Healsville Sanctuary, open daily. This 32 ha reserve is very popular with adults and children alike. A variety of native animals and birds live in a largely natural bushland setting. Key attractions are the Platypus Research Station, the subterranean display of nocturnal animals and dense fern glades which have been constructed to simulate a natural habitat for lyrebirds. There is a nature trail, barbecue and picnic facilities, a restaurant and toilet facilities with a fully equipped mother's room. There is a pottery, lapidary and art gallery at Nigel Court, off Badger Creek Road, which is open daily. Other interesting drives from Healesville include a tour of the Toolangi State Forest, criss-crossed with logging roads, a trip through the forests to Myer's Creek Reserve and Falls, and to Steavenson's Falls 31 km east. The drive north to Marysville, via the Black Spur, takes you past the Maroondah Reservoir where there are picnic and barbecue areas, and on through towering stands of mountain ash and lush tree fern glades. There are other scenic picnic areas just off this road. **Accommodation:** 2 hotels, 5 motels, 3 caravan/camping parks.
Map ref. 154 I8, 159 R10, 160 D10, 173 J4

Heathcote Population 1214.
In attractive countryside on the McIvor Highway, Heathcote is set along the McIvor Creek, 47 km south of Bendigo. **Of interest:** Lake Eppalock, 10 km west, one of the state's largest lakes and popular for motor boat racing. The hilly country gives excellent views, particularly from Viewing Rock Lookout and Mount Ida Lookout. Don't miss the Pink Cliffs, created by eroded spoil from gold sluices, with their brilliant mineral staining. The McIvor Range Reserve has an historic powder magazine and the old Heathcote Hospital, built in 1859, is listed for preservation by the National Trust. Tourist information can be obtained at the Reserve, and there are picnic and barbecue facilities. **Accommodation:** 1 caravan/camping park.
Map ref. 154 D2, 166 F10

Hopetoun Population 832.
A small Mallee town just south of the Wyperfeld National Park, it was named after the seventh Earl of Hopetoun who was the first Governor-General of Australia. Hopetoun was a frequent visitor to the home of Edward Lascelles, who was largely responsible for opening up the Mallee area. **Of interest:** Hopetoun House, built for Lascelles, and classified by the National Trust. Lake Lascelles is a good spot for boating, swimming and picnics. **In the area:** To the north, the Wyperfeld National Park. **Accommodation:** 1 hotel, 1 motel, 1 caravan/camping park.
Map ref. 164 I2, 162 I13

Horsham Population 12 034.
At the junction of the Western, Wimmera and Henty Highways, Horsham is generally regarded as the capital of the Wimmera region. Its location makes it a good base for tours of the region, particularly to the Little Desert National Park 40 km west and to the Grampians some 50 km south-east. **Of interest:**

The Mallee

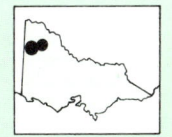

The Mallee region takes its name from an Aboriginal word given to the many-stemmed eucalyptus scrub which once covered most of this extreme north-west corner of Victoria. Vast stretches of mallee scrub still abound in the area, and stretch down into the Wimmera, but today most of the region has been developed for grain production.

The landscape seems to stretch for ever with grain lands and semi-arid sand plains. The Mallee is not the place for 'pretty' scenery. It is well worth exploring, though, as parts of it are so typical of the Australian inland landscape as it has been since time immemorial. The other parts are an incredible testament to the work of the pioneers who painstakingly turned most of this scrubland into the state's second largest grain treasury.

One of Victoria's largest national parks, Wyperfeld, is a wonderful illustration of the variety of animal and plant life which can thrive in this apparently arid terrain. The park has been set aside to protect the Mallee fowl — a fascinating sight to watch, as it tirelessly works to perfect its incubator style nesting mound — and to preserve an area of typical Mallee country. Emus, parrots and kangaroos are plentiful. The road from **Albacutya** (164 G3) leads to the park entrance and then you take a sealed road to the central 'tourist' area, which has camping and picnic facilities.

The main Mallee towns are **Nhill**, **Sea Lake** and **Ouyen**, all serving primarily as centres for the grain areas. The Hattah-Kulkyne National Park, 34 kilometres north of Ouyen, has a large population of water birds.

A welcome sight in this region is Lake Hindmarsh, the state's largest natural freshwater lake. It has very pleasant beaches and picnic spots and is popular for swimming, water-skiing and fishing.

A word of warning — the Mallee does get extremely hot in high summer. Spring or autumn are probably better times to visit the area — particularly spring for the wild flower bloomings.

The Blue Dandenongs

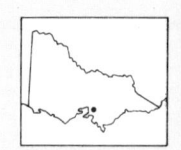

These ranges, 50 kilometres from the centre of Melbourne, are a renowned beauty area and tourist attraction. Heavy rainfall and rich volcanic soil have created a lush vegetation with spectacular hills and gullies crowded with creepers, tree ferns and soaring mountain ash. The area is fairly closely settled and there are a number of pretty townships dotted about the hills.

It has long been a traditional summer retreat for people from Melbourne and many of the gracious old homes have now been converted into guest houses and restaurants.

The entire area is famous for its beautiful gardens and for its great variety of European trees, particularly attractive in spring and autumn. Many excellent restaurants, art and craft galleries, antique shops and well-stocked plant nurseries add to the charms of these hills, ideally placed for a relaxed day's outing from Melbourne. At 633 metres, Mount Dandenong (147 E6) is the highest point of the ranges, and at its summit there are excellent views, picnic facilities and the 'Skyhigh' restaurant from which a magnificent night-time view of Melbourne can be seen.

Ferntree Gully National Park is quite small but includes, among its lush trees and ferns, a wide variety of flora and fauna. The lyrebird and eastern whipbird can be heard here. Sherbrooke Forest Park, on the road from **Belgrave** (147 E10) to **Kallista** (147 E9) is also unspoiled bushland with many lyrebirds. A tourist road runs through the park areas from **Ferntree Gully** (147 A9) to **Montrose** (147 D5). William Ricketts Sanctuary (open daily), on Mount Dandenong Road, is a natural forest area in which Ricketts, a musician and naturalist, has sculpted in clay a number of Aboriginal figures and symbolic scenes. Near **Sherbrooke** (147 D9), the Nicholas Memorial Gardens, 13 hectares of formerly private garden, are open daily.

'Puffing Billy', one of the Dandenongs' most famous attractions, leaves from Belgrave and travels 13 kilometres to Emerald Lake. This little train, loved by children, is pulled by the only surviving locomotive designed for narrow gauge tracks at the turn of the century. The Puffing Billy Museum at Menzies Creek, open on Sundays, displays some restored locomotives and rolling stock. Puffing Billy runs at weekends and on Tuesdays and Thursdays throughout the year and daily, except on fire ban days, from November to early April. A timetable is available from Victour, 230 Collins St, or telephone 870 8411 for information.

Emerald (147 H12) was the first settlement in the area and is situated on a high ridge. It has a number of interesting galleries and in the surrounding countryside there are lavender farms and some attractive picnic spots. **Olinda** (147 D8) is a pretty township with some good restaurants. The home of one of Victoria's first settlers, Edward Henty, is here on Ridge Road. It was originally sited at 501 St Kilda Road, and is constructed from original pre-fabricated sections brought from England. Inside, there are a number of historic domestic items and furnishings. It is open daily except Friday. Also of interest is the National Rhododendron Garden, especially in spring, when the annual show is held. Another spring flower festival is held at **Silvan** (147 G6) where tulip bulbs are cultivated. Ferntree Gully, at the foot of the ranges, is now virtually an outer suburb of Melbourne.

Horsham Art Gallery, McLachlan St, has a good collection of photography and of Australian art. 'Olde Horsham' is a collection of historic buildings and exhibits, a zoo, a restaurant, and a tea room in a tramcar. The Wimmera River provides attractive picnic spots and good fishing for trout, redfin and Murray cod. The Apex fishing contest is held each March. The Victorian Crops Research Institute is located at Horsham and inspection of the Longerenong Agricultural College cereal research centre, 13 km north-east, can be arranged. **In the area:** Rocklands Reservoir, 90 km south on the Glenelg River, was built to supplement the Wimmera-Mallee irrigation scheme and is very popular for water sports and general recreation. There are launching and picnic facilities, plus caravan and camping areas at the lake's western edge. 14 km from Balmoral. Green Lake, 13 km south-east of the city and Lake Natimuk, 24 km north-west, are attractive and have picnic and barbecue facilities. **Accommodation:** 7 hotels, 12 motels, 2 caravan/camping parks.
Map ref. 164 H9

Inglewood   Population 674.
North along the Calder Highway from Bendigo are the towns of Inglewood and Bridgewater. Sizeable gold nuggets have been found in this area — the largest being the 'Welcome Stranger' which weighed 65 kg. Midway between Inglewood and St Arnaud are the Melville Caves, once the haunt of the notorious bushranger, Captain Melville. The Loddon River, at Bridgewater, is a popular spot for fishing and water skiing and has barbecue and picnic facilities. **Accommodation:** Limited.
Map ref. 165 Q8, 166 A8

Inverleigh   Population 252.
On the Leigh River, this little town west of Geelong has a number of historic buildings. **Of interest:** The former Horseshoe Inn and the two-storey hotel opposite. Also the Church of England, the Presbyterian church and the State School. **In the area:** Barunah Plains homestead, west of the town. **Accommodation:** Limited.
Map ref. 155 B7, 172 B7

Inverloch   Population 1523.
This is a small seaside resort on Anderson Inlet, east of Wonthaggi. It has good surf, long stretches of excellent beach and is very popular in summer. **In the area:** Spear fishing and surfing at Cape Patterson. **Accommodation:** 1 hotel, 1 motel, 4 caravan/camping parks.
Map ref. 173 K11

Jeparit   Population 533.
This little town in the Wimmera, north of Dimboola, is famous as the birthplace of Sir Robert Menzies; there is a thistle-bedecked spire to commemorate this fact. It is on the shores of Lake Hindmarsh, which is the largest natural freshwater lake in Victoria and has many kilometres of safe, sandy beaches, good fishing and an interesting variety of birdlife. **Of interest:** The Wimmera/Mallee Pioneer Museum, a 4 ha complex of colonial buildings at the southern entrance to the town, furnished in the period with displays of restored farm machinery. **In the area:** Near Antwerp, 20 km south of Jeparit, is the Ebenezer Mission, which is being restored by the National Trust. It was founded in 1859 by Moravian missionaries to bring Christianity to the Aborigines. The Wyperfeld National Park lies 44 km to the north. **Accommodation:** 2 hotels, 1 caravan/camping park.
Map ref. 164 G5

Kaniva   Population 956.
Kaniva in the west Wimmera, 43 km from Bordertown, SA, is just north of the Little Desert, which is famous for its wild flowers in spring. **Of interest:** The historical museum has a large collection of items of local history. **In the area:** The railway station at Serviceton, 23 km west, is classified by the National Trust. **In the area:** The Billy-Ho Bush Walk begins some 10 km out of town. It is a 3 km walk in the Little Desert, with numbered pegs denoting various species of desert flora. Safaris to the Big and Little Deserts can be arranged from Kaniva, Nhill and Dimboola. **Accommodation:** 2 hotels, 1 motel, 1 caravan/camping park.
Map ref. 164 C7

Kerang   Population 4049.
Some 30 km from the Murray and 60 km from Swan Hill, Kerang is the centre of a productive rural area and lies at the southern end of a chain of lakes and marshes. Some of the largest breeding grounds in the world for ibis and other waterfowl are found in these marshes. The ibis is closely protected because of its value in controlling locusts and other pests. **Of interest:** Korina Park, on Riverwood Drive, has over 100 species of birds and an assortment of animals. Strathclyde Cottage, corner Wellington and Victoria Sts, is an arts and crafts centre in a restored building. Of the three Reedy Lakes, the first has the Apex Park recreation area, the second has a large ibis rookery and the third is popular for water sports. All the lakes in the Kerang area are popular for sailing and boating and have picnic facilities. **In the area:** Lake Boga, 16 km from Swan Hill, has good sandy beaches. Murrabit, 29 km to the north, is situated on the Murray and surrounded by picturesque river forests. It holds a country market on the first Saturday of each month, selling local produce and arts and crafts. Australian Tractor Pull Championships are held at Quambatook every Easter Sunday. **Accommodation:** 4 hotels, 2 motels, 2 caravan/camping parks.
Map ref. 163 Q13, 165 Q2, 166 A2

Koo-wee-rup   Population 1046.
Well known for its annual Potato Festival every March, this town is in the middle of a rich market garden area, near Westernport Bay. **Of interest:** Bayles Flora and Fauna Park, just north of the town. **In the area:** Tooradin, 10 km west, situated on Sawtell's Inlet, is popular with fishing and boating enthusiasts. **Accommodation:** Limited.
Map ref. 173 J8

The Wimmera

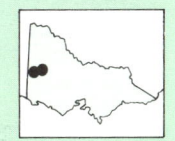

Travelling through the Wimmera on a hot summer's day is an unforgettable experience. The Wimmera is the granary of the state; the wheatfields stretch as far as the eye can see, an endless golden plain broken only occasionally by a gentle ripple in the terrain. In the south-east corner, however, are the Grampians, surrounded by a network of lakes, understandably popular with anglers and watersports lovers.

The region takes its name from the Aboriginal word for spear thrower. Signs left by the original inhabitants, the Wotjobaluk and Jardwa tribes, can still be seen: trees have had their bark stripped off to make canoes and baskets and there are many cave paintings in the Grampians. The Ebenezer Mission Station at Antwerp, near **Dimboola**, founded by Czechoslovakian missionaries to care for the Aboriginal population, is currently being restored by the National Trust and local inhabitants.

Horsham is the area's only city; with its delightful gardens and an excellent art gallery it makes a good base from which to explore the whole region. If you are visiting in March, don't miss the famous annual 'Wimmera machinery field days', held at the Longerenong Agricultural College nearby. The agricultural life of the last century has been remembered at **Warracknabeal**, the largest wheat receiving centre in the state, where an agricultural machinery museum houses huge steam-powered chaff cutters, headers and tractors and depicts the history of the wheat industry. Near Dimboola, set along the banks of the Wimmera River, is the entrance to the Little Desert National Park. 'Little Desert' is something of a misnomer as it is neither 'little', nor does it look like a 'desert' as there is a proliferation of plant and animal life, particularly in spring when the heath and scrublands come into bloom.

The Prom.

Wilsons Promontory, at the southernmost tip of the Australian mainland, is one of Victoria's largest and most spectacular national parks. 'The Prom', as it is affectionately known to Victorians, has an impressive range of landscapes, tall forested ranges, luxuriant tree fern valleys, open heaths, salt marshes and long drifts of sand dunes. Its wide, white sandy beaches are magnificent, some dominated by towering granite cliffs and washed by spectacular rolling surf. There are also very safe swimming beaches, particularly at Norman Bay near the main camping area at Tidal River and also the aptly named Squeaky Beach where the sands squeak underfoot.

Birds and wildlife abound on The Prom; flocks of lorikeets, rosellas and flame robins, kookaburras and brilliant blue wrens are in evidence, even in the main general store area, and for the more dedicated and patient bird-watcher, sightings of tree creepers, herons and lyrebirds can be the reward.

Emus 'graze' unperturbed on the open heath by the side of the main road as you enter the actual park area and kangaroos and wallabies seem unimpressed by their human observers. At night wombat-spotting by torchlight is a favourite pastime with children staying in the Tidal River area; these animals, and indeed most birds and wildlife here, seem surprisingly tame.

There are more than 80 kilometres of walking tracks in the Wilsons Promontory National Park. Some cover short walks, such as the nature trail in Lilly Pilly Gully, where the vegetation varies from bushland, inhabited by many koalas, to rainforest, with ancient tree ferns and trickling streams; other longer walks can be taken to places such as Sealers Cove or to the tip of The Prom, where there is a lighthouse dating from 1859.

At the visitors' information centre and park office at **Tidal River** (161 E10), leaflets are available detailing walking tracks and the flora and fauna of the park. During summer and Easter, information officers give talks and spotlight tours as well as leading children's nature activities.

Koroit Population 988.
Koroit is 18 km west of the coastal resort of Warrnambool in the south-west of Victoria. It is a quiet agricultural town with a number of churches and some interesting hedge topiary. **In the area:** The Tower Hill volcanic area just south of the town towards Warrnambool is well worth a visit. The nearby coast between Port Fairy and Warrnambool offers some delightful scenery. **Accommodation:** 1 caravan/camping park.
Map ref. 171 J9

Korumburra Population 2798.
The giant Gippsland earthworm, sought by fishermen and geologists alike, is found in the Korumburra area. Situated on the South Gippsland Highway, 116 km south-east of Melbourne, the area surrounding the town is given to dairying and agriculture, and the countryside is hilly with a high rainfall. **Of interest:** The Coal Creek Historical Park is a re-creation of a nineteenth century coal mining village. Black coal was first discovered in this area in 1872 but, due to the inaccessibility of the area, it was not until the 1890s that the Coal Creek mine began. Black coal was very important to the development of the Victorian railway system, and Korumburra's last mine closed down in 1958. The Historical Park is located on the original site of the Coal Creek Mine and is open daily. **In the area:** To the south, Leongatha and excellent fishing and beaches at Waratah Bay and Corner Inlet. There are good views from Cooks Hill and Mt Eccles over the surrounding area and Wilson's Promontory. Tourist information available at the Historical Park. **Accommodation:** 1 hotel, 1 motel, 1 caravan/camping park.
Map ref. 173 L10

Kyabram Population 5413.
A prosperous town in the Murray-Goulburn, just 40 km north-west of Shepparton, Kyabram is in a rich dairying and fruit growing district. **Of interest:** A community-owned fowl and fauna park on Lake Road at the southern end of the town is open daily. It comprises five lakes with varieties of duck, ibis, swans and pelicans and has a 16 ha enclosure for emus and kangaroos. **Accommodation:** 3 hotels, 2 motels, 2 caravan/camping parks.
Map ref. 166 H6

Kyneton Population 3815.
Little more than an hour's drive from Melbourne, along the Calder Highway in Central Victoria, Kyneton is an attractive and well preserved town with several interesting bluestone buildings. It holds an antique fair each Easter. Farms around the town prospered during the gold rushes, supplying large quantities of fresh food to the diggings at Ballarat and Bendigo. **Of interest:** The Historical Centre Collection is housed in what was a two-storey bank, built in 1855; the collection contains a comprehensive array of Victoriana. There is a drop-log cottage in the grounds. The Botanic Gardens, in an area of 8 ha above the river, contains 500 ancient trees. Interesting historic

Gippsland's Lakes

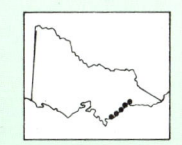

Many people regard the area of the Gippsland Lakes as Victoria's most outstanding holiday area. Dominated, as it is, by Australia's largest system of inland waterways, it certainly does live up to all the superlatives accorded it. With the foothills of the high country just to the north and the amazing stretch of the Ninety Mile Beach separating the lakes from the ocean, the region offers an incredible variety of natural beauty and recreation activities. Here the choice really is yours — lake, river or ocean fishing, boating, cruising, surfing, bird watching or just lazy sunning.

Within easy reach of the Lakes area, the high country begins, so it's possible to vary a waterside trip with days exploring the alpine reaches and some of the fascinating little old townships like **Walhalla** (173 O6) and **Dargo** (174 C5). The road across the Dargo High Plains and the Omeo Highway leading to Hotham Heights both pass through some stunning country.

Check your car thoroughly before you set off — service stations are scarce along the way. If you are visiting the area in spring, do try to make the Omeo Highway trip.

Wellington, King, Victoria, Tyers, Reeve and Coleman — these six lakes cover more than 400 square kilometres and stretch parallel to the Ninety Mile Beach for almost its entire length. **Sale**, at the western edge of the region, is currently enjoying boom town status due to the development of the Bass Strait oilfields. **Bairnsdale**, further east, on the northern shores of Lake King, makes an excellent base for alpine trips. The main resort towns are **Lakes Entrance**, at the mouth of the Lakes, **Paynesville**, a mecca for boating and fishing enthusiasts, and **Metung** (174 F8), where a cruising holiday on the Lakes can be commenced. There are many cruises available around the Lakes, and their sheltered waters are a haven for birdlife. The book *Explore Victoria's Waterways* includes a comprehensive section on the Lakes.

The Lakes National Park, the Glenaladale National Park and the hills and valleys of the alpine foothills to the north all provide plenty of opportunities for bushwalking or for simply watching the wildlife and enjoying the peace and quiet.

---

buildings include the town's churches, Mechanic's Institute and the old police depot. Two-storey bluestone mills stand on either side of the town.
In the area: The Barringo Wildlife Reserve and the Lauriston and Malmsbury Reservoirs are nearby. Malmsbury, 11 km to the north-west, has an historic bluestone railway viaduct. Willis Flour Mill in Piper Street has been restored to operational condition and is open for inspection at weekends. **Accommodation:** 5 hotels, 2 motels, 1 caravan/camping park.
Map ref. 154 C5, 158 G5, 166 D13, 172 D1

Lake Bolac Population 211.
In the Western District plains area, this small town on the Glenelg Highway is by a large freshwater lake which has good sandy beaches and is very popular for fishing, boating and swimming. There are several boat launching ramps and an aquatic club. A four day yachting regatta is held here each Easter. **Accommodation:** 1 motel, 1 caravan/camping park.
Map ref. 171 L5

Lakes Entrance Population 3414.
This extremely popular holiday town is at the eastern end of the Gippsland Lakes, which form the largest inland network of waterways in Australia. They cover an area of more than 400 sq km and are separated from the ocean by a thin sliver of sand dunes which form a large part of the Ninety Mile Beach which stretches down to Port Albert. A bridge across the Cunningham Arm gives access to the surf beach from Lakes Entrance. The town is very well developed for the holiday maker and caters both to seaside recreation and exploration of the mountain country to the north. It is the home port for a very large fishing fleet and also for many pleasure craft. Large cruise vessels conduct regular sightseeing tours of the lakes throughout the year. Boats can also be hired. Fishing, both ocean and beach, is popular, as are swimming and surfing on a variety of good beaches.
Of interest: The Shell Museum on the Esplanade. The Gippsland Aboriginal Art Museum, 3 km north-east on the Princes Highway. An Antique Car and Folk Museum is also on the Princes Highway.
In the area: The sheltered waters of Lake Tyers are popular for fishing, swimming and boating and there are holiday flats and caravan parks here. The Buchan Caves to the north are well worth a visit. At Sperm Whale Head, the Lakes National Park is a wooded area with a variety of native animals and birds. It has picnic facilities and a camping area at Point Wilson. Day trips can be made to the old mining areas around Omeo. Boats may be hired at Metung, about 15 km by road to the west. Lakes Entrance has a variety of hotels serving counter meals, motels with licensed restaurants, cafes and take-away food shops. It is wise to pre-book in holiday seasons. Tourist information from South East Coast Tourism Limited, Silkstone Road, Korumburra 3950. **Accommodation:** 3 hotels, 16 motels, 22 caravan camping parks.
Map ref. 174 G8

Leongatha Population 3736.
Near the foothills of the Strzelecki Ranges, 14 km east of Korumburra, Leongatha, the centre of a dairying area, is a good base from which to make trips to Wilson's Promontory National Park and the seaside and fishing resorts which stretch from Phillip Island to the south-western end of the Ninety Mile Beach. **Of interest:** The Murray Goulburn Co-operative, which provides milk for Melbourne and dairy produce for export, is one of Australia's largest dairy factories. **In the area:** Along the coast road there are impressive plantations of English trees, areas of natural bushland, picnic and camping facilities. To the north, the Grand Ridge Road offers excellent scenic driving and can be followed across into the Tarra Valley and Bulga National Parks. Korumburra, with its Coal Creek Historic Park, is 14 km west along the South Gippsland Highway. **Accommodation:** 2 motels, 1 caravan/camping park.
Map ref. 173 L10

Lorne Population 893.
The approaches to Lorne along the Great Ocean Road, whether from east or west, are quite spectacular. The town is one of Victoria's most attractive coastal resorts, with the superb mountain scenery of the Otways behind, and a mild, year-round climate. Tragically in the 1983 bushfires several homes and areas of bush land were destroyed. Captain Loutit gave the district the name of Loutit Bay. The village of Lorne was established in 1871, became popular with pastoralists from

inland areas, and developed rather in the style of an English seaside resort. When the Great Ocean Road opened in 1932 Lorne grew more popular until it became a lively and well-maintained resort with attractive art and craft shops, restaurants and many take-away food shops. The town itself remained relatively unspoiled with good beaches, surfing and excellent bushwalking in the hills behind added to its charm. **Of interest:** Teddy's Lookout, behind the town, offers good bay views. Lorne's foreshore reserve has a children's playground, pool, amusement centre, trampolines and picnic ground. Pedal boats can be hired. **In the area:** Attractive waterfalls such as Kalimna, Phantom and Erskine. River rapids at Erskine. A few km south-west, Mt Defiance. The Cumberland River Valley has good walking areas and a camping ground. Allenvale is also an attractive walking area and has barbecue and picnic facilities. At Wye River, 17 km west, there is good shooting, fishing and surfing. This tiny but attractive settlement has limited accommodation. **Accommodation:** 2 hotels, 4 motels, 6 caravan/camping parks.
Map ref. 155 A13, 171 R10, 172 B10

Macedon   Population 1057.
Situated on the Calder Highway 20 km from Kyneton, the Macedon area was renowned for its many beautiful private gardens and splendid old homes. On Ash Wednesday, 1983 terrible bushfires destroyed a large percentage of these old homes, including the historic 26-room mansion Derriweit Heights and the Mount Macedon church which was restored only six years ago. Mount Macedon is an extinct volcano, 1013 m high. At its summit, there is a memorial cross, which was erected in honour of those who died in World War I. **In the area:** Woodend is an attractive old township and hill resort. The Hanging Rock made famous by Joan Lindsay's story, 8 km from Woodend, is a massive volcanic rock formation which makes for interesting climbing; picnic reserve at its base. The race meeting at Hanging Rock is an annual event each January. **Accommodation:** 1 motel.
Map ref. 158 H7, 172 E2

Maffra-Heyfield   Pop. 3822, 1635.
The Shire of Maffra includes both these towns and extends from the fertile farming lands of the Macalister Irrigation Area north to the magnificent mountain scenery of the Great Dividing Range. **Of interest:** The Glenmaggie Weir, 11 km north of Heyfield, is a popular water sports venue and has camping facilities. The forest road north (partly closed in winter) to Licola and Jamieson is unsealed but has a fairly good surface and passes through some spectacular scenery. Watch out for logging trucks. This road leads to Mt Tamboritha and Mt Howitt and gives access to alpine country and the snowfields. The road north from Maffra, via Briagalong, leads over the Dargo High Plains. **Accommodation:** Maffra, 3 hotels, 1 motel, 1 caravan/camping park. Heyfield, 2 hotels, 1 motel.
Map ref. 173 R6, 174 B9

Maldon   Population 1009.
The National Trust has declared Maldon the 'First Notable Town' in Victoria, on the basis that no other town has such an interesting collection of nineteenth century buildings, nor such a collection of European trees. Situated north-west of Castlemaine, in central Victoria, Maldon is very popular with tourists, especially during the annual 'Back to Maldon' Easter Charity Fair, and in spring when the wild flowers are in bloom. The deep reef gold mines were among Victoria's richest and at one stage 20 000 men worked on the nearby Tarrangower diggings. Enthusiasts still search for gold in the area. **Of interest:** Many of the town's buildings, mostly constructed of local stone, in particular, Maldon Hospital, the post office, St Brigid's Church, the old council offices (now converted into a folk museum containing many interesting relics) and Dabb's General Store in the main street, where the old storefront has been faithfully restored. The Eagle Hawk Restaurant, in a restored hotel in the main street, offers good food and wines. Also in the main street are the Cumquat Tea Rooms. **In the area:** The Mount Tarrangower Chinese Cemetery, Cairn Curran Lake, 10 km from Maldon, popular for water sports, fishing and picnics, the Koala Sanctuary on Mount Alexander (26 km) and the wild flower sanctuary (3 km). The district also offers delightful bush walks. A little south of the town is Carman's Tunnel, open for inspection, a vivid reminder of the hardships of gold-mining days. The whole district is noted for its

The Great Ocean Road

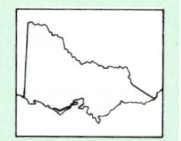

Very few roads in Australia can offer more than 300 kilometres of breath-taking scenery, with not one boring stretch, but the Great Ocean Road, along Victoria's south-west coast, does exactly that. This area suffered devastation on Ash Wednesday 1983 as bushfires burned from Lorne through to Airey's Inlet and Anglesea.

Built to honour the servicemen of World War 1, and completed in 1932, it has dramatic stretches of precipitous cliffs, idyllic coves and wide beaches.

The Great Ocean Road begins at **Torquay**, not far from **Geelong**. This is a popular surfing spot and the Road leads past a collection of famous surfing and safe swimming beaches and resorts. **Lorne** is one of the most charming of these. Despite offering modern holiday amenities and plenty of seaside entertainment for families, its gracious old hotels and guest-houses remain as a reminder of days gone by. Behind the town, the Otway Ranges, which stretch from **Anglesea** to Cape Otway, offer beautiful hills, waterfalls, excellent walking tracks and lovely picnic spots. At **Apollo Bay**, the Road leaves the coast and winds through the ferny slopes of Cape Otway. This is rainforest country — silent and untouched — and well worth exploring. Many of the roads are unsealed but quite adequate for standard cars. Do try to visit the Melba Gully State Park and the tiny township of **Lavers Hill (171 O12)**.

At **Princetown (171 N12)**, the Great Ocean Road returns to hug the coastline along the entire length of the Port Campbell National Park. This stretch makes compulsive viewing and many an avid photographer can be seen risking life and limb to take advantage of the dramatic coastal scenery. It is advisable, however, for the driver to keep his or her eyes firmly on the road. The coastline takes on tortured, twisted shapes, with amazing rock formations like 'The Twelve Apostles' — huge stone pillars looming out of the surf — and 'London Bridge', a rocky promontory arch carved out by the incessantly boiling sea.

The Road leaves the coast at **Peterborough (171 L11)**, where the Curdies River enters the sea, in a wide sandy inlet beloved of fishermen. It's well worth following this river inland to see how the countryside changes to a more tranquil rolling terrain, typical of the Western District to the north.

interesting rock formations. Tourist information from the Maldon Progress Association, Phoenix St. **Accommodation:** 1 caravan/camping park.
Map ref. 154 A3, 158 C1, 165 R11, 166 B11

Mallacoota Population 725.
On the Gippsland coast, at the mouth of a deep inlet of the same name, Mallacoota is a seaside and fishing township growing in popularity as a holiday centre. It offers the remote and beautiful countryside of the Alfred, Lind and Croajingolong National Parks to explore, as well as good beaches and excellent fishing. Mallacoota's specialities are oysters and abalone and there are some excellent restaurants serving delicious seafood. **In the area:** Gipsy Point, a few km north, is set in attractive countryside. Genoa, on the Princes Highway, is the last township before entering NSW and nearby Genoa Peak has some magnificent coastal views. A trip to Gabo Island, a few km offshore, is an interesting diversion. **Accommodation:** Mallacoota, 2 motels, 5 caravan/camping parks. Genoa, 1 motel, 1 caravan/camping park.
Map ref. 175 O6

Mansfield Population 1920.
A popular inland resort at the junction of the Midland and Maroondah Highways, Mansfield is 3 km east of the northern arm of Eildon Weir. It is the nearest sizeable town to the Mt Buller Alpine Village. **Of interest:** In the town is a marble obelisk, erected to the memory of three police officers shot by Ned Kelly at Stringybark Creek, near Tolmie, in 1878. Their graves are in the Mansfield cemetery. Apart from its interest as a resort, Mansfield is also a timber town and boasts six sawmills, some open for inspection. **In the area:** The road north-east over the mountains to Whitfield in the King River Valley passes through spectacular scenery. To the south are the Goulburn and Jamieson Rivers, both offering trout fishing and gold fossicking. **Accommodation:** 3 hotels, 1 motel, 1 caravan/camping park.
Map ref. 167 M11

Maryborough Population 7858.
First sheep farming, then the gold rush, contributed to the development of this small city on the northern slopes of the Great Dividing Range, 48 km west of Castlemaine. Modern Maryborough is in the centre of an agricultural and timber area and is quite highly industrialised. **Of interest:** Pioneer Memorial Tower, Bristol Hill. Worsley Cottage, Palmerston St, an historical museum. The splendid Maryborough railway station and the Civic Square buildings. Princes Park, with good sports facilities. **In the area:** A few km north is Bowenvale-Timor, once a thriving gold town, with the Miners' Right Gallery and Store, an early brick building, now housing a museum and arts and crafts shop. The annual Golden Wattle Festival is held for a fortnight during August/September. Tourist information from the Municipal Offices, Neil St. **Accommodation:** 4 motels, 1 caravan/camping park.
Map ref. 165 P11, 166 A11

Marysville Population 593.
The peaceful and attractive town of Marysville, which owes much of its existence to timber milling, is 37 km north from Healesville, off the Maroondah Highway. It is surrounded by attractive forest-clad mountain country and is a popular resort in summer and winter. **Of interest:** L. J. Gould Sawmill, open for inspection. Nicholl's Lookout for excellent views. Numerous bushwalking tracks to beauty spots in the area, including the 1-hour walk to Keppel's Lookout, a 1½-hours walk to Mt Gordon and a 2-hours walk to Steavenson's Falls. Lake Eildon and the Cumberland Valley Forests are within easy driving distance. **In the area:** Lake Mountain often has sufficient snow for tobogganing and sightseeing in winter. **Accommodation:** 1 hotel, 5 motels, 1 caravan/camping park.
Map ref. 160 G8, 173 K3

Mildura Population 15 762.
Sunny mild winters and picturesque locations on the banks of the Murray make Mildura and neighbouring towns popular tourist areas. Mildura, on the Sunraysia Highway 544 km north of Melbourne, is a small and pleasant city which developed along with the irrigation of the area. Alfred Deakin, statesman and advocate of irrigation, persuaded the Chaffey brothers, Canadian born irrigation experts, to visit this region. They recognised its potential and selected Mildura as the first site for development. The early days of the project were fraught with setbacks but by the turn of the century the citrus growing industry was well established and, with the locking of the Murray completed in 1928, Mildura soon afterwards became a city.
Of interest: W.B. Chaffey remained in the town and became its first Mayor; his statue is in Deakin Avenue. The Mildura Arts Centre includes 'Rio Vista', the original Chaffey home, and the first irrigation pump. 'Rio Vista' is now a museum with an interesting collection of colonial household items. Paddle steamers leave from Mildura Wharf for trips on the Murray and Darling Rivers. The *P.S. Melbourne* does 2-hour round trips, 10.50 am and 1.50 pm weekdays and Sundays. *P.S. Avoca* has 2-hour luncheon cruises, 7 days a week, a 4-hour Disco cruise on Friday nights and a 4-hour Cabaret cruise on Saturday nights. Adjacent to the Mildura Airport is War Birds Aviation Museum, open weekends. The Mildura Lock Island and Weir can be inspected. One of the longest bars in the world is housed in the Mildura Workingman's Club.
In the area: Many vineyards, including Lindemans (which is the largest winery in the Southern Hemisphere), Mildara and Murray Valley wineries are open weekdays for tastings and sales. Capogreco Wines, Riverside Avenue, Mildura, are open Monday to Saturday. Mildura has an excellent range of holiday entertainment facilities and special events include the annual Marching Girls' Championship in June and the three-day Mildura Show in October. Tourist information from the

Skiing in Victoria

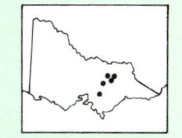

Victoria has seven ski resorts, all within easy reach of Melbourne. Before setting off, read the motoring section earlier in this book. Special attention should also be given to clothing. It is essential to wear clothes which provide insulation — warm winter underwear, woollen jumpers, waterproof parkas, thick woollen socks and gloves, balaclavas or wool hats which cover the ears, and goggles. Children particularly must be kept generously warm at all times.

Falls Creek (168 C10) 379 km from Melbourne, via Wangaratta. Four-wheel drive vehicles not permitted near alpine village. Access by tracked vehicles from car park beyond Mount Beauty. Protected ski runs for novices, intermediate and advanced skiers; good cross-country skiing.
Lake Mountain (173 L3) 109 km from Melbourne, via Healesville. Sightseeing and novice skiing.
Mount Baw Baw (173 N5) 177 km from Melbourne, via Drouin. Beginners, novices and cross-country skiing.
Mount Buffalo (167 Q10) 331 km from Melbourne, via Myrtleford. Includes Dingo Dell and Cresta. Beginners, families and cross-country skiing. Ski hire and instruction.
Mount Buller (167 O12) 241 km from Melbourne, via Mansfield. For beginners to advanced skiers. Ski hire and instruction.
Mount Donna Buang (173 K4) 95 km from Melbourne, via Warburton. Sightseeing and novice skiing.
Mount Hotham (168 C11) 367 km from Melbourne, via Wangaratta. The 'powder snow capital' of Australia. For experienced downhill skiers; unlimited cross-country skiing. Ski hire and instruction.

Mildura Tourist Information Centre, Deakin Avenue. **Accommodation:** 2 hotels, 26 motels, 16 caravan/camping parks.
Map ref. 162 H2

Moe   Population 18 158.
Situated on the Princes Highway 135 km east of Melbourne, Moe is a rapidly growing residential city in the Latrobe Valley. Nearby, what was the State Electricity Commission town of Yallourn has been demolished to make way for an extension on the enormous brown coal open-cut mine, and most of Yallourn's residents have been moved to other towns in the area. **Of interest:** The 'Old Gippsland' folk museum, Princes Highway, is a re-creation of a nineteenth-century community, with restored buildings brought from surrounding areas. There are barbecues and picnic facilities and an adventure playground. The nearby Power Station is open for guided inspections. A scenic road leads north to the old mining township of Walhalla, and through the mountains to Jamieson. A little further north, the Baw Baw plateau and the Mt Baw Baw ski village. The plateau is the highest alpine point in central Gippsland and in the summer has abundant wild flowers and is excellent for bushwalking. **Accommodation:** 1 hotel, 3 motels, 1 caravan/camping park.
Map ref. 173 N8

Morwell   Population 16 438.
Morwell, 150 km east of Melbourne, has grown to become one of the main cities of the Latrobe Valley. This valley contains one of the world's largest deposits of brown coal. Electricity generated by the State Electricity Commission's power stations on the coal fields at Morwell, Hazelwood, Churchill and Yallourn accounts for more than 85 per cent of Victoria's power needs. Morwell is an industrial town with a number of secondary industries. The immense open-cut mining projects, powerhouses and briquette-making plants are open daily for guided inspections. **In the area:** Many scenic day tours can be made from the three main cities in the Latrobe Valley, Morwell, Moe and Traralgon. Coalville and Narracan offer panoramic views of the valley. Lake Narracan and the Hazelwood pondage, a few km from Morwell, are ideal for water sports and picnics. There are views of Moe, Yallourn North and the valley between the Strzelecki Ranges and the Baw Baw mountains at Narracan Falls. Old Tanjil is interesting for its gold history and gold panning and the Bulga and Tarra Valley National Parks are very beautiful with fern glades, waterfalls, rosellas and, if you are lucky, lyrebirds and koalas. To the north, dense mountain country and the interesting old mining township of Walhalla, also Moondarra Reservoir and the beautiful Tanjil and Thomson river valleys. At Tyers, a few km north of Traralgon, is the Wirilda Environment Park. Information on the area can be obtained from South East Coast Tourism Limited, Silkstone Road, Korumburra 3875. **Accommodation:** 3 hotels, 7 motels, 3 caravan/camping parks.
Map ref. 173 O8

Murtoa   Population 946.
Murtoa is situated on the edge of picturesque Lake Marma, 45 km north-east of Horsham on the Wimmera Highway. It is in the centre of Victoria's wheatbelt and with two other old wheat towns, Minyip and Rupanyup, makes up the Shire of Dunmunkle. **Of interest:** A huge wheat storage silo, and an old railway water tower, built in 1886, with a museum below which houses the district's past with James Hill's taxidermy collection of some 500 birds completed more than 50 years ago. Open Sundays 2-5 pm. Lake Marma has trout and redfin fishing, water sports and caravan park on its eastern side. Rupanyup, 16 km east, is an attractive old township and is the administrative centre of the Shire. The Barrabool Forest Reserve, 7 km south of Murtoa, has an attractive spring display of plain-type wild flowers. **Accommodation:** 1 caravan/camping park.
Map ref. 165 J8

Myrtleford   Population 2815.
On the Ovens Highway, 45 km south-east of Wangaratta, the town of Myrtleford is surrounded by a rich hops and tobacco growing area. It also has some of the largest walnut groves in the southern hemisphere. The Ovens Valley was opened up by miners flocking to the area and creeks in the area are still popular for gold panning and gem fossicking. **Of interest:** Reform Hill Lookout, 1½ km from the town. The Jaycees Historic Park and Swing Bridge has picnic facilities and a display of antique steam engines and machinery. **In the area:** Lake Buffalo, Lake Catani, the Ovens River and the Buffalo River all offer good fishing. The Mt Buffalo National Park is within easy driving distance, as are the old towns of Beechworth and Bright. Tourist information and fishing permits from Sam's Sports Tourist Information Centre, 61 Clyde St, and the Ponderosa Cabins. This centre can arrange visits to hop and tobacco farms. **Accommodation:** 2 motels, 2 caravan/camping parks.
Map ref. 167 Q8, 169 D1

Nagambie   Population 1102.
Between Seymour and Shepparton on the Goulburn Valley Highway, Nagambie is on the shores of Lake Nagambie, which was created by the construction of the Goulburn Weir in 1891. Rowing and yachting regattas, speedboat and water-ski tournaments are held here throughout the year. There is a 65 metre slide at one of the swimming areas. **Of interest:** The town has some interesting old buildings classified by the National Trust and there is an Historical Society display of colonial Victoriana and early horse-drawn vehicles. **In the area:** Two of Victoria's best-known wineries, Chateau Tahbilk and Mitchelton. To get to Chateau Tahbilk, turn on to the Heathcote Road and follow the signposts. The underground cellars here have been classified by the National Trust and the National Estate and are open for tastings, inspections and sales. The Mitchelton Winery is 10 km south-west of Nagambie, and is open every day. It has cellar sales and tastings, and three licensed restaurants. There are river bank lawns, children's playgrounds, swimming pools and a 60 m observation tower. At Graytown, 24 km west of Nagambie, is Osicka's Vineyard. **Accommodation:** 2 motels, 2 caravan/camping parks.
Map ref. 154 G2, 166 H9

Natimuk   Population 432.
This Wimmera town, 27 km west of Horsham, is close to the striking Mt Arapiles, a 356 m sandstone monolith which has been described as 'Victoria's Ayers Rock'. You can drive to the summit where there is a lookout and a telecommunications relay station. The mountain was first climbed by Major Mitchell in 1836 and is popular with climbing enthusiasts. **Of interest:** The Arapiles Historical Society has a museum in the old court-house. **In the area:** There is a group of lakes north of Natimuk and near to Lake Natimuk is the John Smith Memorial Sanctuary, a fauna and flora reserve with up to 106 species of native plants. **Accommodation:** 1 caravan/camping park.
Map ref. 164 G9

Nhill   Population 2067.
The name of this town is possibly derived from the Aboriginal word 'nyell' meaning 'white mist on water'. A small wheat town on the Western Highway exactly half-way between Melbourne and Adelaide, it claims to have the largest single bin silo in the southern hemisphere. **Of interest:** The cottage of John Shaw Neilson, lyric poet, in the Shaw Neilson Park, also the Draught Horse Memorial in Goldsworthy Park, built to the memory of the famous Clydesdales who were so indispensable in the opening up of the Wimmera region. Nhill's Post Office, built in 1888, is classified by the National Trust. **In the area:** Nhill is in easy reach of the Little Desert National Park and Lake Hindmarsh, the largest freshwater lake in Victoria, 45 km north. **Accommodation:** 2 hotels, 4 motels, 2 caravan/camping parks.
Map ref. 164 E6

Numurkah   Population 2713.
Numurkah, 34 km north of Shepparton on the Goulburn Valley Highway, is only a half-hour drive from some excellent beaches and fishing spots on the Murray River. The town is in an irrigation area which concentrates on fruit growing and dairying, and which was originally developed through the Murray Valley Soldier Settlement Scheme. **Of interest:** Steam and Vintage Machinery Display, Numurkah. **In the area:** The Barmah Red Gum Forest is the largest of its type in the world, to the north-west along the Murray. Monichino's Winery on the Goulburn Valley Highway, Katunga, 11 km north of the town. At Strathmerton, 21 km north, is the Ulupna Island flora and fauna reserve. **Accommodation:** 2 motels, 1 caravan/camping park.
Map ref. 167 J4

Parks & Gardens

Melbourne is a city which has grown to become a place of dignity and beauty, designed, as it was, with wide, tree-shaded streets and magnificent public gardens. The feeling for greenery and open space has been maintained by individual residents, many of whom take great pride in their gardens, whether they be planted with European species or with the increasingly popular native trees and shrubs.

The jewel of the 'Garden State' is the Royal Botanical Gardens, situated beside the Yarra River, close to the city of Melbourne. Here there are 43 hectares of plantations, flower beds, lawns and ornamental lakes, so superbly laid out and cared for that they are considered to be among the best in the world.

The site for the Gardens was selected in 1845 but the main work of their development was carried out by Baron Sir Ferdinand von Mueller who was appointed Government Botanist in 1852. He was succeeded by W. R. Guilfoyle, a landscape artist, who further remodelled and expanded the gardens. The gardens and the riverside are now a favourite place for Melburnians on Sundays. Families flock to picnic, feed the swans and water birds on the lakes or simply to take a pleasant stroll. In the south-west corner of the gardens is the National Herbarium which contains an enormous variety of sub-tropical, tropical and temperate zone flora.

Adjoining the gardens and flanking St Kilda Road is another large area of parkland, the Kings Domain, which comprises 43 hectares of tree-shaded lawns and contains the Shrine of Remembrance, La Trobe's Cottage, which was the first Government House, and the Sidney Myer Music Bowl, an unconventional aluminium and steel structure which creates a perfect amphitheatre for outdoor concerts. This vast garden area is completed by the adjoining Alexandra and Queen Victoria gardens, a further 52 hectares of parkland.

BELOW: *The Floral Clock in Melbourne's Alexandra Gardens has its display of colourful blooms changed four times a year.*

BELOW: *Melbourne's programme of Free Entertainment in Parks, started in 1972, has become the biggest free entertainment programme in the world. Daytime concerts at the Sidney Myer Music Bowl are part of it.*

Victoria

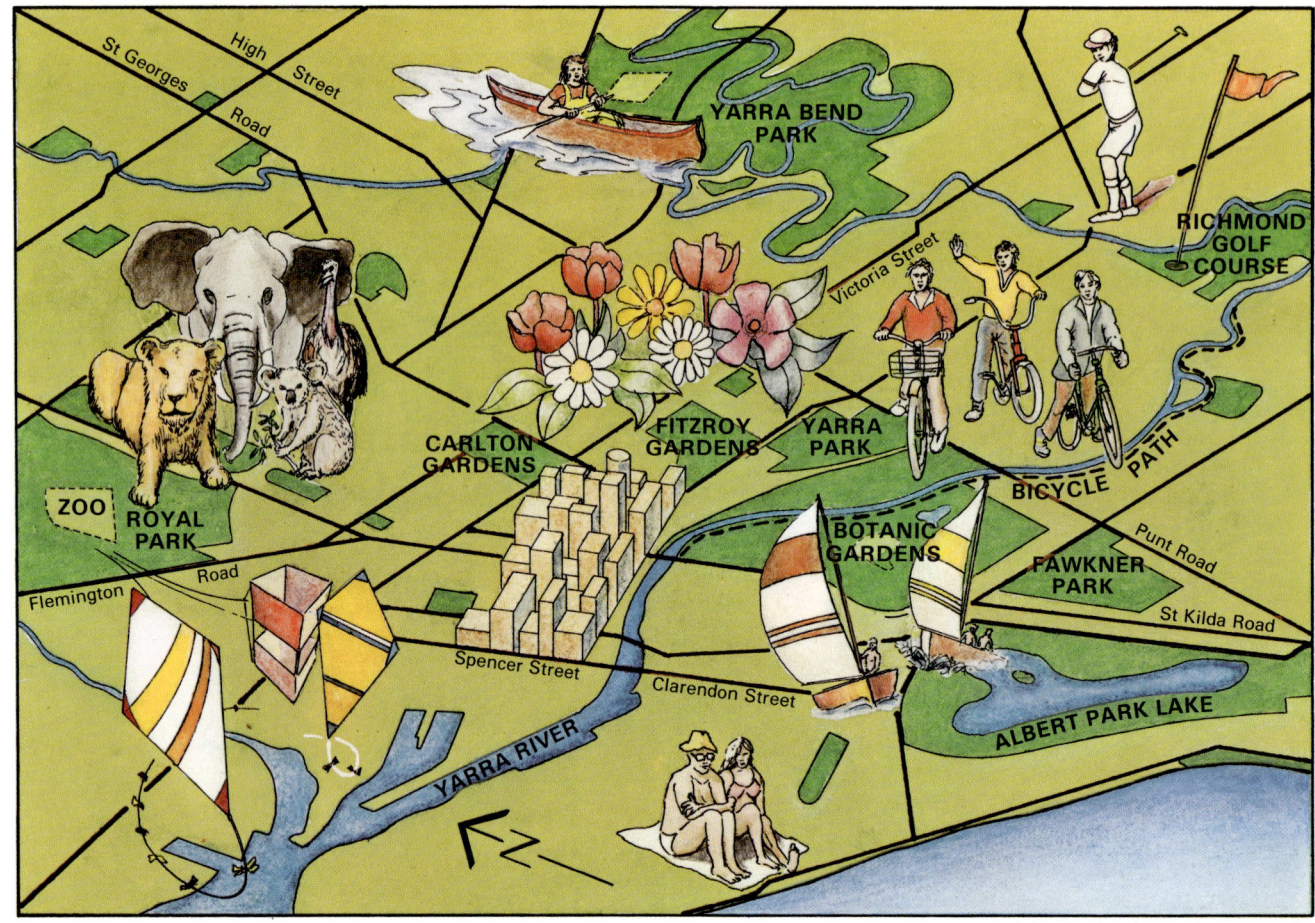

The city's first public gardens were the Flagstaff Gardens at William Street, West Melbourne. A monument in the gardens bears a plaque describing how the site was used as a signalling station to inform settlers of the arrival and departure of ships at Williamstown. On the other side of the city, not far from the centre, in East Melbourne are the Treasury and Fitzroy Gardens close by the State Government offices. In the Fitzroy Gardens is Captain Cook's cottage, which was transported in 1934 from the village of Great Ayton, Yorkshire, where Cook was born, and which was re-erected to commemorate Melbourne's centenary. Also in these gardens is a model Tudor village, laid out near an ancient tree trunk — a fairy tree, carved with tiny figures by the late Ola Cohn. Another garden close to the city is the Exhibition Gardens in which the domed Exhibition Buildings are situated. They were erected for the Great Exhibition of 1880. The building was, for 27 years, the meeting place of the Federal Parliament.

Apart from these formal gardens — and every Melbourne suburb is endowed with large municipal garden areas — Melbourne also has large recreational areas around the city and throughout the urban regions and these are always expanding to meet the demands of a sport-loving populace. The most notable is Albert Park, where there are golf courses, indoor sports centres, two major cricket and football grounds and many other ovals, and a lake for sailing and rowing. Another large sporting area in East Melbourne contains the famous Melbourne Cricket Ground which has been established for more than 100 years as a venue for test cricket and football and which has stands that

ABOVE: *This 'bird's eye view' of the many parks and recreation areas of Melbourne gives some idea of the great variety of sports and pastimes it is possible to enjoy.*

BELOW LEFT: *Captain Cook's Cottage, in the Fitzroy Gardens.*

BELOW: *Rippon Lea has some superb English-style gardens with roaming peacocks.*

Parks and Gardens

ABOVE: *The Fairy Tree, carved by Ola Cohn, has delighted Melbourne's children since the 1930s.*

ABOVE: *Cricket has been played at Melbourne's famous MCG for more than a hundred years. As well as this, the Ground has been the venue for many Australian Rules football matches, including the annual Victorian Grand Final, and for the 1956 Olympic Games.*

BELOW: *Immaculate green lawns, colourful floral displays and varied trees and shrubs are featured in most of the public parks and gardens throughout Victoria.*

BELOW: *Small yachts make a colourful scene at Albert Park Lake only three kilometres from the centre of the city. The path around the lake is a favourite route for joggers.*

can accommodate more than 120 000 people. Nearby are the Olympic Swimming Pool and various sports grounds which were established for the Olympic Games held in Melbourne in 1956.

The man-made beauty of Melbourne is surpassed by nature in the Dandenong Ranges, about 48 kilometres from the city. The heavily forested ranges have trees like the tall, straight mountain ash, grey gums, messmate, peppermint and box eucalypts interrupted by spectacular fern gullies. A network of good roads connects the many small towns in the Dandenongs, most of which blend pleasantly into their bushland surroundings. The private gardens in the district are beautifully maintained and a drive through the hills is delightful at any time of the year, but particularly so in spring when fruit trees and ornamentals are in blossom, or in autumn when the European trees which have been extensively planted in the private gardens in the hills are at their most colourful.

There are a number of natural forests in the Dandenongs with tracks for bushwalkers. The best known is Sherbrooke Forest Park which seems beautifully unspoiled despite the fact that it is visited by tens of thousands of people

Victoria

every year. It is a bird sanctuary and a home of the famous, but shy, lyrebird. A rare delight is to see the elaborate mating dance and display of these birds and to hear their brilliant mimicking calls.

A fascinating way to see the Dandenongs is to take a trip on the Puffing Billy, a delightful narrow-gauge steam railway maintained by a preservation society. It runs from Belgrave to Emerald Lake through bushland and flower farms. Visits to art galleries, antique shops, restaurants, sanctuaries or plant nurseries can add to the pleasure of a visit to the Dandenongs.

There are many other spectacular natural areas throughout Victoria and over the years the Government has been active in preserving many of these for the people. Places like the Wilson's Promontory National Park with its secluded beaches and superb coastal scenery; the Tarra Valley National Park in the Strzelecki Ranges, with its mountain ash trees and rainforest vegetation; the Wyperfeld National Park in the north-west, with its spring wild flowers and dry country birdlife; the alpine parks like Mount Buffalo National Park and Mount Buller Alpine Reserve and many others.

The quality of Victoria's public gardens is exceptional wherever you go, and most major towns have large, meticulously maintained areas, each with its own special quality. The Ararat Gardens are noted for their begonia hothouses. The gardens at Ballarat have a famous begonia house which is the centre of the festival held every year in March. Benalla conducts a rose festival every year. The small town of Bright attracts visitors to see the superb autumn leaves in the surrounding countryside. Details of various garden festivals and displays may be obtained from Victour, 230 Collins Street, Melbourne.

ABOVE LEFT: *An outdoor art show at the National Rhododendron Garden, Olinda.*

ABOVE: *Children take in the view as Puffing Billy rounds a curve in the beautiful Blue Dandenongs.*

ABOVE: *Wilsons Promontory*

ABOVE: *Tarra Valley National Park.*

BELOW: *Floral displays in Ballarat's parks attract many visitors, especially at begonia time.*

Ocean Grove-Barwon Heads Population 6776.

At the mouth of the Barwon River, the resort of Ocean Grove offers fishing and surfing, while nearby Barwon Heads offers safe family relaxation along the shores of its protected river. Both resorts are very popular in the summer months as they are the closest ocean beaches to Geelong, 22 km to their north. **Of interest:** The Ocean Grove Nature Reserve, Finnigans Irish Donkey Stud and Zoo. There are many riding schools in the district. **In the area:** To the north, Lake Connewarre, mangrove swamps. **Accommodation:** Ocean Grove, 2 motels, 5 caravan/camping parks. Barwon Heads, 1 hotel, 1 motel, 2 caravan/camping parks.
Map ref. 155 G9, 172 E8

Omeo Population 272.

The high plains around Omeo were opened up in 1835 when overlanders from the Monaro region moved their stock south to these lush summer pastures. Its name is an Aboriginal word meaning mountains, and the township is set in the heart of the Victorian Alps at an altitude of 643 m. It is used as a base for winter traffic approaching Mt Hotham from Bairnsdale, 120 km to its south, and for bushwalking and fishing expeditions to the Bogong High Plains in summer and autumn. A scenic road leads to Corryong, past the new lake being created by the Dartmouth Dam project, but it is difficult to negotiate in bad weather. Motorists should be alert for timber trucks and wandering cattle. The Tambo River valley is well worth a visit, and is especially beautiful in autumn. Omeo has suffered several natural disasters — it was devastated by earthquakes in 1885 and 1892 and was destroyed by the 'Black Friday' bushfires of 1939. Nevertheless, several old buildings remaining in the area are of historic interest, including the log gaol and police station and the old courthouse, at the rear of the present courthouse. Omeo has a gold-rush history and the high cliffs, left after sluicing for gold, can be seen at the Oriental Diggings. Gold panning is still popular along Livingstone Creek and pans can be hired from the Shire Offices. **Accommodation:** 1 hotel, 1 motel, 1 caravan/camping park.
Map ref. 168 E12, 174 E3

Orbost Population 2586.

Situated on the banks of the Snowy River, this Gippsland timber town is on the Princes Highway surrounded by spectacular coastal and mountain territory. It is the most easterly town served by the Victorian Railways. **Of interest:** The beautiful Bonang Highway, unsealed in parts, leads north through the mountains to Delegate in NSW and makes a pleasant drive, as does the road to Buchan and on to the Little River Falls and McKillop's Bridge on the Snowy River. To complete a round trip, follow the road towards Bonang and then back to Orbost along the Bonang Highway. For a coastal drive, take the Cape Conran Road just west of Orbost, which leads to the attractive fishing village of Marlo, at the mouth of the Snowy River. The road on to Cape Conran offers lovely views of the coast. There is good shooting on the nearby lakes and lagoons. Marlo has one hotel, holiday flats and caravan parks. Bemm River, on the Sydenham Inlet, a few km further up the coast, is a very popular centre for bream fishermen. It has several caravan and camping grounds. **Accommodation:** 2 hotels, 3 motels, 2 caravan/camping parks.
Map ref. 174 I7

Ouyen Population 1527.

On the Sunraysia Highway, Ouyen is about 100 km south of Mildura, north-east of the Big Desert area. Hattah-Kulkyne National Park, 34 km to the north, has large populations of waterbirds, especially ibis and pelicans, as well as birds of the Mallee, emus and red and grey kangaroos. Excellent for bird watching and photography, it is best visited in winter and spring, because of the extremely hot temperatures in summer. **Accommodation:** 1 hotel, 2 motels, 1 caravan/camping park.
Map ref. 162 J9

Paynesville Population 1597.

A popular tourist resort 18 km from Bairnsdale on the McMillan Straits, Paynesville is a mecca for the boat enthusiast, and is famous for yachting and speedboat racing as well as water-skiing. It is the headquarters of the Gippsland Lakes Yacht Club, and speedboat championships are held each Christmas and Easter. There are five boat ramps and excellent picnic facilities. The Ninety Mile Beach can be reached by boat, and a punt crosses the Straits to Raymond Island. **Accommodation:** 3 caravan/camping parks.
Map ref. 174 E8

Port Albert Population 267.

This tiny and historic township on the south-east coast, 120 km from Morwell, was the first established port in Victoria. Sailing boats from Europe and America once docked at the large timber jetty here. Boats from China brought thousands of Chinese to the Gippsland goldfields. Originally established for trade with Tasmania, Port Albert was the supply port for Gippsland pioneers for many years until the railway line from Melbourne to Sale was completed in 1878. The timber jetty is still crowded with boats as it is a commercial fishing port and its sheltered waters are very popular with fishermen and boat owners. Some of the original stone buildings are still in use and are classified by the National Trust. **Of interest:** Buildings in the main street include original government offices and stores, the Bank of Victoria (1861), the Maritime Museum, with photographs and relics of the area, and Christ Church, built 1858, first church in Gippsland. The Port Albert Hotel, close by the water, is possibly the oldest hotel still operating in the state, first licensed in 1842. There is a wildlife sanctuary on St Margaret Island. **In the area:** To the north-east, Yarram and Alberton, once the administrative capital of Gippsland. **Accommodation:** 1 hotel, 1 caravan/camping park.
Map ref. 173 P11

Portarlington Population 1863.

Named after an Irish village and with a history of Irish settlement in the area, Portarlington is a popular seaside resort on the Bellarine Peninsula, 31 km east of Geelong. It has a safe bay for children to swim, good fishing and a variety of water sports. Of special interest is the historic flour mill, built in 1857, which has been restored by the National Trust. **Accommodation:** 1 motel, 3 caravan/camping parks.
Map ref. 155 I7, 172 F7

Port Fairy Population 2276.

The home port for a large fishing fleet and an attractive rambling holiday resort, Port Fairy is on the Princes Highway, 29 km west of Warrnambool. The town's history goes back to whaling days and at one time it was one of the largest ports in Australia. Many of its small cottages and bluestone buildings have been classified by the National Trust — over fifty in all. **Of interest:** The Historical Centre, Banks St. Battery Hill, an old fort and signal station at the mouth of the river. The splendid timber home of Captain Mills, a whaling skipper, and Mott's Cottage, 5 Sackville St, both have National Trust classifications. The cottage is open in the afternoons during school holidays. Other attractive buildings include the Old Caledonian Inn, Seacombe House, the stone court-house and the ANZ Bank building. Good beaches, rock fishing and extensive camping areas make Port Fairy a very popular location in the summer months. **In the area:** Griffiths Island, connected to the town by a causeway, has a lighthouse and mutton bird rookeries. Lady Julia Percy Island, about 10 km off the coast, is a home for fur seals, but is only accessible by experienced fishermen in calm weather. These waters also attract big game fishing for the white pointer shark. Tower Hill, a fascinating area with an extinct volcano, crater lake and islands, is a few km east of the town. The town has a number of take-away food shops and cafes and a couple of licensed restaurants. Tourist information from Borough Chambers, Bank St. **Accommodation:** 5 motels, 6 caravan/camping parks.
Map ref. 170 I10

Portland Population 9353.

Portland, situated about 75 km east of the SA border, is the most western of Victoria's major coastal towns and is the only deep water port between Melbourne and Adelaide. It was the first permanent settlement in Victoria, founded by the Henty brothers in 1834 and today it is an important industrial and commercial centre and also a popular summer resort. Good beaches, surfing and outstanding coastal and forest scenery make it an excellent holiday stopping point. **Of interest:** The town has many early and attractive buildings, some classified by the National Trust. Among them, the Customs House and Court House in Cliff St, several interesting old inns, including the Steam Packet Hotel, Mac's Hotel, the Portland Club and Foresters Hall. Portland's historic museum is in the old

town hall. **In the area:** Some beautiful old homesteads, including Maretimo and Burswood. To the south, the Cape Nelson Park, with spectacular coastal scenery and a lighthouse classified by the National Trust. Petrified forest and blowholes at Cape Bridgewater, as well as interesting walks to Discovery Bay and Cape Duquesne. Good swimming and surfing. The Mt Richmond National Park, 45 km to the north-west, has excellent spring wild flowers. The Princes Highway swings inland at Portland but 70 km west along the coastal road is the tiny and charming hamlet of Nelson. This is a favourite resort, particularly for people from Mt Gambier, over the border. The nearby Princess Margaret Rose Caves are worth a visit and pleasant river trips up the Glenelg River can be arranged. The Lower Glenelg National Park is notable for its huge gorges, wild flowers and native birds. The area is very popular for its excellent fishing but offers only limited accommodation. Tourist information at Cliff St. Portland. **Accommodation:** 10 motels, 6 caravan/camping parks.
Map ref. 170 F9

Pyramid Hill Population 539.
A small country town some 40 km south of Cohuna and the Murray River, Pyramid Hill was named for its unusually shaped hill, 187 m high. **Of interest:** Pyramid Hill township has an historical museum which features a display of old farm machinery. A climb to the top of Pyramid Hill itself gives a good view of the surrounding irrigation and wheat district. **In the area:** To the east, at Terrick Terrick, the 2833 ha Murray Pine forest can be seen, with its numerous granite outcrops. The southernmost outcrop, Mitiamo Rock, has an adjacent picnic ground, and walks through the forest reserve will reveal a variety of birdlife. Kangaroos can be seen at times. **Accommodation:** 1 caravan/camping park.
Map ref. 165 R4

Queenscliff-Point Lonsdale
Population 3420.
Queenscliff, 31 km east of Geelong on the Bellarine Peninsula, was established as a commercial fishing centre in the 1850s and still has a large fishing fleet based in its harbour. The town looks out across the famous and treacherous Rip at the entrance to Port Phillip Bay. **Of interest:** Many old buildings, including Fort Queenscliff, the Black Lighthouse and some grand old hotels such as the Ozone and the Queenscliff with excellent cuisine in sumptuous surroundings. A steam train operates between Queenscliff and Drysdale on weekends and daily in summer holidays. In summer and school holidays a regular ferry service operates between Queenscliff and Portsea across the bay. Point Lonsdale has been extensively developed as a holiday and tourist resort and offers very good swimming and surfing. There are excellent golf courses at Swan Island and Point Lonsdale. **Accommodation:** Queenscliff, 2 hotels, 4 caravan/camping parks. Point Lonsdale, 2 caravan/camping parks.
Map ref. 152 A5, 154 D12, 155 I9, 172 F8

Rainbow Population 700.
This Wimmera township, 70 km north of Dimboola, is almost equidistant from Lake Hindmarsh and Lake Albacutya, both of which are popular for fishing, boating and water-skiing. It is also within easy reach of the Wyperfeld National Park. The Big Desert, to the west, is now mainly farming land but also has a wide variety of flora and fauna. Because of the wild flowers, it is best seen in spring. **Of interest:** Yurunga homestead, National Trust classified, situated on the northern edge of the town, has a large selection of antiques and original fittings. Rainbow Tours run half and full day bus tours to places of interest around the area. Tourist Information Centre in Federal St. **Accommodation:** 2 hotels, 1 motel, 1 caravan/camping park.
Map ref. 164 G3

Robinvale Population 1751.
This small, well-laid-out town on the NSW border, 80 km from Mildura, is almost entirely surrounded by bends in the Murray River, and the surrounding area is ideal for the production of citrus, dried fruit and wine grapes. It is a picturesque town, and water sports and fishing are popular along the river. **Of interest:** McWilliams Wines and the Lexia Room, with historical exhibits, in Moore St. **In the area:** The state's largest olive plantation at Tol Tol, 8 km from the town. The weir and lock is 2.5 km downstream and nearby is one of the country's largest windmills. Robinvale Wines, a Greek style winery, 5 km south on the Sea Lake Road. **Accommodation:** 1 hotel, 1 motel, 2 caravan/camping parks.
Map ref. 163 K5

Rochester Population 2396.
On the Campaspe River, 28 km south of Echuca on the Northern Highway, Rochester is the centre for a rich dairying and tomato growing area. A small, busy town, it has some attractive older buildings and boasts the largest dairy factory in Australia, which processes over 900 000 litres of milk a day. **Of interest:** Just out of town is an engineering achievement, the Campaspe Siphon, where the Waranga-Mallee irrigation channel runs under the Campaspe River. These district channels are popular with fishermen and cod and bream are plentiful. **In the area:** Pleasant lakes in the district for fishing and water sports, including the newly made Thunderbird Lake and the Corop Lakes, 14 km south-east. The Mt Camel Range attracts gem fossickers and has some good scenery. **Accommodation:** 1 motel, 1 caravan/camping park.
Map ref. 166 F6

Rushworth Population 994.
Rushworth is 20 km off the Goulburn Highway, between Seymour and Shepparton, and still shows traces of its gold-rush days. Many of the attractive original buildings still stand, witness to the days when Rushworth was the commercial centre for the surrounding mining district. Rushworth's local history museum is open at weekends. The Glasgow Gallery sells arts and crafts and has tourist information. The Nuggety Hill Tea Rooms in the main street serve refreshments and Devonshire teas. **In the area:** Nearby Lake Waranga is popular for fishing and water sports and has picnic facilities. Around the town of Whroo, a few kilometres south, remains of the old open-cut mines are still visible. **Accommodation:** 2 hotels, 2 caravan/camping parks.
Map ref. 166 G8

Rutherglen Population 1454.
This is the centre of the most important wine growing area in Victoria. There is a cluster of vineyards around Rutherglen and the wine growing country stretches south to the Milawa area. Of particular interest is the winery building at All Saints, 10 km north-west of Rutherglen, which has a National Trust classification. Rutherglen holds a Winery Walkabout every Queen's Birthday weekend but most wineries are open from 9 am to 5 pm Monday to Saturday, with two of them open 12-5 pm Sunday.
In the area: Lake Moodemere, 8 km west of the town, is popular for water sports and there is a pleasant fauna sanctuary nearby. The old Customs House at Wahgunyah is a relic of the days when duty was payable on goods coming from NSW. Rutherglen is conveniently situated for day trips to Yarrawonga, Lake Mulwala, Beechworth, Bright and Mt Buffalo. Tourist information from Jasper's Garage and the Vintage Cellar, both in Main St. **Accommodation:** 2 motels, 1 caravan/camping park.
Map ref. 167 O4, 176 D3

St Arnaud Population 2720.
Many of the historic iron lacework decorated buildings in this old gold-mining town have been classified by the National Trust. It is on the Sunraysia Highway between Donald and Avoca and is surrounded by attractive forest and hill country. The town's sporting facilities at the local sports stadium include squash, basketball, badminton, table tennis and indoor tennis. Queen Mary Gardens are pleasant for picnics. **Of interest:** Good fishing to be found in the Avoca River and Teddington Reservoir. At Lake Batyo Catyo, some 35 km north-west, fishing and water sports. The Melville Caves, between St Arnaud and Inglewood, are famous as a haunt of the bushranger, Captain Melville, and have picnic facilities nearby. **Accommodation:** 2 hotels, 2 motels, 1 caravan/camping park.
Map ref. 165 N8

St Leonards Population 900.
A small beach resort, south-east of Portarlington, on the Bellarine Peninsula, St Leonards has excellent coastal fishing, and calm waters for boating and yachting. It is popular for family summer holidays, as is the neighbouring resort of Indented Head, further up the coast. It was in this area that Matthew Flinders landed in 1802 and John Batman and his party in 1835; a memorial in the town commemorates these occasions. **Accommodation:** 1 hotel, 2 caravan/camping parks.
Map ref. 152 B2, 155 I7, 172 F8

The Mornington Peninsula

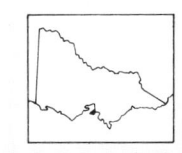

This boot-shaped promontory separates Port Phillip and Westernport Bays and provides Melburnians with a beachside playground. It is a mixture of resort towns, varying in size and tourist development, and inland countryside which is still rural. As well as safe bayside beaches, there are excellent surf beaches, particularly along the stretch of rugged coast between **Portsea** and **Cape Schanck** (172 G10) at the end of the Peninsula. The Cape Schanck Coastal Park includes the key beaches in this area — Portsea, **Sorrento, Diamond Bay, Koonya** and **Gunnamatta**. A number of walking tracks are being developed through the park. Swimming is considered unsafe in these areas unless they are controlled by the Surf Lifesaving Association.

The Westernport Bay side of the Peninsula is less developed, much of its foreshore having remained relatively unspoiled and being still devoted to farming and grazing land. **French Island**, which is set in the centre of this bay, was a Victorian penal settlement for 40 years and is now administered by the Department of Youth, Sport and Recreation as a holiday and sports centre.

A ferry service links Portsea and Sorrento with the town of **Queenscliff**, across Port Phillip Bay, during the summer months.

The Peninsula is well developed for tourists, with good sporting facilities and many art galleries, craft shops, restaurants and take-away food shops. Because of its popularity, it is advisable to book accommodation, whether hotel or campsite, well ahead during the summer and Easter seasons. The foreshore from **Dromana** to **Blairgowrie** (152 D8) is almost entirely devoted to campers and caravans during these peak seasons. The resorts also offer a wide variety of hotel, motel, holiday flat and guest house accommodation. The Peninsula is an ideal destination for day trips from Melbourne as most of it is within easy driving distance. Beware of bumper to bumper traffic jams, especially on the way home, in the summer and of the hazards of speeding on the long straight roads in the inland areas.

Dromana (172 G9) rests at the foot of Arthurs Seat, the 305 m mountain that provides the Peninsula with panoramic views over both bays. A good road leads to the summit and a chairlift operates at weekends and holidays during the summer months. At the summit, there is a lookout tower, picnic reserve and licensed restaurant.

Flinders (172 G10) The most southerly Peninsula township, on Westernport Bay, this is a fishing and holiday resort, with good surfing, swimming and fishing. Cape Schanck lighthouse, the Blowhole and Elephant Rock are worth visiting.

Frankston (172 H8) Now mainly a residential area for Melbourne commuters, Frankston is a thriving town within easy reach of good beaches at Daveys Bay, Canadian Bay and Mount Eliza. It is served by rail from Melbourne or a 40 km drive down the Nepean Highway.

Hastings (172 H9) This attractive fishing port and holiday centre has a seawater swimming pool, yacht club and boat launching ramps south of the pier.

McCrae (152 G7) is a small resort centre, noted for the McCrae Homestead, built in 1843, now a National Trust property, open daily. It was the first homestead on the Peninsula and is situated on the slopes of Arthurs Seat. Safety Beach has boat launching ramps and trailer facilities.

Mornington (172 H8) The deep safe harbour at Point Schnapper first attracted settlers to this area and the township of Mornington was established in 1864. It has been a popular resort town ever since and today it is a pleasant commercial, farming and recreational centre. Between the town and nearby Mount Martha stretches a fine coastline with sheltered sandy bays separated by rocky bluffs and backed by steep wooded slopes. There are a number of historic buildings in the town, including the gaol and court-house on the Esplanade, and the old post office on the corner of the Esplanade, which is now an historic museum. Fossil Beach, between Mount Martha and Mornington, is one of only two exposed fossil plains in the world.

Portsea (152 B6) Situated at the end of the Nepean Highway, Portsea is an attractive resort with excellent deep water bayside beaches and first-class surfing on its Back Beach. Victoria's first Quarantine Station (now an Army training camp) was built here in 1856 after 82 deaths from smallpox on the vessel *Ticonderoga* anchored in Weroona Bay. Panoramic views of the impressive rocky coastline abound and near the Back Beach is London Bridge, a spectacular rock formation created by sea erosion.

Rosebud (172 G9) A busy commercial centre with wide foreshore camping areas. Just outside the town is the Peninsula Gardens Sanctuary, set back from the Nepean Highway.

Rye (152 E8) A township with extensive camping, picnicking and recreational foreshore areas, together with boat launching facilities.

Shoreham (172 H10) is a sprawling holiday settlement on Stony Creek, close to a pleasant stretch of seafront. Five kilometres from Shoreham is Point Leo which has one of the safest surf beaches on the Peninsula. Between Point Leo and Balnarring, short access roads from the main Flinders–Frankston Road lead to very pleasant beaches at Merricks, Coles, Point Sumner and Balnarring.

Somers (172 H9), a quiet village with many holiday homes, has good beaches, excellent fishing, tennis and yacht clubs. Between Somers and Crib Point is *HMAS Cerberus,* a Royal Australian Navy training establishment.

Sorrento (152 C7) In 1803, Col. Collins landed in this area and founded Victoria's first settlement. The early settlers' graves and a memorial to Collins can be found in the cliff top cemetery overlooking Sullivans Bay. Sorrento was energetically developed as a 'watering place' by a George Coppin in the 1870s. At nearby Point King, the Union Jack was raised for the first time in Australia.

Sale Population 12 968.

The main administrative city in Gippsland, Sale is expanding rapidly, due to the concentration of off-shore oil development in nearby Bass Strait. It is just over 200 km east of Melbourne on the Princes Highway. Only 25 km from Lake Wellington, Sale is conveniently located for exploration of the whole Gippsland Lakes area which stretches from Wilson's Promontory to Lakes Entrance and is bordered most of the way by the famous Ninety Mile Beach. There is an excellent up-to-date shopping centre and pleasant lake and park areas in its city area.

Of interest: The Oil and Gas Display on the Princes Highway at the western approach to the city has displays depicting the story of the development of the off-shore oil reserves. The Port of Sale, a thriving spot during the days of the paddle steamers, is on the right side as you approach the city from Traralgon. It has barbecue and picnic facilities, also boat launching ramps. Cruises can be arranged from here for 100 km to Lakes Entrance, through the lakes system. Lake Guthridge, in the city centre, is a popular picnic and barbecue spot and has a fauna park and aviary. The city has a number of attractive and substantial buildings, including Our Lady of Sion Convent, the gaol and the Criterion Hotel, with beautiful lacework verandahs. The Historical Museum is located on the Princes Highway near the Commodore Motel.

In the area: To the north, the towns of Maffra and Heyfield, in intensively cultivated country, and the Glenmaggie Weir. The road from Stratford leads across the Dargo High Plains to Mt Hotham, and offers a stunning drive through the high country. To the south, Seaspray on the Ninety Mile Beach, 32 km from Sale, has excellent surfing and fishing. Marlay Point, 25 km from Sale, on the shores of Lake Wellington, has extensive launching facilities. The yacht club here sponsors the annual overnight yacht race to Paynesville each March. Popular fishing rivers include the Avon, near to Marlay Point, and the Macalister, Thomson and Latrobe, all of which flow into the lakes system. Tourist information from the Oil and Gas Display Centre, Princes Highway. **Accommodation:** 5 motels, 2 caravan/camping parks.
Map ref. 173 R7, 174 B10

Seymour Population 6492.

On the Goulburn River, at the junction of the Goulburn Valley and Hume Highways, Seymour is a busy commercial, industrial and agricultural town, serving the local rural community. The area was recommended by Lord Kitchener as being particularly suitable for a military base, during his visit in 1909. Nearby Puckapunyal was an important training base for troops during World War 2 and it is still used by the army. Seymour marks the start of the 'Boomerang Way', an alternative route to Sydney via the Goulburn Valley and Newell Highways, through Tocumwal, bypassing the busy Hume Highway. **Of interest:** The Royal Hotel featured in Russell Drysdale's famous painting, 'Moody's Pub'. The Old Log Cabin, Goulburn Park has picnic and swimming areas, and a caravan park. Glengariff Vineyard, open Monday to Saturday, tastings and sales only. **In the area:** The Mitchelton and Chateau Tahbilk Vineyards, near Nagambie. **Accommodation:** 4 motels, 3 caravan/camping parks.
Map ref. 154 G3, 159 N1, 166 H11

Shepparton-Mooroopna
Population 26 369.

The 'capital' of the rich Goulburn Valley, this thriving, well-developed city, 181 km north of Melbourne, has 4000 ha of orchards within a 10 km radius and 4000 ha of market gardens along the river valley nearby. The area is irrigated by the Yarrawonga and Eildon reservoir schemes and is on the junction of the Goulburn and Broken Rivers. The central shopping area of Shepparton is surrounded by 68 ha of parkland including an open-air music bowl and a new Civic Centre housing an art gallery, town hall, theatre and municipal centre. Shepparton's multi-deck car park includes a lounge and baby feeding room. **Of interest:** The Art Gallery at the Civic Centre has traditional Australian paintings and a collection of Australian ceramics. On Parkside Road, the International Village, a tourist, educational and cultural centre. A Gem Display and Tourist Inspection Centre, open afternoons, on Nixon St. Historical Museum, open Sunday afternoons. The Redbyrne Pottery, on the Old Dookie Road, a few km out of town, sells a wide variety of locally made pottery and ceramics. The 20 ha Victoria Lake Park offers yachting, water sports and a caravan park. The Shepparton Preserving Company, the largest cannery in the southern hemisphere, offers guided inspections during the canning period from January to Easter. **In the area:** There are a number of vineyards including the Gravina Winery, Old Dookie Road. South down the Goulburn Valley Highway, the 1860-built Chateau Tahbilk near Nagambie, recorded by the National Trust, is worth a visit. Historic Brookfield Homestead is 20 km north along the Goulburn Valley Highway, with old farm machinery and shearing sheds; open for inspection by appointment. Victoria's Irrigation Research Institute is just east of Tatura. **Accommodation:** Shepparton, 3 hotels, 9 motels, 4 caravan/camping parks. Mooroopna, 2 motels, 5 caravan/camping parks.
Map ref. 167 J6

Stawell Population 6160.

North-east of Halls Gap, and 123 km north-west of Ballarat on the Western Highway, Stawell is well sited for tours to the northern Grampians. It is the home of the Stawell Easter Gift, Australia's most famous footrace, held annually. **Of interest:** Big Hill, local landmark and the place where gold was first discovered. Sites of famous mines are marked. World in Miniature Tourist Park is a re-creation in miniature of scenes of life in Australia and Pacific countries, using indoor and outdoor scale working models with dioramas and commentaries, is open daily and has play areas and refreshments. The

---

RIVERLAND
The Murray crosses into SA and at **Renmark** begins its splendid flow down to its mouth at Lake Alexandrina. The banks are lined with historic river towns such as **Renmark, Morgan, Murray Bridge** and **Goolwa**, at its mouth, which has a strong tradition of shipbuilding, originating from the busy riverboat days. Renmark, like Mildura, is famous for its year-round sunshine and all these towns make attractive and interesting places for a holiday. This South Australian stretch of the Murray offers splendid river scenery and birdlife, excellent fishing and water sports and the chance to enjoy the many wineries in the area. The Riverland winelands produce more than 40 per cent of the entire national vintage in an average year.

SUNRAYSIA
Proud residents of **Mildura** may mention to you that the city enjoys 400 more hours of sunshine a year than does Surfers Paradise! This beautiful climate supports flourishing citrus and wine growing industries as well as attracting countless holiday-makers to the Mildura area during both the summer and winter seasons. Upstream is **Red Cliffs,** an interesting town which was founded after World War 1 by soldiers, who turned it into a model irrigation town, and the surrounding areas into prosperous winelands. At the junction of the Murray and the Darling lies **Wentworth**, one of the oldest of the river towns, with a historic gaol and a beautifully preserved paddle steamer called *Ruby*.

As a modern-day explorer, a trip following the course of the Murray gives you a chance to discover a rich cross section of Australian country and history, as well as the infinite variety of natural beauty and wildlife the river itself supports.

Stawell — Tallangatta VIC. 141

The Mighty Murray

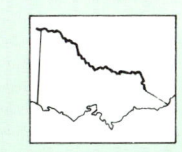

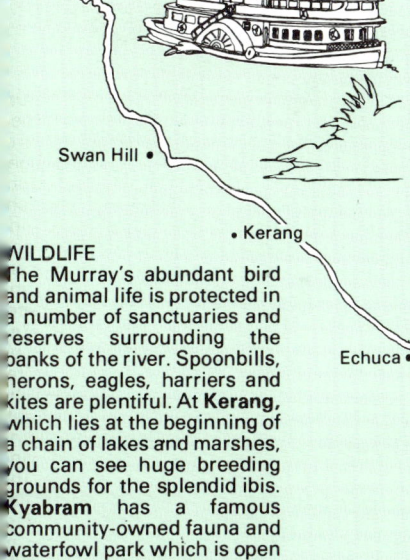

THE HEYDAY OF THE RIVERBOATS
Famous river towns like **Wentworth, Swan Hill** and **Echuca** have carefully preserved much of the history of this colourful era. The Port of Echuca and the Swan Hill Pioneer Settlement are a must if you are in the area. Children, especially, will delight in the 'living museum', where original buildings, paddle steamers and old wharves have been restored.

LAKES, BEACHES AND REDGUMS
As it flows towards the aquatic playgrounds of Lakes Hume and Mulwala, the Murray becomes a wide and splendid river. Lined with magnificent redgums, in the region around **Cobram**, banks are transformed into wide sandy beaches. This is ideal holiday country, with the pleasant resort towns around the conurbation of **Albury** and **Wodonga**, and the towns of **Yarrawonga** and **Tallangatta**.

THE SOURCE
The Murray has its source in the slopes of Mount Pilot, high in the Alps. Here it is just a gurgling mountain stream, rushing through some breathtaking mountain scenery. This is the area of the Snowy Mountains scheme, the great Australian snowfields and the rich grazing lands of Morgan country, named for the famous bushrangers.

WILDLIFE
The Murray's abundant bird and animal life is protected in a number of sanctuaries and reserves surrounding the banks of the river. Spoonbills, herons, eagles, harriers and kites are plentiful. At **Kerang**, which lies at the beginning of a chain of lakes and marshes, you can see huge breeding grounds for the splendid ibis. **Kyabram** has a famous community-owned fauna and waterfowl park which is open daily and almost all of Gunbower Island is a protected sanctuary for wildlife.

WINE COUNTRY
Victoria's main wine growing area is centred around **Rutherglen** and extends down to the wineries of the Ovens and Goulburn Valleys. The wineries welcome visitors and many offer conducted tours.

THE OVENS VALLEY
Nestling in the foothills of the Victorian alps, this beautiful valley has an all year round charm. It's transformed by wattles in the spring and in the autumn by the magnificent colours of its groves of European trees.

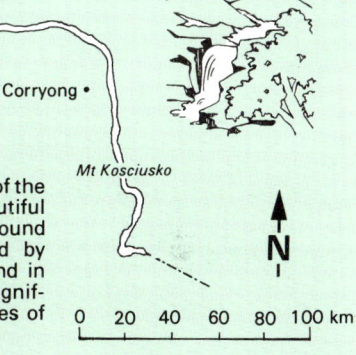

North Western Woollen Mills offer conducted tours on working days at 10.30 am. **In the area:** Bunjil's Cave, with Aboriginal rock paintings in ochre, is off the Pomonal Road, 11 km from the town. The Sisters Rocks are a collection of huge granite boulders, beside the Western Highway south-east of Stawell. They were saved from demolition in 1867 by a local resident who bought the land on which they rest, and fenced it off. Overdale Station, Landsborough Road, is a working farm which gives guided tours during school holidays. Farm holidays are also available there. Roses Gap Deer Park and Wildlife Reserve, open daily, 34 km from Stawell, off the Western Highway. Tottington Woolshed, which is a National Trust property and a rare example of a nineteenth-century woolshed, is 55 km north-east on the road to St Arnaud. Lake Fyans, near Halls Gap, allows both power and other boats, and has picnic and camping facilities. Sailing and rowing boats are permitted on Lake Bellfield, where there are picnic facilities. Tourist information from the Stawell and Grampians Information Centre, London Road, which publishes a 'Stawell and Grampians Visitor Guide'. **Accommodation:** 9 hotels, 13 motels, 8 caravan/camping parks.
Map ref. 165 K12

Swan Hill   Population 8398.
When explorer Thomas Mitchell camped on the banks of the Murray, he named the spot Swan Hill because of the black swans which had kept him awake all night. The township became a busy nineteenth-century river port and today it is a small, pleasant city and major holiday centre on the Murray Valley Highway, 189 km north-west of Bendigo. The climate is mild and sunny and the river offers good fishing, boating and water sport relaxation. **Of interest:** Swan Hill Pioneer Settlement is a 4 ha development built around the Murray's largest paddle steamer *Gem*, preserved as a relic of the days when such craft were the Murray Valley's main form of transport. The restoration of this old boat and the recreation of buildings of the period — shops, blacksmiths, a Cobb and Co. coach office and homesteads — makes the settlement a fascinating excursion and it is worth setting a whole day aside to see and enjoy it all. There is a collection of horse-drawn vehicles and old locomotives as well, plus a pottery. The sound and light show in the evening tells the story of the town and area and visitors are taken around the settlement in horse-drawn carriages. Refreshments are available from the General Store and Bakery and the Lower Murray Inn offers steaks for barbecueing and traditional meals and drinks. There are also picnic and barbecue facilities. The settlement is open daily; an entrance fee is charged. Swan Hill Regional Art Gallery, Horseshoe Bend. The Swan Hill Military Museum has an extensive collection of military arms, uniforms and flags. **In the area:** Lake Boga, 16 km to the south, is popular for water sports and picnicking. The historic Tyntynder Homestead, classified by the National Trust, is 17 km north, on the Murray Valley Highway. Murray Downs Homestead, 2 km away on the Moulamein Road, is an historic sheep, cattle and irrigation property. Tourist Information Centre, Campbell St. **Accommodation:** 10 motels, 4 caravan/camping parks.
Map ref. 163 O11

Tallangatta   Population 953.
The old town of Tallangatta was submerged due to the construction of the Hume Weir but many of its buildings were moved to a new location above the shore line. Today, situated 42 km from Wodonga on the Murray Valley Highway, the town has the benefit of this large lake and boasts an attractive inland beach. It is the most eastern of the main Murray River towns and is directly north of the beautiful alpine region of Victoria. **Of interest:** 'The Hub', Tallangatta's Community Centre, sells arts and crafts. **In the area:** A number of forest drives are recommended by the Forests Commission. They begin at Mitta Mitta, south down the Omeo Highway and include trips to Cravensville, Mt Benambra, Tawonga and Omeo via the Snowy Creek Road. Dartmouth Dam, 58 km from Tallangatta, has good trout fishing, boating, picnic and barbecue facilities. Further information from the North East Tourism Limited, P.O. Box 250, Wangaratta 3677. Tourist information in Tallangatta at 'The Hub'. **Accommodation:** 2 hotels, 1 motel, 1 caravan/camping park.
Map ref. 168 C5

The Grampians

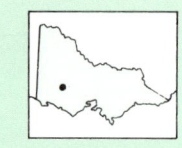

The massive sandstone ranges of the Grampians (165 J13) in Western Victoria provide some of the state's most spectacular scenery. Rising in peaks to heights of over 1000 metres, they form the western extremity of the Great Dividing Range. Major Mitchell climbed and named the highest peak, Mt William, in July 1836 and gave the name 'The Grampians' to the ranges because they reminded him of the Grampians in his native Scotland.

On July 1, 1984 these rugged mountain ranges, famous for their spectacular wild flowers, became Victoria's newest (and largest) national park. It is a superb area for scenic drives on good roads, bushwalking and rock climbing being some of the most popular activities; Lake Bellfield provides for sailing and rowing, and there is excellent trout-fishing in the lake and in Fyans Creek.

There is plenty of wildlife to be seen; koalas, kangaroos and deer are numerous, and echidnas, possums and duck-billed platypus can be found, while more than 100 species of birds have been identified.

Apart from their scenic grandeur, the Grampians are best known for the beauty and variety of their wild flowers. There are more than one thousand species of ferns and flowering plants native to the region and they are at their most colourful from August to November, the most popular time for a visit to the Grampians.

Halls Gap, which takes its name from a pioneer pastoralist who settled in the eastern Grampians in the early 1840s, is the focal point of the area; its wide variety of accommodation includes motels, guest houses, holiday flats, a youth hostel and caravan and camping parks. Further information from the Halls Gap newsagency and from the Stawell and Grampians Tourist Information Officer, Central Park, **Stawell**.

Terang Population 2111.
A well laid out town with good sports facilities, including a polo ground, in an area which is rich in wool and dairy produce. **Accommodation:** 4 hotels, 2 motels, 1 caravan/camping park.
Map ref. 171 M8

Torquay Population 2879.
The popularity of this resort, 22 km south of Geelong, is well-known. Close to the town, the excellent surfing beaches, Bells and Jan Juc, attract surfers from all over the world. The Torquay Surf Lifesaving Club is the largest in the state. Torquay also marks the eastern end of the Great Ocean Road, which offers spectacular drives west to Anglesea, Lorne and Apollo Bay. **Accommodation:** 1 motel, 4 caravan/camping parks.
Map ref. 155 E10, 172 D9

Trafalgar Population 2109.
This small dairying centre in the Latrobe Valley, a few km from Moe, is conveniently situated for trips to the Upper Latrobe and Tanjil River Valleys in the mountainous area to the north and for scenic drives along the beautiful Grand Ridge Road. **In the area:** Trafalgar South Lookout, Narracan Falls and Henderson's Gully. The area offers good trout fishing and shooting. **Accommodation:** 1 hotel.
Map ref. 173 M8

Traralgon Population 18 059.
Situated on the Princes Highway 160 km from Melbourne, Traralgon is one of the Latrobe Valley's main cities, the others being Moe and Morwell. It is a residential area based on an industrial core, but has a variety of light industries. The dense forests of the mountain country to the north have made Traralgon the centre of the paper-making industry in Victoria. The huge new Loy Yang power station is being constructed for the State Electricity Commission 5 km from the town. Tourist and Industrial information can be obtained from the City of Traralgon Offices, Kay Street. **Accommodation:** 2 hotels, 5 motels, 4 caravan/camping parks.
Map ref. 173 P8

Wangaratta Population 16 202.
The Ovens Highway to Bright and the Victorian Alps, through the Ovens Valley, branches off the Hume Highway at Wangaratta, 66 km south-west of Wodonga. The surrounding fertile area produces wool, wheat, tobacco, hops and table and wine grapes. The city is well-planned with good areas of parkland, including one park with a 'man-size' chess set.

Of interest: 'Bontharambo' historic homestead on the Boorhaman Road, 8 km from Wangaratta, classified by the National Trust, open school and public holidays. In the local cemetery, the grave of Daniel 'Mad Dog' Morgan, the bushranger can be seen. His headless body was buried here, the head having been sent to Melbourne for examination as Morgan was believed to be abnormal.

In the area: Glenrowan, 16 km south-west, is famed for its Kelly history. Ned

was captured here after a bloody gunfight at the local hotel and was subsequently condemned and hanged in Melbourne. The tourist centre in the town focuses on the history of the Kelly Gang. Eldorado, 20 km east, is an interesting old gold township with the largest gold dredge in the country, built in 1936. There is an historical museum, a general store with tourist information and a pottery open at weekends. Nearby Reedy Creek is popular with gold panners and gem fossickers. The road south to Moyhu leads to the beautiful King Valley and Paradise Falls. This area includes the tiny townships of Whitfield, Edi, Myrrhee, Cheshunt and Carboor and a network of minor roads allows exploration of an area which is still unspoiled and well worth visiting in all seasons. There are many vineyards in the area. These include: Brown Bros Milawa Vineyards, 16 km south-east, a family winery since 1889; Baileys Bundarra Vineyards, 7 km north of Glenrowan, offers tastings. It was established in 1870 and now has a collection of vineyard antiques; Booth Bros, 4 km north of Baileys. They are all open Monday to Saturday. Moyhu and Whitfield, south of Wangaratta are also worth a visit and have accommodation. Tourist information from the North East Visitors Centre, Hume Highway, Wangaratta. Phone (057) 21 5711. **Accommodation:** 7 hotels, 10 motels, 3 caravan/camping parks.
Map ref. 167 N6, 176 D9

Warburton   Population 2009.
This popular tourist town, surrounded by the foothills of the Great Dividing Range, is only about an hour's drive from Melbourne. **Of interest:** The Acheron Way, just beyond Warburton, gives access to views of Mt Donna Buang, Mt Victoria and Ben Cairn. Mt Donna Buang, 7 km north-west, is a popular day trip destination from Melbourne and is sometimes snow-covered in winter. There are two toboggan runs at the summit. The Upper Yarra Dam, 16 km north-east, has picnic facilities. To the south is an attractive area of vineyards. The countryside around Warburton is ideal for bushwalking, riding and bird watching. **Accommodation:** 1 hotel, 3 motels, 1 caravan/camping park.
Map ref. 160 F12, 173 K5

Warracknabeal   Population 2735.
On the Henty Highway, 350 km north-west of Melbourne, Warracknabeal is in the centre of a rich wheat growing area. The name is Aboriginal, meaning 'the place of the big red gums shading the water course'. **Of interest:** The Historical Centre, 81 Scott St, contains many items and displays of the history of the area. Leaflets are available suggesting a tour of the interesting and historic buildings in the town. Some of these have been classified by the National Trust, including a couple of attractive old hotels with iron lacework and the original log lock-up, built when Warracknabeal acquired its first permanent policeman. The North Western Agricultural Machinery Museum has a unique collection of farm machinery used over the past century. There are picnic and barbecue facilities in the grounds. At the Lions Park, situated in a bend of the Yarriambiack Creek, are picnic spots and a fauna park. **In the area:** Sections of the dog-fence remain, some 30 km north. This was a vermin-proof barrier erected in 1883 from the Murray near Swan Hill to the border. Jeparit, 45 km west, has the Wimmetra-Mallee Pioneer Museum and, a few km north, Lake Hindmarsh. Lake Buloke, 56 km east, provides duck shooting in season. **Accommodation:** 4 hotels, 2 motels, 1 caravan/camping park.
Map ref. 164 I6

Walhalla

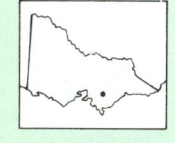

The tiny gold mining ghost town of **Walhalla** (173 O6) is tucked away in dense mountain country in south-east Gippsland. The 46 kilometres drive from **Moe** passes through some spectacular scenery, making a visit to this interesting little township a very worthwhile day trip.

Walhalla is set in a narrow, steep valley, with sides so sheer that its cemetery has graves that have been dug lengthways into the hillside.

Historic buildings and relics of the gold boom days have been preserved, including the Long Tunnel Mine, once the most successful in the state. The town's historic museum is in the old fire station, which still houses a hand-operated fire engine. Spett's Cottage, built in 1871, is furnished in the period and is open at weekends and on public holidays. The old bakery, the oldest surviving building in the town, was built in 1865 and stands near the hotel. The Museum, Spett's Cottage, the Band Rotunda and the two-storey Windsor House have all been classified by the National Trust.

The Long Tunnel Mine is open at weekends and holidays and there are guided tours to inspect its underground workings. There is an hotel at Walhalla and a camping ground and motel at **Erica**, 14 kilometres south.

Warragul   Population 7715.
Most of Melbourne's milk comes from this prosperous dairy farming area, on the edge of the Latrobe Valley 103 km from Melbourne. The state dairying festival is held here every February. **Of interest:** The West Gippsland Arts Centre, recently completed. Wild flower sanctuary at Labertouche, nature reserves and picnic spots at Glen Cromie, Glen Nayook and Toorongo Falls. To the north, interesting mountain country and good trout fishing in the Tarago Reservoir at Neerim South. For further information see entries for Morwell and Moe. **Accommodation:** 4 hotels, 2 motels, 1 caravan/camping park.
Map ref. 173 L8

Warrnambool   Population 21 415.
This flourishing coastal resort 190 km west of Geelong has some excellent beaches and impressive scenery in the surrounding area. Its name is a corrupt version of an Aboriginal word meaning 'plenty of water'. **Of interest:** In the 1880s, Australia was preparing for a Russian invasion and gun emplacements erected at the time can be seen on Flagstaff Hill near the lighthouse. This is now the site of the Port of Warrnambool Maritime Village, a re-creation of a port as it was in the days of sail. It has a museum and visitors can tour restored sailing ships and typical port buildings of the era. There are some impressive buildings in the town, together with an antique vehicle museum, a zoo and a reptile park. **In the area:** Just to the west, Tower Hill. This large lava plain area, with volcanic cone and crater, can be viewed from the road which winds through the area. It is also a state game reserve, and gregarious emus greet arriving cars. Information can be obtained from 600 Raglan Pde. Warrnambool holds a number of annual events, a seaside bowling carnival in February and March, the Warrnambool Cup and Grand Steeplechase in May and the 'Melbourne to Warrnambool' cycling classic in October. **Accommodation:** 11 hotels, 17 motels, 8 caravan/camping parks.
Map ref. 171 J9

Wedderburn   Population 868.
Once one of Victoria's richest gold-mining towns, Wedderburn is on the Calder Highway 74 km north-west of Bendigo. Gold can still be found in and around the town — nuggets worth $20 000 were discovered in a local backyard in the 1950s. **Of interest:** The museum and general store, a restored building furnished and stocked as it was at the turn of the century. There is also a coach building factory and an old bakery has been converted into a kiln for a group of potters, using local clay. Gundawarra Boomerang Park, Main St, is a boomerang factory where visitors can participate in throwing. The Wychitella Forest Reserve, a wildlife sanctuary, is 16 km north. Wedderburn holds an annual Gold Dig Festival in March and a Folk and Country Music Festival in November. Tourist Information Centre in the main street. **Accommodation:** 1 hotel, 1 motel, 1 caravan/camping park.
Map ref. 165 P7

Welshpool-Port Welshpool
Population 514.
Welshpool is a small dairying town and Port Welshpool is a deep-sea port servicing fishing and oil industries. Barry Beach Marine Terminal, 8 km south of the South Gippsland Hwy, services the offshore oil rigs in Bass Strait. There is excellent fishing and boating in the area. **Of interest:** Agnes Falls, the state's highest, are a spectacular sight and panoramic views from Mt Fatigue, just off the South Gippsland Hwy at Toora, are worth visiting. At Port Welshpool, a Maritime Museum. The Tarra Valley and Bulga National Parks lie to the north. **Accommodation:** 1 motel, 2 caravan/camping parks.
Map ref. 173 O11

Winchelsea Population 825.
This township is in the centre of a farming area, on the Barwon River, 37 km west of Geelong. It originated as a watering place and shelter for travellers on the road to Colac from Geelong. **Of interest:** Barwon Bridge; with its graceful stone arches, was opened in 1867 to handle increasing westward traffic. The Barwon Hotel, built in 1842, houses a museum of Australiana which is worth a visit. Nearby, the Barwon Park homestead, a National Trust property, is open daily. Lake Modewarre offers good fishing and is ideal for swimming or any water sports. **Accommodation:** 1 motel, 1 caravan/camping park.
Map ref. 155 B9, 171 R8, 172 B8

Wodonga Population 22 000.
Wodonga is the Victorian section of the Twin City complex astride the Murray in north-east Victoria. Albury-Wodonga is a fast growing city being developed as a decentralised region by the Vic. and NSW State Governments and, with the attractions of the Murray and nearby Lake Hume, makes a good base for a holiday. **Of interest:** Folk Museum at the Turk's Head Hotel; Drage's Aircraft Museum, a private collection of vintage aircraft; the Ettamogah Sanctuary, with native animals, birds and reptiles; 10 km north of Albury on the Hume Highway. The sanctuary has barbecues and picnic facilities. A short drive south leads to the picturesque historic township of Yackandandah. The towns of Beechworth, Wangaratta and Rutherglen are all well worth visiting. Tourist information from the Golden Fleece Roadhouse, Hume Highway, and the Albury Visitors and Travel Centre, 550 Dean St, Albury. **Accommodation:** Albury/Wodonga 27 motels, 9 caravan/camping parks.
Map ref. 167 Q5, 168 A5, 173 H3

Wonthaggi Population 4796.
Once the main supplier of black coal to the Victorian Railways, Wonthaggi, situated 8 km from Cape Patterson in south Gippsland, is now primarily a pastoral and dairying centre. There is excellent scenery in the area and there are good beaches at Inverloch, Walkerville and Tarwin Lower. **Accommodation:** 2 hotels, 1 motel, 1 caravan/camping park.
Map ref. 173 J11

Wycheproof Population 938.
A railway line runs down the middle of the main street of this little township on the edge of the Mallee, 140 km from Bendgo. **Of interest:** A boomerang factory in the town, 'Mt Wycheproof', a mere 43 m high (above the surrounding plains. On the second Saturday in October, is the 'Australian Eagle King of the Mountain' contest is held. Contestants carry a 63.5 kg bag of wheat up Mt Wycheproof. **Accommodation:** 1 motel, 1 caravan/camping park.
Map ref. 165 N4

Yackandandah Population 461.
About 27 km south of Wodonga, this exceptionally attractive township, with avenues of English trees and traditional verandahed buildings, has been classified by the National Trust. Yackandandah is in the heart of the north-east goldfields country, but today it is more famous for its strawberries and has in fact become known as the 'Strawberry Capital of Victoria', with strawberry wine-making a local feature. The wine is on sale at Allans Flat Strawberry Farm.
Of interest: A number of original buildings, including the post office, courthouse, several banks and general stores. The Bank of Victoria (1850) is now an historical museum. Yackandandah has a number of arts and crafts shops, including the Yackandandah Workshop, John Dermer's Workshop (ceramics) and the Antwerpia Art Gallery. There is also a Herb Nursery in the township, with tearooms and a restaurant.
In the area: Indigo Valley, 6 km from Yackandandah, has been classified by the National Trust. The creeks and old diggings still yield specimens of alluvial gold to amateur prospectors. At Dederang, 25 km from Yackandandah, there are arts, crafts and plants for sale; Devonshire teas are available at Clifton Cottages. At Leneva, 12 km away, the Wombat Valley Tramways small gauge railway operates on the last Sunday of each month. Every New Year's Day, Yackandandah holds a country music festival. Tourist information can be obtained from Shaws Tearooms. **Accommodation:** 1 caravan/camping park.
Map ref. 167 Q6

Yarram Population 2085.
This old-established south Gippsland town 225 km by road from Melbourne, has some interesting original buildings and a pleasant golf course, inhabited by relatively tame kangaroos. It is situated between the Strzelecki Ranges and Bass Strait. **Of interest:** To the south, the historic towns of Alberton, Tarraville and Port Albert. The Ninety Mile Beach begins just north of Port Albert. The beach itself is a stunning sight and is very popular with surfers and sea fishermen. Woodside and Seaspray beaches are good and are patrolled during the summer season. For fishing, try Manns, McLoughlins or Robertsons beaches. To the north is the Australian Omega Navigation Facility with its 427 metre high steel tower. In the Strzelecki Ranges, are the Tarra Valley and Bulga National Parks. This is very hilly country, densely forested with mountain ash, myrtle and sassafras, with spectacular fern glades and splendid river and mountain views. Rosellas and lyrebirds can be seen, as can the occasional koala. There are walking tracks in both parks and two caravan parks at Tarra Valley. If approaching the parks from the north, the Midland Highway from Morwell leads through, or the road from Traralgon, which links up with the scenic and beautiful Grand Ridge Road. At Hiawatha, a short drive from Yarram, are the appropriately named Minnie Ha Ha Falls on the Albert River, with picnic facilities. Horses may be hired at the Hiawatha Horse Stud. At Wron Wron Forest, on the Hyland Way, wild flowers can be seen in spring in a dense foothill forest, and native birds and animals. Yarram holds the Tarra Valley Festival each April. **Accommodation:** 2 hotels, 3 motels, 3 caravan/camping parks.
Map ref. 173 P11

Yarrawonga Population 3442.
A pleasant stretch of the Murray plus beautiful Lake Mulwala have made this border town an extremely pleasant and popular holiday resort. The lake was created in 1939 during the building of the Yarrawonga Wier, which controls the irrigation waters in the Murray Valley. Around the lake and along the river, sandy beaches and still waters provide an ideal environment for all kinds of water sports, picnicking, barbecues and general relaxation. The town has excellent sports facilities, including a golf course. The islands and backwaters of the lake contain abundant bird life. Cruises can be taken on the lake and Glenloth Farm conducts trail rides along the river. The Yarrawonga foreshore area has well tended green lawns and willows and its facilities include a children's playground, kiosk, barbecues and boat ramps. Tourist information from 48 Belmore St. **Accommodation:** 6 hotels, 8 motels, 8 caravan/camping parks.
Map ref. 167 M4

Yea Population 996.
The town, 58 km north of Yarra Glen, stands beside the Yea River, a tributary of the Goulburn. Set in attractive pastoral and dairy farming land, it is well situated for touring to Mansfield, Eildon and the mountains and to the gorge country between Yea and Tallarook, as well as south-east to Marysville. There are some beautiful gorges and fern gullies close to the Yea-Tallarook Road and easy access to the mountain country south of Eildon Weir. **Of interest:** Kinglake National Park, south-west of the town, has a number of beautiful waterfalls, tall eucalypts, fern gullies and impressive views. Wildlife includes wombats, platypuses and lyrebirds. North of the town, off the back road to Euroa, there are mineral springs at Dropmore. There is a grotto at Caveat and an ibis rookery at Kerrisdale. There are several good campsites along the Goulburn River. **Accommodation:** 2 motels, 1 caravan/camping park.
Map ref. 159 Q4, 160 C4, 166 I3

Maps of Victoria
Location Map

VINEYARDS CLOSE TO MELBOURNE	154
GEELONG	156
BALLARAT	157
VICTORIAN ALPINE RESORTS	169
VINEYARDS OF NORTH EASTERN VICTORIA	176
FOR APPROACHES TO MELBOURNE SEE	172 - 173
FOR ROUTES TO CANBERRA AND SYDNEY SEE	102 - 103

146 Central Melbourne

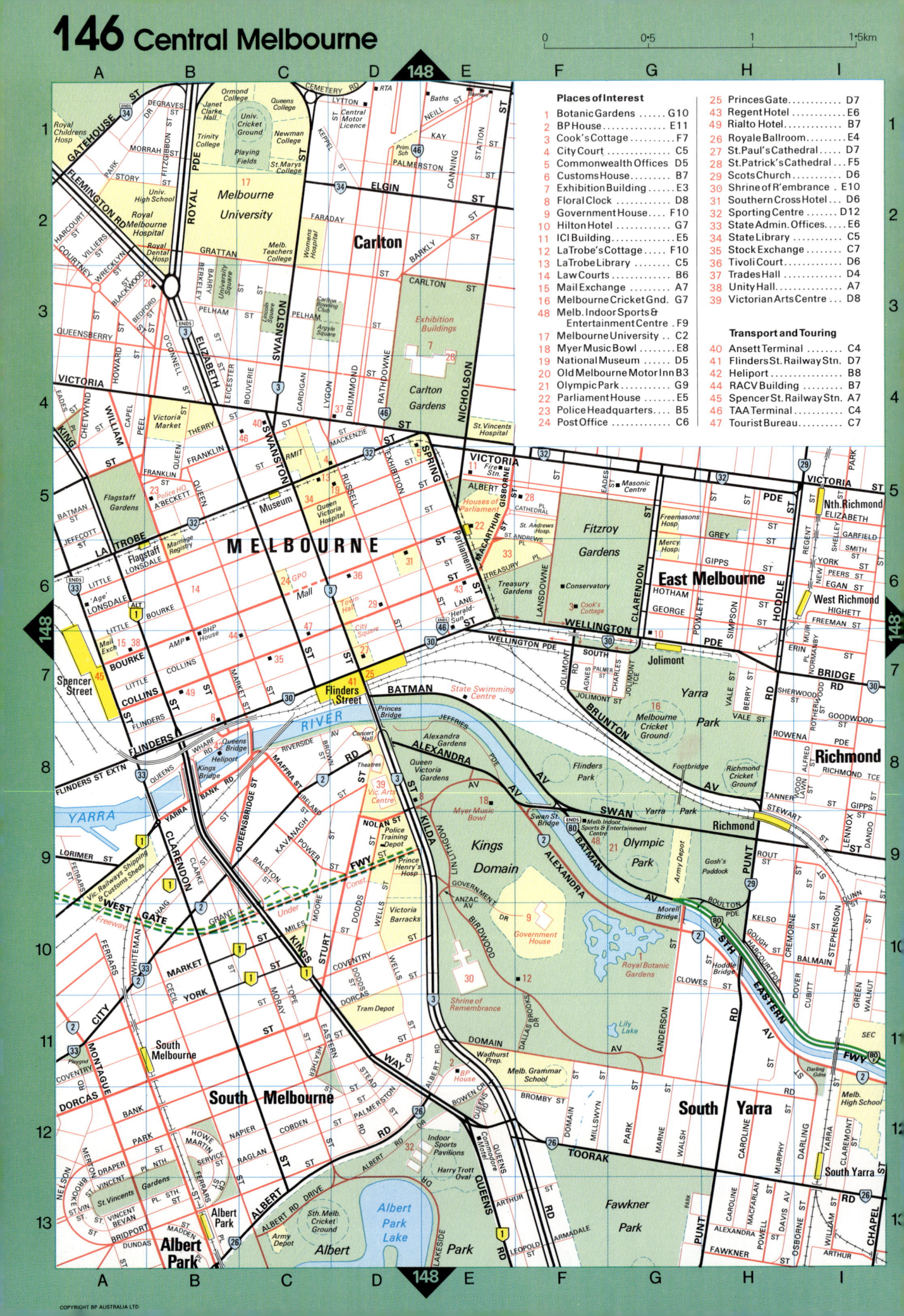

Places of Interest

1. Botanic Gardens G10
2. BP House E11
3. Cook's Cottage F7
4. City Court C5
5. Commonwealth Offices .. D5
6. Customs House B7
7. Exhibition Building ... E3
8. Floral Clock D8
9. Government House F10
10. Hilton Hotel G7
11. ICI Building E5
12. LaTrobe's Cottage ... F10
13. LaTrobe Library C5
14. Law Courts B6
15. Mail Exchange A7
16. Melbourne Cricket Gnd. G7
48. Melb. Indoor Sports & Entertainment Centre . F9
17. Melbourne University .. C2
18. Myer Music Bowl E8
19. National Museum D5
20. Old Melbourne Motor Inn B3
21. Olympic Park G9
22. Parliament House E5
23. Police Headquarters... B5
24. Post Office C6
25. Princes Gate D7
43. Regent Hotel E6
49. Rialto Hotel B7
26. Royale Ballroom E4
27. St. Paul's Cathedral . D7
28. St. Patrick's Cathedral. F5
29. Scots Church D6
30. Shrine of R'embrance . E10
31. Southern Cross Hotel . D6
32. Sporting Centre D12
33. State Admin. Offices . E6
34. State Library C5
35. Stock Exchange C7
36. Tivoli Court D6
37. Trades Hall D4
38. Unity Hall A7
39. Victorian Arts Centre . D8

Transport and Touring

40. Ansett Terminal C4
41. Flinders St. Railway Stn. D7
42. Heliport B8
44. RACV Building B7
45. Spencer St. Railway Stn. A7
46. TAA Terminal C4
47. Tourist Bureau C7

The Dandenongs 147

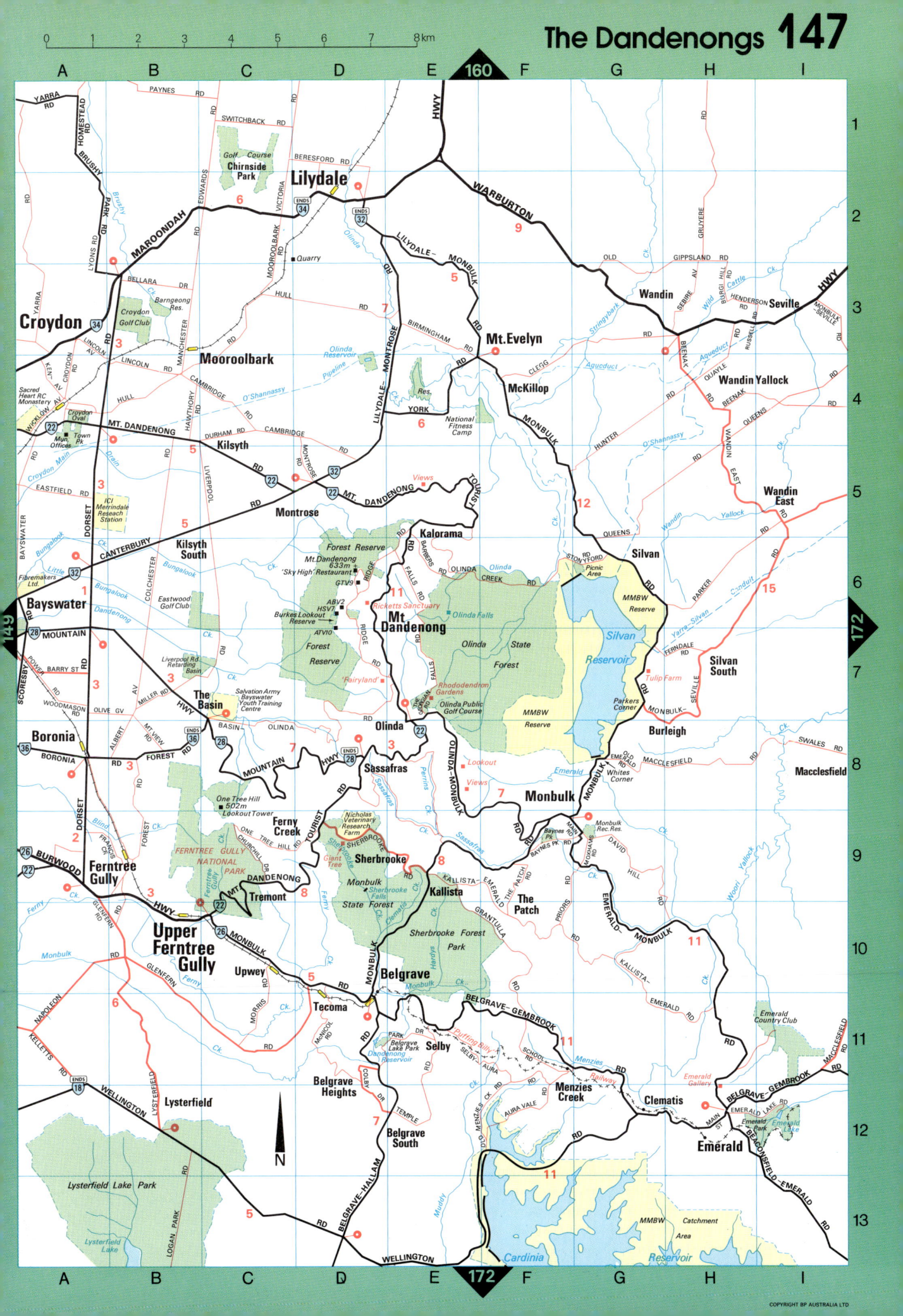

148 Melbourne & Suburbs

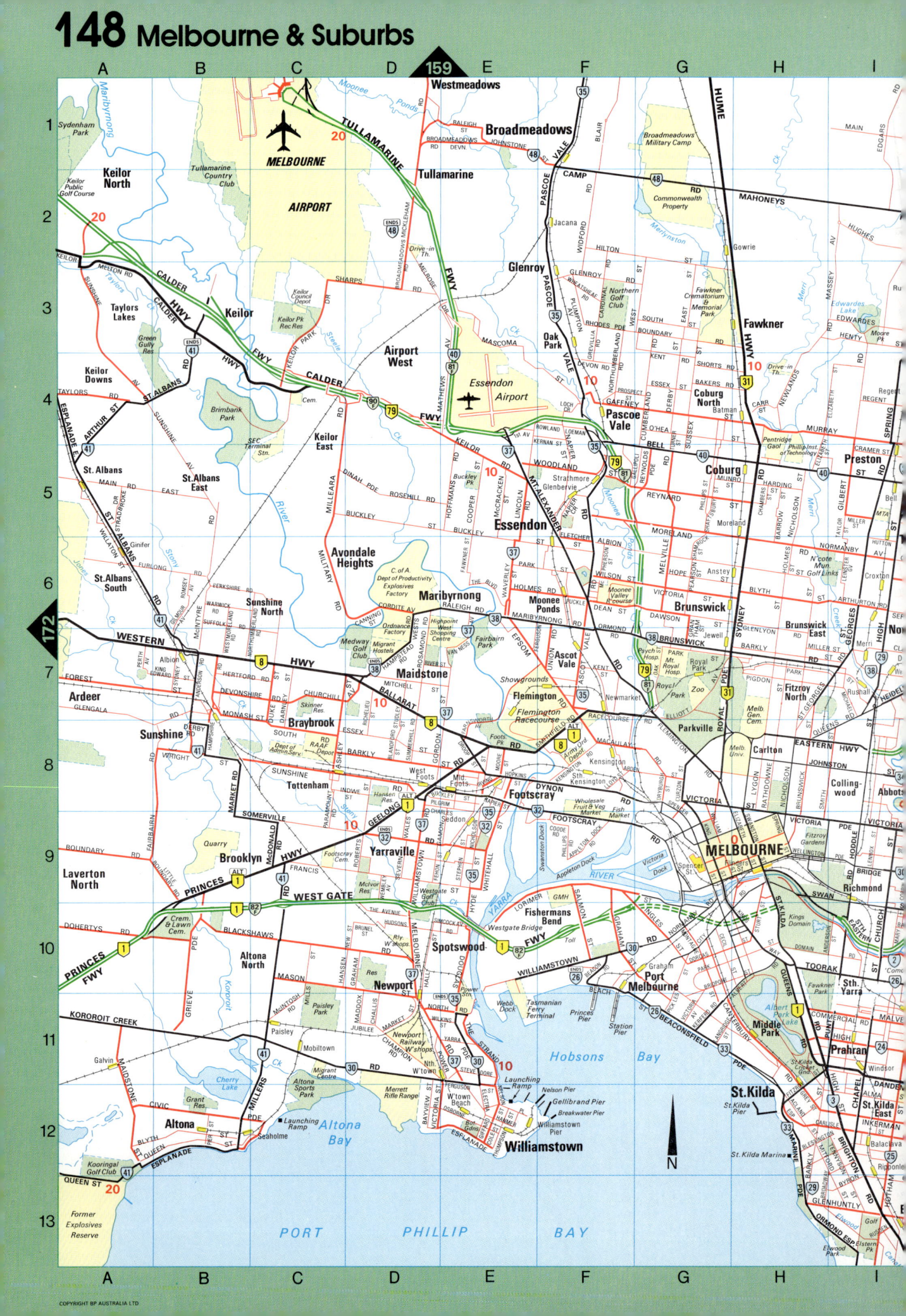

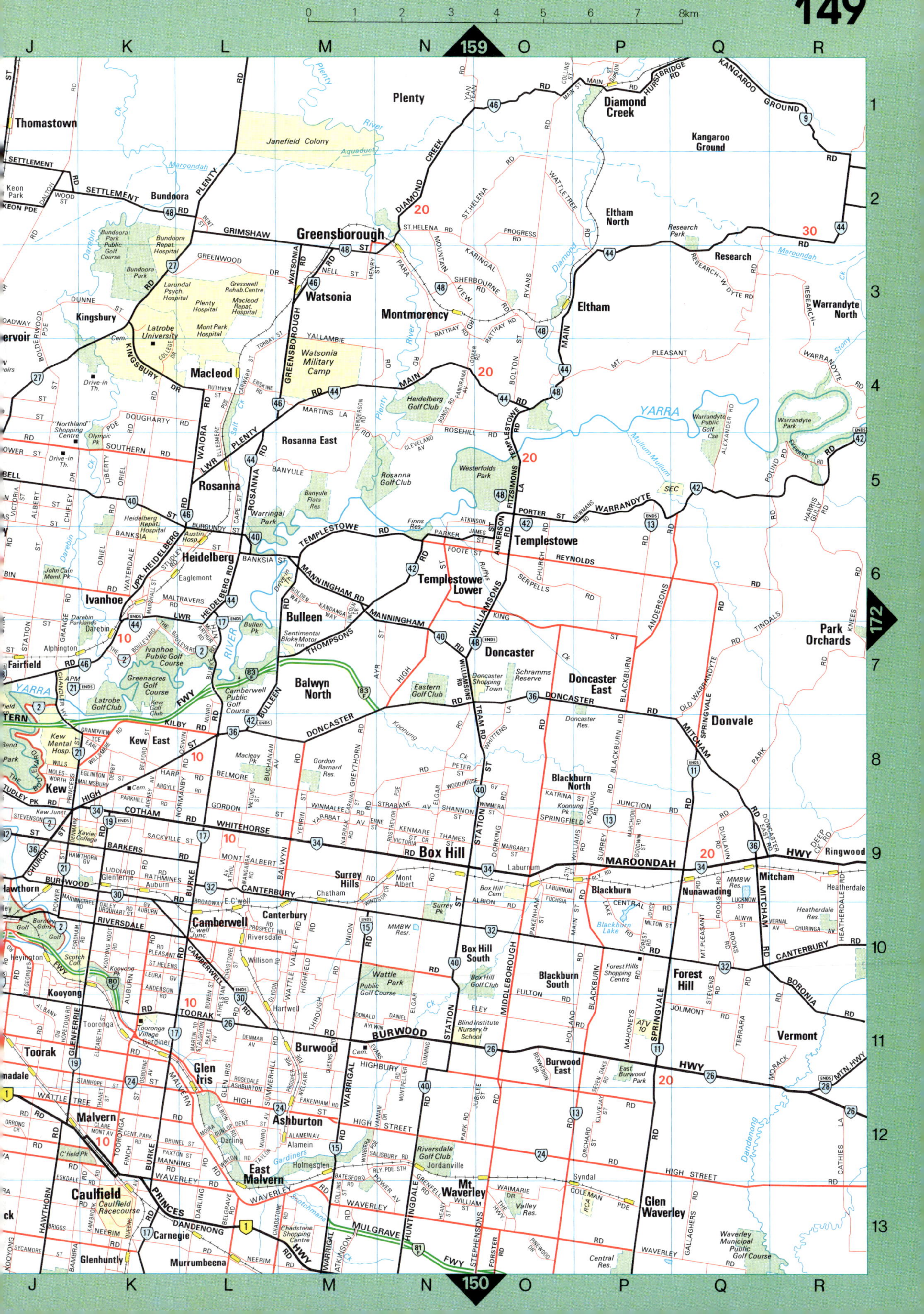
0 1 2 3 4 5 6 7 8km
J K L M N O P Q R
159
150
172
1 2 3 4 5 6 7 8 9 10 11 12 13
Thomastown
Plenty
Janefield Colony
Aquaduct
Diamond Creek
Kangaroo Ground
Keon Park
Bundoora
Bundoora Park Public Golf Course
Bundoora Repat. Hospital
Bundoora Park
Larundal Psych. Hospital
Gresswell Rehab.Centre
Plenty Hospital
Macleod Repat. Hospital
Mont Park Hospital
Kingsbury
Latrobe University
Greensborough
Watsonia
Watsonia Military Camp
Montmorency
Eltham North
Research Park
Research
Eltham
Warrandyte North
Macleod
Rosanna East
Heidelberg Golf Club
Westerfolds Park
Warrandyte Public Golf Cse
Warrandyte Park
Rosanna
Rosanna Golf Club
Banyule Flats Res
Warringal Park
Finns Res
Heidelberg Repat Hospital
Austin Hosp.
Heidelberg
Eaglemont
John Cain Meml. Pk
Templestowe
Templestowe Lower
Ivanhoe
Darebin Parklands
Darebin
Alphington
Fairfield
Bulleen
Bulleen Pk
Sentimental Bloke Motor Inn
Ivanhoe Public Golf Course
Greenacres Golf Course
Latrobe Golf Club
Kew Golf Club
Camberwell Public Golf Course
Balwyn North
Doncaster
Doncaster Shopping Town
Schramms Reserve
Doncaster East
Eastern Golf Club
Park Orchards
Donvale
Doncaster Res.
Kew Mental Hosp.
Kew East
Macleay Pk
Gordon Barnard Res.
Kew
Xavier College
Blackburn North
Box Hill
Surrey Hills
Mont Albert
Chatham
Laburnum
Blackburn
Nunawading
Mitcham
Ringwood
Heatherdale
Heatherdale Res.
Hawthorn
Glenferrie
Auburn
Canterbury
Camberwell
C'well Junc.
Riversdale
Box Hill Cem
Surrey Pk
MMBW Resr.
Blackburn Lake
Forest Hills Shopping Centre
Forest Hill
Box Hill South
Box Hill Golf Club
Wattle Park
Wattle Park Public Golf Course
Blackburn South
Vermont
Kooyong
Scotch Coll.
Willison
Hartwell
Blind Institute Nursery & School
ATV 10
Toorak
Tooronga
Tooronga Village
Gardiner
Glen Iris
Burwood
Burwood East
East Burwood Park
Malvern
Ashburton
Alamein
Darling
Holmesglen
Riversdale Golf Club
Jordanville
Mt Waverley
Valley Res.
Syndal
Glen Waverley
East Malvern
Caulfield
Caulfield Racecourse
C'field Pk
Carnegie
Chadstone Shopping Centre
Murrumbeena
Glenhuntly
Central Res.
Waverley Municipal Public Golf Course
YARRA
Plenty River
Darebin Ck
Salt Ck
Diamond Ck
Mullum Mullum
Stony Ck
Koonung
Gardiners
Scotchmans
Dandenong
FWY
HWY
MAROONDAH HWY
BURWOOD HWY
PRINCES HWY
DANDENONG RD
MULGRAVE FWY
WARRANDYTE RD
DONCASTER RD
MANNINGHAM RD
TEMPLESTOWE RD
HEIDELBERG RD
WHITEHORSE RD
CANTERBURY RD
RIVERSDALE RD
TOORAK RD
WAVERLEY RD
HIGH STREET RD
SPRINGVALE RD
STATION ST
MIDDLEBOROUGH RD
BLACKBURN RD
GRIMSHAW ST
PLENTY RD
DIAMOND CREEK RD
MAIN RD
FITZSIMONS LA
WILLIAMSONS RD
TRAM RD
BULLEEN RD
BURKE RD
WARRIGAL RD
HUNTINGDALE RD
STEPHENSONS RD
10 20 30

150 Melbourne & Southern Suburbs

0 1 2 3 4 5 6 7 8km
J K L M N O P Q R
172
153
1 2 3 4 5 6 7 8 9 10 11 12 13
Lyndhurst
Lyndhurst South
Dandenong South
Proposed SEC Lyndhurst Terminal Station
Skye North
HASTINGS-DANDENONG RD
FRANKSTON-CRANBOURNE RD
PEARCEDALE RD
Carrum Downs North
Carrum Downs
Skye
Dandenong Sanitary Depot
HAMMOND RD
BANGHOLME RD
MMBW South Eastern Purification Plan
Frankston Sewerage Authority Treatment Works
Dept. of Agriculture Vegetable Research Station
Keith Turnbull Research Station
McCORMICKS RD
WORSLEY RD
McCLELLAND DR
FRANKSTON-DANDENONG RD
Bangholme
Carrum North
THOMPSON RD
Frankston North
Karingal
Karingal Shopping Centre
Lloyd Park
Ballam Park
Langwarrin Reserve
WARRANTYTE RD
LINDRUM RD
ROBINSONS RD
MORNINGTON PENINSULA FWY
FRANKSTON FWY
Chelsea Heights
Patterson River Country Club
Peninsula Country Golf Club
Long Island Golf Club
Frankston Golf Club
State Rivers & Water Supply Comm.
Frankston Reservoir
FRANKSTON-FLINDERS RD
NEPEAN HWY
Aspendale
Edithvale
Chelsea
Bonbeach
Carrum
Seaford
Seaford South
Frankston
Rossdale Golf Club
Chelsea Public Golf Course
Olivers Hill
Daveys Bay
Pelican Point
Canadian Bay
Toorak College
OLD MORNINGTON RD
Mt.Eliza
PORT PHILLIP BAY
N

152 The Mornington Peninsula and Westernport

153

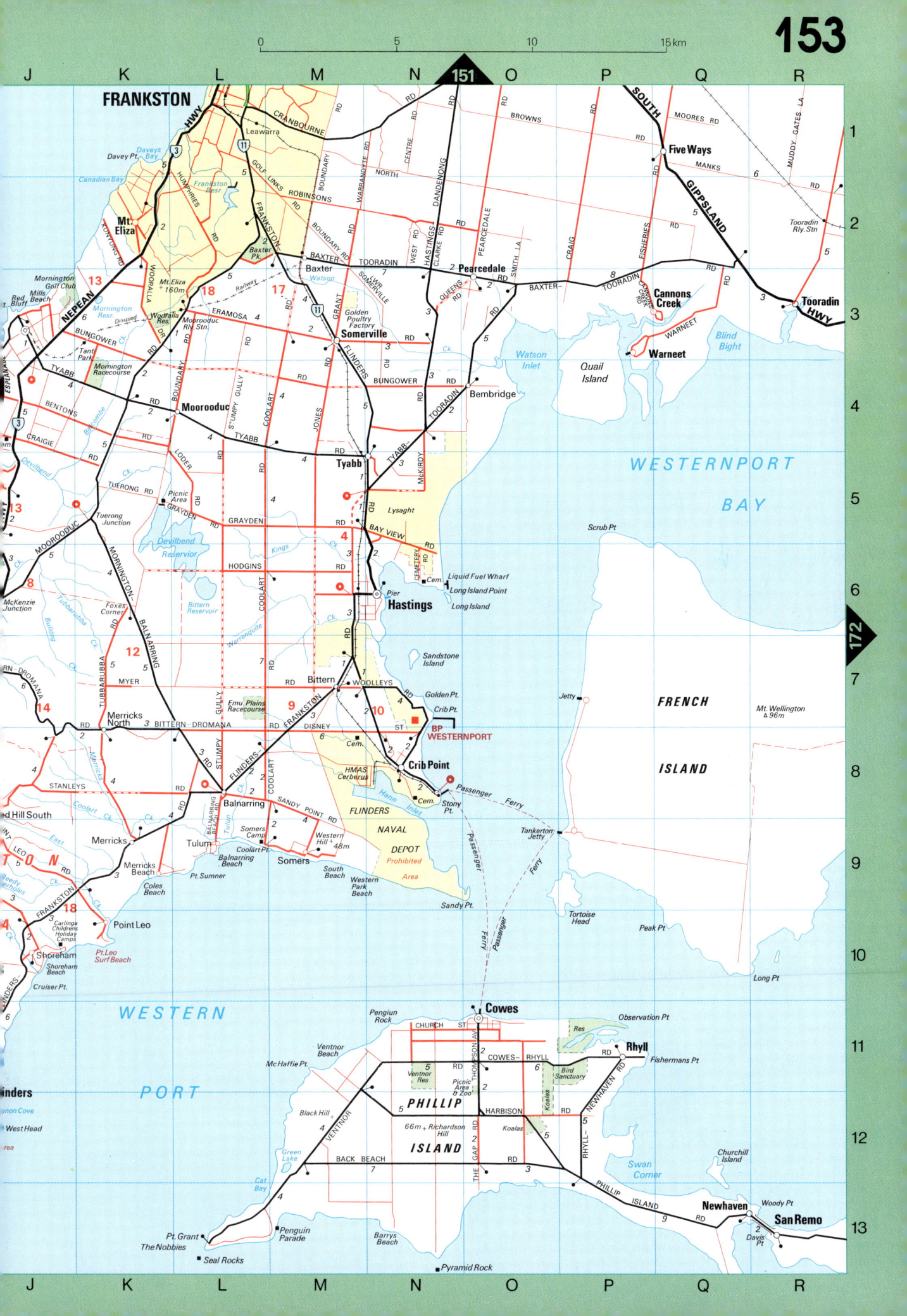

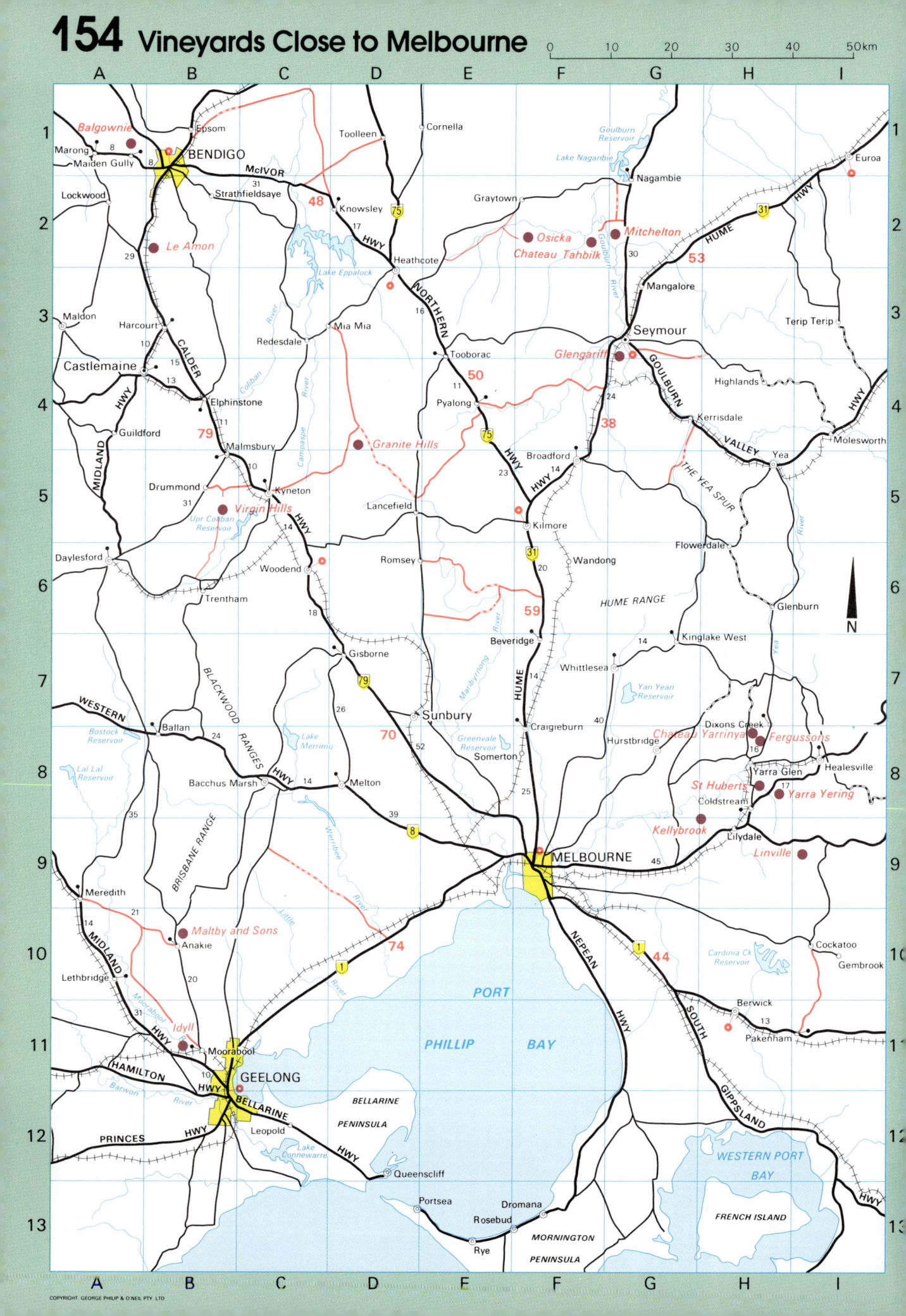

154 Vineyards Close to Melbourne

The Bellarine Peninsula & Great Ocean Road 155

156 Geelong

Places of Interest
1. Barwon Grange E10
2. The Heights C9
3. Geelong Railway Station E8
4. Hospital F9
5. Memorial Art Gallery F9
6. Police Station F9
7. Post Office E9
8. RACV Branch Office E9
9. Tourist Bureau E9
10. Town Hall E9

Ballarat 157

Places of Interest

1. Ballarat Base Hospital D6
2. Ballarat Fine Art Gallery E6
3. Ballarat Railway Station E6
4. Eureka Stockade H6
5. Historical Museum F6
6. Montrose Cottage and Museum F6
7. Old Curiosity Shop G6
8. Police Station E6
9. Post Office E6
10. RACV Branch Office E6
11. Regional Tourist Information Office . E6
12. Sovereign Hill Historical Park F8
13. Town Hall E6

158 Tours from Melbourne

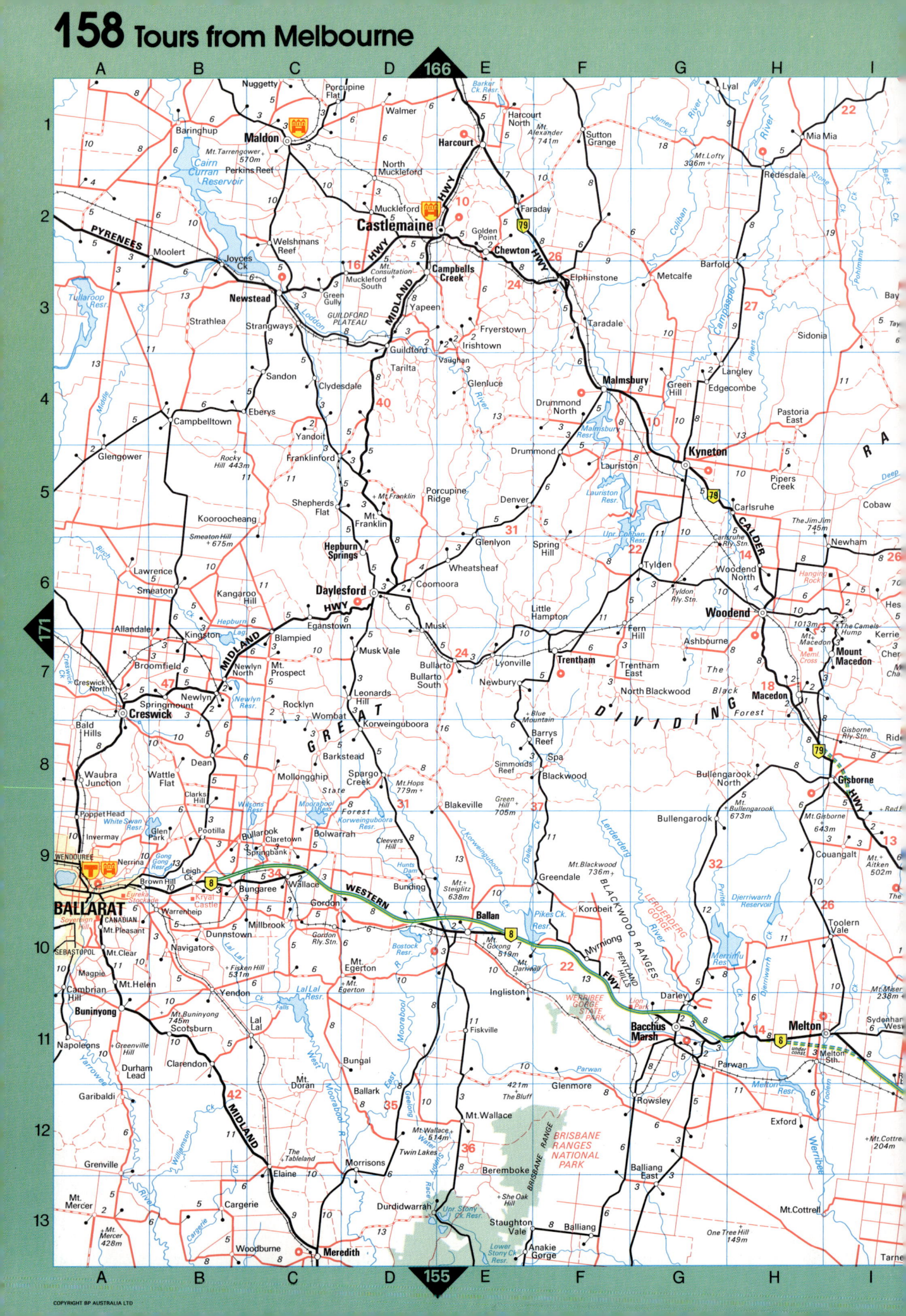

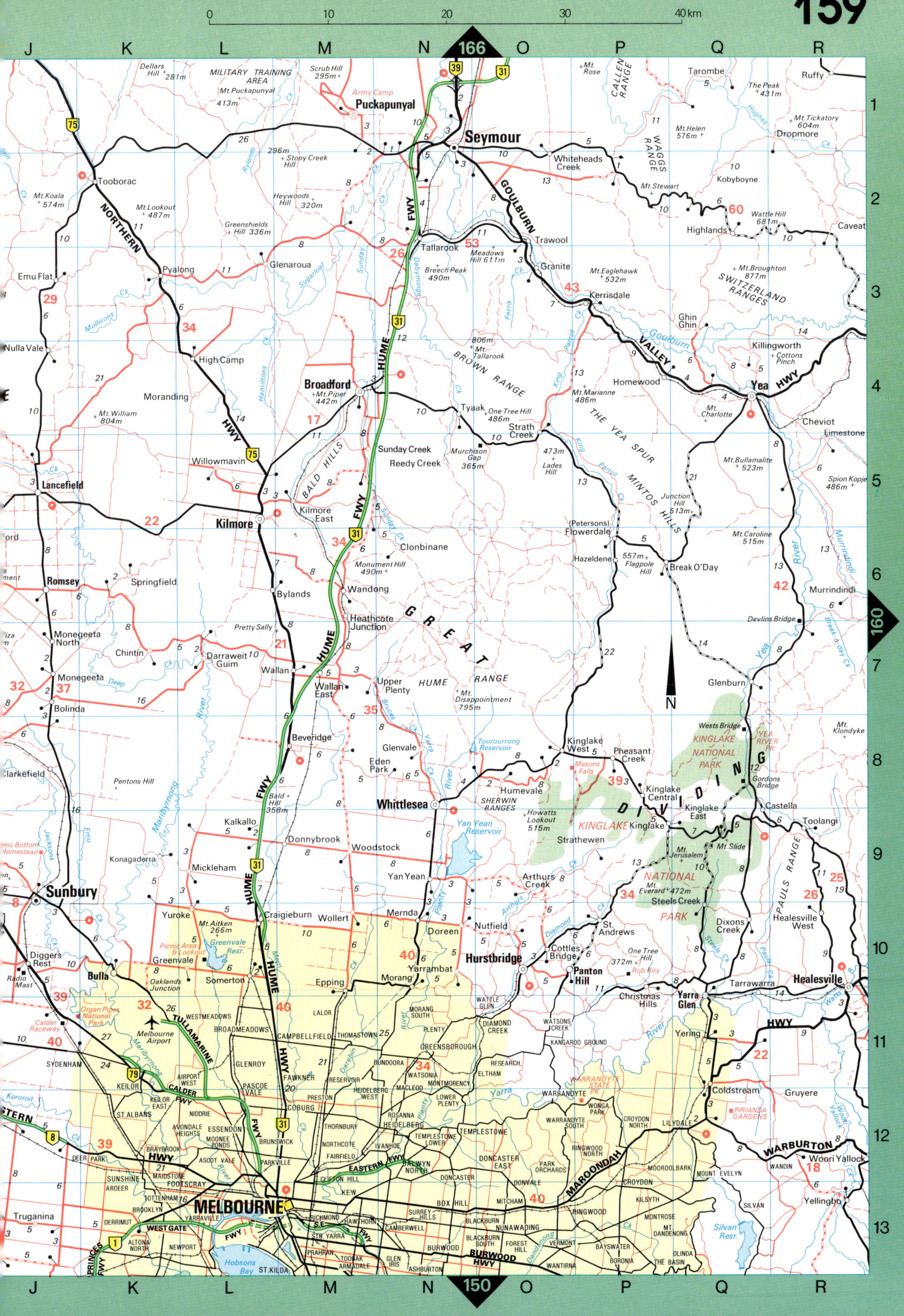

0 10 20 30 40 km
J K L M N O P Q R
1 2 3 4 5 6 7 8 9 10 11 12 13
166
160
150
MILITARY TRAINING AREA
Dellars Hill 281m
Mt.Puckapunyal 413m
Scrub Hill 295m
Army Camp
Puckapunyal
Seymour
Mt. Rose
CALLEN RANGE
Tarombe
Ruffy
The Peak 431m
Mt.Tickatory 604m
Dropmore
Mt.Helen 576m
WAGGS RANGE
Whiteheads Creek
Kobyboyne
Mt.Stewart
Wattle Hill 681m
Highlands
Caveat
Tooborac
Mt.Koala 574m
NORTHERN
Mt.Lookout 487m
Stony Creek Hill
296m
Heywoods Hill 320m
Greenshields Hill 336m
GOULBURN
Trawool
Tallarook
Meadows Hill 611m
Breech Peak 490m
Granite
Mt.Eaglehawk 532m
Mt.Broughton 877m
SWITZERLAND RANGES
Kerrisdale
Emu Flat
Pyalong
Glenaroua
Sugarloaf
Mollisons
Nulla Vale
High Camp
806m Mt. Tallarook
BROWN RANGE
VALLEY
Goulburn
Ghin Ghin
Killingworth
Cottons Pinch
Homewood
Yea
HWY
Mt.Marianne 486m
THE YEA SPUR
Mt. Charlotte
Cheviot
Limestone
Moranding
Mt.William 804m
Broadford
Mt.Piper 442m
HUME
Tyaak
One Tree Hill 486m
Strath Creek
473m Lades Hill
Mt.Bullamalite 523m
Spion Kopje 486m
Willowmavin
BALD HILLS
Sunday Creek
Reedy Creek
Murchison Gap 365m
MINTOS HILLS
Junction Hill 513m
Lancefield
Kilmore
Kilmore East
FWY
(Petersons) Flowerdale
Clonbinane
Hazeldene
557m Flagpole Hill
Break O'Day
Mt.Caroline 515m
Romsey
Springfield
Monument Hill 490m
Wandong
Murrindindi
Bylands
GREAT
Heathcote Junction
Devlins Bridge
Monegeeta North
Pretty Sally
Chintin
Darraweit Guim
Wallan
Monegeeta
Deep
Wallan East
Upper Plenty
HUME RANGE
Mt. Disappointment 795m
Glenburn
Bolinda
N
Wests Bridge
KINGLAKE NATIONAL PARK
YEA RIVER PK
Mt. Klondyke
Beveridge
Glenvale
Toorourrong Reservoir
Kinglake West
Pheasant Creek
Clarkefield
Pentons Hill
Eden Park
Masons Falls
Gordons Bridge
Humevale
Kinglake Central
DIVIDING
Whittlesea
SHERWIN RANGES
Castella
Bald Hill 358m
Howatts Lookout 515m
Kinglake East
Kalkallo
Yan Yean Reservoir
KINGLAKE
Kinglake
Toolangi
Donnybrook
Strathewen
Woodstock
Mt.Slide
Emu Bottom Homestead
Konagaderra
Mickleham
Yan Yean
Mt. Jerusalem
PAULS RANGE
NATIONAL
Arthurs Creek
Mt. Everard 472m
Sunbury
Steels Creek
Healesville West
PARK
Yuroke
Craigieburn
Wollert
Mernda
Nutfield
St. Andrews
Dixons Creek
Mt.Aitken 266m
Doreen
Diamond
Picnic Area & Lookout
Greenvale Resr.
Diggers Rest
Greenvale
Yarrambat
Hurstbridge
Cottles Bridge
One Tree Hill 372m
Radio Mast
Bulla
Oaklands Junction
Somerton
Epping
Morang
Panton Hill
Rob Roy
Tarrawarra
Healesville
Christmas Hills
Yarra Glen
Organ Pipes National Park
TULLAMARINE
WESTMEADOWS
LALOR
MORANG SOUTH
WATTLE GLEN
Calder Raceway
Melbourne Airport
BROADMEADOWS
CAMPBELLFIELD
THOMASTOWN
PLENTY
DIAMOND CREEK
WATSONS CREEK
Yering
KANGAROO GROUND
GREENSBOROUGH
SYDENHAM
GLENROY
BUNDOORA
RESEARCH
ELTHAM
AIRPORT WEST
WATSONIA
MONTMORENCY
WARRANDYTE STATE PK
KEILOR
CALDER
FAWKNER
RESERVOIR
PASCOE VALE
MACLEOD
HEIDELBERG WEST
LOWER PLENTY
WARRANDYTE
Coldstream
Gruyere
Kororoit
KEILOR EAST
NIDDRIE
PRESTON
COBURG
ROSANNA
WONGA PARK
PIRIANDA GARDENS
ST.ALBANS
AVONDALE HEIGHTS
ESSENDON
THORNBURY
HEIDELBERG
TEMPLESTOWE
WARRANDYTE SOUTH
CROYDON NORTH
LILYDALE
MOONEE PONDS
BRUNSWICK
NORTHCOTE
TEMPLESTOWE LOWER
RINGWOOD NORTH
BRAYBROOK
ASCOT VALE
IVANHOE
FAIRFIELD
EASTERN
BALWYN NORTH
DONCASTER EAST
PARK ORCHARDS
MAROONDAH
MOOROOLBARK
WARBURTON
Woori Yallock
DEER PARK
PARKVILLE
SUNSHINE
MAIDSTONE
FOOTSCRAY
CLIFTON HILL
DONCASTER
DONVALE
MOUNT EVELYN
WANDIN
ARDEER
KEW
CROYDON
TOTTENHAM
MELBOURNE
BOX HILL
MITCHAM
RINGWOOD
KILSYTH
SILVAN
Yellingbo
Truganina
BROOKLYN
SURREY HILLS
MONTROSE
DERRIMUT
YARRAVILLE
RICHMOND
HAWTHORN
CAMBERWELL
BLACKBURN
NUNAWADING
MT DANDENONG
Silvan Resr.
WEST GATE
S.E.
STH YARRA
BLACKBURN SOUTH
FOREST HILL
VERMONT
BAYSWATER
ALTONA NORTH
NEWPORT
PRAHRAN
TOORAK
ARMADALE
BURWOOD
Dandenong
BORONIA
OLINDA
Hobsons Bay
ST.KILDA
GLEN IRIS
ASHBURTON
WANTIRNA
THE BASIN
PRINCES FWY

160 Lake Eildon & Southern Ranges

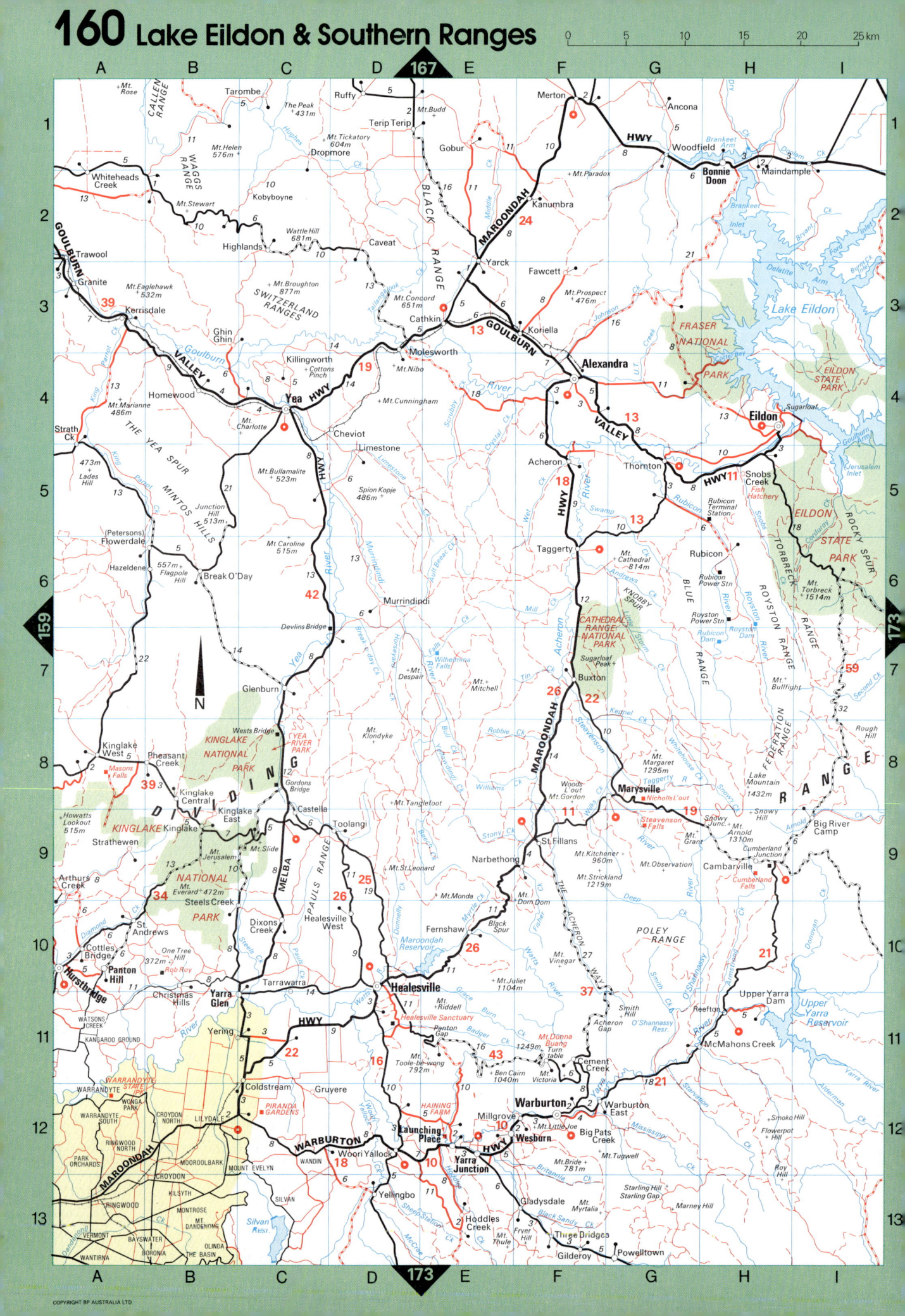

Wilsons Promontory National Park 161

162 North Western Victoria

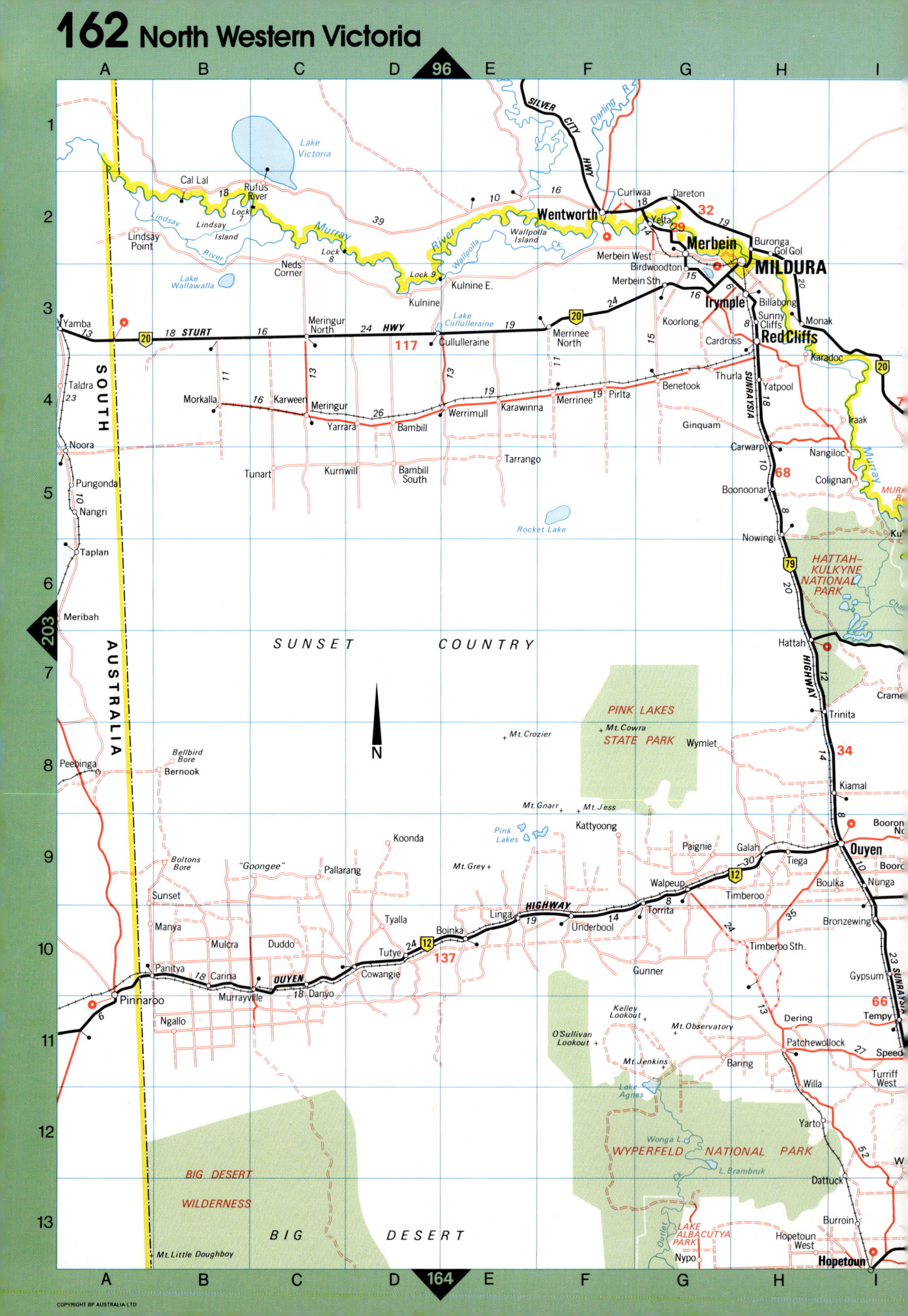

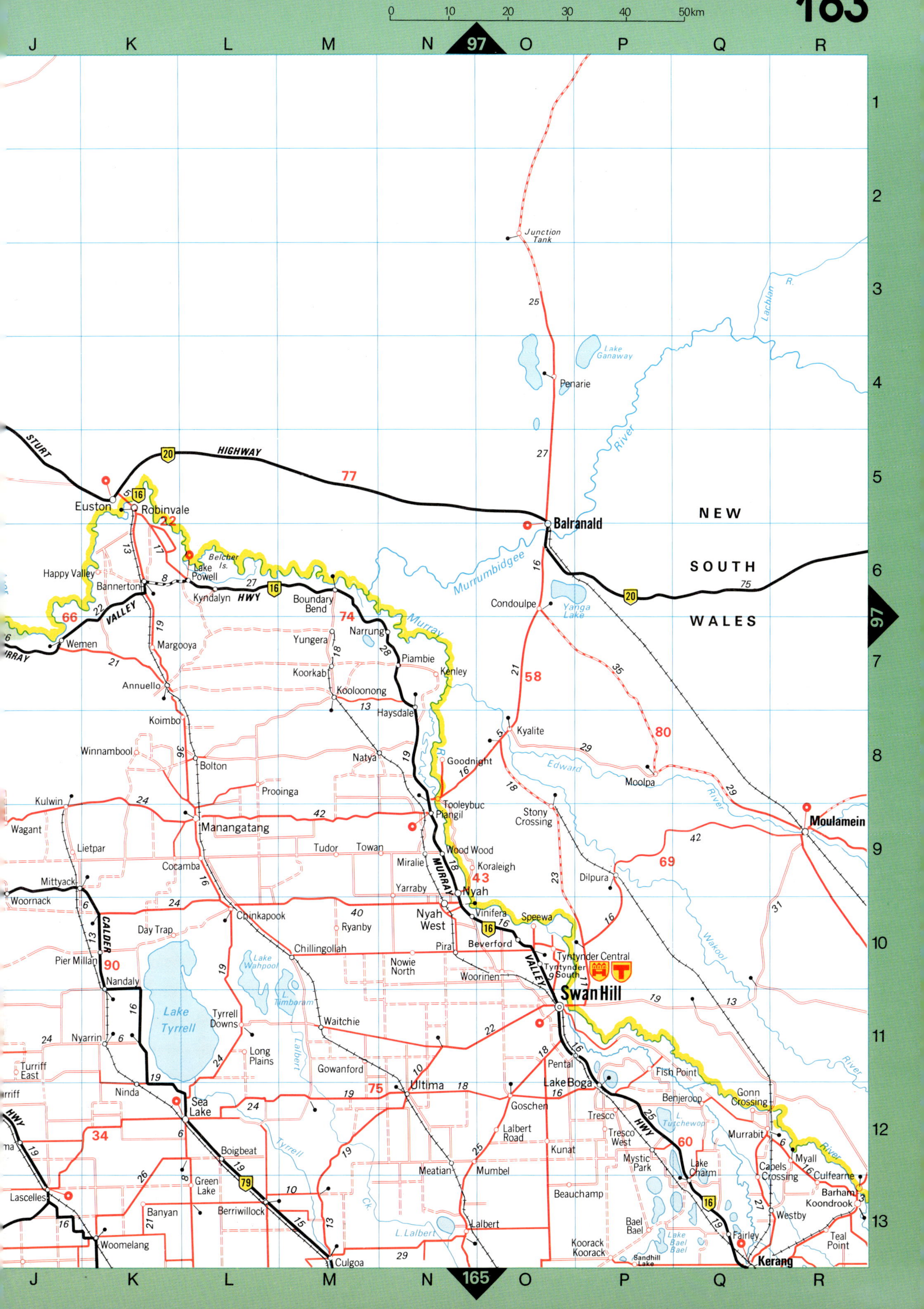

0 10 20 30 40 50km
J K L M N O P Q R
97
165
1 2 3 4 5 6 7 8 9 10 11 12 13
NEW SOUTH WALES
STURT HIGHWAY
20
77
Junction Tank
25
Lake Ganaway
Penarie
27
River
Lachlan R.
Euston
Robinvale
16
22
Balranald
Belcher Is.
Lake Powell
Happy Valley
Bannerton
Kyndalyn HWY
27
Boundary Bend
Murrumbidgee
16
Condoulpe
Yanga Lake
75
66
VALLEY
Wemen
MURRAY
Margooya
Yungera
74
Narrung
Murray
Piambie
Kenley
21
58
35
Koorkab
Kooloonong
Annuello
Haysdale
13
Koimbo
Kyalite
80
Winnambool
Natya
Goodnight
Edward
Moolpa
Bolton
Prooinga
Kulwin
Tooleybuc
Piangil
Stony Crossing
Moulamein
Wagant
Manangatang
42
Lietpar
Tudor
Towan
Wood Wood
Miralie
Koraleigh
43
69
Cocamba
Mittyack
Yarraby
Nyah
Dilpura
Woornack
Chinkapook
Vinifera
Speewa
Nyah West
Ryanby
CALDER
Day Trap
Beverford
Pira
Wakool
Pier Millan
90
Chillingollah
Tyntynder Central
Tyntynder South
Nowie North
Nandaly
Lake Wahpool
Woorinen
Swan Hill
L. Timboram
Lake Tyrrell
Tyrrell Downs
Waitchie
Nyarrin
Lalbert
Long Plains
Turriff East
Gowanford
Pental
Fish Point
Lake Boga
Ninda
Ultima
75
Goschen
Gonn Crossing
Benjeroop
Sea Lake
Tresco
L. Tutchewop
Tresco West
Murrabit
34
Lalbert Road
Kunat
60
Boigbeat
Tyrrell
Mystic Park
Lake Charm
Myall
Capels Crossing
Culfearne
Green Lake
Meatian
Mumbel
Barham
Koondrook
Lascelles
Beauchamp
Westby
Banyan
Berriwillock
Bael Bael
Woomelang
L. Lalbert
Lalbert
Lake Bael Bael
Fairley
Teal Point
Koorack Koorack
Culgoa
Sandhill Lake
Kerang
HWY

164 The Wimmera

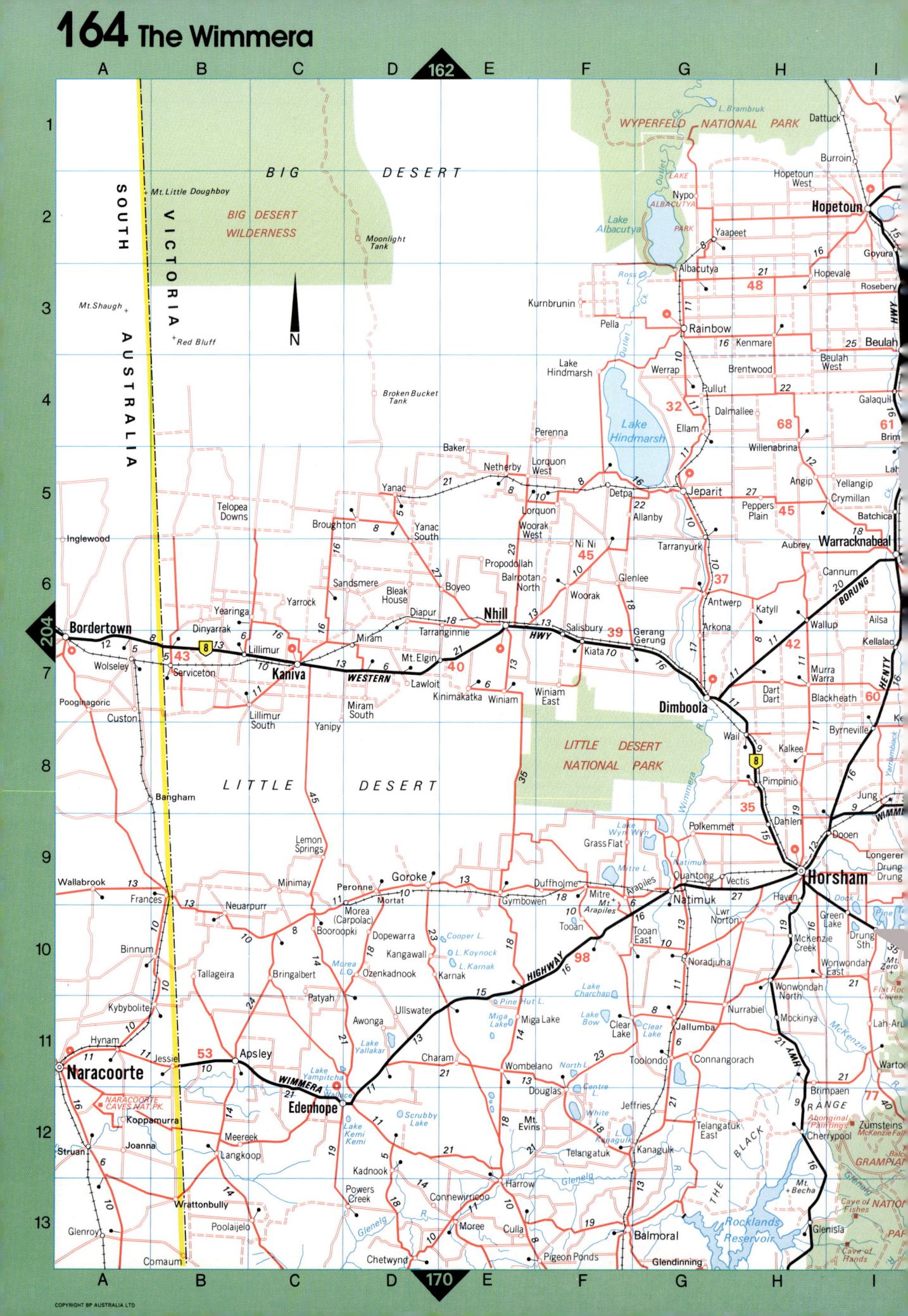

165

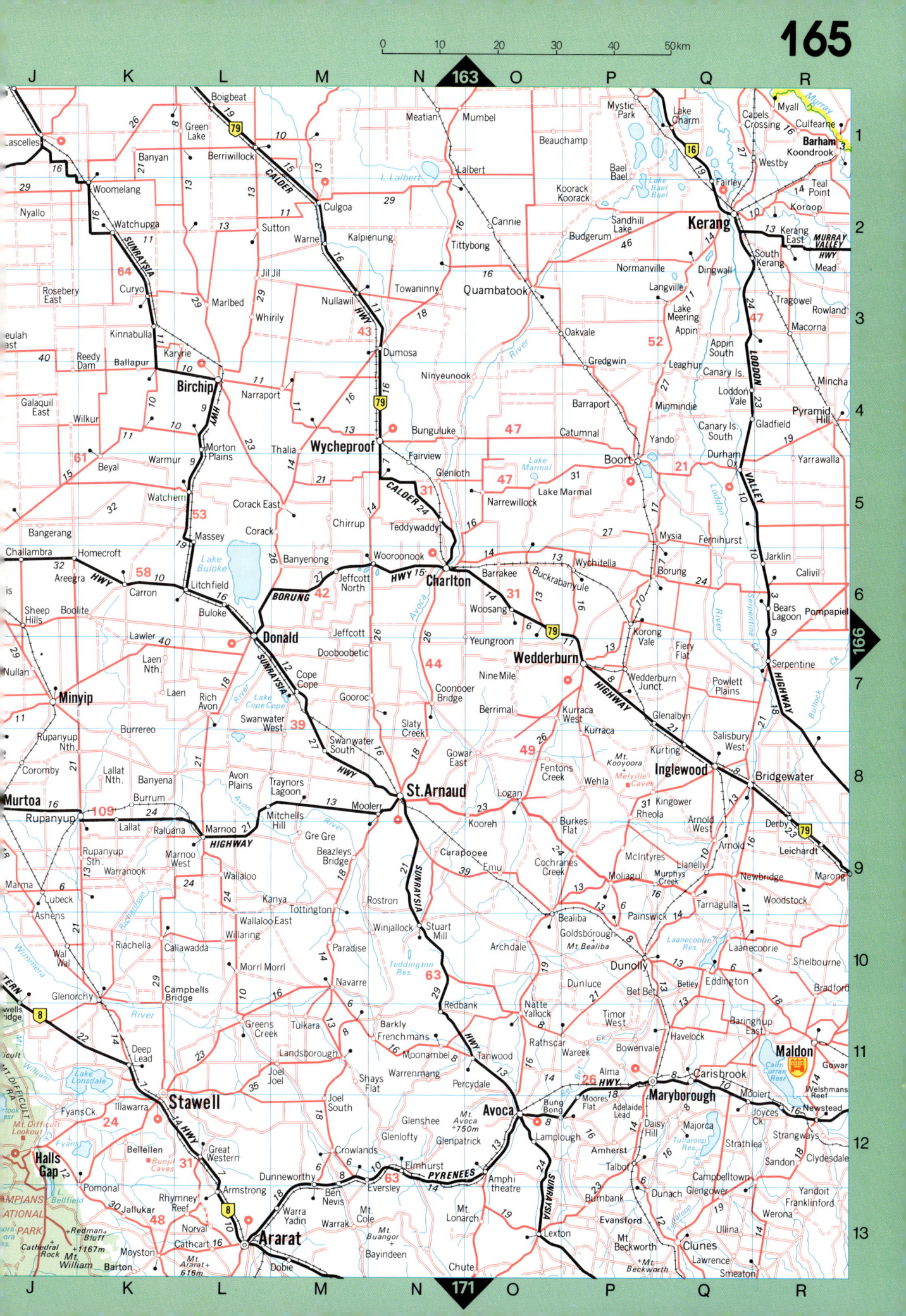

166 North Central Victoria

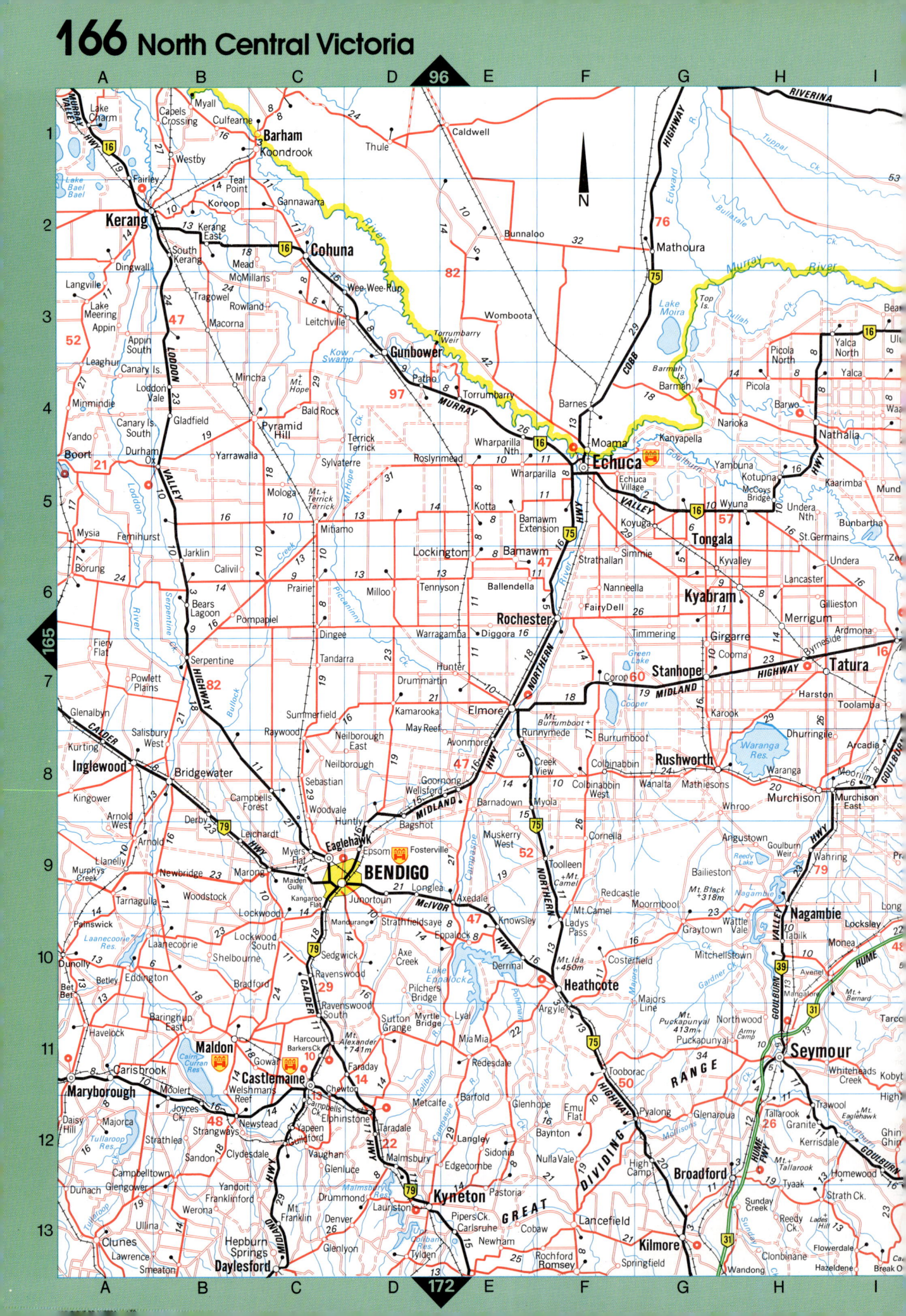

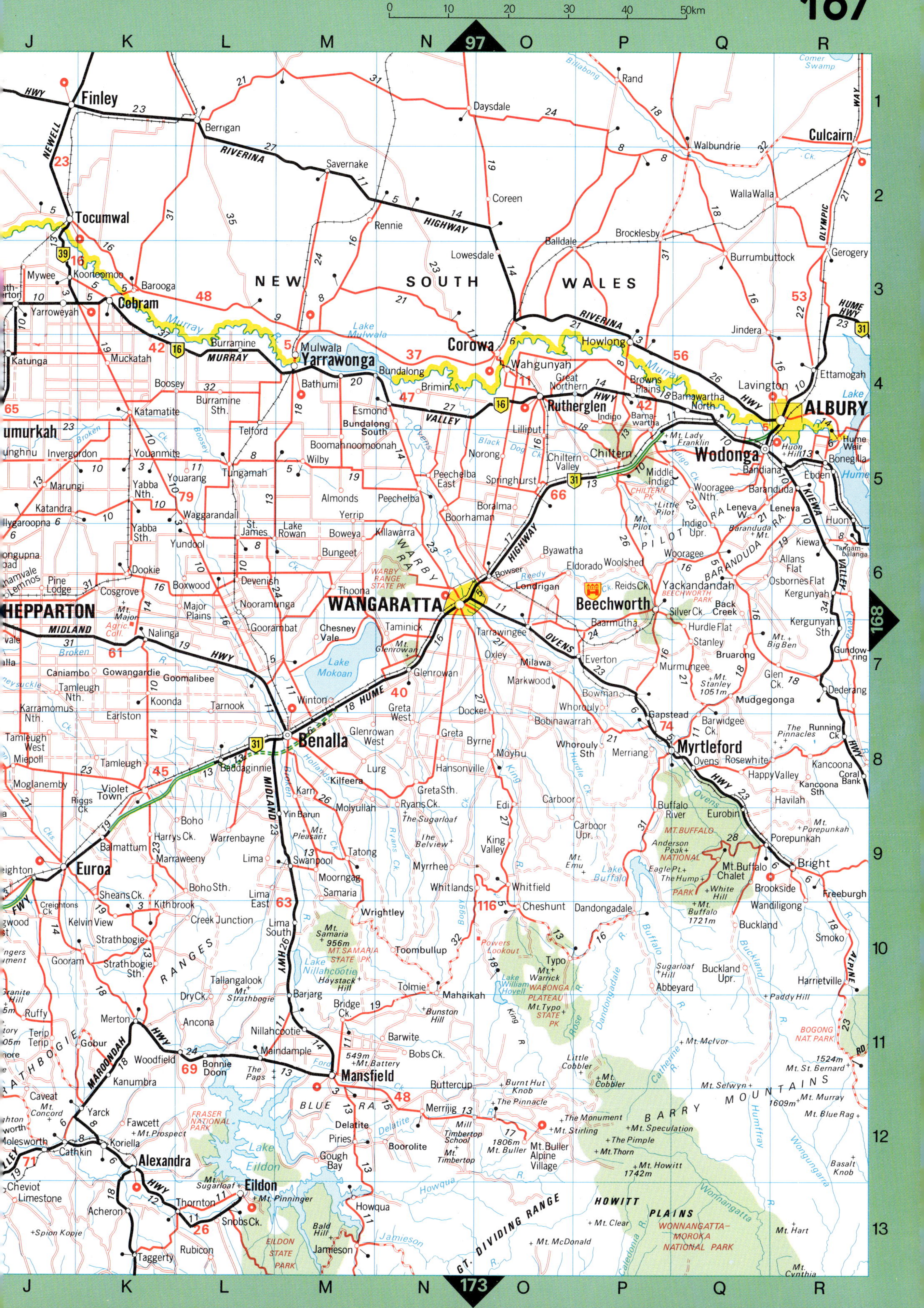
0 10 20 30 40 50km
J
K
L
M
N
97
O
P
Q
R
NEW SOUTH WALES
Finley
Berrigan
Daysdale
Rand
Walbundrie
Culcairn
RIVERINA
Savernake
Coreen
Walla Walla
Tocumwal
Rennie
HIGHWAY
Lowesdale
Brocklesby
Balldale
Burrumbuttock
Gerogery
OLYMPIC
Mywee
Koonoomoo
Barooga
Cobram
Yarroweyah
Katunga
Muckatah
MURRAY
Burramine
Mulwala
Yarrawonga
Lake Mulwala
Bundalong
Corowa
Wahgunyah
Howlong
Jindera
HUME HWY
Lavington
Ettamogah
ALBURY
Bathumi
Boosey
Burramine Sth.
Katamatite
Telford
Esmond
Bundalong South
Brimin
VALLEY
Rutherglen
Great Northern
Browns Plains
Barnawartha North
Barnawartha
Indigo
Wodonga
Chiltern
Mt. Lady Franklin
Huon Hill
Hume Weir
Bonegilla
Bandiana
Barandudu
Ebden
Numurkah
Invergordon
Youanmite
Yabba Nth.
Youarang
Tungamah
Wilby
Boomahnoomoonah
Lilliput
Norong
Chiltern Valley
Middle Indigo
Wooragee Nth.
Leneva
Marungi
Katandra
Waggarandall
St. James
Lake Rowan
Almonds
Peechelba
Peechelba East
Springhurst
Boralma
Boorhaman
Yerrip
Boweya
Bungeet
Killawarra
Yabba Sth.
Yundool
Dookie
Cosgrove
Boxwood
Devenish
Byawatha
Eldorado
Woolshed
Reids Ck.
Yackandandah
Wooragee
Indigo Upr.
Mt. Pilot
PILOT RA.
BARANDUDA RA.
Kiewa
Allans Flat
Osbornes Flat
Kergunyah
Huon
Tangambalanga
SHEPPARTON
Pine Lodge
Mt. Major
Major Plains
Nooramunga
WARBY RANGE STATE PK
Thoona
WANGARATTA
Bowser
Londrigan
Beechworth
BEECHWORTH PARK
Silver Ck.
Back Creek
Hurdle Flat
Stanley
Kergunyah Sth.
Gundowring
MIDLAND
Naringa
Goorambat
Chesney Vale
Taminick
Mt. Glenrowan
Lake Mokoan
Tarrawingee
Oxley
Milawa
OVENS
Everton
Baarmutha
Bruarong
Mt. Big Ben
Caniambo
Gowangardie
Goomalibee
Tamleugh Nth.
Koonda
Tarnook
Winton
Glenrowan
Greta West
Markwood
Whorouly
Bowmans
Murmungee
Mt. Stanley 1051m
Glen Ck.
Mudgegonga
Dederang
Karramomus Nth.
Earlston
Benalla
HUME
Glenrowan West
Greta
Docker
Byrne
Bobinawarrah
Gapstead
Barwidgee Ck.
The Pinnacles
Running Ck
Tamleugh West
Miepoll
Tamleugh
Baddaginnie
Kilfeera
Lurg
Hansonville
Moyhu
Whorouly Sth
Merriang
Myrtleford
Ovens
Rosewhite
Happy Valley
Kancoona
Kancoona Sth
Coral Bank
Moglanemby
Violet Town
Riggs Ck
Karn
Molyullah
Greta Sth.
Ryans Ck.
Edi
Carboor
Buffalo River
Eurobin
Havilah
Boho
Harrys Ck.
Warrenbayne
Yin Barun
Mt. Pleasant
The Sugarloaf
The Belview
King Valley
Carboor Upr.
MT. BUFFALO
Anderson Peak
NATIONAL
Porepunkah
Mt. Porepunkah
Euroa
Balmattum
Marraweeny
Lima
Swanpool
Tatong
Myrrhee
Mt. Emu
Lake Buffalo
Eagle Pt.
The Hump
Mt. Buffalo Chalet
Bright
Brookside
Sheans Ck.
Boho Sth.
Moorngag
Samaria
Whitlands
Whitfield
Cheshunt
Dandongadale
PARK
White Hill
Mt. Buffalo 1721m
Wandiligong
Freeburgh
Creightons Ck
Kithbrook
Creek Junction
Lima East
Lima South
Wrightley
Buckland
Kelvin View
Strathbogie
Gooram
Strathbogie Sth.
RANGES
Mt. Samaria 956m
MT. SAMARIA STATE PK
Toombullup
Powers Lookout
Typo
Mt. Warrick
WABONGA PLATEAU
Mt. Typo STATE PK
Sugarloaf Hill
Abbeyard
Buckland Upr.
Smoko
Harrietville
ALPINE
Granite Hill
Ruffy
Tallangalook
Mt. Strathbogie
Dry Ck.
Lake Nillahcootie
Haystack Hill
Barjarg
Bridge Ck.
Tolmie
Mahaikah
Bunston Hill
Lake William Hovell
Paddy Hill
Merton
Terip Terip
Gobur
Ancona
Nillahcootie
Barwite
Rose
Dandongadale
Buffalo
Catherine
Mt. McIvor
BOGONG NAT. PARK
STRATHBOGIE
MAROONDAH
Woodfield
Bonnie Doon
Maindample
549m Mt. Battery
Bobs Ck.
Little Cobbler
Mt. Cobbler
1524m Mt. St. Bernard
Kanumbra
The Paps
Mansfield
Buttercup
Burnt Hut Knob
The Pinnacle
Mt. Selwyn
MOUNTAINS
1609m Mt. Murray
Mt. Blue Rag
Caveat
Mt. Concord
Yarck
FRASER NATIONAL PARK
BLUE RA.
Merrijig
Fawcett
Mt. Prospect
Delatite
Mill
Timbertop School
Mt. Timbertop
1806m Mt. Buller
Mt. Stirling
The Monument
BARRY
Mt. Speculation
The Pimple
Mt. Thorn
Molesworth
Cathkin
Koriella
Alexandra
Lake Eildon
Pirie
Gough Bay
Boorolite
Alpine Village
Mt. Howitt 1742m
Humffray
Wongungarra
Basalt Knob
Cheviot
Limestone
Mt. Sugarloaf
Eildon
Mt. Pinninger
Thornton
Acheron
Snobs Ck.
Howqua
Bald Hill
HOWITT PLAINS
WONNANGATTA-MOROKA NATIONAL PARK
Wonnangatta
Mt. Clear
Caledonia R.
Mt. Hart
Spion Kopje
Rubicon
Taggerty
EILDON STATE PARK
Jamieson
GT. DIVIDING RANGE
Mt. McDonald
Mt. Cynthia
168
173

168 North Eastern Victoria

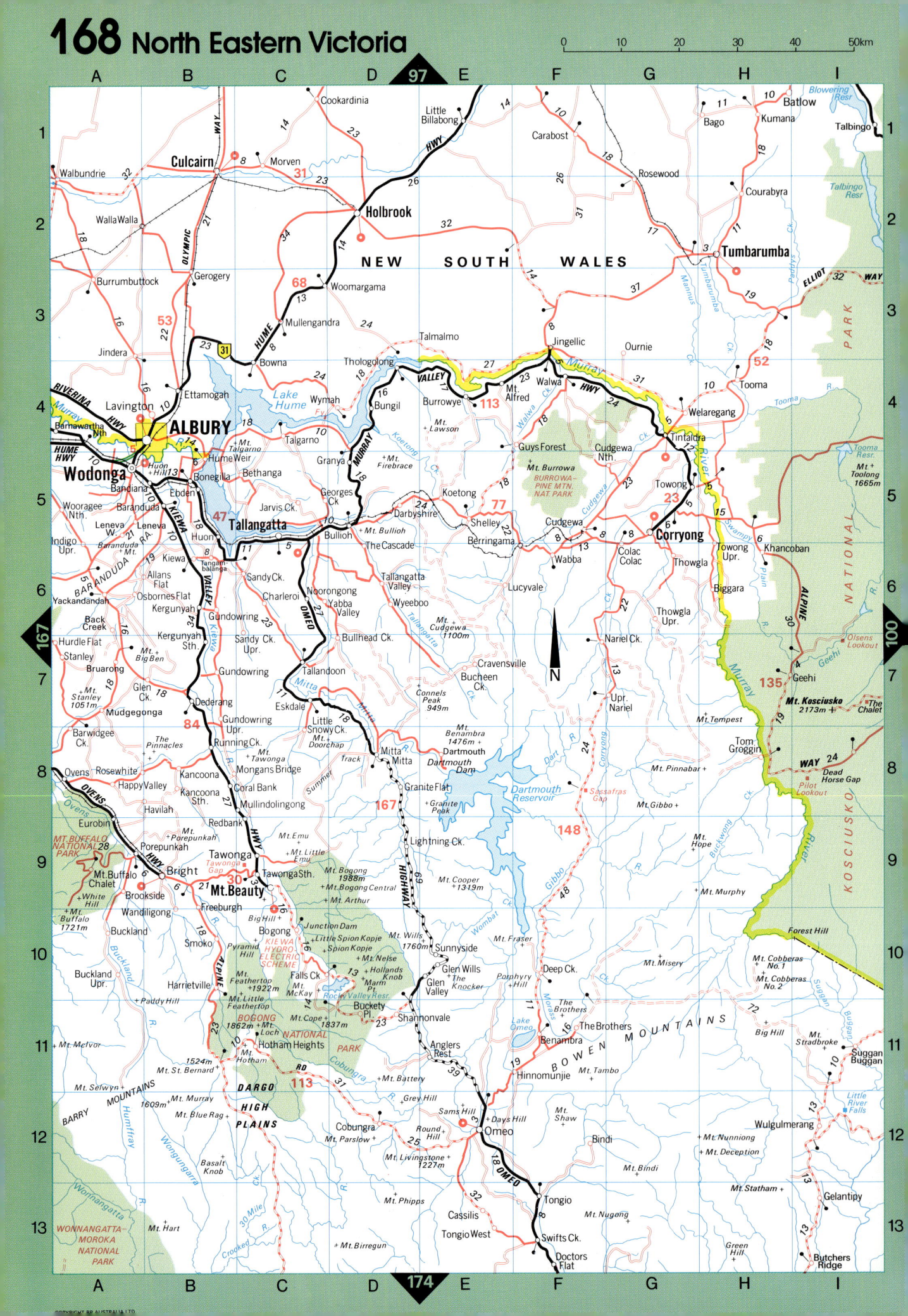

Victorian Alpine Resorts 169

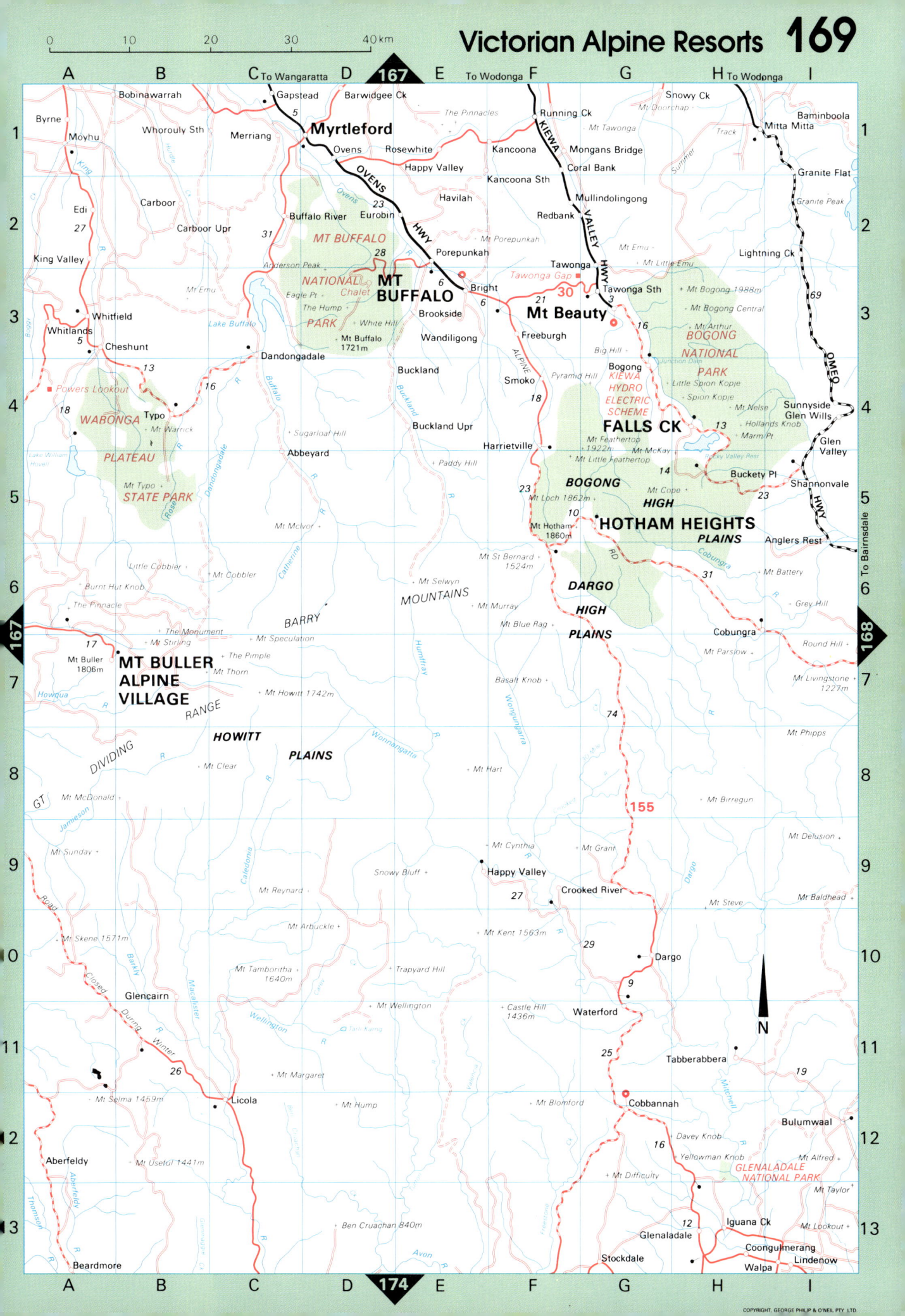

170 South Western Victoria

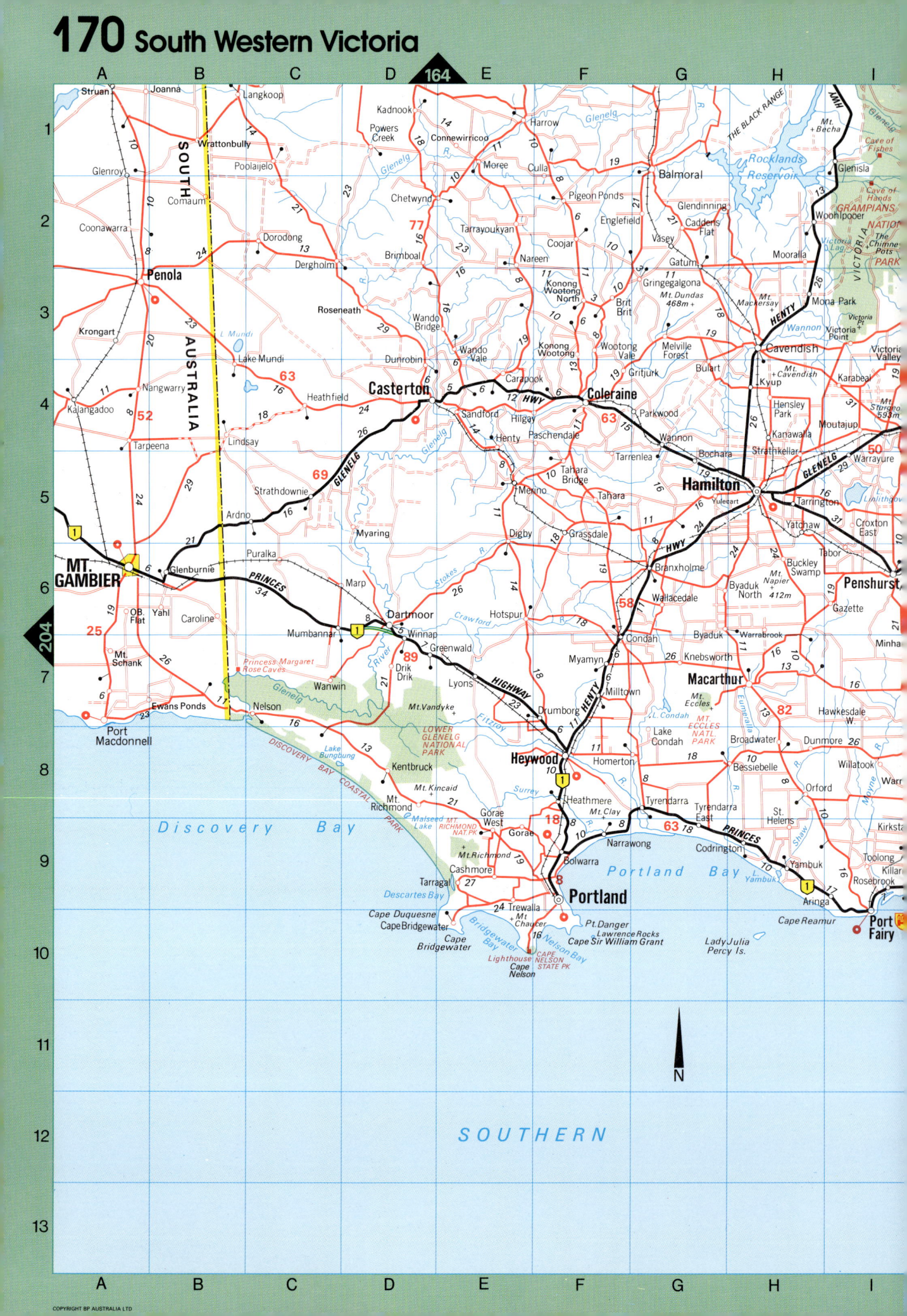

0 10 20 30 40 50km

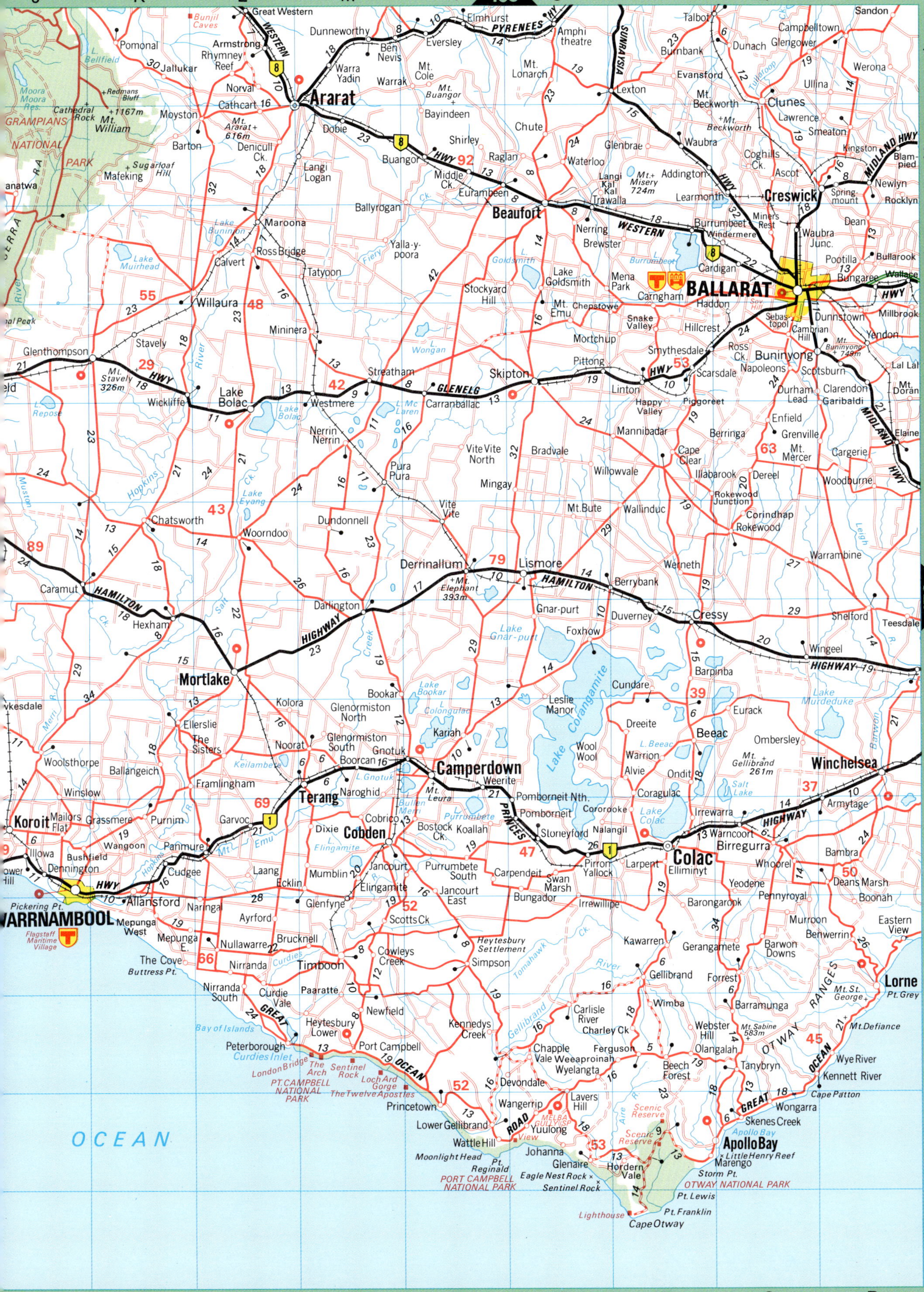

172 South Central Victoria

173

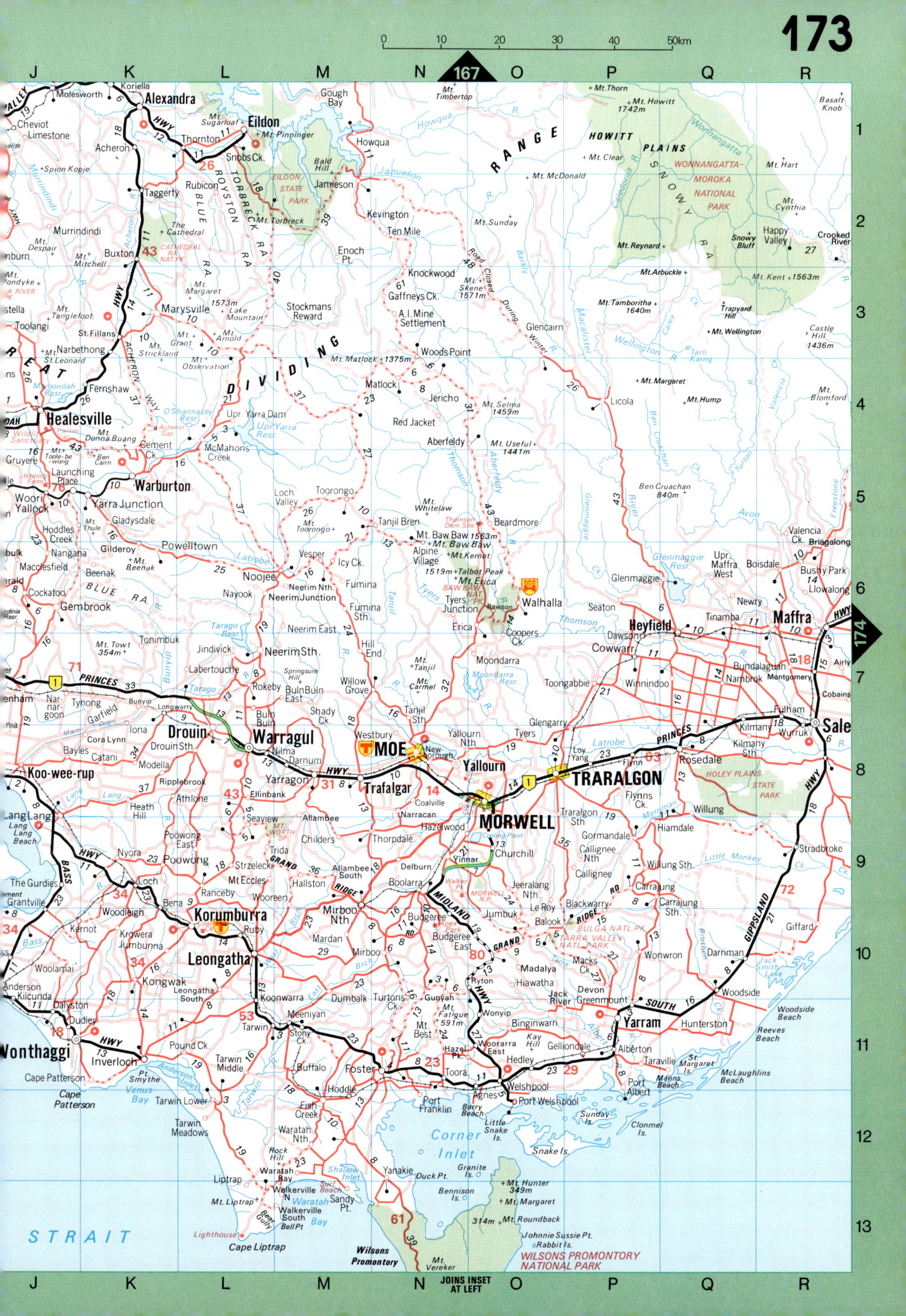

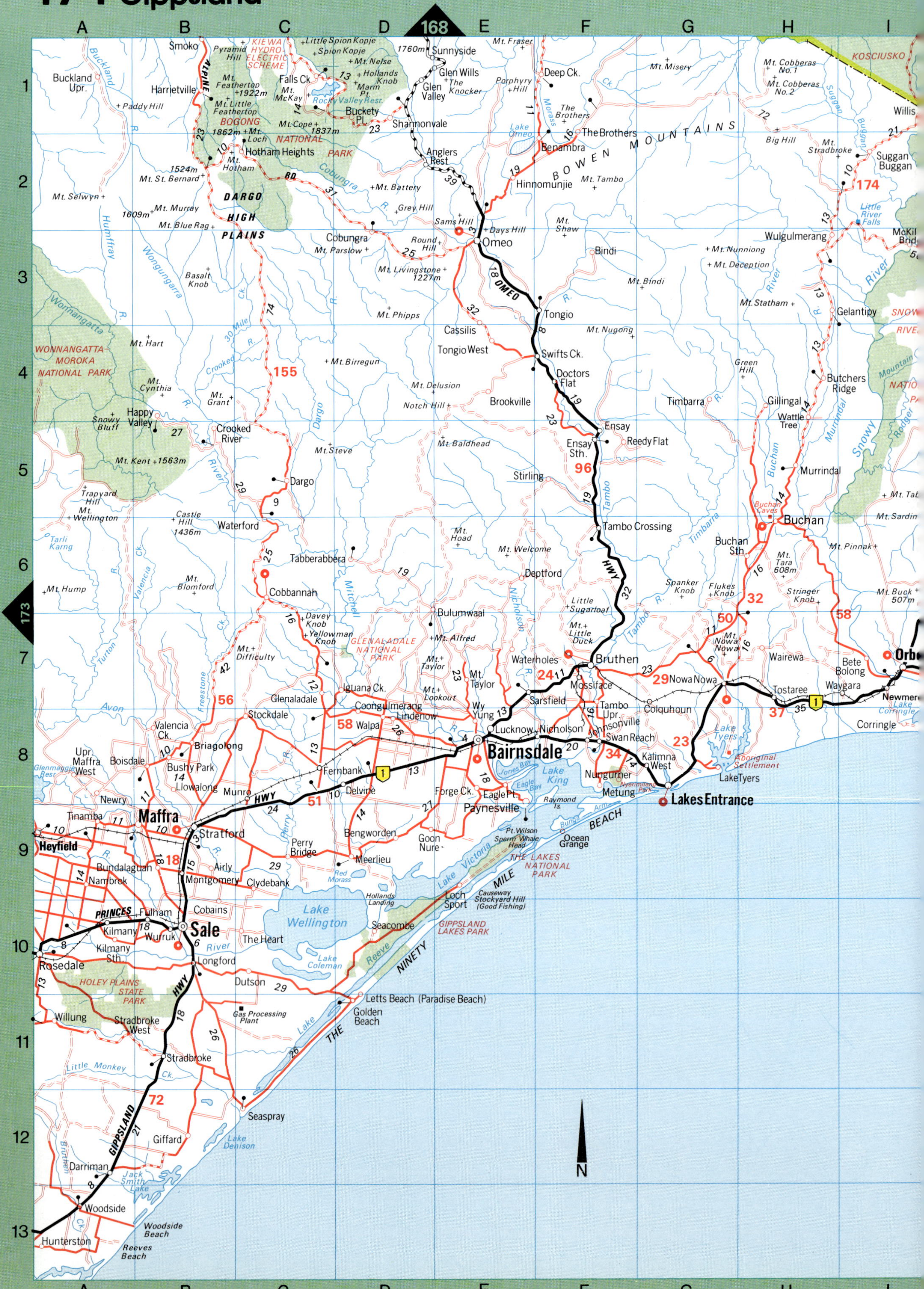

168
173
KOSCIUSKO
Smoko
Pyramid Hill
KIEWA HYDRO ELECTRIC SCHEME
Little Spion Kopje
Spion Kopje
Mt. Nelse
Hollands Knob
Marm Pt.
Rocky Valley Resr.
1760m
Sunnyside
Glen Wills
Glen Valley
The Knocker
Mt. Fraser
Porphyry Hill
Deep Ck.
Mt. Misery
Mt. Cobberas No. 1
Mt. Cobberas No. 2
Willis
Buckland Upr.
Harrietville
ALPINE
Mt. Feathertop +1922m
Mt. Little Feathertop
Falls Ck.
Mt. McKay
Buckety Pl.
Shannonvale
Paddy Hill
BOGONG NATIONAL PARK
1862m
Mt. Loch
Mt. Cope
1837m
Hotham Heights
Mt. Hotham
1524m
Mt. St. Bernard
Anglers Rest
Lake Omeo
Morass
The Brothers
Benambra
BOWEN MOUNTAINS
Big Hill
Mt. Stradbroke
Suggan Buggan
Mt. Selwyn
DARGO HIGH PLAINS
Cobungra
Mt. Battery
Hinnomunjie
Mt. Tambo
174
Little River Falls
1609m
Mt. Murray
Mt. Blue Rag
Grey Hill
Sams Hill
Days Hill
Omeo
Mt. Shaw
Wulgulmerang
McKil Bridge
Cobungra
Mt. Parslow
Round Hill
Bindi
Mt. Nunniong
Mt. Deception
Basalt Knob
Mt. Livingstone 1227m
OMEO
Mt. Bindi
Humffray
Wongungarra
Wonnangatta
Mt. Phipps
Tongio
Mt. Statham
Gelantipy
SNOWY RIVER
Cassilis
Mt. Nugong
Mt. Hart
30 Mile
Tongio West
Swifts Ck.
WONNANGATTA-MOROKA NATIONAL PARK
155
Mt. Birregun
Green Hill
Mountain
Crooked
Mt. Cynthia
Mt. Delusion
Doctors Flat
Butchers Ridge
Mt. Grant
Notch Hill
Brookville
Timbarra
Gillingal
Wattle Tree
Happy Valley
Snowy Bluff
Crooked River
Dargo
Ensay
Reedy Flat
Mt. Baldhead
Ensay Sth.
96
Mt. Steve
Murrindal
Snowy
Mt. Kent 1563m
Stirling
Tambo
Dargo
Trapyard Hill
Mt. Wellington
Castle Hill 1436m
Waterford
Tambo Crossing
Buchan Caves
Buchan
Mt. Tab
Mt. Sardin
Timbarra
Tarli Karng
Mt. Hoad
Mt. Welcome
Buchan Sth.
Mt. Pinnak
Tabberabbera
Mt. Tara 608m
Mt. Hump
Valencia
Mt. Blomford
Cobbannah
Deptford
HWY
Spanker Knob
Flukes Knob
Stringer Knob
Mt. Buck 507m
Mitchell
Nicholson
Little Sugarloaf
32
50
58
Davey Knob
Yellowman Knob
Bulumwaal
Mt. Little Duck
Mt. Nowa Nowa
Turton
Mt. Difficulty
GLENALADALE NATIONAL PARK
Mt. Alfred
Waterholes
Bruthen
Wairewa
Orbost
Mt. Taylor
Mt. Taylor
24
Mossiface
29
Nowa Nowa
Bete Bolong
Freestone
Avon
56
Glenaladale
Iguana Ck.
Mt. Lookout
Sarsfield
Tostaree
Waygara
Newmerella
Lake Corringle
Valencia Ck.
Stockdale
Coongulmerang
Lindenow
Wy Yung
Tambo Upr.
Colquhoun
37
Corringle
58
Walpa
Lucknow
Nicholson
Johnsonville
Lake Tyers
Briagolong
Swan Reach
Upr. Maffra West
Boisdale
Glenmaggie Resr.
Bushy Park
Fernbank
Bairnsdale
34
23
Kalimna West
Aboriginal Settlement
Llowalong
Jones Bay
Lake King
Nungurner
Lake Tyers
Newry
Munro
Delvine
Forge Ck.
Eagle Pt.
Eagle Bay
Metung
Nyerimilang Park
Lakes Entrance
51
Raymond Is.
Tinamba
Maffra
Paynesville
Heyfield
Stratford
Bengworden
Goon Nure
Pt. Wilson
Sperm Whale Head
Bunga Arm
Ocean Grange
BEACH
18
Perry Bridge
Perry
Airly
Meerlieu
Bundalaguah
Nambrok
Montgomery
Clydebank
Red Morass
THE LAKES NATIONAL PARK
MILE
Lake Victoria
Hollands Landing
Loch Sport
Causeway Stockyard Hill (Good Fishing)
Lake Wellington
PRINCES
Fulham
Cobains
Kilmany
Wurruk
Sale
Seacombe
GIPPSLAND LAKES PARK
The Heart
NINETY
Kilmany Sth.
River
Rosedale
Longford
Lake Coleman
Reeve
HOLEY PLAINS STATE PARK
Dutson
HWY
Letts Beach (Paradise Beach)
Golden Beach
Gas Processing Plant
Willung
Stradbroke West
Lake
THE
Stradbroke
Little Monkey
Ck.
72
Seaspray
GIPPSLAND
Giffard
Lake Denison
N
Darriman
Jack Smith Lake
Woodside
Woodside Beach
Hunterston
Reeves Beach
A
B
C
D
E
F
G
H
I
1
2
3
4
5
6
7
8
9
10
11
12
13

175

176 Vineyards of North Eastern Victoria

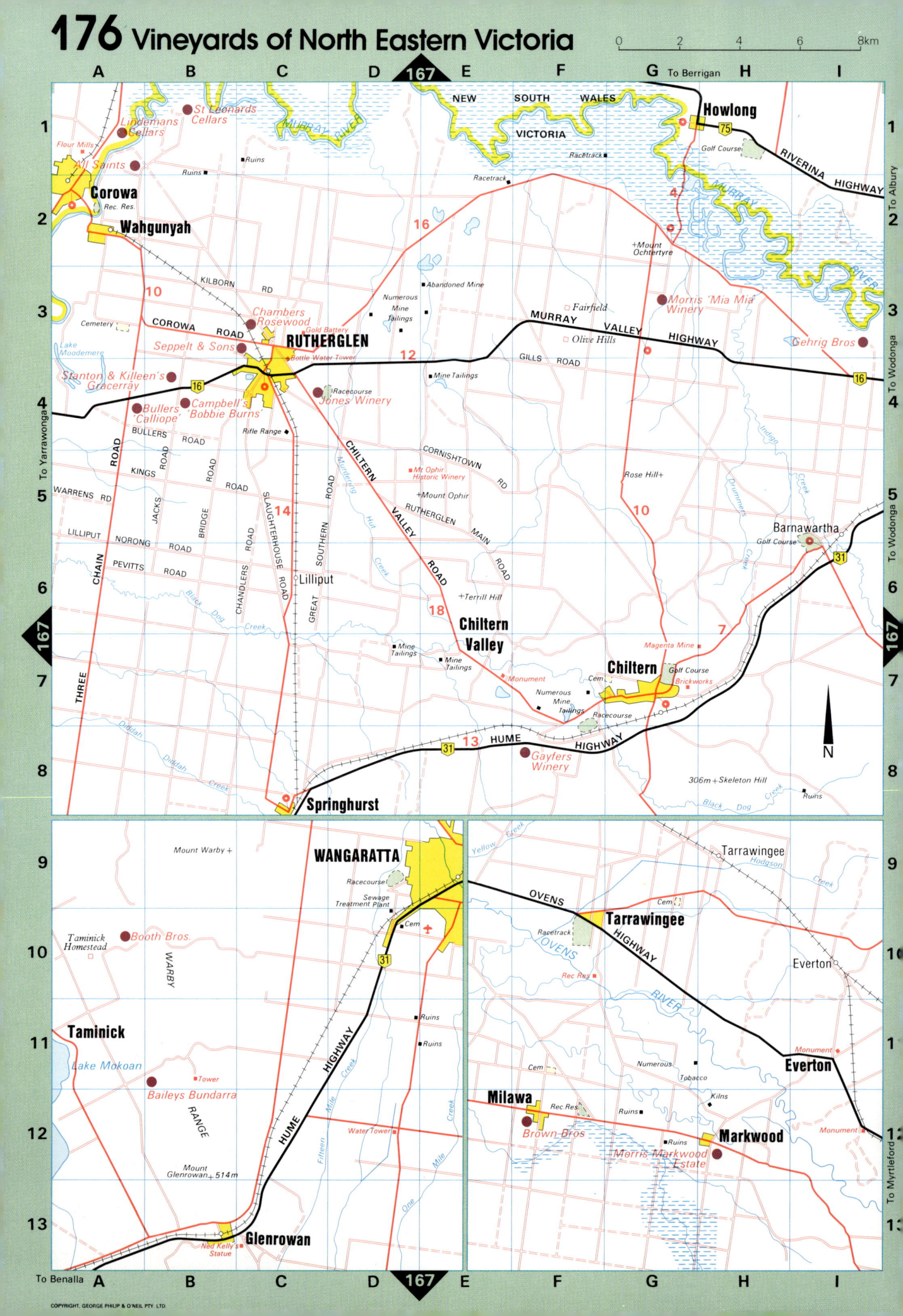

VICTORIA'S WINE REGIONS

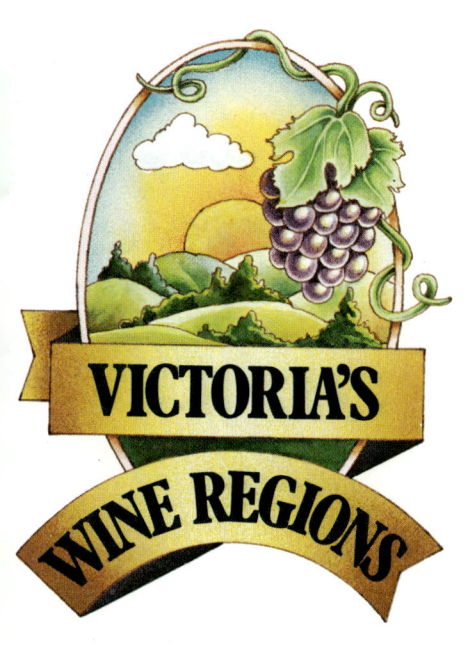

It is more or less by chance that viticulture came to Victoria. In the gold rush years of the 1850s, prospectors who did not strike gold soon found themselves broke and stranded. The European diggers began planting vines as a source of income. Later, two men, Edward Henty and William Rye, brought cuttings to the new colony of Victoria and by 1868 there were more than 1200 hectares of grapes.

The light, dry wines produced in these vineyards won wide acclaim and many gold medals in Europe. At one time, Victoria was looked upon as the future vineyard of the world.

At the end of the last century, the phylloxera mite reduced 14 000 hectares of grapes to just 1350 hectares of weak vines. Vignerons were forced to burn the diseased vines and plant new stocks which were resistant to the disease.

The oldest and most significant wine-growing area in Victoria is found about 270 kilometres north-east of Melbourne, where down-and-out gold diggers first planted their crop. Most of the vineyards in this region are still managed by descendants of the founders. The Rutherglen area is noted for its magnificent wines: top-quality dark reds, superb ports, flor sherries and muscats. Nearby, the Milawa-Glenrowan vineyards produce some distinctive table wines with good body and style. Some of the most famous wineries of Australia are found here: Seppelt's, Lindeman's, Bailey's Bundarra, Booth Brothers, Brown Brothers and All Saints. On the Queen's birthday weekend each June, a winery walkabout is organised for this region so that wine lovers can visit the vineyards and sample some of the fine wines of the north-east.

At the far north-west corner of Victoria, 500 kilometres from Melbourne, are the Mildura-Robinvale vineyards irrigated by the Murray River. The most noted winery here is Mildara, famed for its brandy, for its flor sherry which follows the true Spanish pattern and for its blended Cabernet-Shiraz.

About 200 kilometres west of Melbourne, between Stawell and Ararat, is the little town of Great Western which has given its name to some very fine wines, including the champagne-style Great Western Special Reserve from the House of Seppelt. Dating back to the 1860s, Great Western wineries have produced leading sparkling wines for Australia. Best's winery was also founded in the years following the gold rush, when ex-miners dug underground drives where, today, millions of bottles of champagne are left to mature. The vineyards of Great Western are also noted for their rich red and full-flavoured white table wines. To the south, newer plantations are found at Avoca, which is famous for its brandy, and Drumborg, which specialises in grapes for champagne.

The rich river flats of the Goulburn Valley are ideal for the production of fine table wines. This is one of the most picturesque regions of all Australian vineyards, located just 122 kilometres from Melbourne. The century-old cellars of the Chateau Tahbilk winery have such historical importance that they have earned a National Trust classification. Another well-known winery is just one kilometre away, and is a major tourist attraction. Mitchelton winery comprises a winery, vineyard and restaurant complex on the banks of the Goulburn, and boasts a tower restaurant, observation deck and swimming pool. The wines produced in this area are mainly reds, rosés and dry whites including an unusual one made from the Marsanne grape.

Another of the oldest vineyard districts in Australia is the Geelong and Yarra Valley region. Located only 75 kilometres south-west of Melbourne, wineries such as Idyll, St Huberts, Fergusson and Yarra Yering produce table wines and very fine reds. Linville's is also famed for its fruit wines.

Most wineries are open daily for wine-tasting and buying. For more information contact Victour or the Wine and Brandy Producers' Association of Victoria.

BELOW: *The distinctive buildings at Chateau Tahbilk Winery have been classified by the National Trust.*

BELOW: *Grapes in Victoria's Rutherglen area, ripe for harvesting.*

Far left: The Adelaide Casino is located in the heart of the city.

Left: Majestic gums are typical of the superb landscape of the Flinders Ranges.

Above: The modern city of Adelaide has developed around the original plan drawn up in 1840 by Colonel William Light.

Right: The grape harvest is a big event each year in South Australia.

South Australia
FESTIVAL STATE

The biennial Arts Festival, the Barossa Valley Vintage, Hahndorf, the Kensington Highland Games, the Greek Glendi Festival, the Cornish Kernewek Lowender — from the number and variety of festivities held every year, it seems clear that South Australians enjoy making the most of life. For the visitor, these festivals provide an excellent chance to discover a community at its liveliest.

This energetic spirit also seems to indicate that South Australians have triumphed over what might seem to be rather depressing statistics: it is the driest state in the driest continent, two-thirds is near desert and 83 per cent receives an annual rainfall of less than 250 millimetres. But these facts are easily forgotten when you visit the lush green Barossa Valley or explore the beauty of the Flinders Ranges.

Innovative social changes came about in the 1960s and '70s and today South Australia's conservative image has virtually disappeared. It seems apt that its initial settlement began as the result of one man's ideas of how to create a model colony. Edward Gibbon Wakefield believed that the difficulties of other Australian colonies were caused by the ease with which anyone could obtain land. He claimed that if land were sold at two pounds an acre, only men of capital could buy; those who could not would provide a supply of labour and the finance generated would encourage investment and the development of resources. In 1834, he tested his ideas in the Gulf St Vincent area. Lt-Col Light was dispatched as Surveyor-General to select a site.

Today, more than fifty million dollars worth of iron ore is mined every year and, although South Australia's economy remains traditionally agrarian, secondary industry provides nine out of ten jobs. The Leigh Creek coalfields meet most of the state's power needs.

South Australia also boasts most of the world's opals — although the discretion of the miners prevents an exact estimate of their annual worth.

The gulf lands of South Australia enjoy a Mediterranean climate. The further north you go, the hotter and more inhospitable the temperatures become. Adelaide, with its annual rainfall of 544 millimetres, enjoys a midsummer average maximum temperature of about 29.6°C and a midwinter average maximum of 15°C. Seventy-two per cent of the population lives here, making South Australia the most urbanised of all the states. Adelaide inherited its orderly and pleasant layout from its first Surveyor-General and many of its attractive original stone buildings have survived. Once known as the 'city of churches', it is today more talked about in terms of its Festival Centre, excellent Gallery and Museum and splendid restaurants. The Mt Lofty Ranges make a picturesque backdrop with their dense native forests, vines and orchards.

Given the harsh desert conditions of the north and west, with roads which should be embarked upon only by experienced outback drivers, most tourists will probably remain in the more southerly regions. If you feel intrepid, the opal towns of Coober Pedy and Andamooka are fascinating, but both are well over 500 kilometres from Adelaide along unsealed roads. Temperatures climb to over 50°C in Coober Pedy during summer and much of the town is built underground, so choose a cool period for your trip.

The spectacular Flinders Ranges have passable roads, although some are unsealed. The best way to explore this colourful region of peaks and gorges, carpeted in spring with wild flowers, is by four-wheel drive, on horseback or on foot. Wilpena Pound and Arkaroola are the main resort bases.

Both the Yorke and Eyre Peninsulas have attractive unspoiled coastlines. Port Lincoln, on the Eyre Peninsula, is a popular base for big game fishing and on the Yorke Peninsula the three little towns of Wallaroo-Moonta-Kadina, collectively known as Little Cornwall, with their history of copper mining, are well worth a visit.

South of Adelaide is Victor Harbor, the south coast's largest resort. A little further on is the Coorong National Park, near the mouth of the Murray at Lake Alexandrina. Here, the river completes its 2600 kilometres course. A trip along this Riverland section of the Murray reveals historic river towns, extensive citrus orchards and many hospitable vineyards, all maintained by irrigation from the Murray. The lakes and lagoons at the river's mouth abound with birdlife and offer excellent fishing and seasonal duck shooting. On the southern Victorian border is Mount Gambier, the commercial centre of the south-east which boasts Australia's largest pine forest and the beautiful Blue Lakes.

The fame of South Australia's wine regions now extends well beyond Australian shores. McLaren Vale on the Fleurieu Peninsula produces excellent wines and the Riverland region is responsible for much of the national vintage. In the famed Barossa Valley region, there are more than 30 wineries. The valley was originally settled by German Lutherans who planted orchards, olive groves and vineyards and built charming towns and wineries very much in their native European style. To explore this area, particularly during the Vintage Festival, every odd-numbered year, is to discover a region and lifestyle unique in Australia.

Adelaide
AN ELEGANT CITY

Adelaide is a gracious, well-planned city set on a narrow coastal plain between the rolling hills of the Mt Lofty Ranges and the blue waters of St Vincent's Gulf. A blend of old and new, surrounded by parkland, Adelaide combines the vitality of a large modern city (pop. 990 000) with an easy-going Australian lifestyle.

Thanks to Colonel Light's excellent planning and foresight, Adelaide is well-endowed with greenery. The city centre is completely surrounded by parklands, with beautiful flower beds, playgrounds and sports fields. There are barbecues with tables and chairs under shady trees. At **Rymill Park** there is a children's boating lake with canoes and dinghies for hire. The Riverfront Restaurant is set in parkland overlooking the waters of **Torrens Lake** near the Weir. At **Veale Gardens** there are fountains, rockeries and the Alpine Restaurant; and of course there are the beautiful formal grounds of the **Botanic Gardens**. The Gardens have 16 hectares of Australian and imported plants and man-made lakes where children can feed ducks and swans. While there don't miss the Palm House, an extensive glasshouse brought out from Germany in 1871.

Near the tree-lined boulevard of **North Terrace** on the edge of the city centre there are some fine colonial buildings **Holy Trinity Church** is the oldest church in South Australia. The foundation stone was laid by Governor Hindmarsh in 1838, and the clock was made by Vulliamy, clockmaker to King William IV.

Further along is the old **Legislative Council Chamber** with its arched windows and Dutch gables and, next to it, **Parliament House**. Next to this is the **Constitutional Museum**, which has one of the best audiovisual displays in the world. Nearby is **Government House**, the oldest building in Adelaide, in a beautiful garden setting.

The **State Library**, on the corner of Kintore Avenue, houses over 200 000 volumes and the **Natural History Museum** has an impressive collection of native fauna and Aboriginal artefacts. The **Art Gallery of SA** has an important collection of Australian and overseas paintings, sculpture and artworks.

The **University of Adelaide** is also on North Terrace. Walk through the landscaped grounds to see the blend of classic and contemporary architecture.

The historic Adelaide Railway building, also in North Terrace, has been restored magnificently for the **Adelaide Casino**. From noon to 4 am daily, you can play the many tables, dine at the Pullman Restaurant or visit one of the five bars.

RIGHT: *The Great Hall of the University.*

Opposite the Royal Adelaide Hospital is **Ayers House**, headquarters for the National Trust of South Australia. Sir Henry Ayers bought the property in 1855. The house was extended and became one of the major venues for social functions during Ayers' seven terms as Premier of the state. A charming 19th century residence with slate roof and shuttered bay windows, Ayers House has an elegant formal restaurant and a more relaxed bistro extending into the courtyard, enabling visitors to enjoy the historic surroundings whilst dining.

In King William Street, only a block from North Terrace, is another important reminder of Adelaide's heritage, **Edmund Wright House**. Built in 1878, the building with its elaborate Renaissance facade is used for civil weddings. Other historic buildings in the city include the **Town Hall** in King William Street, with formal portico entrance and graceful tower, the **General Post Office**, and the **Treasury Buildings** on the corner of Victoria Square.

In North Adelaide there are fine old colonial buildings from delightful stone cottages to stately homes and grand old hotels with lace work balconies and verandahs. **St Peter's Cathedral** in King William Road is one of Australia's finest cathedrals and is a fitting backdrop to the beautiful **Pennington Gardens**. There is a particularly fine view from **Light's Vision** on Montefiore Hill. A bronze statue of Colonel Light overlooks the city with its broad streets and spacious parks.

The **Torrens River** flows through many of Adelaide's parks. The banks are landscaped, lined with gums and willows, perfect for a lazy picnic lunch. A fleet of *Popeye* motor launches cruises the river, and they make a delightfully different way of arriving at the **Adelaide Zoological Gardens**. The zoo has an enormous collection of animals and reptiles and is noted for its variety of Australian birdlife. There is a walk-through aviary sheltering many types of unusual land and water birds. The nocturnal house is especially interesting, designed to display animals and birds which are most active at night. The zoo grounds are in a perfect setting with magnificent trees including exotic species, rock beds and rose gardens.

Also situated on the curving banks of the Torrens is the famous **Festival Centre**, hub of Adelaide's biennial festival. This streamlined, modern building contains a 2000 seat lyric theatre, drama and experimental theatres and an imposing amphitheatre for outdoor entertainment. The building has been acclaimed by international critics as one of the finest performing venues in the world. The Southern Plaza incorporates a spectacular environmental sculpture by West German artist O. H. Hajek. There are also some fine contemporary tapestries and paintings hung inside the building. There are licensed bars, restaurants and a terrace café. Or you can buy food from the kiosk and picnic on the lawns. The 'festival complex' has walkways linking it to Parliament House, King William Road, the Adelaide Railway Station and Casino.

Adelaide has a bustling shopping complex centred around **Rundle Mall**. The paved mall has trees and a fountain, modern sculpture, colourful fruit and flower stalls and seats where you can sit and watch the passing parade. Buskers and outdoor cafés give the area a European atmosphere. Surrounding arcades and streets have everything from major department stores to tiny specialist boutiques. King William Street is lined with impressive bank and insurance buildings, and in **Hindley Street** there are clusters of restaurants and continental food shops. A bonus for weary shoppers is the free Bee-line bus service which operates in the inner city area.

Make a trip to **Melbourne Street** in North Adelaide for some of the city's most exclusive shops. **Unley Road** is the place if you are hunting for antiques and **Norwood Parade** for second hand treasures.

A real shopping experience is a visit to the **Central Market** near Victoria Square, with its stalls packed high with fresh produce. Nearby arcades sell clothing, wine and spirits. The **Brickworks Market** at Torrensville sells produce and bric-a-brac, and is part of a complex featuring an amusement park and international restaurants.

One of Adelaide's main attractions is its restaurants. Indian, Spanish, Italian, Mexican, Lebanese — the choice seems endless. Some restaurants are tiny and crowded with fast service and super cheap prices. Others are set in historic buildings, serving international class cuisine in gracious surroundings. Hindley Street in the city has some of the most colourful restaurants with bright red lacquer ducks hanging in the windows and giant pizzas being tossed in the air. Fish is a speciality, of course, fresh from the South Australian waters. Windy Point Restaurant, Belair Road, Belair, has one of the finest views of Adelaide and surrounding suburbs. Some restaurants have court-yards. At Decca's Place in Melbourne Street, North Adelaide, you can enjoy delicious food under a shady grapevine. There are also Japanese, Indian and French restaurants in Melbourne Street; and, being Australia's premier wine-producing state, the capital's restaurants serve first class wines.

Adelaide also has some fine old pubs. Some are friendly 'locals', others incorporate restaurants, wine bars and dance floors. The Old Lion Hotel in North Adelaide is typical: it is a handsome 1880s bluestone building with first class restaurant, sheltered courtyard and popular disco. Adelaide's hotels open until midnight on Fridays and Saturdays and many have late licences for other nights of the week.

Not to be missed in Adelaide are the marvellous beaches, stretching right along the coastline with wide sandy shores and clear blue waters. Most are only a short drive from the city centre. Perhaps the most famous is **Glenelg**. The best way to see it is by taking the famous Bay Tram from Victoria Square to the top of Jetty Road in Glenelg. There is a very good shopping centre. Restaurants abound — Greek food here is a speciality. Grand old homes and guest houses along the foreshore are a reminder of Glenelg's days as a 'toffy' seaside resort for the wealthy. The first settlers came ashore here in 1836 and

RIGHT: *The Old Lion Hotel.*

HOTELS AND MOTELS
Adelaide Parkroyal,
226 South Terrace, Adelaide.
(08) 223 4355
Hilton International Adelaide,
233 Victoria Square, Adelaide.
(08) 217 0711
Meridien Lodge,
21-29 Melbourne St, North Adelaide.
(08) 267 3033

FAMILY AND BUDGET
Botanic,
309 North Terrace, Adelaide.
(08) 223 4411
Kiwi Lodge,
266 Hindley St, Adelaide.
(08) 51 2671
Princes Berkeley,
58 Hindley St, Adelaide.
(08) 51 3236
Producers,
235 Grenfell St, Adelaide.
(08) 223 5026

MOTEL GROUPS: BOOKINGS
Flag (08) 223 6699
Homestead (08) 212 1155
Travelodge (08) 223 6288

This list is for information only; inclusion is not necessarily a recommendation.

proclaimed the colony of South Australia under a gum tree. The Old Gum Tree still remains, with a commemorative plaque. HMS *Buffalo* played a significant part in South Australia's early settlement and a replica of the vessel at Glenelg provides an appropriate setting for a maritime museum and seafood restaurant.

Other beaches include **Marino**, **Henley**, **Brighton** and **Grange**. At **Semaphore**, Fort Glanville is the oldest fortress in South Australia. **West Beach** has a sailing club, golf courses, sandhills and Australia's biggest undercover aquarium, **Marineland**, with performing dolphins, seals and other marine life, as well as 'Mr Percival', a rare trained pelican, who gives a demonstration flight and can be fed by the children. Many beaches have surf boards and catamarans for hire. The jetties are used for promenading, swimming and fishing. Right along the esplanade there are hotels, ideal for a cool drink on a hot day, or cosy retreats to watch the ocean during winter. Most serve counter lunches and teas.

Adelaide's easy-to-reach suburbs have plenty to offer the visitor too. A short drive west towards the beachside suburb of **Grange** is **Sturt's Cottage**, home of Captain Charles Sturt, the famous pioneer and explorer. Period furniture and many of Sturt's belongings recall the early days of South Australia.

In **Port Adelaide** there are many imposing buildings, some in poor repair, but a reminder of the port's heyday in the 1880s. The police station and court-house, town hall, shipping and transport building and Ferguson's bond store are all noteworthy. There is a nautical museum in Vincent Street.

Near the suburb of **Rostrevor**, the Morialta Falls Reserve has a ruggedly beautiful gorge and many walking tracks. The Athelstone Wildflower Garden is a unique Australian flora garden. Brownhill Creek Reservation Park has giant pine and gum trees in a quiet valley setting. There are barbecue facilities and pretty picnic spots. **Belair Recreation Park** has picnic grounds, bushland, a children's playground and the former summer residence of the Governor, **Cleland Conservation Park** shows kangaroos, koalas, wombats and other native fauna in their natural surroundings.

At **St Kilda** there is an **Electrical Transport Museum** where you can take trips on restored trams. **Cowell Jade**, at **Unley**, sells jewellery and carvings made from South Australian jade.

For a magnificent view of Adelaide, follow Unley Road then Belair Road south until Windy Point Lookout. At night the lights of the city look particularly impressive.

Adelaide is now the Formula 1 Grand Prix city of Australia. This exciting race is through city streets, open parklands and the racecourse and the course is regarded by many as the best street circuit in the world. As well, Adelaide offers the sports enthusiasts horseracing at **Victoria Park**, **Morphettville** and **Cheltenham**; greyhound racing at **Angle Park**; tennis; squash; swimming and golf. The municipal Golf Course in North Adelaide commands splendid views of the city.

Tours from Adelaide

One of Adelaide's greatest assets is its close proximity to a number of fascinating regions. Vineyards and wineries, rolling hills and quaint villages, seaside resorts and beautiful wildlife reserves are all within an easy drive of South Australia's capital.

The Barossa Valley, 50 km from Adelaide via the Sturt Highway.

A must for visitors to Adelaide is the Barossa Valley, Australia's premier wine-producing region. In this area to the north-east of Adelaide, there are more than 30 wineries and a multitude of historic buildings and galleries, with restaurants and cafés serving authentic German food. If you plan to take advantage of the 'tasting' facilities at the wineries, make sure that whoever is driving you is happy to forgo this pleasure!

Clare Valley, 135 km from Adelaide via the Sturt Highway and route 32.

This region's wineries may be less well-known than others in South Australia, but they still produce superb wines. Driving north through **Kapunda**, Australia's first mining town, you will pass some of the state's richest pastoral country, noted for its stud sheep. **Clare** produces prize-winning red and white table wines. St Aloysius winery was started by two Jesuit priests in 1848 and still operates today. There are some fine colonial buildings, such as the magnificent Martindale Hall which was used in the film 'Picnic at Hanging Rock'. Wolta Wolta Homestead was destroyed in the Ash Wednesday bush-fires in 1983. In this area there are many charming parks and picturesque picnic areas.

BELOW: *Lutheran Church, Tanunda, Barossa Valley.*

The Southern Vales, 42 km from Adelaide via the South Road.

Another trip for winelovers is the vineyards of the Southern Vales. There are over 30 wineries in the area, often in picturesque bush settings. Most are well signposted and have wine tastings and cellar door sales. Hardy's, D'Arenberg, Seaview and Coriole are some of the names you will recognise. Stop for lunch in **McLaren Vale** at The Barn, a gallery-restaurant complex in an historic old coach station. Your return trip could include a visit to the nearby beaches at Moana, Port Noarlunga and Christies. At Morphett Vale there is a fascinating Pioneer Village, re-creating a 19th century Australian settlement, with thatched roof cottage, blacksmith, general store and horse-drawn vehicles.

The Adelaide Hills and Hahndorf, 25 km from Adelaide via the Princes Highway.

The Adelaide Hills are only half an hour's drive from the city. Stop on the way at **Cleland Conservation Park** where there are native birds and animals in a natural bush setting. Tragically part of this park was destroyed in the Ash Wednesday fires. The hills themselves are a blend of gently rolling mountains, market gardens and orchards with farm buildings nestled in valleys off winding roads. Go off the main highway to visit **Stirling** and **Aldgate**, then **Bridgewater** with its historic water wheel. From Mt Lofty (725 m) there are panoramic views of Adelaide by day or by night.

Hahndorf is probably the best known and most interesting town in the area. A unique German-style village, the main street is lined with magnificent old elms and chestnut trees. Most of the buildings have been carefully restored and the town has a leisurely, old-world feel about it. The Academy has a permanent exhibition by Hans Heysen, who depicted the area's beauty so well. A German folk museum is next door, and both are open daily. The bakeries here sell delicious *apfelstrudel*, cheese cake and Black Forest cake, and small shops offer interesting local handicrafts and home-made preserves. A German beer festival is held each year.

In the little town of **Oakbank**, the Great Eastern Steeplechase, Australia's biggest picnic race meeting, is held with great fanfare every Easter. From Hahndorf you can take the back road through winding hills and farmland to **Echunga**, where gold was mined in the 1800s, and return to Adelaide via the sleepy township of **Mylor**, and **Aldgate**. Stop at the Belair Recreation Park on your return trip to Adelaide. There are some beautiful walks, fireplaces for picnics and a wildlife park.

The Fleurieu Peninsula, 112 km from Adelaide to its furthest point via the South Road.

The Fleurieu Peninsula extends south of Adelaide and has much to offer. Down the length of the west coast there are idyllic, sandy beaches, such as Christies, Maslin and Sellicks, right down to the tip at the wild but beautiful Cape Jervis. Some of the beaches have sheltered coves, some excellent surf, others are ideal for fishing. Inland there are historic buildings, particularly at **Willunga**, where public buildings vie with small cottages for attention. The almond orchards around here are a marvellous sight, especially when they bloom in early spring. There are a number of conservation parks, ideal for keen walkers as well as those looking for a quiet picnic spot. There is a pleasant scenic drive around Myponga Reserve, which is in a park reserve. Only 84 km from Adelaide is **Victor Harbor**, one of the state's most popular seaside resorts. The sandy beach is perfect for swimming. Across the causeway is rugged Granite Island and there is a whaling museum and a licensed restaurant at The Bluff. Further around is **Port Elliot** on splendid Horseshoe Bay. Further east is **Goolwa**, the historic river port at the mouth of the Murray River. A ferry will take you across to Hindmarsh Island for panoramic views of the area. Driving back to Adelaide, don't miss **Strathalbyn** on the banks of the Angas. **Milang**, 20 km to the south-east, is on the shores of Lake Alexandrina. Take your camera — birdlife near these waters is fascinating.

Birdwood Mill Museum, 46 km from Adelaide via the North-East Road.

The Birdwood Mill Pioneer Museum (open daily 10 am to 5 pm) has the largest motor cycle display in Australia. Tea rooms serve light refreshments. At Gumeracha, on Torrens Gorge Ring Route on route from Adelaide, is the 'Toy Factory' which has the largest rocking horse in the world. Drive back to Adelaide through Mt Torrens to the small town of **Lobethal**, which was founded back in the 1840s. The Archives and Historical Museum houses a most remarkable exhibit — the old Lobethal College, complete with shingled roof, which was built in 1845. The museum opens on Tuesday and Sunday afternoons. There is an enjoyable scenic route through Basket Range and Norton Summit back to Adelaide.

South Australia from A to Z

Aldinga Population 2021.
This small coastal town 45 km from Adelaide is on the west coast of the Fleurieu Peninsula. **Of interest:** St Ann's Church of England (1866) and the Uniting Church (1863). **In the area:** Aldinga Beach is 4 km south-west of the town. North along the coast is Maslin, Australia's first nude bathing beach. Take time to visit the nearby Southern Vales wine growing region and McLaren Vale. **Accommodation:** Limited.
Map ref. 198 F5, 202 I 8

Andamooka Population 402.
Andamooka is a lonely, outback mining centre, 610 km from Adelaide to the west of the salt pan Lake Torrens. It is off the beaten track, where conditions are harsh, weather is severe and water precious. There are rough shacks along the dirt road, with many people living in dugouts to protect themselves from the extreme heat. Visitors who have obtained a precious stone prospecting permit from the Mines Department in Adelaide can stake out a claim and try their luck. There are tours of the area and showrooms with opals for sale. The road to Andamooka is fair, but quickly affected by rain. Petrol is available. **Accommodation:** 1 motel, 1 caravan/camping park.
Map ref. 205 H1

Ardrossan Population 961.
Ardrossan, 148 km north-west of Adelaide, is the largest port on the east coast of the Yorke Peninsula. It is an important outlet for wheat and barley. It is an attractive town with excellent crab fishing from the jetty. **Of interest:** The Ardrossan and District Historical Museum, Fifth St. The stump jump plough was invented here in the late 1800s; a restored plough is on display on the cliffs at the eastern end of the town. **Accommodation:** 1 hotel, 1 motel, 1 caravan/camping park.
Map ref. 200 F13, 202 G4

Arkaroola Population under 200.
Founded in 1968, Arkaroola is a remote village settlement in the Flinders Ranges about 500 km north of Adelaide. This privately-owned property of 55 000 ha has been opened as a flora and fauna sanctuary. This is rugged outback country crossed by incredible quartzite ridges, deep gorges, rich mineral deposits, and is a haven for birdlife and rare marsupials. **Of interest:** Mining tracks lead to rockpools at Echo Camp and Bararanna Gorge, and to waterholes at Nooldoonooldoona. There are ruins of old copper mines at Bolla Bollana Springs. **In the area:** Famous Mt Painter; breathtaking views from Freeling Heights overlooking Yudnamutana Gorge and Siller's lookout over Lake Frome (a salt lake). Paralana Hot Springs are the last evidence of volcanic activity in Australia. The Ridgetop Tour is a spectacular four-wheel-drive trip across Australia's most rugged mountains. **Accommodation:** 2 motels, 1 caravan/camping park.
Map ref. 207 P9

Balaklava Population 1306.
Balaklava has a picturesque setting on the banks of the River Wakefield on the northern edge of the Adelaide Plains 91 km from Adelaide. The town was named after a famous battle in the Crimean War. **Of interest:** The National Trust Museum (open on Sundays) has relics of the early days in the district. **In the area:** The quiet beachside town of Port Wakefield, 26 km west at the head of Gulf St Vincent, has a caravan park. **Accommodation:** 2 caravan/camping parks.
Map ref. 200 H12, 202 H3

Barmera Population 2014.
The sloping shores of Lake Bonney make a delightful setting for the Riverland town of Barmera, 227 km north-east of Adelaide. The irrigated land is mainly given over to vineyards but there are also apricot and peach orchards and citrus groves. Soldier settlement after World War 1 marked the beginning of today's community-oriented town. **Of interest:** Napper's Old Accommodation House (1850), built on the overland stock route from NSW, is in ruins but is preserved by the National Trust. National Trust Art Gallery and Museum is worth a visit. The Donald Campbell Obelisk, Lake Bonney, commemorates his attempt on the world water speed record in 1964. Pioneer Park, opposite the police station, has a collection of early farming implements. Lake Bonney is ideal for swimming, waterskiing, sailing, speedboats and fishing. Picnic or sunbake on the sandy shores. Sunset Boulevard Restaurant overlooking the lake offers a varied menu and local wines. **In the area:** Overland Corner Hotel is a restored National Trust museum 19 km west of the town on the Morgan Road. Bonney View Winery opens daily. Tourist information from the Barmera Tourist Office, Barwell Avenue. **Accommodation:** 2 motels, 2 caravan/camping parks.
Map ref. 201 P12, 203 P3

Beachport Population 357.
A quiet little town 51 km south of Robe, nearby Rivoli Bay provides safe swimming beaches and shelter for crayfishing boats. **Of interest:** The old wool and grain store is a National Trust Museum. There are also Museums of Victoriana and military memorabilia. Swim in the Pool of Siloam, a saltwater lake noted for its buoyancy. **In the area:** BMX track, motor bike track, bowls, golf and tennis. Lake George is a haven for water birds as well as being a popular spot for surfcat sailing and fishing. 20 km south is Canunda National Park, a 40 km stretch of spectacular wind-swept sand dunes, virgin bushland, fascinating flora and fauna. Tourist information from the caretakers at caravan parks. **Accommodation:** 1 hotel, 1 motel, 2 caravan/camping parks.
Map ref. 204 E10

The Yorke Peninsula

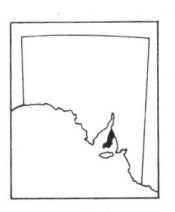

Settled primarily as agricultural country, Yorke Peninsula was put on the map by the discovery of rich copper ore deposits and the influx of thousands of miners including so many from Cornwall that the **Wallaroo/Moonta/Kadina** area became known as Little Cornwall.

The beautiful drive down the highway on the east coast is always within sight of the sea. Many of the east coast towns have excellent fishing.

The west coast of Yorke Peninsula is lined with safe swimming beaches and beautiful coastal scenery. **Port Victoria** was once the main port of call for sailing ships transporting grain. Moonta's solid old stone buildings give it a sense of history and the Moonta mines tell of the mining heyday.

The southern tip of the Peninsula is for the more adventurous and includes Innes National Park with desolate countryside and impressive coastal scenery, with spectacular views across Investigator Straits.

Berri Population 3419.

The commercial centre of the Riverland region, Berri is 227 km from Adelaide. Originally a wood-refuelling stop for the paddle-steamers and barges which plied the Murray, the town was first proclaimed in 1911. This is fruit and vine growing country, dotted with peaceful picnic and fishing areas. A rodeo is held annually. **Of interest:** The tourist lookout, Fiedler St, offers panoramic views of river and town. Wine Barrel Restaurant serves good food and a chance to sample Riverland wines. Olympic pool and sports facilities are surrounded by gardens in Wilkinson St. Martins Bend recreation area for water-skiing and swimming. Nearby is a koala sanctuary. River cruises and houseboats available for hire tie up opposite the Berri Hotel/Motel. Golf and race courses are 1 km from the town. Berri Fruit Juice factory has four tours daily, Monday to Friday. Graziani Winery, Cannery Road, is open for tasting, sales and tours. **In the area:** Karapko Creek, 12 km away, for fishing. Berri Co-operative Winery and Distillery, the largest in Australia, is on the Sturt Highway near the town of Glossop, 13 km west of Berri. It is open for inspection and sales. There are a number of other small wineries in the area. Wilabalangaloo is a residence and reserve with water frontage and excellent views of river cliffs. Tourist information from Berri Tourist Office, Berri Hotel, Riverside Avenue. **Accommodation:** 2 motels, 1 caravan/camping park.
Map ref. 201 P12, 203 P3

Blinman Population under 200.

Blinman, 478 km north of Adelaide in the Flinders Ranges, was a thriving copper mining centre from 1860 to 1890. Today it is a typical, small country town. The friendly hotel is popular with tourists. The countryside is magnificent, particularly when the wild hops bloom. **In the area:** The beautiful Aroona Valley, with the ruins of the old Aroona Homestead. Mt Hayward and Brachina Gorge further south. Great Wall of China, an impressive ironstone-capped ridge. Parachilna Gorge offers a scenic drive to some delightful picnic areas. There is an hotel at Parachilna. The 'almost ghost' town of Beltana has been declared an historic reserve. Old copper mines can be seen at Sliding Rock. **Accommodation:** 1 hotel, 1 caravan/camping park.
Map ref. 207 O10

Bordertown Population 2138.

Bordertown is a quiet town on the Dukes Highway 290 km south-east of Adelaide. The town's growth was stimulated after 1852 when it became an important supply centre for the goldfields of western Victoria. Today the town depends on wool, wheat and dairy farming. **Of interest:** On the eastern edge of town a small stream shaded by gums is a relaxing picnic spot. Nearby is a native wildlife sanctuary. Tourist information from Bordertown Tourist Office, Council Chambers, 43 Woolshed St. **Accommodation:** 2 hotels, 2 motels, 2 caravan/camping parks.
Map ref. 203 Q13, 204 H4

Burra Population 1222.

Nestled in Bald Hills Range 154 km north of Adelaide, Burra is a former copper mining centre. The district of Burra Burra (the name is Hindustani for Great Great) is now famous for stud sheep and Burra serves as the market town for the surrounding farmland. Copper was discovered in 1845 and almost $10 million-worth of copper was extracted before the mine closed in 1877. Along the creek, some of the dugouts remain where more than 2000 people lived during the boom period. There are many relics of the past, unique buildings, old cottages, hotels, vent shafts and chimneys. **Of interest:** The folk museum, Market Square, has mining and farming exhibits. Paxton Square Cottages (1850), a terrace of 33 two-roomed cottages built for Cornish miners, is being restored by the National Trust. The court-house and gaol at Burra North has a shingled roof and stables. Bon Accord Mine buildings (1846); Redruth Gaol (1856). The jinker shed houses the massive jinker which carried the boiler for Morphett's engine house on the three-months trip from Port Adelaide. The creek has many picturesque spots for swimming, canoeing and picnicking. **In the area:** Nearby Kapunda, Australia's oldest mining town. Dangali Conservation Park. A pleasant drive north takes you to Burra Gorge. There are the remains of old gold mines at Mongolata to the north-east. Visit the wineries in the Clare Valley. **Accommodation:** 3 hotels, 1 caravan/camping park.
Map ref. 201 J9

South Australia's National Parks

Nowhere else in Australia can wildlife be seen in such close proximity and in such profusion as in the parks of South Australia. To protect its valuable native animals and birds in their variety of habitats and to conserve the natural features of the landscape, this state has set aside five per cent of its total area as national, conservation and recreation parks.

The range of climatic zones in South Australia enables visitors to enjoy these parks throughout the year; coastal parks are cool in summer and autumn while mountain areas are ideal to visit in winter and spring.

Extending in an unbroken chain for 800 kilometres are the Flinders Ranges, containing the Flinders Ranges National Park which, with its total area of 80 265 hectares, is one of the major national parks in Australia. The Wilpena section, located in the south of the park, comprises the famed **Wilpena Pound** and the Wilpena Pound Range, covering an area of 10 000 hectares. The Pound is one of the most extraordinary geological formations in Australia. Developed in the Cambrian period, it is a vast oval rock bowl, ringed with sheer cliffs and jagged rocks and with a flat floor covered with trees and grass. An old homestead dating back to 1889 still stands. At Arkaroo Rock, Aboriginal rock paintings make this an important area in Aboriginal mythology.

Twenty-five kilometres north of Wilpena is the **Oraparinna** section of the Flinders Ranges National Park. The 68 500 hectares of this section were a sheep grazing station in the 1800s, at one time maintaining more than 20 000 sheep. North, near the Gammon Ranges National Park, **Arkaroola** offers motel accommodation or simple shearers' quarters. Mountains sparkle with exposed formations of quartz, fluorspar, hematites and ochres, making it a gem hunter's paradise. A popular spot is **Paralana**, where the hot springs are one of the few remaining vestiges of volcanic activity in Australia. The Gammon Ranges are a sanctuary for many native birds and animals, paticularly the three species of kangaroo: the big red kangaroo, the grey euro or hill kangaroo and the rare yellow-footed rock wallaby.

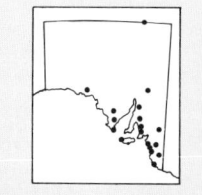

One of the most magnificent national parks in South Australia is the Coorong, 180 kilometres from Adelaide, south of the mouth of the mighty Murray River. The Coorong — a corruption of the Aboriginal word

Ceduna Population 2794.

Near the junction of the Flinders and Eyre Highways, 786 km from Adelaide, Ceduna is the last major town you go through before crossing the Nullarbor from east to west. It is the ideal place to check over your car and stock up with food and water before the long drive west. The port at Thevenard, 3 km east, handles bulk grain, gypsum and salt. The fishing fleet, largely run by Greek fishermen, is noted for its large whiting hauls. Snapper, salmon, tommy ruff and crab are other catches. Ceduna is set on Denial Bay and the sandy coves, sheltered bays and offshore islands of this bay make it an ideal base for a beach holiday. There was a whaling station on St Peter's Island back in the 1850s. **In the area:** McKenzie Ruin, the site of the original township of Denial Bay, built in the 1840s, is 13 km from town. The Overseas Telecommunications Earth Station which links Australia with countries in Asia, Africa and Europe is 34 km to the north. It is open for inspection daily, with tours from Monday to Friday. The spectacular coastline includes the prominent headland at Point Brown, 56 km from Ceduna. The amazing sand dunes and excellent surf at Cactus Beach, near Point Sinclair, are well worth the 195 km drive. Yumbarra Recreation Park, a pleasant drive north, has emus, kangaroos and reptiles in their natural environment. Tourist information from Ceduna Tourist Office, Streaky Bay Road. **Accommodation:** 4 motels, 4 caravan/camping parks.
Map ref. 205 A6, 206 H12

Clare Population 2381.

Set in the midst of rich agricultural and pastoral country, the charming town of Clare was first settled in 1842; it was named after County Clare in Ireland. The area is renowned for its prize-winning table wines. Wheat, barley, fruit, honey, stud sheep and wool are other important regional industries. The first vines were planted by a group of Jesuit priests at Sevenhill in 1848. The priests are still producing communion wines from the St Aloysius Cellars and Winery today. The Clare Valley Wine Festival is held every second year at Easter. **Of interest:** The old police station and court-house, built in 1850, is a National Trust Museum with historical exhibits. Christison Park, a 12 ha flora and fauna sanctuary, has peaceful picnic grounds. Pioneer Memorial Park has walking tracks and barbecue facilities. A plaque here commemorates the arrival of Burke and Wills in 1862. The stately Wolta Wolta Homestead, built by pioneer pastoralist John Hope in 1846, is worth a visit. **In the area:** Most wineries are open for inspection and cellar door sales, but check opening times. Clarevale Co-operative Winery is the largest in the Clare Valley. The Stanley Wine Company was established in 1894, and Wendouree Cellars in 1892. Enterprise Winery, Clare's newest, has been established in the old Enterprise Brewery building. Sevenhill College (1856) and the Church of St Aloysius (1864) are 7 km south. The magnificent classic architecture of Martindale Hall is 21 km east. St Mark's Church at Penwortham is worth visiting and there are pleasant scenic drives south to Neagles Rock Reserve and Spring Gully Conservation Park, which has a stand of rare red stringybarks. **Accommodation:** 2 hotels, 2 motels, 2 caravan/camping parks.
Map ref. 200 I 10, 202 I 1

Cleve Population 827.

An inland town on the Eyre Peninsula, Cleve is surrounded by rich farming country. **Of interest:** The Fauna Park is very interesting and worth a visit. **In the area:** The coastal resorts of Cowell (43 km) and Arno Bay (24 km) both have good swimming beaches and fishing jetties. **Accommodation:** 1 motel, 1 caravan/camping park.
Map ref. 200 A10, 205 G10

Coffin Bay Population 260.

A picturesque little holiday town and fishing village in a sheltered bay, 51 km north-west of Port Lincoln, sailing, waterskiing and swimming are popular here. The coastal scenery in this area is magnificent and fishing is excellent. **In the area:** Drive through the bush along Yangie Trail to Point Avoid for stunning views and good surf beaches. Kellidie Bay Conservation Park has emus, Cape Barren geese and western grey kangaroos. **Accommodation:** 1 caravan/camping park.
Map ref. 205 E12

Coober Pedy Population 2078.

In the heart of South Australia's outback, 925 km north of Adelaide on the Stuart Highway, is the opal mining town of

---

Karangh, meaning 'narrow neck' — is a series of salt water lagoons fed by the waters of the Murray and separated from the sea by the Younghusband Peninsula.

In the park are six island bird sanctuaries, prohibited to the public, but which can be viewed through binoculars. These islands house rookeries of pelicans, crested terns and silver gulls. The ocean beach of the Coorong is a favourite haunt of fishermen, but you may prefer to take the pleasant drive along the coast road beside the waterway where you can stop to camp or picnic. There are more than 160 species of birdlife in the ti-tree and wattle thickets along this road. At dusk, big grey kangaroos and red-necked wallabies come out to feed on the open patches of grass.

On the southern flat plains of South Australia, towards Mount Gambier, just twenty minutes drive from **Naracoorte**, is Bool Lagoon Game Reserve. The lagoon's natural cycle for flooding and drying out provides perfect conditions for the breeding of waterbirds. In spring, when the water is at its deepest, thousands of black swans crowd the lagoon, creating a wildlife spectacle. In summer and autumn, when the water is extremely shallow, waterfowl and waders in large numbers flock to feed on the rich plant life. Bool Lagoon is also the largest permanent ibis rookery in Australia, as dense thickets of paperbark and banks of reeds in its inaccessible central reaches provide safe places for breeding.

A significant national park in South Australia is Flinders Chase, situated on the west end of **Kangaroo Island**. The island was sighted by Matthew Flinders in 1802, and was once inhabited by Aboriginal tribes. The 74 000 hectares of this wild and rugged country, which enjoys mild summers, are popular with bushwalkers who find a challenge in hiking through trackless forests of gum and mallee scrub.

On the Yorke Peninsula is Innes National Park in which there are rocks dating back to Precambrian times. There are also tranquil salt lakes, excellent walking trails and good salmon fishing at the beaches.

Apart from the ten national parks, the National Parks and Wildlife Service also manages 174 conservation parks, 17 recreation parks and 8 game reserves. One of the outstanding conservation parks preserves the Naracoorte Caves, which were discovered in the nineteenth century. There are 60 known caves, three of them open for inspection and tours. These caves enclose a wonderland of delicate cave decorations of stalagmites, stalactites, shawls, straws and other calcite formations. A museum is set up within Victoria Fossil Cave where a conducted tour shows visitors skeletons of the gaint browsing kangaroo, of a hippopotamus-sized wombat and of the Tasmanian tiger.

A unique and successful experiment of familiarising people with native animals is contained in Cleland Conservation Park, located on the slopes of Mount Lofty, overlooking Adelaide. Here, visitors can walk among animals that wander freely in conditions similar to their native habitat.

Coober Pedy. The name is Aboriginal for 'white fellow's hole in the ground'. Very appropriate, since most of the population lives in dugouts as protection from the severe temperatures, often reaching 54°C, and the cold winter nights. There is also a complete lack of timber for building. The countryside is desolate and harsh, and water must be brought in. Opals were discovered here in 1911 and today there are hundreds of mines. Anyone can try their luck after obtaining a precious stones prospecting permit from the Mines Department in Adelaide. There are guided tours and demonstrations of opals being cut and polished. Jewellery and polished stones can be bought. This is one of the last stops for petrol between Kingoonya (285 km south) and the Northern Territory border. **Accommodation:** 2 motels, 1 caravan/camping park. **Map ref. 206 I 6**

Coonalpyn Population 377.
This tiny town on the Dukes Highway 48 km east of Meningie makes a good base to explore the Mt Boothby Conservation Park, which has grey kangaroos, echidnas, emus and mallee fowl in their natural environment. **Accommodation:** 1 hotel, 1 caravan/camping park.
Map ref. 203 N10, 204 E1

Cowell Population 626.
A small pleasant township, 110 km south of Whyalla, Cowell is on the almost-landlocked Franklin Harbour. One of the world's major jade deposits is in the district. The sandy beach is safe for swimming and the fishing is excellent. **Of interest:** Old Post Office, built 1885, a National Trust Museum. The Jade Workshop, West Terrace, is open weekdays. **In the area:** Inland at Cleve there is an interesting fauna park. South along the coast 48 km is Arno Bay, a popular holiday resort with sandy beaches and a jetty for fishing. **Accommodation:** 2 hotels, 1 motel, 2 caravan/camping parks.
Map ref. 200 C10, 205 H9

Crystal Brook Population 1240.
Originally part of a vast sheep station 25 km south-east of Port Pirie. It is now a thriving centre for field peas, barley, wool and beef cattle. **In the area:** Bowman Park, 5 km east of town, has camping and recreation area. There is a caravan park 21 km north-east at the small town of Gladstone, nestled in rich rural country in the Rocky River Valley. Sporting facilities include lawn tennis, bowling greens, hockey fields and a swimming pool. Further north at Wirrabara, there are scenic walks through the pine forests. **Accommodation:** 2 hotels, 1 caravan/camping park.
Map ref. 200 G8

Edithburgh Population 359.
A beautifully located township on the clifftop of the southern tip of the Yorke Peninsula, Edithburgh overlooks Gulf St Vincent and Troubridge Shoals, a chain of very small islands. **Of interest:** Edithburgh Museum has an historical maritime collection. The jetty (1873). The rock pool at the cliff base is excellent for swimming.

Off-shore skin-diving is popular and nearby Sultana Bay is a good spot for boating, fishing and swimming. **In the area:** Coobowie, several km north, is a popular coastal resort with a caravan park. **Accommodation:** 1 caravan/camping park.
Map ref. 202 F7, 205 I 13

Elizabeth Population 32 608.
Located 27 km north of Adelaide, Elizabeth was planned as a satellite city. It was first proclaimed a city in 1964 and was named after Queen Elizabeth II. The city occupies an area of about 2092 ha, with 566 ha set aside for parkland. There are modern theatres, shopping complexes with pedestrian malls and pleasant gardens grouped around the main city centre. There are two large industrial estates with General Motors Holden's having the largest site. The surrounding country has market gardens, poultry farms and produces wheat, wool, fat lambs and dairy produce. **Accommodation:** 4 hotels, 1 motel.
Map ref. 195 G1, 196 H8, 202 I5

Gawler Population 9433.
Settled in the 1830s, Gawler, 40 km north-east of Adelaide, is a prosperous town in a thriving agricultural district producing wine grapes, wool, wheat and dairy products. **Of interest:** Gawler Mill, telegraph station and old post office all reflect Gawler's colonial heritage. **Accommodation:** 1 hotel, 2 caravan/camping parks.
Map ref. 196 I 6, 203 J5

Goolwa Population 1624.
Goolwa is a rapidly growing holiday town 12 km from the mouth of the Murray near Lake Alexandrina. Once a key port in the golden days of the riverboats, the area has a strong tradition of shipbuilding, trade and fishing. The lakes area is ideal for boating, fishing and aquatic sports and popular with bird-watchers and photographers. **Of interest:** There are many historic buildings, including the limestone court-house and the RSL Club which is in the former stables of the Goolwa Railway. The first railway carriage used in South Australia is displayed in the main street. There is a National Trust Museum and the *PS Captain Sturt*, the only Mississippi paddlesteamer in Australia, is now permanently moored as a houseboat. Just east of Goolwa are the Barrages, the desalination points which prevent salt water from reaching the Murray. Nearby is a bird sanctuary with swans, pelicans, waterfowl. The *Aroona* takes pleasure cruises on Lake Alexandrina, offering a good opportunity to see the prolific birdlife close at hand. The stately *Murray River Queen* departs weekly on 5½ day cruises to Swan Reach. (Bookings must be made well in advance.) Fishing here is excellent and catches include the Australian delicacy, yabbies. Captain Sturt Restaurant at the South Lakes Motel serves fine meals and delicious fresh seafood. Tourist information from the Goolwa Tourist Office, 52 Hutchinson St. **Accommodation:** 1 motel, 2 caravan/camping parks.
Map ref. 198 I 9, 203 J9

Hawker Population 351.
This outback town in the centre of the Northern Flinders Ranges is 400 km from Adelaide. Once a railway town, it is now the centre of the unique and world-renowned ranges which attract landscape painters from overseas, who marvel at the colouring and grandeur of the many ranges which together make up the Flinders. **Of Interest:** Museum at Hawker Motors, art galleries, old railway station. Bowls, golf, tennis, swimming. **In the area:** Willow Waters provides fine walking, climbing and a fresh water spring. Moralana Scenic Drive, Yappala, Red Wim Creek and Yourambulla Peak provide views of gorges and valleys. **Accommodation:** 1 motel, 1 caravan/camping park.
Map ref. 200 H1, 207 N11

Innamincka Population under 200.
This tiny settlement 1105 km north-east of Adelaide is on the Strzelecki Track, near Coongie Lake and Cooper Creek. Only experienced outback motorists should attempt the journey. There are no supplies or petrol between Lyndhurst and Innamincka. Stores available. **Accommodation:** 1 motel.
Map ref. 207 R4

Jamestown Population 1384.
Jamestown is an attractive, well-planned country town 205 km north of Adelaide. The surrounding rural country produces stud sheep and cattle, cereals, dairy produce and timber. **Of interest:** The Railway Station Museum has some interesting exhibits. (Open 2 pm to 4 pm Sundays only.) **In the area:** Drive through Bundaleer Forest up towards New Campbell Hill for a panoramic view of the plains stretching towards Mt Remarkable. **Accommodation:** 1 motel, 1 caravan/camping park.
Map ref. 200 I 7

Kadina Population 2943.
The largest town on the Yorke Peninsula, Kadina is the chief commercial and shopping centre of the region. The town's history is related to the boom copper mining era during the 1800s and early 1900s, when thousands of Cornish miners flocked to the area. Part of Little Cornwall, many locals still proudly proclaim their 'Cousin Jack and Jenny' heritage. There are some marvellous old hotels with iron lacework balconies and shady verandahs. Sports facilities are good with tennis courts, a golf course and a trotting track. A Cornish festival, the 'Kernewek Lowender', is held every two years. **Of interest:** The Kadina Museum complex includes Matta House, built for the manager of the Matta Matta Copper Mine in 1863. Agricultural machinery, a printing museum, blacksmith's shop and the old Matta mine are part of the National Trust display. The old Wallaroo mines are adjacent to the town. **In the area:** The towns of Moonta and Wallaroo are both interesting to visit. Tourist information from the Yorke Peninsula Tourist Development Office, Graves St, Kadina. **Accommodation:** 2 hotels, 1 motel, 1 caravan/camping park.
Map ref. 200 F11, 202 F2, 205 I 10

FESTIVAL FUN

As good food and wine go hand-in-hand with festivities, it seems appropriate that South Australia is both the nation's wine capital and her Festival State. During the year, a wide variety of festivals is held throughout South Australia — from the cultural extravaganza of the Adelaide Festival to the country-town carnivals. In October or November each year the city is galvanised by the roar of engines as the world's top car-racing drivers compete in the Formula 1 Grand Prix.

For almost a month of each even-numbered year, Adelaide becomes the cultural centre of Australia, as it stages its Festival of Arts. During this time, the city is like a giant magnet, drawing to it throngs of people from interstate and overseas. Hotels are often booked months ahead; restaurants, taxi services and retailers do a roaring trade.

Since it started in 1960, the Adelaide Festival has grown from a modest 51 performances to an incredible 300, with as many as 30 competing for attention in one day. The cosmopolitan atmosphere and the world-renowned guests have ranked this Festival as outstanding in the world. There have been such illustrious names as Yehudi Menuhin, Vladimir Ashkenazy, Rudolf Nureyev, Sir Donald Wolfit, Philippe Entremont, Dave Brubeck and Shirley Bassey. Overseas companies such as the London and Israel Philharmonic Orchestras, the Royal Shakespeare Company, the Leningrad Ballet, the Janacek String Quartet, the English Opera Group and the Kabuki Theatre of Japan have given some of their best performances at Adelaide. The Australian content is provided by leading symphony orchestras and major drama companies from all over the nation.

Although the Festival emphasises performances in theatre, dance, musical recitals, opera and ballet, it is not confined solely to the visual arts. There are exhibitions, lectures, a writers' week, poetry readings and plenty of outdoor activities to coincide with this three-weeks long cultural feast.

The focal point is the Adelaide Festival Centre which stands on 1.5 hectares on the banks of the River Torrens, just two minutes' walk away from the commercial heart of the city.

RIGHT: *Clowns preparing to entertain the children at Adelaide's Festival.*

BELOW: *The exciting Formula 1 Grand Prix through city streets and parkland is an annual event.*

ABOVE: *Rundle Mall gives a festive atmosphere to the centre of Adelaide.*

South Australia

ABOVE: *Greeks display their national dancing at the Festival Centre's outdoor Amphitheatre.*

ABOVE: *Adelaide's warm climate is ideal for 'continental' style pavement cafes.*

This 21 million dollar performing arts complex contains the Festival Theatre, a multi-purpose concert hall and lyric theatre which seats 2000. This hall is capable of accommodating 100 orchestral players and a choir of 200, making it the largest stage in the country. It also has special acoustic properties. The drama theatre, the Playhouse, seats 600 and is the permanent home of the South Australia Theatre Company, which presents at least ten major productions annually. The Festival Centre also contains The Space, an experimental theatre with seating for 380 and flexible performance areas. The most-used area is probably The Amphitheatre, the open-spaced venue which seats 800 and which is used mainly for free concerts, puppet shows and storytelling for children during the summer months.

When the Festival is not on, Adelaide visitors and residents can make use of the lovely parks and gardens surrounding the centre, and the two restaurants and terrace-style cafe which are open six days a week.

Each odd-numbered year, in May, the Festival Centre organises a youth festival, 'Come Out', which focuses its attention on the arts for children and young people.

The Barossa Valley Vintage Festival, in Australia's premier wine-producing district, just one hour's drive from Adelaide, is also held in odd-numbered years. The mellow autumn weather and picturesque towns of the Barossa Valley

BELOW: *Budding artists at work.*

draw large crowds to this event, which is traditionally a thanksgiving celebration for a successful harvest. The seven-day festival, held during the week after Easter, is strictly *gemutlichkeit* — a gathering of happy people. There is music and dancing, good food, wine tasting, grape-picking and grape-treading competitions, a vintage fair, float processions and a *weingarten* — a big feast with German folk songs. The grand finale takes the form of a spectacular fair held in the oval of Tanunda Park, where dancers in colourful national costumes dance around an 18-metres high maypole, while food and wine is served in the marquees surrounding the oval.

BELOW: *The Scots get their turn to dance.*

Festival Fun

Each 'even' year over Easter weekend, nearby Clare Valley holds a wine festival, with ethnic displays of arts and crafts at a street market and a wonderful *mardi gras*. Another vineyard festival is the McLaren Vale Bushing Festival held annually in October. Here, the wineries of the southern vales offer their best vintage for tasting, while the village green fair comes alive with all forms of entertainment, games, music and dance. The highlight of this festival is an Elizabethan feast at which diners dress up in period costumes and are entertained by jugglers and fire-eaters.

South Australia is a state of many cultures, which accounts for the many ethnic festivals held throughout the year. The largest of these is the *schuetzenfest* held at Hahndorf, an historic German-settled town in the lovely Adelaide Hills. Traditionally a shooting festival to raise funds for the Hahndorf Academy, it has grown into the biggest German-style beer festival held outside Germany. Located just 35 kilometres from Adelaide, the tranquil countryside is transformed into a bustling carnival with 'oompah' music, imported German beer, German folk dancers in colourful national costume and restaurants serving platters of *sauerbraten* and *apfelstrudel*. The hot thirsty month of January is ideal for steins of ice-cold beer while listening to brass bands and waiting for a variety of *wurst* (cold meats) to be served to your table. Another January event is the International Bavarian Festival, held at Valley Lake, Mount Gambier.

In March, the Scottish people hold their Highland Games at Kensington. Pipe bands, highland dancing and tossing the caber are the main features of this occasion. In the same month, the Greek community organises the Glendi Festival to coincide with the Greek National Day. In odd-numbered years in May is the colourful Kernewek Lowender — Cornish family festival — centred around Kadina, Moonta and Wallaroo on the scenic York Peninsula. Quaint old miners' cottages, abandoned mining installations and numerous museums remind visitors of the heyday of copper mining. The streets are filled with music and Cornish dancing, a pasty-making competition and an hilarious wheelbarrow race.

ABOVE: *German dancing is a feature of Hahndorf's* Schuetzenfest.

BELOW: *Vintage time in the Barossa — a grape treading contest.*

BELOW: *Traditional costumes add to the colour of the Kernewek Lowender.*

BELOW: *Part of the Grand Finale of the Barossa Valley Vintage Festival is the traditional Maypole Dance.*

South Australia

In October in even-numbered years, the Italian community launches a festival in the city and country areas to promote its culture and lifestyle.

Perhaps the most popular of all out-of-town festivals is the Riverland Harvest Festival, held biennially in January. This carnival is held at venues throughout the Riverland, which is the great stretch of the Murray reaching down from Renmark through Berri and Loxton, past Barmera to Waikerie and Morgan. Hundreds of people, laden with picnic hampers, flock to the banks of the Murray, to celebrate the citrus and wine harvest of the Riverland. There are re-enactments of the pioneer days, the highlight being a bush banquet at Renmark. The feast includes true Australian dishes such as witchetty grub soup and yabby tails, washed down with the finest Riverland wines. At Berri, there is a fishing competition for all ages. Near Barmera is Monash playground, featuring giant slippery dips. Grape-treading and barrel-rolling contests keep spectators cheering while water-skiers take to the Murray to join in the aquatic carnival.

South Australia boasts many other festivals, among them the Tunerama at the major fishing port and resort of Port Lincoln, held on Australia Day. Australia's biggest fleet of fishing boats gathers to celebrate the opening of the tuna fishing season, while, on the shore, a fair and street procession go on.

During the school holidays in August, Renmark stages an Orange Week festival for family fun, while the old mining town of Burra puts on a carnival every two years to enable visitors to tour the town and join in the carnival in the streets. Each Easter Monday, the Great Eastern Steeplechase is raced at Oakbank race course. This event is billed as the largest picnic meeting in the southern hemisphere, and is a carnival which leads up to the running of the Adelaide Cup in May at Morphettville race course.

One event which is looked forward to by both children and adults alike is the Christmas pageant in the city streets of Adelaide. Floats depicting nursery rhymes and fairy tale characters thrill all those who line the streets to welcome Father Christmas to South Australia.

Information on other festivals can be obtained from the South Australian Travel Centre in your state or at 18 King William Street, Adelaide.

ABOVE: *During the Italian Festival, Rundle Mall, Adelaide's main shopping thoroughfare, is crowded with people.*

BELOW: *Oakbank Races are part of the carnival leading up to the Adelaide Cup Meeting each May.*

ABOVE RIGHT: *Delicious Italian food is prepared for the Italian Festival.*

RIGHT: *A shimmering Christmas tree, complete with fairy, moves on a float through Adelaide's streets as part of the annual Christmas pageant*

Kapunda Population 1340.
Situated 80 km north of Adelaide in the Barossa Valley, Kapunda is a market town for the surrounding farm country. Copper was discovered here in 1842 and Kapunda became Australia's first mining town. At one stage the population was 5000 and there were 16 hotels at one time. A million pounds'-worth ($2m) of copper was dug out before the mines closed in 1878. **Of interest:** Historical Museum. The old mines and chimney recall the mining boom period. Stop for a country-style afternoon tea in the Old Court-house and Gaol Tearooms. **In the area:** Dutton Park has trotting, golf, picnic and barbecue facilities. Pines reserve, 7 km west, has picnic grounds and field camping area. At Marrabel, South Australia's biggest rodeo is held every October. An interesting drive 26 km north through rich sheep, wheat and dairy country takes you to Eudunda. **Accommodation:** 1 caravan/camping park.
Map ref. 197 K2, 201 J13, 203 J4

Keith Population 1147.
Keith is a farming town on the Dukes Highway 241 km from Adelaide. In the centre of the former Ninety Mile Desert, now called Coonalpyn Downs, the area has been transformed from infertile scrubby pasture to productive farming by the use of plant nutrition and modern farming methods. **In the area:** Mount Rescue Conservation Park, 16 km north, is a vast expanse of sand plain with heath, pink gums and native wildlife. **Accommodation:** 1 motel, 1 caravan/camping park.
Map ref. 203 P12, 204 F3

Kimba Population 862.
A small township on the Eyre Highway, Kimba is at the edge of South Australia's outback. This is sheep and wheat-growing country. The Gawler Ranges and Lake Gilles, north-west and north-east of Kimba, are worth visiting. **Accommodation:** 2 motels, 1 caravan/camping park.
Map ref. 200 A7, 205 G8

Kingscote Population 1236.
Kingscote is the largest town and principal port of Kangaroo Island, 110 km south of Adelaide on the northern tip of Nepean Bay. Kingscote was the first settled part of South Australia. There is an airfield nearby and the vehicular ferry arrives here from Port Adelaide. **Of interest:** There is sheltered swimming in a rock-surrounded pool and Brownlow Beach is ideal for swimming and yachting. Fish from the jetty for tommy ruffs, trevally and snook. A cairn on the foreshore marks the state's first post office. National Trust Museum in the historic cottage 'Hope'. The town's cemetery is a fascinating clue to the area's colourful past. **In the area:** The small resort towns of American River, and Penneshaw on the north-east coast of Dudley Peninsula. Flinders Chase National Park is the largest in South Australia. **Accommodation:** 1 hotel, 3 motels, 2 caravan/camping parks.
Map ref. 202 F10

Kingston S.E. Population 1325.
At the southern end of the Coorong in Lacepede Bay, Kingston S.E. is a farming town and seaside resort. It was first named Maria Creek after a ship wrecked in the bay, and later Port Caroline after a brigantine which harboured there. Governor Sir George Strickland Kingston built a house there in 1840. The multitude of shallow lakes and lagoons are a haven for birdlife and a delight for the naturalists and photographers. **Of interest:** National Trust Pioneer Museum; Cape Jaffa Lighthouse (2 pm to 4 pm daily). The Maria Memorial, a granite cairn, commemorates the massacre of 27 shipwrecked Europeans by Aborigines in 1840. **In the area:** Lobster tourist complex. Jip Jip Conservation Park, 45 km to the north-east, has many attractions. Tourist information from the Golden Fleece Service Station, Princes Highway. **Accommodation:** 2 hotels, 2 motels, 1 caravan/camping park.
Map ref. 204 E6

The Coorong

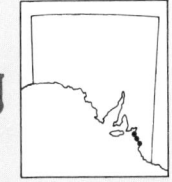

The Coorong is a unique area curving along the south coast of South Australia for 145 kilometres. It has an eerie desolation, a silence broken only by the sound of native birds wheeling low over the scrub and the thunder of the Southern Ocean. It extends from Lake Alexandrina in the north to the small township of **Kingston S.E.** in the south.

The Coorong is a shallow lagoon, a complex of low lying salt pans and clay pans. Never more than three kilometres wide, the lagoon is divided from the sea by the towering white sandhills of Younghusband Peninsula, known locally as the Hummocks.

One of the last natural bird sanctuaries in Australia, giant pelicans, shags, ibis, swans and terns are all at home here. Turn off at Salt Creek, leaving the Princes Highway, and follow the old road along the shore. The coastal scenery is magnificent. Explore the unspoiled stretches of beach where the rolling surf washes up gnarled driftwood and beautiful shells.

For those who enjoy more comforts, **Meningie** in the north or the fishing port of Kingston S.E. have good accommodation and can be used as touring bases.

The Coorong is a national park, with a game reserve within it extending between Policeman's Point and Salt Creek.

Lameroo Population 599.
A quiet little settlement 212 km east of Adelaide on the Ouyen Highway. **In the area:** The Baan Hill Reserve, 20 km south, is a natural soakage area surrounded by sandhills and scrub with picnic and barbecue facilities. **Accommodation:** 1 motel.
Map ref. 203 P8

Leigh Creek South Population 1635.
Leigh Creek South, in the Flinders Ranges, is the largest town north of Port Augusta. The economy is based on the large open-cut coal field. The open-cut eventually consumed the original Leigh Creek township and in 1982, residents moved to the new township about 13 km south. An extensive development and tree planting scheme has transformed the new site into an attractive oasis. **Of interest:** Follow the green arrows for tours of the coal fields. Free bus tours are arranged during school holidays. **In the area:** The small township of Copley, which has a caravan park, is 8 km to the north. Aroona Dam, in a steep-sided valley with richly coloured walls, has a scenic picnic area near the gorge. The rugged Gammon Ranges National Park, 64 km away is very beautiful but recommended for experienced bushwalkers only. A permit is required for entry into the park. **Accommodation:** 1 caravan/camping park.
Map ref. 207 N9

Loxton Population 3100.
Affectionately known as the Garden City of the Riverland region, Loxton is situated 251 km north-east of Adelaide. The surrounding irrigated land supports thriving citrus, wine, dried fruit, wool and wheat industries. The area was first named Loxtons Hut, after a boundary rider from the Bookpurnong Station built a primitive pine and pug hut here. Like all towns in the region, Loxton has a strong sense of community and civic pride. There are many landscaped parks and gardens, a modern shopping centre and extensive sporting facilities. The largest war service settlement scheme in South Australia was carried out here. **Of interest:** The fascinating Historical Village on the river front has recreated 25 buildings, including a bank, bakery, sheds and railway station as well as machinery and implements from the pioneer days of the late 1880s to mid 1900s. Open Mon-Fri 10 am to 4 pm; weekends 10 am to 5 pm. The pepper tree planted by Loxton almost 100 years ago stands nearby. There are a number of art galleries and craft shops that sell local paintings, and hand-crafts. Also a unique wood sculpture exhibition open daily 10 am to 12 pm, 2 pm to 4 pm. Sample excellent wines in the testing and sales facilities at the Loxton Co-operative Winery and Distillery. Open Mon-Sat 9 am to 5 pm. Group tours by arrangement. Enjoy a picnic at Habel's Bend on the sandy shores of the river. Tourist information from Loxton Tourist and Travel Centre, East Terrace. **Accommodation:** 1 hotel, 1 motel, 1 caravan/camping park.
Map ref. 201 P13, 203 P4

Kangaroo Island

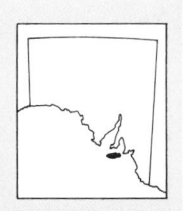

Only 110 kilometres south of Adelaide, Kangaroo Island, Australia's third largest island, shows nature at its wildest and its most majestic in a magical combination of sun and sea, native flora and fauna.

A walk through the bush or over the cliffs may be rewarded with glimpses of koalas nibbling gum leaves, echidnas scuttling across your path, birds and wild flowers in profusion.

At the three main towns, **Kingscote** (202 F10), **American River** (202 F11) and **Penneshaw** (202 G10), there is good accommodation and fishing trips are easily arranged to take advantage of some of Australia's best angling.

The vehicular ferry *Troubridge* journeys twice weekly in winter and three times weekly in summer from **Port Lincoln** to Kingscote. There are three ferry services to **Kangaroo Island**, *The Philanderer III, Valerie Jane* and *H33 Hydraflite.*

American River is a small resort ideal for the fisherman. Pelican Lagoon is a sanctuary for birds and fish. At Penneshaw, which overlooks the passage separating the island from the mainland, penguins can be seen on the esplanade rocks.

The coastline of the island changes from the attractive curved beach at Emu Bay on the north to the rugged cliffs and roaring surf of the south.

At Cape du Couedic is one of the most picturesque of Australia's old lighthouses. Admirals Arch, a huge arch where stalactities are silhouetted against the afternoon sun, is a stunning sight. A colony of seals lives on the Casuarina Inlet, while protected breeding grounds are at Hanson Bay for fairy penguins and at Seal Bay for the Australian sea lion.

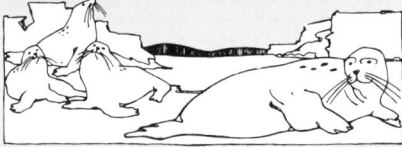

Caves at Kelly Hill have fascinating limestone formations and, to the west, the Flinders Chase National Park is the largest in South Australia. Here, soaring eucalypt forest, native fauna, colourful birds and wild flowers make a visit to this small island a memorable event.

McLaren Vale Population 735.
Centre of the Southern Vale wine growing region, McLaren Vale is only 24 km south of Adelaide. The annual Bushing Fair late October, includes wine tastings, vineyard tours and a medieval ball. **Of interest:** The Barn, originally a coach stop waystation, is now a Bistro and Art Gallery. Taste traditional dishes and local wines. Historic buildings include the Hotel McLaren and Congregational Church. **In the area:** There are about 30 wineries, often in bushland settings. Many are open for inspection, tasting and cellar door sales. Hardy's Tintara is the largest winery in the Southern Vales. (Weekdays 9 to 5.) The interesting Seaview Winery is open for sales weekdays 9 to 5. Not far away, the Chapel Vale Cellars have their sales centre in a restored 114-year old chapel. An exotic treat would be a day tour of local wineries on camelback! The South Australian Tourist Bureau has details. **Accommodation:** 2 motels.
Map ref. 198 G4, 202 I8

Maitland Population 1085.
Maitland is a modern, well-planned town in the centre of the Yorke Peninsula. It serves as the supply centre for the surrounding rich farmland. Wheat, barley, wool and beef cattle are the main primary industries here. The shopping centre is good and there are many pleasant parks. **Of interest:** Maitland National Trust Museum has historical agricultural displays. **Accommodation:** 1 caravan/camping park.
Map ref. 200 F13, 202 F4, 205 I 11

Mannum Population 1984.
Mannum, 82 km east of Adelaide, is one of the oldest towns on the Murray, with an historic and lively past. Picturesque terraced banks overlook the curving river. Wool, beef and cereals are produced in the region and the town is the starting point for the Adelaide water-supply pipeline. The first paddle steamer on the Murray, the *Mary Ann*, left Mannum in 1853 and the first steam car was built here in 1900 by David Shearer. **Of interest:** Riverfront Reserve with picnic spots, barbecue facilities and a lookout tower. There are relics of the *Mary Ann* and its intriguing oblong boiler and a replica of the whaleboat in which Sturt first plied the Murray in 1830. At Arnold Park the *PS Marion*, built 1898, is now a National Trust Museum (10 to 4 daily). The lookout tower off Purnong Road offers sweeping views of the area. **In the area:** The bird sanctuary has a scenic drive which runs parallel to it for 15 km. Cascade Waterfall, 11 km from Mannum, is a pleasant spot for picnics, swimming and beautiful scenic walks. Boats and houseboats are for hire and river cruises are available at weekends during summer. **Accommodation:** 2 hotels, 1 caravan/camping park.
Map ref. 197 P11, 203 L6

Marree Population 334.
Marree is a tiny outback town 645 km north of Adelaide at the junction of the infamous Birdsville Track and the rugged road to Oodnadatta which leads to the Kingoonya-Alice Springs road. There are remnants of the old date palms planted by the Afghani traders who drove their camel trains into the outback with supplies in the 1800s. Desolate saltbush country surrounds the town, with its rough wooden and steel buildings. Marree is the railhead for the Birdsville Track. Petrol is available. **In the area:** 6 km to the north is The Frome, a sandy water course which floods after very heavy rains, surging across the Birdsville Track, often leaving travellers stranded for weeks. **Accommodation:** 1 hotel.
Map ref. 207 N7

Melrose Population under 200.
Melrose is the oldest town in the Flinders Ranges, 268 km north of Adelaide. It is a quiet little settlement, perfect for those who want to 'get away from it all'. **Of interest:** Historical buildings include the old police station and court-house (1862), now a National Trust Museum; Jacka Brewery; a blacksmith's shop; Serendipity art and craft shop; the North Star and Mt Remarkable hotels. There are pleasant walks and picnic spots along the creek. **In the area:** Mt Remarkable National Park, Horrock's Pass and the town of Quorn are close by. **Accommodation:** 2 hotels, 1 caravan/camping park.
Map ref. 200 G5, 207 N13

Meningie Population 807.
Meningie is set on the edge of the freshwater Lake Albert and at the northern tip of the vast salt pans of the Coorong. A small rural township 159 km from

Adelaide, it is a good spot for keen fishermen. The area abounds with birdlife such as ibis, pelicans, cormorants, ducks and swans. Sailing, boating, water-skiing and swimming are popular. **In the area:** An enjoyable drive can be taken to Lake Albert, adjacent to Lake Alexandrina, the largest permanent freshwater lake in Australia (50 000 ha). The channel between Lakes Alexandrina and Albert is crossed by a ferry at Narrung. **Accommodation:** 1 hotel, 1 motel, 1 caravan/camping park.
Map ref. 203 L10, 204 C1

Millicent Population 5255.
A thriving commercial and industrial town, Millicent is situated in the middle of a huge tract of reclaimed land in the south-east of South Australia, 50 km from Mount Gambier. Today wool, oil seed, barley, cattle, fat lambs and a crayfish industry contribute to the area's prosperity. Extensive pine forests support the Apcel and Cellulose paper mills. **Of interest:** On the northern edge of the town, gum trees surround a fine swimming lake and pleasant picnic area. Delicious fresh crayfish can be bought from the Safcol factory. The National Trust Museum and Admella Gallery are in George St. Just nearby is a narrow gauge steam engine on display. The Historical and Maritime Museum has paintings and craftwork. The Shell Garden has an unusual display surrounded by fuchsias, ferns and begonias. There are golf and tennis facilities and a gliding club leases part of the local aerodrome. **In the area:** 21 km south-east is Tantanoola, home of the famous Tantanoola Tiger, shot by Tom Donovan in the 1890s. The 'tiger' — in reality a Syrian Wolf — was stuffed and is now displayed in a glass cage in the Tantanoola Tiger Hotel. The beautiful underground caves at Tantanoola have fascinating limestone formations and are open to view daily, between 9 am and 5 pm. Mt Burr is a short pleasant drive north-east through magnificent pine forests. The saw mill opens for inspection (check times). Canunda National Park is 13 km west. Tourist information from the National Trust Tourist Office, 7 Mt Gambier Road. **Accommodation:** 3 motels, 2 caravan/camping parks.
Map ref. 204 G10

Minlaton Population 865.
Minlaton is a prosperous town serving the nearby coastal resorts of Yorke Peninsula. The town, 209 km west of Adelaide, was originally called Gum Flat because of the giant eucalypts in the area. Pioneer aviator Harry Butler, flier of the 'Red Devil', a 1916 Bristol monoplane, was born here. The plane is displayed at the Harry Butler Museum. **Of interest:** National Trust Museum, Main St. Gum Flat Homestead Gallery, 2 km east of town. **In the area:** Koolywurtie Museum, 11 km west, is a typical pioneer country store. Port Vincent, set on a sweeping bay, 25 km east, provides for swimming, yachting and water-skiing. **Accommodation:** 1 motel, 1 caravan/camping park.
Map ref. 202 E6, 205 I 12

Moonta Population 1924.
Along with Kadina and Wallaroo, Moonta forms the trio of towns known as 'Little Cornwall'. It is a popular seaside resort 163 km north-west of Adelaide, with pleasant beaches and good fishing. Many of the descendants of the 'Cousin Jacks and Jennies' from Cornwall live in the region. A rich copper ore deposit was discovered here in 1861 and soon thousands of miners, including many from Cornwall, flocked to the area. The mines were abandoned in the 1920s with the slump in copper prices and rising labour costs. The town has many solid stone buildings, a charming city square and a picturesque town hall. The 'Kernewek Lowender', a Cornish festival, is held every two years. **Of interest:** All Saints Church (1873). Arts and Crafts Centre in the Old Railway Station. Moonta Mines National Trust Museum, Old Primary School. A typical Cornish miner's cottage (National Trust) is furnished in period style. The old railway station, pump house, various shafts and the mines offices all recall Moonta's heyday as a thriving mining town. The Patio Restaurant offers a panoramic view overlooking Moonta Bay. **In the area:** The towns of Wallaroo and Kadina, whose histories are closely related to that of Moonta, are nearby. **Accommodation:** 1 hotel, 1 motel, 1 caravan/camping park.
Map ref. 200 E11, 202 E2, 205 I 10

Morgan Population 378.
Once one of the busiest river ports in South Australia, Morgan today is just a sleepy little township 164 km north-east of Adelaide. It is the starting point for the Whyalla pipeline. **Of interest:** The impressive wharves built in 1878, standing 12.2 metres high, were constructed for the riverboat industry. Customs and court-houses near the railway station are a reminder of the town's thriving past. **In the area:** White's Dam Conservation Park is 9 km north-west. **Accommodation:** 2 hotels, 1 motel, 1 caravan/camping park.
Map ref. 201 M11, 203 M2

Mount Gambier Population 19 880
Mount Gambier is nestled on the side of an extinct volcano in the centre of the largest pine plantations in Australia and in rich farming and dairy country. It is 460 km from Adelaide on the Princes Highway and is the main commercial centre of the south-east region of South Australia. Wool, wheat, cereals, fat lambs and dairying all contribute to the district's wealth. The local white Mount Gambier stone, used in most of the buildings, together with many fine parks and gardens, give the city a look of solid respectability. Sighted in 1800 by Lt James Grant, Mount Gambier is the first named part of South Australia. The Hentys built the first dwelling in the area in 1841 and by 1850 a weekly postal service to Adelaide was operating. **Of interest:** Mt Gambier is renowned for its four crater lakes, particularly the magnificent Blue Lake, 197 m at its deepest, which changes from a dull grey to brilliant blue each November, mystifying locals and scientists alike. The lake is floodlit at night and the scenic drive 5 km around offers several lookouts. The Pumping Station, providing the town's water supply, can be inspected. Tickets from the Tourist Information Centre. There is a picnic area with barbecue facilities on the wooded slopes of Leg of Mutton Lake. Nearby Valley Lake is ideal for water-skiing and aquatic sports, whilst Browne Lake is a retreat for black swans, waterfowl and coots. The Town Hall (1876) is of pink dolomite and limestone. The Cave Gardens behind the Town Hall are a picturesque setting with creeping ferns and flowers. Black's Museum, featuring Aboriginal artefacts and guns, opens daily. The Old Courthouse Museum opens Sunday afternoons and school holidays. Centenary Tower on the top of Mt Gambier commemorates the first sighting of the volcano. **In the area:** The surrounding pine forests with their large belts of native eucalypts are a sanctuary for wildlife. You can see the pines being felled, trimmed and cut ready for loading at the State timbermill, 2½ km from Mt Gambier. Tours depart at 10 am Mondays and Fridays. Nangwarry Sawmill, 32 km north, opens daily. Limestone Quarries, where the soft Coralline limestone is cut into building blocks with huge mobile saws, is 10 km west of the city in Cafpiro Road. The area is also famous for its locally made cheeses — buy them fresh from the factory at Mt Gambier Co-op Dairy Products Ltd, 3 km west of the Town Hall. Bowling, golf, squash and tennis are all catered for and the town boasts the oldest gun club in Australia. There is also night trotting, fortnightly throughout summer. Tourist information from Mt Gambier Tourist Information Centre, Casterton Road. **Accommodation:** 6 hotels, 18 motels, 6 caravan/camping parks.
Map ref. 170 A6, 204 H11

Murray Bridge Population 8664.
Murray Bridge is South Australia's largest river town. It is only 82 km from Adelaide and there is a modern freeway linking the two cities. First settled in the 1850s, the town overlooks a broad sweep of the Murray and still retains some of the feeling of the time when it was a centre for the bustling riverboat traders. Watersports, river cruises and excellent accommodation make Murray Bridge a perfect holiday spot. **Of interest:** Sturt Reserve, on the banks of the river, is ideal for fishing and swimming, and it has excellent picnic, barbecue and playground facilities. Charter cruises are available on the *MV Kookaburra* and there are houseboats available for hire. Thiele Reserve, east of the river, is popular for water-skiing. Avoca Dell, 5 km upstream, is another pleasant spot for boating, water-skiing and barbecues. Other recommended riverside reserves include Wood Lane, Long Island, Swanport and Wellington. Some places that are worthwhile visiting are the Folk Museum, Johnston Park; Craft Centre and Gallery at the Old Railway Refreshment Rooms. **In the area:** Kooringal Park Wild Life Reserve is 11 km south of the town. The town of Mypolonga, 14 km north, is at the

The Outback of South Australia

Motorists contemplating travel in the outback should prepare their vehicles well and familiarise themselves with expected conditions before setting out.

The outback of South Australia covers almost 60 million hectares and is one of the most remote areas of the world, where conditions are harsh, climate extreme and distances daunting.

The countryside is usually dry, barren and dusty, but occasional freak rains and heavy floods can transform the land. Dry creek beds and water holes fill, wild flowers bloom and bird life flocks to the area. The enormous salt **Lake Eyre** has been filled only twice since white men first reached the desert.

The main road to the Northern Territory is the Stuart Highway. From **Port Augusta** to **Alice Springs** the road is 1368 kilometres, a large section of which is unsealed. The Highway heads north to **Woomera (207 L10)**, a restricted area; turn off here for the **Andamooka** opal fields. Then north-west to **Pimba (205 H3)** and **Kingoonya (205 D3)**, last stop for petrol before the opal mining town of **Coober Pedy**. Petrol, food and supplies are available here before the long drive to **'Kulgera'** just over the Northern Territory border.

The notorious Birdsville Track starts at **Marree**, once a supply outpost for Afghani camel traders, and follows the route originally used to drove cattle from south-west Queensland to the railhead at Marree. The track skirts the fringes of the Simpson Desert with its giant sand dunes and the desolate Sturt's Stony Desert. Artesian bores line the route, pouring out 64 million litres of salty boiling water every day. The road is fair but sometimes washed out by torrential rains and travellers can be left stranded for weeks. Sand storms are another problem. Petrol and supplies are available at Marree, **Mungeranie (207 O5)** and **Birdsville (207 P1)** over the Queensland border.

The Strzelecki Track begins at **Lyndhurst (207 N9)**, a harsh dusty road 494 kilometres to the almost deserted outpost of **Innamincka** with no stops for petrol or supplies.

Only experienced outback motorists should consider driving along the Birdsville and Strzelecki Tracks.

centre of beautiful orange orchards and rich dairying country. Tourist information can be obtained from the Council Office, Sturt Reserve Caravan Park or the Murray Bridge Museum. **Accommodation:** 2 hotels, 4 motels, 5 caravan/camping parks.
Map ref. 199 P3, 203 L7

Naracoorte Population 4758.
Situated 390 km south-east of Adelaide, Naracoorte is one of the oldest towns in South Australia, first settled in the 1840s. The area is world-renowned for its intriguing limestone caves. Dairy cattle, sheep and wheat are the local primary industries. **Of interest:** The Old Mill Museum, the National Trust Museum and the Naracoorte Art Gallery. (Check times.) The Naracoorte Museum and Snake Pit in Jenkins Terrace has the strange combination of gemstones and antiques on display indoors with reptiles in a natural outdoor setting. Two restored locomotives are on display in Pioneer Park. The impressively large swimming lake is shaded by gums and surrounded by lawn. For fishermen, trout and redfin abound in the local streams and creeks. **In the area:** Naracoorte Caves, 11 km to the south-east, are in a wooded conservation park. The Fossil Cave is of world significance, containing unique fossilised specimens of Ice Age animals. The other three caves open to the public have spectacular stalagmites and stalactites. They are open daily for guided tours, check times. Bat Cave, 17 km from the Naracoorte Road, is the hideout for thousands of bats which emerge every evening. Bool Lagoon Reserve 17 km south is a sanctuary for ibis, brolga, Cape Barren geese and other birdlife. Duck shooting in open season. Tourist information from the Naracoorte Tourist Information Centre, 128 Smith St. **Accommodation:** 2 hotels, 4 motels, 2 caravan/camping parks.
Map ref. 204 H7

Old Noarlunga Population 669.
A small village on South Australia's Wine Coast situated 32 km south of Adelaide on the Fleurieu Peninsula. **Of interest:** Old Horseshoe Inn (1843), has a complex of restaurants and a cellar in the original stables. **In the area:** Port Noarlunga and Christies Beach to the west and Moana and Maslins Beach further to the south, all offer good swimming and fishing. The Pioneer Village Museum at Hackham recreates an 1860 settlement with a cottage, smithy, barn, general store and Inn. Also featured in the area are numerous vineyards and wineries producing many fine wines. Accommodation: 1 hotel, 1 motel, 1 caravan/camping park.
Map ref. 198 F4

Oodnadatta Population 229.
A tiny, but famous, outback town 1146 km north-west of Adelaide. Land is arid and water is scarce. It is thought the name Oodnadatta originated from an Aboriginal term meaning 'yellow blossom of the Mulga'. Petrol is available. **Accommodation:** 1 hotel, 1 caravan/camping park.
Map ref. 207 J4

Paringa Population 498.
One of the fastest growing towns in South Australia. Paringa is only 4 km from Renmark in the Riverland region. **Of interest:** Lookout Tower offers fine views of the surrounding irrigated farmland. **In the area:** Margaret Dowling National Trust Park. Old Customs House, 17 km north along the Murtho Road. It is well worth a drive 36 km eastwards to see the delicate blossoms at the Lindsay Point Almond Park in early spring. **Accommodation:** 1 hotel, 1 motel, 1 caravan/camping park.
Map ref. 201 Q12, 203 Q3

Penola Population 1205.
Penola, 52 km north of Mount Gambier near the Victorian border, is surrounded by pine forests and farming country. The Coonawarra vineyards, 10 km north, produce magnificent red table wines. The first vines were planted on the rich terra rossa soils in the 1890s. Today there are eleven wineries as well as 36 private growers. **Of interest:** National Trust Museum, Old Post Office Building. Yallum Park Homestead, an historic two-storeyed Victorian Homestead. All inspections by appointment. **In the area:** Rare species at the fauna sanctuary, 13 km south-east, include the rock wallaby and Parma wallaby (inspection by appointment only). Many wineries are open for inspection, tastings and cellar door sales, including Mildara and Redbank. **Accommodation:** 1 hotel, 1 motel, 1 caravan/ing park.
Map ref. 170 A3, 204 H9

Peterborough Population 2575.
Peterborough is a major railway town 250 km north of Adelaide. It is surrounded by grain-growing and pastoral country. three different rail systems meet here and there are extensive workshop, locomotive sheds and marshalling yards. It is the principal town on the important Port Pirie to Broken Hill railway line. **Of interest:** The old town hall is now a museum and art gallery. Railway enthusiasts can inspect the railway workshops and bogie exchange. Victoria Park has barbecues, picnic facilities and a children's playground. Tourist information can be obtained from the Corporation Office at the Town Hall. **Accommodation:** 1 hotel, 1 motel, 1 caravan/camping park.
Map ref. 201 J6, 207 O13

Pinnaroo Population 731.
This sleepy little township on the Ouyen Highway is only 10 km from the Victorian border. **Of interest:** A small park in the main street has an aviary with native birds and parrots. There is a farm machinery museum. **Accommodation:** 2 hotels, 1 motel, 1 caravan/camping park.
Map ref. 162 A10, 203 R8

Port Augusta Population 15 254.
Port Augusta, a thriving industrial city at the head of Spencer Gulf, is the most northerly port in South Australia. It is 317 km from Adelaide and is a vital supply centre for the outback areas of the state and the large sheep stations of the district. It is

an important link on the east-west 'Indian-Pacific' railway and the famous '*Ghan*' train to Alice Springs which departs from Adelaide. The city has played an intrinsic role in South Australia's development since the State Electricity Trust built a series of major power stations here. Fuelled by coal from the huge open-cut mines at Leigh Creek, the stations generate more than one-third of the state's electricity. **Of interest:** Curdnatta Art and Pottery Gallery is in the town's first railway station. Greenbush Gaol (1869); The Grange (1878) was once a hotel serving bullock and horse teams to the outback and is now a charming, restored residence; the town hall (1887); court-house (1884) with cells built of Kapunda marble; St Augustine's Church with magnificent stained glass windows. Homestead Park pioneer museum includes pleasant picnic areas, a blacksmith's shop, old steam train and crane as well as the rebuilt Yudnappinna Homestead. Many of the motels have excellent restaurants and there is a great range of hotel counter meals, cafes and take-away food shops available in the town. **In the area:** Hancocks Lookout, south towards Wilmington, offers a marvellous view of the surrounding country, Port Augusta and Whyalla. Take care on the turn-off road, which is dangerous when wet. Mt Remarkable National Park has rugged mountain terrain, magnificent gorges and abundant wildlife. A beautiful drive north-east takes you to Pichi Richi Pass, where the Railways Preservation Society runs old steam engines during school holidays. Historic Melrose, 65 km to the south-east, is the oldest town in the Flinders Ranges. There are some fascinating old buildings and a National Trust Museum. **Accommodation:** 9 motels, 2 caravan/camping parks.
Map ref. 200 F4, 205 I7, 207 M12

Port Broughton Population 587.
A small port on the extreme north-west coast of the Yorke Peninsula, Port Broughton is 169 km from Adelaide. On a protected inlet of the sea, the town is a major port for fishing boats and is renowned for its deep sea prawns. **Accommodation:** 1 hotel, 1 motel, 1 caravan/camping park.
Map ref. 200 F9

Port Elliot Population 773.
Only a few kilometres east of Victor Harbor, Port Elliot is a quiet coastal town, and was the first port established on Encounter Bay. The town commands a spectacular view of the coast across to the mouths of the Murray and the Coorong. There are sandy sheltered beaches and many scenic drives. **Of interest:** Port Elliot Art Pottery; the Shell and Doll House, Port Elliot Road; Pine Brae Gallery; Heathfield House, used by Governor Jervois in the 1870s; the old police station and the former Port Elliot and Globe Hotels. **Accommodation:** 2 hotels, 1 caravan/camping park.
Map ref. 198 H9, 202 I 9

Port Lincoln Population 10 675.
Port Lincoln is beautifully sited on the clear waters of Boston Bay, which is three times the size of Sydney Harbour. The port, 250 km due west of Adelaide across St Vincent and Spencer Gulfs, was settled in 1839. It was originally chosen as the State's capital. With its sheltered waters Mediterranean climate, scenic coastal roads and attractive farming hinterland, Port Lincoln is becoming an increasingly popular tourist resort. It is the base for Australia's largest tuna fleet and is also an important export centre for wheat, wool, fat lambs and live sheep, frozen fish, lobster, prawns and abalone. The coastline is deeply indented, offering magnificent scenery from sheltered coves to cliff faces and surf beaches. Nearby offshore islands can be hired for exclusive holiday pleasure and relaxation. The Tunarama Festival, held every Australia Day Weekend, celebrates the opening of the tuna season. **Of interest:** Mill Cottage (1867); Flinders Park; 'Old Mill' lookout, Boston House (1885), overlooks the bay. The Lincoln Hotel (1840), Tasman Terrace, is the oldest hotel on Eyre Peninsula. A couple of restaurants are Robyn's in Tasman Terrace, and Limani on the Lincoln Highway. The bay is ideal for swimming, water-skiing, and yachting; fishing is excellent. **In the area:** There are several pleasant parks close to town and vast natural reserves are no more than a day's outing away, abounding in wildlife. Lincoln National Park, 10 km to the south also has impressive coastal scenery. Hincks Recreation Park (85 km north) and Kellidie Bay Park (30 km west) are well worth a visit. At Poonindie, there is an intriguing church with two chimneys, which was built in 1850. The Koppio Smithy Museum, 38 km away, has a restored smithy, cottage, post office, general store and vintage machinery. Spectacular coastal scenery surrounds Coffin Bay. Tumby Bay, 48 km to the north, is a small beach resort with a marvellous, long crescent beach. Whalers Way, 32 km south-west, has some of Australia's most beautiful coastline. There are a host of offshore islands for boating enthusiasts to visit. Boston Island has farming country and native birdlife, whereas Thistle Island offers unspoiled landscape and memorable walks; Wedge Island is ideas for a relaxing holiday. The whole area is a yachtsman's paradise and Yachtaway holidays are available for the novice as well as the expert. Information from the Tourist Office, Tasman Terrace. **Accommodation:** 5 hotels, 6 motels, 2 caravan/camping parks.
Map ref. 205 F12

Port MacDonnell Population 682.
Port MacDonnell was once a thriving port. Today it is a quiet, well-planned fishing town 28 km south of Mt Gambier, ideal for those wanting to 'get away from it all'. The rock lobster fishing fleet here is the largest in South Australia. **Of interest:** Old Customs House, with a National Trust classification, is now a fine restaurant, or you can enjoy a Devonshire tea at the quaint Ye Olde Post Office Tea Rooms. 'Dingley Dell', home of the poet Adam Lindsay Gordon, is now a museum. **In the area:** The Glenelg River has many scenic spots for fishing and boating. For keen walkers, a track leads to the summit of Mt Schank, crater of an extinct volcano. Picnic and barbecue facilities. Cape Northumberland Lighthouse, on the dramatically beautiful coastline west of the town, is open on Wednesdays and Thursdays from 2 pm to 4 pm. Heading east, there is surf fishing at Orwell Rocks, diving at the crystal clear Ewens Ponds. Tourist information from the District Council Office. **Accommodation:** 1 motel, 2 cara/van camping parks.
Map ref. 170 A7, 204 H12

Port Pirie Population 14 695.
Huge grain silos and smelters' chimneys dominate the skyline of Port Pirie, 227 km north of Adelaide on Spencer Gulf. Situated on a curve of the tidal Port Pirie River, the city is a major industrial and commercial centre. The first settlers came in 1845 and wheat farms were established

The Eyre Peninsula

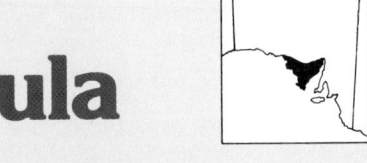

The Eyre Peninsula encompasses a giant triangle, bordered by three major roads, the Lincoln, Eyre and Flinders Highways. In the north-east corner, overlooking the blue waters of Spencer Gulf, is **Whyalla**, famous for its giant iron and steel industry and the largest provincial city in South Australia. Inland at **Iron Knob** (205 H7), iron ore is quarried, providing 50 per cent of the iron used in Australia's steel industry.

The east coast has many quiet seaside resorts such as **Cowell** on sheltered Franklin Harbour, **Arno Bay** (205 G10) and **Port Neill** (205 F11).

South of **Port Lincoln** are impressive sheer cliffs, spectacular crevasses and surf pounding ashore.

Across on the west coast is sheltered **Coffin Bay** (205 E12). Off the main highway, the untouched bushland is a haven for emus and kangaroos.

At Point Labatt you can see the only seal colony on the Australian mainland. The coast is stunning, with magnificent cliffs, secluded coves and bays.

The Barossa Valley

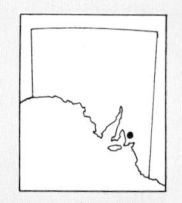

The Barossa Valley, Australia's most famous wine producing area, is a marvellous place to visit, a warm and intimate place of charming old towns, with the vineyards spreading across undulating hills in well tended, precise rows.

The valley is 49 kilometres from Adelaide and, as it is only 29 kilometres long and 8 kilometres wide, its regions and towns are easily accessible.

The largest town in the valley is **Angaston** (208 H4), 100 kilometres north-east of Adelaide, an attractive town with many beautiful old houses and buildings, often constructed with local marble.

Nuriootpa (208 F2) is a small town with a similar historic atmosphere.

Lyndoch (208 B9) is one of the oldest towns in South Australia. Near Lyndoch is the Pewsey Vale Homestead, a superb mansion set in English style landscape. Of all the Barossa towns, **Tanunda** (208 E5) has the greatest German influence, with its Lutheran churches and many German shops and signs.

Some of the more famous wineries are Chateau Yaldara, at Lyndoch, Orlando winery at **Rowland Flat** (208 C8), Chateau Tanunda, Kaiser Stuhl at Nuriootpa, Seppelts at **Seppeltsfield** (208 C3), Penfolds at Nuriootpa, and Yalumba winery at Angaston. Exploration of the many vineyards is the great attraction of a visit to Barossa.

---

in the region. BHP began smelting lead in 1889 and today the largest lead smelters in the world treat thousands of tonnes of concentrates annually from the rich silver, lead and zinc deposits at Broken Hill, NSW. Wheat and barley from the mid-north are exported and there is a thriving fishing industry. Port Pirie is also a vital link in the road and rail routes to Alice Springs and Darwin, Port Augusta and Perth. The city has excellent shopping centres, 10-pin bowling alley, a modern theatre and convention centre in Memorial Park and some fine old hotels in the main street. Wheat and dairy farms, rolling hills sea are all close by. Swimming, water-skiing, fishing and yachting are popular summer sports on the river. **Of interest:** National Trust Museum Buildings, Ellen St, include the old Victorian pavilion-style railway station and former customs house. Broken Hill associated Smelters can be inspected on weekday afternoons. 'Carn Brae', Florence St, is an historic residence with antique exhibits. Visit the waterfront where loading and discharging of Australian and overseas vessels takes place. **In the area:** Weeroona Island, 13 km to the north, has a museum with an excellent Australiana collection. Port Germein is a beach resort 24 km north. There is a caravan park at Port Germein. The south-west reaches of the beautiful Flinders Ranges are close by and a little further east is the ruggedly beautiful Telowie Gorge, lined with giant red river gums. **Accommodation:** 5 motels, 3 caravan/camping parks.
Map ref. 200 G7

Port Victoria   Population 258.
A tiny township on the west coast of the Yorke Peninsula, Port Victoria was once the main port for sailing ships carrying grain from the area. **Of interest:** The maritime museum has interesting relics of sailing ship days. Safe swimming beach and jetty fishing. The island of Wardang can be seen from the town. **Accommodation:** 2 caravan/camping parks.
Map ref. 202 E4, 205 I 12

Quorn   Population 1049.
Nestled in a valley in the Flinders Ranges, 331 km north of Adelaide, Quorn was established as a railway town in 1878. Part of the Great Northern Railway, the line was built by Chinese coolies and British stonemasons. Closed in 1957 for economic reasons, the historic line is gradually being restored. **Of interest:** The mill museum and art gallery are located in an old flour mill, which also has a licensed restaurant. Pottery and Art Gallery, Railway Terrace. A steam locomotive operates during holiday periods, taking passengers on the 25 km round trip through the Pichi Richi Pass which is an interesting journey. The colourful rocky outcrops of Devil's Peak and Dutchman's Stern are nearby. **In the area:** Warren Gorge is popular with climbing enthusiasts, whereas Buckaringa Gorge has plenty of scenic picnic areas. The ruins of the Kanyaka Homestead are 37 km north. This was a settlement which supported 70 families from the 1850s to the 1870s. Kanyaka Death Rock overlooking a permanent waterhole, was once an Aboriginal ceremonial ground. **Accommodation:** 3 motels, 1 caravan/camping park.
Map ref. 200 G3, 207 N12

Renmark   Population 3475.
Renmark is at the heart of the oldest irrigation area in Australia, 260 km north-east of Adelaide on the Sturt Highway. Some of the most beautiful parts of the Murray flow through the Riverland, and red river gums and willows along the river banks form a backdrop for leisurely walks and peaceful picnics. In 1887, the Chaffey brothers from Canada were granted 250 000 acres to test their irrigation scheme. Today lush orchards and vineyards thrive with the water piped from the Murray. There are canneries, wineries and fruit juice factories. Wheat, sheep and dairy cattle are other local industries. The first community-run hotel in the British Commonwealth, the Renmark Hotel, is an impressive three-storeyed building overlooking a sweeping bend of the river. **Of interest:** National Trust Museum 'Olivewood' Renmark Avenue and Renmark Art Gallery, Ral Ral Avenue. An old hand-operated wine press and one of the Chaffeys' original wood-burning irrigation pumps are on display in Renmark Avenue. The town has pleasant riverside gardens, bowling greens, tennis courts, golf course, swimming pool, recreation centre with squash, rollerskating, health and fitness studio with sauna and spa facilities. The paddle-steamer *Industry* built in 1911, is now a floating museum. *Murray Explorer* takes luxury five-day cruises. There are day cruises aboard the *M.V. Barrangul* or you can hire a houseboat. Goat Island, a National Trust property, is a 133 ha koala and wildlife sanctuary. **In the area:** The small township of Paringa is 4 km east. There is a good collection of native animals and reptiles at Bredl's Reptile Park and Zoo, 5 km along the Sturt Highway. Several wineries in the area are open for inspection, tastings and sales, including Angoves, County Hamley and Renmano. Dangali Conservation Park, 60 km north is a vast area of mallee scrub with bluebush and black oak woodland and an abundance of bird and animal life. **Accommodation:** 1 hotel, 4 motels, 3 caravan/camping parks.
Map ref. 201 Q12, 203 Q3

Robe   Population 590.
A small historic town on Guichen Bay, 336 km south of Adelaide (a short detour off the main Princes Highway), Robe is a fishing port and holiday centre. The rugged windswept coast has many beautiful and secluded beaches, sheltered by rugged headlands. Lagoons and salt lakes are all around the area and wildlife abounds. In the 1850s it was a major wool shipping port. In 1857 more than 10 000 Chinese disembarked at Robe before travelling overland to the goldfields to avoid the Victorian Poll Tax. **Of interest:** National Trust buildings and small art and craft galleries. Karatta House was the

summer residence of Governor Sir James Fergusson in the 1860s. The Customs House Museum is open to the public. 'Lakeside' is an historic home worth a visit, and so is the restored old Caledonian Inn which is now a restaurant serving excellent menus, including local seafood. The Obelisk at Cape Dombey is a vantage point for panoramic views of the area. The crayfish fleet anchors in Lake Butler. Fresh crays and fish are available from October to the end of April. Swimming is safe in Guichen Bay, but not recommended in the ocean waters. Waterskiing on Lake Fellmongery is popular and fishing is excellent. **Accommodation:** 2 hotels, 6 motels, 4 caravan/camping parks.
Map ref. 204 D8

Strathalbyn   Population 1756.
An inland town centred on the Angas River, Strathalbyn is 58 km south of Adelaide. Picturesque riverside parks offer shaded picnic grounds and the nearby bakery sells delicious fresh bread, pies and pasties. **Of interest:** National Trust pioneer museum; old police station and court-house; historical folk museum; St Andrew's Church (1848); the Angas flour mill (1852) and the Old Provincial Gas Company (1868). **In the area:** Langhorne Creek, 13 km south-east, is a well-known wine-growing district. **Accommodation:** 3 hotels.
Map ref. 199 K5, 203 J8

Streaky Bay   Population 985.
A holiday resort, fishing port and agricultural centre for the cereal-growing hinterland, Matthew Flinders named the bay because of the streaking effect caused by seaweed. Streaky Bay, 727 km from Adelaide, has pleasant sandy beaches and fishing from the jetty or by boat is good. The town is almost surrounded by small bays, sandy coves and spectacular towering cliffs. **Of interest:** Old School House Museum, Montgomery Terrace. Hospital Cottage, built in 1864, was the first building in Streaky Bay. **In the area:** The Cape Labatt Recreation Park, 40 km south, has the only colony of sea lions on the Australian mainland. Coastal scenery and rugged cliffs along here are really magnificent. Murphy's Haystacks, 20 km inland, are a sculptural group of ancient granite rocks in golden wheatfields. South is the quiet beach town of Port Kenny, which has hotel and camping accommodation. The fishing village of Venus Bay has a caravan park. Don't miss seeing the limestone caves at Talia. **Accommodation:** 1 motel, 1 caravan/camping park.
Map ref. 205 B7, 206 I 13

Swan Reach   Population under 200.
Swan Reach is a quiet little township on the Murray River about 100 km east of Gawler. Picturesque river scenery and good fishing are making it an increasingly popular holiday resort. The *PS Murray River Queen* cruises from Goolwa to Swan Reach on leisurely 5½-day cruises each week. Bookings must be made well in advance. **Accommodation:** 1 caravan/camping park.
Map ref. 203 M5

The Fleurieu Peninsula

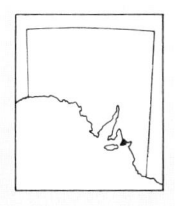

Touring is easy on the Fleurieu Peninsula. You can take the excellent main roads, or wind through the countryside on gravel byways.

Starting 52 kilometres south of Adelaide, the region stretches from **Aldinga Beach** on the west coast around the vast fresh waters of Lake Alexandrina.

There are beaches for all tastes, from magnificent cliff faces and roaring surf to wide, sandy, sheltered bays and coves. **Maslin Beach** is renowned as Australia's first nude

Tailem Bend   Population 1677.
A railway workshop town at the junction of the Dukes and Princes Highways, 107 km from Adelaide, Tailem Bend has some excellent views across the Murray as the river bends sharply towards Wellington. **In the area:** A vehicular ferry takes you 2 km across the river to Jervois, then you can drive 11 km south to Wellington where there are some interesting buildings, including an old restored court-house, built in 1864, and an historical museum. **Accommodation:** 2 hotels, 1 motel, 1 caravan/camping park.
Map ref. 199 R5, 203 L8

Tintinara   Population 355.
A quiet little town 206 km south-east of Adelaide in the Coonalpyn Downs. **In the area:** Access to the Mt Rescue Conservation Park. Sand plains with heath, native fauna, Aboriginal camp sites and burial grounds. **Accommodation:** 1 hotel, 1 motel.
Map ref. 203 O11, 204 E2

Tumby Bay   Population 933.
Tumby Bay is a pretty coastal resort 53 km north of Port Lincoln on the east coast of the Eyre Peninsula. The town is noted for its long crescent beach and white sand. The well-kept lawns along the foreshore are always popular for picnics and barbecues. **Of interest:** The National Trust Museum; the old police station (1871). There are two jetties, one of which is more than a hundred years old. **In the area:** Rock and surf fishing in the district. At Poonta and Cowley's Beaches the scenery is rugged but beautiful, and catches include snapper, whiting and bream. Inland through attractive fertile countryside is Koppio, with a National Trust classified smithy and museum. The peaceful town of Port Neill, 34 km north, has a grassed foreshore for picnics and a safe swimming beach. Accommodation at Port Neill includes an hotel, caravan park and holiday cabins. **Accommodation:** 2 hotels, 3 caravan/camping parks.
Map ref. 205 F11

bathing beach. Cape Jervis, at the tip of the Peninsula, commands a spectacular view across Backstairs Passage to **Kangaroo Island.**

The unofficial capital of the Peninsula is **Victor Harbor,** one of South Australia's most popular beach resorts. Offshore **Granite Island** is joined to the mainland by a long causeway.

The fishing is superb around to **Goolwa,** once an historic port, now the starting point for leisurely paddlewheeler cruises up the Murray.

Victor Harbor   Population 4522
A popular coastal resort town and the unofficial capital of the Fleurieu Peninsula, Victor Harbor is only 84 km south of Adelaide. Established in the early days of whaling and sealing, the town has a long and colourful history. Victor, as it is often called, overlooks historic Encounter Bay, protected from the pounding surf by Granite Island. The island is joined to the mainland by a causeway and a train takes visitors across from November to May. The chairlift affords stunning views of land and sea. There are penguin rookeries on the island and seals can be seen sunning themselves on the shore. The Hindmarsh and Inman Rivers provide fishing and peaceful picnic spots. **Of interest:** The Cornhill museum and art gallery; Museum of Historical Art. Whaler's Haven, south at Rosetta Bay, just below the Bluff, has relics of whaling days and colonial artefacts. The nearby cottage restaurant, Whaler's Inn, is licensed. St Augustine's Church of England (1869). Sports facilities are excellent and there is a large modern shopping centre. **In the area:** Native animals and birds can be viewed in their natural habitat at the Urimbirra fauna park, 5 km north. Sample the licensed restaurant and kiosk, or picnic near the lake. Glacier Rock at Inman Valley, 19 km to the north-west, shows the effect of glacial erosion. There are superb views of the valley from the tea rooms. Hindmarsh Valley Falls is a picturesque picnic location with pleasant walks and spectacular waterfalls. Spring Mount Conservation Park is 14 km north-west. Through rolling hills 13 km west is Waitpinga Beach, with dramatic surf and golden sand. For fishermen, big salmon, mulloway, snapper and bream can be caught. At the tip of the Fleurieu Peninsula is Cape Jervis with splendid views across Backstairs Passage to Kangaroo Island. Tourist information from Victor Harbor Tourist Office, Ocean St. **Accommodation:** 3 hotels, 5 motels, 4 caravan/camping parks.
Map ref. 198 H10, 202 I 9

Waikerie Population 1629.

Waikerie is surrounded by an oasis of irrigated orchards and vineyards in mallee scrub country in the Riverland. Situated 170 km north-east of Adelaide, the town has beautiful views of the river gums and magnificent sandstone cliffs along the Murray. The name means 'anything that flies' and the river and lagoons teem with birdlife, whilst mallee scrub is a haven for parrots and other native birds. **Of interest:** The World Gliding Championships were held here in 1974 and the club is the most active in Australia. Take a joy ride for a bird's eye view of the effects of irrigation. The Co-op Fruit Packing House is the largest in Australia, open to view in season. Kangaroo Park is a good spot for picnics and barbecues. The shady Holder Bend Reserve is ideal for water-skiing. Cyrilton (Hardy's) Winery, Waikerie Cellars and Kaluna Winery are open for tastings and cellar door sales. **In the area:** The Pooginook Conservation Park, 12 km north-east, is a sanctuary for mallee fowl, echidnas and hairy-nosed wombats. Tourist information from the Waikerie Tourist Centre, 20 McCoy St. **Accommodation:** 1 motel, 2 caravan/camping parks.
Map ref. 201 N12, 203 N3

Wallaroo Population 2043.

Situated 154 km north-west of Adelaide, Wallaroo is a key shipping port for the Yorke Peninsula, exporting barley and wheat. Processing of rock phosphate is another major industry here. The safe beaches, good fishing and history of the area make it a popular tourist resort. In 1859 vast copper ore deposits were discovered. A smelter was built, thousands of Cornish miners arrived and Wallaroo and surrounding areas boomed until the 1920s when copper prices dropped and the industry gradually died out. The nearby towns of Moonta and Kadina form part of the trio known as 'Little Cornwall', and the area still has many reminders of its colourful past. The 'Kernewek Lowender', a Cornish festival, is held every two years. **Of interest:** There are a number of charming old Cornish-style cottages in the district. The National Trust Museum, in the town's first post office, has a collection of maritime exhibits. The old railway station, the customs house (1862) and Hughes chimney stack (1865), which contains over 300 000 bricks and is more than 7 metres square at its base, are all interesting buildings. There is safe swimming, boat and jetty fishing. **In the area:** The towns of Moonta and Kadina. **Accommodation:** 2 hotels, 2 motels, 2 caravan/camping parks.
Map ref. 200 E11, 202 E2, 205 I 10

Whyalla Population 29 962.

In 80 years, Whyalla has grown from a small settlement known as Hummock Hill to the largest provincial city in the state and an important industrial centre based on steel. It is famous for its heavy industry, particularly the enormous BHP iron and steel works and ore mining at Iron Knob and Iron Monarch in the Middleback Ranges. A ship yard operated from 1939 to 1978 and the largest ship ever built in Australia was launched from here in 1972, though shipbuilding has since ceased. Whyalla is a modern, well-planned city with a good shopping centre, safe beaches, fishing, boating and excellent recreational facilities. The area enjoys a sunny, Mediterranean-type climate. **Of interest:** BHP has guided tours of its steel works leaving from the BHP Visitors Reception, Mon-Fri at 9.30 am, excluding public holidays. Visitors must wear closed footwear. Mount Laura Homestead Museum (National Trust), in Ekblom St, has historical exhibits, open Sundays only. The fauna and reptile park, near the airport, has native animals and a reptile house. The attractive foreshore beach is safe for swimming and has a jetty and lawn area is very popular for picnics. The nearby Ada Ryan Gardens have a mini-zoo, a picnic area with tables, chairs and barbecues under shady trees. Go to Flinders Lookout in Elliot St for fine views of the city and Spencer Gulf. **In the area:** Point Lowly Lighthouse (1883), 20 km from the city, is the oldest building in the area (not open for inspection). At Iron Knob, 50 km north, visitors can see the iron ore quarries. Tours Monday to Friday 10 am and 2 pm, from the BHP town office. Lake Gilles Recreation Park, 72 km west, has kangaroos, western pigmy possums and reptiles. Tourist information from Patterson St. **Accommodation:** 5 hotels, 5 motels, 1 caravan/camping park.
Map ref. 207 M13

Willunga Population 667.

An historic township just south of the famous Southern Vales wine growing regions, Willunga is Australia's major almond growing centre. An Almond Blossom Festival is held late July. There are some pug cottages and fine examples of colonial architecture, including a number of beautiful bluestone houses with slate roofs from the local quarry. **Of interest:** National Trust police station and court-house. Church of England with an Elizabethan bronze bell. Uniting Church. Willunga House. The historic Bush Inn is a delightful place to stop for lunch when touring the wineries. It serves a traditional Australian menu and local wines. (It is advisable to book a table in holiday periods.) **In the area:** Mt Magnificent Conservation Park, 12 km east, has western grey kangaroos in native bushland, scenic walks and picnic areas. **Accommodation:** Limited.
Map ref. 198 G5, 202 I 8

Wilmington Population 227.

A tiny settlement, formerly known as Beautiful Valley, Wilmington is 290 km north of Adelaide in the Flinders Ranges. **In the area:** Just before Wilmington is the turn-off for the Mount Remarkable National Park with its crystal clear mountain pools, dense vegetation and abundant wildlife. Mambray Creek and the spectacular Alligator Gorge are in the park. (**N.B. A total fire ban applies in summer.**) On the road to Port Augusta, turn off to Hancock's Lookout for a view of Spencer Gulf. Melrose, 20 km south, is the oldest town in the Flinders. There are a number of fine old buildings and a National Trust museum. **Accommodation:** 1 hotel, 2 caravan/camping parks.
Map ref. 200 G4, 207 N13

Wilpena Population under 200.

Wilpena is the small settlement outside Wilpena Pound. The Pound is a vast natural amphitheatre surrounded by colossal peaks which change colour as the light falls on them through the day. The only entrance is through a narrow gorge and across Sliding Rock. In 1900 a wheat farmer built a homestead within the Pound, but a flood destroyed the log road and the farm was abandoned. Organised tours and scenic flights are available. **In the area:** The surrounding country is magnificent, ideal for bushwalking and mountain climbing. St Mary's Peak, the highest point, is 1198 metres; Bunyeroo and Brachina Gorges, and Aroona Valley are to the north. To the south at Arkaroo Rock on the slopes of Rawnsley Bluff and at Sacred Canyon are Aboriginal rock carvings and paintings. Rawnsley Park Station has demonstrations of sheep drafting and shearing every Sunday at 10 am in April and May and from August to October. At Appealinna Homestead (1851), 16 km north, are the ruins of the house built of flat rock from the creek bed. Most of this area is within the confines of Flinders Ranges National Park, the headquarters of which is at Oraparinna Station. **Accommodation:** 1 motel, 1 caravan/camping park.
Map ref. 207 O11

Wudinna Population 572.

Wudinna is a small settlement on the Eyre Highway, 571 km north-west of Adelaide. **Of interest:** Tortoise Rock is an ancient granite rock, which looks surprisingly like its namesake. Mt Wudinna is the second largest rock in Australia — climb it for a panoramic view of the countryside. **Accommodation:** 3 motels.
Map ref. 205 E8

Yankalilla Population 321.

A small, quiet settlement just inland from the west coast of the Fleurieu Peninsula, 35 km from Victor Harbor. **Of interest:** Uniting Church built in 1878; the old flour mill at Bungala House on the Victor Harbor Road. The hotel serves good country-style counter meals. **In the area:** The tiny seaside town of Normanville, with its motel and caravan park, is a few kilometres west. Myponga Conservation Park has western grey kangaroos among its steep hillsides and gullies. **Accommodation:** Limited.
Map ref. 198 D8, 202 H9

Yorketown Population 713.

Principal town at the southern end of the Yorke Peninsula, Yorketown's shopping centre services the surrounding cereal growing district. The extensive inland salt lakes are still worked. **In the area:** The rugged coastal scenery and desolate country of the tip of the Peninsula. Innes National Park. **Accommodation:** 1 hotel, 1 motel, 1 caravan/camping park.
Map ref. 202 E7, 205 I 13

the FLINDERS RANGES

The Flinders Ranges are part of a mountain chain which extends almost 800 kilometres from its seaward end at St Vincent's Gulf. The most spectacular of their peaks and valleys are in two areas — the first north-east of Port Augusta and the second north of Hawker. They are similar in scale to many of Australia's other mountain ranges, but are totally different in their colouration and atmosphere.

There is something unique in the contrast of the dry, stony land and richly lined rock faces — the characteristics of a desert range — with the rich vegetation of the river red gums, casuarinas, native pines and wattles which clothe the valleys and cling to hillsides and rock crevices. In spring, after rain, the display of wild flowers is breathtaking — carpeting the whole region with masses of reds, pinks, yellows, purples and white. The wild flowers, together with the natural beauty of the rock shapes, pools and caves and twisted trees which abound in the Flinders Ranges, make them a favourite haunt of photographers and artists. Many of the paintings of Sir Hans Heysen embody the shape and spirit of the ranges.

The Flinders is served by reasonably good roads. A good trip which will take in the best of the scenery is to drive north-east from Port Augusta over Pichi Richi pass to Hawker and from there on the loop road to Parachilna, circling the Wilpena Pound area.

But it is better to stay and explore, preferably on foot or by four wheel drive. There are kilometres of signposted tracks in the ranges, but it is important to be equipped with a good map and to follow a planned route as it is still only too easy to lose the way. Drivers should avoid using the secondary roads after rain as they can be treacherous.

RIGHT: *Many creeks with their source in the Flinders Ranges flow only after heavy rains. They can rise and dry out again surprisingly quickly.*

FAR RIGHT: *There are many rugged gorges in the Flinders. Here, the high cliffs of Warren Gorge make a colourful sight against the blue sky.*

The best known feature of the Flinders is the Wilpena Pound — an immense elevated basin covering about 50 square kilometres and encircled by sheer cliffs which are set in a foundation of purple shale and rise through red stone to white topped peaks. The only entrance is through a narrow gorge, through which a creek sometimes flows. The external cliffs rise to over 1000 metres but inside is a gentle slope to the floor of the plain. The highest point in

BELOW: *The Wilpena Ranges form a dramatic backdrop to this peaceful rural scene.*

South Australia

ABOVE: *Native flora and fauna, are protected at Arkaroola Sanctuary.*

ABOVE: *The peaks of the Wilpena Ranges rising over the Aroona Valley are typical of the superb scenery encountered throughout the Flinders Ranges.*

the pound is St Mary's Peak at 1190 metres which dominates the northern wall and provides a magnificent view over the surrounding mountains. Within the pound are low rounded hills and folded ridges, grasslands and pine-clad slopes which run down to the gums along Wilpena Creek. It is a wonderland of bird life — rosellas, galahs, red capped robins, budgerigars and wedge tailed eagles are common here. Bushland possums and the rare yellow-footed wallabies can also be seen sometimes.

There is a well organised resort at Wilpena, catering for levels of accommodation from camping to modern motel. Near the pound in this central section of the ranges are Warren Gorge, Buckaringa Gorge, Yourambulla Cave, with its Aboriginal drawings, the Hills of Arkaba, considered the most beautiful spur in this region, Bunyeroo and Aroona Valleys and the Flinders Range National Park.

Some features in the northern section of the Flinders are Willow Springs lookout, the Great Wall of China, a long rocky escarpment, and Mount Chambers and Chambers Gorge, which can be reached by vehicle or on foot, are among the most beautiful of all the attractions that can be seen in the Flinders.

Another region of the Flinders — the Arkaroola village in the far north of the ranges — has become a major attraction for visitors. The country of Arkaroola-Mt Painter Sanctuary is composed of quartzite razorback ridges over elongated valleys, once the sea bed of a great continental shelf which has left a legacy of rippled rock and marine fossils embedded in the rock.

There is a mass of wildlife — emus, ducks, parrots, cockatoos and galahs, possums, marsupial mice and the yellow-footed rock wallaby — all abound here. The Paralana Hot Springs are one of the few remaining vestiges of volcanic action on the continent.

BELOW: *The craggy red peaks of Freeling Heights, seen from a ridge top in the north of The Flinders.*

BELOW: *Chambers Gorge can be visited on foot. In places the rock walls have been decorated with Aboriginal carvings.*

Maps of South Australia
Location Map

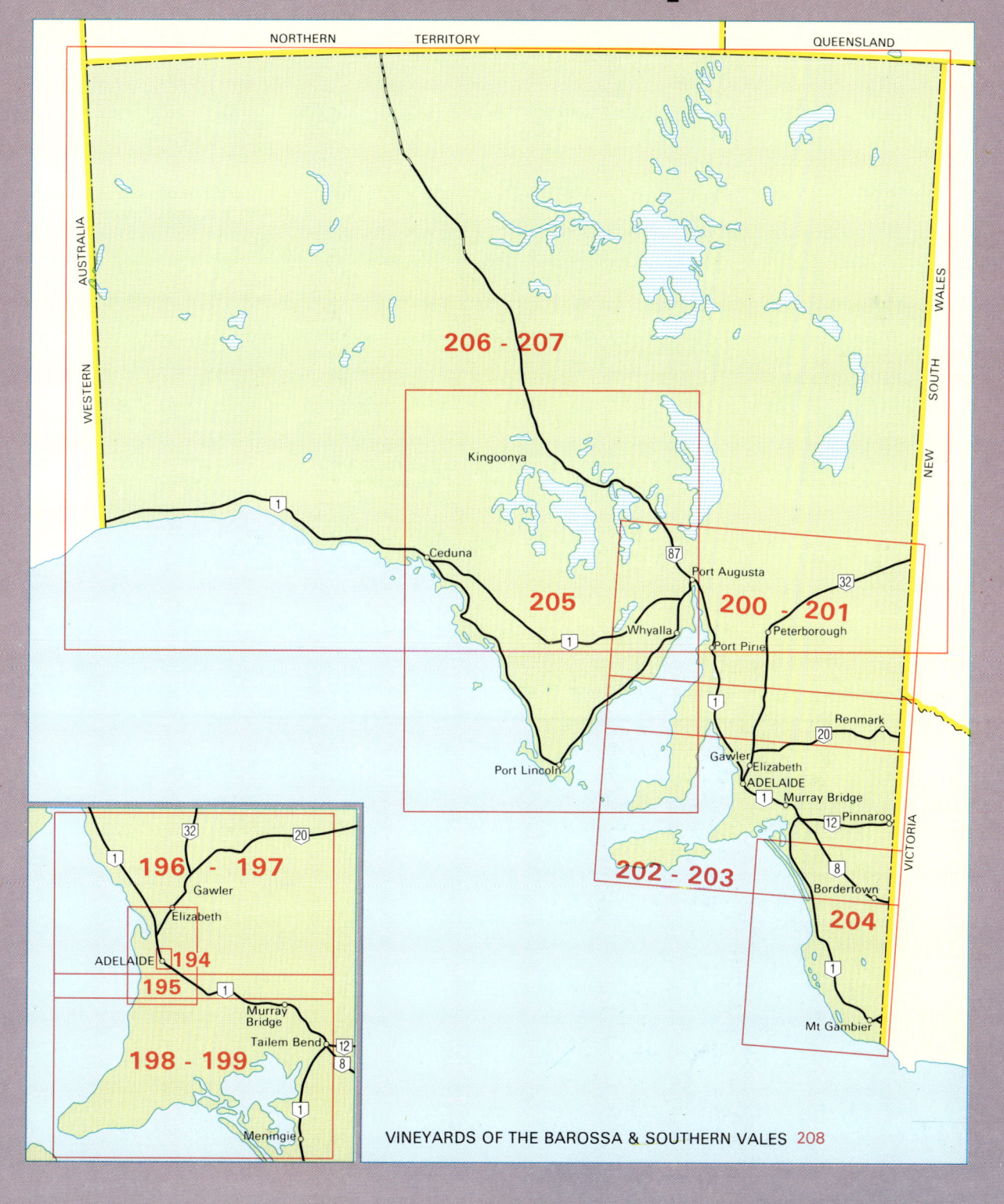

VINEYARDS OF THE BAROSSA & SOUTHERN VALES 208

194 Central Adelaide

Places of Interest

1. Art Gallery of South Aust. F6
2. Ayers House G6
35. Casino E6
3. Central Market E7
4. Festival Centre Complex E6
5. Government House E6
6. Grosvenor Hotel E6
33. Hilton Hotel E7
7. Lights Vision E4
8. Memorial Drive Tennis E5
9. Mosque D8
10. Museum F6
11. Hotel Adelaide E4
12. Parliament House E6
13. Police Headquarters E8
14. Post Office E7
15. Public Library F6
16. Rundle Mall F6
17. St. Francis Xavier Cathedral E7
18. St. Peters Cathedral E5
19. Showgrounds C10
20. South Terrace Travelodge F9
21. State Administration Centre E7
22. Town Hall E7
23. University of Adelaide F6
24. Victoria Park Racecourse H9
25. War Memorial F6
26. Zoological Gardens F5

Transport and Touring

34. Adelaide Rail Passenger Terminal. B9
27. Ansett Terminal E6
28. Glenelg Tram Terminus E7
29. RAA Sth. Aust. Headquarters .. F7
30. Railway Station E6
31. TAA Terminal E6
32. Tourist Bureau E6

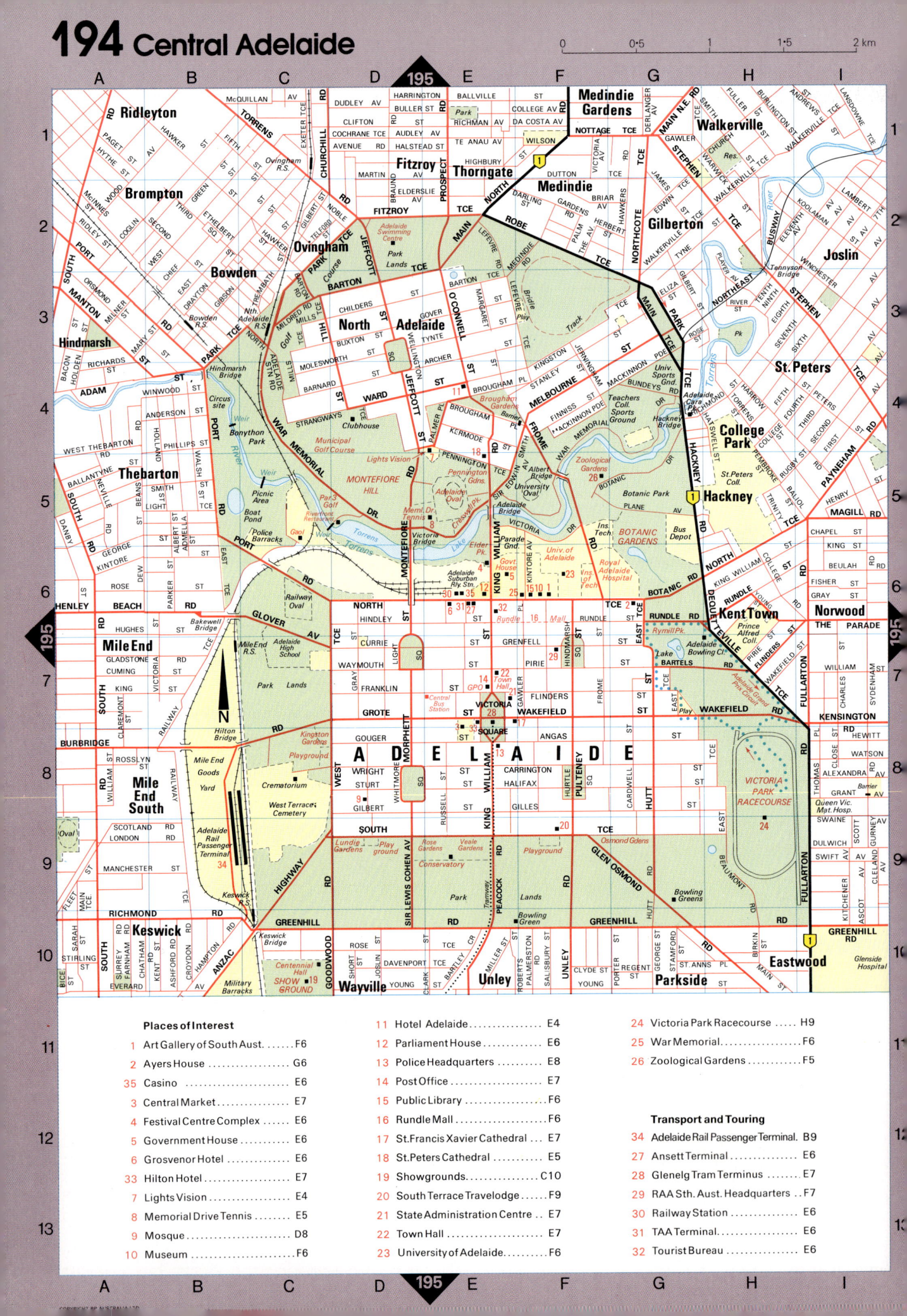

Adelaide & Suburbs 195

196 Tours North from Adelaide

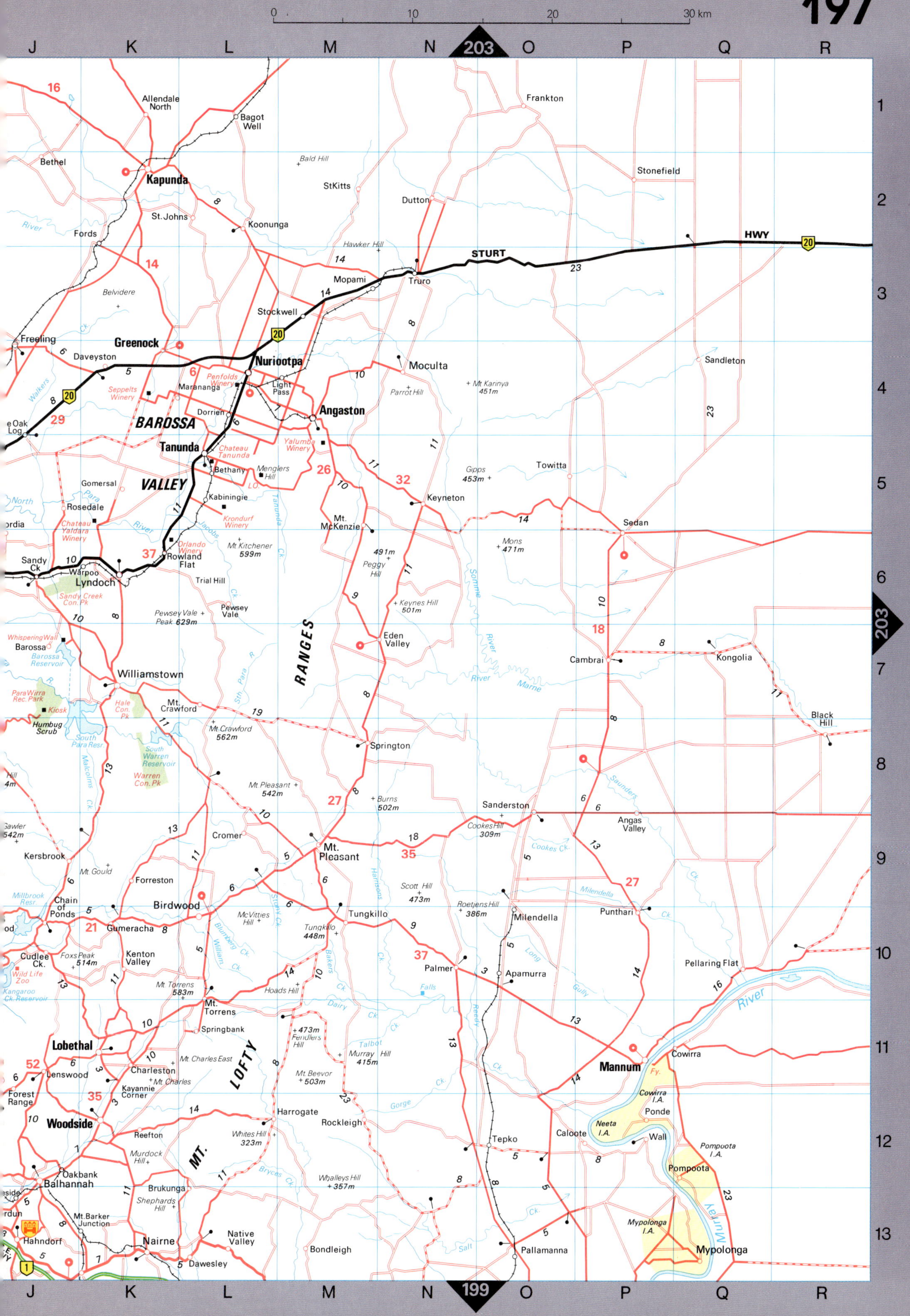
0
10
20
30 km
203
199
J
K
L
M
N
O
P
Q
R
1
2
3
4
5
6
7
8
9
10
11
12
13
Allendale North
Bagot Well
Frankton
Bethel
Kapunda
Bald Hill
Stonefield
StKitts
Dutton
St. Johns
Koonunga
River
Fords
Hawker Hill
STURT
HWY
14
Mopami
Truro
Belvidere
Stockwell
Freeling
Greenock
Daveyston
Nuriootpa
Penfolds Winery
Light Pass
Moculta
Sandleton
Marananga
Seppelts Winery
Parrot Hill
Mt Karinya 451m
Dorrien
Angaston
e Oak Log
BAROSSA
Tanunda
Chateau Tanunda
Yalumba Winery
Bethany
Menglers Hill
Gipps 453m
Towitta
Gomersal
VALLEY
Keyneton
North Para
Rosedale
Kabiningie
Chateau Yaldara Winery
Krondorf Winery
Mt. McKenzie
Sedan
River
Jacobs
Tanunda
Orlando Winery
Mt Kitchener 599m
Mons 471m
Sandy Ck
Warpoo
Rowland Flat
491m
Peggy Hill
Lyndoch
Sandy Creek Con. Pk
Trial Hill
Somme
Keynes Hill 501m
Pewsey Vale Peak 629m
Pewsey Vale
Whispering Wall
Barossa
Barossa Reservoir
RANGES
Eden Valley
Cambrai
Kongolia
Williamstown
River
Marne
Para Wirra Rec. Park
Kiosk
Hale Con. Pk
Mt. Crawford
Humbug Scrub
Mt. Crawford 562m
Sth Para
South Para Resr
Springton
Black Hill
South Warren Reservoir
Warren Con. Pk
Malcolms Ck
Mt Pleasant 542m
Burns 502m
Sanderston
Saunders
Angas Valley
Gawler 542m
Cromer
Cookes Hill 309m
Kersbrook
Mt. Pleasant
Cookes Ck
Mt. Gould
Forreston
Harrisons
Scott Hill 473m
Milendella
Millbrook Resr
Chain of Ponds
Birdwood
Roetjens Hill 386m
Milendella
Punthari
McVitties Hill
Tungkillo
Gumeracha
Stony Ck
Tungkillo 448m
Cudlee Ck.
Foxs Peak 514m
Kenton Valley
Blumberg Ck
William
Palmer
Apamurra
Long Gully
Pellaring Flat
Wild Life Zoo
Kangaroo Ck. Reservoir
Mt Torrens 583m
Hoads Hill
Bakers Ck
Falls
Reedy
River
Mt. Torrens
Dairy Ck
Springbank
473m Fenders Hill
Talbot
Murray Hill 415m
Lobethal
Mannum
Cowirra
Mt. Charles East
Fy.
Lenswood
Charleston
Mt Charles
LOFTY
Mt Beevor 503m
Cowirra I.A.
Forest Range
Kayannie Corner
Ponde
Woodside
Harrogate
Rockleigh
Gorge
Neeta I.A.
Caloote
Wall
Reefton
Whites Hill 323m
Tepko
Pompoota I.A.
Murdock Hill
MT.
Pompoota
Oakbank
Balhannah
Brukunga
Bryces Ck
Whalleys Hill 357m
Shephards Hill
Mt. Barker Junction
Mypolonga I.A.
Murray
Hahndorf
Nairne
Native Valley
Bondleigh
Salt
Pallamanna
Mypolonga
Dawesley

198 Tours South from Adelaide

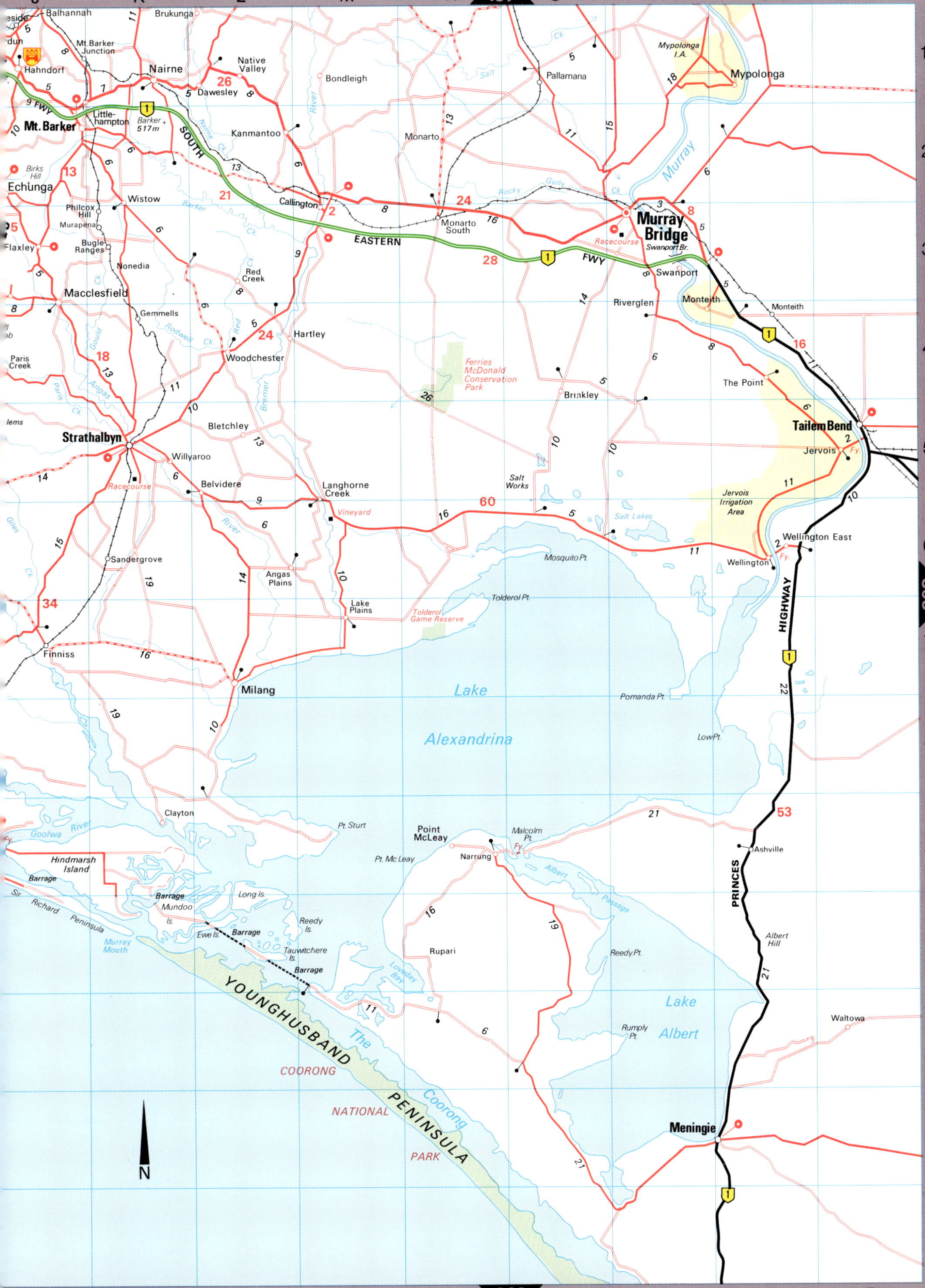

0 10 20 30 km
197
203
Balhannah
Brukunga
Mt. Barker Junction
Hahndorf
Nairne
Native Valley
Dawesley
Bondleigh
Pallamana
Mypolonga I.A.
Mypolonga
Littlehampton
Mt. Barker
Barker 517m
SOUTH
Kanmantoo
Monarto
Murray
Birks Hill
Echunga
Wistow
Philcox Hill
Murapena
Callington
Monarto South
Murray Bridge
Racecourse
Swanport Br.
EASTERN
FWY
Flaxley
Bugle Ranges
Nonedia
Red Creek
Swanport
Riverglen
Monteith
Macclesfield
Gemmells
Hartley
Paris Creek
Woodchester
Ferries McDonald Conservation Park
The Point
Brinkley
Bletchley
Strathalbyn
Tailem Bend
Willyaroo
Jervois
Salt Works
Belvidere
Racecourse
Langhorne Creek
Jervois Irrigation Area
Vineyard
Salt Lakes
Wellington East
Mosquito Pt.
Sandergrove
Wellington
Angas Plains
Tolderol Pt.
Lake Plains
Tolderol Game Reserve
HIGHWAY
Finniss
Milang
Lake Alexandrina
Pomanda Pt.
Low Pt.
Clayton
Goolwa
Pt. Sturt
Point McLeay
Malcolm Pt.
Hindmarsh Island
Barrage
Pt. Mc Leay
Narrung
Ashville
Albert Passage
PRINCES
Long Is.
Mundoo Is.
Sir Richard Peninsula
Ewe Is.
Reedy Is.
Murray Mouth
Tauwitchere Is.
Rupari
Albert Hill
Reedy Pt.
Loveday Bay
YOUNGHUSBAND PENINSULA
The Coorong
Lake Albert
Rumply Pt.
Waltowa
COORONG NATIONAL PARK
Meningie
N

200 North Central South Australia

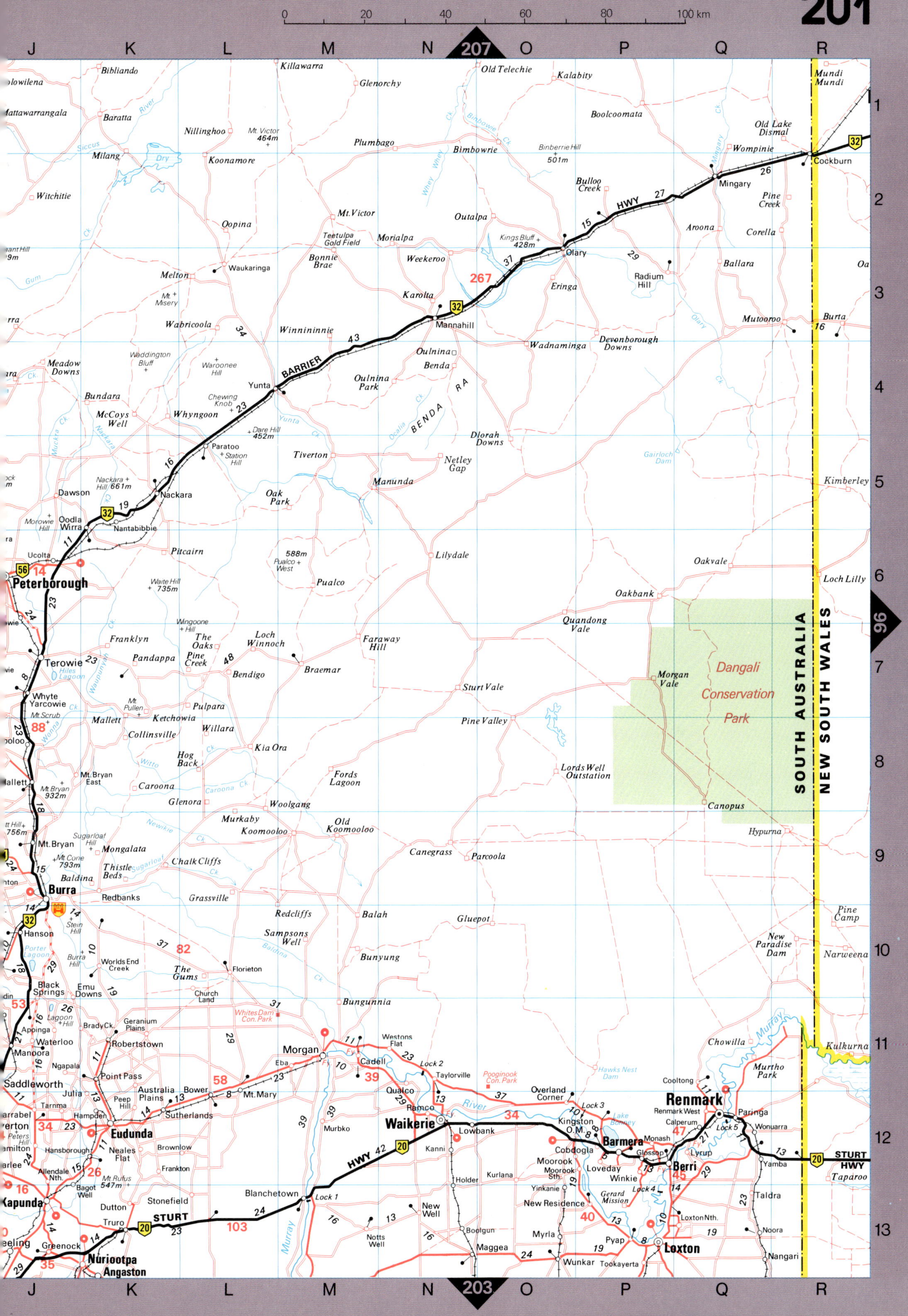
0 20 40 60 80 100 km
207
203
96
J K L M N O P Q R
1 2 3 4 5 6 7 8 9 10 11 12 13
SOUTH AUSTRALIA
NEW SOUTH WALES
Dangali Conservation Park
BARRIER HWY
STURT HWY
Bibliando
Killawarra
Old Telechie
Kalabity
Mundi Mundi
Glenorchy
Baratta
Boolcoomata
Old Lake Dismal
Nillinghoo
Mt. Victor 464m
Plumbago
Bimbowrie
Binberrie Hill 501m
Wompinie
Cockburn
Milang
Koonamore
Bulloo Creek
Mingary
Witchitie
Pine Creek
Mt. Victor
Outalpa
Aroona
Corella
Oopina
Teetulpa Gold Field
Morialpa
Kings Bluff 428m
Olary
Weekeroo
Bonnie Brae
Radium Hill
Ballara
Waukaringa
Melton
Eringa
Karolta
Mt. Misery
Mannahill
Mutooroo
Burta
Wabricoola
Winnininnie
Wadnaminga
Devonborough Downs
Waddington Bluff
Oulnina
Meadow Downs
Waroonee Hill
Benda
Oulnina Park
Yunta
Bundara
Chewing Knob
BENDA RA
McCoys Well
Whyngoon
Dare Hill 452m
Dlorah Downs
Paratoo
Station Hill
Tiverton
Netley Gap
Gairloch Dam
Kimberley
Nackara Hill 661m
Manunda
Nackara
Oak Park
Dawson
Morowie Hill
Oodla Wirra
Nantabibbie
Pitcairn
Ucolta
588m Pualco West
Lilydale
Oakvale
Peterborough
Waite Hill 735m
Pualco
Loch Lilly
Oakbank
Wingoone Hill
Quandong Vale
Franklyn
Loch Winnoch
The Oaks
Faraway Hill
Terowie
Pandappa
Pine Creek
Braemar
Morgan Vale
Hiles Lagoon
Bendigo
Whyte Yarcowie
Sturt Vale
Mt. Pullen
Pulpara
Mt. Scrub
Mallett
Ketchowla
Pine Valley
Collinsville
Willara
Kia Ora
Hog Back
Lords Well Outstation
Mt. Bryan East
Fords Lagoon
Caroona
Caroona Ck
Mt. Bryan 932m
Glenora
Woolgang
Canopus
Murkaby
Old Koomooloo
Koomooloo
Hypurna
Sugarloaf Hill
Mt. Bryan
Mongalata
Canegrass
Parcoola
Mt. Cone 793m
Thistle Beds
Chalk Cliffs
Baldina
Burra
Redbanks
Grassville
Pine Camp
Stein Hill
Redcliffs
Balah
Gluepot
Hanson
Sampsons Well
New Paradise Dam
Narweena
Porter Lagoon
Burra Hill
Worlds End Creek
Bunyung
Black Springs
The Gums
Florieton
Emu Downs
Church Land
Bungunnia
Lagoon Hill
Geranium Plains
Whites Dam Con. Park
Apoinga
Brady Ck.
Westons Flat
Chowilla
Waterloo
Robertstown
Kulkurna
Manoora
Morgan
Cadell
Lock 2
Murtho Park
Ngapala
Eba
Point Pass
Taylorville
Hawks Nest Dam
Pooginook Con. Park
Saddleworth
Australia Plains
Bower
Mt. Mary
Cooltong
Overland Corner
Julia
Qualco
Renmark
Tarnma
Peep Hill
Sutherlands
Lock 3
Renmark West
Paringa
Hampden
Ramco
Lake Bonney
Kingston O.M.
Calperum
Eudunda
Waikerie
Lowbank
Lock 5
Wonuarra
Barmera
Monash
Murbko
Brownlow
Glossop
Hansborough
Kanni
Cobdogla
Lyrup
Yamba
Neales Flat
Moorook
Berri
Taparoo
Frankton
Loveday
Allendale Nth.
Moorook Sth.
Winkie
Holder
Kurlana
Mt Rufus 547m
Gerard Mission
Lock 4
Taldra
Kapunda
Bagot Well
Yinkanie
Stonefield
Blanchetown
Lock 1
New Residence
Dutton
New Well
Loxton Nth.
Truro
Noora
Boolgun
Myrla
Notts Well
Pyap
Maggea
Greenock
Loxton
Nangari
Nuriootpa
Wunkar
Tookayerta
Angaston
Murray
River

202 South Central South Australia

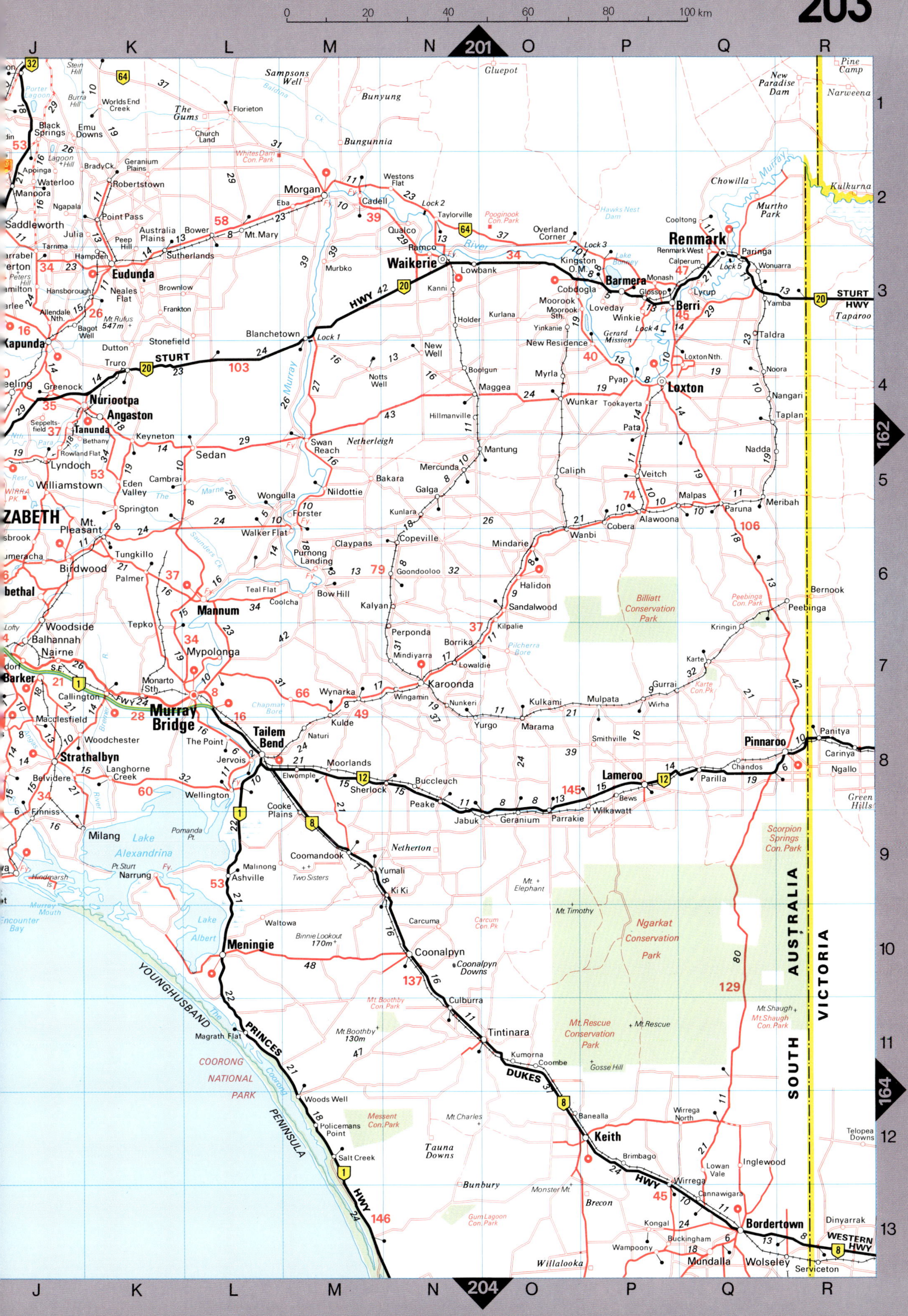
0 20 40 60 80 100 km
J K L M N 201 O P Q R
1 2 3 4 5 6 7 8 9 10 11 12 13
162
164
204
Stein Hill
Burra Hill
Porter Lagoon
Worlds End Creek
Black Springs
Emu Downs
The Gums
Florieton
Church Land
Sampsons Well
Baldina
Bunyung
Bungunnia
Gluepot
New Paradise Dam
Pine Camp
Narweena
Whites Dam Con. Park
Lagoon Hill
Brady Ck.
Geranium Plains
Apoinga
Waterloo
Manoora
Robertstown
Morgan
Westons Flat
Cadell
Lock 2
Taylorville
Pooginook Con. Park
Hawks Nest Dam
Chowilla
Murray
Kulkurna
Murtho Park
Cooltong
Renmark
Renmark West
Paringa
Calperum
Wonuarra
Lock 5
Ngapala
Point Pass
Saddleworth
Julia
Australia Plains
Bower
Mt.Mary
Eba
Qualco
Ramco
River
Overland Corner
Lock 3
Lake Bonney
Kingston O.M.
Barmera
Monash
Glossop
Lyrup
Berri
Tarnma
Peep Hill
Sutherlands
Hampden
Eudunda
Waikerie
Lowbank
Murbko
Kanni
Cobdogla
Moorook
Moorook Sth.
Loveday
Winkie
Yamba
STURT HWY
Taparoo
Hansborough
Neales Flat
Brownlow
Frankton
Allendale Nth.
Mt.Rufus 547m
Bagot Well
Kapunda
Holder
Kurlana
Yinkanie
Gerard Mission
Lock 4
Taldra
Blanchetown
Lock 1
New Well
New Residence
Loxton Nth.
Dutton
Stonefield
Truro
STURT
Notts Well
Boolgun
Myrla
Pyap
Noora
Greenock
Nuriootpa
Angaston
Maggea
Wunkar
Tookayerta
Loxton
Nangari
Seppeltsfield
Tanunda
Bethany
Rowland Flat
Keyneton
Sedan
Hillmanville
Pata
Taplan
Lyndoch
Swan Reach
Netherleigh
Mantung
Nadda
Williamstown
Eden Valley
Cambrai
Marne
Bakara
Mercunda
Caliph
Veitch
Springton
Wongulla
Nildottie
Galga
Malpas
Meribah
Forster
Kunlara
Alawoona
Paruna
ZABETH
Mt. Pleasant
Walker Flat
Saunders Ck
Copeville
Mindarie
Wanbi
Cobera
Tungkillo
Purnong Landing
Claypans
Birdwood
Palmer
Goondooloo
Halidon
Billiatt Conservation Park
Bow Hill
Teal Flat
Coolcha
Sandalwood
Peebinga Con. Park
Bernook
Peebinga
Mannum
Kalyan
Woodside
Balhannah
Tepko
Kilpalie
Kringin
Perponda
Borrika
Nairne
Mypolonga
Pilcherra Bore
Mindiyarra
Lowaldie
Karte
Barker
Monarto Sth.
Karoonda
Gurrai
Karte Con. Pk
Callington
HWY
Chapman Bore
Wynarka
Wingamin
Nunkeri
Kulkami
Mulpata
Wirha
Murray Bridge
Kulde
Yurgo
Marama
Macclesfield
Woodchester
The Point
Tailem Bend
Naturi
Smithville
Panitya
Strathalbyn
Jervois
Moorlands
Pinnaroo
Carinya
Langhorne Creek
Elwomple
Buccleuch
Lameroo
Chandos
Ngallo
Belvidere
Sherlock
Peake
Bews
Parilla
Wellington
Green Hills
Finniss
Cooke Plains
Jabuk
Geranium
Parrakie
Wilkawatt
Milang
Lake Alexandrina
Pomanda Pt.
Netherton
Scorpion Springs Con. Park
Pt.Sturt
Narrung
Fy.
Coomandook
Yumali
Malinong
Ashville
Two Sisters
Hindmarsh Is.
Murray Mouth
Encounter Bay
Ki Ki
Mt Elephant
Mt. Timothy
Waltowa
Carcuma
Carcuma Con. Pk
Lake Albert
Binnie Lookout 170m
Ngarkat Conservation Park
Meningie
Coonalpyn
Coonalpyn Downs
SOUTH AUSTRALIA
VICTORIA
YOUNGHUSBAND
Mt Boothby Con. Park
Culburra
Mt.Shaugh
Mt.Shaugh Con. Park
Mt.Rescue Conservation Park
Mt.Rescue
Magrath Flat
PRINCES
Mt.Boothby 130m
Tintinara
Kumorna
Coombe
COORONG NATIONAL PARK
The Coorong
DUKES
Gosse Hill
Woods Well
Messent Con. Park
Mt.Charles
Baneallla
Wirrega North
PENINSULA
Policemans Point
Keith
Telopea Downs
Tauna Downs
Salt Creek
Brimbago
Lowan Vale
Inglewood
Bunbury
Monster Mt
Wirrega
Brecon
Cannawigara
Gum Lagoon Con. Park
Kongal
Bordertown
Dinyarrak
Buckingham
Wampoony
Mundalla
Wolseley
WESTERN HWY
Serviceton
Willalooka
J K L M N 204 O P Q R

204 South Eastern South Australia

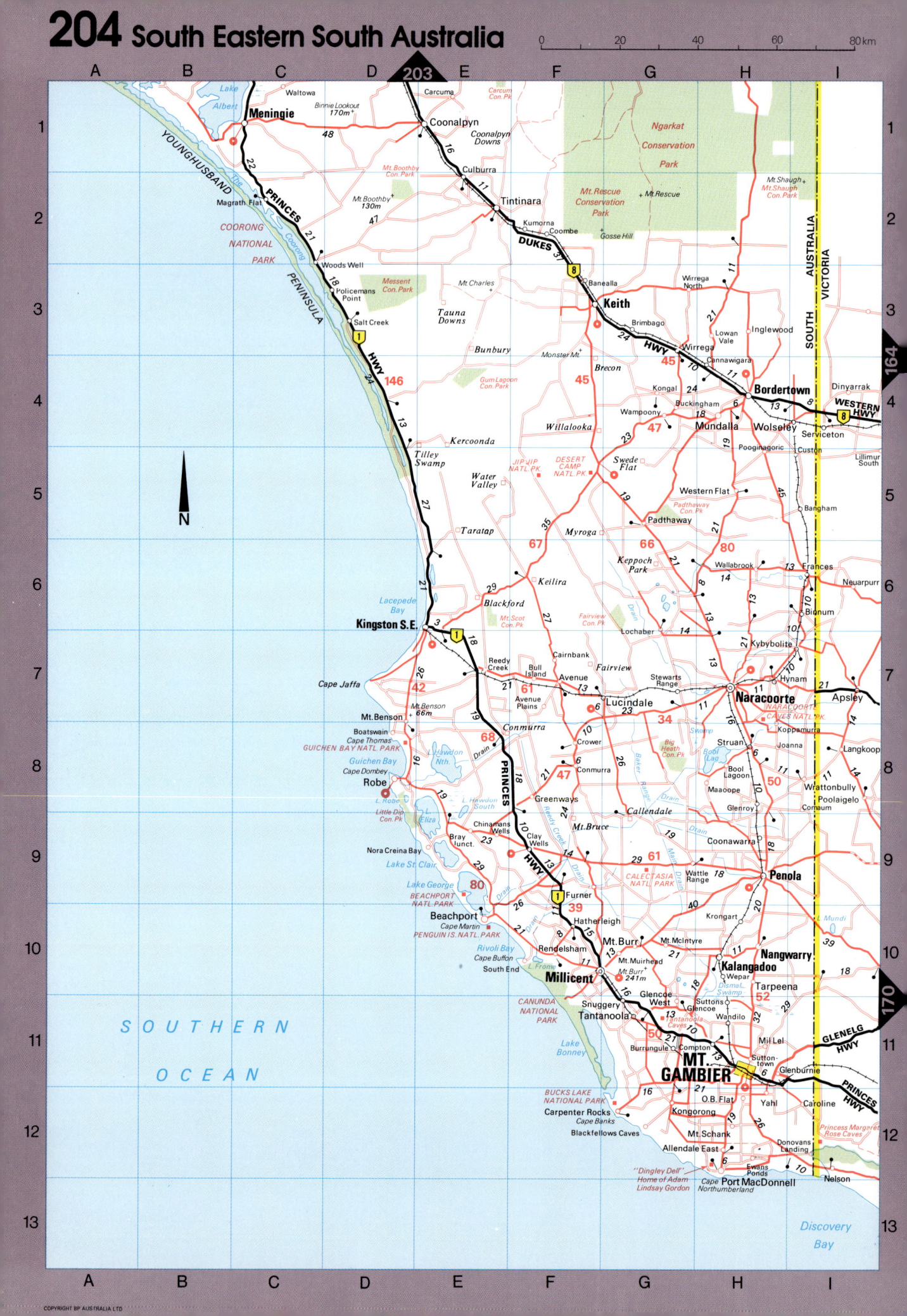

The Eyre Peninsula 205

206 Northern South Australia

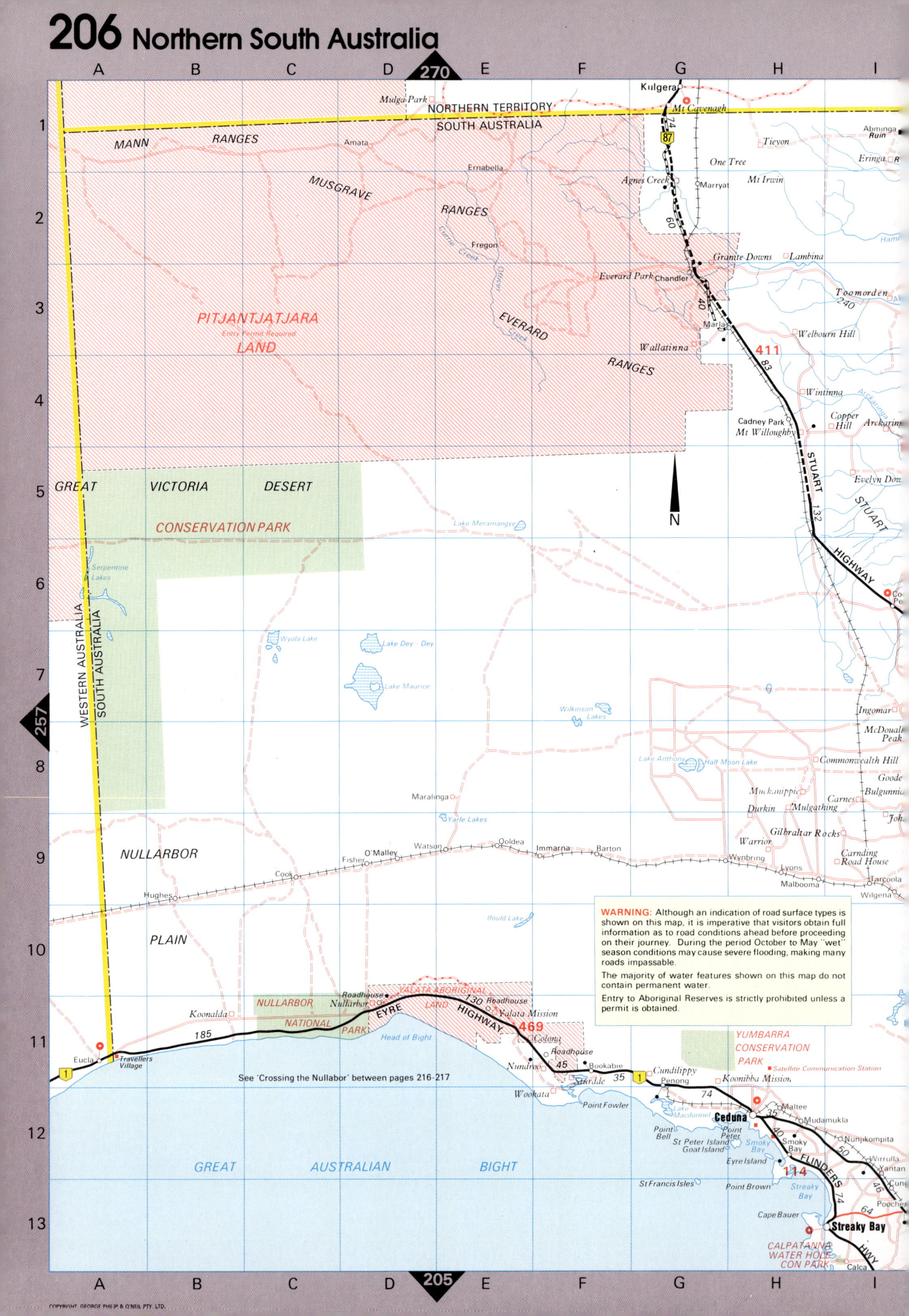

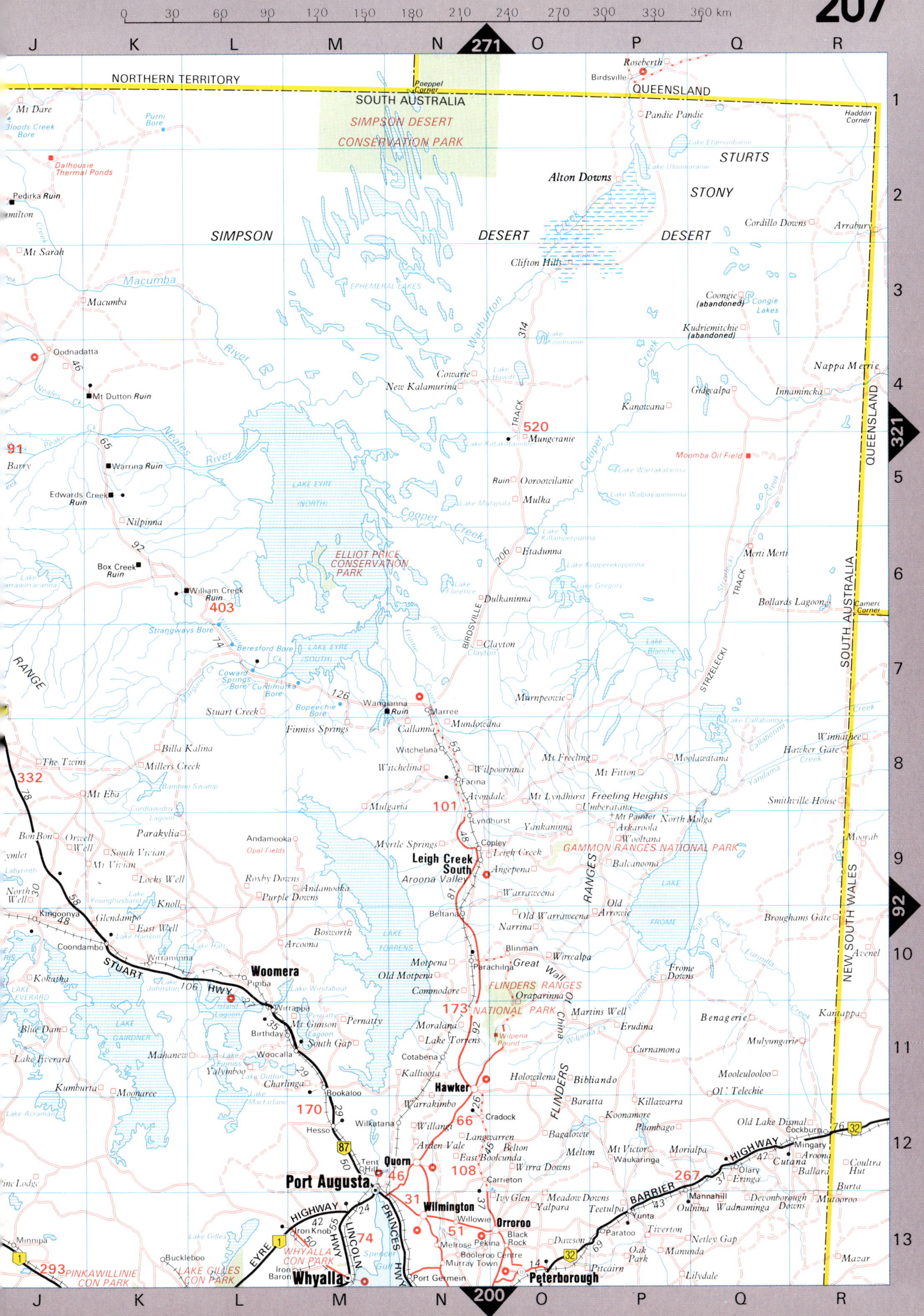

0 30 60 90 120 150 180 210 240 270 300 330 360 km
271
321
92
200
91
NORTHERN TERRITORY
SOUTH AUSTRALIA
QUEENSLAND
NEW SOUTH WALES
Poeppel Corner
SIMPSON DESERT CONSERVATION PARK
Roseberth
Birdsville
Pandie Pandie
Haddon Corner
Mt Dare
Bloods Creek Bore
Purni Bore
Dalhousie Thermal Ponds
Pedirka Ruin
Mt Sarah
SIMPSON
DESERT
STURTS
STONY
DESERT
Alton Downs
Clifton Hills
Cordillo Downs
Arrabury
EPHEMERAL LAKES
Macumba
Coongie (abandoned)
Congie Lakes
Kudriemitchie (abandoned)
Oodnadatta
Warburton
Cowarie
New Kalamurina
Nappa Merrie
Innamincka
Gidgealpa
Kanowana
Mt Dutton Ruin
TRACK
520
Mungeranie
Moomba Oil Field
Warrina Ruin
Neales River
Barry
Edwards Creek Ruin
Ooroowilanie
Mulka
LAKE EYRE (NORTH)
Cooper Creek
Nilpinna
Etadunna
Merti Merti
Box Creek Ruin
ELLIOT PRICE CONSERVATION PARK
William Creek Ruin
403
Dulkaninna
Bollards Lagoon
Strangways Bore
Beresford Bore
LAKE EYRE (SOUTH)
Clayton
BIRDSVILLE
RANGE
Coward Springs Bore
Curdimurka Bore
Stuart Creek
Bopeechee Bore
126
Wangianna Ruin
Marree
Mundowdna
Marnpeowie
STRZELECKI
Finniss Springs
Callanna
Winnathee
Billa Kalina
The Twins
Millers Creek
Witchelina
Wilpoorinna
Farina
Mt Freeling
Mt Fitton
Moolawatana
Hawker Gate
332
Mt Eba
Bamboo Swamp
Mulgaria
101
Avondale
Mt Lyndhurst
Freeling Heights
Umberatana
Smithville House
Lyndhurst
Mt Painter
Arkaroola
Wooltana
North Mulga
Yankaninna
Bon Bon
Orwell Well
Parakylia
Andamooka
Opal Fields
Myrtle Springs
Copley
Leigh Creek
Leigh Creek South
GAMMON RANGES NATIONAL PARK
Moorab
South Vivian
Mt Vivian
Roxby Downs
Aroona Valley
Angepena
Balcanoona
Locks Well
Andamooka
Purple Downs
Warraweena
LAKE FROME
North Well
Knoll
Kingoonya
Glendambo
East Well
Beltana
Old Warraweena
Old Arrowie
Broughams Gate
Lake Hanson
Bosworth
LAKE TORRENS
Narrina
Coondambo
Arcoona
Blinman
Wirrealpa
Wirraminna
Parachilna
Great Wall of China
Avenel
STUART HWY
Woomera
Motpena
Frome Downs
Kokatha
Pimba
Old Motpena
Lake Windabout
FLINDERS RANGES NATIONAL PARK
Oraparinna
LAKE EVERARD
Commodore
173
Martins Well
Island Lagoon
Witrappa
Pernatty
Benagerie
Kalanappa
LAKE GAIRDNER
Birthday
Mt Gunson
Pernatty Lagoon
Moralana
Wilpena Pound
Erudina
Blue Dam
South Gap
Lake Torrens
Mulyungarie
Lake Everard
Mahanewo
Woocalla
Cotabena
Curnamona
Yalymboo
Lake Dutton
Kalliouta
Holowilena
Bibliando
Mooleulooloo
Kumbarta
Moonaree
Charlinga
Hawker
Ol' Telechie
Bookaloo
Baratta
Killawarra
Lake Macfarlane
170
Warrakimbo
Cradock
Koonamore
Lake Acraman
Wilkatana
Willange
66
Plumbago
Old Lake Dismal
Hesso
Langwarren
Bagalowie
Cockburn
87
Arden Vale
Belton
Melton
Mt Victor
Morialpa
Mingary
Aroona
Coultra Hut
HIGHWAY
East Boolcunda
Waukaringa
Cutana
Quorn
Tent Hill
Wirra Downs
Ballara
Port Augusta
46
108
Olary
Eringa
Burta
Carrieton
267
Pine Lodge
31
Ivy Glen
Meadow Downs
Yalpara
BARRIER
Mannahill
Devonborough Downs
Mutooroo
HIGHWAY
Wilmington
Teetulpa
Yunta
Oulnina
Wadnaminga
Willowie
Orroroo
Iron Knob
51
Black Rock
Tiverton
Minnipa
74
Lake Gilles
Melrose
Pekina
Paratoo
Netley Gap
EYRE
WHYALLA CON PARK
Booleroo Centre
Dawson
Oak Park
Buckleboo
LINCOLN HWY
PRINCES HWY
Spencer Gulf
Murray Town
Manunda
Mazar
293
PINKAWILLINIE CON PARK
LAKE GILLES CON PARK
Iron Baron
Whyalla
Port Germein
Peterborough
Pitcairn
Lilydale

208 Vineyards of the Barossa Valley and Southern Vales

Many visitors to South Australia will enjoy a trip to some of the most accessible vineyards in Australia.

There are over 40 wineries in the Southern Vales area just south of Adelaide. Most are centred around McLaren Vale, often tucked away in the countryside, but well signposted so they are easy to find. Don't miss the Bushing Festival, held for a week each October, which includes tastings, tours and an Elizabethan feast.

The Barossa Valley 50 kilometres from Adelaide is also well worth a visit. Scores of beautiful vineyards cover the gently rolling hills and the delightful Germanic-style towns are readily accessible over excellent roads. The Vintage Festival held every second year in April is the highlight of the area.

Vineyards & Wineries

South Australia provides about 65 per cent of the wines and 83 per cent of the brandy made in Australia. In the equable dry climate of the southern and eastern regions of the state, kilometres of vineyards stretch over valleys, plains and hillsides. The state has five distinct grape growing regions: the Barossa Valley, the Southern Vales, the River Murray, the Clare and Watervale district in the mid-north and the Coonawarra area of the south-east. The Southern Vales with their famous wineries, among them Hardy's Tintara, Reynella and Seaview, are on the Fleurieu Peninsula, just south of Adelaide. They are famed for brandies, red table wines, port and sherry.

The largest and most famous wine-region is the Barossa Valley, about 55 kilometres north of Adelaide. The Barossa produces brandy, port, red table wines, riesling, moselle, sauternes, sherry and muscat. Some of the most famous wineries of the Barossa are **Yalumba, Kaiser Stuhl, Orlando, Penfold's and Seppelt's**. Some of these wineries are still run by members of the same families that established them over 100 years ago. Others have been taken over by big international companies, but the distinctive qualities of the wine remain.

The vineyards of Clare and Watervale are about 130 kilometres north of Adelaide and produce fine, light table wines, hock, riesling, chablis and some reds. Some of the better-known wineries of this district are Clarevale, Quelltaler and Stanley. Along the irrigated vineyards of the River Murray, grapes are grown for fine brandies, sherries, sweet dessert wines, table wines and grape alcohol which is used for fortification of dessert wines.

Coonawarra in the south-east produces magnificent red wines from a small area of unique rich, volcanic soil. More vineyards are being established in the south-east at Keppoch and Padthaway.

Most of the South Australian wineries are open for inspection, for tastings and for buying wines at the cellar door. Information about hours of inspection and winery tours can be obtained from the South Australian Government Travel Centre.

ABOVE: *Coonawarra Estates Winery.*

BELOW: *A grape picking competition at the Barossa Valley Vintage Festival.*

ABOVE: *Chateau Yaldara, Lyndoch, houses a superb collection of antiques to view as well as offering wine tastings and sales.*

BELOW: *Wine-making has been carried on for 130 years at Seppeltsfield in the Barossa Valley. This is one of the few areas in the world producing all known wine types.*

Far left: Pink Brachycome makes a colourful display near Albany.

Left: The far north of Western Australia has many spectacular red gorges.

Above: Tower blocks dominate Perth's business district but parkland and the Swan River close at hand make it a most attractive capital.

Right: The jagged peaks of the Stirling Ranges rise above peaceful farmland in the south-west of Western Australia.

Western Australia
WILDFLOWER STATE

Even a casual glance at a map of Australia will quickly reveal that a motor touring holiday in Western Australia requires much thinking about and advance planning. For one thing, for most of us it's a long, long way away, so fly/drive or *Motorail* facilities are well worth investigation; and, given that it is almost half the size of the whole of Australia, unless you have unlimited time and energy, touring by road is only going to get you to certain sections. The south-west region is relatively easily and pleasantly covered by car but much of the unique north and north-east presents a marathon trip, even for an experienced western driver.

Although the state has some 175 000 kilometres of road, the vast distances mean that driving is not always pleasant, so it is worth considering some touring by air in your schedule and budget. Ansett WA operates tours varying in length to all the spectacular remote regions.

Once you've decided by what means you wish to travel, you'll find you have a really amazing state waiting for you. Despite the fact that the Dutch had mapped the western coastline of Australia as early as the 16th century, it wasn't until 1826 that a British party from Sydney landed at King George Sound — and then only for fear of French threats of colonisation. Three years later, Perth, the first non-convict settlement in the country, was founded by Captain James Stirling. Due mainly to the ruggedness and sheer size of the land, the west remained pretty much as it had always been until 1892. In that year, gold was discovered at Coolgardie and the first economic boom for the region began. Today, of course, it is an immensely rich mineral state, its thriving economy still growing in leaps and bounds.

The beautiful city of Perth has the most ideal climate of any Australian capital. It is a true Mediterranean climate, with a midwinter average maximum temperature of 13°C, a year round average of 23°C and an average of 7.8 hours of sunshine a day. The north of the state has a tropical climate and the further south you go, it becomes sub-tropical and then temperate.

It is easy to assume from the map that Perth is a coastal city, though actually it is 19 kilometres inland, up the broad and beautiful Swan River, home of the black swan. A city of over one million people, Perth is large enough to offer a good deal of interest yet compact enough to be seen quite easily. King's Park, 404 hectares of natural bushland, is only a short drive from the city centre and the ocean beaches of Cottesloe, City Beach and Scarborough provide year-round swimming and surfing.

Once you start touring, the Swan Valley is a must, whether or not you're interested in wine. Wandering up to the Darling Range, the valley is lush, fertile and beautiful. The vineyards flourish on the rich, loam soil that is perfect for grape growing and, at the end of a day's drive, you can sample some notable results of these conditions.

Nearby Rottnest Island is low, small and sandy and only 18 kilometres off the coast from Fremantle. Regular air and ferry services from Perth will take you to this wildlife reserve, where even the surrounding sea has been declared a sanctuary. Conditions for skin diving could not be better.

Although Victoria has claimed the title of Australia's 'Garden State', south of Perth is still the 'garden of Western Australia', ablaze every spring with the carpets of wild flowers which give this state its descriptive title. Hardwood forests of massive karri and jarrah trees soar above the hundreds of different species of wild flowers that bloom from September to November. Great surfing beaches and coastal panoramas add to the attractions of the south-west region, with resorts such as Bunbury, Busselton and Yallingup.

North-east of this well-vegetated corner, and 600 kilometres from Perth, is the one time gold boom area around Kalgoorlie, surrounded by ghost towns such as Coolgardie (where it all began) and Broad Arrow. South of Kalgoorlie the modern town of Kambalda owes its prosperity to nickel. Further east you reach the Nullarbor Plain; further north are the Great Victoria and Gibson Deserts.

Up the Brand Highway, 502 kilometres north of Perth, is Geraldton, situated in a farming area. You can sample fresh caught crays here and, a little further north, see an excellent range of fauna in the Kalbarri National Park. From here on for any more exploring to the north, it's probably time to take to the air.

The Pilbara region has some of the most spectacular gorges in the country. This is where Western Australia's second economic boom began — with the exploitation of the dramatic Hamersly Ranges, which are literally, mountains of iron. Despite the fact that the Ranges stretch for 320 kilometres, looking down from the air they seem dwarfed by endless stretches of red sand.

At the state's very top is the Kimberley region, with the spectacular King Leopold Range in the west and an economy also based on iron-ore mining, as well as the more traditional cattle industry, supported by the Ord River irrigation scheme. A visit to this remote dramatic region, with its gorges and rivers, is a unique experience, though infinitely too big for the visitor to get to know — like so much of Australia's largest state.

Perth
A FRIENDLY CITY

Everybody loves easy-going Perth, the capital of Western Australia. The people are friendly, the beaches beautiful, and the climate near perfect. Perth is Australia's sunniest capital with an average of 7.8 hours of sunshine a day.

Beer gardens, barbecues, fishing, surfing and sailing are part of the Perth way of life; one family in every four owns a yacht or power boat — not surprising considering the city's Mediterranean-type climate and river setting. The clear blue **Swan River** winds its way through Perth and its suburbs, widening out to the size of a lake at Perth and Melville Waters; and the Canning River provides another attractive waterway through the southern suburbs.

The city centre, 19 km upstream from the port of Fremantle, is on the Swan River, ringed by a series of gardens, parks and reserves including the magnificent 404 ha **Kings Park**. The green bushland slopes of Mt Eliza in Kings Park contrast dramatically with Perth's impressive skyline, and the serene blue hills of the Darling Ranges can be seen in the distance.

Perth has many new multi-storey buildings which blend attractively with its early colonial architecture. There is also an extremely good range of restaurants but, beneath its sophisticated exterior, Perth is still a big country town at heart. The pace is pleasantly down-beat, traffic jams are minimal and — most noticeable of all — the people are relaxed and cheerful.

Perth was founded by Captain James Stirling in 1829 but the progress of the isolated Swan River Settlement — made up entirely of free settlers — was slow at first and it was not until the first shipment of convicts arrived in 1850 that the colony found its feet. The convicts were soon set to work building roads, bridges and several fine public buildings, and by 1871 Perth was proclaimed a city. Gold discoveries in the state in the 1880s gave Perth another boost and the recent diamond finds in the Kimberley and the reopening of gold mines in the Kalgoorlie region have stimulated new growth.

Perth's citizens live mainly in the pleasant suburbs which stretch to the north and south of the city, bounded by the Indian Ocean on the west and the Darling Ranges on the east. There are quite large Greek and Italian communities and smaller groups from the Netherlands, Germany, Poland and Yugoslavia, although most of the population these days is Australian-born. Perth people make the most of their beautiful city by cooling off on the sandy beaches along the Swan after work in the summer, or heading for the superb silver-sanded surf beaches which stretch for miles along the coast.

For the past few decades Perth has been a pollution-conscious city and a Conservation Board, set up in the sixties, makes sure that the water of the Swan River stays clear and clean. After dusk, you can still scoop out crabs and prawns not far from the city's skyscrapers and, thanks to the foresight of Perth's founding fathers, most of the river's safe beaches and unspoiled reedy backwaters are open to the public.

Major industries have been kept well clear of the city and are mainly concentrated at **Kwinana** (250 F10), 32 km south of the city centre, where there are oil, alumina and nickel refineries with access to the deep water outer harbour in Cockburn Sound.

Perth's city centre is compact, making it easy to find your way around; a free bus service — the **City Clipper** — circles the city every ten minutes during the day. Call in at the **Holiday WA Centre** at 772 Hay Street for the latest information on tours and attractions.

Most of Perth's shops and arcades are in the block bounded by St Georges Terrace, William, Murray and Barrack Streets, centring around the **Hay Street Mall** — closed to traffic — where you can sit under colourful sunshades and watch the passing parade. Perth's unique **London Court** — an Elizabethan-style arcade — runs through the mall to **St Georges Terrace**. At the Hay Street entrance to the arcade, four knights on horseback 'joust' above a replica of Big Ben every 15 minutes, while St George and the dragon do battle above the clock over the St Georges Terrace entrance. Statues of Dick Whittington and Sir Walter Raleigh look down on shoppers from each end of this elaborate turreted and diamond window-paned arcade of exclusive little shops. Perth's decorative **Town Hall** on the corner of Hay and Barrack Streets was built by convicts who left a silent protest in the form of arrows scratched into the brickwork round the clock face.

Stately St Georges Terrace — Perth's financial and professional heart — is worth strolling down for its wealth of historic buildings, cheek by jowl with towering modern glass giants. Start at the west end where you'll see the mellow brickwork of **Barracks Arch** — all that remains of the Tudor-style Pensioner Barracks built in 1863 — in front of **Parliament House**. When Parliament is sitting there are guided tours on weekdays at 11.15 am, and at 3 pm on Mondays and Fridays only.

Continuing along St Georges Terrace you'll come to the charming **Cloisters** — a former boys' school dating back to 1858 — which has been integrated into the modern complex behind, and nearby is an ecclesiastical-looking building — another former boys' school and now the headquarters for the **National Trust**. On weekdays between 12.40 and 1.40 you can get a bird's-eye view of Perth from the **AMP Lookout** on top of the AMP Building at the corner of William Street and St Georges Terrace. The **Palace Hotel**, a grand old Victorian iron-lace balconied

BELOW: *The Merlin Perth Hotel.*

hotel, is on the opposite corner. Further along the terrace is an ornate Victorian church — Trinity Church Chapel — and the arched entrance to London Court. The handsome **Treasury Building** on the corner of Barrack Street overlooks the **Stirling Gardens** — part of the Supreme Court Gardens and a popular picnic spot for shoppers and city workers. **St George's Cathedral** and the **Deanery** are two more interesting old buildings up this end of St Georges Terrace. Tucked behind the imposing modern **Council House** on the opposite side you'll see one of Perth's oldest buildings, the **Old Courthouse**, built in 1836, and the turrets of the Gothic-style **Government House** in its lush private gardens.

Further along is the modern **Perth Concert Hall** which seats 1900 and is used for everything from hard rock to opera. There are a restaurant, a tavern and a cocktail bar inside.

A visit to Perth's **Museum and Art Gallery**, just north of the city centre, could be combined with a meal at one of the many reasonably-priced restaurants which abound in this area. You can choose from Chinese, Indian, French, Italian or Yugoslav cuisines, to name a few. The original **Perth Gaol**, built in 1856, is within the modern complex of the **West Australian Museum** in Francis Street, and cells which once housed prisoners are now used for historical displays. A blue whale skeleton, the Mundrabilla meteorite, Aboriginal artefacts and veteran and vintage cars are among the many exhibits in the modern section of the complex.

The **Art Gallery of Western Australia**, just around the corner in James Street, has a good collection of modern and traditional art.

Kings Park, just west of the city centre, is one of Perth's top attractions. Within this huge natural bushland reserve there are landscaped gardens, lakes, children's playgrounds, lookouts and the **Botanic Gardens** on Mt Eliza Bluff, where you can see a blaze of Western Australian wild flowers in spring. You can drive through the parks by car, or hire a bicycle,

HOTELS
Parmelia Hilton International,
Mill St, Perth.
(09) 322 3622
Sheraton,
207 Adelaide Terrace, Perth.
(09) 325 0501
The Merlin Perth Hotel
99 Adelaide Terrace.
(09) 323 0121

FAMILY AND BUDGET
Freeway,
55 Mill Point Rd, South Perth.
(09) 367 7811
Terminal Motor Lodge,
150 Bennett St, East Perth.
(09) 325 3788
The New Esplanade,
18 The Esplanade, Perth.
(09) 325 2000
YMCA,
119 Murray St, Perth.
(09) 325 2744

MOTEL GROUPS: BOOKINGS
Flag (09) 325 8788
Homestead (09) 325 2588
Travelodge (09) 325 3811

This list is for information only; inclusion is not necessarily a recommendation.

stopping at the many scenic lookouts over the city and river; or you can wander on foot along the many walking trails right to the top of Mt Eliza. Park features include the DNA Lookout tower which offers superb views of the city, suburbs and ocean, and the Pioneer Women's Memorial Fountain.

Other city parks include **Hyde Park** with its wild water birds, ornamental lake and English trees, and the beautiful **Queens Gardens**, with a replica of London's Peter Pan statue.

A pleasant way to visit Perth's **Zoo** — with its natural bushland enclosures — is to catch a ferry from the Barrack Street Jetty. This trip can easily be combined with a visit to the **Old Mill** at the southern end of Narrows Bridge. This picturesque whitewashed windmill built in 1838 now houses an interesting collection of early colonial relics.

Swimming and surfing are part of the joy of Perth and several beautiful Indian Ocean beaches — including **Cottesloe** (250 E9), **Swanbourne** (246 C2), **Port** (246 B7), **City** (244 C10), **Scarborough** (244 C8) and **Trigg Island** (244 B6) — are within easy reach of the city, and the sheltered Swan River beaches dotted along Perth's riverside suburbs are even closer.

There are many other places of interest within a 20 km radius of Perth, including the historic port of **Fremantle** (250 F9), with its fishing harbour, maritime museum, markets and early colonial buildings. **Cottesloe Civic Centre**, in Broome Street, Cottesloe (246 B3), is one of Perth's showplaces and the magnificent grounds of this beautiful Spanish-style mansion are open during office hours. The **University of Western Australia**, with its Mediterranean-style buildings and landscaped gardens in the riverside suburb of Crawley (246 G2), is also worth seeing. The university's new **Fortune Theatre** has been built as a replica of Shakespeare's Fortune Theatre in Elizabethan London.

Perth's sporting facilities are excellent: there are two racecourses, **Ascot** and **Belmont Park**; night pacing at **Gloucester Park** — the famous WACA cricket ground is near here; greyhound racing at **Cannington** and speedcar and motor-cycle racing at the **Claremont Showgrounds**. Major athletics meetings, rugby and soccer matches are held at **Perry Lakes Stadium**, and Australian Rules football finals at **Subiaco Oval**. Hockey is played at the **Commonwealth Hockey Stadium**, the first Astroturf stadium in Australia.

By night Perth offers a wide range of entertainment: there are many restaurants scattered throughout the city and suburbs; discotheques and nightclubs; several theatre restaurants; and a good selection of theatres and cinemas. The modern **Perth Entertainment Centre**, in Wellington Street, seats 8000. Outstanding restaurants include Luis', at Sherwood Court, and Le Normandy at 73 James Street, both French restaurants, and the Wardroom at the corner of Barker Road and Rowland Street, Subiaco, is one of the city's many seafood restaurants. Perth offers an excellent range of accommodation from the five-star Parmelia Hilton, the Sheraton and the Merlin, to dozens of motels and guest houses.

Rottnest Island

Commodore Willem de Vlamingh referred to **Rottnest Island** (243) as a 'terrestrial paradise' when he landed there in 1696, and holidaymakers still flock to the island to enjoy its peace and beauty. A low sandy island, just 19 kilometres northwest of **Fremantle**, Rottnest is a public reserve and wildlife sanctuary. The island is only 11 kilometres long and about five kilometres wide. Vlamingh named it Rottnest, or Rat's Nest, because of the tiny marsupial quokkas, which he believed to be a type of rat. These quaint creatures are protected, as is all wildlife on the island.

The Rottnest Hotel, completed in 1864, was originally the summer residence of the Governors of Western Australia. Commonly known as the Quokka Arms, it's a good place to stay, or enjoy a relaxing drink in the beer garden.

There is no lack of things to do on Rottnest. No cars are permitted (contributing to the wonderful sense of peace) but you can hire a bicycle and explore the island. You may even catch a glimpse of peacocks and pheasants, which were introduced by the governors at the turn of the century. There are special buses which tour the island, offering either a simple morning trip, or a full day out, when you can take a picnic hamper lunch. There are tennis courts, a nine-hole golf course, bowling facilities and horses for hire. You can hire a boat, dinghy or canoe, play mini golf or go trampolining; or you can just laze on the beach in the sunshine.

The *Seaviewer*, a glass-bottomed cruiser, leaves daily from the Main Jetty on pleasure cruises. The boat passes over shipwrecks, coral and a startling array of fish. There are four ferries operating a service to Rottnest, departing daily from Barrack Street Jetty in Perth and also from Fremantle. There are daily flights from Perth and a helicopter service from North Fremantle. Note that all wildlife is protected. No pets are allowed and spear guns may not be taken onto the island.

Further information can be obtained from the Rottnest Island Board and from the Rottnest Island Kiosk, Main Jetty.

Tours from Perth

With the sparkling Indian Ocean surf beaches beckoning from the west, the peaceful Darling Ranges on the east and the Swan River meandering through Perth's attractive suburbs from Fremantle to the Swan Valley vineyards, there are many enjoyable trips within easy reach of Perth.

A delightful way to visit the vineyards is by river. Several cruisers operate wine-tasting tours including the *Lady Houghton* which leaves Barrack Street Jetty at 9.45 am daily. Morning coffee, wine, cheese and biscuits are served on board, stopping at Mulberry Farm for lunch. At Houghtons Winery, you can tour the vineyard and sample a variety of wines.

Other cruises will take you to an historic riverside home 'Woodbridge'. From Wednesday to Saturday nights you can have dinner aboard a cruiser which leaves the Barrack Street Jetty at 6 pm, returning at 12 midnight.

Three ferries operate a service to Rottnest Island — Perth's popular island — once the site of the infamous Rottnest Native Prison.

Travel to **Adventure World** with the M.T.T. — Route 600. Buses depart Perth central bus station daily. Adventure World is open daily from 10 am to 6 pm. Birthday party bookings are available. If you have any enquiries regarding tours, information is available from the Western Australian Government Tourist Centre, 772 Hay Street, Perth.

Fremantle, 19 km from Perth via the Stirling or Canning Highways.

A visit to this fascinating old port can make an interesting round trip if you return via the opposite side of the river. With the old world charm of colonial buildings contrasting with the modern marina facilities, recently completed for the America's Cup, it is worth setting aside a day for this tour.

Historic Guildford in the Swan Valley, 18 km from Perth via Guildford Road.

This pleasant tour takes you past the vineyards of the Swan Valley to Guildford, one of the earliest settlements in the state. Many reminders of the colony's early days remain, including 'Woodbridge', a gracious, towered, two-storey mansion overlooking the river — beautifully restored and furnished by the National Trust. The Mechanics Hall in Meadow Street houses a folk museum, and a rail museum in the nearby suburb of Bassendean is also of interest.

RIGHT: *'Woodbridge', overlooking the beautiful Swan River, can be visited either by river cruise or by road. It was built in 1885 and is run by the National Trust.*

John Forrest National Park, 28 km from Perth on the Great Eastern Highway.

This huge unspoiled bushland park in the Darling Ranges is very popular with tourists. Walking trails, streams, waterfalls and a safe swimming pool for children are among its many attractions. At weekends you could round off the outing with a Devonshire tea at the Old Mahogany Inn, built in 1837 and now an attractive pioneer museum with some rooms furnished in Victorian style.

Mundaring Weir, 42 km from Perth via the Great Southern Highway.

This impressive water catchment area which provides water for the goldfields, more than 500 kilometres away, is surrounded by pleasant picnic areas. A visit to the O'Connor Museum will help you to understand the construction and operation of this complex water scheme.

Cohunu Wildlife Sanctuary, 20 km from Perth via the Albany Highway.

Here you can see wildlife in a natural bushland setting and a miniature railway that operates at weekends.

Pioneer World, Armadale, 29 km from Perth via the Albany Highway.

A reconstruction of the days of the gold rush when every town boasted a blacksmith and a coachhouse. **Elizabethan Village** has 16th century-style buildings and a superb collection of early English oak furniture dating from 1300 to 1690.

Serpentine Dam, 54 km from Perth via the South Western Highway.

Picnic grounds are provided here, overlooking the Serpentine Dam which is set among the peaceful hills and beautiful landscaped gardens of wild flowers.

BELOW: *There are many attractive dams around Perth which are used by visitors and residents for recreational purposes. Serpentine Falls is a popular picnic spot and the nearby dam is one of the most picturesque water catchments in Western Australia.*

Pinjarra, 84 km from Perth on the South Western Highway.

This picturesque old town on the Murray River, only 19 km east of Mandurah, is becoming a popular base for exploring the area. Several historic buildings in the township include the National Trust's 'Old Blythewood', a former coaching house built in the 1830s. Later used as a family homestead it is now open to the public daily from 2 pm to 5 pm, except for Sunday when it opens from 11 am to 1 pm and Thursday when it is closed. A novel way of seeing the surrounding country is on board a steam train which runs from Pinjarra to Dwellingup, a quiet little timber town in the foothills of the Darling Ranges.

Benedictine Abbey, New Norcia, 132 km from Perth via the Great Northern Highway.

Set in the middle of the Australian bush in the isolated Moore Valley, are the imposing Spanish-style buildings of Australia's only Benedictine Abbey.

Originally the site of an Aboriginal mission started by two priests in 1846, this small community of monks — many of them of Spanish origin — now run a boarding school. The mission's museum contains a priceless collection including paintings, and Roman, Egyptian and Spanish artefacts. Some were damaged recently during a robbery.

Toodyay, 85 km from Perth via Toodyay Road.

This tour takes you through the picturesque countryside east of the Darling Ranges to the historic township of Toodyay, in the fertile Avon Valley. You could return via pleasant Northam, the unofficial capital of the area. Toodyay has many interesting old buildings, including the Newcastle Gaol, now a folk museum. After a barbecue at the Toodyay Lookout which overlooks the township and the Avon River, you could sample wines at the 100 years old Coorinja Winery, 4 km out of town.

Yanchep Park and Caves, 51 km from Perth via Wanneroo Road.

One of the most popular day tours, Yanchep Park is a perfect spot for lakeside picnics, with many interesting attractions including native animals, limestone caves, wild flowers, a golf course and a beer garden. Nearby Yanchep Beach, 6 km to the west, is a safe ocean beach protected by reefs.

El Caballo Blanco, 60 km from Perth via the Great Eastern Highway.

At this Spanish-style hotel complex you can watch Andalusian dancing horses; see over the Bodeguero Stud, carriage museum, stables and animal nursery; and ride on the chairlift or water slide. There are barbecue and picnic facilities.

RIGHT: *Fremantle is a thriving modern port but the visitor will also be intrigued by the many historic buildings. Today there are some streets that have changed little since the last century.*

ABOVE: *Perth's waterways offer ample opportunity for the enjoyment of water sports. Swimming in ocean, river or lake, sailing and fishing are all popular activities. These canoeists and swimmers are pictured on the Canning River.*

Rockingham, 46 km from Perth via the Canning Highway and Cockburn Road.

Sheltered swimming and shady lawns along the foreshore make this seaside resort south of Perth a pleasant place for a day trip. At Rockingham Museum you can see documents and memorabilia which give an idea of the town's early days as a busy seaport. It is open daily, except Fridays, 1 pm to 5 pm. Nearby Safety Beach, south of Point Peron, is another attractive resort.

Walyunga National Park, 35 km from Perth via the Guildford Road.

The Swan-Avon River flows swiftly through a narrow gorge of the Darling Ranges in this beautiful bushland park.

Mandurah, 75 km from Perth via the Canning Highway and Cockburn Road.

Mandurah Estuary and Peel Inlet provide a huge expanse of water ideal for boating, swimming and fishing and — in summer — prawning and crabbing. Houseboats and fishing craft can be hired and cruises operate from Mandurah. Further information is available from Mandurah Tourist Bureau in Pinjarra Road. Hall's Cottage, built in the 1830s, is open on Sunday afternoons and Mandurah Marine and Geology Museum opens daily.

York, 96 km from Perth via the Great Eastern and Great Southern Highways.

A visit to the quaint old township of York — the state's oldest inland town — is a must for anyone interested in historic buildings. The incredibly elaborate Romanesque-style Town Hall and the beautifully-proportioned court-house and post office in the main street are reminders of a more gracious age and Faversham House, overlooking the town in Grey Street, is one of the finest colonial mansions in the state. Settlers House, a two-storey mud-brick building, and the Residency Museum, housed in an attractive wide-verandahed old building, are also worth seeing, as are the little cottages sheltering among fruit trees in the quiet side streets. Nearby Mt Brown, an ideal picnic spot with barbecue facilities, has a lookout over the township and surrounding countryside.

Boulder Rock, 47 km from Perth via the Albany and Brookton Highways.

Huge granite boulders frame a popular picnic spot just a few kilometres from the Canning Dam.

Wanneroo Lion Park, 45 km from Perth on the Wanneroo Road.

You can watch families of free-ranging lions here at weekends, school and public holidays. Feeding times are at 11 am and 3.30 pm.

Western Australia from A to Z

Albany Population 15 222.
Albany is Western Australia's oldest town and one of its most picturesque. Situated on the edge of King George Sound and the magnificent Princess Royal Harbour, the town has spectacular views looking out over the coast, and inland towards the historic Stirling and Porongurup Ranges. With its impressive stone colonial buildings and rich countryside, Albany, 402 km south of Perth, has a surprisingly English feel about it. As Western Australia's most important holiday centre, it offers the tourist a wealth of history, beautiful coastal, rural and mountain scenery. The harbours, weirs and estuaries provide excellent fishing. The town dates back to 1826, when a military post was established to give the English a foothold in the west. Whaling was important in the 1840s and in the 1850s Albany became a coaling station for the main steamers from England. **Of interest:** The main street, sloping down to the sea, has some fine Victorian shopfronts. Albany Residency Museum (1850s), originally the home of the Resident Magistrates, has historical and environmental exhibits and is open daily. The Old Farm at Strawberry Hill was the site of the Government Farm for Albany, begun in 1872. Patrick Taylor Cottage (1832) has been faithfully restored and contains an extensive collection of period costume and household goods. Old Gaol and Museum (1851) is now used as a folk museum. Whaling Museum, recalling Albany's colourful past. Old Surrey in Thomas St is a restored colonial home, open for inspection during the summer. The *Amity* is a marvellous full-scale replica of the brig which brought Major Lockyer and a party of convicts to start the settlement of Albany in 1826. The Anzac Light Horse Memorial statue, near the top of Mt Clarence, offers a spectacular view. **In the area:** Jimmy Newhill's Harbour, Emu Point and Oyster Harbour have good beaches for swimming, fishing. Cheyne's Beach Whaling Station, 21 km from Albany, only recently closed down, had a fleet that harpooned about 700 whales each year. There are many beautiful drives and some spectacular coastal scenery. To the south, The Gap and Natural Bridge are massive granite formations. The Blow Holes and Gorge have sheer drops to the sea and Little Beach and Nanarup have sheltered waters. Towards Denmark, west of Albany, is Cosy Corner, Perkins Beach. Take care when exploring along the coast, as dangerous king waves have been known to rush in unexpectedly, causing loss of life. Porongurup National Park, with its huge granite peaks, is 37 km north, and Stirling Range National Park is 80 km north of Albany. Both parks have mountains suitable for climbing, and offer memorable bushwalks. There are many brilliantly coloured wild flowers in the springtime, some unique to this area. Tourist information from the Albany Travel Centre, 171 York St. **Accommodation:** 5 hotels, 11 motels, 10 caravan/camping parks.
Map ref. 249 N13, 256 G13

Augusta Population 588.
Set on the slopes of the Hardy Inlet, the town of Augusta overlooks the mouth of the Blackwood River, the waters of Flinders Bay and rolling, heavily wooded countryside. Augusta is one of the oldest settlements in Western Australia and is a popular holiday resort. Jarrah, karri and pine forests supply the district's hundred years old timber industry. **In the area:** There are some fascinating limestone caves. Jewel Cave, 8 km away, is world famed for its magnificent formations and beautiful colours. Lake Cave and Mammoth Cave are also well worth a visit. Alexandra Bridge, 10 km north, is a charming picnic spot with towering jarrah trees and wild flowers. Cape Leeuwin, the most south-westerly point of Australia, has a lighthouse and a fascinating old waterwheel, both built in 1895. The beaches near Augusta are fine for swimming and surfing. There is plenty of good fishing in both the river and ocean waters. Marron, or freshwater lobster, can be caught in season. Amateur and Inland Fishing Licences are required and obtained from Tourist Bureau head office, Margaret River. **Accommodation:** 1 hotel, 1 motel, 3 caravan/camping parks.
Map ref. 248 C9, 256 E12

Australind Population 1681.
The popular holiday resort of Australind is located 11 km north of Bunbury on the Leschenault Estuary. Fishing, crabbing, swimming and boating on the estuary and the river are the main attractions. The town was established in the 1840s with the aim of becoming a trade link between Australia and India (hence the name Austral-Ind) but the scheme failed. Dairying is the main industry in the region, and the Brunswick Cow, a surprisingly realistic Friesian cow statue in Brunswick Junction, underlines this fact! **Of interest:** Gemstone and Rock Museum, Old Coast Road, has an outstanding collection. Church of St Nicholas (1840s), built originally as a workman's cottage, is said to be the smallest church in Western Australia, while Henton Cottage, opposite, was once the Prince of Wales Hotel. The building is being restored. There is also a Motor Cycle Museum. Boats for crabbing and fishing can be hired. **In the area:** The pleasant beach towns of Binningup and Myalup. The Wellesley Wildlife Park has an extensive collection of native and exotic animals. There are barbecue and picnic facilities and a kiosk. **Accommodation:** 1 caravan/camping park.
Map ref. 248 E3

Balladonia Population under 200.
Balladonia is on the Eyre Highway, 191 km east of Norseman. At this point, the road crosses gently undulating plains surrounding the Fraser Range. Clay pans typical of the region and old stone fences built by the pioneer farmers in the 1800s can be seen. **Accommodation:** 1 motel, 1 caravan/camping park (with limited facilities).
Map ref. 257 L10

Beverley Population 756.
On the Avon River, 158 km east of Perth, is the town of Beverley. **Of interest:** Avondale Research Station an Agricultural Museum, displays farm machinery and equipment from 19th century. An aeronautical exhibition shows the development of aviation in Western Australia. Included is a plane built in 1929 by local aircraft builder Selby Ford. In Hunt Road is the former Settlers Arms Inn, built in 1860. **In the area:** The historic town of York is 38 km north. **Accommodation:** 1 hotel, 1 caravan/camping park.
Map ref. 251 J9, 256 F10

Boyup Brook Population 648.
A small township near the junction of Boyup Creek and the Blackwood River, Boyup Brook is a market centre for the sheep and dairy farming and timber industry of the district. There are some beautiful shaded pools, charming cottages and small rural farms to be seen. Blackboys and huge granite boulders are a feature of the river valley. **Of interest:** Fauna Reserve; old school and teacher's house (1900). Pioneer Garden is a picnic ground with barbecue facilities. **In the area:** Glacial rock formations at Norlup Pool. Vintage engines and the old timber mill at Wilga, 22 km from town. To the north-east is the Old Rose Cottage and Condinup Farm. Tourist information from the Shire Offices. **Accommodation:** 1 hotel, 1 caravan/camping park.
Map ref. 248 H6, 256 F12

Bridgetown Population 1521.
Bridgetown is a quiet spot set in green, undulating country in the south-west corner of WA. The Blackwood River, well-stocked with marron and trout, curves through some of the prettiest country in the state. Bridgetown was first settled in 1857 and the first apple trees were planted soon after. **Of interest:** Blechynden

House (1862), constructed of local clay and timber by the first settler in the area, has been restored by the National Trust. St Paul's Church (1911) has some interesting paintings by a local artist. Memorial Park is a peaceful picnic location. The apple orchards look wonderful in spring, laden with blossom. In the summer the packing sheds are worth a visit. Sutton's Lookout and Hester's Hill offer fine views of the area. **In the area:** Scenic drives take you through rolling green hills, orchards and valleys and into the karri and jarrah timber country for which the south west is famed. **Accommodation:** 2 hotels, 1 motel, 1 caravan/camping park.
Map ref. 248 G7, 256 F12

Brookton   Population 595.
An attractive town at the heart of fertile farming country, Brookton was founded in 1884 when the Great Southern Railway line was opened. Brookton is 137 km south-east of Perth, near the Avon River. **Of interest:** There is a reserve and picnic ground at Boyagin Rock, 18 km from Brookton. **Accommodation:** 1 hotel, 1 caravan/camping park.
Map ref. 251 K11, 256 F10

Bunbury   Population 21 749.
Bunbury is the third largest urban area in Western Australia and serves as the major port and commercial centre for the south-west region. Situated 189 km south of Perth on the Leschenault Estuary, at the junction of the Preston and Collie Rivers, it is one of the state's most popular tourist resorts, with a warm temperate climate, beautiful beaches along the coast, and the foothills of the Darling Ranges in the distance. Bunbury, originally called Port Leschenault, was first settled in 1838, and the whalers who anchored in Koombana Bay provided a market for the pioneer farmers. Today the port is the main outlet for the thriving timber industry, mineral sands and the produce of the fertile hinterland.
Of interest: King Cottage is a fascinating historical museum (open weekends) built in 1880. The Shell Museum, Mangles St, has a collection of shells from around the world, Aboriginal artefacts and minerals. Tree-lined pathways lead to Boulder's Lookout, a vantage point for views of the city and suburbs, surrounding hills and farmland. The Bunbury Lighthouse is a notable landmark, painted in bold black and white checks. The Art Gallery has some fine Australian paintings. Centenary Gardens, in the city centre, is a peaceful picnic spot and has a kiosk. The grassed foreshore along the banks of the estuary is also popular for picnics and family outings. There are barbecue facilities, a children's playground and a boat launching ramp. Bunbury has some excellent beaches and a Surf Club at Ocean Beach. Koombana Bay — the ideal for water-skiing and yachting. There is plenty of good fishing with bream, flounder, tailor and whiting in the bay and deep sea fishing as well. Succulent blue manna crabs can be caught in season in the estuary. There is a great variety of birdlife in the bush near the waters of the inlet. The *Leschenault Lady* and *Koombana Queen* are two vintage steam locomotives, built in the 1890s, which have been faithfully restored.
In the area: St Mark's, Picton, the oldest church in Western Australia, opened in 1842. Although now mostly restored, the church still retains part of the original structure and timber. Australind, 11 km north, is worth a visit. There is a pleasant scenic drive off the Old Coast Road with some good crabbing and picnicking spots. Wirrawee Adventure Playground, at Stratham, 17 km south, is a perfect place for children. Spring Hill Homestead (1855) is 26 km from Bunbury, off the Old Coast Road. Wellington Dam has some pretty bush walks, fishing area and grassy picnic spots. Tourist information can be obtained from the Information Centre, Corner Stirling and Spencer Streets. **Accommodation:** 6 hotels, 9 motels, 5 caravan/camping parks.
Map ref. 248 E4, 256 E11

Busselton   Population 6463.
First settled in the 1830s, Busselton is one of the oldest established areas in Western Australia. Nowadays it is a pleasant seaside town at the centre of a large rural district. Situated 238 km south of Perth, on the sweeping shores of Geographe Bay and the picturesque Vasse River, the town is a very popular holiday resort. Inland there are jarrah forests which supply the local timber industry, and agricultural land carrying dairy and beef cattle and vineyards. Fishing is also important, with crayfish and salmon in season. **Of interest:** Prospect Villa (1855) is a two-storey colonial building, which was previously a museum, with antiques. Opposite the villa is the first steam locomotive used in Western Australia. Also here is St Mary's (1844), the oldest stone church in the state. Allan Jones Cinema Museum houses an historic collection of cinema equipment. Ivanhoe Museum, Peel Terrace, has some interesting relics of bygone days. The Old Butter Factory, on the banks of the river, has some interesting exhibits including antiquated butter and cheese making equipment. Wonnerup House (1859), a National Trust Museum, is a building which is a fine example of colonial Australian architecture and is completely furnished in period style. The old school and teacher's house are restored buildings of local, undressed timber. The Busselton Jetty was the longest timber jetty in Australia, but was partially destroyed by a cyclone in 1978. It is still very popular with fishermen. Vasse River Parkland has barbecue and picnic facilities. The bay has good sheltered beaches for swimming and the western coast is ideal for surfing. **In the area:** Yallingup, 32 km south-west, is the place for surfing enthusiasts, though there is also a sheltered rock pool. Yallingup Cave, with its colourful formations, is open for inspection. Bannamah Wildlife Park houses native animals in natural bushland. There are many scenic drives in the area. Cape Naturaliste, Eagle Bay and Sugar Loaf Rock all offer excellent views of the rugged coast. Tourist information from the Busselton Tourist Bureau, Civic Centre. **Accommodation:** 3 hotels, 8 motels, 13 caravan/camping parks.
Map ref. 248 D5, 256 E12

Caiguna   Population under 200.
This is the first stop for petrol and food after the long straight drive from Balladonia, 145 km west along the Eyre Highway. Between here and Balladonia there are natural rock hole dams, where camel drivers used to stop and rest in the 1890s. **Accommodation:** 1 motel.
Map ref. 257 N10

Carnamah   Population 422.
Carnamah is a small, typically Australian country town, 290 km north of Perth. Wheat and sheep farming are the local

Broome

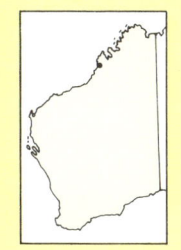

Broome (255 K5) was once a boisterous town with six hotels, three picture shows and plenty of small industries, including a soy sauce factory!

The discovery of rich pearling grounds off the coast in the 1880s lead to the foundation of Broome township in 1883. By the early 1900s, 400 luggers plied the coast in search of pearls. Today, however, Broome is a quiet, scattered settlement, though tradition lives on in its population of 2920, and the multi-racial community is proud of its town.

There are fascinating old buildings, and to walk through Chinatown, with its tropical timber buildings, is to walk back in time. The beaches are white and sandy and known for their beautiful shells. Cable Beach, which stretches for 22 kilometres, was named after the underwater cable which links Broome to Java. The Cable House, later the court-house, was built in 1888 to house the transmitting equipment. At Gantheaume Point, when the tide is out, one can see giant dinosaur tracks, believed to be 130 million years old.

An interesting phenomenon, visible several times a year, is the Golden Staircase to the Moon, when the moonlight reflects on the ocean bed at low water spring tides. The best place to see this is from the southern end of Dampier Terrace.

Each August, the Shinju Matsuri, or Festival of the Pearl, recalls Broome's heyday.

industries. **Of interest:** The Yarra Yarra Lake lies a little to the west and is surrounded by beautiful wild flowers in season. The lake attracts many varieties of migratory birds. **In the area:** Perenjori is a short drive north-east. There are several old gold mining and ghost towns nearby and the area here is rich in minerals and popular with gem stone enthusiasts. Lake Indoon is suitable for water-skiing. **Accommodation:** 1 motel, 1 caravan/camping park.
Map ref. 252 F9, 256 E7

Carnarvon Population 5053.
Bumper crops of bananas, tropical weather, brilliant flowers and excellent fishing: this is Carnarvon, at the mouth of the Gascoyne River, 983 km north of Perth. Carnarvon is the commercial centre of the highly productive Gascoyne region. The district was sighted as long ago as 1616 by Dirk Hartog. Another explorer, Willem de Vlamingh, landed at Shark Bay in 1697. The first pioneers arrived in 1876 and Carnarvon was established seven years later. Today, most of the land is used for pastoral activities, with sheep and beef cattle. The Gascoyne River often flows beneath its bed, and its resources have been tapped for irrigation. The Overseas Telecommunications Commission (OTC) earth station and Radio Australia base are both located at nearby Browns Range. The USA National Aeronautics and Space Administration (NASA) operated here between 1964 and 1974. Carnarvon has warm winters and hot summers and takes on a tropical appearance when the bougainvilleas and hibiscus bloom. The main street, built in the 1880s, is a gracious 40 metres wide, to enable camel trains to turn. **Of interest:** The museum in Civic Centre. Jubilee Hall (1887), Pioneer Park. Rotary Park. Dwyer's Leap is popular with water-skiers. One Mile Jetty on Babbage Island is almost 1500 metres long. Boats can be chartered to go game fishing for marlin or sailfish. **In the area:** Pelican Point, 5 km away, is a good spot for picnics and swimming. OTC Station with its mammoth 157 metres diameter reflector (known as the 'big dish') can be inspected on weekdays. Six kilometres along the highway is the turn-off at South River Road to the plantations. In season you can buy fresh-picked bananas, melons and other fruit and vegetables. At the Research Station you can inspect experimental farmings. Miaboolya Beach, 22 km from town. The hot water from Bibbawarra artesian bore, 16 km north, surfaces at 70°C. Dampier Salt Mines, near Lake McLeod. Ask at the Tourist Bureau, Civic Centre, Robinson St, about inspection. There are blowholes 70 km north, where the water is dramatically forced through holes, sometimes 20 metres into the air and more. About 1 km south of the blowholes is a superb sheltered beach, where you can search for oysters on the rocks. At Cape Couvier, 30 km north, giant Japanese ships pull in below the cliffs to be loaded with salt. Cape Couvier also has excellent fishing. If you drive 55 km inland from Carnarvon along the Gascoyne Road, then turn off to the Rocky Pool, you will come upon a picturesque waterhole. **Accommodation:** 2 hotels, 2 motels, 7 caravan/camping parks.
Map ref. 256 C2

Cocklebiddy Population under 200.
The old ruins of an Aboriginal mission station can still be seen at this tiny settlement on the Eyre Highway, between Madura and Caiguna, about 280 km from the South Australian border. **Accommodation:** 1 motel, 1 caravan/camping park (with limited facilities).
Map ref. 257 O10

Collie Population 7667.
Collie plays an integral part in Western Australia's development as it is the centre of the state's only coal producing region. The town is set in thick jarrah forest 197 km south of Perth, near the winding Collie River, and has an abundance of attractive parks and gardens. The drive into Collie from the South West Highway climbing the Darling Scarp offers some of the finest views in Western Australia. **Of interest:** The historical museum, in the Old Shire Countil buildings, traces the history of the area and of the coal industry. Opposite is the steam locomotive museum with some fine restored trains. All Saints' Church, built in the Norman style, is an impressive building. The art gallery has a collection of Australian paintings. Wildlife roams in a natural bush setting at the flora and fauna sanctuary where the freshwater spring attracts a variety of water fowl. Soldiers Park on the banks of the Collie River has shady trees, flower beds and lawns, ideal for a picnic. Minninup Pool is also a popular spot, surrounded by bushland and, in season, beautiful wild flowers. Wellington Dam, in the heart of the Collie River Irrigation Scheme, is a major tourist attraction with pleasant bushwalking tracks and recreation areas. The delicious marron, or freshwater crayfish, abounds in the dam between December and April. (An Inland Fishing Licence is required.) The Blue Pool is an old open-cut mine which has filled with water, making it an enjoyable swimming and picnic area. **In the area:** The Muja open-cut mines and the Muja Power Station. The name *Muja* is an Aboriginal word used to describe the bright yellow Christmas tree which grows in the area. Tourist information from the Shire Offices, Throssell St. **Accommodation:** 4 hotels, 3 motels, 1 caravan/camping park.
Map ref. 248 G4, 256 F11

Coolgardie Population 891.
The old gold mining town of Coolgardie is one of the best known ghost towns in Australia or possibly the world. Alluvial gold was discovered in 1892 and Coolgardie grew from nothing to a booming town of 15 000 people, 23 hotels, six banks and two stock exchanges in just ten years. The main street was wide enough for camel trains to turn, handsome public buildings were erected and ambitious plans were made for the future. Sadly, the gold soon petered out, and today there are less than 1000 people in Coolgardie. Many of the old buildings are gone without trace, but there is still plenty left to recall the gold boom days, and Coolgardie remains an important tourist attraction. **Of interest:** Goldfields Museum, in the largest building in Coolgardie, built in 1898, has an excellent display of relics from the gold rush; post office (1898); Denver City Hotel (1898), with handsome verandahs; Prior's Park Museum has vintage cars, covered wagons, horse and camel driven vehicles. The railway station (1896), has a transport exhibition and a display of the famous Varischetti mine rescue. A cairn 2 km east marks the site of the first gold find in 1892 at Fly Flat. **Accommodation:** 1 hotel, 3 motels, 1 caravan/camping park.
Map ref. 257 J8, 258 G12

Coral Bay Population under 200.
Site of WA's only coral reef, this development 150 km south of Exmouth is popular with fishermen. **Accommodation:** 1 motel, 2 caravan/camping parks.
Map ref. 254 C12

Corrigin Population 841.
Rich farming country surrounds Corrigin, 230 km east of Perth. **Of interest:** Folk museum in the old Roads Board office has historical exhibits including photographs. Enquire at the Shire Office about inspection. The arts and craft shop also caters for Tourist Information. **In the area:** An observation tower west of the town affords good views. **Accommodation:** 1 hotel, 1 motel, 1 caravan/camping park.
Map ref. 251 N11, 256 G10

Cranbrook Population 316.
In the 1800s sandalwood was exported from Cranbrook to China, where it was used as incense. Today, this attractive town near the foothills of the Stirling Range, 320 km south-east of Perth, is noted for its quality wool and beautiful wild flowers. **In the area:** Stirling Range National Park. The rugged peaks of the Stirling Range are one of the state's most important tourist attractions. Lake Poorarrecup is very popular in summer. Some excellent wines have been produced from the vineyards to the west, near Frankland. Tourist information from the Shire Offices. **Accommodation:** 1 hotel, 1 caravan/camping park.
Map ref. 249 M9, 256 G12

Cue Population 258.
Cue grew up as a gold boom town, an important centre for the Murchison goldfields. Today its well-kept stone buildings are a silent testimony to those frenzied days. Cue is 640 km north-east of Perth on the Great Northern Highway. **Of interest:** The bandstand in the main street was built over a well that was said to have started a typhoid epidemic. There is an impressive government office and an old Masonic Lodge, built largely of corrugated iron. **In the area:** Day Dawn, where a town was established on the site of a gold reef. The town disappeared when the reef died out in the 1930s. The ghost town of Big Bell is another crumbling reminder of the gold boom. **Accommodation:** 1 hotel, 1 caravan/camping park.
Map ref. 256 G4

CROSSING THE NULLARBOR

The trip from Adelaide to Perth along the Eyre Highway is one of Australia's great experiences. It is far from monotonous, with breathtaking views of the Great Australian Bight only a few hundred metres from the road in many places. There is nothing quite like a long straight road stretching as far as the eye can see ahead and in the rear vision mirror.

If planning a return journey it is well worth considering driving one way and placing the car on the train for the return. There is a limited amount of space for cars though, so train bookings need to be made well in advance, even at off peak times. (For booking information on the Indian Pacific and Trans Australia see page 16.)

The Eyre Highway is now bitumen for its entire length, with the South Australian section being the most recently sealed. The Highway is extremely well signposted, with signs telling how far it is to the next place with petrol and other services.

If the journey is undertaken at a sensible pace, it can be surprisingly relaxing, especially during the quieter times of year. The standard of accommodation is good and reasonably priced, with a friendly atmosphere in the bars and dining rooms of the large motel/roadhouses which are strategically situated along the Highway. Many friendships have been made during the trip across the Eyre Highway as you can't avoid meeting up with the same carloads of travellers each night. It is wise to book during holiday periods.

Although the Highway is bitumen, there certainly are hazards to avoid. The Highway is quite narrow, with bad breakaways along its shoulders. This makes overtaking quite dangerous and it can be very difficult to overtake the big semi-trailers thundering along the Highway, particularly when they 'tailgate' to save fuel. Overtaking is even more hazardous in damp conditions when the spray from the vehicle in front completely cuts visibility ahead. On the other hand, the semi-trailer drivers are usually courteous and signal when it's safe to overtake.

Another serious problem is kangaroos

BELOW: *OTC's Ceduna 2 earth station, beside Ceduna 1. These transmit telecommunications traffic between Australia and Europe. Visitors are welcome.*

BELOW: *The Nullarbor Cliffs on the Great Australian Bight. There are several well-signposted places between Nullarbor and Eucla with spectacular views of the Bight.*

ABOVE: *The Nullarbor Plain section of the Eyre Highway. This section takes only a day to cross.*

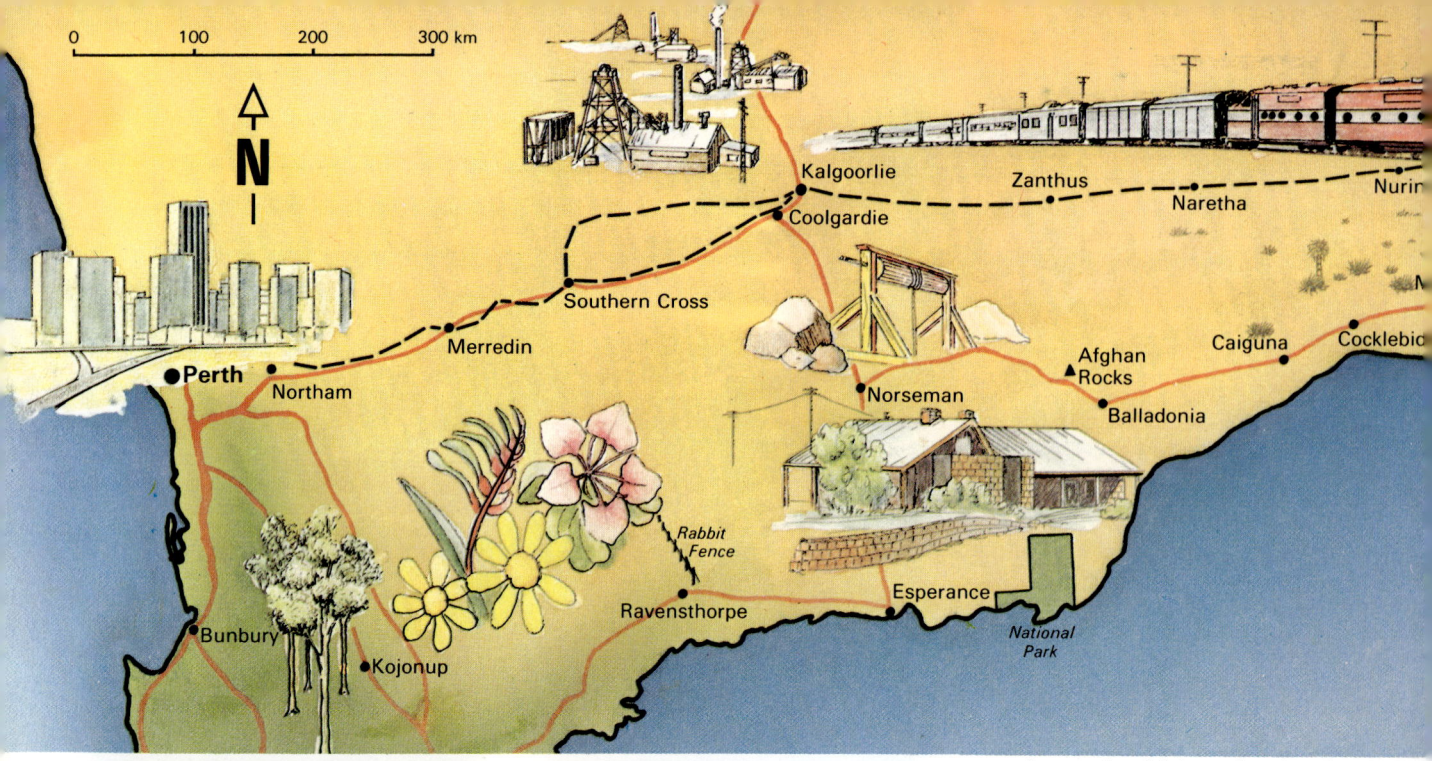

ABOVE: *An unusual road sign!*

ABOVE: *Check-point at Norseman.*

BELOW: *Typical landscape of the Nullarbor section.*

on the road, which makes it wise to avoid travelling at dusk and at night.

When you are travelling in a westerly direction the setting sun can make driving very unpleasant. Also don't forget the time changes that you will encounter on the way!

Above all, it's most important to have a safe, reliable car. The settlements along the Highway are mainly motels with a garage and roadhouse, with few first aid facilities. It could be a very long wait for mechanical or medical help.

The trip begins properly at Port Augusta, 330 kilometres north-east of Adelaide at the head of Spencer Gulf, a town of bare streets which services a vast area of semi-arid grazing and wheat growing country to the north and west. As you head out of Port Augusta on the Eyre Highway you see behind it the last hills of any size for 2500 kilometres, the red peaks of the Flinders Ranges soaring above the sombre blue bush plains. Through the little towns of Kimba and Kyancutta the scenery can vary from mallee scrub to wide paddocks of wheat. This area was once called Heartbreak Plains, a reminder of the time when farmers walked off their land in despair, leaving behind them the crumbling stone homesteads which dot the plains.

The highway meets the sea at Ceduna, a small town of white stone buildings and limestone streets against a background of blue-green sea. The waters of the Great Australian Bight here are shallow and unpredictable, but they yield Australia's best catches of its most commercially prized fish, whiting. On the outskirts of Ceduna is a warning sign about the last reliable water. This marks the end of cultivated country and the beginning of the deserted, almost treeless lands that creep toward the Nullarbor Plain. The highway stays close to the coast and there is always a little scrub and vegetation on the plains or on the sand dunes which lie between the highway and the ocean.

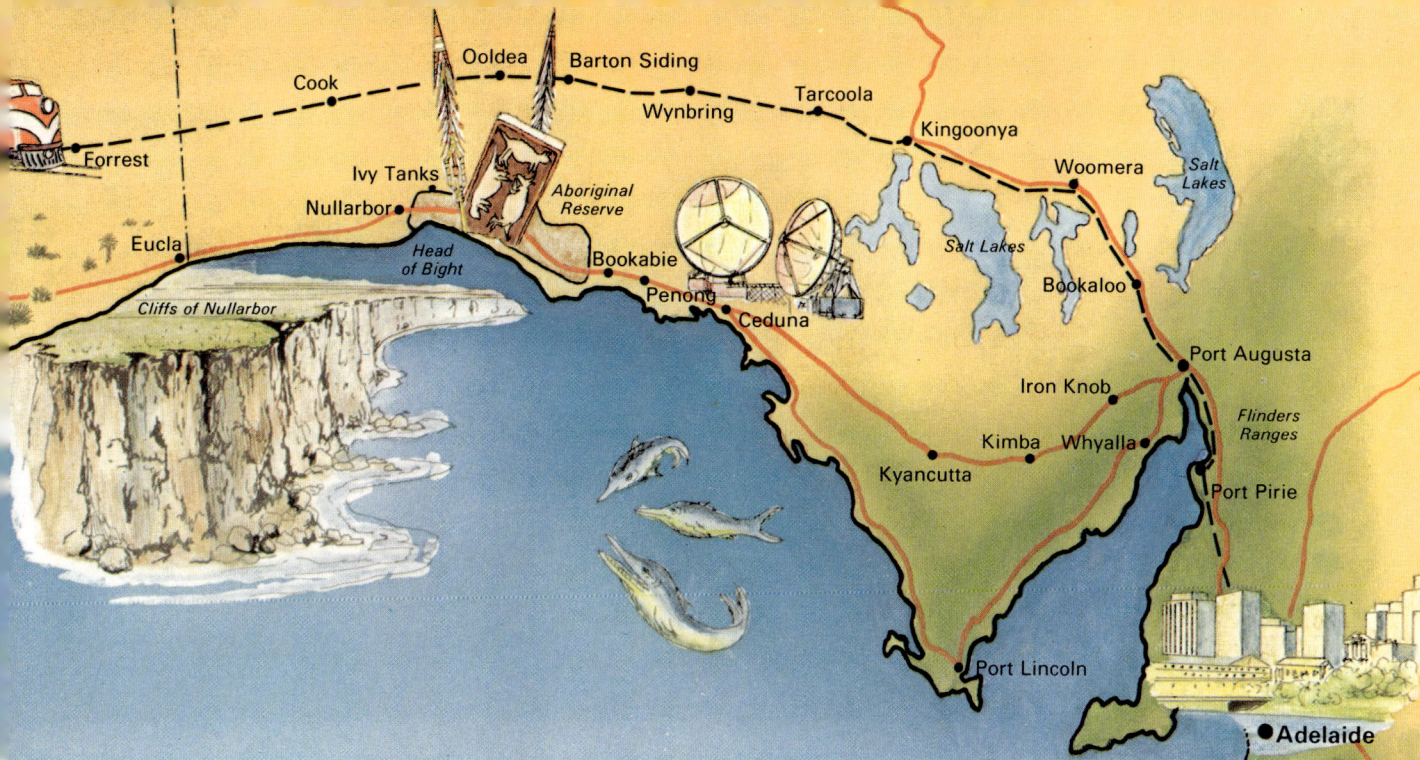

Further north the Nullarbor Plain covers an area greater than the state of Victoria. The name Nullarbor is a corruption from Latin for 'not any trees' and the name is more than apt. Geologists believe that the completely flat plain was once the bed of a prehistoric sea which was raised to dry land by a great upheaval of the earth.

While the road skirts only the edge of the plain, the country it runs through is no less sombre or deserted. Even the smallest sign of civilisation becomes an 'event'. The tiny township of Penong, a wayside petrol pump at Nundroo, the settlement at Nullarbor, the small motels that now give the weary motorist rest and comfort, the shacks of a few desert nomads and huts of road building gangs are comforting signs of life.

The Western Australian border is signalled by the tiny town of Eucla — a place of stone ruins among the sand dunes, once a station on the telegraph line between east and west. Now there is a motel and petrol station at the top of the pass near the town. The telegraph line has gone, shifted to the parallel railway line across the Nullarbor, 150 kilometres to the north. The stone ruins of an Aboriginal mission remain at Cocklebiddy, at Balladonia are the stone fences of the sheep station, then the road passes desolate flats and dry lake beds before it reaches the first real town in more than 1200 kilometres, Norseman. The town is an ideal stopping place on the road to Perth.

From here you turn north to Kalgoorlie or south to Esperance on the coast. Most travellers to Perth prefer to go north after those endless stretches of sand and scrub, and there they will see the buildings and smokestacks of one of the longest lived and most prosperous gold mining centres in WA. After more than 70 years' working, the mines around Kalgoorlie still produce more than 70 per cent of Australia's gold. Set in harsh ugly plains, denuded by the miners who 'rushed' Kalgoorlie in the 1890s, the town is picturesque in its frontier style.

The desert takes over again for a further 250 kilometres until the road reaches the wheat and wool growing lands around the towns of Southern Cross and Merredin. The farmland becomes increasingly rich as it rises into the Darling Range, the beautiful wooded mountain country which overlooks Perth. At the end of this long and tiring journey Perth glitters like a jewel on the Indian Ocean — a place of civilisation and style, of beaches, waterways and greenery.

For more information on the Eyre Highway see South Australian entries on **Kimba, Wudinna, Ceduna** and **Penong**; Western Australian entries on **Eucla, Madura, Cocklebiddy, Caiguna, Balladonia.** See also the maps on pages 205, 206, 257, 258.

BELOW: *Famous Hannan Street, Kalgoorlie, has seen the lively days of the gold rush come and go.*

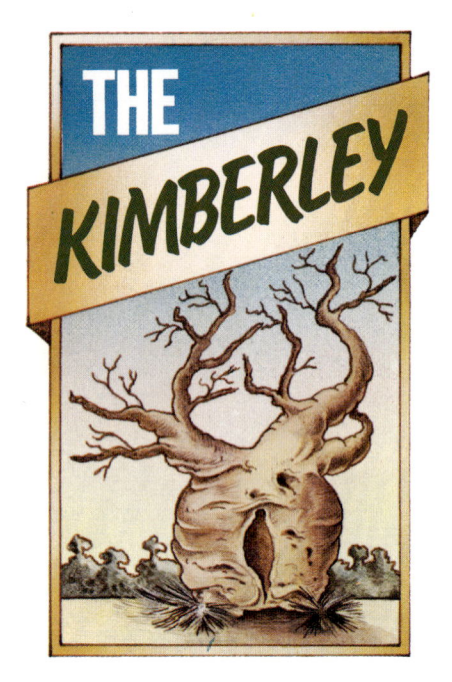

THE KIMBERLEY

ABOVE: *In 1914, there were 400 pearl luggers in Broome. Today the fleet numbers only ten or twelve.*

ABOVE: *The natural quartz outcrop of the China Wall looks as though it could have been constructed by man.*

The Kimberley region in the far north of Western Australia was, until relatively recently, only a place for hardened pioneers and prospectors. Now, with improved communications, it is on Australia's travel map and it can offer a lot of interest and adventure.

From April to November is the most comfortable time to visit the Kimberley, when day temperatures are around 30°C and the nights are pleasantly cool, but the area looks its best during the wet, from December to March.

The gateway to the Kimberley is the old pearling town of Broome. In the boisterous days of the early nineteen hundreds the pearling fleet numbered some 400 luggers and 3000 crewmen. Broome today is a sleepy, rambling town, a place of shuttered windows, deep verandahs and many corrugated iron buildings. There are many points of interest including the dinosaur tracks believed to have been embedded in sandstone more than 120 million years ago; the pioneer cemetery; the Japanese cemetery and Buccaneer Rock, reputed to be the place where Dampier was wrecked in the *Roebuck* in 1699.

Further north-east is Derby, on King Sound near the mouth of the Fitzroy River. It is a centre for the beef cattle industry of the Fitzroy Valley and the King Leopold Ranges. Just 12 kilometres south of the town is a centuries-old boab tree. Shaped like an inverted wine glass, 14 metres in diameter, it is hollow, and is reputed to have been used as a cell for Aboriginal prisoners.

East of Derby is Windjana Gorge, in the Napier Range, and to the west of Derby, on the Fitzroy River, is Geike Gorge near the tiny town of Fitzroy Crossing. These are among the most colourful and spectacular of all the river gorges of northern Australia.

The old gold settlement of Halls Creek was the scene of the first goldrush in Western Australia in 1885. Scores of diggers perished of hunger and thirst and very little gold was found. Nearby is the meteorite crater at Wolf Creek, the second largest in the world, with an average depth of 50 metres and a diameter of 850 metres. The meteorite is believed to have struck the earth about one million years ago. Also near Halls Creek is the China Wall, a completely natural white stone wall above a beautiful creek.

The most northerly port in Western Australia is Wyndham, the terminus of the Great Northern Highway and now also the port for the Ord River irrigation area as well as for the east Kimberley cattle stations. A 104 kilometre road from Wyndham to Kununurra winds through spectacular ancient gorge country. Kununurra is then linked to Darwin by a good dry weather 'beef road', which is being used more and more by travellers making a 'round trip' of Australia.

FAR LEFT: *The tranquil waters of Geikie Gorge are a home for stingrays, sharks and sawfish.*

LEFT: *Created by the Ord River Dam, Lake Argyle, south of Kununurra, contains nine times as much water as Sydney Harbour.*

Cunderdin Population 731.
This progressive town 156 km east of Perth is situated in the heart of rich wheat and sheep farm country. The district was first settled in the 1890s. **Of interest:** The agricultural museum is in an historic building, once a pumping station which was part of C. Y. O'Connor's Goldfields Water Scheme and tourist information is available here. **Accommodation:** 1 motel, 1 caravan/camping park.
Map ref. 251 L7, 256 G9

Dampier Population 2471.
Dampier lies on King Bay, facing the unique islands of the Dampier Archipelago. Hamersley Iron Pty Ltd established the town as a port outlet for the ore mined from two of the world's richest iron ore deposits at Mt Tom Price and Paraburdoo. Dampier is a model town with all modern conveniences. The deepwater port with its export facilities sees over 400 million tonnes of ore loaded each year. A solar salt works has been established with Japan the largest market. **Of interest:** The works and port facilities can be inspected. Permission is needed from the Hamersley Iron Company. **In the area:** Chichester Range National Park. **Accommodation:** 1 motel.
Map ref. 254 F9

Denham Population 402.
Denham is the most westerly town in Australia and the main centre of the Shark Bay region, 911 km north of Perth. Dirk Hartog, the Dutch navigator, landed on an island at the entrance to Shark Bay in 1616. Pearling developed as the main industry and the population was a mixture of Malays, Chinese and Europeans. Shark Bay is renowned for its magnificent fishing. There is a large export processing works for prawns. **In the area:** Monkey Mia, where dolphins can be seen playing in the water. Nanga Bay, 48 km south, has a sheep station and tourist resort. **Accommodation:** 1 motel, 2 caravan/camping parks.
Map ref. 256 C3

Denmark Population 985.
The attractive coastal town of Denmark, 55 km west of Albany, is at the foot of Mt Shadforth, overlooking the tranquil Denmark River. The town is known for its good fishing, sandy white beaches and scenic drives through farming country and karri forests. The dense hardwood forests supply timber for the mills in the area. **Of interest:** Winniston Park is a modern house containing one of Australia's best collections of English antiquities, dating back to the 16th century. Furniture, rare china and coins and over 600 paintings comprise the collection. Open daily. (Children under 12 years not admitted.) Copenhagen House, opposite the Tourist Bureau, has local handcrafts, including jewellery and pottery, for sale. Esplanade Parkland, along the riverbank, has shaded picnic areas, recreation and sports facilities. **In the area:** Mt Shadforth Lookout has magnificent views of the countryside. William Bay, a sheltered swimming beach, Parry Beach for fishing with salmon in season and Ocean Beach for surfing. The picturesque town of Albany with its rich history and beautiful beaches is a short drive away. Another pleasant drive is through the Valley of the Giants revealing the massive karri and tingle trees. Tourist information from the Denmark Tourist Bureau, Stickland St. **Accommodation:** 1 hotel, 2 motels, 3 caravan/camping parks.
Map ref. 249 L12, 265 G13

Derby Population 2933.
Derby operates as administrative centre for the north-west, and centre for the oil industry of the West Kimberley region. Derby is located on King Sound, 216 km north-east of Broome, and is a popular base for expeditions into the outback regions of the Kimberley with its network of rivers and gorges. Roads have been greatly improved in recent years, including a road through Oscar Napier and King Leopold Ranges to Gibb River and further north to the mouth of the King Edward and Drysdale Rivers. The Boab Festival, featuring a corroboree, bushman's festival and more, is held every June or July. **Of interest:** The Museum in the Derby Cultural Centre includes collections of Aboriginal artefacts and a photographic display. **In the area:** Prison Tree, 7 km from town, is a weird boab (or baobab) tree reputedly used as a prison for Aborigines in the early days. Close by is Myall's Bore, an enormous cattle trough, 120 m long and 1.2 m wide. Mowanjum Aboriginal Mission is just south of town. The Fitzroy River empties into King Sound, not far

The Hamersley Range

Stretching more than 300 kilometres through the heart of the mineral-rich Pilbara, the Hamersley Range forms a wild and magnificent panorama. The mountains slope gently up from the south to the flat-topped outcrops and Western Australia's highest peak, Mt Meharry. In the north they rise majestically from golden spinifex plains.

Although the main activity in the area these days is centred on mining towns like **Tom Price** (254 G11), **Paraburdoo** (254 F12) and **Newman** (254 I12) visitors will find plenty of other areas to interest them.

The waters of the Fortescue and other rivers have carved spectacular gorges. Precipitous walls of rock are layered in colours from reddish brown to green and blue to pink with the changing sunlight. The gorges are up to 100 metres deep with the water flow at the base sometimes only one metre wide. Others have wide crystal-clear pools reflecting the colour of the sky. Lush green vegetation thrives and the gorges are a cool oasis in the harsh climate.

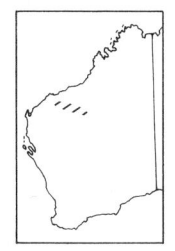

Wittenoom, 322 kilometres inland from Port Hedland, is a good base from which to explore the area. The Wittenoom Gorge is a popular spot because it is so easily accessible. At Yampire Gorge is a watering well once used by Afghani camel drivers in the 1800s. The breathtaking Dales Gorge, approached through Yampire Gorge, is 45 kilometres long, but less than two kilometres of it is accessible. Here, you'll find the splendid Fortescue Falls and crystal-clear pools. The small but intriguing Rio Tinto Gorge and Hamersley Gorge with its folded bands of coloured rock, are also quite beautiful.

One particularly stunning oasis in the Hamersley Range is the tropical paradise of Millstream, on the Fortescue River, inland from **Roebourne** (254 F9). Thousands of birds flock to the beautiful spot, where ferns, lilies, palms and rushes grow in abundance. There are two long, deep, natural pools. The springs produce over 36 million litres of water a day from an underground basin. This is channelled to Roebourne, **Dampier**, **Karratha**, **Wickham** and **Cape Lambert** to supply much-needed water. Visitors are welcome at Millstream Station. Call at the homestead to ask permission to view the lily ponds.

The Hamersley Range is rugged, forbidding country, but it can be enticing and often beautiful. Old roads are being improved and new ones constructed in an effort to open up one of the oldest areas in the world.

from Derby. The spectacular Windjana Gorge and the intriguing Tunnel Creek, with its colonies of flying foxes, are 145 km and 175 km east respectively. **Accommodation:** 2 hotels, 1 caravan/camping park.
Map ref. 255 M5

Dongara Population 1155.
A small settlement 359 km north of Perth, Dongara has superb beaches, reef-enclosed bays and an abundance of delicious rock lobster. **Of interest:** The Old Mill Motel has a very good, fully-licensed restaurant. Historic buildings include the Police Station, Old Mill and Russ Cottage. **In the area:** Port Denison, south along the coast and the historic hamlet of Greenough is 40 km north. **Accommodation:** 1 hotel, 1 motel, 1 caravan/camping park.
Map ref. 252 B7, 256 D7

The South-west

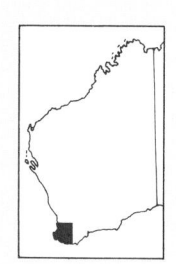

The south-west corner of Western Australia is a lush green land. Its gently rolling hills are crossed by rivers winding through deep-sided valleys. The soils are fertile and the farms prosperous. Along the coast there are beautiful bays and inland are majestic towering karri and jarrah forests. The countryside is dotted with picturesque fruit orchards and in any season the vibrant colours of many flowers can be seen; Western Australia is one of the richest areas of flora in the world. The Mediterranean climate ensures warm, dry summers and mild, wet winters.

Pinjarra, 84 kilometres south of Perth, is one of the state's oldest districts.

Near **Harvey** there is fine agricultural land and the undulating farms stretch to the foothills of the Darling Range. To the north-west is Yalgorup National Park where the lakes attract a wide variety of birdlife. The Old Coast Road, which edges down the coast to Bunbury, is a perfect choice if you want to 'get off the beaten track'.

The coast of the south-west is fascinating: a strange mixture of craggy outcrops and promontories, sheltered bays with calm waters and beaches pounded by rolling surf. From Cape Leeuwin it is possible to see the unique sight of the sun rising over one ocean and setting over another. The length of the coast, together with the many rivers and estuaries, makes the south-west an angler's paradise.

Donnybrook Population 1197.
The township of Donnybrook is at the heart of the oldest apple growing area in Western Australia, 210 km south of Perth. Gold was discovered here in 1898, but it was only mined for three years. Today the delicious Granny Smith apples are know as Donnybrook's 'Green Gold'. The colourful Apple Festival is held every year at Easter. **Of interest:** The Anchor and Hope Inn (1865), once a staging post for mail coaches. Glen Karaleea Deer Park, open 9.30 am-5 pm daily. **Accommodation:** 2 hotels, 1 motel, 1 caravan/camping park.
Map ref. 248 F5, 256 E12

Dumbleyung Population 274.
Dumbleyung lies in the central south of Western Australia, 217 km east of Bunbury and 224 km north of Albany. **Of interest:**

The Murray, Harvey and Brunswick and their tributaries are just some of the streams annually stocked with trout.

The main port for the south-west, **Bunbury** rests on Geographe Bay looking out over the Indian Ocean. It is a perfect holiday town flanked by golden beaches and peaceful rural farmland. One of the oldest towns in the state, **Busselton** is perfectly sited on the Vasse River and has a wealth of pioneer homes, many restored and open to the public.

Cape Leeuwin-Naturaliste National Park combines a scenic coast with magnificent wild flowers and the tall timbers of karri and jarrah forests.

Yallingup (248 C6) is known for its excellent surf and spectacular limestone caves. Dripping water has created strange shapes in the limestone, with magic colours reflected in the glittering underground water.

Bridgetown, Donnybrook and **Greenbushes** (256E12) are small townships tucked away in green hilly country and pretty apple orchards. Gold flourished briefly here at the turn of the century. **Manjimup** and **Pemberton** are world famous for their timber, the giant karri and jarrah trees. Here, some of the world's tallest trees reach straight up, often 80 and 90 metres, to the sky. The Pemberton, Scott, Warren and Brockman National Parks are all near here, introduced to protect the unique environment.

There is an historical museum. **In the area:** At nearby Lake Dumbleyung, Sir Donald Campbell broke the world water speed record in 1964. The area is ideal for swimming and picnicking. **Accommodation:** 1 hotel, 1 caravan/camping park.
Map ref. 249 N4, 256 G11

Dunsborough Population 329.
Dunsborough is a quiet town on Geographe Bay, west of Busselton, popular because of its fine beaches. **Of interest:** Greenacres a shell museum; Bannamah Wild Life Park, 2 km from town. There are good beaches at Meelup, Eagle and Bunker Bays. **Accommodation:** 1 hotel, 1 motel, 2 caravan/camping parks.
Map ref. 248 C5

Dwellingup Population 453.
This quiet little town east of Pinjarra is 109 km from Perth. The road into Dwellingup offers some marvellous views of the Indian Ocean and the Peel Inlet. The impressive jarrah and karri forests supply the local timber mill and bauxite is mined nearby. **Of interest:** Enjoy a real country-style meal in the friendly Dwellingup Community Hotel. The Hotham Valley Railway runs an old-style steam-train between Pinjarra and Dwellingup. **Accommodation:** 1 hotel.
Map ref. 250 G12, 256 F11

Esperance Population 6375.
Wide sandy beaches, scenic coastline and the off-shore islands of the Recherche Archipelago are all attractions of Esperance on the south coast of Western Australia. The town, 760 km from Perth, via Wagin, is both port and service centre for the highly productive agricultural and pastoral hinterland. The first permanent settlers came in 1863. The town boomed during the 1890s as port for the goldfields, but it was not until the 1950s, when scientists realised that the heath plains could be transformed into fertile pasture and farming country, that the town's development began in earnest. **Of interest:** The Municipal Museum has a fine collection of machinery, furniture and farm equipment. Public Library, Windich St, has a collection of books on the history of Esperance. The arts and crafts centre, in the youth centre, has pottery, paintings and handcrafts for sale. Visit the Kurrawong Mission, 2 km from town, to see genuine Aboriginal artefacts. There are also handcrafts, drawings and carvings for sale. Pink Lake is a dense salt water lake and it really is pink. Twilight Bay is a pretty spot for swimming, fishing. A little further on is Picnic Cove with a sheltered swimming beach. At Observatory Point and Lookout near here you can look out over the bay and islands. Rotary Lookout, or Wireless Hill, offers excellent views of the bay, township and farmlands. The Recherche Archipelago, or Bay of Isles, consists of almost 100 small islands. These unspoiled islands are a haven for native fauna, and many unusual species of birds can be seen. There are regular cruises during January and February. There are also trips to Woody

Island which is being developed as an animal sanctuary. **In the area:** Cape Le Grand National Park, 56 km to the east, includes spectacular coastline and many attractive beaches. There are scenic walks and the beautiful wild flowers for which the west is famous. Frenchmans Peak, in the park, has a magnificent view. The huge granite rock can be climbed, but is dangerous when wet. Orleans Farm, 103 km east, is a property specialising in Santa Gertrudis cattle. Visitors may drive on to the property. The homestead has a fine collection of paintings by some of Australia's best known artists. Enquire at the tourist bureau in Dempster St for more details. **Accommodation:** 1 hotel, 4 motels, 5 caravan/camping parks.
Map ref. 257 K12

Eucla Population under 200.
Eucla is just 13 km from the Western Australia/South Australia border, on the Eyre Highway. The ruins of the old telegraph station, once one of the busiest in Australia, can be seen, though they are gradually being covered by sand. The road east, descending Eucla Pass, offers a stunning view of the white sand plains stretching ahead. **Accommodation:** 1 hotel, 2 motels, 1 caravan/camping park.
Map ref. 257 Q9

Fitzroy Crossing Population 428.
In the Kimberley, where the road north crosses the Fitzroy River, is the tiny settlement of Fitzroy Crossing, 270 km inland from Derby. **In the area:** There are picturesque waterholes, supporting an abundance of fish and wildlife. The magnificent Geikie Gorge is 20 km away. Sharks and sawfish, which have adapted to the fresh water, and freshwater crocodiles swim here. Regular boat trips are available during the tourist season at 9.00 am and 2.30 pm. **Accommodation:** 1 motel, 1 caravan/camping park.
Map ref. 255 O6

Fremantle Population 24 000.
The largest port in the state, and known as the 'Western Gateway to Australia'. Fremantle is a bustling city 20 km south of Perth. It is a city of contrasts, with galleries and museums, beautiful sandy white beaches and many historic buildings as a reminder of the city's heritage. Captain Charles Fremantle arrived in May 1829, to take possession of 'the whole of the west coast of New Holland' and was followed one month later by Captain James Stirling who arrived in 1829 with a small group of settlers to found the first colony in Australia made up entirely of free settlers. The engineer C.Y. O'Connor, who instigated the Goldfields Water Scheme, was also responsible for building the artificial harbour which turned Fremantle into an important port. The city was the first stop for many migrants arriving in Australia and as a result has a large European population. **Of interest:** Fremantle Art Gallery, Pioneer Reserve. The Maritime Museum, Finnerty St, was built in the 1860s as a lunatic asylum, and is a fine example of colonial Gothic architecture. Fremantle Arts Centre, in a wing of the Museum complex, has paintings and handcrafts. During the summer the courtyard is used as an outdoor theatre. Cliff Street Art Gallery, 34 Cliff St, is in an early colonial warehouse. Potter's Shed, near the Round House, is a pottery workshop in a converted boatshed. Round House (1830) is the oldest building in Western Australia. The twelve-sided building was constructed as a gaol. Fremantle Gaol (1851-9), a forbidding building of local stone, is still used as a prison. Fremantle Prison Museum, an historic building with displays recording the penal system in Western Australia, is adjacent to the prison. Warders' Quarters is a Georgian terrace, still used by the prison today. Old Customs House (1853) in Cliff St is also in the Georgian style. St John's Church and Square (1882). The gracious Town Hall in the centre of the town was opened in 1887.

The Great Southern

The Great Southern is bounded by a dramatically rugged coastline and the roaring Southern Ocean. The coast gives way to an amazingly beautiful hinterland, rivers winding through forests, ancient mountain ranges and gentle valleys.

The district has an important historical heritage, too. **Albany** was the first town in Western Australia, established two and a half years before the Swan River colony. Major Edmund Lockyer landed in 1826, to claim the western half of the continent as British territory.

Albany is the unofficial capital of the area, and retains a charming English atmosphere from the colonial days. The town looks out over the magnificent blue waters of Princess Royal Harbour in King George Sound. Albany has a number of fine old homesteads, museums and galleries. There are numerous scenic drives around the coast, to the Gap and Natural Bridge, to Dog Rock and the Blowholes. There are also stretches of

The quaint old building at No. 5 Mouat St originally housed the German Consulate and shipping offices. Fremantle Markets, Henderson St, an impressive building, sells food, delicious seafoods, handcrafts, antiques, clothing and more. Adjacent to Marine Terrace and The Esplanade are the modern marina facilities developed for the first Australian Defence of the America's Cup, yachting's most prestigious trophy. Fremantle's large fishing fleet, which works Australia's most valuable fishery, mainly lobster, and its considerable Italian community, give the city a Mediterannean flavour with sidewalk cafes and excellent restaurants. The new Lombardo's restaurant complex is on Fishing Boat Harbour. Port Leighton and South Beaches are all good for swimming. South Beach is especially good for families. Ferries to golden sand and secluded bays. The fishing is superb. **Denmark**, a holiday resort, lies on the banks of the tranquil Denmark River and the little village of **Nornalup** (249 J13) nestles near the Frankland River. Near **Walpole** (248 I 12) is the awe-inspiring Valley of the Giants, tingle and karri trees towering over the tangled undergrowth and vivid splashes of flowers.

The Great Southern has a new industry — viticulture. The vineyards around Mt Barker have already produced award-winning wines. Mt Barker itself is gateway to the Stirling and Porongurup mountain ranges, both within the confines of national parks. The Porongurup Range has granite peaks dominating giant hardwood trees and a maze of wild flowers and creepers. There are many easy climbs, rewarded by panoramic views: Castle Rock, Howard's Peak and Devil's Slide are three of the most popular.

The Stirling Range has high jagged peaks (the highest is Bluff Knoll at 1037 metres) which tower over virgin bushland. From a distance the vegetation changes from heathery shades to blues and reds with the changing light. The peaks can sometimes be seen mysteriously shrouded in mist, and sometimes even tipped with snow.

There are more than 100 species of birds in the park and a great deal of native wildlife. Look for the beautiful wild orchids, Stirling banksia and mountain bells.

The inland area of the Great Southern is dotted with small friendly towns. **Boyup Brook**, noted for its blackboy trees, **Wagin** with its fine Victorian buildings, and the thriving town of **Katanning. Kojonup** (249 K6), **Gnowangerup** (249 O7) and **Ongerup** (249 Q7) are all surrounded by peaceful rural farmland.

Rottnest Island leave from the wharf daily during summer. **In the area:** South of Fremantle is the Kwinana Industrial Complex. Tours can be arranged, including inspection of the oil refinery, alumina and steel works. **Accommodation:** 9 hotels.
Map ref. 246 C8, 250 F9, 256 E10

Geraldton Population 20 895.
The key port and administration centre for the mid-west region, Geraldton enjoys a sunny year-round climate. The mild winter makes it one of the state's most popular winter holiday resorts. Geraldton is 503 km north of Perth on Champion Bay. The city itself is flourishing with a modern shopping centre, interesting museums and excellent accommodation. The beaches are sandy and white and the fishing is good. Rich agricultural land surrounds Geraldton and the district is noted for its beautiful spring wild flowers and picturesque countryside. The Houtman Abrolhos Islands lie 64 km off the coast. They were first sighted and named in the 16th century. There have been many tragic shipwrecks off the coast since then, and coins and other relics have been discovered. **Of interest:** St Francis Xavier Cathedral, designed by an architect-priest who is responsible for some fine buildings in Geraldton. Gem and Mineral Museum. The Geraldton Museum has a good collection of earthenware pots and wine vessels, bronze cannon and coins and other relics from shipwrecks. Tourist Lookout and Wishing Well on Waverley Heights has panoramic views. Point Moore Lighthouse, built in 1878. The Abrolhos Islands are used mainly as a base for the rock lobster fishermen. Fishing is popular and many varieties can be caught. Drummond's Cove, Sunset Beach, the Greenough River mouth and the town's breakwater are all good locations. At Fisherman's Wharf, during the season which is from mid November until the end of June, you can watch the huge hauls of lobster being unloaded. **In the area:** Greenough River is a favourite place for picnics and has safe swimming for children. Ellendale Bluffs and Pool, a permanent waterhole at the base of a steep rock face. Chapman Valley, where there are brilliant wild flowers in spring. From Mill's Lookout, on the Waggrakine Cutting, you can look out over the Moresby Range and coastal pain towards Geraldton. Kalbarri National Park. The sheer coastal rock faces and deep gorges of the Murchison River are stunningly beautiful. **Accommodation:** 6 hotels, 7 motels, 4 caravan/camping parks.
Map ref. 252 A5, 256 D6

Gingin Population 382.
Gingin is situated 82 km north of Perth and 30 km from the coast. It is mainly concerned with sheep, wheat and cattle farming. **In the area:** At the mouth of the Moore River is the popular holiday resort of Guilderton, 93 km from Perth. Guilderton is popular with fishing enthusiasts. Yanchep National Park is to the south. **Accommodation:** 1 hotel, 1 caravan/camping park.
Map ref. 250 F6, 256 E9

Western Australia's National Parks

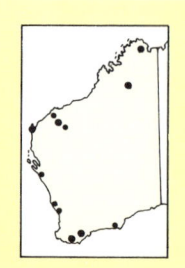

The national parks of Western Australia are tourist attractions in themselves: their spectacular displays of wild flowers create a paradise for photographers and a colourful wonderland for bushwalkers and campers.

Western Australia has more than 3000 species of wild flowers, of all colours and sizes, growing undisturbed in their natural surroundings. One quarter of these species cannot be found anywhere else in the world and they lure admirers from interstate and overseas.

The best months to see them are from August to October. This is also the best time for camping and walking.

Stirling Range National Park, 322 kilometres south-east of Perth, is one of Australia's outstanding reserves. Surrounded by a flat, sandy plain, the Stirling Ranges rise abruptly over 100 metres, their jagged peaks veiled in swirling mists. The cool, humid environment created by these low clouds is responsible for the survival of more than 500 species of plants, some of which, like the Mountain Bell, are found nowhere else in the world.

In the Pilbara, 1000 kilometres north of Perth, is Hamersley Range, a massive block of weathered rock over 450 kilometres long. Within this

Goldsworthy Population 923.
Goldworthy is 112 km from Port Hedland in the Pilbara region of Western Australia. It was the first town in the north-west built for iron ore. Mt Goldworthy itself, once 132 metres high, has been mined into a deep pit. A railway line has been built by Goldsworthy Mining Ltd to Port Hedland on the north-west coast where the iron ore is exported overseas. **Accommodation:** None.
Map ref. 254 H8

Halls Creek Population 966.
In the heart of the Kimberley, 2832 km from Perth, at the edge of the Great Sandy Desert, is Halls Creek, site of Western Australia's first gold discovery, back in 1885. Within a year over 2000 miners had arrived, but there was little gold, and the harsh conditions and hostile Aborigines defeated most of them. The original townsite is 14 km from the present location. Halls Creek is now a centre for the large beef industry. **Of interest:** Crumbling mud brick ruins of the original settlement. China Wall, a natural quartz wall, 6 km north near the creek. Wolf Creek Meteorite Crater, 148 km south, is almost 1 km wide and 49 metres deep and the second largest meteorite crater in the world. **Accommodation:** 1 hotel, 1 motel, 1 caravan/camping park.
Map ref. 255 Q6

Harvey Population 2479.
The thriving town of Harvey is set amidst some of the finest agricultural country in Australia, 139 km south of Perth. Bordered by the Darling Range and the Indian Ocean, the fertile coastal plains make perfect dairying country. The irrigation storage dams have become a popular tourist attraction with their cool water and recreation areas. **Of interest:** J. Knowles' House and Store. Built as the first business premises in Harvey in 1890, the store is now a museum with a fascinating collection of old prints showing the pioneer history of the area. The dwelling is furnished in period style. **In the area:** Wellesley Road Wildlife Park. The Logue Brook Dam, 10 km north, is a popular venue for swimmers, water-skiers and trout fishermen. There are tracks for bushwalking enthusiasts. Myalup and Binningup beaches are wide and sandy, ideal for swimming, fishing and boating. North-west is the Yalgorup National Park. Tourist information from the Harvey Shire Tourist Bureau, Young St. **Accommodation:** 1 hotel, 2 caravan/camping parks.
Map ref. 248 F2

Hopetoun Population under 200.
Hopetoun is a peaceful holiday resort that overlooks the Southern Ocean. The town is 55 km south of Ravensthorpe and offers some rugged but beautiful coastal scenery. The town was once called Mary Anne Harbour and has a colourful history. **Of interest:** The beaches with their white sand, the sheltered bays and the excellent fishing from the jetty, beaches and boats are the main attractions. **In the area:** Fitzgerald River National Park, including the Barrens, is a series of rugged mountains, undulating sand plain and steep narrow gorges. Take care fishing from the

617 606 hectares park are four well-known gorges, including Dales Gorge, whose layers of strata, in horizontal stripes of blue, mauve, red and brown, date back almost 2000 million years.

Western Australia's coastal parks are extremely popular, due to the sunny days and cool sea breezes. Along the south coast are many outstanding parks including Cape Le Grand, located 32 kilometres east of **Esperance**.

One of the loveliest sections of the south coast of Western Australia is Fitzgerald River National Park. The 242 803 hectares comprise undulating sand plains, valleys, precipitous cliff edges, narrow gorges and beaches for swimming and rock fishing.

Along the lower south-west coast is Walpole-Nornalup National Park, 18 858 hectares of wilderness where creeks gurgle under tall eucalypts, rivers meander between mountains, and inlets rich in fish create a haven for anglers and boat enthusiasts. An intricate network of roads and walking tracks, through forests of karri and tingle, attracts bushwalkers who can enjoy the many species of native animals and seabirds.

The wild beauty of landscapes is unsurpassed at Kalbarri National Park, with its 186 076 hectares encompassing the lower reaches of the Murchison River which winds its way to the Indian Ocean. Sea cliffs in layers of multi-coloured sandstone loom over the crashing white foam at Red Bluff.

Unusual rock formations are found at Nambung National Park, 200 kilometres north of Perth on the south-west coast. Here, a flat, sandy open space is studded with strange-looking limestone pillars ranging in size from stony 'twigs' to columns more than six metres tall. This is the Pinnacle Desert, a favourite subject for photographers.

Also on the south-west coast, on the belt of coastal limestone is Yanchep National Park, with its forests of massive tuart trees and popular 'wildflower walks'. Located 51 kilometres north of Perth, this park houses Loch McNess with its little islands which are waterfowl sanctuaries. Yanchep is also famed for its beautiful underground caves.

In the far north of Western Australia are national parks of the Kimberley region — mountain ranges formed millions of years ago. The largest of these parks, Geikie Gorge, has an area of 3136 hectares 21 kilometres north-east of **Fitzroy Crossing**. The multi-coloured cliffs are reflected in the placid waters of the Fitzroy River, which flows through the gorge down the centre of the park. In the dry season, the river forms a series of waterholes fringed with freshwater mangrove and leichhardt trees. The river is inhabited by fish-eating Johnston crocodiles, tortoises, sawfish and many other species of fish. This area is too rugged for walking but there are organised boat trips which go up the river through the gorge, enabling visitors to view one of Australia's most beautiful waterways.

For more information on Western Australia's national parks, contact National Parks Authority of Western Australia, Hackett Drive, Nedlands, WA 6009.

rocks — king waves can roll in unexpectedly. **Accommodation:** 1 hotel, 1 caravan/camping park.
Map ref. 256 I 12

Hyden Population under 200.
Hyden is in the Shire of Kondinin, 351 km from Perth, in the eastern wheat growing area of Western Australia. The country is semi arid, but has some fascinating rock formations nearby, the most famous of which is Wave Rock 3 km from Hyden, an incredible 15 metres high granite rock which hangs over like a giant wave. The rock is streaked with colour from deep grey and ochres to reds and a sandy tint. Studies have shown the rock to be 2700 million years old. There is a wildlife park next to Wave Rock with many native animals and birds. **In the area:** Follow the signposted 81 km round tour to see the natural attractions of the region. At Bates Cave there are Aboriginal rock paintings. **Accommodation:** 1 hotel, 1 motel, 1 caravan/camping park.
Map ref. 251 R11, 256 H10

Jurien Population 449.
On the shores of an attractive sheltered bay between Perth and Geraldton, Jurien is important as a lobster fishing centre. **In the area:** There are spectacular sand dunes along the coast. Nambung National Park is to the south. Check about road conditions before leaving Jurien if you take the coastal track. The main, signposted route further inland is recommended. **Accommodation:** 1 motel, 1 caravan/camping park.
Map ref. 252 C12

Kalbarri Population 820.
This popular holiday resort is ideally located between Geraldton and Carnarvon, 661 km north of Perth. The town's picturesque setting on the estuary of the Murchison River, its year-round sunny climate and the spectacular gorges of the river running through the Kalbarri National Park attract a growing number of tourists each year. Kalbarri is also renowned for its excellent fishing and the brilliance and beauty of the more than 500 species of wild flowers which grow in the district. **Of interest:** Doll and Marine Museum. The All Seasons Restaurant is fully-licensed, serves fresh seafood, overlooking the river. Freshwater and ocean fishing are good. **In the area:** Kalbarri National Park, 186 623 ha of magnificent virgin bushland. Within the park are the spectacular Murchison River gorges and an abundance of wildlife and native flora. There are picnic and barbecue facilities. Camping is not permitted. Red Bluff, 4 km south of town, is ideal for swimming, fishing, exploring the rocks. A cairn at Wittecarra Creek marks the spot where it is believed the first permanent landing of white men in Australia — two Dutchmen sent ashore for their part in the *Batavia* mutiny — took place in 1629. Coastal gorges, with precipitous red cliffs dropping to the Indian Ocean below, are a majestic sight. Coach tours of the National Park and coastal gorges can be arranged with the Kalbarri Travel Service, Grey St. **Accommodation:** 1 hotel, 1 motel, 5 caravan/camping parks.
Map ref. 256 C5

Kalgoorlie-Boulder Pop. 19 848.
At the heart of Western Australia's largest gold mining area are the twin towns of Kalgoorlie and Boulder, centred on the famous Golden Mile, reputed to be the richest square mile in the world. Nearly 1000 tonnes of gold have been mined from this small area. Paddy Hannan discovered gold in 1893 and the rush began. By 1902 the population was 30 000 and there were 93 hotels operating. Men made fortunes overnight and the impressive stone buildings and magnificent wide streets recall the town's fabulous boom past. Rather than walk daily to the Great Boulder Mine, the miners set up their tents on the other side of the Golden Mile, which soon grew into the town of Boulder. Kalgoorlie is 597 km east of Perth on the western fringes of the Nullarbor Plain and the Great Victoria Desert. One of the greatest difficulties facing the miners in this semi-desert area was lack of water. Determination and the brilliant scheme of the engineer C. Y. O'Connor saved the day. A pipeline was established, carrying water an incredible 563 km from a reservoir near Perth. The water began flowing in 1903. Gold mining continues, with renewed vigour now that the price of gold has risen steeply. Rich nickel deposits at Kambalda, 55 km south-east, have also given the district a new lease of life. The Kalgoorlie region is an important pastoral district, too, with high quality wool being produced. **Of interest:** Some fine examples of early Australian architecture are to be seen. Buildings worthy of note include the Exchange Hotel, Australia House, the Government Building and Kalgoorlie

The Goldfields

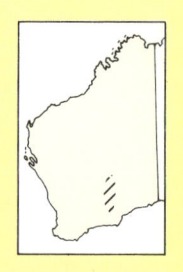

The land of the first gold mining boom in Western Australia is almost as forbidding as that of the far northwest. This is the vast semi-desert region to the east of Perth which contains the fabled towns of **Kalgoorlie, Coolgardie, Boulder, Norseman, Leonora, Gwalia** and **Laverton**. Some towns, like Gwalia, are colourful but nearly deserted reminders of the great rush days. Others, like Kalgoorlie, remain centres for farming and still-worked gold mines; or, like **Kambalda**, are newborn, growing out of new riches found in nickel.

The western gold rush began in 1892 with strikes around Coolgardie. The town sprang up from nowhere and enjoyed a boisterous but short life. With great optimism diggers flocked to the area. In 1900 there were 15 000 people, 23 hotels and six banks. The main street was wide enough for camel trains to turn. By 1905 the gold was petering out and today Coolgardie is a ghost town. The grand old courthouse, built at the height of the boom, is used as a museum and has a fascinating record of life as it was.

In 1893 the Irishman Paddy Hannan made an even bigger strike of gold at Kalgoorlie. The area became known as the Golden Mile, reputedly the richest square mile in the world. Kalgoorlie, and its twin town Boulder, boasted a population of 30 000 in 1902. Magnificent wide streets and impressive, stately stone buildings were erected.

Kalgoorlie, with a population of over 20 000, is still a prosperous gold mining centre, producing 70 per cent of the gold mined in Australia. It is also an important centre for the district's wheat farms. The Hainault Tourist Mine, built in 1895, gives an indication of the hardships endured by the miners in their search for gold. To the south is Kambalda, a new boom town,

---

Post Office. In the main street is a delightful bronze statue of Paddy Hannan. The distinctive Kalgoorlie Town Hall, built in 1908, has a beautiful staircase and paintings by local artists on display. The Golden Mile Museum, in the old British Arms Hotel (1899) has a fascinating display recalling the heyday of the gold rush boom. Close to the museum is Paddy Hannan's Tree, marking the spot where gold was first found in Kalgoorlie. The School of Mines Museum has a world class display, including most of the minerals found in Western Australia. Hainault Tourist Mine, Boulder Block Road, is a real gold mine, constructed in 1895, in the heart of the Golden Mile. Visitors can ride in the car, 60 metres down the mine shaft, to see how gold was extracted, and inspect the underground tunnels. There are daily tours. The Golden Mile Scenic Drive, a trip around the richest gold-endowed mile in the world. Only a few of the old mine heads remain. Take care as there are still dangerous open shafts. Boulder Block once included a brewery, businesses, stores and six hotels which opened 24 hours a day. Boulder Town Hall (1908) and the picturesque Cornwall Hotel (1898) are both of interest. The Eastern Goldfields Historical Society can be located at Boulder city railway station. The Royal Flying Doctor Base serves one of the largest areas in Australia. Tours are conducted here from 2.30 to 3 pm weekdays. Hammond Park is a wildlife sanctuary with small lake, waterfall and scale model of a Bavarian castle. The Lions Club Lookout offers a panoramic view of the old goldfields, the township and pastoral countryside. Mt Charlotte Reservoir and Lookout is the storage for Kalgoorlie's vital fresh water supply. **In the area:** Kalgoorlie is an ideal base from which to visit old gold mining towns, some of them now ghost towns, in the district. Coolgardie, Broad Arrow, Ora Banda (no supplies), Kookynie and Leonora-Gwalia are all within a day's drive. Tourist information can be obtained from the Kalgoorlie Boulder Tourist Bureau, Hannan St, Kalgoorlie. **Accommodation:**
Kalgoorlie, 16 hotels, 4 motels, 3 caravan/camping parks.
Boulder, 8 hotels, 1 caravan/camping park.
Map ref: 257 J8, 258 D3

Kambalda Population 4950.
Kambalda's gold mining history lasted from 1897 to 1906, during which time 30 000 ounces of gold were produced. When the gold petered out, so did the town. In 1966, however, rich nickel deposits were discovered and the town has since boomed. Today Kambalda is a large, well-planned city, noted for its environmental protection policy and attractive modern buildings. There are plenty of sporting facilities and pleasant picnic areas in the centre of town. Kambalda is 616 km east of Perth. **Of interest:** Tours of the massive Western Mining Nickel Plant. Red Hill Lookout has excellent views of the area, including the vast Lake Lefroy. Land yachting on the salt lake is popular, and day trips can be arranged. Tourist information from the Kambalda Tourist Bureau, Salmon Gums Road. **Accommodation:** 1 hotel.
Map ref. 257 J9

Karratha Population 8341.
The rapidly growing town of Karratha, on Nickol Bay, is being developed as the regional centre of the Roebourn Shire. It lies 40 km west of the port of Dampier. The town houses the work force of Hamersley Iron, Dampier Salt, the northwest shelf gas project and other major industrial enterprises. There are modern residential and recreational facilities.
Accommodation: 1 hotel, 4 caravan/camping parks.
Map ref: 254 F9

Katanning Population 4413.
A thriving township 186 km north of Albany, Katanning's well-planned streets have some impressive Victorian buildings. The countryside is given over to grain-growing and pastoral activities, and is noted for its fine merino sheep. **In the area:** Norring Lake. The Stirling Range National Park is about 80 km south. **Accommodation:** 3 hotels, 2 motels, 2 caravan/camping parks.
Map ref. 249 M6, 256 G12

Kellerberrin Population 1091.
Kellerberrin is on the Great Eastern Highway, 200 km from Perth, in wheat farming country. The town dates back to 1897. The hill overlooking the town was originally called 'Killabin' by the Aborigines and referred to the fierce ant called a keela, which had a large colony on the hill. **Of interest:** The Historical Museum in Leake Street is in the former court-house building, erected in 1897.
Accommodation: 1 hotel, 2 motels.
Map ref: 251 N7, 256 G9

Kondinin Population 326.
The small settlement of Kondinin is 278 km east of Perth. There are sheep stud farms nearby. **In the area:** The Kondinin Lake, 8 km from town, is popular with water-skiing and yachting enthusiasts. Kondinin Lions tourist area and museum.
Accommodation: 1 hotel, 1 motel, 1 caravan/camping park.
Map ref: 251 P11, 256 G10

Kulin Population 346.
Centre for the sheep and grain growing farms of the district, Kulin lies 283 km south-east of Perth. The silvery Macrocarpa flowering gums which grow here are an attractive feature. **In the area:** Native orchids grow in the bush. Jilakin Rock and Lake are 18 km from Kulin.
Accommodation: 1 hotel, 1 caravan/camping park.
Map ref: 251 O12

Kununurra Population 2081.
Kununurra (the name is Aboriginal for 'big water') lies at the heart of the Ord River Scheme, in the far north of the East Kimberley. The surrounding country is

founded on the rich nickel deposits, and noted for its modern facilities and tree-lined streets.

The towns north of Kalgoorlie are desolate now, but retain rich vestiges of their mining days. The little town of **Menzies** (257 J7) continues as a pastoral and mining town, a shadow of its former self. The superbly renovated, stately old Gwalia Hotel is one of the few buildings left in what was once one of the state's most prosperous gold mining centres. Herbert Hoover, later President of the United States, was manager of the mine in 1897. Gold is still crushed at the State Battery.

Kanowna once boasted a population of 12 000. Now crumbling ruins are all that remain. **Siberia**, **Broad Arrow** (257 J8), **Niagara** and **Bulong** are the exotic names of some of the towns that flourished and died in a few short years.

majestically beautiful, with rugged coloured hills and valleys and, to the north, the lush green of irrigated fields. Diamonds have been found in the area recently. The Ord Festival is held each August. **In the area:** Kelly's Knob Lookout is a good vantage point for viewing the irrigated land. Kimberley Research Station. Cruises on Lake Kununurra and upstream past the Everglades and beautiful gorges which are teeming with birdlife. Fishing near here is good, with barramundi a prized catch. At Lake Argyle, 72 km south in the Carr Boyd Range, is a tourist village with hotel, caravan park, camping area. The lake, created by the Ord River Dam, is ideal for boating and swimming. Argyle Homestead, the stone home of the famous pioneering Durack family, was moved to this site in 1971, and is now a pioneer museum and memorial to the settlers of this district. **Accommodation:** 1 hotel, 2 motels, 4 caravan/camping parks.
Map ref. 255 R3

Kwinana Population 12 355.
Kwinana, 20 km south of the port of Fremantle, symbolises Western Australia's rapidly developing industrial strength, and is one of the nation's major industrial centres. Construction of the complex, built on Cockburn Sound, one of the world's finest natural harbours, was begun in 1951. The BP Oil Refinery, the vast BHP Steel Works and Alcoa's Alumina Works are all part of Kwinana.

Of interest: Escorted tours of many industries can be arranged. The hull of the wrecked ship, SS *Kwinana*, has been filled with cement and is now used as a diving platform for swimmers at Kwinana Beach. **In the area:** The resort town of Rockingham; trips to the offshore islands, Cape Peron, Penguin and Graden Islands. **Accommodation:** Parmelia, 1 hotel.
Map ref. 250 F10, 256 E10

Lake Grace Population 575.
A pleasant country town 252 km north of Albany in the peaceful rural countryside of the central south wheat belt, Lake Grace derives its name from the shallow lake just west of the settlement. **Of interest:** The wildlife sanctuary. **Accommodation:** 1 hotel, 3 motels, 1 caravan/camping park.
Map ref. 249 Q2, 256 H11

Lancelin Population 399.
This quiet little fishing town on the shores of Lancelin Bay is 130 km north of Perth. A natural breakwater extends from Edward Island to Lancelin Island providing a safe harbour and perfect breeding ground for fish. There are plenty of rock lobsters to be caught on the offshore reefs outside the bay. Lancelin is at the end of the main road along the coast, until the Brand Highway turns in at Dongara, almost 200 km north. **In the area:** There is a track leading north to Nambung National Park, but check about road conditions before setting out. **Accommodation:** 1 hotel, 4 caravan/camping parks.
Map ref. 250 D4, 256 E9

Laverton Population 872.
Laverton has developed as a modern satellite town for the important nickel ore deposits near Mt Windarra. The now famous Poseidon Ltd was involved in this project during the nickel-mining boom of the late 1960s. The Windarra Mine is not open for inspection, but can be seen clearly from Mt Windarra, which is adjacent. Wedgetailed eagles fly overhead, and camels, emus and kangaroos abound.
WARNING: DRIVING ON DESERT ROADS
● There is no water except after rains.
● Unmade roads can be extremely hazardous when wet.
● Traffic is almost non-existent except on main roads.
Accommodation: 1 hotel, 1 caravan/camping park.
Map ref. 257 K6

Leonora Population 524.
A former gold mining town 240 km north of Kalgoorlie, Leonora has a typical Australian country town look with its wide main streets and verandahed shopfronts. The town's importance today is as a railhead for the nickel from Leinster and Windarra. Just 4 km away is the ghost town of Gwalia, with a population of about 80, and many reminders of the gold boom days. **Of interest:** Sons of Gwalia Gold Mine. An early manager was Herbert Hoover, later a President of the United States. Gwalia Historical Gallery. The impressive old Gwalia Hotel (1903) is now the regional office for Western Mining. **In the area:** The small gold mining town of Menzies, 110 km south. Most of the country is flat mulga scrub, but after good rains there are brilliant flowers in August and early September. **Accommodation:** 2 hotels, 1 motel, 1 caravan/camping park.
Map ref. 257 J6

Madura Population under 200.
The hills of the Hampton Tablelands form a backdrop to Madura, 195 km from the Western Australia/South Australia border, on the Eyre Highway. The town's settlement dates back to 1876. **Accommodation:** 1 motel, 1 caravan/camping park.
Map ref. 257 O10

Mandurah Population 10 978.
The popular holiday resort of Mandurah is located on the coast only 80 km south of Perth. The Murray, Serpentine and Harvey Rivers meet here, forming the vast inland waterway of the Peel Inlet and Harvey Estuary. The river waters and the Indian Ocean offer excellent conditions for yachting, boating, swimming, water-skiing and fishing, and the town becomes a mecca for tourists in holiday periods. **Of interest:** Hall's Cottage, a small whitewashed cottage, built in 1845 by two of the colony's earliest settlers. Geological Museum has an extensive collection of shells, coral and gemstones. Christ Church (1870) has hand-carved wood furnishings. Boats can be hired and there are cruises on the river. Watch for dolphins which can often be seen in the estuary. The water also attracts an abundance of bird life. The Mandurah Estuary Bridge is a particularly good fishing spot. **In the area:** There are pleasant picnic areas near the numerous storage dams in the nearby Darling Range. Boating and swimming are permitted in the Waroona and Logue Brook dams. Hamel Forestry Department Nursery is open for inspection. Lakes Clifton and Preston, 20 km to the south, are two long, narrow salt lakes running parallel to the coast. This is a good trip for birdwatchers and photographers. **Accommodation:** 2 hotels, 4 motels, 11 caravan/camping parks.
Map ref. 250 E12, 256 E10

Manjimup Population 4150.
Fertile agricultural country and magnificent karri forests surround Manjimup, 309 km south of Perth. This is the commercial centre of the south-west corner of Western Australia, and the state's largest apple-growing area. Dairying, beef, sheep and vegetable farming are other pastoral activities. The wood chip mill and cannery are flourishing industries contributing to the town's more recent growth. The first settlers arrived here in 1856 and Manjimup's history has been closely tied to the timber industry since then. **Of interest:** The Timber Museum has an excellent display illustrating the development of the timber industry in Western Australia. A wildlife sanctuary which has kangaroos and emus in a pleasant natural bush setting. **In the area:** The Diamond Tree Mill and the

Co-operative Cannery can both be inspected. The Diamond Tree Fire Lookout, 9 km south, provides a very impressive view of the countryside. Warren National Park is an ideal spot for bushwalkers and a peaceful picnic location. One Tree Bridge is 22 km from town. A pleasant walk along the river edge to Four Aces; four magnificent karri trees, standing in line, are believed to be between 300 and 400 years old. The 19 km round trip to Dingup takes you through farmland and forest. Dingup Church (1896) is worth viewing and historic Dingup House (1870) can be seen from the road, Tourist information from the Manjimup Tourist Bureau, Giblett St. **Accommodation:** 2 hotels, 3 motels, 3 caravan/camping parks.
Map ref. 248 G8, 256 F12

Marble Bar Population 357.
Reputedly the hottest place in Australia, Marble Bar lies 200 km south-east of Port Hedland on the Great Northern Highway. From October to March the daytime temperatures regularly exceed 38°C. The town takes its name from the unique bar of red coloured jasper which crosses the Coongan River, 3 km from town. Alluvial gold was discovered in 1891, and in 1931 at the Comet Mine. Today gold is still mined and crushed in the State Battery nearby. Marble Bar still serves as a centre for the pastoral and gold mining industries. Tin is also mined. Marble Bar is a very typical Western Australian outback town.
Of interest: Government Buildings, built of locally-quarried stone in 1895, are impressively sturdy, and still used by the police and mining registrar.
In the area: Marble Bar and Chinaman's Pool 3 km from town; the jasper deposit. The country is surprisingly scenic, with beautiful ranges, plains, gorges, pools and many natural scenic spots. The town of Nullagine, 120 km south, is in a mineral rich area. Old gold mines dot the area, and there is some fascinating scenery. **Accommodation:** 1 hotel, 1 caravan/camping park.
Map ref. 254 I9

Margaret River Population 798.
Margaret River is a pretty township nestled on the side of a river near the coast 280 km from Perth. The town is noted for the magnificent coastal scenery, surfing beaches, wineries and spectacular cave formations in the district. Guesthouse and chalet holidays are available.
In the area: Leeuwin Estate Winery features an especially welcoming tasting room, a splendid function room with Australian paintings and picnic and barbecue facilities. Mammoth Cave, 19 km south-west, has fossils of prehistoric animals. Another 3 km on is the Lake Cave. Tourist information from the Tourist Bureau, Cnr Wallcliffe Road and Bussel Highway. **Accommodation:** 1 hotel, 1 motel, 4 caravan/camping parks.
Map ref. 248 C7, 256 E12

Meekatharra Population 989.
Meekatharra lies 768 km north-east of Perth on the Great Northern Highway. Gold, copper and other minerals are mined, and there are huge sheep and cattle stations in the area. Meekatharra was once important as the railhead for cattle which had travelled overland from the Northern Territory or the East Kimberley. The Royal Flying Doctor Service base is here.
Of interest: Old gold mining towns and the relics of equipment and shafts can be seen. Since the upturn in gold prices several mines such as Peak Hill, Gabanintha, Nannine and Quinns have re-opened. Wiluna, 180 km west, is another of the West's ghost gold towns. In 1920s and '30s the town boomed, with a population of over 7000. **Accommodation:** 3 hotels, 2 motels, 1 caravan/camping park.
Map ref. 256 H3

Merredin Population 3520.
A main junction on the important Kalgoorlie-Perth railway line, Merredin is situated 261 km north from Perth. During the late 1800s Merredin grew up as a shanty town, as miners stopped on their way to the goldfields. The town has excellent parks and recreation facilities.
Of interest: Harling Memorial Library, and the Old Railway Station Museum. **In the area:** The famous Wave Rock near Hyden. **Accommodation:** 3 hotels, 3 motels, 2 caravan/camping parks.
Map ref. 251 P6, 256 G9

Mingenew Population 368.
The little township of Mingenew is in the wheat growing district of the mid-west, 378 km north of Perth. The town was established back in the 1880s as a railway terminal for stock heading south.
Of interest: Mingenew Museum is in the small, original Roads Board office. Western Australia's first coal shafts were built here and can be seen at the nearby Coalseam Park. **In the area:** Dongara, 53 km west, has superb beaches and excellent fishing. **Accommodation:** 1 motel, 1 caravan/camping park.
Map ref. 252 D7, 256 E7

Morawa Population 694.
Renowned for its plentiful grain harvests, the progressive town of Morawa is situated in the mid-west, 394 km north of Perth. Spring is the perfect time to visit, when the wildflowers are in brilliant bloom. **In the area:** Koolanooka Springs and Koolanooka Hills 24 km east are ideal for picnics. **Accommodation:** 1 hotel, 1 motel, 1 caravan/camping park.
Map ref. 252 G7, 256 E7

Mount Barker Population 1519.
Mount Barker is a quiet, friendly town in the Great Southern district of Western Australia. It is 360 km from Perth, with the Stirling Ranges to its north, and the Porongurups to the east. Mt Barker was discovered in 1829, and the first settlers arrived in the 1830s. Vineyards in the area, though relatively new, have produced some top quality wines. **Of interest:** The old police station and gaol (1868) is now used as a museum. **In the area:** The privately-owned St Werburgh's Chapel (1872) is a small mud-walled chapel overlooking the Hay River Valley. The Lookout, 5 km south-west on Mt Barker Hill, gives panoramic views. The TV tower is the tallest free-standing structure in the southern hemisphere. The historic town of Kendenup is 16 km north of Mt Barker. Western Australia's first gold was discovered here. The Porongurup National Park, 24 km east, has granite peaks and brilliant seasonal wildflowers. Stirling Range National Park, 80 km north-east, has tall peaks, picturesque plains, native flora and fauna. Lake Poorrarecup, 50 km north-west of Mt Barker. The area is also noted for the orchids and brown and red boronia which bloom from September to November. Tourist information from Mount Barker Tourist Bureau, Lowood Road. **Accommodation:** 1 hotel, 2 motels, 1 caravan/camping park.
Map ref. 249 M11, 256 G13

Mount Magnet Population 618.
The former gold mining town of Mount Magnet is now a popular stopping place for motorists driving north to Port Hedland. The surrounding land is used for pastoral farming. Mount Magnet is 562 km from Perth on the Great Northern Highway. **In the area:** Fossick for gemstones, but take care as there are dangerous old mine shafts. **Accommodation:** 3 hotels, 1 motel.
Map ref. 253 N1, 256 G5

Mullewa Population 918.
Gateway to the Murchison goldfields, Mullewa is 96 km from Geraldton. **Of interest:** Our Lady of Mount Carmel Church. Kembla Zoo, in Stock St, has native animals. **In the area:** Water Supply Reserve, Main Road, is a delightful spot with native plants and flowering bushes. Waterfalls near the airport. A drive 58 km north takes you to the beautiful wild flowers at Tallering Peak and Gorges. **Accommodation:** 2 hotels, 1 caravan park.
Map ref. 252 E3, 256 E6

Mundaring Population 823.
The picturesque Mundaring Weir is about 40 km north-east of Perth, set in wooded mountain country. This is the source of water for the eastern goldfields. The original dam was opened in 1903, and the pumping station used until 1955. **Of interest:** The attractive bush setting makes the weir a popular picnic spot in summer. The C. Y. O'Connor Museum has an intriguing collection of models and diagrams of the Goldfields Water Supply. **In the area:** The Old Mahogany Inn, a museum and tearooms. Built in 1837, the inn served as a military outpost to offer protection to travellers from hostile Aborigines. John Forrest National Park, on a high point of the Darling Range, is 26 km east of Perth. **Accommodation:** 2 hotels, 1 caravan/camping park.
Map ref. 250 G8

Mundrabilla Population under 200.
A tiny settlement on the Eyre Highway where you can stop for a meal, to break the long journey across the continent. There is an interesting bird sanctuary behind the motel. **Accommodation:** 1 motel, 1 caravan/camping park.
Map ref. 257 P10

Western Wildflowers

The sand plains, swamps, flats, scrub and woodlands of south-western Australia light up with colour in spring as the 'wildflower state' puts on its brilliant display. The plains can become, almost overnight, carpeted with the gold of everlastings or feather flowers or the reds and pinks of boronia and lechenaultia. The banksia bushes throw up their red and yellow cylinders along the coast and in the woodlands. Grevilleas spill their flowers down to the ground. Orchids cling to rocks and trees. Flowering gums become a mass of red and the felty kangaroo paws invade the plains. There are lilies, banksias, pitcher plants, parrot bushes, flame peas, feather flowers, foxgloves, all displayed in a magnificent abundance.

There are over 3000 different species of wild flowers in the south-west and around 75 per cent of them are unique to the region, although they may have family connections with other plants of northern or eastern Australia. They have been isolated and become individual because of the barrier of plain and desert that separates the west from the eastern states, which has caused the families of plants on both sides to pursue their own evolution. There are, however, some families of plants in the west that are unique in the world.

Visitors on even a short trip to Perth can see a good sample of Western Australian wild flowers. At King's Park close to the city wild flower species abound and give a brilliant display in the July to November period. Tourists in any part of the south-west in that period will see wild flowers all around them. It is in the National Park areas, however, that the full beauty of massed wild flower displays is best seen. Only 25 kilometres east of Perth on the Great Eastern Highway is the John Forrest National Park, situated on the edge of the Darling Range escarpment. On these undulating hills and valleys the undergrowth of the jarrah forest is rich in flowering plants — red and green kangaroo paw, swamp river myrtle, blue lechenaultia and pink calytrix are the most common plants. Fifty kilometres north of Perth is the Yanchep National Park, a place of coastal limestone and sandy plains, covered with many wild flowers.

There are many distant places further north that are worth visiting, if only for the unique quality of their scenery. One such is the Kalbarri National Park, 670 kilometres north of Perth, at the mouth of the Murchison River. It contains magnificent flowering trees,

ABOVE: *Mulla Mulla.*

BELOW: *Plumed Grevillea.*

BELOW: *Spring in the Wildflower State.*

BELOW: *Banksia.*

Western Australia

ABOVE: *Lesser Bottlebrush.*

ABOVE: *Wild flowers in profusion.*

ABOVE: *Blue Leschenaultia.*

banksias, grevilleas, melaleuca and leschenaultia, while the ground beneath is covered with millions of plants of many species.

The Dryandra State Forest, a few kilometres from Narrogin in the south-west, has enormous stands of karri trees reaching well over 65 metres. An important sanctuary for mallee fowl and numbat, this deep forest contains a number of species of dryandra.

Another fascinating area of WA is the Stirling Range National Park, 340 kilometres south of Perth and near the Porongurup Range. The Stirlings are very jagged peaks which rise above flat farmlands. The scenery is magnificent and wild flowers abound, including some unique to the region. There are banksias here as well as dryandra, the fuchsia grevillea and the grevillea wilsonii which has brilliant scarlet flowers, the delicate pink rose cone bush, the lemon scented myrtle, the pink feather flower and many others. The bare granite domes and boulders of the Porongurup Range look down to lower slopes of flowering trees and creepers such as the banksia grandis and clematis.

Also in this region are the many interesting coastal parks around Albany. The Albany Coastline Reserve is an area of coastal hills and cliffs and fascinating scenic features like the gap, the blowhole and the natural bridge. The stunted windswept coastal vegetation has many wild flowers including giant banksia and the Christmas tree with its brilliant orange foliage.

Twenty-five kilometres to the east of Albany is the peaceful and beautiful Two People Bay flora and fauna reserve, which has thickets of mallee, banksia and peppermint together with many flowering shrubs and plants. Further west along the coast from Albany is the Walpole Nornalup National Park, where dense karri forest mingles with other trees like red tingle, jarrah, marri, casuarina and banksia, and with many wild flowers like the tree kangaroo paw, the babe-in-cradle orchid and the potato orchid.

While enjoying Western Australia's wild flower display visitors should remember that all wild flowers of certain areas are protected under the *Native Flower Protection Act.* These include the south-west and Eucla divisions of the state, where most wild flowers exist.

Further information on national parks and wild flower display areas may be obtained from the Holiday WA Centre and National Parks Authority in South Perth.

BELOW: *Cowslip Orchid.*

ABOVE: *Prickly Dryandra.*

BELOW: *Sturt's Desert Pea.*

Nannup Population 552.

Nannup is a quiet friendly town in the Blackwood Valley, 290 km south of Perth. The surrounding countryside is lush, gently rolling pasture, jarrah and pine forests. **Of interest:** Arts and crafts centre, with handcrafts for sale. Colonial House (1895) is a classic example of colonial architecture. Visitors are welcome to inspect the largest jarrah sawmill in the state. **In the area:** Barrabup Pool, 10 km west of town. Tourist information from the Tourist Office, Warren Road. **Accommodation:** 1 hotel, 1 caravan/camping park.
Map ref. 248 F7, 256 E12

Narrogin Population 4969.

Narrogin is important as the centre of prosperous agricultural country and as a major railway junction. Sheep, pigs and cereal farms are the main primary industries. The town is 235 km south-east of Perth on the Great Southern Highway. The name Narrogin is derived from an Aboriginal word meaning 'water-hole'. The Three Day Horse Competition held every November attracts entrants from all over Australia. **Of interest:** Court-house Museum (1894), originally a school and later the district court-house. Foxes Lair, Williams Road, is a five hectare area of natural bushland. Lions Lookout has panoramic views of Narrogin. **In the area:** There are some unusual rock formations 11 km east of town at Yilliminning and Bird Whistle Rocks. Tourist information from the Shire Office. **Accommodation:** 2 hotels, 1 motel, 1 caravan/camping park.
Map ref. 249 K2, 256 G11

New Norcia Population under 200.

The Spanish Benedictine monks established a mission at New Norcia in 1846 to help the Australian Aborigines. Today Salvado College is a secondary school catering for nearly 200 boarders from all over Western Australia. The handsome Spanish-inspired buildings of New Norcia come as a surprise, surrounded by dusty Australian paddocks and distant bushland. The settlement is in the secluded Moore Valley, and wheat, wool and other farm products are produced. The museum and art gallery has a priceless collection including gifts sent by Queen Isabella of Spain, fine paintings and Roman, Egyptian and Spanish artefacts. Some were damaged recently during a robbery. **Accommodation:** 1 hotel.
Map ref. 250 G4, 256 F9

Norseman Population 2029.

Norseman, 200 km south of Kalgoorlie, is the last large town on the Eyre Highway heading east towards South Australia. It is a popular stopping place on the long overland trip. Gold put Norseman on the map back in the late 1890s, and the richest quartz reef in Australia is still being mined today. There is plenty of gold mining history here, with the colossal tailings dump as a reminder of the area's wealth. **Of interest:** The historical and geological museum; the post office (1896); Lookout Hill, 2 km from town, has fine views. The rich mineral deposits make this a good area for amateur propectors and gemstone collectors to fossick. **In the area:** Norseman Tourist reception area has hot showers and barbecue facilities. Travellers can park their caravans here. The Dundas Hills and Lake Dundas are perfect picnic spots. Lady Miller has colourful banded ironstone and is a good place to fossick. It's worth the easy climb of Mararoa or Lookout Hill to see the views. The gemstone lease, 17 km from Norseman, has many fine specimens. **Accommodation:** 2 hotels, 1 motel, 1 caravan/camping park.
Map ref. 257 K10

Northam Population 6791.

The unofficial capital of the fertile Avon Valley at the junction of the Avon and Mortlock Rivers, Northam is an attractive rural town. East of Perth on the Great Eastern Highway, it is an important supply point for the farms of the eastern wheat belt. Northam is also a major railway centre and the main depot for the Goldfields Water Scheme which takes water as far east as Kalgoorlie. Western Australia's largest military training camp on the outskirts of town. **Of interest:** A weir across the Avon River forms a lake which attracts black and white swans and many species of native birdlife. **In the area:** Drive south to Wooroloo to see the famous El Caballo Blanco. This complex comprises a Spanish-inspired homestead, villas and stables and a collection of beautifully restored carriages and coaches. Magnificent Andalusian horses are trained and give performances, Tuesday to Sunday. **Accommodation:** 3 hotels, 1 motel, 1 caravan/camping park.
Map ref. 250 I7, 256 F9

Northampton Population 750.

Northampton nestles amidst gentle hills in the valley of Nokarena Brook, 48 km north of Geraldton. Inland there is picturesque country with vivid wild flowers in spring. The drive west takes you to the coast, with beaches for swimming and fishing. **Of interest:** Chiverton House Museum. Built by convict labour between 1868 and 1875, this stone building now houses historical displays. Gwalia church site and cemetery. **In the area:** At Horrocks Beach, 20 km away, are pleasant bays and sandy beaches. Near the coast at Port Gregory, there was a labour hiring depot for convicts back in the 1800s. The squat building with slits for windows was probably erected as protection from Aborigines. Lake Hutt, near Port Gregory, turns pink in the light of the midday sun. Hutt River Province, which has seceded from Australia and is 'ruled' by 'Prince Leonard' and 'Princess Shirl'. An estimated 60 000 tourists visit this barren, remote, 7400 ha 'province' each year and come away bearing stamps, tea-towels, currency and other souvenirs to commemorate their 'international' visit. **Accommodation:** 1 motel, 1 caravan/camping park.
Map ref. 252 A2, 256 D6

Northcliffe Population 208.

Magnificent virgin karri forests surround the little township of Northcliffe, 32 km south of Pemberton in the extreme south-west corner of the state. **Of interest:** The Pioneer Museum has relics and photographs of the early days in the region. The Warren River is good for fishing. Moons Crossing and the Lane Poole Falls are popular. **In the area:** The sandy beaches of Windy Harbour, to the south, are ideal for fishing and swimming. The cliffs at Point D'Entrecasteaux are popular with climbers. **Accommodation:** 1 hotel, 1 caravan/camping park (summer only).
Map ref. 248 G11, 256 F13

Onslow Population 594.

Onslow, on the north-west coast of the state, is important as the base for the oil fields off the coast at Barrow Island. The town was originally located at the mouth of the Ashburton River, but was moved to its site on Beadon Bay after constant cyclones. The remains of the old townsite can still be seen. Onslow was a bustling pearling centre and in the 1890s gold was discovered. US submarines refuelled here during World War 2, and the town was bombed by the Japanese. In 1952 it was the mainland base for Britain's nuclear experiments at Monte Bello Islands. **Of interest:** The fishing is good. There are many native animals including the mountain devil, or bungarra, and a wide variety of birdlife. In spring, after rain, many wildflowers bloom, including the Sturt Desert Pea and wild hibiscus, which are a brilliant red. **Accommodation:** 1 hotel, 1 motel, 1 caravan/camping park.
Map ref. 254 D10

Pemberton Population 871.

The town of Pemberton is nestled in a quiet valley, surrounded by towering karri forests. This lush rainforest area has some of the tallest hardwood trees in the world, and brilliant flowering bush plants. **Of interest:** The museum has historic photographs and authentic old forestry equipment. The art gallery, in a restored squatter's cottage, has paintings and handcrafts. The trout hatchery supplies fish for Western Australian rivers and dams. Fishing in the local rivers is good. An Inland Fishing Licence is required for trout and marron fishing. Brockman Sawpit was restored to show how timber was sawn in the 1860s. The Pemberton Sawmill is open for inspection. **In the area:** Gloucester Tree, the tallest fire lookout in the world, is over 60 metres high. Brave tourists are welcome to attempt the climb. Further south is the picturesque Lane Poole Falls and at Northcliffe an interesting pioneer museum. At Windy Harbour sandy beaches line the rugged coast. Fishing here is good. Warren, Brockman and Beedelup National Parks are all close by. Tourist information from the Pemberton Northcliffe Tourist Bureau, Brockman St. **Accommodation:** 2 hotels, 3 motels, 1 caravan/camping park.
Map ref. 248 G9, 256 F13

Perenjori Population 257.

On the Northam-Mullewa Highway, 352 km north-east of Perth, Perenjori lies on the fringes of the Murchison Goldfields and the great sheep stations of the west.

Fossickers will find many gemstones in this mineral rich area. **In the area:** The wild flower season lasts from July to September and there are many scenic drives. The salt lakes attract a variety of water birds. Old gold mining and ghost towns include Rothsay, Warriedar, Payne's Find and Crows Nest. Take care as there may be dangerous unfenced pits. At Damperwah Soak, 40 km north-east, are the Aboriginal Stones. **Accommodation:** 1 hotel, 1 caravan/camping park.
Map ref. 252 H8, 256 F7

The Pilbara

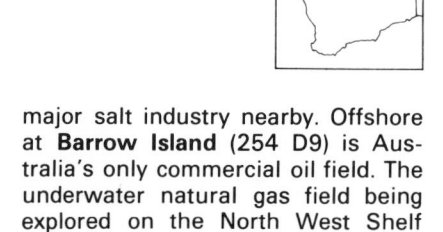

In the far north-west of their state, the Western Australians are moving mountains with giant earth movers that chew their way through the red iron ore. The discovery of vast mineral wealth has created a major economic breakthrough for the state. The arid Pilbara region, one of the most heavily-mineralised areas in the world, is also the biggest exporter of iron ore. The iron ore boom has created jobs in this desolate land of sand spinifex, mulga scrub and massive red mountains. Model towns have sprung up. Gardens, swimming pools, golf courses and communal activities help compensate for the isolation and harsh climate.

The largest towns of the Pilbara are company towns, residential and administrative centres for the iron ore mines, or ports for the export of ore. **Exmouth** (254 C10) is an exception: a modern town, it was built by the Commonwealth and Western Australian Governments as a service centre for the US Navy radio communication base on North West Cape. The sheltered waters of Exmouth Gulf are ideal for all water sports and provide superb fishing, including big game fish. Cape Range National Park nearby is rugged, but startlingly beautiful.

Roebourne (254 F9), the oldest town in the north-west, has been a centre for the pastoral, copper and pearling industries. The old deserted pearling port of **Cossack** is a short drive away. Inland on the Fortescue River, lush ferns, palms and lilies grow near the deep pools at **Millstream** (254 F10), the source of water for many Pilbara towns. The Chichester Range National Park is also well worth a visit. **Dampier**, on King Bay, is a modern iron ore company town, with a major salt industry nearby. Offshore at **Barrow Island** (254 D9) is Australia's only commercial oil field. The underwater natural gas field being explored on the North West Shelf promises immense potential.

Karratha is a modern town and regional centre, as is **Wickham**. Wickham's port at Cape Lambert has the longest and tallest jetty in Australia. It stands 3 kilometres long and 18.5 metres above water. **Port Hedland** is the state's fastest-growing town. Streamlined port facilities cope with more tonnage than any other port in the country. Ore mined inland at **Tom Price** (254 G11), **Newman** (254 I 12), **Paraburdoo** (254 F12) and other centres is railed on giant trains to the ports for export.

The fishing here is good, but swimming is dangerous. Sharks, sea snakes and poisonous fish frequent the waters. **Wittenoom** affords easy access to the magnificent gorges in the Hamersley Range National Park, with their many-coloured walls, deep cool waters and lush green growth. And, of course, there's **Marble Bar**, living up to its reputation as the hottest place in Australia and keeping alive the tradition of 'the great Australian outback'.

Despite great improvements to the main roads in recent years, they are still liable to rapid deterioration, and can have long stretches of rough and dangerous surface. It is wise to check on conditions before setting out.

Pingelly   Population 937.

On the Great Southern Highway, 154 km south-east of Perth, Pingelly is part of the central southern farming district. The cutting of sandalwood was once a local industry, but today the land is given over to sheep and wheat growing. **Of interest:** Apex Lookout, for fine views of town and country. **In the area:** Drive east 10 km to the historic Moorumbyne St Patrick's Church (1873). Tuttanning Flora and Fauna Reserve is 21 km east, with many beautiful species of native plants and indigenous animals. Dryandra Reserve has unique examples of flora and numerous tree types. Animal life found in the reserve includes the numbat, Western Australia's fauna emblem. Timber is also produced in the reserve, which has been called an ecological oasis. Boyagin Rock Picnic Ground and Reserve is north-west. **Accommodation:** 1 hotel, 1 motel.
Map ref. 251 K12, 256 F10

Pinjarra   Population 1336.

Pinjarra is a pleasant drive 84 km south of Perth, along the shaded South Western Highway or the scenic Old Coast Road. The town has a picturesque setting on the banks of the Murray River in one of the oldest established districts in Western Australia. The Alcoa Refinery just north-east of town is the largest alumina refinery in Australia. Pinjarra is becoming increasingly popular with tourists as a base from which to explore the area. **Of interest:** St John's Church (1845), Edenvale and Liveringa (1880). Old Blythewood, built in the 1840s has served as post office, coach stop and family home. The Hotham Valley Railway runs a steam train between Pinjarra and Dwellingup. **Accommodation:** 2 hotels.
Map ref. 250 F12, 256 E11.

Port Denison   Population 900.

This quiet town on the coast, just south of Dongara, is about 362 km north of Perth. **Of interest:** There is an abundance of fish in the waters around Port Denison and a new fishing boat harbour has been built. Rock lobster can be caught in season with a net, or on the reefs at low tide. You need a licence — ask at the Fisheries and Wildlife Office, Carnarvon St. There is a golf course, and the fisherman's lookout gives panoramic views of the harbour. **Accommodation:** 2 caravan parks.
Map ref. 252 B7, 256 D7

Port Hedland   Population 12 948.

As port for the booming iron ore mines of the mineral rich Pilbara, Port Hedland is the fastest growing town in the state. It is built on a narrow island 1953 km north of Perth and is connected to the mainland by three long causeways. The town was named after Captain Peter Hedland who discovered the harbour in 1829. Today Port Hedland handles the largest tonnage of any Australian port. Iron ore from some of the world's biggest mines is loaded on to the world's biggest ore carriers. The town has grown so rapidly that satellite towns, South Hedland and Finucane Island, have been established to cope with the expansion. Gathering of salt is another major industry, with about 2 million tonnes of salt exported per annum. The Spinifex Spree, held each August, is ten days of sport, social and cultural activities. **Of interest:** Drysdales Shell Collection, Richardson St; Lions Park, Hunt St, has pioneer relics. Aboriginal Progress Association, opposite the Tourist Bureau, has Aboriginal artefacts for sale. Visitors are welcome at the wharf, where the ore is loaded on to giant ships. Mt Newman Mining Company tourist bus departs

daily at 2 pm to inspect the company's operations. Opposite the main gate on the limestone ridge are some impressive Aboriginal carvings. An Olympic pool is in McGregor St, next to the Civic Centre. Don't swim in the sea! Sharks, sea snakes, stone fish and blue ringed octopus all frequent the waters. From October to March Port Hedland and the surrounding areas can be subject to severe cyclones. **In the area:** Swim, picnic or fish at Pretty Pool. Six kilometres from the port you can see giant cone-shaped mounds of salt, piled high awaiting export. Fishing near Port Hedland is good. Birdlife is abundant in the district. Watch for bustards, eagles, cockatoos, galahs, ibis, pelicans and parrots. Tourist information from the Tourist Information Centre, 13 Wedge St. **Accommodation:** 3 hotels, 2 motels, 3 caravan/camping parks.
Map ref. 254 G8

Ravensthorpe Population 327.
Ravensthorpe, situated 533 km south-east of Perth, is the centre of the old Phillips River goldfield. Copper mining was also important here, reaching a peak in the late 1960s. Many old mine shafts can be seen around the district. Wheat and sheep are the local industries. **Of interest:** 'Cocanarup', an historic homestead built in 1868, has a display of farm machinery, and barbecue facilities in its grounds. **In the area:** Drive to Ravensthorpe Range and Mt Desmond for panoramic views. A number of unique species of wild flowers grow in the area. Fitzgerald River National Park is close by. **Accommodation:** 1 hotel, 1 motel, 1 caravan/camping park.
Map ref. 256 I 11

Rockingham Population 24 693.
At the southern end of Cockburn Sound, 45 km south of Perth, Rockingham is a coastal town and seaside resort. Begun in 1872 as a port, the harbour fell into disuse with the increasing size of ships and the opening of the Fremantle inner harbour in 1897. Today the magnificent golden beaches and protected waters are Rockingham's main attraction. The Silver Sands Carnival held in March and the Cockburn Yacht Regatta in January draw people from all over the state. **Of interest:** There are regular boat trips to nearby Penguin and Garden Islands. Holiday cottages can be rented on both islands. The Lookout at Point Peron offers panoramic views of the sea and town. **In the area:** Kwinana Industrial Complex. A scenic drive 48 km inland takes you to the Serpentine Dam, Western Australia's major water conservation area. Brilliant wild flowers, gardens and bushland surround the dam and the Serpentine Falls are close by. **Accommodation:** 2 motels, 4 caravan/camping parks.
Map ref. 250 E10, 256 E10

Shay Gap Population 853.
A model town established 84 km east of Mt Goldsworthy, Shay Gap is a mining town for iron ore. A sophisticated planning scheme has houses grouped in shadow-generating enclosures in a unique setting of picturesque hills. **Accommodation:** None.
Map ref. 254 I9

Southern Cross Population 798.
A small but flourishing town on the Great Eastern Highway, 278 km east of Perth, Southern Cross was a gold mining town for a brief period, but owes its prosperity today to agricultural and pastoral activities. **Of interest:** The first court-house in the Eastern Goldfields, built in 1893 is now a history museum, open daily. The streets and town are named after stars and constellations. **In the area:** Beautiful wild flowers bloom on the sand plains during spring. Koolyanobbing, 56 km away, is a model township built for the miners who work with the rich iron ore deposits. Guided tours can be arranged. **Accommodation:** 1 hotel, 1 motel, 1 caravan/camping park.
Map ref. 256 H9

Tammin Population 254.
This tiny town, located in rich wheat and sheep country, 175 km from Perth, is on the Great Eastern Highway. **Accommodation:** 1 hotel, 1 caravan/camping park.
Map ref. 251 M7

Three Springs Population 638.
Sir John Forrest named Three Springs, 170 km south-east of Geraldton. Western Australia's finest talc is mined here from an open-cut mine just a few kilometres

The Ord River Scheme

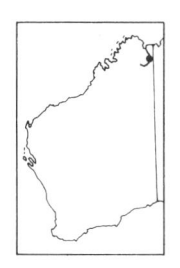

The introduction of the Ord River Scheme was a progressive and far-sighted move to develop the tropical north of Western Australia. During the 'wet' the rivers of the Kimberley become raging torrents and at times the waters of the Ord River empty more than 50 million litres a second into Cambridge Gulf. With the end of the monsoon rain, the rich seasonal pastures die and the land becomes dry again. The Ord River Dam was built to harness this tremendous wealth of water for agriculture.

The Kimberley Research Station was established in 1945 to investigate the potential of the area and the likelihood of producing crops on the black, alluvial soil of the plains. The land was found to be suitable for a variety of tropical crops. By 1963 the Diversion Dam at **Kununurra** (255 R3) was built to divert water from the river into supply channels. Lake Argyle, 72 kilometres south in the Carr Boyd Range, is the main storage reservoir. This is the largest man-made lake in Australia, and holds nine times the volume of water of Sydney Harbour, its normal capacity being 5674 million cubic metres. This vast expanse of water is dotted with islands that were once peaks rising above the surrounding valleys. The water of the Ord is now capable of irrigating 72 000 hectares of land. A third of the projected irrigation area will be along the Keep River Plain in the Northern Territory.

The area is becoming increasingly attractive to tourists. Surrounding Lake Argyle are rugged red slopes, a haven for native animals such as the bungarra lizard, brush-tailed wallabies and grey kangaroos. Looking out over the lake is a tourist village, with a modern hotel-motel, caravan and camping facilities and green, shaded lawn areas. Cruises on the lake can be organised. For the more energetic there are fishing trips, bushwalks or tennis

The Argyle Downs Homestead is also here; once home of the famous pioneering Durack family, the homestead was moved to its present site to prevent it being covered by the waters of the lake. A fascinating memorial to the pioneers of the district, it recreates life as it was once in the Kimberley.

The town of Kununurra — the name means big water — has been established as the residential and administrative centre of the Ord scheme.

east. **In the area:** The Yarra Yarra Lake system attracts many interesting types of migratory birds. **Accommodation:** 1 motel.
Map ref. 252 F8

Toodyay Population 560.
The historic town of Toodyay, nestled in the Avon Valley, has many charming old buildings recalling its pioneering past. Situated 90 km north-east of Perth, Toodyay is surrounded by picturesque farming country and, to the west, virgin bushland. **Of interest:** Classified by the National Trust as an historic town, Toodyay has many buildings of historic significance. Connor's Mill, Piesse St, built in the 1870s, is an imposing structure, now housing the local tourist centre, and a fascinating steam engine, still in working order. The old gaol (1865) and police stables (1870) were built by convicts with random rubble stone. **In the area:** On the Perth Road 4 km from Toodyay is the Coorinja Winery, begun in 1870. Avon Valley National Park, to the south-west has spectacular scenery and beautiful seasonal wild flowers. Northam is 27 km west and a little further on the Avon River Weir is a sanctuary for swans. The grassy river bank makes a delightful spot for a picnic. **Accommodation:** 2 hotels.
Map ref. 250 H6

Wagin Population 1488.
The prosperous rural countryside surrounding Wagin supports grain crops and pastures for livestock, especially sheep. Wagin's development has been tied to its important location as a railway junction town, 177 km east of Bunbury. The annual 'Woolorama' held in Wagin each March is an attraction for sheep farmers from all over Australia. **Of interest:** Art Gallery, with Australian paintings. The town has some fine old Victorian buildings and shop fronts. **In the area:** The granite Mt Latham, 6 km west, affords scenic views and an opportunity for bushwalkers to enjoy the country. Putapin, another rock formation is 6 km south-east of town and is used as a water catchment area. Wild flowers abound in the spring. Lakes Norring and Dumbleyung are nearby. **Accommodation:** 2 hotels, 1 motel, 1 caravan/camping park.
Map ref. 249 L3

Wanneroo Population 6745.
Wanneroo is 45 km north from Perth, in fine vineyard country. **Of interest:** Wanneroo Lion Park, Botanical golf gardens, Vineyards in the area are open for inspection and cellar door sales. Wanneroo Manor. Ocean reef marina. Joondalup, Jandabup and Gnangara Lakes are close by. International competitors are attracted to some of Wanneroo Motor Racing Circuit's regular meetings. **Accommodation:** 4 caravan/camping parks.
Map ref. 250 F8

Wickepin Population 267.
Wickepin dates back to the 1890s when the first settlers came to the district. The town is 214 km south-east of Perth in farming country. **In the area:** To the north are the tiny town of Yealering and the Yealering Lake. Toolbin Lake attracts a variety of water fowl. **Accommodation:** 1 hotel, 1 caravan/camping park.
Map ref. 251 M13

Wickham Population 2387.
A modern company town, Wickham was established to serve as the port for the iron ore mined by Cliffs Robe River Iron Associates. The town is just 11 km north of Roebourne and the port facilities at Cape Lambert. Mining operations are at Pannawonica. **In the area:** Point Samson, with a beautiful beach and excellent game fishing. The ghost town of Cossack, once a pearling port; Roebourne, the oldest town in the north-west. **Accommodation:** 1 hotel, 2 caravan/camping parks.
Map ref. 254 F9

Williams Population 453.
Williams enjoys a picturesque setting on the banks of the Williams River, 161 km south-east of Perth. **In the area:** Dryandra Forest. **Accommodation:** 1 hotel, 1 motel, 1 caravan/camping park.
Map ref. 249 J2

Wittenoom Population 247.
Easy access to the magnificent Hamersley Range National Park and the river gorges have ensured Wittenoom's position as tourist centre for the Pilbara. The town lies 289 km from Roebourne and 322 km from Port Hedland. Wittenoom grew up as a service centre for the workers of the Blue Asbestos Mining Industry, but world demand had declined by 1966 and mining ceased. The Wittenoom Annual Race Meeting is held in September. **In the area:** Magnificent gorges, mostly within the Hamersley Range National Park. Wittenoom Gorge is only 13 km from town. Oxer's Lookout, at the junction of Red, Weano and Hancock Gorges, has a breathtaking view. Yampire Gorge, Fig Tree Well, which camel drivers used as a water spot, and an old asbestos mine. Dales Gorge. Less than 2 km of the 45 km Yampire Gorge are accessible, but at its mouth are the beautiful Fortescue Falls and enticing crystal clear pools. Rio Tinto Gorge, 43 km away, and Hamersley Gorge, 47 km away, are also interesting. Tourist information from the Wittenoom Tourist Centre, Second Avenue. **Accommodation:** 1 hotel, 1 motel, 1 caravan/camping park.
Map ref. 254 G11

Wyndham Population 1509.
Wyndham, the most northerly port in Western Australia, was once landing point for the prospectors heading for the goldfields. Today it is port for the irrigated area of the Ord River. Wyndham is just 64 km from the Timor Sea and 97 km from the Northern Territory border. The tropical summer heat is extremely humid. **Of interest:** The meat works can be inspected in season. There is abundant bird life at Crocodile, Police and Marlgu Lagoons. The Grotto, a rock edged waterhole near town, is a cool, shaded oasis. The modern sealed road 108 km to Kununurra passes through splendid gorge country. **Accommodation:** 1 motel, 1 caravan/camping park.
Map ref. 255 Q3

Yalgoo Population under 200.
Yalgoo lies 216 km east of Geraldton along an excellent road in real Australian outback country. Alluvial gold was discovered in the 1890s and recently the 'Emerald' mine has been re-opened. Small traces of gold are still found in the district which keeps locals and travellers fossicking. **Of interest:** Court-house Museum and restored Dominican Convent Chapel. Enquire at the Shire Offices if you wish to view them. The area harbours abundant native wildlife and there are prolific wild flowers in season. **Accommodation:** 1 motel.
Map ref. 252 I2

Yanchep Population 486.
Within easy driving distance, 51 km north of Perth is the resort of Yanchep. The Sun City marina, the largest in Australia, and the Yanchep National Park are Yanchep's popular attractions. The Museum (Gloucester Lodge) has a wide range of exhibits from the area, open Sat. 12 pm-4 pm; Sun, Tues, Wed, and Public Holidays 10.20 am-4 pm. **Of interest:** Yanchep National Park, covering 2891 ha, has natural bushland, caves, a wildlife sanctuary and the freshwater Loch McNess. The Crystal and Yonderup Caves have startling limestone formations. Launches take cruises on Loch McNess. At Two Rocks there is Atlantis Marine Park and a marina. Don't miss the Waugul monoliths, giant limestone sculptures depicting figures from Aboriginal mythology. **In the area:** Gnangara Lake is a favourite spot with water-skiing enthusiasts. **Accommodation:** 1 motel, 1 caravan/camping park.
Map ref. 250 E7

York Population 1136
Founded in 1830, York is the oldest inland town in Western Australia, set on the banks of the Avon River in the fertile Avon Valley. The town has a wealth of historic buildings, carefully preserved. The York Fair is held annually. **Of interest:** Faversham House, a beautifully preserved building over 130 years old. The post office, court-house and police station were built of local stone in 1895. Settlers' House, a two-storey mud brick building, erected in 1850, has been restored beautifully and offers accommodation. Castle Hotel is a fine example of an early coaching inn and York's first licensed hotel. The Romanesque-style Town Hall has impressive dimensions. The railway station was built in 1886; the old hospital has its original shingle roof (now a recreation camp). Residency Museum has colonial furniture and early photographs. The Motor Museum has a superb collection of cars, bicycles and motorbikes. The Suspension Bridge across the river was erected in 1906. Follow the signs from the Castle Hotel to Pioneer Drive to Mt Brown. The lookout has a marvellous view and there are picnic and barbecue facilities. **Accommodation:** 2 hotels, 1 motel.
Map ref. 251 J8, 256 F10

Far left: Heat and dust are no deterrent to enthusiastic riders and spectators at Harts Range Races.

Left: Palm trees add a tropical air to Mitchell Street, Darwin.

Above: Northern Territory homesteads can be hundreds of kilometres from their nearest neighbour.

Right: Many roads in the Northern Territory, like this one to The Olgas, are unsurfaced red dirt.

Northern Territory
OUTBACK AUSTRALIA

There are only three main highways that take motorists into the Northern Territory: the Barkly Highway from Mount Isa in Queensland, the Stuart Highway from South Australia and the Victoria Highway from the extreme north-east of Western Australia. Given the enormous distances involved, you may well decide to fly, either to Darwin or to Alice Springs, and then hire a car. Alternatively, airlines, coach companies and tour operators offer day and extended coach tours, coach camping tours, adventure and safari trek tours which allow you to discover this unique, relatively uninhabited and exciting Territory in experienced hands.

Six times the size of Great Britain, with a population similar to that of Newcastle, NSW, and boasting the famous 'red centre' and the world's largest monolith, the Northern Territory abounds with staggering statistics.

The first, unsuccessful, attempt to settle this huge, forbidding region was, in fact, not on the mainland at all, but on Melville Island, in 1825, but it wasn't until 1869 that a town called Palmerston was established on the coast, the town which was later to become Darwin. Originally the Territory was part of New South Wales, when that state's western boundary extended to the 129th east meridian. Later, it was annexed to South Australia and it did not come under Commonwealth control until 1911. In July 1978, the Territory attained self-government.

In terms of monetary value, the Territory's main industry is mining. Gold, bauxite, manganese ore, copper, silver, iron ore and uranium all contribute to this industry, but beef cattle farming is by no means unimportant, even though 16 hectares or more are often required to support one animal. Poor soil, huge distances from markets and winter droughts all combine to render commercial crop growing virtually impossible.

The 'dry season', between the months of April and October, is the best time to visit the Northern Territory; and 'dry' means dry — during the 'wet season' Darwin has an average annual rainfall of 1500 mm, while only 25 mm falls in the 'dry season'. July is the Territory's coolest month. Temperatures in Darwin range then between 20° and 30°C. In 'The Alice' (as Alice Springs is affectionately known) the average maximum in August is 22.5°C, cooling at night to lows of around zero.

The Northern Territory's two main centres are more than 1500 kilometres apart. Darwin, at the 'Top End', has a population of about 60 000. It suffered extensively from cyclone Tracy in 1974 and has since been virtually rebuilt. It is renowned for its relaxed lifestyle and beautiful beaches. Its 34 hectares Botanic Gardens are splendidly tropical and at Yarrawonga Park, 21 kilometres south, you can see crocodiles and meet water buffalo, snakes and brolgas. Darwin makes a perfect jumping-off spot for exploring the Top End region.

If, however, you are 'going it alone' by car, you should research your trip thoroughly before setting out; read the section on 'Outback Motoring' and bear in mind that the dry season is definitely the most pleasant weather for touring. Always be sure to make full enquiries as to conditions before leaving sealed roads. Both the Stuart and Barkly Highways are now all weather roads, sealed for their entire length. Even so, any driving at night should be undertaken with care.

East of Darwin is the spectacular Kakadu National Park. Further east is Arnhem Land which can be explored by extended coach tour or adventure tour. Many Aboriginal reserves require entry permission from an Aboriginal Land Council; these reserves belong to the Aborigines; much of the land is sacred to them and should be respected by visitors.

South of Darwin is Katherine with its spectacular gorge, on the southern fringe of Arnhem Land. Freshwater crocodiles are common in the Katherine River, so its dramatic beauty is best viewed from either bank! From Katherine, the Stuart Highway continues south through the Tanami Desert to Alice Springs. The only town of any size along the way is Tennant Creek. South of this desert outpost are the Devil's Marbles, a random pile of granite boulders, some of which are almost perfect spheres. The Aboriginal legend about them is that they are eggs laid by the mythical Rainbow Snake.

Many people outside Australia think of Alice Springs as one of the most important towns in Australia. Certainly, it has been immortalised on film and snapshot countless times and no other town, or even tiny settlement, is nearer to the geographic centre of the country. In 1872, Alice Springs was simply a repeater station for the Overland Telegraph Service. Today, it is not only the centre for the outback cattle industry but also a lively tourist centre with a population of over 18 000.

Ayers Rock, 470 kilometres to its south-west in Uluru National Park, is the world's biggest monolith: one, enormous rock, 9 kilometres in circumference and rising 350 metres above the plain on which it stands. The Aborigines made it a part of their sacred rituals, and guides will explain the mythology of the cave paintings.

The magnificent Olgas and, closer to the Alice, the prehistoric palms at Palm Valley, the dramatic Kings Canyon, Standley Chasm and Ormiston Gorge, all add their own fascination to the many wonders of the Northern Territory.

Darwin
A RELAXED CITY

The first coastal town established in the Northern Territory was Palmerston, in 1864. Located at the mouth of the Adelaide River, it was quickly abandoned after a disastrous wet season in 1865.

Another expedition, led by Surveyor-General George Goyder, established a base at Adam Bay about 50 kilometres east of present day Darwin. After surveying the area, he recommended that Port Darwin, which had been discovered in 1839 and named after Charles Darwin, would be the best place for a settlement. The town was officially called Palmerston, but the locals referred to it as Port Darwin to distinguish it from the old original settlement. The name was officially changed to Darwin in 1911 when the Federal Government took control of the Territory.

In its early days, Darwin's development was hampered by its isolation. During World War 2, however, the Stuart Highway was completed, linking Darwin with the railhead at Alice Springs, but after recovering from bomb damage in the war, growth was still slow.

The new Darwin's prosperity is based largely on the mineral wealth of the Northern Territory. It is the exploitation of this that has finally led to the city being developed to the modern standard it has today, despite the major setback when Cyclone Tracy struck in 1974.

A new Darwin has grown out of the ruins of the cyclone, as befits the city's role as the capital of a self-governing territory. Until recently, Darwin had been largely maintained by the Commonwealth Government because of its strategic location, as much as for its function as a route centre and supply base for a grazing and mining area by no means yet fully developed.

Life for the early citizens was hard and changed very little until the Second World War. Graziers and agriculturalists could only hope to cope with the violent climatic changes. Development of modern techniques saw the population grow to 45 000 in 1974, when Cyclone Tracy struck. Now, after the storm, the figure has pushed past 56 000 which says something either for the hardiness of its people, or the desirability of the city as a place to live, or maybe a bit of both. With Broome, in Western Australia, Darwin is one of Australia's most 'foreign' settlements, embracing people of 47 different racial and cultural backgrounds. Chinese people have always formed a major part of the city's population and, in more recent years, Timorese and South-east Asian refugees have been arriving in Darwin and many have stayed. Quite large contingents of military and airforce personnel are also stationed at bases around Darwin.

Temperatures in the city area itself average around 28°C; there is very little or no rain. In the 'wet', temperatures average close to 34°C with high relative humidity that can be uncomfortable for people from more equable climes. But always Darwin is good for sailing, swimming, water-skiing or soaking up the sun.

The city has developed its own style of dress. Daytime rig is shorts with short-sleeved, open-neck shirts, long socks and shoes for men, while the ladies wear light dresses or shorts and a shirt or blouse. Full 'Territory Rig' for evenings is long trousers with long-sleeved shirt (sometimes plus jacket and tie) for men: the ladies wear afternoon or evening cocktail fashions.

BELOW: *The restored Victoria Hotel.*

City sightseeing is conveniently done from air-conditioned motor coaches that make regular tours. The main features to see are the **Botanical Gardens**, the few surviving historic buildings, churches, memorials, the **Reserve Bank**, the **Law Courts** and Darwin's busy **harbour** area. Darwin's airport and harbour are most important these days as the city serves as Australia's northern gateway.

The city's business district is much like any other similar sized city, but the relaxed and tropical atmosphere adds a distinct character of its own. Modern air-conditioned shopping centres now serve Darwin's suburbs which are in two main sections, divided by the airport.

Christchurch Cathedral was completed and consecrated in March 1977. It incorporates the porch from its predecessor which was destroyed by Cyclone Tracy. During the war it was a Garrison Church and came under fire from Japanese bombers. The new Cathedral was built at a cost of $800 000 and features a stained glass window in memory of the trawlermen lost at sea during the Cyclone. The altar, weighing 2.5 tonnes, has been hewn from a solid jarrah log believed to be more than 400 years old.

There are several other interesting places of worship in Darwin, particularly the **Chinese Temple**, the inside of which visitors are permitted to inspect.

One of Darwin's most historic hotels, **The Old Victoria** in Smith Street, has been restored into a modern shopping complex, at the same time retaining its colonial character with 'punkahs' to cool the Balcony Bar. The shops in the complex are varied, and the **Northern Territory Tourist Bureau** office is also located here.

BELOW: *Christchurch Cathedral.*

For those with cultural interests, the city boasts a theatre group which welcomes visitors' participation in its workshops held in **Brown's Mart**, another building that survived Tracy. The Arts Council also presents live theatre performances in Darwin. Cinemas are located in Mitchell Street, at Parap and at Nightcliff.

Several Art Galleries, including some which feature the art and craft of the Aboriginal people can be seen in the city area and the **East Point War Museum** at **Fannie Bay** displays artillery, war planes and other militaria close to the gun turrets that were constructed during the Second World War. Fannie Bay is also the site where Ross and Keith Smith landed their Vickers Vimy aircraft in 1919, completing the first flight from the UK to Australia. It is also one of the most beautiful spots in the world for a prison!

Darwin's best known annual event is probably the beer can regatta, held each June, when boats and other floating craft are constructed out of beer cans, a commodity of which there never seems to be a shortage in this city!

Darwin's restaurants offer an excellent choice of cuisine, from simple steak houses to French, Italian and Indonesian menus. There are also some wine bars which offer varied menus and pleasant settings for lunch and dinner.

To the north of the city area, Darwin's suburbs have been virtually rebuilt since 1974. Visitors will see what a remarkable achievement this has been. Because of the tropical climate, the lush vegetation has quickly developed new gardens of beautiful bougainvillea, hibiscus and alamander beside the newly designed houses which, it is hoped, will better withstand any future cyclonic onslaught. These suburbs too enjoy similar modern facilities to their southern Australian equivalents, even down to American-style fast food outlets and large supermarkets.

HOTELS
Diamond Beach Casino,
Gilruth Ave, Darwin.
(089) 81 7755
Telford International,
Dashwood Crescent, Darwin.
(089) 81 5333
Travelodge,
122 The Esplanade, Darwin.
(089) 81 5388

FAMILY AND BUDGET
Darwin,
10 Herbert St, Darwin.
(089) 81 9211
Telford Top End,
Cnr Daly St and Esplanade, Darwin
(089) 81 6511
Poinciana, Cnr McLachlan and Mitchell Sts, Darwin. (089) 81 8111
YWCA,
119 Mitchell St, Darwin.
(089) 81 8644

MOTEL GROUP: BOOKINGS
Homestead (089) 81 9200
Travelodge (089) 81 5388
This list is for information only; inclusion is not necessarily a recommendation.

BELOW: *There is great fun for all at the Beer Can Regatta held in Darwin each June!*

Sporting interests are well served. There is a golf course, speedway track, a racecourse at Fannie Bay, and the usual facilities for tennis, squash, bowls, football (Aussie Rules and Rugby) and so on. An **Olympic Pool** is located on Ross Smith Avenue — swimming in the sea for much of the year is not recommended as sea wasps are common in the waters off Darwin.

Darwin is the natural jump-off point for touring the Top End. The good hotels and motels are as well-found as their counterparts in other Australian capitals. The pressure on these is often great and lots of alternative, less luxurious, accommodation has developed which can still be very comfortable. Quite a number of the many caravan parks in Darwin are occupied by permanent residents, so it is worthwhile booking ahead.

The **Diamond Beach Casion** in Darwin is built a few metres from the shores of Mindil Beach. This new thirty million dollar complex offers luxury accommodation, restaurants, discos, plus gambling, sporting and convention facilities.

Future state

The floral emblem of the Northern Territory is Sturt's Desert Rose, a bushy plant which produces beautiful mauvish-pink flowers during late winter and spring.

In Alice Springs it can be cultivated as a garden shrub and is found wild mainly in the southern part of the Territory. It is often called the Darling River Rose, the Cotton Rosebush or Australian Cotton. As it is, in fact, a member of the cotton genus these are the most accurate common names.

To mark its new status as a self-governing territory, the Northern Territory now has its own flag.

The flag incorporates the floral emblem of the Territory, Sturt's Desert Rose, with the Southern Cross from the Australian flag. The colours of the flag are those of the Territory, black, white and red ochre.

The seven petals and seven-pointed star in the flower emblem represent the six state governments and the government of the Northern Territory. The flag was designed by Robert Ingpen.

The Northern Territory's faunal emblems are the red kangaroo, found in great numbers throughout the Territory, and the wedge-tailed eagle, Australia's largest bird of prey.

THE TOP END

A new Darwin has arisen from the old city which was devastated by Cyclone Tracy on Christmas Eve 1974. Business and industry has been re-established, houses and public buildings are being rebuilt, the gardens are flourishing and the attractive layouts of street plantations, reserves and public gardens give the city an air of colour and well-being. The free and friendly spirit and the open community life in this city, which swelters in summer and has the best winter climate in Australia, is again in evidence.

With improved roads and the vast increase in tourism in Australia, Darwin has become a major tourist destination. Rebuilding has brought a number of high quality hotels and motels to the city and there is accommodation to suit either luxury or family means. Darwin itself is a winter haven, with its excellent beaches, abundance of fish and warm weather, but its real attraction is as a base for exploring the wild and fascinating country at the 'Top End'. Here you might see wide billabongs covered with lilies, herds of buffalo on the plains or standing knee-deep in waterholes, clouds of geese wheeling above the trees, crocodiles sunning themselves on waterside rocks, plunging waterfalls, rows of pillar-like ant hills, spectacular cliff and rock features, caves and cliffs carrying the Aboriginal cave paintings of the past.

The Northern Territory Administration has created a number of reserves to preserve the features of the region and

ABOVE RIGHT: *This residence of the Northern Territory Administrator has withstood wartime bombings and the ravages of Cyclone Tracy.*

RIGHT: *The Diamond Beach Casino in Darwin.*

Northern Territory

ABOVE: *Kakadu National Park is in the dense and wild country between the South and East Alligator Rivers, 220 kilometres east of Darwin. This huge park covers an area of 6000 square kilometres and has a rich natural and cultural heritage. The vegetation ranges from pockets of rainforest through dwarf shrubland, to open forests and swamps.*

ABOVE: *The Jim Jim Falls are considered by many to be the most spectacular feature in Kakadu National Park. The Park's dramatic landscape is the result of continual weathering erosion and sedimentation over some two million years.*

to make them accessible to travellers. The most spectacular of them, in an area destined to become one of the top natural tourist attractions in Australia, is the new Kakadu National Park in the dense and wild country along the East Alligator River, bordering the Arnhem Land Aboriginal Reserve.

The park is rich in vegetation, ranging from pockets of rainforest through dwarf shrubland, to open forest and swamps. The abundant wildlife includes several animals unique to the area, such as the banded pigeon, the rock possum and a species of rock wallaby. There are emus, a rich variety of pigeons and parrots, many marsupials, freshwater crocodiles and rivers teeming with fish. The most spectacular point in the park is the Jim Jim Falls — 215 metres high and with a sheer drop of 152 metres of water pouring over the rugged and colourful escarpment which is a feature of the area.

North of Jim Jim Falls is Death Adder Valley, where Death Adder Creek winds through narrow, deeply-cleft rock walls. There is a wealth of Aboriginal

LEFT: *Aboriginal stockmen. Although the days of long distance droving are gone, men and cattle still go along the back trails from station to station, in the north of the Territory.*

The Top End

ABOVE: *One of the many examples of Aboriginal art which decorate the rocks and caves of the Northern Territory. The subject matter is usually animals, ritual or totemic symbols.*

BELOW: *Katherine Gorge where the river flows swiftly through towering cliffs to form fascinating river canyons. Boat tours through the gorge offer the chance to see freshwater crocodiles.*

cave paintings here. North again, one reaches the East Alligator River, a well-known fishing ground where barramundi can be caught in plenty and where the river reaches wind through spectacularly beautiful country. The park includes black soil plains, the habitat of water buffalo and water birds, stone country where a massive rock escarpment rises to Nourlangie Rock and Mount Brockman. The park can be reached on the main Jabiru highway, east of Darwin.

Two small parks close to Darwin are Berry Springs and Howard Springs. Berry Springs is noted for its warm water, a continual 20°C for pleasant and safe swimming, and its marvellous birdlife. More than 120 species of birds have been recorded, the most colourful ones including rainbow lorikeets, the northern rosellas, red-winged parrots, rainbow birds and blue-faced honeyeaters. At Howard Springs, the pool is surrounded by forest, including pandanus palms, milkwood, red ash, white cedar, wild nutmeg and camphorwood trees. Again, the park abounds in birds and wildlife.

Along the Stuart Highway, known as 'the track', 354 kilometres south of Darwin are the town of Katherine and the spectacular Katherine Gorge National Park. Here, the clear river flows between towering, brilliantly coloured walls to form one of the most fascinating river canyons in Australia. Boat tours through the gorge are a popular experience, guaranteed to be an exciting highlight of any holiday.

Northern Territory

Further south is the Mataranka Pool Reserve, near the Mataranka Homestead, where thermal springs are surrounded by lush tropical forest and the water is permanently at body temperature. Four wheel drive wildlife safaris can be arranged in Darwin and they are an ideal way to see the country and to experience something of life in the Top End.

There are major roads to all these interesting places around the Top End, but it is vital that travellers should not stray into unknown areas where they may get into difficulties. Read the earlier section on outback driving if you are contemplating a tour of this area. Further information about the Top End can be obtained from the Northern Territory Government Tourist Bureau and in Darwin from the Territory Parks and Wildlife Commission.

ABOVE: *The Stuart Highway north of Tennant Creek. Watch out for kangaroos, cattle and wild donkeys and, north of Katherine, the odd buffalo or wild pig!*

ABOVE RIGHT: *Robin Falls look invitingly cool in this mainly arid, sparsely vegetated landscape.*

RIGHT: *Ant hills grow to the height of small trees in the 'Top End'. These extraordinary mounds of digested mud are constructed by termites.*

BELOW RIGHT: *Visitors to Kakadu National Park can take a cruise on the Alligator River and are likely to see many different species of wildlife, particularly the buffalo, wallaby, crocodile and many kinds of water birds.*

BELOW: *Nourlangie Rock in the Kakadu National Park, Arnhem Land. This rocky outcrop serves as a vast Aboriginal art gallery, with scores of rock paintings expressing the rituals and beliefs, the heroes and creatures of the Dreamtime.*

Tours from Darwin

The eight million hectares of the Arnhem Land Aboriginal Reserve, one of Australia's most fascinating wilderness areas, lie to the east of Darwin. It is a land that changes from broken mountains to vast plains, irrigated by constantly flowing rivers. An entry permit is required which tourist agencies arrange through local government. In the 'dry' many tours of places of interest in and around the city are available, by bus or hire car. Safaris by air and four-wheel-drive take sportsmen to less accessible areas for sightseeing, shooting and fishing. Buffalo and barramundi are the popular quarry.

The best month for the bush is July when, on a clear night, the stars seem to get in your eyes and you would not swap the finest dish in the world for a cutlet of barramundi grilled in the traditional manner on a shovel over an open fire. Almost any time from April to September is suitable for getting back to nature. When you do it is hard to conceive that Darwin, serving all this barely touched vastness, has an airport that can take not only jumbo jets, but also supersonic Concorde.

Fogg Dam, 70 km from Darwin via the Arnhem Highway.

A sunrise or sunset wildlife tour offers the best way to visit this area. Wildlife is close by and these are the best times to see it, as animals and birds are on the move between feeding grounds and where they sleep.

Fogg Dam is a likely spot to see a crocodile, and you will certainly see lots of wallabies. The nearby swamps are about the closest spot to the city where you may see the elegant jabiru stork. Other birds in abundance are the pelican, egret, galah, cockatoo and kitehawk. The usual tour route then pushes on to the Marakai Plains for more birds and perhaps buffalo. Millions of dollars were lost in this area when the rice irrigation scheme at **Humpty Doo** (266 E5) failed.

Kakadu National Park, 250 km from Darwin via the Arnhem Highway.

Apart from abundant wildlife, the scenery here is dramatic and there are many fine examples of ancient Aboriginal art. The five to seven hours of driving in and out are fascinating, topped off by a cruise on the Alligator River. You would be unlucky not to see crocodiles as well as buffalo, wallaby and many kinds of birdlife. The Arnhem Highway is sealed all the way to **Jabiru** (266 H5), and you could do the trip in your own car or a hire car. **Jim Jim** (266 H5) is only 55 km to the south-east and there is pleasant motel accommodation there. The safari guides have local knowledge and can show you far more than if you explore on your own.

Arnhem Land produces the skeletal type of Aboriginal art — animals, birds, fish and reptiles drawn with bones and internal organs showing. There are paintings in hundreds of caves, and you can buy bark paintings, carved figures and huge didgeridoos on location.

BELOW LEFT: *Melaleuca swamp, Arnhem Land.*

ABOVE: *Agile wallabies can be seen at Fogg Dam.*

Howard Springs, 36 km from Darwin via the Arnhem Highway.

There are safe swimming holes in the creek here and any birdwatcher who has done his homework can spot 50 or more species in a few hours, and varieties of reptiles abound. Picnic areas, kiosk and toilet facilities are provided.

Berry Springs, 58 km from Darwin via the Stuart Highway.

This nature park offers everything that Howard Springs has plus a fascinating walking track. Kiosk, toilets, and picnic areas provided.

RIGHT: *Many air tours are available from Darwin.*

ABOVE: *Arnhem Land is a region of great beauty. This scene is at Jim Jim Falls.*

Ferry trips to the Cox Peninsula

Daily trips depart from the wharf in Darwin Harbour either to Mandorah Inn or the Golden Sands Holiday Resort, ideal for a relaxed day on the beach, swimming or fishing. From Mandorah, it is possible to arrange a tour of Woods Everglades where dense tropical growth overhangs a narrow waterway.

Air tours

Several tours by air from Darwin are available, including day or weekend trips to Jim Jim Falls and fishing and shooting trips. A three-day air tour into Western Australia including a jungle cruise at Lake Kununurra, the Hidden Valley, the Carr Boyd Ranges, Lake Argyle and the Ord River makes a most enjoyable trip, if you can spare the time.

Northern Territory from A to Z

Adelaide River Pop. under 200.
A small settlement set in pleasant country, 112 km south of Darwin on the Stuart Highway, Adelaide River is a good jump-off point for visits to Rum Jungle, an old uranium mining area; the Daly River district; and the Batchelor and Tipperary experimental farming areas. **Accomodation:** 1 motel.
Map ref. 266 E6

Aileron Population under 200.
On the Stuart Highway, 139 km north of Alice Springs. **Accommodation:** 1 motel.
Map ref. 270 I5

Alice Springs Population 18 395
Alice Springs is at the heart of the Red Centre of Australia, almost 1000 kilometres from the nearest capital city. It is the gateway to the NT's biggest single tourist attraction, Ayers Rock. A modern and well maintained town, right in the heart of the Macdonnell Ranges, close to 250 000 visitors a year pass through between May and September. In this period cloudless skies and warm days usher in refreshingly cool nights. The rest of the year is very hot, with dust storms. Rains, usually brief, can come at any time of year. While there is plenty to see in the town itself, many natural wonders lie within a day's journey.

Like any other big town, the Alice, as it is affectionately called, offers a variety of restaurants, a new international hotel-casino, sports grounds, a swimming pool, laundromats and so on. There is a good variety of shops and a number of art galleries, including some which specialise in Aboriginal art.

The Todd River, which runs through the town, is dry except after flash floods, but this does not stop the locals holding their annual 'Henley-on-Todd Regatta'. The boats are carried, or wear wheels, for the occasion.

The few areas of land that can be irrigated support small dairy and fruit growing enterprises but the main produce of the area is beef cattle from huge runs.

The site of the town was discovered by William Whitfield Mills in 1871. He was at the time surveying a route for the Overland Telegraph Line. He named the Todd river after the South Australian Superintendent of Telegraphs, Sir Charles Todd, and a nearby waterhole was named Alice Springs after his boss's wife. The first settlement was at the repeater station, built for transmitting messages across the continent. Most of the thick-walled stone buildings have been restored and can be viewed.

About ten years before Mills, John McDouall Stuart records in his diary that he passed about 50 kilometres west of the site. Stuart also discovered and named Central Mount Sturt (since renamed Central Mount Stuart) in 1860. He named it after Captain Sturt who had commanded an earlier expedition in which he (Stuart) had taken part, but the South Australian Government renamed it in Stuart's honour after he had completed his successful expedition to the northern coast of Australia.

John Ross, a pastoralist, was also active in the area seeking new grazing lands. He also helped look for a route for the telegraph line.

Touring the Territory

Many people will not want to embark upon a tour of the Northern Territory's outback areas alone. Fortunately, an enormous variety of accompanied tours leave from all capital cities enabling the least intrepid visitor to see Australia's magnificent centre. These range from quite basic holidays under canvas, travelling by coach or four-wheel drive between overnight stops or, for those who prefer a few 'home comforts', air conditioned coaches choose a route served by motel, hotel or tourist camp accommodation.

The main tourist season operates from approximately April to September, but the Northern Territory Tourist Bureau also now exhorts you to 'See Alice while she's hot' and offers excellent reductions for travel and accommodation costs during the 'off season' months between October and March. This is the 'hot season' and if you do not like intense heat you may be better off to save up until you can afford the high season prices.

On camping tours, it is usual for campers to help in the putting up of tents, preparation, serving and washing up of meals and general cleaning up, but all this lends itself to making the holiday a truly 'different' experience. It does also mean, however, that adaptability is an advantage as you will not be choosing the people who accompany you on the holiday.

Another way to tackle the outback is to join a convoy expedition, using your own vehicle, but guided by experts. Motoring organisations arrange such tours, but departure times are limited and your own vehicle must be in an acceptable condition before you will be allowed to join the tour.

If you do decide to travel alone on roads that are off the beaten track, it is wise to take a few precautions for your own security. It is not advisable to pick up hitchhikers or to camp, other than in a lockable caravan, outside organised sites.

The new 'Ghan' train is another way of avoiding the long boring stretches of road. To travel one way by train and return by air is a time-saving way of seeing the centre — a great variety of coach tours based on Alice Springs will convey you to the main tourist attractions of the region once you are there and this is an excellent way of seeing the centre. Coach operators also combine a one-way rail trip with a return coach journey. The rail trip takes approximately 22 hours. 'The Alice' is a new direct rail service from Sydney to Alice Springs. The trip takes two nights and three days.

Carrying a camera

If you are making a 'once in a lifetime' trip to the Red Centre, you will probably want to preserve the memories of it on film, so it's wise to check a few points before setting out.

1. If your equipment is new, try one 'test' film so that you know how the camera reacts in different weather and light conditions.
2. As weather conditions may vary on your trip, it is a good idea to take different speeds of film. If you're not an expert, talk to your local dealer about the varieties of film available.
3. Before you leave home, check that you have plenty of film, a lens brush, flash holder and bulbs. Other useful accessories are close-up lens, exposure meter, lens hood and filters.
4. When you are travelling, try to safeguard your equipment from water, heat, sand and dust. Ideally, protect your equipment in a camera bag. Remember how hot it can get in a closed car and always keep the camera in the shade. The best place to keep it in the car is on the floor, on the opposite side to the exhaust pipe. Make sure, however, that the strap or bag is secured.
5. High temperatures and humidity can damage colour films. Store your film in the coolest spot available and don't break the watertight vapour seal until just before use. Once the film is used, remove it from the camera and send it for processing as soon as possible.
6. Filming in hot conditions: even with automatic exposure, it will probably be necessary to allow one, or one-half of a stop down to compensate for the brilliance. If in doubt about light conditions, consult the instruction sheet included with your film.

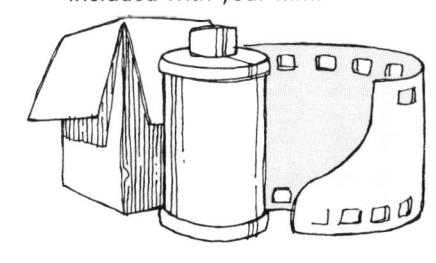

The repeater station was for many years the only reason for the existence of a handful of people in this remote area but in 1888 the South Australian Government became eager to open up the country and sent surveys north seeking suitable sites for railheads. The township of Stuart, 3.2 km from the telegraph station, was gazetted in that same year; but the railway remained unbuilt and Stuart stagnated. Regular supply was maintained by camel train from Port Augusta, which was both expensive and slow. Even the discovery of gold at Arltunga, 96 km east of the settlement, did little to develop it.

The Federal Government took control of the Northern Territory from South Australia in 1911. From that time the township began to develop steadily, if still slowly.

The Australian Inland Mission stationed Sister Jane Finlayson there in 1916. She was supposed to stay only one year but the growing needs of the area led to the establishment of Adelaide House nursing hostel in 1926. The railway was finally completed in 1929 and the first train reached Stuart in August that year. The service became known as 'The Ghan', after the Afghan camel drivers it had replaced.

The white population increased from 40 in 1926 to 200 in 1931 as the supply of materials became more reliable and less expensive. As the township grew there came need for better identification. There was too much confusion between Stuart and the telegraph station Alice Springs, only 3 km apart. So Stuart was dropped and the name of the township changed to Alice Springs. Now it is the jump-off point for tourists who visit the Red Centre. **Of interest:** Royal Flying Doctor Service base tours, half-hourly daily except Sundays. A demonstration 'lesson' at the School of the Air in Head St can be seen Mondays to Fridays, 1.30 to 3.30 pm. Art Exhibition, Government Centre. The Araluen Arts Centre, the focal point for performing and visual arts. John Flynn Memorial Church, Todd St, which was built in memory of the founder of the RFDS. Craft workshop, Todd St, where you can see spinners, weavers and potters at work. The old gaol, Parsons St. **In the area:** View the town from the top of Anzac Hill at the north end of the town. The old telegraph station is 3 km north of the town, off the Stuart Highway. There is a display of early photos, papers and documents relating to the original settlement. Old Timers' Homes museum of pioneer equipment, 5 km south of the town. Pitchi Richi, 3 km from town, is a native bird and flower sanctuary as well as an open-air pioneer museum. **Accommodation:** 2 hotels, 7 motels, 5 caravan/camping parks.
Map ref. 261, 263 M5, 271 J8

Alyangula Population 1181.*
Situated on the Groote Eylandt Aboriginal Reserve in the Gulf of Carpentaria.
Map ref. 267 O7

---

*Denotes population centres where visitors are not encouraged; permits are sometimes required; no accommodation.

Gove

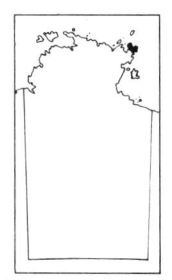

The Gove Peninsula, named after W. H. J. Gove, an Australian airman killed in the area during World War 2, is situated at the far north-east point of Arnhem Land.

The whole of the peninsula is set aside as an Aboriginal Reserve and the main centres are **Yirrkala** and **Nhulunbuy**. To the west of Nhulunbuy, near Dundas Point, is Melville Bay which the explorer Matthew Flinders described as the best natural harbour on the Gulf of Carpentaria. Ships up to nine metres draught can use it. Accommodation is limited.

The Yirrkala Mission, near Mount Dundas, provides a residential base for many of the Aborigines in the area. Its name has become familiar in recent years because of the struggle by its people to win title to their land. The *Aboriginal Land Rights (Northern Territory) Act* was finally assented to on 16 December 1976. It represents to the people of Yirrkala the culmination of years of struggle to win recognition for their claims to land on which their people have lived for many thousands of years.

The Yirrkala area is noted for carvings of birds and fish. The most spectacular cave art in this area is at Obiri Rock, close to the East Alligator River. The climb is easy, the reward two long galleries of paintings — plus a glorious view.

No great encouragement is given to tourists but trips to Gove can be arranged through the Northern Territory Government. The practical way is by charter aircraft.

Tours from Alice Springs

An ideal way to see the multitude of tourist attractions in the red centre is to base yourself in Alice Springs and to take advantage of the many and varied coach tours which operate from there.

Of course the one you won't want to miss is **Ayers Rock**. About 450 kilometres south-west of the Alice, its great bulk curves up from the desert, challenging you to climb it. If you succeed, you can buy yourself a tee-shirt to commemorate the event — 'I've climbed Ayers Rock'. It is actually no mean feat to complete the climb and it is best omitted by the elderly or unfit. If you can't make the climb, be content to stay below and just observe the sunrise or sunset to see the fantastic colours of the rock. Around the nine-kilometres perimeter you can see weirdly eroded caves that contain Aboriginal paintings in charcoal and ochre. At the southern side, Maggie Springs is a permanent waterhole, but after rain the whole rock becomes veiled in waterfalls, which appear and disappear with great rapidity.

About 32 kilometres further west are **The Olgas**, a more rounded group of rocks which rise abruptly from the spinifex covered plain. The Rock and The Olgas together form the greatest single tourist attraction in the Northern Territory. Accommodation for visitors available at Yulara Tourist Village. There are no facilities at The Olgas.

Ross River Homestead, 80 kilometres east of Alice Springs, is a delightful place to base yourself for exploration of the East Macdonnells. The homestead features old-style cooking and horse rides and swimming are available. The bar has an interesting display of antiques. **Trephina Gorge**, the **John Hayes Rockholes, N'Dhala Gorge** and **Arltunga** are the principal attractions in the area.

Trephina Gorge nature park is home for many creatures, including fairy martins and wasps, bats, lizards and many species of parrots and other birds.

Arltunga Historical Reserve has been set aside to preserve memories of the gold mining era in the region. Little evidence remains of the shanty town which grew up after 1887 when alluvial gold was found there. In 1897 a government battery and cyanide works were constructed west of the town and the ruins of these and of the old police station remain. Facilities are limited — it is best to come prepared with your own wood or gas barbecue if you wish to cook.

If you take advantage of the organised Ross River tour from Alice Springs, you will be able to visit these attractions as well as learn much of the folklore relating to the Eastern Aranda Aborigines, learn how to throw a boomerang and sample billy tea and damper.

A turning off the Stuart Highway about 130 kilometres south of Alice Springs leads to the **Henbury meteorite craters** and, a further 200 kilometres west, the spectacular beauty of **Kings Canyon**. The **Wallara Ranch** is a good accommodation base from which to see these attractions.

The Henbury craters are believed to have been formed less than 4700 years ago when a meteor hit the earth. The largest crater is 183 metres wide, its rim is six metres above the ground and its depth is 12 metres. There are barbecues at the reserve, but no supplies of water or wood.

Kings Canyon is located on private property and visitors are asked to treat the area with care and not to leave litter. The climb to the rim of the Canyon is fairly arduous, but well worth it. Even more spectacular views can be obtained by crossing the tree trunk bridge — a nerve-racking experience, as there is no handrail — to the north wall. The Lost City and the Garden of Eden are the superb sights here.

Within easy reach of Alice Springs for a day tour is the beautiful Standley Chasm. Located about 50 kilometres from Alice Springs to the west, this colourful cleft in the West Macdonnells is only five metres wide. At midday when the sunlight reaches to its floor it is a memorable sight.

Simpsons Gap National Park can be visited on this same trip.

Further west, about 136 kilometres from Alice Springs on the Namatjira Drive are **Glen Helen** and **Ormiston Gorges**. Located on the Finke River, their colours were captured by Aboriginal artist Albert Namatjira and today lend themselves to photography, as does the sunrise on Mount Sonder which can be seen to the west. Glen Helen Tourist Camp is an accommodation base for this area, or a coach tour lasting approximately ten hours is available from Alice Springs.

A 12 hour tour from Alice Springs will take you to **Palm Valley** and the **Finke River Gorge**. The Finke River is one of the oldest water courses in the world and to walk along its bed is a memorable experience, the spectacular red walls towering above you.

Palm Valley, with its rock pools, cycad palms and *Livistona* palms unique to the area, is yet another of the incredible sights of the centre and seems like a trip back in time, the plant life has such a 'prehistoric' appearance.

These two places can also be visited by taking a two-day tour from Alice Springs, staying overnight at Glen Helen.

Much nearer 'home', the Alice Springs **Telegraph Historical Reserve** is a most interesting area only three kilometres from town. It is the site of the original township and all its buildings still stand. The Territory Parks and Wildlife Commission has restored the site to its original period of 1890 to 1900. The Reserve occupies 444 hectares and an amazing number of birds, amphibians and reptiles have been sighted there. Emus and kangaroos can be easily seen wandering in wildlife enclosures.

The telegraph station was originally built to link Port Augusta to Darwin, thence by submarine cable to Java. The line was completed in 1872 and was used from then until 1932 when operations were transferred to the site at the corner of Parsons Street and Railway Terrace in Alice Springs.

Amoonguna Population under 200.*
An Aboriginal settlement about 12 km east of Alice Springs.
Map ref. 271 J8

Angurugu Population 597.*
Situated on the Groote Eylandt Aboriginal Reserve in the Gulf of Carpentaria.
Map ref. 267 O8

Areyonga Population under 200.*
This Aboriginal Reserve is situated about 50 km due west of Palm Valley.
Map ref. 270 G9

Bamyili/Beswick Population 685.*
These settlements are on the Beswick Aboriginal Reserve, north of Mataranka.
Map ref. 266 H9

Barrow Creek Pop. under 200.
On the Stuart Highway, 283 km north of Alice Springs. **Accommodation:** 1 hotel.
Map ref. 269 J13, 271 A3

Barry Caves Population under 200.
On the Barkly Highway, 283 km east of Tennant Creek. **Accommodation:** 1 motel.
Map ref. 269 O10

Bathurst Island Population 1032.*
This island north of Darwin is set aside as an Aboriginal Reserve.
Map ref. 266 D3

Borroloola Population 420.*
Situated on the Carpenteria Highway in the far north-east of the Territory.
Map ref. 267 O12, 269 O2

Croker Island Population 244.*
An Aboriginal Reserve on the north-west tip of Arnhem Land.
Map ref. 266 H2

Daly River Population 430.*
A small township and Aboriginal Reserve on Joseph Bonaparte Gulf.
Map ref. 266 D7

Daly Waters Population under 200.
At the junction of the Stuart and Carpentaria Highways. **Accommodation:** 1 motel, 1 caravan/camping park.
Map ref. 266 I 12, 268 I 2

Docker River Population 217.*
This settlement is in the Petermann Ranges almost on the Western Australian border.
Map ref. 270 A10

Dunmarra Population under 200.
At the junction of the Stuart and Buchanan Highways, 363 km north of Tennant Creek. **Accommodation:** 1 motel, 1 caravan/camping park.
Map ref. 266 I 13, 268 I 3

Elliott Population under 200.
On the Stuart Highway, 254 km north of Tennant Creek. **Accommodation:** 1 motel, 2 caravan/camping parks.
Map ref. 269 J5

Galiwinku Population 987.*
Situated on Elcho Island off the north coast of Arnhem Land.
Map ref. 267 N3

Glen Helen Population under 200.
On Namatjira Drive, 136 km west of Alice Springs, this tourist camp is an excellent base for exploring some superb scenery. Ormiston Gorge is known as the 'jewel of the centre'. At Glen Helen Gorge you can walk along the Finke River bed and see towering, rugged red cliffs. Finke River Gorge has amazing rock formations known as the 'amphitheatre', the 'sphinx' and the 'battleship'. Nearby Palm Valley is a sudden contrast with its beautiful rock pools and palm trees. In the early morning the changing colours of the sunrise on the slopes of Mt Sonder are a remarkable sight. **Accommodation:** Glen Helen Tourist Camp.
Map ref. 270 H8

Goulburn Island Population 277.*
An Aboriginal Reserve off the north-west coast of Arnhem Land.
Map ref. 266 I 3

Hermannsburg Population 541.*
Hermannsburg Mission is situated on Larapinta Drive, north of Palm Valley. Although no permit is required to visit Hermannsburg, visitors are not encouraged and no facilities are provided for them. Information can be obtained from the Finke River Mission Office, Gap Road.
Map ref. 262 E7, 270 H8

Hooker Creek Population 671.*
This Aboriginal Reserve is located south of Wave Hill.
Map ref. 268 D7

Howard Springs Population 1368.*
Off the Stuart Highway, 33 km from Darwin. **Accommodation:** 1 caravan/camping park.
Map ref. 266 E4

Katherine Population 3737.
In times of drought — sometimes for years on end — you can travel northern Australia for 2000 kilometres and more before you see the sheen of flowing water in a permanent river. Perhaps it is the instant impact of incredible contrast between unending arid plain and Katherine Gorge that heightens its dramatic beauty. The town of Katherine is 337 km south of Darwin, by a stretch of boring bitumen that reaches from horizon to horizon in an almost ruler-straight line. Nowadays Katherine's economic mainstay is tourism, but still this neat township is the centre of scientific agricultural experiments designed to improve the

---

*Denotes population centres where visitors are not encouraged; permits are sometimes required; no accommodation.

Northern Territory National Parks

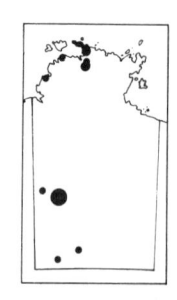

The 22 parks and reserves of the Northern Territory are grouped into two sections, separated by 200 kilometres of road. One group is at the Top End close to **Darwin** and the other at the southern end around **Alice Springs**. Best known of all the parks is Uluru, which contains the monolith of Ayers Rock and The Olgas rising abruptly from the surrounding plains. Ayers Rock, the Aboriginal people's sacred dreaming place, is not a rock but the tip of a huge bed of comglomerate pebbles laid down on the floor of an inland sea in the Cambrian period some 600 million years ago. It is properly described as a monolith, and is the world's largest such formation. It is also the Territory's single biggest tourist attraction.

The Rock changes colour with the time of day and the mood of weather. Like molten metal flowing from a blast furnace it flares from fiery red right through the spectrum until the sun goes down and it cools into earth colour again. One good way to see the Rock without any drama is to join the guided tour parties which take you around the nine-kilometres base to examine fascinating features such as the Sound Shell, Brain and Kangaroo Tail and caves containing elaborate Aboriginal rock paintings.

The climb to the 348-metres high summit is strictly for people with a good head for heights, and even though you're assisted by a rope-walk part of the way, you'll still need plenty of energy! The view from the top is well worth it, though: a great red plain stretching to the horizon, often covered in wild flowers after a thunderstorm. At the base of the rock is Maggie Springs, a true oasis for wildlife. Animals such as the big red kangaroo, the smaller euro and marsupial mouse depend upon it for water, as do some 130 species of birds.

Further west, the 28 great domes of The Olgas are separated by deep clefts that hold sweet water and support abundant wildlife. The Olgas are venerated by the Aborigines as Katatjuta, the many-headed one.

The town of Alice Springs lies in the Macdonnell Ranges, the land of the Aranda tribe and a paradise for photographers and artists. Cutting through the ranges are spectacular gorges holding some of the finest rock scenery in Australia — crimson and ochre rock walls bordering deep blue pools and slopes covered with spring wild flowers.

Within the West Macdonnells are five scenic parks. The best-known is Ormiston Gorge and Pound National Park, where fish bury themselves as a string of waterholes shrinks to puddles, waiting for the rains to brim them again. The deepest part of Ormiston Creek is a magnificent permanent pool the Aranda believed to be inhabited by a great water snake. At the far end of the gorge, the walls are curtained by a variety of ferns and plants, including the lovely Sturt's desert rose and the relic macrozamia.

Finke Gorge National Park also lies in this part of the Macdonnells. It is a scenic wilderness that straddles the Finke River and includes the picturesque Palm Valley. This valley is a refuge for cycad palms and the ancient *Livistona mariae*, estimated to be about 5000 years old. This park is particularly rugged and visitors who do not join tours are advised to use four-wheel-drive.

The East Macdonnells contain five parks and reserves, all rich in Aboriginal history and culture. Corroboree Rock Conservation Reserve protects the sacred grounds of the Aranda.

In N'Dhala Gorge National Park there are engravings foreign to the present day Aborigines of central Australia.

The six hectares of Ewaninga Rock Carvings Conservation Reserve are just 35 kilometres from Alice Springs. They contain a small group of rock outcrops on which prehistoric carvings trace a maze of wavy lines, circles and animal tracks. Anthropologists believe this art form was the work of an indigenous people who antedate the modern Aboriginal.

Further south from Alice Springs are the Henbury meteorite craters, which were formed about 4700 years ago. This is a haunt of the ferocious-looking, but harmless, bearded dragon lizard.

At the Top End of the Territory are two impressive national parks — Katherine Gorge and Kakadu. Located 348 kilometres south of Darwin, Katherine Gorge is a favourite spot for people who want to get away from the city. When the Katherine River flows peacefully in 'the dry', anglers will be delighted with good catches of barramundi, perch and the other 30 or so species of fish that are found there in the long, deep pools. Eight walking tracks run through forests of pandanus and ti-tree. Wildlife abounds — the antelope kangaroo, euro, echidna, black flying fox and dingo. Rainbow birds, red-shouldered parrots and the big bustard are all common among some 30 species of birds in the area. On the gorge walls, high above flood level, Aboriginal rock paintings key into each other to make big murals. The best way to see the river is from flat-bottomed boats, which are available for hire with or without a guide. Three of the gorges are usually fairly easy to get at, but the aluminium boats do have to be carried or dragged over the rock bars between the stretches of water.

Kakadu, one of the most scenic parks in Australia, contains two kinds of wilderness: the blacksoil flood plains and paperbark lagoons of the Alligator River system, and the rugged walls of the Arnhem Land escarpment which is deeply indented with gorges, streams and waterfalls.

At the northern end of Kakadu is a series of shallow lagoons and billabongs which attract thousands of water birds and hundreds of thousands of magpie geese. In this area is Cannon Hill, the Aboriginal 'art gallery' of Arnhem Land. There is good camping along the Alligator River, but perhaps the best spot is at Muirella Park, where the Nourlangie Creek affords deep and clean stretches of water for swimming and fishing. **Note:** Outside tourist areas in national parks and reserves it is wise to take local advice about swimming because of the possibility of crocodiles. The saltwater crocodile, found mainly in river estuaries, is highly dangerous, but the freshwater Johnstone river crocodile is generally regarded as harmless — it lives on fish and there is no reported case of it having ever interfered with man.

efficiency of the traditional beef cattle industry on which it was founded. Indeed it is sited in some of the NT's most promising agricultural and grazing country, 340 km south of Darwin. The township is located on the southern side of the Katherine River and has good facilities, including several churches, parks, a golf course and Showground.

The Katherine River was named after a beautiful daughter of one of the sponsors of John McDouall Stuart who was the first white man to find it, in 1862. The gorge sides tower above the sparkling, slow-moving water in the dry season. The ancient rock walls are dotted with caves. Aboriginal paintings, from miniatures to huge murals, decorate both faces above the floodline. The scene changes in the wet when the water level often rises 18 metres as the river boils through. The caves are swamped and a bigger flood than average may wash away another piece of an irreplaceable art form that was developed thousands of years ago. The rock is grey, black and ochre: the vegetation bright green.

Fifty-eight species of reptiles and amphibians have been identified in the area. They include a burrowing frog, the freshwater crocodile (harmless), a tortoise with a neck so long it looks like a snake when its body is submerged, three kinds of frog that climb trees, a lizard without legs, pythons that often grow to two metres — and lots of poisonous snakes. In the higher reaches of the gorge kangaroos and wallabies in mobs of hundreds at a time crowd in to drink. You may catch a barramundi — if you don't hook a tortoise or crocodile.

The only way to see the gorge properly is by flat-bottomed boat. You can hire one yourself or take a guided tour. Cruises take place daily. For information, contact the Katherine Gorge Tourist Agency, Katherine Terrace. There are three easily-reached pools in the gorge, so a party is better because the aluminium craft need portage over the rock bars. The weather is always hot, but there is little humidity for the nine not-quite-so-hot months of the year. You will need a cardigan on top of cotton clothes for early morning and nights from about mid-April to mid-July. **In the area:** Historic Springvale Homestead is 8 km from town. It is the oldest remaining homestead in the Northern Territory, having been built in 1879. Visitors will enjoy watching the Aboriginal Corroboree which is performed here three times a week. Edith Falls, for picnics, swimming and camping, 82 km north-east of Katherine. Mataranka Homestead, 115 km from town, has a thermal pool believed to have therapeutic powers. The tourist resort here has excellent facilities. At Mataranka, several tours are available, including four-wheel drive safaris, barramundi fishing and trail rides. Tours of Cutta Cutta Cave, 26 km from town. **Accommodation:** 3 motels, 3 caravan/camping parks.
Map ref. 266 G9

---

*Denotes population centres where visitors are not encouraged; permits are sometimes required; no accommodation.

Kulgera Population under 200.
About 20 km from the South Australian border on the Stuart Highway. **Accommodation:** 1 hotel.
Map ref. 270 I 12

Larrimah Population under 200.
On the Stuart Highway, 90 km north of Daly Waters. **Accommodation:** 1 hotel, 1 caravan/camping park.
Map ref. 266 I 11, 268 I 1

Maningrida Population 702.*
This settlement is located on the north coast of Arnhem Land.
Map ref. 267 K3

Mataranka Population under 200.
This settlement 103 km south-east of Katherine has a very well developed tourist resort with a thermal spring pool nearby. Trail riding, four-wheel drive safaris and barramundi fishing are all available in the area. It is a delightful area for camping. **In the area:** Elsey Cemetery and National Reserve. The graves of outback pioneers are at the cemetery. Mrs Aeneas Gunn who lived at Elsey Station Homestead from 1902-3 immortalised these pioneers in her classic, *We of the Never-Never*. **Accommodation:** 1 hotel, 1 motel (tourist resort), 2 caravan/camping parks.
Map ref. 266 I 10

Melville Island Population 554.*
This large island off the coast of Darwin is an Aboriginal Reserve.
Map ref. 266 D2

Milingimbi Population 564.*
This small island settlement is off Arnhem Land in Castlereagh Bay.
Map ref. 267 L4

Ngukurr Population 391.*
This settlement is on the Roper Highway on the southern boundary of the Arnhem Land Aboriginal Reserve.
Map ref. 267 L9

Nhulunbuy Population 3879.*
This centre for the bauxite mining operations on the Gove Peninsula is served by regular air service from Darwin.
Map ref. 267 P4

Noonamah Population under 200.
On the Stuart Highway, 38 km south of Darwin. **Accommodation:** 1 motel.
Map ref. 266 E5

Numbulwar Population 422.*
This settlement is on the south-east coast of the Arnhem Land Aboriginal Reserve.
Map ref. 267 N8

Oenpelli Population 452.*
This settlement is on the Arnhem Land Aboriginal Reserve is just north-east of the Kakadu National Park.
Map ref. 266 I 4

Papunya Population 635.*
This settlement on the Haasts Bluff Aboriginal Reserve is north-west of Glen Helen.
Map ref. 270 F7

Sportsman's Territory

Even though the Northern Territory has an area of 135 million hectares — six times the size of Great Britain and one-sixth of the Australian continent — there are few places where you can legally shoot game. Even fishing is restricted in some areas, too.

Every kind of firearm must be registered. The possession of high-powered rifles and pistols is tightly controlled. A visitor with a high-powered weapon properly licensed in his home state or country may be allowed it in the Territory if a valid certificate or licence is produced at a police station. The police must be satisfied that the weapon is safe, that the applicant is over 21 years and that there is a 'substantial reason' for carrying the weapon. The term 'substantial reason' does *not* include sporting purposes. All visitors must report any firearms to police within two days of entering the NT.

Firearms are prohibited in the main sanctuaries and protected areas. Sanctuaries now in existence are: Cobourg Peninsula, Tanami Desert, Woolwonga Aboriginal Reserve, Daly River Aboriginal Reserve, Murgenella River and the Arnhem Land Aboriginal Reserve. All Aboriginal reserves are protected areas. It is an offence to take firearms or traps into any reserve or protected area. Penalties range from fines up to $400 to imprisonment for up to 12 months. Maps showing existing sanctuaries and protected areas can be seen at police stations.

Property owners will rarely give permission for strangers to shoot on their land because of the danger and disturbance caused to stock. Shooters on private property without permission from the owner are liable themselves to be shot at — trigger-happy tourists have caused serious stock losses. Even some fish are protected in some areas, but fishing is otherwise unrestricted both inland and in the sea. The visitor who wants to mount a hunting, shooting and fishing expedition in the Territory could well save himself heavy fines and confiscation of guns and gear by booking into an organised safari through a hometown travel agency.

Pine Creek Population 214.
On the Stuart Highway, 92 km north-west of Katherine, Pine Creek was originally a centre for gold mining. This has now given way to copper mining as the main industry. **In the area:** Scenic areas at Oenpelli, Waterfall Creek and Muiralla Park. **Accommodation:** 1 hotel.
Map ref. 266 F7

Port Keats Population 819.*
This settlement on the Daly River Aboriginal Reserve looks out across Joseph Bonaparte Gulf.
Map ref. 266 B8

Renner Springs Pop. under 200.
On the Stuart Highway, 161 km north of Tennant Creek. **Accommodation:** 1 motel, 1 caravan/camping park.
Map ref. 269 J6

Ross River Population under 200.
It is well worth visiting this settlement 85 km east of Alice Springs by means of a two or three days tour. **Of interest:** Trephina Gorge, John Hayes Rock Hole where there are magnificent rock scenery, ghost gums and Aboriginal paintings. At N'Dhala Gorge there are superb Aboriginal carvings believed to be more than 30 000 years old. **In the area:** Bird-life and animals abound. Ancient fossils dating from when the inland was covered by sea can be found. **Accommodation:** Ross River Homestead.
Map ref. 263 R4, 271 K8

Tennant Creek Population 3118.
The story goes that Tennant Creek was founded when a beer wagon broke down and the drivers stayed to drink the cargo. Since the township is 420 kilometres north of Alice Springs, on the Stuart Highway, this might sound plausible enough. Gold, copper and bismuth deposits are the reason for its development today. From April to October it is clear and warm by day, cool at night. **Of interest:** Visitors can see the old gold mines of Warrego and Nobles Nob, the biggest open-cut gold mine in Australia. There is also Attack Creek, site of an unfortunate encounter between early settlers and Aborigines, the old telegraph station 10 km north of the township where there are two unnamed graves. The junction of the Stuart and Barkly Highways, known as the Three Ways Corner, is 26 km north. Here stands the memorial to Flynn of the Inland, Australia's great pioneer Flying Doctor. **In the area:** No road traveller along the Stuart can miss the Devil's Marbles, 96 km to the south. They are huge red, black and sand-coloured boulders piled up on each other, looking exactly like old-fashioned cottage loaves. Less well-known but equally impressive are the Devil's Pebbles, similar rock formations only 10 km north-west of the township. Because of its location and climate the area is relatively rich in flora and fauna. **Accommodation:** 1 hotel, 3 motels, 1 caravan/camping park.
Map ref. 269 K9

Victoria River Crossing
Population under 200.
Located where the Victoria Highway crosses the Victoria River, between Timber Creek and the junction with Delamere Road. **Accommodation:** 1 motel.
Map ref. 266 E11, 268 E1

Victory Downs Pop. under 200.
Situated on the border with South Australia, just off the Stuart Highway, 316 km from Alice Springs. **Accommodation:** 1 motel.
Map ref. 270 I 13

Wallara Population under 200.
This settlement, 97 km off the Stuart Highway, south-west of Alice Springs, serves as the tourist centre for visitors to the spectacular Kings Canyon, 100 km to the north-west. A climb to the rim of the Canyon will be rewarded with a view of the 'Lost City', weathered buttresses of rock which resemble ruins of an ancient city, and the 'Garden of Eden', a valley where permanent waterholes are overgrown with cycad palms. A log bridge which is solid and safe takes visitors to the north wall of the Canyon, from which the best views may be gained. To the east, near the Stuart Highway, are the Henbury Meteorite Craters. **Accommodation:** Wallara Ranch.
Map ref. 262 A13, 170 G10

Wauchope Population under 200.
On the Stuart Highway, 115 km south of Tennant Creek, Devil's Marbles closeby. **Accommodation:** 1 hotel.
Map ref. 269 K12, 271 K1

Yulara Population 500 approx.
About 25 km from Ayers Rock and The Olgas this luxurious tourist resort offers comfortable air-conditioned accommodation in all price brackets. **Of interest:** Visitors Centre displays excellent information on Uluru National Park. Audio Visual shows held at 8, 9 and 10 pm in the outdoor amphitheatre. **Accommodation:** 2 hotels, lodge units, caravan/camping ground.
Map ref. 270 E11

---

*Denotes population centres where visitors are not encouraged; permits are sometimes required; no accommodation.

Maps of Western Australia
Location Map

CENTRAL PERTH — 242
ROTTNEST ISLAND — 243
PERTH & NORTHERN SUBURBS — 244 - 245
PERTH & SOUTHERN SUBURBS — 246 - 247
KALGOORLIE & COOLGARDIE — 258
SWAN VALLEY VINEYARDS — 259

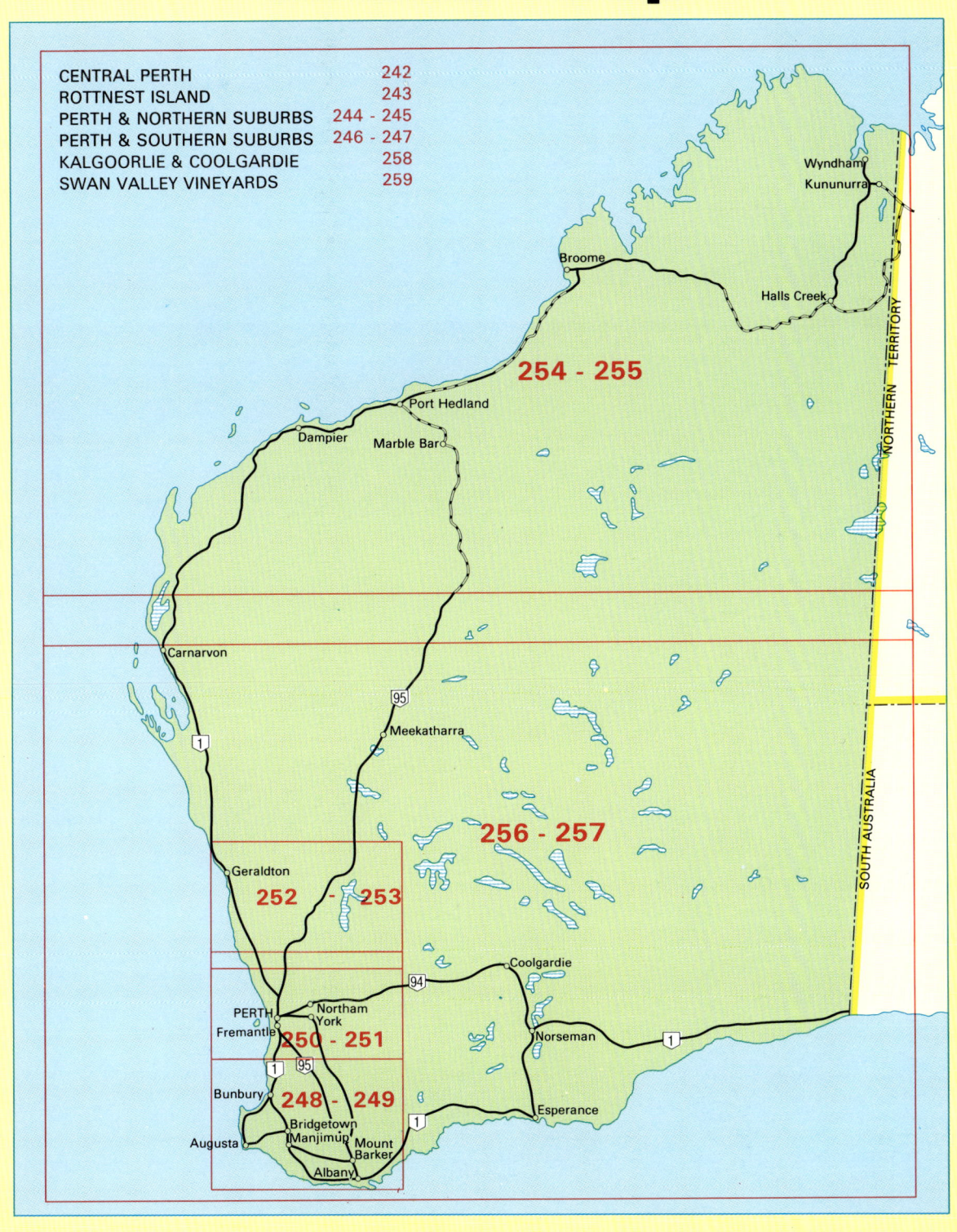

242 Central Perth

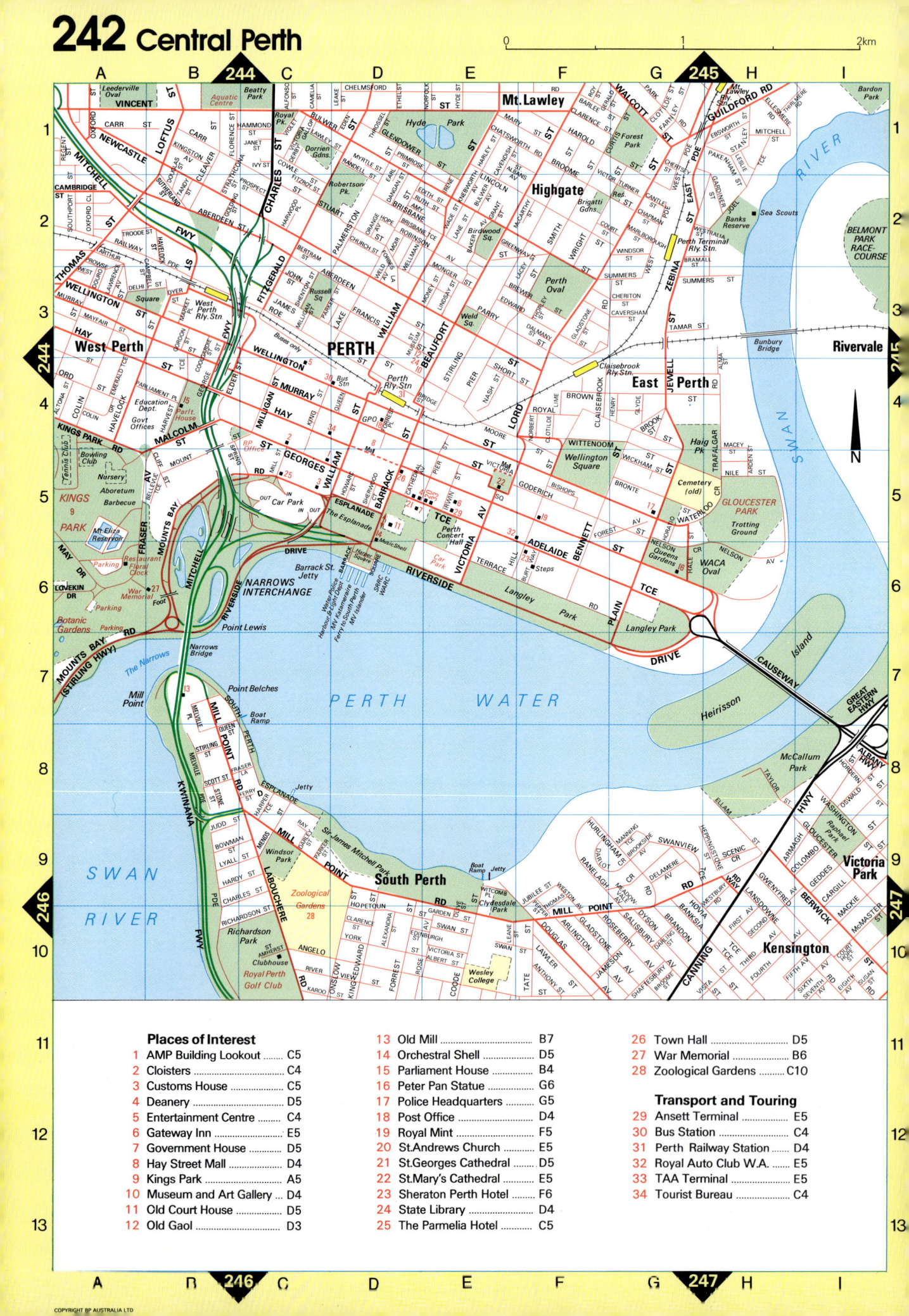

Places of Interest
1. AMP Building Lookout ... C5
2. Cloisters ... C4
3. Customs House ... C5
4. Deanery ... D5
5. Entertainment Centre ... C4
6. Gateway Inn ... E5
7. Government House ... D5
8. Hay Street Mall ... D4
9. Kings Park ... A5
10. Museum and Art Gallery ... D4
11. Old Court House ... D5
12. Old Gaol ... D3
13. Old Mill ... B7
14. Orchestral Shell ... D5
15. Parliament House ... B4
16. Peter Pan Statue ... G6
17. Police Headquarters ... G5
18. Post Office ... D4
19. Royal Mint ... F5
20. St. Andrews Church ... E5
21. St. Georges Cathedral ... D5
22. St. Mary's Cathedral ... E5
23. Sheraton Perth Hotel ... F6
24. State Library ... D4
25. The Parmelia Hotel ... C5
26. Town Hall ... D5
27. War Memorial ... B6
28. Zoological Gardens ... C10

Transport and Touring
29. Ansett Terminal ... E5
30. Bus Station ... C4
31. Perth Railway Station ... D4
32. Royal Auto Club W.A. ... E5
33. TAA Terminal ... E5
34. Tourist Bureau ... C4

COPYRIGHT BP AUSTRALIA LTD

Rottnest Island 243

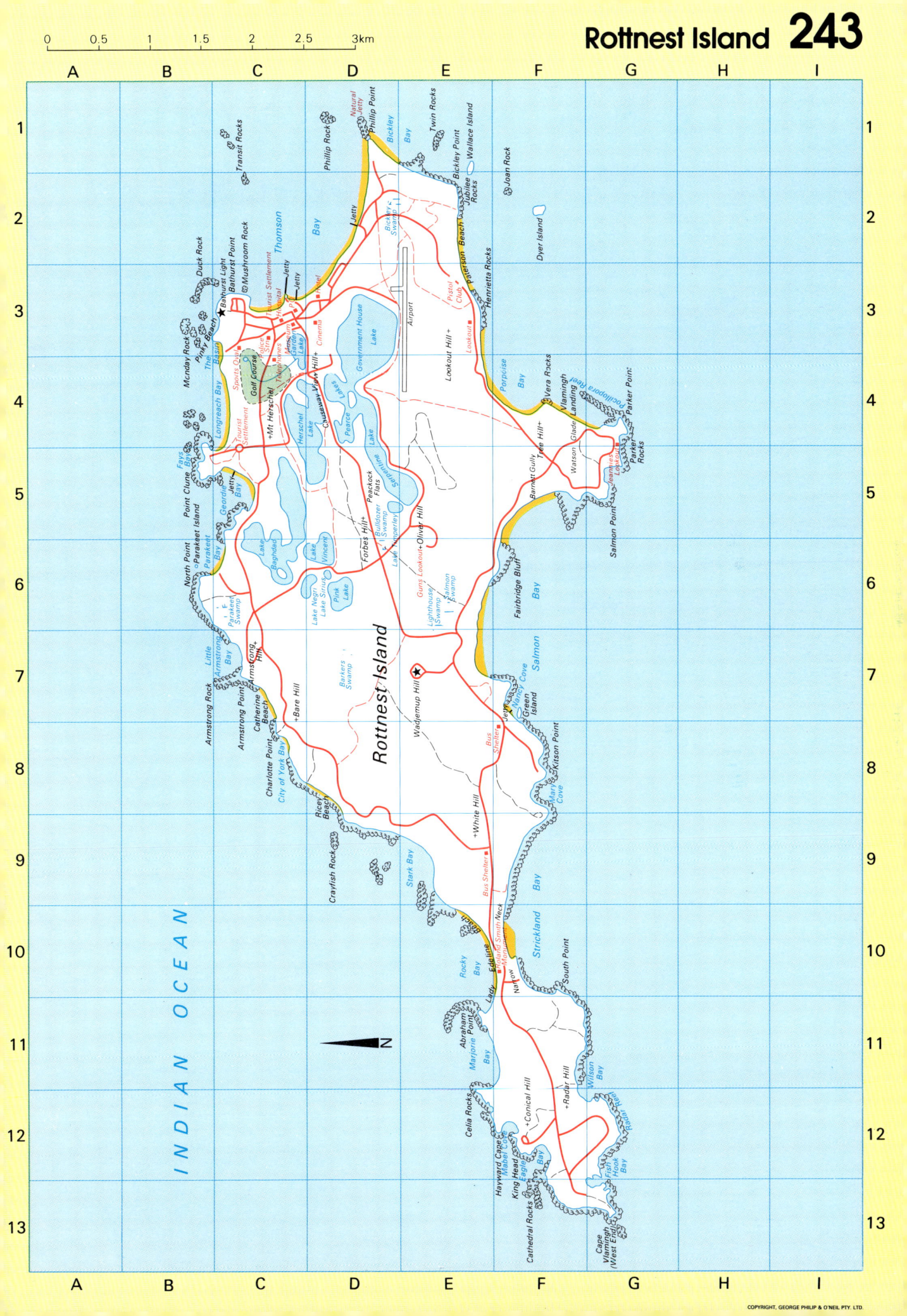

244 Perth & Northern Suburbs

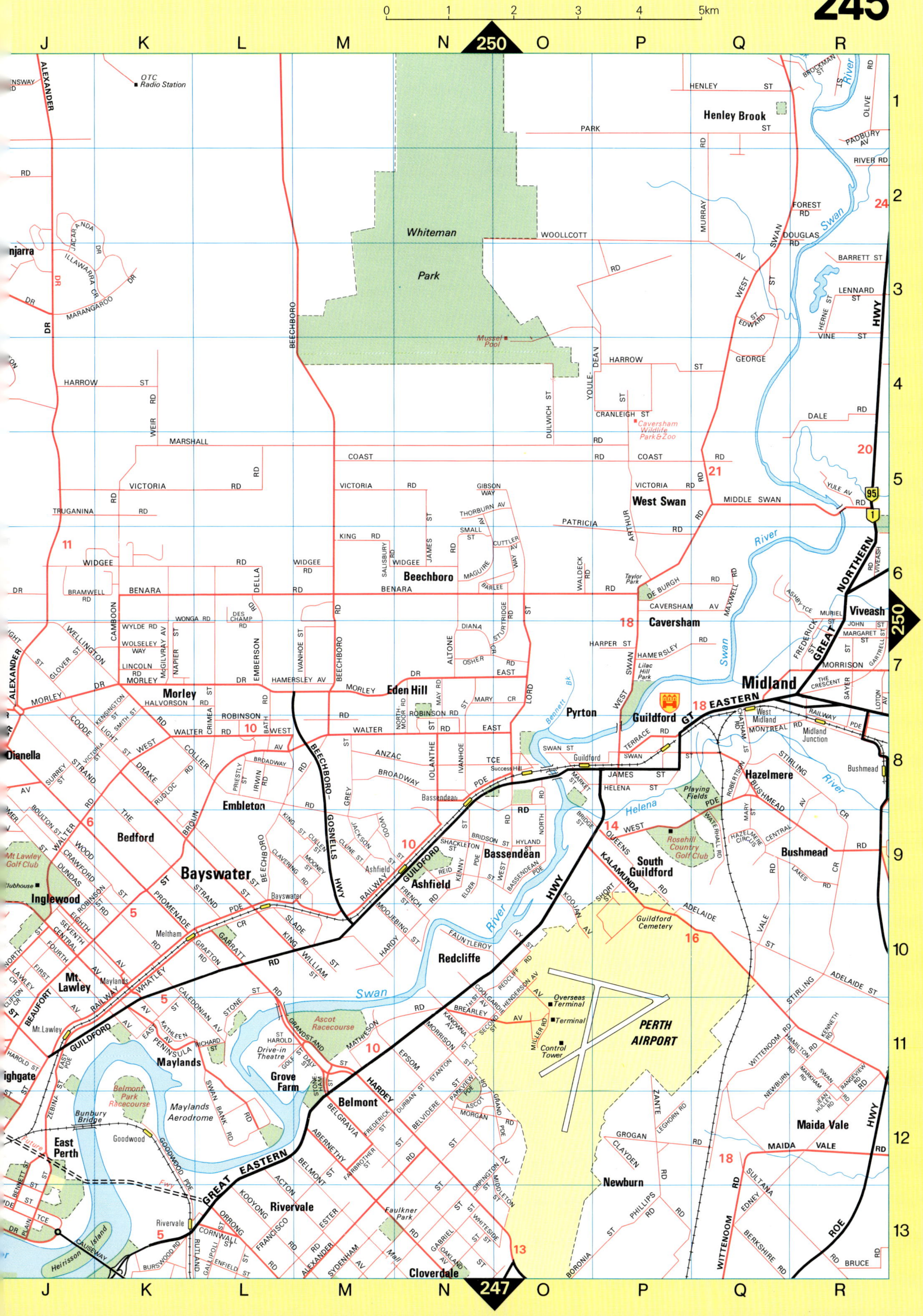
0 1 2 3 4 5km
250
247
Whiteman Park
Mussel Pool
Henley Brook
West Swan
Caversham Wildlife Park & Zoo
Beechboro
Caversham
Taylor Park
Viveash
Midland
Midland Junction
West Midland
Eden Hill
Morley
Pyrton
Guildford
Hazelmere
Bushmead
Embleton
Bedford
Bayswater
Bassendean
Ashfield
South Guildford
Rosehill Country Golf Club
Playing Fields
Guildford Cemetery
Dianella
Inglewood
Mt Lawley Golf Club
Mt. Lawley
Maylands
Maylands Aerodrome
Belmont Park Racecourse
Ascot Racecourse
Drive-in Theatre
Grove Farm
Belmont
Redcliffe
PERTH AIRPORT
Overseas Terminal
Terminal
Control Tower
Newburn
Maida Vale
Rivervale
Cloverdale
Faulkner Park
East Perth
Heirisson Island
Bunbury Bridge
Swan River
Helena River
Bennett Bk
OTC Radio Station
GREAT EASTERN HWY
GREAT NORTHERN HWY
ROE HWY
BEECHBORO-GOSNELLS HWY
ALEXANDER DR
GUILDFORD RD
BENARA RD
MORLEY DR
WALTER RD
COAST RD
MARSHALL RD
VICTORIA RD
HARROW ST
WOOLLCOTT
PARK ST
HENLEY ST
MIDDLE SWAN RD
CAVERSHAM AV
KALAMUNDA RD
ADELAIDE ST
STIRLING CR
MAIDA VALE RD
WITTENOOM RD
HARDEY RD
ABERNETHY RD
BELGRAVIA ST

246 Perth & Southern Suburbs

247

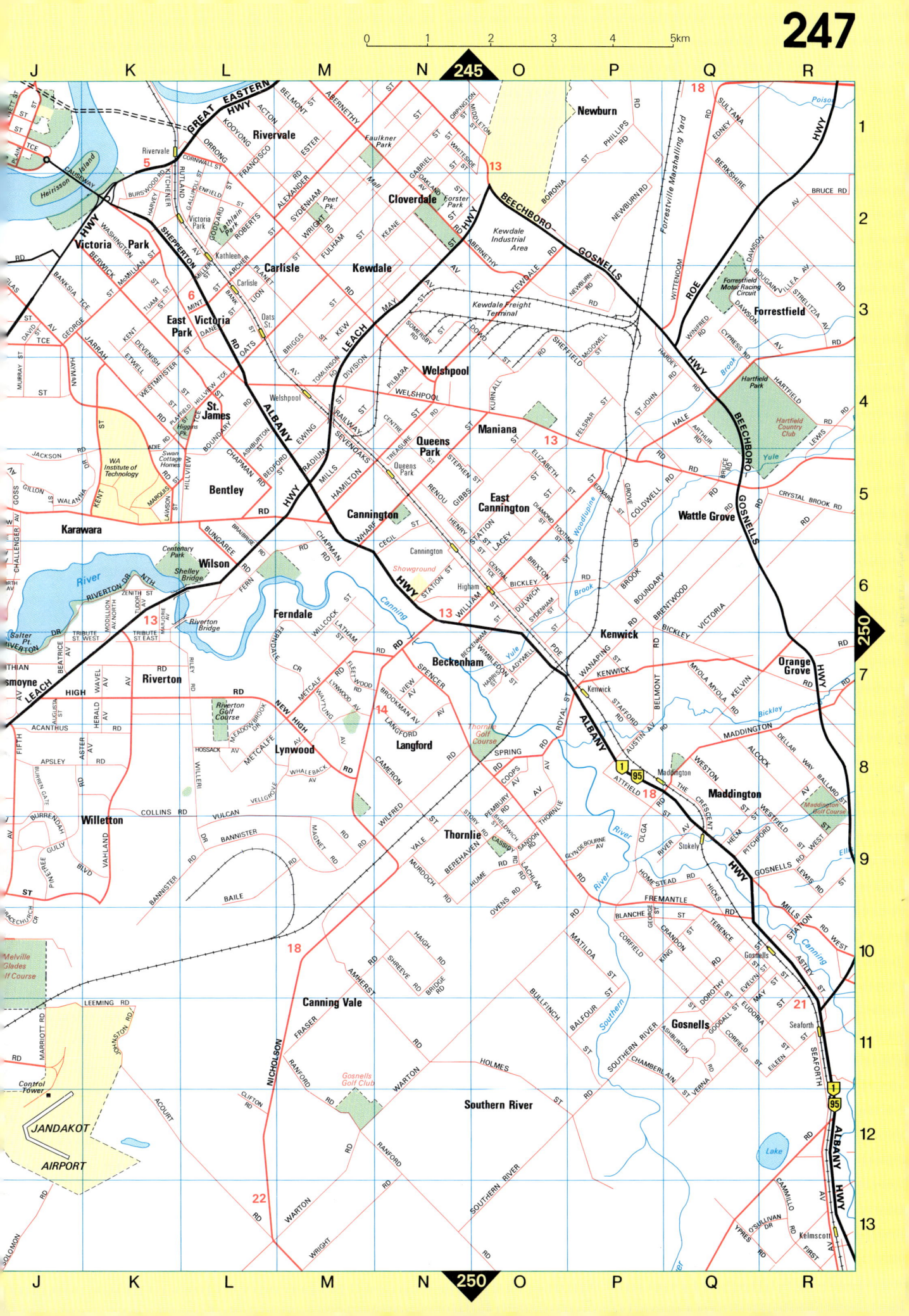

248 The South West Corner

249

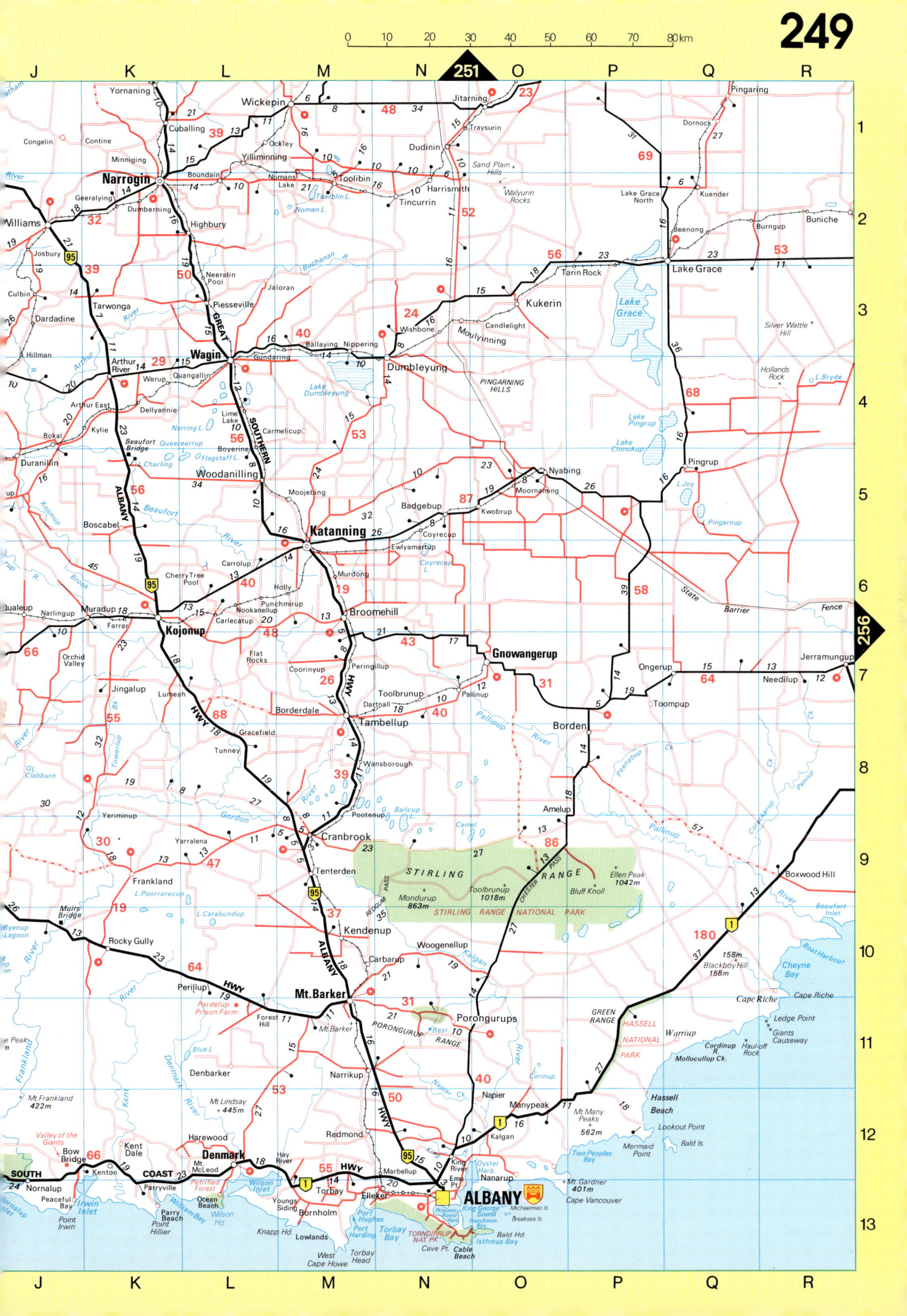

250 Tours from Perth

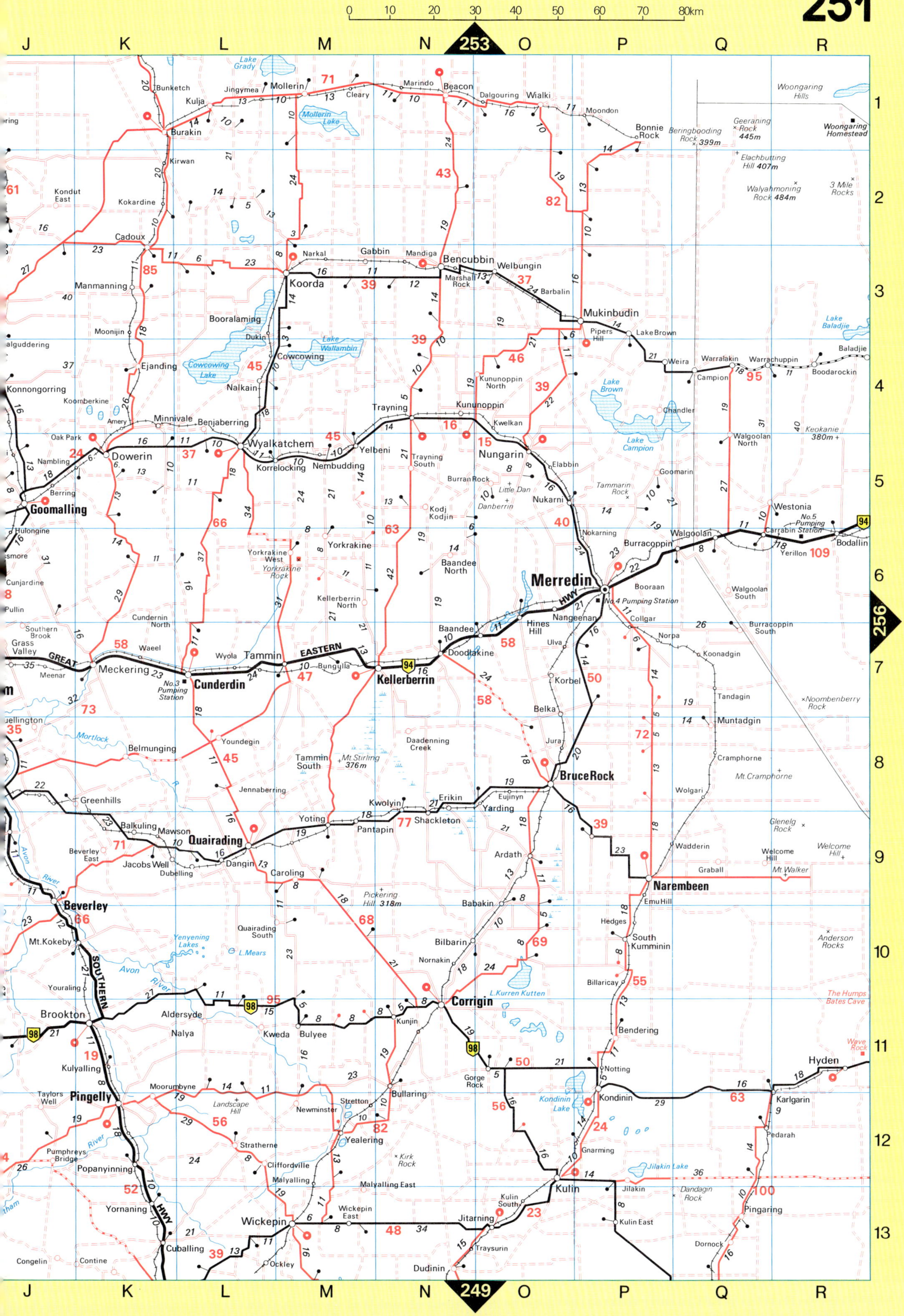
0 10 20 30 40 50 60 70 80km
J K L M N O P Q R
253
249
256
Lake Grady
Bunketch
Kulja
Jingymea
Mollerin
Cleary
Marindo
Beacon
Dalgouring
Wialki
Moondon
Bonnie Rock
Beringbooding Rock 399m
Geeraning Rock 445m
Woongarring Hills
Woongarring Homestead
Mollerin Lake
Burakin
Kirwan
Elachbutting Hill 407m
Walyahmoning Rock 484m
3 Mile Rocks
Kondut East
Kokardine
Cadoux
Narkal
Gabbin
Mandiga
Bencubbin
Welbungin
Marshall Rock
Barbalin
Manmanning
Koorda
Mukinbudin
Booralaming
Moonijin
Dukin
Cowcowing
Lake Wallambin
Pipers Hill
Lake Brown
Lake Baladjie
Baladjie
alguddering
Cowcowing Lake
Ejanding
Nalkain
Weira
Warralakin
Campion
Warrachuppin
Boodarockin
Kununoppin North
Konnongorring
Koomberkine
Trayning
Kununoppin
Lake Brown
Chandler
Amery
Minnivale
Benjaberring
Kwelkan
Oak Park
Dowerin
Wyalkatchem
Yelbeni
Nungarin
Lake Campion
Walgoolan North
Keokanie 380m
Nambling
Korrelocking
Nembudding
Trayning South
Elabbin
Goomarin
Berring
Burran Rock
Little Dan
Tammarin Rock
Goomalling
Kodj Kodjin
Danberrin
Nukarni
Westonia
No.5 Pumping Station
Carrabin Station
Hulongine
Nokarning
Walgoolan
Bodallin
Burracoppin
Yerillon
Yorkrakine
smore
Yorkrakine West
Yorkrakine Rock
Baandee North
Merredin
Cunjardine
Booraan
Kellerberrin North
Walgoolan South
Pullin
No.4 Pumping Station
Nangeenan
HWY
Cundernin North
Hines Hill
Collgar
Southern Brook
Baandee
Burracoppin South
Norpa
Grass Valley
Waeel
Ulva
GREAT
Tammin
EASTERN
Doodlakine
Koonadgin
Meenar
Meckering
Wyola
Bungulla
Kellerberrin
No.3 Pumping Station
Cunderdin
Korbel
Tandagin
Noombenberry Rock
Belka
Muntadgin
uellington
Mortlock
Youndegin
Daadenning Creek
Jura
Belmunging
Tammin South
Mt Stirling 376m
Cramphorne
Mt Cramphorne
Bruce Rock
Jennaberring
Wolgari
Greenhills
Kwolyin
Erikin
Eujinyn
Yarding
Balkuling
Mawson
Yoting
Shackleton
Glenelg Rock
Quairading
Pantapin
Ardath
Wadderin
Welcome Hill
Beverley East
Jacobs Well
Dubelling
Dangin
Caroling
Graball
Mt Walker
Avon
River
Narembeen
Pickering Hill 318m
Emu Hill
Beverley
Babakin
Hedges
Mt.Kokeby
Yenyening Lakes
Quairading South
L.Mears
South Kumminin
Anderson Rocks
Avon
River
Bilbarin
Nornakin
Youraling
SOUTHERN
Billaricay
L.Kurren Kutten
The Humps Bates Cave
Brookton
Aldersyde
Kunjin
Corrigin
Nalya
Kweda
Bulyee
Bendering
Wave Rock
Kulyalling
Gorge Rock
Notting
Hyden
Moorumbyne
Landscape Hill
Taylors Well
Pingelly
Bullaring
Kondinin
Kondinin Lake
Karlgarin
Newminster
Stretton
Yealering
Pedarah
Stratherne
Kirk Rock
Gnarming
Pumphreys Bridge
River
Clifforddville
Jilakin Lake
Popanyinning
Malyalling
Malyalling East
Kulin
Jilakin
Dandagin Rock
Kulin South
Pingaring
Yornaning
HWY
Wickepin
Wickepin East
Jitarning
Kulin East
Cuballing
Trayssurin
Dornock
Congelin
Contine
Ockley
Dudinin

252 Tours from Geraldton

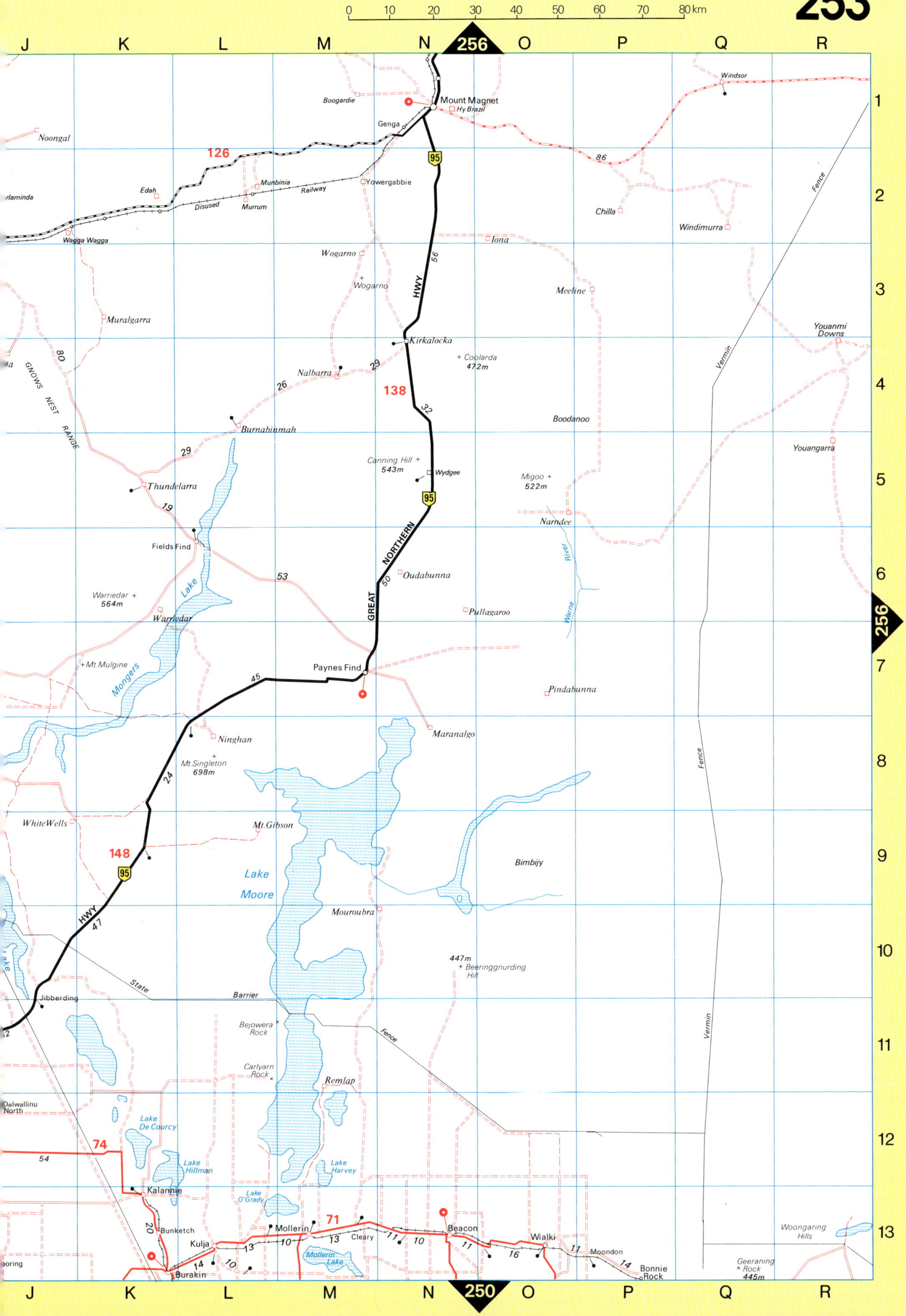
0 10 20 30 40 50 60 70 80 km
J K L M N O P Q R
256
1 2 3 4 5 6 7 8 9 10 11 12 13
250
Windsor
Boogardie
Mount Magnet
Hy Brazil
Genga
Noongal
126
95
86
Munbinia
Yowergabbie
Edah
Railway
Disused
Murrum
rlaminda
Chilla
Fence
Windimurra
Wagga Wagga
Iona
Wogarno
Wogarno
56
HWY
Meeline
Muralgarra
Youanmi Downs
Kirkalocka
Coolarda 472m
80
GNOWS NEST RANGE
Nalbarra
29
26
138
Vermin
32
Boodanoo
Burnabinmah
Youangarra
29
Canning Hill 543m
Wydgee
Migoo 522m
Thundelarra
19
Narndee
Fields Find
River
GREAT NORTHERN
Oudabunna
53
50
Lake
Warriedar 564m
Warriedar
Pullagaroo
Warne
Mt.Mulgine
Mongers
Paynes Find
45
Pindabunna
Ninghan
Maranalgo
Mt.Singleton 698m
24
Fence
White Wells
Mt.Gibson
148
Bimbijy
Lake Moore
HWY
47
Mouroubra
447m Beeringgnurding Hill
State
Barrier
Jibberding
Bejowera Rock
Fence
Vermin
Carlyarn Rock
Remlap
Dalwallinu North
Lake De Courcy
74
54
Lake Hillman
Lake Harvey
Kalannie
Lake O'Grady
71
20
Bunketch
Mollerin
Beacon
Kulja
13
10
13
Cleary
11
10
11
16
Wialki
11
Moondon
Woongaring Hills
14
10
Mollerin Lake
14
Bonnie Rock
Geeraning Rock 445m
Burakin
ooring

254 Northern Western Australia

INDIAN OCEAN

Port Hedland
Poissonnier Point, Cape Keraudren, Eighty
Larrey Point
Spit Point, Pardoo
De Grey, Goldsworthy
DAMPIER ARCHIPELAGO — Legendre Island, Cape Thouin
Mundabullangana, Mulyie
Cape Bruguieres, Rosemary Island, Dolphin Island, Point Samson, Pippingarra, Strelley, Carlindie, Coongan
Montebello Islands
Karratha — Enderby Island, Dampier, **Wickham Roebourne**, Sherlock, 201, Tabba Tabba, Wallareenya, Lalla Rookh, Eginbah, Muccan, Yarri
Barrow Island WILDLIFE SANCTUARY — Cape Preston, Sholl Island, Regnard Bay, Cooya Pooya, Whim Creek, Kangan, **Marble Bar**
Cape Poivre, Boodie Island, Pyramid, Yandeurra, Abydos, Corunna Downs
Airlie Island — Mardie Roadhouse, MILLSTREAM CHICHESTER RANGE NATIONAL PARK, Woodstock, Hillside, Nullagine
Thevenard Island — Beadon Point, Yarruloola, Pannawonica, Yalleen, Millstream, Mt Florance, Hooley, White Springs
North Muiron Island, South Muiron Island, Old Onslow (Ruins), Onslow, Red Hill, Cane River, Hamersley, Mt Brockman, Hamersley Gorge, Wittenoom, Bamboo Springs, Bonney Downs
Point Murat
Exmouth — Minderoo, Mt Stuart, HAMERSLEY RANGE, Dales Gorge, Marillana, Roy Hi
CAPE RANGE NAT PARK — Shothole Canyon, Exmouth Gulf, Koordarrie, Nanutarra, Wyloo, 956m Mt Wall, **Tom Price**, NATIONAL, Juna Downs, OPTHALMIA RANGE
Learmonth, Sandy Point, Yanrey, Kooline, Rocklea, PARK, Mt Meharry 1245m, Newman
Norwegian Bay, Ningaloo, Girawa, Bullara, Barradale Roadhouse, Uaroo, Glenflorrie, Paraburdoo, Tropic
Point Cloates, Marrilla, Winning, Nyang, WILDLIFE SANCTUARY, Ashburton Downs, Ullawarra, Mininer, Turee Creek, Prairie Downs
Point Maud, Cardabia, Mia Mia, Towera, Maroonah, Edmund, Pingandy, 683m Mt Bresnahan, Bullo Downs, Weelarr
Tropic Of Capricorn — Warroora, Minilya, Lyndon, Wandagee, Lyndon, Williambury, Wanna, Tunnel
Cape Farquhar, Gnarraloo Bay, Minilya Roadhouse, Middalya, Mangaroon, Gifford Creek, Mt Vernon 584m, Tangadee Ck
Gnarraloo, Minilya, Manberry, Moogoonee, Minnie Creek, Cobra, Dooley Downs, Mt Vernon, Brumby
Quobba, Lake Macleod, Hillsprings, Mardathuna, Mt Augustus, Mt Phillip
Point Quobba, Cooralya, Eudamullah

NORTH WEST COASTAL HIGHWAY
GREAT NORTHERN HIGHWAY

COPYRIGHT, GEORGE PHILIP & O'NEIL PTY. LTD.

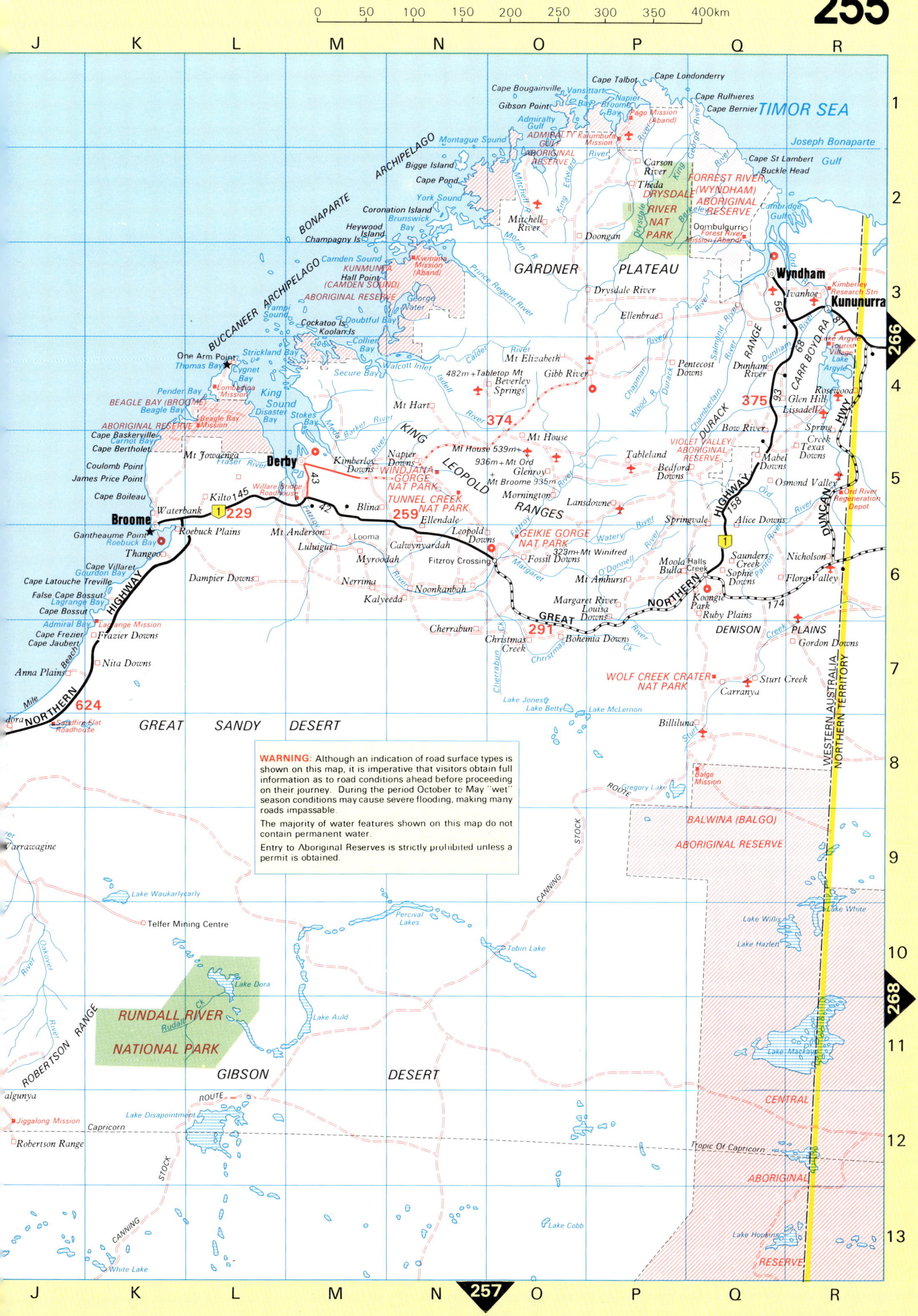

WARNING: Although an indication of road surface types is shown on this map, it is imperative that visitors obtain full information as to road conditions ahead before proceeding on their journey. During the period October to May "wet" season conditions may cause severe flooding, making many roads impassable.

The majority of water features shown on this map do not contain permanent water.

Entry to Aboriginal Reserves is strictly prohibited unless a permit is obtained.

256 Southern Western Australia

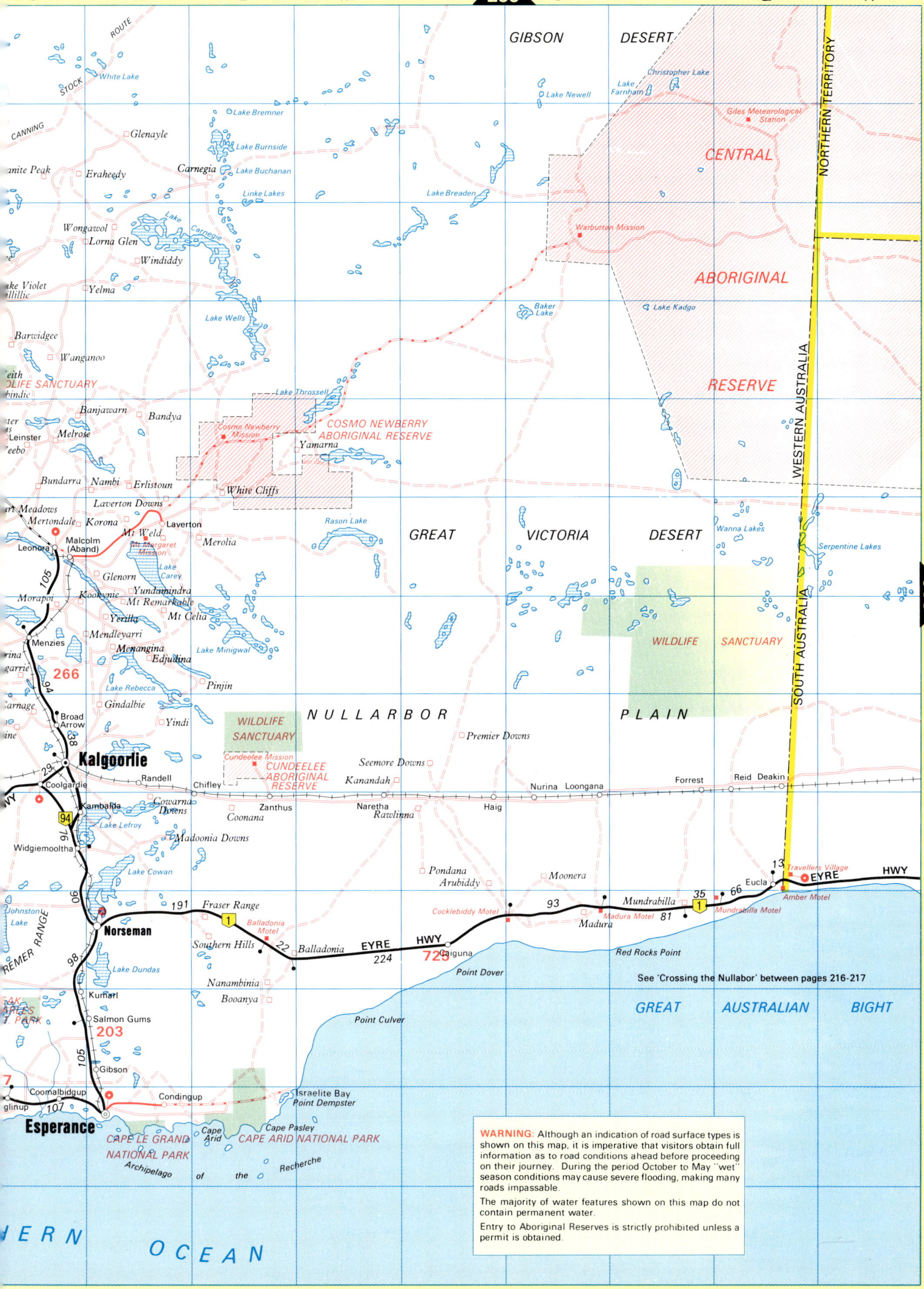

258 Kalgoorlie and Coolgardie

WARNING
Desert Roads

Once leaving the main towns in this area, there are only infrequent towns and station homesteads. Traffic is almost non existent, except on main roads. All rivers and most lakes are dry and the area is waterless, except during rain. After heavy rain the unsurfaced roads can be impassable in patches and the rain can be confined to a very local area, so it is difficult to judge whether it may be wet in an area only a relatively short distance away.

It can be difficult to obtain spares for your car, even in Kalgoorlie.

You are advised to make every effort possible to ensure that conditions are suitable for your vehicle before setting out.

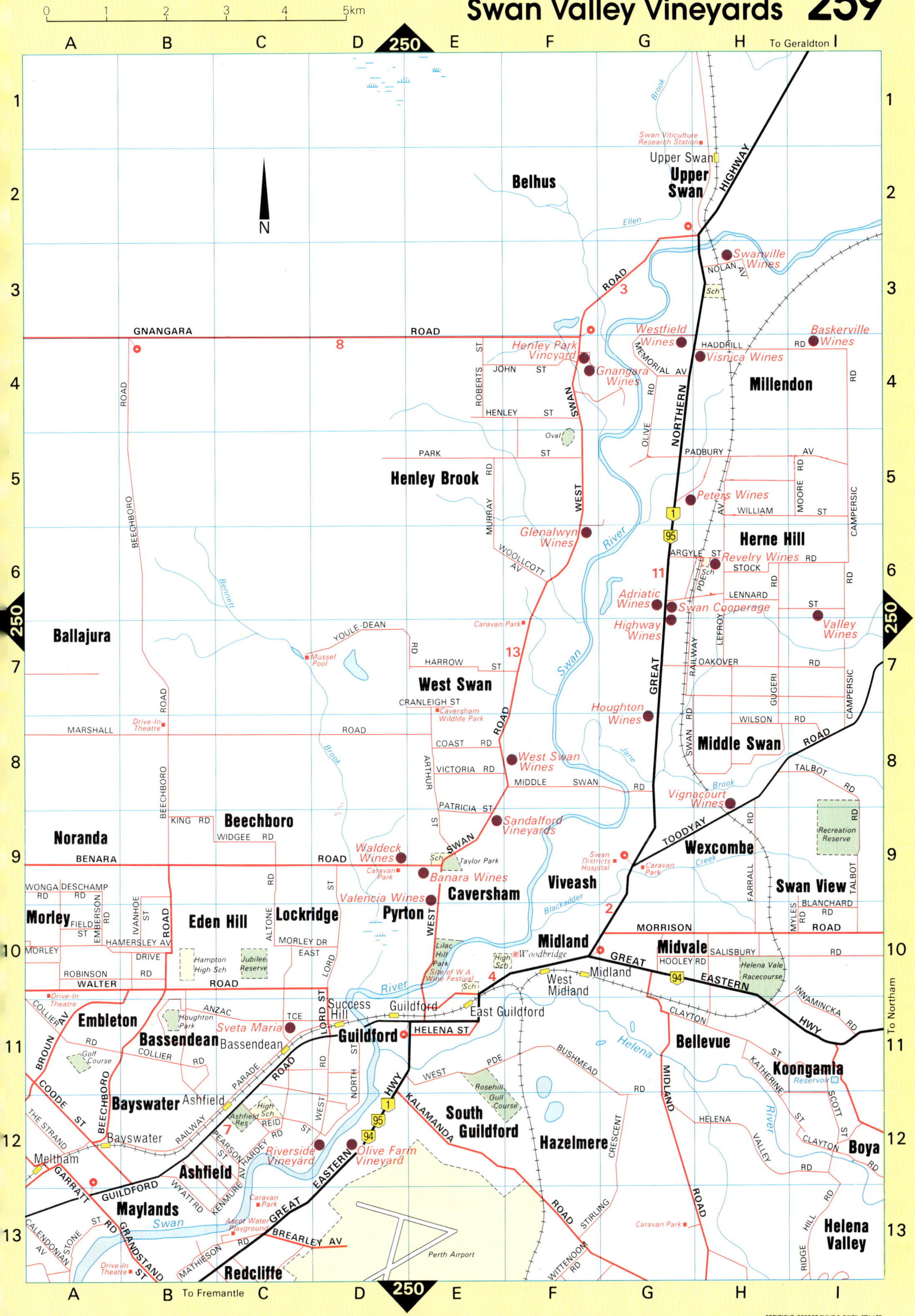
0 1 2 3 4 5km
A B C D E F G H I
250
To Geraldton
To Northam
To Fremantle
N
Swan Viticulture Research Station
Upper Swan
Upper Swan
Belhus
HIGHWAY
Brook
Ellen
Swanville Wines
NOLAN AV
Sch
ROAD
3
GNANGARA
ROAD
8
Westfield Wines
Baskerville Wines
Henley Park Vineyard
Gnangara Wines
HADDRILL
Visnica Wines
MEMORIAL AV
Millendon
ROBERTS ST
JOHN ST
SWAN
HENLEY ST
Oval
OLIVE
NORTHERN
PARK ST
PADBURY
AV
Henley Brook
MURRAY RD
WEST
Peters Wines
WILLIAM ST
MOORE RD
CAMPERSIC
Glenalwyn Wines
River
1
95
Herne Hill
ARGYLE ST
Revelry Wines RD
STOCK
WOOLLCOTT AV
11
PDE
LENNARD
Adriatic Wines
Swan Cooperage
Highway Wines
Valley Wines
Bennett
Ballajura
YOULE-DEAN
Caravan Park
RD
HARROW ST
13
Mussel Pool
Swan
LEFROY
RAILWAY
OAKOVER RD
West Swan
GREAT
CRANLEIGH ST
Caversham Wildlife Park
Houghton Wines
GUGERI
WILSON RD
Drive-In Theatre
MARSHALL
ROAD
COAST RD
Middle Swan
Brook
West Swan Wines
Jane
VICTORIA RD
MIDDLE SWAN RD
TALBOT RD
ARTHUR ST
Brook
Vignacourt Wines
BEECHBORO ROAD
KING RD
Beechboro
PATRICIA ST
Sandalford Vineyards
Recreation Reserve
Noranda
WIDGEE RD
TOODYAY
Wexcombe
BENARA ROAD
Waldeck Wines
Sch
Taylor Park
Swan Districts Hospital
Caravan Park
Creek
Banara Wines
Viveash
Swan View
WONGA RD
DESCHAMP RD
EMBERSON RD
IVANHOE ST
ALTONE RD
Valencia Wines
Caversham
Blackadder
BLANCHARD RD
Morley
FIELD ST
Eden Hill
Lockridge
Pyrton
2
MYLES RD
FARRALL
MORRISON ROAD
HAMERSLEY AV
MORLEY DR EAST
Midland
Midvale
SALISBURY RD
MORLEY
DRIVE
Hampton High Sch
Jubilee Reserve
Lilac Hill Park
Site of W A Wine Festival
High Sch
Woodbridge
GREAT
HOOLEY RD
Helena Vale Racecourse
ROBINSON RD
West Midland
Midland
94
EASTERN
WALTER ROAD
River
4
Sch
INNAMINCKA RD
Drive-In Theatre
ANZAC
Success Hill
Guildford
East Guildford
CLAYTON
HWY
COLLIER AV
Embleton
Houghton Park
TCE
LORD ST
Sveta Maria
Bassendean
Bassendean
Guildford
HELENA ST
Bellevue
BROUN
RD
Golf Course
COLLIER RD
NORTH ST
Helena
BUSHMEAD RD
Koongamia
Reservoir
PDE
WEST
Rosehill Golf Course
KATHERINE ST
PARADE
ROAD
HWY
MIDLAND
COODE ST
Bayswater
Ashfield
High Sch
Ashfield Res
REID RD
WEST
KALAMANDA
South Guildford
Hazelmere
CRESCENT
HELENA
SCOTT ST
THE STRAND
7
RAILWAY
PEARSON ST
HARDEY
Riverside Vineyard
Olive Farm Vineyard
EASTERN
VALLEY
River
CLAYTON
Boya
Bayswater
Meltham
GARRATT RD
GUILDFORD
WYATT RD
KENMURE AV
Ashfield
Caravan Park
GREAT
STIRLING
Caravan Park
ROAD
ROAD
RD
HILL
Maylands
Swan
Ascot Water Playground
BREARLEY AV
Helena Valley
CALEDONIAN AV
STONE ST
GRANDSTAND ST
RD
MATHIESON RD
Redcliffe
Perth Airport
WITTENOOM RD
RIDGE
Drive-In Theatre
1 2 3 4 5 6 7 8 9 10 11 12 13

Maps of Northern Territory

Location Map

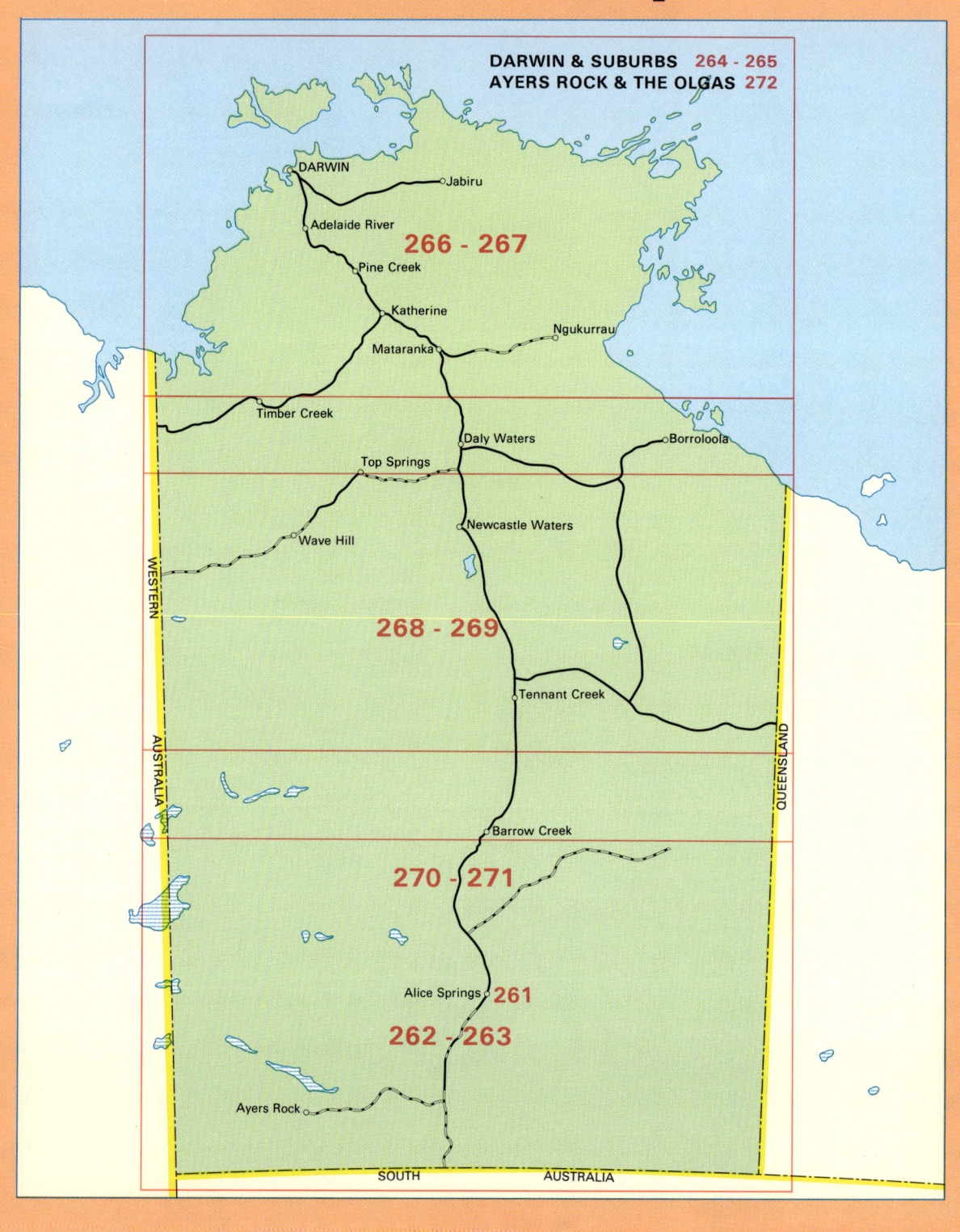

DARWIN & SUBURBS 264 - 265
AYERS ROCK & THE OLGAS 272

266 - 267
268 - 269
270 - 271
261
262 - 263

Alice Springs 261

Places of Interest

#	Name	Grid
1	Administration Offices	F6
3	ANZ Bank	F6
6	Bowling Club	D11
7	Billy Goat Hill	E7
2	Casino	E12
8	Commonwealth Bank	F6
9	Court House	F6
10	Fire Station	F6
11	Flying Doctor Base	E8
16	John Ross Memorial	F5
13	Lands Department	F6
14	National Bank	F6
12	Melanka Lodge	F7
15	Memorial Club	F8
17	Old Police Station	A13
18	Police Station	F6
19	Post Office	F6
20	Power House	H9
21	Pitchi Ritchi Sanctuary	B13
22	RSL Club	F4
23	Stuart Memorial	E7
24	Swimming Pool	D9
5	Westpac Bank	F6

Transport & Touring

#	Name	Grid
27	Airlines of North. Aust.	F6
30	Alice Springs Regional Tourist Association	C6
25	Alice Springs Rly. Stn.	E6
26	Ansett Airlines–Pioneer	F6
28	TAA	F6
29	Tourist Bureau	F6

COPYRIGHT BP AUSTRALIA LTD

262 Tours from Alice Springs

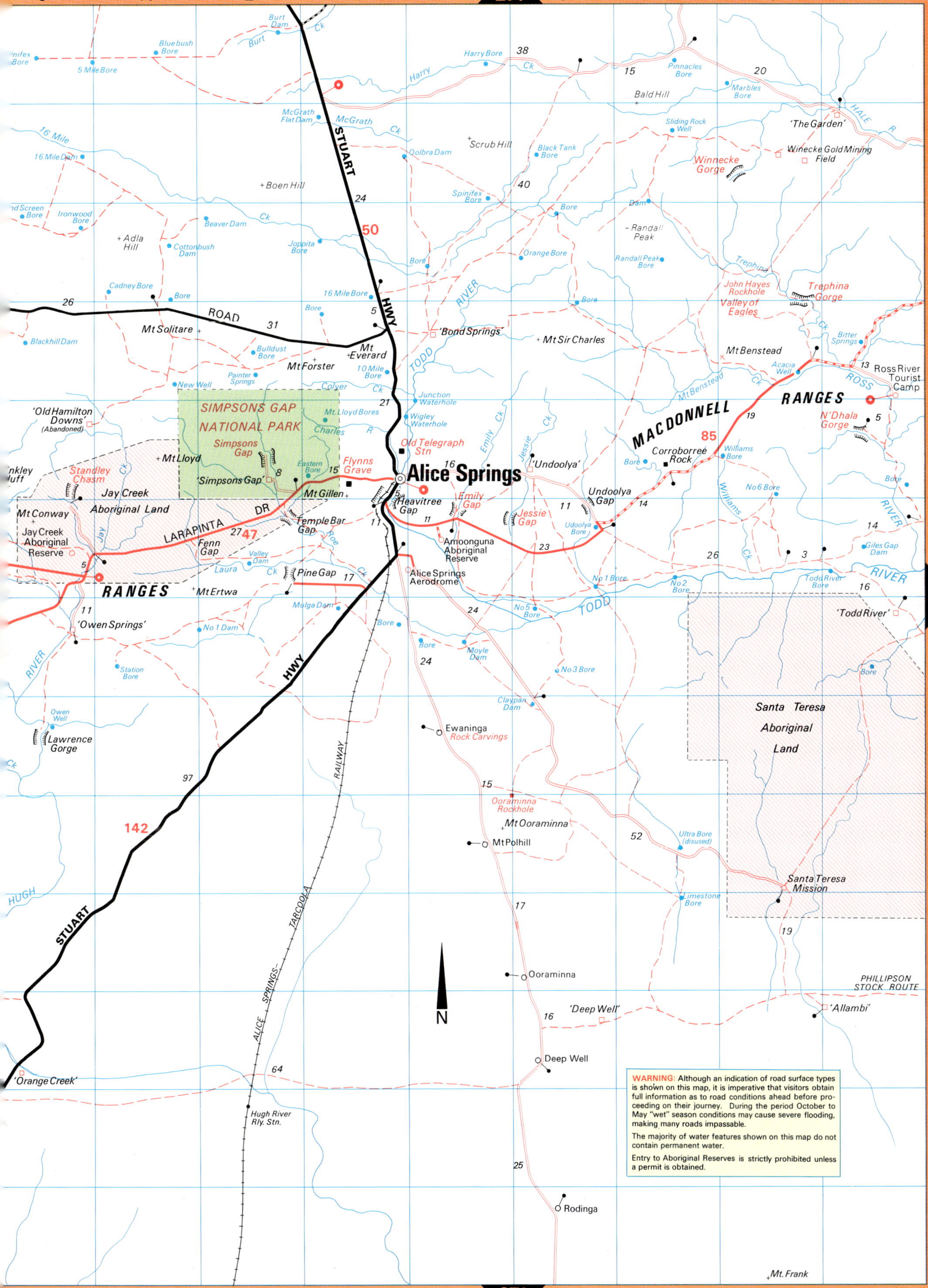

264 Darwin & Suburbs

265

Places of Interest

1	Administration Offices	Q8
14	Amphitheatre	N9
2	Botanical Gardens	M9
3	Casino	N10
4	Catholic Cathedral	P9
5	Chinese Cemetery	M6
6	Chinese Temple	Q7
7	Christchurch Cathedral	Q7
8	Civic Centre	Q7
23	Darwin Cultural Centre	P9
9	Don Motel Hotel	Q7
10	Government Residency	R7
11	Historical Cemetery	L8
12	Leichhardt Memorial	P9
28	Municipal Golf Course	N9
13	Museum & Art Gallery	L9
15	Olympic Pool	J8
16	Police Headquarters	Q8
17	Port Authority	Q7
18	Post Office	Q8
19	Public Library	Q8
20	Ross Smith Memorial	I9
21	Smith Street Mall	Q8
22	Telford Intl. Hotel	O9
24	Travelodge Hotel	P9
25	War Memorial	Q7

Transport and Touring

26	Office/Terminal for Ansett, Airlines of Northern Aust. & Airlines of Western Australia	Q8
27	Bus Terminal	Q7
29	Qantas	Q8
30	TAA Terminal	Q7
31	Tourist Bureau	Q8

266 The Top End

0 50 100 150 200 250 km
J K L M N O P Q R
1 2 3 4 5 6 7 8 9 10 11 12 13
ARAFURA SEA
Cape Wessel
WESSEL ISLANDS
Marchinbar Island
Cumberland Strait
Guluwuru Island
Drysdale Is
North West Crocodile Island
Cuthbert Pt
Braithwaite Pt
Junction Bay
Rolling Bay
Hawkesbury Pt
Nth East Pt
Boucaut Bay
Maningrida
Cape Stewart
Mooroongga Is
ELCHO ISLAND
Galiwinku
Cunningham Islands
Wigram Island
Alger Is
Pt Napier
The English Company's Islands
Malay Road
Cape Wilberforce
Ingis Is
Milingimbi
HOWARD ISLAND
Castlereagh Bay
Flinders Pt
Buckingham Bay
Bremer Is
Nhulunbuy
Yirrkala
Melville Bay
GOVE PENINSULA
Cape Arnhem
Mallison Is
Arnhem Bay
Nangalala
Ramingining
Gapuwiyak
Lake Evella
Port Bradshaw
FREDERICK HILLS
Camburinga
Pt Alexander
Mt Caledon
Caledon Bay
Cape Grey
Trial Bay
Bald Pt
MITCHELL RA
Koolatong
ARNHEM LAND
Arnhem Land Aboriginal Land
RANGE
BATH RA
Mt Flemming
Jalma Bay
Isle Woodah
Cape Shield
Nicol Is
Morgan Is
GULF OF
PARSONS
Mt Ranken
Blue Mud Bay
Burney Is
Cape Barrow
Bennett Bay
Winchelsea Is
Port Langdon
Bickerton Is
Alyangula
Umbakumba
Angurugu
GROOTE EYLANDT Aboriginal Land
GROOTE EYLANDT
Tasman Pt
South Pt
Cape Beatrice
'Weemol'
'Bullman'
Mt Marumba
Mt Weir
Mt Stretton
Black Mtn
Mt Gatt
Mt Bridges
Mainoru
Mt Leane
'Mountain Valley'
'Mainoru'
Mt Bray
Mt Throsby
Three Graces
Whamelk Bluff
Mt Furner
Numbulwar
Mt Karmain
Mt Bagster
Mt Phillip
Mt Favenc
DOWNERS RA
187
Edward Is
Mt Chapman
COLLERA MTNS
CARPENTARIA
Mt Warrington
Ngukurr
'Moroak'
Roper Bar Police Stn
Urapunga
'St Vidgeon'
Port Roper
Limmen Bight
Maria Is
HWY
ROPER
213
65
Mt Price
Mt Eclipse
Mt Boxall
Mt Harriet
'Roper Valley'
Mt St Vidgeon
Mt Forrest
Mt Hughes
Limmen Bight Aboriginal Land
Mt Davidson
Mt Kelly
'Hodgson Downs'
The Four Archers
'Nathan River'
SIR EDWARD PELLEW GROUP
West Is
North Is
'Bing Bong'
'Rosie Creek'
S.W. Is
Centre Is
Vanderlin Is
Port McArthur
'Nutwood Downs'
'Cox River'
80
Borroloola Aboriginal Land
Borroloola
PO
Mt Feathertop
'Manangoora'
74
24
18
'Greenbank'
31
'Bauhinia'
'Tawallah'
'Seven Emu'
CARPENTARIA
171
HWY
'Tanumbirini'
'Broadmere'
'OT Downs'
21
CARPENTARIA
HWY
'McArthur River'
269

268 Central Northern Territory

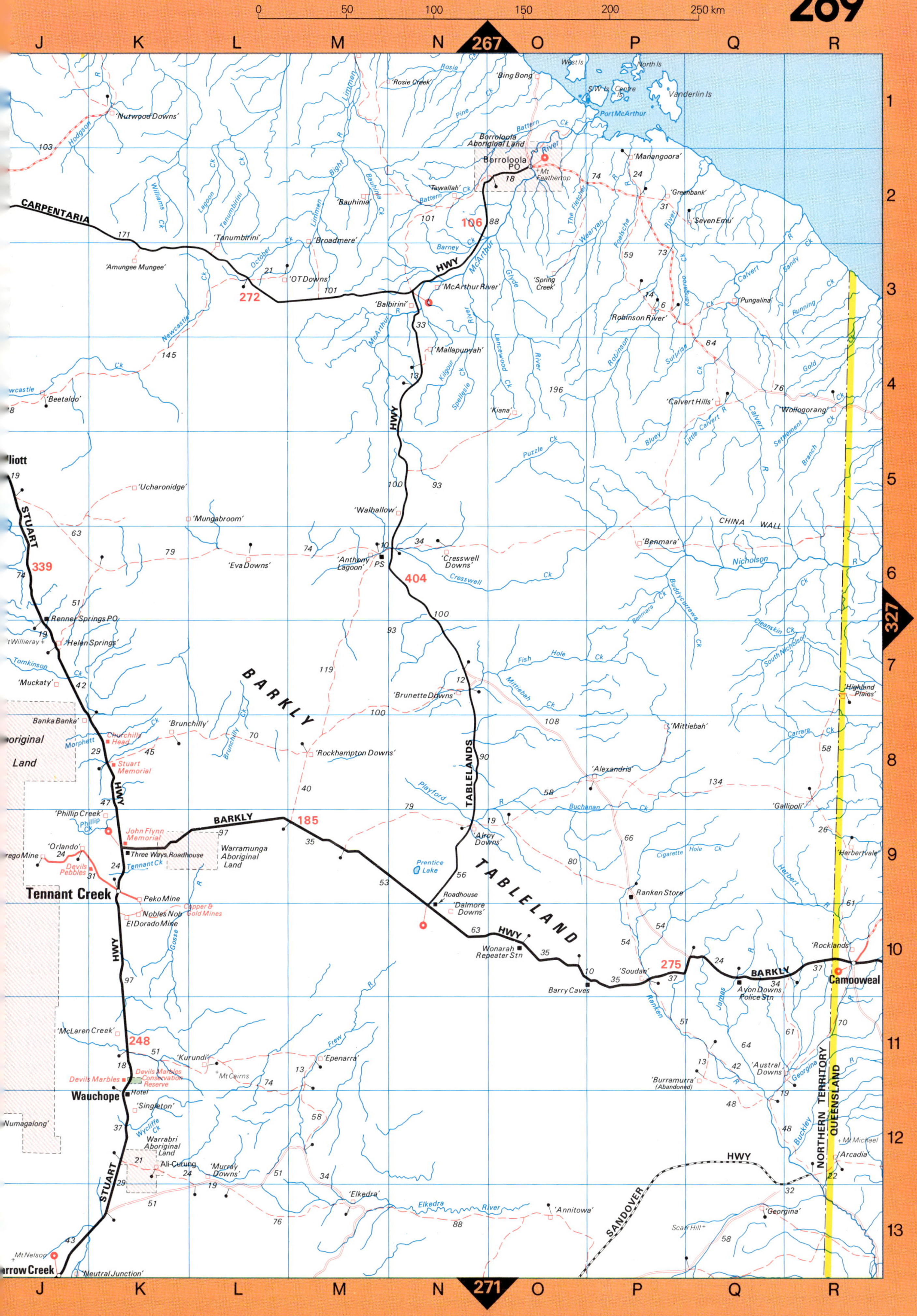

0 50 100 150 200 250 km
J K L M N O P Q R
267
1 2 3 4 5 6 7 8 9 10 11 12 13
327
271
West Is
North Is
S/W Is
Centre Is
Vanderlin Is
Port McArthur
'Bing Bong'
'Rosie Creek'
'Nutwood Downs'
Borroloola Aboriginal Land
Borroloola PO
Mt Featherstop
'Manangoora'
'Greenbank'
'Seven Emu'
'Tawallah'
'Bauhinia'
CARPENTARIA
HWY
'Tanumbirini'
'Broadmere'
'Amungee Mungee'
'OT Downs'
'McArthur River'
'Spring Creek'
'Balbirini'
'Robinson River'
'Pungalina'
'Mallapunyah'
'Beetaloo'
'Kiana'
'Calvert Hills'
'Wollogorang'
Elliott
STUART
'Ucharonidge'
'Mungabroom'
'Walhallow'
CHINA WALL
'Benmara'
'Eva Downs'
'Anthony Lagoon' PS
'Cresswell Downs'
Renner Springs PO
'Helen Springs'
'Muckaty'
BARKLY
'Brunette Downs'
'Highland Plains'
Banka Banka'
Aboriginal Land
'Brunchilly'
Churchills Head
'Rockhampton Downs'
'Mittiebah'
Stuart Memorial
TABLELANDS
'Alexandria'
'Gallipoli'
'Phillip Creek'
John Flynn Memorial
BARKLY
Three Ways Roadhouse
Warramunga Aboriginal Land
'Alroy Downs'
Prentice Lake
TABLELAND
'Orlando'
Devils Pebbles
Tennant Creek
'Herbertvale'
Peko Mine
Nobles Nob
Copper & Gold Mines
El Dorado Mine
Roadhouse
'Dalmore Downs'
Ranken Store
Wonarah Repeater Stn
'Soudan'
Barry Caves
Avon Downs Police Stn
'Rocklands'
Camooweal
'McLaren Creek'
'Kurundi'
Mt Cairns
'Epenarra'
Devils Marbles
Devils Marbles Conservation Reserve
Wauchope
Hotel
'Singleton'
'Burramurra' (Abandoned)
'Austral Downs'
Numagalong'
Warrabri Aboriginal Land
Ali-Curung
'Murray Downs'
NORTHERN TERRITORY
QUEENSLAND
Mt Michael
'Arcadia'
HWY
SANDOVER
'Elkedra'
Elkedra River
'Annitowa'
'Georgina'
Scarr Hill
Mt Nelson
Barrow Creek
'Neutral Junction'
Rosie
Limmen
Pine
Batten
Hodgson
Williams
Lagoon
Tanumbirini
Bight
Bauhinia
Barney
October
Newcastle
McArthur
Glyde
Kilgour
Spellesie
Lancewood
Fletcher
Wearyan
Foelsche
Calvert
Sandy
Running
Gold
Settlement
Branch
Little Calvert
Bluey
Puzzle
Nicholson
Buddycurrawa
Benmara
Cleanskin
South Nicholson
Fish Hole
Mittiebah
Carrara
Morphett
Brunchilly
Playford
Buchanan
Cigarette Hole
Herbert
Tomkinson
Phillip
Tennant Ck
Gosse
Frew
Wycliffe
Ranken
James
Georgina
Buckley

270 Southern Northern Territory

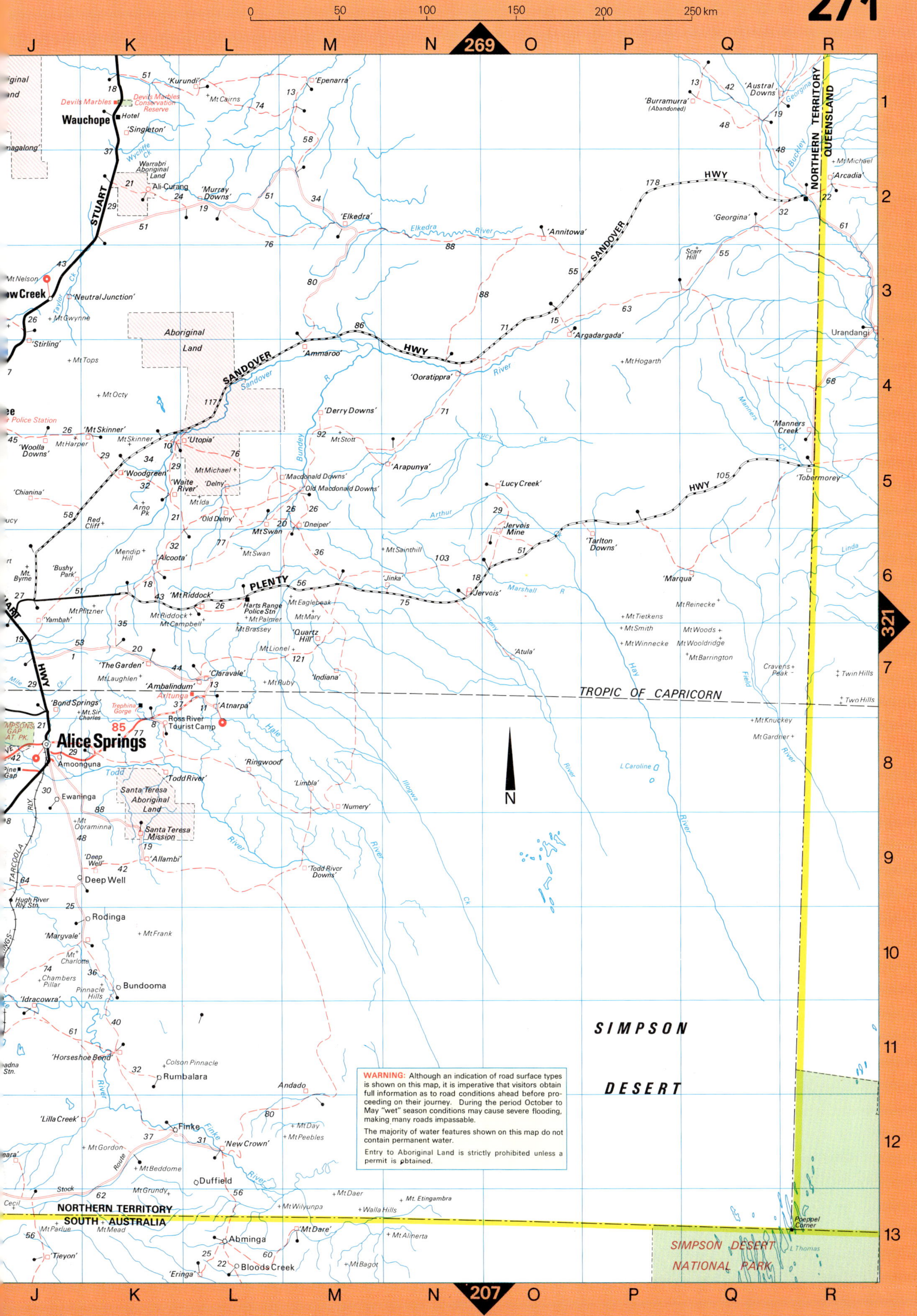
0 50 100 150 200 250 km
J K L M N O P Q R
269
207
321
1 2 3 4 5 6 7 8 9 10 11 12 13
Wauchope
Hotel
Devils Marbles
Devils Marbles Conservation Reserve
'Singleton'
'Kurundi'
Mt Cairns
'Epenarra'
Warrabri Aboriginal Land
Ali-Curung
'Murray Downs'
STUART
'Elkedra'
Elkedra River
'Annitowa'
'Burramurra' (Abandoned)
'Austral Downs'
Georgina
Buckley
NORTHERN TERRITORY
QUEENSLAND
HWY
SANDOVER
Mt Michael
'Arcadia'
'Georgina'
Scarr Hill
Mt Nelson
Creek
'Neutral Junction'
Taylor Ck
Mt Gwynne
'Stirling'
Mt Tops
Aboriginal Land
'Ammaroo'
Sandover
'Ooratippra'
River
'Argadargada'
Urandangi
Mt Hogarth
Mt Octy
Police Station
'Mt Skinner'
Mt Skinner
Mt Harper
'Woolla Downs'
'Utopia'
'Derry Downs'
Bundey R
Mt Stott
'Arapunya'
Lucy Ck
Manners
'Manners Creek'
'Tobermorey'
'Woodgreen'
Mt Michael
'Waite River'
'Delny'
Mt Ida
'Chianina'
'Macdonald Downs'
'Old Macdonald Downs'
'Lucy Creek'
Arthur
Arno Pk
'Old Delny'
Red Cliff
Mt Swan
'Dneiper'
'Jervois Mine'
'Tarlton Downs'
Linda
Mendip Hill
'Alcoota'
Mt Swan
Mt Sainthill
'Bushy Park'
Mt Byrne
'Mt Riddock'
PLENTY
'Jinka'
'Jervois'
Marshall R
'Marqua'
Harts Range Police Stn
Mt Palmer
Mt Eaglebeak
Mt Mary
Mt Pfitzner
'Yambah'
Mt Riddock
Mt Campbell
Mt Brassey
'Quartz Hill'
Plenty
'Atula'
Mt Tietkens
Mt Smith
Mt Winnecke
Mt Reinecke
Mt Woods
Mt Wooldridge
Mt Barrington
Mt Lionel
'The Garden'
Mt Laughlen
'Claravale'
'Indiana'
Mt Ruby
Hay
Field
Cravens Peak
Twin Hills
'Ambalindum'
Arltunga
TROPIC OF CAPRICORN
Two Hills
'Bond Springs'
Mt Sir Charles
Trephina Gorge
'Atnarpa'
Ross River Tourist Camp
Hale
Mt Knuckey
Mt Gardner
Alice Springs
Amoonguna
Todd
'Ringwood'
'Todd River'
'Limbla'
Illogwa
River
L Caroline
River
N
Santa Teresa Aboriginal Land
Ewaninga
'Numery'
Mt Oraminna
Santa Teresa Mission
'Allambi'
'Deep Well'
Deep Well
'Todd River Downs'
Hugh River Rly Stn
TARCOOLA
Rodinga
'Maryvale'
Mt Frank
Mt Charlotte
Chambers Pillar
Pinnacle Hills
Bundooma
'Idracowra'
SIMPSON
'Horseshoe Bend'
Colson Pinnacle
Rumbalara
DESERT
Andado
'Lilla Creek'
Finke
'New Crown'
Mt Day
Mt Peebles
Mt Gordon
Route
Mt Beddome
Duffield
Stock
Mt Grundy
Mt Daer
Mt. Etingambra
Mt Wilyunpa
Walla Hills
NORTHERN TERRITORY
SOUTH AUSTRALIA
Mt Parlue
Mt Mead
'Mt Dare'
Mt Alinerta
Poeppel Corner
Abminga
'Tieyon'
Bloods Creek
'Eringa'
Mt Bagot
SIMPSON DESERT NATIONAL PARK
L Thomas
Alice Springs
WARNING: Although an indication of road surface types is shown on this map, it is imperative that visitors obtain full information as to road conditions ahead before proceeding on their journey. During the period October to May "wet" season conditions may cause severe flooding, making many roads impassable.
The majority of water features shown on this map do not contain permanent water.
Entry to Aboriginal Land is strictly prohibited unless a permit is obtained.

272 Ayers Rock & The Olgas

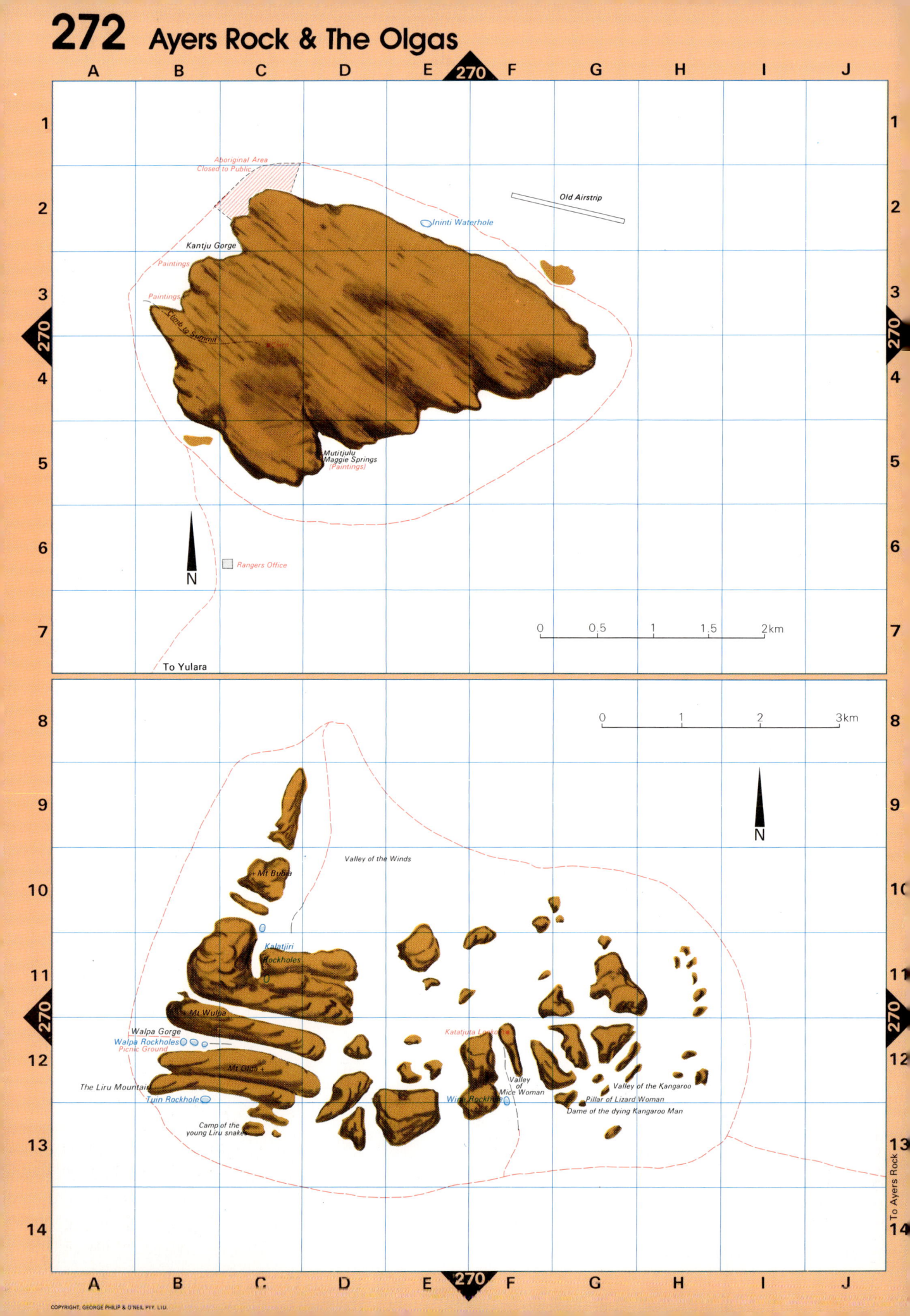

Aboriginal Area Closed to Public

Old Airstrip

Ininti Waterhole

Kantju Gorge

Paintings

Paintings

Climb to Summit

Mutitjulu Maggie Springs (Paintings)

N

Rangers Office

0   0.5   1   1.5   2 km

To Yulara

0   1   2   3 km

N

Valley of the Winds

Mt Bubia

Kalatjiri Rockholes

Mt Wulpa

Walpa Gorge
Walpa Rockholes
Picnic Ground

Mt Olga

Katatjuta Lookout

The Liru Mountain
Tuin Rockhole

Wina Rockhole

Valley of Mice Woman

Valley of the Kangaroo
Pillar of Lizard Woman
Dame of the dying Kangaroo Man

Camp of the young Liru snake

To Ayers Rock

COPYRIGHT, GEORGE PHILIP & O'NEIL PTY. LTD.

THE RED CENTRE

ABOVE: *The Yulara International Tourist Resort at Ayers Rock.*

BELOW: *The more athletic visitor can climb up the spine of the rock at the western end.*

In the 'red centre' of Australia, 451 kilometres south-west of Alice Springs, Ayers Rock, the world's greatest monolith, rises majestically 348 metres above a wide, sandy floodplain which is covered in spinifex and desert oak. The rock is nine kilometres in circumference and, as the sun shines on it during the day, it changes colour through shades of fiery red, delicate mauve, blues, pinks and browns. When rain falls, it veils the rock in a torrent of silver, before running into the waterholes and desert beneath.

The Yulara International Tourist Resort has transformed facilities at Ayers Rock. About 20 minutes drive from the rock, it offers a range of accommodation: the top class Sheraton Hotel; the Four Seasons 4-star resort; Ayers Rock Lodge units; and well-equipped campgrounds.

It is a self-contained township with accommodation for its staff (about 500), a supermarket, a pub and a few other shops and services. Naturally shopping is not cheap as everything has to be freighted in but a surprisingly wide range of goods and services can be obtained.

The prize-winning design of Yulara means that it does not intrude into the landscape but blends in to the ochre colours of the desert around. If you have time, allow at least 3 days at Yulara. This will give you time to see a sunrise, a sunset, to climb the rock and visit the Olgas. Do not attempt the climb unless you are reasonably fit and, if you are doubtful, study the bronze plaques at the base of the chain before setting out! Do take something to drink with you as you can quickly get dehydrated when expending unaccustomed energy in the warm climate.

For those who do make it, the feeling of achievement and the view from the top are well worth the effort; although the trip down may not seem as arduous, do watch your step.

The Aboriginal name for Ayers Rock is Uluru and the National Park there now carries this name. There are cave paintings and carvings made thousands of years ago by members of the Loritja and Pitjanjatjara tribes. It is not hard to understand that this is a sacred place of ancient times. The rock has a quality which cannot be dimmed by the click of cameras or the sight of tourists making their way to its summit along the spine at the western end.

Walking around the rock you will see the 'sound shell', a cavity as smooth as if formed by the sea, the 'brain', an eroded and honeycombed wall, and the 'kangaroo tail', a 160 metre strip of stone hanging at one end of the rock.

Some 32 kilometres away to the west are the Olgas — a cluster of rounded, massive rocks, equally mysterious. They are similarly dramatic and vividly coloured, lacking only the majesty of Ayers Rock's great bulk. The tallest of the Olgas, Mount Olga itself, is 546 metres above the oasis-like 'valley of the winds' that runs through the rock system. Ernest Giles, who first saw Mount Olga and named it after the Queen of Spain, described the rocks as 'minarets, giant cupolas and monstrous domes... huge memorials of the ancient times to the earth'.

Far left: Mossman. Long stretches o beach-lined coast look out to the islands of the Great Barrier Reef.

Left: Cedar Creek, Proserpine. Lush areas of rainforest cover much of Queensland's north coast.

Above: Brisbane is spread on both sides of the Brisbane River, upstream from the river's entry into Moreton Bay.

Right: The beautiful Glasshouse Mountains, north of Brisbane, were named by Captain Cook in 1770.

Queensland
SUNSHINE STATE

To visitors from other states as well as to many Queenslanders, the Sunshine State is holiday country, evoking dreams of long golden days, tropical islands set in jewel blue seas and the chance to get 'a really good tan'. The first settlers in the tropical north, however, were there for grimly practical reasons.

In 1821, Sir Thomas Brisbane, Governor of New South Wales, sent Oxley, his Surveyor-General, to explore the almost unknown country north of the Liverpool Plains. Oxley's job was to find suitable sites for prison camps and he decided on Moreton Bay. In 1824, troops and convicts arrived at Redcliffe but the hostility of the Aborigines persuaded them to move south and they settled at the present site of Brisbane. By 1859, the settlement was well established and free settlers were keen to be separated from New South Wales, so that, on 10 December, the state of Queensland was proclaimed.

Having gained legislative independence, the population of just 23 000 then set about achieving economic independence. Fortunately, the new state was well endowed with excellent farming land and wool and beef production were soon established in the western plains and tablelands. It wasn't long before sugar production, worked by 'kanaka' labour from the Pacific Islands, became much more important and has remained so.

As well as the fertile land which produces grain, sugar, dairy produce, wool, mutton, beef, cotton, peanuts and timber, Queensland is immensely rich in minerals and the vast Mount Isa mining complex in the west produces copper, lead and zinc in enormous quantities.

Over the years, Queensland has been developing another, very different form of industry — tourism. Its attraction as a holiday destination is very much due to its climate.

In the west, it's very similar to the arid Red Centre, with fierce daytime heat, but on the coast the temperature rarely exceeds 38°C and for seven months or so every year the weather is extremely pleasant. If you're unused to humidity, however, the period from December to April can be uncomfortably damp.

The popular coastal region is one of the four geographic and climatic regions which run north to south, neatly dividing the state. In the west is the Great Artesian Basin, flat and hot. Parched and bare during drought, it becomes grassy after rain, thanks to a complex system of boreholes which distribute water through channels and allow grazing; the tablelands to the east are undulating and sparsely timbered, broken up by slow, meandering rivers; and the backbone of Queensland is the Great Dividing Range — most spectacular in its extreme north and south, where it comes closest to the coast. Although the coastal region is the most popular with visitors, Queensland's hinterland is lushly beautiful and its national parks, with many species of bird, animal and plant life unique to the state, total more than a million hectares. The highway and road system is good in the south-east and in the near vicinity of the larger northern towns, but elsewhere roads tend to be narrow and poorly graded and worse during drought or heavy rain conditions.

The two main towns of the tropical northern region are Townsville and Cairns. The more northerly Cairns is fast becoming a fashionable holiday centre and makes an excellent base for deep-sea fishing and for exploring the region, with its lush sugarlands, mountainous jungle country and the wilds of the Cape York Peninsula. The Atherton Tableland is a rich volcanic area west of Cairns, with superb lakes, waterfalls and fern valleys. Stretching all along this northern coastline are the famous islands, from Lizard, north of Cooktown, to Green Island, Dunk, Hinchinbrook, Magnetic, the beautiful cluster in Whitsunday Passage, Great Keppel, Heron and finally Fraser Island. Most can be reached by launch or helicopter from the mainland. If you are planning to stay, make sure your choice fits in with your idea of a tropical paradise. Some are extensively developed for tourism, others are quiet and offer simple accommodation. Beyond, and protecting them from the South Pacific, is the Great Barrier Reef, the world's largest and most famous coral formation.

South of the Reef is the 'Sunshine Coast'. Less developed than the Gold Coast, it has superb beaches; and Bribie Island, the weird and wonderful shapes of the Glasshouse Mountains and the beauties of the Lakes District are within easy reach.

Brisbane, Australia's third city, is a comfortable, far-spreading capital, built on both sides of the Brisbane River. An easygoing, friendly city, with lush parks and gardens full of sub-tropical plants, Brisbane has a year-round average of seven and a half hours of sunshine a day and the Gold Coast 75 kilometres to its south. This is the heart of holiday country, luxuriously developed, offering a wide range of accommodation, nightlife, seemingly endless golden beaches and incessant sun. Inland is rich wheat and dairy farming country, rolling and peaceful — a far cry from the tropical north or the mining areas of Mount Isa — but it goes to prove once more that the Sunshine State is a very diverse place indeed.

Brisbane
A SUB-TROPICAL CITY

The best place from which to see and understand Brisbane's layout is from the lookout on Mt Coot-tha, 8 km south-west of the city centre and easily distinguished by its television towers. Brisbane sprawls over the series of small hills below, with the Brisbane River wandering lazily through the suburbs and city and out into **Moreton Bay**, 32 km down river. Surprisingly little use is made of the river for public transport, and most riverside houses back on to rather than face it.

BELOW: *Busy Queen Street Mall.*

Moreton and **Stradbroke Islands** look like a protective mountain range against the Pacific Ocean, far to the east. On a good day you can see to the rugged mountains behind the Gold Coast to the south, and north to the strange **Glasshouse Mountains** towards the Sunshine Coast.

The **City Hall**, Brisbane's best-known building, is now lost among the clean new cluster of high-rise office buildings that dominate the skyline. Brisbane has at last grown up and is, perhaps reluctantly, losing its 'big friendly country town' image.

Brisbane still doesn't bustle like the large southern capitals, and the suburban architecture, except for the newer, western areas, is predominantly the traditional galvanised-iron roofed timber houses on stumps that residents think sensible and visitors find quaint. What is often lacking in paint is more than made up for by colourful sub-tropical trees and shrubbery.

Brisbane started inauspiciously as a convict settlement as far removed from Britain, and even from Sydney, as possible. In 1799 Matthew Flinders sailed into Moreton Bay on the sloop *Norfolk*. In 1823 John Oxley, then Surveyor-General, sailed the cutter *Mermaid* up the river that flowed into the bay and called it the Brisbane, after the Governor of New South Wales, Sir Thomas Brisbane.

The first troops and convicts arrived in 1824 in the brig *Amity*. The original settlement at Redcliffe was soon abandoned, mainly because of a lack of fresh water, and barracks were built on the present site of the city centre, previously investigated by Oxley. The penal settlement was closed in 1839 and the region was opened for free settlement in 1842.

Today, Brisbane is a busy city with modern freeways, quite an extensive public transport system, a good selection of restaurants, entertainment and nightlife, parks and gardens which thrive in the sub-tropical climate, and a population of over one million.

There are many interesting early buildings which remain. The **Observatory** or **Old Windmill** on Wickham Terrace, overlooking the city, was built in 1828 but never really worked, so convicts were pressed into service on a treadmill to crush grain. In 1934 a picture of the mill was the first television picture in Australia, transmitted to Ipswich, 33 km away.

RIGHT: *The Observatory was built as a windmill in convict days.*

The **Old Government Stores**, or Commissariat Building, at North Quay below the **State Library**, was built by convicts in 1829 and is now being restored. The nearby **Treasury Building** at the top of Queen Street, an impressive Italian Renaissance structure built of local grey sandstone, was commenced in 1888 **Newstead House**, a charming building overlooking the river at Breakfast Creek, was built in 1846 by Patrick Leslie, the first settler on the Darling Downs. He sold it to his brother-in-law Captain John Wickham, RN, resident of the Moreton Bay Colony, and it was the centre of official and social life in Brisbane until the first **Government House** was built in 1862. It is Brisbane's oldest home and is now being restored by a Trust to illustrate a bygone past. Government House was a classic colonial building with additions made between 1882 and 1895 and it was also the original University. It is now part of the **Queensland Institute of Technology** complex at the bottom of George Street and is the home of the National Trust of Queensland. Nearby **Parliament House** was designed by Charles Tiffin in a 'tropical Renaissance' style and was opened in 1868. The new **Parliament House Annexe** (irreverently called the 'Taj Mahal') is a modern tower block behind Parliament House overlooking the river. The exclusive **Queensland Club** is diagonally opposite Parliament House and was built during the 1880s.

The **General Post Office** in Queen Street was built between 1871 and 1879 on the site of the female convict barracks. The small church behind the Post Office in

Elizabeth Street beside **St Stephen's Catholic Cathedral** is the third oldest building in Brisbane, having been dedicated in 1850. The **Customs House** at Petrie Bight at the bottom of Queen Street was built in 1884. The **Deanery**, built in 1849, behind **St John's Anglican Cathedral** in Ann Street, became a temporary residence for the first Governor of Queensland, Sir George Bowen. The proclamation announcing Queensland as a separate colony was read from its balcony in 1859. It became the residence of the Dean of Brisbane in 1910. Further south along Ann Street is **All Saints' Church**, which dates from 1861.

Earlystreet Historical Village is a particularly fine collection of Queensland buildings and architecture at 75 McIlwraith Avenue, Norman Park, east of the city centre. It is open daily from 10 am to 4.30 pm and is well worth a visit. Among the buildings are reconstructions of the ballroom and billiard room of

BELOW: *Brisbane's riverside expressway.*

'Auchenflower' and 'Stromness', one of the first houses at Kangaroo Point. Afternoon teas are served on Sundays.

To the north of the city, another building open to the public is **'Miegunyah'**, a traditional Queensland house with verandahs and ironwork at Jordan Terrace, Bowen Hills. It is the home of the Queensland Women's Historical Society.

There are very few terrace houses in Brisbane but a row at the **Normanby Junction** has been lovingly restored and incorporates a restaurant. A similar development has occurred on **Coronation Drive**. Brisbane's more impressive houses tend to be scattered through the inner city suburbs on the tops of hills, and a quiet drive around to seek them out will be rewarding. Many small cottages in the **Spring Hill**, **Paddington** and **Red Hill** areas are being fashionably restored. The **Regatta Hotel** on the river at Coronation Drive is worth a visit, and the **Breakfast Creek Hotel** has a popular beer garden.

HOTELS
Sheraton Brisbane Hotel and Towers
249 Turbot St.
(07) 835 3535
Gateway Inn,
85-87 North Quay, Brisbane.
(07) 221 0211
Gazebo Terrace,
345 Wickham Terrace, Brisbane.
(07) 221 6177

FAMILY AND BUDGET
Parkview,
128 Alice St, Brisbane.
(07) 31 2695
Queensland Countrywomen's Association,
89-95 Gregory Terrace, Brisbane.
(07) 221 8188
Regal,
132 Alice St, Brisbane.
(07) 31 1541
Southern Cross,
721 Main St, Kangaroo Point.
(07) 391 2881

MOTEL GROUPS: BOOKINGS
Flag (07) 221 0900
Homestead (07) 221 3611
Travelodge (07) 221 8586

This list is for information only; inclusion is not necessarily a recommendation.

The main city department stores are located in Queen Street which, between Edward and Albert Streets, is now a mall. A modern plaza containing 57 specialist shops is at the corner of George, Ann and Adelaide Streets.

For the sports enthusiast, Brisbane's famous 'Gabba' ground at Woolloongabba hosts cricket matches and greyhound racing. There are four horse racing venues at Albion Park, Doomben, Eagle Farm and Bundamba. The new **Queen Elizabeth II Jubilee Sports Centre** at Nathan and the Chandler aquatic centre, indoor sports hall and velodrome were all built for the 1982 Commonwealth Games.

The City Square facing the City Hall is a popular spot for 'watching the world go by'. The **Anzac Memorial and Eternal Flame** is opposite the **Central Railway Station** with its towering backdrop, the **Sheraton Brisbane Hotel and Towers**.

BELOW: *The Cultural Centre.*

ABOVE: *The Story Bridge.*

For the art lover, the **Queensland Art Gallery**, Queensland Cultural Centre, is on the south side river bank. This stunning new gallery includes significant Australian, British and European collections. The Cultural Centre also has an auditorium and a three-theatre performing arts complex, and in 1986 will have a library and the Queensland Museum. The **Civic Art Museum** in the City Hall and the **University of Queensland Art Museum** at St Lucia are both excellent. Private galleries include the Philip Bacon Gallery at New Farm, the Ray Hughes Gallery at Red Hill, the Victor Mace Gallery at Bowen Hills, Para Galleries at South Brisbane, which specialises in Queensland artists, and the New Central Galleries, the Town Gallery, the Don McInnes Galleries, Barry's Gallery and two Aboriginal galleries in the city proper. The **Leichhardt Street** area of Spring Hill has developed as a centre for arts and crafts enthusiasts, and is well worth a browse.

The **Queensland University** is built mainly from Helidon freestone on a superb site on the river at St Lucia. A second university, **Griffith**, is at Nathan. The **Brisbane College of Advanced Education** is an amalgamation of four campuses. Government House at Bardon was built in 1865 for Johann Heussler, who brought German farmworkers to the state, and became the official residence in 1920.

The **Queensland Museum** is an ornate building on the corner of Bowen Bridge Road and Gregory Terrace. Both the Queensland Museum and State Library are being moved to the Queensland Cultural Centre. The main **Post Office** in Queen Street has a museum of telegraphic material.

The old **Botanic Gardens** next to Parliament House are particularly magnificent. In contrast, **New Farm Park**, which is close to the city via the Valley, has 12 000 rose bushes that are at their best between September and November,

RIGHT: *University of Queensland.*

Mount Coot-tha

Only eight kilometres from Brisbane's city centre, Mt Coot-tha offers city dwellers an attractive 'breathing space' and the Brisbane City Council has plans for an ambitious development scheme which will make the best recreational use of the area.

Brisbane's new Botanic Gardens are being developed in the foothills of Mt Coot-tha. The tropical display house, in the form of a futuristic looking dome, has a superb display of tropical plants and is open from 9.30 am to 4.30 pm daily. The arid zone garden and cactus house are nearby. The first stage also includes a lagoon and pond, a demonstration garden, ornamental trees and shrubs and areas of Australian and tropical rainforest. The gardens will include a large collection of Australian native plants.

Situated in the Botanic Gardens is the Sir Thomas Brisbane Planetarium. This is the largest planetarium in Australia, accommodating 144 people. The planetarium is named after the 'founder of organised science in Australia'. When Sir Thomas Brisbane was Governor of New South Wales in 1821, he set up an astronomical observatory at Parramatta. His observations from 1822 to 1826 resulted in the publication he called the *Brisbane Catalog of Stars*.

Various programmes are shown at the Planetarium's Star Theatre. A representation of the night sky is projected on to the interior of the dome and the movements of sun, moon and stars are described as they occur. Special effects can also be obtained by additional projectors to demonstrate more unusual 'happenings' in the sky.

The planetarium complex also contains an observatory which can be used by members of the public, by prior arrangement, to view the day or night sky.

Programmes at the planetarium are at 3.30 pm and 7.30 pm Wednesdays to Sundays, with an additional show at 1.30 pm at weekends. Children under six are not admitted. **NB No admission after the start of the programme**.

Outside again, there are many picnic areas at Mt Coot-tha, including a particularly attractive spot at the J. C. Slaughter Falls. The Mount Coot-tha Restaurant (BYO) on Sir Samuel Griffith Drive is open daily for lunches and morning and afternoon teas. The view from this vantage point is superb, across the city and Moreton Bay, and sometimes as far as the Lamington Plateau in the south and the Glasshouse Mountains in the north.

Perhaps the best view of all from Mt Coot-tha is at night. The lights of the city of Brisbane spread out before you in a breathtaking sight and, even if you have only one evening in Brisbane it is worth making the short trip to the lookout to take in this memorable scene.

jacaranda trees that blossom in October and November, and poinciana trees in November and December. The new **Mt Coot-tha Botanic Gardens**, 5 km from the city, feature a Tropical Display Dome and the superb Sir Thomas Brisbane Planetarium. (Bookings for the planetarium can be made by phoning 370 8513.) The nearby **J. C. Slaughter Falls Park** is popular for picnics, barbecues and walks.

Facilities for evening entertainment and eating out in Brisbane have improved, particularly over the last ten years, with a great many new restaurants being opened up. The local press lists a great choice in its entertainment pages and a comprehensive booklet is available from the **Queensland Government Travel Centre** in Adelaide Street.

Brisbane is famous for its seafood, and several good restaurants let you come to grips with the awesome Queensland mudcrab, Moreton Bay bugs, tiger prawns and delicious reef fish and barramundi.

ferries operate from the city to Kangaroo Point, East Brisbane and New Farm Park. Hayles operate river and bay cruises from North Quay, including the *Captain Cook*, a new floating restaurant.

There are plenty of hotels and motels offering accommodation in and near Brisbane, together with a number of caravan parks within easy reach of the central city area. And, of course, the tourist mecca of the Gold Coast is only a relatively short distance away.

Several of Brisbane's attractions lie just outside the main city area. Views from the surrounding hills are good, particularly from Bartley's Hill lookout at Hamilton. The *Southern Cross*, Sir Charles Kingsford Smith's famous Fokker tri-motor aircraft, is on proud display at Eagle Farm airport. One of Brisbane's most famous attractions is

BELOW: *Newstead House.*

ABOVE: *The Botanic Gardens have a beautiful display of palms and tropical plants which thrive in Brisbane's climate.*

Lone Pine Sanctuary 11 km away at Fig Tree Pocket with its photogenic koalas. At the Oasis Gardens at Sunnybank there are good swimming pools and tropical trees and shrubs 14 km from the city. Bunya Park, 14 km north at Cash's Crossing has a maze, wildlife sanctuary and picnic facilities. Tours of the Golden Circle tropical fruit cannery at Northgate are available.

For further information when in Brisbane, the Queensland Government Travel Centre, 196 Adelaide Street in the city, is extremely helpful. The phone number is 31 2211. The Royal Automobile Club of Queensland has an office at 300 St Pauls Terrace (phone number 253 2444), and offers reciprocal services to members of other Australian Automotive Associations. Their maps are highly recommended.

ABOVE: *Sir Charles Kingsford Smith's Southern Cross is on display at Eagle Farm airport.*

Baxter's, 14 km from the city at Deagon, has been serving seafood since 1861.

Other popular venues are Rags, a garden restaurant with an all weather roof, Gambaro's in Caxton Street Petrie Terrace, Antico's in the Valley and Muddie's in Edward Street. The Coral Trout at Breakfast Creek, Aquarius at Woolloongabba, and the Boathouse in Upper Roma Street. The Arts and Battledress in Petrie Terrace, Ardrossan Hall in Bowen Hills, The Milano in Queen Street as well as Baguette at Ascot, are all known to have good reputations.

Because of its vast size (the Brisbane City Council controls an area of 1220 sq. km), the city's public transport network is extensive and adequate. Council buses take most of the load, with trains running only to certain areas. Brisbane's famous trams were pensioned off in 1969. An excellent pocket map is produced by the Metropolitan Transit Authority. Small

Tours from Brisbane

There is such a variety of things to see and do around Brisbane that many of these trips will overlap. Most can be done in one day, but some will be better enjoyed if you plan an overnight stop.

The Brisbane forest parks concept is being developed as breathing space for the city, and many new national parks have been declared in the surrounding area so, as well as the famous beaches, take advantage of these parks — they're well worth a visit.

The Gold Coast, 70 km from Brisbane via the Pacific and Gold Coast Highways.

About an hour's drive south of Brisbane begins the huge holiday area of the Gold Coast, which comprises a strip along the coast from Southport to Coolangatta and includes the famous Surfers Paradise. Excellent surfing beaches and glorious weather have always been the major attractions of the Gold Coast, but a day trip, or several days, can be spent enjoying some of the incredible range of tourist attractions that have developed in this area.

Gold Coast Hinterland, about 100 km from Brisbane via the Pacific Highway and Nerang.

If it is possible to be bored on the Gold Coast simply drive west. The nearby McPherson Ranges have some of Australia's finest scenery. Rainforest, deep ravines, waterfalls, refreshingly quiet mountain air, and a spectacular view of the coast.

Redcliffe, 34 km from Brisbane via the Gympie Road.

Drive to Redcliffe via Petrie and a detour to the North Pine Dam. The whole Redcliffe Peninsula is almost completely surrounded by the waters of Moreton Bay. The stretches of sandy beaches are safe for swimming and the fishing is good. Catch spectacular views high on the volcanic red cliffs — after which the area was named —far across Moreton Bay to Moreton and Stradbroke Islands. These are famous worldwide for their natural surroundings and mountainous sand dunes. The Redcliffe jetty is a favourite spot for local anglers and a pleasant place for a stroll.

O'Reilly's Green Mountains, Lamington National Park, 112 km from Brisbane via the Mt Lindesay or Pacific Highways and Canungra.

The thickly wooded Lamington National Park is one of the wildest and finest in Queensland. On a plateau at the top is O'Reilly's Green Mountains resort, and it is worth making this a full weekend's trip, though advance booking should be made. There is plenty to see and do with a maze of walking tracks in the area, but if walking isn't for you just sit in the sun and admire the superb mountain scenery or feed the birds. In the sub-tropical rainforest there is an abundance of wildlife which has been protected for many years. Obtain information for the area at the tourist centre in Canungra or from the ranger at O'Reilly's.

Toowoomba, 135 km from Brisbane via the Warrego Highway.

A comfortable distance from Brisbane for a day trip, this drive takes you past some pretty small towns and old farmhouses. Stop at Marburg on the way to

City of the Gold Coast

Population: 178 800

To a great many Australians, the Gold Coast is happily linked with the word holiday. It is the most developed, colourful, publicised, commercialised, criticised and popular holiday area in Australia, an hour's drive south of Brisbane via the Pacific and Gold Coast Highways. The main beaches, coming from Brisbane, are **Southport, Surfers Paradise, Broadbeach, Mermaid Beach, Miami, Burleigh Heads, Tallebudgera, Currumbin, Tugun, Kirra,** and **Coolangatta** on the New South Wales border.

Surfers Paradise is undoubtedly the brightest star along the 30-odd kilometres of beaches, relaxation and development. In 1936 Mr Jim Cavill built an hotel at a quiet spot 9 kilometres south of Southport, between the Nerang River and the beach. The place was called Umbi-Gumbi by the Aborigines, meaning 'the place of the ant'. Mr Cavill, however, called his establishment the Surfers Paradise Hotel and until a generation ago the modest two-storeyed white stucco building and its famous beer garden was still the most impressive landmark in the area.

It is still there, on the corner of the Pacific Highway and Cavill Avenue, looking somewhat lost among the spectacular high-rise development that exploded in the late 1950s and 1960s.

The building boom generally showed more enthusiasm than good taste, being an amazing mixture of Miami, Florida, St Kilda Vic., Kings Cross NSW, and Disneyland, USA.

The strip between Southport and Coolangatta is now officially called the City of the Gold Coast, and is one of the fastest growing areas in Australia; in particular it attracts many southerners as permanent residents. At least 3000 places have accommodation available. The staff at the Gold Coast Visitors' Advisory Centre on the Pacific Highway at Surfers Paradise are extremely knowledgeable and helpful, and the Queensland Government Tourist Bureau has offices at Coolangatta and Surfers Paradise.

The excellent surfing beaches and friendly weather have always been the main attractions of the Gold Coast, but a bewildering range of man-made attractions has been opened to entice the visitor out of the water, particularly when the tall buildings overshadow the beach in the afternoons. These are the most popular; and most of them are open every day:

Tours from Brisbane 279

admire the old timber pub with its latticed verandah, a fine example of early hotel architecture. Toowoomba's most popular tourist attraction is its parks and gardens with a touch of England in the magnificent oaks, elms, plane trees and poplars. The gardens are best seen during September when the city has its Carnival of Flowers. The carnival is usually held over the last week of September, and includes a procession, dancing and entertainment in the streets. The Blue Arrow Drive around the city, laid out by the city council, is a must for the tourist. You could return to Brisbane via the New England and Cunningham Highways.

Binna Burra, Lamington National Park, 108 km from Brisbane via the Mt Lindesay or Pacific Highways and Canungra.

If you chose to walk from O'Reilly's to Binna Burra Lodge it would be a distance of some 22 km, but it is much further to go by road. Binna Burra Lodge is a good centre from which to enjoy the great variety of walks in the area but a sensible pair of shoes is a must. Bring a sweater too — it can get cold even in summer. If you plan to spend a weekend 'wilderness camping' in the mountains a permit is necessary and can be obtained from the Chief Ranger at Binna Burra. Information is available in Canungra for the many walks and places of interest on the way. Those who prefer a few more comforts can plan to stay overnight at the Binna Burra Lodge, but make sure accommodation is available in advance.

ABOVE: *Lamington National Park is a haven for bushwalkers.*

Tamborine Mountain, 70 km from Brisbane via the Pacific Highway.

Tamborine Mountain, some 30 km from Oxenford, is a wonderful retreat from the bustle of Brisbane. Here palms, staghorns, elkhorns, ferns and orchids grow in profusion. Watch out for scrub turkeys, especially if you're travelling in the area around dawn or dusk. There are many national parks in the area including the Joalah, Franklin and Palm Grove National Parks. Take comfortable shoes if you're planning to walk through Palm Grove, one of the prettier parks.

Wynnum, Manly and Redland Bay, 35 km from Brisbane via Route Nos 23, 30 and 44.

You won't have to drive very far to enjoy the bayside suburbs of Wynnum and Manly, south-east of Brisbane on the shores of Moreton Bay. Wynnum has an excellent small boat harbour where the Royal Queensland Yacht Squadron has its headquarters. There is also a very good golf course at Wynnum, and a variety of other sporting facilities. Continue on to Redland Bay, a peaceful tourist resort. The area is famed for its market gardens and the Strawberry Festival (on the first Saturday of each September). Wayside stalls sell fruit and flowers at weekends. Boats can be hired all along this coast so that you can do your own exploring or fishing.

The Jondaryan Woolshed Historical Museum and Park, 185 km from Brisbane via the Warrego Highway.

The Jondaryan Woolshed was built in 1859, with space for 88 blade shearers to handle some 200 000 sheep a season. Now an ideal outing for all the family, it is being restored as a working memorial to the early pastoral pioneers. As well as the Woolshed, see the blacksmith's shop, the one-roomed school house, and the

At Southport:
Sea World, on the Spit at Main Beach, is very good, with performing dolphins, water-ski ballet, a paddle-wheel steamer, helicopter and speedboat rides, hand-feeding of sharks, *Endeavour* replica and Old Fort. Andalucia Park, on the Spit, where the Royal Spanish Dancing Stallions are a spectacular feature. The Laserama Planetarium is nearby. Macintosh Park at Narrowneck has picnic areas and wildlife. Australiana Display on Main Beach Parade has coins, banknotes and bottles.
At Surfers Paradise:
The Grundy Entertainment Centre on the beachfront with a large water slide. Wax Museum and Chamber of Horrors. Surfers Paradise International Raceway has regular motor sport. Joy flights in a Tiger Moth biplane. Famous restaurants, night club entertainment, shopping and 'people-watching'.
At Broadbeach:
Pacific Fair shopping centre and cosmopolitan attractions. Cascades Park and Gardens.
At Mermaid Beach:
Traintasia model train exhibition, Chairlift to 'Magic Mountain Castle' a fun park on Nobbys Beach headland.
At Miami:
Gold Coast Zoo.

At Burleigh Heads:
Burleigh Knoll Environmental Park and Burleigh Head National Park are both worth a visit. At Mudgeeraba, further inland, is the Gold Coast War Museum and Battle Playground, together with Hawes Boomerang Factory.
At Tallebudgera:
Tally Valley Market has country arts and crafts. Chewing Gum Field Air Museum has vintage aircraft and displays.
At Currumbin:
Feed the thousands of lorikeets at the famous sanctuary, now a National Trust property. The Land of Legend is a fairytale and fable exhibition. Santaland is a popular children's attraction.
At Coomera:
Dreamworld is situated 23 km north of Surfers Paradise on the Pacific Highway. It is a fun park for families, packed with hours of excitement and fantasy.
At Coolangatta:
Several famous old guesthouses. Captain Cook Memorial and Lighthouse at Point Danger.
At Tweed Heads:
Across the border try your luck on the poker machines — illegal in Queensland — at one of the country clubs.

ABOVE: *The Thunderbolt Rollercoaster ride at Dreamworld Coomera.*

dairy. There is also a fascinating collection of old agricultural machinery. Open from 10 am every day except Good Friday and Christmas Day. Conducted tours operate on the hour.

Brookvale Park, Oakey, 183 km from Brisbane on the Warrego Highway.

For those interested in native flora and fauna, Brookvale Park is a comprehensive botanical garden with a unique display of Australian native shrubs and trees collected from throughout the continent. A road train leaves every hour for tours around the area, and the tour leader gives an excellent descriptive commentary. Koalas, emus and kangaroos can also be seen. The gardens are open each day from 9 am to 5 pm.

Mt Glorious, 40 km from Brisbane via Waterworks Road.

One of the more interesting short drives from Brisbane through mountainous country due west of the city is to Mt Glorious, via Mt Nebo, and then back via Samford. There are many spectacular views of the mountainous Brisbane Forest Park. Stop at McPhee's and Jolly's Lookouts before arriving at the pretty town of Mount Nebo. Hear bellbirds and whipbirds in the Manorina National Park. In the Maiala National Park at Mt Glorious there are many well documented short and long walks through the lush rainforest.

The Sunshine Coast, 100 km from Brisbane to its nearest point via the Bruce Highway.

The Sunshine Coast is a 200 kilometres-long series of magnificent beaches, punctuated by rocky headlands and river mouths that stretch north from Bribie Island to Tin Can Bay, one to two hours driving from Brisbane. Follow the coastal highway from Caloundra to the main beaches of Currimundi, Mooloolaba, Alexandra Headland, Maroochydore, Mudjimba, Marcoola, Coolum, Peregian, Sunshine Beach and Noosa Heads. Surf-Surfing is excellent almost anywhere. The Sunshine Coast, often called the North Coast by Brisbane people, tends to be quieter and more natural than the more highly-developed Gold (or South) Coast strip, with interesting and varied scenery in the hinterland.

The Bunya Mountains, 250 km from Brisbane via the Warrego and Brisbane Valley Highways.

This three hour drive is often spectacular, but hairpin bends make the journey unsuitable for cars towing caravans or trailers. Because there is so much to see along the way it would be wise to stay overnight either camping or at an hotel. On the way Savages Crossing is a good place for a picnic, and the Bellevue Homestead at Coominya is worth a detour. A major National Trust project, the homestead has been moved from its original site and rebuilding and restoration is continuing. Further on, stop at Maidenwell to see the Coomber Falls and King House. There are many more places to visit on the way to the mountains and all are fully signposted. Most of the area is set aside as the Bunya Mountains National Park; there are two major camping sites in the park. Bushwalkers will enjoy the excellent graded tracks. If you have time, and don't want to camp, continue on to Kingaroy, the peanut growing area, where there is plenty of accommodation.

The Cooloola Coast, 259 km from Brisbane via the Bruce Highway and Gympie.

A round trip which takes in the beautiful Mary Valley and the golden city of Gympie where you turn out to the coast on the Tin Can Bay road. For more information contact the Cooloola Coast Visitors' Bureau, Tin Can Bay. (071 86 4389)

Beerwah and Buderim past the Glasshouse Mountains, 100 km from Brisbane via the Bruce Highway.

Travel past the Glasshouse Mountains where you will see ten spectacular trachyte peaks named by Captain Cook as he sailed up the coast in 1770. The sun shining on the rock faces reminded him of glasshouses in his native Yorkshire. Further on you will reach the Queensland Reptile Park, reputed to be one of the best such parks in Australia. Taipans, lizards of all sizes, and crocodiles can be seen. Continue on through Landsborough to Buderim. Visit the art galleries and the Pioneer Cottage, one of Buderim's earliest houses, which retains much of its original furnishings from last century. The Foote Sanctuary would make a good spot for a picnic or barbecue lunch.

The Big Pineapple and Sunshine Plantation, 115 kilometres from Brisbane via the Bruce Highway.

Seven kilometres south of Nambour, the Sunshine Plantation is the largest and most popular tourist attraction on the Sunshine Coast. On the pleasant drive up the Bruce Highway you can pass colourful roadside stalls offering tropical fruit at prices that amaze the southern visitor.

The Big Pineapple itself is a 16 metres high replica of a pineapple, with a top floor observation deck which looks out on the plantation of tropical fruit below. Two floors of audio-visual displays tell the story of the pineapple and there is a Polynesian-style restaurant and tropical market.

For a small charge you can ride on a sugar cane train through more than 40 hectares of pineapples, mangoes, avocados, sugar cane, and nuts and spices. An attractive miniature farm is fun for children. The 'Nutmobile' will take you, for a small charge, to Australia's largest macadamia processing factory, which is next door to the Sunshine Plantation. Visitors can see the complete process from cracking the nut to the final product.

Admission to the Big Pineapple and the industry display is free.

ABOVE: *A full day can be enjoyed at the Big Pineapple.*

Miva Station, 202 km from Brisbane, and Susan River Homestead, 284 km from Brisbane, both via the Bruce Highway.

Here's a weekend with a difference and an opportunity for city people to sample life on one or other of these cattle stations. At Miva Station via Gympie (071 84 8452), you can camp in your own tent, although an extra charge will secure one already erected on site. Trail riding and hay rides are popular, or go canoeing or fishing. If you are very quiet you may see lungfish or platypuses in the creek. The area is a bird and animal sanctuary. At the Susan River property (071 21 6846), 15 km past Maryborough on the Hervey Bay Road, you stay at the homestead where full board is provided. Here you can join in with mustering, swim in the pool, or simply feed the emus and wallabies. For further information about station and farm holidays contact the Queensland Government Tourist Bureau.

The Great Barrier Reef

The Great Barrier Reef is a living phenomenon. Its coloured coral branches sit upon banks of limestone polyps which have been built up slowly over thousands of years from the sea-bed. The banks of coral are separated by channels of water, shading from the delicate green of the shallows to the deepest blue. The reef area is over 1200 kilometres long, stretching from near the coast of western Papua to Breaksea Spit, east of Gladstone on the central Queensland coast. It is only between 15 and 20 kilometres wide in the north but south of Cairns the reef area can extend up to 325 kilometres out to sea. With over 700 islands scattered through the tropical sea, and the banks of reefs darkening the water, this sun-drenched, tropical paradise attracts thousands of visitors each year to its resorts.

The coral presents an incredibly beautiful picture to those who see it through glass-bottomed boats or, even better, swim around in it using snorkels or diving gear. The colours of purples, pinks, yellows, whites and reds are intermixed and made more startling by the spectacular shapes of the coral. There are more than 340 varieties of coral identified, but the most common are the staghorns, brain corals, mushroom corals, organ pipes and blue corals. Spread among these are waving fields of soft coral, colourful anemones, sea urchins and sea slugs. Shellfish of all kinds, ranging from great clams to tiny cowries, cling to the reef while shoals of brightly coloured tropical fish — among them red emperors, coral trout, sweetlip, angel fish, parrot fish and demoiselles — glide and dart through the coral gardens. Multitudes of sea birds nest on the islands of the reef through spring and summer.

Two island resorts, Green Island and Heron Island, are coral cays — actually part of the reef — and at low tide it is possible to walk on the coral ledges which surround them. Other resort islands are continental islands — having once been part of the mainland — and are generally more wooded and mountainous.

BELOW: *Bushes of soft pink coral grow in the deep water.*

BELOW: *The brilliant beauty of a yellow feather star.*

BELOW: *This purple hard coral adds to the colour of the Barrier Reef.*

Queensland

The resort islands off the reef and the Queensland coast offer different styles of living to suit various tastes in holidays and entertainment. Their common denominator is their beautiful setting and a consistency of climate, broken only by the sudden and shortlived downfalls of the wet season from December to February.

Heron Island, 70 kilometres off Gladstone, on the central Queensland coast, is ideal for the reef observer, snorkel-swimmer or diver. It is a true coral cay with part of the reef and lagoon emerging at low tide, and more than 1000 varieties of fish inhabit its reefs. It is also the nesting place for grey and white herons, white capped noddy terns, gulls, seagulls and mutton birds. Turtles lay their eggs from October to January and hatching can be seen from late December to May. It is a quiet 'natural' resort with high standard accommodation, swimming pool, entertainment area, snorkelling and skindiving lessons.

Quoin Island, about four kilometres from Gladstone, is a quiet resort, popular with day-trippers. The accent here is on relaxation and there is no organised entertainment. The island is heavily wooded and there are peaceful nature walks along a network of tracks.

Great Keppel Island is the 'swinging' island for young people, 48 kilometres north-east of Rockhampton. It is ideal for a holiday if you are young, single and would enjoy a nightly disco and well-organised activities like tennis, water-skiing, island safari trips, skindiving and coral viewing. The wooded island has many secluded bays with white surf beaches.

The collection of islands in the magnificent Whitsunday Passage is reached from Shute Harbour, Proserpine or Mackay. These include **Hamilton Island** which has a floating marina and a range of accommodation including Polynesian-style units and the luxurious Bougainvillaea Lodge. Most watersports are catered for and there are tennis and squash courts, gymnasium, hot spas and a huge swimming pool.

Whitsunday 100 on **Long Island** is for the young at heart. There are walks in the national park, a glass-bottom boat for viewing the coral and organised nightly entertainment.

South Molle Island, in the middle of the Whitsunday Passage, has a large swimming pool, tennis courts and a golf course. For evening entertainment

TOP: *Heron Island is an ideal base for a Barrier Reef holiday.*

CENTRE: *Island cruises leave from the jetty at Shute Harbour.*

LEFT: *North and South Molle Islands lie offshore from Shute Harbour.*

there is a cocktail lounge and dance floor, with a band on most nights, and an island bistro. There are several beaches on this hilly island, which is clothed in grassland and rainforest.

Daydream Island is one of the more lavish resorts in the Whitsunday group. Life centres around the free-form salt-water swimming pool more than 8 metres long. The cabaret room, main bar, dining room and holiday units are designed in Polynesian style and are surrounded by landscaped gardens. The island has lavish tropical vegetation and is crested by hoop pines. Badminton, fishing cruises, coral viewing and diving are organised. There is entertainment with a dance band every night.

Hayman Island is the best known resort of the Whitsunday group and is noted for its organised and extensive entertainment, its high standard accommodation and food, and for its beautiful island lagoon, which makes a perfect aquatic playground in front of the Royal Hayman Hotel. There are walks to lookouts, beaches and picnic spots, tennis, bowls, badminton, deck tennis, aquaplaning, even a betting shop and a secluded beachfront nightclub.

Magnetic Island, 4 kilometres off Townsville, is a large island with permanent residents, holiday houses and a series of six resorts nestling in bays around its coastline. The island has golf, tennis, bowls, and many walking tracks through forests where koalas and wallabies may be seen. There are excellent fishing and diving facilities.

Orpheus, in the Palm Island group, 80 kilometres north of Townsville, is a secluded, quiet resort, catering for a small number of guests in holiday bungalows and cabins. There is an island lounge and bar, but no organised evening entertainment.

ABOVE: *Hamilton Island is one of the newest resorts in the Whitsunday group.*

ABOVE: *The mainland bordering the beautiful Whitsunday Passage is set aside as the Conway Range National Park.*

BELOW: *Daydream Island, a popular holiday resort in the Whitsunday group.*

ABOVE: *Sea anemone.*

BELOW: *Bushy Cay.*

Queensland

The holiday resort on mountainous **Hinchinbrook Island** offers self-contained bungalows where guests can do their own cooking as an alternative to eating island style in the resort dining area. The island is a National Park of mountainous peaks and forest areas and is home for a great variety of animal and bird life. Cape Richards has a beautiful beach. Guests gather at the bar and recreation area, but there is no organised entertainment.

Dunk Island is a magnificent tropic isle off the coast from Tully, and has become a major, high quality resort. Not far from the beach, holiday lodges built of stained timber blend into the tropical surroundings, and nearby is a swimming pool, dining room, bar, dance floor and recreation area. There is a bistro, boutique and general store and facilities for golf, tennis, horse-riding, clay pigeon shooting, diving and water-skiing. There are many graded paths through the island's forests for pleasant walks.

Green Island, 27 kilometres from Cairns, is a coral cay surrounded by beautiful patches of reef and crested with thick tropical vegetation. It has holiday units and an hotel with dining and recreation facilities, but is better known as the daily host to visitors from Cairns, who can see the reef through glass-bottomed boats and at the underwater observatory. There is a theatrette showing colour films of the reef and a display of coral, marine and animal life.

Lizard Island, 95 kilometres northeast of Cooktown, caters for a small number of guests in a resort built in homestead style, facing a beautiful lagoon. The island is rather barren but it has beautiful beaches, surrounded by fringing coral, and is ideal for big game fishing. There are facilities for catamaran cruising and water-skiing.

For those who sail or want to cruise the Great Barrier Reef there are passenger cruises, charter yachts and launches available at various centres. The best sailing and cruising time is in the months outside the December-February period, when the weather is more stable.

For further information on the Barrier Reef resorts contact the Queensland Government Travel Centre, the Great Barrier Reef Marine Park Authority (Townsville), and the Queensland National Parks and Wildlife Service.

TOP RIGHT: *A relaxing time can be spent at Dunk Island's resort, rebuilt in 1978.*

CENTRE RIGHT: *The beautiful corals of the Great Barrier Reef.*

RIGHT: *Windsurfing at Hayman Island, one of the most popular resorts of the Great Barrier Reef.*

Queensland from A to Z

Airlie Beach Population 1705.
The 3.2 million-dollar Wanderer's Paradise tourist resort at Airlie Beach, operated in conjunction with TAA, can accommodate 600 people in various styles, from luxury units to tents. Situated on the coast north-east of Proserpine, facilities include an air-conditioned restaurant and bar, tennis courts, an 18-hole golf course and a shopping centre. The annual Whitsunday Village Fun Race is claimed to be the largest cruising yacht race in Queensland (generally held in late August) with special classes for luggers and square-rigged boats. Other general festivities include the 'Miss Figurehead' beauty contest (traditionally topless!). **In the area:** Shute Harbour, the islands of the Whitsunday Passage, Conway National Park, renowned for its natural beauty and butterflies. **Accommodation:** 1 hotel, 4 motels, 3 caravan/camping parks.
Map ref. 331 E4

Allora Population 661.
North of Warwick on the Toowoomba Road, Allora's historical museum is open on Sunday afternoons. **In the area:** Main Range National Park, about 50 km to the east, has rich vegetation including hanging gardens of rock lilies and staghorns. Wildlife includes possums and bowerbirds. Approximately 22 km of walking tracks go through the dense rainforest and eucalypts of the park. **Accommodation:** 1 caravan/camping park.
Map ref. 323 O11

Alpha Population 516.
Alpha on the Capricorn Highway is a small cattle town on the railway 136 km east of Barcaldine. **Accommodation:** 1 hotel, 1 motel, 1 caravan/camping park.
Map ref. 322 H3

Aramac Population 428.
This small, pastoral township, 67 km north of Barcaldine, is on the western side of the Great Dividing Range. It was named by explorer William Landsborough and the name was devised as an acronym of Sir Robert Ramsay Mackenzie, Colonial Secretary in 1866 and Premier of Queensland from 1867 to 1868. **Accommodation:** Limited.
Map ref. 322 F2

Atherton Population 4197.
Huge maize silos interrupt the landscape around this market town on the Atherton Tableland, 100 km south-west of Cairns on the Kennedy Highway. The town is 760 m above sea level and was named after John Atherton, a pioneer pastoralist. The Atherton Maize Festival is held during September. Peanuts are also grown. **In the area:** Lake Tinaroo and the Tinaroo Falls, Lake Eacham and Lake Barrine. **Accommodation:** 5 motels, 5 caravan/camping parks.
Map ref. 324 F4, 326 I13, 335 C12

Ayr Population 8783.
This busy sugar town on the north side of the Burdekin delta is surrounded by intensively irrigated sugar cane fields which are the most productive in Australia. Visitors are welcome at the three main sugar mills during the crushing season June-December. Townsville, 82 km to the north, is the outlet for the bulk sugar. Rice is also grown and production should increase dramatically when the proposed giant dam on the Burdekin is built, as more irrigation is needed. **Of interest:** The House of Australian Nature in Wilmington St contains what is probably Australia's finest collection of butterflies, shells and beetles; the beautiful Cooktown orchid blooms from March till August. **In the area:** Home Hill on the opposite side of the Burdekin is Ayr's sister town. Alva Beach for fishing. Ashworth's Rock Shop and historical museum.
Accommodation: 4 motels, 2 caravan/camping parks.
Map ref. 324 I8

Babinda Population 1389.
A lovely swimming hole and picnic area known as the Boulders is 10 km west of this small sugar town 57 km south of Cairns in the Bellenden Ker National Park. This park has Queensland's two highest mountains, Mt Bartle Frere (1611 m) and Mt Bellenden Ker (1591 m), as well as the Josephine Falls. **Accommodation:** 1 hotel.
Map ref. 324 G4, 335 H13

Barcaldine Population 1432.
A pastoral and rail town on the Capricorn Highway from Rockhampton, 108 km east of Longreach. All the streets are named after trees and citrus fruits thrive on local bore water. The 'tree of knowledge', a ghost-gum in the main street, was the meeting place of the 1891 shearers' strike which resulted in the formation of the Australian Labor Party. The historical museum is open daily. **Accommodation:** 1 motel, 2 caravan/camping parks.
Map ref. 322 F3

Bargara Population 1718.
This popular surf beach 13 km east of Bundaberg is patrolled by one of Queensland's top surf clubs. Nearby is Neilson Park and Mon Repos beach, the only mainland beach where turtles come ashore to lay their eggs, between October and March. In 1912 Bert Hinkler, then an engineering apprentice, flew to a height of some nine metres in a home-made glider off Mon Repos beach, marking the start of his distinguished aviation career. **Accommodation:** 5 motels, 1 hotel, 3 caravan/camping parks.
Map ref. 323 P6

Beaudesert Population 3779.
Beaudesert is a major market town on the Mount Lindesay Highway 66 km south-west of Brisbane, near the New South Wales border. A road west leads to the Cunningham Highway, and the road east leads to the Gold Coast via Tamborine. The district is noted for dairying, agriculture and beef cattle. Beaudesert race meetings are popular. **In the area:** Mt Barney National Park. **Accommodation:** 3 motels.
Map ref. 317 K5, 323 Q11

Beenleigh Population 7839.
Midway between Brisbane and the Gold Coast, Beenleigh is now almost a satellite town of Brisbane. The Beenleigh Distillery on the Albert River has been producing rum from local sugar since 1884. Bullen's African Lion Park and Zoo, open daily, is excellent and popular. Rocky Point Sugar Mill, 20 km east, is Australia's only privately owned mill, also open weekdays July to December. **Accommodation:** 1 motel, 3 caravan/camping parks.
Map ref. 317 N1, 323 Q11

Biloela Population 4643.
This modern, thriving town in the fertile Callide Valley is situated at the crossroads of the Burnett and Dawson Highways 142 km south-west of Rockhampton. The name is Aboriginal for white cockatoo. Underground water is pumped and irrigated for lucerne, cotton and sunflower crops. The unique Biloela buffel grass has been developed for the local pastoral industry. **Of interest:** Cotton Ginnery, tours March till July. Callide Power Station. Meatworks. **In the area:** Boating and swimming at Callide Dam. Callide open-cut coal mine. Mt Scoria, 14 km south, is an interesting solidified volcano core. Thangool's Memorial Park. **Accommodation:** 2 hotels, 5 motels, 3 caravan/camping parks.
Map ref. 323 M5

Birdsville Population under 200.
The well known Birdsville Track starts here on its long path into and across South Australia. The first settlers arrived in Birdsville, nearly 2000 km by road west of Brisbane, in the 1870s and at the turn of the century it was quite a thriving settlement, with three hotels, three stores, several offices and a doctor. When the toll on cattle crossing the border near the town

was abolished after Federation in 1901, prosperity declined and the population diminished. **Of interest:** The ruins of the Royal Hotel in Adelaide St are left as a reminder of Birdsville's boom days. The Birdsville Pub still survives and comes into its own each August or September when the Birdsville Races are held. The normal population of less than 100 grows to about 3000 and they have been known to consume about 50 000 cans of beer over the period of the race meeting! The hotel was burnt down, but has been replaced by another, built in the image of the old one. It is an important overnight stop for tourists travelling down the Track, west across the Simpson Desert (four-wheel drive country), north to Mount Isa or east to Brisbane.

Travel in this area can be hazardous, especially in the 'wet' season (approximately October to March). Supplies of food and water should always be carried as well as petrol, oil and spare parts. You should check the board at the Police station before setting out. The section on Outback Motoring, at the front of this book, gives more details.

The famous 'Flynn of the Inland' founded the first Australian Inland Mission at Birdsville and there is still a well-equipped medical outpost in the town. Birdsville's water comes from a 1219 metres-deep artesian bore, one of the hottest in Queensland. The water comes from the ground almost at boiling point and four cooling ponds bring it to a safe temperature. Electricity is supplied by two diesel-run generators. **Accommodation:** 1 hotel, 1 caravan/camping park.
Map ref. 207 P1, 321 D7

Blackall Population 1609.
Centre of some of the most productive sheep and cattle country in Central Queensland, Blackall has many studs in its vicinity. In recent years more than half a million hectares of gidyea scrub have been cleared and planted with buffel grass for improved grazing. In bygone days Captain Starlight roamed the district, and in 1892 the legendary Jackie Howe set the almost unbelievable record of shearing 321 sheep with blade shears, in a day, at Alice Downs station. Blackall had the first artesian bore in Queensland and still pumps up 6.82 million litres of very hot water daily. **Of interest:** The state's only wool scour outside Brisbane. Bottle trees in the main street. Millions of years old petrified tree stump. **In the area:** 'Black's Palace', a sandstone cliff with Aboriginal ochre paintings, and caves; check locally in case of restricted access. **Accommodation:** 2 motels, 1 caravan/camping park.
Map ref. 322 F5

Blackwater Population 5433.
This major mining town is 195 km west of Rockhampton on the Capricorn Highway. The name comes from the way ti-

Atherton Tableland

Few people visiting the peaceful and productive Atherton Tableland realise just what a wild and remote place it was only a hundred years ago, when most of southern Australia was settled and fairly civilised. The area was unknown until a colourful and aptly named prospector called James Venture Mulligan led several expeditions south-west from **Cooktown** between 1874 and 1876, having previously discovered the spectacular Palmer River goldfields in 1873. The northern Aboriginal tribes bitterly resented their land being over-run with settlers, cattle, and particularly miners. During the 1860s and 1870s there were a great many skirmishes and several outright massacres.

In 1874 Mulligan, leading a party from Cooktown, named the Hodgkinson and St George Rivers and Mt Mulligan, north of the tobacco town of **Dimbulah**. He returned in 1875 and found a beautiful river flowing north, which he presumed was the Mitchell before it swung west to the Gulf of Carpentaria. He had in fact discovered the Barron River, which eventually flows east to the Pacific coast. Mulligan travelled up the Barron and camped at Granite Creek, where **Mareeba** now stands. He travelled over rich basaltic plains, now the tobacco fields on the Kuranda Road, until stopped by dense impenetrable jungle near what is now **Tolga** (335 C12). He marvelled at huge cedar and kauri trees, but skirted the jungle westwards and camped three kilometres from the site of Atherton. In the ranges nearby he discovered the Wild River and traces of tin. Mulligan thought the area too isolated for tin mining as the nearest ports were Cooktown and **Cardwell**, some 500 kilometres away.

Convinced there was gold in the Hodgkinson River valley, Mulligan set off again and found extensive strikes as he prospected the valley. The Hodgkinson gold rush started as soon as he reported his find, most of the diggers coming from Cooktown and the Palmer River. The towns of **Kingsborough** and **Thornborough** quickly sprang up in 1876 between Mt Mulligan and Mareeba. In two years

trees discolour the local water holes. Coal from the three mining companies is railed to Gladstone for use at the power station of for export. The town's population is made up of workers of many nationalities and displays what is claimed to be the most varied collection of national flags this side of the United Nations. Cattle is the traditional industry. The Utah mine may be inspected but you should telephone Utah first on 82 5166. **In the area:** The picturesque Expedition Range, 732 m, discovered by Ludwig Leichhardt. **Accommodation:** 4 motels, 2 caravan/camping parks.
Map ref. 323 K3

Boonah   Population 1874.
South-west of Brisbane between Warwick and Ipswich, Boonah is the main town in the Fassifern district, a highly-productive agricultural and pastoral area. The 'beautiful vale' was noted by Captain Logan in 1827, and by explorer Allan Cunningham in 1828. **Of interest:** Annual Potato Festival first week in September. **In the area:** Moogerah Dam, 20 km south-west. Fassifern Valley National Park. Coochin-Coochin historic homestead. **Accommodation:** Limited.
Map ref. 316 G5, 323 P11

Boulia   Population 292.
At the junction of the Diamantina and Kennedy Development Roads, Boulia is the capital of the Channel Country. The mysterious Min Min light has been seen within 24 km of the town and this phenomenon attracts an increasing number of visitors. Boulia is on the Burke River, and Wills Creek, north of the town, is another reminder of the explorers who first went there. **Travel by road in the 'wet' season is not possible. Outback motoring guide-lines should be observed. Accommodation:** 1 hotel, 1 motel, 1 caravan park.
Map ref. 321 D2, 327 D13

Bowen   Population 7660.
A relaxed town exactly half-way between Mackay and Townsville, Bowen was named after Queensland's first Governor. The town started in 1861 on the protected shores of Port Dennison and was the first settlement in North Queensland. It boasts an excellent climate and an average of eight hours sunshine daily throughout the year. Bowen is famous for its tomatoes and, particularly, for its tropical mangoes, in season from November to January. Don't wear your best clothes when eating them; they're delicious and very, very juicy. **Of interest:** Sign-posted 'Golden Arrow' tourist route starting of the Salt Works. Historical Museum (recommended). Delta shell display and museum. **In the area:** Collinsville, with its important coal mines and power station, is 85 km inland. **Accommodation:**   3 hotels,   5 motels, 7 caravan/camping parks.
Map ref. 325 J9, 331 A1

the population was some 10 000, but the field was not as golden as the Palmer.

This caused an unusual situation with the interior opened up before a direct route to the coast had been discovered and a port founded. During 1876 several difficult tracks were cut down the steep densely-jungled coastal ranges towards **Port Douglas** and **Trinity Bay**. Rivalry developed between the two anchorages, with Trinity Bay eventually being dominant and becoming **Cairns**. Some epic hauls up the range were recorded. A double team of bullocks, yoked four abreast, took ten tonnes of mining machinery from Port Douglas to Kingsborough; in 1881, 80 bullocks hauled up the complete battery for the Great Northern tin mine at **Herberton** (324 F4). An impressive monument at the foot of the Cairns-Kuranda Road, the Kennedy Highway, commemorates the trailblazers who opened tracks from the Tableland to the coast and the outlet for the Hodgkinson gold.

The railway line from Cairns to **Kuranda**, on the edge of the Tableland, is only 34 kilometres long but took four years to build, cost 20 workers their lives, and has 15 tunnels. It was completed in 1888, and the prosperity of the Atherton Tableland, and Cairns, was assured.

In April 1877, John Atherton settled at the junction of Emerald Creek and the Barron River, and formed Emerald End station. When he found alluvial tin in the headwaters of the creek he reputedly yelled 'tin-hurroo' to his mate; hence the name of the area, **Tinaroo**. Atherton was interested in cattle, not tin, but he led others to major tin lodes on the Wild River, discovered by Mulligan four years earlier. Mining commenced and the town of Herberton came into existence. The Tate River field was also important. Tin was more influential in the development of the area than the short-term excitement of gold.

In 1880, Atherton built a wide-verandahed shanty at Granite Creek, a popular camping ground half-way between Port Douglas and Herberton used by men flocking to the new field. This became Mareeba. Eventually the railway linked Herberton and Ravenshoe with Cairns. Today, Herberton is an interesting historic town which holds a Tin Festival every September. The local museum, called the Tin Pannikin, is in a classic old (unlicensed) pub, and is a tourist 'must'.

Ravenshoe (324 F5) (pronounced Ravens-ho, not Raven-shoe) is on the Palmerston Highway 93 kilometres west of **Innisfail**, and is 30 kilometres south of Atherton on the Kennedy Highway. It is noted for its gemstones and the fine cabinet timbers grown and milled in the area. The Torimba Festival shows off the district's products every August.

Mount Garnet (324 F5), 47 kilometres west of Ravenshoe, is an old copper mining town where tourists can 'pan the tailings' for alluvial tin.

The rich dairy country around **Malanda** (324 F4), 14 kilometres south-east of Atherton, supplies milk for what is known as the longest milk run in the world; to **Weipa, Mount Isa, Darwin,** and into Western Australia. A Dairy Festival is held every August.

Millaa Millaa (324 F4), 24 kilometres south of Malanda, has a cheese factory, and the nearby Millaa Millaa, Zillie and Elinjaa waterfalls. McHugh Lookout gives an excellent view of the southern Tableland.

Tinaburra is a popular tourist settlement on Tinaroo Dam. Nearby on the Malanda-Yungaburra (335 D12) road is the amazing and much-photographed curtain fig tree.

Queensland's National Parks

The diverse regions of the Queensland national parks lure visitors by the million each year. Not only are visitors drawn to the endless stretches of sandy beaches and magnificent Great Barrier Reef cays of the east coast, but also to the cooler mountainous regions of the southern border ranges, the arid western desert areas, and to the islands and rainforests of Cape York.

Most of the reserves are accessible by private vehicle; their main attraction is a climate which is suitable for recreation all year round. Certainly, daytime temperatures in the north and west can reach a searing 40°C, yet, in 1984, snow fell in several areas! The wet season (October-May) brings the occasional cyclone and rainfall that can be measured in metres but, other than these extremes, the climate is pleasant for day visits and for extended hiking, camping, and other nature-orientated activities.

Today Cape York Peninsula is like a magnet to tourists, even though the only aim of many of the thousands of visitors may be simply to stand at the tip. The area excels in rugged river gorges, spectacular waterfalls, placid lakes, lush rainforests and a wide variety of wildlife. A growing number of visitors divert to Lakefield, the state's second largest national park, encompassing 537 000 hectares. Its rainforests, open forests, plains, and coastal flats leading to mangroves fringing Princess Charlotte Bay, offer a variety of attractions for the most demanding visitor. Basic campsites are found along the many watercourses. A fly-in resort is proposed.

Within a several hundred kilometre radius of **Cairns** are scores of national parks catering for all tastes. Chillagoe National Park, four and a half hours' drive from Cairns, is dominated by weird castle-like pinnacles of limestone outcrops, housing a wonderland of colourful caves with exquisite underground rock formations. Guided tours around the caves take place twice a day, more frequently during holidays on request. This area, once Queensland's leading mineral producing area, is now popular with fossikers. Fishing is excellent at the Tate and Walsh Rivers.

About 50 kilometres from Cairns is the Atherton Tableland, within which lie several national parks. Here visitors can take excellent walking tracks through rainforest, or can visit the 65-metres wide Millstream Falls, or the crater lakes of Eacham and Barrine.

A north Queensland trip would not be complete without a train trip to Kuranda via Barron Falls National Park, or a visit to the Bellenden Ker, Cape Tribulation, and Daintree National Parks; such areas of undeveloped mountainous country, scenic waterfalls and lush rainforest should not be missed.

One of the most breathtakingly beautiful scenic reserves in Australia is Carnarvon National Park, 720 kilometres north-west of Brisbane. Carnarvon Gorge is a dramatic twisted chasm with sandstone walls of rust and yellow. Bushwalkers can hike through forests of eucalypt, she-oaks, tall cabbage palms and relic macrozamia palms, ferns, vines, moss gardens, and an array of orchids and spring wildflowers. In the pools and streams, schools of perch and catfish can be seen. There are caves with Aboriginal rock paintings of great sacred and ceremonial significance. During holidays there are limits on campsites; booking is essential. Mount Moffat, Salvator Rosa, Ka Ka Mundi, and Blackdown National Parks are also popular reserves.

Queensland's coastal islands range from large steep continental types to genuine coral cays, many of them lying in the vast lagoon between the mainland and the outer limit of the Great Barrier Reef; this makes access by launch or light aircraft easy. The larger islands are developed for tourism. Their popularity means heavy bookings during holiday periods. Check with the rangers if you wish to camp; many island parks do not permit camping. If you plan to camp, it is essential to take sufficient drinking water with you. **Dunk Island**, just south of **Innisfail**, is famed for its tranquility and unspoiled beauty. Further south is **Hinchinbrook**, the largest island off the Queensland coast, an area of wilderness and quiet beaches. Access is by launch from **Cardwell** and **Lucinda**. More than 90 per cent of the 100 islands in the Whitsunday/Cumberland Group (including Conway National Park) is national park and a number of these islands are resorts. Sail-yourself-yachts are a novel way for the experienced to visit some of the more isolated spots.

Eungella National Park, 83 kilometres west of Mackay, is the Aboriginal 'Land of the Clouds'. One of Queensland's wildest andd most majestic parks, the cool, fresh atmosphere under the canopy of rainforest makes it perfect for a day trip. Many, however, choose to camp in these superb surroundings: deep gorges, fast-flowing streams, towering mountains, and over 100 species of birds. In the long pools beside the camping grounds, visitors can often see platypuses swimming, surprisingly tolerant of their human audience.

A launch from **Gladstone** will take the visitor to **Heron Island**, rich in coral and marine life, and a paradise for snorkellers and scuba divers. It is one of the few breeding places of the giant eastern turtle and the nesting grounds for thousands of mutton birds returning from their long migratory flights from the northern hemisphere.

Off **Tin Can Bay** is the world's largest sand island, **Fraser**. The northern third of the island is national park; contact the ranger at **Dundubara** (336 H6) for camping and driving permits. Mount Tempest (**Moreton Island**) and Cooloola National Parks require four wheel drive vehicles for access; the latter offers excellent boating opportunities, particularly on Noosa River. All three parks are served by barges.

Noosa National Park, 160 kilometres north of Brisbane, offers the visitor a wide variety of vegetation and coastal scenery. From lookouts, you can see unusual rock formations such as 'Hell's Gates', 'Boiling Pot' and 'Fairy Pool'.

Further south towards Brisbane, lies the Glasshouse Mountains area — eroded volcanic plugs rising suddenly from the landscape. They were first sighted by Captain James Cook in 1770, and today they provide a challenge for rock climbers.

Bunya Mountains National Park, 250 kilometres north of Brisbane, was established to preserve the last remaining community of bunya pines. Here, Aboriginies used to gather every third year to feast on the nuts of the bunyas — these towering giants of the forest.

The crescent of national parks, or 'Scenic Rim', around Brisbane includes (among the many) Mount Mistake, Main Range, Mount Barney, and Lamington National Parks and those within the Springbrook area. These offer Brisbane dwellers and visitors great recreational opportunities. Lamington National Park, for instance, located 600 metres above sea level, attracts visitors by the thousands to its cool rainforest, rich in elkhorn and staghorn ferns and over 700 species of orchids of all sizes and colours. A number of graded walking tracks fan out and lead to panoramic views of the valleys below.

Eight national parks at **Tamborine** also attract many day visitors to their rainforests, waterfalls, and lookouts.

The Girraween National Park, south of **Stanthorpe** and close to the New South Wales border, offers visitors the best floral displays in the state, with its rare ground orchids, the Wallangarra white gums and barren white mallee. It is a photographer's paradise and the massive granite tors and boulders provide a challenge for the rockclimber.

For more information about Queensland's national parks, contact the National Parks and Wildlife Service, 293 George Street, Brisbane, Qld 4000.

Buderim Population 4015.

Buderim is a delightful town just inland from the Sunshine Coast in a high area of fertile red soil between the Bruce Highway and Mooloolaba on the coast. It is unique in *not* having a hotel! Strawberries, avocados, citrus and tropical fruit are grown as well as ginger. It is a popular residential and retirement area. **Of interest:** There is a deer sanctuary at Forest Glen. Visit the Super Bee; here you can see honey in the making. A genuine pioneer timber cottage in Ballinger Road, one of Buderim's earliest houses, has been faithfully restored to its 1876 style retaining much of its original furnishings. The cottage is open daily. **In the area:** Buderim Zoo and Koala Park at Buderim, turn-off on Bruce Highway. Dino Fun Park which features a fibreglass dinosaur, at the Buderim turn-off. Footes Sanctuary rainforest area off the Mooloolaba road. **Accommodation:** 4 motels, 2 caravan/camping parks.
Map ref. 307 G9, 313 L10

Bundaberg Population 32 560.

Bundaberg, 374 km north of Brisbane, is an important provincial city in the centre of the fertile Burnett river plains, with some good surf beaches nearby. Sugar is the main crop, along with tobacco, tropical fruit, peanuts, pineapples, vegetables and dairy products. Bundaberg's most famous son was Squadron-Leader H. J. L. (Bert) Hinkler who, in 1928, became the first man to fly solo from England to Australia. It is a city of wide, tree-lined streets with bauhinias and poincianas making a brilliant display in the spring. Sugar has been grown in the area since 1866, and two important sidelines of the industry are the distilling of the popular Bundaberg rum and the manufacture and export of advanced sugar harvesting equipment. **Of interest:** Hinkler House Memorial Museum displays items of aviation history. The Hummock, 100 metres high, is the only hill in the area. Versatile Toft Pty Ltd, manufacturers of the world's largest range of cane harvesting equipment, are in North Bundaberg. (Ph. 72 2622 ext 291 for tour.) Millaquin Sugar Mill offers a most interesting tour of the Rum Distillery and Sugar Refinery. It is unique in Australia and is one of only three places in the world where a sugar mill, refinery and distillery can be seen on the same site. Boyd's Antiquatorium in Bourbong St has a replica of George Stephenson's *Rocket*. Allamanda Art Gallery. Around the World Doll Museum. The Tourist Office is situated in the School of Arts building in Bourbong St. **In the area:** Dream Time Reptile Reserve, 4 km south, Avocado Grove Tourist Gardens, 9 km south. Bingera Weir, a popular picnic area, is 20 km south-west. Bargara, an excellent surf beach 13 km east; turtles nest on nearby Mon Repos beach between October and March. Moore Park surf beach, 23 km north. Fishing at Burnett Heads, 15 km east, at the river mouth. **Accommodation:** 15 hotels, 23 motels, 6 caravan/camping parks.
Map ref. 323 P6

Burketown Population under 200.
Situated on the Albert River, 65 km inland from the coast of the Gulf of Carpentaria, Burketown is at the centre of rich beef country. During the 'wet', from December to March (sometimes longer), Burketown can be isolated for weeks on end. Long sections of road in this area are unsealed and are suitable only for experienced outback motorists. **Of interest:** The Barramundi championships held Easter Weekend with prize money of $15 000. The Gregory Downs Hotel, 117 km south of Burketown, is the only supply stop on this road. **Accommodation:** 1 caravan/camping park.
Map ref. 327 C3

Burrum Heads Population 895.
This pleasant holiday resort on Hervey Bay offers excellent fishing. It is 17 km from the town of Burrum on the Bruce Highway, 27 km north of Maryborough. The Burrum River and Woodgate National Parks are close by. **Accommodation:** 2 caravan/camping parks.
Map ref. 323 P6

Caboolture Population 6451
A major dairying centre just off the Bruce Highway 46 km north of Brisbane, Caboolture is noted for its butter, yoghurt and cheese. Fruit, tobacco, cattle and poultry are also useful to the economy. The name comes from the Aboriginal word for carpet snake, and the area is rich in Aboriginal history and relics. The district was opened up in the 1860s for grazing, sugar and cotton. **In the area:** The distinctive landmarks of the Glasshouse Mountains. Bribie Island. The fishing resorts of Toorbul, Donnybrook, Beachmere and Deception Bay. **Accommodation:** 1 caravan/camping park.
Map ref. 315 K41, 323 Q10

Cairns Population 48 531.
Cairns the capital of tropical far north Queensland is Queensland's most casual, exciting and colourful city. Almost 2000 km north of Brisbane, Cairns is an enticing destination for young and old alike. There is reef fishing for the amateur out to catch a Red Emperor or Wrasse or big game fishing for the more famous anglers doing battle with the giant Black Marlin. The week-long 'Fun in the Sun' Festival is held every October. Tropical far north Queensland is Australia's highest rainfall area and during the summer months conditions become humid. Cairns is the northern terminal of the airconditioned *Sunlander* rail service from Brisbane. It is also the end of coastal Highway 1, although the scenic Captain Cook Highway continues on to Mossman. Further north, the road leads to the beautiful Daintree River Valley and the magnificent rainforest country at Cape Tribulation. About half of the 335 km road to Cooktown is now bitumen sealed offering a safe half-day drive from Cairns to historical Cooktown. Sugar cane growing was established in the 1880s. Kanaka labour from the Pacific Islands was brought into the country as it was considered too hot for Europeans to work in the canefields. Early development included a rail line to Herberton beyond the Atherton Tableland for the haulage of tin and other ore produces. Cairns was proclaimed a town in 1903 and a city in 1923. Today, the Cairns district still relies heavily on sugar for its prosperity. There are 4 sugar mills, one each at Mossman, Gordonvale, Babinda and Edmonton and the complete production passes through the bulk sugar terminal at Smith's Creek. The Visitors' Information Centre in McLeod St is open on weekdays from 9 am to 5 pm. The Cairns Botanical Gardens are rated among the best in Australia, while nearby Centenary Lakes is a popular picnic and area for visitors. The Civic Centre, Florence and Sheridan Sts, is the Arts and Cultural Centre. **Of interest:** Cairns Reef World on the Esplanade has an outstanding display of fish and coral. Feeding time daily is at 2 pm. Laroc Coral Jewellery Factory conducts a similar dive under the reef at its technicolour theatre. Cairns is the home base of Air Queensland, formerly Bush Pilots, and flights are conducted daily over the Great Barrier Reef, rainforests and to Cooktown and Lizard Island. The Royal Flying Doctor Service has a major base at Edge Hill, which incorporates 'School of the Air' a service for children living in remove areas. A weighing gantry at the Marlin Public Jetty is used each year for the weigh-in of game fish. **In the area:** Coach tours to Port Douglas, the Atherton Tablelands and

Southern Reef Islands

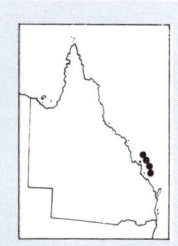

Great Keppel Island (329) is 48 kilometres east of **Rockhampton** and, though not a Barrier Reef island, its beauty and facilities are better than some of the more well-known islands. There are 17 beaches of squeaky-clean sand and unspoiled tropical island scenery. An excellent resort caters for 194 guests. Camping is allowed on several islands; contact the Queensland National Parks and Wildlife Service. There is a good coral reef between Great Keppel and **Humpy** Islands, best seen through a glass-bottomed boat. Take a light plane from Rockhampton, or a launch from **Rosslyn Bay** near **Yeppoon**.

Heron Island (329) is a very small, genuine coral island 72 kilometres offshore from **Gladstone**. Heron is only about one kilometre across, with a continuous white sand beach and coral reef. The island has dense palms, pandanus, pisonia, tournefortia and she-oaks, and is world famous for its bird life, including sea eagles, noddy terns, mutton birds and, of course, herons. Over 1150 types of fish have been recorded in the lagoon. The island and reefs are a national park and wildlife sanctuary, and there is a Marine Biological Research Station. It is a mecca for divers and scuba gear may be hired. Turtles come ashore to lay eggs between October and April. Accommodation is for 205 in sensible rather than luxurious cabins. Transport is by launch or helicopter from Gladstone.

Barrier Reef Cruises

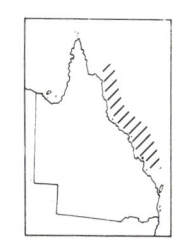

The Barrier Reef is Australia's most beautiful tourist attraction, and the best way to see it is by boat. If you don't have your own yacht, and the holiday budget won't stretch to chartering one, taking one of the many excellent cruises available through the reef and its islands is the obvious answer. The information below is intended as a basic guide only: seasonal and demand variations may apply.

From Rosslyn Bay near Yeppoon
The *Oceanus* and the *Fiesta* leave Rosslyn Bay Tourist Terminal every day for cruises and visits to Great Keppel Island. Visitors may choose to disembark on the island, spending about three hours ashore, or they may prefer to stay on board for the cruise around the island. Boom net riding is a popular pastime and you can view the coral, either through a mask if you're prepared to don snorkel and flippers, or by visiting the underwater observatory on Middle Island (tickets available on board). These two boats are also available for group bookings. Contact Great Keppel Cruises, PO Box 295, Yeppoon, Qld 4703; phone (079) 39 1825.

From Mackay
The *Elizabeth E* is a 34-metre 24-passenger ocean-going cruiser that offers four day/three night cruises through the Whitsunday Passage, visiting Hayman, South Molle and Hamilton Islands as well as the outer Barrier Reef. Contact *Elizabeth E* Coral Cruises, 102 Goldsmith Street, Mackay, Qld 4740; phone (079) 57 4281.

Roylen Cruises operate five day/four night cruises from Mackay to Brampton, Lindeman, Hayman and Whitsunday 100 – also to the outer Barrier Reef (weather permitting). A cruise leaves every Monday at noon. Charters can be arranged and 'cruise and stay' holidays at Brampton Island may be booked. Contact McLeans Roylen Cruises Pty Ltd, River Street (PO Box 169), Mackay, Qld 4740; phone (079) 57 2595.

Day cruises to Newry Island leave from Seaforth near Mackay at 11 am Wednesdays, Saturdays and Sundays; phone (079) 59 0214.

From Shute Harbour near Proserpine
Boats leave here for the Whitsunday Group, including the *Telford Capricorn* which does a three island cruise to Hook, South Molle and Daydream Islands. Other cruises visit Lindeman, Hayman, Happy Bay and South Molle Islands. Contact the Whitsunday Travel Centre, PO Box 98, Airlie Beach, Qld 4741; phone (079) 46 6224.

Charter boats and fishing trips are also available at Shute Harbour.

From Townsville
The *MV Reef Link* is a luxurious 22-metre, catamaran which cruises to John Brewer Reef, via Magnetic Island. The 'semi-submarine' offers a panoramic view of the reef's unique marine life. Snorkelling equipment may also be hired. Contact Reef Link Pty Ltd, 7 Tomlin Street, Townsville, Qld 4810; phone (077) 72 5733.

From Port Douglas
Another high speed catamaran is based at Port Douglas – the *MV Quicksilver* travels at 26 knots past Schnapper Island and Undine Cay to St Crispin Reef. A glass-bottomed boat offers views of the coral and refreshments are served on board. Contact Cairns Tour Service (070) 51 5547 or Port Douglas Tourist and Service Centre (070) 98 5373.

From Cairns
MV Coral Seatel (the 'Big Cat') cruises daily to Michaelmas Cay, the island of birds. You can see the colonies of sooty terns, crested terns and noddies or you may prefer to go snorkelling and discover the giant clams and coral of the Cay. The *Coral Islander* offers cruises to Green Island. For a different sort of cruise, the *SS Louisa* is a 15-tonne paddlewheel steamer that takes a two hour daily cruise around Admiralty Island in Trinity Inlet. Contact Great Barrier Reef Cruise Centre, PO Box 1763, Cairns, Qld 4870; phone (070) 51 7777.

A quicker way to see the reef and islands is by air. Several companies operate regular and charter flights.

TAA's *Coralair* service is by Twin Otter from Mackay to their own strip near Shute Harbour, and Brampton Island.

Lindeman Aerial Services fly between Mackay and Lindeman Island.

Air Whitsunday have scenic flights over the islands in the Whitsunday Group by small seaplanes, and you can land by remote Haslewood Island and swim and explore. Phone (079) 46 9133.

Air Queensland have regular interesting flights from Cairns to Cooktown and Lizard Island.

Innisfail and the spectacular train trip past the Barron Falls to Kuranda are among the tourist highlights. **Accommodation:** 17 hotels, 29 motels, 6 caravan/camping parks.
Map ref. 324 G3, 334, 335 F8

Calliope   Population 728.
Near the junction of the Bruce and Dawson Highways, a large aluminium smelter is at Boyne Island. **Accommodation:** 1 motel, 2 caravan/camping parks.
Map ref. 323 N4

Caloundra   Population 16 758.
This very popular beach resort on the Sunshine Coast is the closest one to Brisbane. It is 96 km north via a turn-off from the Bruce Highway. The main beaches are Kings, Shelley, Moffat and Dickey. The main shipping channel to Brisbane is just offshore, and the lighthouse is prominent. Caloundra Harbour is safe for fishing and for private boats, and Pumicestone Passage between Bribie Island and the mainland has sheltered water for fishing and water-skiing. Shopping and recreational facilities are excellent. **Of interest:** The *Endeavour* at Seafarer's Wharf is an authentic 2/3 scale replica of Captain Cook's ship. Open daily 9 am to 5 pm, this is a very interesting exhibit and well worth inspection. **In the area:** The Glasshouse Mountains. **Accommodation:** 3 hotels, 12 motels, 3 caravan/camping parks.
Map ref. 307 I12, 313 M12, 323 Q9

Camooweal   Population 251.
On the Barkly Highway 188 km west of Mount Isa, Camooweal is the last Queensland town reached before crossing the Northern Territory border. **Accommodation:** Limited.
Map ref. 327 A7

Cannonvale   Population 1216.
First of the three seaside resorts along the Shute Harbour Road from the Proserpine turn-off. **In the area:** Airlie Beach, Shute Harbour, Mandalay Coral Gardens, Conway National Park, Whitsunday Islands. **Accommodation:** 1 motel, 4 caravan/camping parks.
Map ref. 325 K9, 331 E4

Cardwell   Population 1249.
From Cardwell, 58 km north of Ingham, a beautiful view is obtained of Rockingham Bay and many islands, including the well known Hinchinbrook, all of which may be visited by boat from Cardwell. Even more spectacular coastal scenery may be seen from a lookout on the Cardwell Ranges to the west. Local fishing is generally excellent. **Accommodation:** 2 motels, 3 caravan/camping parks.
Map ref. 324 G6

Charleville   Population 3523.
Charleville marks the terminus of the *Westlander* rail service and is at the centre of a rich pastoral district carrying some 800 000 sheep and 100 000 cattle. The town has some interesting history. Charleville's river, the Warrego, was explored by Edmund Bourke in 1847, and in 1862 William Landsborough camped nearby when searching for Burke and Wills. By the 1890s Charleville was a frontier town with its own brewery, ten pubs and 500 registered bullock teams. Cobb and Co. has a coach-building factory here in 1893. The last coach on Australian roads ran to Surat in 1923. A monument 19 km north of the town marks the spot where Ross and Keith Smith landed with engine trouble on the first flight from London to Sydney in 1919. Amy Johnson also landed here in 1920. Qantas started flights from Charleville in 1922.

Charleville proudly calls itself the heart of the Mulga Country. The trees provide welcome shade and in times of drought are cut down and used as sheep fodder. The town has a Flying Doctor base, a school of the air, a pastoral research laboratory, well-attended winter cattle sales, picnic races and the annual 'Booga Woongaroo Festival' in September. **Of interest:** A tree blazed by Landsborough in 1862 is 19 km downstream from the town. Historical museum in the restored (1880) Queensland National Bank building in Albert St and an Art and Crafts shop is opposite. The amazing 5 metres long 'vortex gun' was used in unsuccessful rainmaking experiments in 1902. The 'Weary Willie' swagman statue is in main street. **Accommodation:** 6 hotels, 3 motels, 2 caravan/camping parks.
Map ref. 322 G8

Charters Towers   Population 6823.
This peaceful and historic city once had a gold rush population of some thirty thousand. Between 1872 and 1916 Charters Towers produced ore worth 25 million pounds ($50m). On December 25, 1871 a young Aboriginal boy called Jupiter found the first 'strike' while looking for horses that had bolted during a thunderstorm. He brought some quartz back to his boss. Hugh Mosman, rode to Ravenswood to register his claim, and the gold rush was on. The Government rewarded Mosman with £1000, and he in turn adopted and educated young Jupiter.

Charters Towers is 135 km inland from Townsville on the road and rail line to Mount Isa. Cattle is the main industry, in the Dalrymple Shire, together with citrus and grapes. Much of the classic early Australian architecture with its verandahs and lacework still remains. The city is regarded as the educational centre of North Australia with several boarding schools. **Of interest:** The Tourist Information Centre and Military Museum in Gill Street. The old Stock Exchange has been restored. Old Venus treatment battery. Buckland's Hill lookout. **In the area:** Ravenswood, a small mining town. **Accommodation:** 2 hotels, 4 motels, 2 caravan/camping parks.
Map ref. 324 G9

Childers   Population 1406.
Childers is a small sugar town, 53 km south of Bundaberg. The cane is crushed at the Isis Central Sugar Mill at Cordalba. **Of interest:** The Taur-Aries Leather-arts Centre in North St is housed in an old butcher's shop, built in 1896. Many of the original chopping blocks and implements remain. **Accommodation:** 3 motels, 1 caravan/camping park.
Map ref. 323 P6

Chillagoe   Population under 200.
Once a thriving mining town for copper, silver-lead, gold and wolfram, the smelters stopped in 1943. A museum recalls the town's mining heyday. The rugged castle-like limestone outcrops in the Chillagoe-Mungana Caves National Park contain many fascinating caves. Regular guided tours are offered through three of them, including one which takes some two hours through the floodlit Donna Cave (9 am and 1.30 pm). Further information from the Ranger, National Parks and Wildlife Service, PO Box 38, Chillagoe, 4871 (Ph. Chillagoe 13). Bring torch. Situated about 120 km inland from Atherton, Chillagoe can also be reached by following an interesting 98 km dirt road from Dimbulah on the Atherton Tableland. **Accommodation:** 2 motels, 2 caravan/camping parks.
Map ref. 324 E4, 326 G12

Chinchilla   Population 3092.
Chinchilla is a prosperous and interesting town in the western Darling Downs, 354 km west of Brisbane and 81 km north-west of Dalby on the Warrego Highway. Ludwig Leichhardt named the area in 1847 from 'Jinchilla', the local Aboriginal name for cypress pines. Grain growing is the traditional industry, plus cattle, sheep, pigs, timber and, more recently, grapes and watermelons. **Of interest:** Chinchilla Folk Museum is worth a visit. There's a Polocrosse and Picnic Race Day in May. Fishing on Charley's Creek and the Condamine River. **In the area:** Barakula State Forest, 40 km north, is Queensland's largest commercial forest. Petrified wood, fossils and gemstones are found near Eddington, 20 km south-west. **Accommodation:** 1 hotel, 1 motel, 1 caravan/camping park.
Map ref. 323 M9

Clermont   Population 1659.
Centre of a fertile region which breeds cattle and sheep, and grows wheat, sorghum safflower and sunflower as well as hardwood timber, Clermont is 108 km north west of Emerald on the Gregory Highway. Nearby is the Blair Athol opencut mine, the largest seam of steaming coal in the world. About 170 houses were built in 1982 in Clermont for Blair Athol coal workers. The town takes its name from Clermont in France. **Accommodation:** 2 motels.
Map ref. 322 I2, 324 I13

Clifton   Population 659.
Just off the highway between Toowoomba and Warwick in the Darling Downs, Clifton is the centre of a rich grain-growing and dairying area. **Of interest:** Arthur Hoey Davis, 'Steele Rudd', who wrote the famous Dad and Dave stories *On Our Selection*, grew up in the area. Sister Kenny, remembered for her method of treating poliomyelitis, is buried at the nearby rural settlement of Nobby. **Accommodation:** Limited.
Map ref. 323 O11

The GOLD COAST

One hour's drive from Brisbane takes you to Australia's favourite and most famous playground, the Gold Coast, so named for its sunshine and golden beaches.

At the turn of the century, the Gold Coast was solely for the rich, who came to escape Brisbane's hot summers. Today, it is the most intensively developed and highly publicised tourist resort in Australia.

This 34-kilometres strip of beachland, located between Southport and Coolangatta, welcomes more than three million people each year. The beaches range from the still waters of Labrador to the surfing centres at Main Beach, Northcliffe and Surfers Paradise. There are also cove-and-headland style beaches at Nobby's, Miami and Currumbin.

Although most visitors head straight for the sun and surf, the Gold Coast offers many other activities such as boating, fishing, horse riding, golf, bowling and even roller skating. There is also a wide range of holiday attractions for the whole family — Grundy's at Surfers Paradise, the bird sanctuary at Currumbin, and the national park at Burleigh Heads. At Nobby's Beach, you can take a scenic ride in open chairs up to the headland where a fairytale castle provides a panoramic view of the white sands below. 'Sea World' at The Spit, Southport, Dreamworld at Coomera. Southport also has the only laserama in the southern hemisphere.

At night there is a great variety of restaurants, nightclubs and discos, and a casino to attract the visitor.

There should be no problem finding somewhere to stay as the Gold Coast has more than three thousand accommodation places, ranging from modest guesthouses to luxury penthouse suites. For more information, contact the Queensland Government Travel Centre or the Gold Coast Visitors' Advisory Centre at Surfers Paradise.

ABOVE: *Looking towards Surfers Paradise on the beautiful Nerang River.*

BELOW: *Friendly parrots at Currumbin Bird Sanctuary.*

BELOW: *Holidaymakers enjoy the beach at Burleigh Heads.*

ABOVE: *Cavill Mall, a popular meeting place at Surfers Paradise.*

SUNSHINE COAST

A chain of sun-gold beaches bathed by the blue Pacific stretches from Rainbow Beach southward to Bribie Island to form Queensland's Sunshine Coast. This scenic coastal region, with its average winter temperature of 20°C, its leisurely pace, wide variety of natural attractions and sporting facilities, offers an alternative to the more commercialised Gold Coast.

While huge waves thunder in on to white sand beaches to provide year-round surfing, the calmer waters of protected beaches ensure safe swimming, boating and water-skiing. Rivers and streams are alive with fish to lure the angler and forest-fringed lakes become perfect picnic spots for the family.

The Sunshine Coast is blessed with many wonders of nature. The coloured sands of Teewah in Cooloola National Park, between Tewantin and Rainbow Beach, rise in multi-coloured cliffs to over 200 metres. Geologists say that these sand cliffs are over 40 000 years old, and claim the main colouring agent is from oxide or from the dye of vegetation decay. But the Aboriginal legend is that the colours come from a rainbow which came to the rescue of a black maiden and was killed by a boomerang.

Another marvel of nature are the Glasshouse Mountains formed by giant cores of long extinct volcanoes.

BELOW: *Noosa Heads and Laguna Bay.*

Noosaville and Tewantin, at the northern end of the main area, have facilities for fishing, boating and golf. Poised on the edge of Laguna Bay is the resort of Noosa Heads, with its 382-hectares National Park. This coastal park contains a network of walking tracks that wind through rainforests, giving spectacular ocean views of unusual rock formations such as Hell's Gates, Paradise Caves, Lion's Rock, Devil's Kitchen and Witches' Cauldron. The park also houses an animal sanctuary and coastal lakes, inhabited by elegant black swans, pelicans, ducks and cranes.

The southernmost town of the Sunshine Coast is Caloundra, 'the beautiful place', where Aboriginals once came down from the hills to feast on seafood.

South of Caloundra is Bribie Island, the quiet corner of the Sunshine Coast. Situated just 72 kilometres from Brisbane, this enchanting island, with its beautiful surroundings and wildlife, is easily accessible via a bridge at Toorbul Point.

The hinterland of the Sunshine Coast is like a huge cultivated garden, covered with pineapples, sugar cane, ginger and citrus, dotted with dairy farms and enclosing within its folds cascading waterfalls, lush rainforests and bubbling

BELOW: *Rolling hills near Nambour in the Blackall Ranges, just inland from the Sunshine Coast.*

streams. Looming majestic behind this garden of plenty are the Blackall Ranges, with picturesque mountain resorts at Montville, Mapleton and Maleny. A particular attraction is the Kondalilla Falls, tumbling 75 metres into a valley of rainforest and palms. Nambour is conveniently located on the Bruce Highway for trips to the mountains of the Blackall Ranges or to the beach.

The Sunshine Coast has a wide range of accommodation to suit every budget. There are also caravan parks and camping areas established near both beach and inland resorts. For more information about the Sunshine Coast, contact the Queensland Government Travel Centre or the Sunshine Coast Tourist Board at Buderim.

BELOW: *The cliffs at Teewah change colour as the sun rises and sets.*

Cloncurry Population 1957.

An important mining town 124 km east of Mount Isa, Cloncurry has an interesting history. In 1861, John McKinley of Adelaide, leading an expedition to search for Burke and Wills, reported distinctive traces of copper in the area. Six years later, pioneer pastoralist Ernest Henry discovered the first copper lodes. A rail link to Townsville was built in 1908. During World War 1, Cloncurry was the centre of a copper boom and in 1916 it was the largest source of copper in Australia, with four smelters operating. After copper prices slumped following the war, a pastoral industry took its place. In 1920 a new Qantas air service linked Cloncurry to Winton and in 1928 the town became the base for the famous Royal Flying Doctor Service. In 1974 a rare type of exceptionally pure 22 carat gold, resembling crystallised straw, was discovered. It is now used for jewellery making. **Of interest:** The court-house; the Chinese and Afghan cemeteries; Cloister of Plaques (Flying Doctor Service memorial). Outdoor museum in Ramsay St. Indoor museum in Scarr St. Merry Muster Rodeo is held each August. **In the area:** Alluvial gold workings at Soldier's Cap, 48 km to the south-west Kuridala ghost town. Burke and Wills cairn at Corella River. **Accommodation:** 3 hotels, 1 motel.
Map ref. 327 E8

Cooktown Population 908.

Captain James Cook beached the *Endeavour* here in 1770 to repair damage after running aground on a coral reef. In 1874 Cooktown was a booming, brawling gold rush port for the up-country field at Palmer River, with a transient population of some 30 000 (including 2500 Chinese) and 94 busy pubs. Ten years and five million pounds-worth ($10m) of gold later, it was all over. In 1907 a cyclone flattened much of what was left of the original town. Today Cooktown is still a fascinating spot, even if there are only 3 pubs left! Access is by launch or by air from Cairns, or by a half gravel, half bitumen road inland 330 km from Mossman, via Mt Molloy. **Of interest:** Bank of New South Wales (classified building); Sir Joseph Banks Gardens; James Cook Museum; Hopevale Aboriginal Mission; Endeavour River National Park, west of Cooktown; and the Cooktown Discovery Festival (June) when Cook's landing is re-enacted. **Accommodation:** 3 hotels, 4 motels, 3 caravan/camping parks.
Map ref. 324 F1, 326 I9

Coolangatta Pop. part of Gold Coast.

The most southerly of Queensland's coastal towns, Coolangatta's twin town of Tweed Heads is across the border in NSW. All the typical Gold Coast attractions are here: lovely beaches, bowls, roller skating, ten pin bowling and even croquet. **Of interest:** At Tweed Heads there is Waterworld which has a water slide, paddle boats and a pin ball parlour. There is also a display of coral and a sea-lion show twice daily. At Point Danger is the Captain Cook Memorial and Lighthouse. **In the area:** Coolangatta aerodrome, a short distance from town, offers joyflights, or for those who prefer to keep their feet on the ground, the Razorback lookout behind Tweed Heads offers splendid views of the shore, the mountains and Terranora Lakes. **Accommodation:** 3 motels.
Map ref. 317 R8, 319 P4, 323 Q12

Cooroy Population 1429.

At this small township and railway station on the Bruce Highway between Nambour and Gympie is the turn-off to Noosa Heads, 24 km away on the Sunshine Coast. **Accommodation:** Limited.
Map ref. 307 C2, 313 J6

Crows Nest Population 1037.

This small town 45 km north of Toowoomba acquired its name from one Jim Crow, an Aboriginal from the Kabi-Kabi tribe who once made his home in a hollow tree near what is now the police station. A life-size memorial commemorates this legend. **Of interest:** An authentic split timber and shingle pioneer's hut is on the Crows Nest to Cooyar road. **In the area:** Crows Nest Falls National Park, 6 km (look for the roadsign to 'Valley of Diamonds'). Several km of walking track lead to the falls and gorge. Picnic and camping (above falls) facilities available. **Accommodation:** 1 caravan/camping park.
Map ref. 323 O10

Cunnamulla Population 1627.

A western sheep town renowned for its friendliness and hospitality. It is on the Warrego River 122 km north of the NSW border and is the biggest wool loading station on the Queensland railway network, with some 2 million sheep in the area, plus beef cattle and Angora goats. Explorers Sir Thomas Mitchell and Edmund Kennedy were the first white visitors in 1846 and 1847, and by 1879 it had become a town with regular Cobb and Co. services. In 1880 a daring but disorganised villain called Joseph Wells held up the local bank and tried to escape with the loot but couldn't find his horse. Irate locals bailed him up in a nearby tree, demanding justice, and their money back. The tree is still a landmark. **In the area:** Large varieties of wild flowers after rain. Yowah opal fields, 144 km west via Eulo on the Paroo River. Wildlife, including black swans, brolgas, seagulls, pelicans and eagles. Shearing sheds may be visited when working. **Accommodation:** 5 hotels, 2 motels, 1 caravan/camping park.
Map ref. 322 F11

Currumbin Pop. part of Gold Coast.

Situated at the mouth of the Currumbin Creek, this part of the Gold Coast has many attractions for visitors. At the famous Currumbin Bird Sanctuary, which is now owned by the National Trust of Queensland and is open 8 am to 5 pm, you can hand-feed colourful rainbow lorikeets and wander freely among other native animals and birds within the 20 ha reserve. There is a modern cafeteria at the Sanctuary which has indoor and outdoor settings and a ride around the Sanctuary on the miniature railway is both informative and pleasurable. The Land of Legend has thousands of dolls displayed in fairytale settings and there is an interesting sea shell museum, where shells and ornaments made from them can be purchased. **Accommodation:** 3 motels, 1 caravan/camping park.
Map ref. 317 Q8, 319 O7

Dalby Population 8784.

Dalby is a pleasant well-planned country town at the cross-roads of the Warrego, Bunya and Moonie Highways, 84 km north-west of Toowoomba on the Darling Downs. It is the centre of Australia's richest grain growing area, and cattle, pigs and sheep further add to the wealth of the district. **Of interest:** An obelisk in Edward St marks the spot where explorer Henry Dennis camped in 1841. The Cactoblastis Memorial Cairn in Myall Creek picnic area pays homage to the voracious Argentinian caterpillar which eradicated the dreaded prickly pear cactus in the 1920s. **In the area:** Jimbour House, not open for inspection, but you can enjoy a walk through the extensive gardens. Dalby Pioneer Park. Broadway Lagoon 29 km south-west is a pleasant spot for boating and water-skiing. **Accommodation:** 3 motels, 8 hotels, 2 caravan/camping parks.
Map ref. 323 N10

Dirranbandi Population 430.

A small pastoral township and railhead on the Balonne River, Dirranbandi is south-west of St George, close to the New South Wales border. **Accommodation:** 1 hotel, 1 caravan/camping park.
Map ref. 323 J12

Dysart Population 3257.

This new town in the Denham Range, east of Clermont, has been built near the coal centre of Moranbah to service the Utah open-cut coal mines of Saraji and Norwich Park. The coal is railed to Hay Point for shipment. **Accommodation:** 1 hotel, 1 motel, 1 caravan/camping park.
Map ref. 323 J2

Eidsvold Population 613.

The Eidsvold gold field was extremely productive for twelve years from 1888 and remains an attractive haunt for fossickers. The district is recognised as the state's best producer of quality beef cattle. Situated on the Burnett Highway 205 km north of Kingaroy, the Wuruma Dam, on the Nogo River 32 km to the north, is a popular spot for swimming, sailing and water-skiing. **Accommodation:** 1 caravan/camping park.
Map ref. 323 N7

Emerald Population 4628.

An attractive town, 266 km west of Rockhampton at the junction of the Capricorn and Gregory Highways, Emerald is rightly called the hub of the Central Queensland Highlands. As well as the long-established cattle industry, grain, oilseeds, soybeans and cotton are important. **Of interest:** Shady Moreton Bay fig trees line the main streets. The railway station was built in 1901 and is classified by the National Trust. Emerald Pastoral College. **In the area:** The new Gregory coal fields to the north. Fairbairn Dam,

19 km south, for picnics and water sports. Be careful of kangaroos and emus on the roads around Emerald. **Accommodation:** 6 motels, 6 caravan/camping parks.
Map ref. 323 J3

Emu Park Population 1429.
On the way to this pleasant seaside resort, 45 km north-east of Rockhampton, is St Christopher's Chapel, built by the US Army in 1942. Emu Park has excellent picnic spots and a safe beach. On a headland overlooking Keppel Bay is the unusual and graceful 'singing ship' memorial to Captain Cook, who sailed past in May, 1770. The memorial represents a billowing sail, mast and rigging. Hidden organ pipes create musical sounds in the sea breezes. **Accommodation:** 1 motel, 3 caravan/camping parks.
Map ref. 323 N3

Esk Population 676.
A small township in the Upper Brisbane Valley, Esk is near the Somerset Dam, source of Brisbane's main water supply, and Wivenhoe Dam. **Accommodation:** 1 hotel, 1 caravan/camping park.
Map ref. 314 D6, 323 P10

Darling Downs

The 72 500 square kilometres of black volcanic soil on the Darling Downs produce 90 per cent of the state's wheat, 50 per cent of its maize, 90 per cent of its oilseeds, two-thirds of its fruit and one-third of its tobacco, as well as oats, sorghum, millet, cotton, soybeans and navy beans. It is a major sheep and dairying area and the home of several famous bloodstock studs.

Allan Cunningham was the first white man to ride across these fertile plains in 1827.

The Darling Downs is rural Australia at its best, with a touch of England in the magnificent oaks, elms, plane trees and poplars of **Toowoomba**'s parks, and the colourful rose gardens of **Warwick** in the south. The climate is cooler and more bracing than in the rest of the state.

Driving across the Downs with its neat strips of grainfields, lush pastures, patches of forest and national parks, and well-established homesteads, gives the visitor a feeling of beauty and quiet prosperity.

The Warrego Highway leads north-west from Toowoomba to the wheat fields and silos of **Dalby**, the 'hub of the Downs'. Gowrie Mountain is a popular lookout, and historic Old Gowrie Homestead is on the **Kingsthorpe** road, just off the Warrego Highway. The Georgian-style house was built between 1866 and 1873 from imported English and American timbers and Italian marble, and paid for by profits made from selling wool. Conducted tours take place at 3 pm (Wednesday to Sunday). A little further on at **Mount Tyson** you can buy samples of locally made cheese on Saturday or Sunday mornings.

The New England Highway, the main Sydney to Brisbane route, turns into the Cunningham Highway at Warwick, and descends from the Downs towards the coast through Cunninghams Gap, discovered in 1827. Main Range National Park has lovely rainforest, palms and native wildlife. Another lesser used, but scenic, route is the Heifer Creek Way through the Lockyer Valley from near **Greenmount East** to **Gatton**.

Gatton Population 4190.
This thriving agricultural town in the Lockyer Valley is mid-way between Ipswich and Toowoomba, and 96 km west of Brisbane on the Warrego Highway. **Of interest:** The Queensland Agricultural College, opened 1897. **In the area:** Helidon, 14 km west, is noted for its spa water and Helidon freestone, used in many Brisbane buildings, including the University of Queensland. A Pioneer Village at Laidley, 20 km south-east, is open on Sunday afternoons only. **Accommodation:** 2 motels, 1 caravan/camping park.
Map ref. 314 B11, 323 P10

Gayndah Population 1703.
Gayndah claims to be Queensland's oldest town, having been founded in 1848. It is on the Burnett River and the Burnett Highway, just over 100 km due west of Maryborough. The district is famous for citrus fruit, particularly oranges, lemons, mandarins and grapefruit. The orchards are irrigated and use modern machinery. An Orange Festival is held every second (or odd) year, on the Queen's Birthday weekend. **Of interest:** The original school (1863) is still in use, and there are several homesteads in the district built in the 1850s. The main street was used as a location for the film, *The Mango Tree*. **In the area:** Ban Ban Springs, 26 km south of Gayndah, is a natural spring and popular picnic area. **Accommodation:** 3 motels, 2 caravan/camping parks.
Map ref. 323 O7

Georgetown Population 319.
This small township is on the Gulf Developmental Road to Croydon and Normanton. Once a goldfield, Georgetown is now noted for its gemstones, especially agate and onyx. It is also a trans-shipping centre for beef road trains. **In the area:** Ambo hot springs. **Accommodation:** 1 hotel, 1 caravan/camping park.
Map ref. 324 C6

Gin Gin Population 865.
Some of Queensland's oldest cattle properties are in the area of this pastoral town on the Bruce Highway, 52 km west of Bundaberg. Gregory Blaxland, one of the three explorers who first crossed the Blue Mountains, settled here in 1846. **In the area:** The Mystery Craters, 17 km along the Bundaberg Road, are a curious formation of 27 craters, estimated to be about five million years old. On the Kolan River north of Gin Gin is the Fred Haigh Dam, Queensland's second largest, where there are picnic facilities and a boat ramp. **Accommodation:** 2 motels, 1 caravan/camping park.
Map ref. 323 O6

Gladstone Population 22 080.
Matthew Flinders discovered Port Curtis, Gladstone's impressive deep-water harbour, in 1802. But it was not until the 1960s that its potential began to be utilised, and Gladstone developed boom-town status. In fact it has made a spectacular transition from a quiet coastal country town to a major industrial shipping complex. Gladstone is one of Australia's most prosperous seaboard cities as an outlet for Central Queensland's mineral and agricultural wealth. Its harbour is one of Australia's busiest, handling more shipping tonnage per annum than Sydney. The reason for this growth is the opening-up of the almost inexhaustible coal supplies in the hinterland. Coal from the Blackwater open-cut mine (Utah) is railed to and loaded from Auckland Point, and coal from Moura (Theiss-Peabody-Mitsui) is exported from Barney Point. The recently opened Clinton coal handling facilitiy, ships coal received from the Gregory Mine and the Blackwater Mine. The Auckland Point facilities also handle most of Central Queensland's rich wheat and sorghum crops, meat, and pyrites from Mount Morgan. Another reason for Gladstone's rapid expansion is that the world's largest single alumina plant is at Parsons Point, operated by the multinational backed Queensland Alumina Limited. Some four million tonnes of bauxite from Weipa on the Gulf of Carpentaria are processed annually into two million tonnes of alumina, the 'half-way stage' of aluminium. Comalco has built an aluminium

Capricornia

This is the rich and diverse slice of Queensland stretching inland from Rockhampton and Gladstone out to Emerald, and straddling the Tropic of Capricorn. The area includes the Central Queensland Highlands, and is drained by the Fitzroy, Mackenzie, Comet, Nogoa and Dawson Rivers. The district was first opened up by gold and copper mining around **Emerald** in the 1860s, and the discovery of sapphires around **Anakie** (322 I 3). The original owners of the land have left their heritage in superb and mysterious rock paintings on the silent stone walls of the Carnarvon Ranges to the south. Since European settlement cattle have been the economic mainstay, but vast tracts of brigalow scrub were cleared after World War 2 to grow wheat, maize, sorghum and safflower. These days coal has become king with mainly American companies gouging out enormous deposits for local and Japanese markets. On a smaller scale, professional and amateur fossickers are still finding gems, and a great deal of enjoyment.

For a good tour of Capricornia, drive west from **Rockhampton**, the commercial and manufacturing capital, along the Capricorn Highway. Detour to Blackdown Tableland National Park; the turn-off is between **Blackwater** and **Dingo** (323 L3). A permit is needed from the Forestry Department in **Duaringa**, or the Forestry Office in Rockhampton, to enter Blackdown Tableland Forestry Reserve. There are waterfalls, rock pools and camping areas. At Emerald turn south to **Springsure** (323 J4), then east to **Biloela** on the Dawson Highway. Continue on to **Gladstone** or north on the Burnett Highway via **Mount Morgan** back to Rockhampton.

Mt Hay Gemstone Tourist Park, 41 kilometres from Rockhampton, lets visitors fossick for thunder eggs and rhyolite, which may be cut and polished at the factory. Utah's Blackwater coal mine produces four million tonnes of coking coal and almost three million tonnes of steaming coal annually. Tours can be arranged.

Emerald is the main town in the western Capricornia region, with the central-western railway continuing much further west to **Longreach** and the Channel Country. **Clermont** and the **Blair Athol** (322 I 2) coalfields are 106 kilometres to the north-west. The gemfields of Anakie, **Rubyvale** (322 I 3), **Sapphire** (322 I 3), **Willows** (322 I 3) and **Tomahawk Creek** are west of Emerald, and are popular with tourists seeking a different holiday. A 'Miner's Right' is required. An informative map/brochure is produced by the RACQ.

Springsure, 63 kilometres south of Emerald, is one of Queensland's oldest towns, having been surveyed in 1854. It produces beef and grain. Nearby is Old Rainworth Fort at **Burnside**, a fascinating piece of Australiana, where early farm equipment, wool presses and the like are on display. It was built in 1853 from local stone. (Phone Springsure 74S first.)

Rolleston (323 K5), 70 kilometres to the south-east, is the turn-off to the magnificent Carnarvon National Park, 103 kilometres further south. The park is some 28 000 hectares of rugged mountains, forests, caves and deep gorges, some of which are Australia's earliest 'art galleries' with countless Aboriginal paintings and carvings, which in places extend in a colourful frieze for more than 50 metres.

Moura (323 M5) is a modern town closely associated with the coal mine, which has the world's second largest dragline that 'works as it walks'. Each step is two metres, with a scoop capacity of 200 tonnes. Tours start at 10 am weekdays from the main office except in wet weather. The mine is operated by Thiess Dampier Mitsui.

Another open-cut mine is the **Callide** (323 M5) near Biloela, the principal town in the Callide Valley. The nearby Callide Power Station supplies the Rockhampton, Moura and Blackwater districts as well as Biloela. Inspection can be arranged through the Station Engineer.

Mount Larcom (323 N4), between Gladstone and Rockhampton, is a rich area for dairying and fruit and tomato crops. **Yarwun** (323 N4) is noted for its delicious papaws.

What are known as 'Snowy Mounts' are actually huge piles of salt in the Fitzroy River delta between **Bajool** (323 N4) and **Port Alma** (323 N3). Underground salty water is pumped to the surface into pools called crystallisers, and the salt is 'harvested' during October/November after solar evaporation.

smelter at Boyne Island. A $500-million power station has been built in Gladstone to supply power to the alumina plant, as well as feeding into the state's electricity grid. Two rivers flow into Port Curtis, the Boyne and the Calliope; Auckland Creek, at the bottom of the main street, is the finishing line for the annual Brisbane to Gladstone yacht race, one of Australia's most important blue water classics. This is the highlight of the week-long Harbour Festival held every Easter. **In the area:** Quoin Island and Tannum Sands resorts in the harbour; Heron Island, 80 km by launch or helicopter, the most southerly of the Great Barrier Reef resorts. **Accommodation:** 21 motels, 5 caravan/camping parks.
Map ref. 323 N4, 328 G9

Goondiwindi   Population 3575.
This attractive and busy country town on the Cunningham Highway (which continues from the Newell) is on the Queensland/New South Wales border and the Macintyre River, which was discovered by explorer Allan Cunningham in 1827. The Aboriginal word 'goonawinna' means 'resting place of the birds'. The district's economy is based on cattle and grain growing industries, supported by irrigation in the area. The Australian Sheepdog Trials are held at Goondiwindi every year, and the Spring Festival coincides with the blooming of oleanders, jacarandas and silky oaks. **Of interest:** A sculpture of the famous racehorse *Gunsynd*, the 'Goondiwindi Grey', is in Apex Park. University of Queensland Pastoral Veterinary College. Boobera Lagoon is a wildlife sanctuary. The Victoria Hotel has interesting architecture. A museum is in the old Customs House. **In the area:** Callandoon artesian bore. **Accommodation:** 5 motels, 2 caravan/camping parks.
Map ref. 323 M12

Gordonvale   Population 2372.
This town just off the Bruce Highway in the sugar belt is only 24 km south of Cairns. The Gillies Highway with its 295 bends leads west up to the Atherton Tableland. Nearby is the Bellenden Ker National Park and the prominent landmark of Walsh's Pyramid. **Accommodation:** 4 hotels, 1 caravan/camping park.
Map ref. 324 G4, 335 G10

Gympie   Population 10 765.
The city of Gympie started with the 'Great Australian Gold Rush', 1867 version, led by James Nash. The field proved extremely rich, and some four million ounces were found by the time the gold petered out in the 1920s. By then dairying and agriculture were well established and Gympie continued to prosper. Gympie is on the Mary River, 182 km north of Brisbane by the Bruce Highway. It is an attractive city, with jacarandas, flowering silky oaks, cassias, poincianas, flame trees and civic pride very much in evidence. Its heritage can be seen at the Historical Museum, and the nearby cottage of Andrew Fisher, the first Queenslander to become Prime Minister (1908) may be inspected. The annual Gympie Gold Rush Week is held mid-October. A signposted tour starts at the Tourist Information Centre (look for the Big Pineapple on the main road through). **In the area:** Borumba Dam, for picnics and water sports, is 51 km south-west via Imbil. Mothar Mountain rock pool. The fishing resort of Tin Can Bay and the excellent small resort of Rainbow Beach is 77 km northeast through vast pine forests. The ferry to Fraser Island operates near Rainbow Beach. The Cooloola National Park and Coloured Sands of Tewantin are to the south. **Accommodation:** 3 hotels, 6 motels, 3 caravan/camping parks.
Map ref. 312 G3, 323 P8

Hervey Bay   Population 13 569.
Hervey (pronounced Harvey) Bay is the large area of water between Maryborough and Bundaberg that is protected by Fraser Island. It is usually used to describe the pleasant strip of seaside resorts along its southern shore, some 34 km north-east of Maryborough, including Gatakers Bay, Pialba, Scarness, Torquay and Urangan. Maryborough is the commercial and administrative centre for the Hervey Bay and Wide Bay Burnett region. An ideal climate makes the area popular with residents of Maryborough and Bundaberg as well as with country people. During the winter months there is a regular influx of visitors from the south and it is especially popular for those with caravans. Hervey Bay is known as 'the caravan capital of Australia'. As there is no surf, swimming is safe even for children. Fishing is the main recreation and boats may be hired and fresh yabbies caught for bait. **Of interest:** The Hervey Bay Historical Society Museum recalls pioneer days and is located at Scarness. Matthew Flinders landed in 1799 and a cairn at Dayman Point, Urangan, commemorates the event. The 1 km long pier at Urangan is used by fishermen as well as by large tankers discharging at the Caltex terminal. There is an historical museum at Pialba. There are bowling greens, tennis courts, croquet lawns, squash courts, a golf course and a skating rink in the area. A yachting regatta is held at Scarness every Easter. **Accommodation:** Pialba, 2 motels, 2 caravan/camping parks. Point Vernon, 2 caravan parks. Scarness, 3 motels, 2 caravan/camping parks. Torquay, 5 motels, 6 caravan/camping parks. Urangan, 2 motels, 4 caravan/camping parks.
Map ref 323 Q6

Holloways Beach   Population 1602.
This popular little seaside spot is 11 km north of Cairns. **Accommodation:** 1 motel.
Map ref. 335 F6

Home Hill   Population 3138.
Sister town to Ayr, Home Hill is on the south side of the Burdekin River. The towns are joined by a high-level bridge as the river is liable to flood. **Of interest:** Rice refinery; rock shop and museum. **In the area:** Groper Creek, 16 km away, is noted for its fishing and giant mud crabs.

Gulf Country

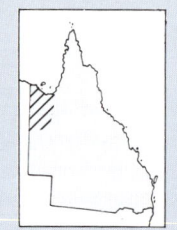

The Gulf Country is a vast, remote, thinly-populated region stretching north from **Mount Isa** and **Cloncurry** to the mangrove covered shores of the Gulf of Carpentaria, and west to the Queensland/Northern Territory border. The unfortunate Burke and Wills were the first white visitors, although the waters of the Gulf itself were first charted by Dutch navigators almost 400 years ago. The country is flat and open and has more rivers than roads. June to September is the recommended time to see the Gulf Country as the 'Big Wet', generally from November to April, closes the dirt roads and often floods the sealed roads from Cloncurry and **Julia Creek**. Motorists should realise that this is not 'Sunday-driving' country and should plan accordingly. It is, however, an ideal corner of Australia if you want to get-away-from-it-all, and the people are exceptionally friendly and helpful.

Normanton (327 F3) is the main town, with a population of 817, although in the gold days of 1891 it counted some 3000 people. The former gold-mining town of **Croydon** (327 H4) is 152 kilometres to the east. The strangely isolated railway between the two towns is not connected to any other system. It is used once a week by the *Gulflander*, a quaint, but practical, vintage rail motor. It leaves Normanton every Wednesday, and Croydon every Thursday. Many of Croydon's buildings have been classified by the National Trust and the Australian Heritage Commission.

Karumba (327 E2), 69 kilometres north of Normanton on the mouth of the Norman River, is the centre of a major prawning industry as well as the fishing and hunting attractions of the Gulf. Keen fishermen from Mount Isa who do not mind the long drive

Home Hill — Ipswich QLD 293

Accommodation: 1 motel, 2 caravan/camping parks.
Map ref. 324 I8

Hughenden Population 1652.
The explorer William Landsborough camped at this spot on the Flinders River in 1862, while unsuccessfully searching for the missing Burke and Wills expedition. A year later a cattle station was established, and Hughenden came into existence. The town is on the Townsville-Mount Isa rail line and the Flinders Highway, 250 km west of Charters Towers. **In the area:** Porcupine Gorge National Park, often described as a 'mini-Grand Canyon'. **Accommodation:** 4 motels, 1 caravan/camping park.
Map ref. 324 D10

Ingham Population 5589.
A major sugar and sightseeing town near the mouth of the Herbert River, Ingham is on the Bruce Highway 113 km north of Townsville. The town has a strong Italian and Spanish Basque cultural background. CSR's Victoria Mill is the largest in the southern hemisphere. The sugar is shipped from Lucinda 29 km north, with its amazing 5.8 km long jetty and conveyor belt. Tobacco, timber and Brahman cattle are also important to Ingham. **Of interest:** Victoria Mill. Macknade Mill is the oldest still operating in Australia. **In the area:** An hour's drive to the west through vast cane fields and rainforest is the Wallaman National Park (be careful, loaded timber trucks have right of way). The park has spectacular jungle and excellent swimming and picnic spots, and the 300-metres high Wallaman Falls are possibly Australian's finest. Jourama Falls National Park; the Herbert River Gorge with its 600-metres high cliffs (charter aircraft available); Mt Fox, a dormant volcano; Taylor's beach. Forrest beach. Everglades cruises from Cardwell are popular through the Hinchinbrook Channel. Dunk and Orpheus Islands are also close. **Accommodation:** 8 hotels, 2 motels, 2 caravan/camping parks.
Map ref. 324 G6

Inglewood Population 984.
An early hostelry called Brown's Inn has grown into the town of Inglewood, in the south-western corner of the Darling Downs, 108 km west of Warwick. Beef cattle and sheep are raised, and lucerne, grain and fodder crops are irrigated from nearby Coolmunda Dam, which attracts boating enthusiasts as well as many pelicans and swans. **Accommodation:** 2 motels, 3 caravan/camping parks.
Map ref. 323 N12

Injune Population 407.
This small cattle and timber town 89 km north of Roma is the southern gateway to the magnificent Carnarvon National Park and gorges. The park is 154 km north of Injune and has some of Australia's most important Aboriginal 'art galleries' hidden along the cliffs of the beautiful gorges. Explorer Ludwig Leichhardt called the region 'Ruined Castle Valley'. The Carnarvon Gorge resort and caravan park is at the park's entrance; check with the resort for camping inside the park. Camping also in Mount Moffat section. The RACQ has produced an excellent brochure/map of the area. **Accommodation:** 1 caravan/camping park.
Map ref. 323 J7

Innisfail Population 7934.
Innisfail is a prosperous, colourful town on the Johnstone River 92 km south of Cairns. Sugar has been grown here since the early 1880s, with a major boost by Italian immigrants after World War 2. The annual gala Sugar Festival is held for 9 days from the last Saturday in August. The famous Opera Festival happens every December. Besides sugar, bananas and other tropical fruit are grown, beef cattle are raised, and the milling of black walnut, Queensland maple, silky oak and red cedar is important. Big game fishing is growing in popularity. **Of interest:** Goondi, Mourilyan and South Johnstone Sugar Mills. Chinese Joss House in Owen St. **In the area:** Australia's only tea plantation at Nerada, 35 km west, is open daily except Mondays. Flying Fish Point for swimming and camping. Mt Bartle Frere (1611 m) is Queensland's highest peak, with a hiking track to the top. Mourilyan, 7 km south, has a comprehensive tourist information service for far North Queensland, and a sugar museum. Palmerston National Park. Innisfail is an excellent base for exploration of the quieter lagoons and islands of the Great Barrier Reef, and a good road leads up to the Atherton Tableland. **Accommodation:** 5 motels, 3 caravan/camping parks.
Map ref. 324 G4

Ipswich Population 65 346.
In 1827 a convict settlement was established on the Bremer River to work the limestone deposits in the nearby hills. The limestone was ferried down-river to Brisbane in whaleboats. In 1828 explorer Allan Cunningham used Limestone Hills, as the settlement was known, as the starting point for his exploration of the Darling Downs to the west. In 1842 it was renamed Ipswich after the city in Suffolk, England, and the enormous coal deposits in the area speeded development. The railway from Brisbane arrived in 1876, displacing the busy river trade and Cobb and Co. services. Ipswich is 40 km south-west of Brisbane on the way to both Toowoomba and Warwick. Coal mining, earthenware works, sawmills, abattoirs and foundries make it a major industrial centre. **In the area:** Mt Crosby, Kholo Crossing, Lake Manchester and College's Crossing are popular swimming and picnic spots. Swanbank Power Station. Redbank Railway Museum, 10 km towards Brisbane, is open daily except Mondays. Wolston House is a restored historic homestead at Wacol open Wednesday to Sunday. **Accommodation:** 3 hotels, 4 motels, 4 caravan/camping parks.
Map ref. 314 H12, 323 P11

---

generally use the Karumba Lodge and its facilities.

The famous North Queensland barramundi can be caught throughout the Gulf rivers. Experts consider this one of Australia's finest fish, and eaten fresh they are absolutely superb. Prawns are snap frozen in Karumba and freighted to markets in the south and overseas. They are almost impossible to buy locally, except as bait.

The almost forgotten town of **Burketown** (327 C3), close to the Gulf, usually only makes the headlines during round-Australia car trials or when it is flooded. It can be isolated for long periods during the wet. Explorers Leichhardt and Landsborough termed the surrounding area the 'Plains of Promise', and today, like most of the Gulf Country, it is cattle country. Barramundi, wild pigs and ducks attract sportsmen; a well-equipped four wheel drive vehicle is advisable.

The newly created Lawn Hill National Park is to the west of the **Gregory Downs** (327 C5) bush pub, a welcome 'waterhole' to the traveller.

Motorists on the sealed beef-road from Cloncurry to Normanton should visit the curious Bang Bang Jump-up, a lonely hill 29 kilometres north of the Donors Hill station turn-off.

Bush Pilots Airways operate regular flights and this is probably the best way to appreciate the vast beauty of the Gulf Country and its many sleepy winding rivers.

Motorists travelling in this area should ensure that they have sufficient supplies for themselves and their vehicle. Road conditions should be checked before departure and, if possible, you should notify someone of your destination and expected arrival time there.

The Channel Country

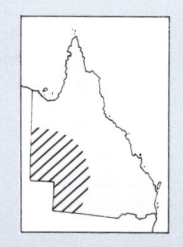

The remote Channel Country is an endless horizon of sweeping plains in Queensland's far-west and south-west corner. It seldom rains in the Channel Country itself but, after the northern monsoons, the Georgina, Hamilton and Diamantina Rivers and Cooper Creek completely take over the country as they flood through hundreds of channels in their futile effort to reach Lake Eyre. There is scarcely any gradient. After the 'wet without rain' the enormous quantities of water carried by these rivers vanish into waterholes, salt pans and desert sands; lush grass, wild flowers and bird and animal life miraculously appear, and cattle are moved in for fattening.

The region is sparsely populated except for large pastoral holdings and scattered settlements, linked by very essential beef-roads. The Diamantina Developmental Road runs south from **Mount Isa** through **Dajarra** (327 D10) and **Boulia** (327 D13) to **Bedourie** (321 D4), then swings east across the many channels of the Diamantina River and Cooper Creek through **Windorah** (321 I6) to the railhead at **Quilpie** (322 D8), then on to **Charleville** (322 G8), a journey of some 1335 kilometres.

Boulia, which proclaims itself the capital of the Channel Country, was first settled in 1877, and has a population of 300. It is 305 kilometres south of Mount Isa and 365 kilometres west of **Winton**. It is a friendly relaxed town on the Burke River; Burke and Wills filled their water bags here. The name comes from the Aboriginal for clear water. The first mail service was by horse from Cloncurry, and a telegraph station was established in 1884.

Bedourie, 198 kilometres further south, is the administrative centre for the Diamantina Shire, and has a store, school, police station and Flying Doctor medical clinic. It has

---

Julia Creek Population 602.
A small cattle and rail township on the Flinders Highway, Julia Creek is 134 km east of Cloncurry. A sealed road runs north to Normanton in the Gulf Country. **Accommodation:** 2 hotels, 2 motels.
Map ref. 324 A10, 327 G8

Killarney Population 699.
This attractive small town is on the Condamine River 34 km east of Warwick, and very close to the NSW border. There is excellent mountain scenery in the area, and Queen Mary, Dagg's and Brown's waterfalls are all worth viewing. Cherribah Mountain Resort offers riding, golf, sailing and bushwalking. **Accommodation:** 1 caravan/camping park.
Map ref. 316 B10

Kingaroy Population 5135.
This prosperous agricultural town in the South Burnett is famous for its peanuts and for its best-known citizen, Johannes (Joh) Bjelke-Petersen, Premier of Queensland. Maize, barley, oats, wheat, soy and navy beans are grown, and specialised agricultural equipment is manufactured. Kingaroy is 233 km north-west of Brisbane and its giant peanut silos make a distinctive landmark. **Of interest:** The Peanut Marketing Board has an audio-visual display for visitors, by arrangement. **In the area:** Mt Wooroolin scenic lookout, 3 km west. Gordonbrook Dam for water-skiing. Bunya Mountains National Park, 56 km to the south. **Accommodation:** 4 motels, 2 caravan/camping parks.
Map ref. 323 O9

Kuranda Population 661.
This township at the top of the Macalister Range is best known to tourists who have taken the scenic rail trip from Cairns, 29 km away. **Of interest:** The railway station with its platforms surrounded by lush ferns and orchids. Barron Falls are spectacular after heavy rain. They have been harnessed to produce hydro-electric power. The town's motel displays bees in glass hives and, adjacent to it, a 1911 homestead has been relocated to show the early way of life in the Atherton Tableland. **Accommodation:** 2 motels, 1 caravan/camping park.
Map ref. 335 E6

Landsborough Population 533.
Just off the Bruce Highway, Landsborough is 9 km south of the Caloundra turn-off. It has an Historical Museum open on Sunday afternoons. A bottle gemstone and shell museum. **Accommodation:** 1 caravan/camping park.
Map ref. 307 E12, 313 K12

Longreach Population 2970.
Longreach may have a relatively small human population, but if you count the 800 000 sheep and 20 000 beef cattle in the area, it becomes the most important and prosperous town in the Central-West. It's a friendly modern town of broad streets (and broad hats!) on the Thomson River, some 700 km by road or rail west of Rockhampton. Some of Australia's most interesting history was made here. In 1870, a Mr Harry Redford, better known as Captain Starlight, with four mates rounded up 1000 head of cattle and drove them 2400 km into South Australia over wild unmapped country that, only ten years before, had been the downfall of Burke and Wills. There Starlight sold the cattle. Unfortunately, since they didn't belong to him, he was arrested in Adelaide and brought back to Queensland to be put on trial at Roma. Despite the evidence, the jury found him not guilty: probably because of the pioneer philosophy that if you are daring enough to carry out that sort of deed, you deserve to get away with it! The events were the basis for Rolf Boldrewood's novel *Robbery Under Arms*. Although Qantas (Queensland And Northern Territory Air Services) actually started in Winton, it soon moved its base to Longreach and there commenced regular operations. The same hangar used then became Australia's first aircraft factory and the first of six DH 50 biplanes was assembled there in 1926. The world's first Flying Surgeon Service started from Longreach in 1959. **Of interest:** Stockman's Hall of Fame and Outback Heritage Centre. Longreach Pastoral College. The Folk Museum at Ilfracombe, 27 km east. **Accommodation:** 7 hotels, 2 motels, 2 caravan/camping parks.
Map ref. 322 D3

ample artesian water, without the usual pungent smell, and swimming is popular. The hotel serves petrol as well as beer.

South of Bedourie the Diamantina Road swings east for the partly-sealed drive to Windorah, on Cooper Creek. The name means 'place of large fish'. During drought the area is a dustbowl; during the wet it's a lake. It's got a good pub. Sheep is the industry.

A good but narrow sealed road leads 237 kilometres east to Quilpie, the eastern gateway to the Channel Country. Cattle, sheep and wool are railed to the coast from here. The name derives from the Aboriginal word for stone curlew, and all but one of the streets have birds' names. Opals have been found here since 1880. Although it is on the Bulloo River, the town's water supply is near-boiling artesian.

The Kennedy Developmental Road from Winton to Boulia is sealed for most of its 256 kilometres. There are two welcome stops, the Middleton and Hamilton bush pubs. Visitors are sure to be told about the Min Min light, a totally unexplained phenomenon that often appears at night near the old Min Min pub, some 96 kilometres from Boulia. Some people think it is an earth-bound UFO that chases cars, then disappears.

Betoota (321 F7) has two buildings, a store and a pub, that bask in the centre of a very large, very boring, gibber plain. It is the only stop on the lonely 394 kilometres drive from Windorah to Birdsville, and Betoota can be beautifully welcome. The store is open every day and sells fuel.

Birdsville, the most isolated settlement in Queensland, is 11 kilometres from the South Australian border, with the Simpson Desert to the west. It is the top end of the Birdsville Track to Marree in South Australia.

Thargomindah (322 D11) is a small settlement on the eastern fringe of the Channel Country 187 kilometres from **Cunnamulla**. Camels were once used to carry wool to **Bourke**. Around the turn of the century Cobb and Co. were operating regularly to Cunnamulla, Hungerford, Charleville, Nocundra and Eromanga.

Nocundra, 142 kilometres even further west, has a permanent population of three, but they can put you up at the pub and sell you petrol and car parts. Waterholes on the nearby Wilson River are the places for yellow belly and catfish, brolgas, pelicans, emus and red kangaroos.

Tourists to the Channel Country should realise that summer is unbearable, so April to September is best, particularly for wild flowers.

Lucinda Population 663.
Ingham's sugar terminal port, 29 km away via Halifax. Lucinda's major feature is the amazing 5.8 km long jetty and conveyor belt which loads 2000 tonnes of sugar an hour on to ships. This jetty won the 1979 Australian Construction Achievement Award. The Dungeness boat harbour nearby, for fishing and trips to the islands. **Accommodation:** 1 hotel, 1 motel, 1 caravan/camping park.
Map ref. 324 G6

Mackay Population 35 356.
Mackay is often called the 'sugar capital' of Australia, producing one-third of the nation's tonnage. Seven mills operate in the area, and the bulk sugar loading terminal is the world's largest. Mackay became a major port only in 1939 when an ingenious breakwater was built, making it one of Australia's largest artificial harbours. The nearby Hay Point coal loading terminal handles the massive output from the Central Queensland fields of Peak Downs Goonyella and Norwich Park. Sugar was first grown in 1865, a mill was built and in the same year Mackay became a town. It became a city in 1918, it is now an attractive and progressive city. Besides sugar and coal, Mackay's economy depends on beef cattle, dairying, timber, pigs, and the growing of tropical fruit. Tourism is important, with cruises to Brampton, Lindeman and the Whitsunday Islands. **Of interest:** Bayersville Zoo. Harbour Beach. Mt Bassett and Rotary lookouts. Hay Point terminal. Pleystowe Sugar Mill (tours June-December). Queen's Park. Mackay/Whitsunday tourism council beside Nebo Road has a Taiwanese fishing junk as a kiosk. Good beaches are Blacks, Bacasia, Illawong, Lamberts and Shoal Point. Historical buildings: old town hall, Commonwealth Bank, National Bank, court-house and customs house. **In the area:** The 'Hibiscus Coast' drive to Mt Jukes lookout, Cape Hillsborough National Park, Seaforth, and Mt Blackwood. Eungella (pronounced Younggella) National Park, 84 km west via Marian and Mirani, has a tricky climb up from Finch Hatton for a spectacular view of the Pioneer Valley. There are tours of the bulk sugar terminal at 10.15 am Mon.-Fri. **Accommodation:** 2 hotels, 21 motels, 8 caravan/camping parks.
Map ref. 325 L11, 331 H11

Maleny Population 552.
A steep road climbs west to Maleny, 50 km south-west of Maroochydore on the Blackall Range. This is excellent dairy country with a New England look. The Mary Cairncross Park has thick rainforest and a fine view of the Glasshouse Mountains to the south. These ten spectacular trachyte peaks were named by Captain Cook as he sailed up the coast in 1770, and the sun shining on the rock faces reminded him of glasshouses in his native Yorkshire. **In the area:** The scenic drive from Maleny through Montville and Flaxton to Mapleton is one of the best in south-east Queensland. Most of the Sunshine Coast can be seen, right across to Moreton Island, plus closer slopes of pineapples. Montville has an excellent pottery and art gallery, both open daily, and Flaxton has a model English village, a clock museum, and a large model train exhibition. There are various other museums, antique shops, fruit stalls, afternoon tea places and tourist attractions along the way. The Kondalilla National Park has rainforest, palms, swimming holes and a waterfall. **Accommodation:** 2 hotels, 1 motel.
Map ref. 307 B11, 323 Q9

Mareeba Population 6306.
This town is at the centre of the main tobacco growing region of Australia. Farms in the Mareeba/Dimbulah area are irrigated from Lake Tinaroo, a giant lake created by damming the Barron River. Another local crop, rice, is processed at the mill at Home Hill on the lower Burdekin. Timber, mining and cattle are also important. **Of interest:** The famous Mareeba Rodeo attracts many visitors each July. **In the area:** A dirt road via Dimbulah crosses the Great Dividing Range to Chillagoe, an old mining town with some fine limestone caves. It's a 145 km trip, but most interesting. **Accommodation:** 4 hotels, 2 motels, 3 caravan/camping parks.
Map ref. 324 F3, 326 I12, 335 B8

Maroochydore Population 17 457.
A well-established and popular beach resort, Maroochydore is in the centre of the Sunshine Coast, 112 km north of Brisbane. The surf beaches are famous and the Maroochy River offers safe swimming and fishing amongst pelicans, swans and seagulls. Cotton Tree has been popular camping area for 50 years. **Of interest:** Bern Kemp's Gallery of Sand Paintings, in Bradman Avenue. This is a gallery of unique natural coloured sand paintings depicting local Aboriginal legends and scenes. **In the area:** Yacht Harbour, beach and Pilot Station at Mooloolaba, 5 km south. Cane fields inland. Fairytale Castle at Bli Bli, 10 km north. Suncoast Pioneer Village, 13 km north, has excellent exhibits of vintage cars and Australiana. Mooloolah River National Park, 10 km south (access difficult). Maroochy airport has daily flights to and from Sydney by East-West Airlines and Airlines of NSW. **Accommodation:** 6 motels, 4 caravan/camping parks.
Map ref. 307 H8, 313 L10, 323 Q9

Maryborough Population 20 107.
Maryborough is an attractive, provincial city near the mouth of the Mary River. The area produces sugar, timber, dairy products, grain and fruit and vegetables. Secondary industries include sawmills, engineering works, a sugar mill and a butter factory. The local fish board is the state's largest outside Brisbane, some 300 km to the south. The Mary River was discovered in 1842, and a village and port soon grew to handle wool being grown inland. It was officially proclaimed a port in 1859, and a municipality in 1861. The city itself is well-planned, as are its parks: Queen's Park with its unusual domed fernery and waterfall; Elizabeth Park, noted for its roses; Anzac Park; and Ululah Lagoon, near the golf links, is a scenic waterbird sanctuary where black swans, wild geese and ducks, and waterhens may be fed by hand. Ships too large for the Mary River berth at Urangan, 35 km away on Hervey Bay. The climate is sub-tropical with warm moist summers and mild winters, and the seaside resorts of Pialba, Scarness, Torquay and Urangan offer pleasant, unsophisticated holidays and fishing. The city is connected by road to the resorts of Rainbow Beach and Tin Can Bay, some 90 km to the south. **Of interest:** St Paul's bell tower, built in 1887, has one of the first sets of cathedral bells in Queensland. Pioneer grave sites in Alice St, Baddow; historic time gun in Queen's Park; Ululah Lagoon. **In the area:** Hervey Bay seaside resorts; Fraser Island; Teddington Weir, 15 km south; Tuan Forest, 24 km south-east. Brooweena, 49 km west on the Biggenden road, has a pioneer museum. **Accommodation:** 1 hotel, 7 motels, 4 caravan/camping parks.
Map ref. 323 P7, 336 C10

Mary Kathleen
Well known to many Australians because of the controversial issue of uranium mining, Mary Kathleen was once a small mining town on the Barkly Highway between Mount Isa and Cloncurry. The area has now been returned to its natural state, leaving no trace of the former inhabitants. In late 1982 the mine was shut down and by the end of 1983 the houses were sold and removed to new areas. **In the area:** Mount Frosty off the Mount Isa Road is a popular swimming hole and a well-known fossicking area for minerals and gemstones. **Note:** The hole is not suitable for children to swim in, as the depth is about 9 metres with no shallow areas.
Map ref. 327 D9

Miles Population 1264.
Ludwig Leichhardt passed through the Miles district on three separate expeditions. He named the place Dogwood Creek, after the shrub that grows on the banks of the creek. In 1878 the western railway line reached 'Dogwood Crossing', and Cobb and Co. continued the journey on to Roma. The town was renamed Miles after a local member of parliament. Miles is 340 km west of Brisbane on the Warrego Highway where it intersects with the Leichhardt Highway. The area has always been good sheep country but today the emphasis is on cattle, mainly Herefords, and wheat. Tall silos dominate the surrounding plains. Timber is also important. After the spring rains the wild flowers are magnificent. **Of interest:** The historical museum, in the form of an exceptionally interesting 'pioneer settlement' with all types of early buildings and a war museum, vehicles and implements on display. **Accommodation:** 1 motel, 2 caravan/camping parks.
Map ref. 323 M9

Millaa Millaa Population 302.
Located 75 km inland from Innisfail, Millaa Millaa is renowned for the many spectacular waterfalls in the area. Millaa Millaa Falls, Zillie Falls and Elinjaa Falls can all be viewed from the 15 km gravel road which leaves and rejoins the Palmerston Highway east of the town. The road is not suitable for cars in wet weather. The town's main industry is cheese-making. **In the area:** A lookout to the west of the town offers an excellent panoramic view of the district. **Accommodation:** Limited.
Map ref. 324 F4

Milmerran Population 1107.
The main product of this town on the Condamine River is eggs. It is also a centre for cotton, grain, vegetables, fat cattle and wool. **Accommodation:** 1 hotel, 1 motel, 1 caravan/camping park.
Map ref. 323 N11

Mission Beach Population 640.
This quiet tropical 8 km long beach is backed by coconut palms and heavy rainforest, close to Tully. Day trips to Dunk and other beautiful islands can be taken from the jetty. At the southern end of the beach, a cairn at Tam O'Shanter Point commemorates the ill-fated 1848 Cape York expedition of Edmund Kennedy. Bingil Bay and Clump Point are nearby. **Accommodation:** 3 motels, 2 caravan/camping parks.
Map ref. 324 G5

Mitchell Population 1171.
This typical western country town, with its broad tree-lined streets, lies on the Warrego Highway between Roma and Charleville. On the Maranoa River, the town was named after Sir Thomas Mitchell, explorer and Surveyor-General of NSW who visited the region in 1845. An unsealed tourist road leads north into the Great Dividing Range and the former stronghold of local bushrangers, the Kenniff brothers, who murdered a constable and a station manager at Lethbridge Pocket in 1902. The region behind the Carnarvon National Park is interesting and little known, but sufficient petrol and supplies must be carried for the 516 kilometre return trip to Mitchell. **Accommodation:** 5 hotels, 1 motel, 1 caravan/camping park.
Map ref. 323 J8

Thursday Island

An unusual place with a magnificent winter climate, **Thursday Island** is Queensland's most northerly administration centre, off the tip of Cape York Peninsula in the Torres Strait. It is 2200 kilometres by air north of Brisbane. It is a colourful outpost with Europeans in the minority amongst the native islanders, Malays, Polynesians, Chinese and Japanese. It has an excellent harbour, once the base for 150 pearling luggers. The Harbours and Marine Department operate the Torres Strait Pilot Service from here.

THE FAR NORTH

Sitting in a tropical garden through dusk and into lush evening, dining superbly on king prawns, Queensland mud crabs and a chilled bottle of white wine, it is hard to believe you are at 'the end of the line' — Port Douglas, the most northerly of the easily accessible coastal towns of Queensland.

This sort of surprise is part of the continuing joy of travelling in the north — a region larger than most European countries and considered by many to be the most diversely beautiful and exciting part of Australia.

This Port Douglas scene typifies the beauty of coastal Queensland; the restaurant looks down from a jungle-covered hill which looms over the small town and the seven kilometres of ocean beach. By day the dense tropical forest is revealed in showers of coloured flowers against the intense green of the jungle. The lavish rainforest and the rush of sparkling mountain streams are lasting impressions for the traveller in the north.

Cairns, 1766 kilometres from Brisbane, is the stepping-stone to a variety of sight-seeing excursions. A major city for tourism, Cairns is often known as the 'capital of Far North Queensland'. Nestling beside Trinity Bay, this scenic city is an ideal base for visiting the surrounding tourist attractions. From Cairns, you can relax on a launch cruise which takes you to see the wonders of the Great Barrier Reef or to explore uninhabited islands. Aerial tours from Cairns take you over the Great Plateau, with its lush tablelands and spectacular waterfalls.

The pleasant climate in winter and early spring is one of the main attractions of this city. Visitors can enjoy snorkelling or other water sports while fishermen flock to Cairns from September to December to catch the big black marlin. Cairns itself is a picturesque city. Delicate ferns, tropical shrubs and fragrant flowers thrive in the Botanical Gardens, where a walking track joins the Centenary Lakes Parkland, created in 1976 to mark the city's hundredth anniversary. Two lakes, one salt water and the other fresh water, provide a haven for wildlife among native trees and shrubs. You can also see orchids growing to perfection in orchid nurseries, which form the basis of one of Cairns' important export industries.

ABOVE: *North of Cairns, this beautiful stretch of deserted ocean beach at Port Douglas, overlooked by thick tropical forest, is typical of the beauty of this far northern area of Queensland.*

BELOW: *Tree-lined streets and a magnificent tropical backdrop make Cairns an attractive city. These palm trees lend a tropical air to the formal colonial-style architecture of some of Cairns' buildings.*

Queensland

ABOVE: *Sugar cane is burned off in preparation for harvesting.*

ABOVE: *The fertile countryside around Mareeba is used for tobacco and rice growing.*

RIGHT: *A cool scene at Mossman Gorge National Park.*

Other places of interest for visitors are the 'House on the Hill' at Mooroobool, an historic landmark built in 1896, now a restaurant and motel; the Laroc coral jewellery factory; the bulk sugar terminal; the 'Big Boomerang'; and the Crystal Cave, a mineral, gemstone and agate museum, where jewellery souvenirs can be purchased.

There are dozens of places around Cairns, all within easy driving distance on good roads, that will claim the traveller's attention. Port Douglas is only one of them. The 76 kilometre journey from Cairns passes through a magnificent stretch of coastal scenery as the Cook Highway winds past white, coral beaches, through archways of tropical forest, and past the islands which dot the azure northern waters.

Just inland from Port Douglas (and don't forget to stop at the cemetery that contains the graves of many pioneer settlers who were lured north by the Palmer River gold rush) is the sugar town of Mossman, where the crushing plant can be inspected from July to November. During these months, when the sugar cane grows to its full height, the cane farmers create raging fires as they burn the thick leaves to prepare the cane for harvesting. These days the fabled strong men of the north, the cane cutters, are seldom seen, having exchanged their machetes for a seat on one of the ingenious machines which cuts the cane and throws it, in a shower of short sticks, into the hopper which trails behind. Sugar growing is a major industry of the north and the waving fields of cane wind through the vaulting blue mountains for hundreds of kilometres down the lush coastal plain.

Near Mossman is one of those perfect places that seem so prevalent in the north, the Mossman River Gorge. A short walk under the dense green canopy of the rainforest leads to the boulder-strewn river which rushes in a series of cascades through the jungle-sided gorge. It is a place to picnic, to swim or simply to bask in the rays of the North Queensland sun.

RIGHT: *Ravenswood today is almost a ghost town. The stairs in the foreground used to lead into the hotel. The old store still remains.*

ABOVE: *Lake Eacham was formed by a volcano.*

ABOVE: *Hinchinbrook Island off the coast near Ingham.*

There are many such places — particularly on the edge of the tableland where the mountains have thrown up fascinating geological oddities and where waterfalls spill. In the Cairns area are the two rainforest volcanic lakes Barrine and Eacham, where walking tracks through the forest give beautiful water views and a chance to see the abundant wildlife — parrots, waterfowl, turtles, platypuses, goannas and many marsupials.

Nearby is the Crater National Park, where one can walk beneath huge rainforest trees, past staghorn ferns and orchids, along the Dinner Creek to the falls and up to the crater — a funnel of sheer granite walls which fall away into dark and forbidding water.

Near the Malanda Falls, where water cascades over a fern-swathed precipice into a delightful swimming pool, is the Curtain Fig Tree, a huge affair, which has resulted from a strangling fig taking over its host tree, climbing higher and higher and throwing down showers of roots to support its massive structure. There are dozens of other delightful waterfalls in this area. Near Millaa Millaa is Falls Circuit, where one can see the Millaa Millaa Falls and Elinjaa Falls amid a panorama of rainforest mountains and plains.

There are four main highways linking the tablelands with the coast. They are all magnificent scenic routes, although the roads are narrow and winding in some parts. Undoubtedly, however, the most novel and popular way of getting up to the tableland is by the scenic railway to Kuranda, built to serve the Herberton tin mine in the 1880s, and now regarded as one of the most difficult feats of engineering achieved in Queensland. The track climbs 300 metres in twenty kilometres to traverse the Barron Gorge and part of it runs over a viaduct along the edge of a 200 metre precipice. The lovely old carriages have rear platforms where travellers can lean against the decorative iron railings and take in the superb

BELOW: *The beautiful waterfall at Millaa Millaa.*

BELOW: *The Mossman Road at Cassowary is almost the most northerly of Queensland's sealed roads.*

Queensland

uninterrupted view. The Kuranda railway station, festooned in tropical plants, ferns and shrubs, is a much-photographed stopover before the descent to Cairns.

The Atherton and Evelyn Tablelands are areas of volcanic land at altitudes between 600 and 1000 metres, mild in climate and supporting dairying, maize and tobacco farming. Gradually the tablelands change into dry, rough country, where tin, copper, lead and zinc mining used to take place. Beyond the main tableland settlement of Atherton is the fascinating mining town of Herberton — its old houses proclaiming its boom days of the late nineteenth century.

Southward from Cairns the plain is flanked by the Malbon Thompson Range on the seaward side and the Bellenden Ker Range, with its superb rainforest. A turn off the highway beyond the town of Innisfail leads into the tropical holiday resort area, where many small towns nestle in the encroaching forest and peep through palms across the sand to the Barrier Reef islands. Further south is the Hinchinbrook Channel, opposite the large, continental island of Hinchinbrook.

The southern city of North Queensland is Townsville, a large and growing city which has an air of prosperity and endeavour. It is a city with many handsome historic buildings, particularly in the waterfront park area around Cleveland Bay.

Charters Towers, 130 kilometres inland from Townsville, in hot, dry cattle country, is one of the most interesting places to visit away from the popular coast area. It has retained all the character of its past, which began with the discovery of gold in the 1880s. The public buildings, the long verandahed main street, the roofed-over railway station and the Venus gold battery, lovely private houses like Ayot Lookout, the hotels, schools and churches have been refurbished or preserved as they were in the past. In the leafy streets are Victorian houses and cottages with steeply pitched roofs and deep verandahs — often shuttered to keep out the sun, but opened to create breezeways in the cooler evening air. The pepperpot fans on many roofs are another tropical innovation — the slightest swing of a breeze is an important thing in Charters Towers.

It is hard to believe that this expression of opulence and style in high Victorian tradition has been built on a hot plain in such a remote part of the world.

RIGHT: *The Mall in Townsville, the unofficial capital of north Queensland. Townsville combines an historic past with many multi-million dollar developments.*

ABOVE: *A peaceful scene in the agriculturally productive Atherton Tableland, originally opened up in the 1870s by explorer James Mulligan.*

ABOVE: *Colonial grandeur in Charters Towers.*

ABOVE: *The railway station at Kuranda is beautified with tropical foliage.*

Monto Population 1397.
Monto, on the Burnett Highway, inland from Bundaberg, is the centre of a rich dairying, beef cattle and agricultural district. The Monto Dairy Festival is held on the Queen's Birthday weekend every second (or even) year. The Cania Gorge National Park, 25 km north, has spectacular geological formations, rock pools, caves, and dense vegetation. Gold was discovered in Cania in 1875 and some may still be found. **Accommodation:** 2 motels, 1 caravan/camping park.
Map ref. 323 N6

Moranbah Population 4362.
On the Peak Downs Highway 200 km south-west of Mackay, this town services the huge open-cut coal mines of Goonyella and Peak Downs operated by the Utah Development Company. Coking coal is railed to the Hay Point export terminal just south of Mackay. The Peak Downs mine may be inspected at 1.30 pm, Tuesdays and Thursdays. **Accommodation:** 1 motel.
Map ref. 325 J12

Mossman Population 1614.
On the scenic Cook Highway 75 km north of Cairns, Mossman is Australia's most northerly sugar town. **Of interest:** Good Shepherd Rock on Mt Demi (1158 m). Waterfalls at Mossman Gorge, 5 km away. Superb beach at Wonga, 25 km north. The Mossman/Daintree area has most spectacular scenery, and should not be missed. Port Douglas and Hartleys Creek Zoo are passed on the journey from Cairns. **Accommodation:** 1 motel.
Map ref. 324 F3, 326 I 11

Mount Isa Population 23 664.
In 1923 John Campbell Miles discovered a rich silver-lead deposit on the western edge of the Cloncurry field. Today the progressive city of Mount Isa is the most important industrial, commercial and administrative centre in north-west Queensland. The 'Isa' is a company town, with Mount Isa Mines operating one of the largest silver-lead mines in the world. Copper and zinc are also mined and processed. Ore trains run 900 km east to Townsville for shipment. The 'Isa' is an oasis of civilisation with excellent amenities and facilities in the otherwise hot and monotonous spinifex and cattle country surrounding it. **Of interest:** The new $3 million Civic Centre. The silver smelter stack, Australia's tallest free-standing structure (265 m). The Rotary Mining Museum is fascinating. Surface mine tours are conducted daily and the extremely interesting underground tour is available by appointment. For tour times and appointments contact the information centre in Centenary Park, Marian Street. The famous Rotary Rodeo, held every August, attracts rough-riders from all over Queensland and almost doubles the population of Mt Isa for the period of the festivities. **In the area:** The man-made Lake Moondarra, 20 km north, is popular, as is Julius Dam, 105 km to the north. Aboriginal rock paintings in the area. Carpentaria Air Charter provides flights to the excellent barramundi fishing grounds of Birri Beach on Mornington Island. Mount Frosty, an old limestone mine and swimming hole; a popular area for fossikers. There is now no trace of the former mining town of Mary Kathleen, between Mount Isa and Cloncurry, which was sold and dismantled in 1983. Nearby Lake Corella has a Burke and Wills memorial cairn. Camooweal, 188 km west of the 'Isa' on the Barkly Highway, is the last Queensland town before crossing the Northern Territory border. **Accommodation:** 5 hotels, 7 motels, 6 caravan/camping parks.
Map ref. 327 C8

Mount Morgan Population 2874.
The crater of the Mount Morgan open-cut gold, silver and copper mine is one of the world's largest man-made holes, measuring some 800 m across and 274 m deep. Inspections can be made at 9.30 am and 1.30 pm daily. The mine still produces, but not as profitably as in its golden heyday when the town had 15 000 people. The museum in East St is particularly interesting. **Of interest:** The superior court-house, gold bullion store and other buildings have National Trust classifications. **In the area:** The Big Dam for swimming, boating and picnics. **Accommodation:** Limited.
Map ref. 323 M3

Mourilyan Population 494.
Located 7 km south of Innisfail, Mourilyan has a good tourist information centre with an excellent audio-visual guide to the many attractions of North Queensland. **Of interest:** The Australian Sugar Museum, open daily. Nearby Mourilyan Harbour handles the sugar from Innisfail. Tours of the bulk sugar terminal take place at 10 am daily during the crushing season. A quiet tropical beach is Etty Bay. **Accommodation:** Limited.
Map ref. 324 G5

Mundubbera Population 1102.
Centre of an important citrus growing area, Mundubbera is on the Burnett Highway, 410 km north-west of Brisbane. **Of interest:** The Golden Mile Orchard, 13 km west of Mundubbera, is one of the best in Australia, and the largest of its type in the world. It is open weekdays for inspection but phone (071) 65 4555 first. The rare Neoceratodus, or lung fish, is found in the Burnett River nearby. **In the area:** Jones Weir, Auburn River National Park. Gurgenna Plateau, a peanut, maize and bean growing area. **Accommodation:** 1 motel, 2 caravan/camping parks.
Map ref. 323 N7

Murgon Population 2327.
Murgon, known as the 'Hub of the South Burnett', is one of the most attractive inland towns in southern Queensland. Settlement dates back to 1843 and the name comes from the Aboriginal word for 'lily pond'. Dairying and mixed crops are the main industries. The town is 101 km inland from Gympie and 46 km north of Kingaroy. The Cherbourg Aboriginal Community is nearby. **Accommodation:** 1 motel.
Map ref. 323 O8

Nambour Population 7965.
Nambour is a busy provincial town 106 km north of Brisbane on the Bruce Highway. The district was settled in the 1860s, mainly by disappointed miners from the Gympie goldfields, and sugar has been the main crop since the 1890s. Small locomotives pulling trucks of sugar cane regularly trundle across the main street to Moreton Central Mill during the crushing season. Pineapples and tropical fruit are grown extensively. Nambour is the Aboriginal name for the red-flowering ti-tree which grows locally. **In the area:** The spectacular Glasshouse Mountains lie to the south, and the scenic Blackall Ranges to the west. The major tourist attractions of The Big Pineapple and the new CSR Macadamia Nut Factory are 6 km south; The Big Cow is 6 km north. Wappa Dam is a picnic retreat 7 km north; 4 km south is the Sunshine Waterslide, a thrill-packed 120 m ride down the hillside. The beach resorts of Maroochydore and Mooloolaba are 20 km east at the mouth of the Maroochy River. **Accommodation:** 4 motels, 3 caravan/camping parks.
Map ref. 307 E8, 313 K9, 323 Q8

Nanango Population 1830.
Gold was found here from 1850 to 1900, but the area now relies on beef cattle, beans and grain. **In the area:** Bunya Mountains National Park. The 1400 megawatt Tarong Power Station, 18 km out of town. The old gold digging grounds. **Accommodation:** 3 motels, 6 caravan/camping parks.
Map ref. 323 O9

Nerang Population 4356.
This small township in the Gold Coast hinterland is 10 km from Southport. A road leads inland to the Numinbah Valley, Advancetown, and the new Hinze Dam lake. **Accommodation:** 2 hotels, 1 caravan/camping park.
Map ref. 317 O5

Noosa-Tewantin Population 9965.
Noosa Heads is the most northerly of the Sunshine Coast resorts, and is unique in terms of its natural scenery and atmosphere. A combination of the Noosa National Park, a protected main beach facing north, the interesting Noosa River and lakes system, and Queensland sunshine, has grown into a fashionable resort with excellent accommodation and restaurants, without Gold Coast-style high-rise development. Tewantin is a quiet country town a few km up the river, first settled in the 1870s as a base for timber-getters. Noosaville is a relaxed family-style resort on the river between the two centres. **Of interest:** Walking and surfing in the National Park between Noosa Heads and Sunshine Beach, with its rocky headlands, sandy coves and patches of rainforest. View of the river and lakes from Laguna lookout. Tourist information available from the Noosa Information Centre, Noosaville. House of Bottles, has an interesting display at Tewantin. **In the area:** Teewah coloured sandhills, the stranded freighter *Cherry Venture*, everglades and Cooloola National Park may be visited by four

wheel-drive vehicles and boat tours go out from Noosaville. The Noosa Lakes system is ideal for boating and sailing fanatics, being navigable for 50 km into the National Park. Boats may be hired on a daily basis or houseboat holidays are available. Boreen Point is a quiet holiday and sailing centre on Lake Cootharaba, 21 km north of Tewantin. **Accommodation:** 1 hotel, 14 motels, 2 caravan/camping parks.
Map ref. 307 H1, 313 L6, 323 Q8

Oakey Population 2857.
On the Warrego Highway 29 km from Toowoomba, this town is the base for Australian Army Aviation. **Of interest:** A bronze statue of the racehorse *Bernborough* who was bred nearby in 1939. **In the area:** Brookvale Park, 8 km west of Oakey, is a popular picnic and barbecue spot, where you can also see koalas, emus and kangaroos. North of Oakey on the Warrego Highway is Jondaryan Woolshed built in 1859 with space for 88 blade shearers. It has been restored as a working memorial and you can see shearing demonstrations, try billy tea and damper, or buy items from the wool store. The Australian Heritage Festival is held at Brookvale park and the Woolshed during a ten day period beginning on the last weekend in August. **Accommodation:** 4 hotels, 2 motels.
Map ref. 323 O10

Pittsworth Population 1817.
Pittsworth is a typical Darling Downs town with streets shaded by flowering silky-oaks. Situated 40 km south-west of Toowoomba on the road to Milmerran, it is the centre of a rich grain and dairying district and produces excellent cheeses. Cotton is grown with the help of irrigation. **Of interest:** Folk Museum open on Sunday afternoons features a pioneer cottage, blacksmith's shop and early school. **Accommodation:** 1 motel, 1 caravan/camping park.
Map ref. 323 O11

Pomona Population 757.
This small farming centre and railway station is in the northern hinterland of the Sunshine Coast, just off the Bruce Highway 33 km south of Gympie. Mt Cooroora (439 m) dominates the town. **In the area:** Lake Cootharaba is north-east of Pomona. This is a large, shallow, saltwater lake on the Noosa River where Mrs Eliza Fraser spent her time with the Aborigines after the wreck of the *Stirling Castle* on Fraser Island in 1836. **Accommodation:** 1 hotel.
Map ref. 313 J5, 323 Q8

Port Douglas Population 675.
A small, peaceful seaside town 67 km up the Cook Highway from Cairns, near Mossman, Port Douglas was originally a gold rush port, but fishing now provides the main occupation. **Of interest:** Daily boat trips to Low Island, a classic coral cay with its own lighthouse. Flagstaff Hill. Seafood. Mocka's Pies. **In the area:** Feed Charlie, a very large,

The Whitsunday Islands

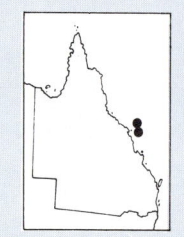

The islands in the magnificent Whitsunday Passage include Lindeman, Brampton, Hamilton, Long, South Molle, Daydream and Hayman. **Hamilton Island**, with its floating marina designed for 400 yachts and excellent service facilities, is a yachtsman's dream. A wide range of accommodation and sporting activities is catered for. Go by launch from Mackay.

Brampton Island (330) is a mountainous island of 8 square kilometres in the Cumberland Group, 32 kilometres from **Mackay** Harbour. It is a national park and wildlife sanctuary with lush forests, palm trees and fine white beaches. The island is surrounded by coral reefs, particularly in the passage between Brampton and Carlisle Islands. A well-developed tourist resort can accommodate 218 people in 95 units, and features a salt water swimming pool. There are glass-bottomed boats for coral browsing, speedboats for water-skiing, and a 15 metre launch for fishing available for hire. The outer reef is 8 hours' cruising away. Air and launch services operate from Mackay.

A famous resort island, **Lindeman** (325 K9) is 67 kilometres north of **Mackay**. It is one of the **Cumberland Group** (331 H5), which is more than 90 per cent national park. It is some 20 square kilometres in area and 70 islands in the Whitsunday Group can be seen from the 1112 metre Mt Oldfield. The island, noted for its birds and butterflies, is covered by 19 kilometres of walking tracks. The Nicolson family have looked after tourists here since 1923, but the large resort complex for 259 people is now operated by P & O.

Swimming, sailing, suntanning, fishing, water-skiing and golf are the main recreations, and trips to several other islands and reefs are available. Daily transport by launch or air from Mackay.

Long Island (331 F5) is in the Whitsunday Group, 8 kilometres from **Shute Harbour** and 43 kilometres from **Proserpine**. An excellent walking track climbs up through the rainforest to give 'postcard' views of the other islands. Scrub turkeys are friendly and common. **Whitsunday 100** is a relaxed resort housing guests in cabins among palms and casuarinas, and a smaller resort at **Palm Bay** has family cabins. Transport is by launch or Ansett helicopter from Shute Harbour. Most holiday activities are available and oysters are yours for the opening.

very live crocodile at Hartleys Creek Zoo. **Accommodation:** 4 motels, 3 caravan/camping parks.
Map ref. 324 F3, 326 I 11

Proserpine Population 3058.
A sugar town, Proserpine is also an important stepping-off point for visitors making for Airlie Beach, Shute Harbour and the islands of the Whitsunday Passage. **Of interest:** Folk museum and bulk sugar terminal. **In the area:** Visit the Aquarium, wildlife sanctuary, Mandalay Coral Gardens, and diving centre. Conway National Park is mostly undeveloped, and offers spectacular views across the islands of the Whitsunday Passage. **Accommodation:** 4 motels, 2 caravan/camping parks.
Map ref. 325 K9, 331 D5

Ravenswood Population under 200.
Ravenswood is a friendly, 'not-quite a ghost town' 70 km east of Charters Towers via Mingella. One hundred years ago it was the classic gold rush town. Visitors will find interesting old buildings and workings and, perhaps, a little gold along with the nostalgia. **Accommodation:** 2 hotels.
Map ref. 324 H9

Redcliffe Population 39 073.
Redcliffe was actually the first settlement in Queensland. Matthew Flinders landed in 1799 while exploring Moreton Bay and it was simply named for what was found: red cliffs. In 1824 John Oxley and Commandant Miller arrived with the first convicts and troops to set up the new Moreton Bay penal colony. It was abandoned the following year in favour of Brisbane. The Aborigines, one of the reasons for the move, called the place Humpybong, meaning 'dead houses', and the name is still used for the Redcliffe Peninsula which comprises the towns of Woody Point, Margate, Clontarf, Scarborough and Redcliffe. The City of Redcliffe was proclaimed in 1959 and is a fast-growing separate-but-satellite area of Brisbane, 35 km away via the 2.6 km long bridge known as the Hornibrook Highway. Fishing and boating are popular pastimes. **Accommodation:** 2 hotels, 1 caravan/camping park.
Map ref. 315 M6, 323 Q10

Redland Bay Population 1325.
Some 30 km south-east of Brisbane on the shores of Moreton Bay, the famous red soil of this area grows excellent vegetables and strawberries, mainly for the Brisbane market. It is a popular Sunday afternoon drive from the city. Nearby Cleveland is the main centre of the Redland area and beaches at Wellington, Victoria Point and Redland Bay offer safe swimming and boating, when the tide is in. This was nearly the capital for the new colony of Queensland, but when Governor Gipps and his official party arrived for an inspection the tide was out and the trudge over the mud flats created a less than favourable impression.

South Molle (331 F4) is a well-known island situated in the heart of the Whitsunday Passage 8 kilometres from **Shute Harbour**. New management has recently spent $1 million modernising the resort, but it is still the ideal place for an unpretentious and unsophisticated holiday. Accommodation for 190 is fully air-conditioned, night-life is good, with toad racing an unusual attraction. Four launches are available, including the *Lady Ruby*, a top marlin boat. The island is only four kilometres by 2.4 kilometres, lightly timbered, with numerous inlets, quiet bays, coral gardens and reefs. Mt Jefferies, 198 metres high, is strictly for the energetic. Access is by launch from Shute Harbour, or by helicopter from **Proserpine** or **Mackay**.

Daydream Island (331 E4) is a small island (1.2 kilometres by half a kilometre) of volcanic rock and coral 5 kilometres from **Shute Harbour**. Foliage is dense and tropical. The Polynesian Village resort is exciting and sophisticated, with a magnificent freeform swimming pool large enough to have an exotic bar in the middle, and the night-life is well-organised. Management says swimsuits are optional and Sunlover's Beach is the place to get that all-over tan to impress your close friends. The resort caters for 184 guests. Launch from Shute Harbour or helicopter from **Proserpine** or **Mackay**.

Just south of **Hayman**, **Hook Island** (331 F2) is 1½ hours by launch from **Shute Harbour**. A spectacular underwater observatory, the world's largest, lets visitors see the famous Barrier Reef coral and marine life ten metres below the surface without getting their feet wet. Highly recommended. Refreshments available but no accommodation. Launches leave Shute Harbour daily at 9 am and return at 5 pm. Most cruises from and through the Whitsunday Islands visit Hook Island.

Ansett operate a large and highly-developed resort on **Hayman Island** (331 F2) for over 500 guests. The island itself is 4.8 by 1.6 kilometres, and is the most northerly of the Whitsunday Group and the closest to the outer reef. It is mountainous with some 80 varieties of birds in the tropical bushland. At low tide the lagoon in front of the resort becomes a series of shallow pools, making coral exploration easy. There are also Hayman's own coral gardens and famous Blue Pool. Glass-bottomed boats are available, and cruising and fishing trips can be arranged on one of the resort's seven launches. Access is by launch from **Shute Harbour** (29 kilometres), or by helicopter from **Proserpine** or **Mackay**.

Cape York

The Cape York Peninsula is a vast triangular area as large as Victoria, with **Cairns** in the lower east corner, **Normanton** in the lower west, and **Thursday Island** as a dot at the northern tip. It is virtually uninhabited except for isolated cattle stations, several Aboriginal communities, and a string of small settlements along the overland telegraph line to **Bamaga** (326 C1) at the northern tip. Many rivers flow east of the Great Dividing Range to the Coral Sea, or west to the Gulf of Carpentaria.

Cape York was first explored during the 1840s and the 1860s by the Jardine Brothers, John Bradford, Robert Jack, and the ill-fated Edmund Kennedy and his famous Aboriginal guide Jackey Jackey. Little has changed since then. Vegetation varies from gums and ant hills in the south to swamps and jungle in the north. The Cape is a sanctuary for much of Australia's unique wildlife including crocodiles, orchids, and insect-eating pitcher plants.

There are two distinct seasons: the wet and the dry. During the wet virtually all road transport stops and the only movement is by regular Air Queensland flights, often in veteran DC 3s. **There are almost no sealed roads or bridges in the area.**

All Aboriginal communities are self-sufficient and may be visited, but it is essential that a permit be obtained in writing beforehand. It is no use just turning up. The main settlements are Lockhart River and Portland Roads on the east coast; Bamaga at the tip; and Edward River, Weipa South, and Aurukun on the Gulf.

For the motorist with an adventurous spirit, the Cape is the ideal place to go exploring. A reliable and well-equipped four wheel drive vehicle is essential for this area, preferably with a winch. It is possible to drive north from Cairns or **Mareeba** to Bamaga through **Laura** (326 G10) and **Coen** (326 E7). The Royal Automobile Club of Queensland provide an excellent map and information sheet and it is essential reading before an expedition north is planned. **Conditions on the track are unpredictable and the RACQ or Police at Cairns should be contacted before heading north.** August to October are the recommended travel months. It should be realised that there are virtually no facilities or petrol north of Coen. You can drive for days without seeing another car. The Laura, Kennedy, Stewart, Archer, Wenlock, Dulhunty and Jardine Rivers must be forded. During good dry conditions it is possible to take a conventional car, with care, north to Coen and west to Weipa.

Weipa, on the Gulf of Carpentaria, has the world's largest deposits of bauxite, the raw material for aluminium. It is mined and shipped to the huge alumina plant at Gladstone on the central Queensland coast. The red bauxite cliffs were first seen by the Dutch explorer Captain Willem Jansz in 1606. Comalco offer conducted tours of the operation. Direct access to Weipa is by regular Ansett flights from Cairns.

Ormiston House at Cleveland is a superb example of colonial architecture. It was built in 1862 for Captain Louis Hope who pioneered the sugar industry in Queensland. It is open from March to November on Sunday afternoons. The old court-house at Cleveland is now a restaurant and dates from 1853. **Accommodation:** 1 caravan/camping park.
Map ref. 315 O12

Richmond   Population 784.
This small town on the Flinders Highway, serves the surrounding properties. A tourist resort is in the area. **Accommodation:** 2 hotels, 2 motels.
Map ref. 324 C10, 327 I10

Rockhampton   Population 50 146.
Rockhampton is often called the beef capital of Australia, with some two and a half million cattle in the region. Gold was discovered at Canoona, 60 km north-west of Rockhampton in 1858. Cattle became the major industry, with English Shorthorns and Herefords the main breeds, since successfully cross-bred with more exotic breeds to produce disease-resistant herds. On the Fitzroy River, Rockhampton is right on the Tropic of Capricorn. It is a prosperous provincial city with considerable architectural charm. Many of the original stone buildings and churches remain, set off by yellow flowering peltophorum, bauhinia and brilliant bougainvilleas. The Capricana Springtime Festival is held each September; Camp Draft and Rough Riding Championships are an annual feature. The city has several well-established secondary industries, including two of Australia's largest meat processing and exporting factories. **Of interest:** Victorian buildings in Quay St; Botanic Gardens on Athelstane Range contain what is probably the finest tropical display in Australia. A Japanese-style garden has been added as well as a walk-in aviary. The Fitzroy River Barrage provides 63 700 million litres of water and separates tidal salt water from upstream fresh water. Rainbow Fountain in Central Park takes 30 minutes to display its full colour cycle. The 14 m high Capricorn Spire at Curtis Park marks the exact line of the Tropic of Capricorn (Tourist Information Centre is here.) St Aubin's Village, has an historic 1870 homestead. **In the area:** The rugged Berserker Range has spectacular limestone caves. Olsen's and Cammoo Caves have conducted tours every hour. There is a pleasant drive to the top of Mount Archer. Mount Morgan Mine and Museum, 38 km south-west; thunder eggs prospecting at Mt Hay Gemstone Tourist Park, 41 km west of Rockhampton on the Capricorn Highway; Gemland, 9 km to the north. Port Alma, Rockhampton's harbour, is located 34 km to the south. Great Keppel Island tourist resort 13 km off the Capricorn Coast; Yeppoon and Emu Park beaches with the musical singing ship memorial to Captain Cook who discovered Keppel Bay in May 1770 and the new Underwater Observatory off Middle Island. **Accommodation:** 11 hotels, 18 motels, 5 caravan/camping parks.
Map ref. 323 M3, 328 B7

Roma Population 5706.

Roma was named after the wife of Sir George Bowen, Queensland's first Governor. In 1859 it became the first gazetted settlement after the separation from New South Wales. It is a progressive, comfortable town with some interesting history and achievements. Mt Abundance cattle station was set up in 1857 and sheep and cattle have been the economic mainstay ever since. The famous trial of Harry Redford, alias Captain Starlight, was held in Roma in 1872. In 1863, S. S. Bassett brought vine cuttings to Roma and Queensland's first wine making enterprise got under way. Australia's first natural gas strike was made at Hospital Hill in 1900, and the gas from this source was used, briefly, to light the town. Further deposits were found periodically, and 'oil' (actually gas and condensate) caused excitement in the area in the early 1960s. Roma now supplies Brisbane with gas via a 450 km pipeline. There are several abandoned oil rigs to be seen and a small crude oil refinery 10 km west of town supplies petrol for local consumers. Roma is on the Warrego Highway, 261 km west of Dalby, with the Carnarvon Highway going south to St George, and north to Injune and the Carnarvon Gorges. The town has excellent sporting and recreational facilities. **Of interest:** Romavilla Winery, open every day. Campbell Park for natural gas barbecues. Bassett Park showgrounds and sporting complex. **Accommodation:** 5 hotels, 5 motels, 3 caravan/camping parks.
Map ref. 323 K8

St George Population 2203.

Situated at a major road junction, St George is in the centre of a rich cotton growing district. It is on the Balonne River, 118 km north of Mungindi by the Carnarvon Highway, and 292 km southwest of Dalby by the Moonie Highway. As St George has a rainfall of only 500 mm a year, an extensive irrigation programme is carried out by means of a new dam and three weirs. Cotton growing and harvesting is completely mechanised; planting is from October to November, and harvesting is from April to June. The cotton ginnery may be inspected by appointment during the harvesting months. Wheat, barley, oats and sunflowers are also irrigated, and sheep and cattle are raised. Fishing for Murray cod, yellow-belly and fresh-water jew is popular on the Balonne River. **Accommodation:** 3 hotels, 1 motel, 2 caravan/camping parks.
Map ref. 323 J11

Sarina Population 2815.

In the sugar belt, Sarina lies 37 km south of Mackay on the Bruce Highway. Its many fine beaches, including Sarina, Armstrongs, Campwin, Grasstree, Half Tide and Perpetua Point, are sometimes referred to as the 'Sugar Coast'. Sarina produces molasses and ethyl alcohol as by-products of the sugar industry. **Of interest:** Plane Creek Central Sugar Mill; the Geranium Gardens; Barton's lookout; Hay Point coal terminal. **Accommodation:** 2 motels, 2 caravan/camping parks.
Map ref. 325 L11

Moreton Bay Islands

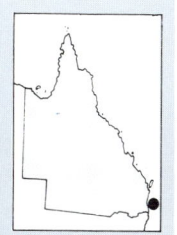

Bribie Island (315 M2) is a largely undeveloped island 69 kilometres north of Brisbane, reached via a turn-off on the Bruce Highway and a one-kilometre bridge across Pumicestone Passage. Bribie is about 31 kilometres long, the northern tip being opposite **Caloundra** on the Sunshine Coast. Matthew Flinders landed on the southern tip in 1799. Apart from the townships of **Bongaree** on the mainland side and **Woorim** on the surf side, little has changed since those days. Bribie is a wildlife sanctuary, with excellent fishing, boating and crabbing. Accommodation available is 1 hotel, 2 motels and 3 caravan/camping parks.

Moreton Island (315 P4), predominantly national park, is a remarkable wilderness island only 35 kilometres east of Brisbane, though seldom visited by the residents of that city. Apart from rocky headlands the island is mostly huge sand hills, native scrub, banksias and undisturbed freshwater lakes which attract over 125 types of birds. A lighthouse at the northern tip was built in 1857 and still guides shipping into Brisbane. There are no roads on the island but occasional four wheel drive vehicles use tracks and the magnificent 40 kilometres long beach. Mt Tempest (280 m) is probably the highest permanent sandhill in the world. The pleasant tourist resort of **Tangalooma** is on the leeward side and can accommodate 225 guests; it is a popular base for big-game fishing. There are several camp sites in the park. Transport is by launch or air from Brisbane.

North Stradbroke Island (315 Q10) or 'Straddie', as it is affectionately called, is a large and fairly unspoiled island directly east of Brisbane across Moreton Bay. It is a popular spot for fishermen, surfers, and weekenders. The small settlements of **Dunwich** and **Amity Point** are on the leeward side, and **Point Lookout** is on the north-east corner. Dunwich started as a quarantine station for the port of Brisbane in 1828, and a typhoid plague in 1850 resulted in some historic local gravestones. Point Lookout has the only hotel on the island, some impressive rocky headlands, and great fishing and surfing. The Blue Lake and Brown Lake are interesting. Vehicular ferries sail regularly from **Redland Bay** and **Cleveland** to Dunwich.

South Stradbroke Island (317 P3) was separated from North Stradbroke Island by a cyclone in 1896, and the channel between them is called Jumpinpin. South Stradbroke stretches down to Southport on the Gold Coast, the protected Broadwater being a well-used boating playground. The island is almost uninhabited. Day cruises operate from **Southport**.

Tropical Islands

Only 35 minutes by launch or vehicular ferry across Cleveland Bay, **Magnetic Island** (333) is almost a seaside 'suburb' of Townsville, with some 1800 permanent residents. 2709 hectares of this mountainous island is a national park and bird sanctuary, with good walking tracks. Trees are mostly pines, with she-oaks, pandanus, poincianas and banyans giving variety. There are four hotels and one motel on the island. Resorts are at **Picnic Bay, Nelly Bay, Arcadia, Radical Bay** and **Horseshoe Bay**, with Nelly Bay having the most accessible coral reef. Buses and taxis operate on the island. **Of interest:** The Fernery at Arcadia. Marine Gardens, Shark World and Coral Observatory at Nelly Bay. Koala Park Oasis, a wildlife refuge at Horseshoe Bay. Fishing is good almost anywhere.

A small, volcanic island surrounded by coral reefs, **Orpheus Island** (324 H6) is 80 kilometres north of Townsville and 16 kilometres off Lucinda Point. The island is a densely wooded national park, and some 50 varieties of birds have been seen. Turtles regularly nest on the beaches. There is a friendly family-run resort that can accommodate 24 guests. Game fishing is a particular attraction, and the resort can arrange fishing excursions to the outer reef, only 19 kilometres away. Visitors arrive by launch from **Townsville** or from **Dungeness** near **Ingham**, or fly from Townsville to **Palm Island** and continue by launch.

Hinchinbrook Island (334) is the largest island national park in the world: all of its 642 square kilometres are totally protected. Even insecticides are banned. There are rugged mountain ranges with thick tropical vegetation and waterfalls, which contrast with long sandy beaches and secluded coves on the eastern side. A Marine Research Station has been set up at Cape Ferguson to study the ecology of mangroves. Permits to camp on the island may be obtained from the National Parks and Wildlife Service in **Cairns** or **Cardwell**. A small pleasant resort at **Cape Richards** has 15 self-contained family units, and offers natural unsophisticated holidays. The resort's launch collects visitors from Cardwell.

Five kilometres off the coast near Tully, **Dunk Island** (334) is one of the most popular of the resort islands. In 1978 TAA spent $2.5 million improving their resort village at **Brammo Bay**. This is one of the finest holiday complexes in Australia, and can accommodate 200 guests in various degrees of luxury. The island is the largest of the Family Group, with superb rainforest and scenery. More than 90 varieties of birds have been identified. Butterflies and wild orchids complete the tropical picture. The writer E. J. Banfield ('Beachcomber') lived on the island from 1897 to 1913, and the film 'Age of Consent' was made here. Access is by launch from **Clump Point**, or by air from **Townsville** or **Cairns**.

A popular tourist attraction 27 kilometres north-east of Cairns, **Green Island** (335 H2) is a true coral cay, 13 hectares in area, and a marine national park. Launches depart from Cairns every morning, and day trippers can visit the famous Underwater Observatory; Marineland Melanesia with its fish, coral, crocodiles and Papua New Guinea primitive art; see Barrier Reef films at Castaway Theatre; study the coral from a glass-bottomed boat or hire a mask and snorkel; swim or go for walks. The Coral Cay Hotel resort can accommodate 100 holidaymakers.

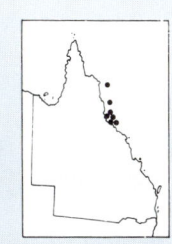

Bedarra Island is a very small heavily-wooded island 6 kilometres from the mouth of the Hull River near Tully. Transport is by launch from the mainland or via nearby Dunk Island. The resort can accommodate 10 people. Fishing, swimming, sunbaking, beachcombing and bushwalking are the main attractions.

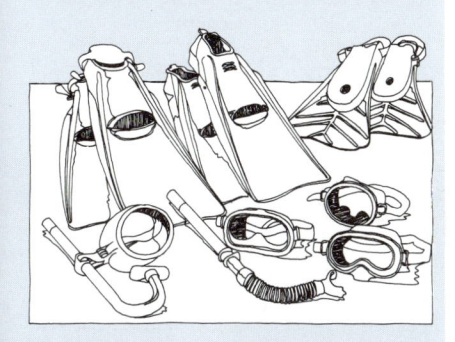

Lizard Island (326 I8) is the most northerly of the Barrier Reef resort islands, being 97 kilometres north-east of Cooktown and 50 minutes from Cairns by Air Queensland. Despite its somewhat unromantic name, it is a rather special island with an excellent newly developed resort that takes only 20 guests, ideal for people wanting a more secluded holiday. The reefs around this national park are magnificent, with excellent fishing including the famous black marlin. The first 'tourist' was Captain James Cook in August 1770. He landed and climbed Cook's Look (359 metres) to spy out a safe passage through the reefs to the open sea. The island takes its name from the large but harmless monitor lizards he found.

Shute Harbour   Pop. under 200.
The jetty at Shute Harbour, 36 km north-east of Proserpine, is the best place to start exploring the 100 or so tropical islands that bask in the spectacularly beautiful Whitsunday waters. Hayman, Daydream, South Molle and Lindeman are the best known. Every morning big and small launches, yachts and glass-bottomed boats take tourists on board for a memorable day out. Try boom net riding on one of the three-island tours available daily. You can even fly by seaplane to Hardy's Lagoon on the outer Barrier Reef for a few hours' snorkelling amongst the coral. **In the area:** Airlie Beach. Conway National Park. **Accommodation:** 2 motels.
Map ref. 331 E4

Southport   Pop. part of Gold Coast.
At the northern end of the Gold Coast strip, Southport is packed with attractions to suit the holidaymaker. It also serves as the commercial and administrative centre for the Gold Coast. **Of interest:** Sea World at the Spit is a marine park where a full day can happily be spent. Dolphins give marvellous displays to delight visitors. A play is acted out on a replica of the *Endeavour*. Queensland's first train is on display in the grounds. Other tourist attractions are Andalucia Park, on the spit, where the Royal Spanish Dancing Stallions are a spectacular feature. For the sportsman, Southport offers facilities for bowls, croquet, golf, greyhound coursing, trotting and racing, tennis, squash and rifle shooting. **In the area:** The many other attractions of the Gold Coast and its hinterland. **Accommodation:** 1 hotel, 4 motels, 2 caravan/camping parks.
Map ref. 317 P5, 318 D12, 323 Q11

Stanthorpe   Population 3966.
The main town in the Granite Belt, 225 km south-west of Brisbane, in the mountain ranges along the border between Queensland and New South Wales, Stanthorpe came into being after the discovery of tin at Quartpot Creek in 1872. Silver and lead were discovered in 1880, but the minerals boom did not last. The area has produced excellent wool for more than a century, but is best-known for large-scale growing of apples, pears, plums, peaches and grapes. Stanthorpe is 915 metres above sea level and is often the coolest part of the state. Spring is particularly beautiful with fruit, wattles and flowers in bloom. There are 90 varieties of wild orchids found in the area. There are six wineries in the district. **In the area:** Storm King Dam is popular for canoeing and water-skiing. Mt Marlay has excellent views of the town and district. Biltmore Wine Cellars at Thulimbah. Angelo's Cellars at Ballandean. Undercliffe, Boonoo Boonoo and Jolly's waterfalls. Sundown National Park is a wilderness area with a basic camping ground on the Severn River in the south-west of the park. Girraween National Park with spectacular granite outcrops and wildflowers; popular for walking, rock-climbing and camping. **Accommodation:** 1 hotel, 5 motels, 2 caravan/camping parks.
Map ref. 323 O12

Taroom   Population 688.
Taroom is almost 300 km due west of Maryborough, on the Dawson River and Leichhardt Highway. Cattle is the main industry. **Of interest:** A coolibah tree in the main street was marked 'L.L.' by Ludwig Leichhardt on his 1844 trip from Jimbour House near Dalby to Port Essington (Darwin). Rare Livistona palms can be seen near the highway 14 km north. **Accommodation:** 2 hotels, 2 motels.
Map ref. 323 L7

Texas   Population 807.
Quite the opposite in size to its United States namesake, Texas lies on the Dumaresque River and the New South Wales border, 55 km south of Inglewood. Tobacco is the main crop. The Historical Museum is in the old police station, built 1893. **In the area:** Glenlyon Dam. **Accommodation:** 1 caravan/camping park.
Map ref. 323 N12

Theodore   Population 543.
Grain and cotton are the main crops around this town on the Leichhardt Highway 220 km north of Miles. It was named after Edward Theodore, a Premier of Queensland. **In the area:** Isla Gorge, National Park. Glebe Weir, Dawson Folk Museum. Cracow, 49 km south-east, produced gold from the famous Golden Pleateau mine from 1932 to 1976. **Accommodation:** 1 hotel, 1 caravan/camping park.
Map ref. 323 M6

Tin Can Bay   Population 883.
Popular for fishing, prawning and crabbing on Tin Can Inlet, south of Inskip Point and Fraser Island. **In the area:** The Teewah Coloured Sands and Rainbow Beach. **Accommodation:** 1 hotel, 1 motel, 4 caravan parks.
Map ref. 323 Q8

Toowoomba   Population 63 401.
The garden city of Toowoomba has a distinctive charm and graciousness, due to its wide, tree-lined streets, colonial architecture, and many fine parks and gardens. It is at its best every September for the Carnival of Flowers. Toowoomba is 138 km west of Brisbane, on the rim of the Great Dividing Range, and the start of the fertile Darling Downs. It began in 1849 as a village near an important staging-post for teamsters and travellers, and was known as The Swamp. Aborigines pronounced this as T'wamp-bah, or Toowoomba. Today it is the commercial centre for the Downs, with butter and cheese factories, sawmills, flour mills, tanneries, engineering and railway workshops, a modern iron foundry, clothing and shoe factories. It has an active cultural and artistic life. **Of interest:** The main parks are Lake Annand, Laurel Bank, Queens, and Webb Park. The Blue Arrow Scenic Drive starts at Mt Kynoch, 6 km out towards Crow's Nest. Mt Lofty lookout. Prince Henry Drive from the end of Bridge St. Picnic Point, 5 km east, for mountain views, Camera Obscura observatory, and Carnival Falls. Steele Rudd Memorial in Brisbane St. The

Bull's Head Inn, Drayton Road, has been fully restored by the National Trust. Early Settler's Museum, Parker St, Drayton. The City Hall Gallery and Gould Gallery, Ruthven St. Lionel Lindsay Gallery, Jellicoe St. Willow Springs Adventure Park. Downs Art Centre, Margaret St behind the Greyhound terminal. And last, but by no means least, a Teddy Bear Museum in Bell St. **Accommodation:** 5 hotels, 11 motels, 5 caravan/camping parks.
Map ref. 320, 323 O10

Townsville Population 86 106.
In 1864, a sea captain named Robert Towns commissioned James Melton Black to build a wharf and establish a settlement on Cleveland Bay to service the new cattle industry inland. Townsville was gazetted in 1865 and declared a city in 1903. Today, Townsville has an international airport and is expanding rapidly with The Breakwater Island Casino Hotel recently completed and the Great Barrier Reef Wonderland Project being developed. Its busy port handles the minerals from Mount Isa and Cloncurry; beef and wool from the western plains; sugar and timber from the rich coastal region; and its own manufacturing and processing industries. It is the administrative, commercial and manufacturing capital of northern Queensland with some impressive new public buildings, including the James Cook University. Next door to the University is the Institute of Education. The climate is tropical. See the Great Barrier Reef through the underwater windows of the semi-submerged craft, the *Manta*, moored at John Brewer Reef off Townsville. You can take a pleasant 40-minute trip across the bay to Magnetic Island National Park and resort, or walk the length of the Strand with its tropical parks, waterfall and overhanging bougainvillea gardens. Flinders pedestrian mall in the heart of the city has a lot to offer. A major annual attraction is the ten-day 'Pacific Festival' each June.
Of interest: Civic Theatre; Perc Tucker Regional Art Gallery; James Cook University. Lavarack Army Barracks, Garbutt RAAF Base, Coral Gardens, South Townsville. Tobruk and Kokoda Memorial Baths. The Ross River and Alligator Creek meatworks are Australia's largest. Copper Refinery at Stuart has tours daily. Queen's Gardens.
In the area: Magnetic Island. Palm Island Aboriginal Settlement, 51 km to the north. Mt Spec, Hidden Valley, and Paluma Dam, 85 km north-west. Mt Elliot National Park, 22 km north-west. Pangola Park and Stud, 60 km south. **Accommodation:** 3 hotels, 21 motels, 8 caravan/camping parks.
Map ref. 324 H7, 332

Tully Population 2728.
Huddled under Mt Tyson, Tully receives the highest annual rainfall in Australia, some 4400 mm. Sugar is the main crop, together with tea, bananas and timber. **In the area:** Fishing and white-water canoeing on the Tully River. American-owned King Ranch to the west. Spectacular rainforests at Mission Beach, Clump Point, Bingil Bay, Kareeya Gorge and Murray Falls. There are daily launch trips to Dunk Island, and regularly to the Great Barrier Reef. **Accommodation:** Limited.
Map ref. 324 G5

Warwick Population 5852.
An attractive city on the Darling Downs, 162 km south-west of Brisbane on the Cunningham Highway, and 82 km south of Toowoomba on the New England Highway. Allan Cunningham was the first explorer in 1827, and in 1840 the Leslie brothers arrived from the south and established a sheep station at Canning Downs, and other pastoralists followed. The New South Wales Government asked Patrick Leslie to select a site for a township, and in 1849 Warwick was surveyed and established. It was the first town, after Brisbane, in what became Queensland. The railway line from Ipswich was opened in 1871, and Warwick became a city in 1936. What seemed to be a minor incident in 1917 led to the formation of the Commonwealth Police Force. Prime Minister Billy Hughes was hit by an egg while addressing a crowd on the controversial conscription issue of the day. He asked a local policeman to arrest the man and the policeman refused. As a result the Commonwealth Police Force was soon established. Warwick is on the willow-shaded Condamine River, 453 m above sea level, and calls itself the 'Rose and Rodeo City'. The surrounding rich pastures support many famous horse and cattle studs, and produce some of Australia's finest wool and grain. Fruit, vegetables and timber grow well, and its dairy products and bacon are famous. It has many well-known schools. **Of interest:** Leslie Park in the main street, and Jubilee Gardens for superb displays of roses. The celebrated Warwick Rodeo in October. Pringle Cottage, built 1863, and now a museum. The Doll Museum. Highland dancing and pipe band competition on Boxing Day. Rock-Swap Festival at Easter. The Tourist Information Centre is at the Warwick Town Hall. **In the area:** Leslie Dam, 15 km west, for water sports and picnics. Queen Mary Falls National Park, 45 km east via Killarney, and Carr's Lookout 14 km further on. Main Range National Park, 50 km north-east. Cherribah Mountain Resort, 35 km east near Killarney. **Accommodation:** 11 hotels, 5 motels, 3 caravan/camping parks.
Map ref. 323 O11

Weipa Population 2436.
Two-thirds of the way up the west coast of the Cape York Peninsula, Weipa is a company mining town, where bauxite is mined by Comalco. **Of interest:** There is a modern township including a branch of the Commonwealth Bank in the town, and a service station where some mechanical repairs can be carried out. The roads, once out of the town, however, are not suitable for other than experienced outback motorists. Most visitors arrive by air. Conducted tours of the mining operations are available. The huge trucks used to transport the bauxite are probably the best known feature of the town to outsiders. Some women are now employed to drive these massive vehicles. In the town, all traffic must give way to heavy mine trucks which travel at about 60 km per hour. **Accommodation:** Limited.
Map ref. 326 C4

Winton Population 1259.
Banjo Paterson wrote Australia's most famous song, 'Waltzing Matilda', on Dagworth Station near Winton in 1895. Combo Waterhole was then part of Dagworth, and the ballad had its first public airing in Winton. The town is 173 km north-west of Longreach on the Landsborough Highway, and at the headwaters of the Diamantina River. A major sheep area, Winton is also a large trucking centre for the giant road-trains bringing cattle from the Channel Country into the rail head. The town's water supply comes out of deep artesian borees at 70°C. **Of interest:** Swagman statue near the swimming pool; Qantilda pioneer museum; gift and gem centre; bottle museum. **In the area:** Combo Waterhole, 141 km south-east off Landsborough Highway. Opalton gemfields, 115 km to the south. Rugged scenery and abundant wildlife. Aboriginal paintings and ceremonial grounds. Lark Quarry Environmental Park preserves footprints of a dinosaur 'stampede'. **Accommodation:** 1 hotel, 1 motel, 1 caravan/camping park.
Map ref. 322 B1, 324 B13, 327 I11

Wondai Population 1024.
This typical, small country town in the South Burnett is 23 km south of Murgon, and 31 km north of Kingaroy. **Accommodation:** 1 motel, 1 caravan/camping park.
Map ref. 323 O8

Yeppoon Population 6447.
This popular coastal resort, 40 km north-east of Rockhampton, lies on the shores of Keppel Bay. Yeppoon and the strip of beaches to its south — Cooee Bay, Rosslyn Bay, Causeway Lake, Emu Park and Keppel Sands — are known as the Capricorn Coast. Great Keppel Island tourist resort is 13 km offshore. **Of interest:** Yeppoon shell museum. The Yeppoon Pineapple Festival is celebrated every September. **In the area:** Cooberrie Park, 15 km north, is a noted flora and fauna reserve, with peaceful picnic facilities. Byfield State Forest, 17 km further north, is the home of the extremely rare Byfield fern. Yeppoon is the site of a 9000 hectares Japanese development which will be known as the Iwasaki International Resort. **Accommodation:** 5 motels, 5 caravan/camping parks.
Map ref. 323 N3

Yungaburra Population 452.
On the edge of the Atherton Tableland, inland from Cairns, the name Yungaburra is Aboriginal for fig tree. The region was once volcanic, and lakes have formed in the old craters. Lakes Eacham and Barrine are said to be linked by subterranean channels. **Accommodation:** 1 motel, 1 caravan/camping park.
Map ref. 335 D12

Maps of Queensland

Location Map

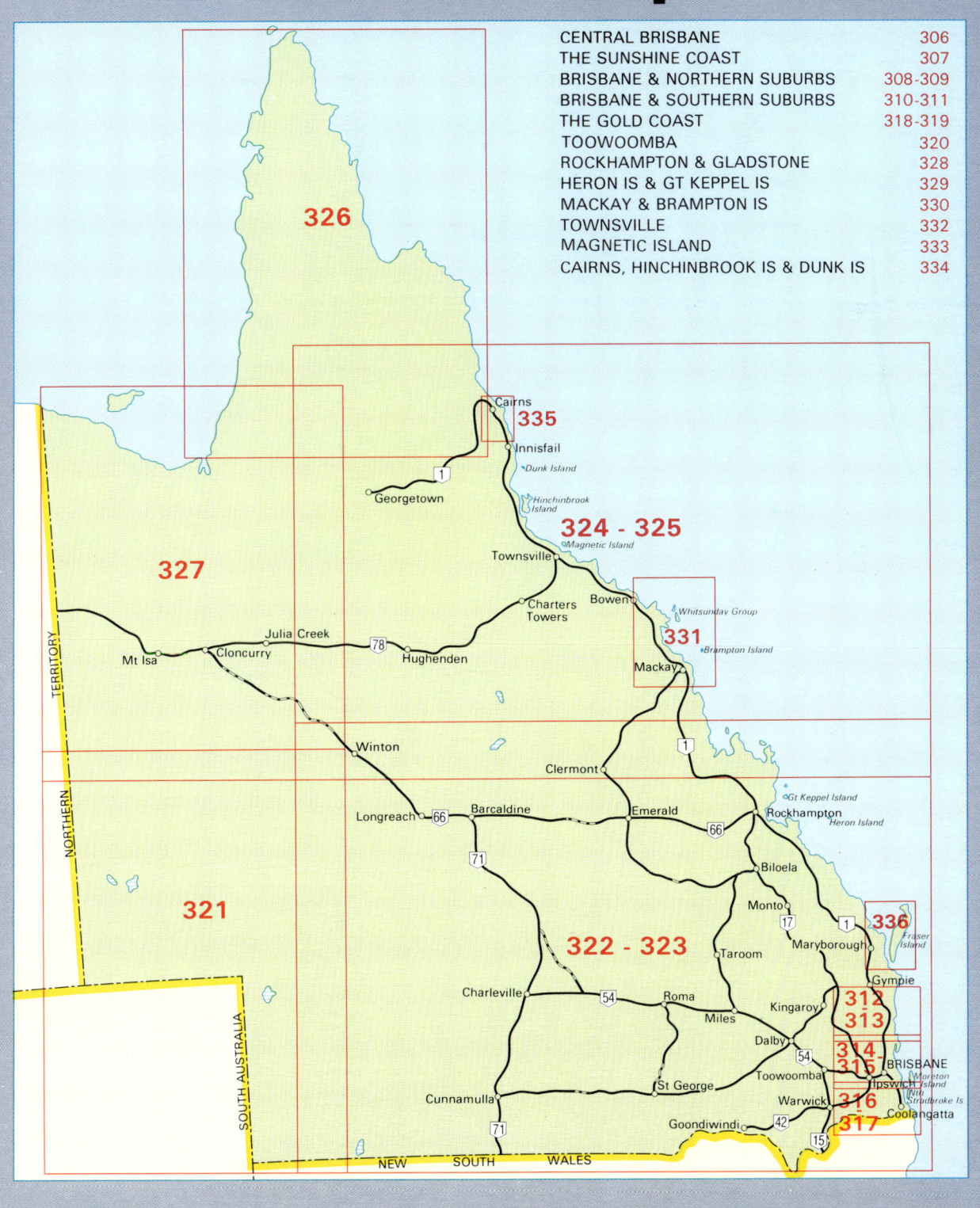

CENTRAL BRISBANE	306
THE SUNSHINE COAST	307
BRISBANE & NORTHERN SUBURBS	308-309
BRISBANE & SOUTHERN SUBURBS	310-311
THE GOLD COAST	318-319
TOOWOOMBA	320
ROCKHAMPTON & GLADSTONE	328
HERON IS & GT KEPPEL IS	329
MACKAY & BRAMPTON IS	330
TOWNSVILLE	332
MAGNETIC ISLAND	333
CAIRNS, HINCHINBROOK IS & DUNK IS	334

306 Central Brisbane

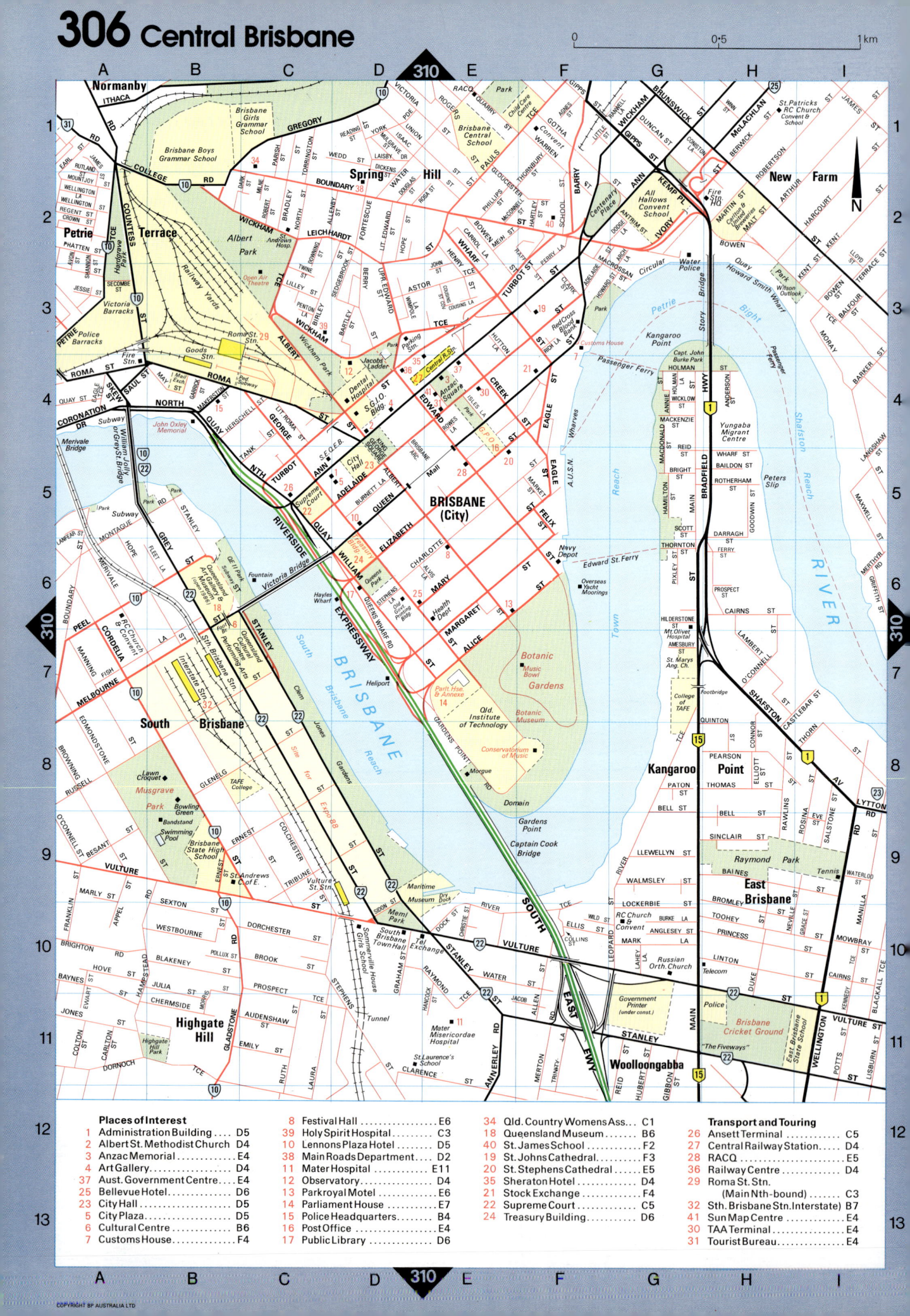

Places of Interest
1. Administration Building D5
2. Albert St. Methodist Church D4
3. Anzac Memorial E4
4. Art Gallery................ D4
37. Aust. Government Centre.... E4
25. Bellevue Hotel............. D6
23. City Hall.................. D5
5. City Plaza................. D5
6. Cultural Centre............ B6
7. Customs House.............. F4
8. Festival Hall E6
39. Holy Spirit Hospital C3
10. Lennons Plaza Hotel D5
38. Main Roads Department D2
11. Mater Hospital E11
12. Observatory D4
13. Parkroyal Motel E6
14. Parliament House E7
15. Police Headquarters B4
16. Post Office E4
17. Public Library D6
34. Qld. Country Womens Ass.... C1
18. Queensland Museum B6
40. St. James School F2
19. St. Johns Cathedral F3
20. St. Stephens Cathedral E5
35. Sheraton Hotel D4
21. Stock Exchange F4
22. Supreme Court C5
24. Treasury Building D6

Transport and Touring
26. Ansett Terminal C5
27. Central Railway Station.... D4
28. RACQ E5
36. Railway Centre D4
29. Roma St. Stn.
    (Main Nth-bound) C3
32. Sth. Brisbane Stn.Interstate B7
41. Sun Map Centre E4
30. TAA Terminal E4
31. Tourist Bureau............. E4

The Sunshine Coast 307

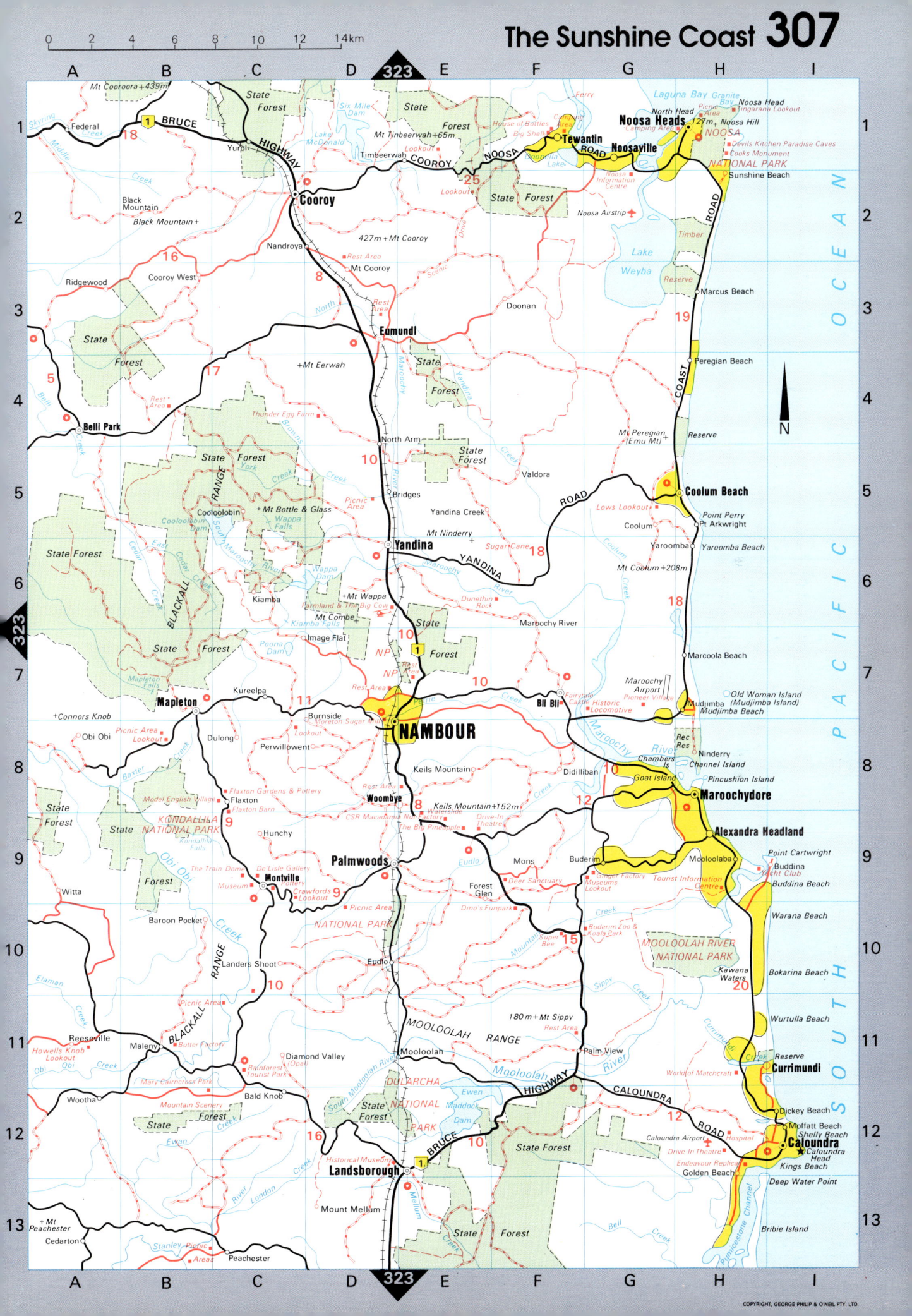

308 Brisbane & Northern Suburbs

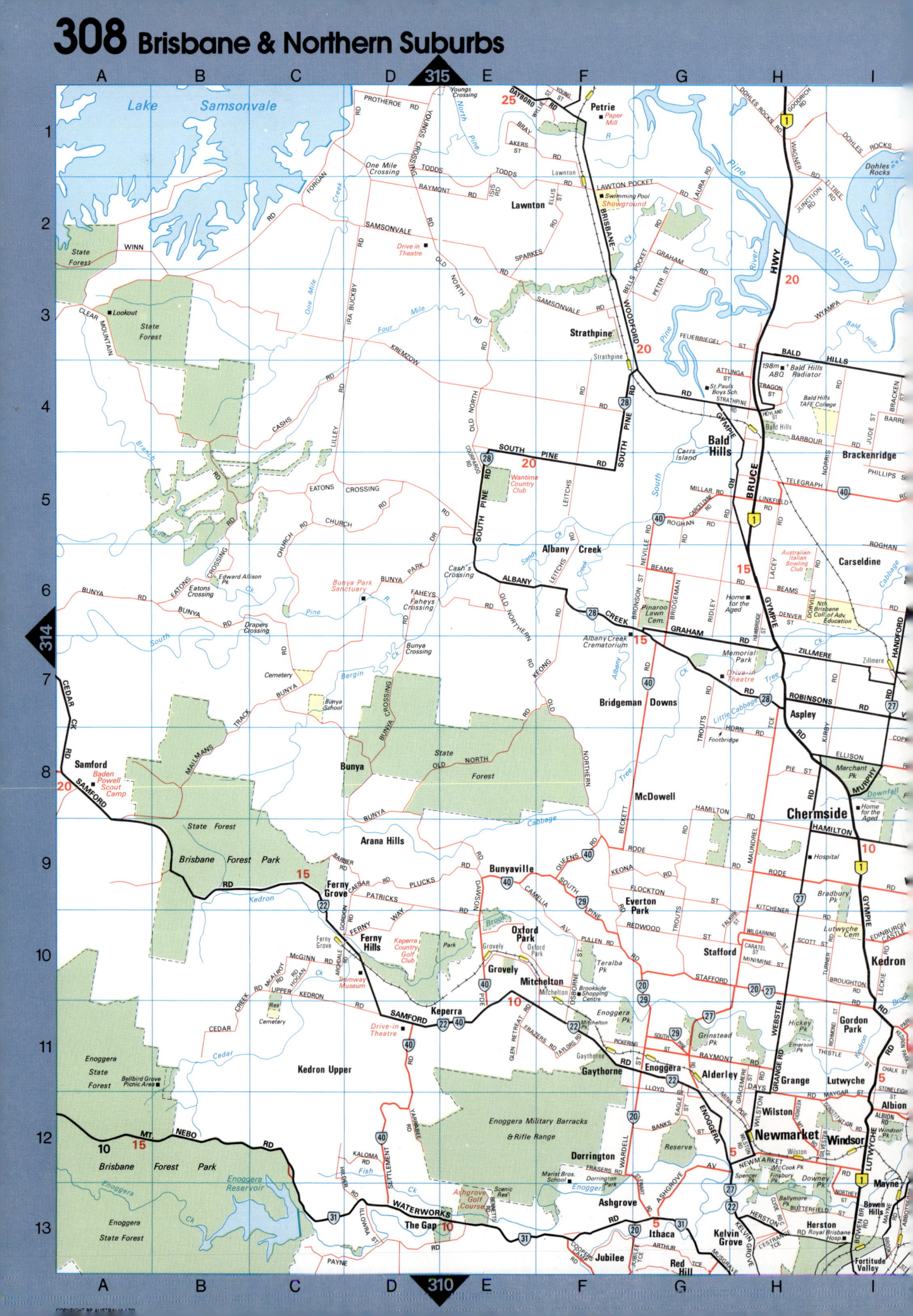

0 1 2 3 4 5km
315
311
J K L M N O P Q R
MORETON BAY
Bramble Bay
Brighton
Nashville
Sandgate
Shorncliffe
Deagon
Boondall
Nudgee Beach
Nudgee
Banyo
Virginia
Northgate
Lower Nudgee
Nundah
Toombul
Eagle Junc.
Wooloowin
Clayfield
Hendra
Ascot
Doomben
Hamilton
Whinstanes
Eagle Farm
Pinkenba
Meeandah
BRISBANE AIRPORT
New International Terminal
Under Construction
Myrtletown
Juno Point
Luggage Point
FISHERMAN ISLANDS
Whyte Island
Bulwer Island
Gibson Island
Lindum
Lytton
Wynnum North
Hemmant
Wynnum
Wynnum Sth
Oyster Pt
Darling Point
Bulimba
Newstead
Queensport
Cabbage Tree Head
Sandgate Pier
Baxters Jetty
Signal Station
Bishop Island
Fisherman Point
Container Terminal
Export Coal Terminal
Boat Passage
Oil Refinery
Quarantine Station
Fort Lytton
Brisbane Abbatoir
Cairncross Graving Dock
Royal Queensland Golf Club
Eagle Farm Racecourse
Doomben R'course
Virginia Golf Course
Nudgee Golf Club
Deagon Racecourse
Boondall Sports & Entertainment Complex
BRISBANE RIVER
Lytton Reach
Hamilton Reach
Bretts Wharf
Gateway Bridge

310 Brisbane & Southern Suburbs

0 1 2 3 4 5km

J K L M N 309 O P Q R

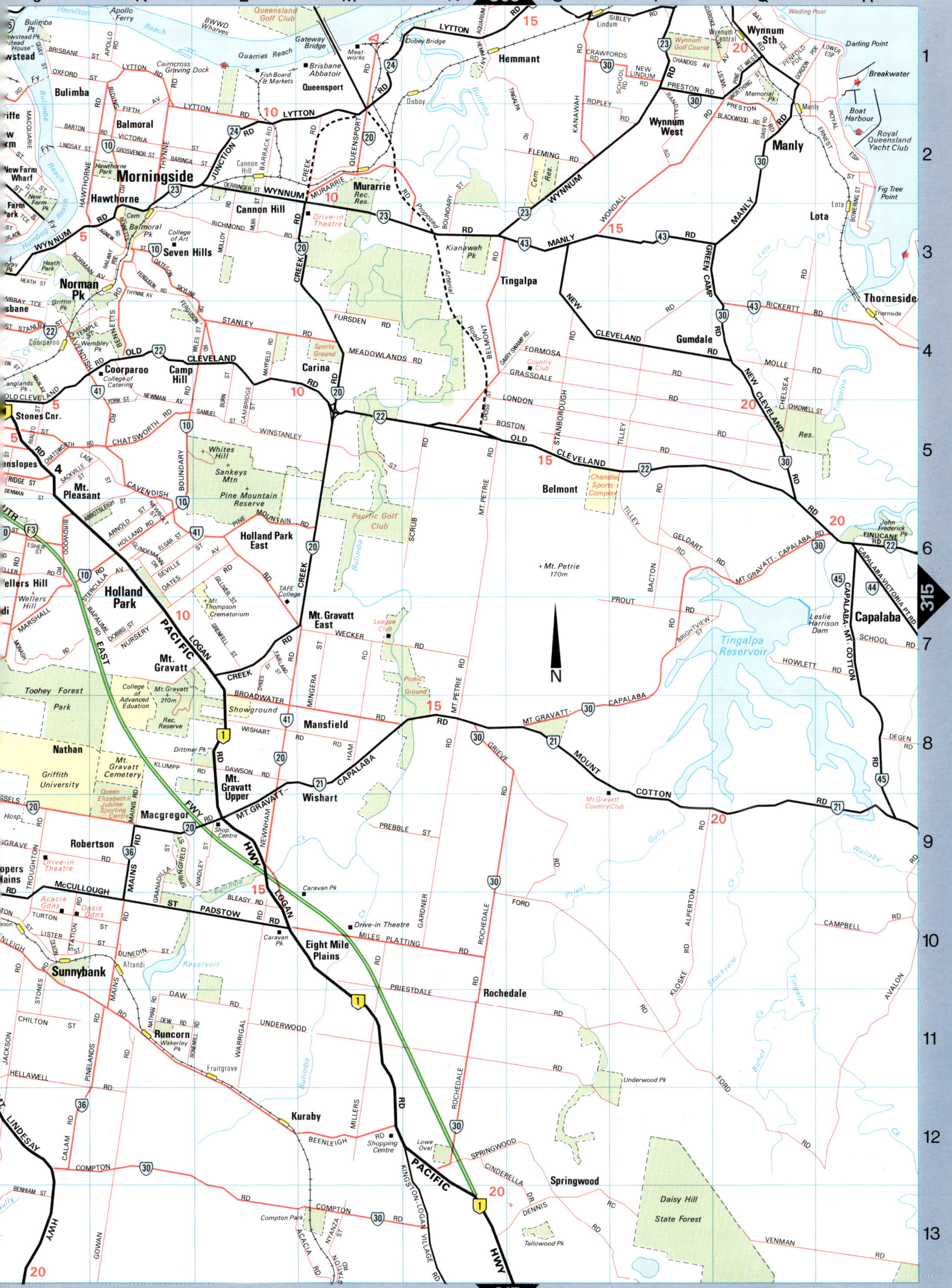

1 2 3 4 5 6 7 8 9 10 11 12 13

J K L M N 315 O P Q R

312 Tours North from Brisbane

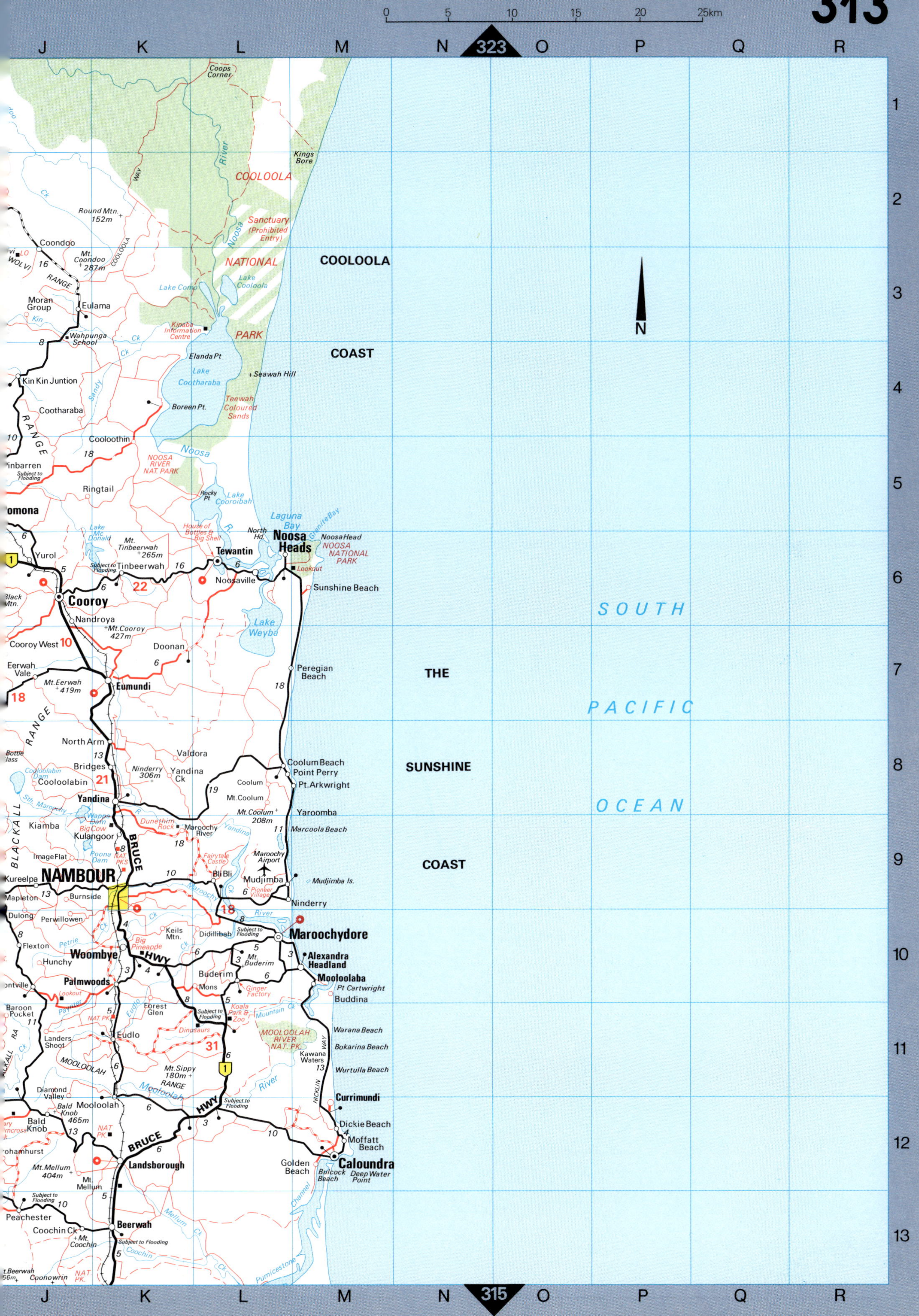
0 5 10 15 20 25km
323
315
COOLOOLA
COAST
THE
SUNSHINE
COAST
SOUTH
PACIFIC
OCEAN
N
COOLOOLA
NATIONAL
PARK
Sanctuary (Prohibited Entry)
Coops Corner
Kings Bore
Round Mtn. 152m
Coondoo
Mt. Coondoo 287m
WOLVI
RANGE
Moran Group
Eulama
Wahpunga School
Kin Kin Juntion
Cootharaba
Cooloothin
Pinbarren
Ringtail
Pomona
Lake Como
Lake Cooloola
Kinaba Information Centre
Elanda Pt
Lake Cootharaba
Seawah Hill
Boreen Pt.
Teewah Coloured Sands
Noosa
NOOSA RIVER NAT. PARK
Rocky Pt
Lake Cooroibah
Laguna Bay
Granite Bay
House of Bottles & Big Shell
Mt. Tinbeerwah 265m
Tinbeerwah
North Hd
Noosa Heads
Noosa Head
NOOSA NATIONAL PARK
Lookout
Tewantin
Noosaville
Sunshine Beach
Yurol
Cooroy
Nandroya
Mt. Cooroy 427m
Lake Weyba
Cooroy West
Doonan
Eerwah Vale
Mt. Eerwah 419m
Eumundi
Peregian Beach
North Arm
Valdora
Coolum Beach
Point Perry
Pt. Arkwright
Bridges
Ninderry 306m
Yandina Ck
Coolum
Mt. Coolum
Mt. Coolum 208m
Yaroomba
Marcoola Beach
Cooloolabin
Yandina
Kiamba
Kulangoor
Dunethin Rock
Maroochy River
Fairytale Castle
Maroochy Airport
BLACKALL
RANGE
BRUCE
ImageFlat
Poona Dam
NAT. PKS
Kureelpa
NAMBOUR
Bli Bli
Mudjimba
Mudjimba Is.
Pioneer Village
Ninderry
Mapleton
Burnside
Dulong
Perwillowen
Keils Mtn.
Didillibah
Subject to Flooding
Maroochydore
Flaxton
Woombye
Big Pineapple
HWY
Mt. Buderim
Alexandra Headland
Hunchy
Buderim
Mooloolaba
Pt Cartwright
Buddina
Palmwoods
Mons
Ginger Factory
Montville
Lookout
Baroon Pocket
Forest Glen
Koala Park & Zoo
Landers Shoot
Eudlo
Dinosaurs
MOOLOOLAH RIVER NAT. PK.
Warana Beach
Bokarina Beach
Kawana Waters
Wurtulla Beach
MOOLOOLAH
Mt. Sippy 180m
RANGE
NICKLIN WAY
Currimundi
Diamond Valley
Mooloolah
Bald Knob 465m
Bald Knob
Dickie Beach
Moffatt Beach
Glasshouse
Mt. Mellum 404m
Mt. Mellum
Landsborough
Golden Beach
Caloundra
Bulcock Beach
Deep Water Point
Peachester
Coochin Ck
Mt. Coochin
Beerwah
Subject to Flooding
Mt. Beerwah
Coonowrin
NAT. PK.
Pumicestone
Channel
Mellum Ck
Coochin Ck

314 Brisbane & Hinterland

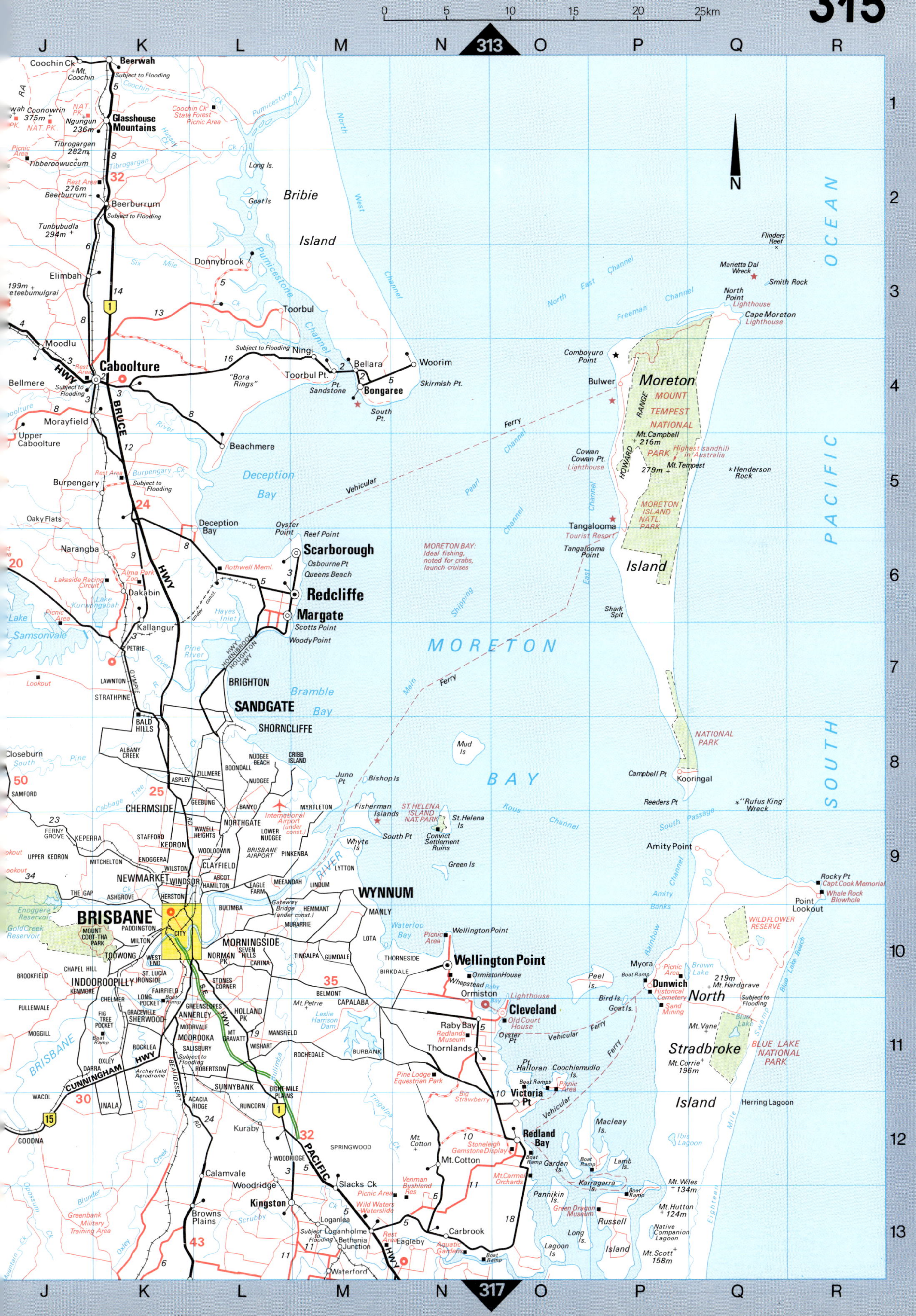

316 Tours South from Brisbane

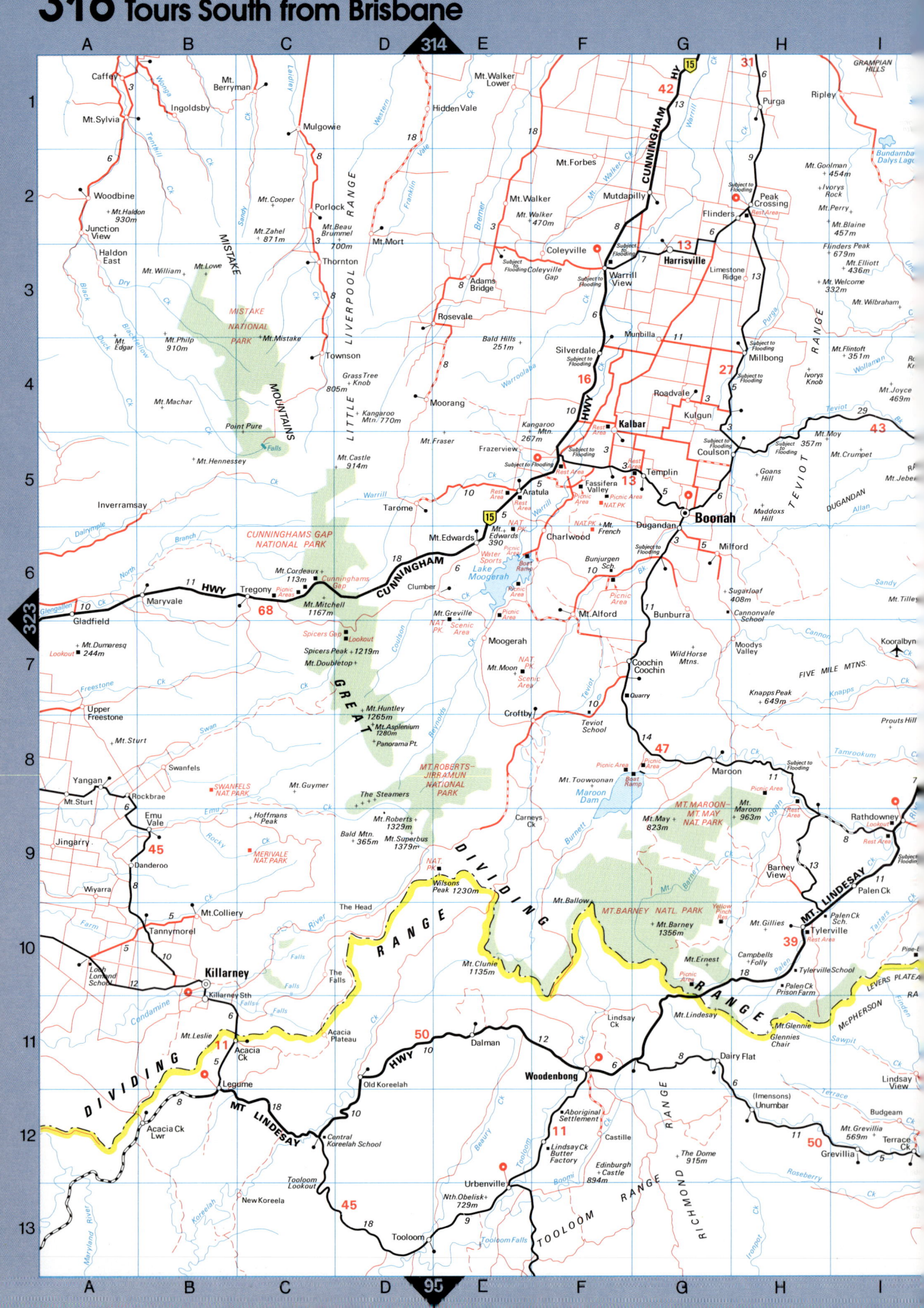

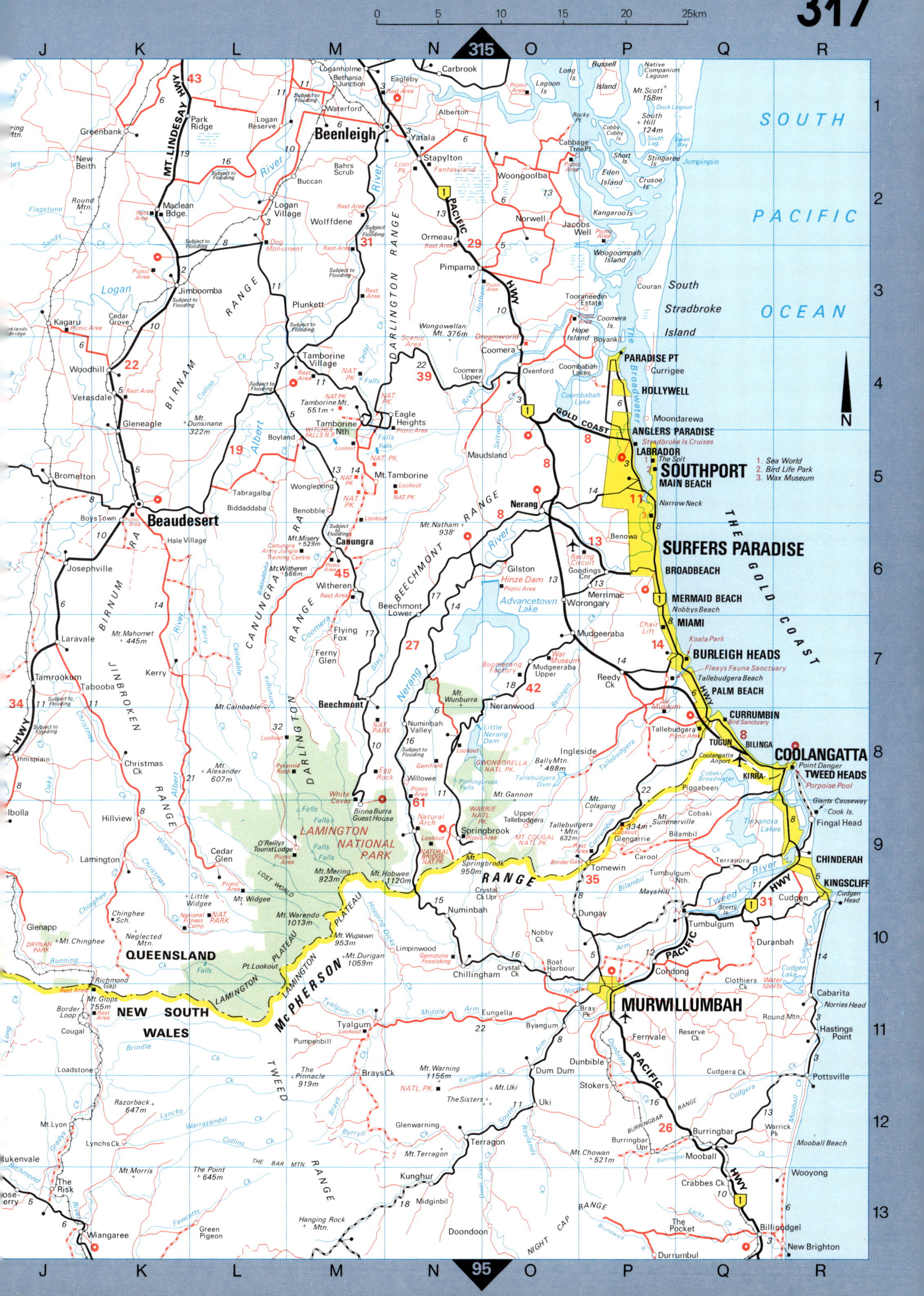

0 5 10 15 20 25km
315
95
J K L M N O P Q R
1 2 3 4 5 6 7 8 9 10 11 12 13
SOUTH PACIFIC OCEAN
South Stradbroke Island
THE GOLD COAST
N
1. Sea World
2. Bird Life Park
3. Wax Museum
Beenleigh
Loganholme
Bethania Junction
Eagleby
Carbrook
Waterford
Logan Reserve
Yatala
Alberton
Stapylton
Woongoolba
Bahrs Scrub
Buccan
Logan Village
Wolffdene
Ormeau
Pimpama
Norwell
Jacobs Well
Russell Island
Long Is.
Lagoon Is.
Native Companion Lagoon
Mt.Scott 158m
South Hill 124m
Duck Lagoon
Swan Bay
Rocky Pt.
Cobby Cobby Is.
Cabbage Tree Pt
Short Is.
Eden Island
Stingaree Is.
Jumpinpin
Crusoe Is.
Kangaroo Is.
Woogoompah Island
Couran
Tooraneedin Estate
Coomera Is.
Hope Island
Boyankil
PARADISE PT
Currigee
HOLLYWELL
The Broadwater
Coombabah Lakes
Coombabah Lake
Moondarewa
ANGLERS PARADISE
Stradbroke Is. Cruises
LABRADOR
The Spit
SOUTHPORT
MAIN BEACH
Narrow Neck
SURFERS PARADISE
BROADBEACH
MERMAID BEACH
Nobbys Beach
MIAMI
Chair Lift
Koala Park
BURLEIGH HEADS
Fleays Fauna Sanctuary
Tallebudgera Beach
PALM BEACH
CURRUMBIN
Bird Sanctuary
TUGUN
BILINGA
COOLANGATTA
Coolangatta Airport
KIRRA
Point Danger
TWEED HEADS
Porpoise Pool
Giants Causeway
Cook Is.
Fingal Head
CHINDERAH
KINGSCLIFF
Cudgen Head
Cudgen
Cudgen Lake
Duranbah
Terranora
Terranora Lakes
Tweed River
Cabarita
Norries Head
Round Mtn.
Hastings Point
Pottsville
Cudgera Ck
Mooball
Mooball Beach
Warrick Pk
Wooyong
Crabbes Ck
Billinudgel
New Brighton
The Pocket
Durrumbul
Burringbar
Burringbar Upr
Burringbar Range
Mt. Chowan 521m
MURWILLUMBAH
Condong
Clothiers Ck
Water Sports
Reserve Ck
Fernvale
Dunbible
Stokers
Bray Pk
Byangum
Dum Dum
Uki
Eungella
Tumbulgum
Tumbulgum Nth.
Mays Hill
Cobaki
Cobaki Broadwater
Piggabeen
Bilambil
Carool
Glengarrie
Mt. Summerville
Mt. Colagang
Tomewin
Border Gate
Tallebudgera Mtn. 632m
Upper Tallebudgera
Tallebudgera
Tallebudgera Dam
Ingleside
Bally Mtn. 488m
Mt. Gannon
Reedy Ck
Mudgeeraba
Mudgeeraba Upper
War Museum
Boomerang Factory
Neranwood
Worongary
Merrimac
Goodings Cnr
Racing Circuit
Benowa
Nerang
Gilston
Hinze Dam
Advancetown Lake
Maudsland
Oxenford
Coomera
Upper Coomera
Dreamworld
Wongawallan Mt. 376m
GOLD COAST
PACIFIC HWY
Beechmont
Beechmont Lower
BEECHMONT RANGE
Mt. Nathan 938'
Numinbah Valley
Little Nerang Dam
GWONGORELLA NATL. PK.
Purlingbrook Falls
Springbrook
Natural Arch
NATURAL BRIDGE NAT.PK
WARRIE NATL. PK.
MT. COUGAL NATL. PK.
Mt. Springbrook 950m
Mt. Wunburra
Willowie
Egg Rock
Binna Burra Guest House
White Caves
LAMINGTON NATIONAL PARK
O'Reillys Tourist Lodge
LOST WORLD
Mt. Merino 923m
Mt. Hobwee 1120m
Mt. Warendo 1013m
Mt. Wupawn 953m
Mt. Durigan 1059m
LAMINGTON PLATEAU
McPHERSON RANGE
Numinbah
Crystal Ck Upr
Dungay
Nobby Ck
Boat Harbour
Crystal Ck
Chillingham
Limpinwood
Gemstone Fossicking
Tyalgum
Pumpenbill
The Pinnacle 919m
Brays Ck
Mt. Warning 1156m
NATL. PK.
The Sisters
Mt. Uki
Glenwarning
Mt. Terragon
Terragon
Kunghur
Midginbil
Doondoon
NIGHT CAP RANGE
Hanging Rock Mtn.
THE BAR MTN RANGE
TWEED RANGE
Tamborine Village
Tamborine Mt. 551m
Tamborine Nth
Eagle Heights
Mt. Tamborine
WITCHES FALLS N.P.
Boyland
Wonglepong
Benobble
Canungra
Canungra Army Jungle Training Centre
Mt. Misery 529m
Mt. Witheren 566m
Witheren
Flying Fox
Ferny Glen
DARLINGTON RANGE
CANUNGRA RANGE
Plunkett
Mt. Dunsinane 322m
BIRNAM RANGE
Albert River
Tabragalba
Biddaddaba
Beaudesert
Boys Town
Hale Village
Bromelton
Gleneagle
Veresdale
Woodhill
Kagaru
Cedar Grove
Jimboomba
Logan River
Flagstone
Maclean Bdge.
Greenbank
Park Ridge
MT. LINDESAY HWY
New Beith
Round Mtn.
Josephville
Laravale
Mt. Mahomet 445m
Tamrookum
Tabooba
Kerry
JINBROKEN RANGE
BIRNUM RA
Mt. Cainbable
Christmas Ck
Mt. Alexander 607m
Hillview
Innisplain
Lamington
Cedar Glen
Mt. Widgee
Little Widgee
NAT. PARK
National Fitness Camp
Chinghee Sch.
Neglected Mtn.
Mt. Chinghee
Glenapp
DRYNAN PARK
QUEENSLAND
NEW SOUTH WALES
Richmond Gap
Mt. Gipps 755m
Border Loop
Cougal
Loadstone
Razorback 647m
Mt. Lyon
Lynchs Ck
Kunkenvale
The Risk
Mt. Morris
The Point 645m
Green Pigeon
Wiangaree

318 The Gold Coast

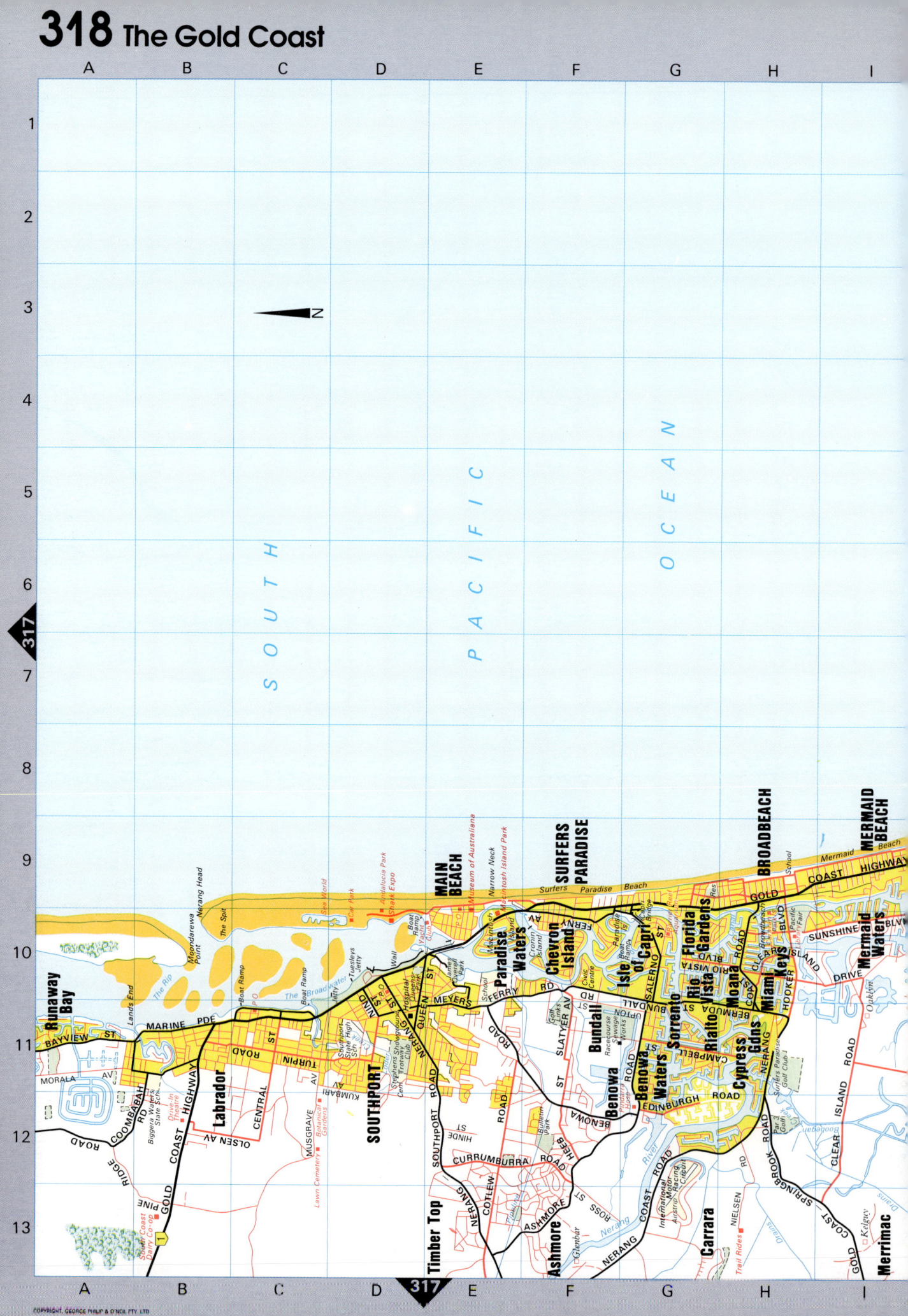

SOUTH PACIFIC OCEAN

Runaway Bay · Morala Av · Bayview St · Marine Pde · Coombabah Rd · Gold Coast Highway · Pine · Ridge Road · Labrador · Olsen Av · Central Av · Turpin Road · Kumbari Av · Musgrave · Lawn Cemetery · Biggera Waters State School · Drive In Theatre · Moondarewa Point · Nerang Head · Lands End · The Rip · The Spit · Sea World · Boat Ramp · Andalucia Park · Shark Expo · Car Park · The Broadwater · Tuesleys Jetty · Boat Ramp · P.O. · Stephens Showgrounds · Southport State High School · Southport · Nerang St · Queen St · Meyers · Hospital · Hinde St · Southport Road · Currumburra Road · Cotlew St · Nerang St · Ashmore · Ross St · Glenbar · Timber Top · Nerang · Museum of Australiana · Narrow Neck · McIntosh Island Park · Main Beach · Surfers Paradise Beach · Surfers Paradise · Ferry Rd · Paradise Waters · Cronin Island · James · School · Ferry Rd · Slatyer Av · Upton St · Bundall · Racecourse Sewage Works · Benowa · Pindara Hosp · Butterfly Park · Chevron Island · Civic Centre · Bundall Rd · Salerno St · Isle of Capri · Bermuda St · Campbell · Benowa Waters · Edinburgh Road · International Moto Airstrip Racing Circuit · Carrara · Nielsen · Nerang Coast Rd · Trail Rides · Florida Gardens · Rio Vista Blvd · Moana · Miami Keys · Hooker Blvd · Sunshine Blvd · Mermaid Waters · Broadbeach · Gold Coast Highway · School · Pacific Fair · Clear Island · Sorrento · Rialto · Cypress Gdns · Surfers Paradise Golf Club · Clear Island Road · Boodgeroi · Par 3 Golf · Oakhri · Kalgru · Springbrook · Gold Coast Highway · Mermaid Beach · Mermaid Waters · Merrimac

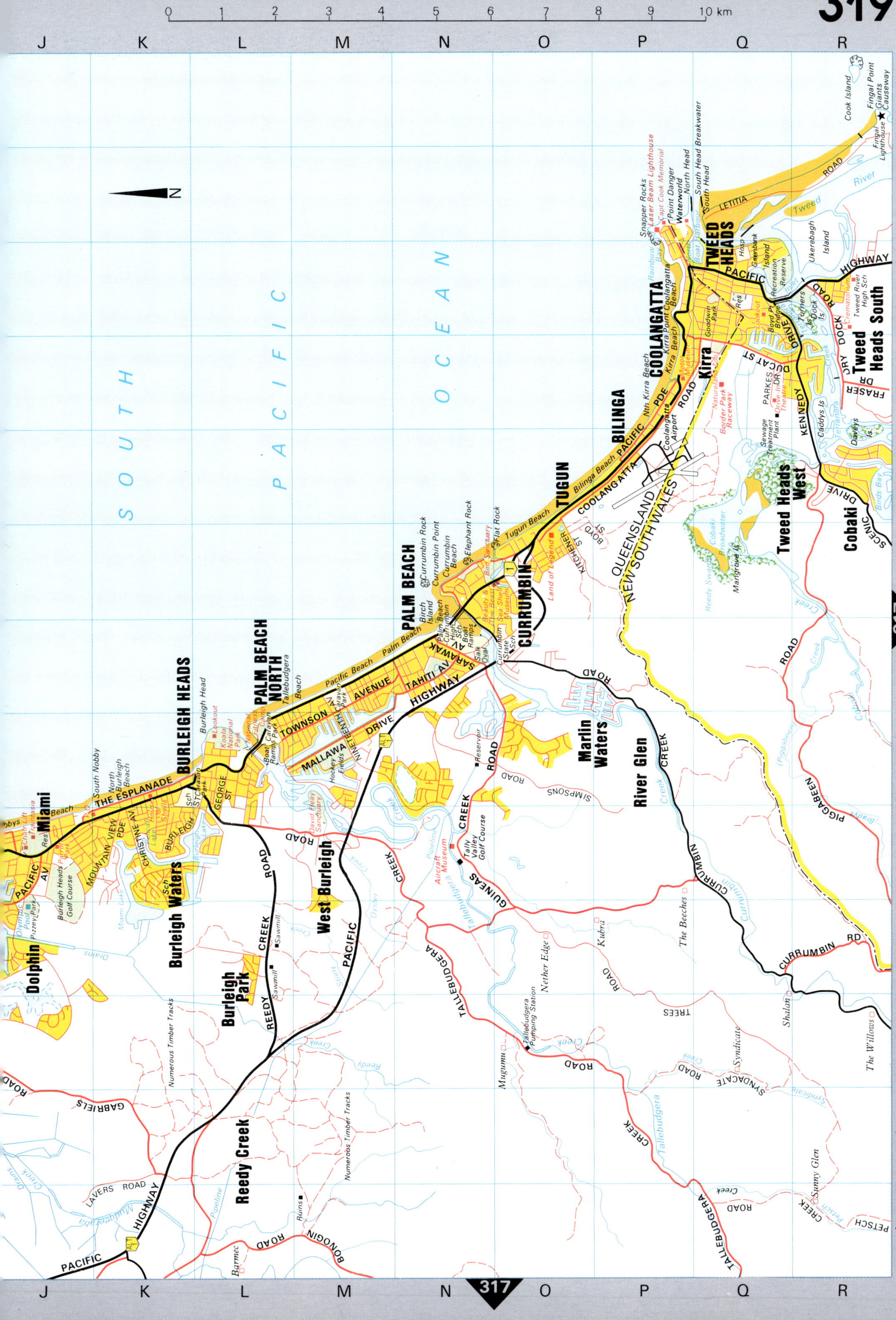
0 1 2 3 4 5 6 7 8 9 10 km
J K L M N O P Q R
1 2 3 4 5 6 7 8 9 10 11 12 13
N
SOUTH
PACIFIC
OCEAN
Fingal Point
Giants Causeway
Fingal Lighthouse
Cook Island
Tweed River
Ukerebagh Island
Snapper Rocks
Laser Beam Lighthouse
Capt Cook Memorial
Point Danger
Waterworld
North Head
South Head Breakwater
South Head
LETITIA ROAD
TWEED HEADS
COOLANGATTA
Rainbow Bay
Coolangatta Beach
Kirra Point
Kirra Beach
Kirra
Greenbank Island
Recreation Reserve
PACIFIC HIGHWAY
Goodwin Park
Boyd Pk
Turners Is
Dry Dock Is
Crematorium
Tweed River High Sch
Tweed Heads South
DRY DOCK ROAD
FRASER DR
DUCAT ST
PARKES DR
Drive-In Theatre
Border Park Raceway
Sewage Treatment Plant
KENNEDY DRIVE
Caddys Is
Daveys Is
Terranora Inlet
Tweed Heads West
Cobaki Broadwater
Mangrove Is
Reedy Swamp
Cobaki
SCENIC DRIVE
Birds Bay
Nth Kirra Beach
PACIFIC PDE
Coolangatta Airport
AIRPORT ROAD
BILINGA
Bilinga Beach
COOLANGATTA ROAD
TUGUN
Tugun Beach
BOYD ST
KITCHENER ST
Land of Legend
QUEENSLAND
NEW SOUTH WALES
Flat Rock
Bird Sanctuary
Elephant Rock
Currumbin Beach
Currumbin Point
Currumbin Rock
CURRUMBIN
Beauty & the Beast
Sea Shell Museum
Currumbin State Sch
PALM BEACH
Birch Island
Palm Beach
Currumbin High Sch
Boat Ramps
SARAWAK AV
TAHITI AV
Pacific Beach
TOWNSON AVENUE
NINETEENTH AV
Caravan Park
MALLAWA DRIVE
Hockey Fields
David Fleay Sanctuary
PALM BEACH NORTH
Tallebudgera Beach
Boat Ramps
Caravan Park
BURLEIGH HEADS
Burleigh Head
Lookout
Koala National Park
THE ESPLANADE
South Nobby
North Burleigh Beach
GEORGE ST
Sch
Miami
Beach
Res
Christine Lake
MOUNTAIN VIEW AV
CHRISTINE AV
PACIFIC PDE
BURLEIGH
Burleigh Lake
Burleigh Heads Golf Course
Olympic Pool
Pizzey Park
Miami Lake
Burleigh Waters
Sch
West Burleigh
Dolphin
Drains
PACIFIC HIGHWAY
Burleigh Park
REEDY CREEK ROAD
Sawmill
Numerous Timber Tracks
Reedy Creek
Oyster Creek
Aircraft Museum
Tally Valley Golf Course
GUINEAS CREEK ROAD
Reservoir
SIMPSONS ROAD
Marlin Waters
River Glen
CURRUMBIN CREEK ROAD
Currumbin Creek
The Beeches
Kubra
Nether Edge
TALLEBUDGERA CREEK ROAD
Tallebudgera Pumping Station
Mugumu
TREES ROAD
SYNDICATE ROAD
Syndicate
Shalan
PIGGABEEN ROAD
Piggabeen Creek
CURRUMBIN RD
The Willows
GABRIELS ROAD
LAVERS ROAD
Mudgeeraba Creek
Pipeline
Ruins
BONOGIN ROAD
Barmec
PACIFIC HIGHWAY
Sunny Glen
PETSCH CREEK ROAD
Tallebudgera Creek

317
317

320 Toowoomba

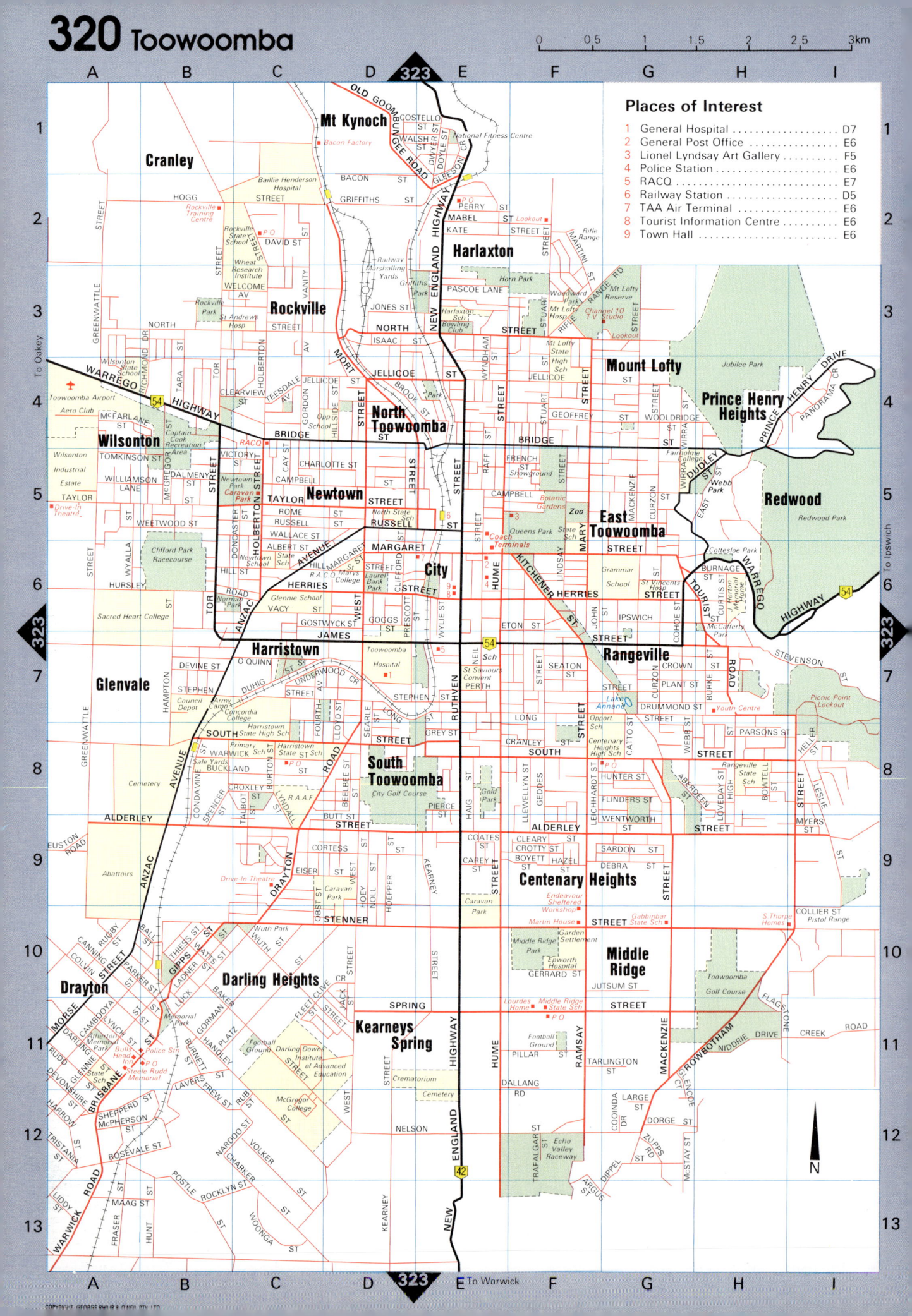

Places of Interest

1. General Hospital ... D7
2. General Post Office ... E6
3. Lionel Lyndsay Art Gallery ... F5
4. Police Station ... E6
5. RACQ ... E7
6. Railway Station ... D5
7. TAA Air Terminal ... E6
8. Tourist Information Centre ... E6
9. Town Hall ... E6

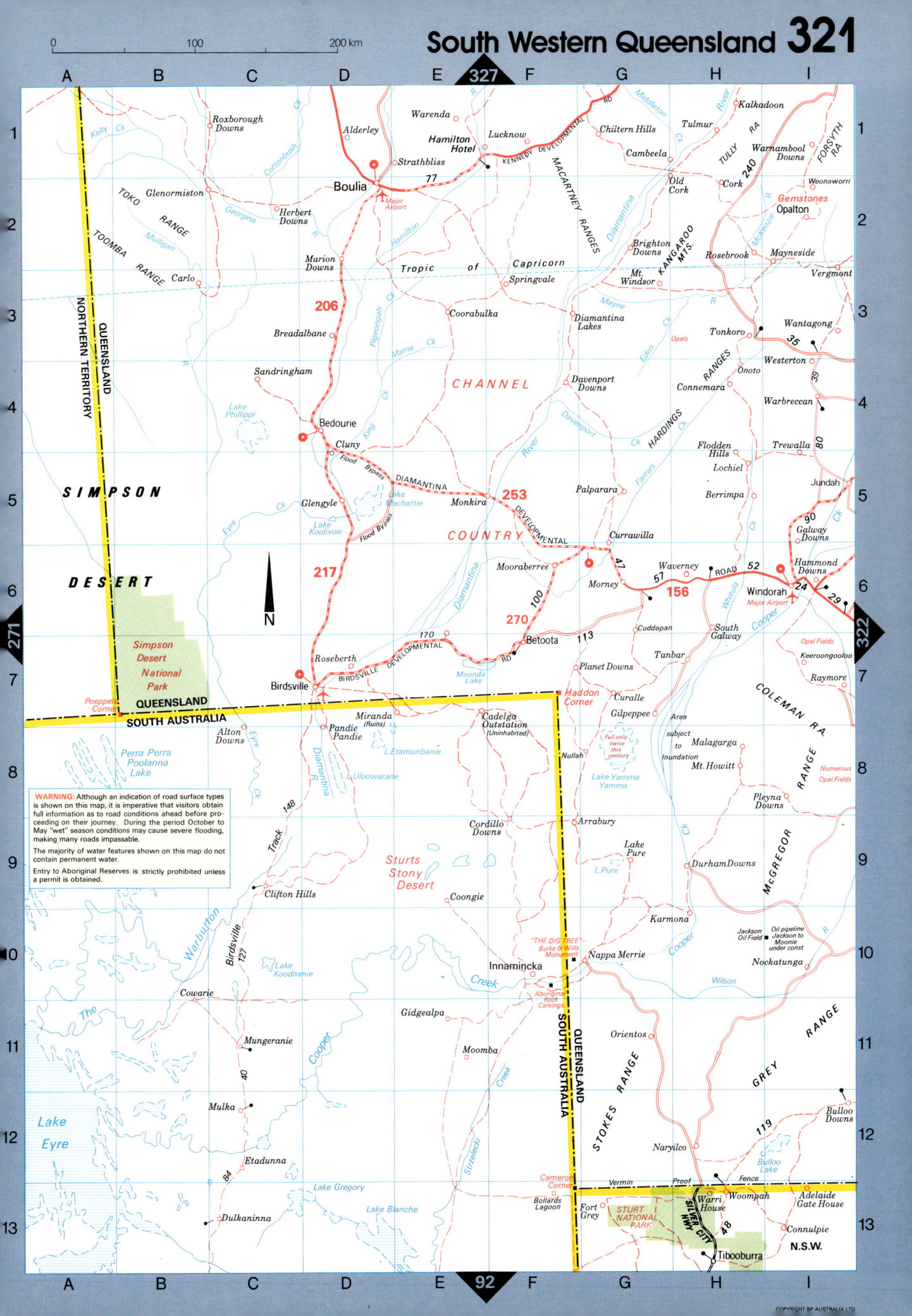

South Western Queensland 321

322 South Eastern Queensland

0
100
200
300 km
325
95
SOUTH PACIFIC OCEAN
GREAT BARRIER REEF MARINE PARK– CAPRICORN SECTION
GREAT BARRIER REEF MARINE PARK– CAPRICORNIA SECTION
GREAT BARRIER REEF REGION BOUNDARY
Tropic of Capricorn
Capricorn Channel
Broad Sound Channel
Shoalwater Bay
MILITARY TRAINING AREA SEAWARD BOUNDARY
MILITARY TRAINING AREA
Prohibited Area
Heron Island
Lady Elliot Island
Curtis Island
Sandy Cape
GREAT SANDY NAT. PARK
Fraser Island
Hervey Bay
ROCKHAMPTON
Yeppoon
Shell Museum
Great Keppel Island
Emu Park
Keppel Sands
Gladstone
Mt. Morgan
Biloela
Monto
Theodore
Taroom
Wandoan
Roma
Miles
Chinchilla
Dalby
Kingaroy
Gayndah
Mundubbera
Eidsvold
BUNDABERG
MARYBOROUGH
Pialba
Gympie
Noosa Heads
Nambour
Maroochydore
Caloundra
THE SUNSHINE COAST
Caboolture
Redcliffe
Sandgate
BRISBANE
Ipswich
Beenleigh
Beaudesert
THE GOLD COAST
SOUTHPORT
Surfers Paradise
Coolangatta
Murwillumbah
Tweed Heads
Brunswick Heads
Byron Bay
Ballina
LISMORE
Casino
Kyogle
Tenterfield
Stanthorpe
WARWICK
TOOWOOMBA
Gatton
Goondiwindi
Boggabilla
Inglewood
Texas
Millmerran
St.George
Dirranbandi
Mungindi
Surat
Mitchell
Emerald
Springsure
Capella
Blackwater
Rolleston
Injune
Banana
Moura
Baralaba
Dingo
Duaringa
Marlborough
St. Lawrence
Dysart
CAPRICORN HWY
BRUCE HWY
DAWSON HWY
BURNETT HWY
LEICHHARDT HWY
WARREGO HWY
CUNNINGHAM HWY
NEW ENGLAND HWY
BRUXNER HWY
NEWELL HWY
CARNARVON HWY
MOONIE HWY
BARWON HWY
PACIFIC HWY
GREAT DIVIDING RANGE
J K L M N O P Q R
1 2 3 4 5 6 7 8 9 10 11 12 13

324 North Eastern Queensland

325

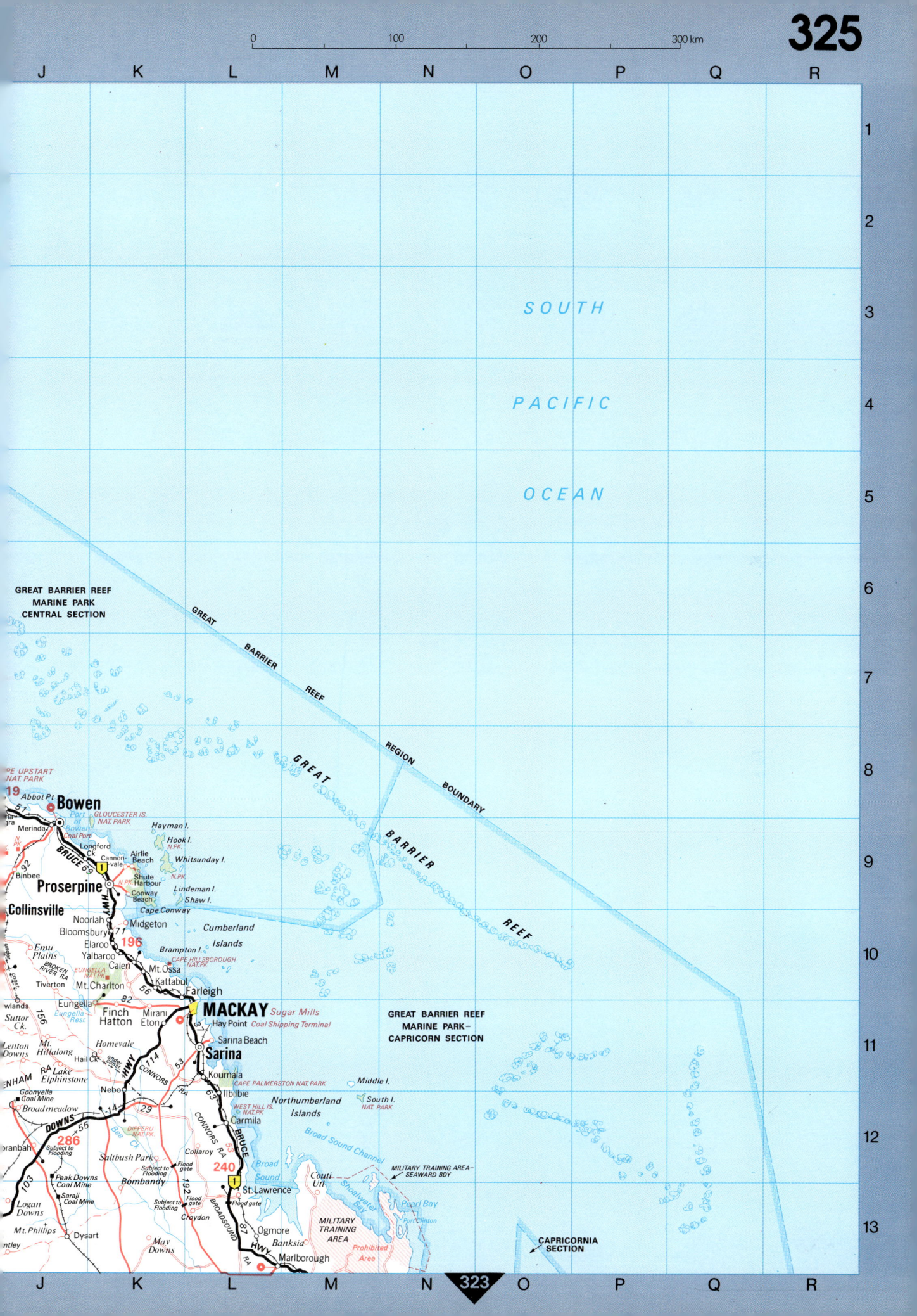

SOUTH PACIFIC OCEAN

GREAT BARRIER REEF MARINE PARK CENTRAL SECTION

GREAT BARRIER REEF REGION BOUNDARY

GREAT BARRIER REEF

GREAT BARRIER REEF MARINE PARK – CAPRICORN SECTION

CAPRICORNIA SECTION

- Abbot Pt
- Bowen
- Port of Bowen Coal Port
- Merinda
- Gloucester Is. Nat. Park
- Longford Ck
- Hayman I.
- Cannonvale
- Airlie Beach
- Hook I. N.P.
- Binbee
- Whitsunday I.
- Proserpine
- Shute Harbour
- Lindeman I.
- Collinsville
- Conway Beach
- Shaw I.
- Noorlah
- Cape Conway
- Bloomsbury
- Midgeton
- Cumberland Islands
- Emu Plains
- Elaroo
- Yalbaroo
- Brampton I.
- Broken River R.A.
- Calen
- Cape Hillsborough Nat. Pk
- Tiverton
- Mt. Ossa
- Eungella Nat. Pk
- Mt. Charlton
- Kattabul
- Eungella
- Finch Hatton
- Farleigh
- Suttor Ck
- Eungella Resr.
- MACKAY
- Sugar Mills
- Mt. Hillalong
- Mirani
- Eton
- Hay Point Coal Shipping Terminal
- Lenton Downs
- Lake Elphinstone
- Sarina Beach
- Sarina
- Hail Ck
- Homevale
- Koumala
- Goonyella Coal Mine
- Nebo
- Ilbilbie
- Cape Palmerston Nat. Park
- Broadmeadow
- West Hill I. Nat. Park
- Middle I.
- Carmila
- Northumberland Islands
- South I. Nat. Park
- Saltbush Park
- Dipperu Nat. Pk
- Collaroy
- Broad Sound Channel
- Peak Downs Coal Mine
- Bombandy
- Subject to Flooding
- Military Training Area – Seaward Bdy
- Saraji Coal Mine
- Croydon
- St. Lawrence
- Broad Sound
- Couti Utti
- Logan Downs
- Flood gate
- Ogmore
- Pearl Bay
- Port Clinton
- Mt. Phillips
- Dysart
- May Downs
- Banksia
- Military Training Area Prohibited Area
- Marlborough

326 Cape York Peninsula

North Western Queensland 327

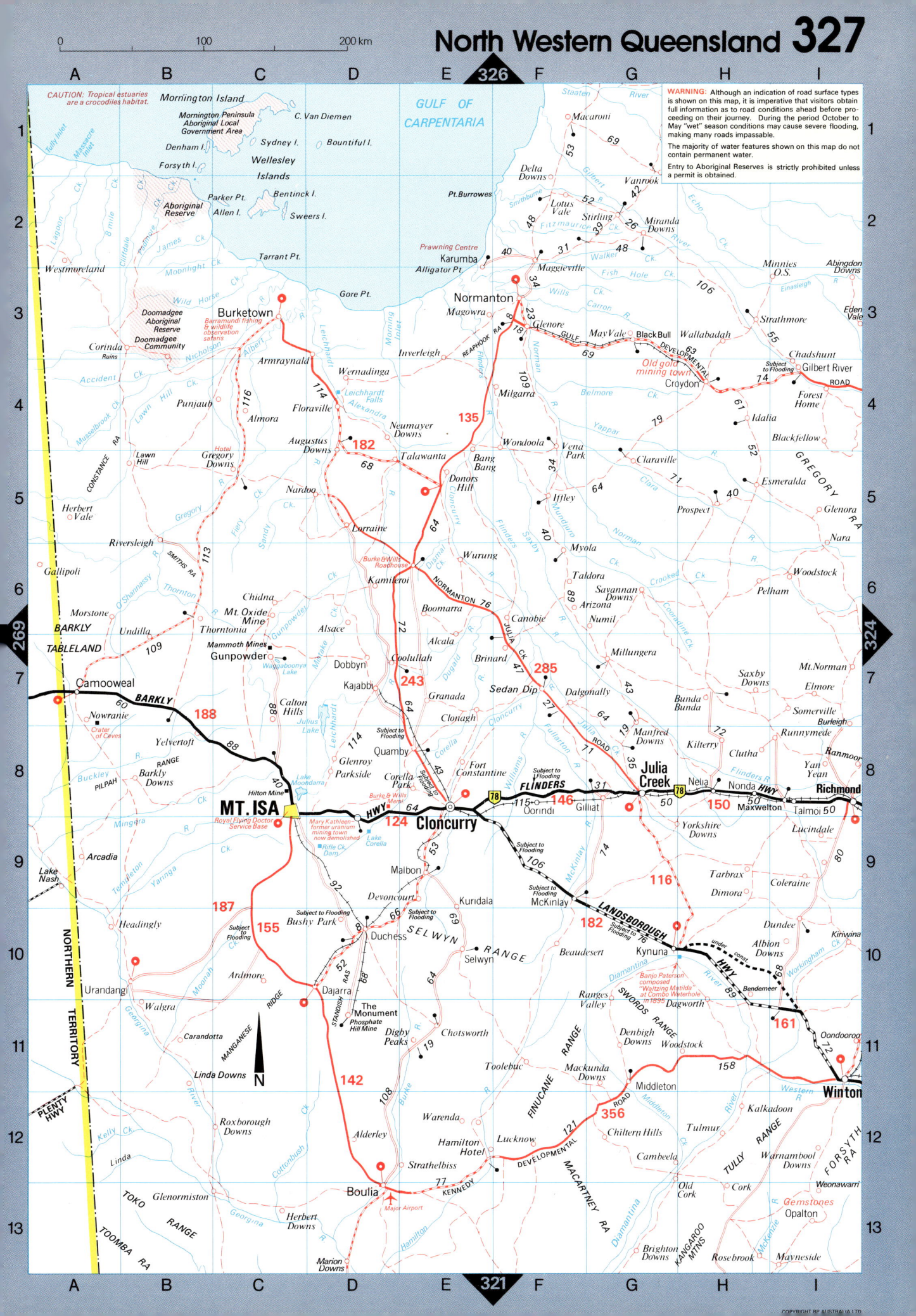

328 Rockhampton and Gladstone

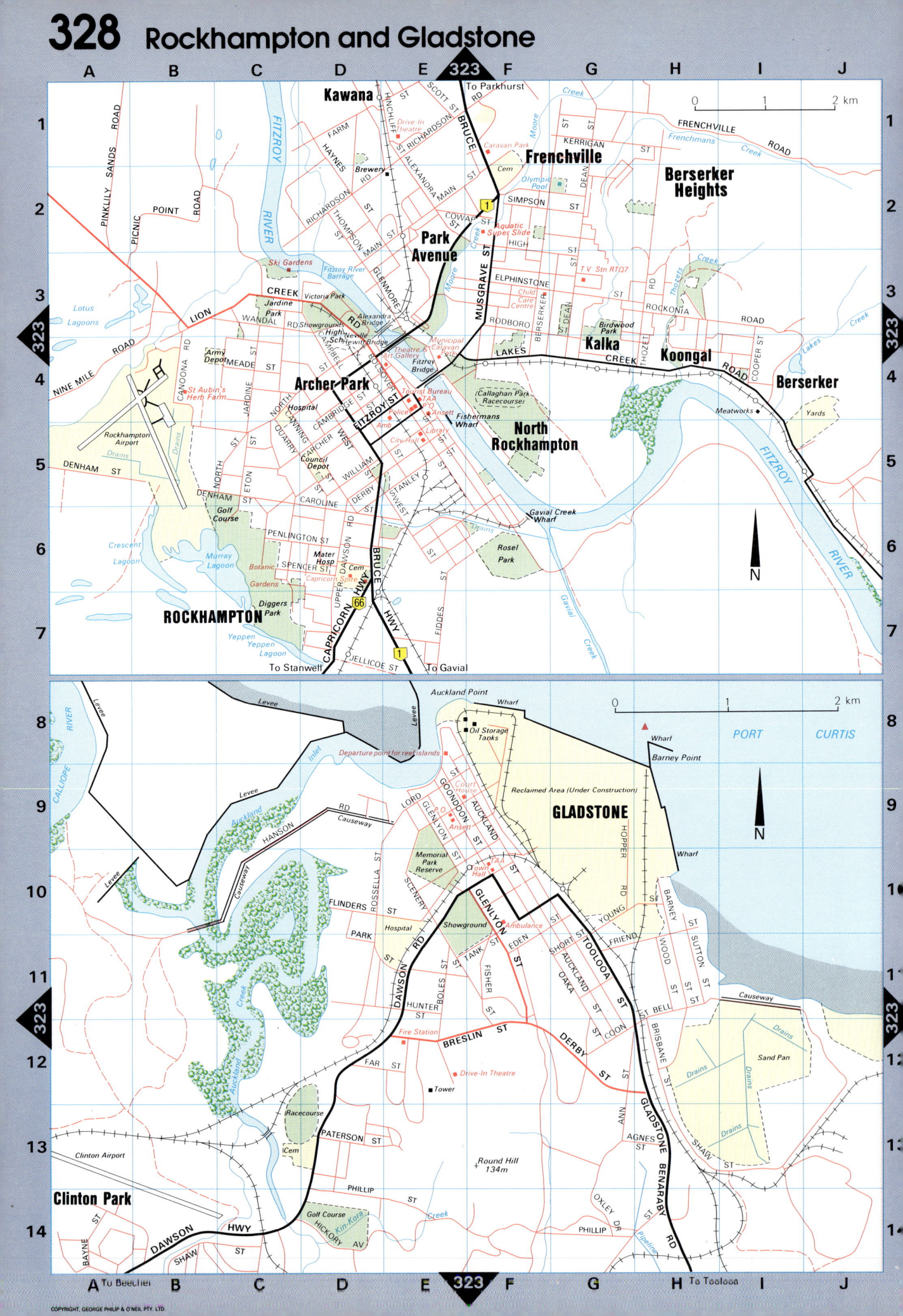

Heron Island and Great Keppel Island 329

330 Mackay and Brampton Island

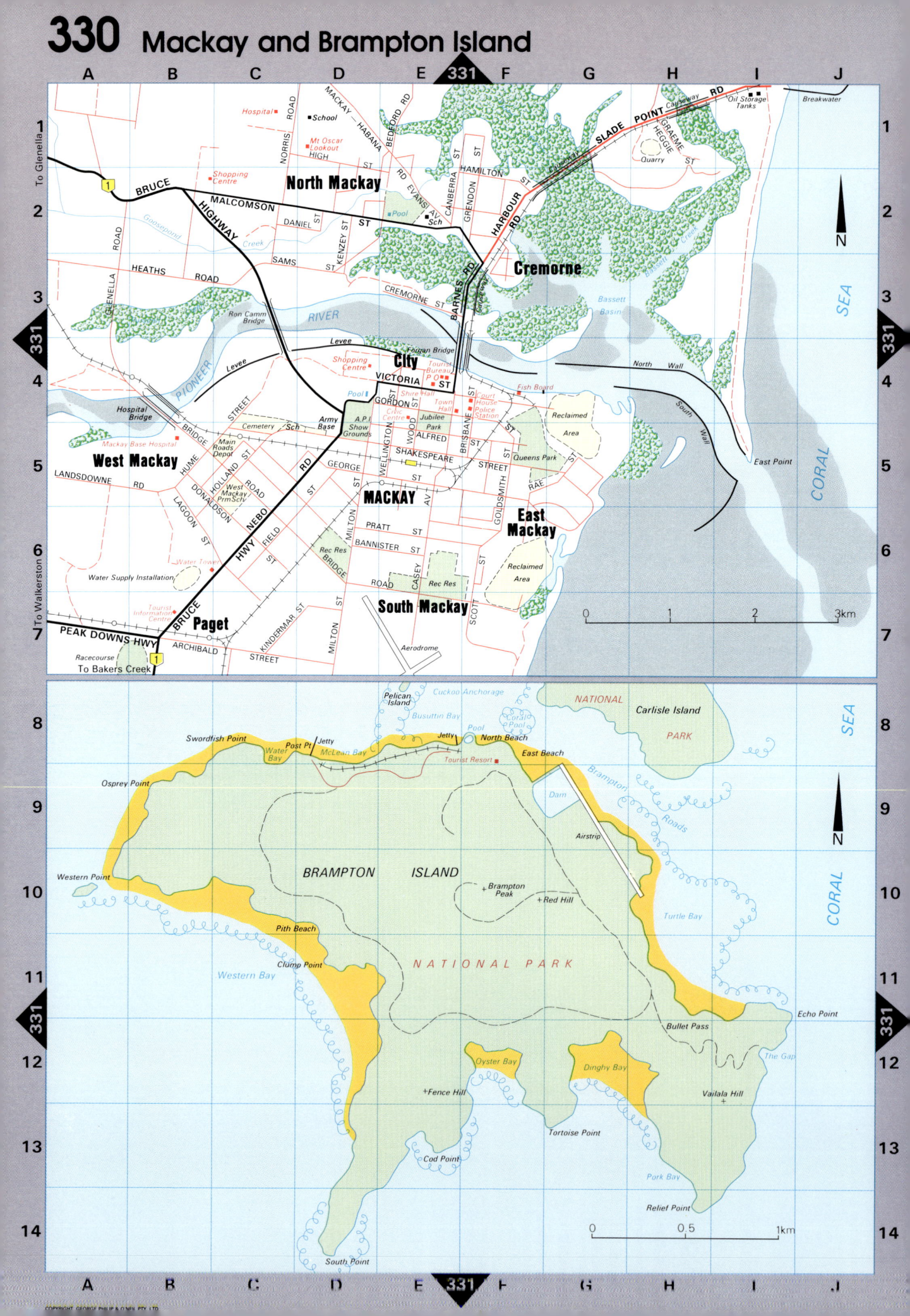

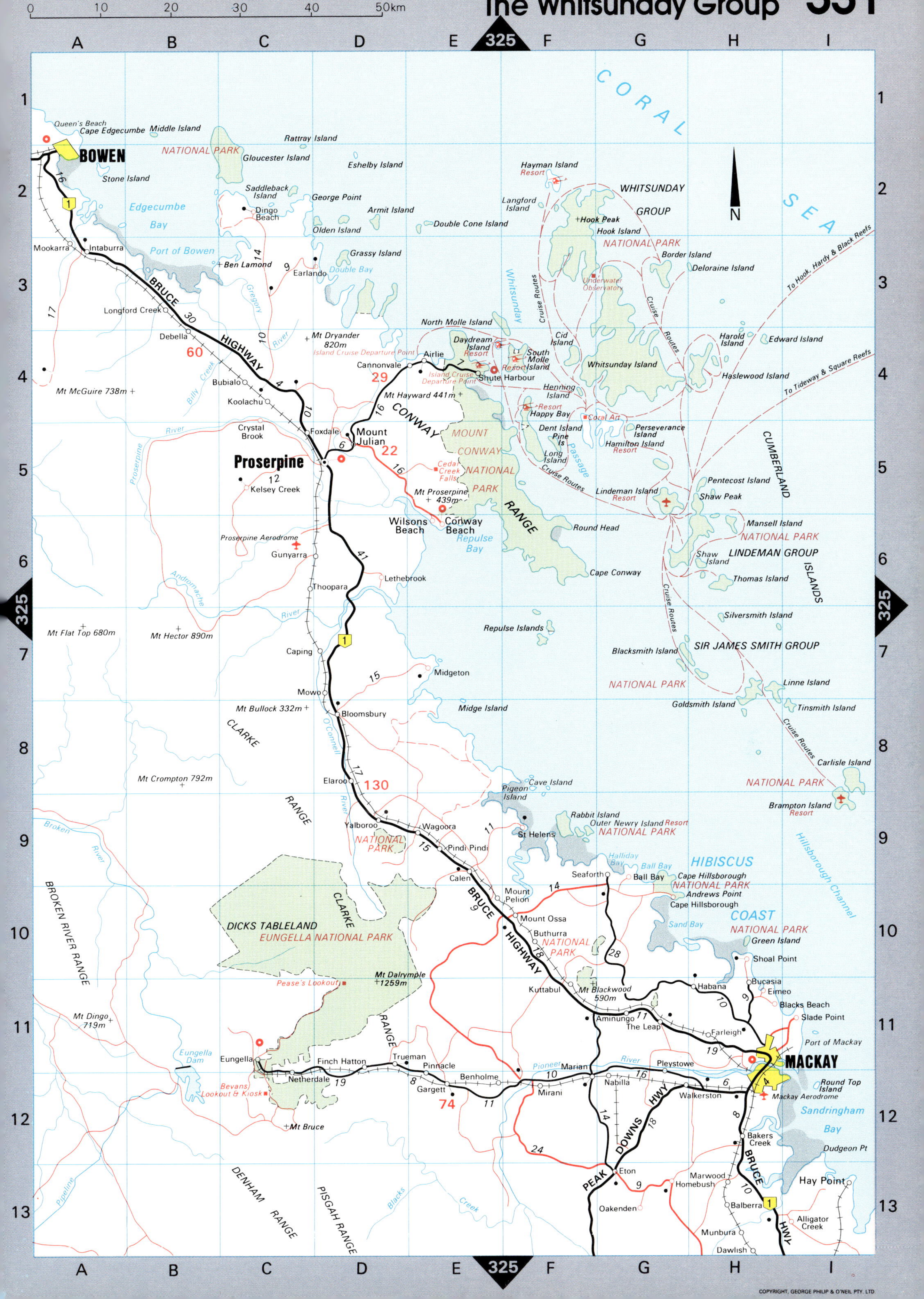

332 Townsville

Places of Interest
1. Ansett G3
2. Sacred Heart Cathedral G3
3. Centenary Fountain H2
4. Fire Brigade G3
5. Government Tourist Bureau G3
6. Police Station G3
7. RACQ F4
8. Supreme Court G3
9. St James Cathedral G3
10. Townsville Central P O F4
11. Town Hall G3
12. Townsville P O G3

Magnetic Island 333

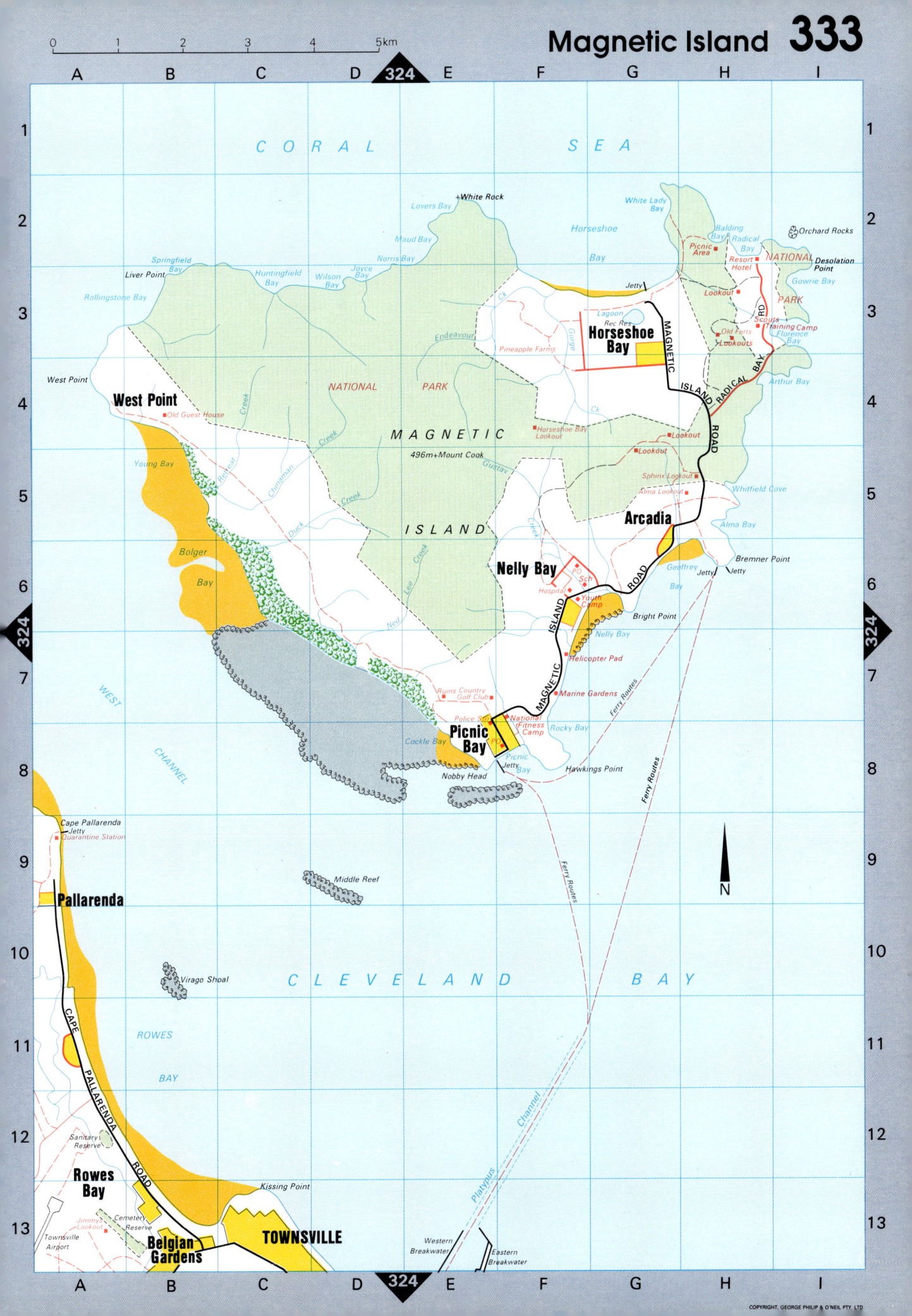

334 Cairns, Hinchinbrook Island and Dunk Island

Tours from Cairns 335

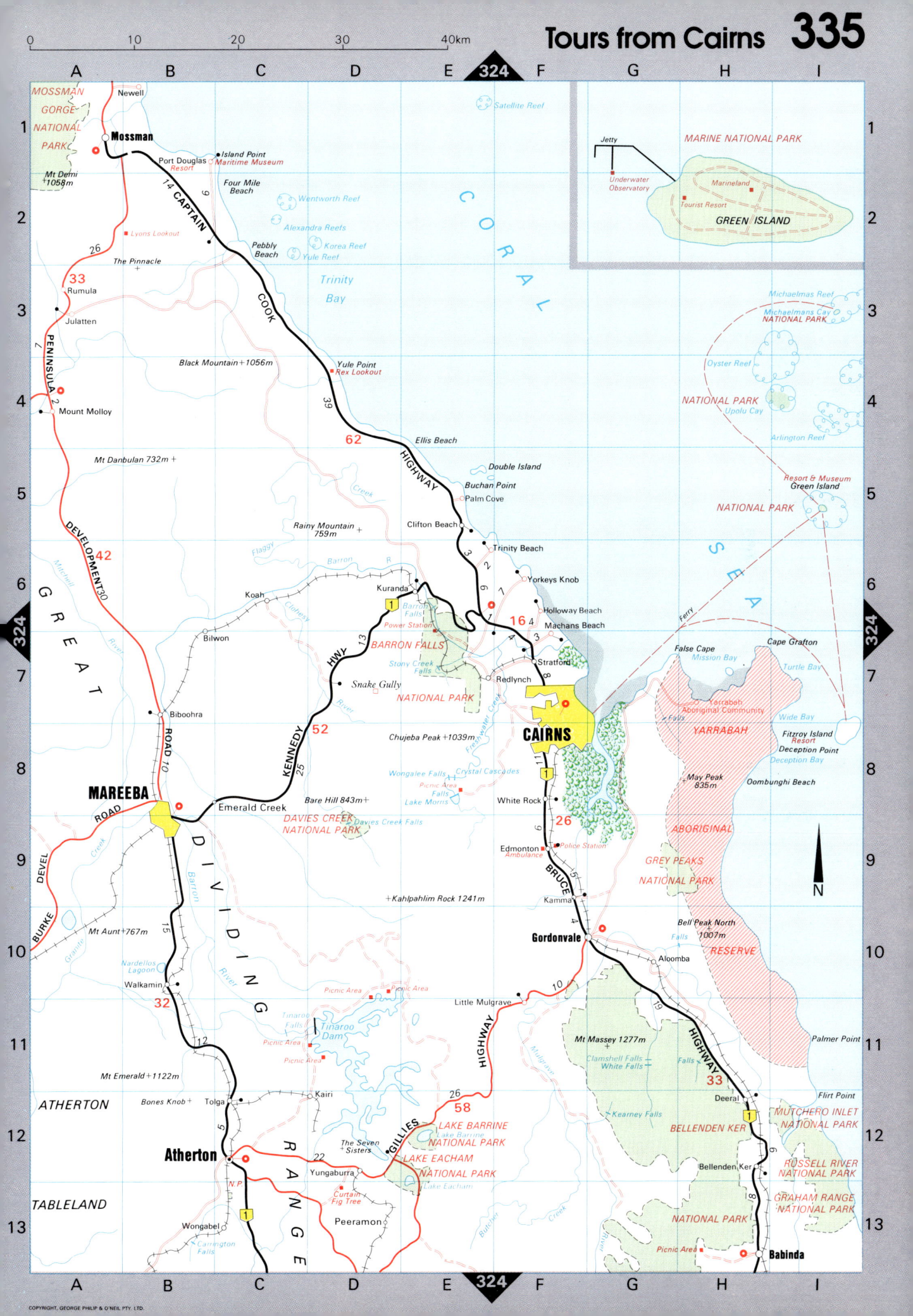

336 Fraser Island

CAUTION: DRIVING ON FRASER ISLAND SHOULD BE UNDERTAKEN ONLY IN FOUR WHEEL DRIVE VEHICLES. LOCAL KNOWLEDGE SHOULD BE SOUGHT. BEACH DRIVING REQUIRES EXTREME CARE ESPECIALLY ON INCOMING TIDES.

FRASER ISLAND

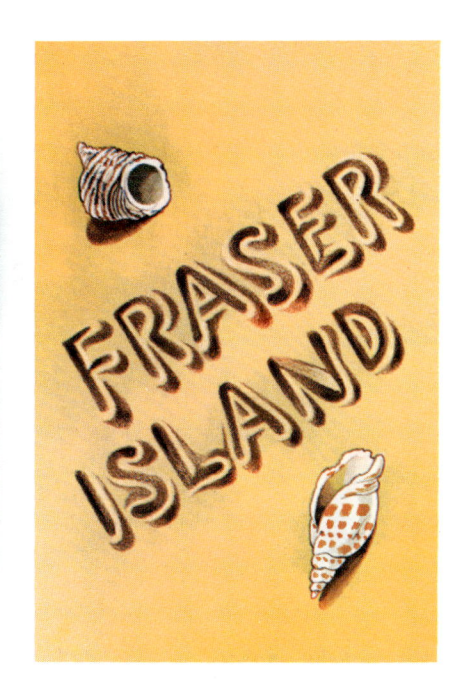

If you like sand, sea, sailing, fishing and plenty of peace and quiet, Fraser Island would be your ideal holiday place. One hundred and twenty-three kilometres long, Fraser is the largest sand island in the world and the largest island on Australia's east coast. It acts as a breakwater, protecting the coast from Bundaberg to well south of Maryborough, and forms the eastern shores of Hervey Bay, a magnificent stretch of sheltered water which is ideal for sailing and which also attracts hundreds of fishermen each year for the annual tailor season.

Fraser's remote and abundant sand dunes are particularly attractive to those with 4-wheel drives and beach buggies, but the island is large enough to accommodate them in certain areas without upsetting the peace and quiet.

Apart from its long stretches of beautiful beach, Fraser Island has a unique area of freshwater lakes and tangled rainforests. There are over 40 lakes on the island, all of them above sea level, and the dense forests surrounding them attract a wide range of bird and animal life.

An odd geological feature of the island is its ever moving creeks which may run parallel to the ocean for several kilometres, then spill through a dune, carving a new course through the sand to the sea.

The island is accessible by air service from Brisbane, Maroochydore, Maryborough, Hervey Bay or Toowoomba or by barge from Inskip Point (Rainbow Beach).

There are three areas of accommodation on the ocean side of Fraser Island, at Orchid Beach, Happy Valley and Eurong.

The Orchid Beach island village is at the northern end of the island, overlooking the 32 kilometre sweep of Marloo Bay and the main surf beach — a rarity on Queensland islands as those further north are sheltered from the surf by the Barrier Reef. All these holiday centres offer family accommodation.

Several settlements on the coastal shores of Hervey Bay have also been developed as holiday resorts. Swimming, fishing and boating are the main recreations, but there are also facilities for sporting activities.

The two large cities in the region, Maryborough and Bundaberg, serve an area rich in primary production,

BELOW: *Wide expanses of beautiful beach are the best-known feature of Fraser Island, the largest sand island in the world.*

ABOVE: *A creek flows by lush ferns.*

particularly of sugar, tobacco, pineapples and other tropical fruit, seed crops and dairy produce. They are both handsome cities where tropical trees and flowering shrubs make a brilliant display in the spring.

The climate in this central coastal region of Queensland is warm, moist and equable, varying little in temperature between winter and summer. Because of the rainfall distribution, May to October is the best time of the year for holidaymakers.

Further information on Fraser Island and the Hervey Bay district can be obtained from the Queensland Government Tourist Bureau.

BELOW: *Four wheel drive vehicles are ideal for Fraser Island.*

Far left: The colourful crop of the Huon Valley is the reason why Tasmania is sometimes called the 'Apple Isle'.

Left: The tower of the Wrest Point Hotel-Casino is the most prominent building in Hobart.

Above: Attractive rural scenes like this abound in Tasmania's countryside.

Right: Ruined sandstone walls at Port Arthur are a grim reminder of Tasmania's past.

Tasmania
HOLIDAY ISLAND

Tasmania has certainly won many more hearts than it can claim square kilometres. It has only 68 000 of the latter, but it crams into them its rugged west, a central plateau broken by steep mountains and narrow river valleys, and an eastern coastal region offering a soft 'English' pastoral beauty. Its diverse charms have made it a popular tourist attraction for Australians from 'the mainland' for many years.

This pretty island, however, has a far from pretty early history. First sighted by Abel Tasman in 1624, it was later claimed by Cook for the English and was first settled in 1803. For the next fifty years, it was maintained primarily as a penal colony, although settlement developed quite prosperously around Hobart and New Norfolk. The convicts did the hard labour and lived in brutal conditions at Port Arthur. The only people treated more harshly than the convicts were the Aborigines, who resisted the takeover of their tribal lands and were systematically wiped out. Political separation from New South Wales was granted in 1825 and transportation of convicts ceased in 1852. Today, the ruins of Port Arthur have taken on a mellow charm and Tasmania is an infinitely more hospitable place.

Tasmania was first called Van Diemen's Land; these days it is known as the 'holiday island', 'treasure island' or the 'apple isle'. Its economy is basically agricultural but secondary industry now contributes goods worth over 200 million dollars a year. It produces half of Australia's tin and the largest zinc refinery in the world is near Hobart. The Tasmanian hydro-electric system has a greater output than that of the Snowy Mountains Scheme. Tasmania's high rainfall helps in this area. The climate offers mild summers and cool winters, with much of the mountain regions receiving heavy winter snowfall. Mid-December to late January is very popular with visitors and it is worth considering late spring or autumn when the weather is just as pleasant and the countryside is picturesque with pear and apple blossom or autumn colours.

Another consideration when planning a trip to Tasmania is the heavy booking for the ferry service from Melbourne from December to April. Either book far in advance or consider fly/drive which can be a relaxing and economic alternative.

Tasmania's roads are well suited to relaxed meandering, many of them being winding and narrow. In a fortnight, however, you can happily complete what is virtually a round tour of the island, taking in some interesting detours on the way.

Built on either side of the Derwent River, Hobart, capital of Tasmania, is dominated by Mt Wellington. The Wrest Point Casino, with its lavish entertainments and International Convention Centre, is now competing for first place as the city's best known landmark, towering over Hobart's many colonial buildings which reflect its early days. Port Arthur, Richmond with its beautiful bridge — the oldest in Australia — and the early settlements of Bothwell and New Norfolk are all within easy reach.

The Derwent Valley with its hop fields and apple orchards, lovely in blossom time, lies to the west, and further west is Lake Pedder. The flooding of this spectacular country was a source of great controversy when it was made part of the Tasmanian hydro-electric scheme. The surrounding country makes up the South West National Park, Tasmania's largest. The Lyell Highway then leads to the stunning Cradle Mountain-Lake St Clair National Park, with its 'European' style alpine scenery and deep, still lakes. Queenstown, surrounded by eerie white mountains, is the largest settlement in this wild, forested region. Nearby coastal Strahan was once a mining boom town and is the starting point of the October to May Gordon River cruises. North of Queenstown, the town of Zeehan is currently enjoying a mining revival, with the re-opening of the Renison Bell Tin Mine.

The north coast is yet another contrasting area. Burnie is one of the larger towns and Stanley is a classified 'historic town' situated on The Nut, an unusual peninsula. East of Burnie, the Bass Highway hugs the coast as far as Devonport, the terminal of the Bass Strait passenger/vehicle ferry and the centre of a productive apple growing area. Inland from here is Launceston, Tasmania's second largest city. Situated on the River Tamar, Launceston has many well-preserved old buildings. Only minutes from the city centre is the beautiful Cataract Gorge and the nearby colonial villages of Evandale, Hagley, Westbury, Carrick, Perth, Longford and Hadspen are well worth a visit.

A mild climate, good surfing beaches and sheltered seaside resorts add to the attraction of the green and lovely east coast region. St Helens, 160 kilometres east of Launceston, is the principal resort town. Don't miss Bicheno, a picturesque old port and one-time whaling town. Further south, the Hazards, a red granite mountain range, tower up behind Coles Bay, at the entrance to the Freycinet Peninsula National Park, with its beautiful beaches. Nearby Swansea offers top class sea and freshwater fishing.

Whether you complete a round trip or only explore parts of this island state, it's very likely that, by the time you come to leave, Tasmania will have won yet another heart.

Hobart
AN HISTORIC CITY

Hobart is an enchanting little city built around a beautiful yacht-studded harbour in the shadow of majestic Mt Wellington. A strong sea-faring flavour and sense of the past give Hobart an almost European air. This feeling is heightened in winter when Mt Wellington is snow-capped and temperatures drop to a crisp 5°C. The rest of the year Hobart gets plenty of sparkling blue days but temperatures rarely exceed 25°C.

Many of Hobart's beautiful early colonial sandstone buildings were erected by the sweat and blood of the unfortunate convicts who formed the majority of the first settlers in 1803.

Hobart's deepwater harbour on the broad estuary of the Derwent River soon became a thriving seaport and by 1842 Hobart was proclaimed a city. The harbour is still Hobart's lifeblood and the port is always busy — especially in autumn when the state's annual apple crop is loaded for export around the world. The suburbs nestle right up to the lower slopes of **Mt Wellington** and the city's population of 172 500 spreads both sides of the graceful **Tasman Bridge**, which made tragic world headlines in January 1975, when it was rammed by a cargo ship.

From the bridge you will see **Government House** and the **Royal Botanical Gardens** set in the Queen's Domain — a large parkland with sporting facilities and an adventure playground. Within the lovely old Botanical Gardens is a children's playground and a restaurant which serves lunch and teas.

In a matter of minutes from here you are in the heart of Hobart which has been bypassed by the usual pressures of modern city life. Parking is no problem but most of the narrow city streets are one-way.

Hobart's waterfront retains much of its early character and it is not hard to imagine it in the early whaling days when Hobart Town was a lusty, brawling seaport known to sailors all round the world. Foreign ships tie up almost in the centre of town — battered whalers now replaced by neat Japanese fishing trawlers. Wander around to **Constitution Dock**, the haven for the yachts in the famous annual Sydney to Hobart Yacht Race; you can buy live seafood from the fishermen just in with their catch.

Just around the corner, in Argyle Street, is the **Tasmanian Museum and Art Gallery**, which has a fine collection of early prints and paintings, Aboriginal artefacts and convict relics. From here it's but a short stroll to the **Theatre Royal**, which was built in 1837 and is the oldest theatre in Australia. It is worth going inside to glimpse its charming dolls'-house scale Georgian interior. Dame Sybil Thorndike rated it as the finest theatre she had played in outside London.

Heading back towards the centre of the city you will see Hobart's imposing sandstone old **Town Hall**, built on the site of the original **Government House**, on the corner of Macquarie and Elizabeth Streets.

Australia's second oldest capital, Hobart has a wealth of beautiful Georgian buildings — mostly concentrated in Macquarie and Davey Streets. More than 90 of them have National Trust classification and the **Anglesea Barracks**, in Davey Street, is the oldest military establishment in Australia still used by the Army. The Tasmanian Government Tourist Bureau in Elizabeth Street has produced an excellent free brochure called *Let's Talk About Hobart's Historic Buildings*.

Several large modern complexes blend in with the old buildings without destroying the overall scale and atmosphere. The largest landmark is the tower of Australia's first hotel-casino, **Wrest Point**, built on a promontory in the elite suburb of **Sandy Bay**, just out of town. Back towards the waterfront is the famous **Salamanca Place**, which displays the finest row of early merchant warehouses in Australia. Dating back to the whaling days of the 1830s, the whole area has been sympathetically restored and the warehouses are now used as art and craft galleries, restaurants and a puppet theatre. In summer a colourful open-air crafts market is held here on Saturdays, which, in winter, takes refuge in one of the old warehouses. Children will particularly enjoy the nearby **Post Office Museum**, in Castray Esplanade, where they can see old telephones, letter boxes and a small post office.

The steep **Kelly's Steps**, wedged between two old warehouses in Salamanca Place, lead to the heart of Hobart's unique **Battery Point** — a former mariners' village which has miraculously retained its nineteenth century character. If you like seafood, head for Mure's Fish House, in Knopwood Street, and try their fisherman's basket (brimming with such delicacies as crayfish, mussels, squid and scallops) while dining under colourful sunshades in a small courtyard. Battery Point has many other attractive licensed restaurants and several quaint cottage tearooms.

The area is also Hobart's mecca for antique hunters. Just round the corner is the **Van Diemen Folk Museum**, with its interesting collection of colonial relics housed in 'Narryna', a gracious old town house, complete with an ornamental fountain and shady old gardens. A short walk from here is the graceful old St George's Anglican Church, which was built between 1836 and 1847 and designed by two of Tasmania's most prominent colonial architects, John Lee Archer and James Blackburn. The **Tasmanian Maritime Museum**, behind the church, has a good collection of old seafaring relics and documents.

Back towards the city, **St David's Park**, with its beautiful old trees, is an ideal place for a rest. One side of this park was Hobart Town's first burial ground and the pioneer gravestones — dating from 1804 — make fascinating reading. Across the road, in Murray Street, is **Parliament**

RIGHT: *These charming cottages are typical of the quaint architecture of Battery Point.*

House, one of the oldest buildings in Hobart. Originally used as the Customs House, it was built by convicts between 1835 and 1841. Visitors may ask to see the tiny **Legislative Council Chamber**, which is exactly as it was when it was first inaugurated. The ceiling has recently been painstakingly repainted in its original ornate pastel patterns and the benches have been refurbished in plush red velvet.

The **Allport Library and Museum of Fine Arts** — a library of rare books and a collection of antique furniture, china and silver — is also in Murray Street, within the State Library.

The main shopping area of Hobart is centred round the Elizabeth Street Mall, between Collins and Liverpool Streets and in Murray Street. The **Cat and Fiddle Arcade and Square** is in the middle. Shoppers can relax in the modern square with its fountain and animated mural which 'performs' on the hour.

Hobart offers a sophisticated nightlife with the **Wrest Point Casino**, cabaret and revolving restaurant, and a wide range of licensed restaurants — from Japanese and Mexican to colonial-style. For a touch of 'olde-worlde' class you can sip cocktails in the drawing room of **'Lenna'**, an Italianate former mansion (now a distinctive hotel-motel) in Battery Point, before dining in the lavishly decorated restaurant. There's a more boisterous atmosphere at 'The Ball and Chain' in Salamanca Place, where you'll be served by 'wenches' in period dress. Fresh seafood is a speciality of many of the city's restaurants. Hobart also has several interesting old pubs with a nautical flavour such as the old Customs House Hotel on the corner of Murray and Morrison Streets, and the Hope and Anchor on the corner of Macquarie and Market Streets.

The suburbs of Hobart have plenty to offer the tourist. Nearby Sandy Bay is the site for the **University of Tasmania**, one of the oldest established universities in Australia, and for a **model Tudor village**. Beyond this, just out of **Taroona**, is a convict-built shot tower, from the top of which you can get a superb view of the Derwent Estuary. North of the city in the suburb of New Town is **'Runnymede'**, a National Trust homestead. Beautifully restored, it commands an attractive view over New Town Bay and Risdon where Hobart's first settlement was pioneered. **Rokeby** and **Bellerive** on the eastern shore of the Derwent have many fascinating old buildings. The ruins of an old fort at **Kangaroo Bluff**, built to guard Hobart against a feared Russian invasion late last century, are worth seeing. Some of Hobart's best beaches, including **Lauderdale**, **Cremorne** and **Seven Mile Beach**, are in this area. For surfers there is a wild ocean beach at **Clifton**, where the Australian surfing championships have been held.

There are dozens of scenic drives and lookouts around Hobart, with spectacular views from the pinnacle of Mt Wellington and from the old Signal Station on top of **Mt Nelson**. The **Waterworks Reserve** is an attractive picnic area only a few minutes' drive from town.

HOTELS
Four Seasons Downtowner,
96 Bathurst St, Hobart.
(002) 34 6333
Inkeepers Lenna
20 Runnymede St, Battery Point.
(002) 23 2911
Wrest Point Hotel-Casino,
410 Sandy Bay Rd, Sandy Bay.
(002) 25 0112

FAMILY AND BUDGET
Hobart Pacific
Kirby Court, West Hobart.
(002) 34 6733
Hobart Tower,
300 Park St, New Town.
(002) 28 4520
Panorama,
Tasman Highway Rosny Hill.
(002) 43 8555
Taroona
178 Channel Highway, Taroona.
(002) 27 8748

MOTEL GROUPS: BOOKINGS
Homestead (003) 31 9366
Innkeepers (002) 23 4264

This list is for information only; inclusion is not necessarily a recommendation.

The hundreds of yachts moored near the prestigious **Royal Yacht Club** in Sandy Bay are evidence of one of Hobart's most popular sports. Other sports are well catered for with a public golf course at **Rosny Park**, racing and trotting at **Glenorchy**, and public squash courts at Sandy Bay, New Town and Bellerive. The Tasmanian Cricket Association Grounds and the Southern Tasmanian Tennis Association Courts and an Olympic swimming pool are in **Queen's Domain**.

Hobart offers a complete range of accommodation from modern Wrest Point Hotel-Casino — with superb views from its 21-storey tower — to tiny Georgian cottage guest houses in Battery Point. Between these two extremes there are about 36 hotels, 15 motels and five guest houses recommended by the tourist bureau, as well as three caravan parks and several holiday flats and cottages.

BELOW: *Whalers used to tie up their ships within a few steps of these stone warehouses at Salamanca Place.*

Battery Point

The most delightful part of Hobart is the former maritime village **Battery Point** — perched between the city docks and Sandy Bay. Battery Point goes back to Hobart Town's earliest days — when it soon became a lively mariners' village with fishermen's cottages, shops, churches, a village green and a riot of pubs with evocative names such as The Whalers' Return and the Neptune Inn. Miraculously it has hardly changed since those days. Strolling through its narrow hilly streets — with enchanting glimpses of harbour, yachts and mountains at every turn — it looks almost like a Cornish fishing village.

Quaint **Arthurs Circus** is built around the former village green — now a children's playground. A profusion of old-fashioned flowers such as sweet william, honeysuckle, daisies and geraniums grow in pocket-sized gardens.

Pubs still bearing names such as The Lord Nelson and The Shipwright's Arms add to the feeling that time has stood still. Place names like Knopwood Street and Kelly's Steps are reminders of two pioneer settlers: The Reverend Bobby Knopwood (Battery Point's first landowner) and the adventurer James Kelly who owned a whaling fleet and undertook a daring voyage round Van Diemen's Land.

Battery Point gets its name from a battery of guns set up on the promontory in front of a small guard house in 1818. This soon became a signalling station and is now the oldest building on Battery Point.

Today the area has many inviting restaurants, tea rooms and antique shops to explore, but it is still mainly residential. Most of the houses are tiny dormer-windowed fishermen's cottages with a few grander houses such as Secheron, Stowell, Narryna and Lenna. An attractive leaflet with a detailed map called 'Let's Talk About Battery Point' is available from the tourist bureau, and the National Trust organises walking tours of the area — leaving from the Wishing Well, Franklin Square at 9.30 am each Saturday.

Tours from Hobart

Hobart is within easy reach of a marvellous range of tourist attractions. To appreciate its superb natural setting it is worth going on a scenic flight over the city and its surroundings — taking in the beautiful Derwent estuary, the patchwork of fields of the Midlands, the Tasman Peninsula and the spectacular lakes and mountains of central and south-western Tasmania. Flight bookings are made at the Government Tourist Bureau, Hobart, which also arranges half and whole day coach tours in this most interesting area.

Mt Wellington, 22 km from Hobart via the Huon Road.

The most popular short trip from Hobart is to the pinnacle of Mt Wellington, 1271 metres above the city, which commands panoramic views of the Derwent Valley to the north and the D'Entrecasteaux Channel to the south. A novel way to see the stunning views is the half-day tour 'Mt Wellington Downhill': a bus to the top and a bike ride down.

Cadbury's Factory, Claremont, 14 km from Hobart on the Lyell Highway.

Visits to this beautifully-sited model factory — the biggest chocolate and cocoa factory in Australia — are another popular short trip. Coach tours leave the Tourist Bureau on Tuesdays and Thursdays and private car trips may be made on Tuesdays, Wednesdays and Thursdays, but these must be pre-paid and booked at the Bureau. The factory is usually closed from the end of December to mid-January.

Richmond, 26 km from Hobart via the Eastern Outlet Road.

Tasmania's oldest and most famous historic village, Richmond has the oldest bridge in Australia, and a wealth of mellow old colonial buildings including Tasmania's oldest gaol, two historic churches and Prospect House, built in 1830, now a licensed restaurant open daily, except Mondays.

New Norfolk, 32 km from Hobart on the Lyell Highway.

This historic town, in the centre of Tasmania's beautiful hop-growing country, is particularly delightful in autumn when the many English trees planted last century turn to beautiful golden hues. Quaint old oast-houses are a feature of the landscape and the town's attractions include the historic Old Colony Inn — now a licensed restaurant set in charming grounds, and the Plenty Salmon Ponds, 11 km to the west — the first successful trout hatchery in Australia. A delightful way to visit New Norfolk in the summer is by taking a full day cruise up the Derwent River. Bookings for the cruises, which operate on Wednesdays and Saturdays during the summer only, can be made at the Government Tourist Bureau.

Mt Field National Park and Russell Falls, 72 km from Hobart via the Lyell Highway and Gordon River Road.

The road from New Norfolk to Mt Field passes through some of the loveliest parts of the Derwent Valley. The Russell Falls — beautiful cascades dropping 32 metres into a gorge of rainforest and tree ferns — are near the park entrance. This large scenic wildlife reserve, sheltering many native birds and animals including the elusive Tasmanian devil, is under heavy snow from July to October. There are several ski club huts in the area.

Lake Pedder and Lake Gordon, 170 km from Hobart via the Lyell Highway and Gordon River Road.

In clear weather, the road from Mt Field National Park to the township of Strathgordon is probably the most spectacular stretch of mountain highway in Australia. Unfortunately from the tourist's point of view, there is a very high rainfall in the area and motorists are advised to cancel trips on overcast days. Man-made Lakes Pedder and Gordon — part of the Hydro-Electric Commission's giant Gordon River power development — are liberally stocked with trout. You can hire boats and fishing tackle, and charter scenic cruises from **Strathgordon** where there is a chalet available for overnight accommodation. Inquiries should be directed to the Tourist Bureau in Hobart.

The Tasman Peninsula and Port Arthur, 151 km from Hobart via the Arthur Highway.

There is so much to see on this fascinating trip that it would be well worth staying overnight at the narrow isthmus of **Eaglehawk Neck** or at **Port Arthur**. Once guarded by a line of tethered hounds to prevent convicts escaping, Eaglehawk Neck is now a base for game fishing charter boats, with modern accommodation and a nearby camping ground. There are four unique coastal formations in the area — the spectacular Devil's Kitchen, the Blowhole, Tasman's Arch and the Tessellated Pavement. The ruins of the old penal settlement of Port Arthur are Tasmania's number one tourist attraction. The Port Arthur Marine Park at Taranna is open seven days a week.

BELOW: *Oast-houses near New Norfolk.*

Huonville, 37 km from Hobart via the Huon Highway.

You can make a scenic trip to Huonville — the centre of Tasmania's picturesque apple-growing district — via the shoulder of Mt Wellington on the Huon Highway, returning via the coastal town of **Cygnet** and along the Channel Highway which commands spectacular vistas of the coastline and rugged Bruny Island.

Hastings Caves, 110 km from Hobart via the Huon Highway.

These three caves, 10 km from the small Hastings township, are another popular attraction. There are daily guided tours of the only illuminated cave — Newdegate Cave — regarded as one of the most beautiful limestone caves in Australia. A restaurant and a natural thermal swimming pool with an average temperature of 27°C are near the cave entrance. Motorists are warned that Dover is the last place to buy petrol en route to Recherche Bay. The Ida Bay Railway is another popular tourist attraction near Hastings.

BELOW: *St John's Church, Buckland.*

Tasmania from A to Z

Avoca Population 207.
This small town, on the Esk Main Road, serves the communities of Rossarden and Storeys Creek, in the foothills of the Ben Lomond National Park. **Of interest:** Historic buildings include St Thomas's Church and parish hall; just out of town is one of Tasmania's most attractive historic houses, 'Bona Vista', which has sadly fallen into disrepair. It may be inspected by contacting the caretaker. **Accommodation:** Limited.
Map ref. 361 O10

Beaconsfield Population 898.
The ruins of impressive brick buildings with Romanesque arches dominate this quiet town on the West Tamar Highway, 43 km from Launceston. Formerly a thriving gold township (called Cabbage Tree Hill), the ruins are the remains of buildings erected at the pithead of the Tasmanian Gold Mine in 1904. When the mine closed ten years later due to water seepage, more than six million dollars-worth of ore had been won from the reef. Work is being carried out at present to re-open the mine. In 1804 a party of officers established a settlement north of the town, called York Town. **Of interest:** Old mine buildings; York Town memorial, on Kelso/Greens Beach Road; the 'auld kirk' at Sidmouth, built in 1846. **Accommodation:** Limited.
Map ref. 361 K6, 363 B5

Beauty Point Population 998.
This popular fishing and water sports centre on the West Tamar Highway, 48 km from Launceston, is the oldest deepwater port in the area and was constructed to serve the Beaconsfield gold mine. Today cargo is loaded at Bell Bay on the eastern shore of the Tamar River. **Of interest:** Nearby Sandy Beach for safe swimming. **In the area:** The small resorts of Kelso, which dates back to the early York Town settlement, and Greens Beach, at the mouth of the River Tamar, where there is a fine beach, golf course and a caravan and camping area. **Accommodation:** 1 hotel, 1 motel
Map ref. 361 K5, 363 B5

Bicheno Population 674.
Crayfish can be caught by hand in this beautiful fishing port and holiday resort on the east coast, 195 km from Hobart. Surf, rock, spear, sea and estuary fishing are all available. The town's mild climate, outstanding fishing, nearby sandy beaches safe for children, and picturesque setting make it one of Tasmania's most popular holiday resorts. Licensed sea-food restaurants and outstanding accommodation add to its appeal. Originally a whaling town in about 1803, it later became a coal-mining port in 1854. Today crayfishing is the main local industry. On a Saturday night, go to the 'craybake'; an outdoor barbecue style dinner where the crays are cooked in a large cauldron (previously a whale blubber pot!). **Of interest:** Hundreds of varieties of fish may be viewed in their natural habitat at the Sea Life Centre on the foreshore. Dinghies and charter boats available for hire for fishing and tours down the scenic Freycinet Peninsula. Fairy penguins can be seen at Diamond Island at low tide. Easily reached lookouts at the top of the town's twin hills. **In the area:** Beautiful bushwalks. Shells and wild flowers abound. Water-skiing, surfing. Duck shooting at Moulting Lagoon. Grave of Waubedar, an Aboriginal heroine. **Accommodation:** 1 hotel, 3 motels, 1 caravan/camping park.
Map ref. 361 R10

Boat Harbour Population 280.
The clear water and rocky points of this attractive resort make it an ideal spot for skin-diving and spear-fishing. Situated on the north-west coast, 3 km off the Bass Highway, it serves one of the richest agricultural areas in the state. **Of interest:** Safe swimming from a crescent-shaped white sandy beach, sheltered by hills. Plentiful marine life in the pools at low tide. Fishing, water-skiing, bushwalking. **In the area:** Rocky Cape National Park. Good fishing and swimming at the small coastal resort of Sisters Beach, to the west. Sisters Island (½ km off-shore) has unique flora and fauna. **Accommodation:** 2 motels, 1 caravan/camping park.
Map ref. 360 E4

Bothwell Population 356.
This peaceful old country town in the beautiful Clyde River valley north of Hobart has been proclaimed an historic village. It has 18 buildings classified by the National Trust, and many more which have been recorded as 'worthy of preservation'. Surveyed in 1824 and named by Governor Macquarie after the Scottish town of the same name, it is now the centre of quality sheep and cattle country. It is possible that the first golf in Australia was played on the links at the nearby homesteads of Ratho and Logan during

Rural Landscapes

Tasmania's homesick early settlers were amazingly successful in their attempts to tame their strange new Antipodean home. They systematically set about clearing the more accessible lowlands of all traces of native bush, replacing it with neatly tilled fields fringed by hedge-rows and shaded English trees. Georgian farm houses set in gardens with flower beds and borders completed the picture.

Tasmania's main pastoral district is the beautiful Midlands area between **Oatlands** and **Perth** (361 M8), noted for its high-quality merino wool and stock-raising. This was one of the first farming areas established in Tasmania and its gently undulating plains are offset by mellow farm houses, historic villages and a wealth of old English trees. The historic township of **New Norfolk** is the centre of Tasmania's long-established hop-growing district, which is a main supplier of hops for Australian beer. This enchanting countryside is enhanced by huge old English trees and quaint old oast houses, or hop-drying kilns. Apples and dairy products are also produced in the Derwent Valley, and apricots and vegetables are grown extensively along the Derwent River between New Norfolk and **Bellerive** (357 J7).

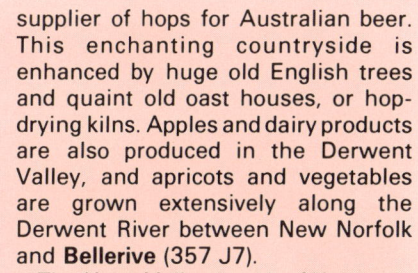

The Huon Valley, south of Hobart, is the centre of Tasmania's famous apple-growing industry, which goes back to the early 19th century when Lady Franklin, the wife of the Governor, started a farm at Franklin.

Tasmania's richest and most highly productive farmland lies on the north-west coast where the main industries are potato-growing, prime beef and dairy cattle.

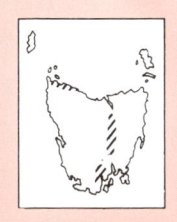

Tasmania's National Parks

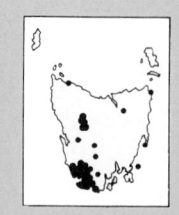

Tasmanians recognised early on that their state had some of the most splendid scenery in Australia, and legislation was introduced in 1863 to preserve certain districts for their scenic value. Today, the National Parks and Wildlife Service of Tasmania manages not only national parks but state reserves and their caves, gorges, waterfalls and rivers, Aboriginal areas and historic sites which date back as far as 1803, when settlers first landed on the island.

Despite the small size of this state, almost 7 per cent of its total area has been set aside for a dozen or so national parks, all of which are easily accessible from **Hobart** or **Launceston**. The best time to visit these parks is in summer, when the climate is more reliable, and when wild flowers bloom in profusion, flowering trees and shrubs are alive with birdlife, native animals roam freely at dusk, rivers and streams gurgle and waterfalls crash over steep drops. This island — the world's most mountainous — embraces hidden treasures for its visitors: rugged peaks with many limestone caves and deep valleys holding sparkling glacial lakes.

The two areas to be declared the first national parks of Tasmania were Mount Field, just 80 kilometres from Hobart, and Freycinet, on the central east coast. Mount Field is one of the most popular venues, as it offers activities for everyone: climbing, boating, bushwalking. It also provides the only developed skiing area in southern Tasmania. There are several delightful waterfalls within the park, the best known being Russell Falls, which was discovered in 1856. The cascading water plunges in two stages into deep gorges shaded by tree ferns which filter sunlight to create a mosaic effect. There are two levels of forest, including the ancient Huon pine, 250 years-old gum trees, sassafras, giant man ferns, the unique horizontal scrub and a variety of mosses, ferns, lichens and fungi. There is a wide range of walks, leisurely or strenuous, including the famed Lyrebird Walk where you may see the black currawong, native to Tasmania, and hear the noisy yellow wattle bird or perhaps the endless repertoire of the lyrebird's mimicry.

Near Freycinet National Park is **Coles Bay**, a fishing and swimming resort with delightful coastal scenery. The park offers the nature lover wide stretches of white sands, rocky headlands, granite peaks, quiet beaches and small caves, with windswept eucalypt forests on its slopes and excellent short or long walking tracks. One of its important features is Moulting Lagoon, which is the breeding ground of the lovely black swan and a refuge for other waterfowl. This park also includes Schouten Island, separated from the Freycinet Peninsula by a one-kilometre wide passage, and reached only by boat.

---

the 1820s. These courses still operate and are open to visitors with golf club membership elsewhere. **Of interest:** Many historic buildings including the glorious St Luke's Church (1831) in Alexander St; the Coffee Palace in Dalrymple St, which is now a colonial museum; and the Georgian brick cottage 'Slate House' in High St, which has been restored and furnished in the style of the day. **In the area:** Excellent deer shooting, golfing and fishing in areas such as Arthurs Lake, Penstock Lagoon, Great Lake and Lake Echo. There are many interesting old homesteads, and two mills, Thorpe Mill and Nant Mill, in the district. **Accommodation:** Limited.
Map ref. 359 L3

Branxholm   Population 273.
This small, former tin-mining town on the Tasman Highway, 26 km from Scottsdale, now serves the surrounding agricultural district. Pine plantations nearby extend north to the slopes of Mt Horror. **Of interest:** Pine plantations and Firth Memorial Grove, Mt Horror Road; Mt Horror; old tin mine workings and lapidary. **Accommodation:** Limited.
Map ref. 361 O6

Bridgewater   Population 6880.
This important market town, only 19 km north of Hobart, is situated on the bank of the main northern crossing of the Derwent River. The causeway was built by 160 convicts in chains in the early 1830's, barrowing two million tonnes of stone and clay. The original bridge was opened in 1849, and the present one dates from 1946. **Of interest:** The Old Watch House, Granton (now a petrol station) was built by convicts in 1838 to guard the causeway. It has the smallest cell used in Australia (50 cm square and 2 m high) which was used to punish convict laggards, together with other harsh penal devices. The Black Snake, erected in 1833, is another convict building in Granton. Formerly an inn, its licence lapsed in 1860. **Accommodation:** Limited.
Map ref. 356 H5

Bridport   Population 951.
Bridport is a popular holiday resort and fishing town on the north-east coast, 85 km from Launceston. **Of interest:** Fine beaches and excellent river, sea and lake fishing. A fine old homestead near the town, 'Bowood', built in 1839, is still standing. View across the sand dunes from PMG tower at Waterhouse, to the east. **In the area:** Views from Waterhouse Point and Ranson's Beach are breathtaking. **Accommodation:** 1 caravan/camping park.
Map ref. 361 N4, 363 I2

Brighton   Population 650.
This town near Hobart on the Midland Highway has always been an important military post. It was first established in 1826 and today the Brighton Army Camp is the main military base in Tasmania. It was named after the English resort by Governor Macquarie in 1821. **In the area:** The historic township of Pontville to the north. **Accommodation:** Limited.
Map ref. 356, I4, 359 M6

Many of Tasmania's national parks are important wildlife reserves. One such park, Mount William, with its 10 595 hectares in north-east Tasmania, is a sanctuary for an abundance of native animals, including the Forester kangaroo, Tasmania's only kangaroo, echidna, wombat, pademelon, Bennetts wallaby and the Tasmanian devil. Spring brings a carpet of wild flowers to this park: the red and white heaths provide a beautiful background for the contrasting colours of the golden wattle and the guinea flower. At Lookout Point, thousands of rock orchids creep and cover the granite rocks.

The central north coastal strip of Asbestos Range National Park is an important refuge for the rare ground parrot and the rufous wallaby. Its islands off **Port Sorell** provide an important breeding area for fairy penguins and the tidal and mud flats are ideal feeding grounds for a variety of migratory seabirds. On the unspoiled beaches of this park, white sands come to life with thousands of platoons of soldier crabs.

Covering some of Tasmania's highest country is Cradle Mountain-Lake St Clair National Park. Cradle Mountain has a variety of fine bushwalks, including one of Australia's best-known walking routes, the 85-kilometres Overland Track. Here, walkers can hike through forests of deciduous beech, Tasmanian 'myrtle', pandani, King Billy pine and a wealth of wild flowers. The tranquil Lake St Clair, with a depth of over 200 metres, occupies a basin gouged out by two glaciers more than 20 000 years ago. This lake was discovered as early as 1826, and is now a popular spot for trout fishing, boating and picturesque campsites.

Although **Maria Island** (359 Q5), off the east coast, is not easily accessible it is well worth a visit. You can get there either by taking a light aircraft or by charter boat from Triabunna. On arrival, it seems as if you have stepped into another world, for on Maria Island, except for one car belonging to the rangers, there are no vehicles; hence there is no pollution and no noise other than the sounds of nature. The island embraces magnificently coloured sandstone cliffs and is refuge for over 80 species of birds. The Forester kangaroo, emus and Cape Barren geese roam freely in this totally unspoiled landscape. Its intriguing history and historic buildings date back to the convict era of 1825 and provide a contrast to the now peaceful surroundings.

Tasmania's largest national park is South West National Park, which has 403 240 hectares of mainly remote wilderness country. There are dolerite and quartzite capped mountains, sharp ridges and steep valleys left by glaciers; its dense forests are of giant mountain ash, eucalypts, ancient Huon pines, shrubs and limbs of the Antarctic beech, all covered with mosses, ferns and lichens and the pink-flowered climbing heath. Mountain climbers will find a challenge in Federation Peak, Mount Anne and Precipitous Bluff, while anglers will be kept busy with trout fishing at Lakes Pedder and Gordon. There are also plenty of facilities for visitors, whether they are on a day trip or camping out.

On the 15 state reserves, limestone caves are popular with both locals and tourists. The cave interiors are dramatically lit to enhance the wonderland of limestone-derived calcite formation. The Hastings Caves, located 110 kilometres from Hobart, enclose a thermal swimming pool, with year-round warm temperature. It is set in a fern glade, surrounded by lawns and picnic areas. Other caves on state reserves are King Solomon, Marakoopa and Gunns Plains.

State reserve rivers are also established for their unique beauty and surrounding vegetation. Of these, Gordon River is specially protected for its forests of ancient Huon pine and its unusual buttongrass vegetation which grows right to the edge of the water and stains it the colour of tea.

Other important features on state reserves include the Tasman Arch, the Blowhole and the Tessellated Pavement, all on the Tasmanian Peninsula. Several Aboriginal sites are of particular interest to visitors. There are many Aboriginal rock carvings found at The Bluff, Sundown Point, West Point and Rocky Cape National Park in the far north-west.

Bruny Island   Population 340.

Almost two islands, separated by a narrow isthmus, Bruny was named after the French Admiral Bruni d'Entrecasteaux, who surveyed the channel between the island and the mainland of Tasmania in 1792. Abel Tasman discovered the island in 1642 but did not land. Other early visitors included Furneaux (1773), James Cook (1777) and William Bligh (1788 and 1792). The first apple trees in Tasmania are said to have been planted here by a botanist with the Bligh expedition. **Of interest:** Bligh Museum, open daily, at the attractive holiday township of Adventure Bay, exhibits much of the island's recorded history. A memorial to the early explorers is nearby. The lighthouse on South Bruny was built in 1836 and is the second oldest in Australia. Walking tracks around Mt Bruny. Scenic reserve at Waterfall Creek is administered by National Parks and Wildlife Service. On North Bruny, the remains of a convict-built church are on private property near the airstrip. Visitors can be shown around by the keeper on Tuesday and Thursday 10 am-12 noon and 2-4 pm. **Accommodation:** 1 hotel, 2 caravan/camping parks.
Map ref. 359 M9, 359 M11

Buckland   Population under 200.

A stained glass window dating back to the fourteenth century is in the church in this tiny township, 64 km north-east of Hobart. History links the window with Battle Abbey, England, which stands on the site of the Battle of Hastings. The abbey was sacked by Oliver Cromwell in the seventeenth century but the window was hidden before it could be destroyed. Two centuries later it was given to Dean Cox, Buckland's first rector, by Lord Robert Cecil, the Secretary of State for the Colonies. It is now set into the east wall of the church of St John the Baptist, which was built in 1846. Although the window has been damaged and restored several times in its long life, the original figure-work is intact. **Accommodation:** Limited.
Map ref. 357 M3, 359 O5

Burnie   Population 20 368.

The rapid expansion of Burnie, now Tasmania's fourth largest town, is based on one of the state's largest industrial enterprises, Associated Pulp and Paper Mills Ltd. Situated on Emu Bay, 148 km west of Launceston, Burnie has a busy deep water port which serves the west coast mining centres. Other important industries include plants for the manufacture of titanium oxide pigments, dried milk, chocolate products and cheese. **Of interest:** The Pioneer Village Museum is a reconstruction of Burnie's small tradesmen's shops at the turn of the century. 'Burnie Inn', the town's oldest remaining building, has been re-erected in Burnie Park and is open for inspection in the summer. **In the area:** Local beauty spots include Round Hill, for panoramic views; the Guide Falls at Ridgley; Fern Glade, for riverside walks and picnics; and, further afield, the Upper Natone Forest Reserve for picnics. **Accommodation:** 8 hotels, 4 motels, 1 caravan/camping park.
Map ref. 360 G5, 362

Campbell Town Population 879.
Campbell Town, on the Midlands Highway, 66 km south of Launceston, is a national centre for selling stud sheep. The area's links with the wool industry go back to the early 1820s when Saxon Merinos were introduced to the Macquarie Valley, west of town. Timber and stud beef are also important primary industries. The town was named by Governor Macquarie for his wife, the former Elizabeth Campbell, in 1921. **Of interest:** Many National Trust 'A' classified buildings including Balmoral Cottage (1840s); St Luke's Church (1839); The Grange, which is a large brick and stone house owned by the National Trust and leased to the Adult Education Board; Campbell Town Inn (1840); and St Michael's Roman Catholic Church (1857). The town's red brick bridge was built by convicts in 1836-8. **In the area:** Fishing in local rivers and lakes. Deer and duck shooting in the hills, in season. **Accommodation:** 1 hotel. At Lake Leake 1 hotel.
Map ref. 359 N1, 361 N11

Coles Bay Population under 200.
This beautiful unspoiled bay, 39 km south of Bicheno on the Freycinet Peninsula, is a good base for visitors to the Freycinet National Park, a 6500 ha reserve and wildlife sanctuary. **Of interest:** Fine beaches, rocky cliffs and bush paths, ideal for swimming, fishing and bushwalking. Abundant birdlife and flora, including more than 60 varieties of the small ground orchid. **Accommodation:** Limited.
Map ref. 359 R2, 361 R12

Cygnet Population 715.
A vineyard and a winery are among the many varied attractions of this centre which is in a fruit-growing district, 54 km from Hobart. Originally named by the French Admiral D'Entrecasteaux *Port de Cygne*, meaning Swan Port, because of the number of swans in the bay. **Of interest:** Good beaches and boat launching facilities at Verona Sands. Randalls Bay and Eggs and Bacon Bay. **In the area:** Chateau Lorraine Winery, 4 km from town. Tahune woodturning at Gardeners Bay. Boating, fishing, bushwalks and gem fossicking. The unique Lymington lace agate can sometimes be found at nearby Drip Beach, Lymington. **Accommodation:** 3 hotels, 1 caravan/camping park. Host Farm and hostel operate at Balfes Hill.
Map ref. 356 G11, 359 L9

Deddington Population under 200.
In 1830 well-known artist John Glover arrived from England and bought land on the site of this little town, about 37 km south-east of Launceston. He named his property Deddington after the village in the English Lake District, where he had lived. Many of his oils and water colours remain in Tasmania today. **Of interest:** A chapel, built in 1840, and possibly designed by Glover, has been restored by the National Trust. An old inn, which is still licensed, remains, as well as the ruins of a police station. **In the area:** A John Batman re-enactment each year commemorates the fact that the founder of Melbourne lived for many years in a convict-built cottage on the property known as 'Kingston', about 25 km beyond town. The cottage is still standing. **Accommodation:** Limited.
Map ref. 361 N8, 363 I 12

Deloraine Population 1923.
Scenic Deloraine, with Bass Strait to its north and the Great Western Tiers to its south, is an ideal base for exploring the many attractions of northern Tasmania. The rich surrounding countryside is used mainly for dairying and mixed farming. **Of interest:** Many interesting old buildings remain including the Deloraine Folk Museum and Cider Bar, which is housed in a former inn classified by the National Trust; St Mark's Church of England; the Church of the Holy Redeemer. The new Military Museum is entered from the Hobby Horse Toy Shop in a row of small brick cottages originally built to house officers of the army detachment stationed in town. The museum contains militaria ranging from Boer War times to the present. Deloraine has a good variety of restaurants and cafes. **In the area:** Bowerbank Mill Gallery, 2 km east of town, was built in 1853 and is now an art gallery. Famous 'Calstock', just out of town, once supplied Australia's best racehorses. Visitors are welcome at the Tasmanian Smokehouse, 10 km from town, where gourmet fish and poultry are processed. The Tasmanian Wildlife Park, 2 km beyond Chudleigh, has a specially-designed 'noctarium' for displaying nocturnal animals. There are several falls in the area including Liffey, Meander and Montana Falls, and the scenic drive to the Central Highlands and the power station is worthwhile. There is excellent trout fishing in the Mersey River and many other sites within a few kilometres of town. Further afield is the Great Lake, the highest body of water in Australia. There are conducted tours of the Marakoopa and King Solomon limestone caves. (See Mole Creek.) **Accommodation:** 3 hotels, 1 caravan/camping park.
Map ref. 361 J8

Derby Population 202.
Derby is a small tin-mining town on the Tasman Highway, 34 km from Scottsdale in the north-east. In its heyday, tin mining was a flourishing industry, but there has been a gradual swing to rural production, although tin is still worked. **Of interest:** Several old mine workings and dams; lapidary. Cheese factory on Tasman Highway near Winnaleah. Cheeses may be bought. Visitors welcome. **Accommodation:** Limited.
Map ref. 361 P5

Devonport Population 21 424.
As the terminal for the vehicular ferry from Melbourne, Devonport has become a busy industrial and agricultural export town, as well as a major tourist centre. Devonport has its own airport, and is ideally suited for seeing scenic northern Tasmania. **Of interest:** There are tourist information centres at the ferry terminal and in Rooke St; Gallery and Art Centre; Wheel House, an early pedal-power museum; Maritime Museum; Bramich's Early Motoring and Folk Museum; and 'Tiagarra', a Tasmanian Aboriginal Culture and Art Centre at Mersey Bluff, a parklands and beach resort promontory at the mouth of the river. Rock carvings made by the now extinct Tasmanian Aborigines are outside the display area. **In the area:** Braddon's Lookout, near Forth, offers a panoramic view of the coastline; Port Sorell, 20 km north-east on the Rubicon River estuary, has a wildlife reserve; Bell's Parade is a picturesque reserve on the banks of the Mersey at Latrobe; the Mersey-Forth hydro-electric scheme. **Accommodation:** 7 hotels, 6 motels, 1 caravan/camping park.
Map ref. 354, 360 I5

Dover Population 570.
This attractive fishing port, south of Hobart, was once a convict station. The original Commandant's office still stands, but the cells are buried just up from the wharf. Quaint old cottages and English trees give the town an old-world atmosphere. The three islands in the bay are called Faith, Hope and Charity. There are several old graves on Faith Island. **Of interest:** Fishing trips may be arranged with private boat captains. The picturesque scenery and unspoiled white beaches make it ideal for bushwalking and swimming. Counter lunches are available at the hotel. Drivers should stock up on petrol and provisions if planning to continue south, as these shops are the last on the road. **In the area:** Southport, 21 km south, is another old fishing port, established since the days of sealers and whalers. It is good for fishing, swimming, surfing and bushwalking. **Accommodation:** 1 hotel, 1 caravan/camping park.
Map ref. 359 L10

Dunalley Population 203.
This prosperous fishing village stands on the narrow isthmus connecting the Forestier Peninsula to the rest of Tasmania. The Denison Canal, spanned by a swing bridge, gives much quicker access to the east coast for small vessels. **In the area:** The Tasman Memorial, which marks the first landing by white men on 2 December 1642, is a few kilometres from town near Cape Paul Lamanon. **Accommodation:** 1 motel.
Map ref. 357 N7, 359 O7

Eaglehawk Neck Pop. under 200.
In convict days this narrow isthmus which separates the Tasman from the Forestier Peninsulas, was guarded by a line of ferocious tethered dogs. Soldiers and constables also stood guard, to make sure that no convicts escaped from the notorious convict settlement at Port Arthur. The only prisoners to escape did so by swimming. Today, in complete contrast, it is a pleasant fishing resort. A tuna fishing fleet operates from the Neck jetty. **Of interest:** Boats for hire. **In the area:** Within about 4 km of Eaglehawk are four unusual natural features: Tasmans Arch, the Devils Kitchen, the Blowhole and the Tessellated Pavement. **Accommodation:** 1 motel.
Map ref. 357 P9, 359 P8

SCENIC ISLAND STATE

Wherever you start or finish your holiday journey in Tasmania you will be sure to see brilliant scenery and to have lots of fascinating experiences along the way. Most travellers start their Tasmanian holiday in the north, where they can take their cars off the ferry from the mainland or hire cars or mobile homes.

Probably the best way to see what Tasmania has to offer is to take the circle route, with as many diversions along the way as time permits to see some extra scenic or historic highlights. Such a tour of the island, which is small enough to allow a visitor to see most of it in a short space of time, will take you through some of the most fascinating country that Australia has to offer. The incomparable wildness of the west coast, the towering mountains of the central district, the gentle pastoral landscapes of the midlands, the lavish orchard country around Launceston and on the Huon Peninsula, the snug beaches, bays and villages of the east coast, are all relatively accessible on good roads.

You will soon find that not everything about Tasmania is small; the trees are taller here than on the mainland, nurtured by the temperate climate; mountains vault to the skies from wild forest land. The great inland lakes in the mountains feed savage rivers, some of which harness the state's great hydro-electric schemes. The hills and valleys are harshly carved by the weather and become gentle only in the rolling pastoral lands of the midlands and the north.

In this romantic landscape, more reminiscent of Scotland than Australia, are set the remnants of a rich past of convict and colonial life — the prisons, churches, cottages and court-houses, the barracks, mansions and homesteads from the earliest days of settlement.

From Devonport, the coast road west runs with the northern railway along the sea's edge, beneath the impressive cliffs that face Bass Strait. Along this road are the thriving industrial towns of Ulverstone, Burnie, Wynyard and Stanley, and the impressive headlands of Table Cape, Rocky Cape and the Nut. They are worth a special trip, as is a detour down the side road from Penguin, to the peaceful mountain

TOP: *Gunns Plains, a rich pastoral area south of Ulverstone is reminiscent of the patchwork-like terrain of the English countryside.*

LEFT: *The business centre of Hobart, capital city of Tasmania, has modern tower buildings which contrast strongly with its historic past. Sandy Bay in the foreground is popular with yachtsmen, overlooked by the tower on Wrest Point.*

Tasmania

farmland of Gunns Plains and the Gunns Plains caves. The road from Forth into the vast wilderness areas of the magnificent Cradle Mountain and Lake St Clair National Park is also well worth a visit but the turn-off to follow the circle route is at Somerset, from where you head south down the Murchison Highway through the rich farmlands towards the increasingly mountainous country of the west coast. An interesting diversion leads to Corinna, a small town on the spectacularly wild and beautiful Pieman River not far from its mouth. Launches from Corinna travel through deeply-cut river gorges west to the Indian Ocean.

Back on the main road, the mountain scenery is unique and quite spectacular. The towns here developed only as a result of their mineral wealth. Zeehan now has only a tiny population but at the turn of the century there were more than 10 000 inhabitants when tin mining was at its height. Many buildings of those days still stand, including the Gaiety Theatre where Dame Nellie Melba is said once to have sung. The larger town of Queenstown has grown up around the Mount Lyell copper mine, in a valley beneath bare, bleached hills, streaked and stained with the hues of minerals, chrome, purple, grey and pink. Nearby is Strahan on Macquarie Harbour, the only coastal town in the west. The harbour can be reached only by shallow draught vessels through the notorious passage called Hell's Gates. Visitors can cruise through fantastic country along the Gordon River, past

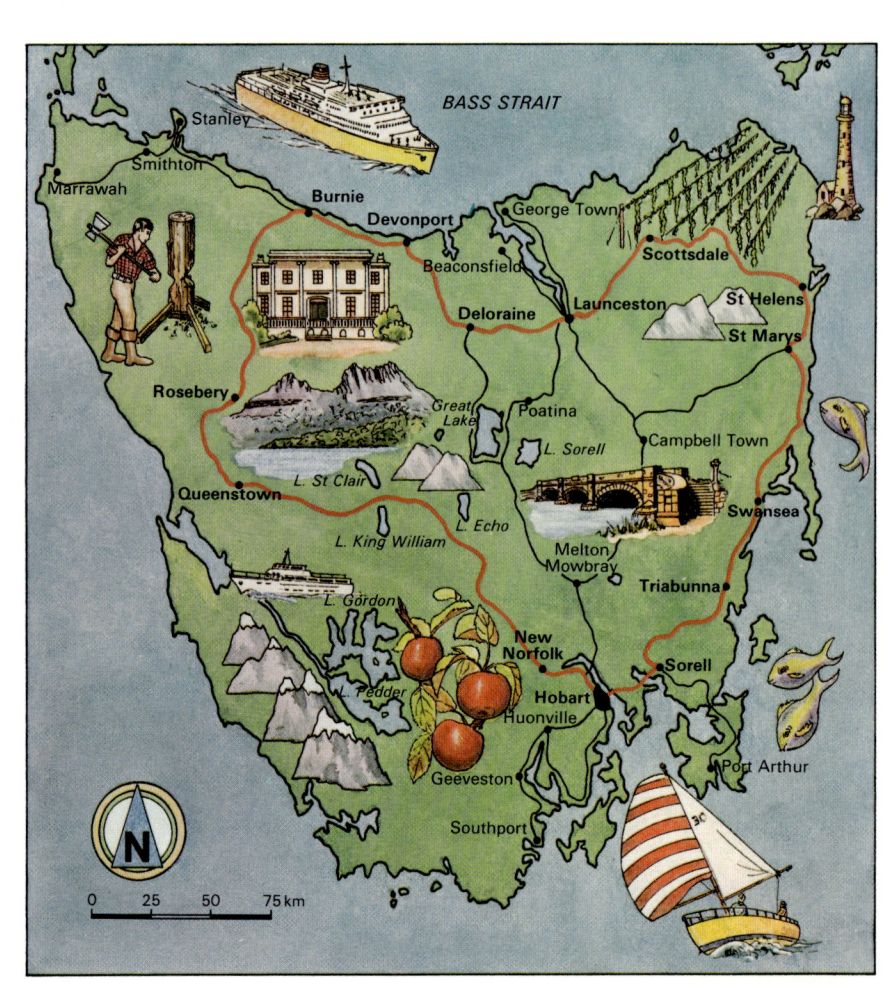

ABOVE: *Whether you spend a week or two simply following the 'Great Circle Route' around Tasmania, or decide to spend your holiday in one of the many pleasant towns, the 'Island State' probably offers more variety in a small area than any other state in Australia.*

BELOW: *Strahan, the only port on the rugged west coast of Tasmania. The harbour can be reached only by shallow vessels through a notorious passage called Hell's Gates.*

BELOW: *The bare mountains around Queenstown give the area a rather eerie feeling. Logging to provide firewood for the copper smelters, bushfires and heavy rainfall were the cause of this, but the Mt Lyell Company, which mines copper in the area, and on which the town depends for its livelihood, is now assisting in a programme of regeneration.*

ABOVE: *Richmond Bridge reflected here in the tranquil waters of the Coal River is Australia's oldest bridge. Built by convicts between 1823 and 1825, it is said to be haunted by their cruel overseer whom they killed.*

BELOW: *Russell Falls, in the Mount Field National Park cascade into a gorge of rainforest and tree ferns.*

ABOVE: *The Shot Tower at Taroona, once used for making lead pellets. It has been a landmark for over a 100 years.*

the ruins of the world's most remote convict settlement on Sarah Island.

The road turns inland from these towns, avoiding the almost inaccessible south-west, and travels down the Derwent river valley through the town of New Norfolk, centre of the Tasmanian hop growing industry. This valley, brilliantly coloured with foliage in autumn, is both scenic and historically interesting. It was settled in 1808, the site having been chosen by Governor Macquarie. The Bush Inn Hotel in New Norfolk is the oldest licensed public house in Tasmania and St Matthew's Church of England, the oldest church still standing.

A detour from the Hobart road leads to the lovely old town of Richmond, one of the many historic towns off the Midlands Highway which are not visited if the 'circle-route' is followed. (Some of the others are Ross, Oatlands, Campbell Town, Bothwell and Longford, all set in the charming rolling countryside of the midlands with their English trees framing or hiding the landowners' mansions.) Richmond is probably the best example, its old Georgian houses and cottages clustered together with its bridge, convict-built and the oldest freestone bridge still in use in Australia. The gaol pre-dates Port Arthur as a penal settlement; there are two churches, a court-house, a school-house, a rectory, the hotel granary, a general store and a flour mill, all built in the eighteen twenties and thirties.

Hobart, Australia's second oldest and most southerly city, is most attractively sited on the Derwent River with Mt Wellington looming above it. It is a fascinating place, The old port area at Salamanca Place, where the old bond stores and warehouses are, is a reminder of the dangerous days when the whaling fleet and the timber ships tied up, and sailors went out on the town. Battery Point with its barracks, workers' cottages and Arthur's Circus — its Georgian-style houses built around a circular green — are part of Hobart's early beginnings.

There are many fine public buildings in the city which help it to retain something of the feeling of its colonial days. There is modern-day fun in Hobart, too, since the Wrest Point casino and hotel developed as Hobart's best-known entertainment complex.

In complete contrast, the grim but beautiful penal settlement of Port Arthur is not far from Hobart, on the Tasman Peninsula. Here, within the

Tasmania

forbidding sandstone walls visitors will feel something of the hopelessness and isolation of the thousands of convicts who passed through this settlement during its 47 years of existence.

South of Hobart is the scenic Huon Peninsula, where a fascinating day can be spent, particularly when the apple trees are in blossom.

North on the circle route from Hobart the Tasman Highway traverses the east coast — a region which enjoys a mild and equable climate throughout most of the year and which has a number of attractive seaside resorts. Most are on sheltered inlets but within easy reach of surf beaches and fishing grounds — towns like Orford, Triabunna, Swansea, Bicheno, St Marys, Scamander and St Helens.

Off the Tasman Highway near Bicheno is the Freycinet National Park on the Freycinet Peninsula. There are many walking tracks through this park, which is dominated by the Hazards, a red granite mountain range. More than 68 varieties of the small ground orchid have been identified in the unspoiled bush of the park, and bird life is prolific.

The road cuts across the less developed farming country of the north and goes west to Launceston, the northern capital of Tasmania, 64 kilometres from the north coast at the junction of the North Esk, South Esk and Tamar rivers. It is a smaller, more provincial city than Hobart, set in pleasant hilly countryside, and makes an excellent base for exploring the rich coastal plain of the Tamar Valley and the mountain country to the north of the island's central plateau. Cataract Gorge, historic Franklin House and Entally House, and the hydro-electric station built in 1895 are all within easy reach of Launceston.

On to Devonport, where this description of the circle route began. Many of Tasmania's magnificent national parks are not far away from the circle route highway and it is worth a close scrutiny of the map which will lead to many other interesting diversions. For further information contact the nearest Tasmanian Government Tourist Bureau.

TOP: *The Tamar River at Launceston is a popular spot for mooring small craft.*

CENTRE LEFT: *The Penny Royal Watermill, Launceston, built in the 1840s, is now a unique motel.*

CENTRE RIGHT: *Franklin House, South Launceston, built in 1838, is now owned by the National Trust.*

RIGHT: *The Freycinet Peninsula has rugged granite rocks strewn around its coast. The whole peninsula is a National Park.*

Evandale Population 614.
This little township, 19 km from Launceston, has been proclaimed an historic village. Founded in 1829, some of its buildings date from as early as 1809. Originally it was named Collins Hill, but was renamed in 1836 in honour of Tasmania's first Surveyor-General, G. W. Evans. It remains unspoiled by progress and still retains many buildings of architectural significance. **Of interest:** many historic buildings including original shop fronts, old hotels and St Andrew's Church. There is a Sunday market and a licensed restaurant. Solomon House, built in 1836 by Joseph Solomon offers Devonshire teas and overnight accommodation. **In the area:** 'Pleasant Banks', open for inspection; Clarendon, 8 km out of town, at Nile. Designed in the grand manner and set in extensive formal gardens, it is now owned by the National Trust. Extensive restoration has been carried out. The old inn at Nile is also of historic interest. **Accommodation:** 1 hotel.
Map ref. 361 M8, 363 G11

Exeter Population 353.
In the midst of a large fruit growing area, 24 km north-west of Launceston, Exeter serves the district surrounding it. **In the area:** A high rocky outcrop used by the notorious bushranger Matthew Brady, known as Brady's Lookout, is 5 km south of the town. Nearby river resorts of Gravelly Beach, Paper Beach and Blackwell and, at the mouth of the Supply River, the ruins of the first water-driven flour mill in Tasmania. The Notley Fern Gorge, at Notley Hills, is the last of the heavy rainforests which once covered much of the area. The 10 ha reserve is also a sanctuary for wildlife. John Batman's ship *Rebecca*, in which he undertook his historic trip across Bass Strait to the Yarra River, was built at the once busy shipyards at Rosevears, further south. **Accommodation:** 1 hotel.
Map ref. 361 L6, 363 D7

Fingal Population 424.
Fingal is situated 21 km inland from St Marys on the east coast, on the South Esk River, and is the headquarters of the state's coal industry. The first payable gold in Tasmania was found at The Nook, near Fingal. **Of interest:** Historic buildings including the homestead 'Malahide' (1828), which has a National Trust 'A' classification; St Peter's Church and the Roman Catholic Church; Lord Carrington Lodge and the Fingal Hotel, which has a collection of over 280 different brands of Scotch whisky. **In the area:** Mathinna, an extensive forestry development area which was once the scene of an important gold strike. **Accommodation:** Limited.
Map ref. 361 P9

Franklin Population 479.
This timber milling town south-west of Hobart was the site of the first settlement in the Huon district in 1804. It was named after Governor Sir John Franklin, who took up 259 ha on the banks of the Huon River. Timber milling has been an important local industry since the very early years. Orcharding and dairy farming are the other main industries. **Accommodation:** Limited.
Map ref. 356 F10, 359 L8

Geeveston Population 860.
This important timber town is the gateway to the rugged Hartz Mountains National Park. Timber has always been an important industry in the area and the huge reserves feed the Australian Paper Mills pulp mill at Hospital Bay, about 3 km from the town. Appointments can be made to inspect the mill. **Accommodation:** 1 hotel.
Map ref. 356 E11, 359 K9

George Town Population 5592.
Situated at the mouth of the River Tamar, George Town was first settled in 1811, when it was named for King George III. Today it is a flourishing commercial centre, mainly due to the Comalco plant at Bell Bay, and some other industrial developments in the area. **Of interest:** A monument on The Esplanade commemorates an unintentional landing in 1804, when Lieutenant-Colonel William Paterson and his crew in HMS *Buffalo* ran aground in a gale. Morning and afternoon teas and lunches are served at The Grove, a beautifully restored old house, built in the 1820s, and open to the public. There is a licensed restaurant in Macquarie St. **In the area:** The ghost town of a former gold-mining township at Lefroy, which was a thriving town in the 1870s. All that remains today are ruins of brick buildings, old diggings and an interesting cemetery. In Hillwood, south of town, there is a large strawberry farm where visitors may pick their own fruit in season. High quality apples are also produced in this important fruit growing centre. Low Head, 5 km north of the town, has a good surf beach and a safe river beach. The old lighthouse is sometimes open for inspection. Inspections of the Comalco plant at the important industrial port of Bell Bay can be made by arrangement. **Accommodation:** 1 hotel, 1 caravan/camping park.
Map ref. 361 K5, 365 B4

Gladstone Population under 200.
The small township of Gladstone is one of the few communities in the far north-east which still relies on tin mining. The district was once a thriving tin and gold mining area, with a colourful early history. Many Chinese worked in the mines. Now many of the townships are ghost towns or near-ghost towns. **Of interest:** Geological formations in the Gladstone/South Mt Cameron area. **In the area:** Remains of the once-substantial township of Boobyalla to the north-west of the town; and Moorina to the south-west. Little remains at Moorina today except a post office and shop. The Chinese section of the graveyard is interesting. The township of Pioneer still mines tin and has an artificial lake suitable for water sports. Further south is another former tin-mining town, Weldborough, which was once the headquarters for 900 Chinese miners. Today Weldborough is on the main highway between Scottsdale and St Helens; petrol and provisions are available. **Accommodation:** Limited.
Map ref. 361 Q4

Hadspen Population 908.
Charming Entally House (1820), one of Tasmania's most famous historic homes, is just beyond Hadspen, on the banks of the South Esk River. Lavishly furnished with antiques and set in beautifully kept gardens planted with old English trees, it has its own chapel and a collection of horse-drawn vehicles in its outbuildings. It is open daily. The township of Hadspen, which was first settled in the early 1820s, has many other interesting historic buildings. **Of interest:** A row of Georgian buildings, including 'The Red Feather Inn', an 1845 coaching house, where a theatrical production 'The Story of Red Feather Inn' is presented. Seats and a four-course supper must be booked in advance through the tourist bureau. The adjoining 'Red Feather Tea Shoppe' serves lunches and Devonshire teas. The Hadspen gaol and nearby Church of the Good Shepherd are also well worth a visit. **Accommodation:** 1 caravan/camping park.
Map ref. 361 L8, 363 E10

Hastings Population under 200.
This small township, about 100 km from Hobart, attracts many tourists because of its famous limestone caves, local gemstones and nearby scenic railway. **In the area:** The Hastings Caves are about 10 km from town, on the right hand road. One of them, Newdegate Cave, has daily guided tours. A restaurant and heated pool are opposite the entrance. The Lune River (take the left hand road past Hastings) is a haven for gem collectors. Beyond the river is the Ida Bay Railway, originally built to carry limestone but now a tourist railway. It carries passengers along the 7 km track to the Deep Hole and back. There are picnic facilities at both ends of the track. **Accommodation:** Limited.
Map ref. 359 K10

Huonville Population 1347.
Huonville is an important commercial centre serving the surrounding townships, and is the largest apple producing centre in the area. In the early days, the valuable softwood, now known as Huon pine, was discovered in the district. Some is still grown. **In the area:** Scenic drive to townships of Glen Huon, Judbury and Ranelagh. **Accommodation:** Limited.
Map ref. 356 F9, 359 L8

Kettering Population 288.
The Bruny Island ferry leaves several times daily from the terminal at Kettering. Extra services are provided during holiday periods. This township on the Channel Highway serves a large fruit-growing district. **In the area:** The Oyster Cove Inn and marina; pleasant walks in the Snug Falls Track area, near the small township of Snug and good swimming and boating at Coningham Beach. A monument to the French explorer, Bruni d'Entrecasteaux, is at Gordon, to the south. **Accommodation:** Limited.
Map ref. 365 H11, 359 M8

Stately Homes

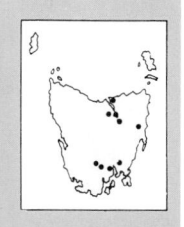

One of Tasmania's big attractions is its wealth of beautiful stately homes with a distinctly English air. You can dine in style in some — such as Prospect House in the historic township of **Richmond**, or the Old Colony Inn in **New Norfolk** — and stay in others.

Several of Tasmania's grand old mansions like Malahide and Killymoon — both in **Fingal** — are privately owned and cannot be inspected, but many of the state's finest homesteads are open to the public.

Superb Clarendon House, near **Nile** (361 M9), and a short drive from Launceston, is probably Australia's grandest Georgian mansion. Built in the late 1830s, it is now owned by the National Trust and has been meticulously restored and beautifully furnished.

For an even closer contact with the past, you could stay at another of Tasmania's stately homes — Pleasant Banks in nearby **Evandale**. Built in 1838 on land granted in 1809, Pleasant Banks is Tasmania's oldest superfine merino stud, with stock based on sheep imported in 1823. Today the imposing two-storey homestead doubles as a guest house providing antique-furnished rooms, breakfast and dinner.

Three other stately homesteads open to the public and within easy reach of **Launceston** are Franklin House, just six kilometres south of Launceston; Entally House at **Hadspen**; and Brickendon in **Longford**. Franklin House is another elegant Georgian mansion, beautifully furnished, restored and owned by the National Trust, and open daily. Built in 1838, it is a fine example of the period. Charming Entally House has been furnished with antiques dating back to 1600 and is set in spacious grounds with avenues of English trees, walled gardens, rolling lawns and neatly pruned hedges. Controlled by the National Parks and Wildlife Service, it is open daily.

Two-storeyed, shuttered Brickendon, with its graceful metal front porch, has a French look but its long stretches of hawthorn hedges and its many old chestnuts, oaks, ash and junipers make it look like part of an English farm.

The Grove in **George Town**, north of Launceston, is another privately-owned historic house which is open daily (except during July). Built during the 1820s, it has been painstakingly restored by the present owners who dress in period costume. Lunch and teas are served.

The White House, in **Westbury**, near **Deloraine**, was built in 1841-2 as a general store. Today it contains an antique collection and the coach house and stables house horse-drawn vehicles and vintage cars.

Hobart has two historic homes open for inspection — the National Trust property, Runnymede, in the suburb of New Town, and Narryna in Battery Point. Graceful Runnymede, built in 1844, has been restored and furnished with antiques by the Trust. Narryna, also known as the Van Diemen's Land Memorial Folk Museum, has interesting collections of early colonial ornaments, handcrafts and clothes. The fine freestone gentleman's town house, built in 1836, is open daily.

The misleadingly-named Old Colony Inn in **New Norfolk** serves lunches — with fresh trout as a speciality — and Devonshire teas. This beautiful old building set in delightful grounds has become one of Tasmania's most photographed tourist attractions. Despite its name it was never used as an inn.

Kingston-Blackmans Bay
Population 8336.
Kingston Beach, 11 km south of Hobart, was discovered by Scottish botanist Robert Brown in 1804. The beach, and those at Blackmans Bay and in the Tinderbox-Howden area, have excellent facilities. Kingston has a major shopping centre. **Of interest:** The Kingston Cultural Centre, in Windsor St. Sporting complex with a variety of facilities. **In the area:** Scenic drives through Blackmans Bay. Tinderbox and Howden, with magnificent views of Droughty Point and Bruny Island from Piersons Point. The small blowhole at Blackmans Bay, on the reserve on Talone Road, is spectacular in stormy weather. Margate and Snug both have fish processing factories. There are pleasant walks in the Snug Falls Track area **Accommodation:** Limited.
Map ref. 356 I9, 359 M7

Latrobe   Population 2401.
Situated on the Mersey River, 9 km from Devonport, Latrobe was once a busy town with its own shipyards. In the 1880s it had three local newspapers and in 1888 the English cricket team played a match there. Today it is the site of one of the biggest cycling carnivals in Australia, the Latrobe Wheel Race, which is held every Christmas. The Latrobe Bicycle Race Club was established in 1896. **Of interest:** Many early buildings, including some with National Trust classifications; Bell's Parade offers attractive parklands and picnic areas along the riverbank. The town has one licensed restaurant. **In the area:** 'Frogmore', an old homestead with a National Trust classification, and now a host farm, is just out of town. **Accommodation:** 2 hotels.
Map ref. 360 I6

Launceston   Population 64555.
Although it is Tasmania's second largest city and a busy tourist centre in its own right, Launceston manages to retain something of the air of a sleepy provincial town. Nestling in hilly country where the Tamar, North Esk and South Esk rivers meet, Launceston is centrally placed for exploring the rest of the state. It is at the junction of four main highways and has direct air links with Melbourne and Hobart. Launceston is sometimes known as the Garden City because of its beautiful parks and gardens. European trees such as oaks and elms thrive in the mild climate.

Officially proclaimed in 1824, Launceston's architecture, though not outstanding, is certainly of great interest. In particular, St John and George Streets, Trustee Court and Prince's Square, with its fountain and fine surrounding buildings, are well worth seeing. The main shopping area is around The Mall. A good starting point for visitors is the Government Tourist Bureau at the corner of Paterson and John Sts. One of Launceston's best-known tourist attractions is in Paterson St: the Penny Royal Watermill complex is a collection of buildings originally situated at Barton, and moved stone by stone to Launceston. The complex includes modern accommodation, restaurants and a tavern, as well as a museum, a working cornmill and a graceful windmill. It is open daily from 9-5.30. The mill complex is linked by a restored tramway to the Penny Royal Gunpowder Mill at the old Cataract Quarry site. Children will enjoy the many attractions here — a boat trip on the artificial lake and the chance to light the fuse on a cannon are among them.

One of Launceston's outstanding natural attractions is the spectacular Cataract Gorge, only a few minutes' drive from the city centre. Cataract Cliff Grounds Reserve, on the north side of the deep canyon, is a formal park with lawns, European trees, peacocks and a licensed restaurant, which also served Devonshire teas. The area is linked to the south side by a scenic chairlift. For the strong-stomached, the view from this vantage point is breath-taking; the less adventurous can cross by a suspension bridge. On the south side there is a swimming pool and kiosk; there are delightful walks on both sides of the Gorge. Other parks in Launceston include the 5 ha City Park, which has a small zoo and a conservatory; Royal Park, a formal civic park fronting on to the South Esk River; and, south of the city, the Launceston Wildlife Sanctuary, which has native and European fauna in natural surroundings, and the Rhododendron Gardens. The landscaped grounds around the Trevallyn Dam, make an attractive picnic spot.

The Queen Victoria Museum and Art Gallery, situated in Royal Park, is worth visiting. It has exhibits of historical interest; native flora, fauna and minerals; early china and glassware and colonial and modern art. The Design Centre of Tasmania, on the outskirts of City Park, displays contemporary arts and crafts. Launceston's entertainment includes a theatre, a cinema, a drive-in; and the usual sporting fixtures and facilities including three 18-hole golf courses. The Launceston Country Club Casino was opened early in 1982 and has provided a wonderful complement to the Hobart complex, as the Launceston Casino provides an 18 hole golf course, tennis courts, squash courts, gymnasium, sauna facilities, horse riding and a heated indoor swimming pool. Situated only 7 km from Launceston, it has provided the city with an excellent mix of entertainment and provided the international accommodation required by overseas and interstate visitors. River cruises on the *MV Goondooloo* leave the terminal at Royal Park. Bookings are made at the tourist bureau. Launceston has several good licensed restaurants including the Old Masters, in Elizabeth St; the Owl's Nest at the Penny Royal Watermill; and El Matador in York St.

Three outstanding historic houses are within easy reach of Launceston. Franklin House, 6 km from town, is a classical two-storey Georgian house, now owned by the National Trust and furnished in the style of the day; Entally House is 13 km from town at Hadspen; and the National Trust property, Clarendon, is in the township of Nile, near Evandale. For sheer grandeur Clarendon must be ranked as one of the great houses of Australia. All these houses are open daily, but Clarendon is closed for the whole of July.

Visitors to Launceston have a wide range of accommodation to choose from, including 15 hotels, some modern and some historic but modernised; 10 motels; colonial cottages and holiday apartments; and a caravan and camping park.
Map ref. 361 L7, 362, 363 F9

Lilydale Population 308.
At the foot of Mt Arthur, 27 km from Launceston, the township of Lilydale has many nearby bush tracks and picnic spots. **In the area:** Lilydale Falls Reserve, 3 km from town. Two oak trees which were grown from acorns from the Great Park at Windsor were planted here on Coronation Day, 12 May 1937. There are scenic walks to the top of Mt Arthur. Hollybank Forest Reserve is a plantation area with large stands of ash and pine and barbecue facilities, located at Underwood. La Provence Vineyards, which were established by Frenchman John Miguet in 1962, are located at Lalla, 4 km west of Lilydale. At weekends fresh produce can be bought at the Lalla Market. The Appleshed, alongside it, sells locally made arts and crafts. There is an old Rhododendron Nursery, established by the Walker family on the northern slopes of Brown Mountain. The nursery has been handed over to the Government on a long term lease for use by the Public. The only Lavender Farm in the Southern Hemisphere is located at Nabowla, 26 km North east of Lilydale. The lavender plants flower in January each year and provide a splendid view. The area under cultivation is 52 ha (130 acres) and the farm produces 2 tonnes of lavender oil yearly. **Accommodation:** 1 caravan/camping park.
Map ref. 361 M6, 363 G6

Longford Population 2200.
This quiet country town, 22 km south of Launceston, was first settled in 1813 when former settlers of Norfolk Island were given land grants in the area. Since then it has had three changes of name, having previously been known as Norfolk Plains and Latour. Now classified as an historic town, it serves a rich agricultural district. The municipality of Longford carries the largest head of stock in the state. **Of interest:** There are many historic buildings, some of them built by convicts. Christ Church, in the centre of the town, was built in 1839. It is noted for its outstanding stained glass window, made in Newcastle-upon-Tyne, England, and for the interesting pioneer gravestones in its grounds. Other historic buildings include Jessen Lodge, the Queens Arms Hotel, Blenheim Inn and the Roman Catholic and Methodist churches. 'Brickendon', just 2 km from the centre of town, a two-storey house built by William Archer in 1824, is still owned by his descendants. Longford Wildlife Park is a conservation area for fallow deer and for Australian fauna and flora. There are barbecue facilities and a man-made lake in the grounds. **In the area:** Perth, 5 km from town, also has many historic buildings including Eskleigh Home (now a home

The Bass Strait Islands

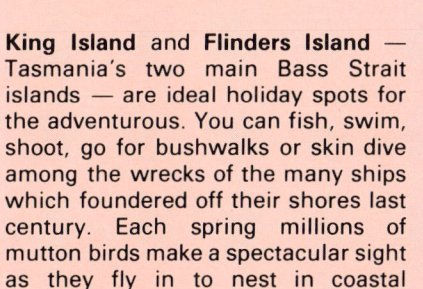

King Island and **Flinders Island** — Tasmania's two main Bass Strait islands — are ideal holiday spots for the adventurous. You can fish, swim, shoot, go for bushwalks or skin dive among the wrecks of the many ships which foundered off their shores last century. Each spring millions of mutton birds make a spectacular sight as they fly in to nest in coastal rookeries on the islands.

King Island, on the western end of the strait, is a picturesque, rugged island with an unspoiled coastline of beautiful sandy beaches on the east and north coasts, contrasting with the forbidding cliffs of Seal Rocks and the lonely coast of the south.

Once famous for its great number of seals and now almost extinct sea-lions, its main industries today are scheelite mining and farming. Only about half the island has been cleared. The island's unofficial capital is **Currie** (358 A2); accommodation includes a motel and holiday cottages.

Flinders Island is renowned for its excellent fishing, its magnificent granite mountains and its gemstones, including the Killiecrankie 'diamonds' which are really a kind of topaz. Mt Strzelecki, near the civic centre, **Whitemark** (358 A5), provides challenging rock-climbing. Accommodation on the island includes two hotels, one guest house and holiday farms.

In the 1830s the last of the Tasmanian Aborigines were settled near **Emita** (358 A5), in a belated attempt to save them from extinction. All that remains today is the graveyard and chapel — Wybalenna — which has been restored by the National Trust.

Fishing is the main industry of the tiny community on **Cape Barren Island** to the south — the home of the protected Cape Barren Goose.

for the aged), the Jolly Farmer, the Old Crown Inn and the Leather Bottell Inn, now a licensed French-style restaurant. Cressy, to the south of town, has several old buildings and long-established sheep stations, including 'Connorville', which was established by an early settler, Roderic O'Connor. His descendants still produce superfine wool there. **Accommodation:** 3 hotels, 1 guest house, 1 caravan/camping park.
Map ref. 361 L8, 363 F12

Mole Creek Population 303.
The unique Tasmanian leatherwood honey is produced in this town at the foot of the Great Western Tiers. It is made by bees from the blossom of the leatherwood tree which grows only in the rainforests of the west coast of Tasmania. Each summer apiarists transport hives to the leatherwood forests. The town serves an important farming and forestry district. **In the area:** One of the finest limestone caves in Tasmania, Marakoopa, is 7 km from the town, and the smaller, but still spectacular, King Solomon Cave is a further 2 km away. Both caves are electrically lit and have daily guided tours. Marakoopa is the only cave with glow-worms in Tasmania which is open to the public. **Accommodation:** Limited.
Map ref. 360 I8

New Norfolk Population 6243.
Mellow old buildings set among English trees and hop fields dotted with oasthouses give this classified historic town a decidedly English look. The beautiful surrounding countryside has often been compared to that of Kent in England. On the Derwent River, 38 km from Hobart, New Norfolk owes its name to the fact that displaced settlers from the abandoned Norfolk Island settlement were granted land in this area. Although the New Norfolk district produces a majority of the hops used by Australian breweries, the chief industry today is paper manufacture. The Australian Newsprint Mills, established in 1941 at Boyer, used to produce the only newsprint made in Australia (now made at Albury, New South Wales). **Of interest:** The Old Colony Inn, in Montague St, is one of Tasmania's outstanding historic attractions. Built in 1835 and set in delightful grounds, it contains fine antiques and a collection of items dating back to the penal era. Open daily, it serves lunches and Devonshire teas. The Oast House, now a hops museum and art gallery is worth a visit. St Matthew's Church of England, built in 1823, is the oldest church still standing in Tasmania; and the adjoining Close is now a craft centre. The Bush Inn, built in 1815, claims the oldest licence in the Commonwealth, although this is contested by the Launceston Hotel. **In the area:** The famous Plenty Salmon Ponds, 11 km from town, where the first brown and rainbow trout in the southern hemisphere were bred in 1864, are open to the public. There are lawns for picnickers, a tea room, a kiosk and a freshwater fish museum. **Accommodation:** 1 hotel, 1 motel, 1 caravan/camping park.
Map ref. 356 F5, 359 L6

Oatlands Population 545.
This classified historic town on the shores of Lake Dulverton, 84 km north of Hobart, attracts both history lovers and fishermen. It was named by Governor Macquarie in 1821, and surveyed in 1832. Many of its buildings were constructed in the 1830s and it is said that almost everyone in the town lives in an historic building. **Of interest:** The convict-built court house (1829), one of the oldest buildings in town; Holyrood House, known as the Doctor's House is now a restaurant with an 1840s atmosphere. St Peter's Church of England (about 1838); and the Oatlands Mill (1837). Lake Dulverton is good for fishing. **In the area:** Lake Sorell, 29 km from town, and adjoining Lake Crescent are well-stocked with trout. Table Mountain, to the south-west of Lake Crescent. **Accommodation:** 2 hotels.
Map ref. 359 M3, 361 M13

Orford Population 378.
Views from this popular holiday resort at the estuary of the Prosser River, on the Tasman Highway, are dominated by Maria Island, which is 20 km off shore. **Of interest:** Bushwalks, river and sea fishing, scuba diving and golf. **In the area:** The beautiful fourteenth century stained glass window in the Church of St John the Baptist at Buckland. **Accommodation:** 2 motels, 1 caravan/camping park.
Map ref. 357 O2, 359 P5

Penguin Population 2616.
The Dial Range rises over this quiet town on the north coast situated on the three bays. It is a good base for exploring the surrounding country. **Of interest:** St Stephen's Church and the Uniting Church both have National Trust classifications. **In the area:** Magnificent view from summit of Mt Montgomery and the Dial Range, only 5 km from town; Gunns Plains Caves; a wildlife bird sanctuary; a drive to Ulverston via the coast road, through Lonah, passes the Three Sisters Islands. Myora Park, near the Detention River bridge, is a good picnic spot. **Accommodation:** 2 hotels, 1 caravan park.
Map ref. 360 G5

Poatina Population 213.
This modern plateau town, south-west of Launceston, was built to house the construction team working on the hydro-electric power station. **In the area:** Guided tours of the Poatina underground power station about 5 km from town. **Accommodation:** Limited.
Map ref. 361 L10

Pontville Population 980.
Much of the freestone used in Tasmania's old buildings was quarried near this classified historic township. With a revival in restoration work, two quarries are still operating. Pontville was founded in 1830 and many of its early buildings remain. On the Midland Highway, 27 km north of Hobart, it is the seat of local government for the Brighton Municipality. **Of interest:** Historic buildings include St Mark's Church of England, built in 1841; 'The Sheiling' behind the church, which was built in 1819 and restored in 1953; the old post office; the Crown Inn; and 'The Row', recently restored, which is thought to have been built in 1824 as soldiers' quarters. **In the area:** There are many old townships nearby, with interesting old buildings: Bagdad, to the north, with a wildlife sanctuary; Kempton, beyond Bagdad; also Tea Tree and Broadmarsh. **Accommodation:** Limited.
Map ref. 356 I4, 359 M5

Port Sorell Population 859.
Sheltered by hills, this well-established holiday resort at the estuary of the Rubicon River near Devonport has a mild climate. It is a fully protected wildlife sanctuary. Named after Governor Sorell in 1822, it is the oldest township on the north-west coast. Unfortunately many of its old buildings were destroyed by bushfires early this century, after it had been almost deserted for the thriving new port of Devonport. **Of interest:** Abundant flora and fauna; sheltered swimming, fishing, boating and bushwalking. Good views from Watch House Hill, once the site of the old gaol and now a bowling green. **Accommodation:** 1 motel, 2 caravan/camping parks.
Map ref. 361 J5

Queenstown Population 3714.
The discovery of gold and mineral resources in the Mt Lyell field last century led to the almost overnight emergence of the township of Queenstown. It is a town literally carved out of the mountains, which tower starkly around it. Mining has

---

Tasmania's West Coast

The beautiful but inhospitable west coast, with its wild mountain ranges, lakes, rivers, eerie valleys and dense rainforests, is one of Tasmania's most fascinating regions. The majestic untamed beauty of this coast is in complete contrast to the state's pretty pastures. The whole area has a vast mineral wealth and a colourful mining history, reflected in its towns. The discovery of tin and copper in 1879 and 1883 started a rush to the west coast, booming at the turn of the century. Today **Queenstown** — the largest town — still depends almost entirely on the Mt Lyell copper mine and the other main towns — **Zeehan**, **Rosebery**, **Waratah** and **Strahan** — also owe their existence to mining.

It was not until 1932 that a rough road was pushed through the mountainous country between Queenstown and **Hobart**. Fortunately modern road-making techniques have improved the situation and today west coast towns are linked by the Murchison, Zeehan and Waratah Highways and the Lyell Highway — the original road to Hobart — has been brought up to modern standards. Driving round the west coast road circuit and seeing the superb mountain scenery and colourful towns of the area is an unforgettable experience. The only drawback is the area's exceptionally heavy rainfall — even in summer and autumn.

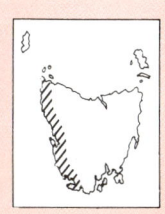

The little township of Zeehan, south-west of Rosebery, typifies the changing fortunes of mining towns. After rich silver-lead ore discoveries in 1882 its population swelled to 10 000 and the town boasted 26 hotels and the largest theatre in Australia — the Gaiety — where Dame Nellie Melba sang. Many of these fine buildings from the boom period can still be seen, including the Gaiety Theatre and the Grand Hotel, now flats. Zeehan's West Coast Pioneers' Memorial Museum, housed in the former School of Mines, is a very popular tourist attraction with a first-class collection of minerals. Next to the museum is a display of steam locomotives and carriages used on the west coast.

Driving into Queenstown you get one of the most spectacular views on any highway in Australia. As the narrow road winds down the steep slopes of Mt Owen, you can see the amazing bare hills — tinged with pale pinks, purples, golds and greys — which surround the town. At the turn of the century the trees from these hills were cut down to provide fuel for the copper smelters and heavy rains eroded their topsoil, revealing the strangely hued rocks beneath.

The first European settlement of the west coast was in 1821 when the most unruly convicts from Hobart were dispatched to establish a penitentiary on **Sarah Island** (358 E4) in Macquarie Harbour, and to work the valuable Huon pine forests around the Gordon and King Rivers. Sarah Island soon became a notorious prison and most of the unfortunate convicts who managed to escape died in the magnificent, but unyielding, surrounding bush. The horrors of that time are echoed in the name of the entrance to the harbour — Hell's Gates. Today thousands of tourists visit Strahan each year to go on the spectacular Gordon River cruise. Launches make frequent trips up the mouth of the Gordon River — one of Tasmania's largest and more remote rivers — from late August to early June. On the return trip launches pass close enough to Sarah Island to see or photograph the grim old court-house. Another interesting trip from Strahan is to Ocean Beach — 6 kilometres from the town. This long, lonely stretch of beach lashed by enormous breakers somehow typifies the magnificent wild west coast.

been continuous in Queenstown since 1888, and the field has so far produced more than 670 000 tonnes of copper, 510 000 kg of silver, and 20 000 kg of gold. The Mt Lyell Company, which employs most of the town's inhabitants, is now engaged in a scheme to establish large-scale underground mining. The town now has modern shops and facilities but its wide streets, remaining old buildings and unique setting give it an old mining town flavour. In certain lights the bare peaks surrounding the town turn to amazing shades of pink and gold. **Of interest:** Information about guided tours of Mt Lyell is available from the Tourist Information Centre, 39 Orr St. A photographic museum at the corner of Sticht and Driffield Sts depicts the history of the area. **In the area:** Spectacular views on the Lyell Highway as it climbs steeply out of town; ghost town of Linda on the Lyell Highway; and the satellite town of Gormanston, 6 km from town, which was the original mining settlement. **Accommodation:** 3 hotels, 3 motels.
Map ref. 358 E1, 360 E11

Railton Population 857.
This substantial country town south of Devonport owes its existence to the Goliath Portland Cement Company — one of Tasmania's major industries. Raw materials are taken from a huge quarry on the site and carried by an overhead conveyor to the crusher. **In the area:** Scenic drive of 14 km through an area known as Sunnyside. **Accommodation:** Limited.
Map ref. 360 I7

Richmond Population 587.
Charming Richmond, 26 km from Hobart, is one of the oldest and most important historic towns of Australia. The much-photographed Richmond Bridge is the oldest bridge in Australia, and many of the town's buildings were constructed in the 1830s or even earlier. Some of these graceful structures, including the bridge, were built by convicts under appallingly harsh conditions. Legend has it that the ghost of an overseer, who was murdered by the convicts, still haunts the bridge. **Of interest:** The old gaol, which was built five years before Port Arthur in 1825, is open to the public. John Lee Archer added the square and gaoler's house between 1832 and 1834. The court-house, which is still in use, was built in 1825-6. St John's (1837) is the oldest Roman Catholic church in Australia. St Luke's Church of England was built between 1834 and 1836. It is noted for its fine ceiling and gallery. The two-storey general store and former post office was built in 1829 and is the oldest postal building in Australia. Georgian Prospect House is now a licensed restaurant with a courtyard, saddlery and outdoor display of horse-drawn vehicles, many of which are still in use. Meals are also served at the old Richmond Arms Hotel. Galleries featuring local crafts and paintings include Saddlers Court, Honeysuckle Cottage and the Granary. One of the town's oldest buildings, Bridge Inn, displays veteran vehicles. **Accommodation:** 1 hotel, 1 caravan park.
Map ref. 357 J5, 359 N6

Ringarooma Population 223.
Farming and timber milling support this north-eastern town which dates back to the 1860s. **In the area:** Mathinna Hill offers charming views of Ringarooma and surrounding towns; pleasant drives of New River Road and Alberton Road; the Old Tin Mining Road to Branxholm gives a glimpse of the area as it was in the days of the early tin miners and pioneers.
Accommodation: Limited.
Map ref. 361 O6

Rokeby Population 3495.
This old township on the eastern shore of the River Derwent was first settled in 1809. The first apples to be exported from Tasmania were grown here, as was the first wheat ever produced in Tasmania. Rokeby's rural character is now rapidly changing with the expansion of the Clarence Municipality. The town has been earmarked for a State Housing development for 30 000 people over the next 15 years. **Of interest:** Rokeby has one of the few village greens in Australia; a few historic buildings remain, including Rokeby Court, Rokeby House and St Matthew's Church. Some of the chairs in the church's chancel were carved from one of the ships in Nelson's fleet, and the organ, brought from England in 1825 and first installed in what is now St David's Cathedral, Hobart, is still in use here. **In the area:** Rokeby is on the road to the boating and swimming townships of the South Arm. Clifton Beach is excellent for surfing. **Accommodation:** Limited.
Map ref. 357 K7, 359 N7

Fisherman's Paradise

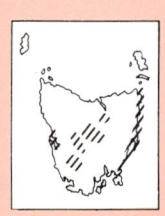

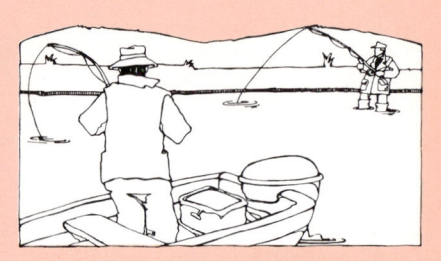

Fish are biting all year round in Tasmania — a fisherman's paradise by any standards, and famous for three species of fish. These are trout in the fresh water, bream in the estuaries, and tuna off the coast.

One area alone contains hundreds of lakes and lagoons stocked with trout of world class size. This is the inaccessible area, known as 'The Land of Three Thousand Lakes'. You are more likely, however, to choose from the huge range of developed areas brimming with trout in the central highlands region — such as Great Lake, Bronte Lagoon, Lake Sorell and Arthurs Lake. The Brumby Creek Weirs, just 25 kilometres from Launceston and 8 kilometres from Poatina chalet, are rapidly gaining a reputation as one of the great trout waters of Australia.

As the brown trout season closes in May (and the rainbow trout season in June), game fish begin to swarm down the mild east coast and fishermen start hauling in the big ones: bluefin tuna often weighing in at over 45 kilograms. Then, as the bluefin leave in the mid-winter months, schools of barracouta arrive in their thousands, and large Australian salmon schools return to the estuaries and along the shoreline — providing great sport for rock and beach fishermen.

In spring, one of the great sport fish of Tasmania — the silver bream — arrives in the river estuaries. Many anglers regard this tasty fish as one of the best fighting fish for its size.

Of course, in summer the whole island is an angler's dream. January and February are peak inland trout fishing months, and from February to March schools of Australian salmon swim close to the shoreline of Tasmania's many river estuaries, providing exciting fishing for the angler using a silver flash lure from the beach or rocks.

Rosebery Population 2675.

Gold was discovered in Rosebery in 1893 in what is now called Rosebery Creek. Today the town owes its existence to the huge Electrolytic Zinc Co. **In the area:** At Williamsford, 7 km from town, ore is carried from the mine to the refinery by a spectacular system of aerial buckets. The Montezuma Falls, the highest waterfall in the state, are 5 km west. Mt Murchison lies to the east. **Accommodation:** 2 hotels, 1 caravan/camping park.
Map ref. 360 E9

Ross Population 289.

One of the oldest and most beautiful bridges in Australia spans the Macquarie River at this attractive historic township. The bridge was designed by colonial architect John Lee Archer and built by convicts in 1836. The convict stonemason who worked on the bridge received a free pardon in recognition for his fine carvings. Ross was established in 1812 as a military post for the protection of travellers who once stopped there to change coaches. Today it is still an important stopover on the Midland Highway between Launceston and Hobart. The district is famous for its superfine wool. Beef cattle are also raised. **Of interest:** The Scotch Thistle Inn, a former coaching house, is now a high class licensed restaurant. Built in 1826, a plaque by the front door was presented by the National Trust in recognition of the faithful restoration work. An avenue of English trees in the main street complements other historic buildings such as Sherwood Castle Inn, Macquarie Store and the Church of England Sunday school. The old barracks has been restored by the local National Trust group, and now houses a wool and craft centre. Three fine churches are among the many other historic buildings. **In the area:** The Beaufort Deer Park and Wildlife Sanctuary, 6 km from town, has deer and native fauna in 400 ha of natural bushland, with barbecue facilities and a kiosk. It is open daily except for Tuesdays and Wednesdays. Some of the state's best trout fishing lakes, Sorell, Crescent, Tooms and Leake, are within an hour's drive of Ross. **Accommodation:** 1 hotel, 1 caravan/camping park.
Map ref. 359 N1, 361 N11

St Helens Population 1005.

This popular resort on the shores of Georges Bay is renowned for its crayfish and flounder. The largest town on Tasmania's east coast, it has three freezer works in or near the settlement to handle the catch of the crayfishing and scallop fleet based in its harbour. **Of interest:** The beautiful bayside beaches are ideal for swimming and fishing and the coastal beaches are good for surfing. Charter boats are available for deep sea fishing. The Scamander River offers excellent fishing for bream. Many of the local restaurants specialise in fish dishes. **In the area:** There are many attractive bushwalks around the district, with abundant wild flowers and birds. Scamander, 19 km south of town, also has good fishing and beaches and the little township of Binalong Bay, 11 km north of town, offers surf and rock fishing. **Accommodation:** 4 hotels, 1 motel, 3 caravan/camping parks.
Map ref. 361 R7

St Leonards Population 18 307.

St Leonards, just east of Launceston, abounds in history. The district was first opened up as pasturelands as early as 1806, when it was known as Paterson's Plains. In 1866 it was proclaimed a town and given its present name. **Of interest:** Many of the original homes remain, and are still owned by the same families. The town's noted woollen mills, which were among the first in the state to be electrically lit, may be inspected. **In the area:** A riverside picnic ground, just ½ km from town, has a kiosk, children's playground and is good for swimming. The surrounding farmlands, with their hawthorn-edged country lanes, have an old English air. **Accommodation:** Limited.
Map ref. 361 M7, 363 F10

St Marys Population 653.

The position of this small township, at the junction of the Tasman Highway and the Esk Main Road, makes it a busy thoroughfare. At the head waters of the South Esk River system, St Marys is about 10 km inland from the attractive east coast. **In the area:** The small coastal township of Falmouth, 4 km off the main highway, is an early settlement of historical interest with several convict-built structures. It has fine beaches, attractive rocky headlands and good fishing. There are many spectacular mountain and coast views to the south through Elephant Pass. **Accommodation:** Limited.
Map ref. 361 Q8

Savage River Population 1141.

This township in the rugged north-west serves the workers on the major Savage River iron ore project, which has been financed by a consortium of American, Japanese and Australian interests. Ore deposits are formed into a slurry and pumped through an 85 km pipeline north to Port Latta on the coast, where they are pelletised and shipped to Japan. **Of interest:** Inspections of the mine complex may be arranged. **In the area:** The near-ghost town of the former gold-rush township of Corinna, to the south-west, has good fishing and spectacular scenery. Regular launch excursions operate from here to Pieman Head. Dinghies may be hired. Old graves with Huon pine headstones are reminders of the past. Luina, to the north-east, is an important mining

township, with the second largest tin mine in Australia. Copper is also produced. **Accommodation:** 1 hotel.
Map ref. 360 D8

Scamander Population under 200.
This well-developed resort town midway between St Marys and St Helens offers excellent sea and river fishing, and has good swimming beaches. **Of interest:** There are many scenic walks and drives through the forestry roads and plantations. The Scamander River is noted for its bream fishing and beautiful scenery. Trout are taken in the upper reaches. Licensed restaurant. **In the area:** Beaumaris, 5 km north of the town, also has excellent beaches and lagoons and a licensed restaurant. **Accommodation:** 1 hotel, 1 motel, 1 caravan/camping park.
Map ref. 361 R8

Scottsdale Population 2573.
Scottsdale is the major town of Tasmania's north-east and serves some of the richest agricultural and forestry country on the island. A large food-processing factory specialises in the deep freezing and dehydrating of vegetables grown in the district. **Of interest:** The town has modern shops and most sports facilities. **In the Area:** The beach resort of Bridport of 23 km to the north. A lookout at the 'Sideling', elevation of 557 m above sea level. The lavender farm near the small farming township of Nabowla, west of town, is worth visiting in the main flowering period in late December. **Accommodation:** 2 hotels, 1 caravan/camping park.
Map ref. 361 N5

Sheffield Population 945.
This town, 30 km south of Devonport, stands in the foothills of the spectacular Great Western Tiers, in one of the most scenically attractive areas in the state. Rugged mountain gorges, quiet streams and rivers stocked with fish, and waterfalls and forests make it an ideal base for tourists. The town's economy is based on farming but has recently been given an additional boost by the construction of the vast Mersey/Forth Power Development Scheme. **In the area:** The lakes and dams of the scheme are about 10 km out of town. Lake Barrington, created by the scheme, has picnic facilities, a lookout, and is ideal for fishing and swimming. The spectacular Devil's Gate Dam is 13 km from town. The beautiful Cradle Mountain National Park is 61 km away. **Accommodation:** 1 hotel, 1 caravan/camping park.
Map ref. 360 I7

Smithton Population 3378.
This substantial township is the administrative centre of Circular Head in the far north-west. It serves the most productive dairying and vegetable growing area in the state, and is the centre of one of Tasmania's most important forestry areas. The town has the most modern butter and casein factory in Tasmania as well as several large sawmills. Fishing is another important industry. **Of interest:** Fishing and boating in the river and Duck Bay.

Inspections of the dairy and timber mills may be arranged. There is a lookout tower on Tier Hill, at the end of Massey St. **In the area:** The classified historic township of Stanley is 22 km to the east. **Accommodation:** 1 hotel.
Map ref. 360 C3

Somerset Pop. part of Burnie.
At the junction of the Bass and Waratah Highways, Somerset has become a satellite town for Burnie, which is about 6 km to its east. **In the area:** The small rural settlement of Yolla serves the surrounding rich pastoral country. **Accommodation:** 1 hotel, 2 motels.
Map ref. 360 F5

Sorell Population 2544.
Named after Governor Sorrell, this town not far from Hobart was founded in 1821. It played an important part in early colonial history by providing most of the grain for the state from 1816 to 1860. It also provided grain for NSW for more than 20 years. The area is still an important agricultural district, specialising in fat lambs. **In the area:** Many Hobartians have holiday homes in the extensive beach area around Carlton and Dodges Ferry and many of these are available for rental. It is the largest grouping of popular beaches in the state. Carlton Beach has a surf life saving club. **Accommodation:** 2 hotels, 1 caravan/camping park.
Map ref. 357 L6, 359 N6

Stanley Population 603.
This quaint little village nestling under the huge rocky outcrop called The Nut is steeped in history. It was the site for the headquarters of the London-based Van Diemen's Land Company, set up in 1825 to cultivate land and breed high-class sheep, when its wharf handled old whalers and sailing ships. Today these are replaced by modern crayfish and shark fishing fleets, but little else has changed. The birthplace of Australia's only Tasmanian Prime Minister, the Hon. J. A. Lyons, Stanley has recently been declared an historic town. **Of interest:** Many old buildings can be found round the wharf, including a bluestone grain store and a former customs house, designed by colonial architect John Lee Archer, who lived in the township. Archer's own home, now known as Poet's Cottage, is situated at the base of The Nut. Other historic buildings include the quaint Union Hotel (1849) which has a nest of cellars and narrow stairways, and serves counter meals; two historic inns, the Commercial Inn (1842), which is now a private home, and the Plough Inn (1843), which has been restored and furnished in the style of the day and is open for inspection. It has a cider bar. Next to this is the Discovery Centre, a folk museum and art gallery. The old cemetery has interesting headstones, including those of John Lee Archer and the explorer Henry Hellyer. **In the area:** 'Highfield', the old homestead of the agent for the Van Diemen's Land Company, is just out of town. Built in 1835, it has unfortunately fallen into disrepair. The family chapel and the remains of the servants' quarters are

Dams for Power

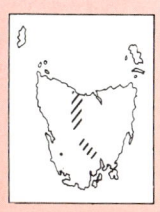

Tasmania has the largest hydro-electric power system in Australia, producing nearly ten per cent of the nation's electrical energy. Tasmania's first dam for hydro-electric power was built at Great Lake in 1911.

It is Tasmania's mighty highland rivers which produce the immense volume of water necessary for these extensive hydro-electric systems. The Derwent, Mersey, Forth and Gordon Rivers have already been harnessed for power production.

Stage one of the Gordon River power development involved four major dams, the creation of Lakes Gordon and Pedder, and an underground power station. These lakes are liberally stocked with trout and have already become tourist attractions.

The next major development involves the construction of four major dams — Murchison, Mackintosh, Bastyan and Lower Pieman — and the creation of four new lakes. A spectacular rockfill dam will create Lake Pieman on the Lower Pieman River and supply water for the third and biggest power station in the complex.

Driving between Hobart and Queenstown, you can see much of the Derwent power scheme — the most extensive of the hydro-electric developments — consisting of ten power stations. The Derwent River rises in Lake St Clair, 738 metres above sea level, and all but the last 44 metres of its fall is utilised.

There are public viewing galleries at Tungatinah, Tarraleah, Liapootah and Trevallyn power stations, and overnight accommodation is available at HEC chalets at **Bronte Park** (358 I2), **Tarraleah** (360 I13) and **Poatina** (361 L10). Tours can be arranged through the Government tourist bureau.

The power developments on the Mersey and Forth Rivers — although producing only half the power of the Derwent scheme — are far more spectacular as the whole system lies within a very steep river valley. Day trips can easily be arranged from any north-west coast centre and the construction roads built by the HEC are open to the public. This scheme encompasses seven power stations and rises at Lake Mackenzie, 1121 metres above sea level.

nearby. Two arched gates by the road are all that remain of a former deer park. There is a popular picnic area at the Dip Falls, off the highway, south-east of town. The pelletising plant of the Savage River Mines is at Port Latta, to the east, where ore is moved by conveyor to the enormous jetty and loaded into Japanese carriers. **Accommodation:** 1 hotel, 1 caravan/camping park.
Map ref. 360 D3

Strahan   Population 402.
This pretty little port in Macquarie Harbour is the only town on Tasmania's forbidding west coast. Originally a Huon pine timber milling town, its growth was boosted by the copper boom at the Mt Lyell mine. When the Strahan-Zeehan railway opened in 1892, it became a busy port. Today it handles freight to and from Queenstown and is used by crayfish, abalone and shark fishermen, but the use of the harbour is limited because of the formidable bar at Hell's Gates, the mouth of the harbour. **Of interest:** Mineral and gemstone museum, near the entrance to the West Strahan caravan park. Water Tower Hill gives an excellent view of the township and harbour. **In the area:** The Botanical Creek Park and Hogarth Falls are just out of town. The spectacular Ocean Beach, with its enormous surf and high sand dunes, is 6 km west of town. Launch trips up the Gordon River pass the Marble Cliffs and the infamous Sarah (or Settlement) Island, Tasmania's first and most brutal penal establishment. Another cruise goes across Macquarie Harbour to Hell's Gates. **Accommodation:** 1 hotel, 1 motel.
Map ref. 358 D2, 360 D12

Swansea   Population 428.
Swansea is a small town of historical interest in Oyster Bay in the centre of Tasmania's east coast. It is the administrative centre of Glamorgan, the oldest rural municipality in Australia. The original council chambers are still in use. **Of interest:** Bark Mill and East Coast Museum, c. 1885, has excellent displays and tea rooms; Morris's general store which was built in 1838 now houses an historical display; Schouten House; the Institute, now a pioneer museum; and the Lyne family's log cabin, which was built in 1826. **In the area:** Safe swimming, beach and rock fishing, surfing at Waterloo Point, trout fishing at Lake Leake. **Accommodation:** 1 hotel, 2 caravan/camping parks.
Map ref. 359 Q2, 361 Q12

Taroona   Population 4000.
A convict-built shot tower is the main attraction of this residential area near Hobart. **Of interest:** The tower, which is set in 3 ha of grounds, is open to the public. There is also a museum and tea room, both housed in old buildings (1855) as well as the original owner's house, which was built in 1835. At Taroona Park a tombstone marks the grave of James Batchelor, first officer of the ship *Venus*, who was buried in 1810. **In the area:** Extensive views over the Derwent Estuary from Bonnet Hill. **Accommodation:** Limited.
Map ref. 356 I8, 359 M7

Triabunna   Population 924.
When Maria Island was a penal settlement, Triabunna, 86 km north-east of Hobart, was a garrison town and whaling base. Today it is a fishing port, with an important export wood chipping mill just south of the town. **Of interest:** Fishing trips and visits to Maria Island National Park may be arranged. Charter boats are available for hire. Local beaches are good for swimming, water-skiing and fishing. **Accommodation:** 2 hotels, 1 caravan/camping park.
Map ref. 359 P4, 357 P1

Ulverstone   Population 9413.
Situated 19 km west of Devonport near the mouth of the Leven River, Ulverstone is a well-equipped tourist centre. **Of interest:** Riverside Anzac Park has an outer space children's playground with a rocket and flying saucer, electric barbecues, attractive walks and views. A giant water slide situated near Fairway Park provides thrills for all ages. 'Westella', an early home built in 1886, houses a variety of crafts and fine antiques which are on sale to the public. **In the area:** Extensive beaches east and west of town are safe for children. Beach, river and estuary fishing is good. Two nearby coastal areas are Turners Beach and Leigh. Further afield are the Gunns Plains Caves, Preston Falls, Level Canyon and Waldheim. **Accommodation:** 3 hotels, 3 motels, 4 caravan/camping parks.
Map ref. 360 H5

Waratah   Population 342.
This lonely little settlement set in mountain heathland 100 km north of Queenstown was the site of the first mining boom in Tasmania. In 1900 it had a population of 2000 and Mount Bischoff was the richest tin mine in the world. The deposits were discovered in 1872 by James 'Philosopher' Smith, a colourful local character, and the mine closed in 1935, with dividends totalling £200 for every £1 of original investment. Today the town is experiencing a revival of mining activity at nearby Luina and Savage River and at its own mine in the North Valley. **Of interest:** A few 'boom' buildings remain, including the court-house, the Atheneum Hall and the old church. **In the area:** The mining townships of Luina, Savage River and the fascinating former gold township of Corinna are worth a visit. **Accommodation:** Limited.
Map ref. 360 E7

Westbury   Population 1161.
A village green gives this town, 16 km east of Deloraine, a decidedly English air. Situated on the Bass Highway, Westbury was surveyed in 1828, and has several fine old buildings. **Of interest:** Facing the green is 'the White House', actually a group of buildings built in the early 1840s which now house a wide collection of antique furniture, prints and paintings, and a toy museum. The outbuildings include a bakehouse and stable with a display of vintage vehicles. The former 'Olde English Inn', built in 1833, is now privately run and contains a fine antique collection. **In the area:** The beautiful St Mary's Church in Hagley, 5 km east, is noted for its fine east window. It was donated by Lady Dry, the wife of Sir Richard Dry, who, in 1858, was the first Australian to be knighted and who was Tasmania's first Speaker and native-born Premier eight years later. The Liffey Falls are south of town. **Accommodation:** 1 hotel.
Map ref. 361 K8, 363 B11

Wynyard   Population 4345.
This small fishing port at the mouth of the Inglis River, west of Burnie, has daily flights between its airport and Melbourne. Situated within short driving distance of many varied attractions, it has become well-developed as a tourist centre, offering excellent accommodation and sporting facilities. The Wynyard municipality is a prosperous dairying and mixed farming district and the town has a large modern dairy factory. One of its motels has a licensed restaurant. **Of interest:** Excellent trout, fly and sea fishing in the river, sea and estuary. Sporting facilities include two golf courses. **In the area:** The oldest marsupial fossil in Australia was found at Fossil Bluff, 7 km from town. Nearby Table Cape offers panoramic views. Boat Harbour, 11 km from town, has one of the best beaches on the coast. Sisters Beach, which has a National Park with abundant flora, is a further 7 km away. The small Rocky Cape National Park is about 31 km west of town. **Accommodation:** 3 hotels, 1 motel, 2 caravan/camping parks.
Map ref. 360 F4

Zeehan   Population 1750.
Named after Abel Tasman's ship, this former mining town has had a chequered history. Situated 38 km from Queenstown, silver-lead deposits were discovered here in 1882. By 1901 it had 26 hotels and a population of 5014 — making it Tasmania's third largest town. Just seven years later the mines began to fail and Zeehan became a virtual ghost town. In the boom period between 1893 and 1908, 8 million dollars-worth of ore had been recovered. Now the town is once again on an upward swing with the re-opening of the tin mine at Renison Bell. Zeehan is the main town for this mine and many new houses are now being built. **Of interest:** Many 'boom' buildings remain, including the fabulous Gaiety Theatre, where Nellie Melba once sang, the Grand Hotel, the post office, bank and St Luke's Church. The West Coast Pioneers' Memorial Museum is now an important tourist attraction and has an outstanding mineral collection, together with historical and geological sections. Beside the museum is a unique display of steam locomotives and rail carriages used on the west coast. **In the area:** Dundas, 13 km from town, was once the site of a large mining town, but has reverted to bush. The old mine workings can still be seen. Trial Harbour, 23 km from town, is a popular fishing area but roads to both these areas are often in poor condition and tourists should check locally before going. **Accommodation:** 2 hotels, 1 motel, 1 caravan/camping park.
Map ref. 360 D10

TASMANIA'S CONVICT PAST

Despite their grim history, the ruins of the infamous Port Arthur settlement are the greatest single tourist attraction in Tasmania. The fact that they were a place of isolated incarceration for more than 12 000 prisoners has been blurred by time but it is still possible, particularly in bleak weather, for the ruins to create something of the atmosphere of hopelessness and misery which existed there about 130 years ago.

Port Arthur is on the Tasman Peninsula which extends from the Forestier Peninsula south-east of Hobart, screening Pitt Water and the Derwent estuary from the Tasman Sea. The whole area of both peninsulas is very beautiful, with sweeping pasture, timbered areas and a coastline of sheltered bays and towering cliffs. Many secondary roads and tracks and a host of secluded beauty spots make it an ideal place for bushwalking.

Eaglehawk Neck is on the isthmus between the two peninsulas. In the days of the penal colony, hounds were tethered in a tight line across the Neck to prevent escapes. The line was continually patrolled and guard posts were established in the nearby hills. No prisoner ever broke through this fearful barrier, although some did swim to freedom. Near Eaglehawk Neck are four incredible rock formations, the Tasman Arch, the Devil's Kitchen, the Blow Hole and the Tessellated Pavement.

TOP: *Port Arthur was once a notorious penal settlement. Now in its natural parklike setting it is Tasmania's most popular tourist attraction.*

LEFT: *The gaol at Port Arthur. If stones could speak these crumbling walls would have many a harrowing tale to tell of this infamous place.*

Tasmania

Many of Port Arthur's ruins have been preserved and some have been restored. The many-spired church, said to have been designed by the convict James Blackburn; the model prison which, like Pentonville Prison in England, was wheel-shaped so that a warder standing in the centre could observe activities in all the cells around him; the exile cottage, originally a hospital and then the home of the exiled Irish rebel, William Smith O'Brien; and the guard house are among the ruined buildings still standing. Some which have been restored are the lunatic asylum and the commandant's residence, now privately owned. The prison was established by Governor Arthur in 1830 and, although transportation ceased in 1853, the prison was not abandoned until 1877.

Many buildings were demolished by contractors and others were badly damaged by a bushfire which swept through the peninsula in 1897.

In the middle of Port Arthur Bay stands the Island of the Dead, with its 1769 graves, all of which are unnamed: the only exceptions are the 180 additional graves of prison staff and the military.

ABOVE RIGHT: *The asylum at Port Arthur which housed mentally ill convicts.*

RIGHT: *The prison hospital, now a ruin. Patients who died here were buried on the Island of the Dead.*

BELOW RIGHT: *Smith O'Brien's Cottage, occupied by him for only a few months.*

BELOW: *The Guard Tower at Port Arthur viewed through a beautiful archway crafted by convict workmen.*

Maps of Tasmania

Location Map

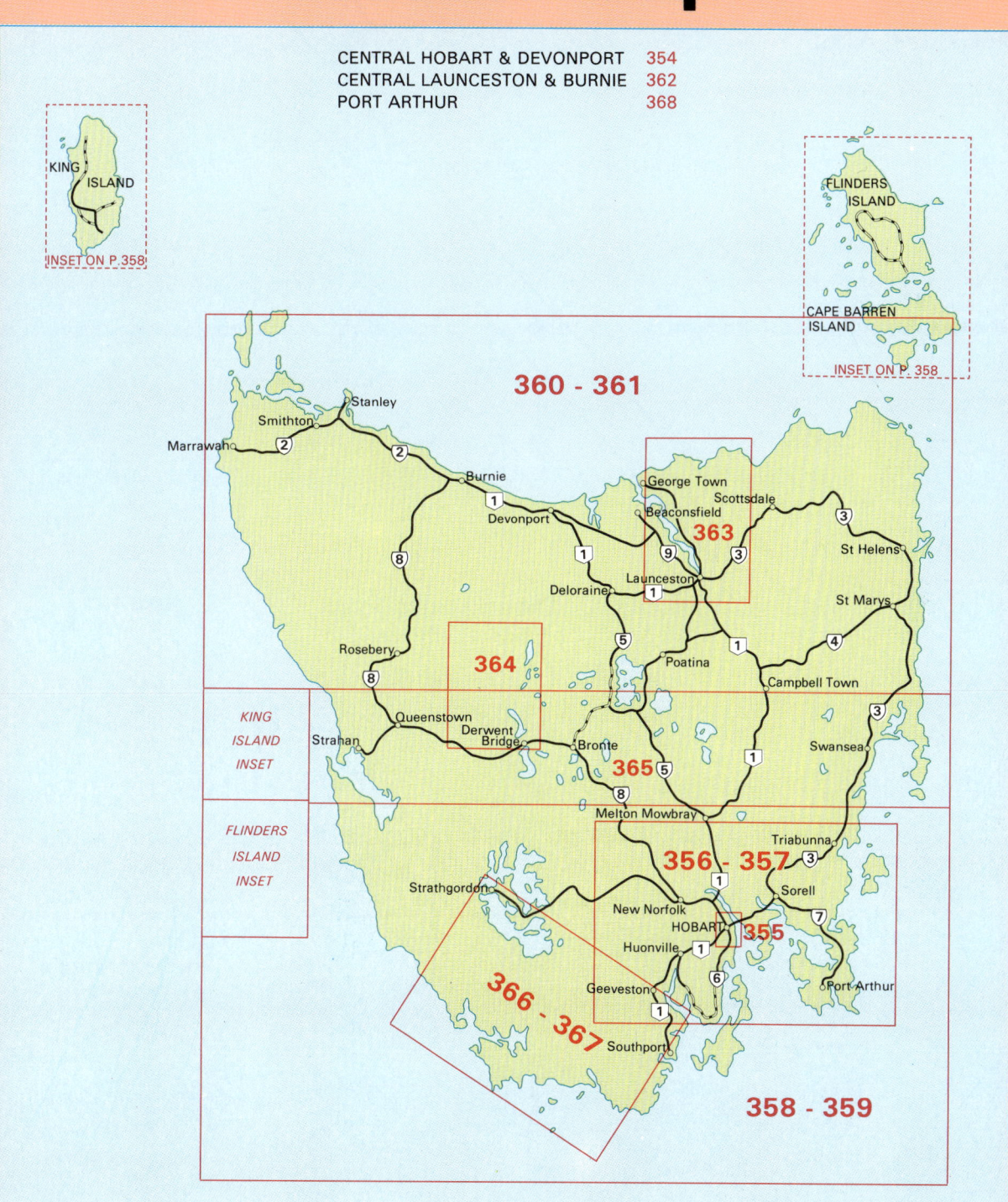

CENTRAL HOBART & DEVONPORT 354
CENTRAL LAUNCESTON & BURNIE 362
PORT ARTHUR 368

KING ISLAND INSET ON P.358

FLINDERS ISLAND
CAPE BARREN ISLAND
INSET ON P.358

360 - 361

Stanley
Smithton
Marrawah
Burnie
Devonport
George Town
Scottsdale
Beaconsfield
363
St Helens
Launceston
Deloraine
St Marys
Rosebery
364
Poatina
Campbell Town
Queenstown
Strahan
Derwent Bridge
Bronte
Swansea
365
Melton Mowbray
Triabunna
356 - 357
Strathgordon
New Norfolk
Sorell
HOBART
355
Huonville
Port Arthur
366 - 367
Geeveston
Southport
358 - 359

KING ISLAND INSET

FLINDERS ISLAND INSET

354 Central Hobart & Devonport

HOBART
Places of Interest
1. Cat and Fiddle Arcade E4
2. Folk Museum (Narryna) F7
3. Hadley's Hotel E5
4. Hobart Hospital F3
5. Holy Trinity Church C1
6. Lenna Motor Inn H6
7. Museum and Art Gallery F4
8. Parliament House F6
9. Police Headquarters E3
10. Post Office F4
11. St. Davids Cathedral E5
12. St. Mary's Cathedral B4
13. State Library D4
14. Town Hall F4
15. Wrest Point Hotel & Casino ... F7
21. Centrepoint Arcade D5

Transport & Touring
16. Ansett Terminal D5
17. National Trust Information Office ... F6
18. Royal ACT Headquarters C3
19. TAA Terminal F2
20. Tourist Bureau D4

DEVONPORT
Places of Interest
1. Don River Tramway A8
15. City Council Chambers D11
2. Gallery and Art Centre D11
3. Library D11
16. Maritime Museum D9
4. Police D11
5. Post Office E11
6. Railway Museum A12
17. Tiagarra (Aboriginal Museum) . C8
7. Town Hall D11

Transport & Touring
8. Ansett Terminal D11
9. Coach Depart D11
10. Ferry Terminal E11
11. RACT E11
12. Railway Station E11
13. TAA Terminal D11
14. Tourist Bureau D11

Hobart & Suburbs 355

356 Tours from Hobart

0 5 10 15 20 25 km
359
J K L M N O P Q R
1 2 3 4 5 6 7 8 9 10 11 12 13
Rhyndaston
Woodsdale
Eldon
Mt. Hobbs 821m
Mt. Douglas
Blue Tier 593m
Triabunna
A3
Colebrook
Levendale
Cape Bougainville
Lords Bluff
Moreys Hill
Okehampton Bay
Louisville
Pt. Horne
Prosser Bay
Mt. Bains 334m
Boomer Hill
Orford
Quarry Pt.
Spring Beach
Stapleton Pt.
Johnson Pt.
Isle Du Nord
Cape Boullanger
Convict Ruins
Darlington
Danby Siding
Brown Mt. 792m
Historic Church
HWY
Three Thumbs 549m
Passage
Mt. Maria 709m
Beaching Bay
Lowdina
Campania
Runnymede
TASMAN
Buckland
Burst My Gall Hill
Mt. Gatehouse
Griffiths
Rheban
Carrickfergus Bay
MARIA ISLAND NATIONAL PARK
Mistaken Cape
Lachlan I.
Booming Bay
Rekuna
Mt. Morrison 471m
Brushy Plains Rivt
Prossers S. L. 647m
Shoal Bay
Riedle Bay
MARIA ISLAND
Longs Hill 315m
Earlham Hill
Pt. Des Galets
Cockle Bay
Mercury
Nugent
Jacob Hill
Middle Peak
Cape Bernier
Cape Maurouard
Australias oldest bridge
Richmond
Orielton
Pawleena
Walking Track
Cape Peron
Duck Hole
Mt. Lord 279m
Gordon S. L. 415m
Kellevie
Penna
Wattle Hill
Sorell
Marion Bay
Midway Pt.
Forcett
Bream Creek
Flagstaff Hill
Water
ARTHUR
SEA
Lindisfarne
Cambridge
Hobart Airport
Lewisham
Copping
Seven Mile Beach
Dodges Ferry
Cape Paul Lamanon
Bellerive
Mt. Rumney 378m
Tiger Hd.
Carlton
Tasman Memorial
North Bay
Fine coastal views.
Fishing
Blackman Bay
Cape Frederick Hendrick
Howrah
Rokeby
Roches Beach
Carlton Bluff
Primrose Sands
Primrose Pt.
Tasman Monument
Dunalley
Boomer Id.
Humper Bluff
Lauderdale
Surfing
Fulham Id.
Dunalley Bay
Mt. Forestier 320m
High Yellow Bluff
River
Frederick
Green Hd.
HWY
FORESTIER
Sandford
Henry
Droughty Pt.
Smooth Id.
King George Id.
Murdunna
Cape Surville
Crayfish Pt.
Cremorne
Sloping Id.
Whitehouse Pt.
PENINSULA
Gellibrand Pt.
Ralphs
Bay
Chronicle Pt.
Mt. Augustus 163m
Pipe Clay Lagoon
Convict Coal Mine Ruins
Norfolk
Macgregor Peak 592m
Opossum Bay
Cape Deslacs
Sloping Main
Flinders Bay
Flinders
Clifton Beach
North West Hd.
Gwandalon
Bay
Derwent
South Arm
Cape Contrariety
Saltwater River
Deer Pt.
Tessellated Pavement
Pirates Bay
Eaglehawk Bay
Eaglehawk Neck
Hope Beach
Premaydena Pt.
Blow Hole
Devils Kitchen
Cape Direction
Betsey Island
Iron Pot
Mt. Communication
Premaydena
Taranna
Tasmans Arch
Waterfall Bay
Cape Delasorte
Koonya
Outer North Hd.
O'Hara Bluff
Auk Pt.
Signal Hill
TASMAN
One Tree Pt.
Nubeena
TASMAN
PENINSULA
Storm
Oakwood
Thumb Pt.
Wedge Bay
The Yellow Bluff
Wedge Id.
Hippolyte Rocks
Trumpeter Bay
Highcroft
Radnor
Port Arthur
Denman
Fortescue Bay
The Lanterns
Cape Hauy
Bay
Trumpeter Pt.
Mt. Fortescue
Stormlea
Remarkable Cave
Munroe Bight
Variety Bay
NORTH BRUNY ISLAND
Church Hill 178m
Salters Pt.
Mt. Raoul
West Arthur Hd.
Black Hd.
Cape Pillar
Raoul Bay
Maingon
Bay
Cape Queen Elizabeth
Cape Raoul
Tasman Id.
Bligh Museum
Capt. Cooks Landing Place
Adventure Bay
A9
62
26
74

358 Southern Tasmania

359

360 Northern Tasmania

0 10 20 30 40 50 km
J K L M N O P Q R
1 2 3 4 5 6 7 8 9 10 11 12 13
Cape Barren Island
Kent Bay
Sloping Pt
Clarke Island
Snug Cove
Forsyth I.
Passage I.
Look Out Heads
Moriarty Bay
Moriarty Point
STRAIT
N
Banks Strait
Cape Portland
Swan I.
Waterhouse I.
Waterhouse Pt
Croppies Pt
Ringarooma Bay
Mussel Roe Bay
Poole
Cape Naturaliste
Mt. William
MT. WILLIAM NATIONAL PARK
Eddystone Pt
Tomahawk
Waterhouse
Boobyalla
Gladstone
South Mt.Cameron
Ansons Bay
West Sandy Cape
East Sandy Cape
Anderson Bay
Stony Head
Noland Bay
Bridport
Five Mile Bluff
Lulworth
Beechford
Weymouth
Bellingham
Low Head
Lighthouse
West Head
Badger Head
Greens Beach
Kelso
Port Dalrymple
GeorgeTown
ASBESTOS RANGE NAT. PK
York Town
Port Sorell
Beauty Point
Bell Bay
Lefroy
Pipers River
Pipers Brook
Beaconsfield
Rowella
The Glen
Retreat
Lebrina
Golconda
Lietinna
Scottsdale North
Jetsonville
Scottsdale
Nabowla
Scottsdale West
Springfield
Springfield South
Forester
Winnaleah
Warrentinna
Herrick
Pioneer
Moorina
Telita
Derby
Branxholm
Weldborough
Kamona
Legerwood
Ringarooma
Bay of Fires
The Gardens
SEA
Lottah
Goulds Country
Goshen
Priory
Binalong Bay
Grants Pt
St.Helens Pt
Georges Bay
Stieglitz
St.Helens
St.Helens I.
Sidmouth
Devoit
Hillwood
Robigana
Turners Marsh
Lower
Karoola
Bangor
Lilydale
Lisle
TASMAN
Flowery Gully
Winkleigh
Holwell
Harford
Sassafras
East Sassafras
Frankford
Glengarry
Exeter
Rosevears
Dilston
Notley Hills
Legana
Notley Fern Gorge
Bridgenorth
Mt Arthur 1187m
Myrtle Bank
Targa
Paterson
Tayene
Nunamara
Mt Barrow National Park
Rocherlea
Riverside
LAUNCESTON
Trevallyn P.S.
St.Leonards
Birralee
Rosevale
Selbourne
Parkham
Elizabeth Town
Reedy Marsh
Weetah
Green Pea Farms
Deloraine
Westbury
Hagley
Westwood
Entally House
Hadspen
Relbia
White Hills
Breadalbane
Carrick
Western Junction
Evandale
Perth
Longford
Cressy
Exton
Quamby Brook
Cluan
Whitemore
Bishopsbourne
Toiberry
Golden Valley
Meander
Quamby Bluff 1226m
Bracknell
Jackeys Marsh
Drys Bluff 297m
Liffey
Liffey Falls
Blackwood Creek
WESTERN TIERS
Poatina
Poatina P.S.
Delmont
Burns Creek
Musselboro
Blessington
Upper
Castle Hill 699m
Deddington
Nile
Ben Nevis 1367m
Mt Saddleback
Esk Upper
Roses Tier
Legges Tor 1573m
Skiing
BEN LOMOND NATIONAL PARK
Stacks Bluff 1527m
Storys Creek
Rossarden
Mathinna
Tower Hill
Mt Nicholas 869m
Cornwall
St Patricks Head
St.Marys
Fingal
Gray
Elephant Pass
Lagoons
Piccaninny Pt
Mt Young 903m
St. Columba Falls
Pyengana
Legunia
Alberton
Talawah
Trenah
Mt Victoria
Mt Maurice 1120m
Didleum Plains
Scamander Upper
Beaumaris
Scamander
Henderson Lagoon
Falmouth
Mangana
MAIN ROAD
Ormley
Avoca
St Pauls Dome 1027m
Royal George
Seymour
Long Point
Douglas River
Maclean Bay
Waubs Harbour
Bicheno
Cape Lodi
Apslaw
Cranbrook
Moulting Lagoon
Nine Mile Beach
Swansea
Coles Bay
Great Oyster Bay
Cape Tourville
Sleepy Bay
The Hazards
Wineglass Bay
Cape Forestier
Mt Freycinet +614m
FREYCINET NATL. PARK
FREYCINET PENINSULA
Cape Degerando
Schouten Passage
Schouten Island
Cape Baudin
Cape Faure
Mayfield Bay
Buxton Point
Mayfield
Little Swanport
Pontypool
Mt Tooms
Epping Forest
Cleveland
MIDLAND HWY
Conara Junction
Llewellyn Siding
Campbell Town
Snow Hill
Lake Leake
Mt Hobgoblin
Mt Connection
Ross
Old Bridge
Mona Vale
Tunbridge
Woodbury
Antill Ponds
York Plains
Pawtella
Nala
Lemont
Oatlands
Andover
Parattah
Fadden Tier
Tooms Lake
Bradys Lookout 1371m
Trout fishing and hydro-electric scheme.
Millers Bluff 1212m
Auburn
Goldsmith
Mt Franklin 1102m
Interlaken
Old Mans Head
Table Mt 1095m
Rutland
Lake Sorell
Lake Crescent
Woods Lake
Lag. of Islands
Arthurs Lake
Tods Corner P.S.
Pump
952m
Mt Penny 1115m
Wihareja
Steppes
Waddamana
Shannon
Miena
Barren Tier 1188m
Dam
Great Lake 1030m
Reynolds I.
Rats Castle 1393m
Bernacchi
Liaweeny
Breona
Augusta
Lake Echo 846m
Dee Lagoon
Power Stn
Dee
Hermitage
Victoria Valley
Osterley
Blue Hill
HIGHWAY
LAKE HWY
TAMAR HWY
EAST TAMAR HWY
WEST
ESK
HWY
A3 A4 A5 A7 A8
359

362 Launceston & Burnie

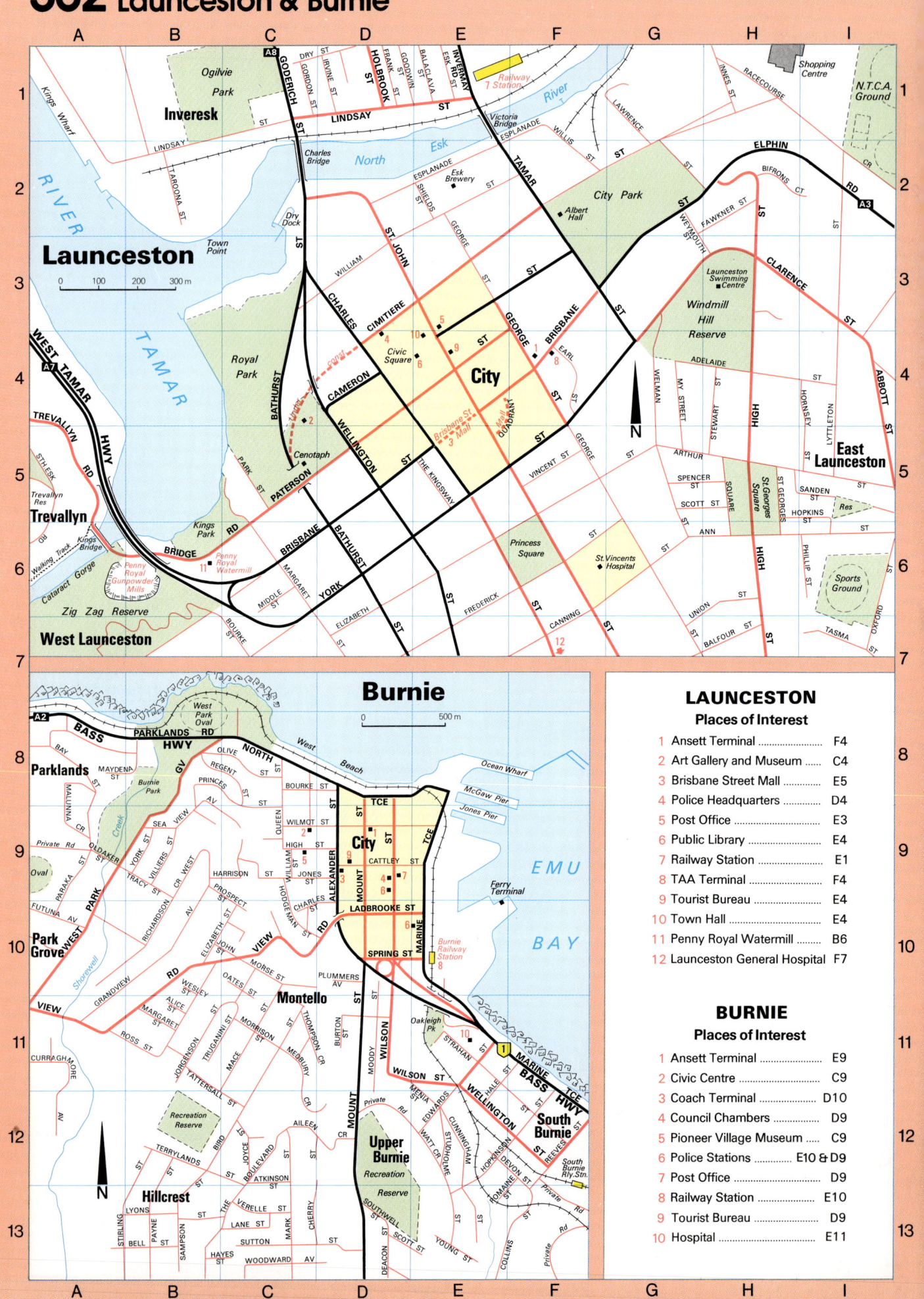

LAUNCESTON
Places of Interest
1. Ansett Terminal F4
2. Art Gallery and Museum C4
3. Brisbane Street Mall E5
4. Police Headquarters D4
5. Post Office E3
6. Public Library E4
7. Railway Station E1
8. TAA Terminal F4
9. Tourist Bureau E4
10. Town Hall E4
11. Penny Royal Watermill B6
12. Launceston General Hospital F7

BURNIE
Places of Interest
1. Ansett Terminal E9
2. Civic Centre C9
3. Coach Terminal D10
4. Council Chambers D9
5. Pioneer Village Museum C9
6. Police Stations .... E10 & D9
7. Post Office D9
8. Railway Station E10
9. Tourist Bureau D9
10. Hospital E11

Tours from Launceston 363

364 Cradle Mountain & Lake St Clair National Park

0 2·5 5 7·5 10 12·5 15 17·5 20km
J K L M N O P Q R
360
To Hobart
To Queenstown
1 2 3 4 5 6 7 8 9 10 11 12 13
MOUNTAINS OF JUPITER
RANGE
TRAVELLERS
MERSEY
RIVER
TRACK
Narcissus
River
CANE
RANGE
THE LABYRINTH
THE GUARDIANS
NATIONAL PARK
LAKE ST CLAIR
CRADLE MOUNTAIN —
LAKE ST CLAIR
MT OLYMPUS
OVERLAND
TRACK
Ida Bay
Narcissus Bay
Cynthia Bay
Derwent Bridge
Hotel
LAKE ST CLAIR
RD
LYELL
HWY
Frankland Beaches
Boat Ramp
Rangers Cottage
CHEYNE
RANGE
MURCHISON
RIVER
Mt Gould 1491m
Mt Byron 1378m
Mt Cuvier 1380m
Mount Manfred 1402m
Mt Massif 1470m
Mt Geryon 1509m
The Acropolis 1471m
Walled Mountain 1410m
Mount Nereus 1180m
High Dome 1320m
Pyramid Mountain 1250m
Mt Hugel 1397m
Mt Rufus 1416m
Mt Gell 1442m
Mt Charles 1050m
Mt Ida 1253m
Eldon Bluff 1200m
Lake Dorothy
ELDON RANGE
Pine Valley Hut
Windy Ridge Hut
Narcissus Hut
Echo Point Hut
Gingerbread Hut
Joe Slater Hut
Kia Ora Hut
Du Cane Hut
Nichols Junction
Collingwood
Cardigan
River
Balaclava
Franklin
Navarre
LYELL
HIGHWAY
Lake King William
Transmission
Lines
Power
Weir
Dam
Derwent Basin
Travellers Rest Lagoon
Travellers Rest
Lake Marion
Lake Helios
Lake Elysia
Lake Meston
Lake Payanna
Lake Ewart
Lake Sappho
Eldon
South
George
Cephissus
Patons
Inserman

366 South West National Park

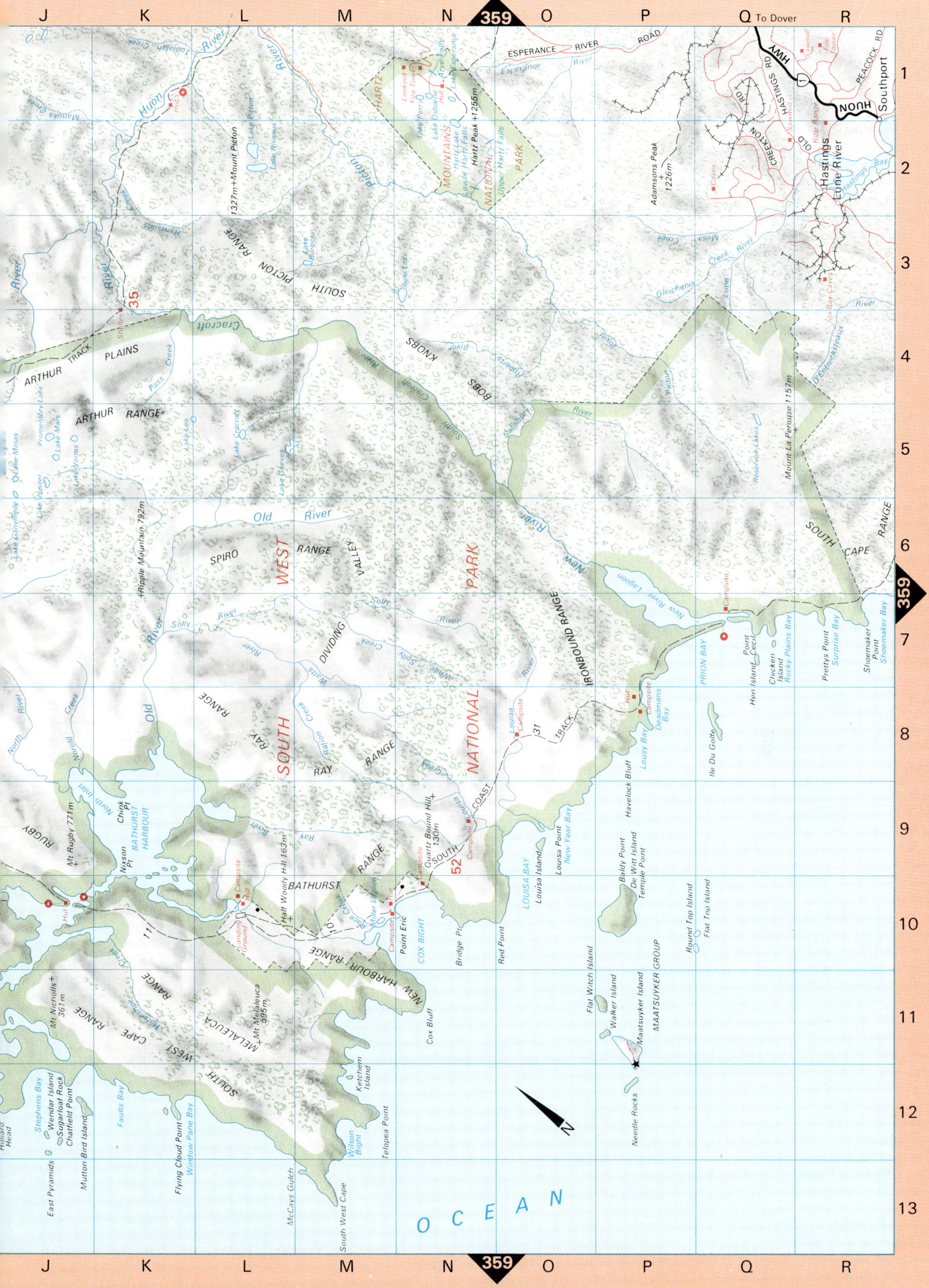
0 5 10 15 20 25 30 35 40km
J K L M N O P Q R
359
To Dover
1 2 3 4 5 6 7 8 9 10 11 12 13
ESPERANCE RIVER ROAD
Esperance River
HARTZ MOUNTAINS NATIONAL PARK
Hartz Peak 1255m
Arve Falls
Lake Osborne
Lake Perry
Hartz Lake
Lower Hartz Falls
Upper Hartz Falls
Lake Esperance
HUON HWY
HASTINGS RD
PEACOCK RD
OLD CREEKTON RD
Southport
Hastings
Lune River
Hastings Bay
Adamsons Peak 1226m
Mosa Creek
Gleichenia Creek
Lune River
Huon River
Tolosah Creek
Manuka Creek
Hut
Mount Picton 1327m
Lake Picton
Lake Riveaux
Picton River
Hartnett Rivulet
PICTON RANGE
SOUTH PICTON
Craycroft
ARTHUR PLAINS
TRACK
ARTHUR RANGE
Pass Creek
Lake Oberon
Lake Mars
Promontory Lake
Lake Ganymede
Lake Sirona
Lake Leo
Lake Cygnus
Lake Geeves
Lake Craycroft
BOBS KNOBS
Salisbury River
Roberts
SOUTH CAPE RANGE
Picton
Reservoir Lakes
Mount La Perouse 1157m
D'Entrecasteaux River
Old River
SPIRO RANGE
WEST VALLEY
SOUTH WEST NATIONAL PARK
Ripple Mountain 792m
Solly River
White Solly Creek
DIVIDING RANGE
IRONBOUND RANGE
New River
New River Lagoon
Campsite
PRION BAY
Point Cecil
Hen Island
Chicken Island
Rocky Plains Bay
Prettys Point
Surprise Bay
Shoemaker Point
Shoemaker Bay
Ile Du Golfe
Deadmans Bay
Lousy Bay
Hut
Havelock Bluff
Louisa Creek
Louisa Campsite
TRACK
31
SOUTH COAST
RAY RANGE
Ray River
Rallon Creek
Watts Creek
RUGBY RANGE
Mt Rugby 771m
North Inlet
Chink Pt
Nixson Pt
BATHURST HARBOUR
Norold Creek
North River
Old River
BATHURST RANGE
Woody Hill 163m
Quartz Bound Hill 130m
Landing Ground
Campsite
Hut
Point Eric
COX BIGHT
Bridge Pt
Red Point
LOUISA BAY
Louisa Island
Louisa Point
New Year Bay
Baldy Point
De Witt Island
Temple Point
Round Top Island
Flat Top Island
Flat Witch Island
Walker Island
Maatsuyker Island
MAATSUYKER GROUP
Needle Rocks
35
52
NEW HARBOUR RANGE
Cox Bluff
Ketchem Island
MELALEUCA RANGE
Mt Melaleuca 395m
SOUTH WEST CAPE RANGE
Mt Nicholls 361m
Stephens Bay
Wendar Island
Sugarloaf Rock
Chatfield Point
Faults Bay
Mutton Bird Island
Hilliard Head
East Pyramids
Flying Cloud Point
Window Pane Bay
McCays Gulch
Wilson Bight
Telopea Point
South West Cape
OCEAN
N

368 Port Arthur

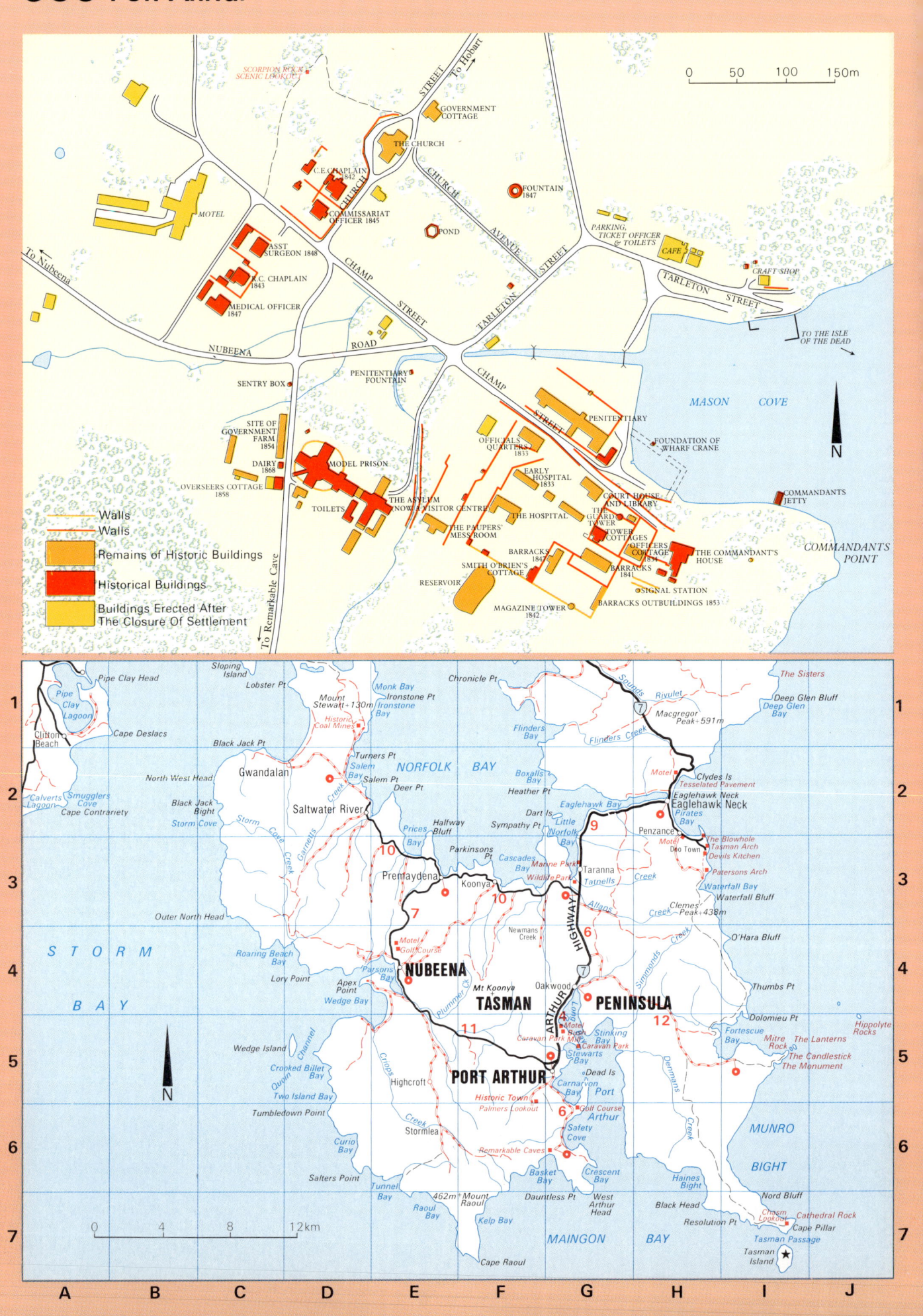

Gazetteer of place names

ACT Australian Capital Territory
Ck Creek
Cons. Park Conservation Park
Hwy Highway
Is. Island
L. Lake
Lwr Lower
Nat. Park National Park
NSW New South Wales
NT Northern Territory
Pt Point
Qld Queensland
Res. Reserve
SA South Australia
St Saint
Stn Station
Tas. Tasmania
Vic. Victoria
WA Western Australia

Note: Words starting with Mac, Mc or M' are indexed as though they were spelt Mac.

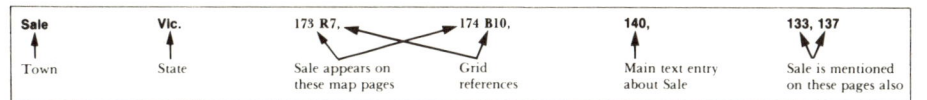

Sale → Town
Vic. → State
173 R7, → Sale appears on these map pages
174 B10, → Grid references
140, → Main text entry about Sale
133, 137 → Sale is mentioned on these pages also

A

Abbeyard Vic. 167 P10
Abbotsford NSW 72 I3
Abbotsford Vic. 148 I8
Abbotsham Tas. 360 H6
Abercorn Qld 323 N6
Abercrombie NSW 98 G7, 100 E2
Aberdeen NSW 95 J13, 99 J1, **40**
Aberfeldy Vic. 173 N4
Aberglasslyn NSW 83 E2
Abermain NSW 83 D4, 99 L3
Abernethy NSW 83 D5
Abminga SA 206 I1, 271 L13
Acacia Creek NSW 316 C11
Acacia Gap NT 266 E5
Acacia Plateau NSW 316 C11
Acacia Ridge Qld 310 H11
Acheron Vic. 160 F5, 167 K13, 173 K1
Acton ACT 109 K6
Adaminaby NSW 100 D8, 104 H3, **40**
Adamsfield Tas. 358 I6
Adamstown NSW 82 C8, 83 H5
Adavale QLD 322 E7
Addington Vic. 171 P2
Adelaide SA 194-9, 202 I6, 178-9, **180**
Adelaide Airport SA 195 B9, 196 F12
Adelaide Lead Vic. 165 P12
Adelaide River NT 266 E6, **234**
Adelong NSW 97 R11, 98 C11, 100 B6, **40**
Adjungbilly NSW 98 D10, 100 C5
Admiralty Gulf Aboriginal Reserve WA 255 O1
Advancetown Qld 317 N7, **297**
Adventure Bay Tas. 359 M10, **343**
Agery SA 200 F12, 202 F3
Agnes Vic. 173 O11
Agnes Banks NSW 77 J5
Agnes Creek SA 206 G2
Aileron NT 270 I5, **234**
Ailsa Vic. 164 I6
Ainslie ACT 109 M3
Aireys Inlet Vic. 155 C12, 172 C10, **120**
Airlie Beach Qld 331 E4, 281, 287, 288, 299, 303
Airly Vic. 173 R7, 174 B9
Airport West Vic. 148 D3
Alanwick NSW 83 H3
Alawa NT 264 A1
Alawoona SA 203 P5
Albacutya Vic. 164 G3, **129**
Albany WA 249 N13, 256 G13, **214, 217, 219**
Albany Creek Qld 308 F6
Albert NSW 93 Q13, 97 Q2, 98 B2
Albert Hill SA 199 Q10
Albert Park Vic. 146 B13, **116**
Alberton Qld 315 N13, 317 N1
Alberton Tas. 361 O6
Alberton Vic. 173 P11, **137, 144**
Albion Qld 308 I12
Albion Vic. 172 F5
Albion Park NSW 91 N7
Albury NSW 97 P13, 167 R4, 168 B4, **40, 141**
Alco WA 248 G8
Alcomie Tas. 360 C4
Alderley Qld 308 G11, 321 D1
Aldersyde WA 251 L11
Aldgate SA 196 I13, 198 I1, 203 J7, **180**
Aldinga SA 198 F5, 202 I8, **181, 191**
Aldinga Beach SA 198 E5
Alectown NSW 98 D4
Alexandra Vic. 160 F4, 167 K12, 173 K1, **120**
Alexandra Bridge WA 248 C8
Alexandra Headland Qld 307 H9, 313 M10, **280**
Alexandria NSW 73 M6
Alford SA 200 F10, 202 F1
Alfred Cove WA 246 F7
Alfred National Park Vic. 100 E13, 175 M6, **135**
Alice NSW 95 O3
Alice Springs NT 261-3, 271 J8, **234-5, 188**
Allambee Vic. 173 M8
Allambie Heights NSW 71 N8
Allanby Vic. 164 F5
Allandale NSW 83 D3
Allandale Vic. 158 A7
Allans Flat Vic. 167 R6, 168 B6, **144**
Allansford Vic. 171 K9
Allanson WA 248 G4
Allawah NSW 72 I12, 97 L6
Alleena NSW 97 P7, 98 A7
Allendale East SA 204 H12
Allendale North SA 197 K1, 201 J12, 203 J3
Allies Creek Qld 323 N8
Alligator Creek Qld 324 H8, 331 I13
Alligator Gorge National Park SA 200 G5, **192**
Allora Qld 323 O11, **281**
Alma SA 196 G1, 200 I12, 202 I3
Alma Vic. 165 P11
Almaden Qld 324 E4, 326 G13
Almonds Vic. 167 M5
Alonnah Tas. 359 M10
Aloomba Qld 335 G10
Alpha Qld 322 H3, **281**
Alpine NSW 91 K5
Alstonville NSW 95 Q3, **54**
Alton Qld 323 K11
Altona SA 208 C9
Altona Vic. 148 B12, 172 F6
Alton Downs SA 321 C8
Alvie Vic. 171 P8
Alyangula NT 267 O7, **235**
Amamoor Qld 312 G5
Ambania WA 252 C4
Ambleside SA 197 J13, 199 J1
Ambrose Qld 323 N4
Amby Qld 323 J8
Ambyne Vic. 175 J2
Amelup WA 249 P9
American River SA 202 F11, **186, 185**
Amery WA 251 K4
Amherst Vic. 165 P12
Aminungo Qld 331 G11
Amity Point Qld 315 Q9, **301**
Amoonguna NT 271 J8, **237**
Amoonguna Aboriginal Reserve NT 263 N6
Amosfield NSW 95 N2, 323 O12
Amphitheatre Vic. 165 O12, 171 O1
Anakie Qld 322 I3, **291**
Anakie Vic. 154 D10, 155 D4, 172 C6, **128**
Anakie Gorge Vic. 155 E3, 158 E13
Anarel NSW 76 A6
Ancona Vic. 160 G1, 167 L11
Andamooka SA 205 H1, **181, 188**
Anderson Vic. 173 J10
Ando NSW 100 E10
Andover Tas. 359 N3, 361 N13
Andrews SA 200 I9
Angas Plains SA 199 L6
Angaston SA 197 M4, 201 K13, 203 K4, 208 H4, **190**
Angip Vic. 164 H5
Angledool NSW 323 J13
Anglers Paradise Qld 317 P5
Anglers Reach NSW 104 G3
Anglers Rest Vic. 168 E11, 174 D2
Anglesea Vic. 155 D11, 172 C9, **120, 126, 134, 142**
Angle Vale SA 196 H7
Angourie NSW 95 Q5, **54, 64**
Angurugu NT 267 O8, **237**
Angus Place NSW 76 B2
Angustown Vic. 166 H9
Anna Creek SA 207 K6
Annandale NSW 73 K5
Annangrove NSW 77 M6
Annerley Qld 310 I5
Annuello Vic. 96 F10, 163 K7
Antechamber Bay SA 202 G11
Antill Ponds Tas. 359 N2, 361 N12
Antwerp Vic. 164 G6, **131**
Anzac Village NSW 77 M10
Apamurra SA 197 O10
Apoinga SA 201 J11, 203 J2
Apollo Bay Vic. 171 Q12, **120, 134, 142**
Appila SA 200 H6
Appin NSW 91 N2, 99 J8, 100 I3
Appin Vic. 165 Q3, 166 A3
Applecross WA 246 G5
Apple Tree Creek Qld 323 P6
Apple Tree Flat NSW 98 G3
Apslawn Tas. 359 Q1, 361 Q11
Apsley Tas. 359 L4
Apsley Vic. 164 B11, 204 I7
Araluen NSW 100 F7, **41**
Aramac Qld 322 F2, **281**
Aramara Qld 323 P7
Arana Hills Qld 308 D9
Aranda ACT 108 G2
Arapiles Vic 164 F9
Ararat Vic. 165 L13, 171 M1, **120, 126**
Aratula Qld 316 E5
Arcadia NSW 77 N4
Arcadia Vic. 166 I8
Arcadia Vale NSW 83 G8
Archdale Vic. 165 O10
Ardath WA 251 O9
Ardeer Vic. 148 A7
Ardingly WA 252 D4
Ardlethan NSW 97 P8, **40**
Ardmona Vic. 166 I6
Ardmory Qld 314 F9
Ardno Vic. 170 C5
Ardross WA 246 G6
Ardrossan SA 200 F13, 202 G4, **181**
Areegra Vic. 165 J6
Areyonga Aboriginal Reserve NT 262 A8, 270 G9, **237**
Argalong NSW 98 D11, 100 C6
Argyle Vic. 166 F11
Argyle WA 248 F5
Ariah Park NSW 97 P8, 98 B8
Aringa Vic. 170 I9
Arkaroola SA 207 P9, **181, 182**
Arkona Vic. 164 G7
Armadale Vic. 149 J11, 150 A12, **117**
Armadale WA 250 G10, **212**
Armatree NSW 94 E10

Armidale — Baxter

Armidale NSW 95 L8, 40
Armstrong Vic. 165 L13, 171 L1
Armstrong Creek Qld 314 I6
Armstrong Heights NSW 83 H6
Armytage Vic. 171 R9, 172 B9
Arncliffe NSW 73 K9
Arnhem Land NT 267 J6, 233, 239, 240
Arnhem Land Aboriginal Res. NT 267 J6, 234
Arno Bay SA 200 A11, 202 A2, 205 G10, 183, 184, 189
Arnold Vic. 165 Q9, 166 A9
Arrabury Qld 321 F9
Arrilalah Qld 322 D3
Arrino WA 252 E8
Artarmon NSW 71 L11
Arthur East WA 249 K4
Arthur River WA 249 K4
Arthurs Creek Vic. 159 O9, 160 A9, 172 H3
Arthurs Lake Tas. 361 K11, 342, 350
Arthurs Seat Vic. 152 H7, 139
Arthurton SA 200 F12, 202 F3, 205 I11
Arumvale WA 248 C8
Arwakurra SA 200 H6
Ascot Qld 309 K12
Ascot Vic. 171 Q2, 172 A2
Ascot Vale Vic. 148 F7
Ashbourne SA 198 I5, 203 J8
Ashbourne Vic. 158 G7
Ashburton Vic. 149 M12, 150 B8
Ashbury NSW 72 I7
Ashens Vic. 165 J10
Ashfield NSW 73 J6
Ashfield WA 245 N9, 259 B12
Ashford NSW 95 K4, 323 N13, 40
Ashgrove Qld 308 F13, 310 F1
Ashley NSW 94 H4, 323 L13
Ashton SA 196 I12
Ashville SA 199 Q9, 203 L9
Aspendale Vic. 151 J8
Aspley Qld 308 H7
Asplin WA 248 H6
Asquith NSW 70 G4
Atherton Qld 324 F4, 326 I13, 335 C12, 281, 282, 288
Athlone Vic. 173 K8
Attadale WA 246 F6
Attunga NSW 95 J9
Aubrey Vic. 164 H6
Auburn NSW 72 C4
Auburn SA 200 I11, 202 I2
Auburn Tas. 359 M1, 361 M11
Auchenflower Qld 310 G3
Audley NSW 77 O12, 44
Augathella Qld 322 H7
Augusta WA 248 C9, 256 E12, 214
Aurukun Mission Qld 326 B6, 300
Austinmer NSW 91 P3
Austral NSW 77 L10
Australian Capital Territory 112, between 56-7, opp. 112, 39
Australia Plains SA 201 K11, 203 K2
Australind WA 248 E3, 214, 215
Avalon NSW 79 M2
Avenel Vic. 166 I10
Avenue SA 204 F7
Avoca NSW 91 K8
Avoca Tas. 361 O10, 341
Avoca Vic. 165 O12, 120
Avoca Beach NSW 77 R2
Avoca Vale Qld 312 B11
Avon SA 196 D1, 200 H12, 202 H3
Avondale NSW 83 E8, 91 N6
Avondale Heights Vic. 148 C6
Avonmore Vic. 166 E8
Avon Plains Vic. 165 L8
Awaba NSW 83 F7
Awonga Vic. 164 D11
Axe Creek Vic. 166 D10
Axedale Vic. 166 E9
Ayers Rock NT 270 E11, 272
Aylmerton NSW 91 K5
Ayr Qld 324 I8, 281
Ayrford Vic. 171 L10
Ayton Qld 324 F2, 326 I10

B

Baan Baa NSW 94 H8
Baandee WA 351 O7
Baarmutha Vic. 167 P7
Babakin WA 251 O9
Babinda Qld 324 G4, 335 H13, 281, 286
Bacchus Marsh Vic. 154 C8, 158 G11, 172 D4, 120 119
Back Creek NSW 97 R6, 98 C6
Back Creek Tas. 363 F3
Back Creek Vic. 167 Q6, 168 A6
Backwater NSW 95 M6, 49
Baddaginnie Vic. 167 L8
Baddera WA 252 A2
Baden Tas. 359 N4
Badgebup WA 249 N2
Badgerys Creek NSW 77 K9
Badgingarra WA 250 E1, 252 E13, 256 E8
Badjaling WA 251 M9
Bael Bael Vic. 163 P13, 165 P1
Baerami NSW 94 I13, 98 I2
Bagdad Tas. 356 H3, 359 M5, 348
Bagnoo NSW 95 O11
Bago NSW 168 H1
Bagot Well SA 197 L1, 203 J3
Bagshot Vic. 166 D9
Bahrs Scrub Qld 317 M2
Bailieston Vic. 166 G9
Bailup WA 250 H7
Bairnsdale Vic. 174 E8, 121, 133, 137
Bajool Qld 323 N4, 291
Bakara SA 203 M5
Baker Vic. 164 E5
Bakers Creek Qld 331 H12
Bakers Hill WA 250 H8
Bakers Swamp NSW 98 F3
Balaam Hill Qld 318 C9
Baladjie WA 251 R4
Balaklava SA 200 H12, 202 H3, 181
Balbarrup WA 248 G8
Balberra Qld 331 H13
Balcatta WA 244 G6
Balcolyn NSW 83 F8
Balcombe Vic. 153 J5, 172 H8
Bald Hills Qld 308 G4
Bald Hills Vic. 158 A8
Bald Knob NSW 95 M5
Bald Knob Qld 307 C12, 313 J12
Bald Rock NSW 166 C4
Baldry NSW 98 E3
Balfour Tas. 360 B6
Balga WA 244 I5
Balgowan SA 200 E13, 202 E4, 205 I11
Balgowlah NSW 71 O9
Balgowlah Heights NSW 71 P10
Balgownie NSW 91 O4
Balhannah SA 197 J12, 203 J7
Balingup WA 248 G6
Balkuling WA 251 K9
Balladonia WA 257 L10, 214, 215
Balladoran NSW 94 E12
Ballajura WA 259 A7
Ballaba NSW 100 F6
Ballan Vic. 154 B8, 158 E10, 172 C4, 121, 119
Ballandean Qld 95 M2, 303
Ballangeich Vic. 171 K8
Ballapur Vic. 165 K4
Ballarat Vic. 157, 158 A9, 171 Q3, 172 A3, 121, 118, 122
Ballark Vic. 155 C1, 158 D12, 172 C5
Ballaying Vic. 249 M3
Ballbank NSW 96 I11
Balldale NSW 97 O12, 167 O3
Ballendella Vic. 166 E6
Balliang Vic. 155 E3, 158 F13, 172 D5
Ballidu WA 251 J2
Ballimore NSW 94 F13
Ballina NSW 95 R3, 323 Q13, 40
Bally Bally WA 251 K10
Ballyrogan Vic. 171 N2
Balmain NSW 73 L3
Balmattum Vic. 167 K9
Balmoral NSW 71 O11, 83 G7, 91 K4
Balmoral Qld 311 K2
Balmoral Vic. 164 F13, 170 G1, 126, 131
Balnarring Vic. 153 L8, 172 H9, 139
Balook Vic. 173 O10
Balranald NSW 96 H9, 163 O6, 40
Balrootan North Vic. 164 F6
Balumbah SA 205 F8
Balwina Aboriginal Reserve WA 255 Q9
Balwyn North Vic. 149 M7
Bamaga Qld 326 C1, 300
Bamarang NSW 91 L12
Bamawm Vic. 166 E6
Bambaroo Qld 324 G7
Bambill Vic. 162 D4
Bambra Vic. 155 A10, 171 R9, 172 B9
Bamganie Vic. 155 A7
Baminboola Vic. 168 E8
Bamyili NT 266 H9, 237
Banana Qld 323 M5
Bancroft Qld 323 N6
Bandiana Vic. 167 R5, 168 B5
Bandon Grove NSW 95 L13, 99 L2
Banealla SA 203 O12, 204 F3
Bangalow NSW 95 Q2, 323 Q12
Bang Bang Qld 327 E4
Bangerang Vic. 165 J5
Bangham SA 164 A8, 204 I5
Bangholme Vic. 151 K4
Bangor SA 200 G6
Bangor Tas. 361 L6, 363 F6
Banksia NSW 73 K10
Banksiadale WA 250 G12
Banksmeadow NSW 73 M10
Bankstown NSW 72 D9
Bannaby NSW 98 H8, 100 G3

Bannerton Vic. 96 F9, 163 K6
Bannister NSW 98 G9, 100 E4
Bannister WA 250 I12
Bannockburn Vic. 155 C6, 172 C7
Bantry Bay NSW 71 N9
Banyan Vic. 163 K13, 165 K1
Banyena Vic. 165 K8
Banyenong Vic. 165 M6
Banyo Qld 309 K8
Barabba SA 196 G2
Baradine NSW 94 F9, 46
Barakula Qld 323 M8
Baralaba Qld 323 L4
Baranduda Vic. 167 R5, 168 B5
Barbalin WA 251 O3
Barberton WA 250 G2
Barcaldine Qld 322 F3, 281
Bardon Qld 310 E2, 276
Bardwell Park NSW 73 J9
Barellan NSW 97 O8
Barfold Vic. 158 H2, 166 E12
Bargara Qld 323 P6, 281, 285
Bargo NSW 91 L3, 98 I8, 100 H3
Barham NSW 96 I12, 163 R13
Barham Vic. 165 R1, 166 C1
Baring Vic. 162 G11
Baringhup Vic. 158 B1
Baringhup East Vic. 165 R11, 166 B11
Barjarg Vic. 167 M11
Barkly Vic. 165 N11
Barkstead Vic. 158 C8, 172 C3
Barmah Vic. 166 G4, 127, 136
Barmedman NSW 97 Q7, 98 B7
Barmera SA 201 P12, 203 P3, 181
Barmundu Qld 323 N4
Barker Creek Reservoir Vic. 158 E1
Barnadown Vic. 166 E8
Barnawartha Vic. 167 P5, 176 I5
Barnes NSW 97 K13, 166 F4
Barnes Bay Tas. 357 J11, 359 M8, 343
Barney View Qld 316 H9
Barngeong Reservoir Vic. 147 B3
Barnsley NSW 83 F6
Barongarook Vic. 171 P10
Barooga NSW 97 M13, 167 K3
Baroon Pocket Qld 307 B10, 313 J11
Baroota SA 200 F6
Barossa SA 197 J7
Barossa Valley SA 197 K4, 208, 190, 180
Barpinba Vic. 171 P7
Barraba NSW 95 J7, 40, 51
Barrabarra WA 253 J12
Barrabool Vic. 155 D7
Barrakee Vic. 165 O6
Barramunga Vic. 171 Q11, 172 A11
Barraport Vic. 165 P4
Barrengarry NSW 91 L9
Barrington NSW 95 M12, 99 M1
Barrington Tas. 360 I7
Barrington Lower Tas. 360 H6
Barrington Tops National Park NSW 95 L12, 99 L1, 48
Barringun NSW 93 M3, 322 F13
Barrogan NSW 98 E5
Barron Falls National Park Qld 335 E7, 288, 294
Barrow Creek NT 269 J13, 271 A3, 237
Barronhurst WA 248 G9
Barrow Island WA 254 D9, 225, 226
Barry NSW 98 F6, 100 E1
Barry Caves NT 269 O10, 237
Barrys Reef Vic. 158 E8, 172 D3
Barton ACT 109 L9
Barton SA 206 F9
Barton Vic. 165 J13, 171 K2
Barunga Gap SA 200 G10, 202 G1
Barwidgee Creek Vic. 167 Q8, 168 A8
Barwite Vic. 167 N11
Barwo Vic. 166 H4
Barwon Downs Vic. 171 Q10, 172 A10
Barwon Heads Vic. 155 G9, 172 E9, 137, 128
Baryulgil NSW 95 O4, 323 P13
Basket Range NSW 196 I12, 180
Bass Vic. 173 J10
Bassendean WA 245 O9, 259 B11, 212
Bass Hill NSW 72 C8
Batchelor NT 266 E6, 234
Batchica Vic. 164 I5
Bateau Bay NSW 83 F13
Batehaven NSW 100 G7, 41
Bateman WA 246 H8
Batemans Bay NSW 100 G7, 41, 61
Batesford Vic. 155 E6, 172 D7, 128
Bathumi Vic. 167 M4
Bathurst NSW 98 G5, 101, 41
Bathurst Island NT 266 D3, 237
Batlow NSW 97 R11, 98 D11, 100 B6, 41
Battery Point Tas. 355 F10, 339, 338, 346
Battle Creek Qld 323 O5
Baulkham Hills NSW 70 B9
Bauple Qld 323 P7
Baw Baw National Park Vic. 173 N6, 125
Bawley Point NSW 100 H6
Baxter Vic. 153 M2, 119

Bayindeen Vic. 165 N13, 171 N2
Bayles Vic. 173 J8
Baynton Vic. 158 I3, 166 F12
Bayswater Vic. 147 A6, 160 A13
Bayswater WA 245 L9, 259 B12
Bayview NSW 77 Q5
Beachmere Qld 315 L5, 286
Beachport SA 204 E10, 181
Beachport National Park SA 204 E9
Beacon WA 251 N1, 253 N13, 256 G8
Beacon Hill NSW 71 O7
Beaconsfield NSW 73 M7
Beaconsfield Tas. 361 K6, 363 B5, 341
Beaconsfield Vic. 172 I7
Beaconsfield WA 246 C10
Beagle Bay Aboriginal Reserve WA 255 L4
Bealiba Vic. 165 O10
Bearbung NSW 94 E11
Beardmore Vic. 173 O5
Beargamil NSW 98 D4
Bearii NSW 166 I3
Bears Lagoon Vic. 165 R6, 166 B6
Beatty WA 252 E3
Beauchamp Vic. 163 O13, 165 O1
Beaudesert Qld 317 K5, 323 Q11, 281
Beaufort SA 200 G11, 202 H2
Beaufort Vic. 171 O3, 121
Beaumaris Tas. 361 R7, 351
Beaumaris Vic. 150 H10
Beaumont NSW 91 L11
Beauty Point NSW 71 O11
Beauty Point Tas. 361 K5, 363 B5, 341
Beazleys Bridge Vic. 165 M9
Bebeah NSW 83 C9
Beckenham WA 247 N7
Beckom NSW 97 P8
Bedarra Island Qld 324 G5, 303
Bedford WA 245 K9
Bedgerebong NSW 98 C5
Bedourie Qld 321 D4, 294-5
Beeac Vic. 171 P8
Beebo Qld 323 N12
Beechboro WA 245 N6, 259 C9
Beechford Tas. 361 L5, 363 D2
Beech Forest Vic. 171 P11
Beechmont Qld 317 M7
Beechworth Vic. 167 P6, 121-2, 136, 138, 144
Beechworth Park Vic. 167 Q6
Beecroft NSW 70 E8
Beedelup National Park WA 248 F9, 225
Beela WA 248 F3
Beenak Vic. 173 K6
Beenam Range Qld 312 I3
Beenleigh Qld 317 N1, 323 Q11, 281
Beenong WA 249 Q2
Beerburrum Qld 315 K2
Beermullah WA 250 F5
Beerwah Qld 313 K13, 315 K1, 323 Q9, 280
Beetaloo Valley SA 200 G7
Bega NSW 100 F10, 41, 61
Beggan Beggan NSW 98 D9, 100 B4
Bejoording WA 250 I6
Belair National Park SA 195 F11, 198 H1, 179, 180
Belalie SA 200 I7
Belanglo NSW 90 H8
Belaringar NSW 93 Q11, 94 B11
Belbora NSW 95 N12, 99 N1
Belconnen ACT 106 F9, 108 C1
Belfield NSW 72 H7
Belford NSW 83 B2
Belgrave Vic. 147 E10, 172 I6, 130
Belhus WA 259 F2
Belka WA 251 O7
Bell NSW 76 E4, 98 I5
Bell Qld 323 O9
Bellambi NSW 89 G1, 91 O4
Bellara Qld 315 M4
Bellarine Vic. 155 H7, 172 E8
Bellarwi NSW 98 A7
Bellata NSW 94 H6
Bellawongarah NSW 91 M10
Bell Bay Tas. 361 K5, 363 C4, 345
Bellbird NSW 83 C5, 99 K4
Bellbird Creek Vic. 100 D13, 175 K7
Bellbrae Vic. 155 D10, 172 C9
Bellbrook NSW 95 O9
Bellellen Vic. 165 K12
Bellenden Ker National Park Qld 335 H12, 281, 284, 288
Bellerive Tas. 355 I7, 357 J7, 359 M7, 339, 341
Bellevue WA 259 G11
Bellevue Hill NSW 67 P8, 73 P4
Bellingen NSW 95 P8, 41
Bellingham Tas. 361 M4, 363 F2
Belli Park Qld 307 A4, 312 I8
Bellmere Qld 315 J4
Bellmount Forest NSW 98 F10, 100 E5
Bell Park Vic. 156 C3
Bells Beach Vic. 155 E10, 172 D9, 142
Bells Bridge Qld 312 F2
Bellthorpe Qld 312 G13
Belltrees NSW 95 K12, 99 K1
Belmont NSW 83 H7, 99 L4, 59

Belmont Qld 311 O5
Belmont Vic. 156 C13
Belmont WA 245 M12
Belmore NSW 72 H8
Belmunging WA 251 K8
Belrose NSW 71 M5
Beltana SA 207 N10, 182
Belton SA 200 I2
Belvidere SA 199 L5, 203 J8
Bemboka NSW 100 E10
Bembridge Vic. 153 O4
Bemm River Vic. 100 D13, 175 L7, 137
Bena NSW 97 P5, 98 A5
Bena Vic. 173 K9
Benalla Vic. 167 M8, 122
Benambra Vic. 168 F11, 174 F2
Benandarah NSW 100 G7
Benaraby Qld 323 N4
Ben Boyd Nat. Park NSW 175 Q3, 100 F11, 48
Ben Bullen NSW 76 A1
Bencubbin WA 251 N3, 256 G8
Bendalong NSW 100 H6, 62
Bendemeer NSW 95 K9
Bendering WA 251 P11
Bendick Murrell NSW 98 D7, 100 C2
Bendigo Vic. 154 B1, 166 C9, 122
Bendoc Vic. 100 D11, 175 L3
Bendolba NSW 95 L13, 99 L2
Benetook Vic. 162 G4
Benger WA 248 F3
Bengworden Vic. 174 D9
Benholme Qld 331 E12
Beni NSW 94 E13
Benjaberring WA 251 L4
Benjeroop Vic. 163 Q12
Benjinup WA 248 H6
Benlidi Qld 322 E5
Ben Lomond NSW 95 L6
Ben Lomond National Park Tas. 361 O8, 341
Bennelacking WA 248 I4
Ben Nevis Vic. 165 M12, 171 M1
Benobble Qld 317 M5
Benowa Qld 317 P6, 318 F12
Benowa Waters Qld 318 G11
Bensville NSW 77 Q2
Bentleigh Vic. 150 D11
Bentley NSW 95 P2
Bentley WA 247 L5
Benwerrin Vic. 155, A12, 171 R10, 172 B10
Berakin WA 250 H9
Berala NSW 72 E5
Berambing NSW 76 G4, 100 H1
Beremboke Vic. 155 D2, 158 E12, 172 C5
Berendebba NSW 98 C7, 100 A1
Beresfield NSW 83 G4
Bergalia NSW 100 G8
Bergins Pocket Qld 312 H6
Berkeley NSW 91 O5
Berkeley Vale NSW 83 E12
Berkshire Valley WA 250 G1
Bermagui NSW 100 G9, 41, 61
Bernook Vic. 162 B8, 203 R6
Berowra NSW 77 O5, 79 M13
Berowra Heights NSW 79 L13
Berri SA 96 A8, 201 P12, 203 P3, 182
Berridale NSW 100 D9, 104 I8
Berriedale Tas. 356 H6
Berrigan NSW 97 M12, 167 L1
Berrima NSW 90 I7, 98 I8, 100 G3, 41
Berrimah NT 266 D4
Berrimal Vic. 165 O7
Berrimpa Qld 321 H5
Berring NSW 251 J5
Berringa Vic. 171 Q5, 172 A5
Berringama Vic. 168 F6
Berriwillock Vic. 163 L13, 165 L1
Berry NSW 91 N10, 99 J9, 100 H4, 41
Berrybank Vic. 171 P6
Berry Springs NT 266 E5, 233
Berwick Vic. 154 H11, 172 I7
Bessiebelle Vic. 170 H8
Beswick Aboriginal Reserve NT 266 I8, 237
Beta Qld 322 G3
Bet Bet Vic. 165 P10, 166 A10
Bete Bolong Vic. 174 I7
Bethanga Vic. 168 C5
Bethania Junction Qld 315 M13, 317 M1
Bethany SA 197 L5, 208 E6
Bethungra NSW 98 C9, 100 A4
Betley Vic. 165 Q10, 166 A10
Betoota Qld 321 F7, 295
Beulah Tas. 360 I7
Beulah Vic. 96 E13, 164 I3
Beulah Lower Tas. 360 I7
Bevendale NSW 98 F8, 100 D3
Beverford Vic. 163 O10
Beveridge Vic. 154 F7, 159 M8, 172 G3
Beverley WA 251 J9, 256 F10, 214
Beverley Hills NSW 72 H10
Beverley Park NSW 73 K12
Bews SA 203 P8
Bexhill NSW 95 Q2

Bexley NSW 73 J10
Bexley North NSW 72 I9
Beyal Vic. 165 K5
Biala NSW 98 F9, 100 E4
Biarra Qld 314 C5
Bibbenluke NSW 100 E10, 175 N1
Bibllup WA 248 E7
Biboohra Qld 335 B7
Birra Lake WA 246 G11
Bicheno Tas. 361 R10, 341
Bicton WA 246 E6
Biddaddaba Qld 317 L5
Biddon NSW 94 E11
Big Desert Wilderness Vic. 162 B12, 164 B2, 138
Bigga NSW 98 F7, 100 E2, 47
Biggara Vic. 168 H6
Biggenden Qld 323 O7
Biggs Flat SA 198 I2
Big Heath National Park SA 204 G8
Big Hill NSW 90 F8
Big Pats Creek Vic. 160 G12
Big River Camp Vic. 160 I9
Bilambil NSW 317 Q9
Bilbarin WA 251 N10
Bilinga Qld 317 Q8, 319 P5
Billabong WA 162 H3
Billaricay WA 251 P10
Billiatt National Park SA 203 P6
Billinudgel NSW 317 Q13, 95 Q2
Billys Creek NSW 95 O7
Billys Lookout NSW 98 A6
Biloela Qld 323 M5, 281, 291
Bilpin NSW 76 G4, 98 I5
Bilyana Qld 324 G5
Bimbi NSW 97 R7, 98 C7, 100 B2
Binalong NSW 98 E9, 100 C4
Binalong Bay Tas. 361 R6, 350
Binbee Qld 325 J9
Binda NSW 98 F8, 100 E3, 47
Bindi Vic. 168 F12, 174 F3
Bindi Bindi WA 250 H2, 256 F8
Bindle Qld 323 K10
Bindoon WA 250 G6
Bingara NSW 95 J5, 41, 51
Bingera Qld 323 P6, 285
Binginwarri Vic. 173 O11
Biniguy NSW 94 I4
Binjour Qld 323 O7
Binnaway NSW 94 G11
Binningup WA 248 E3, 214, 220
Binnu WA 252 A1
Binnum SA 164 B10, 204 I6
Binya NSW 97 N7
Birchgrove NSW 68 E13, 73 L3
Birchip Vic. 96 F13, 165 L4, 123
Birchs Bay Tas. 356 H12
Birdsville Qld 207 P1, 321 D7, 281-2, 188, 295
Birdsville Track Qld 321 D7, 295
Birdsville Track SA 207 N7-P1, 186, 188
Birdwood NSW 95 N10
Birdwood SA 197 L10, 203 J6, 180
Birdwoodton Vic. 162 G3
Birralee Tas. 361 K7, 363 B9
Birrego NSW 97 O10
Birregurra Vic. 171 Q9, 172 A9, 126
Birriwa NSW 94 G12
Birrong NSW 72 D7
Birru Qld 314 F12
Birthday SA 205 H4, 207 L11
Bishopsbourne Tas. 361 L8, 363 D12
Bishops Bridge NSW 83 E3
Bittern Vic. 153 M7, 172 H9
Blackall Qld 322 F5, 282
Blackalls Park NSW 83 G7
Blackburn Vic. 149 P9
Blackbutt Qld 327 G3
Blackfellows Caves SA 204 G12
Blackheath NSW 76 E6, 80 B2, 98 I6, 100 G1, 53
Blackheath Vic. 164 I7
Black Hill NSW 83 G4
Black Hill SA 197 R8
Black Hill Vic. 157 F4
Black Hills Tas. 356 F4
Blackmans Bay Tas. 356 I9, 359 M8, 346
Black Mountain NSW 95 L7
Black Mountain Qld 307 B2, 312 I6
Black River Tas. 360 D3
Black Rock SA 200 I5, 207 O13
Black Rock Vic. 150 G11, 172 G6
Blacks Beach Qld 331 H11
Blacksmiths NSW 83 H8
Black Springs NSW 98 G6, 100 F1
Black Springs SA 201 J10, 203 J1
Black Swamp NSW 95 N3
Blacktown NSW 75 N2
Blackville NSW 94 I11
Blackwall NSW 77 Q2, 78 F3
Blackwarry Vic. 173 P10
Blackwater Qld 323 K3, 282-3, 290, 291
Blackwood SA 195 E12
Blackwood Vic. 158 F8, 172 D3
Blackwood Creek Tas. 361 K9
Blackwood Ranges Vic. 158 F9

Blair Athol Qld 322 I2, 324 I13, **288, 291**
Blairgowrie Vic. 152 D8, 172 F9, **139**
Blakehurst NSW 72 I13
Blakeville Vic. 158 E8, 172 C3
Blampied Vic. 158 C7, 172 B2
Blanche Town SA 201 M13, 203 M3
Bland NSW 97 Q7, 98 B7, 100 A2
Blanket Flat NSW 98 F7, 100 E2
Blaxland NSW 76 I7, 80 I5
Blaxlands Ridge NSW 77 J3
Blayney NSW 98 F5, **42**
Bleak House Vic. 164 D6
Blenheim Qld 314 C12
Blessington Tas. 361 N8, I11
Bletchley SA 199 L5
Blewitt Springs SA 198 G3, 208 I11
Bli Bli Qld 307 F7, 313 L9, **296**
Blighty NSW 97 L12
Blinman SA 207 O10, **182**
Bloods Creek SA 271 L13
Bloomsbury Qld 325 K10, 331 D8
Blow Clear NSW 98 C4
Blue Gum Forest NSW 91 P1
Blue Mountains NSW 76, 80, **53, 37, 39**
Blue Mountains National Park NSW 76 F5, 80, 98 I6, 100 H1, **53, 44**
Bluff SA 202 E6
Bluff Rock NSW 95 M4
Blyth SA 200, I10, 202 I1
Boambee NSW 95 P7
Boara NSW 98 D8, 100 B3
Boat Harbour NSW 317 O10
Boat Harbour Tas. 360 E4, **341, 352**
Boatswain SA 204 D8
Bobadah NSW 93 O13, 97 O1
Bobbin Head NSW 71 J1, 79 O12
Bobin NSW 95 N11
Bobinawarrah Vic. 167 O8
Bobs Creek Vic. 167 N11
Bochara Vic. 170 G5
Bodalla NSW 100 G8, **56**
Bodallin WA 251 R6, 256 H9
Boddington WA 248 H1, 250 H13, 256 F11
Bogan Gate NSW 97 R4, 98 C4
Bogantungan Qld 322 I3
Boggabilla NSW 94 I2, 323 M12
Boggabri NSW 94 H8
Bogolong NSW 97 R6, 98 C6, 100 B1
Bogong Vic. 168 C10, 169 G5, **137**
Boho Vic. 167 L9
Boigbeat Vic. 163 L12, 165 L1
Boinka Vic. 162 E10
Boisdale Vic. 173 R6, 174 B8
Bokal WA 249 J4
Bolangum Vic. 165 L9
Bolganup WA 249 N11
Bolgart WA 250 I5
Bolinda Vic. 159 J7, 172 F2
Bolivar SA 196 G9
Bolivia NSW 95 M4
Bollon Qld 322 I11
Bolong NSW 91 N11
Bolton Vic. 163 L8
Bolwarra NSW 83 F2
Bolwarra Vic. 170 F9
Bolwarrah Vic. 158 C9
Bomaderry NSW 91 M12, 98 I9, 100 H4, **57**
Bombala NSW 175 N2, 100 E11, **42**
Bombo NSW 91 O8, 99 J9, 100 I4
Bomera NSW 94 H11
Bonalbo NSW 95 O2
Bonang Vic. 100 C11, 175 K3, **137**
Bonaparte Archipelago WA 255 M2
Bonbeach Vic. 151 L7
Bondi NSW 73 Q5
Bondleigh SA 197 M13, 199 M1
Bonegilla Vic. 167 R5, 168 B5
Boneo Vic. 152 F9, 172 G10
Bongaree Qld 315 M4, 323 Q10, **301**
Bonnells Bay NSW 83 F8
Bonnie Doon Vic. 160 H1, 167 L11, **128**
Bonnie Rock WA 251 P1, 253 P13, 256 G8
Bonnyrigg NSW 77 M9
Bonshaw NSW 95 L3, 323 N13
Bonville NSW 95 P7, **59**
Booborowie SA 201 J9
Boobyalla Tas. 361 P4, **345**
Boodarockin WA 251 R4
Boogardie WA 253 N1
Bookabie SA 206 F11
Bookaloo SA 200 D1, 205 I5, 207 M11
Bookar Vic. 171 M7
Bookara WA 252 B6
Booker Bay NSW 77 Q2, 78 F2
Bookham NSW 98 E9, 100 C4
Boolading WA 248 I4
Boolaroo NSW 83 G6
Boolarra Vic. 173 N9
Boolba Qld 323 J17
Boolboonda Qld 323 O6
Booleroo SA 200 H5
Boolgun SA 201 N13, 203 N4
Booligal NSW 97 K6

Boolite Vic. 165 K6
Bool Lagoon SA 204 H8, **183 188**
Booloumba Qld 312 G10
Boomahnoomoonah Vic. 167 M5
Boomi NSW 94 G2, 323 L12
Boomleera NT 266 F7
Boonah Qld 316 G5, 323 P11, **283**
Boonah Vic. 155 A11, 171 R10, 172 B10
Boonangar Qld 323 L12
Boonoonar Vic. 162 H5
Boondall Qld 309 K6
Boonoo Boonoo NSW 95 N3
Booraan WA 251 P6
Booragoon WA 246 G7
Booral NSW 99 M2
Booralaming WA 251 L3
Boorcan Vic. 171 M8
Boorhaman Vic. 167 N5
Boorindal NSW 93 N7
Boorolite Vic. 167 N12
Boorongie Vic. 162 I9
Booroobin Qld 312 H12
Booroopki Vic. 164 C10
Booroorban NSW 97 K10
Boorowa NSW 98 E8, 100 C3
Boors Plain SA 200 F11, 202 F2
Boort Vic. 165 P5, 166 A4, **123**
Boosey Vic. 167 L4
Bootenal WA 252 A5
Boothby SA 200 A10, 202 A1
Boowillia SA 200 H11, 202 H2
Booyal Qld 323 O6
Bopeechee SA 207 M7
Borallon Qld 314 G11
Boralma Vic. 167 O5
Borambil NSW 94 H12
Boraning WA 248 I2
Borden WA 249 P8, 256 H12
Borderdale WA 249 M7
Bordertown SA 203 Q13, 204 H4, **182**
Boree NSW 98 E4
Boree Creek NSW 97 O10
Bornholm WA 249 M13
Boro NSW 98 G10, 100 F5
Boronia Vic. 147 A8, 160 A13
Boronia Park NSW 71 J 12, 73 J1
Bororen Qld 323 O5
Borrika SA 203 N7
Borroloola NT 267 O12, 269 O2, **237**
Borung Vic. 165 P6, 166 A6
Boscabel WA 249 K5
Bostobrick NSW 95 O7
Bostock Creek Vic. 171 N9
Bostock Reservoir Vic. 158 D10, 172 C4
Boston Island SA 205 F12 **189**
Botany NSW 73 N9
Botherling WA 251 J4
Bothwell Tas. 359 L3, **341-2**
Bouddi State Park NSW 78 H2, **49, 60**
Boulder WA 258 E7, **221-2**
Boulia Qld 321 D2, 327 D13, **283, 294, 295**
Boulka Vic. 162 I9
Boundain WA 249 L2
Boundary Bend Vic. 96 G9, 163 M6
Bourke NSW 93 M6, **42 295**
Bow NSW 94 I13
Bow Bridge WA 249 J12
Bowden SA 194 B3
Bowelling WA 248 I4
Bowen Qld 325 J9, 331 A1, **283**
Bowenfels NSW 76 C4
Bowen Hills Qld 308 I13, 310 I1, **275, 277**
Bowen Mountain NSW 76 I5
Bowenvale Vic. 165 P11, **135**
Bowenville Qld 323 O10
Bower SA 201 L12, 203 L2
Boweya Vic. 167 M6
Bowgada WA 252 G7
Bow Hill SA 203 M6
Bowling Alley Point NSW 95 K10
Bowman NSW 99 M1
Bowman Vic. 167 P7
Bowmans SA 200 H12, 202 H3
Bowna NSW 97 P13, 168 C4
Bowning NSW 98 E9, 100 D4
Bowral NSW 91 J6, 98 I8, 100 H3, **42**
Bowraville NSW 95 P8, **54**
Bowser Vic. 167 O6
Box Creek Qld 322 G8
Box Creek SA 207 K6
Box Hill Vic. 149 N9, 172 H5
Box Tank NSW 92 D13, 96 D2
Boxwood Vic. 167 L6
Boxwood Hill WA 249 R9, 256 H12
Boya NSW 259 I12
Boyacup WA 249 L8
Boyankil Qld 317 P4
Boyanup WA 248 F4, 256 E12, **215**
Boydtown NSW 100 F11, 175 P3, **48, 61**
Boyeo Vic. 164 E6
Boyer Tas. 356 G5, 359 L6, **348**
Boyerine WA 249 L4

Boyland Qld 317 M5
Boys Town Qld 317 K5
Boyup Brook WA 248 H6, 256 F12, **214, 219**
Bracalba Qld 314 I3
Brackendale NSW 95 L10
Brackenridge Qld 308 I5
Bracknell Tas. 361 K9, 363 C13
Bradbury SA 198 I2
Braddon ACT 109 L4
Bradford Vic. 165 R10, 166 B10
Bradvale Vic. 171 O5
Brady Creek SA 203 K2
Braefield NSW 95 J11
Braemar NSW 91 K6
Braeside Vic. 150 H7
Braidwood NSW 98 G11, 100 F6, **42**
Bramfield SA 205 D9
Brammo Bay Qld 334 G1, **302**
Brampton Island Qld 325 L10, 330, 331 I9, **298, 287, 295**
Brandon Qld 324 I8
Bransby Qld 321 H11
Branxholm Tas. 361 O6, **342, 349**
Branxholme Vic. 170 G6
Branxton NSW 83 C2, 99 K3
Brawlin NSW 98 C9, 100 B4
Braybrook Vic. 148 C8
Bray Junction SA 204 E9
Bray Park NSW 317 P11
Brays Creek NSW 317 M11
Brayton NSW 90 E10
Breadalbane NSW 98 G9, 100 E4
Breadalbane Qld 321 D3
Breadalbane Tas. 361 M8, 363 F11
Breakfast Creek NSW 98 E7, 100 D2
Breakfast Creek NSW 98 H3
Breakfast Creek Qld 309 J12
Break O'Day Vic. 159 P6, 160 B6
Breakwater Vic. 156 G13
Bream Creek Tas. 357 O6, 359 O6
Breamlea Vic. 155 F9, 172 D9
Bredbo NSW 100 D8
Breelong NSW 94 E11
Breeza NSW 94 I10
Bremer Bay WA 256 H12
Brentwood SA 202 E6, 205 I12
Brentwood Vic. 164 H4
Brentwood WA 246 H7
Breona Tas. 361 J10
Bretti NSW 95 M12
Brewarrina NSW 93 O6, 94 A6, **42**
Brewster Vic. 171 P3
Briagalong Vic. 173 R6, 174 B8, **134**
Bribbaree NSW 97 R7, 98 C7, 100 A2
Bribie Island Qld 307 F13, 315 M2, **301, 286, 288**
Bridge Creek Vic. 167 M11
Bridgenorth Tas. 361 L7, 363 D8
Bridges Qld 307 D5, 313 K8
Bridgetown WA 248 G7, 256 F12, **214-15, 218**
Bridgewater SA 196 I13, 198 I1, **180**
Bridgewater Tas. 356 H5, **342**
Bridgewater Vic. 165 Q8, 166 B8, **131**
Bridport Tas. 361 N4, 363 I3, **342, 351**
Brigalow Qld 323 N9
Bright Vic. 167 R9, 168 B9, **123, 136, 138**
Brighton Qld 309 J3, 315 L7
Brighton SA 195 B12, 196 F13, 198 F1, **179**
Brighton Tas. 356 I4, 359 M6, **342**
Brighton Vic. 150 D13
Brighton Downs Qld 321 G2
Brighton-le-Sands NSW 73 L11
Brightview Qld 314 E10
Brightwaters NSW 83 F9
Brim Vic. 164 I4
Brimbago SA 203 P12, 204 G3
Brimboal Vic. 170 D2
Brimin Vic. 167 N4
Brimpaen Vic. 164 H11
Brindabella NSW 98 E11, 100 D6
Brinerville NSW 95 O8
Bringagee NSW 97 M8
Bringalbert Vic. 164 C10
Bringelly NSW 77 K10
Brinkley SA 199 O4
Brinkworth SA 200 H10
Brisbane Qld 306, 308-17, 323 Q10, **274-7, 278-80**
Brisbane Airport Qld 309 L11
Brisbane Ranges National Park Vic. 155 D3, 158 E13, 172 D5, **128**
Brisbane Water National Park NSW 77 P2, 78, 99 K5, **39, 44, 49, 64**
Brit Brit Vic. 170 F3
Brittons Swamp Tas. 360 B4
Brixton Qld 322 E3
Broad Arrow WA 257 J8, **222, 223**
Broadbeach Qld 317 P6, 318 H9, **278, 279**
Broad Creek SA 200 G7
Broadford Vic. 154 F5, 159 M4, 166 G12, 172 H1, **123**
Broadmarsh Tas. 356 G3, 359 L5, **348**
Broadmeadows Vic. 148 E1
Broadwater NSW 95 Q3, **40**
Broadwater Vic. 170 H8

Brocklehurst NSW 94 E13
Brocklesby NSW 97 O12, 167 P2
Brockman WA 248 G10
Brocks Creek NT 266 E7
Brodies Plains NSW 95 K5
Brodribb River Vic. 175 J7
Brogo NSW 100 F10
Broke NSW 99 K3
Broken Bay NSW 77 Q3, 63
Broken Hill NSW 92 B12, 96 B1, 42
Bromelton Qld 317 J5
Brompton SA 194 A2
Bronte NSW 73 Q5
Bronte Tas. 358 I2, 360 I12
Bronte Park Tas. 358 I2, 360 I12, 351
Bronzewing Vic. 162 I10
Brookfield Qld 310 A3
Brookhampton WA 248 F5
Brooklyn NSW 77 P3, 78 I9
Brooklyn Vic. 148 B9
Brookside Vic. 167 Q9, 168 A9
Brookton WA 251 K11, 256 F10, 215
Brookvale NSW 71 P7
Brookville Vic. 174 E4
Brooloo Qld 312 G7
Broome WA 255 K5, 215
Broomehill WA 249 M6, 256 G12
Broomfield Vic. 158 A7
Brooms Head NSW 95 Q5
Broughton Vic. 164 D5
Broughton Vale NSW 91 N10
Broughton Village NSW 91 O10
Broula NSW 98 E6, 100 C1
Broulee NSW 100 G7
Brown Hill Vic. 157 H4, 158 A9
Brownlow SA 201 L12, 203 L3
Brownlow Hill NSW 77 J12
Brown Range Vic. 159 N4
Browns Plains Qld 315 L13
Browns Plains Vic. 167 P4
Brownsville NSW 91 O6
Bruarong Vic. 167 Q7, 168 A7
Bruce ACT 106 I12, 108 G1
Bruce SA 200 G4
Brucefield SA 200 F10, 202 F1
Bruce Rock WA 251 O8, 256 G10
Brucknell Vic. 171 M10
Bruckunga SA 197 L13, 199 L1
Brundee NSW 91 N12
Brungle NSW 98 D10, 100 B5
Brunkerville NSW 83 E6
Brunswick Vic. 148 G6
Brunswick Heads NSW 95 R2, 323 Q12, 42
Brunswick Junction WA 248 F3, 214
Bruny Island Tas. 359 M9, 343, 340, 345
Brush Creek NSW 83 C10
Bruthen Vic. 174 F7
Bryant Park WA 252 G11
Bryden Qld 314 F7
Buangor Vic. 171 N2, 120
Buaraba Qld 314 C8
Buaraba Creek Qld 314 D9
Bubialo Qld 331 C4
Bucasia Qld 331 H11
Buccan Qld 317 M2
Buccaneer Archipelago WA 255 L3
Buccarumbi NSW 95 O6
Buccleuch SA 203 N8
Buchan Vic. 174 H6, 123, 137
Buchanan NSW 83 F4
Bucheen Creek Vic. 168 E7
Buckaroo NSW 98 G2
Buckenderra NSW 100 C8, 104 H5, 40
Bucketty NSW 83 A9, 99 K4
Buckety Place Vic. 168 D11, 174 D1
Buckingham SA 203 P13, 204 G4
Buckingham WA 248 H4
Buckland Tas. 357 M3, 359 O5, 343, 348
Buckland Vic. 167 Q10, 168 A10
Buckleboo SA 205 F8, 207 K13
Buckley Vic. 155 C8, 172 C8
Buckleys Swamp Vic. 170 H6
Buckrabanyule Vic. 165 O6
Bucks Lake National Park Vic. 204 G12
Buddabuddah NSW 93 P12, 94 A12
Buddina Qld 307 I9, 313 M10
Buderim Qld 313 L10, 280, 285
Budgeam NSW 316 I12
Budgee Budgee NSW 98 G2
Budgeree Vic. 173 N10
Budgerum Vic. 165 P2
Budgewoi NSW 83 G10, 99 L5
Buffalo Vic. 173 M11
Buffalo River Vic. 167 P9
Buff Point NSW 83 F10
Bugaldie NSW 94 F9
Bugilbone NSW 94 E6
Bugle Ranges SA 199 K3
Bugong Gap NSW 91 K11
Builyan Qld 323 O5
Bukalong NSW 100 E10
Bukkulla NSW 95 K4
Bulahdelah NSW 99 N2, 42

Bular Qld 312 C1
Bulart Vic. 170 G4
Buldah Vic. 175 L4
Bulga NSW 95 N11, 99 K3
Bulga National Park Vic. 173 P10, 133, 136, 144
Bulgandramine NSW 98 D2
Bulgandry NSW 97 O12
Bulgobac Tas. 360 E8
Bulimba Qld 309 J13, 311 J1
Bulla Vic. 159 K10, 172 F4
Bullaburra NSW 76 G7, 80 D8
Bullarah NSW 94 F4, 323 K13
Bullaring WA 215 N11
Bullarook Vic. 158 B9, 171 R3, 172 B3
Bullarto Vic. 158 E7, 172 C2
Bulls Creek SA 198 I5
Bull Creek WA 246 I9
Bulleen Vic. 149 M6
Bullengarook Vic. 158 G9
Bullfinch WA 256 H9
Bullhead Creek Vic. 168 D7
Bulli NSW 91 P3, 99 J8, 100 I3
Bullio NSW 90 G5, 100 G3
Bullioh Vic. 168 D5
Bull Island SA 204 F7
Bullock Creek Qld 324 E5, 326 G13
Bulloo Downs Qld 321 I12
Bullsbrook WA 250 G7
Buln Buln Vic. 173 L7
Buloke Vic. 165 L6
Bulumwaal Vic. 174 D6
Bulyee WA 251 M11
Bumbaldry NSW 98 D7, 100 C1
Bumberry NSW 98 E4
Bumbunga SA 200 H11, 202 H2
Bunburra Qld 316 G6
Bunbury WA 248 E4, 256 E11, 215, 218
Bundaberg Qld 323 P6, 285
Bundalaguah Vic. 173 R7, 174 B9
Bundaleer Qld 93 O2
Bundall Qld 318 F11
Bundalong Vic. 167 N4
Bundanoon NSW 90 I9, 98 I9, 100 G4, 42
Bundarra NSW 95 K6
Bundeena NSW 77 P11
Bundella NSW 94 H11
Bunding Vic. 158 D9, 172 C3
Bundook NSW 95 M12, 99 M1
Bundooma NT 271 K10
Bundoora Vic. 149 K2, 172 H4
Bundure NSW 97 N10
Bunga NSW 100 G9
Bungador Vic. 171 O9
Bungal Vic. 155 C1, 158 C11, 172 C4
Bungarby NSW 100 D10
Bungaree Vic. 158 B9, 171 R3, 172 B3
Bung Bong Vic. 165 O12
Bungeet Vic. 167 M6
Bungendore NSW 98 G11, 100 E6
Bungil NSW 168 D4
Bungonia NSW 90 E13, 98 H9, 100 G4
Bungulla NSW 95 M3
Bungulla WA 251 M7
Bunguluping WA 251 P9
Bunguluke Vic. 165 N4
Bungunya Qld 323 L12
Bungwahl NSW 99 N2
Buniche WA 249 R2
Buninyong Vic. 158 A11, 171 Q4, 172 A4
Bunjil WA 252 H9
Bunker Bay WA 248 C5
Bunketch WA 251 K1, 253 K13
Bunnaby NSW 90 E7
Bunnaloo NSW 97 J12, 166 E2
Bunnan NSW 95 J12, 99 J1
Buntine WA 252 I11
Bunya NSW 95 N13, 99 N2
Bunya Qld 308 D8
Bunyan NSW 100 D8
Bunyaville Qld 308 E9
Bunyip Vic 173 K7
Burabadji WA 251 J5
Burakin WA 251 K1, 253 K13
Buranda Qld 310 I4
Burcher NSW 97 P5, 98 B5
Burekup WA 248 F4
Burges Siding WA 251 J8
Burgooney NSW 97 O5
Burkes Flat Vic. 165 O8
Burketown Qld 327 C3, 286, 293
Burleigh Vic. 147 G8
Burleigh Heads Qld 317 Q7, 319 K8, 278, 279
Burleigh Park Qld 319 L10
Burleigh Waters Qld 319 K10
Burnbank Vic. 165 P13, 171 P1
Burngup WA 249 Q2
Burnie Tas. 360 G5, 362, 343, 351
Burns NSW 92 A13, 96 A1
Burns Creek Tas. 361 N6
Burnsfield SA 200 H10
Burnside Qld 307 D7, 313 J9
Burnside SA 195 F9
Buronga NSW 96 D8, 162 H2, 135

Burpengary Qld 315 K5
Burra SA 201 J9, 182
Burra Bee Dee NSW 94 G10
Burraboi NSW 97 J11
Burracoppin WA 251 Q6, 256 H9
Burradoo NSW 91 J7
Burraga NSW 98 G7, 100 F2
Burragate NSW 100 F11, 175 O2
Burramine Vic. 167 L4
Burran Rock WA 251 O5
Burrawang NSW 91 K8
Burraway NSW 94 D12
Burrell Creek NSW 99 N1
Burrendong Dam NSW 98 F3, 56, 63
Burren Junction NSW 94 F6
Burrereo Vic. 165 K8
Burrier NSW 91 K12
Burrill Lake NSW 98 I11, 100 H6
Burringbar NSW 95 Q1, 317 Q12
Burrinjuck NSW 98 E10, 100 C5, 64
Burroin Vic. 162 I13, 164 I1
Burrowapine National Park Vic. 168 F5
Burrowye Vic. 168 E4, 100 A8
Burrum Vic. 165 K8
Burrumbeet Vic. 171 P3
Burrumbool Vic. 166 F8
Burrumbuttock NSW 97 O12, 167 Q3, 168 A3
Burrum Heads Qld 323 P6, 286
Burrungule SA 204 G11
Burtundy NSW 96 D7
Burwood NSW 72 H5
Burwood Vic. 149 M11, 150 A8, 172 H5
Bushfield Vic. 171 J9
Bushmead WA 245 R9
Bushy Park Tas. 356 E4, 359 K6
Bushy Park Vic. 173 R6, 174 B8
Busselton WA 248 D5, 256 E12, 215, 218
Butchers Ridge Vic. 168 I13, 174 H4
Bute SA 200 G10, 202 G1
Buthurra Qld 331 F10
Butler WA 205 F11
Buttercup Vic. 167 N12
Buxton NSW 91 K3
Buxton Vic. 160 F7, 173 K2
Byaduck Vic. 170 G6
Byangum NSW 317 O11
Byawatha Vic. 167 O6
Byford WA 250 G10
Bylands Vic. 159 L6, 172 G2
Bylong NSW 94 H13, 98 H2
Bymount Qld 323 J8
Byrne Vic. 167 O8
Byrneside Vic. 166 H7
Byrnestown Qld 323 O7
Byrneville Vic. 164 I8
Byrock NSW 93 N8
Byron Bay NSW 95 R2, 323 Q12, 45
Bywong NSW 98 F10, 100 E5

C

Cabanda Qld 314 F12
Cabarita NSW 317 R11
Cabawin Qld 323 M10
Cabbage Tree Creek Vic. 175 K7
Cabbage Tree Point Qld 317 O2
Caboolture Qld 315 K4, 323 Q10, 286
Caboonbah Qld 314 E5
Cabramurra NSW 100 C8, 104 D2
Caddapan Qld 321 G6
Caddens Flat Vic. 170 G2
Cadelga Outstation SA 321 E7
Cadell SA 201 M11, 203 M2
Cadney Park SA 206 H4
Cadoux WA 251 K3, 256 F8
Caffey Qld 314 A13, 316 A1
Cahills Crossing NT 266 H4
Caiguna WA 257 N10, 215
Cairnbank SA 204 F7
Cairns Qld 324 G3, 334, 335 F8, 286-8, 283, 284, 287, 300, 302, 303
Cairns Bay Tas. 356 E12, 359 K9
Calamvale Qld 315 L12
Calca SA 205, C8, 206 I13
Calcarra WA 250 H4
Calder Tas. 360 E5
Calderwood NSW 91 N7
Caldwell NSW 97 J12, 166 E1
Calectasia National Park SA 204 G9
Calen Qld 325 K10, 331 E9
Calga NSW 77 P1, 99 K5
Calgardup WA 248 C7
Calico Creek Qld 312 G4
Calingiri WA 250 H4, 256 F9
Caliph SA 203 O5
Calivil Vic. 165 R6, 166 B6
Cal Lal NSW 96 B7, 162 B2
Callawadda NSW 165 K10
Calleen NSW 97 P6, 98 A7
Callen Range Vic. 159 P1
Callide Qld 323 M5, 291, 281

Callignee Vic. 173 P9
Callington SA 199 M3, 203 K7
Calliope Qld 323 N4, 288
Calomba SA 196 E3
Caloona NSW 94 G2
Caloote SA 197 P12
Caloundra Qld 307 I12, 313 M12, 323 Q9, 288, 280, 301
Calpatanna Water Hole Cons. Park SA 206 I13
Calperum SA 201 Q12, 203 Q3
Caltowie SA 200 H7
Calvert Qld 314 E13
Calvert Vic. 171 L3
Cambarville Vic. 160 H9
Cambeela Qld 321 G1
Camberwell Vic. 149 L10
Cambewarra NSW 91 L11
Cambrai SA 197 P7, 203 L5
Cambray WA 248 E7
Cambrian Hill Vic. 158 A10, 171 Q4, 172 A4
Cambridge Tas. 357 J6, 359 N7
Camburinga NT 267 P5
Camden NSW 77 K12, 99 J7, 100 H2, 45, 38
Camellia NSW 70 D13, 72 D2
Camena Tas. 360 G5
Camira Creek NSW 95 P4
Cammeray NSW 69 L1, 71 M12, 73 N1
Camooweal Qld 269 I10, 327 A7, 288, 286, 293, 297
Campania Tas. 357 J4, 359 N5
Campbell ACT 109 N7
Campbells Bridge Vic. 165 K10
Campbells Creek Vic. 158 D3, 166 C12
Campbells Forest Vic. 166 C8
Campbells Pocket Qld 314 I4
Campbelltown NSW 77 L12, 99 J7, 100 I2, 45, 38
Campbelltown SA 195 G7, 196 H11
Campbell Town Tas. 359 N1, 361 N11, 344
Campbelltown Vic. 158 B4, 165 R12, 166 B12, 171 R1, 172 B1
Camperdown NSW 73 L6
Camperdown Vic. 171 N8, 123-4, 126
Camp Hill Qld 311 K4
Campion WA 251 Q4
Camp Mountain Qld 314 I9
Campsie NSW 72 I8
Campup WA 249 K8
Camurra NSW 94 H4
Canadian Vic. 157 H8, 158 A10
Canary Island Vic. 165 Q4, 166 A4
Canbelego NSW 93 N11
Canberra ACT 98 F11, 100 D6, 105-11, opp. 57, 39
Canberra Airport ACT 109 N7
Candelo NSW 100 F10, 175 P1, 41
Candlelight WA 249 O3
Cangai NSW 95 O5
Caniambo Vic. 167 K7
Canimbla NSW 98 E6, 100 C1
Canna WA 252 F5
Cannawigara SA 203 Q13, 204 H4
Cannie Vic. 165 O2
Cannington WA 247 M5, 250 F9
Canning Vale WA 247 M11
Cannon Hill Qld 311 L3
Cannons Creek Vic. 153 Q3
Cannonvale Qld 325 K9, 331 E4, 288
Cann River Vic. 100 D13, 175 L6, 124
Cannum Vic. 164 H6
Canoelands NSW 77 N3
Canonba NSW 93 Q10, 94 B10
Canowie SA 200 I8
Canowie Belt SA 200 I7
Canowindra NSW 98 E6, 45
Canterbury NSW 72 I8, 73 J8
Canterbury Vic. 149 L10, 152 D8
Canunda National Park SA 204 F11, 181, 187
Canungra Qld 317 M6, 278, 279
Canyon Leigh NSW 90 G9
Caoura NSW 90 H12
Capacabana NSW 77 R2
Capalaba Qld 311 R7
Cape Arid National Park WA 257 L12
Cape Barren Island Tas. 358 A6, 361 Q1, 347
Cape Borda SA 202 B11
Cape Bridgewater Vic. 170 E10
Cape Clear Vic. 171 P5
Cape Hillsborough Qld 331 G10
Cape Howe NSW 100 F12
Cape Jaffa SA 204 D7
Cape Jervis SA 198 A11, 202 G10, 180, 191
Capel WA 248 E5
Cape Leeuwin-Naturaliste National Park WA 248 C9, 218
Cape Labatt Recreation Park SA 205 B8, 191
Cape Le Grand Nat. Park WA 257 K12, 219, 221
Capella Qld 323 J3
Capels Crossing Vic. 163 Q3, 165 R1, 166 B1
Cape Nelson State Park Vic. 170 F10
Cape Patterson Vic. 173 K11, 131
Cape Range National Park WA 254 C11, 226
Capercup WA 249 J5
Capertee NSW 98 H4
Cape Schanck Vic. 172 F10, 125, 139

Cape York Peninsula Qld 326, 300
Caping Qld 331 D7
Capital Hill ACT 109 K9
Capricorn Coast Qld 323 N3, 304
Capricornia Qld 323, 291
Captains Flat NSW 100 E7
Carabost NSW 97 Q12, 100 A7, 168 F1
Caragabal NSW 97 R6, 98 C6, 100 A1
Caralue SA 205 F9
Caramut Vic. 171 J6
Carapooee Vic. 165 N9
Carapook Vic. 170 E4
Carbarup WA 249 M10
Carboor Vic. 167 P8, 143
Carbrook Qld 315 D13, 317 N1
Carbunup WA 248 C5
Carcoar NSW 98 F6, 100 E1, 42
Carcuma SA 203 N10, 204 E1
Cardiff NSW 83 G5
Cardigan Vic. 171 Q3
Cardinia Vic. 173 J8
Cardinia Creek Reservoir Vic. 147 F13
Cardross Vic. 162 G3
Cardup WA 248 H7
Cardwell Qld 324 G6, 288, 282, 284, 293, 302
Carey Gully SA 196 I12
Cargerie Vic. 155 A2, 158 B13, 171 R5, 172 B5
Cargo NSW 98 E5
Caribbean Lake Vic. 150 D2
Carina Qld 311 M4
Carina Vic. 162 B10
Carinda NSW 93 Q7, 94 C7
Carine WA 244 E5
Caringbah NSW 77 P11
Carinya Vic. 203 R8
Carisbrook Vic. 165 Q11, 166 A11
Carlecatup WA 249 L6
Carlingford NSW 70 D10
Carlisle WA 247 M3
Carlisle River Vic. 171 O11
Carlo Qld 321 B3
Carlotta WA 248 F8
Carlsruhe Vic. 158 H5, 166 E13, 172 E1
Carlton NSW 73 J11
Carlton Tas. 357 M7, 359 O7, 351
Carlton Vic. 146 D2, 117
Carmelicup WA 249 M4
Carmila Qld 325 L12
Carnamah WA 252 F9, 256 E7, 215-16
Carnarvon WA 256 C2, 216
Carnarvon National Park Qld 323 J5, 285, 293, 296
Carnegie Vic. 149 K13, 150 C10
Carneys Creek Qld 316 F9
Carnegham Vic. 171 P4
Caroda NSW 94 I6
Carole Park Qld 310 D12
Caroline SA 170 B6, 204 I12
Caroling WA 251 M9
Caron WA 252 H9
Carool NSW 317 P9
Caroona NSW 94 I10
Carpa SA 200 B10, 202 B1
Carpendeit Vic. 171 N9
Carpenter Rocks SA 204 G12
Carrabin WA 251 Q6
Carrajung Vic. 173 P9
Carranballac Vic. 171 N4
Carrara Qld 318 G13
Carrathool NSW 97 L8
Carrick NSW 90 D11
Carrick Tas. 361 L8, 363 D11
Carrickalinga SA 198 D8
Carrieton SA 200 I3, 207 N12
Carrington NSW 82 F4
Carroll NSW 94 I9
Carroll Gap NSW 95 J9
Carrolup WA 249 L6
Carron Vic. 165 K6
Carrow Brook NSW 95 K13, 99 K2
Carrowidgin NSW 100 D11
Carrum Vic. 151 M7, 172 H7
Carrum Downs Vic. 151 M3
Carters Ridge Qld 312 H7
Carwarp Vic. 162 H4
Cary Bay NSW 83 G7
Cascades Tas. 355 B10
Cashmore Vic. 170 E9
Casino NSW 95 P3, 323 Q13, 45
Cassilis NSW 94 H12, 55
Cassilis Vic. 168 E13, 174 E3
Cassowary Qld 324 F3, 326 I11
Castambul SA 196 I10
Castella Vic. 159 Q8, 160 C9, 173 J3
Casterton Vic. 170 D4, 124, 126
Castillo NSW 316 F11
Castle Cove NSW 71 N9
Castlecrag NSW 71 N10
Castle Forbes Tas. 359 K8
Castle Forbes Bay Tas. 356 E11
Castle Hill NSW 70 B7
Castlemaine Vic. 154 A4, 158 E2, 166 C11, 124, 119

Castlereagh NSW 77 J6
Castra Upper Tas. 360 H6
Casula NSW 77 M10
Catagunya Tas. 359 J4
Catamaran Tas. 359 K11
Catani NSW 173 K8
Cathcart NSW 100 E10, 175 N1
Cathcart Vic. 165 L13, 171 L2, 120
Cathedral Range National Park Vic. 160 F7, 173 K2, 125
Cathedral Rock Vic. 165 J13
Catherine Field NSW 77 K11
Catherine Hill Bay NSW 83 G9
Cathkin Vic. 160 E3, 167 J12
Cathundral NSW 93 R12, 94 C12
Cattai NSW 77 L4, 64
Catterick WA 248 G6
Catumnal Vic. 165 P4
Caulfield Vic. 149 K13, 150 B11
Cavan NSW 98 E10, 100 D5
Caveat Vic. 159 R2, 160 D2, 167 J12, 144
Cavendish Vic. 170 H3
Cave of Fishes Vic. 170 I1
Cave of Hands Vic. 170 I2
Caversham WA 245 P7, 259 E9
Caves Beach NSW 83 H8
Caveside Tas. 360 I8
Cawdor NSW 77 J12
Cawongla NSW 95 P2
Cecil Park NSW 77 L9
Cecil Plains Qld 323 N10
Cedar Brush NSW 83 C10
Cedar Glen Qld 317 L9
Cedar Grove Qld 317 K3
Cedar Pocket Qld 312 H3
Cedarton Qld 307 A13
Ceduna SA 205 A6, 206 H12, 183
Cement Creek Vic. 160 F11, 173 K4
Centennial Park NSW 67 M13, 73 O5
Central Aboriginal Reserve WA 255 Q10, 257 Q2
Central Castra Tas. 360 H6
Central Mangrove NSW 83 C12
Central Tilba NSW 100 G9
Ceratodus Qld 323 N6
Ceres NSW 94 D13
Ceres Vic. 172 D8, 128
Cervantes WA 250 C1, 252 C13
Cessnock NSW 81 H12, 83 C5, 99 K3, 45, 39
Cethana Tas. 360 H7
Chadoora WA 248 G1, 250 G13
Chain of Ponds SA 197 J10
Chain Valley NSW 83 G9
Chakola NSW 100 E8
Challambra Vic. 165 J6
Chambigne NSW 95 O5
Chandada SA 205 C7
Chandler SA 206 G3
Chandler WA 251 P4
Chandlers Creek Vic. 100 E12, 175 M4
Chandlers Hill SA 208 I8
Chandos SA 203 Q8
Channel Country Qld 321, 322, 327, 294-5, 283, 291
Chapel Hill Qld 310 D4
Chapman ACT 110 B3
Chapple Vale Vic. 171 O11
Charam Vic. 164 E11
Charbon NSW 98 H3
Charlerol Vic. 168 C6
Charleston SA 197 K11
Charlestown NSW 82 A13, 83 H6
Charleville Qld 322 G8, 288, 294, 295
Charley Creek Vic. 171 P11
Charleyong NSW 98 H11, 100 F6
Charlton NSW 93 O6
Charlton Vic. 165 N6, 124
Charlwood Qld 316 F6
Charmhaven NSW 83 F10
Charnwood ACT 106 D7
Charters Towers Qld 324 G9, 288
Chatsbury NSW 98 H9, 100 F3
Chatswood NSW 71 L11
Chatsworth Qld 312 F2
Chatsworth Vic. 171 K6
Cheeple Qld 322 E9
Cheesemans Creek NSW 98 E4
Cheethams Flats NSW 76 B5
Chelmer Qld 310 F6
Chelsea Vic. 151 L7, 172 H7
Cheltenham NSW 70 F8
Cheltenham SA 195 C6
Cheltenham Vic. 150 G10
Chepstowe Vic. 171 O4
Chermside Qld 308 H8
Cherokee Vic. 158 I7
Cherry Gardens SA 198 H2
Cherrypool Vic. 164 H12
Cherry Tree Pool WA 249 L6
Cherryville SA 196 I11
Cheshunt Vic. 167 O10, 143
Chesney Vale Vic. 167 M7
Chester Hill NSW 72 C7
Chetwynd Vic. 164 D13, 170 D2

Cheviot — Coonawarra   375

Cheviot Vic. 159 R4, 160 D4, 167 J13, 173 J1
Chevron Island Qld 318 F10
Chewton Vic. 158 E2, 166 C11, **124**
Chichester Range National Park WA 254 F10, **217**, **226**
Chidlow WA 250 H8
Chifley ACT 110 F3
Chifley NSW 73 P10
Chifley NSW 257 L8
Childers Qld 323 P6, **288**
Childers Vic. 173 M9
Chillagoe Qld 324 E4, 326 G12, **288**, **295**
Chillingham NSW 95 Q1, 317 N10
Chillingollah Vic. 163 M10
Chiltern Vic. 167 P5, 176 G7, **124-6**, **121**
Chiltern Hills Qld 321 G1
Chiltern Park Vic. 167 P5
Chiltern Valley Vic. 176 E6
Chilwell Vic. 156 D11
Chinamans Wells SA 204 E9
Chinchilla Qld 323 M9, **288**
Chinderah NSW 95 R1, 317 R9
Chinkapook Vic. 96 I11, 163 L10
Chinocup WA 249 P5
Chintin Vic. 159 K7, 172 F2
Chippendale NSW 66 A13
Chipping Norton NSW 72 A10
Chirnside Park Vic. 147 C1
Chirrup Vic. 165 M5
Chisholm ACT 111 J12
Chiswick NSW 73 J3
Chittaway Point NSW 83 F12
Chittering WA 250 G6
Chorkerup WA 249 M12
Chorregon Qld 322 C2, 324 C13
Chowerup WA 248 I8
Chowilla SA 96 A7
Christies Beach SA 198 F3, 208 F10
Christmas Creek Qld 317 K8
Christmas Hills Tas. 360 C4
Christmas Hills Vic. 159 P10, 160 B10, 172 I4
Chudleigh Tas. 360 I8, **344**
Chullora NSW 72 E7
Churchill Qld 314 H12
Churchill Vic. 173 O9, **136**
Churchill National Park Vic. 150 F1, 172 I6
Church Land SA 201 I10, 203 L1
Churchlands WA 244 E10
Church Point NSW 77 Q5, 79 N5
Chute Vic. 165 O13, 171 O2
Cinnabar Qld 312 A2
City Beach WA 244 C10, **211**
Clackline WA 250 I7
Clandulla NSW 98 H4
Clara Creek Qld 322 H8
Clare Qld 324 I8
Clare SA 200 I10, 202 I1, **183**, **180**
Claremont Tas. 356 H5, 359 M6, **340**
Claremont WA 246 E3, 250 E9
Clarence NSW 76 D4
Clarence Town NSW 99 L3
Clarendon NSW 77 K5
Clarendon Qld 314 E9
Clarendon SA 198 H2, 202 I7
Clarendon Tas. 363 G12
Clarendon Vic. 155 A1, 158 B11, 171 R4, 172 B4
Claretown Vic. 158 C9
Clare Valley SA 200 I10, **180**, **182**, **183**
Clareville Beach NSW 77 Q4
Clarkefield Vic. 159 J8, 172 F3
Clarke Island Tas. 361 Q1
Clarks Hill Vic. 158 B8
Claude Road Tas. 360 H7
Clayfield Qld 309 J11
Claymore WA 248 E6
Claypans SA 203 M6
Clayton Qld 323 P6
Clayton SA 199 K9
Clayton Vic. 150 E6
Clay Wells SA 204 F9
Clear Lake Vic. 164 F11
Clear Ridge NSW 98 B6
Cleary WA 251 M1, 253 M13
Cleland National Park SA 195 G10, **179**, **180**, **183**
Clematis Vic. 147 G12
Clements Gap SA 200 G9
Clempton Park NSW 72 I8
Clermont Qld 322 I2, 324 I13, **288**, **291**
Cleve SA 200 A10, 205 G10, **183**, **184**
Cleveland Qld 315 O11, **299**, **300**, **301**
Cleveland Tas. 361 N10
Cliffordville WA 251 L12
Clifton NSW 91 P2
Clifton Qld 323 O11, **288**
Clifton Tas. 357 K9
Clifton Beach Qld 335 E5
Clifton Beach Tas. 359 N8, **339**, **349**
Clifton Gardens NSW 71 O13, 73 O1
Clifton Hill Qld 310 I6
Clifton Springs Vic. 155 H7, 172 E8, **127**
Clinton Centre SA 200 F12, 202 G3
Clintonvale Qld 323 O11
Clonbinane Vic. 159 N6, 166 H13, 172 H2

Cloncurry Qld 327 E8, **289**, **292**, **293**
Clontarf NSW 71 P11
Closeburn Qld 314 I8
Clothiers Creek NSW 317 Q11
Clouds Creek NSW 95 O6
Clovelly NSW 73 Q6
Cloverdale WA 245 N13, 247 N2
Cluan Tas. 361 K8, 363 B12
Club Terrace Vic. 100 D12, 175 L6
Clumber Qld 316 E6
Clunes NSW 95 Q2
Clunes Vic. 165 Q13, 166 A13, 171 Q1, 172 A1, **126**
Clwydd NSW 76 D5
Clybucca NSW 95 P9
Clyburn NSW 72 D3
Clyde NSW 72 C3
Clyde Vic. 172 I8
Clydebank Vic. 174 C9
Clydesdale Vic. 158 C4, 165 R12, 166 B12, 172 C1
Coal Point NSW 83 G7
Coalcliff NSW 91 P2
Coal Creek Qld 314 D5
Coaldale NSW 95 O4
Coalstoun Lakes Qld 323 O7
Coalville Vic. 173 N8, **136**
Cobains Vic. 173 R7, 174 B10
Cobaki NSW 317 Q9, 319 R6
Cobar NSW 93 M11, **45-6**
Cobargo NSW 100 F9, **41**
Cobark NSW 95 L12, 99 L1
Cobaw Vic. 158 I5, 166 E13, 172 E1
Cobbadah NSW 95 J7
Cobbannah Vic. 174 C6
Cobbitty NSW 77 J11
Cobbora NSW 94 F12
Cobden Vic. 171 M9, **124**
Cobdogla SA 201 P12, 203 P3
Cobera SA 203 P5
Cobourg Peninsula NT 266 G2, **234**
Cobram Vic. 97 M13, 167 K3, **126**, **141**
Cobrico Vic. 171 M9
Cobungra Vic. 168 D12, 174 D3
Coburg Vic. 148 G5, 172 G5
Cocamba Vic 163 L4
Cochranes Creek Vic. 165 P9
Cockaleechie SA 205 F11
Cockatoo Vic. 154 I10, 173 J6
Cockatoo Island NSW 68 B12
Cockburn SA 92 A13, 96 A1, 201 R2, 207 R12
Cocklebiddy WA 257 O10, **216**
Coconut Grove NT 264 C6
Cocoparra National Park NSW 97 N7, **49**
Cocoroc Vic. 172 E6
Coen Qld 326 E7, **300**
Coffin Bay SA 205 E12, **183**, **189**
Coffs Harbour NSW 84, 95 P7, **46**
Coghills Creek Vic. 171 Q2, 172 A2
Cohuna Vic. 96 I12, 166 C2, **126**
Colac Vic. 171 P9, **126**
Colac Colac Vic. 168 G5
Colbinabbin Vic. 166 F8
Coldstream Vic. 154 H8, 159 Q11, 160 C11, 172 I5
Coleambally NSW 97 M9, **46**
Colebrook Tas. 357 J1, 359 M5
Coledale NSW 91 P3, 99 J8, 100 I3
Coleraine Vic. 170 F4, **126**
Coles Bay Tas. 359 R2, 361 R12, **344**, **342**
Coleyville Qld 316 F3
Colignan Vic. 162 I5
Colinroobie NSW 97 O8
Colinton NSW 100 D7
Colinton Qld 314 C1
Collarenebri NSW 94 E4
Collaroy NSW 71 Q6, 94 H12
Collector NSW 98 G10, 100 E5
College Park SA 194 H4
Collerina NSW 93 O5
Collgar WA 251 P7
Collie NSW 94 D11
Collie WA 248 G4, 256 F11, **216**
Collieburn WA 248 G4
Collie Cardiff WA 248 G4
Collingullie NSW 97 P10, 98 A10
Collins WA 248 G9
Collins Cap Tas. 356 G6, 359 L7
Collinsfield SA 200 H9
Collinsvale Tas. 356 H6, 359 M7
Collinsville Qld 325 J10, **283**
Collombatti Rail NSW 95 O9
Colly Blue NSW 94 H10
Colo NSW 77 K2
Colo Heights NSW 77 J1, 99 J5
Colo Vale NSW 91 K5
Colquhoun Vic. 174 G7
Colton SA 205 D9
Comara NSW 86 I11, 95 N9
Comaum SA 164 B13, 170 A2, 204 I8
Combara NSW 94 G9
Combienbar Vic. 175 L5
Comboyne NSW 95 N11
Come-by-Chance NSW 94 E7
Comet Qld 323 J3

Comleroy Road NSW 76 I4
Commissioners Flat Qld 312 I13, 314 I1
Como NSW 77 O10
Como WA 246 I5
Compton SA 204 H11
Compton Downs NSW 93 O7
Conara Junction Tas. 361 N10
Conargo NSW 97 L11
Concord NSW 72 H4
Concordia SA 197 J6
Condah Vic. 170 F7
Condamine Qld 323 M9
Condell Park NSW 72 D9
Condingup WA 257 K12
Condobolin NSW 97 P4, 98 A4, **46**
Condong NSW 317 P10
Condoulpe NSW 163 O6
Condowie SA 200 H10, 202 H1
Congelin WA 249 J1, 251 J13
Congewai NSW 83 C7
Congo Park NSW 100 G8
Congupna Road Vic. 167 J6
Coningham Tas. 356 I10, **345**
Coniston NSW 89 C12, 91 P5
Conjola NSW 98 I11, 100 H6
Conmurra SA 204 F8
Connangorach Vic. 164 G11
Connells Point NSW 72 I13
Connels Peak Vic. 168 D7
Connemara Qld 321 H4
Connemarra NSW 94 H11
Connewarre Vic. 155 F9
Connewirricoo Vic. 164 D13, 170 E1
Connulpie NSW 321 I13
Conondale Qld 312 H11
Contine WA 249 K1, 251 K13
Conway Qld 331 E6
Conway National Park Qld 331 E5, **281**, **288**, **299**, **303**
Coober Pedy SA 206 I6, **183-4**, **188**
Coobowie SA 202 F7, 205 I13, **184**
Coochin Coochin Qld 316 G7
Coochin Creek Qld 313 J13, 315 J1
Cooee Tas. 360 G5
Cooeeinbardi Qld 314 E4
Coogee NSW 73 Q7
Coogee WA 246 C13
Cooinda NT 266 H5
Coojar Vic. 170 F2
Cook ACT 108 E2
Cook SA 206 C9
Cookamidgera NSW 98 D4
Cookardinia NSW 97 P12, 98 A11, 168 C1
Cooke Plains SA 203 M9
Cookernup WA 248 F2
Cooks Gap NSW 94 G13, 98 G2
Cooktown Qld 324 F1, 326 I9, **289**, **282**, **286**, **287**, **303**
Cookville Tas. 359 M10
Coolabah NSW 93 O9
Coolabine Qld 312 H9
Coolac NSW 98 D10, 100 B5
Cooladdi Qld 322 F9
Coolah NSW 94 H12
Coolamatong NSW 104 H8
Coolamon NSW 97 P9, 98 A9
Coolana Qld 314 E11
Coolangatta NSW 91 N12, **41**
Coolangatta Qld 95 R1, 317 R8, 319 P4, 323 Q12, **289**, **278**, **279**
Coolanie SA 200 B9, 205 G9
Coolatai NSW 95 J4, 323 M13
Coolbellup WA 246 F11
Coolbinia WA 244 I9
Coolcha SA 203 M6
Coolgardie WA 257 J8, 258, **216**, **222**
Coolimba WA 252 C10
Coolongolook NSW 95 N13, 99 N2
Cooloola Coast Qld 313 L3, **280**
Cooloola National Park Qld 313 L3, **292**, **297-8**
Cooloolabin Qld 307 C5, 313 J8
Cooltong SA 98 A8, 201 Q11, 203 Q2
Coolum Qld 307 G5, 313 L8
Coolum Beach Qld 307 H5, 313 L8, **280**
Coolup WA 248 G1, 250 F13
Cooma NSW 100 D8, **46**
Coomalbidgup WA 257 J12
Coomandook SA 203 M9
Coombabah Lakes Qld 317 P4
Coombe SA 203 O11, 204 F2
Coomberdale WA 250 G1
Coombogolong NSW 94 D7
Coombell NSW 95 P3
Coomera Qld 317 O4
Coomingiah Qld 323 N6
Coominya Qld 314 E8, **280**
Coomoora Vic. 158 D6
Coomungla SA 205 E12
Coonabarabran NSW 94 G10, **46**
Coonalpyn SA 203 N10, 204 E1, **184**
Coonamble NSW 94 D9, **46-7**
Coonana WA 257 L9
Coonawarra SA 170 A2, 204 H9, **188**

Coondambo SA 205 E3, 207 K10
Coondoo Qld 313 J3
Coongoola Qld 322 G10
Coongulmerang Vic. 174 D8
Coonong NSW 97 N10
Coonooer Bridge Vic. 165 N7
Cooper Creek SA 207 P5, 184
Coopernook NSW 95 O12
Coopers Creek Vic. 173 O7
Coopers Hill Qld 314 C12
Coopers Plains Qld 311 J9
Cooplacurripa NSW 95 M11
Coorabulka Qld 321 E3
Cooragook Qld 314 D8
Cooran Qld 312 I5
Cooranbong NSW 83 E8, 99 L4
Coorinyup WA 249 M7
Coorong National Park SA 203 L11, 204 C2, 182-3, 185, 186
Coorow WA 252 G10, 256 E7
Cooroy Qld 307 C2, 313 J6, 289
Coorparoo Qld 311 K4
Cootamundra NSW 97 R9, 98 C9, 100 B4, 47
Cooyal NSW 98 H2
Cooyar Qld 323 O9
Cope Cope Vic. 165 M7
Copeville SA 203 N6
Copmanhurst NSW 95 O5
Copping Tas. 357 N6, 359 O7
Corack Vic. 165 M5
Coradgery NSW 98 C3
Coragulac Vic. 171 P8
Coraki NSW 95 Q3, 323 Q13
Coral Bank Vic. 167 R8, 168 B8
Coral Bay WA 254 C12, 216
Coral Ville NSW 95 O12
Cora Lynn Vic. 173 K8
Coramba NSW 95 P7
Cordering WA 248 I5
Corella Qld 312 G2
Corella Dam Qld 327 D9, 297
Corfield Qld 324 C12
Corinda Qld 310 F8
Corindhap Vic. 171 Q6, 172 A6
Corindi NSW 95 P6
Coree South NSW 97 L11
Coreen NSW 97 N12, 167 O2
Corinella Vic. 172 I10
Corinna Tas. 360 C9, 350, 352
Corio Vic. 155 F6, 156 F1, 128
Cork Qld 321 H2
Cornella Vic. 154 D1, 166 F9
Cornwall Tas. 361 Q8
Cornwallis NSW 77 K5
Corny Point SA 202 C7, 205 H13
Corobimilla NSW 97 O9
Coromandel Valley SA 198 H1, 196 H13, 208 I7
Coromby Vic. 165 J8
Coronation Beach Qld 313 L8
Corop Vic. 166 F7
Cororooke Vic. 171 P9
Corowa NSW 97 N13, 167 O4, 176 A2, 47
Corrigin WA 251 N11, 256 G10, 216
Corrimal NSW 89 E3, 91 P4, 99 J8, 100 I3
Corringle Vic. 174 I8
Corryong Vic. 97 Q13, 100 A8, 168 G5, 126, 137
Cortlinye SA 205 G8
Cosgrove Vic. 167 K6
Cosmo Newberry Aboriginal Res. WA 257 M5
Costerfield Vic. 166 F10
Cotabena SA 207 N11
Cottesloe WA 246 B3, 250 E9, 211
Cottles Bridge Vic. 159 O10, 160 A10
Couangalt Vic. 158 I9
Cougal NSW 95 P1, 317 J11
Coulson Qld 316 H5
Coulta SA 205 E11
Countegany NSW 100 E8
Courabyra NSW 100 B7, 168 H2
Courada NSW 94 I6
Couran Qld 317 P3
Couridjah NSW 91 K2
Courtlea Vic. 252 I12
Coutts Crossing NSW 95 P6
Cowabbie West NSW 97 P8
Cowal Creek Mission Qld 326 C1
Cowan NSW 77 O4, 79 K12
Cowangie Vic. 162 D10
Cowaramup WA 248 C6
Coward Springs SA 207 L7
Cowcowing WA 251 L4
Cowell SA 200 C10, 205 H9, 184, 183, 189
Cowes Vic. 153 O11, 172 I10, 126-7
Cowirra SA 197 P11
Cowleys Creek Vic. 171 M10
Cowper NSW 95 P5
Cowra NSW 98 E6, 100 C1, 47
Cowwarr Vic. 173 P7
Coyrecup WA 249 N5
Crabbes Creek NSW 95 Q2, 317 Q13
Crabtree Tas. 356 G8
Cracow Qld 323 M6, 303

Cradle Mountain Lake Saint Clair National Park Tas. 358 G1, 360 G10 264-365, 343, 351, 352
Cradoc Tas. 356 F10, 359 L8
Cradock SA 200 H2, 207 N12
Crafers SA 198 H1, 196 I12
Craigie NSW 100 D11
Craigieburn Vic. 154 F8, 159 L10, 172 G4
Crament Vic. 162 I7
Cramphorne WA 251 Q8
Cranbourne Vic. 172 I7
Cranbrook Tas. 359 Q1, 361 Q11
Cranbrook WA 249 M9, 256 G12, 216
Cranebrook NSW 77 J7
Craven NSW 95 M13, 99 M1
Cravensville Vic. 168 E7, 141
Crawfordville NSW 83 B6
Crawley WA 246 G2
Creek Junction Vic. 167 L10
Creek View Vic. 166 E8
Creighton Vic. 167 J9, 128
Creightons Creek Vic. 167 J10
Cremorne NSW 69 Q2, 71 N13, 73 N1
Cremorne Tas. 357 K8, 359 N7, 339
Cremorne Point NSW 69 R9, 71 O13, 73 O2
Crescent Head NSW 95 P10
Cressbrook Lower Qld 314 D3
Cressy Tas. 361 L9, 363 E13, 348
Cressy Vic. 171 P7
Creswick Vic. 158 A7, 171 R2, 172 B2, 127
Cribb Island Qld 309 N7
Crib Point Vic. 153 N8, 172 H9, 139
Croajingalong National Park Vic. 175 M7, 100 E13, 125, 124, 135
Croftby Qld 316 F8
Crohamhurst Qld 313 J12
Croker Island NT 266 H2, 237
Cromer NSW 71 P6
Cromer SA 197 L9
Cronulla NSW 77 P11
Crooble NSW 94 I3
Crooked River Vic. 173 R2, 174 B5
Crookhaven Heads NSW 91 O12, 99 J10, 100 H5
Crookwell NSW 98 F8, 100 E3, 47
Croom NSW 91 O7
Croppa Creek NSW 94 I3, 323 M13
Crossdale Qld 314 F5
Crossman WA 248 I1, 250 I13
Crotty Tas. 358 E2
Crowdy Bay National Park NSW 95 O12, 60
Crower SA 204 F8
Crowlands Vic. 165 M12
Crow Mountain NSW 95 J7
Crows Nest NSW 69 J3, 71 M12, 73 M1
Crows Nest Qld 323 O10, 289, 280
Crowther NSW 98 D7, 100 C2
Croxton East Vic. 170 I5
Croydon NSW 72 I5
Croydon Qld 324 A6, 327 H4, 292
Croydon Vic. 147 A3, 160 B13, 172 I5
Croydon Park NSW 72 I6
Crymillan Vic. 164 I5
Cryon NSW 94 E6
Crystal Creek NSW 317 O10
Crystal Brook Qld 331 C4
Crystal Brook SA 200 G8, 184
Cuballing WA 249 K1, 251 K13
Cubbaroo NSW 94 F6, 63
Cubbie Qld 322 I12
Cudal NSW 98 E5
Cuddell NSW 97 N9
Cudgee Vic. 171 K9
Cudgegong NSW 98 H3
Cudgen NSW 95 R1, 317 R10
Cudgera Creek NSW 95 Q1, 317 Q11
Cudgewa Vic. 100 A8, 168 F5, 126
Cudlee Creek SA 197 J14
Cudmirrah NSW 100 H6
Cue WA 256 G4, 216
Culbin WA 249 J3
Culburra NSW 91 O13, 99 J10, 47
Culburra SA 203 N16, 204 E2
Culcairn NSW 97 P12, 167 R1, 168 B1
Culfearne Vic. 163 R13, 165 R1, 166 B1
Culgoa Vic 96 G13, 163 M13, 165 M2
Culla Vic. 164 E13, 170 F1
Cullalla WA 250 G5
Cullen NT 266 F8
Cullen Bullen NSW 76 A2
Cullerin NSW 98 G9, 100 E4
Cullulleraine Vic. 96 C8, 162 D3
Cumberland Islands Qld 331 H5, 298
Cumborah NSW 93 R5, 94 C5
Cummins SA 205 E11
Cumnock NSW 98 E3
Cundare Vic. 171 P7
Cundeelee Aboriginal Reserve WA 257 L8
Cunderdin WA 251 L7, 256 G9, 217
Cundinup WA 248 F6
Cungena SA 205 C7, 206 I13
Cunjardine WA 251 J6
Cunliffe SA 200 F12, 202 F2, 205 I11
Cunnamulla Qld 322 F11, 289, 295
Cunningar NSW 98 D8, 100 C3

Cunningham SA 200 F13, 202 F4
Cuprona Tas. 360 G5
Curalle Qld 321 G7
Curara WA 252 E4
Curban NSW 94 E11
Curdie Vale NSW 171 L10
Curdimurka SA 207 M7
Curl Curl NSW 71 P8
Curlewis NSW 94 I9
Curlewis Vic. 155 G8
Curlwaa NSW 96 D7, 162 F2, 63
Curra Qld 312 F1
Currabubula NSW 95 J10
Curramulka SA 202 F5, 205 I12
Currans Hill NSW 77 K12
Currarong NSW 99 J10, 100 I5
Currawang NSW 98 G10, 100 E5
Currawarna NSW 98 A10
Curraweela NSW 90 B4
Currawilla Qld 321 G5
Currency Creek SA 198 I8
Currigee Qld 317 P4
Currimundi Qld 307 I11, 313 M12, 280
Currowan Corner Upper NSW 100 G7
Currumbin Qld 317 Q8, 319 O7, 289, 278, 279
Curtin ACT 108 G11, 110 G1
Curtis Island Qld 323 N3
Curyo Vic. 165 K3
Custon SA 164 A7, 204 I5
Cuttabri NSW 94 F7
Cygnet Tas. 356 G11, 359 L9, 344, 340
Cygnet River SA 202 E10
Cynthia Qld 323 N6
Cypress Gardens Qld 318 H11

D

Daadenning Creek WA 251 N8
Daceville NSW 73 O8
Dadswells Bridge Vic. 165 J11
Daglish WA 244 E12, 246 E1
D'Aguilar Qld 314 I2
Dagun Qld 312 G5
Dahlen Vic. 164 H9
Daintree Qld 324 F2, 326 I11, 297
Dairy Flat NSW 316 G11
Daisey Dell Tas. 360 G8
Daisy Hill Vic. 165 P12, 166 A12
Dajarra Qld 327 D10, 294
Dakabin Qld 315 K6
Dalaroo WA 250 G2
Dalbeg Qld 324 I9
Dalby Qld 323 N10, 289, 290, 303
Dale WA 250 I10
Dale Bridge WA 251 J9
Dale West WA 251 J10
Dalgety NSW 100 D9, 104 I10
Dalgouring WA 251 O1, 253 O13
Dalkeith WA 246 E4
Dallarnil Qld 323 O7
Dalma Qld 323 M3
Dalmallee Vic. 164 H4
Dalman NSW 316 H11
Dalmeny NSW 100 G8
Dalmorton NSW 95 N6
Dalton NSW 98 G9, 100 E4, 51
Dalveen Qld 95 M1
Dalwallinu WA 252 I12, 256 F8
Dalwallinu North WA 253 J12
Dalwood NSW 83 D2
Daly River NT 266 D7, 237
Daly River Aboriginal Reserve NT 266 B8, 234
Daly River Wildlife Sanctuary NT 266 C7
Dalyston Vic. 173 J11
Daly Waters NT 266 I12, 268 I2, 237
Damboring WA 251 J1, 253 J13
Dampier WA 254 F9, 217, 226
Danby Siding Tas. 357 J2
Dandaloo NSW 93 Q13, 94 B13, 97 Q2, 98 B1
Dandaragan WA 250 E2, 256 E8
Dandenong Vic. 150 H3, 172 H6
Dandenong Ranges Vic. 147, 125, 118, 130
Danderoo Qld 316 A9
Dandongadale Vic. 167 P10
Dangarfield NSW 99 K1
Dangarsleigh NSW 95 M8
Dangin WA 251 L9
Danyo Vic. 162 C10
Dapto NSW 91 N6, 99 J8, 100 I3
Darbys Falls NSW 98 E7, 100 D2
Darbyshire Vic. 168 D5
Dardadine WA 249 J3
Dardanup WA 248 F4
Dareton NSW 96 D7, 162 G2
Dargo Vic. 174 C5, 133, 134, 140
Darkan WA 248 I4, 249 J4, 256 F11
Dark Corner NSW 98 H5
Darke Peak SA 205 F9
Darkes Forest NSW 91 O2
Darkwood NSW 95 O8
Darley Vic. 158 G11, 172 D4
Darling Downs Qld 323 N10-O11, 290, 289, 293

Darlinghurst NSW 66 G9, 37
Darling Point NSW 67 L5, 73 O3
Darlington NSW 73 L5
Darlington SA 208 H7
Darlington Tas. 357 Q2, 359 Q5
Darlington Vic. 171 M7
Darlington Point NSW 97 M9
Darnick NSW 96 H3
Darnum Vic. 173 M8
Daroobalgie NSW 98 C5
Darr Qld 322 D3
Darra Qld 310 D9
Darradup WA 248 E8
Darraweit Guim Vic. 159 L7, 172 G2
Darriman Vic. 173 Q10, 174 A12
Dart Dart Vic. 164 H7
Dartmoor Vic. 170 D6
Dartmouth Qld 322 E3
Dartmouth Dam Vic. 168 E8, 137, 141
Dartnall WA 249 M7
Darwin NT 264, 265, 266 D4, 231-3, 283
Dattuck Vic. 162 I12, 164 I1
Davenport Downs Qld 321 F4
Daveyston SA 197 K4, 208 A2
Davidson NSW 71 L6
Davies Creek National Park Qld 335 D9
Davis Creek NSW 99 K1
Davistown NSW 77 Q2, 78 D2
Dawes Qld 323 N5
Dawesley SA 199 L1, 197 L13, 199 L1
Dawesville WA 250 E12
Dawlish Qld 331 H13
Dawn Qld 312 G4
Dawson SA 201 J5
Dawson Vic. 173 P7
Dawson Hill NSW 99 K2
Dayboro Qld 314 I6, 323 P10
Daydream Island Qld 331 E4, 299, 287
Daylesford Vic. 154 A6, 158 D6, 166 C13, 172 C2, 127, 119
Daymar Qld 94 F1, 323 K12
Daysdale NSW 97 N12, 167 N1
Day Trap Vic. 163 K10
Dead Horse Gap NSW 100 B9
Deagon Qld 309 K5, 277
Deakin ACT 108 I10
Deakin WA 257 Q8
Dean Vic. 158 B8, 171 R3, 172 B3
Deanmill WA 248 G8
Deans Marsh Vic. 171 R9, 172 B9
Debella Qld 331 B3
Deception Bay Qld 315 L5, 286
Deddick Vic. 175 J3
Deddington Tas. 361 N8, 363 I12, 344
Dederang Vic. 167 R7, 168 B7, 144
Dee Tas. 361 J13
Deep Creek Vic. 168 F10, 174 F1
Deepdene WA 248 C9
Deep Lead Vic. 165 K11
Deep River WA 248 I12
Deepwater NSW 95 M3
Deep Well NT 263 O11, 271 J9
Deer Park Vic. 172 F5
Deeside WA 248 H9
Dee Why NSW 71 P7
Delacombe Vic. 157 A10
Delamere SA 198 B10
Delaneys Creek Qld 314 I3
Delatite Vic. 167 M12
Delburn Vic. 173 N9
Delegate NSW 100 D11, 175 L3, 137
Delegate River Vic. 100 D11, 175 K3
Dellicknora Vic. 175 K3
Delissaville NT 266 D5
Dellyannie WA 249 K4
Delmont Tas. 361 L9
Deloraine Tas. 361 J8, 344, 346
Delungra NSW 95 J5
Delvine Vic. 174 D8
Denbarker WA 249 L11
Denham WA 256 C3, 217
Denial Bay SA 205 A6
Denicull Creek Vic. 171 L2
Deniliquin NSW 97 K12, 167 K1
Denison Gorge Tas. 363 G5
Denistone NSW 70 G11
Denman NSW 95 J13, 99 J2
Denmark WA 249 L12, 256 G13, 217, 214, 219
Dennes Point Tas. 356 I10, 359 M8
Dennington Vic. 171 J9
Denver Vic. 158 E5, 166 D13, 172 D1
Depot Creek SA 200 F2
Deptford Vic. 174 E6
Derby Tas. 361 P5, 344
Derby Vic. 165 R8, 166 B8
Derby WA 255 M5, 217-8
Dereel Vic. 171 Q5, 172 A5
Dergholm Vic. 170 C2
Dering Vic. 162 H11
Deringulla NSW 94 G10
Derriers Flat Qld 312 G7
Derrinal Vic. 166 E10
Derrinallum Vic. 171 N6

Derriwong NSW 97 Q4, 98 B4
Derwent Bridge Tas. 358 H2, 360 H12
Derwent Park Tas. 355 B3
Desert Camp National Park SA 204 F5
Detpa Vic. 164 F5
Devenish Vic. 167 L6
Devils Marbles National Park NT 269 K11, 271 K1
Devil's Peak SA 200 G3, 190
Devoit Tas. 361 K6, 363 C6
Devon Vic. 173 P10
Devondale Vic. 171 N11
Devonport Tas. 360 I5, 344
Dewars Pool WA 250 H6
Dharug National Park NSW 77 M1, 83 A13, 99 K5, 44, 64
Dhurringie Vic. 166 I8
Diamantina Lakes Qld 321 F3
Diamond Creek Vic. 149 P1
Diamond Tree WA 248 G9
Diamond Valley Qld 307 C11, 313 J11
Dianas Bath Qld 314 G5
Dianella WA 245 J8
Diapur Vic. 164 D6
Dickie Beach Qld 307 I12, 313 M12
Dickson ACT 107 O13, 109 M2
Dicks Tableland Eungella Nat. Park Qld 331 C10
Didillibah Qld 307 F8, 313 L10
Didleum Plains Tas. 361 N6
Digby Vic. 170 E5
Diggers Rest Vic. 159 J10, 172 F4
Diggora Vic. 166 E6
Dilkoon NSW 95 P5
Dilling WA 251 N11
Dilpura NSW 163 P9
Dilston Tas. 363 E7
Dimboola Vic. 164 G7, 127, 131
Dimbulah Qld 324 E4, 326 H12, 282, 288, 295
Dingabledinga SA 198 H5
Dingee Vic. 166 C6
Dingo Qld 323 L3
Dingup WA 248 G8, 224
Dingwall Vic. 165 Q2, 166 A2
Dinninup WA 248 I6
Dinoga NSW 95 J6
Dinyarrak Vic. 164 B6, 203 R13, 204 I4
Direk SA 196 G8
Dirranbandi Qld 94 D1, 323 J12, 289
Discovery Bay Coastal Park Vic. 170 C8
Dixie Vic. 171 M9
Dixons Creek Vic. 154 H7, 159 Q10, 160 C10, 173 J4, 118
Djerriwarrah Reservoir Vic. 158 H9, 172 E4
Dobbyn Qld 327 D7
Dobie Vic. 165 M13, 171 M2
Dobroyd Point NSW 73 J4
Docker Vic. 167 O7
Docker River NT 270 A10, 237
Doctors Flat Vic. 168 F13, 174 F4
Dodges Ferry Tas. 357 L7, 359 O7, 351
Dolls Point NSW 73 K13
Dolphin Qld 319 J10
Donald Vic. 165 L7, 127
Donbakup WA 248 G10
Doncaster Vic. 149 O7
Dongara WA 252 B7, 256 D7, 218, 223, 224
Dongolocking WA 249 N3
Donnelly River Mill WA 248 F8
Donnybrook Qld 315 L3, 286
Donnybrook Vic. 159 M9, 172 G3
Donnybrook WA 248 F5, 256 E12, 218
Donors Hill Qld 327 E5
Donovans Landing SA 204 I12
Donvale Vic. 149 Q7
Dooboobetic Vic. 165 M7
Doodenanning WA 251 K8
Doodlakine WA 251 N7
Dooen Vic. 164 I9
Dookie Vic. 167 K6
Doomadgee Mission Qld 327 B3
Doomben Qld 309 K12, 275
Doonan Qld 307 F3, 313 K7
Doondoon NSW 317 O13
Doonside NSW 77 L7
Dooralong NSW 83 D10
Dopewarra Vic. 164 D10
Dora Creek NSW 83 F8
Doreen NSW 94 G6
Doreen Vic. 159 N10
Dornock WA 249 Q1, 251 Q13
Dorodong Vic. 170 C2
Dorrien SA 197 L4, 208 F4
Dorrigo NSW 95 O7, 48, 41
Dorrigo National Park NSW 86 C7, 48
Dorrington Qld 308 F12
Dorset Vale SA 198 H2
Double Bay NSW 67 N7, 73 O4, 37
Doubleview WA 244 D8
Douglas Vic. 164 F2
Douglas Park NSW 91 L1
Douglas River Tas. 361 R10
Dover Tas. 359 L10, 344, 340
Dover Heights NSW 73 R3
Doveton Vic. 150 H2

Dowerin WA 251 K5, 256 F9
Dowlingville SA 200 F13, 202 G4
Downer ACT 107 O12, 109 M1
Downsfield Qld 312 G1
Downside NSW 98 B10
Doyalson NSW 83 F10, 99 L5
Drake NSW 95 N3
Dreeite Vic. 171 P8
Drik Drik Vic. 170 D7
Drillham Qld 323 L9
Dripstone NSW 98 F3
Dromana Vic. 152 H7, 154 F13, 172 G9, 139
Dromedary Tas. 356 H5, 359 L6
Dropmore Vic. 159 R1, 160 C1, 167 J11, 144
Drouin Vic. 173 L8, 127
Drumborg Vic. 170 F7
Drumcondra Vic. 156 E7
Drummartin Vic. 166 D7
Drummond Vic. 154 B5, 158 F5, 166 D13, 172 D1
Drummoyne NSW 73 J3
Drung Drung Vic. 164 I9
Dry Creek Vic. 167 L11
Drysdale Vic. 155 H7, 172 E8, 127
Drysdale River National Park WA 255 P2
Duaringa Qld 323 L4, 291
Dubbo NSW 94 E13, 98 E1, 48, 59
Dubelling WA 251 L9
Dublin SA 196 D4, 200 H13, 202 H4
Duchess Qld 327 D10
Duckenfield NSW 83 G3
Duckmaloi NSW 76 A8
Dudawa WA 252 E8
Duddo Vic. 162 C10
Dudinin WA 249 N1, 251 N13
Dudley NSW 83 H6
Dudley Vic. 173 J11
Duff Creek SA 207 K5
Duffholme Vic. 164 F9
Duffield NT 271 L12
Duffy ACT 108 B12, 110 B1
Duffys Forest NSW 71 K2
Dugandan Qld 316 G6
Duggan WA 249 O3
Dukin WA 251 L3
Dulacca Qld 323 L9
Dulbolla Qld 317 J9
Dullah NSW 97 P9, 98 A9
Dulong Qld 307 C8, 313 J10
Dululu Qld 323 M4
Dulwich Hill NSW 73 J7
Dumbalk Vic. 173 M10
Dumberning WA 249 K2
Dumbleyung WA 249 N4, 256 G11, 218
Dum Dum NSW 317 O11
Dumosa Vic. 96 G13, 165 N3
Dunach Vic. 165 P13, 166 A13, 171 Q1, 172 A1
Dunalley Tas. 357 N7, 359 O7, 344
Dunbible NSW 317 P11
Duncan WA 250 H12
Duncraig WA 244 D3
Dundas NSW 70 D12, 72 D1
Dundas Qld 314 F7
Dundas Valley NSW 70 E11
Dundee NSW 95 M5
Dundonnell Vic. 171 M6
Dundubara Qld 336 H6, 285
Dundurrabin NSW 95 O7
Dunedoo NSW 94 G12
Dungay NSW 317 O10
Dungog NSW 99 L2, 48
Dungowan NSW 95 K10
Dunheved NSW 77 K7
Dunkeld NSW 98 G5
Dunkeld Vic. 170 I4, 127, 126
Dunk Island Qld 324 G5, 333, 334, 302, 284, 296, 304
Dunluce Vic. 165 P10
Dunmarra NT 266 I13, 268 I3, 237
Dunmore NSW 91 O8, 97 R3, 98 C3
Dunmore Vic. 170 H8
Dunneworthy Vic. 165 M12, 171 M1
Dunns Creek NSW 83 G1
Dunnstown Vic. 158 B10, 171 R4, 172 B4
Dunolly Vic. 165 P10, 166 A10, 127
Dunrobin Tas. 356 C1
Dunrobin Vic. 170 D4
Dunsborough WA 248 C5, 218
Duntroon ACT 109 P8
Dunwich Qld 315 P10, 301
Dural NSW 70 B4
Duranbah NSW 317 Q10
Duranillin WA 249 J5
Durdidwarrah Vic. 155 D2, 158 D13, 172 C5
Durham Downs Qld 321 H9
Durham Lead Vic. 158 A11, 171 Q4, 172 A4
Durham Ox Vic. 165 Q5, 166 B5
Durong Qld 323 N8
Durran Durra NSW 98 H11, 100 F6
Durras NSW 100 G7
Durren Durren NSW 83 E10
Durrie Qld 321 E6
Durrumbul NSW 317 P13
Durundur Qld 314 H2

Dutson Vic. 174 C10
Dutton SA 197 N2, 201 K13, 203 K4
Dutton Park Qld 310 I4
Duverney Vic. 171 P7
Dwarda WA 248 I1, 250 I13
Dwellingup WA 250 G12, 256 F11, **218, 213, 226**
Dwyers NSW 93 N7
Dyliabing WA 249 N5
Dynnyrne Tas. 355 D12
Dysart Qld 323 J2, **289**
Dysart Tas. 356 H2, 359 M5

E

Eagle Bay WA 248 C5
Eagleby Qld 315 N13, 317 N1
Eagle Farm Qld 309 L12, **275, 277**
Eaglehawk Vic. 166 C9
Eaglehawk Neck Tas. 357 P9, 359 P8, 368 H2, **344, 340**
Eagle Heights Qld 317 N4
Eagle Junction Qld 309 J11
Eagle Point Vic. 174 E8, **121**
Earlston Vic. 167 K8
Earlwood NSW 73 J9
Eastbrook WA 248 G9
Eastern Creek NSW 77 L7
Eastern View Vic. 155 B12, 171 R10, 172 B10
East Hills NSW 72 C12
Eastlakes NSW 73 N8
East Melbourne Vic. 146 H6, **117**
East Perth WA 242 G4, 245 J12
East Point NT 264 G11
Eastwood NSW 70 G10
Eastwood SA 194 H10
Eaton WA 248 E4
Eatonsville NSW 95 P5
Eba SA 201 M11, 203 M2
Ebden Vic. 167 R5, 168 B5
Ebenezer NSW 77 L4, **64**
Ebenezer Qld 314 F13
Eberys Vic. 158 B4
Ebor NSW 95 N7
Eccleston NSW 95 L13, 99 L2
Echuca Vic. 97 K13, 166 F5, **127, 141**
Echunga SA 199 J2, **180**
Ecklin Vic. 171 M9
Edah WA 253 K2
Eddington Vic. 165 Q10, 166 A10
Eden NSW 100 F11, 175 P3, **48, 61**
Eden Hill WA 245 N7, 259 B10
Edenhope Vic. 164 C12, **127**
Eden Park Vic. 159 N8
Eden Valley SA 197 N7, 203 K5
Edgecliff NSW 67 L8, 73 O4
Edgecombe Vic. 158 G4, 166 E12, 172 E1
Edgeroi NSW 94 H6
Edgeworth NSW 83 G5
Edi Vic. 167 O8, **143**
Edillilie SA 205 E11
Edith NSW 76 A9, 98 H6, 100 G1
Edithburgh SA 202 F7, 205 I13, **184**
Edith Creek Tas. 360 C4
Edith River NT 266 G8
Edithvale Vic. 151 K7, 172 H7
Edlands NSW 95 N11
Edmonton Qld 335 F9, **286**
Edward River Mission Qld 326 B8, **300**
Edwards Creek SA 207 K5
Eerwah Vale Qld 313 J7
Eganstown Vic. 158 C6
Egelabra NSW 93 R11, 94 C11
Eglinford NSW 83 C6
Eidsvold Qld 323 N7, **289**
Eight Mile Plains Qld 311 M10
Eildon Vic. 160 H4, 167 L13, 173 L1, **128, 144**
Eildon State Park Vic. 167 M13
Eimeo Qld 331 H11
Einasleigh Qld 324 D6
Ejanding WA 251 K4
Ekibin Qld 310 I6
Elabbin WA 251 O5
Elaroo Qld 325 K10, 331 D8
Elaine Vic. 155 B2, 158 C12, 171 R5, 172 B5
Elanora NSW 71 O3
Elanora Heights NSW 79 R6
Elbow Hill SA 200 B10, 202 B1, 205 G10
Elcho Island NT 267 N3
Elcombe NSW 94 I5
Elderslie NSW 83 B1
Elderslie Tas. 356 G3, 359 L5
Eldon Tas. 357 J1, 359 N4
Eldorado Vic. 167 O6, **143**
Eleebana NSW 83 G6
Elgin WA 248 E5
Elgin Vale Qld 312 A6
Elimbah Qld 315 J3
Elingamite Vic. 171 M9
Elizabeth SA 195 G1, 196 H8, 202 I5, **184**
Elizabeth Bay NSW 73 O4, 83 G10, **37**
Elizabeth Town Tas. 361 J7
Ellalong NSW 83 C6
Ellam Vic. 164 G4

Elleker WA 249 N13
Ellenborough NSW 95 N11
Ellendale Tas. 356 C3, 359 J5
Ellen Grove Qld 310 D13
Ellerslie Vic. 171 K8
Ellerston NSW 95 K12
Ellery Gorge NT 262 G6
Elliminyt Vic. 171 P9
Ellinbank Vic. 173 L8
Ellingerrin Vic. 155 A7
Elliott NT 269 J5, **237**
Elliott Tas. 360 F5
Elliot Price Conservation Park SA 207 M6
Elliston SA 205 D9
Elmhurst Vic. 165 N12, 171 N1
Elmore Vic. 166 E7
Elong Elong NSW 94 F12
Elphin WA 250 I3
Elphinstone Vic. 154 B4, 158 F3, 166 D12
Elsinore NSW 93 K11
Elsmore NSW 95 L5
Elsternwick Vic. 150 C12
Eltham NSW 95 Q2
Eltham Vic. 149 P3, 172 H5, **118-19**
Elwomple SA 203 M8
Embleton WA 245 L8, 259 A11
Emerald Qld 323 J3, **289-90, 291**
Emerald Vic. 147 H12, **128, 130**
Emerald Hill NSW 94 I9
Emerald Lake Vic. 147 I12, **128, 130**
Emily Gap NT 263 N6
Emmaville NSW 95 L4
Emmet Qld 322 E5
Empire Bay NSW 77 Q2, 78 E1
Empire Vale NSW 95 Q3
Emu Vic. 165 O9
Emu Bay SA 202 E10
Emu Downs SA 201 J10, 203 J1
Emu Flat Vic. 159 J3, 166 F12
Emu Hill WA 251 P9
Emu Park Qld 323 N3, **290, 300, 304**
Emu Plains NSW 77 J7
Emu Point WA 249 N13
Emu Vale Qld 316 B9
Eneabba WA 252 D10, 256 E7
Enfield NSW 72 H6
Enfield SA 195 E6, 196 G10
Enfield Vic. 171 Q5, 172 A5
Engadine NSW 77 N11
Englefield Vic. 170 G2
Enmore NSW 73 L6, 95 M8
Enngonia NSW 93 M4, 322 G13
Enoch Point Vic. 173 M2
Enoggera Qld 308 G11
Ensay Vic. 174 F3
Enterprise Qld 312 H2
Eppalock Vic. 166 E10
Epping NSW 70 F9
Epping Vic. 159 M10, 172 G4
Epping Forest Tas. 361 M9
Epsom Vic. 154 B1, 166 D9, **122**
Eradu WA 252 C4
Eraring NSW 83 F8
Eribung NSW 98 C3
Erica Vic. 173 O6, **143**
Erigolia NSW 97 N6
Erikin WA 251 N8
Erina NSW 77 R1
Erith SA 200 H12, 202 H3
Ermington NSW 70 E13, 72 E1
Ernabella SA 270 G13
Eromanga Qld 322 C9, **295**
Erriba Tas. 360 H7
Errinundra Vic. 175 L5
Erskine Park NSW 77 K8
Erskineville NSW 73 M6
Esk Qld 314 D6, 323 P10, **290, 280**
Eskdale Vic. 168 C7
Esk Upper Tas. 361 O7
Esmond Vic. 167 N4
Esperance WA 257 K12, **218-19, 221**
Essendon Vic. 148 E5
Eton Qld 325 K11, 331 G13
Ettalong NSW 77 Q2, 78 F3
Ettamogah Vic. 167 R4, 168 B4
Ettrick NSW 95 P2
Euabalong NSW 97 O4
Euchareena NSW 98 F4
Eucla WA 206 A11, 257 Q9, **219**
Eucumbene NSW 100 C8, 104 G5
Eudlo Qld 307 D10, 313 K11
Eudunda SA 201 K12, 203 K3, **185**
Eugowra NSW 98 D5, **48**
Eujinyn WA 251 O8
Eulama Qld 313 J3
Eulin WA 249 J6
Eulo Qld 322 F11, **289**
Eumundi Qld 307 D3, 313 K7
Eumungerie NSW 94 E12
Eungai Creek NSW 95 P9
Eungella NSW 317 O11, 325 K11, 331 C11
Eurack Vic. 171 Q8, 172 A8
Eurambeen Vic. 171 N2

Eureka Vic. 157 H6
Eureka Stockade Vic. 158 A9, **121, 122**
Eurelia SA 200 I4
Euroa Vic. 154 I1, 167 J9, **128, 144**
Eurobin Vic. 167 Q9, 168 A9
Eurobodalla NSW 100 F8, **56**
Euroka NSW 80 A6,
Euroli NSW 97 L9
Eurongilly NSW 97 R10, 98 C10, 100 A5
Euston NSW 96 F9, 163 K5
Evandale Tas. 361 M8, 363 G11, **345, 346, 347**
Evansford Vic. 165 P13, 171 P1
Evans Head NSW 95 Q4, **48**
Evatt ACT 106 H7
Everard Central SA 200 H11, 202 H2
Eversley Vic. 165 M12, 171 N1
Everton Vic. 167 P7, 176 I11
Everton Park Qld 308 G9
Ewaninga NT 263 N8, 271 J8
Ewens Ponds SA 170 A7, 204 H2
Ewlyamartup WA 249 N6
Exeter NSW 90 I9, 100 G4
Exeter Tas. 361 L6, 363 D7, **345**
Exford Vic. 155 H1, 158 H12, 172 E5
Exmouth WA 254 C10, **226**
Exton Tas. 361 J8, 363 A11
Eyre Peninsula SA 205, **189**

F

Fadden ACT 111 J9
Fairfield Qld 310 I5
Fairfield Vic. 149 J7
Fairhaven Vic. 172 C10
Fairholme NSW 97 Q4, 98 A4
Fairley Vic. 163 Q13, 165 Q2, 166 A1
Fairlight NSW 71 P10
Fairney View Qld 314 G10
Fairview Vic. 165 N5
Fairview National Park SA 204 G6
Fairy Dell Vic. 166 F6
Fairy Hill NSW 95 P2
Fairy Meadow NSW 89 D6, 91 P4
Falls Creek NSW 99 I10, 100 H5
Falls Creek Vic. 168 C10, 169 G4, 174 C1, **135**
Falmouth Tas. 361 R8, **350**
Fannie Bay NT 265 K9, **232**
Faraday Vic. 158 E2, 166 D11
Farina SA 207 N8
Farleigh Qld 325 L10, 331 H11
Farley NSW 83 E3
Farmeadow NSW 91 N11
Farnborough Qld 323 N3
Farnham NSW 98 G3
Farrar WA 249 K6
Farrell Flat SA 201 J10, 203 J1
Farrer ACT 110 I6
Fassifern NSW 83 G6
Fassifern Valley Qld 316 F5
Fassifern Valley National Park Qld 316 F5, **283**
Faulconbridge NSW 76 H7, 80 H4
Fawcett Vic. 160 F3, 167 K12
Fawkner Vic. 148 H3
Federal Qld 307 A1, 312 I6
Feilton Tas. 356 E6
Fennell Bay NSW 83 G7
Fentonbury Tas. 356 C3, 359 K5
Fentons Creek Vic. 165 O8
Fenwick Vic. 155 G8
Ferguson Vic. 171 P11
Fergusson River NT 266 G8
Fernbank Vic. 174 C8
Ferndale NSW 97 O12
Ferndale WA 247 M6
Fernhill NSW 89 D4
Fern Hill Vic. 158 F6
Fernihurst Vic. 165 Q5, 166 A5
Fernshaw Vic. 160 E10, 173 K4
Ferntree Tas. 356 H8, 359 M7
Ferntree Gully Vic. 147 A9, **130**
Ferntree Gully National Park Vic. 147 C9, 172 I6, **125, 130**
Fernvale Qld 314 G10, 317 P11
Ferny Creek Vic. 147 C9
Ferny Glen Qld 317 M7
Ferny Grove Qld 308 C9
Fields Find WA 253 L6
Fiery Flat Vic. 165 Q7, 166 A7
Fifield NSW 97 Q3, 98 B3
Fig Tree NSW 71 J13, 73 J2, 89 A11, 91 O5
Fig Tree Pocket Qld 310 D6, **277**
Finch Hatton Qld 235 K11, 331 D11, **295**
Fine Flower Creek NSW 95 O4
Fingal Tas. 361 P9, **345, 346**
Fingal Head NSW 317 R9
Finke NT 271 K12
Finke Gorge National Park NT 262 E9, **237, 238**
Finley NSW 97 M12, 167 J1, **48**
Finniss SA 199 J7, 203 J9
Fish Creek Vic. 173 M12
Fisher ACT 110 D4
Fisher SA 206 D9
Fisherman Islands Qld 309 Q8

Fishermans Bend Vic. 148 E10
Fishermans Pocket Qld 312 F2
Fish Point Vic. 163 P11
Fiskville Vic. 158 E11
Fitzgerald Tas. 356 B5, 359 J6
Fitzgerald River National Park WA 256 I12, 220, 221, 227
Fitzroy SA 194 D1
Fitzroy Crossing WA 255 O6, 219, 221
Fitzroy Falls NSW 91 K9, 99 I9, 100 H4
Fitzroy Vic. 148 H7

Five Dock NSW 72 I4
Five Ways Vic. 153 Q1
Flagpole Hill Vic. 160 B6
Flagstaff Hill SA 208 I7
Flat Rocks WA 249 L7
Flaxley SA 199 J3
Flaxton Qld 307 C8, 313 J10, 295
Flemington NSW 72 F5
Flemington Vic. 148 E7
Fleurieu Peninsula SA 198 D10, 202 H9, 180, 191
Flinders Qld 316 H2
Flinders Vic. 152 I12, 172 G10, 139, 119
Flinders Bay WA 248 C9
Flinders Chase National Park SA 202 B11, 183, 185, 186
Flinders Island Tas. 358 A4, 347
Flinders Peak Vic. 155 F4
Flinders Ranges National Park SA 207 O10, 182, 192
Flinton Qld 323 L11
Flodden Hills Qld 321 H5
Floreat Park WA 244 E11
Florey ACT 106 E9
Florida NSW 93 N11
Florida WA 250 E13
Florida Gardens Qld 318 G10
Florieton SA 201 L10, 203 L1
Flowerdale Tas. 360 F4
Flowerdale Vic. 154 H6, 159 P6, 160 B6, 166 I13
Flowery Gully Tas. 361 K6, 363 B6
Flying Fox Qld 317 M7
Flynn ACT 106 E7
Flynn Vic. 173 P8
Flynns Beach NSW 85 H8
Flynns Creek Vic. 173 P8
Flynns Grave NT 263 M5
Footscray Vic. 148 E8
Forbes NSW 97 R5, 98 C5, 48, 59

Forcett Tas. 357 L6, 359 O6
Fords SA 197 K2
Fords Bridge NSW 93 L5
Forest Tas. 360 D3
Forester Tas. 361 O5
Forest Glen Qld 307 E9, 313 K10
Forest Grove WA 248 C8
Forest Hill Qld 314 C12
Forest Hill Vic. 149 Q10
Forest Hill WA 249 L11
Forestier Peninsula Tas. 357 P8, 359 P7
Forest Range SA 197 J11
Forestville NSW 71 M8
Forge Creek Vic. 174 E8
Forrest ACT 109 K10
Forrest Vic. 171 Q10, 172 A10
Forrest WA 257 P8
Forresters Beach NSW 83 F13, 49
Forrestfield WA 247 R3
Forreston SA 197 K9
Forrest River Aboriginal Reserve WA 255 Q2
Forsayth Qld 324 C6
Forster NSW 95 N13, 99 N2, 48
Forster SA 203 M5
Foster Vic. 173 N11, 128
Fosterville Vic. 166 D9
Fortitude Valley Qld 306 G1, 310 I1
Fort Grey NSW 321 G13
Forth Tas. 360 H6, 344
Fountain Head NT 266 F6
Foxdale Qld 331 C5
Fox Ground NSW 91 O9
Foxhow Vic. 171 O7
Fox Valley NSW 70 G6
Framlingham Vic. 171 K8
Frampton NSW 98 C10, 100 B4
Frances SA 164 B9, 204 I6
Frankford Tas. 361 K7, 363 A8
Frankland WA 249 K9, 256 G13, 216
Franklin Tas. 356 F10, 359 L8, 345, 341
Franklinford Vic. 158 C5, 165 R13, 166 B13, 172 C1
Frankston Vic. 151 P7, 153 L1, 172 H8, 139, 119
Frankton SA 197 O1, 201 K12, 203 K3
Fraser ACT 106 E5
Fraser Island Qld 323 Q6, 336, 284, 292, 296
Fraser National Park Vic. 160 G3, 167 L12, 120
Frazerview Qld 316 E5
Frederickton NSW 95 P9
Freeburgh Vic. 167 R9, 168 B9
Freeling SA 197 J4, 201 J13, 203 J4
Freemans Reach NSW 77 K4
Freemans Waterholes NSW 83 E7
Freestone Upper Qld 316 A7

Fremantle WA 246 C8, 250 F9, 256 E10, 219-20, 211, 212
Frenches WA 250 I7
French Island Vic. 153 Q7, 172 I9, 139
Frenchmans Vic. 165 N11
Frenchmans Cap Nat. Park Tas. 358 F3, 360 F13
Frenchs Forest NSW 71 M7
Freshwater Creek Vic. 155 E9, 172 D8
Freycinet National Park Tas. 359 R2, 361 R13, 342, 344
Freycinet Peninsula Tas. 361 R13
Frogmore NSW 98 F8, 100 D3
Fryerstown Vic. 158 E3, 124
Fulham Vic. 173 R7, 174 B10
Fulham Vale Qld 314 D4
Fullerton NSW 98 H8, 100 F2
Fumina Vic. 173 M6
Furner SA 204 F9
Furracabad NSW 95 L5
Fyans Creek Vic. 165 J12
Fyansford Vic. 155 E7, 156 A8, 128
Fyshwick ACT 109 Q12

G

Gabalong WA 250 H2
Gabbin WA 251 M3
Gabo Island Vic. 175 P6, 134
Gadara NSW 98 D11, 100 B6
Gaffneys Creek Vic. 173 N3
Gailes Qld 310 C12
Galah Vic. 162 H9
Galaquil Vic. 164 I4
Galga SA 203 N5
Galiwinku NT 267 N3, 237
Gallanan Qld 314 D6
Gallangowan Qld 312 C6
Galong NSW 98 E9, 100 C4
Galore NSW 97 P10
Galston NSW 70 C2
Galway Downs Qld 321 I5
Gama Vic. 163 J12
Gammon Ranges National Park SA 207 O9, 185
Gannawarra Vic. 166 C2
Gap NSW 95 J10
Gapsted Vic. 167 P8
Garah NSW 94 G3, 323 L13
Garden Island Creek Tas. 356 G13, 359 L9
Gardner Plateau WA 255 O3
Gardners Bay Tas. 356 G12, 359 L9
Garema NSW 98 C5
Garfield Vic. 173 K7, 127
Gargett Qld 331 E12
Garibaldi Vic. 158 A12, 171 R4, 172 B5
Garie NSW 77 O13, 91 Q1, 99 K8, 100 I2
Garland NSW 98 F6, 100 D1
Garra NSW 98 E4
Garran ACT 108 I13, 111 J1
Garrawilla NSW 94 G9
Garvoc Vic. 171 L9
Gascoyne Junction WA 256 D2
Gateshead NSW 83 H6
Gatton Qld 314 B11, 323 P10, 290
Gatum Vic. 170 G2
Gawler SA 196 I6, 203 J5, 184
Gawler River SA 196 H6
Gayndah Qld 323 O7, 290
Gaythorne Qld 308 F11
Gazette Vic. 170 I6
Geebung Vic. 168 I13, 174 H3
Geehi NSW 100 B9, 104 B9, 168 H7
Geelong Vic. 154 C11, 155 E7, 156, 172 D8, 128
Geeralying WA 249 K2
Geeveston Tas. 356 E11, 359 K9, 345
Geikie Gorge National Park WA 255 O6, 219, 221
Geilston Bay Tas. 355 G4
Gelantipy Vic. 168 I13, 174 H3
Gellibrand Vic. 171 P10
Gelliondale Vic. 173 P11
Gembrook Vic. 154 I10, 173 J6
Gemmells SA 199 K4
Gemstones Qld 321 I2
Genga WA 253 N1
Genoa Vic. 100 E12, 175 N5, 135
Georges Creek Vic. 168 C5
Georges Hall NSW 72 B9
Georges Heights NSW 71 P12, 73 P1
Georges Plains NSW 98 G5
Georgetown Qld 324 C6, 290
Georgetown SA 200 H8
George Town Tas. 361 K5, 363 B4, 345, 346
Georgica NSW 95 Q2
Gerangamete Vic. 171 Q10, 172 A10
Gerang Gerung Vic. 164 F7
Geranium SA 203 O9
Geranium Plains SA 201 K11, 203 K2
Gerogery NSW 97 P12, 167 R3, 168 B3
Gerringong NSW 91 O10, 99 J9, 100 I4, 48
Gerroa NSW 91 O10
Geurie NSW 94 E13, 98 E2
Gheerulla Qld 312 H8
Gheringap Vic. 155 D6, 172 C7

Ghin Ghin Vic. 159 Q3, 160 B3, 166 I12
Gibraltar Range National Park NSW 95 N4, 49
Gibson WA 257 K11
Gibson Desert WA 255 L11, 257 O1
Gidginbung NSW 97 Q8, 98 B8, 100 A3
Giffard Vic. 173 R10, 174 B12
Gilberton Vic. 194 G2
Gilbert River Qld 324 B5, 327 I4
Gilderoy Vic. 160 F13, 173 K6
Gildora Qld 312 G4
Giles Corner SA 200 I12, 202 I3
Gilgai NSW 95 K5
Gilgandra NSW 94 E11, 48
Gilgooma NSW 94 E8
Gilgunnia NSW 93 M13, 97 M2
Gilliat Qld 327 G8
Gillieston Vic. 166 H6
Gillingal Vic. 174 H4
Gillingarra WA 250 G3
Gilmore ACT 111 L11
Gilmore NSW 98 D11, 100 B6, 62
Gilpeppee Qld 321 G7
Gilston Qld 317 O6
Gindie Qld 323 J4
Gin Gin NSW 93 R12, 94 D12
Gin Gin Qld 323 O6, 290
Gingin WA 250 F6, 256 E9, 220
Gingkin NSW 76 A11, 98 H7, 100 G1
Gippsland Lakes Park Vic. 174 E10, 133
Gipsy Point Vic. 100 F12, 175 O5, 135
Giralang ACT 107 J7
Girgarre Vic. 166 G7
Girilambone NSW 93 P10, 94 A9
Girral NSW 97 P6
Girraween National Park Qld 323 O12, 285
Girrawheen WA 244 G4
Giru Qld 324 I8
Gisborne Vic. 154 D7, 158 I8, 172 E3, 128
Gladesville NSW 70 I13, 71 J13, 72 I2, 73 J2
Gladfield Qld 316 A6
Gladfield Vic. 165 Q4, 166 B4
Gladstone Qld 323 N4, 328, 290-2, 283, 284, 286, 291
Gladstone SA 200 H7, 184
Gladstone Tas. 361 Q4, 345
Gladysdale Vic. 160 F13, 173 K5
Glamis NSW 95 M11
Glamorgan Vale Qld 314 F10
Glasshouse Mountains Qld 315 K1, 274, 280, 285, 286, 288, 295, 297
Glastonbury Qld 312 E3
Glaziers Bay Tas. 356 F11
Glebe NSW 73 L5, 37
Glebe Tas. 355 E8
Glenaire Vic. 171 O12
Glenaladale Vic. 174 C7
Glenaladale National Park Vic. 174 D7, 121, 133
Glenalbyn Vic. 165 P7, 166 A7
Glen Alice NSW 98 I4
Glenapp Qld 317 J10
Glenariff NSW 93 O8
Glen Aplin Qld 95 M2
Glenaroua Vic. 159 L3, 166 G12
Glenbrae Vic. 171 P2
Glenbrook NSW 76 I8, 53
Glenburn Vic. 154 H6, 159 Q7, 160 C7, 173 J2
Glenburnie SA 170 B6, 204 H11
Glencairn Vic. 173 P3
Glencoe NSW 95 M6
Glencoe SA 204 G11
Glen Creek Vic. 167 R7, 168 B7
Glendalough WA 244 F10
Glen Davis NSW 98 I4, 59
Glendevie Tas. 356 F13, 359 L9
Glendinning Vic. 170 G2
Glendon NSW 83 B1
Glendon Brook NSW 99 K2
Gleneagle Qld 317 K4
Glen Eagle WA 250 G10
Glenelg SA 195 B11, 196 F12, 179
Glen Elgin NSW 95 N5
Glenelg National Park Vic. 170 D8
Glen Esk Qld 314 E6
Glenfern Qld 314 F2
Glen Fern Tas. 356 F6, 359 L6
Glenfield NSW 77 M10
Glenfield WA 252 A4
Glenfyne Vic. 171 M10
Glengarrie NSW 317 P9
Glengarry Tas. 361 K7, 363 B8
Glengarry Vic. 173 P8
Glen Geddes Qld 323 M2
Glengower Vic. 158 A5, 165 Q13, 166 A13, 171 Q1, 172 A1
Glengyle Qld 321 D5
Glenhaven NSW 70 A5, 77 M6
Glen Helen NT 270 H8, 237
Glen Helen Gorge NT 262 D5, 237
Glenhope Vic. 166 E12
Glenhuntly Vic. 149 L13, 150 C11
Glen Huon Tas. 356 E9, 359 K8, 345
Glen Innes NSW 95 M5, 49, 51
Glen Iris Vic. 149 L11, 150 A9

Glenisla Vic. 164 H13, 170 I1
Glenlee Vic. 164 F6
Glenlofty Vic. 165 N12
Glenloth Vic. 165 N5
Glenluce Vic. 158 E4, 166 C12, 172 C1
Glenlusk Tas. 356 H6, 359 M6
Glenlyon Qld 95 L2
Glenlyon Vic. 158 E5, 166 C13, 172 C1
Glenmaggie Vic. 173 Q6, 134, 140
Glenmaggie Reservoir Vic. 173 Q6, 174 A8
Glenmore NSW 76 I12
Glenmore Vic. 155 F11, 158 F11
Glenmorgan Qld 323 L10
Glen Oak NSW 83 G1
Glenora Tas. 356 E4, 359 K6
Glenoran WA 248 G8
Glenorchy Tas. 356 I6, 359 M7, 339
Glenorchy Vic. 165 K10
Glenore Tas. 363 C11
Glenore Grove Qld 314 D11
Glenorie NSW 77 M4
Glenormiston Qld 321 B2
Glen Osmond SA 195 F10
Glen Park Vic. 149 O2, 158 B9
Glenpatrick Vic. 165 N12
Glenquarry NSW 91 K7
Glenreagh NSW 95 P6
Glenrowan Vic. 167 N7, 176 C13, 142-3
Glenroy SA 164 A13, 170 A1, 204 H8
Glenroy Vic. 148 E3
Glenshee Vic. 165 N12
Glenthompson Vic. 171 K4
Glenvale Vic. 159 N8
Glen Valley Vic. 168 E10, 174 D1
Glenwarning NSW 317 N12
Glen Waverley Vic. 149 P13, 150 B4
Glen Wills Vic. 168 E10, 174 E1
Glenworth Valley NSW 77 O2
Glossodia NSW 77 K4, 64
Glossop SA 201 P12, 203 P3
Gloucester NSW 95 M12, 99 M1, 49
Gloucester Park WA 242 H5
Gnarming WA 251 P12
Gnar-Purt Vic. 171 O7
Gnarraloo WA 254 C13
Gnarraloo Bay WA 254 C13
Gnarwarre Vic. 155 C7
Gnotuk Vic. 171 N8
Gnowangerup WA 249 O7, 256 G12, 219
Goangra NSW 94 D6
Goat Island NSW 68 I13
Gobarralong NSW 98 D10, 100 B5
Gobongo Qld 312 A5
Gobur Vic. 160 E1, 167 K11
Gocup NSW 98 D10, 100 B5
Godfreys Creek NSW 98 E7, 100 C2
Gogango Qld 323 M4
Golconda Tas. 361 M5, 363 H5
Gold Coast Qld 318-19, 278-9, 289, 303
Golden Beach Qld 307 H12, 313 M12
Golden Beach Vic. 174 D11
Golden Grove SA 196 I9
Golden Point Vic. 158 E2
Golden Valley Tas. 361 J9
Goldsborough Vic. 165 P10
Goldsmith Tas. 359 M1, 361 M11
Goldsworthy WA 254 H8, 220
Golf Hill Vic. 155 C5
Gol Gol NSW 96 E8, 162 H2
Gollan NSW 94 F13, 98 F2
Golspie NSW 90 A5, 98 G8, 100 F3
Gomersal SA 197 K5, 208 B6
Gongolgon NSW 93 P7, 94 A7
Gonn Crossing Vic. 163 Q12
Good Hope NSW 98 E10, 100 D4
Goodilla NT 266 E6
Goodings Corner Qld 317 P6
Goodna Qld 310 B12
Goodnight NSW 163 N8
Goodooga NSW 93 Q3, 94 B3, 322 I13
Goodwood Tas. 355 B1
Goolgowi NSW 97 M7
Goolma NSW 94 F13, 98 F2
Goolmangar NSW 95 Q2
Gooloogong NSW 98 D6, 100 C1
Goolwa SA 198 I9, 203 J9, 184, 140, 180, 191
Goomalibee Vic. 167 L7
Goomalling WA 251 J5, 256 F9
Goomarin WA 251 P5
Goomboorian Qld 312 I1
Goomeri Qld 323 O8
Goomong Qld 312 H5
Goondah NSW 98 E9, 100 D4
Goondiwindi Qld 94 I1, 323 M12, 292
Goondooloo SA 203 N6
Goonellabah NSW 95 Q3
Goongerah Vic. 175 K4
Goon Nure Vic. 174 D9
Goonumbla NSW 97 R4, 98 D4
Goonyella Qld 325 J12, 295, 297
Gooram Vic. 167 K10, 128
Goorambat Vic. 167 L7
Goornong Vic. 166 E8

Gooroc Vic. 165 M7
Goovigen Qld 323 M4
Goowarra Qld 323 L3
Gorae Vic. 170 E9
Gordon NSW 71 J8
Gordon SA 200 G2
Gordon Tas. 356 H13, 359 M9, 345
Gordon Vic. 158 C10, 172 C4
Gordon Park Qld 308 I11
Gordon River Tas. 358 F5, 349, 352
Gordonvale Qld 324 G4, 335 G10, 292, 284, 286
Gore Hill NSW 68 D1, 71 L12
Gorge Rock WA 251 O11
Gormandale Vic. 173 P9
Gormanston Tas. 358 E1, 360 E11, 349
Gorokan NSW 83 F11
Goroke Vic. 164 D9, 128
Goschen Vic. 163 O12
Gosford NSW 77 Q1, 78 A2, 83 E13, 99 K5, 49, 39
Gosforth NSW 83 E2
Goshen Tas. 361 Q6
Gosnells WA 247 Q11
Gough Bay Vic. 167 M12, 173 M1
Goulburn NSW 90 C12, 98 G9, 100 F4, 49
Goulburn Island NT 266 I3, 237
Goulburn Weir Vic. 166 H9
Goulds Country Tas. 361 Q6
Gove Peninsula NT 267 P4, 240
Gowanford Vic. 163 M11
Gowangardie Vic. 167 K7
Gowar Vic. 165 R11, 166 C11
Gowrie ACT 110 I10
Gowrie Park Tas. 360 H7
Goyura Vic. 164 I2
Graball WA 251 Q9
Grabben Gullen NSW 98 G8, 100 E3
Gracefield WA 249 L8
Gracetown WA 248 B6
Graceville Qld 310 F6
Gradgery NSW 93 R10, 94 C9
Gradule Qld 94 G1, 323 K12
Grafton NSW 95 P5, 49
Graham NSW 98 E7, 100 D2
Graham Range National Park Qld 335 I13
Grahamstown NSW 98 C11, 100 B6
Grahamvale Vic. 167 J6
Graman NSW 95 K4
Grampians Mountains Vic. 165 J13, 171 J1, 142, 126, 129, 131
Grandchester Qld 314 D13
Grange Qld 308 H11
Grange SA 195 A8, 196 F11, 179
Granite Vic. 159 O3, 160 A3, 166 H12
Granite Flat Vic. 168 D8
Granite Island SA 198 H10, 180 191
Grantham Qld 314 A11
Granton Tas. 356 H5, 359 M6, 342
Grantville Vic. 173 J10
Granville NSW 72 C3
Granville Harbour Tas. 360 C10
Granya Vic. 168 B5
Grassdale Vic. 170 F5
Grass Flat Vic. 164 F9
Grassmere Vic. 171 K9
Grass Valley WA 251 J7
Gravelly Beach Tas. 363 D7
Gravesend NSW 94 I5
Grawin NSW 93 Q5, 94 C4, 62
Gray Tas. 361 Q9
Graylands WA 244 D13, 246 D2
Grays Point NSW 77 O11
Graytown Vic. 154 F2, 166 G10, 136
Great Australian Bight SA 206 B12
Great Keppel Island Qld 323 N3, 329, 286, 287, 300, 304
Great Lake Tas. 361 J10, 342, 344, 350, 351
Great Northern Vic. 167 O4
Great Ocean Road, Vic. 170 L11, 172 A12, 134
Great Palm Island Qld 324 H6
Great Sandy Desert WA 255 L8
Great Victoria Desert WA 257 N6
Great Western Vic. 165 L12, 120, 126
Greenacre NSW 72 F7
Greenbank NSW 317 K1
Greenbushes WA 248 G6, 256 E12, 218
Greendale NSW 77 J10
Greendale Qld. 312 L7
Greendale Vic. 158 F9, 172 D3
Greenethorpe NSW 98 D7, 100 C2
Greengrove NSW 77 O1, 83 B13
Green Gully Vic. 158 C3
Green Head WA 252 B11
Green Hill Vic. 158 G4
Green Hills SA 199 J3
Greenhills WA 251 J8
Green Island Qld 335 H2, 302, 286
Green Lake Vic. 163 L13, 164 I10, 165 L1
Greenmount Vic. 173 P11
Greenock SA 197 K4, 201 J13, 203 J4, 208 C2
Greenough WA 252 B5, 218
Green Pigeon NSW 317 L13
Green Point NSW 77 Q2, 78 C1
Greenridge Qld 312 H5

Greens Beach Tas. 361 K5, 363 A3, 341
Greensborough Vic. 149 M2
Greens Creek Vic. 165 L11
Greenslopes Qld 311 J5
Greenvale Vic. 159 L10
Green Valley WA 249 N12
Greenwald Vic. 170 D7
Greenways SA 204 F8
Greenwell Point NSW 91 O12, 99 J10, 100 H5
Greenwich NSW 68 E10, 71 L13, 73 L2
Greenwich Park NSW 90 E9
Greenwood WA 244 F3
Gredgwin Vic. 165 P4
Greg Greg NSW 100 B8
Gregors Creek Qld 314 D2
Gregory Downs Qld 327 C5, 286, 293
Gre Gre Vic. 165 M9
Greigs Flat NSW 100 F11
Grenfell NSW 98 D6, 100 B1, 49
Grenville Vic. 158 A12, 171 R5, 172 B5
Gresford NSW 99 L2
Greta NSW 83 D2
Greta Vic. 167 N8
Gretna Tas. 356 E4, 359 K5
Grevillia NSW 95 O1, 316 I12
Grey Peaks National Park Qld 335 G9
Griffin WA 248 G4
Griffith ACT 109 M12
Griffith NSW 97 N8, 49, 43
Grimwade WA 248 G6
Gringegalgona Vic. 170 G3
Gritjurk Vic. 170 F4
Grogan NSW 97 R8, 98 C8, 100 A3
Grong Grong NSW 97 O9
Groote Eylandt NT 267 P8
Grose Vale NSW 76 I5
Grose Wold NSW 76 I5
Grosvenor Qld 323 N7
Grove Tas. 356 G9, 359 L8
Grovedale Vic. 155 E8, 172 D8
Grove Farm WA 245 L11
Grove Hill NT 266 F6
Grovely Qld 308 E10
Gruyere Vic. 159 R12, 160 C12, 173 J5
Gubbata NSW 97 O6
Guichen Bay National Park SA 204 D8
Guilderton WA 250 E5, 220
Guildford NSW 72 B5
Guildford Tas. 360 F7
Guildford Vic. 154 A4, 158 D3, 166 C12, 124
Guildford WA 245 P8, 250 F8, 259 D11, 212
Gulargambone NSW 94 E10
Gular Rail NSW 94 E10
Gulf Country Qld 327, 292-3
Gulf Creek NSW 95 J6
Gulgong NSW 94 G13, 98 G2, 49-51
Gullewa WA 252 H4
Gulnare SA 200 H8
Gulpa NSW 97 K12
Gumble NSW 98 E4
Gumbowie SA 201 J6
Gum Creek SA 201 J9
Gumdale Qld 311 P4
Gumeracha SA 197 K10, 203 J6
Gum Lake NSW 96 G3
Gumlu Qld 324 I8
Gumly Gumly NSW 98 B10
Gunbar South NSW 97 L7
Gundagai NSW 97 R10, 98 C10, 100 B5, 51
Gundaring WA 249 L3
Gundaroo NSW 98 F10, 100 E5
Gunderman NSW 77 N2
Gundowring NSW 167 R7, 168 B7
Gundurimba South NSW 95 Q3
Gundy NSW 95 K12, 99 K1
Gunebang NSW 97 O4
Gungal NSW 94 I13, 98 I2
Gunnary NSW 98 E8, 100 D3
Gunnedah NSW 94 I9, 51
Gunner Vic. 162 F10
Gunnewin Qld 323 J7
Gunning NSW 98 F9, 100 E4, 51
Gunningbland NSW 98 C4
Gunning Grach NSW 100 D10
Gunns Plains Tas. 360 G6, 343, 348, 352
Gunpowder Creek Qld 327 C7
Gunyah Vic. 173 N10
Gunyarra Qld 331 D6
Gunyidi WA 252 G11
Gurley NSW 94 H5
Gurrai SA 203 P7
Gurrundah NSW 98 G9, 100 E4
Gutha WA 252 F6
Guthalungra Qld 325 J8
Guthega NSW 104 D8
Guy Fawkes National Park NSW 95 N6, 49
Guyra NSW 95 M7, 51
Guys Forest Vic. 168 F4
Gwabegar NSW 94 F8
Gwalia WA 257 J6, 223, 222, 225
Gwambygine WA 251 J9
Gwandalan NSW 83 G9

Gwandalan — Howqua 381

Gwandalan Tas. 357 M9, 359 O8, 368 D2
Gwelup WA 244 E6
Gwindinup WA 248 F5
Gwongorella National Park Qld 317 O8
Gwynneville NSW 89 D9
Gymbowen Vic. 164 E9
Gymea NSW 77 O11
Gympie Qld 312 G3, 323 P8, **292, 280**
Gypsum Vic. 162 I10

H

Haasts Bluff NT 270 G7
Haasts Bluff Aboriginal Res. NT 262 A7, 270 C8
Habana Qld 331 H11
Haberfield NSW 73 J5
Hackett ACT 107 Q13, 109 O1
Hackham SA 198 F3, 208 G11
Hackney SA 194 H5
Haddon Vic. 171 Q4
Haden Qld 323 O10
Hadspen Tas. 361 L8, 363 E10, **345, 346, 347**
Hagley Tas. 361 K8, 363 C11, **352**
Hahndorf SA 197 J13, 199 J1, 203 J7, **180**
Haig WA 257 N9
Haigslea Qld 314 F11
Hailisdale NSW 87 Q7
Hakea WA 248 H1
Halbury SA 200 I11, 202 I2
Haldon East Qld 316 A3
Hale Village Qld 317 K6
Halfway Creek NSW 95 P6
Halidon SA 203 O6
Halifax Qld 324 G6
Hall ACT 98 F10, 100 D5, 106 H2
Hallett SA 201 J8
Hallett Cove SA 198 F2
Hallidays Point NSW 95 N13, 99 N1
Halls Creek WA 255 Q6, **220**
Halls Gap Vic. 165 J12, 171 J1, **129, 142**
Halls Head WA 250 E12
Hallston Vic. 173 M9
Halton NSW 95 L13, 99 L2
Hamel WA 248 F1, 250 F13
Hamelin Bay WA 248 C8
Hamelin Pool WA 256 C3
Hamersley WA 244 E5, 251 J8
Hamersley Range WA 254 F10
Hamersley Range National Park WA 254 G11, **217, 220-1, 226, 228**
Hamilton NSW 82 E6, 83 H5
Hamilton Qld 309 K12, **277, 295**
Hamilton SA 201 J12, 203 J3
Hamilton Tas. 356 D2, 359 K5
Hamilton Vic. 170 H5, **129, 126**
Hamilton Gate NSW 92 G3
Hamilton Hill WA 246 D11
Hamilton Hotel Qld 321 E1
Hamley Bridge SA 196 H2, 200 I13, 202 I4
Hamlyn Heights Vic. 156 A6
Hammond SA 200 H4
Hammond Downs Qld 321 I6
Hammondville NSW 72 A11
Hampden SA 201 K12, 203 K3
Hampshire Tas. 360 F6
Hampton NSW 76 B7, 100 G1
Hampton Qld 323 O10
Hampton Vic. 150 E12
Hanging Rock Vic. 158 I6, **119, 134**
Hannams Bridge NSW 94 G12
Hansborough SA 201 K12, 203 K3
Hanson SA 201 J10, 203 J1
Hansonville Vic. 167 N8
Hanwood NSW 97 N8
Happy Bay Qld 331 F4, **298, 287**
Happy Valley SA 198 G2, 208 H9
Happy Valley Vic. 163 K6, 167 Q8, 171 P5, 173 R2
Harbord NSW 71 J2
Harcourt Vic. 154 B3, 158 E1, 166 C11, **124**
Harden NSW 98 D8, 100 C3, **51**
Hardwicke Bay SA 205 I13
Hardys Beach NSW 77 Q3
Harefield NSW 98 B10, 100 A5
Harewood WA 249 L12
Harford Tas. 361 J6
Hargraves NSW 98 G3
Harkaway Vic. 172 I7
Harlin Qld 314 C2
Harrietville Vic. 167 R10, 168 B10, 174 B1, **123**
Harrington NSW 95 O12, 99 O1
Harrismith WA 249 N2
Harris Park NSW 72 C2
Harrisville Qld 316 G3
Harrogate SA 197 L12
Harrow Vic. 164 E13, 170 E1, **127**
Harrys Creek Vic. 167 K9
Harston Vic. 166 H7
Hart SA 200 H10, 202 H1
Hartley NSW 76 D5, 98 H6, 100 G1, **51, 54**
Hartley SA 199 L4
Hartley Vale NSW 76 D5
Hartz Mountains National Park Tas. 356 A13, 359 J9, **345**

Harvey WA 248 F2, **220, 218**
Harveys Siding Qld 312 G1
Harwood Island NSW 95 Q4
Haslam SA 205 B7
Hastings Tas. 359 K10, **345, 340**
Hastings Vic. 153 N6, 172 H9, **139, 119**
Hastings Point NSW 317 R11, 95 R1
Hatfield NSW 96 H7
Hat Head National Park NSW **52**
Hatherleigh SA 204 F10
Hattah Vic. 162 H7
Hattah-Kulkyne Nat. Park Vic. 162 H6, **137, 129**
Hatton Vale Qld 314 D11
Havelock Vic. 165 Q11, 166 A11
Haven Vic. 164 H9
Havilah Vic. 167 R8, 168 A8
Hawker ACT 106 D13, 108 C1
Hawker SA 200 H1, 207 N11, **184**
Hawkesbury River NSW 78 H8, **38, 63**
Hawkesdale West Vic. 170 I7
Hawks Nest NSW 99 M3
Hawthorn Vic. 149 J9
Hawthorne Qld 311 K2
Hay NSW 97 K8, **51**
Haydens Bog Vic. 175 K3
Hayes Tas. 356 F5, 359 L6
Hayes Creek NT 266 E7
Hayman Island Qld 325 K9, 331 F2, **299, 287**
Haymarket NSW 66 C10
Hay River WA 249 L12
Haysdale Vic. 163 N7
Hazelbrook NSW 76 G7, 80 F5
Hazeldene Qld 314 F3
Hazeldene Vic. 159 P6, 160 B6, 166 I13, 172 I2
Hazelmere WA 245 Q8, 259 F12
Hazel Park Vic. 173 N11
Hazelwood Vic. 173 N9, **136**
Healesville Vic. 154 I8, 159 R10, 160 D10, 173 J4, **129, 118**
Healesville Sanctuary Vic. 160 D11, **129, 118**
Heartlea Vic. 158 I8
Heathcote Vic. 154 D2, 166 F10, **129**
Heathcote Junction Vic. 159 M6
Heatherton Vic. 150 F8
Heathfield Vic. 170 C4
Heath Hill Vic. 173 K8
Heathmere Vic. 170 F8
Heavitree Gap NT 263 M5
Heavitree Range NT 262 E5
Hebden NSW 95 K13, 99 K2
Hebel Qld 93 R2, 94 C2, 322 I13
Heddon Greta NSW 83 E4
Hedges WA 251 P10
Hedley Vic. 173 O11
Heidelberg Vic. 149 K6
Heigh Ridge Qld 312 H6
Heiling NT 266 G8
Heka Tas. 360 G6
Helena Valley WA 259 I13
Helensburgh NSW 77 N13, 91 P1, **64**
Hemmant Qld 309 O13, 311 N1
Henbury Meteorite Craters NT 262 H13, 270 I10, **236, 238, 240**
Hendra Qld 309 K11
Henley NSW 73 J3
Henley Beach SA 195 A8, 196 F11, **179**
Henley Brook WA 259 E5
Henrietta Tas. 360 F5
Hensley Park Vic. 170 H4
Henty NSW 97 P11
Henty Vic. 170 E4
Hepburn Lagoon Vic. 158 B7
Hepburn Springs Vic. 158 D6, 166 C13, 172 C2, **127**
Herbert Downs Qld 321 C2
Herberton Qld 324 F4, 326 I13, **283, 286**
Herbert Vale Qld 324 G6
Herdsman WA 244 F10
Hermidale NSW 93 O11
Hermannsburg Mission NT 262 E7, 270 H8, **237**
Hermitage Tas. 359 K3, 361 K13
Hernani NSW 95 N7
Herne Hill Vic. 156 B7
Herne Hill WA 259 H6
Heron Island Qld 323 P3, 329, **284, 286, 292**
Herons Creek NSW 95 O11
Herrick Tas. 361 P5
Herring Lagoon Qld 315 Q12
Herston Qld 308 H13, 310 H1
Hervey Bay Qld 323 Q6, **292, 296**
Hesketh Vic. 158 I6
Hesso SA 200 D2, 205 I6, 207 M12
Hester WA 248 G7
Hewetsons Mill NSW 95 O1
Hexham NSW 83 G4
Hexham Vic. 171 K7
Heybridge Tas. 360 G5
Heyfield Vic. 173 Q6, 174 A9, **134, 140**
Heytesbury Lower Vic. 171 M11
Heywood Vic. 170 F8
Hiamdale Vic. 173 P9
Hiawatha Vic. 173 O10, **144**
Hibbard NSW 85 A5.

Hibiscus Coast Qld 323 N3, 325 L11, 331 H11, **287, 295**
Hidden Vale Qld 314 D13, 316 D1
Higgins ACT 106 C10
Higginsville WA 257 J9
Highbury NSW 249 L2, 256 G11
High Camp Vic. 159 L4, 166 G12, 172 G1
Highclere Tas. 360 F6
Highcroft Tas. 357 N11, 359 O9, 368 E5
Highett Vic. 150 F11
Highgate WA 242 F2, 245 J11
Highgate Hill Qld 306 B11, 310 H4
Highlands Vic. 154 H4, 159 Q2, 160 C2, 166 I12
High Range NSW 90 I5, 98 I3, 100 G3
Highton Vic. 155 E7, 156 B10
Highvale Qld 314 I8
Hilgay Vic. 170 E4
Hillary WA 244 B1
Hillcrest Vic. 171 P4
Hill End NSW 98 G4, **41**
Hill End Vic. 173 M7
Hillgrove NSW 95 M8, **40**
Hillman WA 249 J3
Hillmanville NSW 201 N13, 203 N4
Hillsdale NSW 73 O9
Hillston NSW 97 L5
Hilltop NSW 91 K4
Hilltown SA 200 I9
Hillview NSW 93 M11
Hillview Qld 317 K9
Hillwood Tas. 361 L6, 363 D6, **345**
Hilton WA 246 E10
Hinchinbrook Island Qld 324 G6, 333, 334, **302, 284, 288**
Hincks Recreation Park SA 205 F10, **189**
Hindmarsh SA 195 D7, 194 A3
Hindmarsh Island SA 199 J9, 203 J9, **180**
Hindmarsh Valley SA 198 H9, **191**
Hines Hill WA 251 O6
Hinnomunjie Vic. 168 F11, 174 E2
Hinton NSW 83 G2
Hirstglen Qld 323 O11
HMAS Albatross NSW 91 M13
Hobart Tas. 355-7, 359 M7, **338-9, 340, 342, 346**
Hobart Airport Tas. 357 K6
Hobbys Yards NSW 98 F6, 100 E1
Hoddle Vic. 173 M12
Hoddles Creek Vic. 160 E13, 173 J5
Hoffmans Mill WA 248 G2
Holder SA 201 N13, 203 N3
Holly WA 249 M6
Holbrook NSW 97 Q12, 168 D2, **52**
Holder ACT 108 C12, 110 C1
Holey Plains State Park Vic. 174 A10, 173 Q8
Holgate NSW 77 R1, 83 E13
Holland Park Qld 311 K6
Holloways Beach Qld 335 F6, **292**
Hollow Tree Tas. 356 E1, 359 K4
Hollywell Qld 317 P4
Holmesville NSW 83 F5
Holmwood NSW 98 E6, 100 D1
Holt ACT 106 A9
Holts Flat NSW 100 E10
Holwell Tas. 361 K6
Holyoake WA 250 G13
Homebush NSW 72 G5
Homebush Qld 331 G13
Homecroft Vic. 165 J6
Home Hill Qld 324 I8, **292-3, 281, 295**
Homerton Vic. 170 F8
Homestead Qld 324 F9
Homewood Vic. 159 P4, 160 B4, 166 I12, 172 I1
Honiton SA 202 F7
Hooker Creek NT 268 D7, **237**
Hooker Creek Aboriginal Reserve NT 268 C6
Hook Island Qld 325 K9, **299, 284, 287, 295**
Hope Forest SA 198 G5
Hopetoun Vic. 164 I2, 162 I13, **129**
Hopetoun WA 256 I12, **220-1**
Hopevale Vic. 164 H3
Hope Vale Mission Qld 326 H9
Hordern Vale Vic. 171 P12
Hornsby NSW 70 F5, 99 K6
Hornsdale SA 200 H6
Horse Lake NSW 92 D13, 96 D1
Horseshoe Creek NT 266 G8
Horsham SA 198 I4
Horsham Vic. 164 H9, **129-31**
Horsley Park NSW 77 L8
Hoskinstown NSW 98 G11, 100 E6
Hotham Heights Vic. 168 C11, 169 G5, **133**
Hotspur Vic. 170 E6
Houghton SA 196 I10
Howard Qld 323 P7
Howard Island NT 267 M4
Howard Springs NT 266 E4, **233, 237**
Howatharra WA 252 A3
Howden Tas. 359 M8, **346**
Howder Tas. 356 I9
Howes Valley NSW 99 J3
Howley NT 266 E6
Howlong NSW 97 O13, 167 P4, 176 G1
Howqua Vic. 167 M13, 173 M1

Howrah Tas. 357 J7
Hoxton Park NSW 77 L10
Hoyleton SA 200 I11, 202 I2
Huddleston SA 200 H8
Hughenden Qld 324 D10, 293
Hughes ACT 108 H12, 110 H1
Hughes SA 206 B9
Hulongine WA 251 J6
Hume Highway 102, 103
Hume Park NSW 98 E10, 100 D4
Hume Range Vic. 159 N7
Humevale Vic. 159 O8, 172 H3
Hume Weir NSW & Vic. 97 P13, 98 A13, 167 R5, 168 B5, 40
Humpty Doo NT 266 E5, 233
Humula NSW 97 R11, 98 C11, 100 A6
Hunchy Qld 307 C9, 313 J10
Hungerford NSW 92 I3, 322 E13, 295
Hunter Vic. 166 E7
Hunter Island Tas. 360 A1
Hunters Hill NSW 71 J13, 73 J2
Hunterston Vic. 173 Q11, 174 A13
Hunter Valley NSW 99 M3, 43, 39
Huntly Vic. 166 D9
Huon Vic. 167 R5, 168 B5
Huon Valley Tas. 356 G8-F9, 341
Huonville Tas. 356 F9, 359 L8, 345, 340
Hurdle Flat Vic. 167 Q7, 168 A7
Hurlstone Park NSW 73 J7
Hurstbridge Vic. 154 G8, 159 O10, 160 A10, 172 H4
Hurstville NSW 72 I11
Hurstville Grove NSW 72 I12
Huskisson NSW 99 J10, 100 H5
Hutt WA 252 A1
Hyams Beach NSW 99 J10, 100 H5
Hyden WA 251 R11, 256 H10, 221, 222, 224
Hynam SA 164 A11, 204 H7
Hythe Tas. 359 L11

I

Icy Creek Vic. 173 M6
Ida Bay Tas. 359 K11, 340, 345
Iguana Creek Vic. 174 D7
Ilbilbie Qld 325 L12
Ilford NSW 98 H4
Ilfracombe Qld 322 E3, 294
Ilfraville Tas. 363 B4
Illabarook Vic. 171 P5
Illabo NSW 98 C9, 100 A4
Illalong Creek NSW 98 E9, 100 C4
Illawarra NSW 91 K8
Illawarra Vic. 165 K12
Illawarra Coast NSW 99 L10, 54
Illilliwa NSW 97 K8
Illowa Vic. 171 J9
Iluka NSW 95 Q4, 54
Image Flat Qld 307 C7, 313 J9
Imbil Qld 312 G7, 323 P9, 292
Impimi NSW 96 H9
Inala Qld 310 E11
Indarra WA 252 D4
Indented Head Vic. 155 I7, 172 F7, 138
Indigo Vic. 167 P4, 144
Indooroopilly Qld 310 F5
Ingalta SA 162 A4
Ingebyra NSW 100 C10, 104 E12
Ingham Qld 324 G6, 293, 302
Ingleburn NSW 77 M10
Inglegar NSW 93 R10, 94 C10
Inglehope WA 248 G1, 250 G13
Ingleside NSW 71 O2
Ingleside Qld 317 P8
Inglewood Qld 95 K1, 323 N12, 293
Inglewood SA 164 A6, 196 I10, 203 Q12, 204 H3
Inglewood Vic. 165 Q8, 166 A8, 131, 138
Inglewood WA 245 J9
Ingliston Vic. 158 E10, 172 D4
Ingoldsby Qld 314 B13, 316 B1
Injune Qld 323 J7, 293
Inkerman Qld 324 I8
Inkerman SA 196 C1, 200 H12, 202 H3
Inman Valley SA 198 E9,191
Innaloo WA 244 E8
Innamincka SA 207 R4, 321 F10, 184, 188
Innes National Park SA 205 G13, 181, 183, 192
Inneston SA 202 C8, 205 H13
Innisfail Qld 324 G4, 293, 283, 284
Innisplain Qld 317 J8
Innot Hot Springs Qld 324 F5, 326 I13
Intaburra Qld 331 A3
Interlaken Tas. 359 M2, 361 M12
Inveralochy NSW 98 G10, 100 F5
Inverell NSW 95 K5, 52, 51
Invergordon Vic. 167 J5
Inverleigh Vic. 155 B7, 172 B7, 131
Inverloch Vic. 173 K11, 131, 144
Invermay Vic. 158 A9
Inverramsay Qld 316 B5
Iona NSW 83 F2
Iona Vic. 173 K7
Ipswich Qld 314 H12, 323 P11, 293

Iraak Vic. 162 I4
Irishtown Tas. 360 C4
Irishtown Vic. 158 E3
Irishtown WA 250 H7
Iron Baron SA 200 D6, 205 H8, 207 L13
Irondale Vic. 76 A3
Iron Knob SA 200 C5, 205 H7, 207 M13, 192, 189
Iron Range Qld 326 E4
Ironside Qld 310 G5
Irrewarra Vic. 171 P9
Irrewillipe Vic. 171 O10
Irwin WA 252 C7
Irymple Vic. 162 H3
Isaacs ACT 111 J4
Isabella NSW 98 G7, 100 F2
Isabella Plains ACT 110 H12
Isisford Qld 322 E4
Island Bend NSW 100 C9, 104 E7
Isle of Capri Qld 318 G10
Isseka WA 252 A3
Ithaca Qld 308 G13, 310 G1
Ivanhoe NSW 96 I3
Ivanhoe Vic. 149 K6
Ivory Creek Qld 314 C3

J

Jabiru NT 266 H5, 233
Jabuk SA 203 N9
Jackadgery NSW 95 O5
Jackeys Marsh Tas. 361 J9
Jack River Vic. 173 P11
Jackson Qld 323 L9
Jacobs Well Qld 317 P2
Jacobs Well WA 251 K9
Jallukar Vic. 165 K13, 171 K1
Jallumba Vic. 164 G11
Jaloran SA 249 L3
Jamberoo NSW 91 O8, 99 J9, 100 I4
Jambin Qld 323 M4
Jamboree Heights Qld 310 C9
Jamestown SA 200 I7, 184
Jamieson Vic. 167 M13, 173 M2, 128, 134, 136
Jancourt Vic. 171 N9
Jandakot WA 246 H13, 250 F9
Jandakot Airport WA 247 K11
Jandowae Qld 323 N9
Jan Juc Vic. 155 E10
Jardee WA 248 G9
Jarklin Vic. 165 R6, 166 B6
Jarrahdale WA 250 G11
Jarrahwood WA 248 E6, 256 D12
Jarvis Creek Vic. 168 C5
Jaspers Brush NSW 91 N11
Jaurdi WA 256 I8
Jay Creek Aboriginal Reserve NT 265 K5, 270 I8
Jeebropilly Qld 314 G12
Jeeralang North Vic. 173 O9
Jeffcott Vic. 165 M6
Jeffries Vic. 164 G12
Jemalong NSW 98 C5
Jennaberring WA 251 M8
Jennacubbine WA 251 J6
Jenna Pullin WA 251 J6
Jenolan Caves NSW 76 B10, 100 G1, 55, 39, 52
Jeogla NSW 95 N8
Jeparit Vic. 164 G5, 131, 143
Jerangle NSW 100 E7
Jericho Qld 322 G3
Jericho Tas. 359 M4
Jericho Vic. 173 N4
Jerilderie NSW 97 M11, 52
Jerramungup WA 249 R7, 256 H12
Jerrara NSW 91 O9
Jerrawa NSW 98 F9, 100 D4
Jerrys Plains NSW 99 J2
Jerseyville NSW 95 P9
Jervis Bay ACT 99 J10, 100 H5, opp. 57
Jervois SA 199 R5, 203 L8, 191
Jessie SA 164 B11
Jessie Gap NT 263 N6
Jetsonville Tas. 361 N5
Jibberding WA 253 J10
Jigalong Aboriginal Reserve WA 255 J12
Jilakin WA 251 P12
Jilby NSW 83 E11
Jil Jil Vic. 165 L3
Jimboomba Qld 317 K3
Jimbour Qld 323 N9
Jimenbuen NSW 100 D10
Jim Jim NT 266 H5, 233
Jimna Qld 312 D10
Jindabyne NSW 100 C9, 104 G9, 52
Jindalee Qld 310 D7
Jindera NSW 167 Q3, 168 A3
Jindivick Vic. 173 L7
Jindong WA 248 C6
Jingalup WA 249 K7
Jingarry Qld 316 A9
Jingellic NSW 97 Q13, 100 A7, 168 F3
Jinglli NT 264 C2
Jingymea WA 251 L1, 253 L13
Jip Jip National Park SA 204 F5, 185

Jitarning WA 249 O1, 251 O13
Joadja NSW 90 H6, 98 H8, 100 G3, 55
Joanna SA 164 A12, 170 B1, 204 H8
Joel Joel Vic. 165 M11
Joel South Vic. 165 M12
Johanna Vic. 171 O12
Johnberg SA 200 I3
John Forrest National Park WA 250 G8, 212, 224
Johnsonville Vic. 174 F8
Jolimont WA 244 F12
Jondaryan Qld 323 O10, 279, 298
Joondanna WA 244 H9
Josbury WA 249 J2
Josephville Qld 317 J6
Joslin SA 194 I2
Joyces Creek Vic. 158 B2, 165 R12, 166 B12
Jubilee Qld 308 F13, 310 F1
Jubuk WA 251 M11
Judbury Tas. 356 E9, 359 K8, 345
Jugiong NSW 98 D9, 100 C4
Julatten Qld 335 A3
Julia SA 201 K12, 203 K2
Julie Creek Qld 324 A10, 327 G8, 294, 292
Jumbuk WA 173 O10
Jumbunna Vic. 173 K10
Junction View Qld 316 A2
Jundah Qld 321 I5, 322 C6
Junee NSW 97 Q9, 98 B9, 100 A4, 52
Jung Vic. 164 I8
Junortoun Vic. 166 D9
Jupiter SA 198 I3
Jura WA 251 O8
Jurien WA 252 C12, 221

K

Kaarimba Vic. 166 I5
Kabininge SA 197 L5, 208 E7
Kadina SA 200 F11, 202 F2, 205 I10, 184, 181, 187, 192
Kadnook Vic. 164 D12, 170 D1
Kadungle NSW 97 Q3, 98 B3
Kagaru Qld 317 J3
Kahibah NSW 82 C12
Kain NSW 100 F7
Kainton SA 200 F12, 202 F3
Kairi Qld 335 D12
Kajabb Qld 327 D7
Kakadu National Park NT 266 H6, 233, 239
Kalamunda WA 250 G9
Kalangadoo SA 170 A4, 204 H10
Kalangara Qld 314 H1
Kalannie WA 253 K13, 256 F8
Kalbar Qld 316 F4
Kalbarri WA 256 C5, 221
Kalbarri National Park WA 256 C5, 220, 221, 226
Kaldow SA 205 E10
Kaleen ACT 107 K10
Kaleentha Loop NSW 96 F3
Kalgan WA 249 O12
Kalgoorlie WA 257 J8, 258, 221-2, 210, 223
Kalguddering WA 251 J4
Kalimna West Vic. 174 G8
Kalinga Qld 309 J10
Kalkadoon Qld 321 H1
Kalkallo Vic. 159 L9, 172 G3
Kalkee Vic. 164 H8
Kallangur Qld 315 K6
Kallista Vic. 147 E9, 130
Kallora SA 200 H12, 202 H3
Kalorama Vic. 147 E5
Kalpienung Vic. 165 N2
Kalpowar Qld 323 N5
Kalumburu Aboriginal Reserve WA 255 P1
Kalyan SA 203 N6
Kamarah NSW 97 O8
Kamarooka Vic. 166 D7
Kambah ACT 110 D7
Kambalda WA 257 J9, 222, 221
Kamballup WA 249 O10
Kamber NSW 94 E11
Kamona Tas. 361 O5
Kanaguik Vic. 164 G12
Kanangra Boyd National Park NSW 76 C11, 98 H7, 100 G2
Kanappa SA 197 O8
Kanawalla Vic. 170 H4
Kancoona Vic. 167 R8, 168 B8
Kandanga Qld 312 G6
Kandanga Creek Qld 312 G6
Kandos NSW 98 H3
Kangaloon NSW 91 L7
Kangarilla SA 198 H3
Kangarooby NSW 98 D6, 100 C1
Kangaroo Flat NSW 95 N10
Kangaroo Flat SA 196 H5
Kangaroo Flat Vic. 166 C10
Kangaroo Ground Vic. 149 Q1, 160 A11
Kangaroo Hill Vic. 158 B6
Kangaroo Hills Qld 324 F7
Kangaroo Island SA 202 A11, 186, 183, 185, 191
Kangaroo Point Qld 306 G8
Kangaroo Valley NSW 91 L10, 98 I9, 100 H4, 57

Kangawall Vic. 164 D10
Kaniva Vic. 164 C7, **131**
Kanmantoo SA 199 L2
Kanni SA 201 N12, 203 N3
Kanumbra Vic. 160 F2, 167 K11
Kanwal NSW 83 F11
Kanya Vic. 165 M9
Kanyapella Vic. 166 G4
Kaoota Tas. 356 G9, 359 L8
Kapinnie SA 205 E11
Kapooka NSW 98 B10
Kapunda SA 197 K2, 201 J13, 203 J4, **185**, **180**, **182**
Karabeal Vic. 170 I4
Karadoc Vic. 162 H3
Karanja Tas. 356 D4
Karara Qld 323 O11
Karatta SA 202 C12
Karawara WA 247 J5
Karawinna Vic. 162 E4
Karcultaby SA 205 D7
Kardinya WA 246 F9
Kariah Vic. 171 N8
Karingal Vic. 151 P4
Kariong NSW 77 P1, 78 B5
Karkarook SA 205 F9
Karkoo SA 205 E10
Karlgarin WA 251 R11, 256 H10
Karlo Creek Vic. 175 N6
Karmona Qld 321 H10
Karn Vic. 167 M8
Karnak Vic. 164 D10
Karonie WA 257 K8
Karook Vic. 166 G7
Karoola Tas. 361 L6, 363 F6
Karoonda SA 203 N7
Karping WA 251 K12
Karragullen WA 250 G9
Karrakatta WA 246 F2
Karramomus North Vic. 167 J8
Karrandgin WA 251 J5
Karratha WA 254 F9, **222**, **217**, **226**
Karridale WA 248 C8
Karrinyup WA 244 D6
Kars Springs NSW 95 J12
Karte SA 203 Q7
Karuah NSW 99 M3, **58**
Karumba Qld 326 A13, 327 E2, **292-3**
Karumbul Qld 95 J2
Karween Vic. 162 C4
Karyrie Vic. 165 L3
Katamatite Vic. 97 M13, 167 K4
Katandra Vic. 167 J5
Katanning WA 249 M6, 256 G12, **222**, **219**
Katherine NT 266 G9, **237-9**
Katherine Gorge Nat. Park NT 266 G8, **238-9**
Katoomba NSW 76 E7, 80 B5, 98 I6, 100 G1, **52**, **39**, **44**, **53**
Kattabul Qld 325 K10
Kattyoong Vic. 162 F9
Katunga Vic. 97 L13, 167 J4, **136**
Katyil Vic. 164 H6
Kawarren Vic. 171 P10
Kayannie Corner SA 197 K11
Kayena Tas. 363 C5
Kearsley NSW 83 D5
Kebaringup WA 249 O7
Kedron Qld 308 I10
Kerra NSW 95 J6
Keilor Vic. 148 B3, 172 F4
Keils Mountain Qld 307 E8, 313 K10
Keinbah NSW 83 D3
Keiraville NSW 89 B8
Keith SA 203 P12, 204 F3, **185**
Kellalac Vic. 164 I7
Kellerberrin WA 251 N7, 256 G9, **222**
Kellevie Tas. 357 O5, 359 O6
Kellidie Bay Cons. Park SA 205 D12, **183**, **189**
Kellys Creek NSW 98 D7, 100 C2
Kelmscott WA 250 G9
Kelsey Creek Qld 331 C5
Kelso Tas. 361 K5, 363 B4, **341**
Kelville NSW 77 M6
Kelvin NSW 94 I8
Kelvin Grove Qld 308 G13, 310 G1
Kelvin View Vic. 167 K10
Kembla Grange NSW 91 O6
Kembla Heights NSW 91 N5
Kemps Creek NSW 77 K9
Kempsey NSW 95 O10, **52**
Kempton Tas. 356 H13, 359 M4, **348**
Kendall NSW 95 O11
Kendenup WA 249 M10, 256 G13, **224**
Kenebri NSW 94 F8
Kenilworth Qld 312 H9, 323 P9
Kenley Vic. 163 N7
Kenmare Vic. 164 H3
Kenmore NSW 90 C11, 98 G9, 100 F4
Kenmore Qld 310 D5
Kennedy Qld 324 G6
Kennedys Creek Vic. 171 N11
Kennett River Vic. 171 Q11, 172 A11
Kenny Hill NSW 77 L12
Kennys Creek NSW 98 E8, 100 D3

Kensington NSW 73 O7
Kensington WA 242 H10
Kentbruck Vic. 170 D8
Kent Dale WA 249 K12
Kenthurst NSW 70 A3, 77 M5
Kentish West Tas. 360 H7
Kentlyn NSW 77 L12
Kenton WA 249 K12
Kenton Valley SA 197 K10
Kent Town SA 194 H6
Kentucky NSW 95 L8
Kentville Qld 314 D10
Kenwick WA 247 P7
Keperra Qld 308 E11
Keppel Sands Qld 323 N3, **304**
Kerang Vic. 96 I12, 163 Q13, 165 Q2, 166 A2, **131**, **141**
Kerein Hills NSW 97 P3
Kergunyah Vic. 167 R6, 168 B6
Kernot Vic. 173 J10
Kerrabee NSW 98 I2
Kerrie Vic. 158 I7, 172 F2
Kerrisdale Vic. 154 G4, 159 P3, 160 A3, 166 I12, **144**
Kerriwah NSW 93 Q13, 94 B13, 97 Q2, 98 B2
Kerrs Creek NSW 98 F4
Kerry Qld 317 K7
Kersbrook SA 197 J9, 203 J6
Keswick SA 194 A10
Kettering Tas. 356 H11, 359 M8, **345**
Kevington Vic. 173 M2
Kew NSW 95 O11
Kew Vic. 149 J8, 172 H5
Kewdale WA 247 M3
Kewell Vic. 164 I8
Keyneton SA 197 N5, 203 K5
Keysborough Vic. 150 I5
Keysbrook WA 250 F11
Khancoban NSW 100 B8, 104 A6, 168 H6
Kiah NSW 100 F11, 175 P3
Kialla NSW 98 G8, 100 E3
Kialla Vic. 167 J7
Kiama NSW 91 O8, 99 J9, 100 I4, **52**, **54**
Kiamal Vic. 162 I8
Kiamba Qld 307 C6, 313 J9
Kiandra NSW 100 C7, 104 E1, **62**
Kianga NSW 100 G8
Kiata Vic. 164 F7, **127**
Kibbleup WA 249 M6
Kidaman Creek Qld 312 H9
Kielpa SA 205 F9
Kiewa Vic. 167 R6, 168 B6
Ki Ki SA 203 N9
Kikoira NSW 97 O6
Kilcara Heights NSW 77 Q3
Kilcoy Qld 314 F2, 323 P9
Kilcunda Vic. 173 J10
Kilfeera Vic. 167 M8
Kilkerran SA 200 E13, 202 E4
Kilkivan Qld 312 B1, 323 P8
Killara NSW 71 J8
Killarney Qld 95 N1, 316 B10, **294**
Killarney Vic. 170 I9
Killarney Heights NSW 71 M9
Killarney Vale NSW 83 F12
Killawarra Vic. 167 N6
Killingworth NSW 83 F6
Killingworth Vic. 159 Q4, 160 C4, 167 J12
Kilmany Vic. 173 Q7
Kilmore Vic. 154 F5, 159 L5, 166 G13, 172 G1
Kilpalie SA 203 O6
Kilsyth Vic. 147 C4, 160 B13
Kimba SA 200 A7, 205 G8, **185**
Kimberley Tas. 360 I7
Kimberley WA 255, **217**, **220**, **221**, **227**
Kimberley Downs WA 255 M5
Kimbriki NSW 99 N1
Kinalung NSW 92 D13, 96 D1
Kinchega National Park NSW 96 D2, **45**, **55**
Kinchela Creek NSW 95 P9
Kincumber NSW 77 R2
Kindred Tas. 360 H6
Kingaroy Qld 323 O9, **294**, **280**
King Beach SA 198 G11
King Island Tas. 358 A14, **347**
Kinglake Vic. 159 P9, 160 B9, **118**
Kinglake National Park Vic. 159 P9, 172 I3, **125**, **118**, **144**
Kingoonya SA 205 D3, 207 J10, **184**, **188**
Kingower Vic. 165 P8, 166 A8
King River WA 249 N12, 256 G13
Kingsbury Vic. 149 K3
Kings Canyon NT 270 F9, **236**, **240**
Kingscliff NSW 95 R1, 317 R9
Kingscote SA 202 F10, **185**, **186**
Kings Cross NSW 66 H8, 73 N4, **37**
Kingsdale NSW 90 B11, 98 G9, 100 F4
Kingsford NSW 73 N7
Kingsgrove NSW 72 H10
Kingsley WA 244 E1
King Sound WA 255 L4
Kings Park WA 242 A5, 246 G1
Kingston ACT 109 M10
Kingston Qld 315 M13

Kingston Tas. 356 I9, 359 M7, **346**
Kingston Vic. 158 B7, 171 R2, 172 B2
Kingston Beach Tas. 356 I9
Kingston-on-Murray SA 201 P12, 203 P3
Kingston S.E. SA 204 E6, **185**
Kingstown NSW 95 K7
Kingsvale NSW 98 D8, 100 C3
Kingswood NSW 77 J7
Kingswood SA 200 G3
King Valley Vic. 167 O9
Kinimakatka Vic. 164 E7
Kin Kin Qld 313 J4
Kinnabulla Vic. 165 K3
Kioloa NSW 100 H7
Kipper Qld 314 B6
Kirkdune WA 253 J12
Kirkleigh Qld 314 F3
Kirkstall Vic. 170 I9
Kirra Qld 317 Q8, 319 Q4, **278**, **279**
Kirrawee NSW 77 O11
Kirribilli NSW 69 P11, 73 N2
Kirup WA 248 F6
Kirwan WA 251 K2
Kissing Point NSW 70 H8
Kitchener NSW 83 D5
Kitchener WA 257 M8
Kithbrook Vic. 167 K10
Klimpton NSW 98 I10, 100 H5
Knebsworth Vic. 170 G7
Knockrow NSW 95 Q2
Knockwood Vic. 173 N3
Knowsley Vic. 154 D2, 166 E10
Knoxfield Vic. 150 C1
Koah Qld 335 C6
Koallah Vic. 171 N9
Kobble Qld 314 I6
Kobyboyn Vic. 159 Q2, 160 C2, 166 I11
Kodj Kodjin WA 251 N5
Koetong Vic. 168 E5
Kogan Qld 323 N9
Kogarah NSW 73 K11
Koimbo Vic. 163 L8
Kojarena WA 252 B4
Kojonup WA 249 K6, 256 G12, **219**
Kokardine WA 251 K2
Koloona NSW 95 J5
Kolora Vic. 171 L8
Komungla NSW 98 G9, 100 F4
Konanda SA 205 F9
Kondinin WA 251 P11, 256 G10, **222**
Kondut WA 251 J2
Kongal SA 203 P13, 204 G4
Kongolia SA 197 Q7
Kongorong SA 204 G12
Kongwak Vic. 173 K10
Konnongorring WA 251 J4
Konong Wootong Vic. 170 F3
Koojan WA 250 G3
Kookaburra NSW 95 N9
Koolachu Qld 331 C4
Koolanooka WA 252 G7
Koolewong NSW 77 Q2, 78 C3
Kooloonong Vic. 96 G10, 163 M7
Koolunga SA 200 H9
Koolyanobbing WA 256 I8, **227**
Koolywurtie SA 202 F5
Koomberkine WA 251 K4
Koonadgin WA 251 Q7
Koonagaderra Springs Vic. 159 K9
Koonda Vic. 162 D9, 167 K7
Koondoola WA 244 I3
Koondrook Vic. 96 I12, 163 R13, 165 R1, 166 C1
Koongamia WA 259 I11
Koonoomoo Vic. 167 J3
Koonunga SA 197 L2
Koonwarra Vic. 173 L10
Koonya Tas. 357 N10, 359 O8
Koorack Koorack Vic. 163 P13, 165 P2
Koorawatha NSW 98 E7, 100 C2
Koorda WA 251 M3, 256 G8
Kooreh Vic. 165 O8
Koorkab Vic. 163 M7
Koorlong Vic. 162 G3
Kooroocheang Vic. 158 C5
Koo-wee-rup Vic. 173 J8, **131**
Kooyong Vic. 149 J10
Kopi SA 205 E9
Koppamurra SA 164 A12, 204 H8
Koraleigh NSW 163 N9
Korbel WA 251 O7
Koriella Vic. 160 F3, 167 K12, 173 K1
Korobeit Vic. 158 F10, 172 D4
Koroit Vic. 171 J9, **132**
Korong Vale Vic. 165 P6
Koroop Vic. 165 R2, 166 B2
Korora NSW 95 P7, **46**
Korralling WA 251 J3
Korrelocking WA 251 M5
Korumburra Vic. 173 L10, **132**, **133**
Korunye SA 196 F5
Korweinguboora Vic. 158 D8
Korweinguboora Reservoir Vic. 172 C3

Kosciusko National Park NSW 98 D13, 100 C6, 104, 168 I9, 174 I1, **45, 47, 52**
Kotara NSW 82 A11
Kotta Vic. 165 E5
Kotupna Vic. 166 H5
Koumala Qld 325 L11
Kowat Vic. 175 M4
Koyuga Vic. 166 G5
Krambach NSW 95 N12, 99 N1
Kringin SA 203 Q7
Krongart SA 204 H10
Krowera Vic. 173 K10
Kudardup WA 248 C9
Kuender WA 249 Q2
Kuitpo SA 198 H4
Kuitpo Colony SA 198 H5
Kukerin WA 249 O3, 256 G11
Kulangoor Qld 313 K9
Kulde SA 203 M7
Kulgera NT 270 I12, **239, 188**
Kulgun Qld 316 G4
Kulikup WA 248 I6
Kulin WA 251 O12, **222**
Kulja WA 251 L1, 253 L13
Kulkami SA 203 O7
Kulkyr Vic. 162 I5
Kulnine Vic. 162 D3
Kulnura NSW 83 C11, 99 K5
Kulpara SA 200 G11, 202 G2
Kultanaby SA 205 E3
Kulwin Vic. 96 F10, 163 J9
Kulyalling WA 251 K11
Kumarina WA 256 H1
Kumarl WA 257 J11
Kumbarilla Qld 323 N10
Kumbia Qld 323 O9
Kumorna SA 203 O11, 204 F2
Kunama NSW 97 R12, 100 B6, 168 H1
Kunat Vic. 163 O12
Kundabung NSW 95 O10
Kungala NSW 95 P6
Kunghur NSW 95 Q1, 317 N13
Kunjin WA 251 N11
Kunkala Qld 314 F12
Kunlara SA 203 N5
Kunmunya Aboriginal Reserve WA 255 M3
Kununoppin WA 251 N4
Kununurra WA 255 R3, **222-3, 227, 228**
Kunwarara Qld 323 M2
Kuraby Qld 311 L12
Kuranda Qld 335 E6, **294, 283, 288**
Kureelpa Qld 307 C7, 313 J9
Kuridala Qld 327 E9
Ku-ring-gai Chase National Park NSW 77 P4, 79, 99 K6, **39, 44**
Kuringup WA 249 P5
Kurlana SA 203 O3
Kurmond NSW 77 J4
Kurnbrunin Vic. 164 F3
Kurnell NSW 73 O13, **38**
Kurnwill Vic. 162 D5
Kurraca Vic. 165 P8
Kurrajong NSW 76 I4, 99 J6, 100 I1
Kurrajong East NSW 77 J3
Kurrajong Heights NSW 76 I4
Kurri Kurri NSW 83 E4, 99 L3
Kurting Vic. 165 Q8, 166 A8
Kurumbul Qld 323 M12
Kuttabul Qld 331 F11
Kweda WA 251 L11
Kwelkan WA 251 O4
Kwinana WA 250 F10, 256 E10, **223, 210, 220, 227**
Kwobrup WA 249 O5
Kwolyin WA 251 N8
Kyabram Vic. 166 H6, **132, 141**
Kyalite NSW 96 H10, 163 O8
Kyancutta SA 205 E8
Kybeyan NSW 100 E9
Kybong Qld 312 H5
Kybunga SA 200 I11, 202 I2
Kybybolite SA 164 B11, 204 I7
Kydra NSW 100 E9
Kyeamba NSW 97 Q11, 98 B11, 100 A6
Kyeemagh NSW 73 L10
Kyeema National Park SA 198 H5
Kyndalyn Vic. 163 L6
Kyneton Vic. 154 C5, 158 G5, 166 D13, 172 D1, **132-3, 119, 124**
Kynuna Qld 324 A11, 327 G10
Kyogle NSW 95 P2, 323 Q12, **52-3**
Kyup Vic. 170 H4
Kyvalley Vic. 166 G6
Kywong NSW 97 O10

L

Laanecoorie Vic. 165 Q10, 166 A10
Laanecoorie Reservoir Vic. 166 A10
Laang Vic. 171 L9
Labertouche Vic. 173 L7, **143**
Labrador Qld 317 P5, 318 B12
Lachlan Tas. 356 F6, 359 L7
Lady Bay Tas. 359 L10
Lady Julia Percy Island Vic. 170 H10
Ladysmith NSW 97 Q10, 98 B10, 100 A5
Ladys Pass Vic. 166 F10
Laen Vic. 165 K7
Laggan NSW 98 G8, 100 F3, **47**
Lagoon Pocket Qld 312 G4
Lagoons Tas. 361 R9
Laguna NSW 83 A7
Lah Vic. 164 I5
Lah-Arum Vic. 164 I11
Laheys Creek NSW 94 F13
Laidley Qld 314 D12, **290**
Lake Albacutya Park Vic. 162 G13
Lake Albert SA 199 P11, 203 L10, **186-7**
Lake Alexandrina SA 199 N7, 203 K9, **184, 185, 187, 191**
Lake Argyle WA 255 R4, **223, 227**
Lake Barrine National Park Qld 335 E12, **281, 284, 304**
Lake Bathurst NSW 98 G10, 100 F5
Lake Bellfield Vic. 165 J13, **141, 142**
Lake Boga Vic. 96 H11, 163 P12
Lake Bolac Vic. 171 L5, **133**
Lake Brown WA 251 P3
Lake Buloke Vic. 165 L6, **127, 143**
Lake Burley Griffin ACT 109 L7, **39**
Lake Burragorang NSW 76 G11, 90 I1, **38**
Lake Burrumbeet Vic. 171 P3, **121**
Lake Cargelligo NSW 97 N5, **53**
Lake Charm Vic. 96 I12, 165 Q1, 163 Q13, 166 A1
Lake Clarendon Qld 314 C10
Lake Clifton WA 248 E1, 250 E13
Lake Corangamite Vic. 171 O8, **124, 126**
Lake Cowal NSW 98 B6, **63, 59**
Lake Dumbleyung WA 249 M4, **218**
Lake Eacham Nat. Park Qld 335 E12, **281, 284**
Lake Echo Tas. 361 J12, **342**
Lake Eildon Vic. 160 H3, **128**
Lake Eppalock Vic. 166 E10, **129**
Lake Eucumbene NSW 100 C8, 104 G4, **40**
Lake Eyre SA 207 M5, **188**
Lakefield National Park Qld 326 G9, **284**
Lake Frome SA 207 P10, **181**
Lake Fyans Vic. 165 K12, **141**
Lake Gairdner SA 207 K11
Lake George NSW 98 G10, 100 E5
Lake George SA 204 E9, **181**
Lake Gilles Conservation Park SA 207 L13
Lake Ginninderra ACT 106 G10
Lake Goldsmith Vic. 171 O3, **121**
Lake Gordon Tas. 358 H6, 340, 343, 351
Lake Grace WA 249 Q2, 256 H11, **223**
Lake Hindmarsh Vic. 164 F4, **129, 131, 136, 138, 143**
Lake Hinds NSW 250 I2
Lake Illawarra NSW 91 O6, **64**
Lake Jindabyne NSW 100 C9, 104 G8, **52**
Lake Leake Tas. 359 O1, 361 O11, **350, 352**
Lake Lonsdale Vic. 165 K11
Lake MacFarlane SA 200 B1
Lake Mackay Aboriginal Reserve NT 270 B4
Lake Macleod WA 256 C1
Lake Macquarie NSW 83 G7, **59**
Lake Margaret Tas. 358 E1
Lake Marmal Vic. 165 O5
Lakemba NSW 72 G8
Lake Meering Vic. 165 Q3, 166 A3
Lake Menindee NSW 96 D2
Lake Moogerah Qld 316 E6
Lake Mountain Vic. 173 L3, **135, 119**
Lake Mundi Vic. 170 B4
Lake Pedder Tas. 358 H7, 340, 343, 351
Lake Plains SA 199 M7
Lake Powell Vic. 163 L6
Lake Rowan Vic. 167 L6
Lake St Clair Tas. 358 H1, 343, 351
Lakesland NSW 91 K1
Lake Sorell Tas. 361 L12, **348, 350**
Lake Tinaroo Qld 335 D11, **281, 295**
Lake Torrens SA 200 E1, 207 N10, **181**
Lake Tyers Vic. 174 G8, **133**
Lake Victoria NSW 162 C1
Lake View NSW 83 G8
Lake View SA 200 H9
Lake Wallawalla Vic. 162 B3
Lake Wendouree Vic. 157 B5, **121**
Lalbert Vic. 96 G12, 163 N13, 165 N1
Lalbert Road Vic. 163 O12
Lalla Tas. 363 F6, **347**
Lal Lal Vic. 158 C11, 172 B4
Lal Lal Reservoir Vic. 172 B4
Lallat Vic. 165 K9
Lambton NSW 82 A6, 83 H5
Lameroo SA 203 P8, **185**
Lamington Qld 317 K9
Lamington National Park Qld 95 P1, 317 M9, **278, 279, 285**
Lamplough Vic. 165 O12
Lancaster Vic. 166 H6
Lancefield Vic. 154 D5, 159 J5, 166 F13, 172 F1
Lancelin WA 250 D4, 256 E9, **223**
Landers Shoot Qld 307 C10, 313 J11

Landsborough Qld 307 E12, 313 K12, **294, 280**
Landsborough Vic. 165 M11
Lane Cove NSW 68 A1, 71 K12
Lanena Tas. 363 D7
Langford WA 247 N8
Langhorne Creek SA 199 M5, 203 K8, **191**
Langi Kal Kal Vic. 171 O2
Langi Logan Vic. 171 M2
Langkoop Vic. 164 B12, 170 B1, 204 I8
Lang Lang Vic. 173 J8
Langley Vic. 158 G4, 166 E12
Langlo Crossing Qld 322 F8
Langloh Tas. 356 D1
Langshaw Qld 312 F4
Langville Vic. 165 Q3, 166 A3
Langwarrin Vic. 153 M1
Lankeys Creek NSW 97 Q12, 100 A7
Lannercost Vic. 324 G6
Lansdowne NSW 72 B8, 95 O12
Lansvale NSW 72 A8
La Perouse NSW 73 O12
Lapoinya Tas. 360 E4
Lara Vic. 155 F5, 172 D7, **128**
Lara Lake Vic. 155 F5, 172 D7
Larapinta Drive NT 262 G7
Laravale Qld 317 J7
Largs NSW 83 F2
Largs Bay SA 196 F10
Lark Hill Qld 314 F11
Larpent Vic. 171 P9
Larrakeyah NT 265 O12
Larras Lee NSW 98 E4
Larrimah NT 266 I11, 268 I1, **239**
Lascelles Vic. 96 F12, 163 J13, 165 J1
Latham ACT 106 D9
Latham WA 252 H9, 256 F7
Latrobe Tas. 360 I6, **346, 344**
Lauderdale Tas. 357 K7, 359 N7, **339**
Laughtondale NSW 77 M2
Launceston Tas. 361 L7, 362, 363 F9, **346-7, 342, 346, 350**
Launceston Airport Tas. 363 G11
Launching Place Vic. 160 E12, 173 J5
Laura Qld 324 E1, 326 G10, **300**
Laura SA 200 H7
Laurel Hill NSW 97 R12, 100 B7
Laurence Road NSW 95 P4
Laurier WA 249 P7
Laurieton NSW 95 O11, **45**
Lauriston Vic. 158 F5, 166 D13, 172 D1
Lavender Bay NSW 69 K9
Lavers Hill Vic. 171 O12, **120, 134**
Laverton Vic. 172 F6
Laverton WA 257 K6, **223, 222**
Lavington NSW 97 P13, 167 R4, 168 B4
Lawes Qld 314 C11
Lawgi Qld 323 M5
Lawloit Vic. 164 D7
Lawn Hill National Park Qld **293**
Lawnton Qld 308 E2
Lawrence NSW 158 A6, 165 Q13, 171 R2, 172 B2
Lawrenny Tas. 356 C1
Lawson NSW 76 G7, 80 E5, 98 I6, 100 H1
Layard Vic. 172 C9
Leadville NSW 94 G12
Leaghur Vic. 165 Q4, 166 A3
Leam Tas. 363 D6
Learmonth Vic. 171 Q2, 172 A2
Learmonth WA 254 C11
Leasingham SA 200 I11, 202 I2
Leawarra Vic. 153 L1
Ledge Point WA 250 D4
Leederville WA 244 G11
Leeman WA 252 C10
Leeton NSW 97 O8, **53**
Leets Vale NSW 77 L2
Leeville NSW 95 P3
Lefroy Tas. 361 L5, 363 D4, **345**
Legana Tas. 361 L7, 363 E8
Legerwood Tas. 361 O6
Legume NSW 95 N1, 316 B11, 323 P12
Legunia Tas. 361 P6
Leichardt Vic. 165 R9, 166 B9
Leichhardt NSW 73 K5
Leigh Creek South SA 207 N9, **185**
Leigh Creek Vic. 158 B9
Leighton SA 201 J9
Leightonfield NSW 72 B6
Leinster WA 257 J5
Leitchville Vic. 97 J13, 166 C3
Leith Tas. 360 H5, **352**
Lemana Tas. 361 J8
Lemnos Vic. 167 J6
Lemon Springs Vic. 164 C9
Lemont Tas. 359 O3, 361 O13
Lemon Tree NSW 83 D9
Lenah Valley Tas. 355 B6
Leneva Vic. 167 Q5, 168 A5, **144**
Lennonville WA 253 N1
Lenswood SA 197 J11
Leonards Hill Vic. 158 D7, 172 C2
Leongatha Vic. 173 L10, **133, 132**
Leonora WA 257 J6, **223, 222**

Leopold Vic. 154 C12, 155 G8, 172 E8
Leppington NSW 77 L10
Leprena Tas. 359 K11
Lerderderg Gorge Vic. 158 G9
Le Roy Vic. 173 O9
Leslie Manor Vic. 171 O8
Leslie Vale Tas. 356 H8, 359 M7
Lessingham SA 200 I11, 202 I2
Lethbridge Vic. 154 A10, 155 C5, 172 C6
Lethebrook Qld 331 D6
Letts Beach Vic. 174 D11
Leumeah NSW 77 L11
Leura NSW 76 F7, 80 C5, **52**, **37**
Levendale Tas. 357 L2, 359 N5
Lewana Park WA 248 F6
Lewisham NSW 73 K6
Lewisham Tas. 357 L6, 359 O7
Lewiston SA 196 G6
Lexton Vic. 171 P1, 165 O13
Leyburn Qld 323 O11
Liamana NSW 94 G12
Liapootah Tas. 358 I2, **351**
Licola Vic. 173 P4, **134**
Lidcombe NSW 72 D5
Liddell NSW 99 K2, **59**
Lidsdale NSW 76 B3
Liena Tas. 360 H8
Lietinna Tas. 361 N5
Lietpar Vic. 163 J9
Liffey Tas. 361 K9, 363 B13, **352**
Lightning Creek Vic. 168 D9
Lightning Ridge NSW 93 R4, 94 C4, 323 J13, **53**
Light Pass SA 197 M4, 208 G2
Lileah Tas. 360 C4
Lillimur Vic. 164 B7, 203 R13, 204 I4
Lillimur South Vic. 164 C7
Lilli Pilli NSW 77 P11
Lilliput Vic. 167 O5, 176 C6
Lilydale Tas. 361 M6, 363 G6, **347**
Lilydale Vic. 147 D2, 154 H9, 160 B12, 172 I5
Lilyfield NSW 73 K4
Lilyvale NSW 77 N13, 91 P1
Lima Vic. 167 L9
Lime Lake WA 249 L4
Limerick NSW 98 G7, 100 E2
Limestone Vic. 159 R5, 160 D5, 167 J13, 173 J1
Limestone Ridge Qld 316 H3
Limevale Qld 95 K2, 323 N12
Limpinwood NSW 317 N10
Lincolnfields SA 200 G10, 202 G1
Lincoln National Park SA 205 F13, **189**
Linda Downs Qld 321 A1
Lindeman Island Qld 325 K9, **298**, **284**, **287**, **295**
Linden NSW 76 H7
Lindenow Vic. 174 D8
Lindfield NSW 71 K9
Lindisfarne Tas. 355 H4, 357 J6
Lind National Park Vic. 100 D13, 175 L6, **135**
Lindsay Vic. 170 B4
Lindsay Creek NSW 316 F11
Lindsay Point Vic. 162 A2
Lindsay View NSW 95 P1, 316 I11
Lindum Qld 309 O12
Linga Vic. 162 E10
Linley Point NSW 71 J13, 73 J1
Linton Vic. 171 P4
Linville Qld 312 B13
Linwood SA 196 I2
Lipson SA 205 F11
Liptrap Vic. 173 L13
Lisarow NSW 83 E13
Lisle Tas. 361 M6, 363 H6
Lismore NSW 88, 95 Q3, 323 Q12, **53-4**
Lismore Vic. 171 O6
Lismore East NSW 88 D12
Lismore Heights NSW 88 H9
Liston NSW 95 N2
Litchfield Vic. 165 L6
Lithgow NSW 76 C4, 98 H5, **54**
Little Bay NSW 73 Q11
Little Billabong NSW 168 E1
Little Desert National Park Vic. 164 F8, **127**, **128**, **192**, **131**, **136**, **138**
Little Hampton SA 199 K2
Little Hampton Vic. 158 E6
Little Hartley NSW 76 D5
Little Jilliby NSW 83 D11
Little River Vic. 155 G4, 172 E6
Little Snowy Creek Vic. 168 C8
Little Swanport Tas. 359 P3, 361 P13
Little Topar NSW 92 D12
Liverpool NSW 75 O12, 77 M9, 99 J7, 100 I2, **54**
Lizard Island Qld 326 I8, **303**, **287**
Llandillo NSW 77 K6
Llanelly Vic. 165 Q9, 166 A9
Llangothlin NSW 95 M6
Llewellyn Siding Tas. 361 N10
Llowalong Vic. 173 R6, 174 B8
Loadstone NSW 317 K11
Lobethal SA 197 K11, 203 J6, **180**
Lochabar SA 204 G7
Lochiel NSW 100 F11
Lochiel Qld 321 H5
Lochiel SA 200 G11, 202 G2
Lochinvar NSW 83 D2, **54**
Loch Lomond Qld 95 N1
Lochnagar Qld 322 F3
Loch Sport Vic. 174 E9
Loch Valley Vic. 173 M5
Lock SA 205 E9
Lockhart NSW 97 O11
Lockhart River Mission Qld 326 E5, **300**
Lockier WA 252 D7
Lockington Vic. 166 E6
Lockridge WA 259 C10
Lockrose Qld 314 D10
Locksley Vic. 166 I10
Lockwood Vic. 154 A2, 166 C10
Loddon Vale Vic. 165 Q4, 166 B4
Logan Vic. 165 O8
Loganholme Qld 315 M13, 317 M1
Loganlea Qld 315 M13, 317 L1
Logan Reserve Qld 317 L1
Logan Village Qld 317 L2
Loira Tas. 363 C7
Lombardina Aboriginal Reserve WA 255 L4
Lomos WA 251 M11
Londonderry NSW 77 J6
Londrigan Vic. 167 O6
Lone Pine Qld 310 E7
Longerenong Vic. 164 I9, **131**
Long Flats Qld 312 G4
Longford Tas. 361 L8, 363 F12, **347-8**, **346**
Longford Vic. 174 B10
Longford Creek Qld 325 J9, 331 B3
Long Island Qld 331 F5, **298**, **287**
Long Jetty NSW 83 F12
Longlea Vic. 166 D9
Longley Tas. 356 H8, 359 M7
Long Plains SA 196 D2, 200 H13, 202 H4
Long Plains Vic. 163 L11
Long Pocket Qld 310 G6
Longreach Qld 322 D3, **294**, **291**
Longueville NSW 68 A7, 71 K13, 73 K2
Longwarry Vic. 173 K7
Longwood SA 196 I13, 198 I1
Longwood Vic. 166 I9
Lonnavale Tas. 356 D8, 359 K7
Looma WA 255 M6
Loongana WA 257 O9
Lord Howe Island NSW **87**
Lorinna Tas. 360 H8
Lorne NSW 95 O11
Lorne SA 196 B2
Lorne Vic. 155 A13, 171 R10, 172 B10, **133-4**, **128**,
Lorquon Vic. 164 F5
Lostock NSW 95 L13, 99 L2
Lota Qld 311 Q3
Lotta Tas. 361 Q6
Louth NSW 93 K8
Louth Bay SA 205 F12
Loveday SA 201 P12, 203 P3
Lowaldie SA 203 N7
Lowanna NSW 95 P7
Lowan Vale SA 203 Q12, 204 H3
Lowbank SA 201 N12, 203 N3
Lowden WA 248 F5
Lowdina Tas. 357 J3, 359 N5
Lower Acacia Creek NSW 95 N1
Lower Bucca NSW 95 P7
Lower Chittering WA 250 G7
Lower Creek NSW 95 N8
Lower Gellibrand Vic. 171 N12
Lower Glenelg National Park Vic. 170 D8, **138**
Lower Hawkesbury NSW 77 M2
Lower Light SA 196 E5
Lower Mangrove NSW 77 O1
Lower Mookerawa NSW 98 F3
Lower Mount Hicks Tas. 360 F5
Lower Norton Vic. 164 H10
Lower Nudgee Qld 309 M10
Lower Portland NSW 77 L2
Lower Sandy Bay Tas. 355 G13
Lower Wilmot Tas. 360 H6
Lowesdale NSW 97 N13, 167 O3
Low Head Tas. 361 K5, 363 B3, **345**
Lowlands NSW 77 J4, 97 L4
Lowmead Qld 323 O5
Lowood Qld 314 F10
Lowther NSW 76 C6
Loxton SA 201 P13, 203 P4, **185**
Loyetea Tas. 360 G6
Loy Yang Vic. 173 P8
Lubeck Vic. 165 J9
Lucas Heights NSW 77 N11
Lucaston Tas. 356 F9, 359 L7
Lucinda Qld 324 G6, **295**, **284**, **293**
Lucindale SA 204 G7
Lucknow NSW 98 F5, **57**
Lucknow Qld 321 F1
Lucknow Vic. 174 E8
Lucky Bay SA 205 H10
Lucky Flat NSW 94 G8
Lucyvale Vic. 168 E6
Luddenham NSW 77 J9
Ludlow WA 248 D5

Ludmilla NT 264 H5
Lue NSW 98 H3
Lugarno NSW 72 F13
Luina Tas. 360 D7, **350-1**, **352**
Lulworth Tas. 361 L4, 363 E2
Lumeah WA 249 L7
Lunawanna Tas. 359 M10
Lune River Tas. 359 K11
Lurg Vic. 167 M8
Lurnea NSW 77 M10
Lutana Tas. 355 D4
Lutwyche Qld 308 I11
Lyal Vic. 158 G1, 166 E11
Lyalls Mill WA 248 G4
Lyetta Tas. 363 B4
Lymington Tas. 356 F12, 259 L9, **344**
Lynchford Tas. 358 E2
Lynchs Creek NSW 95 P1, 317 K12
Lyndbrook Qld 324 D5
Lyndhurst NSW 98 F6, 100 D1
Lyndhurst SA 207 N9, **184**, **188**
Lyndhurst Vic. 151 K1, 172 I7
Lyndoch SA 197 K6, 203 J5, 208 B9, **190**
Lyneham ACT 107 M13, 109 L1
Lynwood WA 247 M8
Lyons ACT 108 G13, 110 G2
Lyons SA 205 B2, 206 H9
Lyons Vic. 170 E7
Lyonville Vic. 158 E7, 172 C2
Lyrup SA 201 Q12, 203 Q3
Lysterfield Vic. 147 B12
Lysterfield Reservoir Vic. 147 B13
Lytton Qld 309 P12

M

Maaoope SA 204 H8
Mablac WA 249 P2
McAlinden WA 248 H5
McAllister NSW 98 G8, 100 F3
Macarthur ACT 111 L10
Macarthur Vic. 170 H7, **129**
Macclesfield SA 199 J3, 203 J8
Macclesfield Vic. 147 I8, 173 J6
McCoys Bridge Vic. 166 H5
McCrae Vic. 152 K2, **139**
McCullys Gap NSW 99 K1
Macdonnell Ranges NT 262, 263, **238**
Macedon Vic. 158 H7, 172 E2, **134**
Macgillivray SA 202 E11
McGraths Hill NSW 77 K5
Macgregor ACT 106 B8
Macgregor Qld 311 K9
Machans Beach Qld 335 F7
McHarg Creek SA 198 I5
McIntyres Vic. 165 P9
Mackay Qld 325 L11, 330, 331 H11, **295**, **284**, **287**, **298**, **299**
McKees Hill NSW 95 Q3
McKenzie Creek Vic. 164 H10
McKillop Vic. 147 F4
McKillops Bridge Vic. 174 I3
McKinlay Qld 327 F9
McKinnon Vic. 150 D11
Macks Creek Vic. 173 P10
Macksville NSW 95 P8, **54**
McLachlan SA 205 E9
McLaren Flat SA 198 G4, 208 H12
McLaren Vale SA 198 G4, 202 I8, 208 G13, **186**, **180**, **181**
Maclean NSW 95 Q5, **54**
Maclean Bridge NSW 317 K2
McLeay SA 205 H4
Macleod Vic. 149 L4
McMahons Creek Vic. 160 H11, 173 L4
McMahons Point NSW 69 L11
McMahons Reef NSW 98 D9, 100 C4
McMasters Beach NSW 77 R2
McMillans Vic. 166 C3
McMinns NT 266 E4
Macorna Vic. 165 R3, 166 B3
McPhail NSW 98 D3
Macquarie ACT 106 G13, 108 F1
Macquarie Fields NSW 77 M10
Macquarie Harbour Tas. 358 D3, **352**
Macquarie Plains Tas. 356 E4, 359 K6
Macrossan Qld 324 D7
Madalya Vic. 173 O10
Maddington WA 247 Q8
Madura WA 257 O10, **223**
Mafeking Vic. 171 K2, **120**
Maffra Vic. 173 R6, 174 B9, **134**, **140**
Maggea SA 201 N13, 203 N4
Magnetic Island Qld 324 H7, 333, **302**, **304**
Magpie Vic. 158 A10
Magra Tas. 356 F5, 359 L6
Magrath Flat SA 203 L11, 204 C2
Mahaikah Vic. 167 N11
Maharatta NSW 100 E11
Maiala National Park Qld 314 H7, **280**
Mainbar NSW 77 O11
Maida Vale WA 245 R12

Maiden Gully Vic. 154 A1, 166 C9
Maidenwell Qld 323 O9, **280**
Maidstone Vic. 148 D7
Mailors Flat Vic. 171 J9
Maimuru NSW 98 D8, 100 B2
Main Beach Qld 317 P5, 318 E9
Maindample Vic. 160 I1, 167 L11
Main Range National Park Qld 316 C6, 323 P11, **281, 290, 304**
Main Ridge Vic. 152 I9
Maitland NSW 83 F3, 99 L3, **54**
Maitland SA 200 F13, 202 F4, 205 I11, **186**
Majorca Vic. 165 Q12, 166 A12
Majors Line Vic. 166 G10
Malabar NSW 73 P10
Malabar Qld 314 F11
Malagarga Qld 321 H8
Malanda Qld 324 F4, **283**
Malbina Tas. 356 G6, 359 L6
Malbon Qld 327 E9
Malbooma SA 205 B2, 206 H9
Malcolm WA 257 J6
Maldon NSW 91 L2
Maldon Vic. 154 A3, 158 C1, 165 R11, 166 B11, **134-5, 119, 124**
Malebelling WA 251 J8
Maleny Qld 307 B11, 312 I11, 323 Q9, **295**
Malinong SA 203 L9
Mallacoota Vic. 100 F13, 175 O6, **135, 125**
Mallacoota National Park Vic. 100 F12
Mallala SA 196 F3, 200 I13, 202 I4
Mallanganee NSW 95 O3
Malmsbury Vic. 154 B5, 158 F4, 166 D12, 172 D1, **133**
Malmsbury Reservoir Vic. 166 D12, 172 D1
Malpas SA 203 Q5
Maltee SA 205 B6
Malvern Vic. 149 K12, 150 B11
Malyalling WA 251 M12
Mambray Creek SA 200 F5, **192**
Mambray Creek National Park SA 200 G5
Manangatang Vic. 96 F10, 163 L9
Manara NSW 96 G3
Mandagery NSW 98 D4
Mandalong NSW 83 E9
Mandemar NSW 90 I6
Mandiga WA 251 N3
Mandorah NT 266 D4, **233**
Mandurah WA 250 E12, 256 E10, **223, 213**
Mandurama NSW 98 F6, 100 D1
Mangalo SA 200 B9
Mangalore NSW 93 O11
Mangalore Tas. 356 H3, 359 M5
Mangalore Vic. 154 G3, 166 H11
Mangana Tas. 361 P8
Mangerton NSW 89 B11
Mangoplah NSW 97 P11, 98 A11
Mangrove Creek NSW 83 B13
Mangrove Mountain NSW 83 B12
Maniana WA 247 O4
Manifold Heights Vic. 156 C7
Manildra NSW 98 E4
Manilla NSW 95 J8, **54, 51**
Maningrida NT 267 K3, **239**
Manjimup WA 248 G8, 256 F12, **223-4, 218**
Manly NSW 71 Q9, **37, 38**
Manly Qld 311 Q2, **279**
Manly Beach Vic. 153 K9
Manly Vale NSW 71 Q9
Manmanning WA 251 K3
Mannahill SA 201 N3, 207 P12
Mannanarie SA 200 I6
Mannerim Vic. 155 H8
Mannering Park NSW 83 F9
Mannibadar Vic. 171 P5
Manning WA 246 I6
Manns Beach Vic. 173 Q11
Mannum SA 197 P11, 203 L6, **186**
Manoora SA 201 J11, 203 J2
Manor Vic. 155 H4, 172 E6
Manorina National Park Qld 314 H8, **280**
Mansfield Qld 311 M8
Mansfield Vic. 167 M11, **135, 144**
Mantung SA 203 O5
Manumbar Qld 312 B6, 323 P8
Manumbar Mill Qld 312 C6
Manya Vic. 162 B10
Manypeak WA 249 O12
Mapleton Qld 307 B7, 313 J9, **295**
Mapoon Aboriginal Reserve Qld 326 C3
Maralinga SA 206 E8
Marama SA 203 O8
Marananga SA 197 K4, 208 D3
Maranboy NT 266 H9
Marangaroo WA 244 G2
Marathon Qld 324 C10
Maraylya NSW 77 L4
Marble Bar WA 254 I9, **224, 226**
Marburg Qld 314 F11, **278-9**
Marchagee WA 252 G11
Marcoola Beach Qld 307 H7, **280**
Marcus Beach Qld 307 H3
Marcus Hill Vic. 155 H8, 172 E8

Mardan Vic. 173 M10
Mardella WA 250 F10
Mareeba Qld 324 F3, 326 I12, 335 B8, **295, 282, 283, 300**
Marengo Vic. 171 P12
Margaret River WA 248 C7, 256 E12, **224**
Margate Qld 315 M6, **299**
Margate Tas. 356 H9, 359 M8, **346**
Margooya Vic. 163 K7
Maria Island Tas. 357 R4, 359 Q6
Maria Island National Park Tas. 359 Q5, **343, 352**
Marian Qld 331 F12, **295**
Maribyrnong Vic. 148 D6
Marindo WA 251 N1, 253 N13
Marine National Park Qld 335 H1
Marino SA 196 F13, 208 G7, **179**
Marion SA 195 D11, 196 G13, 198 G1
Marion Bay SA 202 C8, 205 H13
Marion Downs Qld 321 D2
Markdale NSW 98 F8, 100 E2
Marks Point NSW 83 G7
Markwood Vic. 167 O7, 176 H12
Marla SA 206 H3
Marlbed Vic. 165 L3
Marlborough Qld 323 L2, 325 L13
Marlee NSW 95 N12
Marlin Waters Qld 319 O8
Marlo Vic. 100 C13, 175 J8, **137**
Marma Vic. 165 J9
Marmion WA 244 B3
Marmong Point NSW 83 G6
Marmor Qld 323 N4
Marne WA 250 I1
Marnoo Vic. 165 L9
Marong Vic. 154 A1, 165 R9, 166 C9
Maroochydore Qld 307 H8, 313 L10, 323 Q9, **296, 280, 297**
Maroochy River Qld 307 F6, 313 K9
Maroon Qld 316 G8
Maroona Vic. 171 J4
Maroondah Reservoir Vic. 160 E10, 173 J4
Maroota NSW 77 L3
Maroubra NSW 73 Q9
Maroubra Junction NSW 73 O9
Marp Vic. 170 C6
Marrabel SA 201 J12, 203 J3, **185**
Marracoonda WA 249 L5
Marradong WA 248 H1, 250 H13
Marrangaroo NSW 76 B3
Marrar NSW 98 B9
Marrawah Tas. 360 A4
Marraweeny Vic. 167 K9
Marree SA 207 N7, **186, 188, 295**
Marrickville NSW 73 K7
Marsden NSW 97 Q6, 98 B6, 100 A1
Marsden Park NSW 77 K6
Marsfield NSW 70 H10
Marshall Vic. 155 F8
Marshall Rock WA 251 N3
Martindale NSW 90 J2
Martins Creek Vic. 175 J5
Martinsville NSW 83 E8
Martin Walker Park Vic. 173 O9
Marulan NSW 90 F11, 98 H9, 100 G4
Marungi Vic. 167 J5
Marvel Loch WA 256 I9
Marwood Qld 331 H13
Maryborough Qld 323 P7, 336 C10, **296, 280**
Maryborough Vic. 165 P11, 166 A11, **135**
Mary Burts Corner SA 196 C1, 200 H13, 202 H3
Mary Creek Qld 312 F3
Maryfields NSW 77 K12
Mary Kathleen Qld 327 D9, **296, 297**
Marysville Vic. 160 G8, 173 K3, **135, 129, 144**
Maryvale NSW 94 F13, 98 E2
Maryvale Qld 316 B6
Maryvale WA 248 E6
Mascot NSW 73 M8
Maslin Beach SA 198 F4, 208 E13, **180, 181, 191**
Massey NSW 165 L5
Matakana NSW 97 M4
Mataranka NT 266 I10, **239**
Matcham NSW 77 R1, 83 E13, **49**
Matheson NSW 95 L5
Mathiesons Vic. 166 G8
Mathinna Tas. 361 P8, **345**
Mathoura NSW 97 K13, 166 G2
Matlock Vic. 173 N4
Matong NSW 97 P9
Matraville NSW 73 P10
Maude NSW 96 I8
Maude Vic. 155 C4, 172 C6
Maudsland Qld 317 N5
Mawbanna Tas. 360 D4
Mawson NSW 83 H8, 110 H4
Mawson WA 251 K9
Maxwellton Qld 324 B10, 327 I8
Maya WA 252 I10
Mayanup WA 248 H7
Mayberry Tas. 360 I8
Maydena Tas. 356 B5, 359 J6
Mayfield Tas. 359 P3, 361 P13, 363 F8
Maylands WA 245 K11, 259 B13

May Reef Vic. 166 E7
Mayfield NSW 82 D4, 83 H5
Mayne Qld 308 I12, 310 I1
Mayneside Qld 321 I2
Mead Vic. 165 R2, 166 C2
Meadowbank NSW 70 G12, 72 F1
Meadow Flat NSW 98 H5
Meadows SA 198 I4, 203 J8
Meandarra Qld 323 L10
Meander Tas. 361 J9
Mears NSW 251 L11
Meatian Vic. 163 I2, 165 N1
Meckering WA 251 K7, 256 F9
Medina WA 250 F10
Medindie SA 194 F2, 199 P12
Medindie Gardens SA 194 F1
Medlow Bath NSW 76 E7, 80 B4
Meeandah Qld 309 M12
Meekatharra WA 256 H3, **224**
Meelon WA 250 F12
Meelup WA 248 C5
Meenar WA 251 J7
Meeniyan Vic. 173 M11
Meereek Vic. 164 B12
Meerlieu Vic. 174 D9
Meerschaum Vale NSW 95 Q3
Megalong NSW 76 E8, 80 A5
Megan NSW 95 O7
Melawondi Qld 312 G6
Melba ACT 106 F7
Melba Gully State Park Vic. 171 O12
Melbourne Vic. 146-151, 154 F9, 172 G5, **114-17, 118**
Melbourne Airport Vic. 148 C1, 159 K11
Mella Tas. 360 C3
Mellis Vic. 165 J6
Melrose NSW 250 E12
Melrose NSW 97 P3
Melrose SA 200 G5, 207 N13, **186, 189, 192**
Melrose Tas. 360 H6
Melrose Park NSW 70 F12, 72 F1
Melton SA 200 G11, 202 G2
Melton Vic. 154 D8, 158 I11, 172 E4
Melton Mowbray Tas. 356 H1, 359 L4
Melton Reservoir Vic. 155 G1, 172 E5
Melville WA 246 F7
Melville Caves Vic. 165 P8
Melville Forest Vic. 170 G3
Melville Island NT 266 D2, **239**
Mena Tas. 359 J1
Menangle NSW 77 K13, **45**
Menangle Park NSW 77 K12
Mena Park Vic. 171 O3
Mendooran NSW 94 F11
Mengha Tas. 360 C4
Menia NSW 77 N11
Menindee NSW 92 E13, 96 E2, **54-5**
Meningie SA 203 L10, 204 C1, **186-7, 185**
Menora WA 244 I10
Mentone Vic. 150 H10, 172 H6
Menzies WA 257 J7, **223**
Menzies Creek Vic. 147 F12, **130**
Mepunga East Vic. 171 K10
Mepunga West Vic. 171 K10
Merah North NSW 94 G6
Merbein Vic. 96 D8, 162 G2, **135**
Mercunda SA 203 N5
Merebene NSW 94 F8
Meredith Vic. 154 A9, 155 B3, 158 C13, 172 B5, **128**
Merewether NSW 82 F8, 83 H6
Meribah SA 162 A6, 203 Q5
Merildin SA 201 J11, 203 J1
Merilup WA 249 O3
Merimal Qld 323 M2
Merimbula NSW 100 F10, 175 P2, **55, 61**
Merinda Qld 325 J9
Meringur Vic. 162 C4
Merino Vic. 170 E5
Merkanooka WA 252 F6
Mermaid Beach Qld 317 P6, 318 I9, **278, 279**
Mermaid Waters Qld 318 I10
Mernda Vic. 159 N10, 172 H4
Meroo Meadow NSW 91 M11
Merredin WA 251 P6, 256 G9, **224**
Merriang Vic. 167 P8, 172 G3
Merricks Vic. 153 K9, 172 H9, **139**
Merrigum Vic. 166 H6
Merrijig Vic. 167 N12
Merrimac Qld 317 P6
Merrinee Vic. 162 F4
Merriton SA 200 G8
Merriwa NSW 94 I13, **55**
Merriwagga NSW 97 M6
Merrygoen NSW 94 F11
Merrylands NSW 72 B3
Merrywinebone NSW 94 E5
Merseylea Tas. 360 I7
Merton NSW 97 N13
Merton Vic. 160 F1, 167 K11
Messent National Park SA 203 M12, 204 D3
Metcalfe Vic. 158 G3, 166 D12
Methul NSW 97 P9, 98 A9
Metricup WA 248 C6

Metung Vic. 174 F8, **121**, **133**
Meunna Tas. 360 E5
Miallo Qld 324 F2, 326 I11
Miami Qld 317 P7, 319 J9, **278**, **279**
Miami WA 250 E12
Mia Mia Vic. 154 D3, 158 H1, 166 E11
Miami Keys Qld 318 H10
Miandetta NSW 93 P11, 94 A11
Michael Creek Qld 324 G7
Michelago NSW 100 E7
Mickleham Vic. 159 L9, 172 G3
Middleback P.O. SA 205 H8
Middle Beach SA 196 E6
Middle Camp NSW 83 G9
Middle Cove NSW 71 M10
Middle Creek Vic. 171 N2
Middle Indigo Vic. 167 P5
Middle Island Qld 325 M11
Middle Park Qld 310 B9
Middle Park Vic. 148 H11
Middle River SA 202 D10
Middle Swan WA 259 H8
Middleton Qld 327 G11, **295**
Middleton SA 198 I9
Middleton Tas. 356 H13, 359 M9
Middlingbank NSW 100 D8, 104 H6
Midgeton Qld 325 K10, 331 E7
Midginbil NSW 317 N13
Midland WA 245 Q7, 250 G8, 259 F10
Midvale WA 259 G10
Midway Point Tas. 357 K6, 359 N6
Miena Tas. 361 J11
Miepoll Vic. 167 J8
Miga Lake Vic. 164 E11
Mila NSW 100 D11
Milang SA 199 L7, 203 J9, **180**
Milawa Vic. 167 O7, 176 F12, **143**
Milbrulong NSW 97 P11
Milchomi NSW 94 E7
Mildura Vic. 96 D8, 162 H2, **135-6**, **140**
Mile End SA 194 A7
Milendella SA 197 O10
Miles Qld 323 M9, **296**
Milford Qld 316 G6
Milguy NSW 94 I4, 323 M13
Miling WA 250 H1, 252 H13, 256 F8
Milingimbi NT 267 L4, **239**
Millaa Millaa Qld 324 F4, **296**, **283**
Millbong Qld 316 H4, 323 P11
Millbrook Vic. 158 C10, 171 R4, 172 B4
Mil Lel SA 204 H11
Millendon WA 259 H4
Millers Forest NSW 83 H3
Millers Point NSW 66 A2
Millfield NSW 83 B6, 99 K4
Millgrove Vic. 160 F12
Millicent SA 204 G10, **187**
Millie NSW 94 G5
Millmerran Qld 323 N11, **296**
Millner NT 264 C5
Milloo Vic. 166 D6
Millstream National Park WA 254 F10
Millthorpe NSW 98 F5
Milltown Vic. 170 F7
Millwood NSW 98 A10
Milman Qld 323 M3
Milner SA 196 E7
Milparinka NSW 92 C5, **61**
Milperra NSW 72 C10
Milsons Point NSW 69 M11
Miltalie SA 200 B9
Milton NSW 98 I11, 100 H6, **62**
Milton Qld 310 G2
Milvale NSW 97 R8, 98 C8, 100 B3
Mimosa NSW 97 Q9, 98 B8
Mimosa Rocks National Park NSW 100 G10, **41**
Minbrie SA 200 C9
Mincha Vic. 165 R4, 166 B4
Mindarie SA 203 O6
Minden Qld 314 E11
Mindiyarra SA 203 N7
Miners Rest Vic. 171 Q3, 172 A3
Mingary SA 201 Q2, 207 R12
Mingay Vic. 171 O5
Mingela Qld 324 H8
Mingenew WA 252 D7, 256 E7, **224**
Mingoola NSW 95 L3
Minimay Vic. 164, C9
Minimbah NSW 83 B2
Mininera Vic. 171 M4
Minjilang NT 266 H1
Minlaton SA 202 E6, 205 I12, **187**
Minmi NSW 83 G5
Minmindie Vic. 165 P4, 166 A4
Minnamurra NSW 91 O8
Minnie Water NSW 95 Q5
Minniging WA 249 K1
Minnipa SA 205 D7, 207 J13
Minnivale WA 251 K4
Minore NSW 94 D13, 98 D1
Mintaro SA 200 I11, 203 J1
Minto NSW 77 M11
Mintos Hills Vic. 159 P5

Minvalara SA 200 I6
Minyip Vic. 165 J7, **136**
Miowera NSW 93 Q11, 94 B11
Miralie Vic. 163 N9
Miram Vic. 164 D7
Miranda SA 321 E8
Mirani Qld 325 K11, 331 F12, **295**
Mirannie NSW 95 L13, 99 L2
Mirboo Vic. 173 N10
Miriam Vale Qld 323 O5
Mirrool NSW 97 P8, 98 A8
Missabotti NSW 95 O8
Mission Beach Qld 324 G5, **296**, **304**
Mistake National Park Qld 316 C3
Mitcham SA 195 A11, 196 G12
Mitcham Vic. 149 Q9
Mitchell ACT 107 N8
Mitchell Qld 323 J8, **296**
Mitchell River Mission Qld 326 B10
Mitchells Flat NSW 83 B1
Mitchells Hill Vic. 165 L8
Mitchellstown Vic. 166 H10
Mitchellville SA 205 H9
Mitchelton Qld 308 F10
Mitiamo Vic. 166 C5
Mitre Vic. 164 F9
Mittagong NSW 91 J6, 98 I8, 100 H3, **55**
Mitta Mitta Vic. 168 D8, **141**
Mittyack Vic. 96 F11, 163 J9
Moama NSW 97 K13, 166 F4
Moana Qld 318 H10
Moana SA 198 F4, 208 F12, **180**
Mockinga Vic. 164 H11
Moculta SA 197 N4
Modbury SA 196 H10
Modella Vic. 173 K8
Modewarre Vic. 155 C9
Moe Vic. 173 N8, **136**, **143**
Moe River NSW 323 O13
Moffatt Beach Qld 307 I12, 313 M12
Mogil Mogil NSW 94 E4, 323 K13
Moglanemby Vic. 167 J8
Mogo NSW 100 G7, **56**
Mogriguy NSW 94 E12
Mogumber WA 250 G4
Moina Tas. 360 G8
Mokine WA 248 I2, 250 I8
Mole Creek Tas. 360 I8, **348**
Mole River NSW 95 M3, 323 O13
Molesworth Vic. 154 I4, 160 D3, 167 J12, 173 J1
Moliagul Vic. 165 P9, **127**
Molka Vic. 167 J9
Mollerin WA 251 M1, 253 M13
Mollongghip Vic. 158 C8
Mollymook NSW 98 I11, **62**
Mologa Vic. 166 C5
Molong NSW 98 E4, **55-6**
Molterna Tas. 360 I7
Molyullah Vic. 167 M8
Mona SA 200 F11, 202 G1
Monak NSW 96 E8, 162 H3
Mona Park Vic. 170 H3
Monarto SA 199 N2
Monash ACT 110 G11
Monash SA 201 P12, 203 P3
Monash University Vic. 150 D6
Mona Vale NSW 71 P1, 79 P3, 99 K6
Mona Vale Tas. 359 N2, 361 N12
Monbulk Vic. 147 F8, 173 J6
Monbulk State Forest Vic. 147 D9
Monea Vic. 166 I10
Monegeeta Vic. 159 J7, 172 F2
Mongans Bridge Vic. 168 B8
Mongarlowe NSW 98 H11, 100 F6
Monkira Qld 321 F5
Monkland Qld 312 G3
Mons Qld 307 F9, 313 L10
Monsildale Qld 312 D10
Montacute SA 196 I11
Montagu Tas. 360 B3
Montagu Bay Tas. 355 G7
Montana Tas. 361 J8
Montarra SA 198 G5
Monteagle NSW 98 D7, 100 C2
Monte Bello Islands WA 254 D9
Monteith SA 199 Q4
Monteith Flat SA 199 P4
Montgomery Vic. 173 R7, 174 B9
Montmorency Vic. 149 N3
Monto Qld 323 N6, **297**
Montrose Vic. 147 D5, 160 B13, **130**
Montumana Tas. 360 E4
Montville Qld 307 C9, 313 J10, **295**
Monument Qld 327 D11
Mooball NSW 95 Q1, 317 Q12
Moockra SA 200 H4
Moodiarup WA 249 J5
Moodlu Qld 315 J4
Moody SA 205 F11
Moodys Valley Qld 316 H7
Moogara SA 356 E5, 359 K6
Moogerah Qld 316 E7
Moojebing WA 249 M5

Mookarra Qld 331 A3
Moolap Vic. 155 F8, 172 D8
Moolerr Vic. 165 N8
Moolert Vic. 158 B2, 165 Q12, 166 B12
Mooliabeenie WA 250 G5
Mooloo Qld 312 F4
Mooloolaba Qld 307 H9, 313 M10, **296**, **280**, **297**
Mooloolah Qld 313 K12
Mooloolah River National Park Qld 313 L11, **296**
Moolpa NSW 163 P8
Moombooldool NSW 97 O8
Moombra Qld 314 E7
Moonah Tas. 355 C5, 356 I6
Moonambel Vic. 165 N11, **120**
Moonan Flat NSW 95 K12, 99 K1
Moona Plains NSW 95 M9
Moonaran NSW 95 J8
Moonbah NSW 100 C9, 104 F10
Moonbi NSW 95 K9
Mondarewa Qld 317 P4
Mondarra Vic. 173 O7
Moondarra Reservoir Vic. 173 O7
Moondon WA 251 P1, 253 P13
Moonee Beach NSW 95 P7
Moonee Ponds Vic. 148 F6, 172 G5
Mooney Mooney NSW 77 O3
Mooney Mooney Creek Nat. Park NSW 83 C13
Mongulla NSW 323 J13
Moonie Qld 323 M11
Moonijin WA 251 K3
Moonta SA 200 E11, 202 E2, 205 I10, **187**, **181**, **184**, **192**
Moonta Bay SA 200 E11, 202 E2
Moonyoonooka WA 252 A5
Moora WA 250 G2, 256 E8
Moorabbin Vic. 150 E11, 172 H6
Moorabbin Airport Vic. 150 G8
Mooraberree Qld 321 F6
Moorabool Vic. 154 B11, 155 E6
Moorabool Reservoir Vic. 158 C8, 172 B3
Mooralla Vic. 170 H2
Moora Moora Reservoir Vic. 165 J13, 171 J1
Moorang Qld 316 D4
Moorbel NSW 98 E5
Moore Qld 312 B13, 314 B1
Moorebank NSW 72 A10
Moore Creek NSW 95 K9
Moorefields NSW 72 H9
Moore Park NSW 67 J13, 73 O6
Moore River National Park WA 256 E9
Moores Flat Vic. 165 P12
Moorilim Vic. 166 I8
Moorina Tas. 361 P5, **345**
Moorland NSW 95 O12
Moorlands SA 203 M8
Moorleah Tas. 360 E4
Moormbool Vic. 166 G9
Moorna NSW 96 C8
Moornaming WA 249 O5
Moorngag Vic. 167 M9
Moorooduc Vic. 153 L4
Moorook SA 201 O12, 203 O3
Moorooka Qld 310 H7
Mooroolbark Vic. 147 C4, 160 B12
Mooroopna Vic. 166 I7, **140**
Moorowie SA 202 E7
Moorumbyne WA 251 K12, **226**
Moorvale Qld 310 I7
Mootai NSW 83 C6
Mootwingee NSW 92 D10, **42**
Mopami SA 197 M3
Moppin NSW 94 H3, 323 L13
Moranbah Qld 325 J12, **297**, **289**
Moranding Vic. 159 L4
Morang Vic. 159 N10
Morangarell NSW 97 Q7, 98 C7, 100 A2
Moran Group Qld 313 J3
Morans Crossing NSW 100 F10
Morans Rock NSW 77 K2
Morawa WA 252 G7, 256 E7, **224**
Morayfield Qld 315 K4
Morbinning WA 251 K9
Morchard SA 200 H5
Mordalup WA 248 I9
Mordetta WA 249 Q1, 251 Q13
Mordialloc Vic. 150 I8, 172 H7
Morea Vic. 164 D9
Moree NSW 94 H4, **56**, **59**
Moree Vic. 164 E13, 170 E1
Moreenia SA 205 F11
Morella Qld 322 D2
Moreton Bay Qld 315 N7, **274**, **278**, **279**
Moreton Island Qld 315 P4, **301**, **274**, **295**
Morgan SA 201 M11, 203 M2, **187**, **140**, **190**
Moriac Vic. 155 D9
Morisset NSW 83 F9, 99 L4
Morkalla Vic. 162 B4
Morley WA 245 K7, 259 A10
Morney Qld 321 G6
Morningside Qld 311 K2
Mornington Vic. 153 J3, 172 H8, **139**
Mornington Island Qld 327 C1, **297**
Mornington Mills WA 248 F3

Mornington Peninsula Vic. 152-3, 172 G10, **139, 119**
Morongla Creek NSW 98 E7, 100 C2
Morpeth NSW 83 G2, **54**
Morphett Vale SA 198 F3, 202 I7, 208 G9, **180, 188**
Morri Morri Vic. 165 L10
Morrisons Vic. 155 C2, 158 D12, 172 C5
Mortana SA 205 C8
Mortat Vic. 164 D9
Mortchup Vic. 171 P4
Mortdale NSW 72 H12
Mortigallup Wa 249 M10
Mortlake NSW 72 H3
Mortlake Vic. 171 L7
Morton National Park NSW 90 I12, 98 H10, 100 G4, **42, 56, 62**
Morton Plains Vic. 165 L4
Morundah NSW 97 N10
Moruya NSW 100 G8, **56**
Moruya Heads NSW 100 G8
Morven NSW 97 P12, 168 C1
Morven Qld 322 H8
Morwell Vic. 173 O8, **136, 144**
Mosman NSW 71 O12, 73 O1
Mosman Park WA 246 C6
Mosquito Creek NSW 94 I4
Mossgiel NSW 97 J5
Mossiface Vic. 174 F7
Mossman Qld 324 F3, 326 I11, **297, 286**
Mossman Gorge National park Qld 335 A1
Moss Vale NSW 98 I9, 100 H4, **56**
Mossy Point NSW 100 G7
Mothar Mountains Qld 312 H4
Mouingba Qld 312 B1
Moulamein NSW 96 I10, 163 R9
Moule SA 205 A5
Moulyinning WA 249 N3
Mount Adrah NSW 98 C10, 100 A5
Mountain River Tas. 356 G8, 359 L7
Mount Aitken Vic. 158 I9
Mount Alexander Vic. 158 F1
Mount Alford Qld 316 F6
Mount Alfred Vic. 168 E4
Mount Anakie Vic. 155 D3
Mount Arthur Tas. 361 M6, **347**
Mount Barker SA 199 J2, 203 J7
Mount Barker WA 249 M11, 256 G13, **224, 219**
Mount Barker Junction SA 197 K13, 199 J1
Mount Barney National Park Qld 95 O1, 316 G10
Mount Barrow National Park Tas. 361 N6
Mount Battery Vic. 167 M11
Mount Baw Baw Vic. 173 N5, **135, 136**
Mount Beauty Vic. 168 C9, 169 G3, **135**
Mount Beckworth Vic. 165 P13, 171 P2
Mount Benambra Vic. 168 E8
Mount Benson SA 204 D8
Mount Beppo Qld 314 D5
Mount Berryman Qld 314 C13, 316 C1
Mount Best Vic. 173 N11
Mount Bindi Vic. 174 G3
Mount Blackwood Vic. 158 F9
Mount Bogong Vic. 168 D9
Mount Boothby National Park SA 203 N11, 204 D2, **184**
Mount Bryan SA 201 J9
Mount Buangor Vic. 165 N13
Mount Buffalo Vic. 167 Q10, 168 A9, 169 D3, **135**
Mount Buffalo Chalet Vic. 167 Q9
Mount Buffalo National Park Vic. 167 Q9, 168 A9, 169 D3, **125, 136, 138**
Mount Buller Vic. 167 O12, 169 B7, **135**
Mount Burr SA 204 G10, **187**
Mount Bute Vic. 171 O6
Mount Camel Vic. 166 F9
Mount Carbine Qld 324 F3, 326 H11
Mount Cavenagh SA 206 G1
Mount Charlton Qld 325 K10
Mount Clear Vic. 157 H11, 158 A10
Mount Colah NSW 70 G2
Mount Cole Vic. 165 N13, 171 N1
Mount Colliery Qld 316 B10
Mount Compass SA 198 G6, 202 I8
Mount Consultation Vic. 158 D3
Mount Coolangatta NSW 91 N11
Mount Coolon Qld 324 I11
Mount Coolum Qld 313 L8
Mount Cooper SA 205 C8
Mount Cooper Vic. 168 E9
Mount Cooroy Qld 307 D3
Mount Coot-tha Qld 310 E4, **276, 277**
Mount Cotterill Vic. 172 E5
Mount Cotton Qld 315 N12
Mount Cottrell Vic. 155 H2, 158 H13
Mount Cougal National Park Qld 317 O9
Mount Crawford SA 197 L7
Mount Crosby Qld 314 I11
Mount Cudgewa Vic. 168 E6
Mount Dandenong Vic. 147 E6, 172 I5, **130**
Mount David NSW 98 G6, 100 F1
Mount Difficult Vic. 165 J11
Mount Direction Tas. 363 D6
Mount Disappointment Vic. 159 N7
Mount Donna Buang Vic. 173 K4, **135, 143**

Mount Doran Vic 155 B1, 158 C12, 172 B5
Mount Druitt NSW 74 I3, 77 K7
Mount Drummond P.O. SA 205 D11
Mount Drysdale NSW 93 M10
Mount Dundas Vic. 170 G3
Mount Duneed Vic. 155 E9, 172 D8
Mount Dusley NSW 89 C6
Mount Dutton SA 207 K4
Mount Eccles Vic. 173 L9
Mount Eccles Nat. Park Vic. 170 G7, **124, 129**
Mount Edwards Qld 316 E6, 323 P11
Mount Egerton Vic. 158 D10, 172 C4
Mount Elgin Vic. 164 D7
Mount Eliza Vic. 151 R8, 153 K2, 172 H8, **139**
Mount Emu Vic. 171 O4
Mount Esk Pocket Qld 314 E5
Mount Evelyn Vic. 147 F3, 160 B13, 172 I5
Mount Evins Vic. 164 F12
Mount Fairy NSW 98 G10, 100 F5
Mount Feathertop Vic. 168 C10, 174 C1
Mount Field National Park Tas. 356 A3, 359 J5, **340, 342**
Mount Flora NSW 91 J5
Mount Forbes Qld 316 F2
Mount Franklin Vic. 158 D5, 166 C13, 172 C1
Mount Gambier SA 170 A6, 204 H11, **187**
Mount Garnet Qld 324 F5, 326 G13, **283**
Mount Glorious Qld 314 H8, **280**
Mount Gorong Vic. 158 E10
Mount Gravatt Qld 311 K7
Mount Hallen Qld 314 D7
Mount Hawthorn WA 244 H10
Mount Helen Vic. 158 A10
Mount Helena WA 250 G8
Mount Hill SA 205 F10
Mount Hope NSW 97 M3
Mount Hope SA 205 E11
Mount Horeb NSW 98 C10, 100 B5
Mount Hotham Vic. 168 C11, 174 B2, **135, 137, 140**
Mount Howitt Qld 321 H8
Mount Howitt Vic. 167 P12
Mount Hunter NSW 77 J12
Mount Isa Qld 327 C8, **297, 283, 292, 294**
Mount Jagged SA 198 G8
Mount Kaputar National Park NSW 94 I6, **40, 56**
Mount Keira NSW 91 N8, 91 O5
Mount Kembla NSW 91 N5, **64**
Mount Kilcoy Qld 312 F13, 314 F1
Mount Kokeby WA 251 K10
Mount Kosciusko NSW 100 B9, 104 C9, 168 I7
Mount Ku-ring-gai NSW 70 H1, 79 O13
Mount Larcom Qld 323 N4, **291**
Mount Lawley WA 242 E1, 245 J10
Mount Lewis NSW 72 F8
Mount Lloyd Tas. 356 E6, 359 K7
Mount Lofty SA 195 H10, 203 J7, **180, 183**
Mount Lofty Vic. 158 G1
Mount Lonarch Vic. 165 O13, 171 O1
Mount Lyon NSW 317 J12
Mount Macedon Vic. 158 I7, 172 E2, **119, 134**
Mount McIntyre SA 204 G10
Mount McKenzie SA 197 M5
Mount McLeod WA 249 L12
Mount Magnet WA 253 N1, 256 G5, **224, 228**
Mount Magnificent Cons. Park SA 198 H6, **192**
Mount Maroon National Park Qld 316 G9
Mount Marshall NSW 91 N7
Mount Martha Vic. 152 I5, 172 G8, **139**
Mount Mary SA 201 L11, 203 L2
Mount Mee Qld 314 H4
Mount Mellum Qld 313 J12
Mount Mercer Vic. 158 A13, 171 Q5, 172 A5
Mount Misery Vic. 158 I10
Mount Molloy Qld 324 F3, 326 I12, 335 A4
Mount Morgan Qld 323 M3, **297, 291, 300**
Mount Moriac Vic. 155 D8, 172 C8
Mount Mori Qld 316 D2
Mount Muirhead SA 204 G10
Mount Mulligan Qld 324 E3, 326 H12, **282**
Mount Murray NSW 91 M7
Mount Murray Vic. 167 R12, 168 B12, 174 B2
Mount Napier Vic. 170 H6
Mount Nebo Qld 314 H9, **280**
Mount Nelson Tas. 355 E13, **339**
Mount Olga NT 270 D11, **272**
Mount Olive NSW 95 Q3, 99 K2
Mount Ommaney Qld 310 C8
Mount Ossa Qld 325 K10, 331 F10
Mount Pelion Qld 318 E10
Mount Perry Qld 323 O6
Mount Pleasant NSW 89 A6
Mount Pleasant Qld 311 J5, 314 H5
Mount Pleasant SA 197 M9, 203 K6
Mount Pleasant Vic. 157 E9, 158 A10
Mount Pleasant WA 246 H6
Mount Polhill NT 263 N9
Mount Pollock Vic. 155 B7
Mount Prospect Vic. 158 C7
Mount Rae NSW 90 B7
Mount Rat SA 202 E5
Mount Remarkable National Park SA 200 G5, **184, 186, 189, 192**

Mount Rescue National Park SA 203 O11, 204 F2, **185, 191**
Mount Richmond Vic. 170 D8
Mount Richmond National Park Vic. 170 E9, **138**
Mount St Bernard Vic. 167 R11, 168 B11, 174 B2
Mount St Thomas NSW 89 B13
Mount Samaria Vic. 167 M10
Mount Samaria State Park Vic. 167 M10
Mount Samson Qld 314 I7
Mount Schank SA 170 A7, 204 H12, **189**
Mount Seaview NSW 95 M10
Mount Selwyn Vic. 174 A2
Mount Seymour Tas. 359 N4
Mount Slide Vic. 172 I3
Mount Sonder NT 262 C4, 270 H8, **237**
Mount Stanley Qld 312 A10
Mount Stanley Vic. 167 Q7, 168 A7
Mount Steiglitz Vic. 158 E9
Mount Stuart Tas. 355 C8
Mount Sturgeon Vic. 170 I4
Mount Sturt Qld 316 A8
Mount Surprise Qld 324 D6
Mount Sylvia Qld 316 A1
Mount Tamborine Qld 317 M5
Mount Tarampa Qld 314 E9
Mount Tarrengower Vic. 158 C1
Mount Taylor Vic. 174 E7
Mount Toolong Vic. 168 I5
Mount Torrens SA 197 L10, **180**
Mount Towrang NSW 90 D12
Mount Victoria NSW 76 E6, 80 A1, 98 I6, 100 G1
Mount Victoria Vic. 160 F11
Mount View NSW 83 C5
Mount Vincent NSW 83 E6
Mount Walker Qld 316 E2
Mount Walker Lower Qld 314 E13, 316 E1
Mount Wallace Vic. 155 D1, 158 E12, 172 C5
Mount Waverley Vic. 149 N13, 150 B6
Mount Wedge P.O. SA 205 D9
Mount Wellington Tas. 356 H7, 359 M7, **338, 339, 340**
Mount White NSW 77 O2
Mount Whitestone Qld 323 O11
Mount William Vic. 165 J13
Mount Willoughby SA 206 H4
Mount Wilson NSW 76 F4
Mount Windsor Qld 321 G3
Mount Worth State Park Vic. 173 M9
Moura Qld 323 M5, **291, 290**
Mourilyan Qld 324 G5, **297, 293**
Moutajup Vic. 170 I4
Mowbray Tas. 363 F9
Mowbray Park NSW 91 K1
Mowen WA 248 C7
Mowo Qld 331 D7
Moyhn Vic. 167 O8, **143**
Moyston Vic. 165 J13, 171 L2
Muchea WA 250 F7
Muckadilla Qld 323 J8
Muckatah Vic. 167 K4
Muckleford Vic. 158 D2
Mudamuckla SA 205 B6
Mudgee NSW 98 G3, **56, 43**
Mudgeeraba Qld 317 O7, **279**
Mudgegonga Vic. 167 Q7, 168 A7
Mudjimba Qld 307 H7, 313 L9, **280**
Muggleton Qld 323 K8
Muja WA 248 H4, **216**
Mukinbudin WA 251 P3, 256 G8
Mulbring NSW 83 E5
Mulcra Vic. 162 B10, 203 R7
Mulgoa NSW 77 J9
Mulgowie Qld 316 C1
Mulgrave NSW 77 K5
Mulgrave Vic. 150 D4
Mulkirri SA 200 I11, 202 I2
Mullaley NSW 94 H9
Mullaloo WA 250 F8
Mullalyup WA 248 F6
Mullaway NSW 95 P6, **64**
Mullengandra NSW 97 P13, 168 C3
Mullengudgery NSW 93 Q11, 94 B11
Mullet Creek Qld 323 P5
Mullewa WA 252 E3, 256 E6, **224**
Mullindolingong Vic. 168 C8
Mullion Creek NSW 98 F4
Mullumbimby NSW 95 Q2, 323 Q12, **56**
Mulpata SA 203 P7
Mulwala NSW 97 N13, 167 M4, **47**
Mumballup WA 248 G5
Mumbannar Vic. 170 C6
Mumbel Vic. 163 N12, 165 N1
Mumbil NSW 98 F3
Mumblin Vic. 171 M9
Mumell NSW 90 A11
Mummulgum NSW 95 P3
Munbilla Qld 316 G3
Munbinia WA 253 L2
Munbura Qld 331 H13
Mundalla SA 203 Q13, 204 H4
Mundaring WA 250 G8, **224**
Mundaring Weir WA 250 G9, **212**
Mundijong WA 250 F10

Mundoona — Niagara Park **389**

Mundoona Vic. 166 I5
Mundoora SA 200 G9
Mundoora National Park SA 200 G9
Mundrabilla WA 257 P10, **224**
Mundubbera Qld 323 N7, **297**
Mungallala Qld 322 I8
Mungana Qld 324 D4, 326 G12
Mungeriba NSW 93 R13, 94 D12
Mungerup WA 249 P8
Mungery NSW 97 R2, 98 C2
Mungindi NSW 94 F3, 323 K13
Munglinup WA 257 J12
Mungungo Qld 323 N6
Munmorah Lake NSW 83 G10
Munro Vic. 174 C8
Muntadgin WA 251 Q8
Muradup WA 249 K6
Murapena SA 199 K3
Murarrie Qld 311 M2
Murbko SA 201 M12, 203 M3
Murchison Vic. 166 H8
Murdinga SA 205 E10
Murdong WA 249 M6
Murdunna Tas. 357 O8, 359 P7
Muresk WA 250 I8
Murga NSW 98 E5
Murgenella NT 266 H2
Murgenella Wildlife Sanctuary NT 266 H3, **234**
Murgheboluc Vic. 155 C7, 172 C7
Murgon Qld 323 O8, **297**
Murmungee Vic. 167 P7
Muronbung NSW 94 F13
Murphys Creek Vic. 165 Q9, 166 A9
Murrabit Vic. 96 I12, 163 Q12, **131**
Murrawal NSW 94 G10
Murra Warra Vic. 164 H7
Murray Bridge SA 199 P3, 203 L7, **187-8**, **140**
Murray Town SA 200 H6, 207 N13
Murrayville Vic. 162 C10, 203 R8
Murrindal Vic. 174 H5
Murrindindi Vic. 159 R6, 160 D6, 173 J2
Murringo NSW 98 D8, 100 C3
Murroon Vic. 171 Q10, 172 A10
Murrumba Vic. 314 E6
Murrumbateman NSW 98 F10, 100 D5
Murrumbeena Vic. 149 L13, 150 C10
Murrumburrah NSW 98 D8, 100 C3, **51**
Murrungowar Vic. 175 K6
Murrurundi NSW 95 J11, **56**
Murtoa Vic. 165 J8, **136**
Murwillumbah NSW 95 Q1, 317 P11, 323 Q12, **56**
Musk Vic. 158 D6, 172 C2
Muskerry West Vic. 166 E9
Musk Vale Vic. 158 D7
Musselboro Tas. 361 N6, 363 I10
Muston SA 202 F11
Muswellbrook NSW 95 J13, 99 J2, **56**, **43**
Mutarnee Qld 324 G7
Mutchero Inlet National Park Qld 335 I12
Mutdapilly Qld 316 G2
Muttaburra Qld 322 E2, 324 E13
Muttama NSW 98 D9, 100 B4, **47**
Myall Vic. 163 R12, 165 R1, 166 B1
Myalla Tas. 360 E4
Myall Lakes National Park NSW 99 N2, **42**, **48**
Myall Mundi NSW 93 R12, 94 C12
Myall Plains NSW 97 M11
Myalup WA 248 E2, **214**, **220**
Myamyn Vic. 170 F7
Myaree WA 246 F7
Myaring Vic. 170 D5
Myers Flat Vic. 166 C9
Mylestom NSW 95 P8
Mylor SA 196 I13, 198 I1, **180**
Myola Vic. 166 E8
Myphree SA 200 G11, 202 G2
Mypolonga SA 197 Q13, 199 Q1, 203 L7, **187-8**
Myponga SA 198 F7, 202 I9
Myponga Beach SA 198 E7
Myra Vale NSW 91 L8
Myrla SA 201 O13, 203 O4
Myrniong Vic. 158 F10, 172 D4
Myrrhee Vic. 167 N9, **143**
Myrtle Bank Tas. 361 M6, 363 H7, **351**
Myrtle Bridge Vic. 166 D11
Myrtleford Vic. 167 Q8, 169 D1, **136**
Myrtle Scrub NSW 95 M10
Myrtletown Qld 309 O9
Myrtleville NSW 90 C7, 98 H8, 100 F3
Mysia Vic. 165 Q5, 166 A5
Mystic Park Vic. 163 P12, 165 P1
Mywee Vic. 167 J3

N

Nabageena Tas. 360 C4
Nabawa WA 252 B3, 256 D6
Nablac NSW 95 N13, 99 N1
Nabilla Qld 331 G12
Nabowla Tas. 361 N5, 363 H5, **351**
Nackara SA 201 K5
Nadda SA 203 Q5
Nadgee Fauna Park NSW 100 F12, 175 P5

Nagambie Vic. 154 G2, 166 H9, **136**, **140**
Nagoorin Qld 323 N5
Nairne SA 197 K13, 199 K1, 203 J7
Nala Tas. 359 N3, 361 N13
Nalangil Vic. 171 O9
Nalbaugh National Park NSW 175 O3
Nalinga Vic. 167 K7
Nalkain WA 251 L4
Nalya WA 251 K11
Namatjira Drive NT 262 E6
Namatjira's Monument NT 262 E8
Namban WA 252 G1, 252 G13
Nambling WA 251 K5
Nambour Qld 307 E8, 313 K9, 323 Q8, **297**, **280**
Nambrok Vic. 173 Q7, 174 A9
Nambucca Heads NSW 95 P8, **56**
Nambung National Park WA 250 C2, **221**, **223**
Nammuldi SA 200 A7, 205 G8
Nana Glen NSW 95 P7
Nanango Qld 323 O9, **297**
Nanarup WA 249 O12
Nandaly Vic. 96 F11, 163 K10
Nandroya Qld 307 D2, 313 J6
Nanga WA 248 G1, 250 G13
Nangana Vic. 173 J6
Nangari SA 201 Q13, 203 Q4
Nangeenan WA 251 O6
Nangiloc Vic. 162 I5
Nangkita SA 198 H6
Nangri SA 162 A5
Nangus NSW 97 R10, 98 C10, 100 B5
Nangwarry SA 170 A4, 204 H10
Nanneella Vic. 166 F6
Nannine WA 256 G4, **224**
Nannowtharra WA 253 K2
Nannup WA 248 F7, 256 E12, **225**
Nanson WA 252 B3
Nantabibble NSW 201 K5
Nantawarra SA 200 H11, 202 H2
Napier WA 249 O12
Napoleons Vic. 158 A11, 171 Q4, 172 A4
Nappa Merry Qld 321 G10
Napperby SA 200 G7
Naracoorte SA 164 A11, 204 H7, **188**, **183**
Naracoorte Caves National Park SA 204 H7, **127**, **183**, **188**
Naradhan NSW 97 N6
Naraling WA 252 B3
Narangba Qld 315 K6
Narara NSW 77 Q1, 83 E13
Narbethong Vic. 160 F9, 173 K3
Narcoona SA 197 L9
Nareen Vic. 170 E2
Narellan NSW 77 K12
Narembeen WA 251 P9, 256 H10
Naremburn NSW 71 M12
Naretha WA 257 M9
Nariel Creek Vic. 168 F7
Naringal Vic. 171 L10
Narioka Vic. 166 H4
Narkal WA 251 M3
Narlingup WA 249 J6
Nar-Nar-Goon Vic. 173 J7
Naroghid Vic. 171 M8
Narooma NSW 100 G9, **56**, **61**
Narrabarba NSW 100 F12, 175 P4
Narrabeen NSW 71 Q4, 79 R4
Narrabri NSW 94 H7, **56**
Narrabundah ACT 109 M13, 111 M1
Narracan Vic. 173 N8, **136**, **142**
Narrandera NSW 97 O9, **56**, **59**
Narraport Vic. 165 M4
Narrawa NSW 98 F8, 100 E3
Narraweena NSW 71 P7
Narrawong Vic. 170 F9
Narrewillock Vic. 165 O5
Narridy SA 200 H8
Narrikup WA 249 M11
Narrogin WA 249 K2, 256 G11, **225**
Narromine NSW 94 D13, 98 D1, **56**
Narrows NT 264 I4
Narrung SA 199 N9, 203 K9, **187**
Narrung Vic. 163 N7
Narwee NSW 72 G11
Naryilco Qld 321 H12
Nashdale NSW 98 F5, **57**
Nashville Qld 309 J3, 312 G3
Nathalia Vic. 97 L13, 166 H4
Nathan Qld 311 J8, **275**, **276**
Natimuk Vic. 164 G9, **136**
National Park Tas. 356 C4, 359 J6
Native Valley SA 197 L13, 199 L1
Natone Upper Tas. 360 G6
Nattai NSW 98 I7, 100 H2
Nattai River NSW 76 H13
Natte Yallock Vic. 165 O11
Natural Bridge National Park Qld 317 N9
Naturi SA 203 M8
Natya Vic. 163 N8
Naval Base WA 250 F10
Navarre Vic. 165 M10
Navigators Vic. 158 B10
Nayook Vic. 173 L6

N'Dhala Gorge NT 263 R5, **240**, **236**
Neales Flat SA 201 K12, 203 K3
Neath NSW 83 D4
Nebo Qld 325 K12
Nectar Brook SA 200 F5
Nedlands WA 246 F3
Neds Corner Vic. 162 C2
Needaling WA 249 P3
Needilup WA 249 R7
Needles Tas. 361 J8
Neeralin Pool WA 249 L3
Neerim Junction Vic. 173 L6
Neerim South Vic. 173 L7, **127**, **143**
Neeworra NSW 94 F3, 323 K13
Neika Tas. 356 H8
Neilborough Vic. 166 C8
Neilrex NSW 94 G11
Nelia Qld 324 A10, 327 H8
Nelligen NSW 100 G7
Nelshaby SA 200 G7
Nelshaby SA 200 O12
Nelson Vic. 170 C7, **124**, **126**, **138**
Nelson Bay NSW 99 M3
Nelsons Plains NSW 83 H2
Nelungaloo NSW 97 R4, 98 C4
Nembudding WA 251 M5
Nerang Qld 317 O5, **297**
Neranwood Qld 317 O7
Nerriga NSW 100 G5
Nerrigundah NSW 100 F8, **56**
Nerrina Vic. 157 H3, 158 A9
Nerring Vic. 171 O3
Nerrin Nerrin Vic. 171 M5
Netherby Vic. 164 E5
Nethercote NSW 100 F11
Netherdale Qld 331 C11
Netherwood WA 249 N4
Neuarpurr Vic. 164 B10, 204 I6
Neurea NSW 98 F3, **63**
Neuroodla SA 200 G1
Neurum Qld 314 G2
Neusa Vale Qld 312 I3
Neutral Bay NSW 69 O7, 71 N13, 73 N1
Nevertire NSW 93 R12, 94 C11
Neville NSW 98 F6, 100 E1
New Angledool NSW 93 R3, 94 C3
New Beith Qld 317 J2
Newborough Vic. 173 N8
Newbridge NSW 98 G6, 100 E1
Newbridge Vic. 165 Q9, 166 B9
New Brighton NSW 95 R2, 317 R13
Newburn WA 245 P12, 247 P1
Newbury Vic. 158 E7, 172 D2
Newcastle NSW 82, 83 I5, 99 L4, **57**
Newcastle Waters NT 268 I4
Newcomb Vic. 156 H11
Newdegate WA 256 H11
Newell Qld 335 B1
Newell Highway NSW 102
New England National Park NSW 86 E11, 95 N8, **44**, **48**
New Farm Qld 306 H2, 311 J2, **275**, **276**
New Farm Park Qld 311 J3
New Farm Wharf Qld 311 J2
Newfield Vic. 171 M11
Newham Vic. 158 I6, 166 E13, 172 E2
Newhaven Vic. 153 Q13, 172 I10
Newington Vic. 157 C7
New Koreela NSW 316 C13
New Lambton NSW 82 A7
Newland SA 198 G10
Newlands WA 248 F5
Newlyn Vic. 158 B7, 171 R2, 172 B2
Newman WA 254 I12, **217**, **226**
Newmarket Qld 308 H12
Newmerella Vic. 174 I7
Newminster WA 251 M12
New Mollyann NSW 94 F11
Newnes NSW 98 I4
Newnes Junction NSW 76 D4
New Norcia WA 250 G4, 256 F9, **225**, **213**
New Norfolk Tas. 356 F5, 359 L6, **348**, **340**, **341**, **346**
Newport NSW 79 O4
Newport Vic. 148 D10
Newport Beach NSW 77 Q5
New Residence SA 201 P13, 203 P4
Newry Vic. 173 Q6, 174 A8
Newrybar NSW 95 Q2
Newry Island Qld 331 F9, **298**, **287**
Newstead Qld 309 J13, 311 J1
Newstead Vic. 158 C3, 165 R12, 166 B12, **124**
Newton Boyd NSW 95 N5
Newtown NSW 73 L6, 77 K5
New Town Tas. 355 D5, 356 I7, **339**, **346**
Newtown Vic. 156 C8, **128**
New Well SA 201 N13, 203 N4
Ngallo Vic. 162 B11, 203 R8
Ngapala SA 201 J11, 203 J2
Ngukurr NT 267 L9, **239**
Nhill Vic. 164 E6, **136**, **129**, **131**
Nhulunbuy NT 267 P4, **239**, **240**
Niagara Park NSW 83 E13

Niangala NSW 95 L10
Nicholls Rivulet Tas. 356 G11, 359 L9
Nicholson Vic. 174 F8
Nierinna Tas. 356 H9
Nietta Tas. 360 G7
Nightcap National Park NSW 95 Q1, 54, 56
Nightcliff NT 264 B6
Nildottie SA 203 M5
Nile Tas. 361 M9, 363 H13, 345, 346, 347
Nillahcootie Vic. 167 M11
Nilma Vic. 173 L8
Nimbin NSW 95 Q2, 54
Nimmitabel NSW 100 E9
Ninda Vic. 163 K12
Ninderry Qld 307 H8, 313 L9
Nindigully Qld 94 F1, 323 K11
Nine Mile Vic. 165 O7
Ninety Mile Beach Vic. 174 C11, 133, 137, 141
Ningana SA 205 E11
Ni Ni Vic. 164 F6
Ninnes SA 200 G11, 202 G2
Ninyeunook Vic. 165 O4
Nipan Qld 323 M5
Nippering WA 249 M3
Nirranda Vic. 171 L10
Noarlunga SA 198 F4, 188
Nobby Creek NSW 317 O10
Nobby Glen Qld 312 G6
Noble Park Vic. 150 G4
Nockatunga Qld 321 I10
Noggerup WA 248 G5
Noggojerring WA 250 I7
Nokarning WA 251 P6
Nollamara WA 244 H7
Nomans Lake WA 249 M1
Nonda Qld 324 B10, 327 H8
Nondiga Qld 312 C1
Nonedia SA 199 K3
Noojee Vic. 173 L6, 127
Nookanellup WA 249 L6
Noonamah NT 266 I2, 239
Noonbinna NSW 98 E6, 100 C1
Noondoo Qld 94 E1, 323 J12
Noora SA 162 A5, 201 Q13, 203 Q4
Nooramunga Vic. 167 L6
Noorat Vic. 171 M8
Noorinbee Vic. 175 M6
Noorlah Qld 325 K10
Noorongong Vic. 168 C6
Noosa Head National Park Qld 313 M6, 285, 297
Noosa Heads Qld 307 H1, 313 L6, 323 Q8, 280, 297-8
Noosaville Qld 307 G1, 313 L6, 297
Nora Creina Bay SA 204 E9
Noradjuha Vic. 164 G10
Norah Head NSW 83 G11, 99 L5, 61
Norahville NSW 83 G11, 61
Noranda WA 259 A9
Nords Wharf NSW 83 G9
Norlane Vic. 156 D2
Normanby Qld 306 A1, 310 H2
Normanhurst NSW 70 F6
Norman Park Qld 311 J3
Normanton Qld 327 F3, 292, 293, 294, 300
Normanville SA 198 D8, 202 H9, 192
Normanville Vic. 165 P2
Nornakin WA 251 N10
Nornalup WA 249 J13, 219, 221
Norong Vic. 167 O5
Norpa WA 251 P7
Norseman WA 257 K10, 225, 222
North Adelaide SA 194 D3, 178, 179
Northam WA 250 I7, 256 F9, 225, 213, 228
Northampton WA 252 A2, 256 D6, 225
North Arm Qld 307 D4, 313 K8
North Balgowlah NSW 71 O9
North Beach WA 244 C4, 250 F8
North Berry Jerry NSW 98 B9
North Blackwood Vic. 158 F7
North Bondi NSW 73 R5
Northbridge NSW 71 M11
Northbrook Qld 314 F8
North Bruny Island Tas. 359 M9, 343
North Canberra ACT 107 R11 109 M2
Northcliffe WA 248 G11, 256 F13, 225
Northcote Vic. 148 I7
North Curl Curl NSW 71 Q7
North Dandalup WA 250 F12
North Deep Creek Qld 312 G1
Northern Gully WA 252 B4
North Fremantle WA 246 B7
Northgate Qld 309 K9, 277
North Haven NSW 95 O11, 45
North Hobart Tas. 355 E7
North Manly NSW 71 P8
Northmead NSW 70 B11
North Motton Tas. 360 H6
North Muckleford Vic. 158 D2
North Parramatta NSW 70 C12, 72 C1
North Perth WA 244 I11
North Pine River Dam Qld 308 B1
North Riverside Tas. 363 E9
North Rocks NSW 70 C10

North Ryde NSW 70 I10
North Shields SA 205 F12
North Shore Vic. 156 F2
North Star NSW 94 I2, 323 M13
North Strathfield NSW 72 G4
North Sydney NSW 69 K6, 71 M13, 73 M2
Northville NSW 83 G6
North West Aboriginal Res. SA 206 B3, 270 D13
North Wollongong NSW 89 E8, 91 O5
Northwood NSW 68 C5
Northwood Vic. 166 H11
Norton Summit SA 196 I11, 180
Norval Vic. 165 L13, 171 L1
Norwell Qld 317 O2
Norwood NSW 90 C11
Notley Hills Tas. 361 K7, 363 C8, 345
Notting WA 251 P11
Notting Hill Vic. 150 C6
Notts Well SA 201 M13, 203 M4
Nourlangie NT 266 H5
Nowa Nowa Vic. 174 G7
Nowendoc NSW 95 M11
Nowie North Vic. 163 N10
Nowingi Vic. 162 H5
Nowley NSW 94 F6
Nowra NSW 91 M12, 98 I10, 100 H5, 57, 54
Nowra Hill NSW 98 I10, 100 H5
Nubba NSW 98 D8, 100 B3
Nubeena Tas. 357 N11, 359 O8, 368 E4
Nudgee Qld 309 L8
Nudgee Beach Qld 309 M6
Nugadong WA 252 I12
Nugent Tas. 357 N4, 359 O6
Nukarni WA 251 O5
Nulkaba NSW 81 H10, 83 C4
Nullagine WA 254 I10, 224
Nullan Vic. 165 J7
Nullarbor Plain WA 206 A9 , 257 M8, 183
Nulla Vale Vic. 159 J4, 166 F12, 172 F1
Nullawarre Vic. 171 L10
Nullawil Vic. 165 M3
Numbla Vale NSW 100 D10, 104 I12
Numbugga NSW 100 F10
Numbulwar NT 267 N8, 239
Numeralla NSW 100 E8
Numinbah NSW 317 N10
Numinbah Valley Qld 317 N8
Numurkah Vic. 97 L13, 167 J4, 136
Nunamara Tas. 361 M7, 363 H8
Nunawading Vic. 149 Q9
Nundah Qld 309 K10
Nundle NSW 95 K11, 60
Nunga Vic. 162 I9
Nungarin WA 251 O5
Nungatta National Park NSW 100 E11, 175 N3
Nungurner Vic. 174 F8
Nunjikompita SA 205 B6, 206 I12
Nunkeri SA 203 N7
Nurina WA 257 O9
Nurinda Qld 314 C1
Nuriootpa SA 197 L4, 201 K13, 203 K4, 208 F2, 190
Nurom SA 200 G8
Nurrabiel Vic. 164 G11
Nurragi SA 199 K7
Nurrondi SA 200 G9
Nutfield Vic. 159 O10
Nyabing WA 249 O5, 256 G12
Nyah Vic. 96 G11
Nyallo Vic. 165 J2
Nyah West Vic. 96 G11, 163 N9
Nyamup WA 248 H9, 256 F13
Nyarrin Vic. 163 K11
Nymagee NSW 93 N12, 97 N1
Nymboida NSW 95 O6
Nymbool Qld 324 E5, 326 G13
Nyngan NSW 93 P11, 94 A11, 57
Nyora Vic. 173 K9
Nypo Vic. 162 G13, 164 G2

O

Oakbank SA 197 J12, 180
Oakdale NSW 76 H13
Oakenden Qld 331 G13
Oakey Qld 323 O10, 298, 280
Oakey Creek NSW 94 H11
Oak Flats NSW 91 O7
Oakhampton NSW 83 F2
Oaklands NSW 97 N12
Oaklands SA 202 F7, 205 I13
Oakleigh Vic. 150 D9, 172 H6
Oak Park Vic. 148 F3
Oak Park WA 251 J5
Oaks Tas. 361 L8, 363 D12
Oakvale Vic. 165 P3
Oakview Qld 312 C1
Oakwood Tas. 357 O11, 359 P8
Oaky Flats Qld 315 J5
Oatlands Tas. 359 M3, 361 M13, 348, 341
Oatley NSW 72 H12
Oberlin Tas. 359 L6
Oberne NSW 97 R11, 98 C11, 100 A6
Oberon NSW 98 H6, 100 F1

O.B. Flat SA 170 A6, 204 H12
O'Bil Bil Qld 323 N7
Obi Obi Qld 307 A8, 312 I9
Obley NSW 98 E3
O.B.X. Creek NSW 95 O6
Ocean Grove Vic. 155 G9, 172 E8, 137, 128
Ocean View NSW 91 M7
Ockley WA 249 L1, 251 L13
O'Connell NSW 98 G6
O'Connor ACT 109 K2
O'Connor WA 246 E9
Oenpelli Aboriginal Reserve NT 266 I4, 239
Ogilvie WA 252 A1
Ogmore Qld 323 L2, 325 L13
O'Halloran Hill SA 208 G8
Olangalah Vic. 171 P11
Olary SA 201 O3, 207 Q12
Old Adaminaby NSW 104 G3, 40
Old Bar NSW 95 O12, 99 O1
Old Beach Tas. 356 I5, 359 M6
Old Bonalbo NSW 95 O2
Old Bowenfels NSW 76 C5
Old Cannidah Qld 323 N6
Old Cork Qld 321 H2
Oldina Tas. 360 F5
Old Junee NSW 97 Q9, 98 B9, 100 A4
Old Koreelah NSW 316 D11
Old Rothbury NSW 81 G4
Old Sydney Town NSW 78 A6, 99 K5, 50, 39
Old Warrah NSW 95 J11
Olga, Mt NT 270 D11, 272
Olgas, The NT 272, 236, 238
Olinda NSW 98 H3
Olinda Vic. 147 D8, 160 B13, 172 I5, 130, 119
Olinda Reservoir Vic. 147 D3
Olinda State Forest Vic. 147 E7
Olio Qld 324 C12
O'Malley ACT 110 I3
Ombersley Vic. 171 Q8, 172 A8
Omega NSW 91 O9
Omeo Vic. 168 E12, 174 E3, 137, 133, 141
Ondit Vic. 171 P8
One Tree NSW 97 J7
One Tree Hill SA 196 N8, 196 I8
One Tree Hill Vic. 155 G3
Ongerup WA 249 Q7, 256 H12, 219
Onoto Qld 321 H4
Onslow WA 254 D10, 225
Oodla Wirra SA 201 K5
Oodnadatta SA 207 J4, 188
Ooldea SA 206 E9
Ooma Creek NSW 98 C6, 100 B1
Oonah Tas. 360 E6
Oondooroo Qld 322 C1, 324 C12
Ooraminna NT 263 O10
Oorindi Qld 327 F8
Ootha NSW 97 Q4, 98 B4
Opalton Qld 321 I2, 322 B3, 327 I13, 304
Opossum Bay Tas. 357 J9, 359 N8
Orama NSW 56
Orange NSW 98 F5, 101, 57
Orange Grove WA 247 R7
Orangeville NSW 76 I12
Oranmeir NSW 100 F7
Oraparinna SA 207 O10, 182
Orbost Vic. 100 C13, 174 I7, 137
Orchard Hills NSW 77 J8
Ord River WA 255 R3, 222-3, 227, 228
O'Reillys Green Mountains Qld 317 M9, 278
Orford Tas. 357 O2, 359 P5, 348
Orford Vic. 170 H8
Organ Pipes National Park Vic. 159 K11, 124
Orielton Tas. 357 K5, 359 N6
Orientos Qld 321 G11
Ormeau Qld 317 N2
Ormesby Qld 312 I3
Ormiston Qld 315 N10
Ormiston Gorge NT 262 D4, 237
Ormley Tas. 361 P9
Ormond Vic. 150 D11
Orpheus Island Qld 324 H6, 302
Orroroo SA 200 I5, 207 O13
Orrvale Vic. 167 J7
Osborne SA 195 A3
Osborne Park WA 244 F8
Osbornes Flat Vic. 167 P6, 168 A6
Osbourne NSW 97 O11
O'Shannassy Reservoir Vic. 173 L4
Osmington WA 248 C7
Osterley Tas. 359 K3, 361 K13
O'Sullivans Beach SA 198 F3, 208 F9
Otford NSW 91 P1
Ottaba Qld 314 D5
Otway Ranges Vic. 171 Q11, 172 A11, 134
Ourimbah NSW 83 E13, 99 K5
Ournie NSW 97 R13, 100 A8, 168 G3
Ouse Tas. 356 C1, 359 J4
Outer Harbor SA 196 E9
Ouyen Vic. 96 E10, 162 I9, 137, 129
Ovens Vic. 167 Q8, 168 A8
Overland Corner SA 201 O12, 203 O2
Ovingham SA 194 C2
Owanyilla Qld 323 P7

Owen SA 196 F1, 200 I12, 202 I3
Owens Gap NSW 95 J12, 99 J1
Oxenford Qld 317 O4, **279**
Oxford Falls NSW 71 N6
Oxford Park Qld 308 E10
Oxley NSW 96 I8
Oxley Qld 310 E9
Oxley Vic. 167 O7
Oyster Bay NSW 77 O10
Oyster Cove Tas. 356 H11, 359 M8
Oyster Point SA 205 I13
Ozenkadnook Vic. 164 D10

P

Paaratte Vic. 171 M10
Pacific Palms NSW 99 N2
Packsaddle NSW 92 C8
Padbury WA 244 C1
Paddington NSW 67 J11, **37**
Paddington Qld 310 G2, **275**
Paddys River NSW 100 G4
Padstow NSW 72 E11
Padthaway SA 204 G5
Page ACT 106 E11
Pagewood NSW 73 O9
Paignie Vic. 162 G9
Painswick Vic. 165 P10, 166 A10
Pakenham Vic. 154 I11, 173 J7
Palen Creek Qld 316 I9
Palgarup WA 248 G8
Pallamallawa NSW 94 I4
Pallamanna SA 197 O13, 199 O1
Pallarang Vic. 162 C9
Pallinup WA 249 N7
Palm Beach NSW 77 Q4, 79 L3, 99 K6, **37, 38**
Palm Beach Qld 317 Q7, 319 N7
Palm Dale NSW 83 E12
Palmer SA 197 N10, 203 K6
Palmers Island NSW 95 Q4
Palmerston Gardens NT 265 M10
Palmerville Qld 324 D2, 326 F10
Palm Grove NSW 83 D12
Palm Islands Qld 324 H6
Palm Valley NT 262 E9, 270 H9, **237**
Palm View Qld 307 F11
Palmwoods Qld 307 D9, 313 K10
Palmyra WA 246 E7
Paloona Tas. 360 H6
Palparara Qld 321 G5
Paluma Qld 324 G7
Pambula NSW 100 F11, 175 P2, **55, 61**
Panania NSW 72 C11
Pandie Pandie SA 321 D8
Panitya Vic. 162 B10, 203 R8
Panketyi NSW 199 K4
Panmure Vic. 171 L9
Pannawonica WA 254 E10, **228**
Pantapin WA 251 M9
Panton Hill Vic. 159 O10, 160 A10
Pappinbarra NSW 95 O10
Papunya NT 270 F7, **239**
Paraburdoo WA 254 F12, **217, 226**
Parachilna SA 207 N10, **182**
Paracombe SA 196 I10
Paradise Tas. 360 I7
Paradise Vic. 165 I6
Paradise Point Qld 317 P4
Paradise Waters Qld 318 E10
Parap NT 265 L7
Paraparap Vic. 155 D9
Paratoo SA 201 L5, 207 P13
Parawa SA 198 D10
Parattah Tas. 359 N3, 361 M13
Para Wirra National Park SA 203 J5
Parham SA 196 C3
Parilla SA 203 Q8
Paringa SA 201 Q12, 203 Q3, **188, 190**
Paris Creek SA 199 J4
Parkdale Vic. 150 H8
Parkes ACT 109 L8
Parkes NSW 98 D4, **57, 59**
Parkham Tas. 361 J7
Park Orchards Vic. 149 R7, 160 A12
Park Ridge Qld 317 K1
Parksbourne NSW 90 A12
Parkside SA 194 G10
Parkville NSW 95 J12, 99 J1
Parkwood Vic. 170 G4
Parndana SA 202 D11
Parragundy Gate NSW 93 J3
Parrakie SA 203 O9
Parramatta NSW 70 C13, 72 C2, 99 J6, 100 I1, **57, 38**
Parrawe Tas. 360 E6
Parryville WA 249 K13
Parsons Beach SA 198 F11
Paruna SA 203 Q5
Parwan Vic. 155 G1, 158 G11, 172 D4
Paschendale Vic. 107 F4
Pascoe Vale Vic. 148 F4
Paskeville SA 200 F11, 202 F2
Pastoria Vic. 166 E13, 172 E1

Pata SA 203 P5
Patchewollock Vic. 162 H11
Pateena Tas. 363 E11
Paterson NSW 83 F11, 99 L3
Patersonia Tas. 361 M7, 363 H8
Patho Vic. 166 D4
Patonga NSW 77 P3, 78 I6
Patonga NT 266 H5
Patrick Estate Qld 314 F9
Patyah Vic. 164 C10
Pauls Range Vic. 159 R9
Paupong NSW 100 C10, 104 H11
Pawleena Tas. 357 L5, 359 N6
Pawtella Tas. 359 N3, 361 N13
Paxton NSW 83 B6
Payneham SA 195 F7
Paynes Crossing NSW 99 K4
Paynes Find WA 253 M7, 256 G7, **226**
Paynesville Vic. 174 E8, **137, 133**
Paytens Bridge NSW 98 D5
Peaceful Bay WA 249 J13
Peachester Qld 307 C13, 313 J13
Peachna SA 205 E10
Peak Crossing Qld 316 H2
Peak Downs Qld 325 J13, **295, 297**
Peake SA 203 N8
Peake Creek SA 207 K5
Peak Hill NSW 98 D3
Peakhurst NSW 72 G11
Peak View NSW 100 E8
Pearce ACT 110 G4
Pearcedale Vic. 153 O3, 172 I8
Pearlah SA 205 E12
Pearl Beach NSW 77 Q3, 78 H4
Peats Ridge NSW 83 C12
Pebbly Beach Qld 335 C2
Pedarah WA 251 Q12
Pedirka SA 207 J2
Peebinga SA 162 A8, 203 R6
Peebinga National Park SA 203 Q6
Peechelba Vic. 167 N5
Peel NSW 98 G5
Peelhurst WA 250 F11
Peelwood NSW 98 G7, 100 E2, **47**
Peep Hill SA 201 J12, 203 K3
Pekina SA 200 I5, 207 N13
Pelaw Main NSW 83 E4
Pelham Tas. 356 F2, 359 L5
Pelican Flat NSW 83 G8
Pella Vic. 164 F3
Pellaring Flat SA 197 Q10
Pelton NSW 83 C5
Pelverata Tas. 356 G10, 359 L8
Pemberton WA 248 G9, 256 F13, **225, 218**
Pembrooke NSW 95 O10
Penarie NSW 95 H8, 163 O4
Penfield SA 196 H8
Penguin Tas. 360 G5, **348**
Penguin Island National Park SA 204 E10
Penna Tas. 359 N6
Pennant Hills NSW 70 F7
Penneshaw SA 202 G10, **186, 185**
Pennyroyal Vic. 171 Q10, 172 A10
Penola SA 170 A3, 204 H9, **188**
Penong SA 206 G11
Penrice SA 200 I13
Penrith NSW 74 B3, 77 J7, 99 J6, 100 I1, **57**
Penrose NSW 90 H10
Penshurst NSW 72 H11
Penshurst Vic. 170 I6, **129**
Pental Vic. 163 O11
Pentland Qld 324 F9
Pentland Hills Vic. 158 F10
Penwortham SA 200 I11, 202 I2, **183**
Penzance Tas. 368 H2
Peppermint Grove WA 246 D4
Peppers Plain Vic. 164 H5
Percydale Vic. 165 O11
Perenna Vic. 164 F4
Peregian Beach Qld 307 H4, 313 M7
Perekerten NSW 96 H10
Perenjori WA 252 H8, 256 F7, **225-6, 216**
Pericoe NSW 100 E11, 175 O3
Perillup WA 249 L10
Peringillup WA 249 M7
Perisher NSW 100 C9, 104 D9, **47, 45, 52**
Perkins Reef Vic. 158 C1
Peronne Vic. 164 D9
Perponda SA 203 N7
Perroomba SA 200 H5
Perry Bridge Vic. 174 C9
Perth Tas. 361 M8, 363 F11, **347-8, 341**
Perth WA 242-247, 250 F9, 256 E10, **210-11, 212-13**
Perth Airport WA 245 P11
Perthville NSW 98 G5
Perwillowent Qld 307 D8, 313 J10
Petcheys Bay Tas. 356 F12
Peterborough SA 201 J6, 207 O13, **188**
Peterborough Vic. 171 L11, **134**
Petermann Ranges Aboriginal Res. NT 270 B10
Petersham NSW 73 K6
Petersons Vic. 159 P6, 166 I13, 172 I2

Petersville SA 200 F13, 202 F4
Petford Qld 324 E4, 326 G13
Petrie Qld 308 F1
Petrie Terrace Qld 306 A2, 310 H2
Pettavel Vic. 155 D8
Pheasant Creek Qld 323 M4
Pheasant Creek Vic. 159 P8, 160 B8, 172 I3
Phegans Bay NSW 77 Q2
Philcox Hill SA 199 K3
Phillip ACT 110 H2
Phillip Bay NSW 73 P11
Phillip Island Vic. 172 I10, **118, 126**
Phils Creek NSW 98 E8, 100 D3
Pia Aboriginal Reserve WA 256 E4
Pialba Qld 323 Q6, **292, 296**
Piallaway NSW 95 J10
Pialligo ACT 109 Q9
Piambie Vic. 163 N7
Piangil Vic. 96 G10, 163 N9
Piawaning WA 250 H3
Pichi Richi Pass SA 200 G3, **189, 190**
Pickering Brook WA 250 G9
Pickettaramoor NT 266 D3
Picnic Point NSW 72 D13
Picola Vic. 166 H4
Picton NSW 91 L1, 98 I7, 100 H2, **57**
Picton Junction WA 248 E4, **215**
Pier Millan Vic. 163 K10
Piesseville WA 249 L3
Pigeon Ponds Vic. 164 F13, 170 F2
Piggabeen NSW 317 Q8
Piggoreet Vic. 171 P5
Pikedale Qld 323 O12
Pilchers Bridge Vic. 166 D10
Pillar Valley NSW 95 P5
Pilliga NSW 94 F7
Pillinger Tas. 358 E3, 360 E13
Pimba SA 205 G3, 207 L10, **188**
Pimbaacla SA 205 C6
Pimpama Qld 317 N3
Pimpinio Vic. 164 H8
Pinbarren Qld 313 J5
Pindar WA 252 F3
Pindi Pindi Qld 331 E9
Pine Creek NT 266 F7, **240**
Pine Gap NT 263 L6, 271 J8
Pine Hill Qld 322 H3
Pine Lodge Vic. 167 J6
Pine Ridge NSW 94 I11
Pine Point SA 202 F5
Pinery SA 196 E1, 200 H13
Pingaring WA 249 Q1, 251 Q13
Pingelly WA 251 K12, 256 F10, **226**
Pingrup WA 249 Q5, 256 H11
Pinjarra WA 250 F12, 256 E11, **226, 213, 218**
Pinkawillinie Conservation Park SA 207 J13
Pinkenba Qld 309 L11
Pinkertons Plains SA 196 H3
Pink Lakes State Park Vic. 162 F7
Pinnacle Qld 331 E11
Pinnaroo SA 162 A10, 203 R8, **188**
Pintharuka WA 252 F6
Pioneer Tas. 361 P5, **345**
Pipers Brook Tas. 361 M5, 363 F3
Pipers Creek Vic. 158 H5, 166 E13, 172 F1
Pipers Flat NSW 76 A3
Pipers Hill SA 251 P3
Pipers River Tas. 361 L5, 363 E4
Pira Vic. 163 N10
Piries Vic. 167 M12
Pirlta Vic. 162 F4
Pirron Yallock Vic. 171 O9
Pithara WA 250 I1, 252 I13
Pittong Vic. 171 O4
Pittsworth Qld 323 O11, **298**
Pitt Town NSW 77 K4
Pittwater NSW 77 Q4, 79 L4, **38**
Plainland Qld 314 D11
Planet Downs Qld 321 F7
Platts NSW 100 E11
Pleasure Point NSW 72 C12
Plenty Tas. 356 E5, 359 K6, **340, 348**
Plenty Vic. 149 N1
Plevna Downs Qld 321 I8
Pleystowe Qld 331 G11
Plumpton NSW 77 L7
Plunkett Qld 317 M3
Plush Corner SA 208 H2
Plympton SA 195 C10
Poatina Tas. 361 L10, **348, 350, 351**
Point Arkwright Qld 307 H5, 313 L8
Point Clare NSW 77 Q1, 78 B3
Point Cook Vic. 172 F6
Point Lonsdale Vic. 155 H9, 172 E9, **138**
Point Lookout Qld 315 R9, **301**
Point McLeay SA 199 N9
Point Pass SA 201 K11, 203 K2
Point Perry Qld 313 L8
Point Piper NSW 67 O3, 73 P3
Point Samson WA 254 F9, **228**
Point Stuart NT 266 F4
Pokataroo NSW 94 E4
Pokolbin NSW 81 C8, 83 B4, **43, 45**

Policemans Point SA 203 M12, 204 D3, **185**
Police Point Tas. 356 F13, 359 L9
Polkemmet Vic. 164 G9
Pomborneit Vic. 171 O9
Pomona Qld 313 J5, 323 Q8, **298**
Pomonal Vic. 165 K13, 171 K1
Pompapiel Vic. 165 R6, 166 B6
Pompoota SA 197 Q12
Ponde SA 197 P12
Pondooma SA 200 C9
Pontville Tas. 356 I4, 359 M5, **348, 342**
Pontypool Tas. 359 P3
Poochera SA 205 D7, 206 I13
Pooginagoric SA 164 A7
Poolaigelo Vic. 164 C13, 170 C1, 204 I8
Pooncarie NSW 96 E5
Pooraka SA 196 G10
Pootenup WA 249 M8
Pootilla Vic. 158 B9, 171 R3, 172 B3
Poowong Vic. 173 K9
Popanyinning WA 251 K12
Poppet Head Vic. 158 A9
Porcupine Flat Vic. 158 C1
Porcupine Ridge Vic. 158 D5
Porepunkah Vic. 167 Q9, 168 A9, **123**
Porlock Qld 316 C2
Porongurup National Park WA 249 N11, **214, 219, 224**
Porongurups WA 249 N11
Port Adelaide SA 195 B5, 196 F10, **179**
Port Albert Vic. 173 P11, **137, 133, 144**
Port Alma Qld 323 N3, **291, 300**
Portarlington Vic. 155 I7, 172 F7, **137, 128**
Port Arthur Tas. 357 O11, 359 O9, 368 G5, **344, 340**
Port Augusta SA 200 F4, 205 I7, 207 M12, **188-9**
Port Broughton SA 200 F9, **189**
Port Campbell Vic. 171 M11, **124**
Port Campbell Nat. Park Vic. 171 N11, **134, 124**
Port Clinton SA 200 G12, 202 G3
Port Davis SA 200 F7
Port Denison WA 252 B7, 256 D7, **226, 218**
Port Douglas Qld 324 F3, 326 I11, 335 B1, **298-9, 283, 286, 297**
Port Elliot SA 198 H9, 202 I9, **189, 180**
Porters Retreat NSW 90 B1, 98 G7, 100 F2
Port Fairy Vic. 170 I10, **137, 129**
Port Franklin Vic. 173 N12, **128**
Port Gawler SA 196 E7
Port Germein SA 200 G6, 207 N13, **190**
Port Gibbon SA 200 B10, 202 B1, 205 G10
Port Hedland WA 254 G8, **226**
Port Hughes SA 200 E12, 202 E2
Port Huon Tas. 356 E11, 359 K9
Port Julia SA 202 F5
Port Keats NT 266 B8, **240**
Port Kembla NSW 91 P5, 99 J8, 100 I3, **64, 54**
Port Kenney SA 205 C8
Portland Vic. 170 F9, **137-8, 129**
Portland Roads Qld 326 E4, **300**
Port Latta Tas. 360 D3, **350, 352**
Port Lincoln SA 205 F12, **189, 186**
Port MacDonnell SA 170 A7, 204 H12, **189**
Port Macquarie NSW 85, 95 P11, **60, 58**
Port Melbourne Vic. 148 G10
Port Minlacowie SA 202 E6
Port Neill SA 200 A12, 202 A3, 205 F11, **191, 189**
Port Noarlunga SA 198 F3, 202 I7, 208 F10, **180, 188**
Port Pirie SA 200 G7, **189-90**
Port Prime SA 196 D5
Port Rickaby SA 202 E5
Portsea Vic. 152 B6, 154 E13, 155 I10, 172 F9, **119, 138, 139**
Port Sorell Tas. 361 J5, **348, 343, 344**
Port Stephens NSW 99 N3, **86, 58, 57**
Port Victoria SA 202 E4, 205 I12, **190, 181**
Port Vincent SA 202 F6, **187**
Port Wakefield SA 200 G12, 202 G3, **181**
Port Welshpool Vic. 173 O12, **144**
Port Willunga SA 198 F5
Pothana NSW 83 B2
Potts Point NSW 66 H4, 73 N4
Pottsville NSW 95 R1, 317 R12
Pound Creek Vic. 173 L11
Powelltown Vic. 160 G13, 173 K6
Powers Creek Vic. 164 D13, 170 D1
Powlett Plains Vic. 165 Q7, 166 A7
Powranna Tas. 361 M9, 363 G13
Prahran Vic. 148 I11, 150 A13, **1.16-17**
Prairie Qld 324 E10
Prairie Vic. 166 C6
Pranjip Vic. 166 I9
Premaydena Tas. 357 N10, 359 O8, 368 E3
Premer NSW 94 H10
Preolenna Tas. 360 E5
Preston Tas. 360 G6
Preston Vic. 148 I5
Preston South Tas. 360 G6
Pretty Beach NSW 77 Q3, 78 G1
Pretty Gully NSW 95 O2
Prevelly Park WA 248 C7
Price SA 200 G13, 202 G3

Primbee NSW 91 P6
Primrose Sands Tas. 357 M7, 359 O7
Princes Highway 103
Princetown Vic. 171 N12, **134**
Priors Pocket Qld 310 A11
Priory Tas. 361 Q6
Prooinga Vic. 163 L8
Propodollah Vic. 164 E6
Proserpine Qld 325 K9, 331 D5, **299, 287, 298**
Prospect SA 195 D7
Prospect Tas. 363 F10
Prospect Hill SA 198 I4
Proston Qld 323 O8
Puckapunyal Vic. 159 M1, 166 H11, **140**
Pudman Creek NSW 98 E9, 100 D4
Pullabooka NSW 97 R6, 98 C6, 100 A1
Pullen Vale Qld 310 C7
Pullut Vic. 164 G4
Pumicestone Qld 315 L3
Pumpenbill NSW 317 M11
Pumphreys Bridge WA 251 J12
Punchbowl NSW 72 F9
Punchmirup WA 249 L6
Pungonda SA 162 A5
Puntabie SA 205 B6
Punthari SA 197 P10
Puralka Vic. 170 C6
Pura Pura Vic. 171 M5
Purfleet NSW 99 N1
Purga Qld 314 H13, 316 H1, 323 P11
Purlewaugh NSW 94 G10
Purnim Vic. 171 K9
Purnong Landing SA 203 M6
Purrumbete South Vic. 171 N9
Putney NSW 70 H13, 72 H1
Putty NSW 99 J4
Pyalong Vic. 154 E4, 159 K3, 166 G12
Pyap SA 201 P13, 203 P4
Pyengana Tas. 361 P6
Pygery SA 205 E8
Pykes Creek Reservoir Vic. 158 E10, 172 D4
Pymble NSW 70 I7
Pyramid Vic. 166 C4
Pyramid Hill Vic. 96 I13, 165 R4, **138**
Pyramul NSW 98 G3
Pyree NSW 91 N12
Pyrmont NSW 66 A8, 73 M4
Pyrton WA 245 O7, 259 D10

Q

Quaama NSW 100 F9
Quail Island Vic. 153 P4
Quairading WA 251 L9, 256 G10
Quakers Hill NSW 77 L6
Qualco SA 201 N11, 203 N2
Qualeup WA 249 J6
Quambatook Vic. 96 H13, 165 O3
Quambone NSW 93 R9, 94 C9
Quamby Qld 327 E8
Quamby Brook Tas. 361 J8, 363 A12
Quandary NSW 97 Q8, 98 B8
Quandialla NSW 97 R7, 98 C7, 100 A2
Quangallin WA 249 L4
Quantong Vic. 164 G9
Queanbeyan NSW 98 F11, 100 E6, 112 G4, **58**
Queenscliff NSW 71 Q9
Queenscliff Vic. 152 A5, 154 D12, 155 I9, 172 F8, **138, 128, 139**
Queens Park WA 247 N4
Queensport Qld 311 M1
Queenstown Tas. 358 E1, 360 E11, **348-9**
Quellington WA 251 J8
Quilergup WA 248 E6
Quilpie Qld 322 D8, **294, 295**
Quindalup WA 248 C5
Quindanning WA 248 I2
Quininup WA 248 H9
Quinns Rock WA 250 E7
Quirindi NSW 95 J11, **58**
Quobba WA 254 C13
Quorn SA 200 G3, 207 N12, **190, 186**
Quorrobolong NSW 83 D6

R

Raby Bay Qld 315 N11
Radium Hill SA 201 P3
Radnor Tas. 357 N11
Raglan Qld 323 N4
Raglan Vic. 171 O2, **121**
Railton Tas. 360 I7, **349**
Rainbow Vic. 164 G3, **138**
Rainworth Qld 310 E2
Raleigh NSW 95 P8
Raluana Vic. 165 K9
Ramco SA 201 N12, 203 N3
Raminea Tas. 359 K10
Ramingining NT 267 M4
Ramsgate NSW 73 K12, 83 F9
Rams Head Corner WA 249 Q9
Ranceby Vic. 173 L9
Rand NSW 97 O12, 167 P1

Randell WA 257 K8
Randwick NSW 73 P7
Ranelagh Tas. 356 F9, 359 L8, **345**
Rankins Springs NSW 97 N6
Rannes Qld 323 M4
Rannock NSW 97 P9, 98 A9
Rapid Bay SA 198 B9
Rapid Creek NT 264 A4
Rappville NSW 95 P3
Rathdowney Qld 95 P1, 316 I9
Rathmines NSW 83 G7
Rathscar Vic. 165 O11
Ravensbourne Qld 323 P10
Ravensdale NSW 83 C10
Ravenshoe Qld 324 F5, 326 I13, **283**
Ravensthorpe WA 256 I11, **227**
Ravenswood Qld 324 H9, **299, 288**
Ravenswood Vic. 166 C10
Ravensworth NSW 99 K2
Rawdon Vale NSW 95 L12, 99 L1
Raymond Island Vic. 174 F8, **137**
Raymond Terrace NSW 83 H3, 99 L3, **58**
Raymore Qld 321 I7
Raywood Vic. 166 C8
Razorback Mountain NSW 91 L1
Recherche Archipelago WA 257 K12, **218-19**
Redan Vic. 157 C9
Redbank Vic. 165 N11, 168 C9
Redbank Plains Qld 314 I12
Red Banks SA 196 G4
Redbanks SA 201 K9
Redbourneberry NSW 83 A1
Redcastle Vic. 166 F9
Redcliffe Qld 315 M6, 323 Q10, **278, 299**
Redcliffe WA 245 N10, 259 C13
Red Cliffs Vic. 96 D8, 162 H3, **140**
Red Creek SA 199 L3
Redesdale Vic. 154 C3, 158 H1, 166 E11
Redfern NSW 73 M6
Redhead NSW 83 H7
Red Hill ACT 109 K13, 111 L1
Red Hill Qld 308 G13, 310 G1, **275**
Redhill SA 200 G9
Red Hill Vic. 152 I8
Red Hill South Vic. 153 J8
Red Island Point Qld 326 C1
Red Jacket Vic. 173 N4
Redland Bay Qld 315 O12, **279, 299-300, 301**
Redlynch Qld 335 E7
Redmans Bluff Vic. 165 J13
Redmond WA 249 M12
Redpa Tas. 360 A4
Red Range NSW 95 M5
Red Rock NSW 95 Q6
Red Rock National Park NSW 95 Q6, **64**
Reedy Creek Qld 317 P7, 319 L12
Reedy Creek SA 204 E7
Reedy Creek Vic. 159 N5, 166 H13, 172 H1, **143**
Reedy Dam Vic. 165 J4
Reedy Flat Vic. 174 F5
Reedy Marsh Tas. 361 J7
Reefton NSW 97 Q8, 98 B7
Reefton SA 197 K12
Reefton Vic. 160 H11
Reesville Qld 312 I11
Reeves Plains SA 196 G5
Regans Ford WA 250 E4
Regatta Point Tas. 358 D2, 360 D12
Regents Park NSW 72 D6
Regentville NSW 77 J8
Reid ACT 109 M5
Reid WA 257 Q8
Reid River Qld 324 H8
Reids Creek Vic. 167 P6, **121**
Reids Flat NSW 98 F7, 100 D2
Reidtown NSW 89 E4
Rekuna Tas. 357 J4, 359 M5
Relbia Tas. 361 M8, 363 F10
Remine Tas. 360 C10
Rendelsham SA 204 F10
Renison Bell Tas. 360 D10, **352**
Renmark SA 96 A8, 201 Q12, 203 Q3, **190, 140**
Renner Springs NT 269 J6, **240**
Rennie NSW 97 N12, 167 M2
Research Vic. 149 Q3
Reservoir Vic. 149 J3
Retreat Tas. 361 M5, 363 F5
Revesby NSW 72 E11
Reynella SA 198 F2, 202 I7, 208 G9
Rheban Tas. 357 P3, 359 P5
Rheola Vic. 165 P8
Rhyll Vic. 153 P11, 172 I10
Rhymney Reef Vic. 165 L13, 171 L1
Rhyndaston Tas. 357 J1, 359 M4
Rhynie SA 200 I12, 202 I3
Riachella Vic. 165 K10
Rialto SA 318 G11
Riana Tas. 360 G6
Richardson Hill Vic. 153 N12
Rich Avon Vic. 165 L7
Richlands NSW 98 H8, 100 F4
Richlands Qld 310 D12

Richmond NSW 77 J5, 99 J6, 100 I1, **59**, **38**
Richmond Qld 324 C10, 327 I8, **300**
Richmond Tas. 357 J5, 359 N6, **349**, **340**, **346**
Richmond Vic. 146 I8, 148 I9, **117**
Ricketts Sanctuary Vic. 147 D6
Riddell Vic. 158 I8, 172 F3
Ridgelands Qld 323 M3
Ridgeway Tas. 356 I8
Ridgewood Qld 307 A3, 312 I7
Ridgley Tas. 360 F5, **343**
Ridleyton SA 194 A1
Riggs Creek Vic. 167 K8
Ringa WA 250 H7
Ringarooma Tas. 361 O6, **349**
Ringtail Qld 313 J5
Ringwood Vic. 149 R9, 160 A13, 172 I5
Rio Vista Qld 318 G10
Ripley Qld 314 I13, 316 I1
Ripplebrook Vic. 173 K8
Risdon Tas. 355 E2, **339**
Risdon Vale Tas. 355 G1, 357 J6, 359 M6
River Glen Qld 319 P8
Riverglen SA 199 P4
Riverhills Qld 310 B9
Riversdale WA 249 J9
Riverside North Tas. 361 L7
Riverstone NSW 77 L6
Riverton SA 201 J12, 203 J3
Riverton WA 247 K7
Rivervale WA 242 I3, 245 L13, 247 L1
Riverview NSW 71 K12, 73 K1
Riverwood NSW 72 F11
Rivett ACT 108 C13, 110 C2
Roadvale Qld 316 G4
Robbins Island Tas. 360 B2
Robe SA 204 D8, **190-1**
Robertson NSW 91 L8, 98 I9, 100 H4
Robertson Vic. 311 J9
Robertstown SA 201 K11, 203 K2
Robigana Tas. 361 L6, 363 C6
Robinvale Vic. 96 F9, 163 K5, **138**
Rochedale Qld 311 N11
Rocherlea Tas. 361 L7, 363 F8
Rochester SA 200 H10
Rochester Vic. 166 F6, **138**
Rochford Vic. 159 J6, 166 F13, 172 F2
Rockbank Vic. 155 I1, 158 I11, 172 F5
Rockbrae Qld 316 A8
Rockdale NSW 73 K10
Rock Flat NSW 100 E9
Rockhampton Qld 323 M3, **328**, **300**, **286**, **287**, **291**
Rockingham WA 250 E10, 256 E10, **227**, **213**, **223**
Rocklands Reservoir Vic. 170 H1, **124**
Rocklea Qld 310 G8
Rockleigh SA 197 M12
Rockley NSW 98 G6, 100 F1
Rocklyn Vic. 158 C7, 171 R2, 172 C3
Rocksberg Qld 314 I4
Rockton NSW 100 E11, 175 N3
Rockvale NSW 95 M7
Rockwell WA 252 B2
Rocky Cape Nat. Park Tas. 360 E3, **341**, **343**, **352**
Rocky Creek NSW 94 I6, **41**
Rocky Dam NSW 95 J3
Rocky Glen NSW 94 G9
Rocky Gully WA 249 K10, 256 F13
Rocky Hall NSW 100 E11
Rocky Hill Vic. 158 B5
Rocky River NSW 95 L8
Rocky Valley Reservoir Vic. 174 D1
Rodinga NT 263 O13, 271 K10
Rodney NSW 100 D10
Roebourne WA 254 F9, **217**, **226**, **228**
Roelands WA 248 F3
Rogans Hill NSW 70 C7
Roger Corner SA 202 E6
Roger River Tas. 360 C4
Rokeby Tas. 357 K7, 359 N7, **349**, **339**
Rokeby Vic. 173 L7
Rokewood Vic. 171 Q6, 172 A6
Rokewood Junction Vic. 171 P5
Roland Tas. 360 A7
Rollands Plains NSW 95 O10
Rolleston Qld 323 K5, **291**
Rollingstone Qld 324 G7
Roma Qld 323 K8, **301**
Romsey Vic. 154 D6, 159 J6, 166 F13, 172 F2
Rookwood NSW 72 E5
Rooty Hill NSW 77 L7
Ropely Qld 314 B12
Rosa Glen WA 248 C7
Rosalie Qld 310 G2
Rosanna Vic. 149 L5
Rose Bay NSW 67 Q6, 73 Q3, **37**
Rose Bay Tas. 355 H6
Roseberry NSW 317 Q13
Roseberth Qld 321 D7
Rosebery NSW 73 N7
Rosebery Tas. 360 E9, **350**, **348**
Rosebery Vic. 164 I3
Rosebrook NSW 83 E2

Rosebrook Qld 321 H2
Rosebrook Vic. 170 I9
Rosebud Vic. 152 G8, 154 F13, 172 G9, **139**, **119**
Rosedale NSW 100 D8, 104 I2
Rosedale Qld 323 O5
Rosedale SA 197 J5
Rosedale Vic. 173 Q8, 174 A10
Rosegarland Tas. 356 E4
Rosehill NSW 72 D2
Roseneath Vic. 170 D3
Roses Tier Tas. 361 O8
Rosevale Qld 316 E3
Rosevale Tas. 361 K7, 363 C9
Rose Valley NSW 91 O9
Rosevears Tas. 361 L6, 363 D7, **345**
Roseville NSW 71 K9
Rosewhite Vic. 167 Q8, 168 A8
Rosewood NSW 97 R12, 100 A7, 168 G2
Rosewood Qld 314 F12
Roseworthy SA 196 I5
Roslyn NSW 90 A8, 98 G8, 100 F3, **47**
Roslynmead Vic. 166 E4
Rosny Tas. 355 G7, **339**
Ross Tas. 259 N1, 361 N11, **350**
Rossarden Tas. 361 O9, **341**
Ross Bridge Vic. 171 L3
Ross Creek Vic. 171 Q4, 172 A4
Rossi NSW 98 G11, 100 E6
Rosslynne Reservoir Vic. 172 E3
Rossmore NSW 77 K10
Rossmore WA 251 J6
Ross Mount Qld 312 H1
Ross River NT 263 R4, 271 K8, **236**, **240**
Rossville Qld 324 F1, 326 I10
Rostrevor SA 195 G7, **179**
Rostron Vic. 165 M9
Rothbury NSW 81 G5, 83 C3
Rothsay WA 253 J7, **226**
Roto NSW 97 L4
Rottnest Island WA 243, 250 E9, 256 E10, **211**, **212**, **220**
Rouchel Brook NSW 99 K1
Roughit NSW 83 A1
Round Corner NSW 70 B4, 77 M6
Round Hill WA 250 H2
Round Mountain NSW 317 R11
Rouse Hill NSW 77 M6
Rowella Tas. 361 K5, 363 C5
Rowena NSW 94 F5
Rowes NSW 100 D11, 175 M2
Rowland Vic. 165 R3, 166 C3
Rowland Flat SA 197 K6, 208 C8, **190**
Rowsley Vic. 155 F1, 158 G12, 172 D5
Rowville Vic. 150 E1, 172 I6
Roxborough Downs Qld 321 C1
Royal George Tas. 361 P10
Royalla NSW 98 F11, 100 E6
Royal National Park NSW 77 O11, 99 K7, **39**, **44**
Rozelle NSW 73 K4
Rubicon Vic. 160 H6, 167 L13, 173 L2
Ruby Vic. 173 L10
Rubyvale Qld 322 I3, **291**
Rudall SA 205 F10
Ruffy Vic. 159 R1, 160 D1, 167 J11
Rufus River NSW 96 B7, 162 C2
Rugby NSW 98 F8, 100 D3
Rukenvale NSW 95 P1, 317 J13
Rumbalara NT 271 K11
Rum Jungle NT 266 E6, **234**
Rumula Qld 335 A3
Runaway Bay Qld 318 A10
Runcorn Qld 311 K11
Rundall River National Park WA 255 K11
Running Creek Qld 323 P8
Running Creek Vic. 167 R8, 168 B8
Running Stream NSW 98 H4
Runnymede Tas. 357 L3, 359 N5
Runnymede Vic. 166 E8
Rupanyup Vic. 165 J8, **136**
Rupari SA 199 N10
Rushcutters Bay NSW 73 O4, **37**
Rushworth Vic. 166 G8, **138**
Rushy Pool WA 249 L2
Russell Lea NSW 73 J4
Russell River Qld 335 I12
Russell River National Park Qld 335 I12
Russell Vale NSW 89 E1
Rutherford NSW 83 E3
Rutherglen Vic. 97 O13, 167 O4, 176 C3, **138**, **141**, **144**
Rutland Tas. 359 M3, 361 M13
Ryanby Vic. 163 M10
Ryans Creek Vic. 167 N8
Rydal NSW 76 B4
Rydalmere NSW 70 D13, 72 D2
Ryde NSW 70 H12, 72 H1
Rye Vic. 152 E8, 154 E13, 172 F9, **139**
Rye Park NSW 98 E8, 100 D3
Ryhope NSW 83 F7
Rylstone NSW 98 H3, **59**
Ryton Vic. 173 O10

S

Sackville North NSW 77 L3
Sackville Reach NSW 77 L3
Saddleworth SA 201 J11, 203 J2
Safety Bay WA 250 E10
Safety Beach Vic. 152 I6
St Albans NSW 99 J5
St Albans Vic. 159 K12
St Andrews Vic. 159 P10, 160 A10, **118**, **119**
St Anthonys NSW 91 M8
St Arnaud Vic. 165 N8, **138**
St Clair NSW 95 K13, 99 K2
St Fillans Vic. 160 F9, 173 K3
St George Qld 323 J11, **301**
St Germains Vic. 166 H5
St Helens Qld 331 F9
St Helens Tas. 361 R7, **350**
St Helens Vic. 170 H9
St Ives NSW 71 J6
St Ives Chase NSW 71 J4, 79 R12
St James Vic. 167 L6
St James WA 247 L4
St Johns SA 197 L2
St Kilda SA 196 F8, **179**
St Kilda Vic. 148 H12, 172 G6, **116**
St Kitts SA 197 M2
St Lawrence Qld 323 L1, 325 L12
St Leonards NSW 68 F2, 71 L12, 73 L1
St Leonards Tas. 361 M7, 363 F10, **350**, **347**
St Leonards Vic. 152 B2, 155 I7, 172 F8, **138**
St Lucia Qld 310 G4, **275**, **276**
St Marys NSW 77 K7
St Marys Tas. 361 Q8, **350**
St Patricks River Tas. 363 H7
St Peters NSW 73 M7
St Peters SA 194 H4, 195 E8
St Peters Island SA 205 A6, 206 H12, **183**
Saints SA 200 H12, 202 H3
Salamander Bay NSW 99 M3, **58**
Sale Vic. 173 R7, 174 B10, **140**, **133**, **137**
Salisbury NSW 95 L13, 99 L2
Salisbury Qld 310 I8
Salisbury SA 195 F2, 196 H9, 202 I6
Salisbury Vic. 164 F7
Salisbury West Vic. 165 Q8, 166 B8
Sallys Flat NSW 98 G4
Salmon Gums WA 257 K11
Salt Creek SA 203 M12, 204 D3, **185**
Salters Springs SA 200 I12, 202 I3
Saltwater River Tas. 357 M9, 359 O8, 368 D2
Salvator Rosa National Park Qld 322 H5
Samaria Vic. 167 M9
Samford Qld 308 A8
Sandalwood SA 203 O6
Sandergrove SA 199 K6
Sanderston SA 197 O8
Sandfire Flat Roadhouse WA 255 J8
Sandford Tas. 357 K8, 359 N7
Sandford Vic. 170 E4
Sandfly Tas. 356 H9, 359 M8
Sandgate NSW 83 G5
Sandgate Qld 309 L4, 315 L7, 323 Q10
Sandhill Tas. 363 F10
Sandigo NSW 97 O10
Sandilands SA 202 F4, 205 I12
Sandhill Lake Vic. 165 P2
Sandleton SA 197 Q4
Sandon Vic. 158 C4, 165 R12, 166 B12, 171 R1
Sandown Park Vic. 150 F5
Sandringham Qld 321 C4
Sandringham Vic. 150 F12
Sandsmere Vic. 164 D6
Sandstone WA 256 H5
Sandy Bay Tas. 355 F11, **338**, **339**
Sandy Creek SA 197 J6
Sandy Creek Vic. 168 C6
Sandy Flat NSW 95 M4
Sandy Hill NSW 95 N3
Sandy Hollow NSW 99 J2, 95 J13
Sandy Point NSW 72 C13
Sandy Point Vic. 173 M13
San Remo Vic. 153 R13, 172 I10, **126**
Sans Souci NSW 73 K13
Sapphire NSW 95 L5
Sapphire Qld 322 I3, **291**
Sapphiretown SA 202 F11
Sarah Island Tas. 358 E4, **349** **352**
Saratoga NSW 77 Q2, 78 D2
Sardine Creek Vic. 175 J6
Sarina Qld 325 L11, **301**
Sarina Beach Qld 325 L11
Sarsfield Vic. 174 E7
Sassafras NSW 100 G5
Sassafras Tas. 361 I6
Sassafras Vic. 147 D8
Savage River Tas. 360 D8, **350-1**, **352**
Savernake NSW 97 N12, 167 M2
Sawtel NSW 95 P7, **59**
Sawyers Gully NSW 83 D4
Sawyers Valley WA 250 H8
Sayers Lake NSW 96 G3
Scamander Tas. 361 R8, **351**, **350**

Scarborough NSW 91 P2
Scarborough Qld 315 M6, 299
Scarborough WA 244 C8, 250 F8, 211
Scarsdale Vic. 171 P4
Schofields NSW 77 L6
School Hill Vic. 152 H10
Schouten Island Tas. 361 R13, 342
Scone NSW 95 J12, 99 J1, 59
Scoresby Vic. 150 D1
Scotsburn Vic. 158 B11, 171 R4, 172 B4
Scott Creek SA 198 H2
Scott National Park WA 248 D9, 218
Scotts Creek Vic. 171 M10
Scottsdale Tas. 361 N5, 351
Scotts Flat NSW 83 B1
Scotts Head NSW 95 P9
Scottsville Qld 324 I10
Scrubby Creek Qld 312 F3
Scrub Creek Qld 314 D3
Scullin ACT 106 D11
Seabird WA 250 D5
Seacombe Vic. 174 D10
Seaford SA 198 F4, 208 F11
Seaford Vic. 151 N7, 172 H7
Seaforth NSW 71 O10
Seaforth Qld 331 G9, 287, 295, 298
Seaham NSW 83 H1, 99 L3
Seahampton NSW 83 F5
Sea Lake Vic. 96 F12, 163 L12, 129
Seal Rocks NSW 99 N2
Seaspray Vic. 174 C12, 140, 144
Seaton Vic. 173 P6
Seaview SA 198 G3
Seaview Vic. 173 L9
Sebastian Vic. 166 C8
Sebastopol NSW 97 Q9, 98 B8, 100 A3
Sebastopol Vic. 157 C12, 158 A10, 171 Q4, 172 A4
Second Valley SA 198 C9, 202 H9
Sedan SA 197 P5, 203 L5
Sedgwick Vic. 166 C10
Sefton NSW 72 C7
Selbourne Tas. 361 K7, 363 C9
Selby Vic. 147 E11
Sellheim Qld 324 H9
Sellicks Beach SA 198 E6
Sellicks Hill SA 198 F6
Selwyn Qld 327 E10
Semaphore SA 196 E10, 179
Seppeltsfield SA 208 C3, 190
Serpentine Vic. 165 R7, 166 B7
Serpentine WA 250 F11
Serpentine Dam WA 250 G11, 212, 227
Serpentine Gorge NT 262 G5
Serviceton Vic. 164 B7, 203 R13, 204 I4, 131
Settlement Point NSW 85 D1
Sevenhill SA 200 I10, 202 I1, 183
Seven Hills Qld 311 K3
Seven Mile Beach Tas. 357 K7, 359 N7, 339
Seventeen Mile Rocks Qld 310 D8
Seville Vic. 147 I3, 173 J5
Seymour Tas. 361 R9
Seymour Vic. 154 G3, 159 N1, 166 H11, 140
Shackleton WA 251 N9
Shady Creek Vic. 173 M7
Shakeshaft NSW 83 B12
Shannon Tas. 359 K1, 361 K11
Shannon River Mill WA 248 H10
Shannons Flat NSW 100 D8
Shannonvale Vic. 168 D11, 174 D1
Shark Bay WA 256 B2, 216, 217
Sharps Well SA 200 G9
Shaw Island Qld 325 K9
Shay Gap WA 254 I9, 227
Shays Flat Vic. 165 M11
Sheans Creek Vic. 167 K9
Sheep Hills Vic. 165 J6
Sheffield Tas. 360 I7, 351
Shelbourne Vic. 165 R10, 166 B10
Shelford Vic. 155 A5, 171 R7, 172 B7
Shelley Vic. 100 A8, 168 E5
Shelley Beach NSW 83 F13
Shellharbour NSW 91 P7, 99 J9, 100 I4, 59, 54
Shelly Beach NSW 85 H9
Shenton Park WA 244 E13, 246 E1
Sheoak Log SA 197 J4
Sheoaks Vic. 155 C4, 172 C6
Shepherds Flat Vic. 158 C5
Shepparton Vic. 167 J6, 140
Sherbrooke Vic. 147 D9, 130
Sherbrooke Forest Park Vic. 147 E10
Sheringa SA 205 D10
Sherlock SA 203 N8
Sherwin Ranges Vic. 159 O8
Sherwood Qld 310 F7
Shipley NSW 80 A3
Shirley Vic. 171 N2
Shoalhaven Heads NSW 91 O11, 99 J9, 100 I4
Shoal Point Qld 331 H10
Shooters Hill NSW 76 A11, 98 H7, 100 F2
Shoreham Vic. 153 J12, 172 H10, 139
Shorncliffe Qld 309 L5, 315 L8
Shotts WA 248 H4

Shute Harbour Qld 331 E4, 303, 287, 288, 298, 299
Sidmouth Tas. 361 K6, 363 C5, 341
Sidonia Vic. 158 H3, 166 E12
Silvan Vic. 147 G6, 160 C13, 173 J5, 130
Silvan Reservoir Vic. 147 G7, 160 C13
Silver Creek Vic. 167 P6
Silverdale NSW 76 I10, 80 I11
Silverdale Qld 316 F4
Silverspur Qld 95 L2
Silverton NSW 92 B12, 96 B1, 42
Silverwater NSW 72 E3, 83 F8
Simmie Vic. 166 F6
Simmonds Reef Vic. 158 E8
Simpson Vic. 171 N10
Simpson Desert National Park SA 207 N1, 271 P13, 321 B7
Simpsons Bay Tas. 356 I13, 359 M10
Simpsons Gap Nat. Park NT 263 L5, 271 J8, 236
Singleton NSW 83 A1, 99 K3, 59
Singleton WA 250 F11
Sir Edward Pellew Group NT 267 P11
Sisters Beach Tas. 360 E4, 341, 352
Sisters Creek Tas. 360 E4
Skenes Creek Vic. 171 Q12, 172 A12

Skipton Vic. 171 O4
Skye Vic. 151 O3
Slacks Creek Qld 315 M12
Slade Point Qld 331 I11
Slaty Creek Vic. 165 N8
Smeaton Vic. 158 B6, 165 R13, 166 B13, 171 R2, 172 B2, 127
Smiggin Holes NSW 100 C9, 104 E8, 47, 45, 52
Smithfield Qld 95 K2
Smithfield SA 196 H7
Smithton Tas. 360 C3, 351
Smithville SA 203 P8
Smoko Vic. 167 R10, 168 B10, 174 B1
Smoky Bay SA 205 B6, 206 H12
Smythesdale Vic. 171 P4
Snake Bay NT 266 D2
Snake Valley Vic. 171 P4
Snobs Creek Vic. 160 H5, 167 L13, 173 L1, 128
Snowtown SA 200 G10, 202 H1
Snowy Mountains NSW 104 C8, 46-7, 40, 52, 61, 62
Snowy River National Park Vic. 174 I3, 125
Snug Tas. 356 H10, 359 M8, 345, 346
Snuggery SA 204 G11
Sodwalls NSW 76 A5
Sofala NSW 98 G4
Soldiers Point NSW 99 M3, 58
Somers Vic. 153 M9, 172 H9, 139
Somersby NSW 83 D13, 50
Somerset Tas. 360 F5, 351
Somerset Dam Qld 314 F4
Somerton NSW 95 J9
Somerton Vic. 154 F8, 159 L10
Somerville Vic. 153 M3, 172 H8
Sommariva Qld 322 H8
Sorell Tas. 357 L6, 359 N6, 351
Sorrento Qld 318 G11
Sorrento Vic. 152 C7, 172 F9, 139, 119
South Arm Tas. 357 J9
South Bexley NSW 73 J11
South Bowenfels NSW 76 C5
South Brisbane Qld 306 A8, 310 H3, 275
South Bruny Island Tas. 359 M11, 343
South Canberra ACT 109 K12
South Coogee NSW 73 Q8
South End SA 204 F10, 181
Southern Brook WA 251 J7
Southern Cross WA 256 H9, 227
Southern River WA 247 O12
Southern Vales SA 208, 198 F3, 180, 181, 186, 192

South Forest Tas. 360 D3
South Fremantle WA 246 B10
South Galway Qld 321 H6
South Granville NSW 72 C4
South Guildford WA 245 P9, 259 E12
South Gundagai NSW 98 C10, 100 B5
South Hobart Tas. 355 C11
South Hummocks SA 200 G11, 202 G2
South Island Qld 325 M12
South Kerang Vic. 165 Q2, 166 B2
South Kilkerran SA 200 E13, 202 E4, 205 I11
South Kincumber NSW 77 Q2
South Kumminin WA 251 P10
South Melbourne Vic. 146 B11, 117
South Molle Island Qld 331 F4, 299, 287
South Mount Cameron Tas. 361 P5
South Oxley Qld 310 F12
South Para Reservoir SA 197 J7
South Perth WA 242 D9, 246 I3
Southport NT 266 E5
Southport Qld 317 P5, 318 D12, 323 Q11, 303, 278-9, 301
Southport Tas. 359 L11, 344
South Riana Tas. 360 G6
South Stradbroke Island Qld 317 P3, 301
South Warren Reservoir SA 197 K8

South West National Park Tas. 356 A13, 358 H8, 366-367, 343
South West Rocks NSW 95 P9
South Yarra Vic. 146 H12, 148 I10, 116
Sovereign Hill Vic. 158 A10, 122-3, 118, 121
Spa Vic. 158 F8
Spalding SA 200 I9
Spalford Tas. 360 H6
Spargo Creek Vic. 158 D8, 172 C3
Spearwood WA 246 C11, 250 F9
Speed Vic. 96 E11, 162 I11
Speers Point NSW 83 G6
Speewa Vic. 163 O10
Spence ACT 106 G6
Spencer NSW 77 O2
Spencers Brook WA 250 I7
Spicers Creek NSW 94 F13, 98 F2
Split Junction NSW 71 O12
Spotswood Vic. 148 E10
Sprent Tas. 360 H6
Spreyton Tas. 360 I6
Springbank SA 197 L11
Springbank Vic. 158 C9
Spring Beach Tas. 357 P2, 359 P5
Springbrook Qld 95 Q1, 317 N9
Springdale NSW 98 C8, 100 A3
Springfield Tas. 361 N6
Springfield Vic. 159 K6, 166 F13, 172 F2
Springfield South Tas. 361 N6
Spring Gully Nat. Park SA 200 I11, 202 I1, 183
Spring Hill Qld 306 D2, 310 H2, 275
Spring Hill Vic. 158 F6
Springhurst Vic. 167 O5, 176 C8
Springmount Vic. 158 B7, 171 R2, 172 B2
Spring Ridge NSW 94 G13, 98 G2,
Spring Ridge NSW 94 I10
Springsure Qld 323 J4, 291
Springton Vic. 197 M8, 203 K5
Springvale Qld 321 F3
Springvale Vic. 150 F6
Springwood NSW 76 H7, 80 H4, 98 I6, 100 H1, 53, 39
Springwood Qld 311 O12
Stafford Qld 308 G10
Stamford Qld 324 D11
Stanborough NSW 95 K6
Standley Chasm NT 263 J5, 236
Stanhope NSW 83 C1
Stanhope Vic. 166 G7
Stanley Tas. 360 D3, 351-2
Stanley Vic. 168 A7, 167 Q7, 168 A7
Stanmore NSW 73 L6
Stanmore Qld 312 H13, 314 H1
Stannifer NSW 95 K6
Stannum NSW 95 M4
Stansbury SA 202 F6, 205 I13
Stanthorpe Qld 95 M2, 323 O12, 285, 303
Stanwell Qld 323 M3
Stanwell Park NSW 91 P2, 99 J8, 100 I3
Stapleton NT 266 E6
Stapylton Qld 317 N2
Staughton Vale Vic. 155 E3, 158 E13, 172 D5
Stavely Vic. 171 K4
Stawell Vic. 165 K12, 140-1
Steels Creek Vic. 159 Q9, 160 B10, 172 I4
Steiglitz Vic. 155 C3, 172 C6, 128
Stenhouse Bay SA 202 C8, 205 H13
Stephens Creek NSW 94 B12
Steppes Tas. 359 K2
Stewarts Range SA 204 G7
Stieglitz Tas. 361 R7
Stirling ACT 110 D2
Stirling Vic. 174 F5
Stirling WA 244 F7
Stirling Range National Park WA 249 O10, 256 G13. 214, 216, 219, 220, 222, 224
Stockdale Vic. 174 C8
Stockinbingal NSW 97 R8, 98 C8, 100 A3
Stockmans Reward Vic. 173 M3
Stockport SA 196 I2
Stockton NSW 83 H3, 83 I5, 99 L4
Stockwell SA 197 M3
Stockyard Creek SA 200 I12, 202 I3
Stockyard Hill Vic. 171 O3
Stokers NSW 317 P12
Stokers Siding NSW 95 Q1
Stokes Bay SA 202 D10
Stonefield SA 197 P2, 201 L13, 203 L3
Stonehaven Vic. 155 D7, 172 C7
Stonehenge NSW 95 M5
Stonehenge Qld 322 C5
Stonehenge Tas. 359 O4
Stone Hut SA 200 H7
Stones Corner Qld 311 J5
Stoneyford Vic. 171 O9
Stonor Tas. 359 M4
Stony Creek Vic. 173 M11
Stony Crossing NSW 96 H10, 163 O9
Stony Point NSW 153 N8, 172 H9
Stoodley Tas. 360 I7
Store Creek NSW 98 F3
Storeys Creek Tas. 361 O9, 341
Stormlea Tas. 357 N12, 359 O9, 368 E6

Stow SA 200 H11, 202 H2
Stowport Tas. 360 G5
Stradbroke Qld 315 Q10
Stradbroke Vic. 173 R9, 174 B11
Stradbroke Island North Qld 315 Q10, 274, 301
Strahan Tas. 358 D2, 360 D12, 352, 348, 349
Strangways SA 207 L7
Strangways Vic. 158 C3, 165 R12, 166 B12
Stratford NSW 95 M13, 99 M1
Stratford Qld 335 F7
Stratford Vic. 174 B9, 140
Strathaird NSW 90 B7
Strathalbyn SA 199 K5, 203 J8, 191, 180
Strathallan Vic. 166 F6
Stratham WA 248 E4, 215
Strathblane Tas. 359 K10
Strathbogie NSW 95 L4
Strathbogie Vic. 167 K6
Strath Creek Vic. 159 O4, 160 A4, 166 H13, 172 I1
Strathdownie Vic. 170 C5
Strathelbiss Qld 321 E1
Stratherne WA 251 L12
Strathewen Vic. 159 P9, 160 A9, 172 I3
Strathfield NSW 72 G5
Strathfieldsaye Vic. 154 B2, 166 D10
Strathgordon Tas. 358 G6, 340
Strathkellar Vic. 170 H5
Strathlea Vic. 158 B3, 165 R12, 166 B12
Strathmerton Vic. 97 L13, 167 J3, 136
Strathpine Qld 308 F3
Strawberry WA 252 D7
Streaky Bay SA 205 B7, 206 I13, 191
Streatham Vic. 171 M4
Stretton WA 251 M12
Strickland Tas. 359 J3
Stroud NSW 99 M2, 59
Stroud Road NSW 95 M13, 99 M2
Struan SA 164 A12, 170 A1, 204 H8
Strzelecki Vic. 173 L9
Strzelecki Track SA 207 N9-R4, 188
Stuart Mill Vic. 165 N10
Stuart Park NT 265 N7
Stuart Town NSW 98 F3
Sturt National Park NSW 92 B3, 45, 61
Sturts Stony Desert SA 207 Q2
Subiaco WA 244 G12, 246 G1
Sue City NSW 100 C7
Suggan Buggan NSW 100 B11, 168 I11, 174 I2
Sulphur Creek Tas. 360 G5
Summerfield Vic. 166 C7
Summerhill NSW 73 J6
Summerholm Qld 314 D12
Summervale NSW 93 P10, 94 A10
Sumner Qld 310 C9
Sunbury Vic. 154 D7, 159 J9, 172 F3
Sundown National Park Qld 323 O13, 303
Sunday Creek Vic. 159 M5, 166 H13, 172 H1
Sunnybank Qld 311 J10, 277
Sunny Cliffs Vic. 162 H3
Sunnyside NSW 95 M3
Sunnyside Vic. 168 E10, 174 E1
Sunnyvale SA 200 F12, 202 F3
Sunset Vic. 162 A9
Sunshine NSW 83 G8
Sunshine Vic. 148 B8
Sunshine Beach Qld 307 H2, 313 M6, 280
Sunshine Coast Qld 307, 280, 297-8, 295-6
Surat Qld 323 K10
Surfers Paradise Qld 317 P6, 318 F9, 323 Q11, 278-9
Surges Bay Tas. 356 E12, 359 L9
Surrey Hills Vic. 149 M9
Surry Hills NSW 66 E12, 73 N5
Sussex Inlet NSW 100 H5
Sussex Mill WA 248 E7
Sutherland NSW 77 N11
Sutherlands SA 201 K12, 203 K3
Sutherlands Creek Vic. 155 D5
Sutton NSW 98 F10, 100 E5
Sutton Vic. 165 L2
Sutton Forest NSW 90 I8, 99 I9, 100 G4
Sutton Grange Vic. 158 F1, 166 D11
Suttons SA 204 H11
Suttontown SA 204 H11
Swanbourne WA 244 C13, 246 C2, 211
Swanfels Qld 316 B8
Swan Hill Vic. 96 H11, 163 O11, 141
Swan Marsh Vic. 171 O9
Swanpool Vic. 167 M9
Swanport SA 199 P3
Swan Reach SA 203 M5, 191, 184
Swan Reach Vic. 174 F8
Swan River WA 246 F5
Swansea NSW 83 G8, 99 L4, 59
Swansea Tas. 359 Q2, 361 Q12, 352
Swan View WA 259 I9
Swanwater South Vic. 165 M8
Sweetmans Creek NSW 83 B6
Swifts Creek Vic. 168 F13, 174 F4
Switzerland Ranges Vic. 159 Q3
Sydenham NSW 73 L7
Sydenham Vic. 172 F4
Sydney NSW 66-77, 99 K7, 34-7, 38-9

Sydney Airport NSW 73 M9
Sydney Cove NSW 73 N3, 34, 39
Sylvania NSW 77 O11
Sylvaterre Vic. 166 C5
Symonston ACT 111 O2

T

Tabbara Vic. 175 J7
Tabberabbera Vic. 174 D6
Tabbimoble NSW 95 Q4
Tabbita NSW 97 M7
Tabilk Vic. 166 H10
Tabooba Qld 317 J7
Tabor Vic. 170 I6
Tabragalba Qld 317 L5
Tabulam NSW 95 O3, 323 P13
Tacoma NSW 83 F11
Taggerty Vic. 160 F6, 167 K13, 173 K2, 120
Tahara Vic. 170 F5
Tahara Bridge Vic. 170 F5
Tahmoor NSW 91 L2
Tailem Bend SA 199 R5, 203 L8, 191
Takone Tas. 360 E5
Talawah Tas. 361 O6
Talbingo NSW 100 B7, 168 I1, 62
Talbot Vic. 165 P12, 171 Q1, 172 A1
Talbot Brook WA 250 I9
Taldra SA 162 A4, 201 Q13, 203 Q3
Talgarno Vic. 168 C4
Talia SA 205 D9
Tallageira Vic. 164 B9
Tallanalla WA 248 G2
Tallandoon Vic. 168 C7
Tallangalook Vic. 167 L10
Tallangatta Vic. 168 C5, 141
Tallangatta Valley Vic. 168 D6
Tallarook Vic. 159 N2, 166 H12, 144
Tallebudgera Qld 317 P8, 278, 279
Tallegalla Qld 314 F12
Tallimba NSW 97 P7
Tallong NSW 90 G11, 100 G4
Tallygaroopna Vic. 167 J5
Talmalmo NSW 97 Q13
Talmoi Qld 324 B10, 327 I8
Talwood Qld 94 G1, 323 L12
Tamarang NSW 94 H10
Tamaree Qld 312 G2
Tambar Springs NSW 94 H10
Tambellup WA 249 M7, 256 G12
Tambo Qld 322 G6
Tambo Crossing Vic. 174 F6
Tamborine Qld 323 Q11, 385
Tamborine Mountain National Park Qld 317 M5, 279, 285
Tamborine North Qld 317 N4
Tamborine Village Qld 317 M4
Tambo Upper Vic. 174 F7
Tamboy NSW 99 N3
Taminick Vic. 167 N7, 176 A11
Tamleugh Vic. 167 K8
Tammin WA 251 M7, 227
Tamrookum Qld 317 J7
Tamworth NSW 88, 95 K9, 60, 51
Tanami NT 268 B10
Tanami Desert Wildlife Sanctuary NT 268 D12, 270 D1, 234
Tanbar Qld 321 H7
Tandagin WA 251 Q7
Tanderra Qld 322 I5
Tandur Qld 312 H4
Tangalooma Qld 315 P5, 301
Tangmangaroo NSW 98 E9, 100 D4
Tangorin Qld 324 D12
Tanina Tas. 356 F3, 359 L5
Tanja NSW 100 F10
Tanjil Bren Vic. 173 N5, 136
Tanjil South Vic. 173 N7
Tankerton Vic. 172 I9
Tannymorel Qld 95 N1, 316 B10
Tansey Qld 323 O8
Tantanoola SA 204 G11, 187
Tanti Park Vic. 153 K3
Tanunda SA 197 L5, 201 J13, 203 J4, 208 E5, 190
Tanwood Vic. 165 O11
Tanybryn Vic. 171 Q11, 172 A11
Tapitallie NSW 91 L11
Taplan SA 162 A6, 203 Q4
Tara Qld 323 M10
Taradale Vic. 158 F3, 166 D12
Tarago NSW 98 G10, 100 F5
Tarago Reservoir Vic. 173 L7
Taragoro SA 205 F10
Taralga NSW 90 C6, 98 H8, 100 F3, 55
Tarampa Qld 314 E10
Tarana NSW 98 H6
Taranna Tas. 357 O10, 359 P8, 368 G3
Tarcombe Vic. 166 I11
Tarcoola SA 205 C2, 206 I9
Tarcoon NSW 93 O7
Tarcowie SA 200 I6
Tarcutta NSW 97 R11, 98 C11, 100 A6
Tardun WA 252 F5

Taree NSW 95 N12, 99 N1, 60
Taren Point NSW 77 P10
Targa Tas. 361 N6, 363 H7
Taringa Qld 310 F4
Tarin Rock WA 249 P3
Tarita Vic. 158 D4
Tarlee SA 196 I1, 201 J12, 203 J3
Tarlo NSW 98 G9, 100 F4
Tarnagulla Vic. 165 Q9, 166 A9
Tarneit Vic. 155 I3, 158 I13
Tarnma SA 201 J12, 203 J3
Tarnook Vic. 167 L7
Tarombe Vic. 159 Q1, 160 C1
Tarome Qld 316 D5
Taronga Zoo Park NSW 73 O2, 38
Taroom Qld 323 L7, 303
Taroona Tas. 356 I8, 359 M7, 352, 339
Tarpeena SA 170 A4, 204 H10
Tarragal Vic. 170 E9
Tarragindi Qld 310 I7
Tarraleah Tas. 358 I3, 360 I13, 351
Tarranginnie Vic. 164 E6
Tarrango Vic. 162 E5
Tarryanurk Vic. 164 G5
Tarra Valley National Park Vic. 173 O10, 133, 136, 144
Tarraville Vic. 173 P11, 144
Tarrawanna NSW 89 C3
Tarrawarra Vic. 159 Q10, 160 C10
Tarrawingee Vic. 167 O7, 176 G10
Tarrayoukyan Vic. 170 E2
Tarrenlea Vic. 170 G5
Tarrington Vic. 170 H5
Tarrion NSW 93 O6, 94 A6
Tarro NSW 83 G4
Tarwin Vic. 173 L11, 144
Tarwin Meadows Vic. 173 L12
Tarwonga WA 249 J3
Tascott NSW 78 C4
Tatham NSW 95 P3
Tathra NSW 100 F10
Tatong Vic. 167 M9
Tatura Vic. 166 H7, 140
Tatyoon Vic. 171 M3
Tawonga Vic. 168 C9, 141
Tayene Tas. 361 N6
Taylors Arm NSW 95 O9, 54
Taylors Flat NSW 98 F8, 100 D3
Taylors Well WA 251 J12
Taylorville SA 201 N11, 203 N2
Tea Gardens NSW 99 M3, 58
Teal Flat SA 203 L6
Teal Point Vic. 163 R13, 165 R2, 166 B1
Teasdale Vic. 155 B5
Tea Tree Tas. 356 I4, 359 M6, 348
Tea Tree Gully SA 196 I10
Tea Tree Well NT 271 A4
Tecoma Vic. 147 D11
Teddington Reservoir Vic. 165 N10
Teddywaddy Vic. 165 N5
Teesdale Vic. 171 R7, 172 B7
Telangatuk Vic. 164 G12
Telarah NSW 83 E3
Telegraph Point NSW 93 O10
Telford Vic. 167 L4
Telita Tas. 361 O5
Telopea NSW 70 D11
Telopea Downs Vic. 164 B5, 203 R12, 204 I3
Telowie Creek SA 200 G6
Temma Tas. 360 A6
Temora NSW 97 Q8, 98 B8, 60
Tempe NSW 73 L8
Templers SA 196 I4
Templestowe Vic. 149 O6
Templin Qld 316 G5
Tempy Vic. 162 I11
Teneriffe Qld 311 J2
Tenindewa WA 252 D4
Ten Mile Vic. 173 N2
Ten Mile Hollow NSW 83 A13
Tennant Creek NT 269 K9, 240
Tennyson NSW 70 H13, 72 I2, 77 J4
Tennyson Qld 310 G7
Tennyson SA 196 E11
Tennyson Vic. 166 D6
Tenterden WA 249 M9
Tenterfield NSW 95 N3, 323 O13, 60
Tenthill Qld 314 B12
Tepko SA 197 O12, 203 K7
Teralba NSW 83 G6
Terang Vic. 171 M8, 142
Teridgerie NSW 94 E9
Terip Terip Vic. 154 I3, 160 D1, 167 J11
Terka SA 200 G5
Termeil NSW 98 I11, 100 G6
Terowie NSW 94 C13, 97 R2, 98 C2
Terowie SA 201 J7
Terrace Creek Qld 316 I12
Terragon NSW 317 N12
Terranora NSW 317 Q9
Terrara NSW 91 M12
Terrey Hills NSW 71 M2, 79 P9
Terrick Terrick Vic. 166 C4, 138

Terrigal — Turriff

Terrigal NSW 77 R1, 60
Terry Hie Hie NSW 94 I5
Tewantin Qld 307 F1, 313 L6, 323 Q8, 297-8, 292
Tewinga NSW 95 P8
Tewkesbury Tas. 360 F6
Texas Qld 95 K2, 323 N12, 303, 292
Thagoona Qld 314 F2
Thalaba NSW 98 G8, 100 E3
Thalia Vic. 165 M4
Thallon Qld 94 F2, 323 K12
Thangool Qld 323 M5, 281
Thargomindah Qld 322 D11, 295
Tharwa ACT 98 F11, 100 D6
Thebarton SA 194 A5, 195 D8, 196 G11
The Basin Vic. 147 C7
The Bluff Vic. 155 D1
The Brothers Vic. 168 F11, 174 F1
The Cascade Vic. 168 D6
The Caves Qld 323 M3
The Cove Vic. 171 K10
The Entrance NSW 83 F12, 99 L5, 60
The Falls Qld 316 C10
The Gap Qld 308 D13, 310 D1
The Glen Tas. 361 L5, 363 E5
The Gold Coast Qld 318-19, 278-9, 289, 303
The Grampians Vic. 165 J13, 171 J1, 142, 126, 129, 131
The Granites NT 268 D11, 270 D1
The Gurdies Vic. 173 J9
The Head Qld 316 D10
The Heart Vic. 174 C10
The Jim Jim Vic. 158 H5
The Lakes WA 250 H8
The Lakes National Park Vic. 174 E9, 133, 125
The Leap Qld 331 G11
The Meadows NSW 76 A7
The Oaks NSW 76 I12, 98 I7, 100 H2
Theodore Qld 323 M6, 303
The Olgas NT 272, 236, 238
The Patch Vic. 147 F9
The Pinnacles Vic. 152 I12
The Pocket Qld 312 G5, 317 Q13
The Point SA 199 Q4, 203 L8
The Range SA 198 G5
Theresa Park NSW 77 J11
The Risk NSW 95 P1, 317 J3
The Rock NSW 97 P11, 98 A11, 60
The Sisters Vic. 171 L8
The Slopes NSW 77 J4
The Spit NSW 71 O11
The Summit Qld 314 H8
The Vale NSW 96 H6
Thevenard SA 205 A6, 183
The Yea Spur Vic. 159 P4
Thirlmere NSW 91 K2, 98 I8, 100 H3
Thirlstane Tas. 361 J6
Thirroul NSW 91 P3
Thistle Island SA 205 F13, 189
Thologolong NSW 168 D4
Thomas Plains SA 200 F11, 202 F2
Thomastown Vic. 149 J1
Thomson Vic. 156 G11
Thoona Vic. 167 M6
Thoopara Qld 331 C6
Thora NSW 95 O7, 41
Thorngate SA 194 E1
Thornlands Qld 315 N11
Thornleigh NSW 70 E7
Thornlie WA 247 N9
Thornside Qld 311 R3
Thornton NSW 83 G3
Thornton Qld 316 C3
Thornton Vic. 160 G5, 167 L13, 173 L1
Thorpdale Vic. 173 N9
Thowgla Vic. 168 G6
Thredbo NSW 100 B9
Thredbo Village NSW 104 C10, 47, 45
Three Bridges Vic. 160 F13
Three Hummock Island Tas. 360 B1
Three Springs WA 252 F8, 256 E7, 227-8
Thrington SA 200 F11, 202 F2
Thuddungra NSW 97 R7, 98 D7, 100 B2
Thule NSW 166 D1
Thulloo NSW 97 O6
Thurla Vic. 162 G4
Thursday Island Qld 326 C1, 296, 300
Tia NSW 95 M10
Tibbuc NSW 95 M12
Tiberias Tas. 359 M4
Tibooburra NSW 92 C4, 321 H13, 322 A13, 61
Tichborne NSW 98 D4
Tickera SA 200 F10, 205 I10, 259 F1
Tidal River Vic. 161 E10, 172 G13, 132
Tiega Vic. 162 H9
Tilba Tilba NSW 100 G9, 56
Tilpa NSW 92 I9
Timbarra Vic. 174 G4
Timber Creek NT 266 D11, 268 D1
Timberoo Vic. 162 H9
Timbertown NSW 87 Q4, 62
Timbillica NSW 100 F12
Timboon Vic. 171 M10, 124
Timmering Vic. 166 G6

Timor NSW 95 K12, 56
Timor West Vic. 165 K12, 135
Tinamba Vic. 173 Q6, 174 A9
Tinana Qld 323 P7
Tinaroo Falls Qld 335 C11, 281
Tinbeerwah Qld 307 E1, 313 K6
Tin Can Bay Qld 323 Q8, 303, 284, 292
Tincurrin WA 249 N2
Tingalpa Qld 311 O3
Tingha NSW 95 K6, 61
Tingiringi NSW 175 K1
Tingoora Qld 323 O8
Tinonee NSW 99 N1
Tintaldra Vic. 100 B8, 168 G4
Tintenbar NSW 95 Q3
Tintinara SA 203 O11, 204 E2, 191
Tipton Qld 323 N10
Tirrannaville NSW 90 B13, 98 G9, 100 F4
Tittybong Vic. 165 N2
Tocal Qld 322 C4
Tocumwal NSW 97 M12, 167 J2, 61, 59
Togari Tas. 360 B4
Toggannoggera NSW 100 F7
Tolberry Tas. 361 L8, 363 D12
Tolga Qld 335 C12, 282
Tolmie Vic. 167 N10, 135
Tomago NSW 83 H4, 58
Tomahawk Tas. 361 O4
Tomboy NSW 98 H11
Tomerong NSW 98 I10, 100 H5
Tomewin Qld 317 P9
Tom Groggin NSW 100 B9, 104 A10, 168 H8
Tomingley NSW 98 D2
Tom Price WA 254 G11, 217, 226
Tone River Mill WA 248 H9
Tongala Vic. 166 G5
Tongarra NSW 91 N7
Tonghi Creek Vic. 175 L6
Tongio Vic. 168 F13, 174 F3
Tonimbuk Vic. 173 K7
Tonkoro Qld 321 H3
Tooan Vic. 164 F10
Toobeah Qld 94 H1, 323 L12
Tooborac Vic. 154 E3, 159 K2, 166 F11
Toodyay WA 250 H6, 256 F9, 228, 213
Toogong NSW 98 E5
Toogoolawah Qld 314 C4, 323 P10
Tookayerta SA 201 P13, 203 P4
Toolamba Vic. 166 I7
Toolangi Vic. 159 R9, 160 D9, 173 J3, 129
Toolbrunup WA 249 N7
Toolern Vale Vic. 158 I10, 172 E4
Tooleybuc NSW 96 G10, 163 N8
Toolibin WA 249 M2
Tooligie SA 205 E10
Toolijoa NSW 91 O10
Toolleen Vic. 154 D1, 166 F9
Toolondo Vic. 164 G11
Toolong Vic. 170 I9
Tooloom NSW 95 O2, 316 D13
Tooloon NSW 94 D9
Tooma NSW 97 R13, 100 B8, 168 H4, 62
Toombul Qld 309 K10
Toombullup Vic. 167 N10
Toomcul Qld 312 C5
Toompine Qld 322 E9
Toompup WA 249 P7
Toongabie Vic. 173 P7
Toongi NSW 94 E13, 98 E2
Toonumbar NSW 95 O2
Tooperang SA 198 I7
Toora Vic. 173 N11
Tooradin Vic. 153 R3, 172 I8, 131, 119
Toorak NSW 149 J11, 150 A11, 116
Toorale East NSW 93 L7
Tooraneedin Estate Qld 317 P3
Tooraweenah NSW 94 F9
Toorbul Qld 315 L3, 286
Toorbul Point Qld 315 M4
Toorongo Vic. 173 M5, 143
Toorourrong Reservoir Vic. 159 O8, 172 H3
Tootgarook Vic. 152 F8
Toowong Qld 310 F3
Toowoomba Qld 320, 323 O10, 303-4, 278-9, 290
Toowoon Bay NSW 83 F12, 60
Top Springs NT 266 F13, 268 F3
Torranlea Qld 323 P7
Torbay WA 249 M13
Toronto NSW 83 G7, 99 L4, 59
Torquay Vic. 155 E10, 172 D9, 142, 128, 134
Torrens ACT 110 G5
Torrens Creek Qld 324 E10
Torrens Vale SA 198 E9
Torrington NSW 95 M4, 323 O13
Torrita Vic. 162 G9
Torrumbarry Vic. 166 E4, 126
Torwood Qld 310 F2
Tostaree Vic. 174 H7
Tottenham NSW 93 Q13, 94 B13, 97 Q1, 98 B1
Tottenham Vic. 148 C8
Tottington Vic. 165 M9, 141
Touche WA 252 F10
Toukley NSW 83 G11, 61

Towallum NSW 95 P6
Towamba NSW 100 F11, 175 O3
Towan Vic. 163 N9
Towaninny Vic. 165 N3
Tower Hill Tas. 361 P8
Tower Hill Vic. 171 J9
Towitta SA 197 O5
Townson Qld 316 C4
Townsville Qld 324 H7, 332, 304, 302
Towong Vic. 97 R13, 100 B8, 168 G5
Towradgi NSW 89 F4, 91 P4
Towrang NSW 90 D11, 98 H9, 100 F4
Trafalgar Vic. 173 M8, 142
Tragowel Vic. 165 R3, 166 B3
Trangie NSW 93 R12, 94 C12, 97 R1
Traralgon Vic. 173 P8, 142, 136, 144
Traveston Qld 312 I5
Trawalla Vic. 171 O3
Trawool Vic. 159 O2, 160 A2, 166 H12
Trayning WA 251 N4, 256 G9
Traynors Lagoon Vic. 165 M8
Traysurin WA 249 N1, 251 N13
Trebonne Qld 324 G6
Treesville WA 248 H3
Treeton WA 248 C6
Tregeagle NSW 95 Q3
Tregony Qld 316 C6
Tremont Vic. 147 C9
Trenan Tas. 361 O6
Trentham Vic. 154 B6, 158 F7, 172 D2
Trephina Gorge NT 263 Q3, 240
Tresco Vic. 163 P12
Trevallyn NSW 99 L2
Trevallyn Tas. 363 F9, 351
Trewalla Qld 321 I5
Trewalla Vic. 170 E9
Trewilga NSW 98 D3
Triabunna Tas. 357 P1, 359 P4, 352, 343
Trial Bay NSW 86 I2, 52
Trida NSW 97 K4
Trida Vic. 173 L9
Trigg WA 244 C6
Trinita Vic. 162 H7
Trinity Bay Qld 335 D3, 283, 286
Trinity Beach Qld 335 E6
Trowutta Tas. 360 C4
Trueman Qld 331 D11
Truganina Vic. 155 I2, 159 J13
Trundle NSW 97 R4, 98 C3
Trunkey Creek NSW 98 F6, 100 E1
Truro SA 197 N3, 201 K13, 203 K4
Tuart Hill WA 244 G8
Tubbul NSW 97 R8, 98 C7, 100 B2
Tubbut Vic. 175 J3
Tuckanarra WA 256 G4
Tucklan NSW 94 G13
Tudor Vic. 163 M9
Tuen Qld 93 M1, 322 F12
Tuena NSW 98 F7, 100 E2, 47
Tuggerah NSW 83 E12
Tuggerah Lake NSW 83 F12, 60
Tuggeranong ACT 110 F8
Tuggerawong NSW 83 F11
Tuglow NSW 76 B12, 98 H7, 100 G2
Tugun Qld 317 Q8, 319 O5, 278
Tulkara Vic. 165 M11
Tullamarine Vic. 148 D1
Tullamore NSW 97 Q3, 98 B3
Tullanaringa Qld 326 C3
Tullaroop Reservoir Vic. 158 A3, 165 Q12, 166 A12
Tullibigeal NSW 97 O5
Tullis WA 248 H1, 250 H13
Tully Qld 324 G5, 304, 302
Tulmur Qld 321 H1
Tulum Vic. 153 L9
Tumbarumba NSW 97 R12, 100 B7, 168 H2, 61-2
Tumbi Umbi NSW 83 F12
Tumbling Waters NT 266 D5
Tumblong NSW 97 R10, 98 C10, 100 B5
Tumbulgum NSW 95 Q1, 317 Q10
Tumby Bay SA 205 F11, 191, 189
Tumorrama NSW 98 D10, 100 C5
Tumut NSW 98 D11, 100 B6, 62
Tunart Vic. 162 C5
Tunbridge Tas. 359 N2, 361 N12
Tuncurry NSW 95 N13, 99 N2, 48
Tungamah Vic. 167 L5
Tungkillo SA 197 M10, 203 K6
Tunkalilla Beach SA 198 D11
Tunnack Tas. 359 N4
Tunnel Tas. 363 F5
Tunnel Creek National Park WA 255 N5
Tunney WA 249 L8
Tuppal NSW 97 L12
Turill NSW 94 H12
Turner ACT 109 K4
Turners Marsh Tas. 361 L6, 363 F6
Turondale NSW 98 G4
Tuross Head NSW 100 G8
Turramurra NSW 70 H6
Turrawan NSW 94 H7
Turrella NSW 73 K9
Turriff Vic. 163 J12

Turton SA 202 E7
Turtons Creek Vic. 173 N11, **128**
Tutunup WA 248 E5
Tutye Vic. 162 D10
Tweed Heads NSW 95 R1, 317 R8, 319 Q3, 323 Q12, **62, 279, 289**
Twelve Mile NSW 98 F2
Twin Lakes Vic. 155 D2, 158 E12, 172 C5
Two Mile Flat NSW 94 G13, 98 G2
Two Wells SA 196 F6, 202 I5
Tyaak Vic. 159 N4, 166 H13, 172 H1
Tyabb Vic. 153 N5, 172 H8
Tyagarah NSW 95 R2
Tyagong NSW 98 D7, 100 B2
Tyalgum NSW 95 Q1, 317 M11
Tyalla Vic. 162 D10
Tycannah NSW 94 H5
Tyenna Tas. 356 B4, 359 J6
Tyers Vic. 173 O8, **136**
Tyers Junction Vic. 173 N6
Tylden Vic. 158 G6, 166 D13, 172 D2
Tylerville Qld 316 H10
Tynong Vic. 173 K7, **127**
Tyntynder Central Vic. 163 O10, **141**
Typo Vic. 167 O10
Tyrendarra Vic. 170 G8
Tyringham NSW 95 O7
Tyrrell Downs Vic. 163 L11

U

Uarbry NSW 94 H12
Ubobo Qld 323 N5
Ucolta SA 201 J6
Uki NSW 95 Q1, 317 O12
Ulamambri NSW 94 G10
Ulan NSW 94 H13, 98 G2
Ulidia NSW 95 O2
Ulinda NSW 94 G11
Ulladulla NSW 98 I11, 100 H6, **62, 54**
Ullina Vic. 165 Q13, 166 B13, 171 R1, 172 B1
Ullswater Vic. 164 D11
Ulmarra NSW 95 P5
Ulong NSW 95 P7
Ulooloo SA 201 J8
Ultima Vic. 96 G12, 163 N12
Ultimo NSW 66 B11
Ulupna Vic. 166 I3
Uluru National Park NT 272, **238**
Ulva WA 251 O7
Ulverstone Tas. 360 H5, **352, 348**
Umbakumba NT 267 P7
Umina NSW 77 Q3, 78 G3
Unanderra NSW 91 O5, 99 J8, 100 I3
Una Voce NSW 77 L2
Undalya SA 200 I11, 202 I2
Undandita NT 270 G8
Undandita Aboriginal Reserve NT 262 A5
Undera Vic. 166 I6
Underbool Vic. 162 F10
Undercliffe NSW 73 K8
Underwood Tas. 363 G7
Ungarie NSW 97 P6
Ungarra SA 205 F11
Union Reef NT 266 F7
Unley SA 194 E10, 195 E9, 196 G12
Unumbar NSW 316 H12
Upper Cedar Creek Qld 314 I8
Upper Coliban Reservoir Vic. 166 D13, 172 D1
Upper Colo NSW 77 J2
Upper Ferntree Gully Vic. 147 B10, 172 I6
Upper Hermitage SA 196 I9
Upper Horton NSW 94 I6
Upper Kangaroo River NSW 91 M9
Upper Laceys Creek Qld 314 H6
Upper Maffra West Vic. 173 Q6, 174 A8
Upper Mangrove Creek NSW 83 B12
Upper Mount Hicks Tas. 360 F5
Upper Myall NSW 95 N13, 99 N2
Upper Nariel Vic. 168 G7
Upper Plenty Vic. 159 M7, 172 H2
Upper Sturt SA 196 H13, 198 H1
Upper Swan WA 250 G8, 259 G2
Upper Yarra Reservoir Vic. 160 I11, 173 L4, **119**
Upwey Vic. 147 C10
Uraidla SA 196 I12
Uralla NSW 95 L8, **62**
Urana NSW 97 N11
Urandangi Qld 271 R3, 327 B10
Urangan Qld 323 Q7, **292, 296**
Urangeline East NSW 97 O11
Urania SA 202 E4
Uranno SA 205 F11
Uranquinty NSW 97 P10
Urbenville NSW 95 O1, 316 E13
Urunga NSW 95 P8, **62**
Uxbridge Tas. 356 D5, 359 K6

V

Vacy NSW 99 L3
Valdora Qld 307 F5, 313 K8

Valencia Creek Vic. 173 R5, 174 B8
Valentine NSW 83 G7
Valley Heights NSW 76 I7, 80 I4
Valley of Eagles NT 263 Q4
Vasey Vic. 170 G2
Vasse WA 248 D5
Vaucluse NSW 73 Q3, **37**
Vaughan Vic. 158 D3, 166 C12, **124**
Vectis Vic. 164 G9
Veitch SA 203 P5
Ventnor Vic. 172 H10
Venus Bay SA 205 C8
Verdun SA 199 J1, 197 J13, 199 J1
Veresdale Qld 317 K4
Vergemont Qld 329 I3
Vermont NSW 83 E10
Vermont Vic. 149 R11, 150 A3
Verran SA 205 F10
Vesper Vic. 173 M6
Victor Harbor SA 198 H10, 202 I9, **191, 180**
Victoria Desert SA 206 B5
Victoria Park WA 242 I9, 247 K2
Victoria Point Qld 315 O12, **299**
Victoria River Crossing NT 266 E11, 268 E1, **240**
Victoria River Downs NT 266 E13, 268 E2
Victoria Valley Tas. 359 J3, 361 J13
Victoria Valley Vic. 170 I4
Victory Downs NT 270 I13, **240**
Villawood NSW 72 B7
Villeneuve Qld 314 G2
Vimy Qld 323 M4
Vimy Ridge SA 196 I13, 198 I1
Vincentia NSW 99 J10, 100 H5
Vine Vale SA 208 F4
Vineyard NSW 77 L5
Vinifera Vic. 163 N10
Violet Town Vic. 167 K8
Violet Valley Aboriginal Reserve WA 255 Q5
Virginia Qld 309 J8
Virginia SA 196 G7, 202 I5
Vite Vite Vic. 171 N6
Viveash WA 245 R6, 259 F9
Vivonne Bay SA 202 D12

W

Waaia Vic. 166 I4
Wabba Vic. 168 F6
Wabonga Plateau State Park Vic. 167 O10
Wacol Qld 310 C11, **293**
Waddamana Tas. 359 K2, 361 K12
Wadderin WA 251 P9
Waddi Forest WA 252 G10
Waddikee SA 205 F9
Waddington WA 250 H3
Waeel WA 251 K7
Wagait NT 266 D4
Wagait Aboriginal Reserve NT 266 C5
Wagant Vic. 163 J9
Wagerup WA 248 F1
Waggarandall Vic. 167 L5
Wagga Wagga NSW 97 Q10, 98 B10, **62**
Wagga Wagga WA 253 J2
Waggrakine WA 252 A4
Waggs Range NSW 159 P1
Wagin WA 249 L3, 256 G11, **228, 219**
Wagonga NSW 100 G9
Wagoora Qld 331 F5
Wagstaffe NSW 77 Q3, 78 G2
Wahgunyah Vic. 167 O4, 176 A2, **138**
Wahring Vic. 166 H9
Wahroonga NSW 70 H5
Waikerie SA 201 N12, 203 N3, **192**
Waikiki WA 250 F11
Wail Vic. 164 H8, **127**
Wairewa Vic. 174 H7
Waitara NSW 70 G5
Waitchie Vic. 163 M11
Waitpinga SA 198 F10, **191**
Waitpinga Beach SA 198 F11
Wakefield NSW 83 F6
Wakool NSW 97 J11
Walbundrie NSW 97 O12, 167 Q2
Walcha NSW 95 L9, **62**
Walcha Road NSW 95 L9
Walebing WA 250 G2
Walgett NSW 93 R6, 94 D6, **62**
Walgoolan WA 251 Q6
Walhalla Vic. 173 O6, **143, 133, 136**
Walkamin Qld 335 B10
Walkaway WA 252 B5
Walker Flat SA 203 M6
Walkerston Qld 331 G12
Walkerville SA 194 H1, 195 E7
Walkerville Vic. 173 M13, **128, 144**
Wallabadah NSW 95 J11
Wallabrook SA 164 A9, 204 H6
Wallace Vic. 158 C9, 171 R3, 172 B3
Wallacedale Vic. 170 G6
Wallacia NSW 76 I9, 99 J7, 100 H1, **38, 57**
Wallaga Lake National Park NSW 100 G9, **41**
Wallalong NSW 83 G2

Wallaloo Vic. 165 L9
Wallan Vic. 159 M7, 172 G2
Wallangarra Qld 95 M3, 323 O13
Wallangra NSW 95 K4, 323 N13
Wallara Ranch Tourist Chalet NT 262 A13, 270 G10, **240, 236**
Wallaroo Qld 323 L4
Wallaroo SA 200 E11, 202 E2, 205 I10, **192, 181, 184, 187**
Wallaville Qld 323 O6
Walla Walla NSW 97 P12, 167 R2, 168 A2
Wall Creek SA 206 I1
Wallendbeen NSW 98 D8, 100 B3
Wallerawang NSW 76 B3, 98 H5
Wall Flat SA 197 P12
Walli NSW 98 E6, 100 D1
Wallinduc Vic. 171 P6
Wallington Vic. 155 G8, 172 E8
Walloon Qld 314 G12
Walloway SA 200 I4
Wallsend NSW 83 H5, 99 L4
Wallumbilla Qld 323 K9
Wallup Vic. 164 H6
Walmer NSW 98 E3
Walmer Vic. 158 D1
Walpa Vic. 174 D8
Walpeup Vic. 162 G9
Walpole WA 248 I12, 256 F13, **219**
Walpole-Nornalup Nat. Park WA 248 I13, **221**
Walsh Qld 324 D3, 326 F12
Waltowa SA 199 R11, 203 L10, 204 C1
Walwa Vic. 97 R13, 100 A8, 168 F4
Wal Wal Vic. 165 J10
Walyunga National Park WA 250 G7, **213**
Wamberal NSW 77 R1, 83 F13, **60**
Wambidgee NSW 98 D9, 100 B4
Wamboyne NSW 98 B5
Waminda NSW 94 D6
Wamoon NSW 97 N8
Wampoony SA 203 P13, 204 G4
Wamuran Qld 315 J3
Wanaaring NSW 92 I5
Wanalta Vic. 166 G8
Wanappe SA 200 H11, 202 H2
Wanbi SA 203 O6
Wandana SA 205 A5
Wandana Heights Vic. 156 A13
Wandandian NSW 98 I10, 100 H5
Wandearah SA 200 G8
Wandering WA 250 I12, 256 F10
Wandiligong Vic. 167 R10, 168 B9
Wandilo SA 204 H11
Wandin Vic. 147 G3, 160 C12
Wandin East Vic. 147 I5
Wandin Yallock Vic. 147 H4
Wandoan Qld 323 L8
Wando Bridge Vic. 170 D3
Wandong Vic. 154 F6, 159 M6, 172 G2
Wando Vale Vic. 170 E3
Wandsworth NSW 95 L6
Wanganella NSW 97 K11
Wangarabel Vic. 100 E12
Wangaratta Vic. 167 N6, 176 D9, **142-3, 144**
Wangary SA 205 E12
Wangerrip Vic. 171 O12
Wanglanna SA 207 M7
Wangi Wangi NSW 83 G8, **59**
Wangoon Vic. 171 K9
Wang Wauk NSW 95 N13, 99 N1
Wanilla SA 205 E12
Wannamal WA 250 G4
Wanneroo WA 250 F8, **228, 213**
Wanniassa ACT 110 H9
Wannon Vic. 170 G4
Wanora Qld 314 G10
Wantabadgery NSW 97 R10, 98 C10, 100 A5
Wantagong Qld 321 I3
Wantirna Vic. 150 A2
Wanwin Vic. 170 C7
Wapengo NSW 100 F10
Waraga NT 267 N4
Waramanga ACT 110 E3
Waranga Vic. 166 H8
Waranga Reservoir Vic. 166 H8
Waratah NSW 82 B4, 83 H5
Waratah Tas. 360 E7, **352, 348**
Waratah Bay Vic. 173 M12, **128, 132**
Waratah North Vic. 173 M12
Warbreccan Qld 321 I4
Warburton Vic. 160 F12, 173 K5, **143, 119, 127**
Warby Range State Park Vic. 167 N6
Wardell NSW 95 Q3
Wards Belt SA 196 H6
Wareek Vic. 165 P11
Wareemba NSW 72 I4, 73 J4
Warenda Qld 321 E1
Wargeila NSW 98 E9, 100 D4
Warge Rock NSW 97 R2, 98 C2
Warialda NSW 95 J4, **62**
Warilla NSW 91 O7
Warkton NSW 94 F10
Warmur Vic. 165 K5
Warnambool Downs Qld 321 I1

Warncoort Vic. 171 Q9, 172 A9
Warne Vic. 165 M2
Warneet Vic. 153 P3, 172 I8
Warner Glen WA 248 C8
Warners Bay NSW 83 G6
Warnertown SA 200 G7
Warnervale NSW 83 E11
Warooka SA 202 E7, 205 I13
Waroona WA 248 F1, 250 F13, 256 E11
Warpoo SA 197 K6
Warra NSW 95 M13, 99 M2
Warra Qld 323 N9
Warrabri NT 269 K12, 271 K2
Warrabri Aboriginal Reserve NT 269 K12, 271 K2
Warrabrook Vic. 170 H6
Warrachie SA 205 E9
Warrachuppin WA 251 Q4
Warracknabeal Vic. 164 I6, **143**, **131**
Warraderry NSW 98 D6, 100 B1
Warragamba NSW 76 I9
Warragamba Vic. 166 E6
Warragamba Dam NSW 80 I9, 98 I7, 100 H2, **38**, **57**
Warragul Vic. 173 L8, **143**
Warrain Beach NSW 100 I5
Warrak Vic. 165 M13, 171 N1
Warralakin WA 251 Q4
Warrambine Vic. 171 Q6, 172 A6
Warramboo SA 205 E8
Warrandyte Vic. 160 A12, 172 H5, **119**
Warranook Vic. 165 K9
Warrawee NSW 70 H6
Warrawee Qld 312 E4
Warra Yadin Vic. 165 M13, 171 M1
Warrayure Vic. 170 I5
Warrell Creek NSW 95 P9
Warren NSW 93 R11, 94 C11, **62**
Warrenbayne Vic. 167 L9
Warrenheip Vic. 158 B10, **121**
Warrenmang Vic. 165 N11
Warren National Park WA 248 F10, **218**, **224**, **225**
Warrentinna Tas. 361 O5
Warrick Park NSW 317 R12
Warrie National Park Qld 317 O9
Warriewood NSW 71 P2
Warri House NSW 321 H13
Warrill View Qld 316 F3
Warrimoo NSW 76 I7, 80 I5
Warrina SA 207 K5
Warrion Vic. 171 P8
Warri Warri Gate NSW 92 C3
Warrnambool Vic. 171 J9, **143**, **129**
Warrong Vic. 170 I8
Warrow SA 205 E11
Warrumbungle NSW 94 E10
Warrumbungle National Park NSW 94 F10, **44**, **46**, **59**
Wartaka P.O. SA 205 H7
Wartook Vic. 164 I11
Warunda SA 205 E11
Warup WA 249 K4
Warwick Qld 95 N1, 323 O11, **304**, **290**
Wasleys SA 196 H4, 200 I13, 202 I4
Watchem Vic. 165 L5
Watchman SA 200 H11, 202 H2
Watchupga Vic. 165 K2
Waterfall NSW 77 N12
Waterford Qld 315 M13, 317 M1
Waterford Vic. 174 C6
Waterholes Vic. 174 E7
Waterhouse Tas. 361 O4, **342**
Waterloo NSW 73 N6
Waterloo SA 201 J11, 203 J2
Waterloo Vic. 171 O2
Waterloo WA 248 F4
Waterloo Corner SA 196 G8
Waterman WA 244 B4, 250 F8
Watervale SA 200 I11, 202 I2
Wathe Vic. 162 I12, 164 I1
Watheroo WA 252 G12, 256 E8
Watson ACT 107 Q11
Watson SA 206 E9
Watsonia Vic. 149 M3, 159 N11
Watsons Bay NSW 71 Q13, 73 Q1
Watsons Creek NSW 95 K8
Watsonville Qld 324 F4, 326 I13
Wattagan NSW 83 B8
Wattamolla NSW 77 P12, 91 M10
Wattamondara NSW 98 E7, 100 C2
Wattening WA 250 I5
Wattle Flat NSW 98 G4
Wattle Flat SA 198 E8
Wattle Flat Vic. 158 B8
Wattle Grove Tas. 356 F11, 359 L9
Wattle Grove WA 247 Q5
Wattle Hill Tas. 357 M5, 359 O6
Wattle Hill Vic. 167 J12, 171 N12
Wattle Range SA 204 G9
Wattle Tree Vic. 174 H4
Wattle Vale Vic. 166 H10
Waubra Vic. 171 P2
Waubra Junction Vic. 158 A8, 171 Q3, 172 A3
Wauchope NSW 95 O11, **62**

Wauchope NT 269 K12, 271 K1, **240**
Waukaringa SA 207 P12
Wauraltee SA 202 E5
Waurn Ponds Vic. 155 E8, 172 D8
Wave Hill NSW 93 O7
Wave Hill NT 268 D5
Wavell Heights Qld 308 I9
Waverley NSW 73 P6
Waverley Tas. 363 F9
Waverney Qld 321 H6
Wave Rock WA 251 R9, **221**, **222**, **224**
Waverton NSW 68 I8, 71 L13, 73 L2
Wayatinah Tas. 358 I3
Waygara Vic. 174 I7
Wayville SA 194 D10
Weam WA 251 K11
Weavers NSW 77 M2
Webbs NSW 94 D13, 98 D1
Webbs Creek NSW 77 L1
Webster Hill Vic. 171 P11
Wedderburn NSW 77 L13
Wedderburn Vic. 165 P7, **143**
Wedderburn Junction Vic. 165 P7
Weddin Mountains National Park NSW 97 R7, 98 C7, 100 B1, **49**
Wedge Island SA 205 G13, **189**
Weeaproinah Vic. 171 P11
Wee Elwah NSW 97 L4
Weegena Tas. 360 I7
Wee Jasper NSW 98 E10, 100 C5, **64**
Weemelah NSW 94 G3
Weeragua Vic. 175 M5
Weerite Vic. 171 N8
Weetah Tas. 361 J7
Weetaliba NSW 94 G11
Weetangera ACT 106 E13, 108 D1
Weethalle NSW 97 O6
Weetulta SA 200 E12, 202 E3, 205 I11
Wee Waa NSW 94 G7, **63**
Wee-Wee-Rup Vic. 166 D3
Wehla Vic. 165 P8
Weilmoringle NSW 93 P3, 94 A3, 322 H13
Weimby NSW 96 G9
Weipa Qld 326 C4, **304**, **283**, **290**, **300**
Weira WA 251 P4
Weja NSW 97 O5
Welaregang NSW 100 B8, 168 G4
Welbungin WA 251 O3
Welby NSW 91 J6
Welcome Hill WA 251 Q9
Weld WA 252 A2
Weldborough Tas. 361 P6, **345**
Wellers Hill Qld 311 J6
Wellingrove NSW 95 L5
Wellington NSW 98 F2, **63**
Wellington SA 199 Q6, 203 L8, **191**
Wellington Mills WA 248 F4
Wellington Point Qld 315 N10
Wellsford Vic. 166 E8
Welshmans Reef Vic. 158 C2, 165 R11, 166 B11
Welshpool Vic. 173 O11, **144**
Welshpool WA 247 N4
Wembley WA 244 F11
Wembley Downs WA 244 D9
Wemen Vic. 96 F9, 163 J7
Wendouree Vic. 155 B3, 158 A9
Wensleydale Vic. 155 B10
Wentworth NSW 96 D8, 162 F2, **63**, **140**, **141**
Wentworth Falls NSW 76 F7, 80 D5, **52**, **53**
Wentworthville NSW 70 A13, 72 A1
Weonawarri Qld 321 I2
Wepar SA 204 H10
Werneth Vic. 171 P6
Werombi NSW 76 I11, 80 I12
Werona NSW 165 R13, 166 B13, 171 R1, 172 B1
Werrap Vic. 164 G4
Werri Beach NSW 91 O9
Werribee Vic. 155 I4, 172 F6, **118**
Werribee Gorge Vic. 158 F11
Werrikimbe National Park NSW 87 O11
Werrimull Vic. 162 E4
Werrington NSW 77 K7
Werris Creek NSW 95 J10
Wesburn Vic. 160 E12
Wesley Vale Tas. 360 I6
Wessel Islands NT 267 O2
West Beach SA 195 A9, **179**
West Burleigh Qld 319 M9
Westbury Tas. 361 K8, 363 B11, **352**, **346**
Westbury Vic. 173 N8
Westby Vic. 163 R13, 165 R1, 166 B1
Westdale NSW 95 J9
West End Qld 310 H4
Western Creek Tas. 360 I9
Western Flat SA 204 G6
Western Hill Vic. 153 M9
Western Junction Tas. 361 M8, 363 G11
Westerton Qld 321 I4
Westerway Tas. 356 C4, 359 K5
West Hobart Tas. 355 C9
Westlake Qld 310 B8
Westleigh NSW 70 E6
Westmar Qld 323 L11

Westmead NSW 70 B13, 72 B1
Westmeadows Vic. 148 E1
Westmere Vic. 171 M4
Weston ACT 108 D13, 110 E1
Weston NSW 83 E4
Weston Creek ACT 108 B13
Westonia WA 251 Q5
Westons Flat SA 201 N11, 203 N2
West Perth WA 242 A3, 244 H12
West Pymble NSW 70 H8
West Ridgley Tas. 360 F5
West Ryde NSW 70 G12
West Swan WA 245 P5, 259 E7
West Wallsend NSW 83 F5
West Wollongong NSW 89 A10
Westwood Qld 323 M3
Westwood Tas. 361 L8, 363 D10
West Wyalong NSW 97 P7, 98 A7, **63**, **59**
Wexcombe WA 259 H9
Weymouth Tas. 361 L4, 363 F2, **342**
Whale Beach NSW 77 Q4
Wharminda SA 205 F10
Wharparilla Vic. 166 E4
Wheatsheaf Vic. 158 E6
Wheeler Heights NSW 71 P4
Wheelers Hill Vic. 150 D3
Wheeo NSW 98 F8, 100 E3
Whetstone Qld 95 K1
Whim Creek WA 254 G9
Whinstanes Qld 309 K12
Whiporie NSW 95 P4, 323 Q13
Whirily Vic. 165 L3
White Cliffs NSW 92 F9, **63**
White Flat SA 205 F12
Whitefoord Tas. 359 N4
White Gum Valley WA 246 C9
Whiteheads Creek Vic. 159 O2, 160 A2, 166 I11
White Hills Tas. 361 M8, 363 G10
White Hut SA 202 C7
Whitemore Tas. 361 K8, 363 K12
White Rock Qld 335 F8
Whitewood Qld 324 C11
Whitfield Vic. 167 O9, 135, **143**
Whitlands Vic. 167 O9
Whitsunday Group Qld 331, **298-9**, **287**, **295**, **303**
Whitsunday Island Qld 325 K9
Whittingham NSW 83 A1
Whittington Vic. 156 H12
Whittlesea Vic. 154 G7, 159 N8, 172 H3
Whitton NSW 97 N8
Whitwarta SA 200 H12, 202 H2
Whoorel Vic. 171 Q9, 172 A9
Whorouly Vic. 167 P7
Whroo Vic. 166 G8, **138**
Whyalla SA 200 E6, 205 I8, 207 M13, **192**, **189**
Whyalla Conservation Park SA 207 M13
Whyte Yarcowie SA 201 J7
Wialki WA 251 O1, 253 O13, 256 G8
Wiangaree NSW 95 P2, 317 J13, **53**
Wicherina SA 252 C4
Wickepin WA 249 M1, 251 M13, 256 G11, **228**
Wickham NSW 82 E4
Wickham WA 254 F9, **228**, **217**, **226**
Wickham Hill SA 198 H4
Wickliffe Vic. 171 K4
Widgee Upper Qld 312 D3
Widgiemooltha WA 257 J9
Widgiewa NSW 97 N10
Wihareja Tas. 359 K1, 361 K11
Wilberforce NSW 77 K4
Wilby Vic. 167 M5
Wilcannia NSW 92 G11, **63**
Wildeloo SA 205 E11
Wildes Meadow NSW 91 L8
Wild Horse Plains SA 196 C2, 200 H13, 202 H4
Wiley Park NSW 72 G9
Wilga WA 248 H6, **214**
Wilgena SA 205 C2, 206 I9
Wilkatana SA 200 F2, 207 N12
Wilkawatt SA 203 P8
Wilkur Vic. 165 J4
Willa Vic. 162 H11
Willagee WA 246 E8
Willamulka SA 200 F11, 202 F2
Willandra National Park NSW 97 K4
Willaring Vic. 165 L10
Willaston SA 196 I6
Willatook Vic. 170 I8
Willaura Vic. 171 L3
Willawarrin NSW 95 O9
Willbriggie NSW 97 N8
Willenabrina Vic. 164 H4
Willetton WA 247 K9
William Creek SA 207 L6
Williams WA 249 J2, 256 F11, **228**
Williamsdale NSW 100 D7
Williamsford Tas. 360 E10, **350**
Williamstown SA 197 K7, 203 J5
Williamstown Vic. 148 E12, 172 G6, **117**
Williamtown NSW 83 I3, 99 M3
Willigam NSW 90 A8
Willina NSW 99 N2
Willis Vic. 100 C10, 174 I1

Willochra — Yallambie

Willochra SA 200 G2
Willoughby NSW 71 M11
Willow Grove Vic. 173 N7
Willowie Qld 317 N8
Willowie SA 200 H5, 207 N13
Willowmavin Vic. 159 L5
Willows Qld 322 I3, **291**
Willow Spring WA 248 F7
Willow Tree NSW 95 J11
Willow Vale NSW 91 O10
Willowvale Vic. 171 O5
Willung Vic. 173 Q8, 174 A11
Willunga SA 198 G5, 202 I8, **192, 180**
Willyabrup WA 248 C6
Willyaroo SA 199 K5
Wilmington SA 200 G4, 207 N13, **192, 189**
Wilmot Tas. 360 H7
Wilpena SA 207 O13, **192**
Wilpena Pound SA 207 O11, **182, 184, 192**
Wilroy WA 252 E4
Wilson Qld 331 E6
Wilson SA 200 H1
Wilson WA 247 L6
Wilsons Downfall NSW 95 N2
Wilsons Pocket Qld 312 I2
Wilsons Promontory Vic. 173 N13
Wilsons Promontory National Park Vic. 161, 172 G12, 173 O13, **132, 125, 133**
Wilston Qld 308 H12
Wiltshire Junction Tas. 360 D3
Wiluna WA 256 I3, **224**
Wimba Vic. 171 P11
Winchelsea Vic. 155 B9, 171 R8, 172 B8, **144**
Winchester WA 252 F10
Windale NSW 83 H6
Windang NSW 91 P6
Windellama NSW 98 H10, 100 F5
Windermere Vic. 171 Q3, 172 A3
Windeyer NSW 98 G3
Windjana Gorge National Park WA 255 N5, **218**
Windomal NSW 96 G9
Windorah Qld 321 F6, 322 B7, **294, 295**
Windsor NSW 77 K5, 99 J6, 100 I1, **63-4, 38**
Windsor Qld 308 I12
Windsor SA 196 D3, 200 H13, 202 H4
Windurong NSW 94 E11
Windy Harbour WA 248 G11, **225**
Wingamin SA 203 N7
Wingeel Vic. 171 Q7, 172 A7
Wingello NSW 90 H10, 100 G4
Wingham NSW 95 N12, **64**
Winiam Vic. 164 E7
Winjallock Vic. 165 N10
Winkie SA 201 P12, 203 P3
Winkleigh Tas. 361 K6, 363 B7
Winnaleah Tas. 361 P5, **344**
Winnambool Vic. 163 K8
Winnap Vic. 170 D7
Winnecke Gorge NT 263 Q2
Winnellie NT 265 K1
Winnindoo Vic. 173 Q7
Winninowie Vic. 200 F4
Winnunga NSW 97 P5
Winslow Vic. 171 J8
Winston Hills NSW 70 A10
Winton Qld 322 B1, 324 B13, 327 I11, **304, 289, 294, 295**
Winton Vic. 167 M7
Winulta SA 200 F12, 202 F3
Winwill Qld 314 A12
Winya Qld 314 F2
Wirha SA 203 P7
Wirrabara SA 200 H6, **184**
Wirraminna SA 205 F3, 207 K10
Wirrappa SA 205 H4, 207 L11
Wirrega SA 203 P12, 204 G3
Wirrimah NSW 98 D7, 100 C2
Wirrinya NSW 97 R6, 98 C6, 100 A1
Wirrulla SA 205 C6, 206 I12
Wisemans Ferry NSW 77 M1, 99 J5, **64, 63**
Wishart Qld 311 M8
Wishbone WA 249 N3
Wistow SA 199 K2
Witchcliffe WA 248 C7
Witchelina SA 207 K8
Witheren Qld 317 M6
Withersfield Qld 322 I3
Witta Qld 307 A9, 312 I10
Wittenbra NSW 94 F9
Wittenoom WA 254 G11, **228, 217, 226**
Wittenoom Gorge WA 254 G11
Wittitrin NSW 95 O10
Wivenhoe Pocket Qld 314 F9
Wiyarra Qld 316 A9
Woden Valley ACT 108 H13
Wodonga Vic. 97 P13, 167 Q5, 168 A5, **144, 141**
Wokurna SA 200 G10
Wolf Creek Crater National Park WA 255 P7
Wolffdene Qld 317 M2
Wolgari WA 251 Q8
Wokalup WA 248 F2
Wollar NSW 94 H13, 98 H2

Wolla Wolla WA 252 I3
Wollert Vic. 159 M10
Wollombi NSW 83 A7, 95 M8, 99 K4, **45**
Wollongong NSW 89, 91 P5, 99 J8, 100 I3, **64, 54**
Wollstonecraft NSW 68 F6, 71 L13, 73 L1
Wollun NSW 95 L9
Wollyllia WA 252 A1
Wolseley SA 164 A7, 203 Q13, 204 H4
Wolvi Qld 312 I2
Wolumla NSW 100 F10, 175 P1
Womalilla Qld 322 I8
Wombarra NSW 91 P2
Wombat NSW 98 D8, 100 B3
Wombat Vic. 158 C7
Wombelano Vic. 164 E11
Wombeyan Caves NSW 90 E5, 98 H8, **42, 55**
Womboota NSW 97 J13, 166 E3
Wonboyn Lake NSW 100 F12, 175 P4
Wondabyne NSW 77 P2, 78 E7
Wondai Qld 323 O8, **304**
Wondalga NSW 97 R11, 98 D11, 100 B6
Wongabel Qld 335 C13
Wonga Lower Qld 312 E1
Wongamine WA 250 I6
Wongan Hills WA 251 J3, 256 F8
Wonga Park Vic. 160 A12
Wongarbon NSW 94 E13, 98 E2
Wongarra Vic. 171 Q12, 172 A12
Wonga Upper Qld 312 D2
Wongawilli NSW 91 N6
Wonglepong Qld 317 M5
Wongulla SA 203 M5
Wonnerup WA 248 D5
Wonning P.O. SA 205 G7
Wonthaggi Vic. 173 J11, **144**
Wonuarra SA 201 Q12, 203 Q3
Wonwondah East Vic. 164 H10
Wonwondah North Vic. 164 H10
Wonwron Vic. 173 P10
Wonyip Vic. 173 O11
Woocalla SA 205 H5, 207 M11
Woodanilling WA 249 L5, 256 G11
Woodbine Qld 316 A2
Woodbridge Tas. 356 H11, 359 M9
Woodburn NSW 95 Q3, 323 Q13, **64**
Woodburn WA 249 N11
Woodburne Vic. 155 A3, 158 B13, 171 R5, 172 B5
Woodbury Tas. 359 M2, 361 M12
Woodchester SA 199 L4, 203 J8
Woodenbong NSW 95 O1, 316 F11, 323 P12
Woodend Vic. 154 C6, 158 H6, 172 E2, **134, 119**
Woodfield Vic. 160 G1, 167 L11
Woodford NSW 76 G7, 80 G5
Woodford Qld 314 H2, 323 P9
Woodgate Qld 323 P6
Woodhill Qld 317 K4
Wood Hill NSW 91 N9
Woodhouselee NSW 90 A9, 98 G9, 100 F3
Woodlands Qld 314 B12
Woodlands WA 244 E9, 248 C6
Woodleigh Vic. 173 K9
Woodridge Qld 315 L12
Woods SA 200 I12, 202 I3
Woodsdale Tas. 357 L1, 359 N4
Woodside SA 197 K12, 203 J6
Woodside Vic. 173 Q10, 174 A13, **144**
Woods Point Vic. 173 N3
Woods Reef NSW 95 J7
Woodstock NSW 98 E6, 100 D1
Woodstock Qld 322 A1, 324 H8
Woodstock Tas. 356 F10, 359 L8
Woodstock Vic. 159 M9, 165 R9, 166 B9, 172 G3
Woodstock WA 254 H10
Woods Well SA 203 M12, 204 C3
Woodvale Vic. 166 C8
Woodville NSW 83 F2, 99 L3
Woodville SA 195 B7, 196 F10
Wood Wood Vic. 163 N9
Woody Point Qld 315 M7, **299**
Woogenellup WA 249 N10
Woohlpooer Vic. 170 H2
Woolamai Vic. 173 J10
Wool Bay SA 202 F7, 205 I13
Woolbrook NSW 95 L9
Woolgoolga NSW 95 P7, **64**
Wooli NSW 95 Q6
Woollahra NSW 67 N11, 73 P5, **37**
Woolloomooloo NSW 66 G7, **37**
Woolloongabba Qld 306 G11, 310 I4
Woolner NT 265 K6
Woolomin NSW 95 K10
Woolooga Qld 312 D1
Wooloowin Qld 309 J11
Woolshed Vic. 167 P6, **121**
Woolsthorpe Vic. 171 J8
Woolwich NSW 68 B10, 73 K2
Woolwonga Wildlife Sanctuary NT 266 H5, **234**
Wool Wool Vic. 171 O8
Woomargama NSW 97 P12, 168 D3
Woombye Qld 307 E8, 313 K10
Woomelang Vic. 96 F12, 163 K13, 165 K2
Woomera SA 205 G3, 207 L10, **188**
Woompah NSW 321 H13

Woondum Qld 312 H4
Woongoolba Qld 317 O2
Woonona NSW 91 P3
Wooragee Vic. 167 Q6
Woorak Vic. 164 F6
Woorarra East Vic. 173 O11
Wooreen Vic. 173 M9
Woorim Qld 315 N4, **301**
Woorinen Vic. 163 O10
Woori Yallock Vic. 159 R12, 160 D12, 173 J5
Woornack Vic. 163 J9
Woorndoo Vic. 171 L6
Wooroloo WA 250 H8, **225**
Wooroonook Vic. 165 N6, **124**
Woosang Vic. 165 O6
Wootha Qld 307 A12, 312 I12
Wootong Vale Vic. 170 F3
Wootoona P.O. SA 205 D8
Wootton NSW 95 N13, 99 N2
Wooyong NSW 317 R13
Worlds End Creek SA 201 K10, 203 K1
Worongary Qld 317 O6
Woronora Reservoir NSW 77 N13
Worrigee NSW 91 M12
Worsley WA 248 G3
Wowan Qld 323 M4
Woy Woy NSW 77 Q2, 78 E3, **64**
Wrattonbully SA 164 B13, 170 B1, 204 I8
Wrest Point Casino Tas. 355 F11, **338, 339**
Wrightley Vic. 167 M10
Wroxham Vic. 175 N4
Wubin WA 252 I11, 256 F8
Wudinna SA 205 E8, **192**
Wulgulmerang Vic. 168 I12, 174 H3
Wundowie WA 250 H8, 256 F10
Wunghnu Vic. 167 J5
Wunkar SA 201 O13, 203 O4
Wuraming WA 248 H1, 250 H13
Wurarga WA 252 H3
Wurdiboluc Vic. 172 B9
Wurdiboluc Reservoir Vic. 172 B9
Wurruk Vic. 173 R8, 174 B10
Wutul Qld 323 O9
Wyadup WA 248 C6
Wyalkatchem WA 251 L5, 256 G9
Wyalong NSW 97 P7, 98 B7
Wyan NSW 95 P3
Wyandra Qld 322 G10
Wyanga NSW 94 D13, 97 R2, 98 D2
Wyangala Dam NSW 98 F7, 100 D2, **47**
Wybong NSW 95 J13, 99 J1
Wycarbah Qld 323 M3
Wycheproof Vic. 96 G13, 165 N4, **144**
Wychitella Vic. 165 P6, **143**
Wyee NSW 83 F10, 99 L4
Wyeeboo Vic. 168 D6
Wyelangta Vic. 171 O11
Wyena Tas. 363 G5
Wyening WA 250 I5
Wye River Vic. 171 R11, 172 B11
Wylie Creek NSW 95 N2
Wymah NSW 97 P13, 168 D4
Wymlet Vic. 162 G8
Wynarka SA 203 M7
Wynbring SA 205 A2, 206 G9
Wyndham NSW 100 F11, 175 O2
Wyndham WA 255 Q3, **228**
Wynnum Qld 309 Q12, 315 M9, **279**
Wynnum South Qld 309 Q13, 311 Q1
Wynyard Tas. 360 F4, **352**
Wyola WA 251 L7
Wyong NSW 83 E11, 99 L5, **64, 49**
Wyongah NSW 83 F11
Wyong Creek NSW 83 D11
Wyperfeld National Park Vic. 162 F12, 164 G1, **125, 129, 131**
Wyuna Vic. 166 H5
Wyuna Downs NSW 93 N7
Wy Yung Vic. 174 E8

Y

Yaamba Qld 323 M3
Yaapeet Vic. 164 G2
Yabba North Vic. 167 K5
Yabba South Vic. 167 K6
Yabba Vale Qld 312 H6
Yabba Valley Vic. 168 C6
Yabmana SA 200 B10, 202 B1
Yacka SA 200 H9
Yackandandah Vic. 167 Q6, **144**
Yagobie NSW 94 I4
Yagoona NSW 72 E8
Yahl SA 170 B6, 204 H12
Yalbarrin WA 251 O9
Yalboroo Qld 325 K10, 331 D9
Yalbraith NSW 90 B5, 98 G8, 100 F3
Yalca Vic. 166 I4
Yalgogrin North NSW 97 O6
Yalgogrin South NSW 97 O7
Yalgoo WA 252 I2, 256 F6, **228**
Yallah NSW 91 O7
Yallambie NSW 83 A8

Yallaroi NSW 95 J3, 323 M13
Yalla-y-poora Vic. 171 M3
Yalleroi Qld 322 G4
Yallingup WA 248 C6, 256 E12, 215, 218
Yallingup Caves WA 248 C5
Yallourn Vic. 173 N8, 136
Yallunda Flat SA 205 F11
Yalwal NSW 91 K13, 100 G5
Yamba NSW 95 Q4, 64, 54
Yamba SA 96 A8, 162 A3, 201 Q12, 203 Q3
Yambuk Vic. 170 H9
Yambuna Vic. 166 G5
Yanac Vic. 164 D5
Yanakie Vic. 161 B2, 173 N12
Yanchep WA 250 E7, 228
Yanchep National Park WA 250 E6, 213, 220, 221, 228
Yanco NSW 97 O9, 53
Yandanooka WA 252 E7
Yanderra NSW 91 L4
Yandiah SA 200 H6
Yandilla Qld 323 N11
Yandina Qld 307 D6, 313 K8
Yandina Creek Qld 307 E5, 313 K8
Yando Vic. 165 Q4, 166 A4
Yandoit Vic. 158 C4, 165 R12, 166 B13, 172 C1
Yangan Qld 316 A8
Yaninee SA 205 D8
Yanipy Vic. 164 C7
Yankalilla SA 198 D8, 202 H9, 192
Yanko Qld 321 H12
Yanmah WA 248 G8
Yantabulla NSW 93 K4, 322 E13
Yantanabie SA 205 C7, 206 I12
Yan Yean Vic. 159 N9, 172 H3
Yan Yean Reservoir Vic. 172 H3
Yaouk NSW 100 D7
Yapeen Vic. 158 D3, 166 C12
Yaraka Qld 322 D6
Yarck Vic. 160 E2, 167 K12
Yardaring WA 255 C7
Yardea P.O. SA 205 E6
Yarding WA 251 O8
Yarloop WA 248 F2
Yaroona SA 198 H3
Yarra NSW 90 B12, 98 G9
Yarrabah Aboriginal Community Qld 335
Yarrabandai NSW 97 Q4, 98 B4
Yarrabin NSW 98 F3
Yarraby Vic. 163 N10
Yarra Glen Vic. 154 H8, 159 Q10, 160 B11, 172 I4, 118
Yarragon Vic. 173 M8
Yarra Junction Vic. 160 E12, 173 K5
Yarralena WA 249 L9
Yarralumla ACT 109 J9
Yarram Vic. 173 P11, 144, 137
Yarramalong NSW 83 C11
Yarraman Qld 323 O9
Yarraman North NSW 94 I11
Yarrambat Vic. 159 N10
Yarramony WA 250 I6
Yarrangobilly NSW 100 C7
Yarrara Vic. 162 D4
Yarras NSW 95 N11
Yarraville Vic. 148 D9
Yarrawalla Vic. 165 R5, 166 B5
Yarrawonga Vic. 97 N13, 167 M4, 144, 138, 141
Yarrie Lake NSW 94 G7
Yarrock Vic. 164 C6
Yarroweyah Vic. 167 J3
Yarrowitch NSW 95 M10
Yarrowyck NSW 95 L7
Yarrunga North NSW 91 K8
Yarto Vic. 162 H12
Yartook Reservoir Vic. 165 J12
Yarwun Qld 323 N4, 291
Yass NSW 98 E9, 100 D4, 64
Yatala Qld 317 N1
Yatchaw Vic. 170 H5
Yatina SA 200 I6
Yatpool Vic. 162 H4
Yatteyatah NSW 98 I11, 100 H6
Yea Vic. 159 Q4, 160 C4, 166 I13, 144
Yeagerup WA 248 G10
Yealering WA 251 M12, 256 G10, 228
Yearinan NSW 94 F9
Yearinga Vic. 164 C6
Yea River Park Vic. 159 Q8
Yedina Qld 323 P9
Yednia Qld 312 F12
Yeelanna SA 205 E11
Yeerongpilly Qld 310 H6
Yelarbon Qld 95 J1, 323 M12
Yelbeni WA 251 M5
Yellangip Vic. 164 I5
Yellingbo Vic. 159 R13, 160 D13
Yellow Rock NSW 91 N8
Yelta SA 200 E12, 202 E2
Yelta Vic. 162 G2
Yelverton WA 248 C6
Yenda NSW 97 N8
Yendon Vic. 158 B10, 171 R4, 172 B4

Yennora NSW 72 A5
Yeodene Vic. 171 Q9, 172 A9
Yeo Yeo NSW 98 C8, 100 B3
Yeoval NSW 98 E3
Yeppoon Qld 323 N3, 304, 286, 287, 300
Yerecoin WA 250 H3
Yerillon WA 251 R6
Yeriminup WA 249 K8
Yering Vic. 159 Q11, 160 B11
Yerong Creek NSW 97 P11, 98 A11
Yeronga Qld 310 H6
Yerranderie NSW 90 G1
Yerrinbool NSW 91 K5
Yerrip Vic. 167 M5
Yetman NSW 95 J2, 323 M13
Yetna WA 252 B4
Yeungroon Vic. 165 O7
Yilki SA 198 G10
Yilliminning WA 249 L1, 251 L13, 225
Yimbun Qld 314 C3
Yin Barun Vic. 167 M9
Yinkanie SA 201 O13, 203 O3
Yinnar Vic. 173 N9
Yirrigan WA 244 I6
Yirrkala NT 267 P4
Yokine WA 244 H8
Yolla Tas. 360 F5, 351
Yongala SA 200 I6
Yoogali NSW 97 N8
Yoongarilup WA 248 D6
York WA 251 J8, 256 F10, 228, 213, 214
Yorke Peninsula SA 202 D5, 205 H12, 181
Yorketown SA 202 E7, 205 I13, 192
Yorke Valley SA 200 F13, 202 F4
Yorkeys Knob Qld 335 F6
York Plains Tas. 359 N3, 361 N13
Yorkrakine WA 251 M6
Yornaning WA 249 K1, 251 K13
Yornup WA 248 G7
Yoting WA 251 M9
Youanmite Vic. 167 K5
Youarang Vic. 167 L5
Youndegin WA 251 L8
Young NSW 98 D8, 100 B3, 64
Younghusband Peninsula SA 204 B1
Youngs Siding WA 249 M13
Youngtown Tas. 363 F10
Youraling WA 251 K10
You Yangs Vic. 172 D6, 128
Yowrie NSW 100 F9
Yuendumu NT 270 F5
Yuendumu Aboriginal Reserve NT 270 F4
Yugar Qld 314 I8
Yulara NT 270 E11, 240
Yuleba Qld 323 L9
Yumali SA 203 M9
Yumbarra Conservation Park SA 206 G11, 183
Yuna WA 252 C2, 256 D6
Yunderup WA 250 F12
Yundi SA 198 H6
Yundool Vic. 167 L6
Yungaburra Qld 335 D12, 304, 283
Yungera Vic. 96 G9, 163 M7
Yunta SA 200 L4, 207 P13
Yurgo SA 203 N8
Yuroke Vic. 159 L10, 172 G4
Yurol Qld 313 J6
Yurpi Qld 307 C1
Yuulong Vic. 171 O12

Z

Zanthus WA 257 L8
Zeehan Tas. 360 D10, 352, 348, 349
Zeerust Vic. 166 I6
Zetland NSW 73 N6
Zillmere Qld 308 I7
Zumsteins Vic. 164 I12

Accident Action
Those vital first moments

Treating an unconscious person

1 CLEAR AIRWAY
Lie victim on his side and tilt head back.

2 CLEAR MOUTH
Quickly clear his mouth using fingers if necessary. If breathing, leave him on his side.

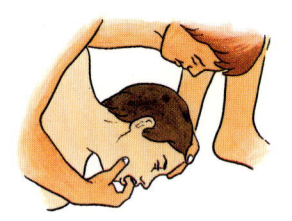

3 TILT
IF NOT BREATHING, place him on his back. Tilt head back. Support the jaw, keeping fingers away from neck.

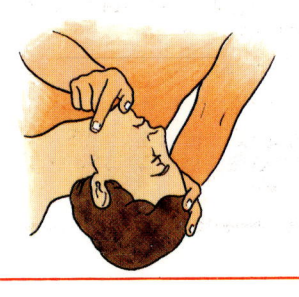

4 BLOW
Kneel beside victim's head. Place widely open mouth over his slightly open mouth, sealing victim's nostrils with cheek. Blow until victim's chest rises.

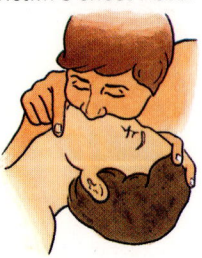

NOTE: With children cover child's mouth and nose with your mouth. Blow until chest rises (20 times per minute).

5 LOOK, LISTEN
Watch chest fall. Listen for air escaping from mouth. Repeat steps 4 and 5, 15 times per minute.

6 RECOVERY POSITION
When breathing begins, place him on his side, head back, jaw supported, face pointing slightly towards ground.

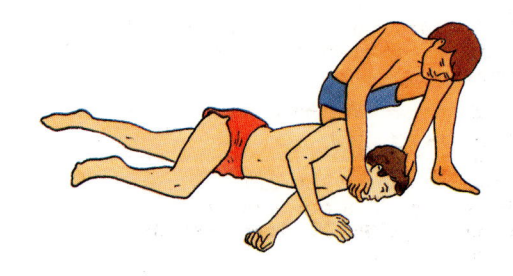

7 IF HE IS UNCONSCIOUS
If he is unconscious and you cannot get him out of the car, still tilt head back and support the jaw.

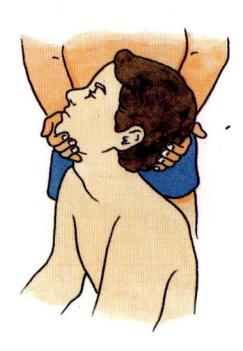

SEND SOMEONE FOR AN AMBULANCE.

DO NOT LEAVE AN UNCONSCIOUS PERSON.